Hutchinson
Dictionary of
Difficult Words

Hutchinson
Dictionary of
Difficult Words

Edited by John Ayto

LONDON NEW YORK SYDNEY TORONTO

This edition published 1993 by BCA
by arrangement with Helicon Publishing

First published (as *A Dictionary of Difficult Words*) 1938
Totally revised edition 1993

Printed and bound in Great Britain by
Mackays of Chatham

CN 9097

Consultant editor	John Ayto
Editorial director	Michael Upshall
Project editors	Emma Callery
	Gillian Haslam
Pronunciation editor	JC Wells MA PhD
Database management	Graham Duncan
Database update and pagination	Helen Bird
Lexicographers	Stephen Curtis
	Sue Lloyd
	Kathy Seed
Text designer	Gwyn Lewis

CONTENTS

6

Pronunciation key

These are given using the International Phonetic Alphabet (IPA). Where required, alternative pronunciations are also given. The pronunciation for foreign names is generally agreed English form, if there is one: otherwise, an approximation using English sounds is given.

ɑ	father ['fɑːðə], start [stɑːt]	m	minimum ['mɪnɪməm]
aɪ	price [praɪs], high [haɪ]	n	nine [naɪn]
au	mouth [mauθ], how [hau]	ŋ	sing [sɪŋ], uncle ['ʌŋkl]
æ	trap [træp], man [mæn]	ɒ	lot [lɒt], watch [wɒtʃ]
b	baby ['beɪbɪ]	ɔ	thought [θɔːt], north [nɔːθ]
d	dead [ded]	ɔɪ	choice [tʃɔɪs], boy [bɔɪ]
dʒ	judge [dʒʌdʒ]	p	paper ['peɪpə]
ð	this [ðɪs], other ['ʌðə]	r	red [red], carry ['kærɪ]
e	dress [dres], men [men]	s	space [speɪs]
eɪ	face [feɪs], wait [weɪt]	ʃ	ship [ʃɪp], motion ['məʃən]
eə	square [skweə], fair [feə]	t	totter ['tɒtə]
ɜː	nurse [nɜːs], pearl [pɜːl]	tʃ	church [tʃɜːtʃ]
ə	another [ə'nʌðə]	θ	thick [θɪk], author ['ɔːθə]
əu	goat [gəut], snow [snəu]	uː	goose ['guːs], soup [suːp]
f	fifty ['fɪftɪ]	u	influence ['ɪnfluəns]
g	giggle ['gɪgl]	ʊ	foot [fʊt], push [pʊʃ]
h	hot [hɒt]	ʊə	poor [pʊə], cure [kjʊə]
iː	fleece [fliːs], sea [siː]	v	vivid ['vɪvɪd]
i	happy [hæpi], glorious ['glɔːrəs]	ʌ	strut [strʌt], love [lʌv]
ɪ	kit [kɪt], tin [tɪn]	w	west [west]
ɪə	near [nɪə], idea [aɪ'dɪə]	x	loch [lɒx]
j	yellow ['jeləu], few [fjuː]	z	zones [zəunz]
k	kick [kɪk]	3	pleasure]'pleʒə]
l	little ['lɪtl]		

Consonants

p b t d k g tʃ dʒ f v θ ð s z ʃ ʒ m n ŋ r l w j x

Vowels and Dipthongs

iː ɪ e æ ɑː ɒ ŋ ɔː uː u ʌ ɜː ə ɪə ʊ aɪ au ɔɪ ɪə eə ʊə əu

Stress marks

' (primary word stress)   , (secondary word stress)

List of abbreviations

abbr.	abbreviated as
adj.	adjective
adv.	adverb
conj.	conjunction
E	East, Eastern (or east, eastern)
e.g.	exempli gratia, for example
etc.	etectera, and other (similar) things
fem.	feminine form
i.e.	id est, that is
masc.	masculine form
N	North, Northern
n.	noun
n. pl.	plural noun
pl.	plural (form)
prep.	preposition
S	South, Southern
sing.	singular (form)
v.i.	intransitive verb
v.i. & t.	verb with transitive and intransitive meaning
v.t.	transitive verb
W	West, Western

PREFACE

The general dictionaries which we all have on our bookshelves and desks, and which we constantly consult, have one significant but little-considered characteristic in common: much of their contents is never used. When was the last time you needed to find out the meaning of *the* or *but*, the spelling of *car* or *dog*? And yet dictionaries compiled for adult native-speakers of English take care to include such straightforward words, which present no difficulty to dictionary users, and which consequently are seldom – if ever – looked up. As dictionaries descend the ladder of size past 'concise' to 'pocket', it is the less frequent and less familiar words that are omitted; the ones we all know are allowed to stay.

We rather take this feature of dictionaries for granted, as if that is how they have always been, and therefore that is how they should always be. But that is *not* how they have always been. In the 17th and 18th centuries, the commonest type of lexical reference book was one that included only those words that might present some difficulty to the user, through unfamiliarity, orthographic irregularity, etc. These are termed 'hard-word dictionaries'. But in the 18th century, the practice began to grow of including more everyday words as well. Confirmed by Dr Johnson's magisterial *English Dictionary* of 1755, this is the tradition that has won out: we now assume that dictionaries will be inventories of all the words of a language.

However, even the huge *Oxford English Dictionary*, with more than half a million entries, would not seriously make that claim. No dictionary, however big, can be a hundred per cent comprehensive – much less a pocket dictionary. As far as the practical needs of users are concerned, it makes much better sense to include only words that they are likely to look up. The space saved by omitting the likes of *and, be, do, house*, and *small* can be much more profitably given to words whose meaning, spelling, pronunciation, etc cause problems.

That is the idea behind the *Hutchinson Dictionary of Difficult Words*. It is a compendium of over 16,000 of the more troublesome and obscure words in the English language. The average non-specialist coming across, say, *capeador* in an article on bullfighting, or *sacroidosis* in a medical text, is unlikely to know their meaning, and would in all probability want to look them up. Such a search in a standard English dictionary may well be unsuccessful (neither word is in the *Concise Oxford Dictionary* or *Collins English Dictionary*, for instance), but the *Hutchinson Dictionary of Difficult Words* will provide the answer. (A capeador, incidentally, is a bullfighter who carries a cape – 'Since Gordito's time ... bandilleros have had most recourse to the aid of capeadors,' Roy Campbell 1932 – and sacroidosis is a disease characterized by the formation of nodules or swellings.) The *Hutchinson Dictionary of Difficult Words* gives you access to the farthest reaches of English vocabulary, including within its modest compass, terms that can otherwise be found only in the largest multi-volume unabridged dictionaries and specialist reference books.

Difficulties with words are not limited to meaning. Spelling can cause problems too, as can pronunciation, grammar, etc. The *Hutchinson Dictionary of Difficult Words* contains a number of special sections designed to provide answers to the most pressing of these: guidance on words whose spelling causes confusion (*practice* or *practise*?); advice on how to pronounce controversial words, like *controversy* (the pronunciation of all the words in the dictionary is given in the International Phonetic Alphabet); and discussions of many contentious or tricky points of grammar, usage, and style, such as the split infinitive and the use of non-sex-specific pronouns.

This book is based on *A Dictionary of Difficult Words* by Robert H Hill, first published in 1938 and revised several times since. The *Hutchinson Dictionary of Difficult Words* brings that collection up to the end of the 20th century. Several hundred obsolete terms have been removed, and over a thousand newly included items – such as *taxeme*, *teleran*, and *triage* – make it an up-to-date interpreter of the English language. It is not a dictionary to be left on the shelf, but a practical problem-solver whose every entry serves a purpose.

John Ayto

A

aardvark ['ɑːdvɑːk] *n.* long-snouted, ant-eating, burrowing mammal of S Africa.

aardwolf ['ɑːdwʊlf] *n.* striped hyena-like, mammal of S Africa.

aasvogel ['ɑːsfəʊgl] (*S African*) *n.* vulture.

aba [ə'bɑː, 'ɑːbə] *n.* coarse, striped, camel-hair or goat-hair fabric of Arabia; loose Arab coat.

abaca [ˌæbə'kɑː] *n.* Philippine Islands plant, yielding fibre for Manila hemp.

abacist ['æbəsɪst] *n.* person using abacus.

abacterial [ˌeɪbæk'tɪəriəl] *adj.* not caused by or containing bacteria.

abaction [æ'bækʃn] *n.* cattle-stealing.

abaculus [æ'bækjuləs] *n.* small tile for mosaic.

abacus ['æbəkəs] *n.* frame with beads for calculation; *Architecture*, flat slab forming uppermost part of capital of column.

abalone [ˌæbə'ləʊni] *n.* ear-shaped marine shellfish, yielding mother-of-pearl; ear-shell.

abandonment [ə'bændənmənt] *n.* *Commerce*, giving over by owner to underwriters of ship or cargo damaged beyond recovery. **abandonee** [əˌbændə'niː], *n.* underwriter to whom such ship or cargo is abandoned.

abapical [æb'æpɪkl] *adj.* at lowest point.

abarthrosis [ˌæbɑː'θrəʊsɪs] *n.* diarthrosis.

abarticular [ˌæbɑː'tɪkjulə] *adj.* not connected with joint.

à bas [ɑː 'bɑː] (*French*) 'down with'.

abasia [æ'beɪziə] *n.* inability to control muscles in walking. **abasic**, *adj.*

abate [ə'beɪt] *v.* *Law*, end (a nuisance); *Law*, abandon (an action).

abatement [ə'beɪtmənt] *n.* *Law obsolete*, unlawful entry by stranger onto land between death of possessor and entry of heir; *Heraldry*, mark on arms to indicate bastardy.

abatis, abattis ['æbətɪs] *n.* barricade of fallen trees.

abatjour [ˌæbæ'ʒʊə] (*French*) *n.* sky-light; device at window to throw light downwards.

abat-sons [ˌæbæ'sɒn] (*French*) *n.* device for directing sound downwards.

abat-vent [ˌæbæ'vɒn] (*French*) *n.* sloping slats to break force of wind.

abat-voix [ˌæbæ'vwɑː] (*French*) *n.* sounding-board.

abaxial [æb'æksiəl] *adj.* distant, or turned away, from axis, as of an organ or organism.

abb [æb] *n.* inferior part of fleece, yarn from this for warp.

abba ['æbə] (*Aramaic*) *n.* father; bishop in Syriac and Coptic churches.

abbozzo [æ'bɒtsəʊ] *n.* rough, preliminary sketch.

abditive ['æbdətɪv] *adj.* remote; hidden. **abditory,**

n. secret hiding-place.

abdominous [æb'dɒmɪnəs] *adj.* having big belly.

abducent [æb'djuːsnt] *adj.* carrying or turning away, especially of nerve or muscle.

abecedary [ˌeɪbiː'siːdəri] *n.* book arranged in alphabetical order; elementary text-book. **abecedarian**, *n.* member of 16th-century German Anabaptist sect who refused to learn to read, **abecedarian** *adj.* alphabetically arranged.

abele [ə'biːl] *n.* white poplar.

aberdevine [ˌæbədɪ'vaɪn] *n.* siskin.

abernethy [ˌæbə'neθi] *n.* a crisp, unleavened biscuit.

aberrant [æ'bərənt] *adj.* wandering; deviating, especially from virtue; abnormal. **aberrance**, *n.*

aberration [ˌæbə'reɪʃn] *n.* deviation; momentary mental lapse; *Astronomy*, apparent deviation from heavenly body's true position due to movement of observer with the earth. **chromatic aberration**, focusing of light of different colours at different points resulting in a blurred image. **spherical aberration** , focusing at different points of rays passing through different parts of spherical lens.

ab extra [æb 'ekstrə, –ɑː] (*Latin*) 'from outside'.

abient ['æbiənt] *adj.* tending to turn away or remove an organism from a stimulus or situation; *Psychology*, turning away or avoiding, as of an answer.

abietic [ˌæbi'etɪk] *adj.* pertaining to fir tree or resin.

abigail ['æbɪgeɪl] *archaic*, a lady's maid.

ab initio [ˌæb ɪ'nɪʃiəʊ] (*Latin*) 'from the beginning'.

abiogenesis [ˌeɪbaɪəʊ'dʒenɪsɪs] *n.* theory of generation of living from inanimate matter. **abiogenetic** [–dʒə'netɪk], *adj.* **abiogenist**, *n.* believer in that theory.

abiological [ˌeɪbaɪə'rɒdʒɪkl] *adj.* not involving or produced by animate things.

abiosis [ˌeɪbaɪ'əʊsɪs] *n.* absence of life. **abiotic**, *adj.*

abiotrophy [ˌeɪbaɪ'ɒtrəfi] *n.* physical degeneration; loss of vitality. **abiotrophic**, *adj.*

abirritate [æb'ɪrɪteɪt] *v.t.* *Medicine*, reduce irritation or sensitiveness. **abirritant**, *n.* such drug. **abirritation**, *n.* loss of sensitiveness in tissues; debility.

abjure [əb'dʒʊə] *v.t.* abstain from; renounce.

ablactate [æb'lækteɪt] *v.t.* wean. **ablactation**, *n.*

ablation [æb'leɪʃn] *n.* surgical removal; wearing away of rock or glacier; melting away of expendable part of spaceship or rocket. **ablator**, *n.* heat shield for re-entry on rockets, etc., which ablates; surgical instrument for removing tissue.

ablative ['æblətɪv] *adj.* signifying agency; *n.* such grammatical case. **ablative absolute,** Latin adverbial phrase formed by noun and adjunct (especially participle), both in ablative.

ablaut ['æblaʊt] *n.* special change or relation in vowel sound, as in vowels of 'ring, rang, rung'.

ablegate ['æblɪgeɪt] *n.* special papal envoy.

ablepsia [eɪ'blepsɪə] *n.* blindness. **–ableptic,** *adj.*

abluent ['æbluənt] *n.* & *adj. Medicine,* cleansing (substance).

ablution [ə'bluːʃn] *n.* act of washing; *pl.* washing the face and hands; washing place. **ablutionary,** *adj.*

abnegate ['æbnɪgeɪt] *v.t.* renounce. **abnegation,** *n.*

aboma [ə'bəʊmə] *n.* S American snake; ringed boa.

abomasum [ˌæbə'meɪsəm] *n.* fourth stomach of ruminants.

aboral [æb'ɔːrəl] *adj.* distant from, or opposite to, mouth.

aborigine [ˌæbə'rɪdʒəni] *n.* inhabitant from earliest times. **aboriginal,** *adj.* indigenous; *n.* aborigine.

abortifacient [əˌbɔːtɪ'feɪʃnt] *n.* drug, etc. which brings about abortion.

aboulia, abulia [ə'buːlɪə, –'bjuː–] *n.* loss of will power. **aboulic,** *adj.* **aboulomania,** *n.* form of insanity marked by aboulia.

ab ovo [æb 'əʊvəʊ] *(Latin)* 'from the egg'; from the beginning. **ab ovo usque ad mala,** 'from the egg to the apples'; from the beginning to the end.

abrade [ə'breɪd] *v.t.* rub off; scrape; cause injury in this way.

abrasion [ə'breɪʒn] *n.* injury caused by, or act of, rubbing or scraping; graze. **abrasive,** *adj.* causing or used in abrasion; *n.* such substance.

abreaction [ˌæbri'ækʃn] *n.* removal of psychological complex.

abreuvoir [ˌæbrɜː'vwɑː] *n.* gap between stones in masonry; *(French.)* watering place for animals.

abrogate ['æbrəgeɪt] *v.t.* cancel formally; repeal. **abrogation,** *n.*

abruption [ə'brʌpʃn] *n.* breaking off of a piece from a mass.

abscind [æb'sɪnd] *v.t.* cut off; pare.

abscissa [æb'sɪsə] *n.* (*pl.* **-ae**), *Mathematics,* horizontal distance of point from fixed line.

abscissin, abscisin [æb'sɪsɪn] *n.* a plant hormone causing the fall of leaves in autumn.

abscission [æb'sɪʃn] *n.* cutting off; separation, especially of cells at base of leaf-stalk.

absconce [æb'skɒns] *n. Roman Catholic,* dark lantern used in night offices.

abseil ['æbseɪl] *v.i.* descend a vertical face by using a rope.

absentee [ˌæbsn'tiː] *n.* one not present; worker absent from work; *adj.* applied to landlord not living in country from which he derives his rent. **absenteeism,** *n.* practice of such landlords; habitual absence from work.

absente reo [æbˌsenti 'riːəʊ] *(Latin) Law,* 'the defendant being absent' (*abbr.* **abs. re.**).

absinth(e) ['æbsɪnθ] *(French) n.* wormwood; liqueur flavoured with wormwood. **absinthism,** *n.* condition due to excessive consumption of absinthe.

absit omen [ˌæbsɪt 'əʊmen] *(Latin)* 'may there be no evil omen'; may no harm result.

absolutism ['æbsəluːtɪzm] *n.* tyrannical government; principle of autocracy.

absolutory [əb'sɒljutri] *adj.* absolving; forgiving.

absorptiometer [əbˌsɔːpʃi'ɒmɪtə, –ˌzɔː–] *n.* instrument measuring solubility of gases in liquid.

absquatulate [əb'skwɒtʃuleɪt] *v.i. jocular,* decamp.

abstemious [əb'stiːmiəs] *adj.* practising temperance; teetotal.

absterge [æb'stɜːdʒ] *v.t. archaic,* wipe clean; purify. **abstergent,** *adj.* cleansing; *n.* such substance. **abstersion,** *n.*

abstinent ['æbstɪnənt] *adj.* abstemious; fasting. **abstinence,** *n.*

abstruse [æb'struːs] *adj.* esoteric; difficult to understand.

abulia *see* **aboulia**

ab urbe condita [æb ˌɜːbi 'kɒndɪtə] *(Latin)* 'from the foundation of the city' (Rome), in c. 753 BC (*abbr.* **A.U.C.**).

abut [ə'bʌt] *v.i.* & *t.* be adjacent to; lean upon. **abutment,** *n.* supporting part of arch, etc.; part of bridge next to land. **abuttals,** *n. pl.* land or parish boundaries. **abutter,** *n.* proprietor of premises adjacent.

aby(e) [ə'baɪ] *v.t. archaic,* pay penalty of; atone for.

abyssal [ə'bɪsl] *adj. Biology,* more than 300 fathoms below surface of sea.

academic [ækəd3m'ɪk] *adj.* pertaining to academy; learned; unpractical. **academical,** *adj.* pertaining to university or other academy. **academicals,** *n. pl.* university costume. **academician** [əkædəmɪʃ'ən], *n.* member of academy, especially of Arts. **academism, academicism,** *n.* formalism. .

acajou ['ækəʒuː] *(French) n.* cashew nut and tree; mahogany tree and timber.

acaleph ['ækəlef] *n.* kind of stinging jelly fish.

acantha [ə'kænθə] *n.* spine, spinous fin. **acanthaceous,** *adj.* spiny or prickly.

acanthus [ə'kænθəs] *n.* kind of prickly herbaceous plant, Bear's Breeches; *Architecture,* leaf decoration used on Corinthian capital.

a cappella, a capella [ˌɑː kə'pelə] *adv., adj. Music* (of singing) unaccompanied by instruments.

acariasis [ˌækə'raɪəsɪs] *n.* infestation with mites or ticks; the itch.

acaricide [ə'kærɪsaɪd] *n.* substance killing mites. **acaricidal,** *adj.*

acarpous [eɪ'kɑːpəs] *adj. Botany,* not yielding fruit.

acatalectic [ˌeɪˌkætə'lektɪk] *adj.* metrically complete; *n.* such verse line.

acatalepsy [eɪ'kætəlepsi] *n.* state of being impossible to understand; *Philosophy,* sceptic doctrine that knowledge cannot be certain. **acataleptic,** *adj.*

acaudate [eɪ'kɔːdeɪt] *adj.* lacking tail.

acaulescent [ˌeɪkɔː'lesnt, ˌæ–] *adj.* lacking a stem.

accelerator [ək'seləreɪtə] *n.* in nuclear physics, a device producing a stream of high energy particles and focusing them on a target atom.

accelerometer [əkˌselə'rɒmɪtə] *n.* instrument measuring acceleration.

accensor [æk'sensə] *n. Roman Catholic,* acolyte.

accentor [æk'sentə] *n.* hedge-sparrow or other bird of genus *Prunella*.

acceptance [ək'septəns] *n. Commerce*, agreement to pay bill of exchange when due. **acceptance-house**, merchant banker. **acceptance for honour**, taking up of bill of exchange by person other than drawer to protect honour of party to bill.

acceptilation [æk,septɪ'leɪʃn] *n. Law*, formal acknowledgement that a claim has been satisfied; *Theology*, God's acceptance of Christ's sufferings as complete atonement for sins of humanity.

accessit [æk'sesɪt, æ'kesɪt] *n.* honourable mention of one who comes nearest to a prize.

acciaccatura [ə,tʃækə'tuərə] *n. Music*, very short note played before a longer note; short appoggiatura.

accidence ['æksɪdəns] *n.* science of gram. inflections.

accident ['æksɪdənt] *n. Logic*, non-essential; attribute not included in definition.

accidental [,æksɪ'dentl] *n. Music*, note made temporarily sharp, flat, or natural; sign indicating such a note.

accipiter [æk'sɪpɪtə] *n.* a kind of hawk, one of genus *Accipiter*. **accipitral, accipitrine**, *adj.* like such bird; rapacious.

accismus [æk'sɪzməs] *n.* rhetorical device of pretending to refuse.

acclivity [ə'klɪvɪti] *n.* slope upward. **acclivitous, acclivous**, *adj.*

accolade ['ækəleɪd] *n.* award or honour, praise; ceremony of knighting; *Music*, vertical line coupling staves; *Architecture*, curved moulding.

accolent ['ækələnt] *adj. obsolete* neighbouring.

accommodation [ə,kɒmə'deɪʃn] *n.* adjustment, especially of eye muscles; adaptation; lodgings; loan. **accommodation bill**, bill of exchange co-signed by a guarantor. **accommodation train**, *American*, train stopping at all or most stations.

accouchement [ə'kuːʃmɒn] *n.* childbirth. **accoucheur, accoucheuse**, *n.* male and female midwife respectively

accoutre [ə'kuːtə] *v.t.* equip; clothe. **accoutrements**, *n. pl.* equipment.

accredit [ə'kredɪt] *v.t.* attribute; gain belief for; attach officially.

accrementition [,ækrɪmen'tɪʃn] *n. Biology* growth by addition of similar matter.

accrescent [ə'kresnt] *adj. Botany*, growing larger even after flowering.

accretion [ə'kriːʃn] *n.* growth, especially by addition from outside.

accrue [ə'kruː] *v.i.* increase by growth or addition.

accubation [,ækju'beɪʃn] *n. obsolete* act or state of reclining at table; *Medicine*, accouchement.

acculturation [ə,kʌltʃə'reɪʃn] *n.* transfer or adoption of the cultural patterns of another group. **acculturate**, *v.t.* cause acculturation in.

accumbent [ə'kʌmbənt] *adj. Botany*, (of plants) lying against something.

accumulator [ə'kjuːmjəleɪtə] *n.* in computers, the electronic circuits that perform the calculations.

accusative [ə'kjuːzətɪv] *adj. Grammar*, objective; *n.* such case in declension of nouns.

accusatorial [ə,kjuːzə'tɔːriəl] *adj. Law*, of a system where the judge is not the prosecutor.

aceldama [ə'keldəmə, ə'se–] *n.* field, or scene, of bloodshed.

acephalous [eɪ'sefələs] *adj.* lacking a head or a leader; lacking the first syllable or foot (of a hexameter). **acephalus** (*pl.* **–li**), *n.* foetus lacking a head.

acerate ['æsəreɪt] *see* **acerose**

acerbity [ə'sɜːbəti] *n.* bitterness, especially of feeling. **acerbate**, *v.t.* to embitter; to make sour. **acerbic** *adj.* harsh, bitter; sour.

aceric [ə'serɪk] *adj.* pertaining to the maple.

acerose, acerate ['æsərəʊs, –eɪt] *adj.* like a needle.

acerous [eɪ'sɪərəs] *adj.* without horns or antennae.

acervate [ə'sɜːveɪt] *adj. Botany*, growing in heaps; clustered. **acervation**, *n.* heaping up. **acervuline**, *adj.* like little heaps.

acescent [ə'sesnt] *adj.* becoming, or tending to be, sour. **acescence**, *n.*

acetabulum [,æsɪ'tæbjuləm] *n.* cuplike hollow on hipbone to receive thighbone.

acetarious [,æsɪ'teəriəs] *adj.* applied to plants used in salads.

acetic [ə'siːtɪk] *adj.* sour; of vinegar. **acetic acid, acid of vinegar. acetate** ['æsɪteɪt], *n.* salt of acetic acid, *adj.* treated wih acetic acid.

acetify [ə'setɪfaɪ, ə'siː–] *v.i. & t.* turn or become sour; make into vinegar. **acetification**, *n.*

acetometer, acetimeter [,æsɪ'tɒmɪtə, –'tɪm–] *n.* instrument measuring strength of acetic acid or vinegar. **acetometry**, *n.*

acetone ['æsɪtəʊn] *n.* liquid obtained from maize or wood spirit, used as solvent, in manufacture of chloroform, etc. **acetonaemia**, *n.* presence of acetone in blood.

acetous, acetose ['æsɪtəs, –əʊs] *adj.* sour; of vinegar.

acetyl ['æsɪtaɪl, –tɪl] *n.* the radical of acetic acid. **acetylsalicylic acid**, aspirin.

achar [æ'tʃɑː] (*Anglo-Indian*) *n.* kind of pickles.

a chara [ə'xærə] (*Irish*) salutation, equivalent of *Dear Sir*, in Ireland.

Achates [ə'keɪtiːz] *n.* a faithful friend.

achene [ə'kiːn, eɪ–] *n.* small one-seeded fruit of plant; naked seed.

à cheval [,ɑː ʃə'væl] (*French*) 'on horseback'; astride; straddling.

Achilles [ə'kɪliːz] *n.* ancient Greek hero; mighty soldier. **Achilles heel**, vulnerable spot. **Achilles tendon**, hamstring; tendon between calf and heel.

achlamydeous [,æklə'mɪdiəs] *adj. Botany* having neither petals nor sepals.

acholous [eɪ'kəʊləs, 'ækələs] *adj.* lacking bile.

achondroplasia [,eɪkɒndrə'pleɪziə] *n.* condition where cartilage does not develop normally, resulting in dwarfism.

achor ['eɪkɔː] *n. Medicine*, *archaic*, eruption on the scalp.

achromat ['ækrəmæt] *n.* achromatic lens; colour-blind person. **achromatic** *adj.* non-coloured; free from chromatic aberration; *Music*, having few accidentals. **achromatin**, *n.* liquid plasmic substance in nucleus of cells resistant to staining agents. **achromatize**, *v.t.* **achromatism**, *n.*

achromatopsia, [eɪ,krəʊmə'tɒpsiə] *n.* colour-blindness, where only white, grey and black are visible.

achromia [eɪ'krəʊmɪə] n. Medicine, pallor. **achromic**, adj.

achrous ['ækrəʊəs] adj. colourless.

acicula [ə'sɪkjʊlə] n. a needle-shaped prickle, spine or crystal. **acicular** adj. **aciculate** adj. having bristles or spines; with scratched appearance.

acidimeter, acidometer [,æsɪ'dɪmɪtə, –'dɒm–] n. instrument for measuring amount and strength of acids. **acidimetry**, n.

acidophilic [,æsɪdə'fɪlɪk, ə,sɪd–] n. easily stained by acid dyes; thriving in acid envoironment.

acidosis [,æsɪ'dəʊsɪs] n. Medicine, excessively acid condition of blood and tissues.

acidulous [ə'sɪdjʊləs] adj. sharp or sour in taste or manner. **acidulate**, v.t.

acierage ['æsɪərɪdʒ] n. process of steel-plating. **acierate**, v.t. make into steel.

aciform ['æsɪfɔːm] adj. needle-shaped.

acinaciform [,æsɪ'næsɪfɔːm] adj. having shape of scimitar.

aciniform [ə'sɪnɪfɔːm] adj. shaped like cluster of grapes; full of seeds, like a grape.

acinous, acinose ['æsɪnəs, –əʊs] adj. containing small seeds or drupes.

acipenser [,æsɪ'pensə] n. sturgeon.

aclastic [ə'klæstɪk] adj. non-refractive.

aclinic [eɪ'klɪnɪk] adj. applied to line passing through all points where there is no magnetic inclination. **aclinic line** magnetic equator.

acology [æ'kɒlədʒi] n. science of medical remedies.

acomia [eɪ'kəʊmɪə] n. baldness.

aconite ['ækənaɪt] n. the monk's-hood or wolf's-bane plant.

aconitine [æ'kɒnɪtiːn, –ɪn] n. poisonous alkaloid obtained from aconite.

acopic [eɪ'kɒpɪk] n. & adj. Medicine, curative of fatigue.

acor ['eɪkɔː] n. Medicine, stomach acidity.

à corps perdu [ɑː ,kɔː peə'duː] (French) 'with lost body'; impetuously; in desperation.

acosmism [ə'kɒzmɪzm] n. doctrine denying existence of universe distinct from God. **acosmist**, n.

acotyledon [,eɪkɒtɪ'liːdn] n. plant without differentiated seed lobes. **acotyledonous** [–'ledənəs, –'liː–], adj.

acoumeter [æ'kuːmiːtə] n. instrument measuring keenness of hearing. **acoumetry**, n.

à coup sûr [ɑː ,ku: 'sjʊə] (French) 'with sure stroke'; certainly.

acousma [ə'kuːzmə] n. ringing noise in head.

acoustic [ə'kuːstɪk] adj. pertaining to the hearing, to sound and its transmission; worked by sound or echoes. **acoustician** [–'tɪʃn], n. expert in acoustics. **acoustics**, n. science of sound laws; properties of audibility of a building.

acquire [ə'kwaɪə] v.t. obtain; gain; come into possession of. **acquired immune deficiency syndrome**, AIDS. **acquired taste**, (liking eventually gained for) something that is not immediately or generally liked. **acquisition**, n. act of acquiring; thing acquired; process of locating by radar, etc., or of re-establishing contact with, a spacecraft, satellite, etc. **acquisitive**, adj. eager to acquire (material possessions).

acquittance [ə'kwɪtns] n. payment of, or release from, debt; full receipt.

acrasy ['ækrəsi] n. obsolete, anarchy, disorder.

acratia [ə'kreɪʃɪə] n. impotence.

acriflavine [,ækrɪ'fleɪviːn] n. a brown-red hydrochloride antiseptic for wounds.

acrimonious [,ækrɪ'məʊnɪəs] adj. bitter; caustic; angry. **acrimony** ['ækrɪməni], n.

acritochromacy [ə,krɪtə'krəʊməsi] n. colour-blindness.

acroamatic [,ækrəʊə'mætɪk] adj. esoteric, told only orally.

acrocephalous, acrocephalic [,ækrə'sefələs, –sɪ'fælɪk] adj. having pointed skull. **acrocephaly** n.

acrodont ['ækrədɒnt] adj. (of a tooth) fused with the jaw; having such teeth.

acrogen ['ækrədʒen, –ən] n. Botany, any flowerless plant where growth takes place at the tip of the main stem. **acrogenous** [–'rɒdʒ–] adj.

acrolith ['ækrəlɪθ] n. statue with wooden trunk and stone head and extremities.

acrologic [,ækrə'lɒdʒɪk] adj. pertaining to initials.

acromegaly [,ækrə'megəli] n. gigantism; enlargement of extremities, head, jaw, etc., due to excess secretion of pituitary gland. **acromegalic**, adj.

acromonogrammatic [,ækrə,mɒnəgrə'mætɪk] adj. applied to verse in which each line begins with letter with which preceding line ended.

acronychal, acronycal, [ə'krɒnɪkl] adj. Astronomy, happening at sunset, especially of star whose rising is at sunset.

acronyx ['ækrənɪks] n. ingrowing nail.

acrophobia [,ækrə'fəʊbɪə] n. dread of heights.

acropolis [ə'krɒpəlɪs] n. fortified elevated part of city, especially of Athens.

acroscopic [,ækrə'skɒpɪk] adj. Botany, facing, or moving to, apex.

acrospire ['ækrə,spaɪə] n. the first real shoot developing in a germinating grain seed.

acroteleutic [,ækrəʊtɪ'ljuːtɪk, –'luː–] n. end of psalm; words added to end of psalm; doxology.

acroter [ə'krəʊtə] n. **acroterion**.

acroteric [,ækrə'terɪk] adj. pertaining to or affecting the extremities.

acroterion [,ækrə'tɪərɪən] n. (pl. **–ria**) Architecture, ornament or its pedestal at angle of pediment.

acrotic [ə'krɒtɪk] adj. pertaining to surface. **acrotism** ['æk–], n. failure of pulse.

actamer ['æktəmə] n. a substance preventing the growth of bacteria in cosmetics and soaps.

actin ['æktɪn] n. a protein found in most cells, especially in muscle. **actinide** n. one of a series of 15 consecutive radio-active elements.

actinism ['æktɪnɪzm] n. property of solar radiation of causing chemical change. **actinic**, adj.; **actinic glass**, glass opaque to actinic rays.

actinium [æk'tɪnɪəm] n. rare radio-active element.

actino-chemistry [,æktɪnəʊ'kemɪstri] n. chemical study of actinism; photo-chemistry.

actinograph [æk'tɪnəgrɑːf] n. instrument for calculating time of photographic exposures.

actinoid ['æktɪnɔɪd] adj. star-shaped; like rays.

actinology [,æktɪ'nɒlədʒi] n. science of chemical effects of light.

actinometer [,æktɪ'nɒmɪtə] n. instrument measuring heating power of the sun's rays; Photography, instrument for calculating exposure times. **actinometry**, n.

actinomorphic,   **actinomorphous**

[ˌæktɪnə'mɔːfɪk, –əs] *adj. Botany*, having symmetrically radiated shape.

actinomycin [ˌæktɪnə'maɪsɪn] *n.* antibiotic produced by a soil fungus.

actinomycosis [ˌæktɪnəmaɪ'kəusɪs] *n.* parasitic disease in men and cattle resulting in inflammation of jaw; 'lumpy jaw'.

actinophone [æk'tɪnəfəun] *n.* instrument in which sound is produced by actinic rays. **actinophonic** [–'fɒnɪk], *adj.*

actinotherapy [ˌæktɪnə'θerəpi] *n.* use of ultraviolet and other actinic rays in medical treatment.

actuary ['æktʃuəri] *n.* expert on insurance statistics and tables of expectation of life. **actuarial**, *adj.*

actuate ['æktʃueɪt] *v.t.* set a machine etc. in motion; be the motive for.

actum ut supra [ˌæktəm ʊt 'suːprə, –ɑː] (*Latin*) 'done as above' (*abbreviatted as* **a.u.s.**).

aculeate [ə'kjuːliət, –ieɪt] *adj. Botany*, bearing many sharp points; *Zoology*, having sting; incisive.

aculeiform [ə'kjuːliɪfɔːm] *adj.* thorn-shaped.

acumen ['ækjumən, ə'kjuː–, –men] *n.* quickness to perceive; shrewdness.

acuminate [ə'kjuːmɪnət, –eɪt] *adj.* pointed; tapering; *v.t.* sharpen; *v.i.* end in point.

acuminulate [ˌækju'mɪnjulət] *adj.* very sharply pointed; ending in minute point.

acupressure ['ækjuːˌpreʃə] *n.* pressing needle across blood vessel to stop haemorrhage.

acushla [ə'kuːʃlə] (*Irish*) *n.* term of address: darling.

acutorsion ['ækjuˌtɔːʃn] *n.* twisting artery with needle to stop bleeding.

acyanopsia [ˌeɪsaɪə'nɒpsiə] *n.* colour blindness towards blue.

acyclic [eɪ'sɪklɪk, –'saɪk–] *adj.* not cyclic: *Botany*, not arranged in whorls; *Chemistry*, not containing a ring of atoms in its molecular structure (of chemical compounds).

acyrology [ˌæsɪ'rɒlədʒi] *n. obsolete*, incorrect diction.

adactylous [ædæk'tɪləs] *adj.* lacking fingers, toes or claws. **adactylia** [eɪdæktɪl'ɪə, æd–], *n.* congenital lack of toes or fingers.

adamant ['ædəmənt] *n.* exceptionally hard substance; *adj.* impenetrable; immovable. **adamantine** [–'mæntaɪn], *adj.*

adaxial [æd'æksiəl] *adj.* on, beside, or turned towards, axis of an organ, organism, or plant.

ad captandum (vulgus) [æd kæp'tændəm, 'vʌlgəs] (*Latin*) 'to capture' the affection or suit the taste (of the crowd).

addendum [ə'dendəm] *n.* (*pl.* **–da**), something added; appendix.

addio [ə'diːəu] (*Italian*) adieu.

additament [ə'dɪtəmənt] *n.* thing added.

addititious [ˌædɪ'tɪʃəs] *adj.* pertaining to, or resulting from, addition; *Astronomy*, applied to force increasing gravitation between planet and satellite.

additive ['ædətɪv] *adj.* pertaining to addition; *Grammar*, signifying addition of similar elements or of new thought; *Philosophy*, marked by addition rather than union; *n.* something added.

address [ə'dres] *n.* in computers, a character or symbol designating a location where information is stored.

adduce [ə'djuːs] *v.t.* bring forward as evidence. **adducent**, *adj.* drawing towards.

adduct, [ə'dʌkt] *v.t.* (of muscles) draw towards a central axis. **adductor** *n.* such a muscle.

adeciduate [ˌeɪdɪ'sɪdjueɪt] *adj.* evergreen.

adelphogamy [ˌædəl'fɒgəmi] *n.* form of marriage in which brothers share a wife or wives.

ademonist [eɪ'diːmənɪst] *n.* person denying existence of demons or the Devil.

ademption [ə'dempʃn] *n. Law*, revoking by testator, donor, etc., of legacy, donation, etc., by previously paying sum or parting with object bequeathed.

adenia [æ'diːniə] *n. Medicine*, enlargement of glands.

adeniform [æ'denɪfɔːm] *adj.* gland-shaped.

adenitis [ˌædɪ'naɪtɪs] *n.* inflammation of glands.

adenoid ['ædɪnɔɪd] *adj.* pertaining to or like gland. **adenoids,** *n. pl.* enlargement of lymphatic tissues at back of throat.

adenology [ˌædɪ'nɒlədʒi] *n.* study of glands. **adenological**, *adj.*

adenoma [ˌædɪ'nəumə] *n.* usually non-lethal tumour of gland. **adenomatous**, *adj.*

adenopathy [ˌædɪ'nɒpəθi] *n.* glandular disease.

adenose ['ædɪnəus] *adj.* gland-like; having many glands.

adenotomy [ˌædɪ'nɒtəmi] *n.* incision into or removal of gland.

adenovirus ['ædɪnəuˌvaɪrəs] *n.* any of several cold-causing viruses.

adephagous [æ'defəgəs] *adj. Medicine*, having morbid appetite for food.

adespoton [ə'despətən] *n.* anonymous saying, poem, etc.

ad eundem (gradum) [æd eɪ'ʊndəm, –iː'ʌn–; 'grɑːdəm, 'greɪ–] (*Latin*) (admitted) 'to same' degree at different university.

à deux [ɑ: 'dɜ:] (*French*) 'for two only'; *Music*, for two hands.

adevism ['ædɪvɪzm] *n.* denial of legendary gods.

ad finem [æd 'fiːnem, –'faɪn–] (*Latin*) 'to the end' (*abbr.* **ad fin.**).

ad hanc vocem [æd ˌhæŋk 'vəukem] 'to this word' (*abbr.* **a.h.v**).

adherent [əd'hɪərənt] *n.* supporter, follower (of a cause, etc.).

adhibit [æd'hɪbɪt] *v.t.* grant admitance to; apply; attach.

ad hoc [ˌæd 'hɒk] (*Latin*) 'to this'; for the present purpose alone; not provable by reference to other phenomena.

ad hominem [æd 'hɒmɪnem] (*Latin*) 'to the man'; appealing to prejudice or passions; illogical.

ad hunc locum [æd ˌhʊŋk 'lɒkəm, –ˌhʌŋk 'ləu–] (*Latin*) *Law*, 'at this place'; on this passage (*abbr.* **ad loc. ; a.h.l.**).

adiabatic [ˌædiə'bætɪk, ˌeɪdaɪə–] *adj.* without losing or gaining heat. **adiabatic gradient**, rate of change in temperature of rising or falling air.

adiabolist [ˌeɪdaɪ'æbəlɪst] *n.* person denying existence of the Devil.

adiactinic [ˌeɪdaɪæk'tɪnɪk] *adj.* not transmitting actinic rays.

adiaphoresis [ˌædiæfə'riːsɪs, ˌeɪdaɪə–] *n.* absence or lack of perspiration. **adiaphoretic** [–'retɪk], *n* & *adj.* (drug) preventing perspiration.

adiaphoron [ˌædiˈæfərɒn] *n.* (*pl.* **-ra**), matter of indifference; *Theology*, religious observance left to conscience; amoral matter. **adiaphorism**, *n.* belief in doctrine of adiaphora. **adiaphorist**, *n.* **adiaphoristic**, *adj.* applied to certain controversies on religious observances. **adiaphorous**, *adj.* neutral; indifferent, neither right nor wrong (of conduct, etc.)

adiapneustia [ˌædiæpˈnjuːstiə, ˌeɪdaɪ–] *n.* defective perspiration.

adiathermic [ˌædiəˈθɜːmɪk, ˌeɪdaɪ–] *adj.* impervious to heat. **adiathermancy**, *n.*

adient [ˈædiənt] *adj.* tending to expose an organism to, or turn it towards, a stimulus or situation.

ad infinitum [æd ˌɪnfɪˈnaɪtəm] (*Latin*) 'to infinity'; for ever; without limit (*abbr.* **ad inf.**).

ad interim [æd ˈɪntərɪm] (*Latin*) 'at interval'; meanwhile; for the present (*abbr.* **ad int.**).

adios [ˌædiˈɒs, –ˈəʊs] (*Spanish*) adieu.

adipescent [ˌædɪˈpesnt] *adj.* becoming fatty.

adipic [əˈdɪpɪk] *adj.* *Chemistry*, pertaining to fatty or greasy substance.

adipocere [ˈædɪpəʊsiə] *n.* fatty substance occurring in dead bodies in moist places. **adipocerous**, *adj.*

adipose [ˈædɪpəʊs] *adj.* fat, fatty. **adipose tissue**, connective fat-storing tissue. **adiposis**, *n.* fatness; fatty degeneration. **adiposity**, *n.*

adipsy, [ˈædɪpsi] *n.* lack of thirst. **adipsous**, *adj.* *Medicine*, quenching thirst.

adit [ˈædɪt] *n.* entrance, especially horizontal passage into mine.

adjunct [ˈædʒʌŋkt] *n.* an addition that is not essential.

adjutator [ˈædʒuteɪtə] *n.* helper.

adjuvant [ˈædʒuvənt] *adj.* helping; *Medicine*, remedial; *n.* such drug.

ad libitum [æd ˈlɪbɪtəm] (*Latin*) 'at one's pleasure'; as much or long as desired; *Music*, according to desire of performer (*abbr.* **ad lib.**). **ad-lib** [–ˈlɪb] *v.i.* & *t.* speak impromptu, especially (of actors) jokes, words, etc., not written or rehearsed, or to replace forgotten lines; *adj.* said on the spur of the moment; *n.* an ad-lib statement.

ad locum [æd ˈlɒkəm, –ˈləʊ–] (*Latin*) 'at the place' (*abbr.* **ad loc.**)

admaxillary [ˌædmækˈsɪləri] *adj.* near or connected with jaw.

admeasurement [ædˈmeʒəmənt] *n.* act or result of measuring; apportionment; dimensions.

admensuration [ˌædmenʃəˈreɪʃn] *n.* admeasurement.

adminicle [ædˈmɪnɪkl] *n.* *Law*, aid; support; corroboration; *Numismatics*, ornament round figure on coin. **adminicular** [–ˈnɪkjʊlə], *adj.* **adminiculate** [–ˈnɪkjuleɪt], *v.t.* corroborate.

admonish [ədˈmɒnɪʃ] *v.t.* reprove gently. **admonition**, *n.*

adnate [ˈædneɪt] *adj.* *Botany* closely attached; related; grown together especially unusually. **adnation**, *n.*

ad nauseam [æd ˈnɔːziæm, –ˈnɔːs–] (*Latin*) 'to nausea'; until disgust is felt.

adnominal [ædˈnɒmɪnl] *adj.* (of noun) functioning as adj.

adnomination [ˌædnɒmɪˈneɪʃn] *n.* *obsolete* punning.

adnoun [ˈædnaʊn] *n.* adjective used as noun.

adobe [əˈdəʊbi] *n.* unburnt sundried brick; dwelling of adobe; clay used for adobe; *adj.* built of adobe.

Adonic [əˈdɒnɪk] *adj.* pertaining to Adonis; applied to metrical foot comprising a dactyl followed by a spondee or trochee.

adonize [ˈædənaɪz] *v.i.* & *t.* ornament; adorn oneself (of men).

adoptionism [əˈdɒpʃn–ɪzm] *n.* doctrine that Christ was Son of God by adoption and not birth. **adoptionist**, *n.* & *adj.*

adoral [ædˈɔːrəl] *adj.* near to mouth.

adosculation [ædˌɒskjuˈleɪʃn] *n.* sexual impregnation by contact only; wind-pollination.

adoxography [ˌædɒkˈsɒɡrəfi] *n.* *Literature*, fine writing on trivial or base subject.

adrectal [ædˈrektl] *adj.* close to rectum.

ad rem [æd ˈrem] (*Latin*) 'to the thing'; to the purpose; pertinent.

adrenal [əˈdriːnl] *adj.* close to kidney; suprarenal, especially applied to ductless glands above kidneys.

adrenalin(e) [əˈdrenəlɪn] *n.* hormone of adrenal gland; preparation from such secretion or synthetic drug used as haemostatic and heart stimulant.

adrenergic [ˌædrəˈnɜːdʒɪk] *adj.* released or activated by adrenalin.

adscititious [ˌædsɪˈtɪʃəs] *adj.* supplementary; auxiliary.

adsorb [ædˈsɔːb, –ˈzɔːb] *v.t.* attract and hold to surface (minute particles of mixture or molecules of gas or liquid). **adsorbate** *n.* substance or molecules adsorbed. **adsorbent**, *n.* & *adj.* (substance) adsorbing. **adsorption**, *n.*

adsum [ˈædsʊm, –sʌm] (*Latin*) 'I am present'.

adulation [ˌædjuˈleɪʃn] *n.* excessive flattery; abject worship. **adulatory**, *adj.*

adumbral [əˈdʌmbrəl] *adj.* shadowy.

adumbrate [ˈædʌmbreɪt] *v.t.* shadow forth; outline; sketch out. **adumbrative**, *adj.* **adumbration**, *n.*

aduncous, aduncate [əˈdʌŋkəs, –ət] *adj.* hookshaped; crooked. **aduncity** [əˈdʌnsəti] *n.* inward curvature.

ad unguem [æd ˈʌŋɡwem, –ˈʊŋ–] (*Latin*) 'to the finger nail'; to a nicety; with great exactitude; to minute detail.

adust [əˈdʌst] *adj.* *archaic*, (sun) burnt or scorched; dried up by heat; gloomy, sad.

ad usum [æd ˈjuːsəm, –ˈuːs–] (*Latin*) 'to usage'; according to custom (abbr. **ad us.**)

ad valorem [ˌæd vəˈlɔːrem] *adj.* in proportion to value, especially of import duties of a percentage of the value of the imports (*abbreviated as* **ad val.**).

advection [ædˈvekʃn] *n.* horizontal movement of an air mass, causing temperature changes.

advehent [ˈædviənt] *adj.* afferent.

advenient [ædˈviːniənt] *adj.* due to outside causes. **advenience**, *n.*

adventitious [ˌædvenˈtɪʃəs] *adj.* *Medicine, Botany*, added from without; not essential; accidental; casual; acquired; adventive.

adventive [ædˈventɪv] *n.* & *adj.* *Botany*, (plant) not completely naturalized or growing out of natural habitat.

ad verbum [æd 'vɜːbəm] (*Latin*) 'to the word'; word for word.

adversaria [ˌædvə'seəriə] *n. pl.* collection of notes and comments; commonplace book.

adversative [æd'vɜːsətɪv] *n.* & *adj. Grammar*, (word or clause) expressing opposition or antithesis.

ad vitam aut culpam [æd ˌviːtæm aut 'kʊlpæm, –ˌvaɪtæm ɔːt 'kʌl–] (*Latin*) 'to life or misdeed'; so long as good behaviour lasts.

advowee [æd'vaʊiː] *n.* ecclesiastical patron; holder of advowson.

advowson [əd'vaʊzn] *n.* the right to present a clergyman to a church living.

adynamic [ˌeɪdaɪ'næmɪk] *adj.* lacking strength; causing weakness. **adynamia** [–'neɪmiə].

adytum ['ædɪtəm] *n.* inner sanctuary of temple; secret room.

adz(e) [ædz] *n.* axe with rounded blade set at right angles to handle.

aedile ['iːdaɪl] *n.* head of ancient Roman office of works. **aedility** [iː'dɪləti] *n.* aedile's office.

aedoeology [ˌiːdi'ɒlədʒi] *n.* study of generative organs.

aegagrus [iː'gægrəs] *n.* mountain goat of Asia Minor.

aegilops ['iːdʒɪlɒps] *n.* stye in inner corner of eye.

aegis ['iːdʒɪs] *n.* protection; shield, especially of classical gods; sponsorship, auspices.

aegrotat ['aɪgrəʊtæt, 'iː–] (*Latin*) *n.* 'he or she is ill'; certificate of student's illness for absence from university lectures or examination. **aegrotat degree,** degree given to student absent from examination by reason of illness.

aeneous [eɪ'iːniəs] *adj.* like brass.

Aeolian [iː'əʊliən] *adj.* pertaining to Aeolus, god of the winds; carried or caused by wind. **Aeolian harp** musical instrument played by wind.

aeolipyle, aeolipile [iː'ɒlɪpaɪl] *n.* first steam engine, with globe made to revolve by steam jets, described in 1st century AD.

aeolistic [ˌiːəʊ'lɪstɪk] *adj.* long-winded.

aeolotropic [ˌiːələ'trɒpɪk] *adj.* having different physical properties in different positions or directions.

aeon ['iːən] *n.* immeasurably long period of time; *Geology* unit of time equal to a thousand million years.

aepyornis [ˌiːpi'ɔːnɪs] *n.* large fossil bird of Madagascar.

aere perennius [ˌaɪri pə'reniəs] (*Latin*) 'more lasting than brass'.

aeriform ['eərɪfɔːm] *adj.* lacking substance, unreal; gaseous.

aerobe, aerobium ['eərəʊb] *n.* (*pl.* **–bia**) organism growing only in presence of oxygen. **aerobic,** *adj.* **aerobiosis,** *n.* such growth or existence.

aerobiology [ˌeərəʊbaɪ'ɒlədʒi] *n.* the biology of airborne particles and organisms.

aerodonetics [ˌeərədə'netɪks] *n.* science of gliding.

aerodynamics [ˌeərəʊdaɪ'næmɪks] *n.* science of forces acting on bodies in motion in air.

aerodyne ['eərədaɪn] *n.* heavier-than-air aircraft kept up by its movement through air.

aerofoil, airfoil ['eərəfɔɪl] *n.* section through aircraft wing, etc.

aerogel ['eərədʒel] *n.* a gel in which the liquid is replaced by a gas.

aerogenic [ˌeərə'dʒenɪk] *adj.* derived from air; gas-forming. **aerogenesis,** *n.*

aerolite, aerolith ['eərəlaɪt, –lɪθ] *n.* meteorite.

aerology [eə'rɒlədʒi] *n.* study of physical properties of atmosphere, especially meteorological.

aeromancy ['eərəmænsi] *n.* divination by the state of the air; weather forecasting. **aeromantic**, *adj.*

aeromechanics [ˌeərəʊmɪ'kænɪks] *n.* science of mechanical properties of gases.

aerometer [eə'rɒmɪtə] *n.* instrument measuring weight or density of gases. **aerometry** *n.* such measurement; pneumatics.

aeronomy [eə'rɒnəmi] *n.* study of chemical and physical phenomena in the upper atmosphere. **aeronomic** [–'nɒmɪk], *adj.*

aeropause ['eərəpɔːz] *n.* level above surface of earth above which ordinary aircraft cannot fly.

aerophagia [ˌeərə'feɪdʒiə] *n.* neurotic habit of swallowing air.

aerophilately [ˌeərəʊfɪ'lætəli] *n.* collecting of airmail stamps and covers.

aerophobia [ˌeərə'fəʊbiə] *n.* fear of air, draughts.

aerophore ['eərəfɔː] *n.* apparatus for inflating lungs, especially of still-born child.

aerophyte ['eərəfaɪt] *n.* plant obtaining all nourishment from the air; epiphyte.

aeropleustic [ˌeərə'pluːstɪk] *adj.* pertaining to aerial navigation.

aeroscopy [eə'rɒskəpi] *n.* observation of varying air conditions.

aerose ['ɪərəʊs] *adj.* brassy.

aerospace ['eərəʊspeɪs] *n.* the Earth's atmosphere and space beyond it.

aerosphere ['eərəsfɪə] *n.* the entire atmosphere surrounding the Earth.

aerostat ['eərəstæt] *n.* lighter-than-air craft. **aerostatic** *adj.* **aerostatics** *n.* science of gases in equilibrium. **aerostation** *n.* navigation of aerostats.

aerotherapeutics [ˌeərəʊθerə'pjuːtɪks] *n.* medical treatment by modifying atmospheric pressure.

aerotrain ['eərəʊtreɪn] *n.* a monorail vehicle operated on principle of hovercraft.

aerugo [ɪ'ruːɡəʊ] *n.* rust, especially of copper and brass; verdigris. **aeruginous** [–'ruːdʒ–], *adj.*

aesculaceous [ˌiːskju'leɪʃəs] *adj.* pertaining to or like horse-chestnut; belonging to the horse-chestnut family of plants.

aesthesia [iːs'θiːziə] *n.* sensibility, sense perception.

aesthesiogenic [iːs,θiːziə'dʒenɪk] *adj.* causing sensation.

aesthesiometer [iːs,θiːzi'ɒmɪtə] *n.* instrument measuring acuteness of sense perception.

aesthesis [iːs'θiːsɪs] *n.* sense perception, aesthesia.

aesthete ['iːsθiːt] *n.* lover of beauty, especially to an exaggerated degree.

aesthetic [iːs'θetɪk] *adj.* pertaining to beauty or appreciation of beauty, or to pure sensation; *n.* science of aesthetic experience. **aestheticism,** *n. Philosophy*, doctrine that principle of beauty is alone fundamental. **aesthetics,** *n.* department of phil. dealing with beauty.

aestival ['iːstɪvl, 'es–, ɪ'staɪvl] *adj.* of summer. **aestivation,** *n. Zoology*, sleepiness in animals during summer; *Botany*, arrangement of organs in flower bud.

aetat, aet ['iːtæt, iːt] (*Latin*) *abbreviation* of **aetatis**, *abbreviation* of **anno aetatis suae**, 'in the year of his or her age'; aged.

aether, *see* **ether.**

aetherial *see* **etherial**

aetiology, etiology [,iːti'ɒlədʒi] *n.* science of causes of natural phenomena. **etiological,** *adj.*

afebrile [eɪ'fiːbraɪl] *adj.* free from fever.

affect [ə'fekt, 'æfekt] *v.t.* have an effect on; influence; move emotionally; (of disease, etc.) attack; damage; make a show or pretence of; adopt the manner or pose of; show a preference for; ['æfekt] *n. Psychology,* emotion, especially as it leads to action (*as opposed to* **effect**). **affectation** [,æfek'teɪʃn], *n.* behaviour, attitude, etc. adopted for effect; pretence. **affected** [ə'fektɪd], *adj.* unnatural; pretentious; contrived. **affecting,** *adj.* touching.

afferent ['æfərənt] *adj.* carrying towards, especially of nerves carrying impulses to centres.

affiche [æ'fiːʃ] (*French*) *n.* poster; placard.

affidavit [,æfɪ'deɪvɪt] *n.* written statement made on oath.

affiliate [ə'fɪlieɪt] *v.t.* attach to; adopt into; unite; fix paternity of or on. **affiliation,** *n.*

affinal [æ'faɪnl] *adj.* related by marriage.

affined [ə'faɪnd] *adj.* closely related; connected.

affinity [ə'fɪnəti] *n.* close relationship; attraction; resemblance; *Law,* relationship by marriage; *Chemistry,* force causing elements to combine.

affirmation [,æfə'meɪʃn] *n. Law,* solemn declaration by person who refuses to take the oath for reasons of conscience. **affirmant,** *n.* person making affirmation.

affix ['æfɪks] *n.* element attached to or inserted in a word, such as a prefix or suffix.

afflatus [ə'fleɪtəs] *n.* divine breath; inspiration. **afflation,** *n.* act of breathing upon; inspiration.

affluent ['æfluənt] *adj. n.* tributary to a river.

afflux ['æflʌks] *n.* flowing towards or together.

affranchise [ə'fræntʃaɪz] *v.t.* liberate from servitude, debt etc.

affreightment [ə'freɪtmənt] *n.* hiring of a ship to carry freight; such a contract.

affricate ['æfrɪkeɪt] *v.t.* rub; grate on; [–ət], *n. Phonetics,* sound, as [tʃ] or [dʒ], comprising a stop developing into a fricative. **affrication,** *n.* **affricative** *n., adj.*

affusion [ə'fjuːʒn] *n.* pouring liquid on, especially in baptismal ceremony or as medical treatment.

aficionado [ə,fɪʃiə'nɑːdəʊ] (*Spanish*) *n.* keen follower of sport; 'fan'.

aflatoxin [,æflə'tɒksɪn] *n.* a toxin produced by a mould on cereals, peanuts, etc.

à fond [ɑː 'fɒn] (*French*) 'to the bottom'; thoroughly.

a fortiori [,eɪ fɔːti'ɔːraɪ, –ʃi'ɔːri] (*Latin*) 'by the stronger'; with better reason; all the more.

afreet ['æfriːt, ə'friːt] *n.* in Arabian mythology, an evil spirit or giant monster.

afrormosia [,æfrɔː'məʊziə] *n.* a dense tropical hardwood resembling teak, used for furniture and panelling.

afterbirth ['ɑːftəbɜːθ] *n.* membrane covering foetus, expelled after birth.

afterdamp ['ɑːftədæmp] *n.* poisonous gas (mixture of carbon dioxide and nitrogen) remaining after explosion of fire-damp in mine; chokedamp.

aga, agha ['ɑːgə] (*Turkish*) *n.* religious leader in Mohammedan community; Turkish chief.

agalactia [,eɪgə'lækʃiə] *n. Medicine,* absence or lack of milk secretion. **agalactic, agalactous,** *adj.*

agami ['ægəmi] *n.* crane-like bird of S America: 'the trumpeter'.

agamic, agamous [ə'gæmɪk, 'ægəməs] *adj.* nonsexual

agamogenesis [,ægəməʊ'dʒenɪsɪs, ,eɪgæm–] *n.* non-sexual reproduction. **agamogenetic** [–dʒə'netɪk], *adj.*

agamy ['ægəmi] *n.* lack of marriage or sexual reproduction.

agape ['ægəpi] *n.* 'love-feast', an early Christian ceremony commemorating the Last Supper.

agar-agar [,eɪgər'eɪgə] (*Malay*) *n.* nutritive jelly obtained from sea-weeds; sea-weed yielding this.

agaric ['ægərɪk, ə'gærɪk] *n.* species of mushroom-like fungus. **agariciform** [–'rɪs–], *adj.* mushroomshaped.

agathism ['ægəθɪzm] *n.* doctrine that ultimate end of all things is good, though means may be evil. **agathist,** *n.*

agave [ə'geɪvi, ə'gɑːvi] *n.* several tropical American fibre-yielding plants; American aloe.

agenesis [eɪ'dʒenəsɪs] *n.* incomplete development of body or part of body. **agenesic** [–'nesɪk], *adj.*

ageotropic [,eɪdʒiə'trɒpɪk] *adj. Botany,* turning away from the earth; apogeotropic.

ageustia [ə'gjuːstiə] *n. Medicine,* absence of sense of taste.

agger ['ægə] *n.* earth rampart or bank, especially Roman.

aggeration [,ædʒə'reɪʃn] *n.* heaping up; mound raised by prehistoric people when erecting standing stones. **aggerose,** *adj.* in heaps; having many heaps.

aggiornamento [ə,dʒɔːnə'mentəʊ] (*Italian*) *n. Roman Catholic,* act or process of bringing up to date.

agglomerate [ə'glɒməreɪt] *v.i. & t.* collect, especially into a mass; *adj.* so collected; clustered; *n. Geology,* rock comprised of angular volcanic fragments.

agglutinate [ə'gluːtɪneɪt] *v.i. & t.* join firmly; thicken; make like glue; coagulate; *Philology,* make compound words by additions. **agglutinin,** *n.* substance in blood causing coagulation. **agglutinogen,** *n.* substance causing production of agglutinin. **agglutinative,** *adj.* applied to agglutinated words or languages containing many such words. **agglutination,** *n.*

agio ['ædʒiəʊ] *n.* charge made when cash is given for paper currency, or one currency is exchanged for another. **agiotage,** *n.* such exchange; speculation; brokerage.

agist [ə'dʒɪst] *v.t. Law,* care for, feed cattle, horses, for payment. **agistment,** *n.* this practice; pastureland available for this.

aglet, aiglet ['æglɪt] *n.* metal tag on lace or as adornment; *Botany,* catkin.

agley [ə'gleɪ, ə'glaɪ] (*Scottish*) *adv.* awry, askew.

aglossal, aglossate [eɪ'glɒsl, –eɪt] *adj. Zoology,* lacking tongue.

aglutition [,eɪglu'tɪʃn] *n.* state of being unable

to swallow.

agminate ['ægmɪnət] *adj*. grouped.

agnail ['ægneɪl] *n*. 'hangnail'; sore at the nail; whitlow.

agnate ['ægneɪt] *adj*. having same male forefather; allied; *Law*, related on father's side; *n*. such relative. **agnation** [æg'neɪʃn], *n*. kinship.

agnathous ['ægnəθəs] *adj*. lacking jaws. **agnathia** [æg'neɪθiə], *n*.

agnomen [æg'nəʊmen] *n*. additional name. **agnomination**, *n*. surname; punning; alliteration.

agnosia [æg'nəʊziə] *n*. loss of ability to recognize familiar things or people.

agnostic [æg'nɒstɪk] *n*. one who denies that there can be any knowledge of God or of supernatural things; *adj*. pertaining to agnostics; non-dogmatic. **agnosticism** [-sɪzm], *n*.

agomphious [ə'gɒmfiəs] *adj*. toothless.

agon ['ægən] *n*. struggle, contest (especially athletic); conflict between main characters in a play, novel etc. **agonist**, *n*. competitor; protagonist in literary work. **agonistic**, *adj*., competitive; striving for effect.

agonic [eɪ'gɒnɪk] *adj*. applied to line drawn through all places where magnetic north is the same as true north.

agoraphobia [ˌægərə'fəʊbiə] *n*. morbid fear of open spaces.

agouti [ə'guːti] *n*. guinea-pig-like S American rodent; *adj*. having the brownish, grizzled colour of the agouti.

agraffe [ə'græf] *n*. hook, especially on pianostring to prevent rattle.

agranulocytosis [əˌgrænjʊləʊsaɪ'təʊsɪs] *n*. a serious blood disease marked by great reduction in the non-granular leucocytes.

agraphia [eɪ'græfiə, æ-] *n*. inability to write due to form of aphasia.

agrarian [ə'greəriən] *adj*. pertaining to agriculture and the land; *n*. believer in a policy of equal distribution of land. **agrarianism**, *n*. such policy.

agrestial [ə'grestiəl] *adj*. growing in country, fields (especially of weeds).

agrestic, [ə'grestɪk] *adj*. of the countryside; rustic, uncouth.

agricolist [ə'grɪkəlɪst] *n. obsolete*, farmer. **agricolous**, *adj*. agricultural.

agriology [ˌægri'ɒlədʒi] *n*. study of customs of primitive peoples.

agrobiology [ˌægrəʊbaɪ'ɒlədʒi] *n*. biology of crop-plants in relation to soil control.

agrology [ə'grɒlədʒi] *n*. scientific study of soils. **agrological**, *adj*.

agronomy [ə'grɒnəmi] *n*. scientific management of land, especially of raising of crops. **agronomic** [ˌægrə'nɒmɪk], *adj*.

agrostology [ˌægrə'stɒlədʒi] *n. Botany*, study of grasses. **agrostologic(al)**, *adj*. **agrostologist**, *n*. **agrostography**, *n*. description of grasses.

agrypnia [ə'grɪpniə] *n*. sleeplessness. **agrypnotic** [-'nɒtɪk], *n*. & *adj*. (stimulant) causing wakefulness.

aguardiente [ˌægwɑː'di'enti] *n*. strong Sp. brandy distilled from potatoes, etc.

agynary ['ædʒɪnəri] *adj. Botany*, lacking female organs.

ahimsa [ə'hɪmsɑː, ə'hɪŋ–] *n*. principle of nonviolence towards any living creature, in Hinduism and Buddhism.

ahypnia [eɪ'hɪpniə] *n*. insomnia.

aide-mémoire [ˌeɪdmem'wɑːr] (*French*) *n*. 'reminder'; memorandum; diplomatic note clearly stating a government's view, policy, etc., on a particular matter.

aiger ['iːgə] *n*. tidal wave in river; bore.

aigrette ['eɪgret] *n*. spray of feathers; any object in that shape; egret.

aiguille ['eɪgwɪl, -iːl] *n*. sharp point; peak.

aikido [aɪ'kiːdəʊ] (*Japanese*) *n*. a Japanese martial art.

ailanthus [eɪ'lænθəs] *n*. Oriental tree, 'tree of heaven', yielding food for silkworms. **ailantery** [-'lænt–], *n*. ailanthus grove.

aileron ['eɪlərɒn] *n*. movable surface of aeroplane, especially of wing, moved in steering.

ailurophile [aɪ'ljʊərəfaɪl, -'lʊə–] *n*. one fond of cats. **ailurophilia** [-'fɪliə], *n*. **ailurophobe**, *n*. one with dread of cats.

aîné ['eɪneɪ] (*French*) *adj*. (*fem*. **aînée**) elder; senior.

aïoli [aɪ'əʊli] (*French*) *n*. garlic mayonnaise.

ait [eɪt] *n*. small island in river or lake; eyot.

à jour [ɑː 'ʒʊə] (*French*) decoratively pierced to admit light, applied to metalwork, lace, etc.

Advice on licensing a practice

The spelling of the pairs *advice/advise*, *licence/license*, and *practice/practise* often gives trouble – particularly the last two, which are not quite the same in British and American English. The easiest to remember is *advice/advise*, because the two are pronounced differently. If you *advise* someone, you pronounce the verb with a /z/ sound. You can't spell /z/ with a *c*, so the verb must be *advise*. Therefore by a process of elimination, the noun is *advice*.

The noun and verb *practice/practise* are pronounced the same, but in British English it is easy to remember that their spelling follows the model of *advice/advise*: *practice* for the noun, *practise* for the verb.

The situation in American English is more complicated: it usually uses *practice* for the noun, but *practise* can occur too; while for the verb both are used, with *practice* being the commoner.

British English follows the same rule with *licence/-ense*: *c* for the noun (*licence*), *s* for the verb (*license*). American English uses either for both noun or verb, although *license* is the commoner spelling for the verb. A complicating factor is the spelling of the adjective *licensed* (as in *licensed premises*). It is generally spelled *licensed* on the grounds that it means 'that has been licensed'. But it could be argued that it is derived from the noun *licence*, in the sense 'that has been given a licence', so *licenced* cannot be unequivocally condemned as incorrect.

akinesia, akinesis [ˌeɪkɪˈniːziə, –sɪs] *n.* paralysis of motor nerves. **akinetic,** *adj.*

à la [æ lɑː, ɑː lɑː] (*French*) 'in the manner as'.

ala [ˈeɪlə] *n.* (*pl.* **–ae**) wing-shaped projection.

alabamine [ˌæləˈbæmiːn] *n.* rare halogen-like element, No. 85, now called astatine.

alabaster [ˈæləbɑːstə, –bæ–] *n.* formerly, carbonate of lime; *modern*, kind of gypsum from which vases and boxes are made; *adj.* of alabaster; very smooth and white. **alabastrine,** *adj.*

à la belle étoile [æ lɑː ˌbel eˈtwɑːl] (*French*) 'under the beautiful star'; in the open air at night.

alalia [əˈleɪliə] *n.* loss of speech.

à la mode [æ lɑː ˈməud] (*French*) 'in fashion'; chic.

alamode [ˈæləməud] *n.* soft, light silk, used in 19th century for shawls, dresses, etc.

à la mort [æ lɑː ˈmɔː] (*French*) 'to the death'; mortally.

alanine [ˈæləniːn] *n.* an amino-acid occuring in protein.

alar(y) [ˈeɪlə, –ri] *adj.* like or pertaining to a wing or shoulder.

alastrim [əˈlæstrɪm] *n.* disease like, or mild form of, smallpox.

alate [ˈeɪleɪt] *adj.* winged. **alation** [eɪˈleɪʃn], *n.* state of having wings; disposition of wings in insect.

alaudine [əˈlɔːdaɪn] *adj.* belonging to bird family which includes the skylark; like or pertaining to skylark.

alb [ælb] *n.* long white priestly garment.

albacore, albicore [ˈælbəkɔː] *n.* several tunny-like marine fishes; tunny.

albedo [ælˈbiːdəu] *n.* degree of whiteness; *Photography*, reflecting power of a surface; *Astronomy*, ratio of light reflected from a body to total amount it receives from the sun. **albedometer** *n.* instrument measuring albedo.

albescent [ælˈbesnt] *adj.* becoming white; whitish.

albicant [ˈælbɪkənt] *adj.* growing white. **albication,** *n.* formation of white patches in plants.

albificative [ˈælbɪfɪkeɪtɪv] *adj.* able to whiten.

albiflorous [ˌælbɪˈflɔːrəs] *adj.* having white flowers.

albino [ælˈbiːnəu] *n.* person or animal with white skin and hair and pinkish eyes; plant deficient in pigment. **albinic** [–ˈbɪnɪk], **albinotic** [–ˈnɒtɪk], *adj.* **albinism** [ˈæl–], *n.*

Albion [ˈælbiən] *n.* old name for Britain.

alborado [ˌælbəˈrɑːdəu] (*Spanish*) *n.* morning song.

albuginea [ˌælbjuːˈdʒɪniə] *n.* white of eye; white fibrous tissue. **albugineous,** *adj.* like white of eye or egg.

albugo [ælˈbjuːgəu] *n.* *Medicine*, white spot on cornea of eye; leucoma; *Botany*, white rust.

albumen [ˈælbjumen, ælˈbjuːmən] *n.* white of egg; substance surrounding embryo in seed.

albumin [ˈælbjumɪn, ælˈbjuːmən] *n.* protein forming chief constituent of animal and plant tissues.

albuminate [ælˈbjuːmɪneɪt] *n.* kind of protein resulting from action of acid or alkali on albumins; compound of albumin with other substance.

albuminoid [ælˈbjuːmɪnɔɪd] *adj.* like albumen; *n.* protein; several substances like protein. **albuminous,** *adj.* pertaining to albumen or albumin.

albuminuria [ælˌbjuːmɪˈnjuəriə] *n.* presence of albumin in urine.

alburnum [ælˈbɜːnəm] *n.* sapwood.

alcahest *see* **alkahest**.

Alcaic [ælˈkeɪɪk] *adj.* written in a four-line verse, each line of which has four feet.

alcaide [ælˈkaɪdɪ] *n.* governor of Spanish, Moorish, etc., prison or fort.

alcalde [ælˈkældɪ] *n.* Spanish sheriff, mayor, etc.

alcazar [ˌælkəˈzɑː, ælˈkæzə] (*Spanish*) *n.* palace; castle; citadel, especially that of Toledo.

alcoholometer [ˌælkəhɒˈlɒmɪtə] *n.* instrument measuring alcoholic strength of liquids.

al dente [æl ˈdenti, –eɪ] (*Italian*) (of pasta) cooked but still firm.

aldrin [ˈɔːldrɪn] *n.* a chemical pesticide the use of which was forbidden in the U.K. in 1964.

aleatoric [ˌæliəˈtɒrɪk, ˌeɪ–] *adj.* (of electronic music) with random elements inside a framework.

aleatory [ˌæliˈeɪtəri, ˈeɪliət–] *adj.* dependent on chance; pertaining to gambling or luck.

ale-conner [ˈeɪlˌkɒnə] *n.* official formerly charged with supervision of selling and testing ale and beer.

alecost [ˈeɪlkɒst] *n.* herb formerly used to flavour ale; costmary.

alectryomachy [əˌlektriˈɒməki] *n.* cock-fighting.

alegar [ˈæligə, ˈeɪ–] *n.* sour ale; malt vinegar.

alembic [əˈlembɪk] *n.* ancient distilling apparatus; purifying or transforming apparatus or act. **alembicate** *v.t.* distil. **alembicated** *adj.* rather too refined (of literary style).

aleph [ˈælef, ˈɑːlɪf] *n.* first letter of the Hebrew alphabet.

alethiology [əˌliːθiˈɒlədʒi] *n.* study of nature of truth.

aleurometer [ˌæljuˈrɒmɪtə] *n.* instrument measuring gluten content of flour.

aleurone [əˈljuərəun, ˈæljurəun] *n.* protein granules in plant seeds; external protein layer of cereal seeds.

alevin [ˈæləvɪn] *n.* young fish, especially salmon just hatched.

alexandrine [ˌælɪgˈzɑːndraɪn, –drɪn] *n.* type of verse having six iambics; kind of mosaic invented by Alexander Severus, emperor of Rome.

alexandrite [ˌælɪgˈzɑːndraɪt] *n.* a gem stone, a green variety of chrysoberyl.

alexia [əˈleksiə] *n.* inability to read due to aphasia.

alexipharmic [əˌleksɪˈfɑːmɪk] *n.* & *adj.* (antidote) against poisoning.

alexipyretic [əˌleksɪpaɪˈretɪk] *n.* & *adj.* (drug) curative of fever.

alexiteric [əˌleksɪˈterɪk] *n.* & *adj.* preventive of contagion; antidote against poison.

alfalfa [ælˈfælfə] *n.* clover-like forage crop; lucerne.

alga [ˈælgə] *n.* (*pl.* **–gae**) [–dʒiː] seaweed; *pl.* division of cryptogamic plants.

algaroba, algarroba [ˌælgəˈrəubə] *n.* carob; mesquite. **algarobin,** *n.* dyestuff obtained from carob tree

algazel [ˌælgəzˈel] *n.* horned antelope of Nigeria.

algedonic [ˌældʒɪˈdɒnɪk] *adj.* pertaining to pain, especially in association with pleasure.

algefacient [ˌældʒɪˈfeɪʃiənt] *adj.* cooling.

algesia [ælˈdʒiːziə] *n.* sensitiveness to pain.

algesic, *adj.* feeling pain. **algesimeter,** *n.* instrument for measuring this. **algetic** [–'dʒetɪk], *adj.* causing pain.

algid ['ældʒɪd] *adj.* chilly, especially during fever. **algidity** [–'dʒɪd–], *n.*

algific [æl'dʒɪfɪk] *adj.* making cold.

alginuresis [ˌældʒɪnjuˈriːsɪs] *n. Medicine,* painful urination.

algivorous [ælˈdʒɪvərəs] *adj.* feeding on algae.

algogenic [ˌælgəˈdʒenɪk] *adj.* producing pain; reducing body temperature.

algolagnia [ˌælgəˈlægnɪə] *n.* taking sexual pleasure in inflicting or enduring pain. **algolagnic,** *adj.* **algolagnist,** *n.*

algology [ælˈgɒlədʒi] *n.* study of algae.

algometer [ælˈgɒmɪtə] *n.* instrument measuring sensitivity to pain. **algometry,** *n.*

algophilia [ˌælgəˈfɪlɪə] *n.* algolagny.

algophobia [ˌælgəˈfəʊbɪə] *n.* morbid dread of pain.

algor ['ælgɔː] *n.* coldness; shivering fit in fever.

algorism ['ælgərɪzm] *n.* art of calculating, especially in Arabic numeration; arithmetic. **algorismic,** *adj.*

algorithm ['ælgərɪðm] *n.* step-by-step system of solving a problem, especially in computers.

algous ['ælgəs] *adj.* pertaining to algae.

alias [ˈeɪlɪəs] *adj.* otherwise called; *n.* assumed name.

alibi ['ælɪbaɪ] *n.* plea that, at the time when act was committed, one was elsewhere than at the place where act was committed; proof of such a plea.

alible ['æləbl] *adj. archaic,* nourishing.

alicyclic [ˌælɪˈsaɪklɪk, –ˈsɪk–] *adj.* denoting organic compounds that are both aliphatic and cyclic, i.e. aliphatic in chemical behaviour but having their carbon atoms in a ring.

alidade ['ælɪdeɪd] *n.* instrument used in surveying & navigation.

alienism ['eɪlɪənɪzm] *n. obsolete,* study of mental disease. **alienist,** *n. obsolete* expert in alienism; *American,* psychiatrist specialising in legal aspects of mental illness.

aliferous [əˈlɪfərəs] *adj.* having wings.

aliform ['ælɪfɔːm] *adj.* like a wing.

aligerous [əˈlɪdʒərəs] *adj.* winged.

aliment ['ælɪmənt] *n.* food; nourishment. **alimental,** [–'mentl], *adj.* affording food. **alimentary,** *adj.* pertaining to food; nourishing; **alimentation,** *n.* act of feeding or being fed. **alimentative,** *adj.* nourishing.

alimentotherapy [ˌælɪmentəʊˈθerəpi] *n. Medicine,* treatment by dieting.

aliped ['ælɪped] *adj.* having winged feet; *n.* such animal.

aliphatic [ˌælɪˈfætɪk] *adj.* pertaining to fat; *Chemistry,* applied to group of organic compounds, including the fats, having open-chain structure.

aliquant ['ælɪkwənt] *n. & adj.* (number) not dividing exactly into another number; not aliquot.

aliquot ['ælɪkwɒt] *n. & adj.* (number) contained an exact number of times in another number; equal share; *v.t.* divide into equal parts.

aliter ['ælɪtə] *(Latin) adv.* 'otherwise'; *Law,* requiring a different rule.

alizarin [əˈlɪzərɪn] *n.* red dye formerly obtained from madder root.

alk [ælk] *n.* resin obtained from turpentine tree.

alkahest ['ælkəhest] *n.* universal solvent sought for by alchemists.

alkalescent [ˌælkəˈlesnt] *adj.* somewhat alkaline.

alkali ['ælkəlaɪ] *n. Chemistry,* substance having property of neutralizing acids.

alkalify ['ælkəlɪfaɪ, ælˈkæl–] *v.t. v.i.,* change into alkali.

alkalimeter [ˌælkəˈlɪmɪtə] *n.* instrument measuring strength or amount of alkali in mixture. **alkalimetry,** *n.*

alkaline ['ælkəlaɪn] *adj.* pertaining to, like or consisting of alkali. **alkalinity** [–'lɪnəti], *n.*

alkalize ['ælkəlaɪz] *v.t.* make alkaline.

alkaloid ['ælkəlɔɪd] *n.* nitrogenous basic compound of vegetable origin. **alkaloidal,** *adj.*

alkalosis [ˌælkəˈləʊsɪs] *n.* abnormally high alkalinity of blood and tissues.

alkanet ['ælkənet] *n.* dyer's bugloss; red dye obtained from that plant.

alkolometry [ˌælkəˈlɒmətri] *n.* measurement of alkaloids; administration and dosage of alkaloids.

allantiasis [ˌælənˈtaɪəsɪs] *n.* sausage poisoning.

allantoic [ˌælənˈtəʊɪk] *adj.* pertaining to allantois; sausage-shaped. **allantoid,** *adj.*

allantois [əˈlæntəʊɪs] *n.* sac-like foetal membrane developing into umbilical cord and forming part of placenta.

allative ['ælətɪv] *n. & adj. Grammar,* (case) expressing motion towards.

allegory ['æləgəri] *n.* story or other representation in which the subject is expressed metaphorically or personified; parable. **allegorical** [–'gɒrɪkl], *adj.* **allegorize,** *v.t.* **allegorism,** *n.* interpreting Scripture as allegory. **allegorist,** *n.*

allele, allelomorph [əˈliːl, –əmɔːf] *n. Biology,* one of a pair of alternative contrasting inheritable characteristics; gene carrying that characteristic. **allelic,** *adj.* **allelism,** *n.*

allergen ['ælədʒen, –dʒən] *n.* substance causing allergy. **allergenic,** *adj.*

allergy ['ælədʒi] *n. Medicine,* abnormal sensitivity towards a substance or germ, due to prior inoculation with that substance or germ; anaphylaxis; abnormal sensitivity to e.g. pollen, dust, etc. **allergic,** *adj.*

alliaceous [ˌæliˈeɪʃəs] *adj.* having smell or taste of garlic; belonging to the onion family of plants.

alligation [ˌælɪˈgeɪʃn] *n.* act or state of attaching or being attached; *Arithmetic,* archaic method of solving 'mixture' problems; 'rule of mixtures'.

allision [əˈlɪʒn] *n.* intentional collision, especially of ships.

alliteration [əˌlɪtəˈreɪʃn] *n.* literary device wherein several or all words in phrase or sentence begin with same sound. **alliterate,** *v.t. & i.* **alliterative,** *adj.*

allocatur [ˌæləˈkeɪtə] *n. Law,* (certificate of) allowance of costs.

allochromatic [ˌæləkrəˈmætɪk] *adj.* pertaining to change of colour; variable in colour.

allochroous [əˈlɒkrəʊəs] *adj.* changing in colour.

allochthonous [əˈlɒkθənəs] *adj.* not autochthonous; formed elsewhere.

allocution [ˌæləˈkjuːʃn] *n.* authoritative or exhortatory address; *Roman Catholic,* formal papal address to College of Cardinals.

allodium [ə'ləudiəm] *n.* property under absolute ownership; freehold; *American*, estates in fee simple. **allodial**, *adj.*

allo-erotism, allo-eroticism [,æləu'erətizm, -ı'rɒtisizm] *n. Psychology*, love of other person or object; opposite of autoerotism.

allogamy [ə'lɒgəmi] *n.* cross-fertilization. **allogamous**, *adj.*

allogeneous [,ælə'dʒi:niəs] *adj.* different in kind. **allegeneity** [-dʒə'ni:əti, -'neı-], *n.*

allograft ['æləgrɑ:ft] *n.* surgical graft from a non-identical donor.

allograph ['æləgrɑ:f] *n.* writing especially signature, for another; opposite of autograph.

allolalia [,ælə'leɪliə] *n.* form of aphasia in which words are spoken at random.

allomerism [ə'lɒmərizm] *n. Chemistry*, variation in constitution without variation in form.

allometry [ə'lɒmətri] *n.* study of growth of a part of an organism in relation to the whole.

allonge [ə'lɒndʒ, ə'lʌndʒ] *n. Commerce*, slip of paper attached to bill of exchange for additional endorsements.

allonym ['ælənim] *n.* other person's name assumed by writer; work published under an allonym. **allonymous** [ə'lɒnıməs], *adj.*

allopathy [ə'lɒpəθi] *n. Medicine*, treatment of disease by remedies producing symptoms different from those of disease treated; opposite of homoeopathy; medical treatment using all methods found successful. **allopathic** [-'pæθık], *adj.* **allopath**, *n.*

allophone ['æləfəun] *n.* any of several speech sounds regarded as variants of a given phoneme.

allopurinal [,ælə'pjuərinɒl] *n.* synthetic drug used against gout.

allosematic [,æləsı'mætık] *adj.* having imitative protective coloration.

allotheism ['æləθi:ızm] *n.* worship of strange gods.

allotropy [ə'lɒtrəpi] *n.* existence of an element in more than one form. **allotrope** ['ælətrəup], *n.* form taken by allotropic element. **allotropic** [-'trɒpık], *adj.*

alluvion [ə'lu:viən, -'lju:-] *n.* impact of water on shore; flood; alluvium.

alluvium [ə'lu:viəm, -'lju:-] *n.* (*pl.* **–viums, –via**) matter deposited by river or flood. **alluvial**, *adj.*

almagest ['ælmədʒest] *n.* comprehensive treatise or textbook, especially on astronomy, generally the treatise of Ptolemy.

alma mater [,ælmə 'mɑːtə, -'meɪtə] (*Latin*) 'fostering mother'; one's school or university.

almandine ['ælməndi:n, –daın, –dın] *n.* kind of violet-coloured garnet.

almira [æl'maırə, əl–] (*Anglo-Indian*) *n.* furniture for storing, *e.g.* cupboard or chest.

almoner ['ɑːmənə, 'ælmənə] *n.* official who distributes alms; *obsolete* hospital official who interviews prospective patients, etc. **almonry**, *n.* place for alms distribution.

almucantar ['ælmjukæntə, ,ælmju'kæntə] *n. Astrononomy*, circle of celestial sphere parallel with horizon; parallel of altitude; telescope that, in rotating, sweeps out curves of this kind.

alnico ['ælnıkəu] *n. trademark*, permanent magnet alloy of aluminium, nickel and cobalt, with some iron and sometimes copper.

aloe ['æləu] *n.* bitter fruit of several plants used in preparation of purgative; *pl.* such purgative. **aloetic** [–əu'etık], *adj.* pertaining to aloe.

alogia [ə'ləudʒiə] *n.* speech defect due to brain lesion, etc.

alogism ['ælədʒızm] *n.* illogical statement.

alopecia [,ælə'pi:ʃə, –iə] *n.* baldness. **alopecia areata**, loss of hair in small patches.

alopecoid [,ælə'pi:kɔıd, ə'lɒpıkɔıd] *adj.* fox-like.

alpenglow ['ælpəngləu] *n.* reddish light at sunset or sunrise on mountain-tops, especially occurring before appearance or after disappearance of sun.

alpestrine [æl'pestrın] *adj.* pertaining to alpine zone.

alpha ['ælfə] *n.* first letter (A, a) of Greek alphabet. **alpha and omega**, first and last; entirely; quintessence. **alpha particle**, positively charged particle, the nucleus of a helium atom. **alpha ray**, a ray or beam of alpha. particles. **alpha wave**, variation in frequency of brain waves associated with drowsiness.

alphanumeric, alphameric [,ælfə(nju)'merık] *adj.* composed of letters and digits.

alphosis [æl'fəusıs] *n. Medicine*, lack of skin pigmentation.

alsike ['ælsık, –aık] *n.* pink-flowered clover, grown as forage.

alsinaceous [,ælsı'neıʃəs] *adj.* like or pertaining to chickweed; belonging to chickweed family of plants.

alt [ælt] *n. & adj. Music*, (note) in first octave above the treble stave.

altarage ['ɔːltərıdʒ] *n.* offerings at altar; payment for masses for dead; certain payments to priest.

altazimuth [æl'tæzıməθ] *n.* instrument measuring altitude and azimuth of heavenly bodies.

alterative ['ɔːltərətıv] *adj.* causing change; *Medicine*, changing gradually to healthy state; *n.* drug or other treatment changing nutritional processes.

altercation [,ɔːltə'keıʃn] *n.* heated argument; quarrel. **altercate**, *v.i.*

alter ego [,æltə 'i:gəu, ,ɔːl–, 'eg–] (*Latin*) 'other self'; close friend; confidant.

alterity [æl'terəti, ɔːl–] *n.* state of being different.

alternator ['ɔːltəneıtə] *n.* machine generating alternating electric current.

althaea, althea [æl'θi:ə] *n.* rose of Sharon; genus containing hollyhock, mallow, etc.

althing ['ɔːlθıŋ] *n.* parliament of Iceland.

altiloquence [æl'tıləkwəns] *n.* pompous, high-sounding speech.

altimeter ['æltı,mi:tə, 'ɔːl–, æl'tımıtə] *n.* instrument for taking or showing altitude.

altisonant [æl'tısənənt] *adj.* high-sounding, pompous.

altissimo [æl'tısıməu] *n. & adj. Music*, (note) in the second octave above the treble stave.

altivolant [æl'tıvələnt] *adj.* flying high.

alto-relievo [,æltəu–rı'li:vəu] *n.* carving in high relief, *i.e.* in which the figures, etc., project more than half their proportions from the background.

altruism ['æltruızm] *n.* principle of regard for others; self-sacrifice. **altruist**, *n.* **altruistic**, *adj.*

alula ['æljʊlə] *n.* part of a bird's wing, corresponding to thumb.

alum ['æləm] *n.* sulphate of aluminium used in dyeing, as an astringent, etc.

alumina [ə'luːmɪnə, -'ljuː-] *n.* oxide of aluminium.

aluminate [ə'luːmɪneɪt, -'ljuː-] *n.* chemical compound of aluminium oxide and another metal.

aluminium [ˌælə'mɪnɪəm, -lju-] *n.* light, malleable white metal, resistant to organic salts, obtained by heating aluminium oxide. **aluminic,** *adj.*

aluminize [ə'luːmɪnaɪz, -'ljuː-] *v.t.* to coat with aluminium.

aluminosis [ə,luːmɪ'nəʊsɪs, -,ljuː-] *n.* lung disease due to inhaling aluminium dust.

aluminous [ə'luːmɪnəs, -'ljuː-] *adj.* pertaining to alumina or aluminium.

aluminum [ə'luːmənəm] (*American*) *n.* aluminium.

alumnus [ə'lʌmnəs] *n.* (*pl.* -**ni**, *fem.* **alumna**, *pl.* -**nae**) graduate of university or college.

alveary ['ælvɪərɪ] *n.* beehive; outer canal of ear.

alveola [æl'viːələ] *n.* (*pl.* —**lae**) *Botany*, small cavity, especially in surface of an organ.

alveolar [æl'viːələ, ˌælvi'əʊlə] *adj.* pertaining to alveolus; bearing alveolae; *Phonetics*, pronounced with tongue and alveolus; *n.* sound so pronounced. **alveolar arch,** tooth-bearing part of upper jaw.

alveolate [æl'viːəleɪt, -ət] *adj.* having many deep cavities; like a honey-comb.

alveolus [æl'viːələs, ˌælvi'əʊləs] *n.* (*pl.* —**li**) *Anatomy*, small cavity; tooth socket; aircell, etc.; *Phonetics*, upper front tooth ridge.

alviducous [ˌælvɪ'djuːkəs] *adj.* purgative.

alvine ['ælvaɪn, -ɪn] *adj. obsolete* pertaining to belly or intestines.

amadelphous [ˌæmə'delfəs] *adj.* gregarious.

amadou ['æməduː] *n.* form of tinder prepared from fungi; punk.

amah ['aːmə, -aː] *n.* female servant or nanny, especially in Far East.

amalgam [ə'mælgəm] *n* alloy of mercury and another metal, especially silver, used to fill teeth; blend.

amandine [ə'mændɪn, ˌaːmən'diːn] *n.* albumin in sweet almonds; cold cream composed of that substance.

amanita [ˌæmə'niːtə, -'naɪ-] *n.* any of the fungi in the genus Amanita, including many highly poisonous ones.

amanous ['æmənəs] *adj.* lacking hands.

amanuensis [ə,mænju'ensɪs] *n.* (*pl.* **amanuenses** [-iːz]), employee who writes from dictation; secretary.

amaranth ['æmərænθ] *n. Mythology*, plant that never fades; love-lies-bleeding; purple colour. **amaranthine,** *adj.* unfading; eternal; purple.

amarthritis [ˌæmaː'θraɪtɪs] *n.* arthritis of several joints.

amaryllis [ˌæmə'rɪlɪs] *n.* belladonna lily; any of several similar plants; poetic name for country girl.

amative ['æmətɪv] *adj.* amorous.

amatol ['æmətɒl] *n.* explosive composed of T.N.T. and ammonium nitrate.

amaurosis [ˌæmɔː'rəʊsɪs] *n.* loss of sight without noticeable change in eye, due to failure of optic nerve; gutta serena. **amaurotic,** *adj.*

ambages [æm'beɪdʒiːz] *n. pl. archaic,* circuitous path or approach; circumlocution. **ambagious,** *adj.*

ambari [æm'baːri] *n.* fibre-yielding plant of E Indies; kenaf.

ambergris ['æmbəgriːs] *n.* substance obtained from intestines of spermwhale, found in the sea and used in perfumes.

ambiance, ambience ['æmbɪəns, 'ɒm-] *n.* particular atmosphere of a place.

ambidextrous [ˌæmbɪ'dekstrəs] *adj.* able to use both hands with equal facility. **ambidexterity** [-'ter-], *n.*

ambient ['æmbɪənt] *adj.* surrounding; *n.* ambiance.

ambiguous [æm'bɪgjuəs] *adj.* of uncertain meaning. **ambiguity** [ˌæmbɪ'gjuːəti], *n.*

ambilaevous [ˌæmbɪ'liːvəs] *adj.* ambisinister.

ambilateral [ˌæmbɪ'lætərəl] *adj.* of both sides.

ambisinister [ˌæmbɪ'sɪnɪstə] *adj.* left-handed in both hands; awkward.

ambit ['æmbɪt] *n.* scope, limits.

ambivalence [æm'bɪvələns] *n.* simultaneous attraction and repulsion. **ambivalent,** *adj.* feeling ambivalence.

ambivert ['æmbɪvɜːt] *n.* someone who is both extroverted and introverted.

amblyopia [ˌæmbli'əʊpiə] *n.* partial loss of sight not due to disease of eye; early stage of amaurosis.

ambo ['æmbəʊ] *n.* raised place or pulpit in early Christian Church.

ambrosia [æm'brəʊziə] *n. Mythology*, food of the gods; any very pleasant food. **ambrosial,** *adj.*

ambry ['æmbri] *n.* niche containing sacred vessels in chancel.

ambsace ['eɪmzeɪs] *n.* double ace; lowest score; bad luck.

ambulant ['æmbjʊlənt] *adj.* walking, continuing active; moving about from place to place. **ambulate,** *v.i.*; **ambulation,** *n.*

ambulatory [ˌæmbju'leɪtəri, 'æmbjʊlətəri] *n.* enclosed space, especially in monastery, for walking; *adj.* pertaining to walking.

ameba *see* **amoeba.**

amebicide [ə'miːbɪsaɪd] *n.* substance killing amoebas.

âme damnée [ˌaːm 'dæneɪ] (*French*) 'lost soul'; dupe; tool; devoted follower.

amelification [ə,melɪfɪ'keɪʃn] *n.* formation of tooth-enamel.

ameloblast [ə'meləblæst] *n.* enamel-producing cell of tooth.

amenable [ə'miːnəbl, -'me-] *adj.* easily persuaded to agree or yield.

amende [æ'mɒnd] (*French*) *n.* fine; reparation. **amende honorable** [ˌɒnɔː'raːbl], public apology; full reparation for dishonour.

amenity [ə'miːnəti, -'me-] *n.* attractiveness; pleasantness; *pl.* pleasant conditions or surroundings; pleasant or useful services.

amenorrhoea [ə,menə'riːə] *n.* abnormal absence or arrest of menstruation.

a mensa et thoro [eɪ ˌmensə et 'θɔːrəʊ, aː-] (*Latin*) 'from table and bed'; applied to judicial separation of husband and wife.

ament, amentum [ə'ment, 'æmənt; ə'mentəm] *n.* catkin. **amentaceous,** *adj.* like or composed of catkins. **amentiferous,** *adj.* bearing catkins. **amentiform,** *adj.* catkin-shaped.

amentia [eɪ'menʃə] *n.* severe, usually congenital, mental deficiency.

amerce [ə'mɜːs] *v.t. obsolete* punish, especially by fine. **amercement,** *n.* **amerciable,** *adj.*

americium [,æmə'rɪsiəm, -'rɪʃ-] *n.* artificial element (No. 95), made by bombarding uranium or plutonium with helium ions.

ametropia [,æmɪ'trəupiə] *n.* abnormality in optical refraction, resulting in inability to focus images on the retina. **ametropic** [-'trɒpɪk], *adj.*

amiantus, amianthus [,æmi'æntəs, -θəs] *n.* asbestos with silky fibres. **amianthine** [-θaɪn], *adj.*

amice ['æmɪs] *n. Roman Catholic,* white linen square covering shoulders of celebrant priest.

amicicide [ə'maɪsɪsaɪd] *n.* murder or murderer of a friend.

amicron [ə'maɪkrɒn] *n.* one of the smallest microscopically detectable particles.

amicus curiae [ə,maɪkəs 'kjuəriiː] (*Latin*) 'friend of the court'; person invited or allowed to assist court on points of law.

amigo [ə'miːgəu] (*Spanish*) *n.* (*pl.* **amigos;** fem. **amiga**) friend

amine ['æmiːn] *n.* compound derived from ammonia.

amino acid [ə,miːnəu 'æsɪd, ,æmɪ-] *n.* one of many acids forming the principal ingredients of protein.

aminobutene [ə,miːnəu'bjuːtiːn, ,æmɪ-] *n.* a synthetic pain-relieving drug, less addictive than morphine.

amitosis [,æmɪ'təusɪs] *n.* direct cell division. **amitotic** [-'tɒtɪk], *adj.*

ammeter ['æmiːtə] *n.* instrument measuring amperage of electric current.

ammonite ['æmənaɪt] *n.* fossil cephalopod with whorled shell.

ammophilous [ə'mɒfɪləs] *adj.* sand-loving

ammotherapy [,æməu'θerəpi] *n.* medical treatment by sand baths.

amnesia [æm'niːziə, -'niːʒ-] *n.* loss of memory. **amnesiac, amnesic,** *n.* **amnemonic** [-nɪ'mɒnɪk], **amnestic,** *adj.*

amniocentesis [,æmniəusen'tiːsɪs] *n.* process of obtaining sample of amniotic fluid from womb of pregnant woman, in order to check for gender or abnormalities.

amnion ['æmniən] *n.* innermost membrane enclosing foetus. **amniota,** *n.pl.* vertebrates having amnion.

amniotic [,æmni'ɒtɪk]

amoeba [ə'miːbə] *n.* (*pl.* **-ae, -as**) unicellular animal, composed of microscopic mass of naked protoplasm; lowest form of animal life. **amoebic, amoeban, amoebous, amoeboid,** *adj.*

amoebaean [,æmɪ'biːən] *adj.* applied to verse in which two persons speak alternately.

amoebiform [ə'miːbɪfɔːm] *adj.* shaped like an amoeba.

amoretto [,æməretəu] *n.* (*pl,* **-ti** [-ti]), in art, plump little boy representing cupid; putto.

amorphous [ə'mɔːfəs] *adj.* without shape; irregularly shaped; *Chemistry,* lacking crystalline structure; *Biology,* lacking differentiation in structure;

Geology, not divided into strata. **amorphism,** *n.*

amortize [ə'mɔːtaɪz] *v.t.* nullify debt, *gen.* by forming a sinking fund. **amortization,** *n.*

amortizement [ə'mɔːtɪzmənt] *n. Architecture,* topmost member of a building; slanting top of buttress, etc.; amortization.

amour [ə'muə, æ-] (*French*) *n.* love-affair, especially illicit. **amourette,** *n.* petty amour.

amour-propre [,æmuə-'prɒprə] (*French*) *n.* self-love; self-respect.

ampelideous [,æmpɪ'lɪdiəs] *adj.* of or like the vine.

ampelotherapy [,æmpələ'θerəpi] *n. Medicine,* grape cure.

amperage ['æmpərɪdʒ] *n.* strength of an electric current measured in amperes.

ampere ['æmpeə] *n.* unit of intensity of electric current (current produced by one volt acting through resistance of one ohm) (*abbr.* **amp.**). **ampere hour,** unit of quantity of electric current (quantity flowing in one hour at one amp).

ampersand ['æmpəsænd] *n.* sign (&) for *and*.

amphetamine [æm'fetəmiːn, -miːn] *n.* drug which stimulates the central nervous system, used in medicine to relieve depression, and to control appetite in cases of obesity: the chief ingredient of 'pep pills'.

amphibian [æm'fɪbiən] *n. & adj.* (animal) able to live both on land and in water; (vehicle) able to alight on or take off from, or to travel on, both land and water.

amphibious [æm'fɪbiəs] *adj.* amphibian.

amphibole ['æmfɪbəul] *n.* rock-forming silicate similar to asbestos and hornblende.

amphibolic [,æmfɪ'bɒlɪk] *adj.* able to turn backwards or forwards, especially of joints and limbs; ambiguous; like amphibole.

amphibolite [æm'fɪbəlaɪt] *n.* rock composed of amphibole; hornblende.

amphibology, amphiboly [,æmfɪ'bɒlədʒi, æm'fɪbəli] *n.* ambiguous speech; equivocation; quibble. **amphibolous** [-'fɪb-], *adj.*

amphibrach ['æmfɪbræk] *n.* metrical foot of one short, one long and one short syllable.

amphichroic, amphichromatic [,æmfɪ'krəuɪk] *adj.* producing two colours. **amphichrome,** *n.* such a plant. **amphichrom** *n.*

amphicoelous [,æmfɪ'siːləs] *adj. Zoology,* having both surfaces concave.

amphictyonic [æm,fɪkti'ɒnɪk] *adj.* applied to ancient Greek council of state-deputies. **amphictyany** [-'fɪktiəni], *n.* league of adjacent states.

amphicyrtic [,æmfɪ'sɜːtɪk] *adj.* with both sides convex.

amphigean [,æmfɪ'dʒiːən] *adj.* occuring in both hemispheres; *Botany,* with flowers arising from root-stock.

amphigony [æm'fɪgəni] *n.* sexual reproduction.

amphigory, amphigouri ['æmfɪgəri] *n.* a nonsense verse or burlesque composition with no meaning.

amphilogism [æm'fɪlədʒɪzm] *n.* circumlocution.

amphimacer [æm'fɪməsə] *n.* metrical foot comprising one long, one short and one long syllable; cretic.

amphimixis [ˌæmfɪˈmɪksɪs] *n.* interbreeding; joining of germ plasm of two individuals in sexual reproduction.

amphipodous [æmˈfɪpədəs] *adj. Zoology*, having both walking and swimming feet.

amphiprostyle [æmˈfɪprəstaɪl, ˌæmfɪˈprəʊ-] *n.* & *adj.* (building) with columns at each end but not at sides.

amphirhinal [ˌæmfɪˈraɪnl] *adj.* with two nostrils.

amphisbaena [ˌæmfɪsˈbiːnə] *n. Mythology* double-headed serpent able to move in both directions; kind of worm-like lizard.

amphiscian [æmˈfɪʃn, -iən] *n.* & *adj.* (inhabitant) of tropics, whose shadow falls in different ways according to the time of year.

amphivorous [æmˈfɪvərəs] *adj.* both carnivorous and herbivorous.

amphora [ˈæmfərə] *n.* (*pl.* **–rae, –ras**) vase with two handles, of Greek or Roman origin; standard liquid measure of nine gallons (Greek) and six gallons. (Roman). **amphoric,** *adj.* applied to sound made by blowing into an amphora, or sound resembling that.

amphoteric [ˌæmfəˈterɪk] *adj.* of both kinds; *Chemistry*, reacting as either alkali or acid.

ampicillin [ˌæmpɪˈsɪlɪn] *n.* an improved form of penicillin taken by mouth.

amplexus [æmˈpleksəs] *n.* the mating embrace of frogs and toads.

ampliative [ˈæmplɪətɪv] *adj.* supplementary.

amplitude [ˈæmplɪtjuːd] *n.* spaciousness; plenty; breadth; amount of displacement of vibrating body or oscillating current; *Astrology*, angular distance between heavenly body at rising or setting and east or west point of horizon; *Astronomy*, arc of horizon between foot of vertical circle through heavenly body and east or west point. **amplitude modulation,** radio transmission by varying the amplitude (height or depth) of carrier wave (*abbr.* A.M.).

ampulla [æmˈpʊlə, -ˈpʌ-] *n.* ancient Roman flask with two handles and globular body; *Anatomy*, sac-like swelling at end of duct. **ampullaceous** [-ˈleɪʃəs], **ampullar,** *adj.* of or like an ampulla.

amyctic [əˈmɪktɪk] *n. Medicine*, irritating.

amygdala [əˈmɪgdələ] *n.* (*pl.* **–lae**) any almond-shaped formation in body, e.g. tonsil.

amygdalin [əˈmɪgdəlɪn] *n.* glucoside in bitter almonds, used as an expectorant. **amygdaline** [-laɪn], *adj.* pertaining to almonds; pertaining to tonsils.

amygdaloid [əˈmɪgdələɪd] *n.* basaltic rock with almond-shaped cavities, *adj.* almond-shaped.

amylaceous [ˌæmɪˈleɪʃəs] *adj.* starchy.

amylase [ˈæmɪleɪz] *n.* enzyme that helps to break down starch.

amyloid [ˈæmɪlɔɪd] *n.* food containing starch; *adj.* starchy; applied to disease in which lardaceous substance arises from degenerated cells.

amylolysis [ˌæmɪˈlɒləsɪs] *n.* conversion of starch into soluble products in digestive process. **amylolytic** [ˌæmɪləˈlɪtɪk], *adj.*

amylopsin [ˌæmɪˈlɒpsɪn] *n.* digestive ferment in pancreatic juice.

amylose [ˈæmɪləʊs] *n.* component of starch.

amyotonia [ˌeɪmaɪəˈtəʊnɪə] *n.* deficiency of muscle tone.

ana [ˈɑːnə] *n.* collection of sayings by, or stories and facts about, a person (often a suffix, *e.g. Dickensiana*).

anabaptist [ˌænəˈbæptɪst] *n.* believer in adult baptism. **anabaptism,** *n.* such belief; re-baptism.

anabas [ˈænəbæs] *n.* African and Asian fish which can leave the water.

anabasis [əˈnæbəsɪs] *n.* (*pl.* **–ses**) upward journey; military advance inland, especially of Persians and Greeks under Cyrus (401 BC); *Medicine*, first phase of disease; increase of fever. **anabatic,** *adj.* ascending; *Meteorology*, (of wind) moving upwards.

anabiosis [ˌænəbaɪˈəʊsɪs] *n.* return to life after seeming death.

anableps [ˈænəbleps] *n.* a tropical American fish that swims with its eyes half out of the water.

anabolic steroid [ˌænəˌbɒlɪk ˈsterɔɪd, -ˈstɪə-] *n.* any of several synthetic hormones used by athletes to improve their strength and muscles, or for medical purposes.

anabolism [əˈnæbəlɪzm] *n.* constructive chem. processes in living creatures. **anabolic,** *adj.* **anabolize,** *v.t.*

anacardic [ˌænəˈkɑːdɪk] *adj.* pertaining to cashew nut.

anacathartic [ˌænəkəˈθɑːtɪk] *n.* & *adj.* (drug) causing vomiting.

anachorism [əˈnækərɪzm] *n.* something out of place in or foreign to a country.

anachronic [ˌænəˈkrɒnɪk] *adj.* out of (chronological) order; out of date.

anachronism [əˈnækrənɪzm] *n.* error in chronology, especially of dating event before its correct date; thing impossible or absurd by reason of such error. **anachronistic, anachronous,** *adj.*

anaclitic [ˌænəˈklɪtɪk] *adj.* (of relationships), marked by dependence on another, or other people; (of sexual desire) dependent on another, non-sexual instinct, such as hunger.

anacoluthon [ˌænəkəˈluːθn] *n. Grammar*, lack of sequence, passing to a new subject, or sentence-construction, without completing first one. **anacoluthia,** *n.* such practice. **anacoluthic,** *adj.*

anaconda [ˌænəˈkɒndə] *n.* python of S America and Sri Lanka; any boa-like snake.

Anacreontic [əˌnækriˈɒntɪk] *adj.* (of verse) in the style of Anacreon, praising love and wine. *n.* such a poem.

anacrusis [ˌænəˈkruːsɪs] *n.* unaccented syllable(s) at beginning of verse-line, or such notes at beginning of piece of music. **anacrustic** [-ˈkrʌstɪk], *adj.*

anadem [ˈænədem] *n.* band; wreath; fillet.

anadiplosis [ˌænədɪˈpləʊsɪs] *n.* rhetorical device of repetition of last word of one clause at beginning of next.

anadipsia [ˌænəˈdɪpsɪə] *n. Medicine*, abnormal thirst. **anadipsic,** *adj.*

anadromous [əˈnædrəməs] *adj.* ascending, especially of fish that ascend rivers to spawn.

anaemia [əˈniːmɪə] *n.* lack of red blood cells; loss of vitality; pallidity. **pernicious** *or* **primary anaemia,** disease resulting in rapid destruction of red corpuscles. **anaemic,** *adj.*

anaemotrophy [ˌænɪˈmɒtrəfi] *n.* insufficient nourishment of blood.

anaeretic, aneretic [ˌænɪˈretɪk] *adj. Medicine* destructive.

anaerobe ['ænərəub, –neə–] *n.* organism able to live without, or unable to live in presence of, oxygen. **anaerobic,** *adj.* **anaerobiosis,** *n.* such existence. **anaerobiotic,** *adj.*

anaerophyte [æ'neərəfaɪt] *n. Botany,* anaerobic plant.

anaesthesia [,ænəs'θiːzɪə, –ʒə] *n.* loss of feeling; unconsciousness; act of causing such state for medical purposes. **anaesthesiology,** *n.* study of anaesthesia. **anaesthetize** [ə'niːsθətaɪz], *v.t.* cause anaesthesia. **anaesthetist** [ə'niːs–], *n., British* doctor specializing in administering anaesthetics.

anagalactic [,ænəgə'læktɪk] *adj. Astronomy,* beyond our galaxy; not galactic.

anagenesis [,ænə'dʒenəsɪs] *n.* tissue regeneration.

anaglyph ['ænəglɪf] *n.* ornament in bas relief; stereoscopic pictures in complementary colours viewed through glasses, etc., of same colours, one to each eye. **anaglyphy** [ə'næglɪfi], **anaglyptics,** *n.* art of carving anaglyphs.

anagnorisis [,ænæg'nɔːrɪsɪs] *n.* denouement in play, arising from recognition.

anagoge, anagogy [,ænə'gəʊdʒi] *n.* spiritual exaltation; mystical interpretation of sacred works such as the Bible. **anagogic(al),** *adj.* mystical.

anal ['eɪnl] *adj.* pertaining to or near the anus.

analects, analecta ['ænəlekts, ,ænə'lektə] *n. pl.* collection of writings; literary gleanings. **analectic,** *adj.*

analemma [,ænə'lemə] *n.* graduated scale in figure-of-eight, showing difference between actual time and that shown by the sun.

analeptic [,ænə'leptɪk] *n. & adj. Medicine,* restorative.

analgesia [,ænəl'dʒiːzɪə] *n.* absence of pain. **analgesic** [–zɪk], *n. & adj.*

analgetic [,ænl'dʒetɪk] *n. & adj.* (drug) arresting pain.

analgia [ə'næld ʒɪə] *n.* analgesia.

anallagmatic [,ænəlæg'mætɪk] *adj. Mathematics,* unchanged in shape by inversion.

analogous [ə'næləgəs] *adj.* similar in some respect; corresponding in function. **analogue** ['ænəlɒg], *n.* (*American*), computers: **analog**) analogous thing; word in other language with same use or meaning *adj* (of a quantity or a device) changing continuously rather than in a series of steps. **analog computer,** one calculating by physical quantities (e.g. voltage) equivalent to numerical variables.

analogy [ə'nælədʒi] *n.* close similarity; a similar case used in reasoning. **analogical** [,ænə'lɒdʒɪkl], *adj.* **analogize,** *v.i & t.* **analogism,** *n.* reasoning by quoting analogies.

analphabet [æŋ'ælfəbet] *n.* illiterate person.

anamnesis [,ænæm'niːsɪs] *n.* act of reminiscence; history of medical case. **anamnestic** [–'nestɪk], *adj.*

anamorphic [,ænə'mɔːfɪk] *adj.* (of optical device or image produced by it) magnifying or being magnified differently in two different directions; changing into a more complex form. **anamorphism,** *n.* such geological change.

anamorphosis [,ænəmɔː'fəʊsɪs, –'mɔːfəsɪs] *n.* distorted image only recognisable if viewed through appropriate device; method of making such images; *Biology,* evolution by slow changes; *Botany,* abnormal change of shape. **anamorphoscope** [–'mɔːf–], *n.* device for viewing anamorphosis.

ananas ['ænənæs] *n.* pineapple.

anandrious [ə'nændrɪəs] *adj.* impotent.

anandrous [ə'nændrəs] *adj. Botany,* without stamens.

ananthous [ə'nænθəs] *adj.* having no flowers.

ananym ['ænənɪm] *n.* name written backwards as pseudonym.

anapaest, anapest ['ænəpiːst] *n.* metrical foot of two short syllables followed by one long syllable. **anapaestic,** *adj.*

anaphora [ə'næfərə] *n.* rhetorical device of repeating word or phrase at beginning of successive clauses. **anaphoric** [,ænə'fɒrɪk], *adj. Grammar,* referring to word occurring earlier.

anaphrodisia [æn,æfrə'dɪzɪə] *n.* absence of sexual desire. **anaphrodisiac,** *n. & adj.* (drug) reducing sexual desire.

anaphroditic [æn,æfrə'dɪtɪk] *adj.* asexually produced.

anaphylaxis [,ænəfɪ'læksɪs] *n.* allergy; extreme sensitivity caused by previous inoculation. **anaphylactic** [–'læktɪk], *adj.*

anaplasia [,ænə'pleɪzɪə, –'pleɪʒə] *n.* reversion of plant or animal cells to a simpler form.

anaplasty ['ænəplæsti] *n.* plastic surgery. **anaplastic,** *adj.* pertaining to anaplasty; pertaining to anaplasia.

anaptotic [,ænəp'tɒtɪk] *adj. Philology,* with weakened or no case inflections.

anaptyxis [,ænəp'tɪksɪs] *n.* insertion of a vowel between two consonants for ease of pronunciation.

anarthrous [æn'ɑːθrəs] *adj. Zoology,* non-jointed; *Grammar,* without the article (of Greek nouns).

anasarcous [,ænə'sɑːkəs] *adj.* dropsical.

anastigmat [æn'æstɪgmæt] *n.* an anastigmatic lens. **anastigmatic** [,ænəstɪg'mætɪk], *adj.* not astigmatic; corrective of astigmatism.

anastomosis [ə,næstə'məʊsɪs] *n.* (*pl.* **-ses**) intercommunication between branches of blood-vessels, nerves, etc., or of rivers; formation of network. **anastomotic** [–'mɒtɪk], *adj.*

anastrophe [ə'næstrəfi] *n.* rhetorical device of reversing natural order of words; inversion.

anathema [ə'næθəmə] *n.* curse, generally by ecclesiastical authorities; act of cursing; thing cursed; object of hatred. **anathematic** [,ænəθɪ'mætɪk], *adj.* **anathematize,** *v.t.*

anatocism [ə'nætəsɪzm] *n.* compound interest; taking such interest.

anatomy [ə'nætəmi] *n.* study of structure of body; art of dissecting; structure; analysis; skeleton; very thin person. **anatomical** [,ænə'tɒmɪkl], *adj.* **anatomize,** *v.t.* dissect; analyse. **anatomist,** *n.*

anaudia [ə'nɔːdɪə] *n.* loss of voice.

anbury, ambury ['ænbəri, 'æm–] *n.* soft tumour of horses; 'finger and toe' disease of turnips; 'club-root'.

anchorite, anchoret ['æŋkəraɪt, –rɪt] *n.* (*fem.* **anchoress, ancress**) hermit, ascetic. **anchoritic(al)** [–'rɪt–], *adj.*

anchusa [æŋ'kjuːsə] *n.* genus including borage and alkanet.

anchylosis [ˌæŋkɪ'ləʊsɪs] *see* ankylosis.

ancien régime [ˌɒnsiæn reɪ'ʒiːm] (*French*) political and social state before the French revolution; former (*generally* evil) times.

ancillary [æn'sɪləri] *adj.* subordinate; auxiliary.

ancipital, ancipitous [æn'sɪpɪtl, –təs] *adj.* having two faces or edges; double-headed; twofold.

ancistroid [æn'sɪstrɔɪd] *adj.* having shape of hook.

ancon ['æŋkɒn] *n. Architecture*, one of a pair of brackets supporting a cornice.

anconal [æn'kəʊnl] *adj.* pertaining to the elbow. anconoid ['æŋkənɔɪd], *adj.* like an elbow.

ancoral ['æŋkərəl] *adj.* like an anchor; hooked.

ancress, ['æŋkres] *see* anchorite.

ancylostomiasis, ankylostomiasis [ˌæŋkɪləʊstə'maɪəsɪs] *n.* infestation with hookworms, leading to anaemia.

andiron ['ændaɪən] *n.* support for logs, fire-irons, or spit; fire-dog.

androcentric [ˌændrəʊ'sentrɪk] *adj.* revolving around men; regarding the male sex as primary.

androcephalous [ˌændrəʊ'sefələs] *adj.* with human head.

androcracy [æn'drɒkrəsi] *n.* domination of society by men. androcratic, [–'krætɪk], *adj.*

androgen ['ændrədʒən, –en] *n. Botany*, substance producing masculine characteristics; male sex hormone. androgenic [–'dʒenɪk], *adj.*

androgyne ['ændrədʒaɪn] *n.* hermaphrodite; effeminate man; masculine woman. androgynism [æn'drɒdʒənɪzm], *n.*

androgynous [æn'drɒdʒənəs] *adj.* hermaphrodite

android ['ændrɔɪd] *n.* machine in form of human being; robot; *adj.* man-like. androidal *adj.*

andromedotoxin [ænˌdrɒmɪdə'tɒksɪn] *n.* a poisonous substance extracted from plants of the heath family and used in medicine to lower high blood pressure.

andromorphous [ˌændrə'mɔːfəs] *adj.* having man's shape or appearance.

androphagous [æn'drɒfəgəs] *adj.* cannibal.

androphilic [ˌændrə'fɪlɪk] *adj.* preferring the male sex, or humans rather than animals.

androphobia [ˌændrə'fəʊbiə] *n.* dread or hatred of men.

androphonomania [ˌændrəfəʊnə'meɪniə] *n.* homicidal mania.

androphorous [æn'drɒfərəs] *adj. Zoology*, having male organs.

androsphinx ['ændrəsfɪŋks] *n.* figure with man's head and lion's body.

androsterone [æn'drɒstərəʊn] *n.* androgenic steroid male hormone.

anecdotage ['ænɪkdəʊtɪdʒ] *n. jocular*, tendency to garrulity in old age.

anechoic [ˌænɪ'kəʊɪk] *adj.* free from echoes and reverberations; sound-absorbent.

anele [ə'niːl] *v.t. archaic* anoint; administer extreme unction to.

anemia, [ə'niːmiə] *see* anaemia.

anemochord [ə'neməkɔːd] *n.* kind of pianoforte having strings vibrated by air currents.

anemograph [ə'neməgrɑːf] *n.* a recording anemometer. anemogram, *n.* record made by an anemograph.

anemometer [ˌænɪ'mɒmɪtə] *n.* instrument measuring strength and speed of wind. anemometry, *n.*

anemophilous [ˌænɪ'mɒfɪləs] *adj. Botany*, pollinated by wind. anemophile [ə'neməfaɪl], *n.* such plant. anemophily, *n.* such pollination.

anemophobia [əˌnemə'fəʊbiə] *n.* morbid dread of high winds, hurricanes, etc.

anemoscope [ə'neməskəʊp] *n.* any instrument indicating direction of wind.

anencephaly [ˌænen'kefəli, –'sef–] *n.* state of lacking a brain or a part of the brain. anencephalic, anencephalous, *adj.*

anent [ə'nent] *preposition archaic* or *jocular*, about, concerning.

anenterous [æn'entərəs] *adj.* lacking intestine or stomach.

anergy ['ænədʒi] *n.* absence of energy; loss of immunity.

aneroid ['ænərɔɪd] *adj.* not using liquid. aneroid barometer, instrument measuring atmospheric pressure by recording the movements of the surface of an air-tight box.

anesis ['ænəsɪs] *n. Medicine*, abatement of symptoms; *Music*, tuning to lower pitch.

aneurin ['ænjərɪn] *n.* thiamine.

aneurysm, aneurism ['ænjərɪzm] *n.* abnormal swelling of blood vessel. aneurysmal [–'rɪz–], aneurismal, *adj.*

anfractuous [æn'fræktjuəs] *adj. Botany*, wavy; snake-like; spiral-shaped. anfractuosity [–'ɒs–], *n.*

angary ['æŋgəri] *n.* right of belligerent to take or destroy property of neutral, subject to compensation.

angelica [æn'dʒelɪkə] *n.* aromatic plant yielding oil used in medicine and cookery; sugared stalks of angelica.

angelolater [ˌeɪndʒə'lɒlətə] *n.* worshipper of angels. angelolatry, *n.* such worship.

angelology [ˌeɪndʒə'lɒlədʒi] *n.* study of angels and their hierarchy.

angelus ['ændʒələs] *n.* prayer(s) said at early morning, noon and sunset. angelus bell, bell calling to prayer at such times.

angiitis [ˌændʒi'aɪtɪs] *n. Medicine*, inflammation of vessel.

angina [æn'dʒaɪnə] *n.* quinsy; any inflammation of throat or trachea. angina pectoris, spasm of the chest resulting from disease of heart or arteries. anginal, anginoid, anginose, anginous *adj.*

angiography [ˌændʒi'ɒgrəfi] *n.* technique for X-raying major blood vessels, using dye opaque to X-rays.

angioid ['ændʒiɔɪd] *adj.* like blood or lymph vessel.

angiology [ˌændʒi'ɒlədʒi] *n.* study of blood and lymphatic system.

angioma [ˌændʒi'əʊmə] *n.* tumour due to dilated blood vessels. angiomatosis, *n.* state of having many angiomas angiomatous, *adj.*

angiospasm ['ændʒiəˌspæzm] *n.* sudden contraction of blood vessels. angiospastic, *adj.*; *n.* substance causing angiospasm.

angiosperm ['ændʒiəspɜːm] *n.* flowering plant with seeds in closed seed-vessel; *pl.* natural division containing plants of such kind, the highest forms of plant life. angiospermous, angiospermal, angiospermatous, angiospermic, *adj.*

angiotomy [ˌændʒi'ɒtəmi] *n.* dissection of or incision into blood vessel.

anglicism, Anglicism ['æŋglɪsɪzm] *n.* characteristic English word or phrase found in another language; characteristic of English people or culture.

anglophone, Anglophone ['æŋgləfəʊn] *adj., n.* (person) speaking English.

angora [æŋ'gɔːrə] *n.* long-haired goat of Asia Minor; material made from angora hair; *adj.* long-haired (of cat, rabbit, etc.).

angostura [,æŋgə'stjʊərə] *n.* Brazilian tree and its bark; tonic fluid extracted from the bark.

angst [æŋst] *n.* general feeling of anxiety or anguish at state of world.

angstrom ['æŋstrəm] *n. Physics*, unit of length of light waves, one hundred-millionth of a centimetre, or of electromagnetic radiations: one tenth of a millimicron.

anguiform ['æŋgwɪfɔːm] *adj.* having shape of snake.

anguilliform [æŋ'gwɪlɪfɔːm] *adj.* having shape of eel.

anguine, anguinous ['æŋgwɪn, –əs] *adj. archaic,* pertaining to or like a snake.

angulation [,æŋgju'leɪʃn] *n.* shape having angles; exact measurement of angles. **angulate,** *adj.* having angles.

anhedonia [,ænhiː'dəʊniə] *n.* inability to be happy.

anhedral [æn'hiːdrəl] *adj.* denoting the angle at which the main planes of an aircraft are inclined downwards to the lateral axis.

anhelation [,ænhɪ'leɪʃn] *n. archaic,* shortness of breath.

anhidrosis [,ænhɪ'drəʊsɪs, –haɪ–] *n.* lack or absence of perspiration. **anhidrotic** [–'drɒtɪk], *n. & adj.* (drug) checking perspiration.

aniconic [,ænaɪ'kɒnɪk] *adj.* without idols; (of objects of worship) portrayed symbolically rather than representationally. **aniconism** [–'aɪkənɪzm], *n.* worship of object symbolising but not representing god; iconoclasm.

anidian [æn'ɪdiən] *adj.* (of an embryo) shapeless.

anil ['ænɪl] *n.* W Indian plant yielding indigo; indigo. **anilic** [ə'nɪlɪk] *adj.*

anile ['ænaɪl, 'eɪ–] *adj.* like a very old woman; imbecile.

aniline ['ænəlɪn, –aɪn] *n.* poisonous substance obtained from indigo, nitro-benzene, etc., used in manufacture of dyes; *adj.* applied to dye prepared with aniline.

anility [ə'nɪləti] *n.* state of being anile.

anima ['ænɪmə] *n. Psychology,* the inner self; the feminine principle as represented in the masculine subconscious.

animadvert [,ænɪmæd'vɜːt] *v.i.* take notice; comment; criticize; reprove. **animadversion,** *n.*

animalcule [,ænɪ'mælkjuːl] *n.* **animalculum** (*pl* –**ula**), *archaic,* microscopic animal, or, *erroneously,* plant. **animalcular,** *adj.*

animatism ['ænɪmətɪzm] *n.* belief that inanimate objects, etc., have personality and will, but not soul.

animative ['ænɪmətɪv, –meɪt–] *adj.* giving life.

animism ['ænɪmɪzm] *n.* belief in the possession of a soul by inanimate objects; belief in existence of soul separate from matter; spiritualism. **animist,** *n.,* **animistic,** *adj.*

animosity [,ænɪ'mɒsəti] *n.* active dislike, hostility.

animus ['ænɪməs] *n.* strong hostility; *Law,* intention: *Psychology* the masculine principle as represented in the feminine subconscious.

anion ['ænaɪən] *n.* negatively charged ion. **anionic** [–'ɒnɪk], *adj.*

anise ['ænɪs] *n.* Egyptian plant yielding aniseed. **anisate,** *v.t.* flavour with aniseed.

aniseed ['ænɪsiːd] *n.* dried fruit of anise; cordial made from it.

anisometropia [æn,aɪsəme'trəʊpiə] *n.* condition of eyes having unequal refractive power. **anisometropic** [–'trɒpɪk], *adj.*

anisosthenic [æn,aɪsə's θenɪk] *adj.* of unequal strength.

anker ['æŋkə] *n.* liquid measure, especially Dutch, of 8½ imperial gallons; cask holding that amount.

ankh [æŋk] *n.* cross with top vertical arm replaced by loop, representing, in ancient Egypt, eternity.

ankus ['æŋkəs] (*Indian*) *n.* elephant goad with hook and spike.

ankylosis, anchylosis [,æŋkɪ'ləʊsɪs] *n.* joining together of bones or hard parts; resulting stiffness. **ankylose** [æŋkɪləʊs], *v.i.* (of bones) to fuse or stiffen in this way.

ankylostoma [,æŋkɪ'lɒstəmə] *n.* lockjaw.

ankylostomiasis *see* **ancylostomiasis**.

ankyroid, ancyroid ['æŋkɪrɔɪd] *adj.* having shape of hook.

anlace ['ænleɪs] *n.* short double-edged sword or long dagger.

anna ['ænə] (*Indian*) *n.* coin valued at sixteenth part of rupee; one-sixteenth.

annates ['æneɪts] *n. pl.* first fruits; *Ecclesiastical,* a year's income of benefice.

annatto [ə'nætəʊ] *n.* reddish dye used for colouring foodstuffs; tropical American tree from seeds of which it is obtained.

anneal [ə'niːl] *v.t.* strengthen; temper, especially by subjecting to great heat and slow cooling.

annectant, annectent [ə'nektənt] *adj.* connecting; *Biology,* linking, especially of species.

annelid ['ænɪlɪd] *n. & adj.* worm; composed of annular segments. **annelidan** [ə'nelɪdən], *adj. & n.* **anneloid,** *adj. & n.*

annihilate [ə'naɪəleɪt] *v.t.* totally destroy; reduce to nothing. **annihilation, annihilator,** *n.* **annihilative, annihilatory,** *adj.*

anno Domini [,ænəʊ 'dɒmɪnaɪ, –iː] (*Latin*) 'in the year of the Lord'; in the Christian era (*abbr.* **A.D.**). *n., jocular,* old age.

anno hegirae [,ænəʊ 'hedʒɪriː, –hɪ'dʒaɪriː] (*Latin*) 'in the year of the hegira'; Mohammedan date (*abbr.* **A.H.**).

annomination [ə,nɒmɪ'neɪʃn] *n.* play on words; pun.

anno mundi [,ænəʊ 'mʊndiː, –'mʌndaɪ] (*Latin*) 'in the year of the world'; dating from creation, fixed by Archbishop Ussher at 4004 BC (*abbr.* **A.M.**).

anno orbis conditi [,ænəʊ ,ɔːbɪs 'kɒndɪtiː, –aɪ] (*Latin*) 'in the year of the creation' (*abbr.* **a.o.c.**).

anno regni [,ænəʊ 'regnaɪ, –niː] (*Latin*) 'in the year of (his/her) reign'.

annos vixit [,ænəʊs 'vɪksɪt] (*Latin*) 'lived (so many) years'; was aged (*abbr.* **a.v.**).

annotine ['ænəʊtaɪn] *n.* one-year-old, especially bird after first moult.

anno urbis conditae [ˌænəʊ ˌɜːbɪs ˈkɒndɪtaɪ, -iː] (*Latin*) 'in the year of the foundation of the city (Rome)', dated at 753 BC (*abbr.* **A.U.C.**). *See* **ab urbe condita**.

annuent [ˈænjuənt] *adj.* nodding, especially of muscles that nod the head.

annuity [əˈnjuːɪti] *n.* yearly income, especially for life. **annuitant**, *n.* person receiving annuity.

annul [əˈnʌl] *v.t.* cancel; invalidate; destroy. **anulment**, *n.*

annular [ˈænjʊlə] *adj.* pertaining to, forming or having shape of a ring. **annular eclipse**, eclipse of sun in which a ring of its surface surrounds the moon. **annulate**, *adj.* marked with rings; having rings of colour; annular. **annulation**, *n.* **annulary**, *n.* ring-finger.

annulet [ˈænjʊlət] *n.* small ring; *Architecture*, fillet or ring round column, especially on Doric capital.

annulism [ˈænjʊlɪzm] *n.* ringed structure.

annulose [ˈænjʊləʊs] *adj.* ringed; composed of rings.

annulus [ˈænjʊləs] (*Latin*) *n.* anything having shape of ring.

annunciate [əˈnʌnsieɪt, -ʃi-] *v.t.* announce; proclaim. **Annunciation**, *n.* announcement of the Incarnation to Mary, mother of Jesus; feast celebrated on Lady Day (March 25); **Annunciation lily**, madonna lily. **annunciative**, **annunciatory**, *adj.*

annus mirabilis [ˌænəs mɪˈrɑːbɪlɪs] (*Latin*) 'wonderful year', especially (in England) 1666.

anoa [əˈnəʊə] *n.* wild ox of Celebes.

anobiid [əˈnəʊbiɪd] *n.* one of the family of beetles which includes the deathwatch and the furniture beetle.

anocathartic [ˌænəkəˈθɑːtɪk] *n.* & *adj.* (drug) causing vomiting or expectoration.

anode [ˈænəʊd] *n.* *Electricity*, positive terminal; electrode by which current enters, or to which electrons flow. **anadal**, **anodic**, *adj.* **anodize**, *v.t.* coat with protective film electrolytically.

anodon [ˈænədɒn] *n.* hingeless and toothless bivalve; freshwater mussel.

anodontia [ˌænəˈdɒnʃiə] *n.* absence of teeth.

anodyne [ˈænədaɪn] *n.* & *adj.* (drug) reducing pain or mental distress. **anodynia**, *n.* absence of pain. **anodynic**, *adj.*

anoesia, anoia [ˌænəʊˈiːziə, əˈnɔɪə] *n.* imbecility.

anoesis [ˌænəʊˈiːsɪs] *n.* *Psychology*, mere reception of impressions without understanding or intellectual effort.

anoestrus [ænˈiːstrəs] *n.* period between two periods of sexual activity in animals. **anoestrous**, *adj.*

anoetic [ˌænəʊˈetɪk] *adj.* pertaining to anoesis.

anogenic [ˌænəˈdʒenɪk] *adj.* *Geology*, formed from below; plutonic.

anole [əˈnəʊli] *n.* chameleon-like W Indian and American lizard.

anolyte [ˈænəlaɪt] *n.* *Electricity*, portion of electrolyte about anode.

anomalism [əˈnɒməlɪzm] *n.* state or instance of being anomalous; anomaly.

anomalistic [əˌnɒməˈlɪstɪk] *adj.* *Astronomy*, pertaining to anomaly. **anomalistic month**, interval between two perigees of moon. **anomalistic year**, interval between two perihelion passages of Earth.

anomaloscope [əˈnɒmələskəʊp] *n.* device for testing for colour blindness.

anomalous [əˈnɒmələs] *adj.* self-contradictory; abnormal; out of harmony; irregular.

anomaly [əˈnɒməli] *n.* something that is anomalous; *Astronomy* the angle between a planet, the sun and the perihelion of the planet.

anomie, anomy [ˈænəmi] *n.* state in a society where normal social standards have deteriorated or been lost; state in an individual lacking usual moral standards, leading to disorientation and isolation. **anomic**, *adj.*

anon [əˈnɒn] *adv.* *archaic*, presently; as soon as possible; at a later date; *n* & *adj. abbreviation* of anonym(ous).

anonym [ˈænənɪm] *n.* anonymous person; pseudonym. **anonymity** [-ˈnɪm-], *n.* act or state of concealing name; unknown authorship. **anonymous** [əˈnɒnɪməs], *adj.* of unknown name or ori-

---

Handling the hyphen

Hyphens have two uses: to join word-parts together to make whole words (as in *word-parts*), and to separate word-parts when the word has to be split over two lines.

As a joining device (*word-part*), the hyphen is a halfway house between a space (*word part*) and complete fusion (*wordpart*). In the main, the way in which such compound words are written does not follow a single coherent set of rules, so it is best to consult a dictionary to find out how a particular compound is generally written. However, there are some principles that can be followed: use a hyphen or space where four or more consonants come together (*muck-spreader* is better than *muckspreader*); use a hyphen when a compound is used adjectivally before a noun (*a hundred-year-old egg*); use a hyphen to dis-

tinguish words that would otherwise be spelled the same (*recover* 'get better' versus *re-cover* 'cover again'); use a hyphen to avoid confusion (*a fine-art expert* is clearly not an art expert who is fine, but *a fine art expert* could be).

Rules and conventions for hyphenating words at the end of a line are also variable, but there are some on which most authorities agree: do not split a single-syllable word (*cal-ves* is not acceptable); do not leave a single letter at the beginning of a word or one or two letters at the end (*a-sleep* is not acceptable); try not to make a break that produces an odd or distracting effect (avoid *the-rapist* for *therapist*); where possible break between two independent consonant or vowel letters (*con-tain, flu-ency*).

gin; unnamed.

anoopsia, anopsia [ˌænəʊ'ɒpsiə, ə'nɒp–] *n.* upward squint.

anopheles [ə'nɒfəliːz] *n.* kind of mosquito. **anopheline,** *adj.*

anopisthographic [ˌænəpɪsθə'græfɪk] *adj.* bearing writing, etc., on one side only.

anorchous [ə'nɔːkəs] *adj.* lacking testicles. **anorchus,** *n.* such person.

anorexia [ˌænə'reksiə] *n.* lack of appetite. pathological refusal to eat, leading to weakness and even death. **anorectic, anorexic,** *adj. & n.*

anorthography [ˌænɔː'θɒɡrəfi] *n.* inability to write correctly due to imperfect muscular coordination.

anosmia, anosphresia [æn'ɒzmiə, ˌænɒs'friːziə] *n.* loss of sense of smell. **anosmic,** *adj.*

anourous [ə'nʊərəs] *adj.* lacking a tail, especially applied to frog.

anovulatory [ˌænɒvju'leɪtəri, æn'ɒvjʊlətəri] *adj.* not associated with ovulation; suppressing ovulation.

anoxaemia [ˌænɒk'siːmiə] *n.* condition resulting from insufficient aeration of blood; mountain sickness. **anoxaemic,** *adj.*

anoxia [æn'ɒksiə] *n.* deficiency of oxygen especially severe; condition due to this, especially in flying at great heights. **anoxic,** *adj.*

anoxybiosis [ˌænɒksɪbaɪ'əʊsɪs] *n.* anaerobiosis. **anoxybiotic,** *adj.*

ansate ['ænseɪt] *adj.* having a handle. **ansate cross, ankh, ansation,** *n.* handlemaking.

anschluss, Anschluss ['ænʃlʊs] (*German*) *n.* political union.

anserine, anserous ['ænsəraɪn, –əs] *adj.* like or pertaining to a goose; foolish.

anta ['æntə] (*pl.* **–s, –ae**), *n.* column forming end of side wall of portico, etc., or pilaster at side of doorway.

antacid [ænt'æsɪd] *n. & adj.* curative of acidity, especially intestinal.

antalgic [ænt'ældʒɪk] *n. & adj.* (drug) alleviating pain.

antalkali [ænt'ælkəlaɪ] *n.* substance neutralising alkali. **antalkaline,** *adj.*

antanaclasis [ˌæntə'nækləsɪs] *n. obsolete,* repetition of word from earlier phrase, especially of same word with different meaning.

ant-apex [ænt'eɪpeks] *n. Astrononomy,* point 180° from that to which sun is moving.

antarthritic [ˌæntɑː'θrɪtɪk] *n. & adj.* (drug) used against gout.

antebellum [ˌænti'beləm] *adj.* existing before the war, especially the US civil war.

antecedaneous [ˌæntɪsɪ'deɪniəs] *adj.* before in time.

antecedent [ˌæntɪ'siːdnt] *adj.* before in time; prior; *n.* event happening prior to; *Music* , subject of fugue stated in first part; *Grammar,* previous word, especially one to which pronoun, etc., refers; *pl.* personal history; ancestry. **antecedence,** *n.* **antecessor,** *n.* predecessor.

antedate [ˌænti'deɪt] *v.t.* date, or assign a date to, a document, etc., earlier than its correct date; precede in point of time; anticipate.

antediluvian, antediluvial [ˌæntɪdɪ'luːviən, –iəl] *adj.* pertaining to period before the Flood; old-fashioned; out of date.

antefix ['æntɪfɪks] *n.* (*pl.* **–xes, –xa**) ornament at end of classical building, hiding ends of roof tiles.

antelucan [ˌænti'luːkən, –'ljuː–] *adj. archaic,* before dawn.

antemeridian [ˌæntimə'rɪdiən] *adj.* in the morning.

antemetic [ˌænti'metic] *n. & adj.* (drug) preventive of vomiting.

ante mortem [ˌænti 'mɔːtem] (*Latin*) 'before death'.

antemundane [ˌænti'mʌndeɪn] *adj.* before the Creation.

antenatal [ˌænti'neɪtl] *adj.* before birth.

antenna [æn'tenə] *n.* (*pl.* **–s, –nae**), *Zoology,* sensitive outgrowth on head of insect, crustacean, etc.; *Radio* aerial, especially complex. **antennal** *adj.* **antennary, antenniferous,** *adj.* bearing antennae. **antenniform** *adj.* antenna-shaped. **antennule** *n.* small antenna or similar appendage.

antenuptial [ˌænti'nʌpʃl] *adj.* before marriage.

antepaschal [ˌænti'pæskl, –'pɑː–] *adj.* before Easter or the Passover.

antepast ['æntɪpæst] *n. archaic,* foretaste, especially a first course.

antependium [ˌæntɪ'pendiəm] *n.* altar frontal; similar cloth on pulpit or lectern.

antepenult [ˌæntɪpɪ'nʌlt] *n.* antepenultimate syllable or word. **antepenultimate,** *adj.* last but two.

antephialtic [ˌæntefɪ'æltɪk] *n. & adj.* preventive of nightmare.

anteprandial [ˌænti'prændiəl] *adj.* before dinner.

anterior [æn'tɪəriə] *adj.* before in time; in front. **anteriority,** *n.*

antetype ['æntɪtaɪp] *n.* prototype.

antevenient [ˌæntɪ'viːniənt] *adj.* preceding.

antevert [ˌænti'vɜːt] *v.t.* to displace a body organ forwards. **anteversion,** *n.*

antevocalic [ˌæntivə'kælɪk] *n.* immediately preceding a vowel.

anthelion [ænt'hiːliən, æn'θiː–] *n.* kind of solar halo opposite sun; antisun.

anthelmintic [ˌænthel'mɪntɪk, ˌænθel–] *n. & adj.* (remedy) used against intestinal worms.

anthemion [æn'θiːmiən] *n.* (*pl.* **–ia**) flat cluster of leaves or flowers as ornament in classical art; *Architecture,* honeysuckle ornament.

anther ['ænθə] *n. Botany,* male, pollen-bearing organ of flower. **antheral,** *adj.* **antherozoid,** *n.* male sexual element in lower plants; spermatozoid.

antheridium [ˌænθə'rɪdiəm] *n.* (*pl.* **–dia**) male organ in cryptogams.

anthesis [æn'θiːsɪs] *n.* the process or period of flowering.

anthology [æn'θɒlədʒi] *n.* collection of literary pieces. **anthological,** *adj.* **anthologize,** *v.t.* anthologist, *n.*

anthomania [ˌænθə'meɪniə] *n.* great love of flowers.

anthophagous [æn'θɒfəgəs] *adj.* feeding on flowers.

anthophilous, anthophilian [æn'θɒfɪləs, ˌænθə'fɪliən] *adj.* flower-loving; feeding on flowers.

anthophorous [æn'θɒfərəs] *adj. Botany,* flower-bearing.

anthotaxy ['ænθətæksi] *n. Botany,* disposition of flowers in cluster.

anthozoan [ˌænθəˈzəʊən] *n.* sea-anemone; coral polyp; any creature of the natural class *Anthozoa*. anthozoan, anthozoic, *adj.* anthozooid, *n.* coral polyp.

anthracoid [ˈænθrəkɔɪd] *adj.* resembling anthrax; resembling carbon, coal or charcoal.

anthracolithic [ˌænθrəkəˈlɪθɪk] *adj.* containing anthracite or graphite.

anthracosis [ˌænθrəˈkəʊsɪs] *n.* presence of coal dust in lungs. anthracotic *adj.*

anthracothere [ˈænθrəkəʊθɪə] *n.* fossil pachyderm.

anthrax [ˈænθræks] *n.* severe infectious disease of cattle and sheep, communicable to human beings; boil cause by this.

anthropic(al) [ænˈθrɒpɪk, -l] *adj.* pertaining to human beings.

anthropocentric [ˌænθrəpəʊˈsentrɪk] *adj.* regarding humanity as centre of universe. anthropocentrism, *n.*

anthropogenesis, anthropogeny [ˌænθrəpəʊˈdʒenəsɪs, -ˈpɒdʒəni] *n.* study of human generation or evolution. anthropogenetic [-dʒəˈnetɪk], *adj.*

anthropogenic [ˌænθrəpəˈdʒenɪk] *adj.* pertaining to the effect of human beings on the natural world.

anthropogeography [ˌænθrəpəʊdʒiˈɒɡrəfi] *n.* study of geographical distribution of human beings.

anthropoglot [ˈænθrəpəʊɡlɒt] *n.* animal with human-like tongue; parrot.

anthropoid [ˈænθrəpɔɪd] *adj.* resembling humans; *n.* such ape. anthropoidal, *adj.*

anthropolatry [ˌænθrəˈpɒlətri] *n.* worship, deification of a human being.

anthropolith, anthropolite [ˈænθrəpəʊlɪθ, -laɪt] *n.* petrified human remains.

anthropology [ˌænθrəˈpɒlədʒi] *n.* science of natural history of human beings. anthropological, *adj.* anthropologist, *n.*

anthropometry [ˌænθrəˈpɒmətri] *n.* measurement of parts and functions of human body, especially as part of study of evolution.

anthropomorphism [ˌænθrəpəˈmɔːfɪzm] *n.* representation of a god in human form; ascribing human characteristics to non-human things. anthropomorphic, *adj.* anthropomorphize, *v.t.* anthropomorphist *n.*

anthropomorphosis [ˌænθrəpəˈmɔːfəsɪs] *n.* transformation into human shape. anthropomorphous, *adj.* resembling human beings in shape.

anthropopathy, anthropopathism [ˌænθrəˈpɒpəθi, -θɪzm] *n.* ascribing human feelings to a god or inanimate object. anthropopathic [-ˈpæθɪk], *adj.*

anthropophagi [ˌænθrəˈpɒfədʒaɪ] *n. pl.* (*sing.* anthropophagus) cannibals. anthropophagous, *adj.* anthropophagy, *n.* anthropophagite, *n.* a cannibal.

anthropophuism [ˌænθrəˈpɒfjuɪzm] *n.* ascribing human nature to God.

anthropopithecus [ˌænθrəpəʊˈpɪθɪkəs] *n.* conjectural animal forming 'missing link' between man and apes.

anthropopsychism [ˌænθrəpəʊˈsaɪkɪzm] *n.* ascribing human-like soul to nature.

anthroposcopy [ˌænθrəˈpɒskəpi] *n.* evaluation of human bodily characteristics by inspection rather than anthropometry.

anthroposociology [ˌænθrəpəʊˌsəʊɪˈɒlədʒi] *n.* study of effect of environment on race, and vice versa.

anthroposophy [ˌænθrəˈpɒsəfi] *n.* knowledge of human nature; human wisdom; form of mysticism akin to theosophy. anthroposophical, *adj.*

anthropotheism [ˌænθrəpəʊˈθiːɪzm] *n.* belief that gods have human nature or are only deified human beings.

anthropotomy [ˌænθrəˈpɒtəmi] *n.* human anatomy.

anthropozoic [ˌænθrəpəʊˈzəʊɪk] *adj. Geology*, characterized by human existence, especially the Quaternary period.

anthus [ˈænθəs] *n.* genus containing meadow pipit.

antibacchius [ˌæntɪˈbækiəs] *n.* metrical foot of two long and one short syllables. antibacchic, *adj.*, *n.*

antibasilican [ˌæntɪbəˈzɪlɪkən, -ˈsɪ-] *adj.* opposed to principle of monarchy.

antibiosis [ˌæntɪbaɪˈəʊsɪs] *n.* association between organisms causing injury to one of them. antibiont [-ˈbaɪɒnt], *n.* organism living in antibiosis.

antibiotic [ˌæntɪbaɪˈɒtɪk] *n.* & *adj.* (substance) active against disease bacteria, obtained from a living organism such as a mould (fungus) or bacterium.

antiblastic [ˌæntɪˈblæstɪk] *adj.* opposing growth, especially of harmful substances; giving natural immunity.

antibody [ˈæntɪˌbɒdi] *n.* substance in blood that neutralizes specific harmful substances.

antibrachial [ˌæntɪˈbreɪkɪəl] *adj.* pertaining to forearm.

anticachectic [ˌæntɪkəˈkektɪk] *n.* & *adj.* (drug) used against cachexy.

anticholinergic [ˌæntɪkəʊlɪˈnɜːdʒɪk, -kɒ-] *adj.* blocking nerve impulses, in order to control intestinal spasms.

antichresis [ˌæntɪˈkriːsɪs] *n.* (*pl.* -es) possession and enjoyment of mortgaged property by mortgagee in lieu of interest payments.

antichthones [ænˈtɪkθəniːz] *n. pl.* inhabitants of antipodes.

anticlastic [ˌæntɪˈklæstɪk] *adj.* having transverse and opposite curvatures of surface.

anticlimax [ˌæntɪˈklaɪmæks] *n.* weak ending; sudden descent to the ridiculous; bathos.

anticline [ˈæntɪklaɪn] *n. Geology*, upward fold. anticlinal [-ˈklaɪnl], *adj.* anticlinorium [-klaɪˈnɔːrɪəm], *n.* arch-shaped group of anticlines and synclines.

anticonvellent [ˌæntɪkənˈvelənt] *n.* & *adj.* (drug) used against convulsions.

anticous [ænˈtaɪkəs] *adj. Botany*, turning away from axis.

anticryptic [ˌæntɪˈkrɪptɪk] *adj. Zoology*, having protective resemblance to environment.

anticyclone [ˌæntɪˈsaɪkləʊn] *n.* area of high atmospheric pressure, from which winds flow outwards in a clockwise direction in N hemisphere.

antidactyl [ˌæntɪˈdæktɪl] *n.* anapaest.

antidetonant [ˌæntɪˈdetənənt] *n.* anti-knock element in petrol.

antidromic [ˌænti'drɒmɪk] *adj.* (of nerve fibres) conducting impulses in the opposite direction to normal; *Botany*, twining towards right and left in members of one species.

antifebrile [ˌænti'fiːbraɪl, -rɪl] *n. & adj.* preventive or curative of fever.

antigalactic [ˌæntigə'læktɪk] *n. & adj.* preventive of milk-secretion.

antigen ['æntɪdʒən, -en] *n.* substance causing production of antibodies.

antihistamine [ˌænti'hɪstəmiːn, -mɪn] *n.* any drug counteracting effect of histamine, especially in treatment of allergies.

antihydropic [ˌæntihaɪ'drɒpɪk] *n. & adj.* (drug) used against jaundice.

anti-icteric [ˌæntiɪk'terɪk] *n. & adj.* (drug) used against dropsy.

antilapsarian [ˌæntilæp'seəriən] *n. & adj.* (person) denying doctrine of the fall of Man.

antilegomena [ˌæntilə'gɒmɪnə] *n. pl.* New Testament books not in early Christian canon.

antilibration [ˌæntilaɪ'breɪʃn] *n.* counterpoising.

antilogarithm [ˌænti'lɒgərɪðm] *n.* number of which logarithm is a power of 10 or other base (*abbr.* **antilog.**).

antilogism [æn'tɪlədʒɪzm] *n. Logic*, statement containing three propositions two of which contradict the third. **antilogistic** *adj.*

antilogy [æn'tɪlədʒi] *n.* self-contradictory statement.

antimatter ['æntiˌmætə] *n.* hypothetical form of matter composed of particles equivalent to particles of normal matter but oppositely charged.

antimetabole [ˌæntime'tæbəli] *n.* repetition of words or ideas in different order.

antimetathesis [ˌæntime'tæθəsɪs] *n.* repetition of parts of antithesis in reverse order. **antimetathetic,** *adj.*

antimony ['æntɪməni] *n.* a brittle, crystalline, whitish mineral; metal obtained from antimony and used in alloys and medicine. **antimonic** [-'mɒnɪk], **antimonious** [-'məuniəs], *adj.* **antimoniferous,** *adj.* yielding antimony.

antineuritic [ˌæntinju'rɪtɪk] *n. & adj.* preventive of neuritis, especially applied to vitamin B or food containing it.

antinomian [ˌænti'nəumiən] *n.* one believing that belief in Christ frees someone from normal legal and moral obligations.

antinomy [æn'tɪnəmi] *n.* legal contradiction; contradiction between logical conclusions. **antinome** ['æntɪnəum], *n.* contradictory law or conclusion. **antinomic** [-'nɒmɪk], *adj.*

antiodontalgic [ˌæntiəudɒn'tældʒɪk] *n. & adj.* (drug) used against toothache.

antiorgastic [ˌæntiɔː'gæstɪk] *n. & adj.* sedative.

antioxidant [ˌænti'ɒksɪdənt] *n.* substance preventing oxidation in food, rubber, petrol etc.

antipaedobaptist [ˌænti,piːdəu'bæptɪst] *n. & adj.* (person) denying validity of infant baptism.

antiparallelogram [ˌænti,pærə'leləgræm] *n.* quadrilateral with two sides parallel and two not parallel.

antiparticle ['æntiˌpɑːtɪkl] *n.* an elementary particle corresponding to another in mass but different in electrical charge. The two destroy each other if they collide.

Antipasch(a) ['æntɪpæsk, -ə] *n.* Low Sunday; first Sunday after Easter.

antipastic [æntɪpæs'tɪk] *adj.* pertaining to or like dishes, aperitifs, etc., served before main courses of dinner. **antipasto,** *(Italian),* *n.* appetizer; hors d'oeuvres.

antipathy [æn'tɪpəθi] *n.* dislike. **antipathetic** [-'θetɪk], **antipathic** [-'pæθɪk], *adj.*

antiperistasis [ˌæntɪpə'rɪstəsɪs] *n. archaic*, opposition; resistance; denying an inference while admitting the fact on which it is based.

antipharmic [ˌænti'fɑːmɪk] *adj.* antidotal.

antiphlogistic [ˌæntiflə'dʒɪstɪk] *n. & adj.* (drug) used against inflammation.

antiphon ['æntɪfən] *n.* a response said or sung as part of the liturgy; a psalm etc. sung alternately by two choirs. **antiphonal,** *adj.* (of music) sung alternately.

antiphrasis [æn'tɪfrəsɪs] *n.* (*pl.* **-ses**), *Rhetoric* use of a word in the opposite sense to its usual one, for humorous or ironic purposes.

antipodagric [æntipə'dægrɪk] *adj.* used against gout.

antipodes [æn'tɪpədiːz] *n. pl.* region on other side of globe; exact opposite. **antipodal,** *adj.* diametrically opposite. **antipodean,** *adj. n.*

antipruritic [ˌæntipru'rɪtɪk] *n. & adj.* (drug) alleviating itching.

antipsychiatry [ˌæntisaɪ'kaɪətri] *n.* treatment of mental illness not relying on drugs, etc.

antipyretic [ˌæntipaɪ'retɪk] *n. & adj.* (drug) preventing or reducing fever; febrifuge. **antipyresis** *n.* treatment of fever with such drugs.

antipyrotic [ˌæntipaɪ'rɒtɪk] *n. & adj.* (treatment) used against burns.

antirachitic [ˌæntirə'kɪtɪk] *adj.* preventive of rickets, especially applied to vitamin D or food containing it.

antiscians [æn'tɪʃnz, -ʃiənz] *n. pl.* persons living on opposite sides of equator but in same longitude.

antiscorbutic [ˌæntiskɔː'bjuːtɪk] *n. & adj.* preventive of scurvy, especially applied to vitamin C or food containing it.

antisemite [ˌænti'siːmaɪt, -'se-] *n.* opponent of Jews. **antisemitic** [-sə'mɪtɪk], *adj.* **antisemitism** [-'semətɪzm], *n.*

antisideric [ˌæntisaɪ'derɪk] *n. & adj.* (substance) counteracting effect of iron.

antispast ['æntɪspæst] *n.* metrical foot comprising an iambus followed by a trochee.

antistrophe [æn'tɪstrəfi] *n.* stanza answering strophe in Greek chorus, recited during movement from left to right. **antistrophic,** *adj.*

antistrumatic [ˌæntistru'mætɪk] *n.* remedy for scrofula.

antithalian [ˌæntiθə'laɪən, -'θeɪliən] *adj.* disapproving of festivity and laughter.

antithesis [æn'tɪθəsɪs] *n.* (*pl.* **-ses**) opposite; contrast; *Literature*, device of parallel but contrasted phrases or sentences, second stage of reasoned argument, opposing the thesis. **antithetical** [ˌæntɪ'θetɪkl], antithetic, *adj.*

antithrombin [ˌænti'θrɒmbɪn] *n.* substance in blood preventing coagulation of blood.

antitoxic [ˌænti'tɒksɪk] *adj.* neutralizing poison. **antitoxin,** *n.* antibody, especially obtained from infected animal.

antitrades ['æntitreidz] *n.pl.* westerly winds prevailing beyond 40°N and S, westerly winds of upper air above trade winds.

antitropic [,ænti'tropik] *adj. Zoology*, symmetrically reversed, as right and left hands. antitrope ['æntitrəup], *n.* such appendage. antitropy, *n.* state of being antitropic.

antitussive [,ænti'tʌsɪv] *n. & adj.* (drug, etc.) that alleviates or prevents coughing.

antitype ['æntitaɪp] *n.* object or person prefigured by the type or symbol. antitypic, antitypical [-'tɪp-], *adj.*

antitypy [æn'tɪtɪpi] *n.* resistance to penetration or alteration.

antivenin, antivenene [,ænti'venɪn, -iːn] *n.* serum used against snake-bite.

antizymic [,ænti'zɪmɪk] *n. & adj.* preventive of fermentation. antizymotic [-zaɪ'mɒtɪk] *n.*

antoecial [æn'tiːʃl] *adj.* applied to places in opposite hemispheres but in same latitude and longitude. antoecians, *n.pl.* persons living in such places.

antonomasia [,æntənə'meɪziə, -ʒə] *n.* literary device of using descriptive epithet or phrase instead of person's name; using proper name as epithet.

antonym ['æntənɪm] *n.* word of opposite meaning. antonymous [æn'tɒnɪməs], *adj.* antonymy, *n.*

antral ['æntrəl] *adj.* pertaining to antrum.

antrorse ['æntrɔːs] *adj. Biology*, turning upward and forward.

antrum ['æntrəm] *n. (pl. -ra)* sinus; cavity, especially leading into nose.

anuran [ə'njʊərən] *n.* any of the order of amphibians which includes frogs and toads.

anuresis [,ænju'riːsɪs] *n.* inability to urinate. anuretic *adj.*

anuria [ə'njʊəriə] *n.* inability to produce urine.

anurous ['ænjʊrəs, ə'njʊərəs] *adj.* lacking a tail, especially applied to frog.

anus ['eɪnəs] *n.* opening at posterior end of alimentary canal.

aorist ['eərɪst] *n. & adj. Grammar*, (tense) signifying happening in unrestricted or unspecified past. aoristic, *adj.* indefinite; pertaining to aorist.

aorta [eɪ'ɔːtə] *n.* main artery from left ventricle of heart. aortal, aortic, *adj.*

à outrance [ɑː 'uːtrɒns] *(French)* 'to the utmost'; to the death.

apaesthesia [,æpiːs'θiːziə] *n.* loss of feeling in limb.

apagoge [,æpə'gəʊdʒi] *n. Mathematics*, argument by reductio ad absurdum. apogogic(-al) [-'gɒdʒ-] *adj.*

apanage *see* appanage.

apandrous [ə'pændrəs] *adj.* having non-functioning male organs (of fungi, etc.).

apartheid [ə'pɑːtheɪt, -haɪt] *(S African) n.* (former) policy of segregating racial groups, especially in S Africa.

apatetic [,æpə'tetɪk] *adj. Zoology*, having protective imitative coloration or shape.

apathy ['æpəθi] *n.* indifference; lack of enthusiasm; intellectual dullness. apathetic [-'θetɪk] *adj.*

aperient [ə'pɪəriənt] *n. & adj.* laxative (medicine). aperitive *adj.*

aperitif [ə,perə'tiːf] *n.* appetizer, generally alcoholic.

apetalous [eɪ'petl-əs] *adj. Botany*, lacking petals.

aphaeresis [ə'fɪərəsɪs] *n.* cutting off beginning of word. aphaeretic *adj.*

aphagia [ə'feɪdʒiə] *n.* inability to swallow.

aphasia [ə'feɪziə, -ʒə] *n.* loss of powers of speech and of memory of words, due to injury to speech area of brain. aphasic, aphasiac, *adj. & n.* (person) so afflicted.

aphelion [æ'fiːliən] *n. (pl. -lia)* point in orbit most distant from sun.

apheliotropic [æ,fiːliə'trɒpɪk] *adj.* growing away from the sun. apheliotropism [-'ɒtrəpɪzm], *n.*

aphemia [ə'fiːmiə] *n.* loss of power of articulate speech; motor aphasia.

aphesis ['æfəsɪs] *n. (pl. -ses)* loss of unaccented vowel at beginning of word. aphetic [ə'fetɪk], *adj.*

aphid ['eɪfɪd] *n.* any of the plant-sucking insects of the family *Aphididae*.

aphis ['eɪfɪs] *n. (pl. -ides ['æfɪdiːz, 'eɪ-], plant-louse; member of genus *Aphis* which includes greenfly, etc. aphidiphagous [-'dɪfəgəs] *adj.* feeding on aphides.

aphonia [eɪ'fəʊniə] *n.* loss of voice. aphonic[eɪ'fɒnɪk], *adj.* voiceless.

aphorism ['æfərɪzm] *n.* brief wise saying; maxim; definition. aphoristic, *adj.* aphorize, *v.i.* speak or write (as if) in aphorisms.

aphotic [eɪ'fəʊtɪk] *adj.* without light.

aphrasia [ə'freɪziə] *n.* inability to speak, or to make intelligible phrases.

aphrodisiac [,æfrə'dɪziæk] *n. & adj.* (drug) inducing sexual desire. aphrodisiacal [-dɪ'zaɪəkl], *adj.* aphrodisian, pertaining to love or Venus.

aphtha ['æfθə] *n. (pl. -ae)* small white spot or small ulceration on mucous membrane, etc. in humans or animals; disease associated with aphthae, such as thrush. aphthic, *adj.* aphthous, *adj.*, pertaining to aphtha; aphthous fever, foot-and-mouth disease.

aphylly [eɪ'fɪli] *n.* absence of leaves. aphyllous, *adj.*

apiaceous [,eɪpi'eɪʃəs] *adj.* parsley-like; belonging to plant family including carrot, parsley, etc.

apian ['eɪpiən] *adj.* pertaining to bees.

apiary ['eɪpiəri] *n.* place where bees are kept; collection of bee-hives. apiarian [-'eər-], *adj.* pertaining to bee-keeping. apiarist, *n.* bee-keeper.

apical ['æpɪkl, 'eɪ-] *adj.* at the summit or tip; *Phonetics* pertaining to a consonant formed with help of tip of tongue. apicad, *adv.* towards the summit.

apiculate [ə'pɪkjuleɪt] *adj.* (of leaves) having short point at tip.

apiculture ['eɪpɪ,kʌltʃə] *n.* bee-keeping. apiculturist, *n.*

apiology [,eɪpi'ɒlədʒi] *n.* study of bees.

apivorous [eɪ'pɪvərəs] *adj.* eating bees.

aplanat ['æplənæt] *n.* aplanatic lens. aplanatic [-'nætɪk], *adj.* free from spherical aberration. aplanatism [ə'plænətɪzm], *n.*

aplasia [ə'pleɪziə, -ʒə] *n. Medicine*, incomplete development. aplastic, *adj.*

aplomb [ə'plɒm] *n.* composure, self-possession.

aplotomy [ə'plɒtəmi] *n.* simple surgical cut.

apnoea [æp'niːə] *n.* temporary cessation of breathing. apnoeic, *adj.*

apocalypse [ə'pɒkəlɪps] *n.* revelation, *generally* of St. John the Divine. **apocalyptic(al)** [–'lɪp–], *adj.* pertaining to apocalypse; prophetic; foretelling disaster; dramatically conclusive.

apocatastisis [,æpəʊkə'tæstəsɪs] *n.* restoration; *Medicine*, relapse; subsidence; *Astrononomy*, reversion to same position; *Theology*, conversion of whole world to Christianity.

apocentre ['æpə,sentə] *n.* point in orbit opposite centre of attraction. **apocentric**, *adj.* different from archetype. **apocentricity**, *n.*

apochromat ['æpəkrəmæt] *n.* apochromatic lens. **apochromatic** [–'mætɪk], *adj.* lacking both spherical and chromatic aberration.

apocope [ə'pɒkəpi] *n.* cutting off end of word. **apocopate**, *v.t. & adj.*

apocrisiary [,æpə'krɪziəri] *n.* papal secretary or nuncio.

apocrustic [,æpə'krʌstɪk] *n. & adj.* astringent (medicine).

apocrypha [ə'pɒkrəfə] *n. pl.* books of unknown authorship; uncanonical books, especially, those of Septuagint and Vulgate. **apocryphal**, *adj.* of doubtful origin.

apocynthion [,æpə'sɪnθɪən] *n.* point in an orbit of the moon which is farthest from the moon's centre.

apodal ['æpədl] *adj. & n.* lacking feet or obvious hind limbs. **apodan**, *n. & adj.* **apodous** *adj.* (of insect larvae.

apodeictic, apodictic [,æpə'daɪktɪk, –'dɪk–] *adj.* evident; demonstrable; incontrovertible.

apodosis [ə'pɒdəsɪs] *n.* (*pl.* –ses) main clause in conditional sentence.

apogaeic, apogaic [,æpə'dʒiːɪk, –'geɪɪk] *adj.* pertaining to apogee.

apogamy [ə'pɒgəmi] *n. Biology*, interbreeding in a separated group which has no characteristic differentiating it from parents; *Botany*, nonsexual reproduction in some ferns.

apogee ['æpədʒiː] *n.* point in orbit, especially moon's, most distant from earth; zenith; climax. **apogean, apogeal,**, *adj.*

apogeny [ə'pɒdʒəni] *n. Botany*, sterility. **apogenous**, *adj.*

apogeotropic [,æpədʒiːə'trɒpɪk] *adj. Botany*, bending up or away from the ground. **apogeotropism** [–'ɒtrəpɪzm], *n.*

apograph ['æpəgrɑːf] *n.* copy; facsimile. **apographal** [ə'pɒgrəfəl], *adj.*

apolaustic [,æpə'lɔːstɪk] *adj.* caring only for pleasure.

apolegamic [,æpəlɪ'gæmɪk] *adj. Biology*, pertaining to selection, especially sexual.

apolitical [,eɪpə'lɪtɪkl] *adj.* not political, politically neutral.

apologetics [ə,pɒlə'dʒetɪks] *n. pl.* defence and proof, *generally* of Christianity; whole body of such writings.

apologia [,æpə'ləʊdʒiə] *n.* formal defence of a cause, one's beliefs, etc.

apologist [ə'pɒlədʒɪst] *n.* one who writes or speaks in defence of a cause or institution.

apologue ['æpəlɒg] *n.* parable, moral tale.

apolune ['æpəluːn, –ljuːn] *n.* point in the orbit of body revolving round the moon that is farthest from the centre of the moon.

apomecometer [,æpəʊmɪ'kɒmɪtə] *n.* instrument measuring height and distance.

apomict ['æpəmɪkt] *n.* organism reproducing by, or formed by, apomixis.

apomixis [,æpə'mɪksɪs] *n.* non-sexual reproduction. **apomictic** *adj.*

apopemptic [,æpə'pemptɪk] *n. & adj.* valedictory (address).

apophasis [ə'pɒfəsɪs] *n.* rhetorical device of emphasizing a fact, by pretending to ignore or deny it.

apophony [ə'pɒfəni] *n.* ablaut.

apophthegm ['æpəθem] *n.* brief wise saying. **apophthegmatic** [–θeg'mætɪk], *adj.*

apophyge [ə'pɒfɪdʒi] *n., Architecture*, curve between shaft and base, or between shaft & capital, in a column.

apophysis [ə'pɒfəsɪs] *n.* offshoot; projecting part, especially of bone. **apophyseal, apophysial** [–'fɪzɪəl], *adj.* **apophysate**, *adj. Botany*, having an apophysis.

apoplexy ['æpəpleksi] *n.* stroke or seizure due to thrombosis or rupture of brain artery. **apoplectic** [–'plektɪk], *adj.* pertaining to, like or symptomatic of apoplexy.

aporia [ə'pɔːriə] *n.* (*pl.* –s, –ae) rhetorical device of pretending not to know what to do or say; passage expressing a doubt or difficulty.

aposematic [,æpəsɪ'mætɪk] *adj. Zoology*, giving warning, applied to coloration, odour, etc., of animals.

aposiopesis [,æpəsaɪə'piːsɪs] *n.* (*pl.* –ses), oratorical device of suddenly stopping in a speech. **aposiopetic**, *adj.*

apostasy [ə'pɒstəsi] *v.i.* desertion from religion or similar body.

apostate [ə'pɒsteɪt] *n. & adj.* (person) committing apostasy. **apostatize** *v.i.* change one's religious allegiance; forsake one's principles.

a posteriori [,eɪ pɒ,steri'ɔːraɪ, ,ɑː–, –stɪə–, –ri] *adj.* derived from experience; empirical; from effect to cause.

apostil(le) [ə'pɒstɪl] *n. archaic*, comment; note in margin.

apostolic [,æpə'stɒlɪk] *adj.* pertaining to apostle. **apostolic fathers**, immediate disciples of the apostles, especially those leaving writings. **apostolic succession**, unbroken derivation of episcopal power from the apostles.

apostrophe [ə'pɒstrəfi] *n.* sign (') that a letter has been omitted, or of possessive case; *Literature*, exclamatory or rhetorical address to absent person, abstract quality, etc. **apostrophic** [,æpə'strɒfɪk], *adj.* **apostrophize** , *v.t.* address in exclamatory or rhetorical fashion; *v.i.* use an apostrophe; omit letter from word.

apotelesm [ə'pɒtəlezm] *n. archaic*, casting of horoscope.

apothecary [ə'pɒθəkəri] *n. archaic*, or *American*, pharmacist.

apothegm *see* **apophthegm**.

apothem ['æpəθem] *n.* perpendicular from centre of regular polygon to any of its sides.

apotheosis [ə,pɒθi'əʊsɪs] *n.* (*pl.* –ses) deification; ascent to glory; personification of ideal. **apotheosise**, *v.t.*

apothesis [ə'pɒθəsɪs] *n. Medicine*, setting of broken limb.

apotropaic [ˌæpətrə'peɪɪk] *adj.* averting or combating evil. **apotropaism** [-'peɪɪzm], *n.* such magical practice.

apotypic [ˌæpəʊ'tɪpɪk] *adj.* differing from type.

appanage, apanage ['æpənɪdʒ] *n.* perquisite; provision, such as land or office, for younger son(s) of king or high official.

apparatchik [ˌæpə'rættʃɪk] (*Russian*) *n.* bureaucrat, official.

apparitor [ə'pærɪtə] *n.* herald; harbinger; officer executing order of ecclesiastical court.

appease [ə'piːz] *v.t.* calm, pacify, allay, satisfy, accede to demands of (especially dishonourably). **appeaser**, *n.* **appeasement**, *n.*

appellant [ə'pelənt] *n.* person appealing to higher court, etc.

appellate [ə'pelət] *adj.* applied to person, court, etc., having power to reverse decision of inferior.

appellation [ˌæpə'leɪʃn] *n.* name; rank.

appellative [ə'pelətɪv] *n.* & *adj. Grammar,* common (noun).

appendage [ə'pendɪdʒ] *n.* something attached to another thing as an extra or subsidiary part; hanger-on. **append**, *v.t.* attach something as an extra.

appendant [ə'pendənt] *n.* & *adj.* (thing) adjunct; attached to; hanging from or to; belonging as of right.

appendicectomy,   **appendectomy** [ə,pendɪ'sektəmɪ, ˌæpən'dektəmɪ] *n.* removal of vermiform appendix.

appendicle [ə'pendɪkl] *n.* small appendage.

appendix [ə'pendɪks] *n.* (*pl.* **-ices**) addition, *generally* to book; vermiform organ in intestines. **appendicitis,** *n.* inflammation of the appendix. **appendicular,** *adj.* pertaining to appendix or an appendage especially a limb.

apperception [ˌæpə'sepʃn] *n.* perception of inner meaning, and of relation of new facts to facts already known; mental assimilation; state of being conscious of perceiving. **apperceptive,** *adj.* **apperceive,** *v.t.*

appersonation [ə,pɜːsə'neɪʃn] *n.* delusion of insane person that he is another, *generally* famous, person.

appertain [ˌæpə'teɪn] *v.i.* belong as of right or according to custom; pertain.

appetence, appetency ['æpɪtəns, -ɪ] *n.* strong desire; craving; powerful instinct. **appetent,** *adj.*

appetible ['æpɪtəbl] *adj.* desirable. **appetition** [-'tɪʃn], *n.* yearning.

applanate ['æpləneɪt] *adj.* flattened. **applanation,** *n.*

appliqué [ə'pliːkeɪ] *n.* & *adj.* (ornament) let into or laid on; *v.t.* to attach or inlay such ornament.

appoggiatura [ə,pɒdʒə'tʊərə, -'tjuə-] *n. Music,* short note placed before a longer one. **short appoggiatura,** acciaccatura.

apport [ə'pɔːt] *n.* tangible object caused to appear by spiritualist medium; production of such object.

appose [æ'pəʊz] *v.t.* to place (things) side by side or next to each other.

apposite ['æpəzɪt] *adj.* appropriate.

apposition [ˌæpə'zɪʃn] *n.* juxtaposition; *Grammar,* putting two nouns or phrases together as attributive or adjunct terms; relationship of such nouns or phrases. **appositive** [ə'pɒz-], *adj.*

appraise [ə'preɪz] *v.t.* set a worth on; evaluate. **appraisal,** *n.*

apprehend [ˌæprɪ'hend] *v.t.* arrest; become aware of; understand; anticipate with fear. **apprehension,** *n.* **apprehensive,** *adj.*

apprise [ə'praɪz] *v.t.* inform.

apprize [ə'praɪz] *v.t.* value, appreciate.

approbate ['æprəbeɪt] (*American*) *v.t.* approve; permit; commend.

approbation [ˌæprə'beɪʃn] *n.* formal approval. **approbatory,** *adj.*

appropinquity [ˌæprə'pɪŋkwətɪ] *n.* nearness, propinquity.

appropriate [ə'prəʊprɪət] *adj.* apt; suitable. *v.t.* [-ieɪt] take exclusively; assign to special use; steal. **appropriation,** *n.* **appropriative,** *adj.* **appropriator,** *n.*

approximate [ə'prɒksɪmət] *adj.* very close to; almost exact; *v.i. & t.* [-meɪt] be or make approximate; approach. **approximation,** *n.* **approximative** [-mətɪv], *adj.*

appulse [ə'pʌls] *n.* act of striking against; *Astronomy,* close approach of two celestial objects.

appurtenance [ə'pɜːtɪnəns] *n.* belonging; appendage; subsidiary right; *pl.* apparatus; paraphernalia. **appurtenant,** *adj.* belonging to by right; accessory.

apraxia [eɪ'præksɪə, ə-] *n.* impaired ability to execute complex muscular movements.

a priori [ˌeɪ praɪ'ɔːraɪ, ˌɑː priː'ɔːrɪ] *adj.* not derived from experience; deductive; lacking proof; arguing from general principle to expected effect. **apriority** [-'ɒrətɪ], *n.*

apriorism [ˌeɪpraɪ'ɔːrɪzm, ˌɑːpriː-] *n.* philosophical belief that knowledge based on general principles may be used to evaluate experience.

apropos [ˌæprə'pəʊ] *adj.* & *adv.* apt; to the point; opportunely. **apropos of,** with reference to.

apse [æps] *n.* rounded extension at end of building, especially at east end of church; *Astronomy,* apsis.

apsidal ['æpsɪdl] *adj.* having shape of apse; pertaining to apsides.

apsis ['æpsɪs] *n.* (*pl.* **-ides**) *Astronomy,* point at which heavenly body is most or least distant from centre of attraction. **higher apsis,** most distant point. **lower apsis,** least distant point.

apteral ['æptərəl] *adj.* (of classical temple) having columns at front or back only; (of church) lacking aisles: apterous.

apterous ['æptərəs] *adj.* lacking wings.

apterygial [ˌæptə'rɪdʒɪəl] *adj.* wingless; finless.

apteryx ['æptərɪks] *n.* tailless, flightless bird of New Zealand; kiwi.

aptyalism [æp'taɪəlɪzm] *n.* lack or absence of saliva.

apyretic [ˌeɪpaɪ'retɪk] *adj.* without fever. **apyrexy** ['æpəreksɪ], *n.* absence or abatement of fever.

apyrous [eɪ'paɪrəs, 'æpərəs] *adj.* non-inflammable.

aqua fortis [ˌækwə 'fɔːtɪs] (*Latin*) *n. obsolete,* nitric acid.

aquamarine [ˌækwəmə'riːn] *n.* gemstone: pale greenish-blue variety of beryl. *adj.* of this colour.

aquanaut ['ækwənɔːt] *n.* an underwater explorer, especially one remaining for extended periods in undersea diving chamber.

aquaphobia [ˌækwə'fəʊbiə] *n.* fear of drowning.

aqua pura [ˌækwə 'pjʊərə] (*Latin*) 'pure water', especially distilled.

aqua regia [ˌækwə 'riːdʒɪə] (*Latin*) 'royal water'; mixture of hydrochloric and nitric acids which dissolves some metals. Used in etching and by alchemists to dissolve gold.

aquarelle [ˌækwə'rel] *n.* method of painting in transparent water-colour; such painting. **aquarellist,** *n.* artist painting aquarelles.

aquarist ['ækwərɪst] *n.* person who studies aquatic life; owner of an aquarium.

aquatic [ə'kwætɪk, ə'kwɒ–] *n. & adj.* (plant) living in or by water.

aquatint ['ækwətɪnt] *n.* (print made by) a method of etching having effect of water-colour drawing.

aquavitae [ˌækwə 'vaɪtiː, –'viːtaɪ] (*Latin*) 'water of life'; strong spirits.

aqueduct ['ækwɪdʌkt] *n.* channel carrying water, especially in shape of bridge.

aqueous ['eɪkwiəs, 'æk–] *adj.* pertaining to water; *Geology,* deposited in or by water.

aquiculture, aquaculture ['ækwi,kʌltʃə, –wə–] *n.* cultivation of water plants and animals for food; hydroponics.

aquiferous [ə'kwɪfərəs] *adj.* carrying, yielding or containing water. **aquifer** ['ækwɪfə], *n.* water-bearing stratum.

aquiline ['ækwɪlaɪn] *adj.* eagle-like; like beak of eagle.

arabesque [ˌærə'besk] *n. & adj.* (decoration) having intertwined scrollwork patterns, especially of leaves, flowers, etc.

arable ['ærəbl] *n. & adj.* (land) used or suitable for ploughing.

arachnid [ə'ræknɪd] *n.* creature of the natural class *Arachnida,* including spiders, mites, etc.; *adj.* of or resembling a spider. **arachnidism,** *n.* condition arising from bite of poisonous spider.

arachnoid [ə'ræknɔɪd] *adj.* like a spider; like a spider's web; *n.* thin middle membrane enveloping brain.

arachnology [ə,ræk'nɒlədʒi] *n.* study of arachnids.

arachnophagous [ə,ræk'nɒfəgəs] *adj.* eating spiders.

araeometer, areometer [ˌeəri'ɒmɪtə] *n.* hydrometer.

araneid, araneidan [ˌærə'niːɪd, –ən] *n.* spider; *adj.* pertaining to spiders. **araneiform,** *adj.* shaped like a spider. **araneology** [ə,reɪni'ɒlədʒi], *n.* study of spiders.

araneous, araneose [ə'reɪniəs, –iəʊs] *adj.* like a spider's web; transparent; delicate.

araphorostic, araphostic [ˌærəfə'rɒstɪk, –'fɒstɪk] *adj.* seamless.

araroba [ˌærə'rəʊbə] *n.* tree of Brazil with striped timber; zebra-wood.

aration [ə'reɪʃn] *n.* ploughing.

araucaria [ˌærɔː'keəriə] *n.* monkey-puzzle tree; genus of conifers including it.

arbalest, arbalist ['ɑːbəlɪst] *n.* cross-bow with mechanism for drawing string.

arbiter ['ɑːbɪtə] *n.* judge, especially one chosen by disputing parties. **arbiter elegantiae,** (*Latin*) 'Judge of taste', especially G. Petronius, supervisor of Nero's entertainments. **arbitral,** *adj.*

arbitrage ['ɑːbɪtrɑːʒ] *n. Commerce,* simultaneously buying stock, etc., in cheaper market and selling in dearer. *v.i.* practise arbitrage. **arbitrageur** [–'ʒɜː] *n.*

arbitrament [ɑː'bɪtrəmənt] *n.* judicial decision; power to make decision.

arbitrary ['ɑːbɪtrəri] *adj.* discretionary; capricious; tyrannical.

arbitrate ['ɑːbɪtreɪt] *v.i. & t.* judge; settle quarrel. **arbitration, arbitrator,** *n.*

arbor ['ɑːbə] *n.* main shaft or beam; spindle or axle (of wheel).

arboraceous [ˌɑːbə'reɪʃəs] *adj.* pertaining to or like a tree; wooded.

arboreal [ɑː'bɔːriəl] *adj.* pertaining to trees, or living in trees.

arboreous [ɑː'bɔːriəs] *adj.* having many trees.

arborescent [ˌɑːbə'resnt] *adj.* branched; having shape or growth like a tree. **arborescence,** *n.*

arboretum [ˌɑːbə'riːtəm] *n.* (*pl.* **–ta**) botanical garden devoted to trees.

arborical [ɑː'bɒrɪkl] *adj.* pertaining to trees.

arboricole [ɑː'bɒrɪkəʊl] *adj.* living in trees.

arboriculture ['ɑːbəri,kʌltʃə, ɑː'bɒr–] *n.* tree-cultivation. **arboricultural,** *adj.* **arboriculturist,** *n.*

arboriform ['ɑːbərifɔːm, ɑː'bɒr–] *adj.* shaped like a tree.

arborist ['ɑːbərɪst] *n.* tree specialist.

arborize ['ɑːbəraɪz] *v.i. & t.* take on or give tree-like shape. **arborization,** *n.*

arborous ['ɑːbərəs] *adj.* pertaining to trees; composed of trees.

arbor vitae [ˌɑːbə 'vaɪtiː, –'viːtaɪ] *n.* a coniferous evergreen shrub.

arbuscle, arbuscula ['ɑːbʌsl, ɑː'bʌskjʊlə] *n.* dwarf tree; shrub-like tree. **arbuscular,** *adj.*

arbuscule [ɑː'bʌskjuːl] *n.* tuft of hairs.

arbustum [ɑː'bʌstəm] *n.* (*pl.* **–ta**) copse; orchard.

arbutus [ɑː'bjuːtəs] *n.* strawberry tree.

arcana [ɑː'keɪnə] *n. pl.* (*sing.* **–num**) mysteries; secrets; *singular* universal remedy; elixir of life. **arcane** [–'keɪn], *adj.* secret.

arcate [ɑː'keɪt] *adj.* shaped like a bow. **arcature** ['ɑːkətʃə], *n.* small or blind arcade.

arc-boutant [ˌɑːk 'buːtɒn] (*French*) *n.* (*pl.* **arcs-boutants**) flying buttress.

archaean [ɑː'kiːən] *adj. Geology,* applied to all pre-Cambrian rocks.

archaeolatry [ˌɑːki'ɒlətri] *n.* worship of archaic customs, expressions, etc.

archaeolithic [ˌɑːkiə'lɪθɪk] *adj.* pertaining to earliest stone age.

archaeology, archeology [ˌɑːki'ɒlədʒi] *n.* study of remains of past human life. **archaeological** *adj.* **archaeologist** *n.*

archaeopteryx [ˌɑːki'ɒptərɪks] *n.* fossil bird with reptilian characteristics.

archaeornis [ˌɑːki'ɔːnɪs] *n.* fossil, beakless, reptile-like bird.

archaeozoic [ˌɑːkiə'zəʊɪk] *adj.* living in the earliest geological era.

archaic [ɑː'keɪɪk] *adj.* ancient; primitive; out of date. **archaism** ['ɑːkeɪɪzm], *n.* such thing, especially word or phrase; use of such thing. **archaistic** [ˌɑːkeɪ'ɪstɪk], *adj.*

archebiosis [ˌɑːkɪbaɪ'əʊsɪs] *n.* abiogenesis.

archecentric [ˌɑːkɪ'sentrɪk] *adj.* pertaining to archetype.

archeology [ˌɑːkɪ'ɒlədʒɪ] *see* **archaeology**.

archetype ['ɑːkɪtaɪp] *n.* original pattern. **archetypal**, *adj.*

archididascalos,   **archididascalus** [ˌɑːkɪdɪ'dæskələs] *adj.* headteacher of school etc. **archididascalian** [–dæ'skeɪlɪən], *adj.*

archiepiscopal [ˌɑːkiː'pɪskəpl] *adj.* pertaining to an archbishop.

archil, orchil ['ɑːkɪl, 'ɔː–] *n.* dye obtained from certain lichens; lichens yielding this.

archimage,   **archimagus**   ['ɑːkɪmeɪdʒ, ˌɑːkɪ'meɪgəs] *n.* (*pl.* **–gi**) great magician.

archimandrite [ˌɑːkɪ'mændraɪt] *n.* superior of large monastery of Greek Church; abbot.

Archimedes' screw [ˌɑːkɪ'miːdiːz] *n.* device for raising water, consisting of a cylinder enclosing a screw.

archipelago [ˌɑːkɪ'peləgəu] *n.* (*pl.* **–goes**, **–gos**) group or string of islands. **archipelagian, archipelagic**, *adj.*

architectonic [ˌɑːkɪtek'tɒnɪk] *adj.* pertaining to architecture, or to the systematization of knowledge; resembling architecture; structural; showing constructive ability; *n . pl.* science of architecture; constructive skill.

architrave ['ɑːkɪtreɪv] *n.* beam resting directly on columns; epistyle; moulding at head and sides of window or doorway.

archives ['ɑːkaɪvz] *n. pl.* public records; place where such are kept. **archival**, *adj.* **archivist** ['ɑːkɪvɪst], *n.* keeper of archives.

archivolt ['ɑːkɪvɒlt] *n.* curved moulding on face of arch.

archizoic [ˌɑːkɪ'zəuɪk] *adj.* pertaining to earliest living things.

archology [ɑː'kɒlədʒɪ] *n.* theory of origins; science of government.

archon ['ɑːkən] *n.* a chief magistrate of ancient Athens. **archontic**, *adj.*

arcifinious [ˌɑːsɪ'fɪnɪəs] *adj.* having a frontier which forms a natural defence.

arciform ['ɑːsɪfɔːm] *adj.* shaped like an arch.

arctogaeal, arctogeal, arctogaean, arctogean [ˌɑːktə'dʒiːəl, –ən] *adj.* pertaining to the region including Europe, Africa, Asia and N America.

arctoid ['ɑːktɔɪd] *adj.* like a bear.

arctophile ['ɑːktəfaɪl] *n.* person who loves or collects teddy bears.

arcuate, arcual ['ɑːkjueɪt, –əl] *adj.* bow-shaped. **arcuation**, *n.*

arcus senilis [ˌɑːkəs sə'naɪlɪs] (*Latin*) 'senile ring'; whitish ring round iris in eyes of old people.

areca [ə'riːkə, 'ærɪkə] *n.* several palm trees, especially the betel. **areca nut**, betel-nut.

arenaceous [ˌærɪ'neɪʃəs] *adj.* like or consisting of sand; growing in sand.

arenarious [ˌærɪ'neərɪəs] *adj.* arenaceous.

areng [ə'reŋ] (*E Indian*) *n.* sago-producing palm.

arenicolous [ˌærɪ'nɪkələs] *adj.* living in sand.

arenilitic [ə,renɪ'lɪtɪk] *adj.* pertaining to sandstone.

arenoid ['ærɪnɔɪd] *adj.* like sand.

arenose ['ærɪnəus] *adj.* sandy; containing much sand.

areography [ˌeərɪ'ɒgrəfɪ] *n.* description of surface of planet Mars; descriptive biogeography.

areola [ə'riːələ] *n.* (*pl.* **–ae**) circular coloured border, especially round pupil of eye, pustule or nipple; small circumscribed space; interstice. **areolar, areolate**, *adj.* **areolation**, *n.*

areology [ˌeərɪ'ɒlədʒɪ] *n.* study of planet Mars.

areometer *see* **araeometer**.

Areopagus [ˌærɪ'ɒpəgəs] *n.* highest legal tribunal in ancient Athens; any important tribunal. **Areopagite** [–gaɪt, –dʒaɪt], *n.* member of such a tribunal.

aretaics [ˌærɪ'teɪɪks] *n.* science of virtue.

aretalogy [ˌærɪ'tælədʒɪ] *n.* relation of wonderful deeds of a god or hero.

arête [ə'reɪt] (*French*) *n.* sharp ridge of mountain.

argal ['ɑːgl] *adv.* therefore (corruption of *ergo*, used to suggest absurd reasoning); *n.* argol.

argali ['ɑːgəli] *n.* Asiatic wild mountain sheep.

argand– ['ɑːgænd, –ənd] *adj.* applied to lamps, burners, etc., having tubular wick or flame.

argent ['ɑːdʒənt] *n. & adj.* silver; silverlike. **argentate, argenteous** [–'dʒen–], **argentic** [–'dʒen–], argentine, argentous, *adj.* **argentiferous** [–'tɪf–], *adj.* yielding silver. **argentine**, *n.* silvery metal. **argentometer** [–'tɒm–], *n.* instrument measuring strength of silver solutions.

argil ['ɑːdʒɪl] *n.* clay, especially used in pottery. **argillaceous** [–'leɪʃəs], **argillous**, *adj.* containing clay; clay-like. **argilliferous** [–'lɪf–], *adj.* yielding or containing clay. **argilloid**, *adj.* like clay.

argol, argal ['ɑːgl] *n.* crust formed on long-kept wine.

argon ['ɑːgɒn] *n.* inert gas contained in very small quantity in atmosphere, used to fill electric light bulbs.

Argonaut ['ɑːgənɔːt] *n.* companion of Jason in the Argo; any heroic sailor; paper nautilus.

argosy ['ɑːgəsi] *n.* large merchant ship; merchant fleet.

argot ['ɑːgəu] (*French*) *n.* slang or jargon, especially of criminals, tramps, etc. **argotic** [–'ɒtɪk], *adj.*

Argus ['ɑːgəs] *n.* monster with a hundred eyes; careful watcher. **Argus-eyed**, *adj.* ever watchful. **argus**, *n .* any of several small brown butterflies with eyespots.

argute ['ɑːgjuːt] *adj.* quick; sharp; shrill; astute; subtle.

argyrocephalous [ˌɑːdʒɪrə'sefələs] *adj.* with silvery or shining head.

aria ['ɑːrɪə] *n.* melody, especially solo for voice in opera or oratorio.

arid ['ærɪd] *adj.* dry, barren (land etc.); dull, unoriginal, lifeless. **aridity** [ə'rɪdəti],.

arietta [ˌærɪ'etə, ˌɑː–] *n.* short aria.

ariose ['ærɪəus] *adj.* characterized by or like melody.

arioso [ˌɑːrɪ'əuzəu, ˌæ–] *n. Music*, song-like instrumental piece; solo pertaining to both aria and recitative; *adj.* melodious.

arista [ə'rɪstə] *n.* (*pl.* **–ae**, **–as**) awn. **aristate**, *adj.*

aristarch ['ærɪstɑːk] *n.* severe critic.

aristology [ˌærɪ'stɒlədʒɪ] *n.* art or science of dining. **aristological**, *adj.* **aristologist**, *n.*

aristulate [ə'rɪstjulət] *adj.* having short arista.

arithmancy ['ærɪθmænsi] *n.* divination by numbers.

arithmogram [ə'rɪθməgræm] *n.* number composed of numerical values assigned to letters in a word. **arithmocracy,** *n.* government by the majority. **arithmography** [ærɪh'mɒgrəfɪ], *n.* representing a number with letters having numerical values. **arithmomania,** *n.* obsession with numbers, especially compulsion to count things. **arithmometer,** *n.* early adding machine.

armadillo [‚ɑːmə'dɪləu] *n.* burrowing animal of S and Central America with bony armour, and able to roll into a ball for protection.

Armageddon [‚ɑːmə'gedn] *n.* devastating conflict; war between good and evil at end of world.

armature ['ɑːmətʃə] *n.* armament; *Botany*, *Zoology*, defensive outgrowth; *Electricity*, piece of iron placed on poles of permanent magnet; piece of iron whose movement, due to magnetic attraction, actuates apparatus or machinery; rotating part of dynamo or electric motor; stationary part of revolving field alternator; framework for sculpture.

armiferous [ɑː'mɪfərəs] *adj.* carrying weapons or arms.

armiger ['ɑːmɪdʒə] *n.* (*pl.* **-s**, **-ri**) armourbearer; knight's squire; person bearing heraldic arms. **armigerous** [ɑː'mɪdʒərəs], armigeral, *adj.*

armillary [ɑː'mɪləri, 'ɑːmɪ–] *adj.* like, pertaining to or composed of rings. **armillary sphere**, celestial globe composed only of rings marking equator, tropics, etc.

armipotent [ɑː'mɪpətənt] *adj.* having strong armament. **armipotence,** *n.*

armisonant, armisonous [ɑː'mɪsənənt, –əs] *adj.* resounding with the clash of arms.

armoire [ɑːm'wɑː] (*French*) *n.* cupboard; wardrobe.

armorial [ɑː'mɔːriəl] *adj.* pertaining, to or bearing heraldic arms. **armorial bearings**, coat-of-arms.

armory ['ɑːməri] *n.* heraldry. **armorist,** *n.* expert in heraldry.

arnatto, arnotto, *see* **annatto.**

arnica ['ɑːnɪkə] *n.* genus of plants including the mountain tobacco; tincture obtained from mountain tobacco used for bruises, etc.

aroint [ə'rɔɪnt] *v.i. archaic*, (imperative) begone!

arpeggio [ɑː'pedʒɪəu, –'pedʒəu] *n. Music*, number of notes sounded in rapid succession; playing in such fashion. **arpeggiando,** *adj.* in such manner. **arpeggiation,** *n.*

arquebus(e), harquebus ['ɑːkwɪbəs, –bjuːz, 'hɑː–] *n.* ancient hand gun supported on tripod. **arquebusier** [–'bjuːzɪə] *n.* soldier armed with arquebus.

arrack ['ærək, ə'ræk] *n.* strong liquor of the East, manufactured from coco-palm, rice, sugar-cane, etc.

arraign [ə'reɪn] *v.t.* call to account; bring before judicial court. **arraignment,** *n.* indictment.

arrant ['ærənt] *adj.* unmitigated; infamous.

arras ['ærəs] *n.* tapestry, especially covering wall. **arrasene,** *n.* embroidery material of silk and wool.

arrect [ə'rekt] *adj.* raised up; attentive.

arrêt [ə'reɪ, ə'ret] (*French*) *n.* judgment; decree; arrest.

arrha ['ærə] *n.* (*pl.* **-ae**) pledge; earnest money. **arrhal,** *adj.*

arrhizal [ə'raɪzl] *adj.* rootless.

arrhythmia [ə'rɪđmɪə, eɪ–] *n.* disturbance of the natural rhythm of the heart. **arrhythmic,** *adj.*

arrière-ban [‚ærɪə'bæn, –'bɒn] (*French*) *n.* summoning by king of his feudatories and their vassals to military service; vassals so called; the nobility.

arrière-pensée [‚ærɪə'pɒnseɪ] (*French*) *n.* hidden meaning; ulterior motive; mental reservation.

arris ['ærɪs] *n.* sharp edge formed by two angled surfaces, especially edge of fluting on column. **arriswise,** *adj.* edgewise.

arriviste [‚ærɪː'viːst] (*French*) *n.* pushful, ambitious person.

arrogate ['ærəgeɪt] *v.t.* take or claim beyond one's rights. **arrogation,** *n.*

arrondissement [‚ærɒn'diːsmɒn] (*French*) *n.* largest subdivision of a French department.

arroyo [ə'rɔɪəu] (*Spanish*) *n.* small stream; dry stream bed; gulley.

arsenal ['ɑːsənəl] *n.* store or factory for weapons; repertory.

arsinotherium [‚ɑːsɪnə'θɪərɪəm] *n.* rhinoceroslike fossil mammal.

arsis ['ɑːsɪs] *n.* (*pl.* **-ses**) *originally*, unstressed part of metrical foot; *modern*, accented syllable; *Music*, unaccented part of bar.

artefact, *see* **artifact.**

arterial [ɑː'tɪərɪəl] *adj.* like an artery; main (of roads). **arterialize,** *v.t.* transform into arterial blood; give arteries to.

artery ['ɑːtəri] *n.* vessel conveying blood from the heart; main channel. **arteriography** [ɑː‚tɪərɪ'ɒgrəfɪ], *n.* x-ray of arterial system. **arteriosclerosis** [ɑː‚tɪərɪəusklə'rəusɪs], *n.* hardening of artery walls. **arteriotomy** [ɑː‚tɪərɪ'ɒtəmɪ], *n.* dissection of arteries.

artesian [ɑː'tiːzɪən, –'tiːʒn] *adj.* applied to wells bored perpendicularly through imporous to porous strata; *American*, applied to any deep well.

arthralgia [ɑː'θrældʒɪə] *n.* pain in a joint.

arthritis [ɑː'θraɪtɪs] *n.* inflammation of joint. **arthritic** [–'ɪtɪk], *adj.* **arthrography,** *n.* x-ray of joint.

arthropod ['ɑːθrəpɒd] *n. & adj.* (creature) of natural division *Arthropoda*, having jointed legs. **arthropodal** [ɑː'θrɒpədl], arthropodan [–'θrɒp–], arthropodous [–'θrɒp–], *adj.*

arthrosis [ɑː'θrəusɪs] *n.* joint or articulation connecting two bones.

articular [ɑː'tɪkjulə] *adj.* pertaining to joints.

articulate [ɑː'tɪkjulət] *adj.* spoken clearly; having power of speech, especially fluent and expressive; divided into syllables; segmented; jointed; *v.t. & i.* [–eɪt] speak clearly; connect or be connected by or at joints. **articulation,** *n.* clear speech; jointing. **articulative, articulatory,** *adj.* **articulator,** *n.*

artifact, artefact ['ɑːtɪfækt] *n.* object of human manufacture; condition caused by human interference. **artifactitious, artifactual,** *adj.*

artifice ['ɑːtɪfɪs] *n.* ingenuity; skill; trickery. **artificer** [ɑː'tɪfɪsə], *n.* craftsman; mechanic in army.

artisan [‚ɑːtɪ'zæn] *n.* workman; journeyman; mechanic.

arum ['eərəm] *n.* large-spathed plant, called 'cuckoo-pint' or 'lords and ladies'. **arum lily,** calla lily.

arundinaceous [ə,rʌndɪ'neɪʃəs] *adj.* like or pertaining to a reed.

aruspex *see* **haruspex**.

arvicoline [ɑː'vɪkəlaɪn] *adj.* living in the fields or countryside. **arviculture**, *n.* cultivation of fields.

Aryan ['eəriən] *n.* & *adj. Philology*, Indo-European (language); (supposed former) speaker of that language; (of) non-Jewish Nordic type considered a superior race in Nazi ideology. **Aryanism**, *n.* such Nazi belief.

as [æs] *n.* (*pl.* **asses**) copper coin of ancient Rome; weight of 12 oz.

asafoetida [,æsə'fetɪdə, -'fiː-] *n.* gum with garlic-like smell obtained from roots of certain E Indian plants.

asbestos [æs'bestəs, æz-] *n.* uninflammable material manufacture from fibrous amphibole. **asbestine, asbestous**, *adj.*

asbestosis [,æsbe'stəʊsɪs, ,æz-] *n.* disease of lungs caused by inhalation of asbestos dust over long periods.

ascarid ['æskərɪd] *n.* (*pl.* *-es*), roundworm. **ascariasis**, *n.* disease caused by infestation with ascarides **ascaricide**, *n.* substance destroying ascarides.

ascendancy, ascendency, ascendance, ascendence [ə'sendənsi, -əns] *n.* domination.

ascendant, ascendent [ə'sendənt] *adj.* rising into power; powerful; *Astronononmy*, moving towards zenith; *Astrology*, immediately above eastern horizon; *n.* powerful or pre-eminent position; *Astrology*, degree of zodiac above eastern horizon at birth of child; horoscope.

ascender [ə'sendə] *n.* part of lower-case letter rising above main part of letter; letter having an ascender.

ascertain [,æsə'teɪn] *v.t.* find out for certain.

ascetic [ə'setɪk] *n.* & *adj.* (person) practising severe abstinence; austere. **asceticism** [-sɪzm], *n.*

ascian ['æʃiən] *n.* inhabitant of torrid zone.

ascidian [ə'sɪdiən] *n.* sea squirt.

ASCII ['æski] *n.* (in computers) *abbreviation* for American Standard Code for Information Exchange; standard system for coding characters etc. in binary form.

ascites [ə'saɪtiːz] *n.* abdominal dropsy.

asclepiad [ə'skliːpiæd] *n.* metrical verse invented by Asclepiades, comprising a spondee, two or three choriambi and an iambus. **asclepiadean**, *n.* & *adj.*

ascribe [ə'skraɪb] *v.t.* attribute or assign to a cause or source. **ascription** [ə'skrɪpʃn], *n.*

aseismic [eɪ'saɪzmɪk] *adj.* free from earthquakes; designed to withstand earthquakes. **aseismatic**, *adj.* reducing or withstanding effect of earthquakes.

asepsis [eɪ'sepsɪs, ə-] *n.* absence of poisonous matter and organisms; method of causing such condition in surgery; sterilising. **aseptic**, *adj.*; *n.* substance causing or in state of asepsis.

asexual [eɪ'seksʊəl, -sju-] *adj.* non-sexual; sexless. **asexuality**, *n.*

ashlar ['æʃlə] *n.* squared building stone; stonework composed of these; thin, dressed stone for facing rough wall. **ashlaring** *n.* partition in attic to cut off angle made by rafters and floor.

asinine ['æsɪnaɪn] *adj.* pertaining to the ass; stupid fatuous. **asininity**, *n.*

askari [ə'skɑːri, 'æskəri] *n.* E African soldier or policeman.

asomatous [eɪ'səʊmətəs, ə-] *adj.* incorporeal; lacking body. **asomatophyte**, *n. Botany*, plant in which body and reproductive cells are undifferentiated.

asparaginous [,æspə'rædʒɪnəs] *adj.* pertaining to, like or eaten like asparagus.

asperate ['æspərət] *adj.* rather rough; *v.t.* [-eɪt] make rough. **asperation**, *n.*

asperge [ə'spɜːdʒ] *v.t.* sprinkle. **asperges** [-iːz], *n. Roman Catholic*, ceremony of sprinkling holy water.

aspergil, **aspergill(um)** ['æspədʒɪl, ,æspə'dʒɪləm] *n. Roman Catholic*, brush-like implement used to sprinkle holy water.

aspergillus [,æspə'dʒɪləs] *n.* (*pl.* *-li*) minute fungus forming mould. **aspergilliform, aspergillosis**, *n.* animal disease caused by aspergilli.

asperity [æ'sperəti, ə-] *n.* roughness, acrimony.

aspermatism, aspermia [eɪ'spɜːmətɪzm, ə-] *n.* failure of male generative powers. **aspermic**, *adj.*

asperse [ə'spɜːs] *v.t.* slander, calumniate. **aspersion** [ə'spɜːʃn], *n.*; *Roman Catholic*, act of sprinkling holy water. **aspersive**, *adj.* **aspersory**, *n.*, aspergil.

aspersorium [,æspə'sɔːriəm] *n. Roman Catholic*, vessel holding holy water; aspergil.

asperulous [ə'sperʊləs, -jʊ-] *adj. Botany*, rather rough.

aspherical [eɪ'sferɪkl] *adj.* (of lens, etc.) free from spherical aberration.

aspheterism [æs'fetərɪzm] *n.* doctrine that there should be no private property.

asphodel ['æsfədel] *n.* kind of liliaceous plant; daffodil; *Literature*, flower of the Elysian fields. **bog asphodel**, British grass-like moorland plant.

asphyxia, asphyxy [æs'fɪksɪə, -si] *n.* suffocation. **asphyxial**, *adj.* **asphixiant**, *n.* & *adj.* (substance) causing asphyxia **asphyxiate**, *v.i.* & *t.* **asphyxiator**, *n.* substance causing asphyxia.

aspidate ['æspɪdeɪt] *adj.* shield-shaped.

aspirant ['æspərənt] *n.* & *adj.* (person) seeking higher position or rank. **aspire** [ə'spaɪə], *v.i.* **aspiration** [,æspə'reɪʃn], *n.*

aspirate ['æspərət] *n.* sound (*h*) made by breathing out; consonant combined with *h* sound; *adj.* so pronounced; *v.t.* [-eɪt] pronounce with initial *h* sound; move or draw by suction. **aspirator**, *n.* any suction machine, especially for withdrawing gas, or for separating corn from chaff; *Medicine*, instrument for withdrawing fluids by suction from body.

aspirin ['æsprɪn] *n.* drug (acetylsalicylic acid) removing pain and fever.

asportation [,æspɔː'teɪʃn] *n.* removal, especially crime of removing property.

assapan(ic) [,æsə'pæn, -ɪk] *n.* flying squirrel of N America.

assart, essart [ə'sɑːt] *v.t. Law*, make arable by clearing trees, etc.; *n.* land so treated; action of assarting.

assary ['æsəri] *n.* small copper coin of ancient Rome; as.

assay [ə'seɪ] *v.t.* analyse or evaluate (ore, etc.); judge the worth of; attempt; *n.* such an analysis; substance analysed.

assecuration [,æsɪkjʊ'reɪʃn] *n.* marine insurance.

assentaneous [,æsen'teɪnɪəs] *adj*. acquiescent.

assentation [,æsen'teɪʃn] *n*. ready, insincere assent. **assentatious**, *adj*. willing to assent. **assentator**, *n*. flatterer; one assenting insincerely or conniving. **assentatory** [ə'sentətəri], *adj*.

assentor [ə'sentə] *n*. *Law*, voter (not proposer or seconder) endorsing nomination of candidate for election.

asseverate [ə'sevəreɪt] *v.t*. affirm; declare. **asseveration**, *n*. **asseverative**, *adj*.

assibilate [ə'sɪbəleɪt] *v.t*. pronounce with sibilant sound or hiss. **assibilation**, *n*.

assiduity [,æsɪ'djuːəti] *n*. unremitting care; unflagging or obsequious attention. **assiduous** [ə'sɪdjuəs], *adj*.

assiento, asiento [,æsi'entəʊ] (*Spanish*) *n*. contract; treaty, especially with Spain for supplying slaves to Spanish America.

assign [ə'saɪn] *v.t*. allot; appoint; select; attribute; transfer legally; *n*. assignee.

assignat ['æsɪgnæt] (*French*) *n*. promissory note secured on state lands, issued during French Revolution.

assignation [,æsɪg'neɪʃn] *n*. appointment to meet; rendezvous; *Law*, formal transference; nomination of assignee; interest transferred; paper money.

assignee [,æsaɪ'niː] *n*. agent; representative; person to whom something is assigned.

assignment [ə'saɪnmənt] *n*. deed of transfer; act of assigning; commission, especially of a journalist.

assignor, assigner [,æsaɪ'nɔː, ə'saɪnə] *n*. person assigning.

assimilate [ə'sɪməleɪt] *v.i*. & *t*. make or become similar; compare; incorporate; digest; absorb; be incorporated, digested, or absorbed. **assimilation, assimilator**, *n*. **assimilative, assimilatory**, *adj*.

assize [ə'saɪz] *n*. legislative assembly; decree, generally one fixing weights, measures and prices, especially of bread and ale; trial; *Scottish*, trial by jury; jury. **assizer**, *n*. person fixing weights and measures; *Scottish*, juror, *n.pl*. court of sessions held periodically in all counties; courtroom for such courts.

assoil(zie) [ə'sɔɪl, –ji] *v.t*. *archaic*, pardon; absolve; acquit; release. **assoilment**, *n*.

assonance ['æsənəns] *n*. similarity between sounds; kind of rhyme in which only vowels are identical. **assonant**, *adj*., *n*. **assonate**, *v.i*.

assuage [ə'sweɪdʒ] *v.t*. soothe; mitigate; appease. **assuasive**, *adj*. **assuagement**, *n*.

assuetude ['æswɪtjuːd] *n*. habituation.

assumpsit [ə'sʌmpsɪt] *n*. *Law*, contract (not under seal); suit for breach of such contract.

assumption [ə'sʌmpʃn] *n*. act of assuming or putting on; pride; supposition; *Roman Catholic*, ascent of Virgin Mary into heaven, and feast (Aug. 15) of that event. **assumptious**, *adj*. assuming. **assumptive**, *adj*. assumed; assuming (too much).

assurgent [ə'sɜːdʒnt] *adj*. ascending; *Botany*, upward curving. **assurgency** *n*.

astasia [ə'steɪzɪə, –ʒə] *n*. inability, due to imperfect muscular co-ordination, to keep erect.

astatic [eɪ'stætɪk] *adj*. unstable; in neutral equilibrium; *Electricity*, not tending to assume a definite position. **astatic pair**, pair of magnetized needles of opposite charges. **astatics**, *n*. study of equilibrium of body under known forces.

astatine ['æstətiːn, –ɪn] *n*. radioactive element of the halogen group.

asteism ['æstiːɪzm] *n*. polite irony.

asteria [æ'stɪərɪə] *n*. gem cut so as to show asterism.

asterial [æ'stɪərɪəl] *adj*. starlike; *n*. a fossil starfish.

asteriated [æ'stɪərieɪtɪd] *adj*. having star-like rays.

A clutch of collectives

A **collective noun** is one that names a group of two or more people, animals, or things. Such groups have a dual existence, as both a single entity and as an aggregate of several individuals, and this is reflected in the grammar of the nouns that name them, particularly in British English. When we think of a group as a unit, we use a singular verb after the noun (*When the ship went down, the crew was lost*). But when we have its individual members in mind, we use a plural verb (*The crew have all signed the petition*). Among other nouns to behave in this way are *audience, committee, company, congregation, gang, government, jury, orchestra, squad, team*. Nouns denoting institutions and places can also take a plural verb when they refer to the people associated with them (*The whole school were down at the sports field*). In American English, however, it is usual to use only a singular verb with such collective nouns.

There is a particular category of collective nouns that names a group of a certain sort of animal or person (or occasionally thing). They are sometimes known as nouns of assemblage.

Lists of the more colourful ones have always found a ready audience, but many of the most outlandish examples (*an exaltation of larks, a murder of crows, a murmuration of starlings*) are at best obsolete and in some instances were probably fanciful coinages that never had any real existence. The main nouns of assemblage for animals still in general use are:

bevy of quails (or, facetiously, attractive young women)
brood of chicks
charm of goldfinches
covey of partridges
flock of sheep/birds
gaggle of geese (on the ground)
herd of cattle/elephants/antelope/wildebeest etc.
litter of cubs/kittens/puppies
pack of hounds/dogs/wolves
pride of lions
school of whales/porpoises/dolphins
shoal of fish
skein of geese (flying)
swarm of insects/flies/bees etc.
troop of monkeys.

asterism ['æstərɪzm] *n.* constellation of stars; group of asterisks; appearance of star-like reflection by certain crystals. **asterismal,** *adj.*

asteroid ['æstərɔɪd] *n.* small planet revolving between Jupiter and Mars; planetoid; any star-like body; *adj.* star-shaped; pertaining to or like a starfish. **asteroidal,** *adj.*

asthenia [æs'θiːnɪə] *n.* debility. **asthenic** [-'θenɪk], *adj.* weak; of slender build; weakening.

asthenopia [,æsθɪ'nəupɪə] *n.* optical weakness, especially muscular. **asthenopic** [-'nɒpɪk], *adj.*

asthenosphere [æs'θenəsfɪə] *n.* hypothetical layer of fluid matter below rigid surface of earth's crust.

astigmatism [ə'stɪgmətɪzm] *n.* defect in curvature of lens or of cornea of eye, causing unequal focusing. **astigmometer** [,æstɪg'mɒmɪtə], *n.* instrument measuring amount of astigmatism. **astigmatic** [,æstɪg'mætɪk], *adj.*

astomatal, astomous [eɪ'stɒmətl, -'stəʊ-, 'æstəməs] *adj.* having no stomata.

astomatous, [eɪ'stɒmətəs] *adj.* lacking mouth or stomata.

astragal ['æstrəgl] *n.* ankle-bone; rounded beading or moulding on column; *pl.*, dice. **astragalar** [ə'strægələ], *adj.* **astragalomancy** [ə'strægələmænsi], *n.* divination by ankle-bones or dice. **astragalus** *n. Medicine,* ankle-bone.

astrakhan [,æstrə'kæn] *n.* closely-curled black or grey fur from fleece of karakul lambs: cloth resembling this.

astral ['æstrəl] *adj.* pertaining to or like stars; heavenly; spiritual; of the non-tangible substance of which astral body is composed. **astral body,** semi-spiritual body believed by theosophists to accompany physical body in life and survive it at death; soul.

astraphobia, astrapophobia [,æstrə'fəubɪə, -rəpə-] *n.* morbid fear of thunder and lightning.

astrict [ə'strɪkt] *v.t.* astringe. **astriction,** *n.* **astrictive,** *adj.*

astringe [ə'strɪndʒ] *v.t.* bind; brace; restrict; constipate.

astringent [ə'strɪndʒənt] *adj.* causing to contract: binding; styptic; tonic; constipating; *n.* such medicine or lotion. **astringency,** *n.*

astrogate ['æstrəgeɪt] *v.t.* guide (spaceship, etc.); *v.i.* navigate in space.

astrognosy [ə'strɒgnəsi] *n.* knowledge of fixed stars.

astrogony [ə'strɒgəni] *n.* theory of the origin of the stars.

astrograph ['æstrəgrɑːf] *n.* photographic telescope. **astrography** [ə'strɒgrəfi], *n.* mapping or describing the stars.

astroid ['æstrɔɪd] *adj.* star-shaped.

astrolabe ['æstrəleɪb] *n.* ancient astronomical instrument for taking altitudes.

astrolatry [ə'strɒlətri] *n.* worship of stars.

astrolithology [,æstrəlɪ'θɒlədʒi] *n.* study of meteorites.

astrologaster [ə'strɒləgæstə] *n.* fraudulent astrologer.

astrology [ə'strɒlədʒi] *n.* study of supposed influence of stars on human life; *archaic,* astronomy. **astrologer,** *n.* one who tells fortunes from the stars. **astrological** [,æstrə'lɒdʒɪkl], *adj.*

astro-meteorology [,æstrəu,miːtiə'rɒlədʒi] *n.* study of supposed effect of heavenly bodies on weather.

astrometry [ə'strɒmətri] *n.* measurement of heavenly bodies.

astronautics [,æstrə'nɔːtɪks] *n.* science of space travel.

astrophile, astrophil ['æstrəfaɪl, -fɪl] *n.* person fond of learning about stars.

astrophysics [,æstrəu'fɪzɪks] *n.* study of composition of heavenly bodies. **astrophysical,** *adj.*

astucious [ə'stjuːʃəs] *adj.* astute. **astucity** [ə'stjuːsəti], *n.*

astute [ə'stjuːt] *adj.* acutely perceptive and shrewd.

astylar [eɪ'staɪlə] *adj. Architecture,* lacking columns.

asymptomatic [eɪ,sɪmptə'mætɪk] *adj.* showing no symptoms (of a disease).

asymptote ['æsɪmptəut] *n.* line approaching a curve but meeting it only at infinity. **asymptotic** [-'tɒtɪk], *adj.*

asynchronous [eɪ'sɪŋkrənəs] *adj.* not occurring at same time. **asynchronism, asynchrony** *n.*

asyndeton [æ'sɪndɪtən] *n.* rhetorical device of omitting conjunctions. **asyndetic** [-'detɪk], *adj.*

asynergy, asynergia [eɪ'sɪnədʒi, ,eɪsɪ'nɜːdʒɪə] *n. Medicine,* lack of co-ordination, especially of muscles.

asyngamy [ə'sɪŋgəmi] *n. Botany,* failure to effect cross-fertilization due to asynchronous development of flowers.

asyntactic [,eɪsɪn'tæktɪk] *adj.* breaking rules of syntax or grammar.

asystole [eɪ'sɪstəli] *n.* cessation of contraction of heart. **asystolic** [-'stɒlɪk], *adj.*

atactic [eɪ'tæktɪk] *adj.* asyntactic; irregular; pertaining to ataxy.

ataghan ['ætəgæn] *n.* yataghan.

ataraxy, ataraxia ['ætəræksi, ,ætə'ræksiə] *n.* tranquillity of mind; imperturbability. **ataraxic, ataraxic** *n. & adj.* (drug) able to calm or tranquillize.

atavism ['ætəvɪzm] *n.* reversion to remote ancestral type; 'throw-back'; recurrence of hereditary feature after an interval of a generation or more. **atavistic** [-'vɪstɪk], *adj.* pertaining to remote ancestor. **atavist,** *n.* person or thing marked by atavism.

atavus ['ætəvəs] *(Latin) n.* remote ancestor whose characteristics recur in atavism.

ataxaphasia [ə,tæksə'feɪzɪə, -ʒə] *n.* inability, due to imperfect muscular co-ordination, to speak sentences.

ataxy, ataxia [ə'tæksi, -sɪə] *n.* inability to co-ordinate muscles; lack of order. **ataxic,** *adj.*

ateknia [ə'teknɪə] *n.* childlessness.

atelectasis [,ætə'lektəsɪs] *n.* incomplete dilatation or collapse of lungs.

atelier [ə'telɪeɪ] *(French) n.* studio; workshop.

ateliosis [ə,teli'əusɪs, -,tiː-] *n.* imperfect development; dwarfism.

atheling ['æθəlɪŋ] *n.* Anglo-Saxon noble; prince, especially heir apparent.

athenaeum [,æθə'niːəm] *n.* club having learned members; library.

athermanous [ə'θɜːmənəs] *adj.* impervious to radiant heat. **athermancy,** *n.*

athermous [ə'θɜːməs] *adj.* without heat.

atherogenic [,æθərəu'dʒenɪk] *adj.* leading to atheroma.

atheroma [‚æθəˈrəumə] *n.* fatty degeneration of the arteries. **atherosclerosis** [–əskleˈrəusɪs], *n.* hardening of the inner lining of the arteries with fatty degeneration. **atheromatous** *adj.*

athetize [ˈæθətaɪz] *v.t.* condemn as spurious.

athetosis [‚æθəˈtəusɪs] *n.* nervous twitching of fingers and toes.

athrepsia [əˈθrepsiə] *n.* complete debility in children. **athreptic,** *adj.*

athymy [ˈæθəmi] *n.* melancholy.

atlantes [ətˈlæntiːz] *n. pl.* male figures used as columns.

atman [ˈɑːtmən] *n. Hinduism,* the soul; universal soul.

atmogenic [‚ætməˈdʒenɪk] *adj. Geology,* of atmospheric origin.

atmology [ætˈmɒlədʒi] *n.* study of laws of watery vapour.

atmolysis [ætˈmɒləsɪs] *n.* method of separating gases of different densities.

atmometer [ætˈmɒmɪtə] *n.* instrument measuring rate of evaporation into atmosphere. **atmometry,** *n.*

atmospherics [‚ætməsˈferɪks] *n. pl.* interference in reception of radio signals due to electrical disturbances in the atmosphere.

atokous [ˈætəkəs] *adj.* lacking offspring.

atoll [ˈætɒl] *n.* island formed of a coral reef surrounding a lagoon.

atom [ˈætəm] *n.* (formerly) ultimate unit of matter; smallest particle of element that can exist alone or as a constituent of molecule; any very small thing or quantity.

atomic [əˈtɒmɪk] *adj.* of atoms. **atom bomb, atomic bomb,** bomb of which the immense destructive power is due to sudden release of energy by nuclear fission. **atomic number, number representing the magnitude of the positive charge on the nucleus of an atom of an element,** *i.e.* the number of protons in the nucleus, or the number of electrons in the atom; numerically equal to the number denoting the position of an element in the periodic table. **atomic pile,** nuclear reactor. **atomic weight,** weight of an atom of an element on a scale on which the weight of an oxygen atom is 16. **atomicity** [‚ætəˈmɪsəti], *n.* number of atoms in molecule of an element.

atomism [ˈætəmɪzm] *n.* theory of atoms. **atomize,** *v.t.* reduce to atoms or a fine spray; treat as individual units rather than as a whole. **atomizer,** *n.* pump-like instrument producing fine spray. **atomistic,** *adj.* of atoms or atomism; divided into units.

atomy [ˈætəmi] *n. archaic,* very small creature; skeleton.

atonal [eɪˈtəunl] *adj. Music,* composed in accordance with theory of atonality. **atonality** [‚eɪtəuˈnæləti], *n. Music,* theory in which the scale consists of twelve semitones of equal value.

atone [əˈtəun] *v.i.* make amends. **atonement,** *n.*

atonic [əˈtɒnɪk, eɪ–] *n. & adj.* unaccented or voiceless (sound); surd; *Medicine,* lacking tone or energy. **atony** [ˈætəni], *n.*

atopic [eɪˈtɒpɪk] *adj. Medicine,* allergic. **atopy** [ˈætəpi], *n.* allergy.

atrabilious [‚ætrəˈbɪliəs] *adj.* very melancholic; hypochondriac.

atrament [ˈætrəmənt] *n.* very dark liquid; *obso-*

lete ink. **atramentous,** *adj.*

atraumatic [‚eɪtrɔːˈmætɪk] *adj.* designed to avoid injury.

atresia [əˈtriːziə, –ʒə] *n.* lack or closing of a passage of the body. **atretic** [əˈtretɪk], *adj.*

atrial [ˈeɪtriəl] *adj.* pertaining to atrium.

atrichia [eɪˈtrɪkiə, ə–] *n.* baldness.

atrium [ˈeɪtriəm] *n.* main courtyard-like room of Roman house; cavity of heart or ear.

atrophy [ˈætrəfi] *n.* wasting or paralysis due to lack of nutrition or exercise; *Biology,* loss of organ due to disuse; *v.i. & t.* suffer or cause atrophy. **atrophic** [əˈtrɒfɪk], *adj.*

atropine [ˈætrəpiːn] *n.* poisonous alkaloid obtained from deadly nightshade roots and leaves.

atrous [ˈeɪtrəs] *adj.* jet black.

attaché [əˈtæʃeɪ] (*French*) *n.* person attached to embassy.

attachment [əˈtætʃmənt] *n. Law,* taking of person or property by order of court.

attain [əˈteɪn] *v.* reach, achieve (a desired goal). **attainment** *n.* accomplishment, achievement.

attainder [əˈteɪndə] *n.* loss of civil rights, formerly result of outlawry or death sentence.

attaint [əˈteɪnt] *v.t. archaic,* pass sentence of attainder on; sully; attach disgrace to; infect; *n.* dishonour; misfortune. **attainture,** *n.*

attar [ˈætə, –ɑː] *n.* oil distilled from rose petals; any perfume derived from flowers.

attemper [əˈtempə] *v.t. archaic,* alter quality by addition or mixture; moderate. **attemperate,** *v.t. archaic,* moderate temperature. **attemporator,** *n.* apparatus for moderating temperature.

attenuate [əˈtenjueɪt] *v.t.* make thin; dilute; weaken; *adj.* thin; tapering; rarified. **attenuation,** *n.* **attenuator,** *n.* resistance diminishing amplitude of oscillations in electric circuit. **attenuant,** *adj.* diluting; *n.* drug diluting the blood.

attestation [‚æteˈsteɪʃn] *n.* witnessing; giving evidence; *British* declaration on oath. **attest** [əˈtest] *v.t.* **attester,** *Law,* **attestor** *n.*

Attic [ˈætɪk] *adj.* of Athens or Attica; classically simple and pure. **atticism** [–sɪzm] *n.* well-turned phrase.

attingent [əˈtɪndʒənt] *adj. archaic,* touching.

atto- [ˈætəu–] *prefix* of measurement meaning one million-million-millionth (10^{-18})

attorney [əˈtɜːni] *n.* accredited agent in law or finance; solicitor; *American,* counsel or solicitor. **power of attorney** authorization to act as agent. **Attorney General,** chief law officer of Crown. **attorneyship,** *n.*

attornment [əˈtɜːnmənt] *n.* acknowledgment by tenant of new landlord's rights. **attorn,** *v.i.*

attrahent [ˈætrəhənt] *adj.* attracting; drawing towards or forward; *n.* such thing or muscle.

attrition [əˈtrɪʃn] *n.* wearing away; rubbing or scraping; *Theology,* incomplete repentance due to fear of punishment. **war of attrition,** campaign of wearing down enemy's morale and resistance. **attritive** *adj.* causing attrition. **attritional** pertaining to, caused by attrition. **attritus** pulverized matter.

atypical [eɪˈtɪpɪkl] *adj.* not typical

aubade [əuˈbɑːd] (*French*) *n.* musical piece performed at or describing dawn.

au courant [əu ˈkurɒn] (*French*) 'in the current'; up-to-date, especially in information.

auctorial [ɔːk'tɔːriəl] *adj.* pertaining to an author.

audile ['ɔːdaɪl] *n.* person whose mental processes are stimulated more strongly by hearing than by other senses; *adj.* pertaining to such persons; auditory.

audio-frequency ['ɔːdiəʊ,friːkwənsi] *n.* frequency between 20 and 20,000 cycles per sec., *i.e.* the frequency of normally audible sound waves.

audiogenic [,ɔːdiə'dʒenɪk] *adj.* caused by sound waves, especially of high frequency.

audiometer [,ɔːdi'ɒmɪtə] *n.* instrument testing sensitivity of hearing and audibility of sounds. **audiometric** [–ə'metrɪk], *adj.* **audiometrist** [–'ɒm–], *n.*

audiophile ['ɔːdiəʊfaɪl] *n.* person interested in high-fidelity sound recordings.

audiphone ['ɔːdɪfəʊn] *n.* instrument for the deaf placed against the teeth.

audit ['ɔːdɪt] *n.* examination, especially of business accounts; report on such examination; *v.t.* make such examination. **audit ale**, special strong ale used at certain Oxford colleges on audit day. **auditor**, *n.* person who audits; listener. **auditorial**, *adj.*

auditory ['ɔːdɪtəri] *adj.* pertaining to hearing; *n. archaic*, audience; auditorium.

au fait [əʊ 'feɪ] (*French*) 'to the fact'; having complete and up-to-date knowledge; conversant.

au fond [əʊ 'fɒn] (*French*) 'at bottom'; fundamentally.

Augean stables [ɔː'dʒiːən] *n. pl.* (place in) filthy condition, from King Augean's stables in Greek mythology, uncleaned for thirty years.

augment [ɔːg'ment] *v.i. & t.* make or become larger or greater in size, etc.

au grand sérieux [əʊ ,grɒn seəri'ɜː] (*French*) 'with great seriousness'; quite seriously.

au gratin [əʊ 'grætæn] (*French*) covered with breadcrumbs (and often cheese) and grilled.

augur ['ɔːgə] *n.* prophet, soothsayer, omen; *v.i. & t.* predict; portend. **augural** *adj.* **augury** *n.* art of prophecy or divination; omen.

august [ɔː'gʌst] *adj.* majestic; venerable; awe-inspiring.

Augustan [ɔː'gʌstən] *adj.* pertaining to Augustus Caesar and his age, especially to the literature of his reign; of any classical or golden age of literature; *n.* writer in such age.

auk [ɔːk] *n.* short-winged seabird, especially the extinct great and the little auk. **auklet**, *n.* small auk.

au lait [əʊ 'leɪ] (*French*,) 'with milk'.

aularian [ɔː'leəriən] *adj.* pertaining to hall; *n.* member of a hall at Oxford or Cambridge.

aulete ['ɔːliːt] *n.* flautist.

aulic ['ɔːlɪk] *adj.* courtly; ceremonious.

aumbry, aumry ['ɔːmbri, 'ɔːmri] *n.* ambry.

au naturel [əʊ ,nætjə'rel] (*French*) 'in natural' (style); simply; without additions, especially of cooking; nude.

aura ['ɔːrə] *n.* emanation; atmosphere surrounding a thing or person; personality; *Medicine,* sensation warning of onset of epileptic fit, hysteria, etc.

aural ['ɔːrəl, 'aʊr–] *adj.* pertaining to ear or hearing; pertaining to aura.

aurantiaceous [ɔː,rænti'eɪʃəs] *adj.* like or per-

taining to orange or plant group containing it.

aurated [ɔː'reɪtɪd] *adj.* gilded.

aurea mediocritas [,ɔːriə miːdɪ'ɒkrɪtæs, ,aʊ–, -meɪ–] (*Latin*) 'the golden mean'.

aureate, aureous ['ɔːrieɪt, -iəs] *adj.* golden-coloured; ornate.

aureity [ɔː'riːəti] *n.* properties of gold.

aureole, aureola ['ɔːriəʊl, ɔː'riːələ] *n.* halo; bright circle of light; *Astronomy,* solar corona.

aureoline, *adj.* gold-coloured.

aureomycin [,ɔːriəʊ'maɪsɪn] *n. trademark,* an antibiotic drug extracted from a soil mould, used in treatment of infections, especially of eyes, skin, etc.

aureus ['ɔːriəs] *n. (pl.* **-ei**)) gold coin of ancient Greece and Rome.

auric ['ɔːrɪk] *adj.* pertaining to, like or composed of gold.

auricle ['ɔːrɪkl, 'ɒ–] *n.* external ear; ear-shaped appendage; upper cavity of heart.

auricomous [ɔː'rɪkəməs] *adj.* having golden hair; making hair golden.

auricular [ɔː'rɪkjʊlə] *adj.* pertaining to hearing, or to the ear; spoken secretly. **auricular finger,** the little finger.

auriculate [ɔː'rɪkjʊlət, -eɪt] *adj.* having ears or ear-shaped outgrowths; lobed; ear-like.

auriferous [ɔː'rɪfərəs] *adj.* containing gold.

auriform ['ɔːrɪfɔːm] *adj.* ear-shaped.

aurify ['ɔːrɪfaɪ] *v.t.* change into gold. **aurific** [ɔː'rɪfɪk] *adj.* producing gold. **aurification** *n.* working with gold.

auriga [ɔː'raɪgə] *n.* charioteer. **Auriga,** constellation in nothern hemisphere. **aurigation** [,ɔːrɪ'geɪʃn], *n.* art of driving a chariot.

auriphrygia [,ɔːrɪ'frɪdʒiə] *n.* gold embroidery. **auriphrygiate,** *adj.*

auriscope ['ɔːrɪskəʊp] *n.* instrument for examining ear.

aurist ['ɔːrɪst] *n.* specialist on the ear and its diseases.

aurochs ['ɔːrɒks] *n.* extinct wild ox.

aurora [ɔː'rɔːrə] *n.* dawn; reddish glow in sky before sunrise. **aurora borealis** [,bɔːri'eɪlɪs], luminosity in sky in Arctic region due to atmospheric electricity; northern lights. **aurora australis** [ɒ'streɪlɪs], same phenomenon in Antarctic region; southern lights. **auroral, aurorean,** *adj.*

aurous ['ɔːrəs] *adj.* pertaining to, containing or made of gold.

aurulent ['ɔːrʊlənt, -jʊ–] *adj.* gold-coloured.

auscultate ['ɔːskltteɪt] *v.i. & t. Medicine,* listen to sounds in human body; examine in this manner. **auscultation,** *n.* **auscultative,** *adj.* **auscultator,** *n.* person practising auscultation; stethoscope. **auscultatory,** *adj.*

auslaut ['aʊslaʊt] (*German*) *n.* final sound of syllable or word.

auspice ['ɔːspɪs, 'ɒ–] *n.* omen, especially of good fortune; *pl.*, observation of such omen; patronage; protection. **auspicate** [–keɪt], *v.i. & t.* predict; give good start to. **auspicious,** *adj.* promising well; favourable; important.

Auster ['ɔːstə] (*Latin*) *n.* south wind; southern latitudes.

austere [ɔː'stɪə, ɒ–] *adj.* strict in moral outlook; extremely simple; without ornamentation; severe;

sharp. **austerity** [ɔː'sterəti], *n.*

austral ['ɔːstrəl, 'ɒ–] *adj.* of the south; moist and warm.

autacoid ['ɔːtəkɔɪd] *n.* hormone. **autacoidal**, *adj.*

autarchy ['ɔːtɑːki] *n.* absolute sovereignty; autocracy. **autarchic** [ɔː'tɑːkɪk], **autarchical** *adj.*

autarky ['ɔːtɑːki] *n.* national economic self-sufficiency. **autarkic** [ɔː'tɑːkɪk] *adj.*

autecology [,ɔːtɪ'kɒlədʒi] *n.* the ecology of the individual organism.

autism ['ɔːtɪzm] *n.* abnormal self-absorption, especially in children. **autistic** [ɔː'tɪstɪk], *adj.*

autocephalous [,ɔːtə'sefələs] *adj.* *Ecclesiastical*, self-governing. **autocephaly** *n.*

autochthon [ɔː'tɒkθən] *n.* native; aboriginal species. **autochthonous**, *adj.* **autochthony**, *n.*

autoclave ['ɔːtəkleɪv] *n.* apparatus for cooking or sterilizing instruments at high pressure.

autocrat ['ɔːtəkræt] *n.* sole ruler; despot. **autocratic**, *adj.* **autocracy** [ɔː'tɒkrəsi], *n.*.

auto-da-fé [,ɔːtəʊdə'feɪ] *n.* (*pl.* **autos-da-fé**) burning of a heretic.

autodidact [,ɔːtə'daɪdækt] *n.* self-taught person. **autodidactic** [–daɪ'dæktɪk], *n.*

autoecious [ɔː'tiːʃəs] *adj.* (of fungus, etc.) passing through all life stages on same species of host.

autoeroticism, autoerotism [,ɔːtəʊ'rɒtɪsɪzm, ,ɔːtəʊ'erətɪzm] *n.* self-induced sexual arousal and/or gratification. **autoerotic**, *adj.*

autogamy [ɔː'tɒgəmi] *n.* self-fertilization. **autogamic** [–'gæmɪk], **autogamous**, *adj.*

autogenesis [,ɔːtə'dʒenəsɪs] *n.* spontaneous generation. **autogenetic** [dʒə'netɪk], *adj.*

autogenous [ɔː'tɒdʒɪnəs] *adj.* self-generated.

autognosis [,ɔːtɒg'nəʊsɪs] *n.* self-knowledge. **autognostic** [–'nɒstɪk], *&ddZ*]

autoimmune [,ɔːtəʊɪ'mjuːn] *adj.* denoting a condition in which antibodies are aroused by a patient's own secretions, etc. **autoimmunity**, *n.*

autointoxication [,ɔːtəʊɪn,tɒksɪ'keɪʃn] *n.* poisoning due to toxins produced in body.

autokinesis [,ɔːtəʊkɪ'niːsɪs, –kaɪ–] *n.* voluntary or automatic movement. **autokinetic** [–'netɪk], *adj.*

autolatry [ɔː'tɒlətri] *n.* self-worship.

automation [,ɔːtə'meɪʃn] *n.* control of machines by other machines, electronic devices, etc., instead of by human beings. **automate** *v.i. & t.*

automaton [ɔː'tɒmətən] *n.* (*pl.* **automata**) automatic mechanism, especially one effecting complex actions; robot; person who acts like a machine. **automatism**, *n.* machine-like action or routine; involuntary action; belief that actions are not controlled by conscious mind.

automorphic [,ɔːtə'mɔːfɪk] *adj.* formed after its or one's own pattern. **automorphism**, *n.*

automotive [,ɔːtə'məʊtɪv] *adj.* self-propelling.

autonomics [,ɔːtə'nɒmɪks] *n.* science of the performance by machines of mental processes such as reading and translation.

autonomy [ɔː'tɒnəmi] *n.* power or right to govern oneself or itself; free-will. **autonomic** [,ɔːtə'nɒmɪk], *adj.* spontaneous; involuntary. **autonomous** [–'tɒn–], *adj.* self-governing.

autonym ['ɔːtənɪm] *n.* writer's own name; work published under own name.

autophagy [ɔː'tɒfədʒi] *n.* devouring of cell constituents by enzymes of same cell. **autophagous**

[–gəs], *adj.*

autophobia [,ɔːtə'fəʊbiə] *n.* fear of solitude.

autophony [ɔː'tɒfəni] *n.* apparent distortion of one's own voice due to infection or stoppage of ears; sound of auscultator's voice as reverberating in patient's chest.

autophyte ['ɔːtəfaɪt] *n.* plant able to organize its foodstuffs; nonsaprophytic plant. **autophytic** [–'fɪtɪk], *adj.*

autoplasty ['ɔːtəplæsti] *n.* grafting tissue from patient's own body. **autoplastic**, *adj.*; *Biology*, pertaining to self-adaptation to environment; pertaining to autoplasty.

autopsy ['ɔːtɒpsi] *n.* personal examination, especially post-mortem. **autoptic**, *adj.* derived from personal observation.

autoschediasm [,ɔːtə'ʃiːdiæzm, –'skiː–] *n.* improvization. **autoschediastic**, *adj.*

autoskeleton ['ɔːtəʊ,skelɪtən] *n.* internal skeleton.

autosome ['ɔːtəsəʊm] *n.* non-sexual chromosome.

autostrada ['ɔːtəʊ,strɑːdə, 'aʊ–] (*Italian*) *n.* motorway.

autotelic [,ɔːtə'telɪk] *adj.* having itself as its only purpose.

autotheism ['ɔːtəʊ,θiːɪzm] *n.* belief in self-subsistence of God the Son; deification of oneself.

autotherapy [,ɔːtəʊ'θerəpi] *n.* treatment of patient by self or by application of own secretions.

autotomy [ɔː'tɒtəmi] *n.* reflex loss of part of the body to save the whole (in lizards, etc.)

autotrophic [,ɔːtə'trɒfɪk] *adj.* *Botany*, nourishing itself; autophytic.

autotropic [,ɔːtə'trɒpɪk] *adj.* *Botany*, tending to grow in straight line.

autotype ['ɔːtətaɪp] *n.* facsimile; true copy. **autotypy**, *n.* process of producing such copies.

autrefois acquit [,əʊtrəfwɑː 'ækiː] (*French*,) 'formerly acquitted'; *Law*, plea that defendant has already been acquitted on the charge.

autres temps, autres moeurs [,əʊtrə 'tɒm, ,əʊtrə 'mɜːs] (*French*) 'other times, other customs'.

auxanometer [,ɔːksə'nɒmɪtə] *n.* instrument measuring rate of growth of plants.

auxesis [ɔːk'siːsɪs] *n.* growth in cell size; hyperbole. **auxetic** [–'setɪk], *adj.*

auxin ['ɔːksɪn] *n.* *Chemistry*, substance increasing growth of plants; plant hormone.

auxograph ['ɔːksəgrɑːf] *n.* instrument recording variations in volume.

auxology [ɔːk'sɒlədʒi] *n.* science of growth.

auxotonic [,ɔːksə'tɒnɪk] *adj.* according or due to growth.

ava ['ɑːvə] *n.* strong liquor of Hawaii; plant from which it is obtained.

avant-garde [,ævɒŋ'gɑːd] (*French*) *n.* artists, etc. in forefront of new ideas in the arts; *adj.* pertaining to such artists or their work; experimental, strange.

avatar ['ævətɑː] *n.* incarnation of deity, especially Hindu; manifestation; deification.

avaunt [ə'vɔːnt] *excl. archaic*, begone!

ave ['ɑːveɪ] (*Latin*) 'hail!'. **ave atque vale**, [–,ætkwi 'vɑːleɪ] hail and farewell. **Ave Maria**

[–mə'riːə], *n.* prayer to the Virgin Mary.

avellaneous [,ævə'leɪnɪəs] *adj.* hazel.

avenaceous [,ævɪ'neɪʃəs] *adj.* pertaining to or like oats. **aveniform** [ə'venɪfɔːm], *adj.* like oats in shape.

avenous [eɪ'viːnəs] *adj.* lacking veins.

aventurine [ə'ventʃəriːn, –ɪn] *n.* glass containing golden or green flecks; quartz containing mica flakes.

aver [ə'vɜː] *v.t.* state as fact, assert. **averment,** *n.*

average ['ævərɪdʒ] *n. Commerce,* loss to owners due to damage to ship or cargo at sea; assessing of incidence of such loss in proportion among interested parties. **average adjuster,** professional assessor of marine insurance claims who apportions them among owners, underwriters, etc.

averaging ['ævərɪdʒɪŋ] *n. Commerce,* operation of increasing transactions on Stock Exchange when market goes against the operator to maintain price at level desired.

averruncate [,ævə'rʌŋkeɪt] *v.t. obsolete,* avert; weed out.

averse [ə'vɜːs] *adj.* strongly disliking. **aversion** [ə'vɜːʃn] *n.* fixed dislike; person or thing arousing this. **aversive,** *adj.* tending to cause aversion.

avian, avine ['eɪvɪən, 'eɪvaɪn] *adj.* pertaining to birds.

avicide ['eɪvɪsaɪd] *n.* killing of birds.

avicular [ə'vɪkjulə] *adj.* pertaining to small birds.

aviculture ['eɪvɪ,kʌltʃə] *n.* rearing of birds.

avifauna ['eɪvɪ,fɔːnə] *n.* birdlife of a region.

avigation [,ævɪ'geɪʃn] *n.* aerial navigation.

avionics [,eɪvɪ'ɒnɪks] *n.* study and use of electronic devices in aviation.

avirulent [eɪ'vɪrulənt, –ju–] *adj.* (of bacteria) not virulent.

avitaminosis [eɪ,vɪtəmɪ'nəʊsɪs] *n.* condition due to vitamin-deficiency. **avitaminotic** [–'nɒtɪk], *adj.*

avocation [,ævə'keɪʃn] *n.* hobby; vocation. **avocational,** *adj.*

avocet, ['ævəset] *n.* long-legged wading bird with upturned beak.

avolitional [,eɪvə'lɪʃənəl] *adj.* involuntary.

avow [ə'vaʊ] *v.t.* openly acknowledge; affirm. **avowal,** *n.*

avulsion [ə'vʌlʃn] *n.* act of pulling away part of body, either by injury or surgery. **avulsive** [ə'vʌlsɪv], *adj.*

avuncular [ə'vʌŋkjulə] *adj.* of or like an uncle.

awn [ɔːn] *n.* 'beard' of grass, barley, etc.; spiky outgrowth; *v.t.* strip of awns.

axenic [eɪ'zenɪk] *adj.* free of parasites and similar forms of life; surgically sterile.

axifugal [æk'sɪfjugl] *adj.* centrifugal.

axil ['æksɪl] *n.* upper angle between leaf and stem, or branch and trunk. **axile** [–aɪl], *adj.*

axilla [æk'sɪlə] *n. (pl.* **-s, -lae,**) armpit; shoulder. **axillary** *adj.* of arm-pit; of or growing in an axil.

axiniform [æk'sɪnɪfɔːm] *adj.* having shape of axe-head.

axiology [,æksɪ'ɒlədʒi] *n.* study of ultimate values. **axiological,** *adj.* **axiologist,** *n.*

axiom ['æksɪəm] *n.* necessary and accepted truth; basic and universal principle. **axiomatic** [–'mætɪk], *adj.*

axolotl [,æksə'lɒtl] *n.* larval salamander of Mexico and W America.

axon ['æksɒn] *n.* projection of nerve cell that passes on nerve impulses.

axonometry [,æksə'nɒmətri] *n.* measurement of or by axes. **axonometric projection** *n.* method of representing three-dimensional object in two-dimensional drawing.

axophyte ['æksəfaɪt] *n.* stem-bearing plant.

axunge ['æksʌndʒ] *n.* medicinal lard or grease.

ayah ['aɪə] *n.* native Ind. nurse or servant.

ayatollah [,aɪə'tɒlə] *n.* in Iran, powerful religious leader.

aye-aye ['aɪaɪ] *n.* species of lemur of Madagascar.

azan [æ'zɑːn] *n.* Muslim call to prayer.

azimuth ['æzɪməθ] *n.* angular distance, measured along horizon, of object from north or south points; angle between meridian and the great circle which passes through both zenith and heavenly body. **azimuth compass,** magnetic compass having sights for taking the **azimuth circle,** quadrant of great circle through zenith and nadir. **azimuthal** [–'mʌθl, –'mjuːθl], *adj.*

azofication [,eɪzəfɪ'keɪʃn] *n.* nitrogenization of soil by bacteria. **azofier,** *n.* bacterium causing azofication.

azoic [ə'zəʊɪk, eɪ–] *adj.* lacking life, especially of geological period.

azoology [,eɪzəʊ'ɒlədʒi] *n.* study of inanimate nature.

azote ['æzəʊt, 'eɪ–] *n. obsolete,* nitrogen. **azotaemia, azotemia** *n.* excess of nitrogen in blood. **azotic,** *adj.* **azotize,** *v.t.* combine with nitrogen.

azoth ['æzɒθ] *n.* alchemists' name for mercury; Paracelsus' postulated panacea.

azulejo [,æθu'leɪxəʊ] *(Spanish) n.* brightly coloured tile of Near East, Spain and Holland.

azygous [eɪ'zaɪgəs, 'æzɪgəs] *adj.* unpaired; odd.

azym(e) ['æzɪm, 'æzaɪm] *n.* unleavened bread; Passover cake; *pl.* feast of such bread.

B

Baal ['beɪəl] *n.* (*pl.* **–im**) local god of ancient Semitic tribes; idol. **Baalism,** *n.* idolatry.

babiroussa, babirussa, babirusa [,bæbɪ'ruːsə] *n.* tusked wild hog of E Indies.

babu, baboo (*Anglo-Indian*) *n.* title of Hindu gentleman; Mr; English-speaking Hindu, especially used contemptuously.

babuina [,bæbu'iːnə] *n.* female baboon.

babul [baː'buːl] *n.* gum-arabic tree of E Indies and Arabia.

babushka [bə'buːʃkə] *n.* woman's head-scarf.

baccaceous [bæ'keɪʃəs] *adj.* like a berry; bearing berries.

baccalaureate [,bækə'lɔːriət] *n.* degree of Bachelor. **baccalaurean,** *adj.* pertaining to a Bachelor.

baccate ['bækeɪt] *adj.* pulpy; like a berry; bearing berries.

bacchanal ['bækənəl, ,bækə'næl] *adj.* pertaining to Bacchus, god of wine, and rites in his worship; *n.* drunkard; reveller; votary of Bacchus. **bacchanalia** [–'neɪliə], *n.pl.* festival of Bacchus; drunken behaviour. **bacchanalian,** *adj.* **bacchanalianism,** *n.* habitual drunken behaviour.

bacchant ['bækənt] *n.* (*pl.* **–es**). priest or votary of Bacchus. **bacchante** [bə'kænti], *n.* such priestess or female votary. **bacchantic,** *adj.*

bacchic ['bækɪk] *adj.* pertaining to Bacchus and bacchanalia; drunken; jovial; *n.* drinking song.

bacchius [bə'kaɪəs] *n.* (*pl.* **–ii**) metrical foot of one long followed by two short syllables.

bacciferous [bæk'sɪfərəs] *adj.* bearing berries. **bacciform** ['bæksɪfɔːm], *adj.* berry-shaped. **baccivorous** [bæk'sɪvərəs], *adj.* feeding on berries.

bacillus [bə'sɪləs] *n.* (*pl.* **–li**) rod-shaped bacterium, especially causing disease. **bacillaemia,** *n.* presence of bacilli in blood. **bacillary,** *adj.* rodshaped; caused by bacillus. **bacillicide,** *n.* substance killing bacilli. **bacilliform,** *adj.* rod-shaped. **bacillosis,** *n.* infection with bacillus. **bacilluria,** *n.* presence of bacilli in urine.

backsheesh *see* **baksheesh.**

backwardation [,bækwə'deɪʃn] *n. Commerce,* postponement by seller of delivery of stock; premium paid to buyer for such postponement.

bacteria [bæk'tɪəriə] *n.pl.* (*sing.* **–rium**) universally present microscopic unicellular organisms. **bacterial, bacterian, bacterious,** *adj.*

bacteriaemia [bæk,tɪəri'iːmiə] *n.* presence of bacteria in blood.

bactericide [bæk'tɪərɪsaɪd] *n.* substance destroying bacteria. **bactericidal,** *adj.*

bacteriogenic,   bacteriogenous [bæk,tɪəriə'dʒenɪk, –i'ɒdʒənəs] *adj.* caused by bacteria.

bacteriology [bæk,tɪəri'ɒlədʒi] *n.* study of bacteria. **bacteriological,** *adj.* **bacteriologist,** *n.*

bacteriolysin [bæk,tɪəriə'laɪsɪn] *n.* antibody causing destruction of bacteria. **bacteriolysis** [–'ɒləsɪs], *n.* decomposition caused by bacteria; destruction of bacteria. **bacteriolytic** [–'lɪtɪk], *adj.*

bacteriophage [bæk'tɪəriəfeɪdʒ] *n.* virus causing destruction of bacteria. **bacteriophagic, bacteriophagous** [–'ɒfəgəs], *adj.* **bacteriophagy** [–'ɒfədʒi], *n.*

bacterioscopy [bæk,tɪəri'ɒskəpi] *n.* examination of bacteria with microscope. **bacterioscopic** [–'skɒpɪk], *adj.* **bacterioscopist,** *n.*

bacteriosis [bæk,tɪəri'əʊsɪs] *n.* bacterial plant disease.

bacteriostasis [bæk,tɪəriə'steɪsɪs] *n.* prevention of growth of bacteria. **bacteriostat,** *n.* agent causing this. **bacteriostatic** [–'stætɪk], *adj.*

bacteriotherapy [bæk,tɪəriə'θerəpi] *n.* medical treatment with bacteria. **bacteriotherapeutic,** *adj.*

bacteriotoxin [bæk,tɪəriə'tɒksɪn] *n.* poison destroying or preventing growth of bacteria; poison produced by bacteria.

bacteriotropic [bæk,tɪəriə'trɒpɪk] *adj.* affecting bacteria.

bacteritic [,bæktə'rɪtɪk] *adj.* caused or marked by bacteria. **bacteroid** ['bæktərɔɪd], *adj.* like bacteria; *n.* irregularly shaped form of bacterium, especially found in plant root-nodules.

baculus ['bækjʊləs] *n.* stick; rod; symbol of power. **baculiferous,** *adj.* bearing canes, reeds, etc. **baculiform,** *adj.* rod-shaped. **baculine,** *adj.* pertaining to rod or punishment therewith.

badigeon [bə'dɪdʒən] *n.* mixture of plaster and ground stone, or glue and sawdust, for repairing masonry and woodwork respectively; *v.t.* repair with badigeon.

badinage ['bædɪnɑːʒ] (*French*) *n.* banter.

baffy ['bæfi] *n.* wooden deep-faced golf club used to give loft to ball.

bagasse [bə'gæs] *n.* dry residue, especially of sugar cane and beet after extraction of juice, and plants after removal of fibre.

bagel ['beɪgl] (*Yiddish*) *n.* hard, ring-shaped bread roll.

baggala ['bægələ, 'bʌgəlɑː] *n.* Arabian two-masted vessel; dhow.

bagheera [bæ'gɪərə] *n.* rough, crease-resistant, velvet-like textile.

bagnio ['bænjəʊ] (*Italian*) *n.* bath house; prison; brothel.

baguette [bæ'get] *n.* long, narrow loaf of French bread; small astragal moulding; narrow rectangular cut gem; *adj.* cut into such shape.

bahadur [bə'hɑːdə, –ʊə] *n.* Indian title of respect; *slang,* self-important official.

Baha'i [bə'l haɪ, baː'haːi] (*Persian*) *n.* member of religion founded by Baha-Ullah in mid-19th century. **Baha'ism,** *n.* **Baha'ist,** *n.*

bailee [,beɪ'liː] *n.* person receiving goods in trust.

bailey ['beɪli] *n.* outer wall of castle; space between outer and inner walls.

bailie, baillie ['beɪli] *n.* Scottish civic officer, equivalent of alderman. **bailiary, bailiery,** *n.* jurisdiction of bailie.

bailiff ['beɪlɪf] *n.* sheriff's officer; agent or steward of estate. **bailiffry,** *n.* office of bailiff. **bum-bailiff,** *n. slang* sheriff's officer.

bailiwick ['beɪlɪwɪk] *n.* jurisdiction of sheriff or bailie.

bailment ['beɪlmənt] *n.* delivery of goods in trust. **bailor** [,beɪ'loː], *n.* person delivering such goods.

bain-marie [,bænmə'riː] *n.* (*pl.* **bains-** ....) vessel holding hot water in which other vessels are placed; double boiler.

bajan *see* **bejan**.

bajra ['baːdʒrə] (*Hindi*) *n.* Indian millet.

baklava ['baːkləvaː] *n.* Middle Eastern pastry filled with nuts and honey.

baksheesh, bakshish [,bæk'ʃiːʃ, 'bækʃiːʃ] (*Persian*) *n.* tip; alms.

balachong, balachan ['bælətʃɒŋ, –ən] (*Indo-Chinese*) *n.* fishy condiment used with rice.

balalaika [,bælə'laɪkə] *n.* triangular guitar-like musical instrument of Russia.

balandra [bə'lændrə] *n.* single-masted Spanish cargo ship.

balaneutics [,bælə'njuːtɪks] *n.* balneology.

balaniferous [,bælə'nɪfərəs] *adj.* bearing acorns.

balanism ['bælənɪzm] *n.* use of suppositories or pessaries.

balanoid ['bælənɔɪd] *adj.* acorn-shaped; pertaining to acorn barnacles; *n.* acorn barnacle.

balata ['bælətə, bə'laːtə] *n.* elastic gum obtained from milk-tree of Brazil.

balatron ['bælətrɒn] *n.* clown. **balatronic,** *adj.*

balaustine [bə'lɔːstɪn] *n.* pomegranate tree.

balbriggan [bæl'brɪgən] *n.* knitted cotton fabric used in underwear.

balbuties [bæl'bjuːʃiiːz] *n. Medicine,* stammering.

baldachin(o), baldakin, baldaquin ['bɔːldəkɪn, 'bæl–, ,bældə'kiːnəʊ] *n.* silk and gold fabric; fabric canopy over throne, altar, etc.; stone canopy over altar.

bald-faced ['bɔːldfeɪst] *adj.* with white face or facial mark.

baldric(k) ['bɔːldrɪk] *n.* shoulder belt for sword, etc.

baleen [bə'liːn] *n.* whalebone.

balefire ['beɪl,faɪə] *n.* bonfire; beacon; funeral pyre.

baline [bə'liːn] *n.* coarse wool or cotton stuff; sacking.

balistarius [,bælɪ'steəriəs] *n.* (*pl.* **–ii**) crossbowman.

balistraria, ballistraria [,bælɪ'streəriə] *n.* cross-shaped opening in fortress wall for discharge of arrows.

balize [bə'liːz] *n.* pole bearing beacon, etc., on sea-shore.

ballade [bæ'laːd] *n.* poem of one or more sets of three-, seven- or eight-lined stanzas, with envoi of four or five lines. **ballade royal,** stanzas of seven or eight decasyllabic lines; rime royal.

balladromic [,bælə'drɒmɪk] *adj.* (of missiles, etc.) maintaining course towards a target.

balletomane ['bælɪtəmeɪn] *n.* person fanatically devoted to ballet. **balletomania,** *n.*

ballista [bə'lɪstə] *n.* (*pl.* **–ae**) ancient military catapult for throwing rocks, fire, etc. **ballistic,** *adj.* pertaining to projectiles. **ballistician,** *n.* student of ballistics. **ballistics,** *n.* science of projectiles.

ballistite ['bælɪstaɪt] *n.* kind of smokeless explosive power.

ballisto-cardiograph [bə,lɪstəʊ'kaːdiəgraːf] *n. Medicine,* instrument for measuring output of heart.

ballon d'essai [bælɔːn'dəseɪ] (*French*) 'trial balloon'; tentative experiment made to discover what the fate of an action would be.

ballonet(te) ['bælənet] *n.* interior, variable-volume gasbag of airship or balloon.

ballote [bə'ləʊt] *see* **bellote**.

ballottement [bə'lɒtmənt] *n.* diagnosis of pregnancy by sharp pressure, causing movement of foetus. **renal ballottement,** diagnosis of floating kidney by same means.

balm [baːm] *n.* aromatic resin; soothing ointment; healing or consoling influence; aromatic herb, especially producing balm.

balmoral [bæl'mɒrəl] *n.* name of Scottish cap, boot and petticoat.

balneal ['bælniəl] *adj.* pertaining to bathing. **balneary,** *n.* bathing-place; medicinal spring. **balneation,** *n.* bathing. **balneatory,** *adj.*

balneography [,bælni'ɒgrəfi] *n.* treatise on baths. **balneographer,** *n.* author of such.

balneology [,bælni'ɒlədʒi] *n.* science of medical application of baths. **balneological,** *adj.* **balneologist,** *n.*

balneotherapy [,bælniə'θerəpi] *n.* treatment by natural waters. **balneotherapeutic,** *adj.* **balneotherapeutics,** *n.*

baluchitherium, baluchithere [bə,luːtʃɪ'θɪəriəm, bə'luːtʃɪθɪə] *n. n.* (*pl.* **–ia**) gigantic rhinoceros-like fossil mammal of Central Asia.

baluster ['bæləstə] *n.* short post supporting a rail.

balustrade [,bælə'streɪd] *n.* rail supported by balusters, especially forming parapet to balcony, terrace, etc.

bambino [bæm'biːnəʊ] (*Italian*) *n.* baby, especially figure of infant Christ.

banal [bə'naːl] *adj.* trivial; trite. **banality** [bə'næləti], *n.*

banausic [bə'nɔːzɪk, –sɪk] *adj.* pertaining to or characteristic of a workshop; utilitarian; materialistic.

bancus superior [,bæŋkəs su'pɪəriɔː, –sju–] (*Latin*) 'upper bench'; *Law,* Queen's (King's) Bench(*abbr.* **banc. sup.**)

bandana, bandanna [bæn'dænə] *n.* coloured spotted handkerchief.

banderilla [,bændə'riːljə] (*Spanish*) *n.* dart stuck into bull at bull-fight. **banderillero** [–ri'eərəʊ], *n.* bull-fighter wielding this.

banderol(e), bandrol ['bændərəʊl, 'bændrəʊl] *n.* small streamer, flag or banner.

bandicoot ['bændɪkuːt] *n.* large Indian rat; small, kangaroo-like Australian animal.

bandobast ['bændəbæst, 'bʌndəbʌst] (*Anglo-*

Indian) *n.* practical, detailed organization; settlement.

bandog ['bændɒg] *n.* fierce dog on chain; mastiff.

bandolier, bandoleer [ˌbændə'lɪə] *n.* shoulder belt carrying cartridges. **bandolero** [-'leərəʊ], *n.* bandit.

bandoline ['bændəlɪn, -iːn] *n.* gummy, scented hair-fixative.

bandonion [bæn'dəʊnɪən] *n.* large concertina.

bandore [bæn'dɔː] *n.* ancient lute-like musical instrument. **bandurria** [-'dʊrɪə], *n.* Spanish instrument of same type.

bandy ['bændi] *n.* any Indian horse-drawn conveyance; form of hockey.

banian ['bænjæn] *see* **banyan**.

banket ['bæŋkɪt] *n.* gold-bearing conglomerate rock of S Africa.

banneret ['bænərət, -et] *n.* knight, especially knighted for valour in battle; such order of knighthood.

bannock ['bænək] *n.* flat, round, unleavened Scottish loaf. **mashlum bannock**, one made of mixed meal.

banquette [bæŋ'ket] *n.* firing-step in trench; narrow seat; raised sidewalk.

banshee ['bænʃiː] *n.* female spirit, especially of Ireland, whose wailing foretells death.

banstickle ['bænstɪkl] *n.* three-spined stickleback.

banteng ['bænteŋ] *n.* wild ox of Malaya.

bantling ['bæntlɪŋ] *n.* brat; illegitimate child.

banxring ['bæŋksrɪŋ] *n.* squirrel-like E Indies mammal.

banyan, banian ['bænjæn] *n.* native Indian trader, especially attached to European firm; Hindu trading case who eat no meat; Indian flannel coat; sacred Indian tree, with aerial roots, covering a vast area. **banyan days**, days when ship's crew received no meat; any period of poor feeding.

banzai [bæn'zaɪ] (*Japanese*) *exclamation.* hurrah! long live (the Emperor)!

baobab ['beɪəbæb] *n.* huge W African, Indian and Australian tree, yielding rope fibre and edible fruit; monkey-bread tree.

baptistery, baptistry ['bæptɪstri] *n.* part of church where baptism is performed, formerly a separate building.

baraesthesia [ˌbærəs'θiːzɪə, -ʒə] *n.* ability to perceive pressure.

baragnosis [ˌbæræg'nəʊsɪs] *n.* loss of ability to perceive weight.

barathea [ˌbærə'θiːə] *n.* worsted fabric with twill hopsack weave; silk or silk-and-worsted fabric with lightly ribbed or pebbled weave.

barbastelle [ˌbɑːbə'stel] *n.* long-eared species of bat.

barbate ['bɑːbeɪt] *adj.* bearded; tufted; barbed; having awns.

barbel ['bɑːbl] *n.* fleshy appendage on head of certain fishes; carplike fish having a barbel. **barbellate**, *adj.* bristly.

barbet ['bɑːbɪt] *n.* brightly plumaged toucan-like tropical bird of Old World; kind of long-haired poodle.

barbette [bɑː'bet] *n.* gun platform behind parapet; armoured protection of gun platform on ship.

barbican ['bɑːbɪkən] *n.* tower on or beyond outer wall of city or castle.

barbicel ['bɑːbɪsel] *n.* small out-growth on barbule.

barbigerous [bɑː'bɪdʒərəs] *adj.* having beard.

barbital ['bɑːbɪtɔːl, -æl] *n. American*, barbitone.

barbiton ['bɑːbɪtɒn] *n.* (*pl.* **-ta**) ancient Greek lyre-like musical instrument.

barbitone ['bɑːbɪtəʊn] *n.* a sleep-inducing drug; veronal.

barbiturate [bɑː'bɪtʃərət] *n.* compound used in preparation of several powerful sleep-inducing and sedative drugs; such a drug. **barbituric** [-'tjʊərɪk], *adj.* denoting acid, from which barbiturates are derived. **barbiturism**, *n.* condition resulting from abuse of barbiturates.

barbotine ['bɑːbətiːn, -ɪn] *n.* kaolin paste used to ornament pottery.

barbule ['bɑːbjuːl] *n.* hooked out-growth on barb of feather. **barbullate**, *adj.* barbellate.

barcarole, barcarolle [ˌbɑːkə'rəʊl] *n.* gondolier's song.

barchan *see* **barkhan**.

bardolatry [bɑː'dɒlətri] *n.* excessive worship of Shakespeare and his works. **bardolater** [-'dɒlətə], *n.* such worshipper.

barège [bə'reɪʒ] *n.* light fabric of silk, or cotton, and worsted; mineral water from Barèges, in the Pyrenees.

barghest ['bɑːgest] *n.* goblin, often dog-like, appearing as portent of death.

bargoose ['bɑːguːs] *n.* sheldrake.

baric ['bærɪk] *adj.* pertaining to weight; barometric; pertaining to barium.

barium ['beərɪəm] *n.* white metallic element. **barium meal**, drink containing a compound of barium which is opaque to X-rays, taken before or during X-ray examination of digestive tract.

bark *see* **barque**.

barkentine *see* **barquentine**.

barkhan, barchan ['bɑːkən] *n.* crescent-shaped sand dune.

barley-break ['bɑːlɪbreɪk] *n.* Old English catching game.

barm [bɑːm] *n.* yeast; froth on surface of fermenting liquor.

Barmecide ['bɑːmɪsaɪd] *n.* giver of illlusory benefits. **Barmecidal**, *adj.*

bar mitzvah [bɑː'mɪtsvə] *n.* (*fem.* **bath** [bɑː-θ-], **bas** [bɑːs-], **bat** [bɑːt-]) Jewish boy attaining age of 13 and religious responsibility; ceremony marking this.

barn [bɑːn] *n.* unit of cross-sectional area of atom or atomic nucleus.

barognosis [ˌbærɒg'nəʊsɪs] *n.* ability to perceive weight.

barogram ['bærəgræm] *n.* recording made by barograph.

barograph ['bærəgrɑːf] *n.* instrument continuously recording atmospheric pressure.

barology [bə'rɒlədʒi] *n.* science of weight and gravitation.

barometer [bə'rɒmɪtə] *n.* instrument registering atmospheric pressure, especially for weather forecasting. **barometric(al)** [-'met-], *adj.* pertaining to atmospheric pressure or barometer. **barometry,** *n.*

baron and feme [ˌbærən ənd 'fiːm] (*French*) *Law*, husband and wife.

baroque [bə'rɒk, -'rəʊk] *adj.* grotesque; extravagant; *n.* contorted style of architecture of late

Renaissance (17th-18th century); similar irregular style of musical composition.

baroscope ['bærəskəʊp] *n.* weather-glass. **baroscopic(al)** [-'skɒp-], *adj.*

barothermograph [ˌbærəʊ'θɜːməgrɑːf] *n.* instrument recording simultaneously pressure and temperature, especially atmospheric.

barothermohygrograph [ˌbærəʊˌθɜːməʊ'haɪgrəgrɑːf] *n.* instrument recording simultaneously atmospheric pressure, temperature and humidity.

barouche [bə'ruːʃ] *n.* four-wheeled four-seater carriage with folding hood and separate driver's seat. **barouchet** [ˌbæru'ʃeɪ], **barouchette** [ˌbæru'ʃet], *n.* light barouche.

baroxyton [bæ'rɒksɪtɒn] *n. Music*, large bass brass wind instrument.

barque, bark [bɑːk] *n.* three-masted vessel with square-rigged mizzen mast; any small ship.

barquentine, barkentine, barkantine ['bɑːkəntiːn] *n.* three-masted vessel with square-rigged foremast and fore-and-aft rigged main and mizzen masts.

barracoon [ˌbærə'kuːn] *n.* enclosure in which slaves or convicts were confined.

barracouta [ˌbærə'kuːtə] *n.* Pacific fish used for food.

barracuda [ˌbærə'kjuːdə, -'kuː-] *n.* pike-like tropical sea fish.

barramundi [ˌbærə'mʌndi] *n.* Australian river fish.

barratry ['bærətri] *n.* unlawful action by captain or seamen injuring owner or freighter of ship; inciting to litigation or riot; simony. **barrator,** *n.* person habitually entering into quarrels and lawsuits. **barratous, barratrous,** *adj.* quarrelsome; guilty of barratry.

barrette [bə'ret] *n.* hair-clip.

barrico [bə'riːkəʊ] *n.* keg.

barrio ['bæriəʊ, 'bɑː-] *n.* Spanish-speaking area of a city in the USA.

bar sinister [ˌbɑː 'sɪnɪstə] *n.* mark of bastardy.

bartizan ['bɑːtɪzən, -zæn] *n.* small overhanging turret.

barton ['bɑːtn] *n.* farmyard; manor farm; fowl-yard.

barycentre ['bærɪsentə] *n.* centre of gravity. **barycentric,** *adj.*

baryecoia [ˌbærɪ'kɔɪə] *n. Medicine,* hardness of hearing.

baryon ['bærɪɒn] *n.* any of the class of subatomic particles known as 'heavy', *e.g.* neutron and proton.

baryphony, baryphonia [bə'rɪfəni, ˌbærɪ'fəʊnɪə] *n.* difficulty of speech. **baryphonic** [-'fɒnɪk], *adj.*

barysphere ['bærɪsfɪə] *n.* area of earth underlying lithosphere.

baryta [bə'ræɪtə] *n.* barium oxide. **barytes,** [bə'ræɪtiz] *n.* barium sulphate.

barythymia [ˌbærɪ'θɪmɪə] *n.* nervous depression.

basal ['beɪsl] *adj.* pertaining to the base; situated at or forming a base; fundamental.

basalt ['bæsɔːlt, bə'sɔːlt] *n.* greenish-black igneous rock, often forming columns. **basaltic, basaltine,** *adj.* **basaltiform, basaltoid,** *adj.* like basalt; column-like.

bas bleu [ˌbɑː 'blɜː] (*French*) 'blue stocking'.

bascule ['bæskjuːl] *n.* balanced lever. **bascule-bridge,** *n.* drawbridge raised by falling counterpoises, as Tower Bridge, London.

base [beɪs] *n. Chemistry,* compound combining with acid to form salt.

bashaw [bə'ʃɔː] *n.* pasha.

bashi-bazouk [ˌbæʃɪbə'zuːk] *n.* Turkish mercenary soldier.

basial ['beɪzɪəl] *adj.* pertaining to kissing. **basiate,** *v.t.* kiss. **basiation,** *n.*

basic ['beɪsɪk] *adj. Chemistry,* applied to salt with base atomically greater than acid; having alkaline reaction. **basicity,** *n.* power of acid to combine with bases.

basifugal [ˌbeɪsɪ'fjuːgl] *adj. Botany,* growing away from base, or at apex only.

basilar ['bæzɪlə, 'bæs-] *adj.* pertaining to or at the base.

basilic [bə'zɪlɪk, -'sɪ-] *adj.* royal;*n.* basilica.

basilica [bə'zɪlɪkə, -'sɪ-] *n.* rectangular building with colonnades along its length, dividing it into nave and aisles; early Christian church; *Roman Catholic,* church having certain liturgical privileges. **basilican,** *adj.*

basilicon [bə'zɪlɪkən, -'sɪ-] *n.* kind of ointment.

basilisk ['bæzɪlɪsk, 'bæs-] *n.* mythical fire-breathing reptile or one whose stare turned persons to stone; cockatrice; tree-lizard of Central America; ancient brass cannon. **basiliscan** [-'lɪskən], **basiliscine** [-saɪn], *adj.*

basipetal [beɪ'sɪpɪtl] *adj. Botany,* growing from top to base.

bas-relief [ˌbɑːrɪ'liːf] *n.* carving in low relief, *i.e.*, in which figures stand out less than half their proportion from background.

basset ['bæsɪt] *n.* short-legged hound used in badger-and harehunting; gambling card game like faro; *Geology,* edge of outcrop. **basset-horn,** tenor clarinet.

bassinet(te) [ˌbæsɪ'net] *n.* hooded cradle or perambulator, especially of wicker.

basso-rilievo [ˌbæsəʊ-rɪli'eɪvəʊ] (*Italian*) *n.* bas-relief.

basta ['bæstə] (*Italian*) *exclamation,* enough!

bastille, bastile [bæ'stiːl] *n.* prison or fortress, especially that of Paris (destroyed by revolutionaries, July 14, 1789).

bastinado [ˌbæstɪ'neɪdəʊ] *n.* (*pl.* **–oes**) beating on soles of feet; *v.t.* administer such punishment to.

bastion ['bæstɪən] *n.* earthwork projecting outwards from fortification.

batata [bə'tɑːtə] *n.* sweet potato.

bateau ['bætəʊ] (*French*) *n.* (*pl.* **–eaux,**) Canadian flat-bottomed river boat. **bateau bridge,** pontoon bridge.

bathetic [bə'θetɪk] *adj.* pertaining to or like bathos.

bathic ['bæθɪk] *adj.* pertaining to depths, especially of sea.

bathmism ['bæθmɪzm] *n.* energy or force of growth. **bathmic,** *adj.*

bath mitzvah *see* **bar mitzvah.**

batholith, batholite ['bæθəlɪθ, –laɪt] *n. Geology,* mass of intruded igneous rock below surface and of great depth. **batholithic, batholitic,** *adj.*

bathometer [bə'θɒmɪtə] *n.* bathymeter.

bathos ['beɪθɒs] *n.* anticlimax with humorous effect; spurious pathos; triteness.

bathyal ['bæθiəl] *adj.* pertaining to zone of sea from 180 metres/600 feet to abyssal zone.

bathybic [bæ'θɪbɪk] *adj.* pertaining to or dwelling in deepest zone of sea.

bathycolpian, bathycolpic [,bæθɪ'kɒlpiən, –ɪk] *adj.* having deep bosom.

bathylimnetic [,bæθɪlɪm'netɪk] *adj.* living at bottom of lake or marsh.

bathymeter [bə'θɪmɪtə] *n.* instrument for deep-sea sounding. **bathymetric** [–'metrɪk], *adj.* pertaining to vertical distribution of organisms in sea. **bathymetry,** *n.* process of measuring depths of sea.

bathyorographical [,bæθɪɒrə'græfɪkl] *adj.* pertaining to or showing depths below and heights above sea level.

bathypelagic [,bæθɪpə'lædʒɪk] *adj.* living in deep sea.

bathyscaph(e) ['bæθɪskeɪf] *n.* submarine-like diving chamber.

bathyseism ['bæθɪ,saɪzm] *n.* earthquake taking place at great depth.

bathysmal [bə'θɪzml] *adj.* pertaining to deepest part or bottom of sea.

bathysophical [,bæθɪ'sɒfɪkl] *adj.* pertaining to knowledge of deep-sea life and conditions.

bathysphere ['bæθɪsfɪə] *n.* kind of diving bell for descending to great depths in sea.

bathythermograph [,bæθɪ'θɜːməgrɑːf] *n.* instrument visually recording the ocean temperature at various depths.

batiste [bæ'tiːst, bə–] *n.* fine linen; cambric; fine cotton or wool fabric, especially as treated for use as antiseptic dressing.

batology [bæ'tɒlədʒɪ] *n.* scientific study of brambles. **batological,** *adj.* **batologist,** *n.*

batophobia [,bætə'fəubiə] *n.* fear of heights, or of being close to high buildings.

batrachian [bə'treɪkiən] *adj.* pertaining to frogs or toads; *n.* a frog or toad. **batrachoid,** *adj.* like a frog or toad. **batrachophagous,** *adj.* eating frogs or toads. **batrachophobia,** *n.* fear of frogs or toads.

battels ['bætlz] *n. pl.* accounts of Oxford college, especially for provisions.

batter ['bætə] *v.i. Architecture,* recede as it rises (of a wall); *n.* such inclination. **batter rule,** plumbline of such walls, falling within base.

battology [bə'tɒlədʒɪ] *n.* an unnecessary repetition. **battological** [,bætə'lɒdʒɪkl], *adj.* **battologize,** *v.i.* **battologist,** *n.*

battue [bæ'tuː, –'tjuː] *n.* driving of game towards guns; shooting-party of that kind; massacre of helpless persons.

batture [bæ'tjʊə] *n.* raised bed of sea or river.

baud [bɔːd] *n.* unit of electrical signalling speed equal to one pulse per second.

baudekyn ['bɔːdɪkɪn] *n.* baldachin.

bauxite ['bɔːksaɪt] *n.* earthy mineral compound yielding aluminium.

bavardage [,bævɑː'dɑːʒ] (*French*) *n.* idle chatter.

bavian ['beɪviən] *n.* poetaster; baboon.

bawd [bɔːd] *n.* procuress. **bawdry,** *n.* obscene talk. **bawdy,** *adj.* obscene.

baya ['baɪə, bə'jɑː] *n.* Indian weaver-bird.

bayadere [,baɪə'dɪə, –'deə] *n.* Hindu dancing girl; *adj.* applied to brightly coloured striped fabrics.

bayberry ['beɪ,beri] *n.* fruit of baytree; *American,* fruit of wax-myrtle; species of W Indies pimento, yielding bay oil or rum.

bayete [baː'jeɪti] (*Zulu*) salutation to king; hail!

bayou ['baɪuː] (*American*) *n.* marshy branch of river, lake or bay; slow-flowing stream.

baysalt ['beɪsɔːlt] *n.* salt obtained from sea-water.

bazigar [,baːzɪ'gaː] *n.* nomadic Indian gypsy.

bazooka [bə'zuːkə] *n.* anti-tank rocket projector.

B.C.G. *abbreviation* for Bacillus Calmette-Guérin, a vaccine giving protection against tuberculosis.

bdellium ['deliəm] *n.* myrrh-like gum-resin; Indian and African tree yielding it.

bdelloid ['delɔɪd] *adj.* pertaining to leech; leech-like in appearance; *n.* leech. **bdellometer,** *n.* cupping-glass for surgical bleeding. **bdellotomy,** *n.* surgical application of leeches.

beadhouse, bedehouse ['biːdhaus] *n.* almshouse housing beadsmen.

beadle ['biːdl] *n.* officer of parish, church, court, etc., for keeping order; mace-bearer. **beadledom,** *n.* petty officialdom.

bead-roll ['biːdrəul] *n. Roman Catholic,* list of persons to be prayed for; any list or catalogue; rosary.

beadsman, bedesman ['biːdzmən] *n.* monk; pensioner or almshouse inmate who prays for benefactor.

beagle ['biːgl] *n.* small hound used in hare-hunting; *pl.* pack of harriers. **beagling,** *n.* hunting on foot with beagles.

beakiron ['biːk,aɪən] *n.* bickern.

beambird ['biːmbɜːd] *n.* spotted flycatcher; garden warbler.

bean-tree ['biːntriː] *n.* Australian chestnut tree; carob tree.

bear [beə] *n. Commerce,* speculator on Stock Exchange who desires a fall in price; *v.t.* cause fall in price of. **bearish** ['beərɪʃ], *adj.* anticipating or associated with a fall in price.

bearing-rein ['beərɪŋreɪn] *n.* rein that compels horse to arch its neck.

beastlings ['biːstlɪŋz] *n. pl.* beestings.

beata [bi'eɪtə, beɪ'aːtə] *n.* (*pl.* **-tae**), *Roman Catholic,* female beatified person.

beatify [bi'ætɪfaɪ] *v.t.* make blessed or happy; *Roman Catholic,* confer title of 'blessed' preliminary to canonization. **beatific** [,biːə'tɪfɪk], *adj.* saintly. **beatification,** *n.*

beatitude [bi'ætɪtjuːd] *n.* blessedness; bliss; *pl.* blessings in Matt. v.

beatus [bi'eɪtəs, beɪ'aːtəs] *n.* (*pl.* **-ti**) *Roman Catholic,* male beatified person.

beau [bəu] *n.* (*pl.* **-x,** [–z]) lover; dandy. **beau geste,** magnanimous action; polite gesture. **beau ideal,** one's highest conception of excellence or virtue. **beau monde,** fashionable society.

beaux-arts [,bəu'zaː] (*French*) *n. pl.* 'fine arts'.

bebeerine [bɪ'bɪəriːn] *n.* bibirine.

beccafico [,bekə'fiːkəu] *n.* European songbird, considered a table delicacy, especially in Italy.

bechamel [,beɪʃə'mel] *n.* white sauce thickened with cream.

bêche-de-mer [,beʃdə'meə] *n.* species of holothurian used for food in China; seacucumber; sea-slug; trepang.

bechic ['bekɪk] *adj.* curative of cough.

becket ['bekɪt] *n.* hook-like device of rope, wood or metal to secure ship's ropes, etc.

bedeguar, bedegar ['bedɪgɑː] *n.* mossy rose-gall; dog rose.

bedel(l) ['biːdl] *n.* beadle at universities.

bedizen [bɪ'dæɪzn] *v.t.* dress gaudily.

bee-bread ['biːbred] *n.* mixture of honey and pollen stored by bees for food.

beele [biːl] *n.* miner's pick with two sharp ends. **beeleman,** *n.* worker using a beele.

beestings ['biːstɪŋz] *n. pl.* first milk of cow after birth of calf.

beeswing ['biːzwɪŋ] *n.* thin crust on old port.

beg [beɪg, beg] *n. (fem.* **begani,** ['beɪgəni]) Turkish and Indian title of honour.

begohm ['begəʊm] *n.* one thousand million ohms.

beguine ['begiːn, bɪ'giːn] *n.* member of religious order of lay sisters, especially of Belgium; rumba-like dance of French W Indies. **beguinage,** *n*] convent of beguines.

begum ['beɪgəm, 'biː–] *n.* Muslim woman of high rank.

behaviourism [bɪ'heɪvjərɪzm] *n.* psychological theory that all mental processes result from external stimuli and association of ideas. **behaviourist,** *adj.*; *n.* believer in such theory.

behemoth [bɪ'hiːmɒθ] *n.* gigantic animal, mentioned in Job xl; hippopotamus.

bejan(t) ['biːdʒən, -t] *n.* freshman at Scottish university.

belay [bɪ'leɪ] *v.i.* & *t.* secure (rope) by coiling round a projection; stop, cease. **belaying pin,** short wooden post to which ropes are secured.

belcher ['beltʃə] *n.* coloured, spotted neckerchief.

belemnite ['beləmnaɪt] *n.* bullet-shaped molluscan fossil. **belemnitic** [–'nɪtɪk], *adj.*

belemnoid ['beləmnɔɪd] *adj.* dart-shaped.

bel esprit [ˌbel e'spriː] *(French) n. (pl.* **beaux esprits,** [ˌboʊz]) genius, witty person, wit.

bel-étage [ˌbel eɪ'tɑːʒ] *(French) n.* main storey of building.

belladonna [ˌbelə'dɒnə] *n.* deadly nightshade; narcotic drug obtained from that plant. **belladonna lily,** bulbous plant of S Africa with lily-shaped flowers.

belle [bel] *n.* beautiful woman; noted beauty. **belle amie,** mistress.

belleric [bə'lerɪk] *n.* kind of myrobalan.

belles-lettres [ˌbel'letr] *n.* writings of solely literary or aesthetic value, especially essays, etc. **belletrist,** *n.* writer or student of these. **belletristic** *adj.*

bellicism ['belɪsɪzm] *n.* war-mindedness.

bellicose ['belɪkəʊs] *adj.* desirous of fighting; warlike. **bellicosity** [–'kɒsəti], *n.*

belliferous [bə'lɪfərəs] *adj.* bringing war.

belligerent [bə'lɪdʒərənt] *adj.* making war; *n.* person or nation engaged in warfare. **belligerence, belligerency,** *n.*

belling ['belɪŋ] *n.* deer's cry at mating time.

bellipotent [be'lɪpətənt] *adj.* powerful in war.

bellonion [bə'ləʊnɪɒn] *n.* mechanical musical instrument consisting of drums and trumpets.

bellote, ballote [bə'ləʊt] *n.* holm-oak acorn.

bell-wether ['bel,weðə] *n.* sheep with bell attached to the neck leading the flock.

beloid ['biːlɔɪd] *adj.* arrow-shaped.

belomancy ['beləmænsi] *n.* divination using arrows.

belonoid ['belənɔɪd] *adj.* needle-shaped.

Beltane ['belteɪn] *n.* ancient Celtic May-day festival.

beluga [bə'luːgə] *n.* white sturgeon; kind of dolphin, also called white whale.

belvedere ['belvədɪə] *n.* turret, or open shelter on roof, giving fine view; summer-house.

bencher ['bentʃə] *n.* senior member of an Inn of Court.

bend sinister [ˌbend 'sɪnɪstə] *n.* diagonal line on coat of arms indicating bastardy.

Benedicite [ˌbenɪ'daɪsəti] *n.* canticle beginning 'O all ye works of the Lord', sung when Te Deum is omitted.

benedick ['benɪdɪk] *n.* newly married husband, especially one formerly a confirmed bachelor.

benediction [ˌbenɪ'dɪkʃn] *n.* blessing; act of blessing; *Roman Catholic,* rite of blessing the people with the monstrance. **benedictional, benedictionary,** *n.* collection of benedictions. **benedictive, benedictory,** *adj.*

Benedictus [ˌbenɪ'dɪktəs] *n.* canticle beginning 'Blessed be the Lord God of Israel'; *Roman*

Best tomato's, 70p a pound

The apostrophe has two basic uses in English: to indicate the possessive form of nouns, and to show that a letter has been omitted.

The possessive of singular nouns is shown by -'s *(the boy's father = the father of the boy)*; the possessive of plural nouns by -s' *(the boys' father = the father of the boys).* (An exception is that plural nouns not ending in s add -'s: *the children's father.)* Most singular nouns ending in s add -'s in the possessive like any other noun *(the boss's daughter)*; but there are some that are traditionally given an apostrophe, with no s *(for Jesus' sake).*

As a mark of omission, the apostrophe is most commonly used in verb forms run together with a neighbouring word, to show where a letter has

been missed out *(weren't = were not, you're = you are, where'd = where did, it's = it is –* not to be confused with *its = of it).* The apostrophe in *o'clock* also indicates omission (it is short for earlier *of (the) clock)* but elsewhere this usage is now mainly restricted to forms that smack of antique poetry *(e'en = even, o'er = over).*

A further use of the apostrophe is to form the plural and other inflections in cases where it is awkward simply to add -s or -d – for example, the plural of numerals *(three 7's)* and the past of abbreviations *(I OK'd her appointment).* But it is traditionally regarded as a mistake to use -'s for the plural of ordinary nouns – as often seen on greengrocers' stalls: *Best tomato's, 70p a pound.*

Catholic , canticle beginning 'Blessed is he who comes in the name of Lord'; section of Mass beginning with this.

benefic [bə'nefɪk] *adj.* favourable, especially astrological.

benefice ['benɪfɪs] *n.* church living; *v.t.* endow with a benefice. **beneficed,** *adj.*, holding a benefice.

beneficent [bə'nefɪsənt] *adj.* doing good; kind; generous. **beneficence,** *n.*

beneficial [,benɪ'fɪʃl] *adj.* advantageous; bringing good. **beneficial interest,** right to enjoy property, though it be legally invested in another. **beneficiary,** *n.* person receiving benefits; legatee under will; holder of benefice; *adj.* holding by feudal tenure.

beneficiate [,benɪ'fɪʃieɪt] *v.t.* prepare for smelting. **beneficiation,** *n.*

Benelux ['benɪlʌks] *n.* Belgium, Netherlands, and Luxembourg (customs union).

beneplacito [,benɪ'plæsɪtəu] (*Latin*) 'during pleasure'.

benet ['benɪt] *n. Roman Catholic,* exorcist.

benevolence [bə'nevələns] *n.* charitableness; former loan demanded by certain English kings. **benevolent,** *adj.*

Bengali, [ben'gɔːli] *adj.* pertaining to Bengal, *n.* native or language of Bengal.

bengaline ['bengəliːn, –'liːn] *n.* silk, silk-and-wool or silk-and-cotton transversely corded fabric.

Bengal light [,bengɔːl 'laɪt] *n.* signal firework, with brilliant blue light.

benighted [bɪ'naɪtɪd] *adj.* overtaken by night; ignorant.

benign [bə'naɪn] *adj.* kindly; favourable; wholesome; *Medicine,* mild; not malignant. **benignant** [–'nɪgnənt], *adj.* **benignance** [–'nɪgnəns], **benignity** [–'nɪgnəti], *n.*

benison ['benɪzən, -sən] *n.* blessing.

benjamin ['bendʒəmɪn] *n.* gum benzoin and tree yielding it; man's tight coat.

Benthamism ['benθəmɪzm] *n.* utilitarian doctrine of Jeremy Bentham (1748-1832) that the greatest happiness of the greatest number is most desirable. **Benthamite** *n.* adherent of Benthamism.

benthos ['benθɒs] *n.* sea-bottom's flora and fauna. **benthic, benthoic** [–'θəuɪk], **benthonic,** *adj.*

ben trovato [,ben trə'vɑːtəu] (*Italian*) 'well invented'; *adj.* well expressed; *n.* such speech or thought.

benzedrine ['benzədriːn, –ɪn] *n.* vasoconstrictor drug, also called amphetamine, which relieves hay fever, catarrh, etc., and, taken internally, increases physical and mental activity.

benzene ['benziːn] *n.* hydrocarbon distilled from coaltar.

benzine ['benziːn] *n.* petrol-like distillate of petroleum, used as solvent; coal-tar oil containing benzene.

benzoin ['benzɔɪn, 'benzəuɪn] *n.* balsamic resin used in perfumery, etc., and in medicine as compound tincture called friar's balsam; bitter-almond-oil camphor, found in gum benzoin. **benzoic** [–'zəuɪk], *adj.*

benzol(e) ['benzɒl, –əul] *n.* benzene; coal-tar oil containing benzene. **benzolate, benzolize,** *v.t.* mix or treat with benzol.

benzoline ['benzəliːn] *n.* benzine; petrol; impure benzene.

berberia [bɜː'bɪəriə] *n.* beri-beri.

berberine ['bɜːbəriːn] *n.* tonic alkaloid obtained from barberry and other plants.

berceuse [beə'sɜːz] (*French*) *n.* cradle-song; lullaby.

bere [bɪə] *n.* four-rowed barley.

beretta *see* **biretta.**

bergamask ['bɜːgəmɑːsk] *n.* kind of country dance.

bergamot ['bɜːgəmɒt] *n.* variety of pear; essence obtained from rind of variety of pear-shaped orange; fruit and tree yielding such essence; snuff scented with such essence; aromatic plant of mint family.

bergère [beə'ʒeə] (*French*) *n.* 'shepherdess'; kind of 18th-century chair and sofa. **bergèrette** [,beəʒə'ret], *n.* kind of country song or dance.

beriberi [,beri'beri] *n.* Eastern disease, similar to peripheral neuritis, due to deficiency of vitamin B1.

berkelium [bɜː'kiːliəm] *n.* radioactive, metallic element made artificially.

berlin [bɜː'lɪn] *n.* four-wheeled, two-seater roofed carriage, with seat or platform behind. **Berlin spirit,** coarse spirit distilled from potatoes, beetroot, etc. **Berlin wools,** fine, dyed wool for tapestry, etc. **berline,** *n.* kind of motor car body with glass partition between driver's and passengers' seats.

berm [bɜːm] *n.* narrow ledge; narrow path by road, canal, etc.; *American,* canal bank opposite towing path.

bernicle ['bɜːnɪkl] *n.* barnacle-goose.

bersaglieri [,beəsəl'jeəri] *n. pl.* (*sing.* **-re**) Italian sharpshooter corps.

berserk [bə'zɜː, –'sɜːk] *adj.* frenzied; wild; especially of fighting. **berserker,** *n.* person fighting thus, especially Norse warrior; *adj.* berserk.

beryllium [bə'rɪliəm] *n.* hard, white metal used in alloys, occurring as an element only in compounds.

bestial ['bestiəl] *adj.* animal-like; base. **bestialize,** *v.t.* **bestiality** [–'æləti]), *n.*; bestial behaviour *Law,* sexual intercourse with animal.

bestiarian [,besti'eəriən] *n.* animal-lover, especially opposed to vivisection. **bestiarianism,** *n.*

bestiary ['bestiəri] *n.* medieval book, especially illustrated, on beasts.

beta ['biːtə] *n.* second letter of Gr. alphabet (B, β). **beta-blocker,** *n.* drug that blocks nerve impulses that stimulate increased cardiac action. **beta particle,** negatively-charged particle; electron. **beta ray,** a beam or stream of beta particles. **betatron,** ['biːtətrɒn] *n.* apparatus in which electrons are accelerated electromagnetically to very high energies to form a beam of beta rays for bombarding atomic nuclei and generating high-voltage x-rays.

betel ['biːtl] *n.* Asiatic palm, yielding nut which is wrapped in leaf of same tree and chewed; areca.

bête noire [,beɪt 'nwɑː] (*French*) 'black beast'; pet abomination; bugbear.

bethel ['beθl] *n.* sacred place; nonconformist chapel.

bêtise [be'tiːz] (*French*) *n.* foolishness; foolish or stupid act.

béton [be'tɒn] *n.* concrete made by mixing gravel with cement and sand.

bettong [be'tɒŋ] *n.* kind of Australian kangaroo-rat.

betulin(ol) ['betjʊlɪn, –ɒl] *n.* resinous extract of birch bark; birch camphor.

bevatron ['bevətrɒn] *n.* synchrotron-like apparatus for accelerating charged particles to an immensely high level.

bey [beɪ] (*Turkish*) *n.* governor; title of honour. **beylic, beylik,** *n.* area of bey's jurisdiction.

bezel ['bezl] *n.* sloping edge of cutting tool; edge and facet of cut gem; flanged groove holding watch- or clock-glass; *v.t.* grind to edge; bevel.

bezoar ['biːzɔː] *n.* stone-like mass found in stomach of ruminants, formerly used in East as antidote to poison. **bezoardic** [–'ɑːdɪk], *adj.*

bhang [bæŋ, bʌn] (*Hindi*) *n.* dried leaves and twigs of cannabis, chewed, smoked and made into infusion or sweetmeat.

bharal ['bʌrəl] (*Hindu*) *n.* Himalayan wild sheep with blue-black coat.

bheesty, bheestie ['biːsti, 'bɪʃti] (*Anglo-Indian*) *n.* servant who draws and carries water.

bhungi(ni) ['bʌŋgi, –ɪni] *n.* Hindu street-sweeper.

bialate [baɪ'eɪleɪt] *adj.* with two wings.

biarchy ['baɪɑːki] *n.* rule by two persons.

bibacious [bɪ'beɪʃəs] *adj.* fond of drinking. **bibacity,** *n.*

bibelot ['bɪbləʊ] *n.* small object of art; trinket; curio.

bibi ['biːbi] (*Hindu*) *n.* lady; Mrs.

bibirine [bɪ'bɪərɪːn] *n.* quinine-like extract of bark of S American greenheart tree.

bibitory ['bɪbɪtəri] *adj.* pertaining to drinking.

biblioclasm ['bɪbliəklæzm] *n.* destruction of books; destructive criticism of Bible. **biblioclast,** *n.* person so destroying or criticizing.

bibliogenesis [ˌbɪbliə'dʒenəsɪs] *n.* production of books.

bibliognost ['bɪbliɒgnɒst] *n.* person having deep knowledge of books. **bibliognostic,** *adj.*

bibliogony [ˌbɪbli'ɒgəni] *n.* bibliogenesis.

bibliography [ˌbɪbli'ɒgrəfi] *n.* list of books on one subject or by one author; list of books referred to in a text or used in its preparation; scientific study of books and writings; historical work on books. **bibliographer,** *n.* compiler of such work. **bibliographical,** *adj.*

biblioklept ['bɪbliəklept] *n.* bookthief. **bibliokleptomania,** *n.* kleptomania towards books.

bibliolater [ˌbɪbli'ɒlətə] *n.* worshipper of books, or of letter of Bible. **bibliolatrous,** *adj.* **bibliolatry,** *n.* such worship.

bibliology [ˌbɪbli'ɒlədʒi] *n.* book-lore; Biblical literature. **bibliological,** *adj.* **bibliologist,** *n.*

bibliomancy ['bɪbliəmænsi] *n.* divination by reference taken at random in book, especially in the Bible.

bibliomania [ˌbɪbliə'meɪniə] *n.* strong desire for collecting books. **bibliomaniac, bibliomane,** *n.* person with such desire.

bibliopegy [ˌbɪbli'ɒpɪdʒi] *n.* art of book-binding. **bibliopegic** [–'pedʒɪk, –'piːdʒɪk], *adj.* **bibliopegist** [–'ɒp–], *n.* book-binder.

bibliophagy [ˌbɪbli'ɒfədʒi] *n.* voracious reading of books. **bibliophagic** [–ə'fædʒɪk], *adj.* **bibliophagist** [–'ɒf–], *n.* voracious reader.

bibliophile ['bɪbliəfaɪl] *n.* lover of books. **bibliophilic** [–'fɪlɪk] *adj.* **bibliophilism, bibliophily** [–'ɒf–], *n.* love of books. **bibliophilist,** *n.* **bibliophilistic,** *adj. adj.*

bibliophobia [ˌbɪbliə'fəʊbiə] *n.* hatred of books. **bibliophobe,** *n.* person hating books. **bibliophobic,** *adj.*

bibliopoesy [ˌbɪbliə'pəʊəzi] *n.* making of books.

bibliopole ['bɪbliəpəʊl] *n.* bookseller, especially of rare books. **bibliopolery** [–'pəʊləri], **bibliopolism, bibliopoly** [–'ɒpəlɪzm, –ɒpəli], *n.* selling of books. **bibliopolar** [–'pəʊlə], **bibliopolic** [–'pɒlɪk], *adj.* **bibliopolist** [–'ɒpəlɪst], *n.* **bibliopolistic,** *adj.*

bibliosoph ['bɪbliəsɒf] *n.* bibliognost.

bibliotaph ['bɪbliətɑːf, –tæf] *n.* person keeping his or her books secret or locked up. **bibliotaphic,** *adj.*

bibliothec(a) ['bɪbliəθek, ˌbɪbliə'θiːkə] *n.* library. **bibliothecal** [–'θiːkl], *adj.* **bibliothecary** [–'ɒθəkəri], *n.* librarian. **bibliothetic,** *adj.* pertaining to arrangement of books.

biblus, biblos ['bɪbləs] *n.* papyrus.

bibulous ['bɪbjʊləs] *adj.* fond of drink; drunken; sponge-like. **bibulosity,** *n.*

bicameral [baɪ'kæmərəl] *adj.* having two Chambers or Houses. **bicameralism,** *n.* **bicameralist, bicamerist,** *n.* person advocating such legislative system.

bicapitate [baɪ'kæpɪteɪt] *adj.* two-headed.

bice [baɪs] *n.* green or blue pigment.

bicentenary [ˌbaɪsen'tiːnəri] *n.* two hundredth anniversary; *adj.* pertaining to two centuries.

bicentennial [ˌbaɪsen'teniəl] *adj.* occurring every two hundred years; lasting two hundred years; bicentenary; *n.* a bicentenary.

bicephalous, bicephalic [baɪ'sefələs, ˌbaɪsɪ'fælɪk] *adj.* having two heads.

bichord ['baɪkɔːd] *adj.* *Music,* having two strings, especially two strings for each note.

bicipital [baɪ'sɪpɪtl] *adj.* pertaining to biceps; bifurcating. **bicipitous,** *adj.* having two heads or extremities.

bickern ['bɪkən] *n.* anvil pointed at both ends.

bicollateral [ˌbaɪkə'lætərəl] *adj.* having two sides the same. **bicollaterality,** *n.*

biconic [baɪ'kɒnɪk] *adj.* having shape of two cones with bases together.

biconjugate [baɪ'kɒndʒugeɪt] *adj.* *Botany,* having a pair each member of which is divided into a pair.

bicorn ['baɪkɔːn] *adj.* having two horns or points. **bicornuate, bicornuous,** *adj.*

bicrural [baɪ'krʊərəl] *adj.* two-legged.

biddery, bidree ['bɪdri] *n.* alloy of several metals on which gold and silver are inlaid.

bident ['baɪdent] *n.* two-pronged instrument; sheep aged two years. **bidental** [baɪ'dentl], **bidentate** [–'denteɪt], *adj.* having two prongs or teeth. **bidenticulate** [–'tɪk–], *adj.* having two small teeth.

biduous ['bɪdjuəs] *adj.* lasting two days.

Biedermeier ['biːdəmaɪə] *adj.* applied to a style of interior decoration, furniture, etc. common in Germany in the first half of the 19th century; bourgeois, conventional.

bien aimé [bi,æn 'eɪmeɪ] (*French*) *n.* (*fem.* **-aimée**) 'well beloved' (person).

bien aise [bi,æn 'eɪz] (*French*) *n.* 'well being'; comfort.

bien-être [bi,æn'eɪtr] (*French*) *n.* 'well being.'

biennial [baɪ'enɪəl] *adj.* lasting two years; occurring every two years; *n.* plant living for two years and flowering in the second. **biennium**, *n.* (*pl. -ia*) two years.

bienséance [bi,æn'seɪɒns] (*French*) *n.* proper, correct or fitting thing; *pl.* the proprieties.

bifacial [baɪ'feɪʃl] *adj.* having distinct upper and lower surfaces; having both sides the same; having two faces.

bifarious [baɪ'feərɪəs] *adj.* in two rows; twofold; pointing in two directions.

bifer ['baɪfə] *n.* plant flowering or fruiting twice a year. **biferous**, *adj.*

bifid(ate) ['baɪfɪd, -eɪt] *adj.* divided into two portions; forked. **bifidity**, *n.*

bifilar [baɪ'faɪlə] *adj.* having two threads, especially of measuring instrument.

bifocal [baɪ'fəʊkl] *adj.* with two foci, especially applied to spectacle lens of which upper part is used for viewing distant and lower part for near objects; *n.* such lens; *pl.* spectacles with such lenses.

biform ['baɪfɔːm] *adj.* having two forms; hybrid.

bifurcate ['baɪfəkeɪt] *v.i. & t.* split into two branches or forks, *adj.* [-'fɜːkət] so divided. **bifurcation**, *n.* forking into two; one of the forks.

bigeminate [baɪ'dʒemɪnət] *adj.* biconjugate. **bigeminal**, *adj.* arranged in pairs.

bigener ['baɪdʒənə, -,dʒiːnə] *n.* hybrid arising from two genera. **bigeneric** [-'nerɪk], *adj.* pertaining to two genera.

bigential [baɪ'dʒenʃl] *adj.* with two races.

bigg [bɪg] (*Scottish*) *n.* four-rowed barley.

bigot ['bɪgət] *n.* person with fixed and intolerant belief. **bigoted** *adj.* **bigotry,** *n.* such belief.

bigrid ['baɪgrɪd] *adj.* applied to thermionic valve having two grids and combining functions of two valves.

bijou ['biːʒuː] *n.* (*pl. -x*, [-z] jewel; piece of jewellery; *adj.* small and well-formed. **bijouterie** [biː'ʒuːtəri], *n.* jewellery.

bijugate, bijugous ['baɪdʒʊgeɪt, -əs] *adj.* having two overlapping heads, said of coin struck to two persons; *Botany* , with two pairs of leaflets.

bilabiate [baɪ'leɪbɪət, -eɪt] *adj.* having two lips. **bilabial,** *adj. Phonetics,* formed with both lips; *n.* such consonant.

bilateral [baɪ'lætərəl] *adj.* having or pertaining to two sides; of two parties or States. **bilateralism, bilaterality,** *n.* bilateral symmetry.

bilbo ['bɪlbəʊ] *n.* sword.

bilboes ['bɪlbəʊz] *n. pl.* fetters, especially long iron bar with sliding shackles used to imprison persons on ship.

Bildungsroman ['bɪldʊŋzrə,maɪn] (*German*) *n.* novel dealing with a person's life and psychological development from youth to maturity.

bile [baɪl] *n.* bitter digestive fluid emanating from liver; melancholy; anger.

bilection [baɪ'lekʃn] *see* **bolection.**

bilge [bɪldʒ] *n.* lowermost part of interior of ship; widest part of barrel; *slang*, nonsense; *v.i. & t.* leak in that part; make hole in bilge. **bilge-water,** foul water in ship's bilge.

bilharzia [bɪl'hɑːzɪə] *n.* worm parasitic in blood; tropical disease caused by its presence. **bilharziasis** [,bɪlhɑː'zaɪəsɪs], *n.* disease of bilharzia.

biliary ['bɪlɪərɪ] *adj.* pertaining to bile.

bilinear [baɪ'lɪnɪə] *adj.* having, pertaining to or between two lines.

biliteral [baɪ'lɪtərəl] *adj.* consisting of or using two letters; *n.* such linguistic root.

bill [bɪl] **bill-broker,** dealer in bills of exchange. **bill of adventure,** declaration that merchandise shipped is not property of shipowner, whose liability is limited to safe delivery. **bill of costs,** solicitor's account of charges. **bill of exchange,** negotiable order to pay cash on or before certain date. **bill of health,** statement of health, especially as to infectious diseases, of persons aboard ship. **bill of indictment,** statement of accusation in criminal court. **bill of lading,** acknowledgement by ship's master that goods have been received on board, and promise of safe delivery. **bill of sale,** document transferring title to goods, especially as security for loan. **bill of sight,** outline description of goods being imported. **bill of sufferance,** permission to load or unload at certain ports without payment of duty. **true bill,** statement by grand jury that there was a prima facie case against accused.

billabong ['bɪləbɒŋ] (*Australian*) *n.* river creek; backwater; watercourse.

billet-doux [,bɪleɪ'duː, -li-] (*French*) *n.* (*pl.* **billets-doux**) 'love-letter'.

billion ['bɪljən] *n.* a thousand millions.

billon ['bɪlən] *n.* alloy of precious metal with larger quantity of base metal.

bilocation [,baɪlə'keɪʃn] *n.* existence, or power to exist, in two places simultaneously.

biloquist ['bɪləkwɪst] *n.* person with power of speaking in two distinct voices.

biltong ['bɪltɒŋ] (*S African*) *n.* strips of dried meat.

bimanous, bimanal ['bɪmənəs, baɪ'meɪn-, -l] *adj.* having two hands; pertaining to human species. **bimanual** [baɪ'mænjuəl], *adj.* requiring or using two hands.

bimarine [,baɪmə'riːn] *adj.* situated between seas.

bimaxillary [,baɪmæk'sɪləri] *adj.* pertaining to both jaws.

bimensal [baɪ'mensl] *adj.* occurring every two months.

bimestrial [baɪ'mestrɪəl] *adj.* occurring every two months; lasting two months.

bimetallism [baɪ'metl–ɪzm] *n.* currency system in which both gold and silver are standard money. **bimetallic** [,baɪme'tælɪk], *adj.* **bimetallist,** *n.* advocate of bimetallism. **bimetallistic,** *adj.*

bimillenary [baɪ'mɪlɪnəri] *n.* space of two thousand years. **bimillennium** [-'lenɪəm], *n.* (*pl. -ia*) two thousand years.

binal ['baɪnl] *adj.* double; twin.

binary ['baɪnəri] *adj.* double; dual. denoting a system of numeration based on 2, and therefore written entirely with 1 and 0, commonly used in digital computers. **binary converter,** machine converting alternating into direct current. **binary fission,** division of cell into two equal parts. **binary measure,** *Music,* common time. **binary star,** two stars revolving round a common centre. **binary**

theory, chem. theory defining every acid as a hydrogen compound with radical, and every salt as hydrogen compound with hydrogen replaced by a metal.

binate ['bameɪt] *adj.* double; in couples. **bination,** *n.* celebration by a priest of Mass twice on the same day.

binaural [baɪ'nɔːrəl] *adj.* pertaining to or for use with two ears.

bine [baɪn] *n.* flexible shoot of climbing plant, especially hop.

binnacle ['bɪnəkl] *n.* fixed case or stand for ship's compass. **binnacle list,** list of sick men on man-of-war.

binocle ['bɪnəkl] *n.* binocular instr.

binocular [bɪ'nɒkjʊlə] *adj.* pertaining to or for two eyes. **binoculate,** *adj.* having two eyes. **binocularity,** *n.* **binoculars,** *n. pl.* field glasses.

binomial [baɪ'nəʊmɪəl] *adj.* having two names, especially of scientific nomenclature giving two names, genus and species, to each species; *Math.*, composed of two algebraic terms joined by + or − . **binomial theorem,** formula for finding any power of a binomial expression. **binomialism,** *n.* use of binomial nomenclature.

binominal [baɪ'nɒmɪnl] *adj.* having two names; binomial, especially of scientific nomenclature. **binominous,** *adj.* having two interchangeable names.

binotic [baɪ'nəʊtɪk, −'nɒ−] *adj.* binaural.

binotonous [baɪ'nɒtənəs] *adj.* consisting of two notes.

binturong [bɪn'tjʊərɒŋ] *n.* Asiatic civet with prehensile tail.

biobibliography [,baɪəʊ,bɪbli'ɒɡrəfi] *n.* bibliography with biographical notes. **biobibliographical,** *adj.*

biocentric [,baɪəʊ'sentrɪk] *adj.* having life as its centre or main principle.

biocide ['baɪəsaɪd] *n.* substance that kills living organisms; pesticide. **biocidal,** *adj.*

biocoenosis, biocenosis [,baɪəʊsɪ'nəʊsɪs] *n.* (*pl.* **-ses**) association of living creatures in a certain area. **biocoenotic** [−'nɒtɪk], *adj.*

biodegradable [,bæɪəʊdɪ'ɡreɪdəbl] *adj.* capable of being broken down by living organisms.

biodynamics [,baɪəʊdaɪ'næmɪks] *n.* study of activities of living organisms. **biodynamic(al),** *adj.*

bioelectric [,baɪəʊɪ'lektrɪk] *adj.* pertaining to plant or animal electricity.

bioengineering [,bæɪəʊ,endʒɪ'nɪərɪŋ] *n.* engineering theories and techniques applied to biological processes; design and use of artificial limbs, pacemakers, etc.; manipulation of living cells to produce desired growth. **bioengineer,** *n.*.

biogen(e) ['baɪədʒən, −dʒen, −dʒiːn] *n.* ultimate component part of protoplasm.

biogenesis [,baɪəʊ'dʒenəsɪs] *n.* theory that life derives only from living matter. **biogenetic** [−dʒə'netɪk], *adj.*; **biogenesic law,** recapitulation theory. **biogenesist,** *n.* adherent of biogenesis.

biogenous [baɪ'ɒdʒənəs] *adj.* produced from living organism; giving life.

biogeny [baɪ'ɒdʒəni] *n.* history of evolution of living organisms; biogenesis. **biogenic,** *adj.*

biogeography [,baɪəʊdʒi'ɒɡrəfi] *n.* study of geographical distribution of plants and animals. **biogeographic(al),** *adj.*

biognosy, biognosis [baɪ'ɒɡnəsi, ,baɪɒɡ'nəʊsɪs] *n.* sciences of life collectively.

biograph ['baɪəɡrɑːf] *n.* early form of cinematograph.

biokinetics [,baɪəʊkɪ'netɪks, −kaɪ−] *n.* study of changes during development of organism.

biolinguistics [,baɪəʊlɪŋ'ɡwɪstɪks] *n.* study of relations between physiology and speech.

biolith, biolite ['baɪəlɪθ, −laɪt] *n.* rock formed by living organisms.

biologism [baɪ'ɒlədʒɪzm] *n.* biological theory; use of biological terms. **biologistic,** *adj.*

bioluminescence [,baɪəʊ,luːmɪ'nesns] *n.* production of light by living creatures. **bioluminescent,** *adj.*

biolysis [baɪ'ɒləsɪs] *n.* destruction of life or organic substance. **biolytic** [−'lɪtɪk], *adj.*

biomagnetism [,baɪəʊ'mæɡnətɪzm] *n.* animal magnetism. **biomagnetic,** *adj.*

biomass ['baɪəʊmæs] *n.* amount of living matter in a unit area or volume of habitat; living matter cultivated as source of energy

biome ['baɪəʊm] *n.* large, naturally occuring community of plants and animals shaped by common patterns of vegetation and climate.

biometrics, biometry [,baɪə'metrɪks, baɪ'ɒmətri] *n.* calculation of length of human life; statistical biology. **biometric,** *adj.* **biometrician,** *n.* student of biometrics.

bionergy [baɪ'nnədʒi] *n.* vital force.

bionics [baɪ'ɒnɪks] *n.* study of the design principles of living organisms and their application to machines.

bionomics [,baɪə'nɒmɪks] *n.* study of relations of living organisms to environment; ecology. **bionomic,** *adj.* **bionomist,** *n.* student of bionomics.

bionomy [baɪ'ɒnəmi] *n.* bionomics; physiology.

biont ['baɪɒnt] *n.* physiologically independent living organism.

biophagous [baɪ'ɒfəɡəs] *adj.* feeding on living organisms. **biophagy** [−'ɒfədʒi], *n.*

biophor(e) ['baɪəfɔː] *n.* biogen.

biophyte ['baɪəfaɪt] *n.* plant consuming living organisms.

bioplasm ['baɪəplæzm] *n.* living protoplasm. **bioplasmic,** *adj.* **bioplast,** *n.* minute portion of bioplasm.

biopsy ['baɪɒpsi] *n.* medical examination of living tissue taken from body.

biorgan ['baɪɔːɡən] *n.* physiological organ.

biorhythm ['baɪəʊ,rɪðm] *n.* rhythmic change in biology and activity patterns of a living organism.

bios ['baɪɒs] *n.* organic life; constituent of yeast, causing its growth.

biosatellite ['baɪəʊ,sætəlaɪt] *n.* artificial satellite carrying living organisms into space for scientific study.

bioscope ['baɪəskəʊp] *n.* form of cinematograph. **bioscopy** [−'ɒskəpi], *n.* med. examination of body for presence of life.

biosis [baɪ'əʊsɪs] *n.* life, as distinguishing living organisms.

biosphere ['baɪəsfɪə] *n.* region of earth, air and water occupied by living organisms.

biostatics [,baɪəʊ'stætɪks] *n.* study of physiological relations between structure and function.

biostatistics [,baɪəʊstə'tɪstɪks] *n.* vital statistics.

biostratigraphy [ˌbaɪəʊstrə'tɪɡrəfi] *n.* determination of age, etc., of sedimentary strata from fossils which they contain.

biosynthesis [ˌbæɪəʊ'sɪnθəsɪs] *n.* synthesis of organic chemicals from inorganic ones by living cells.

biota [baɪ'əʊtə] *n.* flora and fauna of a region.

biotaxy ['baɪətæksi] *n.* biological classification.

biotechnology [ˌbaɪəʊtek'nɒlədʒi] *n.* industrial use of living organisms to manufacture food, drugs, etc. **biotechnologist** *n.*

biotelemetry [ˌbaɪəʊtə'lemətri] *n.* automatic transmission over a distance, for measurements of the condition, functions, etc., of a living creature, *e.g.* of an astronaut on space flight.

biotic [baɪ'ɒtɪk] *adj.* vital; pertaining to life. **bioticism** [–sɪzm], *n.* philosophical theory that ultimate reality is Life. **biotics**, *n.* study of activities of living organisms.

biotin ['baɪətɪn] *n.* growth-promoting vitamin of the vitamin B complex, found in liver and yeast.

biotomy [baɪ'ɒtəmi] *n.* vivisection.

biotope ['baɪətəʊp] *n.* area having uniform conditions and supporting a particular, uniform association of animal life.

biotype ['baɪətaɪp] *n.* all organisms having the same genetic constitution.

biparous ['bɪpərəs] *adj.* bringing forth two offspring at a birth.

bipartile [baɪ'pɑːtaɪl] *adj.* divisible into two parts. **bipartient**, *adj.* so dividing.

bipartisan [ˌbaɪpɑːtɪ'zæn] *adj.* representing or supported by two (political) parties.

bipartite [baɪ'pɑːtaɪt] *adj.* having two parts; between two parties. **bipartition**, *n.*

biped ['baɪped] *n.* & *adj.* (creature) having two feet. **bipedal**, *adj.* **bipedality**, *n.*

bipennate [baɪ'peneɪt] *adj.* having two wings.

bipod ['baɪpɒd] *n.* support or stand with two legs.

bipolar [baɪ'pəʊlə] *adj.* having or pertaining to two poles; occurring in both polar regions; equidistant north and south of equator. **bipolarity**, *n.*

bipropellant [ˌbaɪprə'pelənt] *n.* rocket propellant consisting of fuel and oxidizer stored separately until ignition.

biquadratic [ˌbaɪkwɒ'drætɪk] *adj. Mathematics,* of the fourth power; *n.* number's fourth power; equation involving fourth power of unknown quantity.

biramose, biramous [baɪ'reɪməʊs, -məs] *adj.* divided into two branches.

bireme ['baɪriːm] *n.* & *adj.* (galley) having two banks of oars.

biretta [bə'retə] *n. Roman Catholic,* cleric's square cap.

bis [bɪs] *adv.* twice; in two places; *Music,* direction to repeat; *(French) exclamation* [biːs] encore!; *n.* duplicate.

bise [biːz] *n.* cold, dry north wind of Switzerland, Italy and S France.

biserial [baɪ'sɪərɪəl] *adj.* in two rows.

bisexual [baɪ'sekʃʊəl, –sjuː–] *adj.* of two sexes; hermaphrodite; sexually attracted to both sexes; *n.* bisexual person. **bisexualism, bisexuality**, *n.*

bismarine [ˌbɪsmə'riːn] *adj.* bimarine.

bismillah [bɪ'smɪlə] *(Arabic) exclamation,* in the name of Allah!

bismuth ['bɪzməθ] *n.* hard, brittle, reddish-white metallic element, used in alloys and, as carbonate, for dyspepsia, etc. bismuthic [–'mjuːθɪk, –'mʌθɪk], *adj.*

bisonant [baɪ'səʊnənt] *adj.* having two sounds.

bisontine ['baɪsntaɪn] *adj.* pertaining to bison.

bisque [bɪsk] *n.* point allowed to tennis player; stroke(s) allowed to golfer; extra turn allowed to croquet player; kind of rich thick soup; pottery fired but not glazed.

bissext ['bɪsekst] *n.* intercalary day. **bissextile**, *adj.* containing the bissext; intercalary; *n.* leap-year.

bistort ['bɪstɔːt] *n.* a plant with twisted astringent root; snake-weed.

bistoury ['bɪstəri] *n.* small, narrow surgical knife.

bistournage, *n.* a method of castration.

bistre ['bɪstə] *n.* brown pigment derived from wood soot.

bisulcate [baɪ'sʌlkeɪt] *adj.* with two grooves; cloven.

bisyllabic [ˌbaɪsɪ'læbɪk] *adj.* consisting of two syllables. **bisyllable** [–'sɪləbl], *n.* such word, prefix, etc.

bisymmetrical [ˌbaɪsɪ'metrɪkl] *adj.* having two planes of symmetry at right angles.

bit [bɪt] *n.* in computers, a single character, especially a single binary numeral (0 or 1): *abbreviation* of binary digit.

bitheism [baɪ'θiːɪzm] *n.* belief in two gods.

bitonality [ˌbaɪtəʊ'næləti] *n. Music,* use of two keys simultaneously.

bittern ['bɪtn, –ɜːn] *n.* heron-like wading bird with booming call.

bitts [bɪts] *n. pl.* pairs of posts on deck of ship for fastening ropes.

bitumen ['bɪtʃʊmɪn] *n.* mineral pitch; several partly oxygenated hydrocarbons; asphalt; pigment obtained from asphalt. **bituminate, bituminize** [bɪ'tjuːmɪneɪt, –aɪz], *v.t.* cement with or convert into bitumen. **bituminoid**, *adj.* like bitumen. **bituminous**, *adj.* like or containing bitumen.

biune, biunial ['baɪjuːn, baɪ'juːnɪəl] *adj.* combining two in one. **biunity**, *n.*

bivalent [baɪ'veɪlənt, 'bɪvələnt] *adj. Chemistry,* with valency of two; *n. Biology,* double chromosome. **bivalency**, *n.*

bivariate [baɪ'veərɪət] *adj.* denoting a quantity that depends on two variables.

biventral [baɪ'ventrəl] *adj.* with two bellies.

biverbal [baɪ'vɜːbl] *adj.* relating to two words; punning.

bivious ['bɪvɪəs] *adj.* offering two paths or directions.

bivocal [baɪ'vəʊkl] *n.* diphthong. **bivocalize**, *v.t.* place between two vowels.

bivouac ['bɪvuæk] *n.* temporary camp without tents; *v.i.* **bivouacked, bivouacking**, pitch such camp.

bizarre [bɪ'zɑː] *adj.* fantastic; outlandish; incongruous. **bizarrerie**, *n.*

black [blæk] **blackball** *v.t.* vote against, especially by placing a black ball in the ballot box; reject for membership; exile. **blackcock**, *n.* male of black grouse. **black-fellow**, *n.* Australian aborigine. **blackjack**, *n.* leather wine container; *American,* small oak; life preserver (weapon). **black letter**, Old English or Gothic type. **Black Rod**, chief officer of House of Commons. **blackshirt**, *n.* fascist. **black-strap,** (*American*) *n.* mixture of rum and molasses; cheap wine. **black-water,** *n.* infectious tropical fever.

blain [bleɪn] *n.* sore; blister.

blancmange [blə'mɒndʒ] *n.* gelatinous dessert of milk and cornflour.

blandiloquence [blæn'dɪləkwəns] *n.* complimentary language or speech.

blank verse [ˌblæŋk 'vɜːs] *n.* rhymeless decasyllabic iambic line.

blanquette [blɒŋ'ket] *n.* stew of white meat in white sauce.

blasé ['blɑːzeɪ] (*French*) *adj.* bored; sophisticated; having exhausted all pleasures.

blastogenesis [ˌblæstə'dʒenəsɪs] *n.* reproduction by budding; theory of inheritance of characters through germ-plasm. **blastogenetic** [-dʒə'netɪk], **blastogenic,** *adj.* pertaining to germ cells.

blattnerphone ['blætnəfəun] *n.* system, invented by Ludwig Blattner (*d.* 1935), of recording sound on a steel tape electro-magnetically, and of reproducing sound by same process.

Blaue Reiter [ˌblauə 'raɪtə] group of expressionist painters in Munich in early 20th century.

blauwbok ['blaubɒk] (*S African*) *n.* extinct antelope with bluish coat.

blazon ['bleɪzn] *n.* coat of arms; banner, etc., bearing heraldic device; *v.t.* delineate or describe such object; adorn; announce loudly. **blazonment,** *n.* **blazonry,** *n.* art of delineating such objects; colourful display.

bleak [bliːk] *n.* small fresh-water fish having very silvery scales.

bleeder ['bliːdə] *n.* person suffering from haemophilia.

blende [blend] *n.* zinc sulphide; name of several lustrous metallic sulphides.

blendling ['blendlɪŋ] *n.* hybrid. **blendure,** *n.* mixture.

blennoid ['blenɔɪd] *adj.* like mucus. **blennogenic, blennogenous,** *adj.* generating mucus. **blennorrhoea,** *n.* mucus discharge. **blennorrhoeal,** *adj.*

blennophobia [ˌblenə'fəubɪə] *n.* morbid fear of slime.

blenny ['bleni] *n.* long, slender, spiny-rayed marine fish.

blepharal ['blefərəl] *adj.* pertaining to eyelids. **blepharism, blepharospasm,** *n.* muscular spasm of eyelid. **blepharitis,** *n.* inflammation of eyelids.

blesbok ['blesbɒk] *n.* species of S African antelope with white facial spot.

bletonism ['bletn-ɪzm] *n.* faculty of water divining.

blewits ['bluːɪts] *n.* kind of edible mushroom.

blissom ['blɪsəm] *adj.* with strong sexual desires; in rut.

Blitzkrieg ['blɪtskriːg] (*German*) *n.* swift military campaign.

bloc [blɒk] *n.* group, especially of politically allied countries.

block-system ['blɒkˌsɪstəm] *n.* method of railway signalling by which one section of line never carries more than one train.

bloom [bluːm] *n. Metallurgy,* bar of puddled iron. **bloomary, bloomery,** *n.* place where such bars are manufactured; forge into which iron passes after first melting.

blouson ['bluːzɒn] *n.* blouse-shaped jacket gathered at waist.

blucher ['bluːtʃə, -kə] *n.* leather half-boot.

blue [bluː] : **blue-book,** *n.* Parliamentary publication, bound in blue covers; *American,* book giving particulars of government servants or prominent persons; *adj.* applied to dull, dry literary style. **blue-nose,** *n.* native of Nova Scotia; prudish or puritanical person. **blue-sky,** *n.* having no value; visionary; having no immediate practical aim; theoretical. **blue-sky law,** *American,* law regulating sale of securities. **blue-stocking,** *n.* learned, studious woman, especially with literary pretensions. **blue disease,** cyanosis. **blue laws,** strict Puritanical laws of certain US states; any such laws. **blue peter,** ship's blue flag with white square in centre flown as signal for sailing, etc. **blue pill,** strong purgative containing mercury. **blue ribbon,** highest honour or prize in competition; chief competition of its kind; badge formerly worn by members of teetotal organization.

blunge [blʌndʒ] *v.i.* mix clay and water for pottery; blend. **blunger,** *n.* apparatus for such mixing.

boatel, botel [bəu'tel] *n.* waterside hotel for sailing enthusiasts.

boatswain, bosun ['bəusn] *n.* ship's officer in charge of crew and equipment; skua. **boatswain's chair,** seat suspended by ropes for person working on side of ship, building, etc.

bobbery ['bɒbəri] (*Anglo-Indian*) *n.* disturbance; uproar.

bobbinet, bobbin-net ['bɒbɪnet] *n.* cotton net imitating lace.

bobolink ['bɒbəlɪŋk] (*N American*) *n.* songbird, also called reed-bird, rice-bunting, and skunk-bird.

bob-sleigh ['bɒbsleɪ] *n.* long sports sleigh carrying several persons; *American,* sleigh consisting of two short ones joined together; one of the two sleighs so joined.

bobstay ['bɒbsteɪ] *n.* rope attached to and steadying bowsprit.

bocage ['bəukɑːʒ] *n.* boscage; decorative representation of trees, leaves, etc.

bocking ['bɒkɪŋ] *n.* coarse baize; smoked herring.

bodega [bə'diːgə] (*Spanish*) *n.* wine-shop.

bogey ['bəugi] *n.* in golf, number of strokes in which a good player should play hole or course; score one stroke above this; evil spirit.

bogie ['bəugi] *n.* wheeled undercarriage of a rail vehicle; railway coach; truck for coal, etc.

bohea [bəu'hiː] *n.* cheapest black tea.

bolar ['bəulə] *adj.* pertaining to clay.

bolas ['bəuləs] (*Spanish*) *n.* pair of balls joined by cord, thrown so as to wind round the object of attack.

bolection, bilection [bəu'lekʃn, baɪ-] *n.* projecting part of moulding round panel.

bolero [bə'leərəu; 'bɒlərəu] *n.* lively Spanish dance; waist-length jacket.

bolide ['bəulaɪd, -lɪd] *n.* large meteor; 'fire-ball'.

bolling ['bəulɪŋ] *n.* pollarded tree.

bolometer [bəu'lɒmɪtə, bə-] *n.* instrument measuring small amounts of radiant heat electrically. **bolograph** ['bəuləgrɑːf], *n.* photograph made with a bolometer. **bolometric** [-'metrɪk], *adj.*

bolt *see* **boult.**

bolthead ['bəʊlthed] *n.* long, straight-necked glass vessel for distilling; matrass.

bolus ['bəʊləs] *n.* large pill; any round mass. **bolus alba,** china clay.

boma ['bəʊmə] *n.* large non-venomous snake of W Africa; Brazilian boa; circular fenced-in enclosure in Africa.

bombardon [bɒm'bɑːdn, 'bɒmbədən] *n.* deep bass double-reeded wind instrument

bombasine, bombazine ['bɒmbəziːn] *n.* twilled, black, worsted, worsted-with-silk or worsted-with-cotton dress material. **bombazet(te),** *n.* thin smooth-surfaced worsted fabric.

Bombay duck [‚bɒmbeɪ 'dʌk] *n.* preserved flesh of pike-like marine fish of East.

bombe [bɒm] *n.* frozen dessert made in round mould.

bombé ['bɒmbeɪ] (*French*) *adj.* bulging or curved outward, especially such furniture, embroidery, etc.

bombic ['bɒmbɪk] *adj.* pertaining to silk-worm.

bombilate, bombinate ['bɒmbɪleɪt, –neɪt] *v.i.* buzz; boom. **bombilation, bombination,** *n.*

bombous ['bɒmbəs] *adj.* rounded; convex.

bombycine ['bɒmbɪsɪn] *adj.* bombic.

bona fide [‚bəʊnə 'faɪdɪ, –'fiːdeɪ] (*Latin*) 'with good faith'; genuine; in good faith. **bona fides** [–iːz], *n. pl.* credentials; honesty; sincerity.

bonamano [‚bəʊnə'mɑːnəʊ] (*Italian*) *n.* tip; pourboire.

bonasus, bonassus [bə'neɪsəs, –'næ–] *n.* aurochs.

bona vacantia [‚bəʊnə və'kæntɪə] (*Latin*) *Law,* unclaimed property, especially of a person who has died intestate.

bonbonnière [bɒn'bɒnɪeə] (*French*) *n.* dainty sweetmeat box.

bonce [bɒns] *n.* large playing marble; kind of marbles game.

bond [bɒnd] *n.* in masonry, method of placing bricks or stones. **English bond,** laying of bricks in alternate courses of headers and stretchers. **Flemish bond,** methods in which each course comprises alternate headers and stretchers. **bond-stone,** *n.* stone extending whole depth of wall.

bonded ['bɒndɪd] *adj. Commerce,* applied to warehouse, vaults, etc., where dutiable goods are stored, the goods being not chargeable with duty until removed; applied to such goods.

bongar ['bɒŋgɑː] *n.* kind of poisonous Indian snake; krait.

bongo ['bɒŋgəʊ] *n.* striped antelope of W and E Africa.

bonhomie ['bɒnəmɪ] (*French*) *n.* friendliness; urbane manner.

bonification [‚bɒnɪfɪ'keɪʃn] *n.* betterment; payment of bonus. **boniform,** *adj.* like or seeming good. **bonify,** *v.t.* improve; make good.

boning ['bəʊnɪŋ] *n.* judging level by looking along a line of poles. **boning-rod,** *n.* pole used in boning.

bonito [bə'niːtəʊ] *n.* striped tunny; several fishes of mackerel family.

bon mot [‚bɒn 'məʊ] (*French*) (*pl.* **bons mots**), 'good word'; epigram; witty remark.

bonne [bɒn] (*French*) *n.* female servant.

bonne bouche [‚bɒn 'buːʃ] (*French*) (*pl.* **bonnes bouches**), 'good mouth'; titbit.

bonnet rouge [‚bɒneɪ 'ruːʒ] (*French*) 'red cap', worn by French revolutionaries; a revolutionary, or revolutionary movement.

bonsai ['bɒnsaɪ] (*Japanese*) *n.* art of producing miniature trees by selective pruning; such a tree.

bontebok ['bɒntibɒk] *n.* reddish, white-faced antelope of S Africa.

bon ton [‚bɒn 'tɒn] (*French*) 'good tone'; high society; good breeding.

bon vivant, bon viveur [‚bɒn 'viːvɒn, viː'vɜː] (*French*) (*pl.* **bons vivants, bons viveurs;** *fem.* **bonne vivante,** [–'vɒnt]), 'good living or liver'; lover of good food and drink; gourmet.

bonze [bɒnz] *n.* Buddhist priest. **bonzery,** *n.* Buddhist monastery.

boom [buːm] *n.* long spar extending foot of sail. **boom-sail, boom-sheet,** etc., sail, sheet, etc., attached to boom.

boomer ['buːmə] (*Australian*) *n.* male of largest kangaroo species.

boomslang ['buːmslæŋ] (*S African*) *n.* (*pl.* **-e**) large poisonous snake of S Africa.

boongary [buːn'geərɪ, 'buːŋgərɪ] (*Australian*) *n.* small tree kangaroo.

bora ['bɔːrə] (*Italian*) *n.* cold north wind of N Adriatic.

boracic [bə'ræsɪk] *adj.* pertaining to or derived from borax. **boracic acid,** former name for boric acid. **boracous** ['bɔːrəkəs], *adj.*

borage ['bɒrɪdʒ, 'bʌ–] *n.* rough-stemmed, blue-flowered salad herb.

borasco, borasca, borasque [bə'rɑːskəʊ, –'rɑːskə, –'ræsk] *n.* Mediterranean squall.

borax ['bɔːræks] *n.* a natural salt, also made from soda, used as flux and antiseptic.

borborygmus [‚bɔːbə'rɪgməs] *n.* rumbling of gas in the stomach. **borborygmic,** *adj.*

bordel(lo) ['bɔːdl, bɔː'deləʊ] *n.* brothel.

bordereau [‚bɔːdə'rəʊ] (*French*) *n.* (*pl.* **-x**) invoice; detailed bill; memorandum.

bore [bɔː] *n.* wall of water advancing up narrow estuary at certain tides.

boreal ['bɔːrɪəl] *adj.* pertaining to Boreas, the north wind; cold; of the north.

borecole ['bɔːkəʊl] *n.* kale.

boron ['bɔːrɒn] *n.* non-metallic, non-fusible element, found in borax, etc. **boronic,** *adj.* pertaining to or containing boron; **boric acid,** such acid, formerly called boracic acid, used as preservative and antiseptic. **borise,** *v.t.* preserve with boric acid.

borough-English [‚bʌrə'ɪŋglɪʃ] *n.* custom whereby landed property is inherited by youngest son.

borracha [bə'rɑːʃə] (*Portuguese*) *n.* crude rubber; rubber tree.

bort [bɔːt] *n.* ground diamond fragments, used in polishing, etc. **borty,** *adj.*

bortsch, borsch(t) [bɔːtʃ, bɔːʃ, bɔːʃt] (*Russian*) *n.* mixed soup coloured red with beetroot.

borzoi ['bɔːzɔɪ] (*Russian*) *n.* wolf-hound.

boscage, boskage ['bɒskɪdʒ] *n.* thicket of trees or shrubs.

bosch [bɒʃ, bɒs] (*S African*) *n.* wood; bush. **boschbok,** *n.* bush-buck; kind of antelope. **bosch-man,** *n.* Bushman. **bosch-vark,** *n.* kind of wild pig. **bosch-veldt,** *n.* bush country.

bosket, bosquet ['bɒskɪt] *n.* thicket.

bosky ['bɒski] *adj.* having trees or shrubs; *slang* tipsy.

boson ['bəʊsɒn] *n.* subatomic particle whose spin can only take values that are whole numbers or zero.

bosselated ['bɒsəleɪtɪd] *adj.* covered with or formed into knobs.

bosun *see* **boatswain.**

bot(t) [bɒt] *n.* parasitical maggot of bot-fly; *pl.* disease of horses caused by this.

botargo [bə'tɑːgəʊ] *n.* relish made from tunny's or mullet's roe.

bo-tree ['bəʊtriː] *n.* sacred tree of Sri Lanka, kind of banyan, yielding caoutchouc; peepul tree.

botryoid(al) ['bɒtriɔɪd, -l] *adj.* having shape of cluster of grapes. **botryose,** *adj.* with flowers in clusters that develop upwards from base.

bottine [bɒ'tiːn] *n.* small boot; surgical boot for correcting deformity.

bottomry ['bɒtəmri] *n.* raising loan on ship as security.

botulism ['bɒtjʊlɪzm] *n.* sausage-poisoning; poisoning by any infected preserved meat. **botuliform,** *adj.* sausage-shaped. **botulinic,** *n.* toxin that causes botulism. **botulinus** [,bɒtju'laɪnəs] *n.* bacterium that produces botulism. **botulinic,** *adj.*

bouchée ['buːʃeɪ] (*French*) *n.* small patty; *adj. Music,* muted or stopped.

boucherize ['buːʃəraɪz] *v.t.* preserve by impregnating with copper sulphate.

bouffant ['buːfɒn] (*French*) *adj.* puffed out, as a skirt, hair, etc.

bougie ['buːʒiː, buː'ʒiː] (*French*) *n.* wax candle; flexible medical instrument for insertion into body passages; suppository.

bouillabaisse [,buːjə'bes] (*French*) *n.* fish and vegetable stew.

bouilli ['buːjiː] (*French*) *n.* stewed meat.

bouillon ['buːjɒn] (*French*) *n.* clear soup; broth; stew.

boule [buːl] *n.* roulette-like game.

boule ['buːleɪ] *n.* advisory council or senate of ancient Greece. **bouleuterion,** *n.* (*pl.* **-ia**) assembly-place.

boules [buːl] (*French*) *n.* form of bowls played in France.

boulevard ['buːləvɑːd] (*French*) *n.* wide avenue, especially near park or river; fashionable promenade. **boulevardier** [buːl'vɑːdieɪ], *n.* man-about-town.

bouleversement [buːl'veəsmɒn] (*French*) *n.* overturning, upset.

boulimia *see* **bulimia.**

boult, bolt [bəʊlt] *v.t.* sift. **boultel,** *n.* sifting cloth. **boulter,** *n.* one who sifts; sieve; fishing line with many hooks.

bouquetin ['buːkətæn] (*French*) *n.* ibex of the Alps.

bourasque [buː'ræsk] *n.* borasco.

bourdon ['buədn] *n. Music,* bass drone, as of bagpipe.

bourgeois ['buəʒwɑː] (*French*) *n. & adj.* (person) of middle class. **petit bourgeois,** (person) of lower middle class. **bourgeoisie** [-'ziː], *n.* the middle classes.

bourrée ['buːreɪ] (*French*) *n.* quick dance of S France and Spain

bourse [buəs] *n.* foreign money-market.

boutonnière [bu,tɒni'eə] (*French*) *n.* small bunch of flowers for button-hole.

bouts-rimés [,buː'riːmeɪ] (*French*) *n. pl.* 'rhymed endings'; composition of verses to given rhymes; verses so composed.

bouzouki [bu'zuːki] (*Greek*) *n.* mandolin-like musical instrument.

bovine ['bəʊvaɪn] *adj.* pertaining to cattle; apathetic; stupid. **bovicide,** *n.* killer of cattle; butcher. **boviform,** *adj.* having shape of cattle. **bovoid,** *adj.* like cattle.

bow-chaser ['bau,tʃeɪsə] *n.* ship's gun for firing ahead.

bowdlerize ['baudləraɪz] *v.t.* expurgate, especially too strictly. **bowdlerization, bowdlerism,** *n.*

bower-bird ['bauəbɜːd] (*Australian*) *n.* bird which builds and decorates bower-like runs.

bow-head ['bəʊhed] *n.* Greenland whale.

bowline ['bəʊlɪn] *n.* rope steadying upright edge of sail; knot securing this to sail. **bowline bridle,** rope securing bowline to sail.

bowsprit ['bəʊsprɪt] *n.* spar extending at bows of ship.

bowyer ['bəʊjə] *n.* maker of bows (the weapons).

box-wallah ['bɒks,wɒlə] (*Anglo-Indian*) *n.* itinerant pedlar.

boyar ['bɔɪə] *n.* ancient Russian rank next below prince; Russian land-owner.

boyau ['bwaɪəʊ] (*French*) *n.* (*pl.* **-x**) winding trench; zigzag.

bracciale [,brɑːksi'eɪli] *n.* wall socket or bracket.

brach [brætʃ] *n.* female hunting hound.

brachial ['breɪkiəl] *adj.* pertaining to arm; arm-shaped. **brachiate** *v.i.* swing by arms from place to place; *adj.* having arms. **brachiation,** *n.* **brachiferous** [breɪ'kɪfərəs], *adj.* having arms or branches. **brachiotomy** [-'ɒtəmi], *n.* amputation of arm.

brachistocephalic,   **brachistocephalous** [brə,kɪstəsɪ'fælɪk, -'sefələs] *adj.* having skull of which breadth is 85 per cent or more of length.

brachycatalectic [,brækɪkætə'lektɪk] *adj.* with two syllables lacking from end; *n.* such verse line.

brachycephalic, brachycephalous [,brækɪsɪ'fælɪk, -'sefələs] *adj.* short-headed; having skull of which maximum breadth is 80 per cent or more of maximum length. **brachycephalism,** *n.*

brachycerous [brə'kɪsərəs] *adj.* having short horns or antennae.

brachydactylous,   **brachydactylic** [,brækɪ'dæktɪləs, -dæk'tɪlɪk] *adj.* having short digits. **brachydactylism, brachydactyly,** *n.*

brachygraphy [brə'kɪgrəfi] *n.* short-hand. **brachygrapher,** *n.* stenographer. **brachygraphic(al),** *adj.*

brachylogy [brə'kɪlədʒi] *n.* condensed expression; laconic speech.

brachymetropy,   **brachymetropia** [,brækɪ'metrəpi, -mɪ'trəʊpiə] *n.* shortsightedness. **brachymetropic** [-'trɒpɪk], *adj.*

brachypodous [brə'kɪpədəs] *n.* having short legs or stalk.

brachypterous [brə'kɪptərəs] *adj.* having short wings.

brachyure ['brækɪjʊə] *n.* short-tailed animal, bird, etc. **brachyuran** [,brækɪ'jʊərən], *n.* a crab.

bract [brækt] *n.* leaf from axil of which flower is produced. **bracteal** ['bræktiəl], *adj.* bract-like.

bracteate, *adj.* bearing bracts. **bracteiform**, *adj.* bract-shaped. **bracteole**, *n.* small bract; bract at base of flower. **bracteolate**, *adj.* having bracteoles. **bracteose**, *adj.* having many bracts.

bradycardia [,brædɪ'kɑːdiə] *n.* (abnormally) slow heart rate. **bradykinetic**, [–kɪ'netɪk, –kaɪ–] *adj.* moving slowly.

bradykinin [,brædɪ'kaɪnɪn] *n.* blood hormone causing dilation of blood vessels. **bradytelic** [–'telɪk], *adj.* evolving at a slower rate than normal.

braggadocio [,brægə'dəutʃiəu, –'dəuʃ–] *n.* boasting; braggart. **braggadocian**, *n. & adj.*

brahman ['brɑːmən] *n.* male member of priestly caste of Hindus. **brahmanee, brahmani** [–i], *n.* female member of such caste. **brahmanic(al)** [–'mæn–], *adj.* **brahmanism**, *n.* **brahmany**, *adj.* brahminee.

brahmin ['brɑːmɪn] *n.* brahman; *American,* learned person; pedant. **brahmin ox,** humped ox sacred to Hindus. **brahminic(al)** [–'mɪn–], *adj.* **brahminism**, *n.*

brahminee, brahmany ['brɑːmɪni] *adj.* belonging to Hindu priestly caste. **brahminee bull,** brahmin ox. **brahminee duck,** ruddy sheldrake. **brahminee kite,** sacred Ind. bird of prey.

Braidism ['breɪdɪzm] *n.* hypnotism.

brail [breɪl] *v.t.* truss sail; haul up. **brails,** *n.pl.* cords on edge of sail for trussing.

braille [breɪl] *n.* system of printing for the blind using patterns of raised dots to represent characters.

branchial, branchiac ['bræŋkɪəl, –iæk] *adj.* pertaining to gills. **branchiate**, *adj.* having gills. **branchicolous** [bræŋ'kɪkələs], *adj.* living in gills. **branchiform**, *adj.* gill-shaped.

branchiopod [bræŋ'kɪəpɒd] *n.* kind of crustacean with gills on feet. **branchiopodan, branchiopodus** [–op'ədən, –əs], *adj.*

brandling ['brændlɪŋ] *n.* striped earthworm used by anglers.

brank(s) [bræŋk, –s] *n.* kind of bridle fixed to head of nagging woman as punishment; scold's bridle; *Scottish,* mumps.

brash [bræʃ] *n.* slight sickness; broken pieces of rock or ice; collection of fragments; *adj.* brittle; lifeless; rash. **water-brash,** *n.* pyrosis.

brassage ['brɑːsɪdʒ] *n.* charge for minting coin, difference between value of metal, with cost of minting, and face value.

brassard ['bræsɑːd] *n.* armlet; arm-badge.

brassie ['brɑːsi] *n.* wooden golf-club with brass sole.

brassy ['brɑːsi] *n.* bib.

brattice ['brætɪs] *n.* partition, especially in mine gallery to regulate ventilation or support sides or roof; *v.t.* erect brattice. **brattice cloth,** canvas sheet for regulating ventilation in mine.

bravado [brə'vɑːdəu] *n.* ostentatious show of boldness; braggart.

bravura [brə'vjuərə, –'vu–] *n. Music,* exceptional skill; boldness; brilliance; passage needing this.

braxy ['bræksi] *n.* apoplectic disease of sheep; meat of sheep dead from disease, especially from braxy; *adj.* sick with or dead from this disease.

braze [breɪz] *v.t.* solder with zinc and brass alloy; cover with brass; *n.* joint so soldered. **brazen,**

adj. made of brass; brass-coloured; impudent; shameless.

breastsummer *see* **bressumer**.

breccia ['bretʃiə] *n. Geology,* aggregate of angular rock fragments. **breccial**, *adj.* **brecciation**, *n.* making into brecciae.

breeches buoy ['briːtʃɪz bɔɪ, 'briː–] life-saving device consisting of a lifebuoy with canvas breeches for the legs, suspended between ships by rope.

brehon ['briːhɒn, 'bre–] *n.* judge of ancient Ireland. **brehon law,** ancient Irish legal code.

bressummer ['bresəmə] *n.* beam or girder over opening and supporting a wall.

brettice *see* **brattice**.

breve [briːv] *n.* papal letter; brief; mark indicating a short vowel; *Music,* note equivalent of two semi-breves.

brevet ['brevɪt] *n.* commission giving army officer honorary higher rank. **brevetcy,** *n.* such rank.

breveté ['brevəteɪ] (*French*) *adj.* patented.

breviary ['breviəri, 'briː–] *n.* short prayer-book of Roman Catholic Church.

breviate ['briːvɪət] *n.* summary; precis.

brevicaudate [,brevɪ'kɔːdeɪt] *adj.* having short tail.

brevier [brə'vɪə] *n.* size of type: 8-point.

brevifoliate [,brevɪ'fəulieɪt] *adj.* having short leaves. **brevilingual,** *adj.* having short tongue. **breviloquence** [bre'vɪləkwəns], *n.* laconic manner of speech. **breviped** ['brevɪped], *adj.* having short legs. **brevipennate,** *adj.* having short wings.

brewster ['bruːstə] *n.* brewer. **Brewster Sessions,** court hearing applications for liquor trade licences.

Briarean [braɪ'eəriən] *adj.* pertaining to Briareus [braɪ'eəriəs], monster in Greek legend with hundred hands; having many hands.

bric-à-brac ['brɪkəbræk] *n.* odds and ends of furniture, antiquities, china, art, etc.

bricole ['brɪkl, brɪ'kəul] *n.* indirect stroke, especially in real tennis, in which ball is hit against wall or rebounds from it; and billiards, in which ball hits cushion between the two contacts of a cannon.

bridewell ['braɪdwəl] *n.* prison; house of correction.

brig [brɪg] *n.* two-masted, square-rigged ship.

brigantine ['brɪgəntiːn] *n.* two-masted ship, square-rigged on foremast only.

brilliant ['brɪljənt] *n.* smallest size of type: 3½-point.

brinjal, brinjaul ['brɪndʒəl] (*Anglo-Indian*) *n.* fruit of egg-plant; aubergine.

brinjarry [brɪn'dʒɑːri] (*Anglo-Indian*) *n.* itinerant seller of grain and salt.

brioche [bri'ɒʃ] (*French*) *n.* rich, unsweetened, bread-like roll.

briquette [brɪ'ket] *n.* brick-shaped block of compressed coal dust.

brisling ['brɪzlɪŋ, 'brɪs–] *n.* small, sardine-like fish.

britannia metal [brɪ'tænjə ,metl] *n.* cheap white alloy of copper, zinc, antimony and bismuth, with lead.

British warm [,brɪtɪʃ 'wɔːm] *n.* army officer's overcoat.

britzka ['brɪtskə, 'brɪtʃ-] *n.* single-seated, four-wheeled, hooded Polish carriage.

broach [brəutʃ] *v.t.* introduce; raise for discussion; pierce, tap; *n.* pointed tool; roasting-spit. **broach spire**, octagonal church spire rising from square base.

Brobdingnagian [,brɒbdɪŋ'nægiən] *adj.* pertaining to Brobdingnag, a country of giants in Swift's *Gulliver's Travels*; gigantic; *n.* giant.

brocard ['brəukəd] *(French) n.* axiom; maxim; caustic remark.

brocatel(lo) [,brɒkə'tel, -əu] *n.* kind of variegated marble; thick figured silk used in upholstery.

broch [brɒx] *n.* ancient Scottish stone tower.

broché ['brəuʃeɪ] *(French) adj.* with raised pattern.

brochette [brəu'ʃet] *n.* skewer for grilling food.

brochure ['brəuʃə, brɒ'ʃuə] *n.* booklet; pamphlet.

brock [brɒk] *n.* badger. **brocket**, *n.* stag in its second year; Brazilian pronged deer. **brock-faced**, *adj.* having white mark on face.

broderie ['brəudəri] *(French) n.* embroidery-like pattern. **broderie anglaise** [-'ɒŋgleɪz], mixture of solid and open-work embroidery.

brogan ['brəugən] *n.* coarse, strong shoe; brogue.

brokerage ['brəukərɪdʒ] *n. Commerce,* commission taken by agent, especially on sale or purchase of shares, etc.

bromatology [,brəumə'tɒlədʒi] *n.* treatise on or study of food.

bromide ['brəumaɪd] *n.* compound of bromine; silver bromide, used in photography; sedative drug composed of bromine and potassium hydrate; person using this drug; trite statement; meaningless adjective; dull, tedious person. **bromidic** [-'mɪdɪk], *adj.*

bromidrosis [,brəumɪ'drəusɪs] *n.* strongly smelling perspiration.

bromine ['brəumiːn, -ɪn] *n.* non-metallic chlorine-like element found in seawater and mineral springs. **bromize**, *v.t.* compound with bromine; prepare photographic plate with bromide. **bromism**, *n.* condition due to excessive

use of bromide. **brominated**, *adj.* compounded with bromine.

bromyrite ['brəumɪraɪt] *n.* natural bromide of silver.

bronchi ['brɒŋki] *n. pl. (singular –chus)* divisions of windpipe, one leading to each lung. **bronchial**, *adj.* **bronchiectasis** [-'ektəsɪs], *n.* dilatation of bronchi. **bronchiole**, *n,* minute branch of a bronchus. **bronchitis** [brɒŋ'kaɪtɪs], *n.* inflammation of bronchi. **bronchitic** [-'kɪtɪk], *adj.* **bronchocele**, ['brɒŋkəsiːl], *n* . goitre. **bronchodilator**, *n.* drug that relaxes and dilates the bronchial tubes. **bronchopulmonary** [,brɒŋkəu'pʌlmənəri]), *adj.* pertaining to bronchial tubes and lungs. **bronchos**, [-əs] *n.* temporary loss of voice. **bronchoscope** *n.* instrument for examining the bronchi **bronchoscopic**, *adj.* **bronchotomy**, [brɒŋ'kɒtəmi] *n.* incision into larynx or trachea.

brontephobia, brontophobia [,brɒntɪ'fəubiə, -tə–] *n.* dread of thunder and lightning.

brontide ['brɒntaɪd] *n.* sound like distant thunder, due to seismic causes.

brontograph ['brɒntəgrɑːf] *n.* instr. recording discharges of atmospheric electricity. **brontogram**, *n.* record made by this.

brontology [brɒn'tɒlədʒi] *n.* study of thunder. **brontometer**, *n.* brontograph.

brontosaurus [,brɒntə'sɔːrəs] *n.* gigantic fossil dinosaur.

brose [brəuz] *(Scottish) n.* kind of porridge; broth. **Athole-brose**, mixture of whisky and honey.

brouette [bru'et] *(French) n.* small two-wheeled carriage; kind of four-seater motor car.

brougham ['bruːəm, bruːm] *n.* small, one-horse, four-wheeled closed carriage with unroofed driver's seat; kind of limousine-like motor-car body with driver's seat uncovered.

brouhaha ['bruːhɑːhɑː] *n.* turmoil, uproar, fuss.

Brownian ['brəuniən] *adj.* applied to movement, discovered by Robert Brown (1773–1858), of minute particles suspended in fluid, due to collisions between them and molecules of fluid.

Brownist ['brəunɪst] *n.* follower of Robert Browne (d. 1663), founder of Congregationalism;

Billion

The word *billion* was coined in France in the 16th century to denote a million multiplied by itself once – a million millions. It seems to have been adopted into English in the latter part of the 17th century. However, French mathematicians then decided to change the application of *billion*, so that it denoted not a million millions but only a thousand millions. It was this sense of *billion* that established itself in the U.S.A. in the 19th century, and so a division of usage between the British *billion* (1,000,000,000,000) and the American *billion* (1,000,000,000) was set up which survives to this day. This is a considerable source of potential and actual confusion. It seems to be gradually resolving itself through the adoption by British English of the American convention, which has much wider international currency; but where precision is

vital, the terms *thousand million* and *million million* may be less ambiguous. The American usage will certainly prevail in the end, not only because of the greater prestige of American English, but also because it is simply more useful to have a single word for 1,000,000,000 (not least when referring to inflation-hit money) than it is to have one for the comparatively rarefied 1,000,000,000,000, which is mainly the preserve of astronomers (the 'official' British term for 1,000,000,000, *milliard*, now seems to be obsolete). The status of the high-number words further up the scale (*trillion, quadrillion* etc.) is similar: a British *trillion*, for instance, is officially 1,000,000,000,000,000,000, but it is gradually being overtaken by the American *trillion*, 1,000,000,000,000 (the equivalent of the original British *billion*).

adj. pertaining to his principles; congregationalist; Brunonian. **Brownism,** *n.*

brucellosis [,bru:sɪ'ləʊsɪs] *n.* an undulant fever of cattle.

brucin(e), brucina ['bru:sɪn, -i:n, bru:'saɪnə] *n.* strychnine-like poison derived from nux vomica plant.

bruit [bru:t] *n.* sounds in chest symptomatic of disease; rumour; *v.t.* report; spread abroad.

brumal ['bru:ml] *adj.* pertaining to brume or winter.

brumby, brumbie, brumbee ['brʌmbi] *(Australian) n.* wild horse.

brume [bru:m] *n.* mist or fog. **brumous,** *adj.*

Brummagem ['brʌmədʒəm] *n. slang* Birmingham; *adj.* tawdry; counterfeit.

brunneous ['brʌniəs] *adj.* dark brown.

Brunonian [bru:'nəʊniən] *adj.* applied to theory that disease arises solely from action of external stimuli on body, held by John Brown (1735-88); *n.* Brownist. **Brunoism,** *n.*

brusque [brʊsk, brʌsk] *adj.* blunt in speech or conduct. **brusquerie,** *n.*

brut [bru:t] *(French) adj.* applied to unsweetened wine, especially very dry champagne.

brutum fulmen [,bru:təm 'fʊlmen] *(Latin)* 'unfeeling thunder'; empty threat.

bruxism ['brʊksɪzm, 'brʌ-] *n.* grinding of teeth, especially in sleep.

bryology [braɪ'ɒlədʒi] *n.* study of mosses and liverworts; plant life of such kind of a region. **bryological,** *adj.* **bryologist,** *n.* **bryophyte** ['braɪəfaɪt], *n.* moss or liverwort.

Brythonic [brɪ'θɒnɪk] *adj.* Welsh; of ancient Cambria or Cornwall; of the language group including Breton, Cornish and Welsh.

bubal(is) ['bju:bəl, -ɪs] *n.* kind of African antelope. **bubaline,** *adj.*

bubo ['bju:bəʊ] *n.* (*pl.* **-oes**) swelling with inflammation of lymphatic gland, especially of groin. **bubonalgia,** *n.* pain in groin. **bubonic** [-'bɒnɪk], *adj.*

buccal ['bʌkl] *adj.* pertaining to mouth or cheek.

buccan ['bʌkən, bʌ'kæn] *n.* frame-work over which meat is roasted or dried; *v.t.* dry meat on such.

buccate ['bʌkeɪt] *adj.* with protruding cheeks.

buccinal ['bʌksɪnl] *adj.* having shape or sound of trumpet. **buccinator,** *n.* muscle forming cheek-wall. **buccinatory,** *adj.*

buccula ['bʌkjʊlə] *n.* (*pl.* **-ae**) double chin.

bucentaur [bju:'sentɔ:] *n.* mythical creature, half-man, half-ox; Venetian doges' state barge.

Buchmanism ['bʌkmənɪzm] *n.* religious principles and methods enunciated by F.N.D. Buchman (1878-1961), founder of the 'group movement', including open confession and testimony. **Buchmanite,** *n.* adherent of Buchmanism.

bucolic [bju:'kɒlɪk] *adj.* rustic; pertaining to shepherds; *n.pl.* pastoral poems. **bucoliast** [bju:'kəʊliæst], *n.* writer of bucolics.

Buddhism ['bʊdɪzm] *n.* Asian relig. founded in 5th century BC by Gautama Buddha. **Buddhist,** *adj. & n.* **Buddhistic(al),** *adj.*

buddle ['bʌdl] *n.* sloping trough, etc., for washing crushed ore; *v.t.* wash on a buddle.

budgerow ['bʌdʒərəʊ] *(Anglo-Indian) n.* heavy flat-bottomed Ganges barge.

bufonite ['bju:fənaɪt] *n.* toadstone.

buhl [bu:l] *(German) n.* inlaying of gold, brass, tortoiseshell, mother of pearl, etc., on furniture; piece of furniture so inlaid.

buhrstone *see* **burrstone.**

bulbil ['bʌlbɪl] *n.* small bulb; large, fleshy, axillary bud from which plant may be grown.

bulbul ['bʊlbʊl] *(Persian) n.* song-thrush of Orient; nightingale.

bulger ['bʌldʒə] *n.* parched, crushed wheat.

bulimia, bulimy [bju'lɪmiə, bu-, 'bju:lɪmi] *n.* insatiable hunger; abnormal craving for food. **bulimia nervosa,** excessive overeating compensated for by forced vomiting, periods of fasting, etc. **bulimic** [-'lɪmɪk], *adj.* voracious; pertaining to bulimia (nervosa); *n.* person suffering from bulimia nervosa. **bulimious** [-'lɪmiəs], *&ddZ.* sVfferIg frQm bVIII (nervQs&).).

bull [bʊl] *n. Commerce,* speculator in shares who desires a rise in price; papal edict.

bullace ['bʊlɪs] *n.* small wild plum fruit and tree.

bullary ['bʊⁱɒri] *n.* collection of papal bulls.

bullate ['bʊ eɪt] *adj.* puckered; with blistered appearance. **bullation,** *n.*

bullhead ['bʊlhed] *n.* several small, large-headed spinous marine fishes, especially the miller's thumb.

bulliform ['bʊlɪfɔ:m] *adj.* bullate.

bullion ['bʊljən] *n.* gold or silver in the mass, especially uncoined. **bullionist,** *n.* upholder of metallic currency.

bullish ['bʊlɪʃ] *adj. Commerce,* anticipating or associated with a rise in price.

bullroarer ['bʊl,rɔ:rə] *n.* wooden instrument making a roaring sound, used by Australian and other aborigines, generally to cause rain; whizzingstick; lightning-stick.

bum-bailiff *see* **bailiff.**

bumboat ['bʌmbəʊt] *n.* small harbour boat carrying provisons, etc. to ship.

bumicky ['bʌmiki] *n.* cement mixed with stone fragments for repairing masonry.

bummalo ['bʌmələʊ] *n.* small S Asiatic fish; Bombay duck.

bund [bʌnd] *(Anglo-Indian) n.* quay; esplanade; embankment. **bunder** *n.* quay; harbour; port.

bundobust *see* **bandobast.**

bunt [bʌnt] *n.* kind of fungus attacking wheat; middle of sail or fish-net when slack. **bunt-line,** *n.* furling rope.

buonamano *see* **bonamano.**

buphthalmia [bʌf'θælmiə] *n.* enlargement of eye. **buphthalmic,** *adj.*

buran [bu'rɑ:n] *n.* sudden violent storm of Central Asia.

burbot ['bɜ:bət] *n.* long, slender, freshwater fish of cod family; eel-pout.

bureaucracy [bju'rɒkrəsi] *n.* government by permanent officials; officialdom. **bureaucrat** ['bjʊərəkræt], *n.* **bureaucratic** [-'krætɪk], *adj.* **bureaucratize** [-'rɒk-], *v.t.* **bureaucratism, bureaucratist,** *n.*

burette [bju'ret] *n.* graduated glass measuring tube; *Ecclesiastical,* sacramental cruet.

burgee ['bɜ:dʒi:] *n.* small triangular pennant of yacht, etc.

burgensic [bə'dʒensɪk] *adj.* pertaining to citizen or freeman of borough.

burgeon ['bɜːdʒən] *n. & v.i.* bud; sprout.

burgh ['bʌrə] *n.* Scottish borough.

burgrave ['bɜːgreɪv] *n.* former German commander of a town or castle; title of honour equiv. of count. **burgraviate**, *n.* jurisdiction of burgrave.

burin ['bjuərɪn] *n.* engraver's tool; graver. **burinist**, *n.* engraver.

burlap ['bɜːlæp] *n.* kind of sacking canvas; coarse, vari-coloured curtain fabric.

burletta [bɜːˈletə] (*Italian*) *n.* light comic opera.

burnettize ['bɜːnɪtaɪz] *v.t.* saturate with zinc chloride solution to prevent decay. **burnettizing**, *n.* such process, invented by Sir W Burnett.

burnous, **burnoose** [bɜːˈnuːs] *n.* Moorish hooded cloak.

burra ['bʌrə] (*Hindu*) *adj.* great, used as title of respect. **burra sahib**, important official; manager, chief.

burro ['burəu] (*Spanish-American*) *n.* donkey.

burrow-duck ['bʌrəudʌk] *n.* sheldrake.

burrstone ['bɜː–stəun] *n.* flinty rock used for millstones; millstone made of this.

bursa ['bɜːsə] *n.* (*pl.* **-ae** *or* **-as**) sac, especially fluid-filled at point of friction in joint, etc. **bursal**, *adj.* pertaining to bursa; pertaining to states revenue. **bursitis**, *n.* inflammation of bursa.

bursar ['bɜːsə] *n.* college or school treasurer; holder of bursary. **bursarial** [bɜːˈseəriəl], *adj.* **bursary**, *n.* office of bursar; scholarship at school or university.

burse [bɜːs] *n.* purse; bourse; bursary; *Roman Catholic*, purse-like container of Communion cloth. **bursicle**, *n. Botany*, purse-shaped pod. **bursiculate**, *adj.* having shape of small purse. **bursiform**, *adj.* purse-shaped.

burucha *see* **borracha**.

'bus-bar, **bus** ['bʌsbaː, bʌs] *n. Electricity*, main conductor on printed circuit board.

bush [buʃ] **bush-buck**, *n.* small African spiral-horned antelope. **bushman**, *n.* S African aborigine. **bush-master**, *n.* large S American poisonous snake. **bushcat**, serval. **bushlawyer**, New Zealand bramble.

bushido [buˈʃiːdəu, 'buːʃi–] (*Japanese*) *n.* code of honour of Japanese military class; chivalry.

buskin ['bʌskɪn] *n.* high boot; thick-soled boot (also called cothurnus) worn by actors in ancient Greek tragedy; classic tragedy.

bustard ['bʌstəd] *n.* large crane-like bird of Europe; *American & Canadian*, the Canada goose. **great bustard**, largest European land bird.

but-and-ben [ˌbʌtnˈben] (*Scottish*) *n.* two-roomed dwelling.

butte [bjuːt] (*American*) *n.* steep, isolated hill.

butyric [bjuˈtɪrɪk] *adj.* pertaining to butter. **butyraceous** [ˌbjuːtəˈreɪʃəs], butyrous ['bjuːtɪrəs] *adj.* like, producing or containing butter.

bwana ['bwaːnə] (*Swahili*) *n.* master.

by-blow ['baɪbləu] *n.* side blow; illegitimate child.

byssus ['bɪsəs] *n.* filamentous tuft ('beard') by which molluscs attach themselves; fine flax and fabric woven from it. **byssaceous**, *adj.* consisting of fine threads; like a byssus. **byssal**, *adj.* **byssiferous**, *adj.* having a byssus; tufted. **byssine**, *adj.* silky; the fabric byssus. **byssogenous**, *adj.* producing a byssus. **byssoid**, *adj.* like a byssus; fibrous; cottony.

byte [baɪt] *n.* in computers, a character consisting of eight 'bits'.

bywoner ['baɪwəunə] (*S African*) *n.* sub-tenant of farm; agricultural labourer.

C

caa'ing whale ['kɑːɪŋ weɪl] n. kind of dolphin, also called blackfish or pilot-whale.

cabal [kə'bæl] n. political coterie or intrigue; v.i. form a cabal.

cabala, cabbala [kə'bɑːlə, 'kæbələ] n. occult knowledge; mystery; mystical interpretation of Scriptures. cabalic [–'bælɪk], adj. cabalism, cabalist, n. cabalistic, adj. mysterious.

caballero [ˌkæbə'leərəʊ] (Spanish) n. knight; gentleman.

caballine ['kæbəlaɪn] adj. equine.

cabochon ['kæbəʃɒn] (French) n. convex-cut, polished stone. en cabochon, cut in that manner.

caboose [kə'buːs] n. ship's galley; American, guard's or engineer's van on goods train.

cabotage ['kæbətɑːʒ, –ɪdʒ] n. coastal navigation; restriction of internal air services to a country's own carriers.

cabriole ['kæbriəʊl] n. outward curving leg, with ornamental foot, of Queen Anne furniture.

cabriolet ['kæbriəleɪ] n. one-horse, two wheeled, single- or two-seater carriage; two-door convertible motor car.

cacaesthesia [ˌkækiːs'θiːziə, –ʒə] n. morbid sensation.

ca' canny [kɔː'kæni, kɑː–] (French) v.i. move cautiously; n. extreme caution; limitation of output by workmen; adj. cautious; mean.

cacao [kə'kaʊ, –'keɪəʊ] n. cocoa tree and seed.

cacciatore [ˌkætʃə'tɔːri] (Italian) adj. made with tomatoes, mushrooms and herbs.

cachaemia [kə'kiːmiə] n. poisoned condition of blood. cachaemic, adj.

cachalot ['kæʃəlɒt] n. sperm whale.

cachepot [ˌkæʃ'pəʊ] n. ornamental plant-pot holder.

cache-sexe [ˌkæʃ'seks] n. small cover for the genitals.

cachet ['kæʃeɪ] (French) n. prestige; distinctive mark or quality; seal.

cachexy, cachexia [kə'keksi, –siə] n. generally unhealthy physical or mental state. cachectic, cachexic, adj.

cachinnate ['kækɪneɪt] v.i. laugh harshly and loudly. cachinnation, cachinato, n. cachinatory [kæ'kɪnətəri], adj.

cachou [kə'ʃuː] n. lozenge for sweetening the breath.

cachucha [kə'tʃuːtʃə] n. quick Spanish dance, with castanet accompaniment.

cacique, cazique [kə'siːk] n. S American, Mexican, and W Indian native chieftain.

cacodemon, cacodaemon [ˌkækə'diːmən] n. evil spirit. cacodemonia [–dɪ'məʊniə], cacodemonomania [–mɒnə'meɪniə], n. insanity in which patients believe themselves to be possessed by evil spirit. cacodemoniac [–dɪ'məʊniæk], adj.

cacodoxy ['kækədɒksi] n. heterodoxy.

cacoepy [kæ'kəʊɪpi, 'kækəʊˌepi] n. incorrect pronunciation. cacoepist, n. cacoepistic, adj.

cacoethes [ˌkækəʊ'iːθiːz] n. strong desire; bad habit. cacoethic [–'eθɪk], adj.

cacogastric [ˌkækə'gæstrɪk] adj. dyspeptic.

cacogenics [ˌkækə'dʒenɪks] n. study or process of racial deterioration. cacogenic, adj.

cacography [kə'kɒgrəfi] n. incorrect spelling or writing. cacographer, n. bad speller. cacographic(al) [ˌkækə'græfɪk, –l], adj.

cacology [kə'kɒlədʒi, kæ–] n. incorrect diction.

caconym ['kækənɪm] n. bad or wrongly derived name. caconymic, adj.

cacophony [kə'kɒfəni, kæ–] n. unpleasant, discordant noise. cacophonic [–'fɒnɪk], cacophonous, adj.

cacuminal [kə'kjuːmɪnl] adj. pertaining to point, top or crown. cacuminate, v.t. sharpen. cacumination, n. cacuminous, adj. pointed.

cadastre [kə'dæstə] n. register of lands, their values and owners. cadastral, adj. cadastration, n. making this.

cadaver [kə'dævə] n. corpse. cadaveric [–'dævərɪk], adj. pertaining to corpses. cadaverous [–'dævərəs], adj. deathly pale; gaunt.

cadence ['keɪdns] n. rhythmical fall or modulation; Music, close of phrase, especially final chords. cadential [–'denʃl], adj.

cadenza [kə'denzə] n. Music, virtuoso passage immediately preceding close of work or section.

cadi ['kɑːdi] n. local judge in Islam.

cadre ['kɑːdə] (French) n. permanent trained unit within an organisation forming nucleus for expansion.

caducary, caduciary [kə'djuːkəri, –ʃiəri] adj. Law, passing by forfeiture, lapse, etc.

caduceus [kə'djuːsiəs] n. (pl. –ei) winged wand entwined with snakes, borne by Mercury; herald's wand of office. caducean, adj.

caducous [kə'djuːkəs] adj. of short duration; Botany, dying when function is completed; deciduous. caducity [–səti], n.

caecum ['siːkəm] n. (pl. –ca), blind outgrowth at junction of large and small intestines, terminating in vermiform appendix. caecal, adj. caeciform ['siːsɪfɔːm], adj. shaped like a caecum, caecity, n. blindness.

caenogenesis [ˌsiːnə'dʒenəsɪs] n. development in individual of processes not common to its species. caenogenetic [–dʒə'netɪk], adj.

caesaropapacy [ˌsiːzərəʊ'peɪpəsi] n. secular possession of highest ecclesiastical power.

caesious ['siːziəs] *adj.* pale blue-green.

caespitose, cespitose ['sespitəʊs] *adj.* growing in tufts.

caesura [si'zjuərə] *n.* natural pause in verse-line. **masculine caesura,** one following stressed syllable of foot. **feminine caesura,** one occurring in unstressed part of line. **caesural,** *adj.*

caftan ['kæftæn] *n.* long, wide-sleeved, girdled gown of Asia Minor and Levant.

cahier ['kaɪeɪ] (*French*) *n.* artist's working notes or drawings; report of proceedings.

caiman, cayman ['keɪmən] *n.* Central and S American alligator.

cainozoic [,kaɪnə'zəʊɪk] *n. & adj. Geology,* tertiary.

caique [kaɪ'iːk] *n.* long, narrow, oared Turkish boat.

cairngorm ['keəngɔːm] *n.* yellowish-brown variety of quartz, especially found in Scottish Cairngorm mountains.

caisson ['keɪsn, -ɒn] *n.* underwater water-tight chamber for bridge-building, etc.; hydraulic lift for raising ship; *Military,* ammunition wagon. **caisson disease,** condition, marked by pain, paralysis or death, due to over-rapid lowering of air pressure after working in compressed air; 'the bends'.

cajun ['keɪdʒən] *n. & adj.* (characteristic of) a descendant of French-speaking immigrants to Louisiana.

calabash ['kæləbæʃ] *n.* gourd.

calamary ['kæləməri] *n.* squid.

calamus ['kæləməs] *n.* feather quill; reed used as pen; Malacca and rattan cane palm.

calash [kə'læʃ] *n.* kind of four-seater carriage with hood; *Canadian,* two-wheeled single-seater driving carriage.

calathiform ['kæləθɪfɔːm, kə'læθ-] *adj.* cup-shaped.

calcaneus [kæl'keɪniəs] *n.* (*pl.* **-nei**) heel bone. **calcaneal, calcanean,** *adj.*

calcareous [kæl'keəriəs] *adj.* pertaining to limestone; consisting of carbonate of lime.

calcariferous [,kælkə'rɪfərəs] *adj.* spurred. **calcariform** [-'kærɪfɔːm], **calcarine,** *adj.* spur-shaped.

calceiform ['kælsiɪfɔːm] *adj.* slipper-shaped.

calcicole ['kælsɪkəʊl] *n.* plant thriving on limy soil.

calcicosis [,kælsɪ'kəʊsɪs] *n.* lung disease due to inhaling limestone dust.

calciferous [kæl'sɪfərəs] *adj.* yielding lime or calcite.

calcific [kæl'sɪfɪk] *adj.* forming lime; produced by calcification.

calciform ['kælsɪfɔːm] *adj.* pebble-shaped.

calcifuge ['kælsɪfjuːdʒ] *n.* plant thriving on soil not rich in lime.

calcify ['kælsɪfaɪ] *v.i. & t.* convert or be converted into lime. **calcification,** *n. Medicine,* tissue hardened by lime deposits.

calcimine ['kælsɪmaɪn] *n. & v.t.* whitewash.

calcine ['kælsaɪn, -sɪn] *v.i. & t.* convert or be converted into powder or lime by burning; roast. **calcination,** *n.* **calcinatory,** *adj.*; *n.* vessel for calcination.

calcite ['kælsaɪt] *n.* calcium carbonate; limestone; Iceland spar.

calcitonin [,kælsɪ'təʊnɪn] *n.* hormone secreted by the thyroid gland, controlling the rate of bone destruction.

calcivorous [kæl'sɪvərəs] *adj.* applied to plants thriving on limestone.

calculus ['kælkjuləs] *n.* (*pl.* **-li**), *Medicine,* stone-like concretion; *Mathematics,* method of calculation. **calculary, calculous,** *adj. Medicine* pertaining to a calculus. **calculiform,** *adj.* pebble-shaped.

calèche [kə'leʃ] (*French*) *n.* calash.

calefacient [,kælɪ'feɪʃiənt] *adj.* warming. **calefaction,** *n.* **calefactive,** *adj.* **calefactory,** *adj.*; *n.* warm room or vessel.

calelectricity [,kælɪlek'trɪsəti] *n.* electricity caused by changes in temperature. **calelectric(al),** *adj.*

calendar ['kæləndə] *n.* system determining the length, starting point and subdivisions of the year; table, chart, etc. showing days, weeks and months of a particular year; schedule of events, engagements, etc.; *v.t.* enter in a calendar. **calendric(al)** [kə'lendrɪk, -l], *adj.*

calender ['kæləndə] *n. & v.t.* mangle or press, especially to produce glazed surface.

calends ['kæləndz] *n. pl.* first day of month in ancient Roman calendar. **at the Greek calends,** never. **calendal** [kæ'lendl], *adj.*

calenture ['kæləntʃə] *n.* sunstroke, or other fever or delirium due to heat.

calescent [kə'lesnt] *adj.* becoming warm. **calescence,** *n.*

calicular, caliculate [kə'lɪkjulə, -lət] *adj.* cup-like.

caliduct ['kælɪdʌkt] *n.* conduit for hot fluid.

caligo [kə'laɪgəʊ] *n.* dim-sightedness. **caliginous** [-'lɪdʒɪnəs], *adj.* dim; obscure.

caliology [,kæli'ɒlədʒi] *n.* study of birds' nests. **caliological,** *adj.* **caliologist,** *n.*

calipash ['kælɪpæʃ] *n.* green, glutinous flesh next to a turtle's carapace.

calipee ['kælɪpiː] *n.* yellowish, glutinous flesh next to a turtle's lower shell.

caliph ['keɪlɪf] *n.* ruler of Islam. **caliphate,** *n.* office and succession of caliph.

calix ['keɪlɪks] *n.* (*pl.* **-ices**) cup; chalice.

calligraphy, caligraphy [kə'lɪgrəfi] *n.* handwriting; penmanship. **calligrapher, calligraphist,** *n.* **calligraphic(al)** [,kælɪ'græfɪk, -l], *adj.*

callipygian, callipygous [,kælɪ'pɪdʒiən, -'paɪgəs] *n.* having well-shaped buttocks.

callisection [,kælɪ'sekʃn] *n.* vivisection of anaesthetized animals.

callisteia [,kælɪ'staɪə] (*Greek*) *n. pl.* beauty prizes.

callisthenics, calisthenics [,kælɪs'θenɪks] *n.* strengthening and beautifying exercises.

calodemon, calodaemon [,kælə'diːmən] *n.* good spirit.

calomel ['kæləmel, -məl] *n.* strong purgative, compound of mercury, acting on liver.

caloric [kə'lɒrɪk, 'kælərɪk] *adj.* pertaining to heat. **calorifacient, calorific,** *adj.* producing heat.

calorimeter [,kælə'rɪmɪtə] *n.* instrument for measuring heat. **calorimetry** *n.*

calotte [kə'lɒt] *n.* skull cap, especially of Roman Catholic clergy; small dome.

calque [kælk] *n.* word or phrase directly translated from one language and used in another.

caltrop ['kæltrəp] *n.* spiked device laid on the ground to disable enemy horses or vehicles.

calumet ['kæljʊmet] *n.* American Indian tobacco pipe of peace.

calumniate [kə'lʌmnieɪt] *v.t.* slander. **calumnious, calumniatory,** *adj.* **calumny** ['kæləmni], **calumniation, calumniator,** *n.*

calvarial [kæl'veəriəl] *adj.* pertaining to crown of head.

calvities [kæl'vɪʃiiːz] *n.* baldness. **calvous,** *adj.*

calx [kælks] *n.* (*pl. calces* ['kælsiːz]) lime; oxide.

calyx ['keɪlɪks] *n.* (*pl.* **–lyces**) outer whorl of generally green floral leaves (sepals) in flower. **calycate,** ['kælɪkeɪt] *adj.* having calyces. **calyciform** [kə'lɪsɪfɔːm], *adj.* calyx-shaped. **calycine** ['kælɪsaɪn], *adj.* pertaining to calyces. **calycoid** ['kælɪkɔɪd], *adj.* calyx-like.

camaraderie [ˌkæmə'raːdəri] (*French*) *n.* comradeship; good fellowship.

camarilla [ˌkæmə'rɪlə] *n.* political secret society, especially of king's favourites.

cambism ['kæmbɪzm] *n.* theory of commercial exchange. **cambist,** *n.* person dealing in bills of exchange. **cambistry,** *n.* study of international exchange.

cambium ['kæmbiəm] *n.* soft enveloping tissue of trees from which new tissues are formed. **cambial,** *adj.* **cambiform,** *adj.* like cambium in nature or function. **cambiogenetic,** *adj.* producing cambium.

camelopard [kə'meləpaːd] *n.* giraffe.

cameralism ['kæmərəlɪzm] *n.* economic theory in which public revenue is sole measure of national prosperity. **cameralist,** *n.* adherent of cameralism. **cameralistic,** *adj.* pertaining to public revenue. **cameralistics,** *n.* study of national finance.

camera lucida [ˌkæmərə 'luːsɪdə] *n.* instrument containing prism by which image of object is projected onto flat surface, where it may be traced.

camera obscura [ˌkæmərə əb'skjʊərə] *n.* box or chamber with lens throwing onto screen image of object outside.

camerate(d) [kæm'əreɪt, –ɪd] *adj.* divided into chambers. **cameration,** *n.* division into chambers; vaulting.

cameriere [ˌkæməri'eəreɪ] *n.* (*pl.* **–ri**, *fem.* **cameriera**, *pl.* **–re**) valet; waiter.

camerlingo, camerlengo [ˌkæmə'lɪŋgəʊ, –'leŋ–] *n.* papal treasurer.

camion ['kæmiən] (*French*) *n.* flat, low, four-wheeled truck or dray.

camisade, camisado [ˌkæmɪ'seɪd, –'saːd, –əʊ] *n.* attack by night.

camlet ['kæmlət] *n.* fine dress fabric of silk and camel-hair, or wool and goat's hair. **camleteen, camletine** [ˌkæmlə'tiːn], *n.* imitation camlet of hair and worsted.

camomile, chamomile ['kæməmaɪl] *n.* common daisy-like plant, yielding drug of wide use.

camorra [kə'mɒrə] (*Italian*) *n.* secret terrorist organisation, especially of 19th-century. **camorrism, camorrist,** *n.*

campaniform [kæm'pænɪfɔːm] *adj.* bell-shaped.

campanile [ˌkæmpə'niːli] *n.* free-standing bell-tower.

campanology [ˌkæmpə'nɒlədʒi] *n.* study and knowledge of bells; bell-making; bell-ringing.

campanological, *adj.* **campanologist,** *n.* **campanist,** *n.* expert on bells; bell-ringer.

campanulate, campanular, campanulous [kæm'pænjulət, –lə, –ləs] *adj.* bell-shaped.

campestral, campestrial [kæm'pestrəl, –iəl] *adj.* pertaining to or thriving in open countryside.

canaille [kə'naɪ] (*French*) *n.* the mob; rabble.

canard ['kænaːd] (*French*) *n.* baseless rumour; hoax.

canasta [kə'næstə] *n.* elaborate form of rummy (card-game) with partners.

canaster [kə'næstə] *n.* coarse tobacco.

cancellate(d), cancellous [kæn'sɪleɪt, –ɪd] *adj.* marked with network of lines; having a sponge-like structure.

cancriform ['kæŋkrɪfɔːm] *adj.* crab-shaped; *Medicine*, cancer-like. **cancrivorous,** *adj.* feeding on crabs. **cancrizans,** *adj.* moving crab-wise or backwards; *Music*, having theme repeated backwards. **cancroid,** *adj.* crab-like; cancer-like.

candent ['kændənt] *adj.* white-hot.

candescent [kæn'desnt] *n.* glowing. **candescence,** *n.*

canephorus [kæ'niːfərəs] *n.* (*pl.* **–ri**) sculpture of a young man or woman carrying a basket on head.

canescent [kə'nesnt] *adj.* becoming white; hoary. **canescence,** *n.*

cang(ue) [kæŋ] *n.* wooden yoke, inscribed with list of his offences, hung round criminal's neck in China.

canicular [kə'nɪkjʊlə] *adj.* pertaining to dog star or dog days.

canities [kə'nɪsiiːz] *adj.* whiteness of hair.

cannel ['kænl] *n.* kind of fine, brightly burning coal.

cannellate(d) [kæn'ɪleɪt, –ɪd] *adj.* fluted. **cannelure,** *n.* groove, especially in cartridge.

cannular, cannulate ['kænjʊlə, –lət] *adj.* hollow; tubular.

canon ['kænən] *n.* law; code, especially ecclesiastical; criterion; authentic or accepted books especially of Bible; list; *Music*, part-song in which opening passage is strictly repeated. **canonical** [kə'nɒnɪkl], *adj.* according to ecclesiastical law; authentic; legal. **canonicals,** *n. pl.* clergyman's costume or robes. **canonics,** *n.* study of canon of Bible.

canonist ['kænənɪst] *n.* expert on canon law; strict adherent of rules.

canopus [kə'nəʊpəs] *adj.* (*pl.* **–pi**) ancient Egyptian vase for holding viscera of dead. **canopic,** *adj.*

canorous [kə'nɔːrəs] *adj.* sweet-sounding.

cant [kænt] *n.* jargon or slang of a particular group; hypocritical use of pious phraseology.

cantaloup(e) ['kæntəluːp] *n.* kind of small melon.

cantatory [kæn'teɪtəri, 'kæntə–] *adj.* pertaining to singer or singing.

cantatrice [ˌkæntə'triːs, –'triːtʃeɪ] (*French*) *n.* female singer.

cantharides [kæn'θærɪdiːz] *n. pl.* medical preparation of dried Spanish flies, formerly used as a diuretic or aphrodisiac. **cantharidal,** *adj.* **cantharidate,** *v.t.* treat with this. **cantharidean, cantharidian,** *adj.* made of this. **cantharidism,** *n.* condition due to excessive use of this.

canthus ['kænθəs] *n.* angle between eyelids at corner of eye. **canthal,** *adj.*

canticle ['kæntɪkl] *n.* short psalm; holy song.

cantilena [ˌkæntɪ'liːnə, -'leɪ-] *n.* smooth, flowing melody or vocal style.

cantilever ['kæntɪliːvə] *n.* projecting bracket. **cantilever bridge,** bridge composed of two or more cantilevers, not supporting each other, as Forth Bridge.

cantle ['kæntl] *n.* slice; hinder saddle-bow.

cantonment [kæn'tuːnmənt] *n.* troops' camp or barracks; small military station, especially in British India.

cantor ['kæntɔː] *n.* liturgical singer and leader of prayers in synagogue; precentor. **cantoral, cantorial** [-'tɔːr-], *adj.* pertaining to the north, or precentor's, side of choir.

cantus firmus [ˌkæntəs 'fɜːməs] (*Latin*) *n.* plainchant melody; melodic theme, especially in counterpoint.

canzone [kæn'zəuni] *n.* song; lyric; song-like instrumental piece. **canzonet** [-ə'net], *n.* short song or melody.

caoutchouc ['kautʃuk] *n.* rubber, especially pure. **caoutchoucin(e)** [-sɪn], *n.* rubber oil.

capacitance [kə'pæsɪtəns] *n. Electricity,* ability to store an electric charge; measure of such ability. **capacitor,** *n.* device for accumulating electric charge.

cap-à-pie [ˌkæpə'piː] *adv.* from head to foot.

caparison [kə'pærɪsən] *n.* armour; harness; trappings; *v.t.* place such covering upon.

capeador ['kæpiədɔː, -'dɔː] (*Spanish*) *n.* bull-fighter carrying red cloak.

capercailzie, capercaillie, capercailye [ˌkæpə'keɪli] *n.* largest grouse bird.

capias ['kæpiæs] *n.* writ of arrestment.

capillary [kə'pɪləri] *adj.* pertaining to or like a hair; *n.* minute hair-like blood-vessel. **capillaceous** [ˌkæpɪ'leɪʃəs], capillose ['kæpɪləus], *adj.* hairy; bristly. **capilliform,** *adj.* hair-like. **capillarimeter,** *n.* instrument measuring liquid by action of capillarity. **capillarity** [-'lærəti], *n.* movement of liquid up or down when in contact with solid, due to surface tension.

capistrate [kə'pɪstreɪt] *adj.* hooded.

capitate ['kæpɪteɪt] *adj.* head-like. **capitatim** [ˌkæpɪ'teɪtɪm] *adv.* per head. **capitation,** *n.* counting or levying by the head, *i.e.* per person; poll tax. **capitative,** *adj.* per person.

capitular [kə'pɪtjulə] *adj.* pertaining to cathedral chapter. **capitulary,** *n.* statute or member of such chapter.

capon ['keɪpən] *n.* castrated cock, especially fattened for table. **caponize,** *v.t.* castrate.

caporal [ˌkæpə'ræl] *n.* coarse tobacco.

capote [kə'pəut] *n.* lady's long hooded cloak.

capreolate ['kæpriəleɪt, kə'priː-] *adj.* having tendrils.

capric ['kæprɪk] *adj.* pertaining to goat. **caprid,** *n.* goat.

caprificate ['kæprɪfɪkeɪt] *v.t.* improve (cultivated figs) by artificial pollination from wild figs. **caprification,** *n.*

caprifig ['kæprɪfɪg] *n.* wild fig.

caprifoliaceous [ˌkæprɪfəuli'eɪʃəs] *adj.* pertaining to or like honeysuckle; belonging to honeysuckle family of plants.

caprine, caprinic ['kæpraɪn, kə'prɪnɪk] *adj.* pertaining to or like goat.

capriole ['kæpriəul] *n.* leap and kick by trained horse.

capripede ['kæprɪpiːd] *n.* satyr.

capsicum ['kæpsɪkəm] *n.* plant yielding (*e.g.* red or green) peppers; its fruit.

captation [kæp'teɪʃn] *n.* attempt to obtain applause or recognition.

captious ['kæpʃəs] *adj.* fault-finding.

capybara [ˌkæpɪ'bɑːrə] *n.* the largest rodent, a guinea-pig-like, webbed-footed mammal of S America.

carabiniere [ˌkærəbɪn'jeəri] (*Italian*) *n.* (*pl.* **–ri**) policeman; soldier armed with carbine.

caracal ['kærəkæl] *n.* lynx of Africa and Asia.

caracole ['kærəkəul] *n.* half turn by trained horse; caper; *v.i.* make such turn.

carapace ['kærəpeɪs] *n.* exo-skeleton; protective shell of tortoise, etc. **carapacic,** *adj.*

caravanserai, caravansary [ˌkærə'vænsəraɪ, –ri] *n.* Eastern inn, especially for accommodation of caravans.

caravel, carvel ['kærəvel, 'kɑːvel] *n.* small three- or four-masted ship of 15th and 16th centuries; Turkish battleship.

carbacidometer [ˌkɑːbəsɪ'dɒmɪtə] *n.* instrument measuring quantity of carbon dioxide in air.

carbasus ['kɑːbəsəs] *n.* lint; gauze.

carbomycin [ˌkɑːbə'maɪsɪn] *n.* antibiotic drug obtained from a soil fungus, used chiefly against respiratory infections.

carbonade [ˌkɑːbə'neɪd, -'nɑːd] (*French*) *n.* beef stew made with beer.

carbonado [ˌkɑːbə'neɪdəu, -'nɑː] *n.* piece of meat, fish etc., scored and grilled.

carbonari [ˌkɑːbə'nɑːri] *n. pl.* (*sing.* **–ro**) members of secret 19th-century Italian republican association.

carbonic [kɑː'bɒnɪk] *adj.* pertaining to carbon. **carboniferous** [ˌkɑːbə'nɪfərəs], *adj.* containing coal. **Carboniferous,** *adj. & n. Geology,* (of) a period between 270 and 350 million years ago. **carbonize** ['kɑːbənaɪz], *v.i. & t.* convert into carbon; char.

carborundum [ˌkɑːbə'rʌndəm] *n.* polishing substance compounded of silicon and carbon.

carboy ['kɑːbɔɪ] *n.* large wicker-covered bottle.

carbuncle ['kɑːbʌŋkl] *n.* large boil; garnet cut en cabochon. **carbuncular** [kɑː'bʌŋkjulə], *adj.*

carburet [ˌkɑːbə'ret] *v.t.* combine or charge with carbon. **carburation,** *n.* charging air with enough fuel vapour to render mixture explosive.

carcajou ['kɑːkədʒuː, -əʒuː] *n.* wolverine; cougar; N American badger.

carcanet ['kɑːkənet] *n.* jewelled necklace or collar.

carcinogen [kɑː'sɪnədʒən, -en] *n.* a cancer-causing substance. **carcinogenic** [ˌkɑːsɪnə'dʒenɪk], *adj.*

carcinology [ˌkɑːsɪ'nɒlədʒi] *n.* study of crustaceans. **carcinomorphic,** *adj.* like a crab or crustacean. **carcinophagous,** *adj.* feeding on crabs.

carcinoma [ˌkɑːsɪ'nəumə] *n.* (*pl.* **–mata, –mas**) a form of malignant cancer. **carcinomatous** [-'nɒmətəs, -'nəu-], *adj.* **carcinomatosis,** *n.* condition characterized by multiple carcinomas.

cardamon, cardamom ['kɑːdəmən, -əm] *n.* seeds and fruit of an E Indian plant, used in medicine as stimulant, etc.

cardiac ['kɑːdiæk] *adj.* pertaining to heart; *n.* stimulant for heart or stomach. **cardialgia**, *n.* heartburn.

cardinal ['kɑːdɪnl] *n. & adj.* (applied to) simple numbers, 1, 2, 3, etc.; applied to N, S, E, and W points of compass.

cardiology [ˌkɑːdi'ɒlədʒi] *n.* study of heart and its diseases. **cardiograph** ['kɑː–], *n.* instrument recording heart's movements. **cardiography** [–'ɒg–], *n.* description of heart. **cardioid** ['kɑːdiɔɪd], *adj.* heart-shaped. **cardiometry** [–'ɒm–], *n.* measurement of heart. **cardiopathy** [–'ɒpəθi], *n.* heart disease. **cardiotomy** [–'ɒtəmi], *n.* incision into heart or upper end of stomach. **cardiovascular** [ˌkɑːdiəʊ'væskjʊlə], *adj.* pertaining to heart and blood vessels. **carditis** [kɑː'daɪtɪs], *n.* inflammation of cardiac tissue.

cardophagus [kɑː'dɒfəgəs] *n.* (*pl.* **–gi** [–dʒaɪ]) eater of thistles; donkey.

careen [kə'riːn] *v.i. & t.* heel over; turn on side for repairs.

carême [kæ'rem] (*French*) *n.* Lent.

caret ['kærɪt] *n.* mark (°) indicating omission.

caribou ['kærɪbuː] *n.* N American and Greenland reindeer.

caricology [ˌkærɪ'kɒlədʒi] *n.* study of sedges. **caricography**, *n.* description of sedges.

caricous ['kærɪkəs] *adj.* fig-like.

caries ['keəriz, –iːz] *n.* decay of bone or tooth. **cariogenic**, *adj.* producing caries. **carious**, *adj.* pertaining to caries; decayed.

carillon [kə'rɪljən, 'kærɪlɒn] (*French*) *n.* peal of bells. **carilloneur** [–'nɜː], **carillonist**, *n.* player on carillon.

carinate ['kærɪneɪt] *adj.* like or having a keel. **carinal, cariniform** [kə'rɪnɪfɔːm], *adj.* keel-shaped. **carination**, *n.*

cariole, carriole ['kærɪəʊl] *n.* light one-horse carriage or cart; *Canadian*, kind of sleigh.

caritative ['kærɪtətɪv] *adj.* charitable.

carmagnole [ˌkɑːmæn'jəʊl] (*French*) *n.* wide-lapelled, buttoned jacket of Piedmont; costume of Jacobin French revolutionaries, including the carmagnole, red cap and tricolour sash; French revolutionary song and dance.

carminative ['kɑːmɪnətɪv] *n. & adj.* (medicine) expelling wind.

carnassial [kɑː'næsɪəl] *adj.* (of teeth) adapted for tearing.

carnelian [kɑː'niːliən] *n.* hard, red variety of chalcedony.

carneous ['kɑːnɪəs] *adj.* like or of flesh; flesh-coloured. **carnifex**, *n.* executioner. **carnification**, *n.* conversion into flesh. **carnificial**, *adj.* pertaining to executioner or butcher. **carniform**, *adj.* flesh-like. **carnify**, *v.t.* convert into or become like flesh. **carnivorous** [–'nɪv–], *adj.* flesh-eating. **carnose**, *adj.* fleshy.

carnet ['kɑːneɪ] (*French*) *n.* customs licence for temporary importation of motor vehicle.

carob ['kærəb] *n.* Mediterranean plant yielding edible pulp used *e.g.* as chocolate substitute.

carom ['kærəm] (*American*) *n.* cannon (in billiards); *v.i.* cannon; rebound.

caronamide [kə'rɒnəmaɪd] *n.* substance that prolongs the action of penicillin by preventing its excretion.

carotene ['kærətiːn] *n.* yellowish-red hydrocar-

bon giving colour to carrots, butter, etc., and converted into vitamin A in the body.

carotid [kə'rɒtɪd] *n. & adj.* (artery) conducting blood to head. **carotic**, *adj.* comatose.

carpe diem [ˌkɑːpi 'diːem] (*Latin*) 'enjoy the day'; seize opportunity; 'make hay while sun shines'.

carpel ['kɑːpl] *n. Botany*, pistil; organ forming part of pistil. **carpellary**, *adj.* **carpellate**, *adj.* having carpels. **carpid(ium)**, *n.* small carpel.

carpitis [kɑː'paɪtɪs] *n.* arthritis of carpus.

carpogenous [kɑː'pɒdʒənəs] *adj.* fruit-producing. **carpolith, carpolite**, *n.* fossil fruit or seed. **carpology**, *n.* study of fruit structure. **carpophagous**, *adj.* feeding on fruit.

carpus ['kɑːpəs] *n.* (*pl.* **–pi**) wrist; small bones of wrist. **carpal**, *adj.*

carrack ['kærək] *n.* galleon.

carrageen ['kærəgiːn] *n.* kind of dark red, branched seaweed; Irish moss.

carrel, carrell ['kærəl] *n.* booth for individual study in library.

carronade [ˌkærə'neɪd] *n.* kind of short, light ship's gun.

carron oil ['kærən ɔɪl] *n.* lotion, composed of limewater and linseed oil, formerly used for burns.

carte blanche [ˌkɑːt 'blɑːnʃ] (*French*) 'white card'; permission to act freely.

cartel [kɑː'tel] *n.* association of business organizations, to limit competition and maintain prices; alliance of political parties. **cartelize**, *v.t.* **cartelist**, *n.*

cartilage ['kɑːtəlɪdʒ] *n.* gristle. **cartilaginoid** [–'lædʒɪnɔɪd], *adj.* like cartilage. **cartilaginous** [–'lædʒɪnəs], *adj.* pertaining to or composed of this.

cartogram ['kɑːtəgræm] *n.* map showing statistical information diagrammatically.

cartography [kɑː'tɒgrəfi] *n.* map-making. **cartographer**, *n.* **cartographic**, *adj.*

cartomancy ['kɑːtəmænsi] (*French*) *n.* divination or fortune-telling by playing-cards.

carton pierre [ˌkɑːtɒn pi'eə] (*French*) *n.* kind of papier-mâché imitative of stone or bronze.

cartouch(e) [kɑː'tuːʃ] *n.* scroll- or shield-shaped or oval ornamentation; oval figure containing ancient Egyptian king's name and titles; cartridge-case.

caruncle [kə'rʌŋkl, 'kærəŋkl] *n.* fleshy outgrowth. **caruncular, carunculous** [–'rʌŋk–], *adj.* **carunculate**, *adj.* having caruncles.

carvel-built ['kɑːvlbɪlt] *adj.* (of a ship) with planks meeting flush at the seams.

caryatid [kɑː'tuːʃ] *n.* sculptured female figure acting as pillar. **caryatidal, caryatic**, *adj.*

casaque [kæ'zæk] (*French*) *n.* cassock; blouse.

casease ['keɪsieɪz] *n.* enzyme decomposing the casein in milk and cheese.

casein ['keɪsiːn, –siːn] *n.* essential albumin of milk. **acid casein**, curd. **caseate**, *v.i.* become cheese-like. **caseation**, *n.* **casefy**, *v.i. & t.* become or make cheese-like. **caseous**, *adj.* like cheese.

casemate ['keɪsmeɪt] *n.* bomb-proof room in fortification.

casern(e) [kə'sɜːn] *n.* garrison's barracks.

cassation [kæ'seɪʃn] *n.* annulment. *Music*, a serenade-like instrumental composition for out-

Confusibles

Alcohol doesn't affect me; it has no effect on me at all.
● **affect** is a verb; **effect** is its corresponding noun. But note, there is also a verb *effect*, meaning 'to bring about': *to effect changes*.

a biannual publication; a biennial music festival
● **biannual** means 'twice a year, six-monthly'; **biennial** means 'once every two years'.

The phone's continual ringing got on her nerves. When she picked it up, all she could hear was a continuous tone.
● **continual** means 'happening repeatedly'; **continuous** means 'going on without interruption'.

I wouldn't want to depreciate your talents, but I deprecate your boasting about them.
● To **depreciate** something is to belittle it but if you **deprecate** something you disapprove of it or protest against it.

Even someone of his equable temperament would protest at such lack of equitable treatment.
● **equable** means 'calm, steady, mild'; **equitable** means 'fair, just'.

She flouts my authority, and flaunts her disobedience.
● If you **flout** something you show contempt for it or disregard it; if you **flaunt** something, you show it off ostentatiously or proudly.

the dancer's graceful movements; the antelope's gracile limbs
● **graceful** denotes elegance in form, movement, or style. **gracile**, an unrelated word, is often used in the same sense, but strictly speaking it means 'slender'.

It was a historic moment for the Historical Society.
● **historical** means 'relating to history or past events' or 'having existed a very long time'; **historic** can be used in these senses too but its commonest meaning is probably 'of far-reaching significance, momentous'.

He implied that I was a fool. I inferred from this that he was angry.
● If you **imply** something, you suggest it in a rather roundabout way; if you **infer** something, you deduce it from what someone says or does.

There's to be a judicial review of your case. It would be judicious to attend.
● **judicial** refers to to the proceedings of courts and judges; **judicious** means 'prudent, wise'.

Try to curb your horse from mounting the kerb.
● A **kerb** is the edge of a pavement; to **curb** something is to restrain it or hold it back. (Note that in American English the spelling *curb* is used for both words.)

I laid a wreath on his grave. It lies there still.
● **lay** is a transitive verb. It needs an object. You have to *lay* 'something'. **lie** is an intransitive verb,

so it does not have an object. The two are apt to be confused because the past tense of *lie* is *lay*.

Nothing can mitigate the seriousness of his offence which militates against his acceptance into the society.
● To **mitigate** something is to moderate it or lessen its seriousness; to **militate** against something is to have a strong negative effect on its likelihood.

the foul and noisome exhalations of the pit
● **noisome** has no connection with *noise*. In fact, its nearest relative is *annoy*. It means 'offensive' or 'noxious'.

Your methods are obsolescent; in twenty years time they will be obsolete.
● Something that is **obsolescent** is becoming out of date; something that is **obsolete** already *is* out of date.

The principal reason for her failure is her lack of principles.
● **principal** is an adjective meaning 'main' (and also a noun denoting the leading person or director); **principle** is a noun meaning 'rule of (moral) conduct'.

'I'm ravenous,' said the ravishing blonde; 'let's eat.'
● **ravenous** means 'extremely hungry', **ravishing**, 'extremely beautiful'.

To use solipsism to mean 'mistake' would be a solecism.
● **solipsism** is in fact a philosophical term which denotes the denial of any possibility of knowledge outside one's own experience. A **solecism** is a mistake, especially in the use of language or in good manners.

the long and tortuous road and the torturous pain in his feet.
● **tortuous** means 'winding intricately', and has no direct connection with *torture*; **torturous**, on the other hand, means 'like torture, agonising'.

Sorry to be unsociable but my unsocial working hours mean that I have to be in bed by 5 p.m.
● Someone who is **unsociable** is unfriendly and unwilling to mix with others; **unsocial** working hours are ones that do not fit in with normal social arrangements.

venal judges committing venial sins
● **venal** implies corruption, the compromising of one's honesty for money; **venial** is a much less condemnatory word, used for characterizing sins that are not considered very serious.

By waiving her rights, she waved goodbye to her freedom.
● To **waive** something, such as a right or claim, is to renounce it or defer it willingly. The word should not be confused with **wave** 'to gesture with the hand'.

---

door performance. **court of cassation,** highest French court of appeal.

cassava [kə'sɑːvə] *n.* tropical plant with roots yielding starch used in tapioca making; manioc.

cassideous [kə'sɪdiəs] *adj.* helmet-shaped.

cassidony ['kæsɪdəni] (*French*) *n.* lavender.

cassiterite [kə'sɪtərɑɪt] *n.* native dioxide of tin, the chief ore of tin.

cassowary ['kæsəweəri, –wəri] *n.* emu-like bird of Australasia. **cassowary tree,** casuarina.

castanean, castanian [kæ'steɪnɪən] *adj.* pertaining to chestnut. **castaneous,** *adj.* chestnut-coloured.

castellan ['kæstələn] *n.* castle governor. **castellany,** *n.* jurisdiction of castellan.

castellar [kæ'stelə] *adj.* pertaining to or like a castle.

castellate(d) [kæs'təleɪt, –ɪd] *adj.* battlemented; turreted; castle-like in appearance. **castellation,** *n.*

castigate ['kæstɪgeɪt] *v.t.* punish; reprove; criticize severely. **castigation, castigator,** *n.* **castigative, castigatory,** *adj.*

castor ['kɑːstə] *n.* substance derived from beaver and used in perfumery; hat, especially of beaver fur. **castory,** *n.* brown colour obtained from this.

castral ['kæstrəl] *adj.* pertaining to camp.

castrametation [ˌkæstrəmɪ'teɪʃn] *n.* art of laying out a camp.

castrato [kæ'strɑːtəʊ, kə–] (*Italian*) *n.* (*pl.* –ti) treble or alto male singer whose voice was prevented from breaking by castration.

castrensian [kæ'strensɪən] *adj.* castral.

casualism ['kæʒuəlɪzm, 'kæzju–] *n.* doctrine that all things happen by chance.

casuarina [ˌkæʒju'riːnə, ˌkæzjuə–] *n.* Australian oak.

casuist ['kæzjuɪst, 'kæʒ–] *n.* sophist; resolver of questions of conscience. **casuistic,** *adj.* **casuistry,** *n.* study of rules of right and wrong; application of such rules to particular cases; false reasoning, especially on moral matters.

casus belli [ˌkɑːsʊs 'beliː, ˌkeɪsəs 'belaɪ] (*Latin*) *n.* event which justifies a declaration of war.

catabaptist [ˌkætə'bæptɪst] *n.* opponent of infant baptism.

catabasis [kə'tæbəsɪs] *n.* (*pl.* –ses) decline of disease. **catabatic** [ˌkætə'bætɪk], *adj.*

catabolism [kə'tæbəlɪzm] *n.* destructive chemical processes in living creatures. **catabolic** [ˌkætə'bɒlɪk], *adj.* **catabolize,** *v.t.*

catachresis [ˌkætə'kriːsɪs] *n.* use of wrong words. **catachrestic** [–'krestɪk], *adj.*

catachthonian, catachthonic [ˌkætək'θəʊnɪən, –'θɒnɪk] *adj.* subterranean.

cataclasis [ˌkætə'kleɪsɪs, kə'tækləsɪs] *n.* (*pl.* –ses) *Geology,* deformation of rocks by crushing and shearing. **cataclastic,** *adj.*

cataclasm ['kætəklæzm] *n.* breaking down. **cataclasmic,** *adj.*

cataclysm ['kætəklɪzm] *n.* catastrophe; upheaval. **cataclysmal, cataclysmic** [–'klɪz–], *adj.*

catacoustic [ˌkætə'kuːstɪk] *adj.* pertaining to echoes. **catacoustics,** *n.* study of echoes.

catadioptric [ˌkætədaɪ'ɒptrɪk] *adj.* pertaining or due to both reflection and refraction of light. **catadioptrics,** *n.* study of such phenomena.

catadromous [kə'tædrəməs] *adj.* migrating from fresh to salt water to spawn.

catafalque ['kætəfælk] *n.* fixed bier for lying-in-state.

catakinetic [ˌkætəkaɪ'netɪk] *adj.* destructive of energy.

catalectic [ˌkætə'lektɪk] *adj.* lacking a syllable at end. **catalexis,** *n.*

catalepsy ['kætəlepsi] *n.* rigid or trance-like fit. **cataleptic** [–'leptɪk], *adj.* **cataleptiform,** *adj.* like catalepsy.

catallactic [ˌkætə'læktɪk] *adj.* pertaining to exchange. **catallactics,** *n.* study of commercial exchange.

catalpa [kə'tælpə] *n.* ornamental American and Asiatic tree; Indian bean.

catalysis [kə'tæləsɪs] *n.* alteration in speed of chemical reaction due to introduction of a substance which remains unchanged. **catalyse** ['kætəlaɪz], *v.t.* **catalyst,** ['kætəlɪst], *n.* such introduced substance. **catalytic** [ˌkætə'lɪtɪk], *adj.*; *n.* catalyst; alterative. **catalytic converter,** *n.* device for reducing toxic emissions from internal-combustion engine.

catamenia [ˌkætə'miːnɪə] *n.* *Medicine,* menstruation. **catamenial,** *adj.*

catamite ['kætəmaɪt] *n.* boy kept for homosexual purposes.

catamount(ain) ['kætəmaʊnt, ˌkætə'maʊntɪn] *n.* wild cat.

cataphasia [ˌkætə'feɪzɪə, –ʒə] *n.* speech disorder involving constant repetition of word or phrase.

cataphoresis [ˌkætəfə'riːsɪs] *n.* movement, due to application of electricity, of particles through fluid; injection of drugs electrically. **cataphoretic** [–'retɪk], *adj.*

cataplasm ['kætəplæzm] *n.* poultice.

cataplexy ['kætəpleksi] *n.* catalepsy-like trance or fit due to shock; motionlessness in animals feigning death.

catastaltic [ˌkætə'stæltɪk] *n.* & *adj.* (drug) exercising restraint; astringent.

catastasis [kə'tæstəsɪs] *n.* (*pl.* –ses) climax or culmination of drama.

catastrophe [kə'tæstrəfi] *n.* *Literature,* denouement or unravelling of drama after climax. **catastrophic** [ˌkætə'strɒfɪk], *adj.* **catastrophism,** *n.* *Geology,* theory that sudden isolated upheavals were responsible for geological changes. **catastrophist,** *n.* believer in such theory.

catatonia [ˌkætə'təʊnɪə] *n.* severe mental disturbance marked by catalepsy. **catatonic** [–'tɒnɪk], *adj.*

catchment ['kætʃmənt] *n.* water collection; reservoir. **catchment area,** area draining into reservoir, etc.; area from which institution draws its attendance.

catchpole, catchpoll ['kætʃpəʊl] *n.* bumbailiff.

catechesis [ˌkætɪ'kiːsɪs] *n.* (*pl.* –ses) oral instruction in Christian doctrine. **catechetic(al)** [–'ket–], *adj.*

catechism ['kætɪkɪzm] *n.* teaching by question and answer; summary of religious doctrine in question and answer form. **catechize,** *v.t.* **catechist,** *n.* teacher by catechism; native Christian teacher.

catechu ['kætətʃuː] *n.* astringent substance extracted from fruit, wood or leaves of several tropical plants including acacias and areca palm.

catechumen [ˌkætə'kjuːmən, –en] *n.* person receiving instruction, especially in religion. **catechumenate, catechumenism,** *n.* status of a catechumen **catechumenical** [–kju'menɪkl], *adj.*

categorical imperative [ˌkætə'gɒrɪkl ɪm'perətɪv] *n.* philosophical principle of Kant—an action willed to be good in itself, and not only good as a means to an end.

catena [kə'tiːnə] *n.* chain; series. **catenoid** ['kætɪnɔɪd], **catenular, catenulate** [–'ten–], *adj.* chain-like. **catenarian** [–ɪ'neərɪən], *adj.* pertaining to chain or catenary. **catenary**, *adj.* chain-like; *n.* curve assumed by chain suspended between two points. **catenate** ['kætɪneɪt], *v.t.* join together like a chain; *adj.* chain-like. **catenation**, *n.*

catharsis [kə'θɑːsɪs] *n.* (*pl.* **-ses**) purging; *Literature* purging of emotions by tragedy. **cathartic** [kə'θɑːtɪk], *n.* & *adj.* purgative.

cathedra [kə'θiːdrə] *n.* throne; bishop's or professor's chair. **ex cathedra**, *Latin*, 'from the chair'; authoritative. **cathedratic** [,kæθɪ'drætɪk], *adj.*

catheter ['kæθɪtə] *n.* *Medicine*, tube introduced into bladder through urethra. **catheterize** ['kæθɪtəraɪz], *v.t.*

cathetometer [,kæθɪ'tɒmɪtə] *n.* instrument measuring small vertical distances with great accuracy.

cathode ['kæθəud] *n.* negative terminal; electrode by which current leaves. **cathode particle**, electron. **cathode ray**, stream of electrons from cathode to anode in discharge tube. **cathode ray tube**, vacuum tube in television receiver on fluorescent end of which (the screen) picture is created by cathode rays. **cathodic** [kə'θɒdɪk], *adj.* **cathodograph**, *n.* X-ray photograph.

catholicon [kə'θɒlɪkən] *n.* panacea.

catholyte ['kæθəlaɪt] *n.* portion of electrolyte about cathode.

cation ['kæt,aɪən] *n.* positively charged ion moving towards cathode in electrolysis.

catogenic [,kætə'dʒenɪk] *adj.* *Geology*, formed from above; sedimentary.

catoptric [kə'tɒptrɪk] *adj.* pertaining to reflection of light. **catoptromancy**, *n.* divination by gazing into mirror or crystal. **catoptrics**, *n.* study of reflection.

cattalo ['kætələu] *n.* a cross between domestic cattle and N American bison.

caucus ['kɔːkəs] *n.* small powerful committee, especially in political party; meeting of such committee.

caudal ['kɔːdl] *adj.* pertaining to tail. **caudad**, *adv.* towards tail. **caudate**, *adj.* tailed. **caudiform**, *adj.* tail-like.

caul [kɔːl] *n.* membrane sometimes covering head of new-born infant, and regarded as lucky.

cauline ['kɔːlaɪn] (*Botany*) *adj.* growing on stem. **cauliform**, *adj.* like a stem. **cauligenous**, *adj.* borne on stem. **caulescent**, *adj.* with aerial stem. **caulome**, *n.* stem structure of plant. **caulotaxy**, *n.* disposition of branches on stem.

cause célèbre [,kəuz sə'leb] (*French*) *n.* (*pl.* **causes célèbres**) 'famous lawsuit', especially one creating much public stir.

causerie ['kəuzəri] (*French*) *n.* 'chat'; writing in conversational tone.

cautery ['kɔːtəri] *n.* medical instrument used for searing wounds, etc.; use of such instrument. **cauterant**, *adj.*; **cauterize**, *v.t.*

cavatina [,kævə'tiːnə] *n.* simple song or melody.

cave ['keɪvi, ,keɪ'viː] (*Latin*) 'beware'; look out! **cave canem**, 'beware of the dog'. **keeping cave**, acting as look-out.

caveat ['kæviæt, 'keɪ-] *n.* injunction to stop proceedings; warning. **caveat emptor**, (*Latin*), 'let the purchaser beware'.

cavernicolous [,kævə'nɪkələs] *adj.* living in caves. **cavernulous** [kə'vɜːnjuləs], *adj.* full of small cavities.

cavicorn ['kævɪkɔːn] *adj.* with hollow horns.

cavil ['kævl] *v.i.* find fault; *n.* querulous objection.

cavo-relievo [,kɑːvəurɪ'liːvəu] *n.* sculpture in which highest part is level with surface of stone; hollow relief.

cavy ['keɪvi] *n.* several small rodents; guinea-pig.

cayman *see* **caiman**.

CD-ROM [,siːdiːrɒm] *abbreviation* for compact disc read-only memory: computer storage device using compact-disc technology.

cecidiology [sɪ,sɪdɪ'ɒlədʒi] *n.* study of insect galls. **cecidiologist**, *n.* **cecidiogenous**, *adj.* causing galls.

cecil ['sesl] *n.* forcemeat ball.

cedilla [sə'dɪlə] *n.* comma-like mark (ç) indicating that *c* is pronounced sibilant.

cedrate ['siːdreɪt] *n.* citron.

ceil [siːl] *v.t.* cover with plaster, boarding etc.; give a ceiling to.

ceilidh ['keɪli] (*Scottish*, *Irish*) *n.* informal gathering with music, dancing etc.

ceilometer [siː'lɒmɪtə] *n.* instrument measuring the distance between cloud ceiling and Earth's surface.

celadon ['selədɒn] *n.* porcelain with greyish-green glaze; pale greyish green.

celation [sə'leɪʃn] *n.* concealment. **celative** ['selətɪv], *adj.*

celature ['selətʃə] *n.* process of embossing metal.

celerity [sə'lerəti] *n.* swiftness.

celibatarian [,selɪbə'teəriən] *n.* & *adj.* (person) advocating celibacy.

celidography [,selɪ'dɒgrəfi] *n.* description of sun's or planet's surface markings. **celidographer**, *n.*

cellulosic [,selju'ləusɪk] *n.* plastic made from cellulose.

celoscope ['siːləskəup] *n.* *Medicine*, instrument for examining body cavities.

celt [selt] *n.* prehistoric edged stone, bronze or iron implement. **celtiform**, *adj.* celt-shaped.

cembalo ['tʃembələu] *n.* dulcimer; harpsichord; any musical instrument with hammers to strike strings. **cembalist**, *n.* player on a cembalo.

cenacle ['senəkl] *n.* dining-room, especially room in which the Last Supper was held.

cenobite ['senəbaɪt] *n.* member of religious community; monk. **cenoby**, *n.* convent or monastery. **cenobian** [sɪ'nəubiən], **cenobitical** [-'bɪtɪkl], *adj.* **cenobitism**, *n.* cenobitical state or practice.

censer ['sensə] *n.* receptacle for incense.

cental ['sentl] *n.* measure of weight equivalent to 100 lb.

centenary [sen'tiːnəri] *adj.* pertaining to or lasting 100 years *n.* one hundredth anniversary. **centennial** [sen'teniəl], *adj.* pertaining to or lasting 100 years; *n. American*, centenary. **centenarian** [,sentɪ'neəriən], *n.* person aged 100 years or more.

centesimal [sen'tesɪml] *adj.* counting or counted by hundredths. **centesimate**, *v.t.* punish by punishing (especially executing) every hundredth man. **centesimation**, *n.*

centimetric [,sentɪ'metrɪk] *adj.* less than 1 metre in length (of very short radio and radar waves).

cento ['sentəu] *n.* anthology of short quotations; any patch-work-like composition. **centonical** [-'tɒnɪkl], *adj.* **centonism**, *n.* composition of a cento.

centrifugal [ˌsentrɪ'fjuːgl, sen'trɪfjʊgl] *adj.* tending to move away from centre. **centrifuge** ['sentrɪfjuːdʒ], *n.* machine for separating substances of different densities by centrifugal force; *v.t.* separate by this means. **centripetal** [sen'trɪpɪtl], *adj.* tending to move towards centre.

centrobaric [ˌsentrə'bærɪk] *adj.* pertaining to centre of gravity.

centuple ['sentjʊpl] *adj.* hundredfold; *v.t.* increase a hundredfold.

centuriate [sen'tjʊərɪeɪt] *adj.* divided into hundreds. **centuriation**, *n.*

cepaceous [sɪ'peɪʃəs] *adj.* like an onion.

cephalic [ke'fælɪk, se-] *adj.* pertaining to head. **cephalic index**, 100 times maximum breadth of skull divided by maximum length. **cephalad** ['kef-, 'sef-], *&dv.* towards head. **cephalate** ['kef-, 'sef-], *adj.* having a head.

cephalopod ['sefələpɒd] *n. & adj.* (mollusc, as octopus, squid, etc.) with arm-like tentacles attached to head.

cephalosporin, ceporin [ˌkefələʊ'spɔːrɪn, ˌsef-, 'sepərɪn] *n.* antibiotic drug extracted from cephalosporium mould, of very wide application.

cephalothorax [ˌsefələʊ'θɔːræks] *n.* body, or head with thorax, of spiders, crustaceans, etc. **cephalothoracic** [-θə'ræsɪk], *adj.*

ceraceous [sə'reɪʃəs] *adj.* like wax. **ceral** ['sɪərəl], *adj.* pertaining to wax or cere.

ceramics [sə'ræmɪks] *n.* art of making pottery. **ceramist** [sə'ræmɪst, 'serəm-], **ceramicist** [sə'ræmɪsɪst], *n.* maker of or expert on pottery. **ceramography**, *n.* historical or descriptive work on pottery.

cerate ['sɪəreɪt] *n.* medical unguent composed of wax, lard, etc.; *adj.* having a cere. **cerated**, *adj.* covered with wax.

ceratoid ['serətɔɪd] *adj.* horny; like or shaped like horn.

ceraunoscope [sə'rɔːnəskəup] *n.* ancient instrument used to simulate the sound of thunder.

cercal ['sɜːkl] *adj.* caudal.

cere [sɪə] *n.* wax; wax-like protuberance at base of upper part of bird's bill. **cerous**, *adj.* pertaining to or like a cere.

cerebellum [ˌserə'beləm] *n.* part of brain projecting at back; 'little brain'. **cerebellar**, *adj.*

cerebrotonic [ˌserɪbrə'tɒnɪk, sə,riː-] *adj* having a shy, inhibited temperament associated with ectomorphy. **cerebrotonia** [-'təʊniə], *n.*

cerebrum [sə'riːbrəm, 'serəbrəm] *n.* brain, especially fore part. **cerebral**, *adj.* pertaining to cerebrum; primarily or excessively intellectual. **cerebrate**, *v.i.* think deeply; reason. **cerebration**, *n.* **cerebrospinal**, *adj.* pertaining to brain and spinal cord.

cerements ['sɪəmənts] *n. pl.* grave-clothes.

ceriferous [sə'rɪfərəs] *adj.* yielding wax.

cermet ['sɜːmet] *n.* a strong alloy of a metal with a heat-resisting compound, especially used for turbine blades and similar objects.

cernuous ['sɜːnjuəs] *adj. Botany*, drooping; hanging.

cerography [sə'rɒgrəfi] *n.* writing on wax; painting with wax colours; encaustic painting. **ceroplastics**, *n.* wax modelling.

certes ['sɜːtiz, sɜːts] *adv. archaic* certainly.

certiorari [ˌsɜːʃiə'reəraɪ, ˌsɜːtiɔː-] *n.* writ for transference of hearing to superior court, or calling for production before superior court of records of a lower court.

cerulean [sə'ruːliən] *adj.* sky-blue; dark blue. **cerulescent** [ˌseru'lesnt], *adj.* bluish.

cerumen [sə'ruːmen, -ən] *n.* wax of ear. **ceruminiferous**, *adj.* yielding this. **ceruminous**, *adj.* pertaining to this.

ceruse ['sɪəruːs, sə'ruːs] *n.* white lead.

cervical [sə'vaɪkl, 'sɜːvɪkl] *adj.* pertaining to the neck or cervix.

cervine ['sɜːvaɪn] *adj.* pertaining to or like deer.

cervisial [sə'vɪsiəl] *adj.* pertaining to beer.

cervix ['sɜːvɪks] *n.* (*pl.* **-ices**), neck; narrow mouth.

cesious ['siːziəs] *adj.* blue-grey.

cession ['seʃn] *n.* act of ceding, especially rights, property or territory. **cessionary**, *n.* assignee; grantee.

cetane ['siːteɪn] *n.* an oil found in petroleum. **cetane number,** number representing ignition value of diesel oil, being the percentage of cetane in a mixture used for testing by comparison.

ceteris paribus [ˌketəriːs 'pærɪbəs] (*Latin*) 'other things being equal'.

CFC *abbreviation* for chlorofluorocarbon.

chaconne [ʃə'kɒn, ʃæ-] *n.* quiet old Spanish dance; set of variations on a continuously repeated ground bass.

chad [tʃæd] *n.* small pieces of paper removed by a punch.

chador ['tʃɑːdɔː, 'tʃʌdə] *n.* large cloth worn as head-covering and veil by Moslem women, especially as sign of religious orthodoxy.

chaetophorous [kɪ'tɒfərəs] *adj.* bearing bristles.

chagrin ['ʃægrɪn] *n.* disappointment annoyance; vexation; *v.t.,* disappoint deeply; annoy.

chaise [ʃeɪz] (*French*) *n.* light, two-wheeled carriage, especially with suspended body.

chalastic [kə'læstɪk] *n. & adj.* laxative.

chalcedony [kæl'sedəni] *n.* blue or grey variety of quartz. **chalcedonic** [-'dɒnɪk], **chalcedonous** [-'sedənəs], *adj.*

chalcography [kæl'kɒgrəfi] *n.* engraving on brass or copper. **chalcolithic** [ˌkælkə'lɪθɪk], *adj.* pertaining to copper or bronze age. **chalcotript** ['kælkətrɪpt], *n.* person who takes rubbings of ornamental brasses.

chalicosis [ˌkælɪ'kəʊsɪs] *n.* stone-cutters' lung disease, due to inhaling stone dust.

chalone ['kæləʊn] *n.* glandular secretion curbing activity. **chalonic** [-'lɒnɪk], *adj.* pertaining to this; restraining.

chalybeate [kə'lɪbiət] *adj.* containing salts of iron; *n.* such water, medicine, etc.

chamaecephalic [ˌkæmɪkɪ'fælɪk, -sɪ-] *adj.* having a flattened skull. **chamaecephalus** [-'kefələs, -'sef-], *n.* (*pl.* **-li**) such person. **chamaecephaly** [-'kefəli, -'sef-], *n.* such condition.

chambré ['ʃɒmbreɪ] (*French*) at room temperature (of wine).

chamfer ['tʃæmfə] *n.* groove; (edge with) flat surface between two bevels; *v.t.* cut chamfers in; cut off angles of; round off. **chamfered**, *adj.*

chamma ['tʃæmɑː] *n.* cloak-like Abyssinian garment.

champaign ['tʃæmpeɪn, ʃæm'peɪn] *n.* plain; any level expanse.

champerty ['tʃæmpəti] *n. Law*, crime of aiding another's lawsuit in order to share in gains therefrom. **champertous**, *adj.*

champignon ['ʃæmpiːnjɒn, ʃæm'pɪnjən] (*French*) *n.* mushroom.

champlevé ['ʃɒmləveɪ, ʃæmp–] (*French*) *n.* & *adj.* (enamel) bearing indentations filled with colour.

chancre ['ʃæŋkə] *n.* syphilitic ulcer. **chancriform**, *adj.* like a chancre. **chancroid**, *n.* local sore resembling a chancre. **chancrous**, *adj.* like or having these.

changeling ['tʃeɪndʒlɪŋ] *n.* child substituted secretly for parent's true child, especially ugly or backward child supposedly left by fairies; fickle person.

chantage [ʃɒn'taːʒ] *n.* blackmail.

chanter ['tʃaːntə] *n.* pipe of bagpipe on which the tune is played.

chantry ['tʃaːntri] *n.* chapel, priest or endowment for singing masses.

chaparajos, chaparejos [,ʃæpə'reɪəʊs] (*Spanish-Mexican*) *n. pl.* cowboys' leather leg-coverings, chaps.

chapatti [tʃə'paːti] *n.* Indian unleavened bread or pancake.

chapbook ['tʃæpbʊk] *n.* small popular book, formerly of songs, etc., sold by pedlars. **chapman**, *n.* pedlar.

chapelle ardente [ʃæ,pel aː'dɒnt] (*French*) *n.* 'burning chapel'; framework bearing burning candles over coffin or catafalque.

charcuterie [ʃaː'kjuːtəri, –'kuː–] *n.* (shop selling) cold meats made from pork.

chargé d'affaires [ʃaːʒeɪ dæ'feə] *n.* (*pl.* **chargés** ...) ambassador at minor court; assistant or deputy to ambassador.

charivari [,ʃaːrɪ'vaːri] *n.* medley, especially of noises; mock musical performance with whistles, utensils, etc.

charlatan ['ʃaːlətən] *n.* impostor; quack. **charlatanic** [–'tænɪk], *adj.* **charlatanism, charlatanry**, *n.*

charnel-house ['tʃaːnlhaʊs] *n.* place where dead bodies or bones are deposited.

charpoy ['tʃaːpɔɪ] (*Anglo-Indian*) *n.* light bedstead.

charqui ['tʃaːki] *n.* dried strips of meat; jerked beef. **charqued**, *adj.* cut into strips and dried.

chasmogamy [kæz'mɒgəmi] *n.* opening of flower for fertilization. **chasmogamic** [–'gæmɪk], **chasmogamous**, *adj.*

chasmophilous [kæz'mɒfɪləs] *adj.* fond of crannies and crevices. **chasmophyte** ['kæzməfaɪt], *n.* such plant.

chasuble ['tʃæzjʊbl] *n.* outermost ecclesiastical vestment without sleeves.

chatelaine ['ʃætəleɪn] *n.* woman owner, occupier or caretaker of castle; ring attached to belt for carrying keys, etc.

chatoyant [ʃə'tɔɪənt] *adj.* with lustre that seems different colours in different lights; *n.* stone which shines with a wavy band of light; cat's-eye.

chauffer ['tʃəʊfə] *n.* small portable stove.

chaus ['keɪəs] *n.* wild cat, especially of India and Africa.

chaussure [ʃəʊ'sjʊə] (*French*) *n.* foot covering.

chauvinism ['ʃəʊvənɪzm] *n.* aggressive patriotism; jingoism; implicit belief in the superiority of one's own sex, group, etc. **chauvinist**, *n.* **chauvinistic**, *adj.*

chebec(k) [ʃɪ'bek] *n.* xebec.

chef-d'oeuvre [,ʃeɪ'dɜːvrə] (*French*) *n.* (*pl.* **chefs** ...) masterpiece.

chela ['kiːlə] *n.* (*pl.* **–lae**) pincer-like claw of *e.g.* crab, scorpion. **cheliferous**, *adj.* having pincers. **cheliform**, *adj.*

chelonian [kɪ'ləʊnɪən] *n.* & *adj.* (pertaining to) tortoise or turtle. **chelonid**, *n.* sea turtle.

chemin-de-fer [ʃə,mændə'feə] (*French*) *n.* 'road of iron'; railway; a kind of baccarat.

chemokinesis [,kiːməkaɪ'niːsɪs, –kɪ–] *n.* increase in activity caused chemically. **chemolysis**, *n.* decomposition chemically caused. **chemonuclear**, *adj.* pertaining to or arising from both a chemical and a nuclear reaction. **chemoprophylaxis**, *n.* prevention by means of a chemical drug. **chemoreceptor**, *n.* sense organ that responds to chemical stimuli. **chemotaxis**, *n.* movement of organism towards or away from chemical substance. **chemotherapy**, *n.* medical treatment by chemicals attacking disease-producing organism. **chemotropism**, *n.* growth in response to chemical stimulus.

chemurgy ['kemɜːdʒi] *n.* industrial organic chemistry.

chersonese ['kɜːsəniːs, –iːz] *n.* peninsula.

chert [tʃɜːt] *n.* flint-like concretions in limestone.

chervil ['tʃɜːvl] *n.* a salad herb with curled leaves.

cheval-de-frise [ʃə,vældə'friːz] *n.* (*pl.* **chevaux-** ... [ʃə,vəʊ–]) spiked bar on wall or window-sill. **cheval glass**, full-length mirror in frame.

chevalier [,ʃevə'lɪə] *n.* knight; cavalier; gallant.

chevaline ['ʃevəlɪn] *adj.* equine; *n.* horseflesh.

chevelure [,ʃevə'ljʊə, –'lʊə] (*French*) *n.* head of hair.

chevet [ʃə'veɪ] (*French*) *n.* east end of (especially French Gothic) church or chancel.

cheville [ʃə'viː] *n.* unnecessary word, especially used to extend verse line.

chevrette [ʃə'vret] *n.* kind of thin kid leather.

chevron ['ʃevrən] *n.* V-shaped or Λ-shaped bar or stripe.

chevrotain ['ʃevrəteɪn] *n.* small deer-like mammal of E Indies and Africa; mouse-deer.

chez [ʃeɪ] (*French*) *prep.* at the house or home of.

chiaroscuro [ki,aːrə'skjuːrəʊ, –'skuə–] *n.* use of light and shade in painting; use of similar contrast in writing, etc. **chiaroscurist**, *n.* artist skilled in this.

chiasma [kaɪ'æzmə] *n.* (*pl.* **–mata**) cross-shaped configuration especially in pairing chromosomes.

chiasmus [kaɪ'æzməs] *n.* (*pl.* **–mi**) inversion of order of corresponding elements of two parallel phrases, as in *born under one law, to another bound.* **chiastic**, *adj.*

chibouk, chibouque [tʃɪ'buːk] *n.* long Turkish smoking pipe.

chicane [ʃɪ'keɪn] *n.* chicanery; series of tight bends on motor-racing track; hand of cards without trumps *v.t.* cheat, trick. *v.i.* use subterfuge. **chicanery**, *n.* use of (especially legal) quibbles, sophistry or subterfuge to deceive; trick, quibble.

chicle ['tʃɪkl] (*Spanish*) *n.* rubber-like gum, main ingredient of chewing gum, obtained from Central American sapodilla tree. **chiclero** [tʃɪ'kleərəʊ],

Spanish-American *n*. gatherer of this.

chico ['tʃiːkəu] (*Spanish*) *n*. 'little one'; my friend.

chiffonnier [ˌʃɪfə'nɪə] *n*. sideboard; chest of drawers.

chignon ['ʃiːnjɒn] (*French*) *n*. knot or 'bun' of hair; pad over which hair is arranged.

chigoe ['tʃɪgəu] (*W Indian and S American*) *n*. flea; chigger; jigger.

chiliad ['kɪlɪæd] *n*. one thousand (years). **chiliadal, chiliadic,** *adj*. **chiliagon,** *n*. thousand-sided figure. **chiliarch,** *n*. ancient Greek or Roman officer in charge of a thousand men. **chiliasm,** *n*. belief in second incarnation of Christ as king of world; millenarianism. **chiliast,** *n*. adherent of such belief. **chiliastic,** *adj*.

chillum ['tʃɪləm] (*Anglo-Indian*) *n*. hookah; bowl of hookah; tobacco-smoking. **chillumchee,** *n*. brass wash basin.

chimera, chimaera [kaɪ'mɪərə, kɪ–] *n*. imaginary monster; bogy; impossible idea. **chimerical** [–'merɪkl], *adj*. imaginary; fanciful; fantastic.

chinch [tʃɪntʃ] *n*. bed-bug.

chinchilla [tʃɪn'tʃɪlə] *n*. small, squirrel-like S American rodent; its soft fur; *adj*. applied to soft-furred grey varieties of rabbit, cat, etc.

chine [tʃaɪn] *n*. backbone; cut of meat adjoining backbone; saddle; ridge; small ravine; *v.t.* cut into pieces.

chinkara [tʃɪŋ'kɑːrə] *n*. Indian gazelle or kind of antelope.

chinoiserie [ʃɪn'wɑːzəri] (*French*) *n*. decoration, furniture etc. imitating Chinese design.

chinook [tʃɪ'nuːk] *n*. warm dry wind blowing down E side of Rocky Mountains.

chionablepsia [ˌkaɪənə'blepsɪə] *n*. snow blindness.

chiragra [kaɪ'rægrə] *n*. gout of the fingers.

chiral ['kaɪrəl] *adj*. pertaining to hand; turning to either left or right. **chirality** [–'rælətɪ], *n*. **chirapsia,** *n*. massage.

chiro- ['kaɪrə–] *prefix* of the hand. **chirograph,** *n*. written bond or indenture. **chirography** [–'rɒg–], *n*. handwriting. **chirology** [–'rɒl–], *n*. study of hand. **chiromancy, chirognomy,** *n*. palmistry. **chironomy,** *n*. art of gesture with hands. **chiropractic** [ˌkaɪrə'præktɪk], **chiropraxis,** *n*. manipulation of joints, especially of spine, as medical remedy. **chiropractor,** *n*. **chirothesia,** *n*. laying on of hands in ecclesiastical ceremony. **chirotony** [–'rɒt–], *n*. election by show of hands; *Ecclesiastical*, use of hand.

chirr [tʃɜː] *v.i.* make trill sound like a grasshopper.

chirurgeon [kaɪ'rɜːdʒən] *n*. *archaic*, surgeon. **chirurgery,** *n*. surgery. **chirurgic,** *adj*.

chitin ['kaɪtɪn] *n*. horny substance forming outer surface of most insects, crustaceans, etc. **chitoid,** *adj*. like this. **chitous,** *adj*.

chiton ['kaɪtn, –ɒn] *n*. in ancient Greece and Rome, loose woollen tunic; *Zoology*, small marine mollusc.

chlamys ['klæmɪs, 'kleɪ–] *n*. horse-man's loose cloak of ancient Greece. **chlamydate** ['klæmɪdeɪt], *adj*. having a mantle. **chlamydeous** [klə'mɪdɪəs], *adj*. *Botany*, pertaining to floral envelope.

chloraemia, chloranaemia [klɔː'riːmɪə,

ˌklɔːrə'niːmɪə] *n*. chlorosis.

chloral ['klɔːrəl] *n*. oily liquid obtained from chlorine and alcohol; (properly **chloral hydrate**) sleeping draught obtained from chloral. **chloralism,** *n*. condition due to abuse of this.

chloramphenicol [ˌklɔːræm'fenɪkɒl] *n*. an antibiotic drug originally isolated from a soil microorganism, effective against various bacterial and viral diseases.

chlorochrous ['klɔːrəkrəs] *adj*. greenish.

chlorofluorocarbon [ˌklɔːrəu,fluərəu'kɑːbən] *n*. synthetic gas used as aerosol propellant and refrigerant, thought harmful to the ozone layer.

chlorometer [klɔː'rɒmɪtə] *n*. instrument for measuring chlorine, especially in bleaching powders.

Chloromycetin [ˌklɔːrəumaɪ'siːtɪn] *n*. *Trademark*, name for chloramphenicol.

chlorophyll ['klɒrəfɪl] *n*. green colouring matter of plants. **chlorophyllous, chlorophyllose,** *adj*. **chlorophylloid,** *adj*. like this. **chloroplast(id),** *n*. portion of protoplasm containing this, active in photosynthesis.

chlorosis [klɔː'rəusɪs] *n*. anaemia in young women; green sickness; similar condition of plants, due to lack of light. **chlorotic,** *adj*. lacking chlorophyll.

choanoid ['kəuənɔɪd] *adj*. funnel-shaped.

chokedamp ['tʃəukdæmp] *n*. asphyxiating gas, mainly carbon dioxide, of mines.

cholecyst ['kɒlɪsɪst, 'kəu–] *n*. gall bladder. **cholecystectomy,** *n*. removal of gall bladder. **cholecystitis,** *n*. inflammation of gall bladder. **cholelithiasis** [ˌkɒlɪlɪ'θaɪəsɪs, ˌkəu–] *n*. production of gall-stones.

choler ['kɒlə] *n*. anger; bile. **choleric** [–'lerɪk], *adj*. pertaining to choler; easily angered.

cholesterol [kə'lestərɒl] *n*. sterol found in most animal tissues and fats, thought to contribute to heart disease if present.

choli ['tʃəuli] *n*. short, close-fitting blouse worn under a sari.

choliamb ['kəuliæm] *n*. iambic trimeter having trochee or spondee in third foot. **choliambic** [–'æmbɪk], *adj*.

cholic ['kɒlɪk, 'kəu–] *adj*. pertaining to bile.

choller ['tʃɒlə] *n*. double chin.

chololith ['kɒləlɪθ, 'kəu–] *n*. gall-stone. **chololithic,** *adj*.

chômage [ʃəu'mɑːʒ] (*French*) *n*. work stoppage; slump; unemployment.

chondral ['kɒndrəl] *adj*. cartilaginous. **chondric,** *adj*. **chondrification,** *n*. conversion into cartilage. **chondrogenesis,** *n*. production of cartilage. **chondroid,** *adj*. like cartilage. **chondrosis,** *n*. formation of cartilage. **chondrostean, chondrosteous,** *adj*. with cartilaginous skeleton.

choragus [kɒ'reɪgəs] *n*. leader of chorus in ancient Greek drama; person officiating at festival.

chorale [kɒ'rɑːl] *n*. hymn tune.

chorditis [kɔː'daɪtɪs] *n*. inflammation of vocal cords.

chorea [kɔː'rɪə, kə–] *n*. nervous disease marked by involuntary twitchings. **chorea minor,** St. Vitus's dance. **choreic, choreal,** *adj*.

choree, choreus ['kɔːriː, kɔː'riːəs] *n*. trochee.

choreutic [kə'ruːtɪk] *adj*. pertaining to choral song and dance.

choriamb ['kɒriæmb, –æm] *n*. metrical foot comprising a trochee and an iambus. **choriambic,** *adj.*

choric ['kɒrɪk] *adj.* pertaining to chorus in ancient Greek tragedy.

chorion ['kɔːrɪən, –ɒn] *n.* membrane enclosing amnion. **chorial, chorionic,** *adj.*

choripetalous [ˌkɔːrɪ'petl–əs] *adj.* with petals separated. **chorisepalous,** *adj.* with sepals separated.

chorograph ['kɒrəgrɑːf] *n.* instrument finding position of a place from angles enclosed by lines between it and three other known places.

chorography [kə'rɒgrəfi, kɔː–] *n.* geographical description of a region. **chorology,** *n.* study of geographical distribution. **chorometry,** *n.* surveying of land.

chose jugée [ˌʃəuz 'ʒuːʒeɪ] (*French*) 'judged thing'; settled matter, on which further argument is useless. **chose in action,** *Law*, thing, such as mortgage, debt etc., in respect of which there is a right of legal action. **chose in possession,** thing, as goods and chattels, in ownership.

chota peg [ˌtʃəutə 'peg] (*Anglo-Indian*) *n.* small drink.

choultry ['tʃəultri] (*Anglo-Indian*) *n.* caravanserai; colonnade.

chowder ['tʃaudə] (*American*) *n.* mixed meat, fish, vegetable and clam stew or soup.

chrematistic [ˌkriːmə'tɪstɪk] *adj.* pertaining to gaining of money. **chrematistics,** *n.* study of money.

chrestomathy [kre'stɒməθi] *n.* collection of short written passages, especially in foreign language; phrase-book. **chrestomathic** [–'mæθɪk], *adj.* pertaining to useful knowledge.

chrism ['krɪzm] *n.* holy oil. **chrismal,** *adj.* **chrismation,** *n.* application of this. **chrismatory** ['krɪzmətəri], *n.* vessel holding this; *adj.* pertaining to chrismation.

chromaesthesia [ˌkrəumiːs'θiːzɪə, –ʒə] *n.* mental association of colours with tastes, sights, sounds, figures, etc.

chromascope ['krəuməskəup] *n.* instrument showing colour's effects.

chromatic [krə'mætɪk] *adj.* pertaining to colour; *Music*, using tones outside the key in which it is written, especially the half-tones; *n.* an accidental. **chromaticism,** *n. Music* use of chromatic tones. **chromaticity** [–'tɪsəti], *n.* degree or state of having colour. **chromatics,** *n.* study of colour.

chromatin ['krəumətɪn] *n.* protoplasmic substance in cell nucleus, forming chromosomes and carrying hereditary characters.

chromatism ['krəumətɪzm] *n.* occurrence of abnormal coloration.

chromatography [ˌkrəumə'tɒgrəfi] *n. Chemistry*, separation or analysis of mixtures by adsorption of individual ingredients on filter paper, etc.

chromatopathy [ˌkrəumə'tɒpəθi] *n.* disease causing abnormal coloration of skin.

chromatosis [ˌkrəumə'təusɪs] *n.* chromatism of skin.

chromogen ['krəumədʒən, –en] *n.* substance developing into colouring matter of plants. **chromogenic,** *adj.* producing colour.

chromolithograph [ˌkrəuməu'lɪθəgrɑːf] *n.* coloured lithograph. **chromolithography** [–lɪ'θɒgrəfi], *n.*

chromophilous, chromophilic [krəu'mɒfɪləs,

,krəumə'fɪlɪk] *adj. Chemistry,* readily staining.

chromophobe ['krəuməfəub], *adj.* staining only slightly.

chromophotography [ˌkrəuməfə'tɒgrəfi] *n.* colour photography.

chromoptometer [ˌkrəumɒp'tɒmɪtə] *n.* instrument measuring eye's sensitivity to colour. **chromoptometry,** *n.*

chromosome ['krəuməsəum] *n.* thread-shaped structure occurring in cell nucleus, which transmits hereditary characteristics.

chromosphere ['krəuməsfɪə] *n.* layer of glowing gas surrounding sun or a star.

chromotypography [ˌkrəumətaɪ'pɒgrəfi] *n.* printing in colours. **chromoxylography** [–zaɪ'lɒg–], *n.* printing in colours from wooden blocks.

chronogram ['krɒnəgræm] *n.* phrase or sentence certain letters of which form a date, generally in Roman figures. **chronogrammatic,** *adj.* **chronogrammatist,** *n.* composer of this.

chronograph ['krɒnəgrɑːf] *n.* stop-watch. **chronography** [krə'nɒgrəfi], *n.* recording of intervals of time.

chronology [krə'nɒlədʒi] *n.* science of dates; arrangement in order of time of occurrence. **chronological** [ˌkrɒnə'lɒdʒɪkl], *adj.*

chronometer [krə'nɒmɪtə] *n.* time-piece, especially of exceptional accuracy. **chronometric** [–'metrɪk], *adj.* **chronometry** [–'nɒmətri], *n.* measuring of time and divisions of time.

chronopher ['krɒnəfə] *n.* electrical contact-maker for transmitting time signals.

chronophotography [ˌkrɒnəfə'tɒgrəfi] *n.* taking of a set of photographs of a moving object at regular intervals.

chronoscope ['krɒnəskəup] *n.* instrument measuring very small intervals of time; chronometer in which figures are seen through apertures in dial. **chronoscopy** [–'nɒskəpi], *n.*

chronostichon [krə'nɒstɪkɒn] *n.* chronogrammatic line of verse.

chronothermometer [ˌkrɒnəθə'mɒmɪtə] *n.* chronometer whose rate is altered by temperature changes.

chronotropic [ˌkrɒnə'trɒpɪk] *adj.* affecting rate of pulse. **chronotropism** [–'nɒtrəpɪzm], *n.*

chrysalis ['krɪsəlɪs] *n.* (*pl.* **–ses**) motionless stage of insect's life, in which it has a hard covering; pupa. **chrysalid,** *adj.* **chrysaloid,** *adj.* like a chrysalis.

chrysanthous [krɪ'sænθəs] *adj.* yellow-flowered.

chryselephantine [ˌkrɪselɪ'fæntaɪn] *adj.* made of, or ornamented with, ivory and gold.

chrysoaristocracy, chrysocracy [ˌkrɪsəuær'stɒkrəsi, krɪ'sɒkrəsi] *n.* plutocracy.

chrysocarpous [ˌkrɪsə'kɑːpəs] *n.* having yellow fruit.

chrysochlorous [ˌkrɪsə'klɔːrəs] *adj.* greenish-gold in colour.

chrysochrous ['krɪsəkrəs] *adj.* golden yellow.

chrysography [krɪ'sɒgrəfi] *n.* writing in letters of gold. **chrysographer,** *n.*

chrysolite ['krɪsəlaɪt] *n.* olive-green or yellow crystal used as gem; olivine.

chrysology [krɪ'sɒlədʒi] *n.* economic study of precious metals and their value.

chrysophilist, chrysophilite [krɪ'sɒfɪlɪst, –laɪt] *n.* lover of gold.

chrysopoetics [ˌkrɪsəpəʊ'etɪks] n. manufacture of, or transmutation into, gold.

chrysoprase ['krɪsəpreɪz] n. green variety of chalcedony used as gem.

chrystocrene ['krɪstəkriːn] n. Geology, rock formation resembling glacier.

chthonian, chthonic ['θəʊnɪən, 'θɒnɪk] adj. pertaining to Greek gods of underworld.

chuddar see chador

chukker, chukka ['tʃʌkə] n. one of the periods into which game of polo is divided.

chupatty [tʃə'paːti] n. chapati.

churinga [tʃə'rɪŋgə] n. (pl. –ringa, –ringas) sacred amulet of Australian aborigines.

churrigueresque [ˌtʃʊrɪgə'resk] adj. pertaining to a style of late-17th-century Spanish Baroque architecture.

churrus ['tʃʌrəs] (Indian) n. hemp resin; leather bag for drawing water from well.

chutzpah ['xʊtspə] n. cheek; (shameless) audacity.

chyle [kaɪl] n. milky fat-containing fluid secreted into blood by lactic vessels in small intestine. chylaceous, adj. chylific, adj. producing chyle. chyliform, adj. like chyle. chylocauly, n. Botany, possession of fleshy leaves. chylopoiesis, n. production of chyle. chylous, adj. consisting of chyle.

chyme [kaɪm] n. semi-liquid partly digested food leaving stomach. chymiferous, adj. containing chyme. chymification, n. conversion of food into chyme. chymous, adj.

chypre ['ʃiːprə] n. mixture of resins, etc., used in perfumery.

cibation [saɪ'beɪʃn] n. feeding. cibarian, adj. pertaining to mouth. cibarious, adj. pertaining to food.

cibophobia [ˌsaɪbə'fəʊbɪə] n. dislike for food.

ciborium [sɪ'bɔːrɪəm] n. (pl. –ria) vessel holding consecrated wafers; canopy over altar.

cicada [sɪ'kaːdə] n. insect of warm countries.

cicatrice, cicatrix ['sɪkətrɪs, –ɪks] n. scar. cicatricial, adj. cicatricle, n. small scar. cicatricose, adj. scarred. cicatrise, v.i. & t. heal; grow over.

cicerone [ˌtʃɪtʃə'rəʊni, ˌsɪs–] (Italian) n. (pl. –ni) guide escorting tourists, sightseers. ciceronage, n.

cicisbeo [ˌtʃɪtʃɪz'beɪəʊ] (Italian) n. (pl. –bei) married woman's lover or escort.

ciconine, ciconian ['sɪkənaɪn, sɪ'kəʊnɪən] adj. like or pertaining to a stork.

ci-devant [ˌsiː–də'vɒn] (French) adj. former; ex-.

cilia ['sɪlɪə] n. pl. (sing. –ium) eye-lashes; hair-like outgrowths of microscopic organisms or cells, acting as organs of propulsion. ciliary, adj. ciliary muscle, muscle compressing or extending lens of eye in accommodation. ciliate, adj. having fine hairs.

cilice ['sɪlɪs] n. hair-cloth; hair shirt.

cillosis [sɪ'ləʊsɪs] n. muscular spasm of upper eyelid.

cimex ['saɪmeks] n. (pl. –ices) bed-bug. cimicide, n. substance destroying bed-bugs.

cinchona [sɪŋ'kəʊnə] n. S American tree with bark yielding quinine; Peruvian bark. cinchonic [–'kɒnɪk], adj. cinchonine ['sɪŋkəniːn], n. quinine-like alkaloid extracted from cinchona bark. cinchonism, n. condition due to over-use of quinine and other extracts of cinchona bark.

cincture ['sɪŋktʃə] n. girdle.

cineaste ['sɪniæst] n. devotee of cinema.

cinemograph [sɪ'niːməgraːf] n. instrument recording speed, especially of wind.

cinenchymatous [sɪ'neŋkɪmətəs] adj. laticiferous.

cinerary ['sɪnərəri] adj. pertaining to ashes, especially of cremated body. cinerarium [–'reərɪəm], n. place where ashes of cremated bodies are deposited.

cinerial [sɪ'nɪərɪəl] adj. pertaining to like or coloured like ashes. cinereous, cineritious, adj. like ashes.

cingulate ['sɪŋgjulət] adj. having girdle. cingular, adj. ring-shaped.

cinnabar ['sɪnəbaː] n. natural sulphide of mercury, the chief source of mercury. cinnabaric [–'bærɪk], cinnabarine [–bəriːn], adj.

cinquain ['sɪŋkeɪn, sɪŋ'keɪn] n. group of five, especially five-line stanza.

cinquecento [ˌtʃɪŋkwɪ'tʃentəʊ] (Italian) adj. sixteenth-century; n. work or style of art produced then. cinquecentism, n. cinquecentist, n. Italian artist of 16th century; student of Italian art of that period.

cinquefoil ['sɪŋkfɔɪl, 'sæ–] n. several plants having leaves divided into five lobes; architectural decoration resembling such leaf.

cipolin ['sɪpəlɪn] n. green-streaked white marble.

cippus ['sɪpəs] n. (pl. –pi) small column marking burial-place or landmark.

circa ['sɜːkə] (Latin) prep. 'about' (abbr. c.)

circadian [sɜː'keɪdɪən] adj. pertaining to biological processes occurring regularly at 24 hour intervals.

circinate ['sɜːsɪneɪt] adj. ring-shaped; rolled into a close spiral.

circumambient [ˌsɜːkəm'æmbɪənt] adj. surrounding on all sides. circumambiency, n.

circumambulate [ˌsɜːkəm'æmbjuleɪt] v.t. walk round. circumambulation, circumambulator, n.

circumaviate [ˌsɜːkəm'eɪvɪeɪt] v.t. fly round. circumaviation, circumaviator, n.

circumcrescent [ˌsɜːkəm'kresnt] adj. growing over or round. circumcrescence, n.

circumdiction [ˌsɜːkəm'dɪkʃn] n. circumlocution.

circumferentor [sə'kʌmfərentə] n. surveyor's angle-measuring compass instrument.

circumflex ['sɜːkəmfleks] n. & adj. (applied to) accent (ˆ) indicating length of vowel; curved; arched. circumflexion, n.

circumfluent [sə'kʌmfluənt] adj. flowing round. circumfluence, n.

circumforaneous [ˌsɜːkəmfə'reɪnɪəs] adj. wandering, especially from street to street; vagrant.

circumfulgent [ˌsɜːkəm'fʌldʒənt] adj. shining about or round.

circumfuse [ˌsɜːkəm'fjuːz] v.t. surround with liquid; pour round. circumfusion, n.

circuminsular [ˌsɜːkəm'ɪnsjulə] adj. surrounding an island.

circumjacent [ˌsɜːkəm'dʒeɪsnt] adj. surrounding. circumjacence, circumjacency, n.

circumlittoral [ˌsɜːkəm'lɪtərəl] adj. next to shore.

circumlocution [ˌsɜːkəmlə'kjuːʃn] n. roundabout phrase or talk. circumlocutory [–'lɒkjutəri], adj.

circummigrate [ˌsɜːkəmmaɪˈɡreɪt] *v.i.* wander from place to place. **circummigration**, *n.*

circumnavigate [ˌsɜːkəmˈnævɪɡeɪt] *v.t.* sail round. **circumnavigation, circumnavigator,** *n.* **circumnavigatory,** *adj.*

circumoesophagal [ˌsɜːkəmiːˈsɒfəɡl] *adj.* about or along the gullet.

circumpolar [ˌsɜːkəmˈpəʊlə] *adj.* about or at N or S Pole.

circumscribe [ˈsɜːkəmskraɪb] *v.t.* enclose; limit. **circumscription** [-ˈskrɪp-], *n.* **circumscriptive,** *adj.*

circumsolar [ˌsɜːkəmˈsəʊlə] *adj.* revolving round sun.

circumspect [ˈsɜːkəmspekt] *adj.* cautious. **circumspection** [-ˈspek-], *n.* **circumspective,** *adj.*

circumvallation [ˌsɜːkəmvəˈleɪʃn] *n.* surrounding trench or rampart.

circumvent [ˌsɜːkəmˈvent] *v.t.* outwit; prevent by strategy. **circumvention,** *n.*

circumviate [səˈkʌmvieɪt] *v.t.* travel round.

circumvolant [səˈkʌmvələnt] *adj.* flying round.

circumvolute [səˈkʌmvəluːt] *v.t.* twist; wind round. **circumvolution** [ˌsɜːkəmvəˈluːʃn], *n.* revolution; fold; circumlocution. **circumvolutory** [ˌsɜːkəmˈvɒljʊtəri], *adj.*

circumvolve [ˌsɜːkəmˈvɒlv] *v.i.* & *t.* revolve (round). **circumvolution** [-vəˈluːʃn], *n.*

cirrate [ˈsɪreɪt] *adj.* having tendrils.

cirrhosis [səˈrəʊsɪs] *n. Medicine,* hardened or fibrous condition, especially of liver. **cirrhotic** [-ˈrɒtɪk], *adj.*

cirriped [ˈsɪrɪped] *n.* parasitic marine crustacean, as barnacle. **cirropodous** [səˈrɒpədəs], *adj.*

cirrus [ˈsɪrəs] *n.* (*pl.* **-ri**) tendril; high, fine, thin cloud. **cirrocumulus,** *n.* small cumulus clouds at great height; mackerel sky. **cirrose,** *adj.* cirrate. **cirro-stratus,** *n.* layer of stratus cloud at great height. **cirro-velum,** *n.* sheet of cirrus cloud covering sky.

cisalpine [sɪsˈælpaɪn] *adj.* on this side of the Alps, especially on the southern or Roman side. **cisandine,** *adj.* on this side of the Andes. **cisatlantic,** *adj.* on this side of the Atlantic Ocean. **ciselysian,** *adj.* on this side of Elysium or heaven. **cismarine,** *adj.* on this side of the sea. **cismontane,** *adj.* on this side of mountains; desiring limitation of papal power. **cisoceanic,** *adj.* on this side of ocean. **cispadane,** *adj.* on this (southern) side of the River Po. **cispontine,** *adj.* on this side of bridges, *e.g.* on north side of Thames. **cisrhenane,** *adj.* on this side of the Rhine.

cistron [ˈsɪstrɒn] *n.* segment of DNA required to synthesize a complete polypeptide chain for a particular function.

cistus [ˈsɪstəs] *n.* rock rose.

citation [saɪˈteɪʃn] *n.* summons; quotation; enumeration. **citatory** [saɪˈteɪtəri, ˈsaɪtətəri], *adj.*

cithara [ˈsɪθərə] *n.* ancient lyre-like stringed musical instrument. **citharist,** *n.* player on this.

cither(n) [ˈsɪθə, -n] *n.* lute; cithera; zither, etc. **citheroedic** [ˌsɪθəˈriːdɪk], *adj.*

citreous [ˈsɪtriəs] *adj.* lemon-coloured. **citric,** *adj.* pertaining to or derived from lemons and other acid fruit. **citrine,** *adj.* lemon-coloured. **citron,** *n.* large lemon-like fruit. **citrous, citrus,** *adj.* pertaining to or like citron.

civet [ˈsɪvɪt] *n.* musk-like substance, used as perfume, obtained from civet cat. **civet cat,** banded and spotted cat-like animal of Africa.

cladistics [kləˈdɪstɪks] *n. Biology,* method of animal classification by shared characteristics.

cladoptosis [ˌklædɒpˈtəʊsɪs] *n.* annual shedding of twigs.

clairaudient [kleərˈɔːdiənt] *adj.* able to hear sounds not actually present, as spirit communications, etc. **clairaudience,** *n.*

clair de lune [ˌkleə də ˈluːn] (*French*) *n.* 'moonlight'; greenish-blue colour.

clairsentient [kleəˈsentiənt, -ˈsenʃnt] *adj.* able to perceive sensations not actually present. **clairsentience,** *n.*

clairvoyant [kleəˈvɔɪənt] *n.* & *adj.* (person) able to see objects not actually present; having 'second sight'. **clairvoyance,** *n.*

clamant [ˈkleɪmənt, ˈklæ-] *n.* loud; insistent. **clamatory** [ˈklæmətəri], **clamorous** [ˈklæmərəs], *adj.* loud.

clancular [ˈklæŋkjʊlə] *adj.* clandestine.

clandestine [klænˈdestɪn, ˈklændestaɪn] *adj.* secret; illicit.

clangour [ˈklæŋɡə] *n.* loud, often repeated noise.

claque [klæk] *n.* group of paid applauders. **claqueur** [-ˈkɜː], *n.* member of this.

clastic [ˈklæstɪk] *adj.* detachable into component parts; *Geology,* composed of fragments.

clathrate [ˈklæθreɪt] *adj.* lattice-like. **clathroid,** *adj.,* **clathrose,** *adj.* marked with lattice-like lines or grooves.

claudent [ˈklɔːdnt] *adj.* shutting.

claudicant [ˈklɔːdɪkənt] *adj.* limping. **claudication** [ˌklɔːdɪˈkeɪʃn], *n.*

claustral [ˈklɔːstrəl] *adj.* cloistral. **claustration,** *n.* confinement, especially in convent.

clavate [ˈkleɪveɪt] *adj.* club-shaped. **clavation,** *n.*

clavecin [ˈklævəsɪn] *n.* harpsichord; carillon keyboard.

claviature [ˈklæviətʃə] *n.* keyboard; fingering system.

clavicembalo [ˌklævɪˈtʃembələʊ] *n.* (*pl.* **-li**) harpsichord.

clavichord [ˈklævɪkɔːd] *n.* pianoforte-like musical instrument, preceding pianoforte, with horizontal strings.

clavicle [ˈklævɪkl] *n.* collar-bone. **clavicotomy** [-ˈkɒt-], *n.* incision through this. **clavicular** [kləˈvɪkjʊlə], *adj.* **claviculate,** *adj.* having a clavicle.

clavicytherium [ˌklævɪsɪˈθɪəriəm] *n.* harpsichord-like musical instrument.

clavier [kləˈvɪə, ˈklæviə] *n.* claviature; any stringed musical instrument with keyboard.

claviger [ˈklævɪdʒə] *n.* club-bearer; key-keeper or caretaker. **clavigerous,** *adj.*

clavis [ˈkleɪvɪs] *n.* (*pl.* **-ves**) key; glossary.

clavus [ˈkleɪvəs] *n.* (*pl.* **-vi**) purple stripe worn on toga by persons of high rank in ancient Rome; corn (on foot); intensely painful headache.

claymore [ˈkleɪmɔː] (*Scottish*) *n.* large double-edged sword; *erroneously,* broadsword with basket hilt.

clearance [ˈklɪərəns] *n. Commerce,* official statement that dues have been paid, and permit to sail or move goods. **clearance inwards,** clearance to vessel in port having discharged cargo. **clearance outwards,** clearance to vessel about to sail.

clearcole ['klɪəkəʊl] n. mixture of size and whiting.

cledonism ['kliːdn–ɪzm] n. using circumlocution to avoid speaking words deemed unlucky.

cleek [kliːk] n. golf-club with iron head.

cleg [kleg] n. gad fly; horse-fly.

cleistogamy [klaɪ'stɒgəmi] n. Botany, self-fertilization without opening of flower. **cleistogenous** [–'stɒdʒ–], adj. having such flowers. **cleistogamous**, adj.

clem [klem] (dialect) v.i. & t. starve. **clemmed**, adj. famished.

clemency ['klemənsi] n. mercy; mildness. **clement**, adj.

clepsydra ['klepsɪdrə] n. water-clock.

clerestory ['klɪə,stɔːri] n. windowed part of nave wall rising above aisle roof.

clerihew ['klerɪhjuː] n. short nonsensical or satirical poem, generally of four lines of varying length, and especially biographical, invented by E Clerihew Bentley.

clerisy ['klerəsi] n. educated or literary people collectively.

cleromancy ['klɪərəmænsi] n. divination by casting lots. **cleronomy**, n. inheritance.

clevis ['klevɪs] n. any securing device, U-shaped and with a pin between the extremities.

clew [kluː] n. corner of sail to which ropes are attached; v.t. haul on this when changing sail.

climacteric [klaɪ'mæktərɪk, ‚klaɪmæk'terɪk] adj. critical; forming a turning-point or crisis; n. turning-point, especially in life of individual, generally reckoned at 21, 35, 49, 63 and 81 years of age; 'change of life', menopause. **grand climacteric**, 63rd or 81st year of life. **climacterical**, adj.

climatotherapy [‚klaɪmətəʊ'θerəpi] n. treatment of disease by living in particular climate. **climatotherapeutic** [–,θerə'pjuːtɪk], adj.

clinamen [klaɪ'neɪmen] n. (pl. **–mina**) bias.

clinker-built ['klɪŋkəbɪlt] adj. (of a ship) with overlapping planks.

clinocephalic, clinocephalous [‚klaɪnəʊkɪ'fælɪk, –sɪ–, –'kefələs, –'se–] adj. having a saddle-shaped skull. **clinocephalus** [–'kef–, –'sef–], n. (pl. **–li**) such person. **clinocephaly** [–'kef–, –'sef–], n.

clinodromic [‚klaɪnə'drɒmɪk] adj. moving at an angle, especially of missiles travelling at an angle to a moving target. **clinoscopic** [–'skɒp–], adj. pertaining to missiles travelling in line with a moving target.

clinology [klaɪ'nɒlədʒi] n. study of organism's retrograde development after passing maturity. **clinologic**, adj.

clinometer [klaɪ'nɒmɪtə] n. instrument measuring angle of slope. **clinometric** [–'metrɪk], adj.. **clinometry**, n.

clinophobia [‚klaɪnə'fəʊbiə] n. morbid fear of going to bed.

clinquant ['klɪŋkənt] adj. glittering; showy; n. tinsel; meretricious work of art.

clithridiate [klɪ'θrɪdieɪt] adj. keyhole-shaped.

clitoris ['klɪtərɪs] n. small, erectile, penis-like organ of female, near mouth of vagina. **clitoritis**, n. inflammation of this.

cloaca [kləʊ'eɪkə] n. (pl. **–ae**) sewer; watercloset; Zoology, passage or chamber receiving all bodily excretions in birds, reptiles, etc. **cloacal**, adj.

cloisonné [klwɑː'zɒneɪ] n. & adj. (applied to) enamel with colour applied in spaces partitioned off by wires.

clonic ['klɒnɪk] adj. irregularly spasmodic. **clonicity** [–'nɪs–], n.

closure ['kləʊʒə] n. Parliament, motion that 'the question be now put' which, if carried, ends debate on subject.

cloture ['kləʊtʃə] n. American, closure.

clou [kluː] (French) n. 'nail'; cynosure.

clough [klʌf] n. gully.

clumber ['klʌmbə] n. short-legged heavy kind of spaniel.

clupeoid ['kluːpiɔɪd] n. & adj. (fish) like a herring.

clypeus ['klɪpiəs] n. shield-shaped plate on an insect's head. **clypeate** adj. shaped like a round shield.

clysis ['klaɪsɪs] n. Medicine, washing-out of body cavity.

clysmian ['klɪzmiən] adj. pertaining or due to flood. **clysmic**, adj. cleansing.

clyster ['klɪstə] n. Medicine, enema; v.t. give clyster to.

cnemis ['niːmɪs] n. shin bone. **cnemial**, adj.

coaction [kəʊ'ækʃn] n. compulsion; joint action. **coactive**, adj.

coadjument [kəʊ'ædʒʊmənt] n. mutual aid.

coadjutor [kəʊ'ædʒʊtə] n. (fem. **coadjutrix**) helper; abettor. **coadjutant**, adj.

coadjuvant [kəʊ'ædʒʊvənt] adj. co-operating. **coadjuvancy**, n.

coadunate [kəʊ'ædjuneɪt] v.t. combine into one; [–nət], adj. united. **coadunation**, n. **coadunative**, adj.

coagment [‚kəʊæg'ment] v.t. cement together.

coapt(ate) [kəʊ'æpt, 'kəʊæpteɪt] v.t. join or fit together. **coaptation**, n.

coarctate [kəʊ'ɑːkteɪt] adj. closely pressed together. **coarctation**, n. constriction.

coati [kəʊ'ɑːti] n. raccoon-like animal of S and Central American.

coaxial [kəʊ'æksiəl] adj. having a common axis. **coaxial cable**, cable in which central conductor is surrounded by tubular conductor, the insulation between them being mostly air.

coble ['kəʊbl] n. flat, single-masted North-Sea fishing boat.

cocciferous [kɒk'sɪfərəs] adj. bearing berries.

coccus ['kɒkəs] n. (pl. **cocci** ['kɒksaɪ]) spherical bacterium.

coccyx ['kɒksɪks] n. bone at base of spinal column. **coccygeal** [–'sɪdʒiəl], adj. pertaining to or near this.

cochineal [‚kɒtʃɪ'niːl] n. scarlet dye obtained from dried insects.

cochlea ['kɒkliə] n. (pl. **–ae**) spirally coiled part of ear. **cochlear**, adj. pertaining to the cochlea; spirally shaped. **cochleate**, adj. like a screw or snail's shell.

cochleare [‚kɒkli'eəri] n. Medicine, spoonful. **cochleariform**, adj. spoon-shaped.

cockatrice ['kɒkətraɪs] n. basilisk.

cocket ['kɒkɪt] n. official seal; shipper's clearance; customs duty.

cocotte [kə'kɒt] (French) n. flirt; prostitute; kind of casserole.

coctile ['kɒktaɪl] adj. baked.

codex ['kəudeks] *n.* (*pl.* **-dices**) collection of ancient manuscripts, especially Biblical.

codicil ['kəudɪsɪl, 'kɒd–] *n.* clause added to and altering will; any additional clause or provision. **codicillary,** *adj.*

codon ['kəudɒn] *n.* a character, or group of characters, in the genetic code carried by the living cell, which directs the formation of a particular amino-acid.

coefficient [,kəuɪ'fɪʃnt] *n. Mathematics,* quantitative expression of some characteristic; number by which a variable is multiplied.

coelacanth ['siːləkænθ] *n.* large, spiny, bony-plated fish—probable link between fishes and amphibious reptiles—believed to have become extinct 60 million years ago, live specimens of which were caught in 1952.

coelanaglyphic [,siːlænə'glɪfɪk] *adj.* pertaining to cavo-relievo.

coelialgia [,siːli'ældʒiə] *n.* pain in belly.

coelom ['siːləm] *n.* body cavity. **coelomate** [–eɪt, sɪ'ləumət], *adj.* having this. **coeliac** ['siːliæk], *adj.*

coemption [kəu'empʃn] *n.* gaining monopoly in a commodity by buying all available supplies. **coemptor,** *n.* person practising this.

coenaculous [siː'nækjuləs] *adj.* fond of eating, especially suppers.

coenaesthesis [,siːnəs'θiːsɪs] *n. Psychology,* sensation as a whole.

coenobite ['siːnəbaɪt] *n.* cenobite.

coenotrope ['siːnətrəup] *n. Psychology,* conduct characteristic of a group.

coessential [,kəuɪ'senʃl] *adj. Religion,* formed from same substance.

coetaneous [,kəuɪ'teɪniəs] *adj.* contemporary.

coeval [kəu'iːvl] *n. & adj.* (person or thing) of same age; of same length of time.

cogent ['kəudʒənt] *adj.* compelling; forceful; convincing. **cogency,** *n.*

cogitate ['kɒdʒɪteɪt] *v.i. & t.* think deeply; consider seriously. **cogitable,** *adj.* conceivable. **cogitabund,** *adj.* deep in thought. **cogitation,** *n.* **cogitative,** *adj.* contemplative; having power of thought.

cognate ['kɒgneɪt] *adj.* having same ancestry; closely related; *n.* word of same origin; *Law,* relation on mother's side. **cognation,** *n.* such relationship.

cognisance ['kɒgnɪzns, 'kɒn–] *n.* extent of knowledge; notice, especially judicial; awareness; distinctive badge. **cognisant,** *adj.* taking notice; having knowledge. **cognise,** *v.t.* perceive; take notice of.

cognition [kɒg'nɪʃn] *n.* mental act of perceiving; knowledge. **cognitional,** *adj.* **cognitive,** *adj.* able to perceive or know.

cognomen [kɒg'nəumen] *n.* (*pl.* **-nomens, -nomina**) family name; nickname. **cognominal** [–'nɒmɪnl], *adj.*; *n.* namesake. **cognominate,** *v.t.*

cognoscenti [,kɒgnə'ʃenti, ,kɒnjə–] (*Italian*) *n.pl.* (*sing.* **-te**) connoisseurs.

cognovit [kɒg'nəuvɪt] *n. Law,* admission by defendant of justice of plaintiff's case.

cohabit [kəu'hæbɪt] *v.i.* live together, especially as man and wife. **cohabitant,** *n.* person cohabiting. **cohabitation,** *n.*

cohere [kəu'hɪə] *v.i.* adhere together; be united or consistent. **coherence,** *n.* **coherent,** *adj.* sensible; intelligible. **coherer,** *n. Radio,* early form of detector, based on an imperfect contact.

cohesion [kəu'hiːʒn] *n.* force uniting parts; interdependence. **cohesive** [–sɪv], *adj.*

cohibit [kəu'hɪbɪt] *v.t.* restrain. **cohibition,** *n.* **cohibitive,** *adj.*

cohort ['kəuhɔːt] *n.* company of soldiers, numbering from 300 to 600, in ancient Roman army; band of associates; *American,* associate.

coif [kɔɪf] *n.* close-fitting cap or hood, especially of women; skull cap; any headdress.

coiffeur [kwaː'fɜː, kwæ–] *n.* (*fem.* **coiffeuse,** [–'fɜːz]) hair-dresser. **coiffure,** *n.* hair-dressing; a manner of dressing the hair.

coign [kɔɪn] *n.* corner; angle; viewpoint.

coinstantaneous [,kəuɪnstən'teɪniəs] *adj.* occurring at same instant. **coinstantaneity** [–stæntə'neɪəti, –'niː–] *n.*

coir ['kɔɪə] *n.* fibre obtained from coconut husk.

coition, coitus [kəu'ɪʃn, 'kəuɪtəs] *n.* sexual intercourse. **coitus interruptus** [–,ɪntə'rʌptəs], *n.* withdrawal of the penis before ejaculation.

col [kɒl] *n.* pass between mountain peaks.

colation [kə'leɪʃn] *n.* filtering.

colchicum ['kɒltʃɪkəm, –kɪ–] *n.* meadow saffron;

The colon: its role in the sentence

The main functions of the colon in English are introductory and balancing. It is used to lead into material that follows from the part of the sentence preceding it. This material may be explanatory (*I feel awful: my head's splitting*); it may be interpretative (*I feel awful: it must have been something I ate*); or it may be amplificatory (*I feel awful: get me an aspirin*). In all these cases a full stop could be used instead, but the colon emphasizes more strongly the link with the preceding material. When what follows is only a single word, however, the colon is the only usual option (*He can think of only one thing: food*). The colon is also used to introduce lists (*For this recipe you need: 4 eggs, half a pint of milk, 6 ounces of flour,...*).

The other main function of the colon is to act as a sort of fulcrum for a sentence of two balancing parts. These parts may be parallel or, as in the following example, contrasting: *Many are called: few are chosen.* In such contexts a semicolon or comma is often used in place of a colon.

The colon has a range of other miscellaneous uses, including the introduction of a direct quotation, the separation of chapter and verse in Biblical references and of act number and scene number in plays (*Hamlet* II:i), the denoting of ratio and proportions (*a ratio of 2:1*), the introduction of an example of usage (as in the previous paragraph), and, in American English, the separation of hour and minutes in expressions of time.

autumn crocus. **colchicine** [–si:n], *n.* extract of this used as specific against gout.

coleopterous [ˌkɒli'ɒptərəs, ˌkəʊ–] *adj.* pertaining to beetles and weevils; having hard anterior wings. **coleopteran,** *n.* such insect. **coleopteroid,** *adj.* beetle-like. **coleopterology,** *n.* study of such insects.

colibri ['kɒlɪbri] (*Spanish*) *n.* humming-bird.

colic ['kɒlɪk] *n.* spasmic pain in intestines; *adj.* pertaining to colon.

coliform ['kəʊlɪfɔːm, 'kɒ–] *adj.* like a sieve.

colitis [kə'laɪtɪs] *n.* inflammation of colon.

collage [kɒ'lɑːʒ] *n.* creation of an artistic work by pasting shaped scraps of printed matter and other materials to a surface; such a composition.

collagen ['kɒlədʒən] *n.* gelatinous protein in bones and connective tissue. **collagenic** [–'dʒenɪk], *adj.*

collate [kə'leɪt] *v.t.* compare closely; classify; gather the pages (of a document) into their proper sequence.

collateral [kə'lætərəl] *adj.* derived from same main stock but subsidiary; secondary; *n.* such relative or happening; security for repayment of a loan.

collation [kə'leɪʃn] *n.* act of collating; bestowal of benefice; light meal, especially cold. **collative** [kə'leɪtɪv, 'kɒlətɪv], *adj.* having power to bestow benefice. **collator,** *n.*

collectivism [kə'lɛktɪvɪzm] *n.* theory of communal control of means of production; evolutionary socialism. **collectivist,** *n. & adj.*

collegium [kə'li:dʒiəm] *n.* managing board or committee.

collet ['kɒlɪt] *n.* flange holding a gem; metal collar or sleeve.

colletic [kə'letɪk] *n. & adj.* adhesive (substance).

colliform ['kɒlɪfɔːm] *adj.* neck-like.

colligate ['kɒlɪgeɪt] *v.t.* bind together; collate facts for deduction of principle therefrom. **colligation,** *n.*

collimate ['kɒlɪmeɪt] *v.t.* make parallel; adjust into line; adjust line of sight. **collimation,** *n.* **collimator,** *n.* device in optical instrument for adjusting line of sight or producing parallel rays.

collinear [kə'lɪnɪə, kəʊ–] *adj.* lying along same line. **collineate,** *v.t.* aim at; place in line with. **collineation,** *n.*

collingual [kə'lɪŋgwəl, kəʊ–] *adj.* having same language.

collocal [kə'ləʊkəl] *adj.* in same place.

collocate ['kɒləkeɪt] *v.t.* arrange; place side by side; *n.* word which frequently qualifies another. **collocation,** *n.* **collocative,** *adj.*

collocution [ˌkɒlə'kju:ʃn] *n.* conversation. **collocutor,** *n.* speaker in this.

colloid ['kɒlɔɪd] *n.* mixture between a solution and a fine suspension; jelly-like substance. **colloidal,** *adj.*

colloquy ['kɒləkwi] *n.* conversation; dialogue. **colloquial** [kə'ləʊkwiəl], *adj.* pertaining to ordinary speech. **colloquialism,** *n.* non-literary word or phrase; slang; use of such words or phrases. **colloquize,** *v.i.* converse; use colloquialisms.

collotype ['kɒlətaɪp] *n.* method of printing illustrations from hardened gelatin film.

collusion [kə'lu:ʒn] *n.* secret fraudulent agreement. **collusive,** *adj.*

collutory ['kɒljʊtəri] *n.* mouthwash.

colluvium [kə'lu:viəm] *n. Geology,* mixture of rock fragments. **colluvial,** *adj.*

collyrium [kə'lɪriəm] *n.* (*pl.* **–ia**) eye wash or ointment; suppository.

colocynth ['kɒləsɪnθ] *n.* kind of cucumber forming ingredient of purgative; 'bitter apple'.

colon ['kəʊlən] *n.* part of large intestine from caecum to rectum; punctuation mark (:). **colonic** [–'lɒnɪk], *adj.*

colophon ['kɒləfən] *n.* device, especially printer's or publisher's emblem, on book; statement at end of book of printer's name and other particulars of publication.

colophony [kə'lɒfəni] *n.* rosin.

coloratura [ˌkɒlərə'tjʊərə, –'tʊərə] (*Italian*) *n. & adj.* highly ornamented, virtuoso (musical passage); singer, especially soprano, of such music.

colorimeter [ˌkʌlə'rɪmɪtə] *n.* instrument for measuring quality or intensity of colour.

colostomy [kə'lɒstəmi] *n.* permanent opening made into colon.

colostrum [kə'lɒstrəm] *n.* mother's first milk. **colostral, colostric, colostrous,** *adj.*

colotomy [kə'lɒtəmi] *n.* surgical incision into colon.

colporteur [ˌkɒlpɔː'tɜː] *n.* itinerant seller or giver of books, especially religious literature. **colportage,** *n.*

colubrine ['kɒljubraɪn, –brɪn] *adj.* snake-like; cunning. **colubriform, colubroid,** *adj.* snake-shaped.

colugo [kə'lu:gəʊ] *n.* flying lemur.

columbaceous [ˌkɒləm'beɪʃəs] pertaining to pigeons. **columbarium,** *n.* collection of pigeon-holes; cinerarium. **columbine,** *adj.* like a dove. **columboid** [kə'lʌmbɔɪd], *adj.* like a pigeon.

columniation [kəˌlʌmni'eɪʃn] *n.* use or arrangement of columns in a structure.

colure [kə'lʊə, 'kəʊljʊə] *n.* celestial circle intersecting other at poles. **equinoctial colure,** such circle passing through equinoctial points. **solstitial colure,** such circle at right angles to equinoctial colure.

colytic [kə'lɪtɪk] *adj.* restraining; antiseptic.

comate ['kəʊmeɪt] *adj.* hairy.

comburent [kəm'bjʊərənt] *adj.* burning; *n.* substance aiding combustion. **comburivorous** [ˌkɒmbju'rɪvərəs], *adj.* consuming by burning.

comedo ['kɒmɪdəʊ] *n.* (*pl.* **–dos, –dones**) blackhead.

comestibles [kə'mestəblz] *n. pl.* victuals.

comiferous [kəʊ'mɪfərəs] *adj.* tufted.

comity ['kɒməti] *n.* civility; friendliness. **comity of nations,** *n.* respect for other countries' laws and customs.

commatic [kə'mætɪk] *adj.* divided into short stanzas or lines; pertaining to comma. **commatism,** *n.*

comme ci comme ça [kɒm ˌsi: kɒm 'sɑː] (*French*) *adv.* 'like this like that'; so-so.

comme il faut [ˌkɒm i:l 'fəʊ] (*French*) 'as is necessary'; as it should be; according to good manners; immaculate.

commensal [kə'mensl] *adj.* living and feeding together; *n* such organism; symbiont. **commensalism, commensality,** *n.*

commensurable [kə'menʃərəbl] *adj.* measurable by same standard; proportionate. **commensurate,**

adj. proportionate; *v.t.* make proportionate. **commensuration,** *n.*

commère ['kɒmeə] *(French)* *n.* gossiping woman; female compère. **commèrage** [–'rɑːʒ], *n.* gossip.

commination [ˌkɒmɪ'neɪʃn] *n.* denunciation; cursing; threatening. **comminative** ['kɒm–], **comminatory** [kə'mɪnətəri], *adj.*

comminute ['kɒmɪnjuːt] *v.t.* pulverize. **comminution,** *n.*

commis ['kɒmi] *(French)* *n.* agent; deputy; assistant, especially apprentice waiter or chef.

commissar [ˌkɒmɪ'sɑː] *n.* former title of a chief of a Soviet government department. **commissarial** [–'seəriəl], *adj.* **commissariat** [–'seəriət], *n.* army department of food and stores; supply. **commissary** ['kɒmɪsəri], *n.* commissariat chief; deputy; appointee.

commissure ['kɒmɪsjuə, –ʃuə] *n.* seam; joint; cleft. **commissural,** *adj.*

commodious [kə'məudiəs] *adj.* spacious; convenient.

commonalty ['kɒmənlti] *n.* common people.

commonition [ˌkɒmə'nɪʃn] *n.* warning.

commorant ['kɒmərənt] *n.* & *adj.* (person) residing or dwelling. **commorancy,** *n.*

commorient [kə'mɔːriənt] *adj.* dying together; *n.* such person.

communiqué [kə'mjuːnɪkeɪ] *n.* written communication; dispatch, especially official.

commutation [ˌkɒmju'teɪʃn] *n.* exchange; substitution; *American,* commuter travel. **commutation ticket,** *American,* season ticket.

commutator ['kɒmjuteɪtə] *n. Electricity,* device transforming alternating current produced by dynamo into direct current, especially segmented drum bearing brushes which collect the current.

commute [kə'mjuːt] *v.t.* exchange especially for something less, or many small amounts for one large amount; substitute a lighter penalty for; *v.i.* travel regularly between home and work. **commuter,** *n.*

comose ['kəuməus] *adj.* with tuft of hair. **comoid,** *adj.* like a tuft of hair. **comous,** *adj.* hairy.

compaternity [ˌkɒmpə'tɜːnəti] *n.* relationship in spirit between god-parents, and between them and actual parents.

compeer ['kɒmpiə] *n.* equal; peer.

compellation [ˌkɒmpə'leɪʃn] *n.* calling upon by name; manner in which person is addressed. **compellative** [kəm'pelətɪv], *adj.;* *n.* name by which person is addressed.

compendium [kəm'pendiəm] *n.* (*pl.* –ia) summary; epitome. **compendious,** *adj.* containing much in small space.

competent ['kɒmpɪtənt] *adj.* sufficiently skilful, knowledgeable, qualified, etc.; capable, effective; *Law,* legally qualified; belonging by right (to). **competence,** *n.* ability; *Law,* legal qualification or capacity; income, especially unearned, sufficient to live on; ability of embryonic tissue to react to external conditions.

complaisant [kəm'pleɪznt] *adj.* obliging; desirous of pleasing. **complaisance,** *n.*

complanate ['kɒmpləneɪt] *adj.* level. **complanation,** *n.* act of levelling.

complement ['kɒmplɪmənt] *n.* full number or amount; addition that makes up full number; one of two equal things that complete each

other; *Grammar,* addition to complete a predicate; *v.t.* [–ment] complete. (*as opposed to* **compliment**)**complemental, complementary,** *adj.*

completory [kəm'pliːtəri] *n.* compline.

complicity [kəm'plɪsəti] *n.* fact of being an accomplice.

compliment ['kɒmplɪmənt] *n.* expression of praise or admiration; (*pl.*) formal greetings or expressions of respect; *v.t.* [–ment] praise, congratulate. (*as opposed to* **complement**). **complimentary,** *adj.* expressing praise or admiration; given free of charge.

complin(e) ['kɒmplɪn] *n. Roman Catholic,* last service or prayer of day.

complot ['kɒmplɒt] *n.* plot; conspiracy; *v.i.* & *t.* plot; conspire.

comport [kəm'pɔːt] *v.t.* conduct, behave; *v.i.* accord. **comportment,** *n.*

composite ['kɒmpəzɪt] *n.* & *adj.* (thing) composed of a number of parts; compound. **compositive** [kəm'pɒzɪtɪv], *adj.* synthetic.

compos mentis [ˌkɒmpəs 'mentɪs] *(Latin) adj.* sane. **non compos mentis,** insane; not responsible for actions.

compossible [kəm'pɒsəbl] *adj.* able to coexist or coincide with other thing.

compotation [ˌkɒmpə'teɪʃn] *n.* drinking-party. **compotator,** *n.* **compotatory,** *adj.*

compote ['kɒmpəut] *(French) n.* mixed fruit with syrup; mixed savoury dish. **compotier** [kɒm'pəutieɪ], *n.* dish for this.

comprador(e) [ˌkɒmprə'dɔː] *(Portuguese) n.* native major-domo; Chinese native agent or manager.

comprecation [ˌkɒmprɪ'keɪʃn] *n.* praying together.

compte rendu [ˌkɒnt 'rɒnduː] *(French) n.* 'account rendered'; report.

compunction [kəm'pʌŋkʃn] *n.* remorse; regret. **compunctious,** *adj.*

compurgation [ˌkɒmpə'geɪʃn] *n.* vindication. **compurgatory,** *adj.*

compute [kəm'pjuːt] *v.t.* & *t.* calculate, reckon. **computable,** *adj.* **computation** [ˌkɒmpju'teɪʃn], *n.* **computative** [kəm'pjuːtətɪv], *adj.* using calculation.

con amore [ˌkɒn ə'mɔːreɪ] *(Italian)* 'with love'; with enthusiasm.

conarium [kə'neəriəm] *n.* pineal gland. **conarial,** *adj.*

conation [kəu'neɪʃn] *n.* mental striving. **conative** ['kɒnətɪv, 'kəu–], *adj.;* *Grammar,* expressing endeavour.

concamerated [kɒn'kæməreɪtɪd] *adj.* divided into chambers. **concameration,** *n.* vaulting; vaulted roof.

concatenate [kən'kætəneɪt] *v.t.* link together; form into series; *adj.* linked together. **concatenation,** *n.* chain; sequence; series.

concavo-convex [kɒn,keɪvəu–kɒn'veks] *adj.* with one side concave and other convex. **concavo-concave,** *adj.* concave on both sides.

concede [kən'siːd] *v.t.* admit, acknowledge; allow, grant; surrender; *Sport,* allow opponent to score; *v.i.* admit defeat. **conceder,** *n.*

concelebrate [kɒn'seləbreɪt] *v.t.* celebrate the Eucharist with one or more other priests. **concelebration,** *n.*

concentre [kɒn'sentə] v.t. & i. (cause to) have or converge on a common centre.

concentric [kən'sentrɪk] adj. having a common centre. concentricity [–'trɪs–], n.

conceptualism [kən'septʃuəlɪzm] n. philosophical theory that universal truths exist as mental concepts.

concertante [ˌkɒntʃə'tænti] adj. Music, exhibiting or needing great skill and brilliancy; alternating tutti passages and passages for a group of soloists.

concerto grosso [kən,tʃeətəu 'grɒsəu] n. (pl. concerti grossi [–iː]) concerto, especially of Baroque period, for more than one soloist.

conch [kɒŋk, kɒntʃ] n. (pl. –s, –es) spiral shell. conchate, conchic, adj. having a conch. conchiferous, adj. bearing a conch. conchiform, adj. shell-shaped. conchitic, adj. containing shells. conchitis, n. inflammation of external ear. conchoid, adj. shell-like; n. simple curve. conchology, n. study of shells.

conchyliated [kɒŋ'kɪliːeɪtɪd] adj. obtained from molluscs. conchyliferous [ˌkɒŋkɪ'lɪfərəs], adj. bearing a shell.

concierge ['kɒnsieəʒ] (French) n. door-keeper; caretaker.

conciliabule [kən'sɪliəbjuːl] n. secret meeting of plotters.

conciliar [kən'sɪliə] adj. pertaining to council.

concinnous [kən'sɪnəs] adj. harmonious; fit; elegant. concinnity, n.

concision [kən'sɪʒn] n. conciseness; division; schism.

conclamation [ˌkɒŋklə'meɪʃn] n. shouting together. conclamant [–'klæmənt], adj.

conclave ['kɒŋkleɪv] n. meeting, especially secret or solemn; Roman Catholic, meeting of cardinals for election of pope; rooms in which such meeting is held.

concolorate [kɒn'kʌləreɪt] adj. having same colour on both sides.

concomitant [kən'kɒmɪtənt] n. & adj. accompanying (thing or circumstance). concomitance, n.; Roman Catholic, existence of both body and blood of Christ in one element of Eucharist. concomitancy, n.

concordance [kən'kɔːdns] n. index or listing of words in a book or text; agreement. concordant, adj. agreeing; consistent.

concordat [kɒn'kɔːdæt] n. amicable agreement; treaty.

concordia discors [kɒn,kɔːdiə 'dɪskɔːz] (Latin) n. 'discordant concord'; armed truce.

concours d'élégance [kɔːn'kuə deɪ'leɪgaːns] (French,) 'meeting of elegance'; competition or rally with prizes for neatness, beauty, etc., especially of motor cars.

concresce [kən'kres] v.i. grow together; coalesce. concrescence, n. concrement ['kɒŋkrɪmənt], n. concretion.

concrete [kən'kriːt] v.i. solidify; coalesce. concretion [kən'kriːʃn], n. mass formed by coalescence; stone-like formation in bodily organ. concretionary, concretive, adj.

concubine ['kɒŋkjubaɪn] n. woman living with man without marriage; secondary wife. concubinage [kɒn'kjuːbɪnɪdʒ], n. concubinal, adj.

concubitant [kən'kjuːbɪtənt] adj. marriageable.

concubitancy, n. concubitous, adj. concubitus, n. coition.

concupiscent [kən'kjuːpɪsnt] adj. having strong sexual desires. concupiscence, n lust.

condign [kən'daɪn] adj. deserved; adequate; appropriate.

condominium [ˌkɒndə'mɪniəm] n. joint rule by two states or persons; American, apartment building with apartments under individual ownership. condominate [–'dɒmɪneɪt], adj.

condottiere [ˌkɒndɒti'eəreɪ] (Italian) n. (pl. –ri [–riː]) mercenary soldier; captain of mercenary band.

conductitious [ˌkɒndʌk'tɪʃəs] adj. hired; for hire.

condyle ['kɒndaɪl] n. knuckle-like prominence at end of bone. condylar ['kɒndɪlə], adj. condyloid ['kɒndɪlɔɪd], adj. near or shaped like this.

confabulate [kən'fæbjuleɪt] v.i. chat; hold a discussion; Psychology, replace memory gaps with imagined experiences. confabulation, n.

confect [kən'fekt] v.t. put together (from varied materials). confection, n. fancy sweet dish, sweetened medicinal preparation; elaborate or fanciful creation.

confelicity [ˌkɒnfə'lɪsəti] n. pleasure in other's happiness.

conferva [kən'fɜːvə, kɒn–] n. greenish algae on surface of stagnant water. conferval, confervoid, confervous, adj.

confidant ['kɒnfɪdænt] n. (fem. confidante) confidential friend.

configuration [kən,fɪgjə'reɪʃn, –gə–] n. general outline or appearance; totality of a computer and the devices connected to it. configural, configurate, configurative, adj. configure, v.t.

confiteor [kən'fɪtiɔː, kɒn–] (Latin) 'I confess'; n. prayer confessing sins.

confluent ['kɒnfluənt] adj. flowing together; combining; n. such stream. confluence, conflux, n.

confrère ['kɒnfreə] (French) n. colleague; associate; fellow.

confute [kən'fjuːt] v.t. prove to be wrong; overcome in argument. confutation [ˌkɒnfju'teɪʃn], n.

congé [kɔːn'ʒeɪ] n. leave, especially to go; dismissal; bow. congé d'élire [–deɪlɪə'], permission to elect.

congelation [ˌkɒndʒɪ'leɪʃn] n. act or state of freezing solid.

congener [kən'dʒiːnə, 'kɒndʒɪnə] n. person or thing of same kind. congeneracy [–'dʒenərəsi], n. congeneric [–'nerɪk], congenerous [–'dʒenərəs], adj.

congenetic [ˌkɒndʒə'netɪk] adj. having common origin.

congenital [kən'dʒenɪtl] adj. existing at or dating from birth.

congeries [kɒn'dʒɪəriːz] n. conglomeration; heap or mess.

conglobate [kɒn'gləubeɪt, 'kɒŋgləu–] adj. ball-shaped; v.i. & t. form or be formed into a ball-shaped mass. conglobation, n.

conglobulate [kən'glɒbjuleɪt] v.t. form into a ball. conglobulation, n.

conglomerate [kən'glɒməreɪt] n. Geology, rock formed of rounded fragments; anything composed of particles from diverse sources; v.t. form into mass or balls; [–ət], adj. formed into a mass; concentrated. **conglomeration,** *n.*

conglutinate [kən'gluːtɪneɪt] *v.t.* join together; glue; [–ət], *adj.* stuck together. **conglutinant,** *n.* & *adj.* glueing or healing (substance). **conglutination,** *n.* **conglutinative,** *adj.*

congou ['kɒŋguː] *n.* kind of black China tea.

congruent, congruous ['kɒŋgruənt, –əs] *adj. Geometry,* in agreement or correspondence; exactly coincident. **congruence, congruity** [kən'gruːəti], *n.*

conic ['kɒnɪk] *adj.* pertaining to cone. **conic section,** *Mathematics,* curve formed by intersection of plane and right circular cone.

conifer ['kɒnɪfə, 'kəʊ–] *n.* cone-bearing tree. **conification,** *n.* making or becoming cone-shaped, tapering or pyramidal. **coniform,** *adj.* cone-shaped. **coniferous** [–'nɪfərəs], *adj.*

conjee ['kɒndʒiː] (*Anglo-Indian*) *n.* liquid of boiled rice. **conjee house,** military prison or guard-room.

conjugal ['kɒndʒʊgl] *adj.* pertaining to marriage. **conjugacy,** *n.*, **conjugate,** *v.i.* & *t.* conjoin; *Grammar,* name inflections of verb; *adj.* paired. **conjugation,** *n. Biology,* union of cells in reproduction; groups of verbs with same inflections. **conjugative,** *adj.*

conjunction [kən'dʒʌŋkʃn] *n.* joining together; coincidence; *Grammar,* word used to connect words, phrases or sentences; *Astrononomy,* position of heavenly body when its longitude is same as another's. **conjunctional, conjunctive,** *adj.*

conjunctiva [ˌkɒndʒʌŋk'taɪvə] *n.* membrane lining eyelid and joining it with eyeball. **conjunctival,** *adj.* **conjunctivitis,** *n.* inflammation of this.

connate ['kɒneɪt] *adj.* congenital; joined together from birth. **connation,** *n.* **connatural,** *adj.* congenital; having same nature.

connive [kə'naɪv] *v.i.* permit tacitly; wink (at). **connivance,** *n*

connote [kə'nəʊt] *v.t.* imply; suggest. **connotation** [ˌkɒnə'teɪʃn], *n.* **connotative** ['kɒnəteɪtɪv], *adj.*

connubial [kə'njuːbiəl] *adj.* pertaining to marriage. **connubiality,** *n.*

connumerate [kə'njuːməreɪt] *v.t.* count together. **connumeration,** *n.*

conoid ['kəʊnɔɪd] *n.* & *adj.* somewhat conical (object). **conoidal,** *adj.*

conquistador [kɒn'kwɪstədɔː] *n.* conqueror, especially Spanish conqueror of Central and S America.

consanguinity [ˌkɒnsæŋ'gwɪnəti] *n.* blood-relationship. **consanguineal, consanguineous,** *adj.*

consecution [ˌkɒnsɪ'kjuːʃn] *n.* logical advance in argument; sequence. **consecutive** [kən'sekjutɪv], *adj.* following in uninterrupted or logical order.

consenescence [ˌkɒnsɪ'nesns] *n.* growing old together.

consensus [kən'sensəs] *n.* harmony; agreement; unanimity; general trend. **consension,** *n.* unanimity. **consensual,** *adj.* based on agreement only.

consentaneous [ˌkɒnsen'teɪniəs] *adj.* agreeing; unanimous; suitable. **consentaneity** [–ə'neɪəti, –'niː–], *n.*

consentient [kən'sentiənt, –'senʃnt] *adj.* agreeing; unanimous. **consentience,** *n.*

conservatoire, conservatory, conservatorium

[kən'sɔːvətwɑː, –'sɔːvətəri, –ˌsɔːvə'tɔːriəm] *n.* school of music.

consignificant [ˌkɒnsɪg'nɪfɪkənt] *adj.* synonymous; meaningless unless used with another word. **consignification,** *n.* meaning in context. **consignify,** *v.t.*

consilient [kən'sɪliənt] *adj.* agreeing in inferences drawn from different premises. **consilience,** *n.*

consistory [kən'sɪstəri] *n.* council chamber; papal senate; ecclesiastical court; *adj.* pertaining to this. **consistorial** [ˌkɒnsɪ'stɔːriəl] *adj.*

consonance ['kɒnsənəns] *n.* agreement; harmony. **consonant, consonous,** *adj.* **consonate,** *v.t.* sound in harmony.

conspecies [kɒn'spiːʃiːz] *n.* species belonging to same genus; variety. **conspecific** [ˌkɒnspə'sɪfɪk], *adj.* belonging to same species.

conspectus [kən'spektəs] *n.* general view or outline; summary.

conspue [kən'spjuː] *v.t.* spurn; despise.

constate [kən'steɪt] *v.t.* establish upon positive evidence. **constatation** [ˌkɒnstə'teɪʃn], *n.*

constringe [kən'strɪndʒ] *v.t.* cause to contract; constrict. **constringent,** *adj.* **constringency,** *n.*

construe [kən'struː] *v.t.* translate; interpret; analyse grammatically in order to explain meaning.

consubstantial [ˌkɒnsəb'stænʃl] *adj.* having or formed from same substance. **consubstantiation,** *n.* presence of Christ's body in Holy Communion bread and wine. **consubstantiate** *v.i.* **consubstantiality,** *n.*

consuetude ['kɒnswɪtjuːd] *n.* established custom. **consuetudinal,** *adj.* **consuetudinary,** *adj.*; *n.* book of customs and laws of an association, especially of monastic life.

consummate [kən'sʌmət, 'kɒnsə–] *adj.* perfect; entirely complete; ['kɒnsəmeɪt] *v.i.* & *t.* complete; especially complete (a marriage) by sexual intercourse; fulfil; be or reach culmination. **consummation, consummator,** *n.* **consummative, consummatory,** *adj.*

contabescent [ˌkɒntə'besnt] *adj.* wasting away. **contabescence,** *n.*

contadino [ˌkɒntə'diːnəʊ] (*Italian*) *n.* (*pl.* **–ni;** *feminine* **–na,** *pl.* **–ne**) peasant.

contango [kən'tæŋgəʊ] *n. Commerce,* charge paid by purchaser for postponing payment from one settling day to next; *v.i.* permit such postponement. **contango day,** the day, second before settling day, on which such arrangements are made.

conte [kɒnt] (*French*) *n.* short story. **conte pieux** [ˌkɒnt pi'ɜː], moral story. **conteur** [kɒn'tɜː], writer of these.

contect [kən'tekt] *v.t.* cover. **contection,** *n.*

contemn [kən'tem] *v.t.* treat with contempt; scorn. **contemner, contemnor** [–'temə, –'temnə], *n.*

contemporaneous [kənˌtempə'reɪniəs] *adj.* existing at same time. **contemporaneity** [–rə'neɪəti, –'niː–], *n.* **contemporary** [–'tempərəri], *adj.* of same or present time; *n.* such person; living person; newspaper, etc., published at present day. **contemporize,** *v.t.* cause to occur at same time.

contention [kən'tenʃn] *n.* quarrel; strife; opinion; belief. **contentious,** *adj.* quarrelsome; controversial.

conterminous [kən'tɜːmɪnəs, kɒn–] *adj.* having

common boundary, extent or termination. **conterminant,** *adj.* ending together. **conterminate,** *adj.*

context ['kɒntekst] *n.* words or passages immediately preceding and following a word or passage. **contextual** [kən'tekstjuəl], *adj.*

contiguous [kən'tɪgjuəs] *adj.* adjacent; touching. **contiguity,** *n.*

continence ['kɒntɪnəns] *n.* self-restraint, especially sexual; able to voluntarily control discharge of urine and faeces. **continent,** *adj.*

contingent [kən'tɪndʒənt] *adj.* possible; able to take place; accidental; conditional; *n.* full number of draft of troops. **contingent liability,** *Commerce,* one that may have to be assumed in certain circumstances. **contingency,** *n.* possibility; event that may take place; close relationship.

continuum [kən'tɪnjuəm] *n.* (*pl.* **–nua**) something that is entirely continuous and homogeneous, and can be described only by reference to other things; something containing one common recognisable factor in a multitude of parts or variations. **space-time continuum,** area of four dimensions (three of space, and one of time) in which everything may be determined.

contour ['kɒntuə] *n.* outline; line passing through all places of same altitude.

contraband ['kɒntrəbænd] *n. & adj.* smuggled (goods); goods which it is forbidden to carry or import. **contraband of war,** goods supplied to one belligerent and seizable by another. **absolute contraband,** goods of a kind intended for war use only, *e.g.* armaments. **conditional contraband,** goods which only become contraband of war if specifically intended for war use, *e.g.* food, etc. **contrabandage, contrabandism,** *n.* **contrabandist,** *n.*

contrabass ['kɒntrəbeɪs] *n. & adj.* (voice or instrument) one octave lower than bass; double-bass.

contra bonos mores [ˌkɒntrə ˌbəunəus 'mɔːreɪz, –iːz] (*Latin*) 'against good morals'; harmful to public morality.

contractile [kən'træktaɪl] *adj.* able or causing to grow smaller. **contractility** [ˌkɒntræk'tɪləti], *n.*

contradistinguish [ˌkɒntrədɪs'tɪŋgwɪʃ] *v.t.* differentiate by reference to opposites. **contradistinct,** *adj.* so differentiated. **contradistinction,** *n.*

contrahent ['kɒntrəhənt] *n. & adj.* (party) entering into contract.

contraindicate [ˌkɒntrə'ɪndɪkeɪt] *v.t.* advise against; make unadvisable.

contra mundum [ˌkɒntrə 'mundum, –'mʌndəm] (*Latin*) 'against the world'; in defiance of all accepted belief.

contra pacem [ˌkɒntrə 'pɑːkem, –'peɪsem] (*Latin*) 'against the peace'.

contrapuntal [ˌkɒntrə'pʌntl] *adj.* pertaining to counterpoint. **contrapuntist,** *n.* expert in counterpoint.

contravene [ˌkɒntrə'viːn] *v.t.* infringe; oppose. **contravention** [–'venʃn], *n.*

contretemps ['kɒntrətɒm] (*French*) *n.* unlooked-for mishap; awkward situation.

controvert [ˌkɒntrə'vɜːt] *v.t.* dispute; doubt. **controversial,** *adj.* about which there is dispute. **controversialist,** *n.* disputer. **controversy** ['kɒntrəvɜːsi, kən'trɒvəsi], *n.* dispute.

contubernal [kən'tjuːbənl] *n & adj.* cohabiting (person).

contumacious [ˌkɒntju'meɪʃəs] *adj.* obstinate; rebellious. **contumacy** ['kɒntjuməsi], *n.* **contumacity** [–'æs–], *n.* such act.

contumely ['kɒntjuːmli] *n.* insult; contempt. **contumelious,** [–'miːliəs] *adj.*

contuse [kən'tjuːz] *v.t.* bruise. **contusion,** *n.* **contusive,** *adj.*

conurbation [ˌkɒnɜː'beɪʃn, –nə–] *n.* city surrounded by large number of urban districts.

convection [kən'vekʃn] *n.* conveying; movement of particles of fluid due to alterations in density, especially caused by heat. **convective,** *adj.*

convenances ['kɒnvənɒns, –ɪz] (*French*) *n.pl.* the proprieties; conventions.

conventicle [kən'ventɪkl] *n.* chapel; meeting-house; nonconformist assembly. **conventicular** [ˌkɒnven'tɪkjulə], *adj.*

conventual [kən'ventʃuəl] *adj.* pertaining to convent; *n.* inmate of convent.

conversant [kən'vɜːsnt] *adj.* closely acquainted; having deep knowledge. **conversance,** *n.*

conversazione [ˌkɒnvəsætsi'əuni] (*Italian*) *n.* (*pl.* **–ni**) social gathering.

converse ['kɒnvɜːs] *n. & adj.* opposite.

convexo-concave [kən,veksəukɒn'keɪv] *adj.* convex on one side and concave on other. **convexo-convex,** *adj.*, convex on both sides.

conveyance [kən'veɪəns] *n.* *Law,* act or document by which title to property is transferred. **conveyancing,** *n.* **conveyancer,** *n.* lawyer dealing in such business.

convivial [kən'vɪviəl] *adj.* pertaining to banquet; festive; jolly. **conviviality,** *n.* **convive** ['kɒnvaɪv], *n.* fellow-guest at banquet.

convocation [ˌkɒnvə'keɪʃn] *n.* act of calling together, or assembly of persons; ecclesiastical conference; assembly of graduates of university. **convocational,** *adj.*

convolute ['kɒnvəluːt] *adj.* spiral; *v.i. & t.* twist; contort. **convolution,** *n.* spiral shape; one coil of spiral. **convoluted,** *adj.* intricate and difficult.

cony, coney ['kəuni] *n.* rabbit.

co-opt [kəu'ɒpt] *v.t.* elect by the votes of existing members; commandeer. **co-option,** *n.*

copaiba [kə'paɪbə] *n.* kind of oily resin. **copaibic, copaivic,** *adj.*

copal ['kəupl] *n.* kind of resin used in varnishes, etc.

coparcener [kəu'pɑːsənə] *n.* joint heir. **coparcenary,** *n. & adj.*

cophosis [kə'fəusɪs] *n.* deafness.

copolymer [kəu'pɒlɪmə] *n.* a compound of high molecular weight produced by polymerizing two or more different monomers. **copolymerize** [–'pɒlɪməraɪz] *v.i. & t.* to become or make into a copolymer.

copperas ['kɒpərəs] *n.* sulphate of iron; green vitriol.

copra ['kɒprə] *n.* dried kernels of coconuts yielding coconut oil.

copraemia [kɒ'priːmiə] *n.* poisoning resulting from chronic constipation.

coprolalia [ˌkɒprə'leɪliə] *n.* use of obscene language. **coprolaliac,** person practising this.

coprolite ['kɒprəlaɪt] *n.* fossilized faeces. **coprolith,** *n.* hard mass of faecal matter. **coprolitic** [–'lɪtɪk], *adj.*

coprology [kɒ'prɒlədʒi] *n.* study of filth or faeces, or of obscene literature.

coprophagy [kɒ'prɒfədʒi] *n.* feeding on dung. **coprophagan** [–gən], *n.* dung beetle. **coprophagous** [–gəs], *adj.*

coprophilia [ˌkɒprə'fɪliə] *n.* love of obscenity. **coprophilous** [kɒ'prɒfɪləs], *adj.* living in or feeding on dung.

coprostasis [kɒ'prɒstəsɪs] *n.* constipation.

coprozoic [ˌkɒprə'zəʊɪk] *adj.* living in dung.

copula ['kɒpjʊlə] *n.* link; verb, especially part of *to be*, linking subject and predicate. **copular,** *adj.*

copulate ['kɒpjʊleɪt] *v.i.* unite in sexual intercourse. **copulation,** *n.* **copulative,** *adj.*; *Grammar,* applied to conjunctions which join like terms, implying addition and co-ordination. **copulatory,** *adj.*

copyhold ['kɒpihəʊld] *n.* tenure of manor land at will of lord of manor; land so held. **copyholder,** *n.* holder of such land.

coquillage [ˌkɒkiː'jɑːʒ] *(French) n.* shell-like decoration.

coquito [kəʊ'kiːtəʊ] *n.* Chilean palm yielding sap, seeds and fibre.

coracle ['kɒrəkl] *n.* light round wicker boat covered with skin.

coram populo [ˌkɔːræm 'pɒpjʊləʊ] *(Latin)* 'in the presence of the public'; for appearance's sake. **coram judice** [–'dʒuːdɪsi, –ɪkeɪ], before a judge. **coram paribus** [–'pærɪbəs], before one's equals or peers.

corbel ['kɔːbl] *n.* supporting projection from wall.

corbiculate [kɔː'bɪkjʊlət] *adj.* like a small basket; pertaining to bee's pollen-holding organ.

cordate ['kɔːdeɪt] *adj.* heart-shaped. **cordiform,** *adj.*

cordillera [ˌkɔːdɪl'jeərə] *n.* system of, especially parallel, mountain ranges. **cordilleran,** *adj.*

cordite ['kɔːdaɪt] *n.* smokeless explosive powder compounded of guncotton, nitro-glycerine and vaseline.

cordon bleu [ˌkɔːdɒn 'blɜː] *(French) adj.* 'blue ribbon'; of the highest distinction in cookery.

cordovan ['kɔːdəvn] *n.* Cordova leather, originally of goatskin, later of pig- and horse-skin.

cordwainer ['kɔːdweɪnə] *n.* shoemaker.

coriaceous [ˌkɒri'eɪʃəs] *adj.* like or consisting of leather.

coriander [ˌkɒri'ændə] *n.* plant yielding seeds used in medical and in curries and pickles.

corinne [kə'rɪn] *n.* gazelle.

corkage ['kɔːkɪdʒ] *n.* charge made by hotel keeper for serving bottle of wine, or for consumption in his hotel of bottle purchased elsewhere.

corm [kɔːm] *n.* swollen bulb-like subterranean part of stem, bearing buds. **cormel,** *n.* small corm. **cormoid,** *adj.* like corms. **cormophyte,** *n.* plant with stem and root. **cormous,** *adj.* producing corms.

cornea ['kɔːniə] *n.* transparent horny substance protecting eyeball. **corneal,** *adj.*

cornelian [kɔː'niːliən] *n.* carnelian.

cornemuse ['kɔːnmjuːz] *n.* ancient bagpipe-like instrument.

corneous ['kɔːniəs] *adj.* horny. **corniculate,** *adj.* having horns or horn-like outgrowths. **cornific,** *adj.* producing horn or horns. **corniform,** *adj.*,

horn-shaped. **cornigerous,** *adj.* bearing horns.

corniche [kɔː'niːʃ] *n.* coastal road, especially one running along a cliff face.

cornucopia [ˌkɔːnju'kəʊpiə] *n. (pl.* **–ae, –s)** horn, or source, of plenty; horn-shaped container.

cornute [kɔː'njuːt, 'kɔːnjuːt] *v.t.* cuckold; *adj.* with horn-like outgrowths. **cornuted,** *adj.* horned; horn-shaped.

corolla [kə'rɒlə] *n.* the petals of a flower collectively. **corollaceous** [ˌkɒrə'leɪʃəs], *adj.*

corollary [kə'rɒləri] *n.* fact or proposition that follows naturally from one already proved.

corollate ['kɒrəleɪt] *adj.* having a corolla. **corolliferous,** *adj.* **corolliform, corolline,** *adj.* shaped like a corolla.

corona [kə'rəʊnə] *n. (pl.* **–ae, –as)** coloured ring, due to diffraction, seen round sun or moon; luminous envelope surrounding sun; *Phonetics,* tip of tongue.

coronach ['kɒrənæx] *(Scottish) n.* dirge.

coronagraph [kə'rəʊnəgrɑːf] *n.* astronomical instrument by which the solar corona can be observed in full sunlight.

coronal ['kɒrənl, kə'rəʊnl] *adj.* pertaining to corona or crown of head; *n.* coronet; fillet.

coronary ['kɒrənəri] *adj.* crown-shaped; *Anatomy,* that encircles; *n.* coronary thrombosis. **coronary artery,** artery supplying heart tissues with blood. **coronary thrombosis,** formation of clot in coronary artery.

coronoid ['kɒrənɔɪd] *adj.* beak-shaped.

corozo [kə'rəʊzəʊ] *n.* several tropical New World palms, especially ivory palm.

corporal ['kɔːpərəl] *adj.* pertaining to body. **corporality,** *n.* state of having a body. **corporate,** *adj.*

corporeal [kɔː'pɔːriəl] *adj.* physical; pertaining to or having a body; tangible. **corporeality, corporeity,** *n.*

corposant ['kɔːpəzænt] *n.* flamelike electrical discharge from ship's masts, steeples, etc., in thundery weather; St. Elmo's fire.

corpus ['kɔːpəs] *n. (pl.* **–pora)** body, especially of written works on a certain subject; all of texts gathered for linguistic research. **corpus delicti** [–dɪ'lɪktaɪ], basic fact necessary to prove crime to have been committed; *erroneously,* body of murdered person. **corpus juris,** body of laws of a state. **corpus luteum** [–'luːtiəm], mass of tissue formed after release of an egg in mammals. **corpus vile** [–'vaɪli], worthless thing.

corpuscle ['kɔːpʌsl] *n.* particle; minute portion or body. **corpuscular** [kɔː'pʌskjʊlə], *adj.* **corpusculated,** *adj.* having corpuscles. **corpusculous,** *adj.* containing corpuscles.

corral [kə'rɑːl] *n.* enclosure for horses, cattle, etc.; *v.t.* drive into a corral.

corregidor [kə'regɪdɔː] *(Spanish) n.* magistrate.

correlate ['kɒrəleɪt] *v.i. & t.* have or demonstrate close relationship; bring into relation or accord; *n.* one of two things or propositions that necessitates or implies the other. **correlation,** *n.* **correlative** [kə'relətɪv], *n. & adj.*

correption [kə'repʃn] *n.* shortening in pronunciation.

corrie ['kɒri] *n.* round hollow in hillside.

corrigendum [ˌkɒrɪ'dʒendəm] *n. (pl.* **–da)** thing to be corrected; erratum.

corrigible ['kɒrɪdʒəbl] *adj.* capable of correction.

corrivate ['kɒrɪveɪt] v.t. make to flow together. corrivation, n.

corrobboree [kə'rɒbəriː] n. Australian aborigines' festivity and dance; any noisy gathering; uproar.

corroborant [kə'rɒbərənt] adj. Medicine, tonic; that corroborates; n. tonic.

corroborate [kə'rɒbəreɪt] v.t. confirm. corroboration, n. corroborative, adj.; n. corroborant. corroboratory, adj.

corsage [kɔː'sɑːʒ] n. part of dress over bust; bouquet worn on dress.

corsetier [kɔː'setiei] (French) n. (fem. -ière [-iːə]) corset-maker.

cortège [kɔː'teɪʒ, -'teʒ] n. procession, especially funeral.

cortex ['kɔːteks] n. outer part, rind; grey matter of the brain. corticate ['kɔːtɪkeɪt], corticose, corticous, adj. having cortex or bark. corticiferous [-tɪ'sɪfərəs], adj. forming cortex or bark. corticiform, adj. like bark.

corticosteroid [ˌkɔːtɪkəʊ'stɪərɔɪd, -'ste-] n. (synthetic form of) steroid hormone secreted by the adrenal contex, used against arthritis, allergies, asthma, etc.

cortinate ['kɔːtɪneɪt] adj. cobweb-like. cortinarious, adj.

cortisone ['kɔːtɪzəʊn] n. hormone, essential to life, secreted by cortex of adrenal glands; synthetic equivalent of this obtained from ox-bile or sisal.

corundum [kə'rʌndəm] n. exceptionally hard mineral, crystallized alumina, used, when transparent, as gem.

coruscate ['kɒrəskeɪt] v.i. sparkle; flash. coruscant [kə'rʌskənt], adj. coruscation, n.

corvée ['kɔːveɪ] n. exaction of unpaid labour.

corvette [kɔː'vet] n. flush-decked warship, next below frigate in size; small, fast, submarine-chasing warship.

corvine ['kɔːvaɪn] adj. pertaining to or like a crow. corviform, corvoid, adj.

corybant ['kɒrɪbænt] n. priest, votary or attendant of Cybele, ancient goddess of nature. corybantic, adj. pertaining to wild and noisy rites performed by these; n. wild, frenzied dance.

corymb ['kɒrɪm, -b] n. flat-topped racemelike inflorescence. corymbiate [kə'rɪmbieɪt], corymbiform, corymbose, corymbous, adj. corymbiferous [ˌkɒrɪm'bɪfərəs], adj. bearing these.

coryphaeus [ˌkɒrɪ'fiːəs] n. (pl. -aei) chorus-leader; spokesman. coryphée [-'feɪ], n. leading woman dancer in corps de ballet.

coryza [kə'raɪzə] n. cold in head.

cosaque [kə'sæk] (French) n. cracker.

cosher ['kɒʃə] (Irish) v.t. to be pampered.

cosmesis [kɒz'miːsɪs] n. preservation of bodily beauty, especially of face. cosmetic [-'metɪk], n. & adj. cosmetician [ˌkɒzmə'tɪʃn] n. maker, seller, etc. of cosmetics. cosmetology, n. art of using cosmetics.

cosmic ['kɒzmɪk] adj. pertaining to cosmos. cosmic rays, electrically charged particles of high energy – protons, electrons, mesons, etc.—falling on Earth from outer space.

cosmocracy [kɒz'mɒkrəsi] n. government of whole world. cosmocrat ['kɒzməkræt], n. ruler over world. cosmocratic, adj.

cosmodrome ['kɒzmədrəʊm] n. (Russian) space-exploration centre and rocket-launching installation.

cosmogenic [ˌkɒzmə'dʒenɪk] adj. produced by action of cosmic rays.

cosmogony [kɒz'mɒgəni] n. study or theory of the origin and development of the universe or the solar system. cosmogonal, cosmogonic, adj.

cosmography [kɒz'mɒgrəfi] n. study or description of the makeup of the world or universe. cosmographer, n. cosmographic, adj.

cosmology [kɒz'mɒlədʒi] n. branch of science or philosophy dealing with the origin and structure of the universe. cosmological, adj. cosmologist, n.

cosmonaut ['kɒzmənɔːt] n. (Russian) astronaut.

cosmopolitan [ˌkɒzmə'pɒlɪtən] adj. of all races and regions of world; able to mingle with all races, creeds and classes; n. such person. cosmopolitanism, n. cosmopolite [kɒz'mɒpəlaɪt], n. cosmopolitan person. cosmopolitic, adj. cosmopolitics, n. world politics.

cosmorama [ˌkɒzmə'rɑːmə] n. series of views of different parts of world. cosmoramic [-'ræmɪk], adj.

cosmos ['kɒzmɒs] n. universe; system of universe; order. cosmosophy [ˌkɒz'mɒsəfi], n. theory of cosmos. cosmosphere, n. material universe. cosmotellurian [-te'ljuəriən, -'luə-], adj. pertaining to both heaven and earth. cosmotheism, n. attribution of divinity to the cosmos; identifying God with world.

cosmotron ['kɒzmətrɒn] n. type of proton accelerator.

costal ['kɒstl] adj. pertaining to ribs. costard, n. ribbed variety of apple. costate, adj. having ribs; ridged. costalgia [kɒ'stældʒiə], n. pain in ribs. costectomy, n. removal of rib. costellate, adj. finely ribbed.

costive ['kɒstɪv] adj. constipated.

coteau ['kəʊtəʊ] n. (pl. -x [-z]), divide between valleys; valley-side.

coterie ['kəʊtəri] n. exclusive set of persons; clique.

coterminous see conterminous.

cothurnus [kə'θɜːnəs] n. (pl. -ni), buskin. cothurnal, cothurnian, adj. pertaining to cothurnus or tragedy. cothurnate, adj. wearing cothurnus.

cotillion, cotillon [kə'tɪliən] n. quadrille-like dance.

cotitular [ˌkəʊ'tɪtʃʊlə] n. one of patron saints of a church dedicated to more than one.

cotyledon [ˌkɒtɪ'liːdn] n. first, embryonic seed leaf of plant. cotyledonal, cotyledonary, cotyledonous, adj. cotyloid, adj. cup-shaped.

couchant ['kaʊtʃənt, 'kuːʃnt] adj. Heraldry, lying, especially with head raised.

cougar ['kuːgə] n. large, brown American wild cat; puma.

coulée, coulee ['kuːli] n. steep dry gully; Geology flow of lava.

coulisse [kuː'liːs] (French) n. groove, especially in timber, for thing to slide in; back-stage place; lobby.

couloir ['kuːlwɑː] (French) n. deep cleft in mountain; corridor.

coulomb ['kuːlɒm] n. quantitative unit of electricity: the amount of electrical charge conveyed by current of one ampère in one second. coulometer,

coulombmeter, *n.*

counter-irritant [ˌkaʊntə'ɪrɪtənt] *n.* application or action irritating body surface to relieve internal congestion.

counterpoint ['kaʊntəpɔɪnt] *n.* *Music,* melody added to or woven in with another; combining of melodies; musical composition in which melodies are combined; *v.t.* set in contrast to.

counterpoise ['kaʊntəpɔɪz] *n.* equal and opposite weight or force; *v.t.* counterbalance.

counterpole ['kaʊntəpəʊl] *n.* exact opposite.

coup [kuː] (*French*) *n.* 'stroke'; successful action; **coup d'état. coup de grace** [–də graːs'], finishing blow; fatal blow. **coup de main** [–dəmæn], sudden violent onslaught. **coup d'essai** [–dɜseɪ'], experiment. **coup d'état** [–deɪtaː'], sudden action whereby government is changed; short revolution, especially bloodless. **coup d'oeil** [–dɜɪ'ɪ], swift survey or glance; what is thus seen. **coup de soleil** [–də soleɪ'ɪ], sunstroke. **coup de théâtre** [–dəteɪaː'tr/, sudden dramatic or sensational action.

coupe [kuːp] *n.* (dish of fruit and ice-cream served in) goblet-shaped glass bowl.

coupé ['kuːpeɪ] *n.* small closed four-wheeled carriage with outside driver's seat; two-door saloon motor-car body; moving rapier, in fencing, to other side of opponent's rapier.

courtesan, courtezan [ˌkɔːtɪ'zæn] *n.* high-class prostitute.

couscous ['kuːskuːs] *n.* African gruel-like dish.

couturier [kuː'tjʊərɪeɪ] (*French*) *n.* (*fem.* **ière** [–i'eə] dressmaker.

couvade [kuː'vaːd] *n.* custom among some peoples, whereby the husband of a woman giving birth simulates pregnancy and labour.

couveuse [kuː'vɜːz] (*French*) *n.* incubator for human infants.

couvre-feu [ˌkuːvrə'fɜː] (*French*) *n.* curfew; scuttle-shaped device for covering fire at curfew.

coverture ['kʌvətʃə] *n.* *Law,* status of married woman.

covin(e) ['kʌvɪn] *n.* collusion; fraud. **covinous,** *adj.*

cowrie, cowry ['kaʊrɪ] *n.* small sea shell used as money in E Indies. **cowry bird,** Indian weaver bird.

coxalgy, coxalgia ['kɒksældʒɪ, kɒk'sældʒɪə] *n.* pain in hip. **coxalgic,** *adj.* **coxitis,** *n.* inflammation of hip joint.

coyote [kɔɪ'əʊtɪ, kaɪ–, 'kaɪəʊt] *n.* small N American wolf; prairie wolf.

coypu ['kɔɪpuː] *n.* S American webbed-footed rodent, and its fur; nutria.

cozen ['kʌzn] *v.i. & t.* cheat. **cozenage,** *n.*

crachoir ['kræʃwaː] (*French*) *n.* spittoon.

crambo ['kræmbəʊ] *n.* game in which a rhyme has to be found to a given word. **dumb crambo,** form of crambo in which rhyming words are acted in dumb show.

crampon ['kræmpɒn] *n.* boot-spike for climbing ice; spiked grip for carrying blocks of stone, ice, etc.; *Botany,* aerial root.

cranium ['kreɪnɪəm] *n.* skull, especially part enclosing brain. **cranial,** *adj.* **craniate,** *adj.* having a skull. **craniology,** *n.* study of skulls. **craniometry,** *n.* measurement of skulls. **craniotomy,** *n.* surgical incision in skull; crushing of skull to extract

dead foetus.

crannog ['krænəg] *n.* prehistoric Scottish and Irish lake-dwelling.

crapulent, crapulous ['kræpjʊlənt, –əs] *adj.* (sick through) eating or drinking to excess. **crapulence,** *n.*

craquelure ['krækəlʊə] *n.* fine cracks in surface of old paintings.

crasis ['kreɪsɪs] *n.* constitution; blending; running together of two vowels to form a long vowel.

crassamentum [ˌkræsə'mentəm] *n.* clot of blood.

crassitude ['kræsɪtjuːd] *n.* coarseness; grossness.

cratometer [krə'tɒmɪtə] *n.* instrument measuring power of magnification. **cratometry,** *n.*

craton ['kreɪtɒn] *n.* *Geology,* large, relatively stable section of earth's crust, forming the basis of a continent or ocean.

creancer ['krɪənsə] *n.* guardian; mentor.

creatic [kri'ætɪk] *adj.* pertaining to flesh or meat. **creatophagous** [ˌkriːə'tɒfəgəs], *adj.* flesh-eating.

credence ['kriːdns] *n.* belief; *Ecclesiastical,* small table or sideboard for sacred vessels.

crédit foncier [ˌkreɪdi 'fɒnsɪeɪ] (*French*) *n.* 'landed credit'; loan on mortgage, repaid in annual instalments. **crédit mobilier** [məʊ'biːlieɪ], loan on personal property; banking company for such and other loans.

credo ['kriːdəʊ] *n.* creed; belief.

cremnophobia [ˌkremnə'fəʊbiə] *n.* dread of precipices.

crenate ['kriːneɪt] *adj.* scalloped. **crenation, crenature** ['krenətʃə], *n.*

crenellated ['krenəleɪtɪd] *adj.* having battlements. **crenellation,** *n.*

crenitic [krə'nɪtɪk] *adj.* pertaining to mineral springs. **crenotherapy** [ˌkrenəʊ'θerəpi], *n.* medical treatment by mineral springs.

crenulate ['krenjʊlət] *adj.* minutely crenate. **crenulation,** *n.*

creole ['kriːəʊl] *n.* person born in tropical region of European descent, especially descendant of early French or Spanish settlers; person of mixed ancestry; W Indian language or native. **creolization,** *n.* transformation of a pidgin into a full language.

creophagous [kri'ɒfəgəs] *adj.* carnivorous. **creophagia** [ˌkriːə'feɪdʒiə], **creophagism** [–dʒɪzm], **creophagy** [–dʒi], *n.* eating of flesh. **creophagist,** *n.*

crepitate ['krepɪteɪt] *v.t.* crackle. **crepitant,** *adj.* **crepitation, crepitus,** *n.*

crepuscular [krɪ'pʌskjʊlə] *adj.* pertaining to twilight; appearing or active at twilight. **crepuscle, crepuscule,** *n.* twilight. **crepusculine,** *adj.*

crescograph ['kreskəgraːf] *n.* instrument recording plant growth.

cresset ['kresɪt] *n.* hanging light-giving brazier.

cretaceous [krɪ'teɪʃəs] *adj.* pertaining to or like chalk. **Cretaceous,** *adj. & n. Geology,* (relating to) the last period of the Mesozoic era when chalk deposits were formed.

cretic ['kriːtɪk] *n.* amphimacer.

cretify ['kretɪfaɪ] *v.t.* change into chalk or lime. **cretifaction, cretification,** *n.*

cretin ['kretɪn] *n.* mentally and physically deficient person, generally a large-headed dwarf, whose condition is due to deficient thyroid secretion.

cretinous, *adj.* cretinism, *n.*

crevasse [krə'væs] *n.* deep chasm in glacier.

crewel ['kruːəl] *n.* thin embroidery worsted. crewel needle, *n.* long needle used in embroidery; crewelwork, *n.*

cribriform ['krɪbrɪfɔːm] *adj.* like a sieve. cribrous, cribrose, *adj.* cribration, *n.* sifting.

cri de coeur [,kriː də 'kɜː] (*French*) *n.* 'cry of heart'; deeply-felt, passionate request or complaint.

crime passionel [,kriːm ,pæsiə'nel] (*French*) *n.* 'crime of passion', *i.e.* due to love or jealousy.

criminis ['krɪmɪnɪs] *n.* 'partner in crime'; accomplice.

crimp [krɪmp] *n.* person luring or 'shanghai-ing' sailors aboard vessel; *v.t.* so to obtain sailors for ship. crimpage, *n.* rate paid to crimp.

crinal ['kraɪnl] *adj.* pertaining to hair. crinite, *adj. Biology*, covered in soft hair or tufts.

crinoid ['kraɪnɔɪd, 'krɪ–] *adj.* like a lily in shape; *n. Zoology*, one of a class of sea creatures with round body and feathery arms.

crinose ['kraɪnəus, 'krɪ] *adj.* hairy. crinosity, *n.*

criophore ['kraɪəfɔː] *n.* sculptured figure of man carrying ram. criosphinx, *n.* sphinx with ram's head.

crispate ['krɪspeɪt] *adj.* curled; crisped. crispation, crispature, *n.* curling; shudder.

cristate ['krɪsteɪt] *adj.* bearing crest. cristiform, *adj.* crest-shaped.

criticaster ['krɪtɪkæstə] *n.* inferior critic.

critique [krɪ'tiːk] *n.* written criticism; review.

croceous ['krəuʃəs] *adj.* saffron yellow in colour.

crocidolite [krə'sɪdəlaɪt] *n.* blue asbestos, essentially a sodium iron silicate.

cromlech ['krɒmlek] *n.* prehistoric monument, comprising a flat stone resting horizontally on two vertical stones or circle of stones.

crore [krɔː] (*Anglo-Indian*) *n.* ten million, especially of rupees, *i.e* 100 lakhs.

crosier, crozier ['krəuziə, –ʒə] *n.* shepherd's crook-like staff borne by abbot or bishop.

cross-staff ['krɒsstɑːf] *n.* ancient nautical instrument for taking altitudes.

crotaline ['krɒtəlaɪn, 'krəu–] *adj.* pertaining to rattle-snake. crotalic, crotaliform [–'tæl–], crotaloid, *adj.* like a rattlesnake.

croton ['krəutn] (*E Indian*) *n.* tree with seeds yielding an oil used as purge, etc.

crounotherapy [,kruːnəu'θerəpi] *n.* medical treatment by mineral waters.

crouton ['kruːtɒn] *n.* small piece of fried or toasted bread, served with soup.

croze [krəuz] *n.* groove in the staves of a barrel into which the endpiece fits.

cru [kruː] (*French*) *n.* vineyard; category in classification of certain French wines.

cruciate ['kruːʃiət] *adj.* cross-shaped or Y-shaped; marked with cross; [–eɪt] *v.t* mark with cross. cruciation, *n.* torture; cruciate state.

crucible ['kruːsɪbl] *n.* vessel for fusing metals; melting-pot.

crucifer ['kruːsɪfə] *n.* person bearing cross; cruciferous plant. cruciferous [kruː'sɪfərəs], *adj. Botany*, applied to mustard family of plants (brassicas), in flowers of which four equal-sized petals are arranged in form of cross.

cruciform ['kruːsɪfɔːm] *adj.* cross-shaped.

cruentation [,kruːen'teɪʃn] *n.* oozing of blood, especially from dead body.

cruorin [kruː'ɔːrɪn] *n.* haemoglobin.

crural ['kruərəl] *adj.* pertaining to leg, especially thigh.

cruse [kruːz] *n.* small earthenware pot.

crustacean [krʌ'steɪʃn] *n.* animal with hard shell. crustaceology, *n.* study of these. crustaceous, *adj.* having a shell; like a crust or a crab.

crymodinia [,kraɪmə'dɪniə] *n.* rheumatism due to cold. crymotherapy, *n.* use of cold as medical treatment.

cryogen ['kraɪədʒen, –dʒən] *n.* freezing mixture or agent. cryogeny [kraɪ'ɒdʒəni], *n.* refrigeration.

cryogenics [,kraɪə'dʒenɪks] *n.* study of effects of extremely low temperatures. cryopedology [–pe'dɒlədʒi], *n.* study of action of intense frost on soil. cryostat ['kraɪəstæt], *n.* automatic device for maintaining low temperature. cryosurgery, *n.* performance of surgical operations on heart, brain, etc., which are first cooled to a low temperature, or by instruments maintained at an extremely low temperature. cryostat, *n.* device for producing or maintaining very low temperature.

cryolite ['kraɪəlaɪt] *n.* aluminium-yielding mineral of Greenland.

cryometer [kraɪ'ɒmɪtə] *n.* instrument measuring very low temperatures.

cryonics [kraɪ'ɒnɪks] *n.* practice of freezing a human body at time of death for eventual resuscitation.

cryophorus [kraɪ'ɒfərəs] *n.* instrument demonstrating freezing of water by its evaporation. cryophoric [,kraɪə'fɒrɪk], *adj.*

cryoscopy [kraɪ'ɒskəpi] *n.* determination of freezing points. cryoscope ['kraɪəskəup], *n.* instrument used in this. cryoscopic [,kraɪə'skɒpɪk], *adj.*

cryptaesthesia [,krɪptiːs'θiːziə, –ʒə] *n.* clairvoyance. cryptaesthetic [–'θetɪk], *adj.*

cryptal ['krɪptl] *adj.* pertaining to or like a crypt.

cryptanalysis [,krɪptə'næləsɪs] *n.* study of codes and ciphers. cryptanalytic, *adj.*

cryptic ['krɪptɪk] *adj.* mysterious; secret; concealing.

crypto- ['krɪptəu] *prefix* hidden, secret.

cryptoclastic [,krɪptə'klæstɪk] *adj. Geology*, composed of tiny fragments.

cryptoclimate ['krɪptəu,klaɪmət] *n.* climate of the inside of a building or other enclosed structure.

cryptogam ['krɪptəgæm] *n.* non-flowering or non-seeding plant. cryptogamian, cryptogamic, cryptogamous [–'tɒgəməs], *adj.*

cryptogenic [,krɪptə'dʒenɪk] *adj.* of unknown origin. cryptogenetic [–dʒə'netɪk], *adj.*

cryptogram ['krɪptəgræm] *n.* coded message. cryptogrammic, cryptogrammatic, *adj.*

cryptograph ['krɪptəgrɑːf] *n.* cryptogram; type of code; instrument for encoding or decoding. cryptographer [krɪp'tɒgrəfə], *n.* writer of, expert on codes. cryptography, *n.*

cryptology [krɪp'tɒlədʒi] *n.* science of cryptanalysis and cryptography.

cryptonym ['krɪptənɪm] *n.* secret name. cryptonymous [–'tɒnɪməs], *adj.*

cryptophyte ['krɪptəfaɪt] *n.* plant whose buds or

seeds develop underground or under water.

cryptorchidism [krɪp'tɔːkɪdɪzm] *n.* condition in which one or both testes do not descend normally.

cryptozoic [ˌkrɪptə'zəʊɪk] *adj.* living hidden, or in darkness.

crystallography [ˌkrɪstə'lɒgrəfi] *n.* study of formation of crystals.

crystallomancy ['krɪstl–əmænsi] *n.* divination by a crystal ball.

crystic ['krɪstɪk] *adj. Geology*, pertaining to ice.

crystograph ['krɪstəɡrɑːf] *n.* painting or writing on glass.

ctenoid ['tiːnɔɪd, 'ten–] *adj.* with comb-like edge. **cteniform**, *adj.* comb-like.

ctetology [tiː'tɒlədʒi] *n. Biology* study of acquired characteristics.

cubeb ['kjuːbeb] *n.* dried fruit of a pepper plant, used for catarrh.

cubit ['kjuːbɪt] *n.* measure of length (length of forearm), equivalent of 18 in. (about 0.45 m.). **cubital** *adj.* pertaining to elbow or forearm.

cuculine ['kjuːkjulaɪn] *adj.* pertaining to or like a cuckoo. **cuculiform**, *adj.* like a cuckoo. **cuculoid**, *adj.*

cucullate ['kjuːkəleɪt, kju'kʌleɪt] *adj.* hooded; hood-shaped. **cuculliform**, *adj.* hood-shaped.

cucumiform [kju'kjuːmɪfɔːm] *n.* cucumber-shaped.

cucurbit [kju'kɜːbɪt] *n.* gourd-like chemical vessel, main part of still or alembic. **cucurbitine**, *adj.* like gourd seed in shape.

cudbear ['kʌdbeə] *n.* (dye obtained from) type of orchil.

cui bono? [ˌkuːi 'bəʊnəʊ] (*Latin*) 'to whose good?'; to whose profit?; to what purpose?

cuirass [kwɪ'ræs] *n.* armour for breast and back. **cuirassier**, [ˌkwɪrə'sɪə], *n.* horse-soldier wearing this.

cuisine [kwɪ'ziːn] (*French*) *n.* 'kitchen'; cooking; feeding arrangements. **cuisine minceur,** (*French*) 'cooking for slimness'; health and figure-conscious variant of nouvelle cuisine.

culiciform [kju'lɪsɪfɔːm] *adj.* like a mosquito. **culicifuge**, *n.* substance killing mosquitoes.

culinary ['kʌlɪnəri, 'kjuː–] *adj.* pertaining to cooking.

cullion ['kʌljən] *n.* rascal; orchid root; man orchid.

culm [kʌlm] *n.* grass stem. **culminal**, *adj.*

culminate ['kʌlmɪneɪt] *v.i.* reach peak or climax; *Astronomy*, reach meridian; be directly overhead. **culminant**, *adj.* **culmination**, *n.*

culpable ['kʌlpəbl] *adj.* at fault; criminal. **culpability**, *n.*

cultivar ['kʌltɪvɑː] *n.* variety of plant originated by and kept under cultivation.

cultrate ['kʌltreɪt] *adj.* shaped like a knife blade; sharp-edged.

culverin ['kʌlvərɪn] *n.* kind of ancient small cannon.

culvert ['kʌlvət] *n.* drain; conduit.

culvertage ['kʌlvətɪdʒ] *n.* villeinage.

culvertail ['kʌlvəteɪl] *n.* dovetail.

cum grano salis [kʌm ˌgreɪnəʊ 'seɪlɪs, ˌgrɑːnəʊ 'sælɪs] (*Latin*) 'with a grain of salt'; with caution or incredulity.

cummerbund ['kʌməbʌnd] *n.* wide sash round waist.

cumshaw ['kʌmʃɔː] (*Chinese*) *n.* tip; gratuity.

cumulative ['kjuːmjʊlətɪv] *adj.* increasing; growing by successive additions; gathering strength as it grows; expressing addition.

cumulose ['kjuːmjʊləʊs] *adj.* containing small heaps.

cumulus ['kjuːmjʊləs] *n.* (*pl.* **–li**) rounded, flat-based mass of cloud at middle altitude. **cumulo-cirrus**, *n.* small cumulus at great height. **cumulo-nimbus**, *n.* thunder cloud. **cumulo-stratus**, *n.* cumulus with stratus-like base. **cumulous**, *adj.*

cunabular [kju'næbjʊlə] *adj.* pertaining to cradle or original dwelling; pertaining to incunabula.

cunctation [kʌŋk'teɪʃn] *n.* delay. **cunctator**, *n.* procrastinator.

cuneiform ['kjuːnɪfɔːm, kju'niːɪ–] *adj.* wedge-shaped; applied to such ancient alphabet and inscriptions. **cuneal, cuneate** ['kjuː–], *adj.* wedge-shaped.

cunicular [kju'nɪkjʊlə] *adj.* pertaining to underground passages or burrows; burrow-dwelling.

cupel ['kjuːpl, kju'pel] *n.* small dish, especially of bone ash, or furnace hearth for cupellation. **cupellation**, [ˌkjuːpə'leɪʃn], *n.* refining or separating precious metals.

cupidity [kju'pɪdəti] *n.* avarice.

cupola ['kjuːpələ] *n.* dome, especially small.

cupping ['kʌpɪŋ] *n. Medicine*, drawing blood by causing partial vacuum over surface of skin. **cupping glass**, glass used in this.

cupreous ['kjuːprɪəs] *adj.* pertaining to or like copper.

cupressineous [ˌkjuːpre'sɪnɪəs] *adj.* pertaining to or like the cypress.

cupric ['kjuːprɪk] *adj.* applied to compounds of bivalent copper. **cupro-nickel**, *n.* alloy of copper and nickel used for making 'silver' and 'nickel' coins. **cuprous**, *adj.* applied to compounds of univalent copper.

cupulate ['kjuːpjʊleɪt] *adj.* cup-shaped; having a cup-shaped appendage. **cupuliform**, *adj.* cup-shaped.

curaçao ['kjʊərəsəʊ] *n.* Dutch liqueur made from orange peel.

curare [kju'rɑːri] *n.* vegetable extract used as arrow poison by S American Indians.

curassow ['kjʊərəsəʊ] *n.* turkey-like bird of S and Central America.

curculio [kɜː'kjuːlɪəʊ] *n.* fruit weevil.

curé ['kjʊəreɪ] (*French*) *n.* parish priest; vicar.

curette [kju'ret] *n.* surgical instrument for scraping sides of body cavity; *v.t.* use a curette on. **curettage**, *n.* use of this.

curialism ['kjʊərɪəlɪzm] *n.* ultra-montanism.

curiology [ˌkjʊəri'ɒlədʒi] *n.* picture-writing. **curiologic(al)**, *adj.* **curiologics** [–'lɒdʒɪks], *n.*

curiosa [ˌkjʊəri'əʊsə] *n. pl.* curiosities; erotica.

curium ['kjʊərɪəm] *n.* one of the transuranic elements.

curratow ['kɜːrətəʊ] *n.* fibre from wild pineapple of Brazil.

curricle ['kʌrɪkl] *n.* light two-horse two-wheeled carriage. **curricular** [kə'rɪkjʊlə], *adj.* pertaining to carriages and driving; pertaining to curriculum.

currier ['kʌrɪə] *n.* leather-dresser.

currycomb ['kʌrɪkəʊm] *n.* metal comb for grooming horse.

cursive ['kɜːsɪv] *adj.* running, flowing; *n.* script

with rounded letters joined together.

cursorial [kɜːˈsɔːriəl] *adj.* adapted for walking or running. **cursorious,** *adj.*

cursory [ˈkɜːsəri] *adj.* quick; superficial.

curtal [ˈkɜːtl] *adj.* short; curtailed; *n.* person wearing short garment; animal with docked tail.

curtate [ˈkɜːteɪt] *adj.* shortened; short. **curtate distance,** *Astronomy,* distance of heavenly body from sun or earth in ecliptic plane. **curtation,** *n.* difference between curtate distance and true distance.

curtilage [ˈkɜːtɪlɪdʒ] *n.* courtyard; land attached to house.

curucucu [ˌkuəruːˈkuːkuː] *n.* bush-master.

curule [ˈkjuəruːl] *adj.* applied to curved-legged chair occupied by high officials of ancient Rome. **curule leg,** outward-curving furniture leg.

curvet [ˈkɜːvɪt] *n.* & *v.i.* leap; bound; leap of trained horse with forelegs first raised, immediately followed by raising of hind legs.

curvilinear [ˌkɜːvɪˈlɪniə] *adj.* pertaining to or within curved lines.

curvulate [ˈkɜːvjuleɪt] *adj.* slightly curved.

cushat [ˈkʌʃət, ˈkuː-] *n.* wood-pigeon or ring-dove.

cush-cush [ˈkuʃkuʃ] *n.* kind of yam.

cusp [kʌsp] *n.* prominence; crown of tooth; sharp point; *Astrology,* cross-over point between two signs. **cuspal,** *adj,* **cuspate,** *adj,* having cusps. **cuspid,** *n.* canine tooth. **cuspidal,** *adj.* **cuspidate,** *adj,* coming to a point.

cuspidor [ˈkʌspɪdɔː] (*American*) *n.* spittoon.

custodian [kʌˈstəudiən] *n.* keeper; warden. **custodial,** *adj.* **custodiam** [-iæm], *n.* grant of crown lands.

custos morum [ˌkʌstɒs ˈmɔːrəm, ˌkuː-, -ʊm] (*Latin*) 'keeper of morals'; censor. **custos rotulorum,** keeper of the rolls. **custos sigilli,** keeper of great seal.

cutaneous [kjuːˈteɪniəs] *adj.* pertaining to the skin, especially its surface.

cuticle [ˈkjuːtɪkl] *n.* epidermis; hardened epidermis round nail. **cuticular** [kjuˈtɪkjulə], *adj.* **cuticulate,** *adj.* having this. **cutification,** *n.* formation of this. **cutigeral,** *adj.* skin-bearing.

cutis anserina [ˌkjuːtɪs ˌænsəˈraɪnə] (*Latin*) 'goose-flesh'.

cuvée [ˈkjuːveɪ] (*French*) *n.* vintage.

cyaneous [saɪˈeɪniəs] *adj.* sky-blue.

cyanometer [ˌsaɪəˈnɒmɪtə] *n.* instrument measuring blueness. **cyanometric** [-əˈmetrɪk], *adj.* **cyanometry,** *n.*

cyanopathy [ˌsaɪəˈnɒpəθi] *n.* cyanosis. **cyanopathic** [ˌsaɪənəˈpæθɪk], *adj.*

cyanosis [ˌsaɪəˈnəusɪs] *n.* heart condition or disease causing blueness of surface of body; blue disease. **cyanotic** [-ˈnɒtɪk], *adj.*

cyanotype [saɪˈænətaɪp] *n.* blue-print.

cyathiform [saɪˈæθɪfɔːm] *adj.* cup-shaped.

cybernetics [ˌsaɪbəˈnetɪks] *n.* comparative study of control and communication in living organisms and machines.

cyclarthrosis [ˌsɪklɑːˈθrəusɪs] *n.* (*pl.* **-ses**) pivot joint. **cyclarthrodial,** *adj.*

cyclazocine [saɪˈklæzəsiːn, ˌsaɪkləˈzəusiːn] *n.* synthetic drug protecting against the addictive effects of the morphine group.

cyclitis [sɪˈklaɪtɪs] *n.* inflammation of ciliary muscle.

cyclometer [saɪˈklɒmɪtə] *n.* instrument measuring arcs of circles or revolutions of bicycle wheel.

cyclone [ˈsaɪkləun] *n.* any storm in which wind is rotary; *Meteorology,* area of low pressure into which winds flow in anti-clockwise direction in N hemisphere; hurricane; typhoon; *erroneously* tornado. **cyclonic** [-ˈklɒnɪk], *adj,* **cyclonology,** *n.* study of cyclones.

cyclophoria [ˌsaɪkləˈfɔːriə, ˌsɪ-] *n.* squint due to weakness of an eye muscle.

cycloplegia [ˌsaɪkləˈpliːdʒiə, ˌsɪ-] *n.* paralysis of ciliary muscle. **cycloplegic** [-ˈpliːdʒɪk, -ˈple-], *adj.*

cyclorama [ˌsaɪkləˈrɑːmə] *n.* circular panorama surrounding spectator; curved backcloth of stage used to indicate vast spaces. **cycloramic** [-ˈræmɪk], *adj.*

cyclostyle [ˈsaɪkləstaɪl] *n.* apparatus for printing copies from a handwritten stencil.

cyclothymia [ˌsaɪkləˈθaɪmiə, ˌsɪ-] *n.* mental condition of alternating moods of euphoria and depression. **cyclothyme,** *n.* person having such moods. **cyclothymic,** *adj.*

cyclotomy [saɪˈklɒtəmi, sɪ-] *n.* incision into ciliary muscle. **cyclotome** [ˈsaɪklətəum, ˈsɪ-], *n.* instrument used in this. **cyclotomic** [-ˈtɒmɪk], *adj.*

cyclotron [ˈsaɪklətrɒn] *n.* apparatus in which ions are accelerated to high energies for bombarding atomic nuclei in nuclear fission processes.

cyesis [saɪˈiːsɪs] *n.* pregnancy. **cyesiology,** *n.* medical study of this.

cygnet [ˈsɪgnɪt] *n.* young swan. **cygneous,** *adj.* swan-like.

cyllosis [sɪˈləusɪs] *n.* (*pl.* **-ses**) congenital deformity, especially clubfoot.

cymbiform [ˈsɪmbɪfɔːm] *adj.* boat-shaped. **cymbate,** *adj.* **cymbocephalic, cymbocephalous,** *adj.* having head with forehead receding and back projecting.

cyme [saɪm] *n.* inflorescence in which axes end in single flower only, *e.g.* phlox. **cymiferous,** *adj.* producing these. **cymoid, cymose,** *adj.*

cymograph [ˈsaɪməgrɑːf] *n.* instrument for tracing outlines of projections, profiles, etc.

cymometer [saɪˈmɒmɪtə] *n.* instrument measuring frequency of electric waves. **cymoscope,** *n.* instrument detecting elecrical waves.

cymule [ˈsaɪmjuːl] *n.* small cyme.

cynanche [sɪˈnæŋki] *n.* any inflammatory disease of throat, etc.

cynanthropy [sɪˈnænθrəpi] *n.* form of insanity in which patient has delusions of being a dog.

cynarctomachy [ˌsɪnɑːkˈtɒməki] *n.* bear-baiting with dogs.

cynegetics [ˌsɪnɪˈdʒetɪks] *n.* hunting.

cyniatrics [ˌsɪniˈætrɪks] *n.* study of canine diseases.

cynocephalous, cynocephalic [ˌsɪnəˈsefələs, -səˈfælɪk; ˌsaɪ-] *adj.* having dog-like head or face. **cynocephalus,** *n.* flying lemur; mythological ape with dog's head.

cynoid [ˈsaɪnɔɪd, ˈsɪ-] *adj.* dog-like. **cynopodous,** *adj.* having dog-like claws. **cynorrhodon,** *n.* dog-rose.

cynophobia [ˌsaɪnəˈfəubiə, ˌsɪ-] *n.* morbid fear of dogs.

cynosure [ˈsaɪnəsjuə, ˈsɪ-, -ʃuə] *n.* guiding star;

object of common interest. **cynosural,** *adj.*

cyphonism ['saɪfənɪzm] *n.* pillorying as punishment.

cyprian ['sɪprɪən] *adj.* lecherous; *n.* prostitute.

cyprine ['sɪpraɪn] *adj.* pertaining to the cypress.

cyprinoid ['sɪprɪnɔɪd, sɪ'praɪ–] *adj.* pertaining to or like a carp.

cypseline ['sɪpsəlaɪn] *adj.* pertaining to or like a swift. **cypseloid,** *adj.*

cyst [sɪst] *n.* sac-like outgrowth containing fluid or semi-fluid matter; capsule; vesicle. **cystal, cystic,** *adj*, **cystitis,** *n.* inflammation of bladder. **cystoid,** *adj.* like a bladder. **cystolith,** *n.* stone in the bladder. **cystology,** *n.* study of cysts. **cystoscope,** *n.* instrument for examining bladder. **cystose, cystous,** *adj.*

Cytherean [,sɪθə'riːən] *adj.* pertaining to Venus; *n.* votary of Venus.

cytitis [sɪ'taɪtɪs] *n.* inflammation of skin.

cytoblast ['saɪtəblæst] *n. Biology*, cell nucleus. **cytoderm,** *n.* cell wall. **cytogamy,** *n.* cell conjugation. **cytogenetics,** *n.* study of structural basis of heredity in the cell. **cytogenous,** *adj.* cell-producing. **cytoid,** *adj.* cell-like. **cytology,** *n.* study of cells. **cytolysis,** *n.* dissolution of cells. **cytophagy,** *n.* phagocytosis. **cytoplasm,** *n.* substance of cell excluding nucleus. **cytosome,** *n.* body of cell excluding nucleus. **cytotoxic,** *adj.* (of a drug) poisonous to living cells. **cytotoxin,** *n.* substance poisonous to cells. **cytozoon,** *n.* protozoan parasite within a cell.

czardas ['tʃɑːdæʃ] *n.* Hungarian dance that increases in speed.

czigany [tʃɪ'gɑːni] (*Hungarian*) *n.* gypsy.

D

dabchick ['dæbtʃɪk] *n.* little grebe.
da capo [dɑː 'kɑːpəu] (*Italian*) 'from the beginning'; *Music*, instruction to repeat from start (*abbreviation* **D.C**).
dacha, datcha ['dætʃə] *n.* country cottage or villa in Russia.
dacoit [də'kɔɪt] *n.* brigand of India and Burma. **dacoity,** *n.* robbery by dacoits or by a gang.
dacryops ['dækrɪɒps] *n.* wateriness of eye.
dactyl ['dæktɪl] *n.* metrical foot comprising one long followed by two short syllables; *Zoology*, digit. **dactylate,** *adj.* like a finger, **dactylic,** *adj.*; *n.* verse of dactyls.
dactylioglyph [dæk'tɪlɪəglɪf] *n.* engraver of gems, especially for rings. **dactyliographic,** *adj.* **dactyliography,** *n.* study of gem engraving. **dactyliology,** *n.* study of finger-rings.
dactylitis [,dæktɪ'laɪtɪs] *n.* inflammation of fingers and toes.
dactylogram [dæk'tɪləgræm] *n.* finger-print. **dactylography,** *n.* study of finger-prints.
dactyloid ['dæktɪlɔɪd] *adj.* like a finger.
dactylology [,dæktɪ'lɒlədʒi] *n.* sign language; deaf and dumb language.
dactylomegaly [,dæktɪləu'megəli] *n.* abnormal largeness of fingers and toes.
dactylonomy [,dæktɪ'lɒnəmi] *n.* counting on the fingers.
dactyloscopy [,dæktɪ'lɒskəpi] *n.* comparison of fingerprints for identification.
daedal ['diːdl] *adj.* complicated; showing or needing skill; artistic; variegated. **daedalian** [–'deɪlɪən], **daedalic** [–'dælɪk], *adj.* pertaining to Daedalus, in Greek myth, designer of the labyrinth of Crete and inventor of flying wings; skilful; ingenious; labyrinthine. **daedalist,** *n.* aviator.
daemon ['diːmən, 'daɪ–] *n.* inward spirit; personality; genius. **daemonic** [–'mɒnɪk], *adj.*
dagoba, dagaba ['dɑːgəbə] *n.* shrine holding Buddhist relics.
daguerreotype [də'gerətaɪp] *n.* early 19th-century kind of photograph invented by L. J. M. Daguerre.
dahabeeyah, dahabeah [,dɑːhə'biːə] *n.* sailing house-boat of Nile.
Dáil Éireann [,dɔɪl 'eərən] (*Irish*) lower house of Irish parliament.
daimon ['daɪmɒn, –ən] *n.* daemon.
dairi ['daɪri] (*Japanese*) *n.* mikado and his court.
dak *see* **dawk.**
dalmatic [dæl'mætɪk] *n.* kind of outer ecclesiastical vestment; similar vestment worn by king at coronation.
dalton ['dɔːltən] *n.* unit of mass, equivalent of one-sixteenth of mass of oxygen atom.

daman ['dæmən] *n.* small herbivorous animal of Palestine, called 'cony' in Old Testament.
damascene, damaskeen ['dæməsiːn, –skiːn] *v.t.* ornament (metal) with wavy patterns; *adj.* pertaining to such art or to damask. **damascene blade,** sword made in Damascus or ornamented with damascening.
damassé ['dæməseɪ] (*French*) *n. & adj.* (fabric) with damask-like weave. **damassin,** *n.* damask with patterns in gold or silver.
damier ['dæmieɪ] (*French*) *n.* large-squared pattern.
damine ['deɪmaɪn] *adj.* like a fallow deer or its antlers.
dammar ['dæmɑː, –ə] *n.* kauri gum; several other resins from Australian and E Indian trees.
damnosa hereditas [dæm,nəusə he'redɪtæs] (*Latin*) 'burdensome inheritance'.
damnum fatale [,dæmnəm fə'teɪli, –'tɑːli] (*Latin*) *Law*, loss resulting from act of God.
dapicho, dapico ['dæpɪtʃəu, –kəu] *n.* kind of S American rubber.
dapifer ['dæpɪfə] *n.* bearer of meat to table; steward.
dargah *see* **durgah.**
darnel ['dɑːnl] *n.* tall, awned grass, a weed of corn-fields.
dartre ['dɑːtə] *n.* any eczema-like skin disease. **dartrous,** *adj.*
dashpot ['dæʃpɒt] *n.* shock-resisting device, using air or liquid.
dasymeter [dæ'sɪmɪtə] *n.* device for measuring the density of gases.
dasyphyllous [,dæsɪ'fɪləs] *adj.* with downy leaves.
dasypoedes [,dæsɪ'piːdiːz] *n. pl.* birds having downy young. **dasypoedal, dasypoedic,** *adj.*
dasyure ['dæzijuə, –si–] *n.* small, marten-like Australian marsupial.
datcha *see* **dacha.**
dation ['deɪʃn] *n.* act of giving; conferment.
dative ['deɪtɪv] *adj. Grammar,* signifying indirect object or giving to; *Law,* capable of being given; dismissible; *n.* such grammatical case. **dativist** [də'tarvl], *adj.*
dato, datto ['dɑːtəu] *n.* Malay tribal chieftain.
datura [də'tjuərə] *n.* narcotic, poisonous weed of nightshade family, of India and other countries; jimson weed. **daturism,** *n.* datura poisoning.
daube [dəub] (*French*) *n.* braised meat stew.
dauerschlaf ['dauəʃlɑːf] *n.* long drug-induced sleep, used as psychiatric remedy.
dauphin ['dəufɪn, –æn] *n.* French king's eldest son. **dauphine** [–iːn], **dauphiness,** *n.* his wife.

davenport ['dævənpɔːt] *n.* small writing table; *American*, sort of settee, especially convertible into bed.

davit ['dævɪt] *n.* ship's small crane, especially for lowering boats.

dawk, dak [dɔːk] *n.* Anglo-Indian relay system for post or transport; post. **dawk boat**, mail boat. **dawk bungalow**, rest-house for travellers.

de aequitate [diː ˌekwɪ'teɪtɪ, deɪ-, -'taɪ-] (*Latin*) 'by equity'; by justice if not by right.

dealate [diː'eɪleɪt] *v.t.* rob or divest of wings. **dealation**, *n.*

dealbation [ˌdiːæl'beɪʃn] *n.* whitening.

deambulatory [di'æmbjʊlətəri] *n.* ambulatory; *adj.* wandering.

deasil ['diːsl, 'djeʃl] *adv.* clockwise; towards the right.

deassimilation [ˌdiːəsɪmɪ'leɪʃn] *n.* catabolism.

débâcle [deɪ'bɑːkl] (*French*) *n.* complete rout or failure; stampede; ice-break; flood.

debarrass [dɪ'bærəs] *v.t.* disembarrass.

debellate [dɪ'beleɪt] *v.t.* conquer. **debellation, debellator**, *n.*

debenture [dɪ'bentʃə] *n.* official certificate of right to receive payment; bond; any company security other than shares. **debenture stock**, class of shares, holders of which are guaranteed repayment but cannot demand it until default or winding up of company.

debility [dɪ'bɪləti] *n.* weakness. **debilitant**, *n.* & *adj.* (substance) reducing energy or excitement. **debilitate**, *v.t.* weaken. **debilitation**, *n.* **debilitative**, *adj.*

debouch [dɪ'baʊtʃ, -'buːʃ] *v.t.* issue into open place; *n.* outlet. **debouchment**, *n.* act of debouching; river mouth.

debridement [dɪ'briːdmənt, deɪ'briːdmɒn] *n.* surgical removal of dead tissue from wound.

decachord ['dekəkɔːd] *n.* & *adj.* (musical instrument) having ten strings.

decad ['dekəd] *n.* group of ten. **decadal**, *adj.* **decade** ['dekeɪd, dɪ'keɪd], *n.* period of ten years.

decadescent [ˌdekə'desnt] *adj.* tending to become decadent.

decadic [dɪ'kædɪk] *adj.* pertaining to decimal system.

decagon ['dekəgən] *n.* 10-sided plane figure. **decagonal** [dɪ'kægənl], *adj.*

decahedron [ˌdekə'hiːdrən] *n.* 10-sided solid figure. **decahedral**, *adj.*

decal [dɪ'kæl, 'diːkæl] *n.* decalcomania.

decalcify [diː'kælsɪfaɪ] *v.t.* remove calcium or lime from. **decalcification**, *n.* **decalcifier**, *n.*

decalcomania [dɪˌkælkə'meɪnɪə] *n.* art of transferring a design from paper to another surface; transfer.

decalescence [ˌdiːkə'lesns] *n.* sudden increase at certain temperature in amount of heat absorbed.

decalogue ['dekəlɒg] *n.* Ten Commandments.

decalvant [dɪ'kælvənt] *adj.* depilatory.

decameral [dɪ'kæmərəl] *adj.* divided into ten. **decamerous**, *adj. Botany*, having parts in tens.

decameter [dɪ'kæmɪtə] *n.* verse line of ten feet.

decanal [dɪ'keɪnl] *adj.* pertaining to deacon; on the dean's (*i.e.* south) side of choir.

decapod ['dekəpɒd] *n.* ten-legged crustacean, including shrimps, lobsters, etc. **decapodal, decapodan, decapodous** [-'kæp-], *adj.*

decarch ['dekɑːk] *n.* member of decarchy; commander over ten. **decarchy**, *n.* rule by or ruling body of ten persons.

decarnate [diː'kɑːneɪt] *adj.* divested of bodily form.

decastich ['dekəstɪk] *n.* ten-line poem.

decastyle ['dekəstaɪl] *n.* portico with ten columns.

decasyllable ['dekəˌsɪləbl] *n.* verse line or word of ten syllables. **decasyllabic** [-'læbɪk], *adj.*

decathlon [dɪ'kæθlən] *n.* athletic contest of ten running, jumping and field events.

decatize ['dekətaɪz] *v.t.* cause to uncurl by steaming or damping.

decedent [dɪ'siːdnt] *n. American*, deceased person.

decemvir [dɪ'semvə] *n.* member of decemvirate. **decemviral**, *adj.* **decemvirate**, *n.* ruling body of ten persons.

decennial [dɪ'senɪəl] *adj.* occurring every ten years; consisting of ten years; *n.* tenth anniversary. **decennary**, *adj.* decennial; *n.* decennium. **decennium**, *n.* (*pl.* **-ia**) period of ten years.

decillion [dɪ'sɪljən] *n.* a million nonillions (10⁶⁰); (*American & French*) a thousand nonillions (10³³).

decimate ['desimeit] *v.t.* kill large number of; kill one tenth of; punish by punishing or executing every tenth man chosen by lot. **decimation**, *n.*

decimestrial [ˌdesɪ'mestrɪəl] *adj.* consisting of or lasting ten months.

decimosexto [ˌdesɪməʊ'sekstəʊ] *see* **sextodecimo**.

déclassé [deɪ'klæseɪ] (*French*) *adj.* (*fem.* **-ée**) fallen or degraded from social class.

declension [dɪ'klenʃn] *n.* decline; *Grammar*, group of nouns with same inflection; naming the inflections of nouns. **declensional**, *adj.*

declination [ˌdeklɪ'neɪʃn] *n.* bending; turning aside; angle between magnetic needle and geographical meridian; *Astronomy*, angular distance from equator; (polite) refusal. **declinate** ['dek-], *adj.* bent to one side.

declinometer [ˌdeklɪ'nɒmɪtə] *n.* instrument measuring magnetic declination.

declivity [dɪ'klɪvəti] *n.* downward slope. **declivitous, declivous** [-'klaɪvəs], *adj.*

decoct [dɪ'kɒkt] *v.t.* boil; infuse; extract essence by boiling; reduce. **decoction**, *n.* **decoctive**, *adj.*

decollate [dɪ'kɒleɪt, 'dekə-]] *v.t.* behead.

décolleté [deɪ'kɒleteɪ] *adj.* (*fem.* **-ée**) low-necked; wearing a low-necked dress. **décolletage** [ˌdeɪkɒl'tɑːʒ], *n.* (edge of) low-cut neck; (fact of wearing) such a dress.

decompensation [ˌdiːkɒmpən'seɪʃn] *n. Medicine*, inability of heart to maintain adequate circulation.

decomposer [ˌdiːkəm'pəʊzə] *n. Biology*, organism that breaks down dead tissue.

decorticate [diː'kɔːtɪkeɪt] *v.t.* divest of bark, peel, husk, skin, etc.; flay; [-ət], *adj.* lacking such outer layer. **decortication, decorticator**, *n.*

decoupage, découpage [ˌdeɪkuː'pɑːʒ] *n.* decoration with cut-out shapes or illustrations; example of such work.

decrement ['dekrɪmənt] *n.* decrease; waste.

decrepitate [dɪ'krepɪteɪt] *v.t.* make to crackle by roasting. **decrepitation**, *n.*

decrepitude [dɪ'krepɪtjuːd] *n.* state of being decrepit.

decrescent [dɪ'kresnt] *adj.* decreasing gradually. **decrescence**, *n.*

decretal [dɪ'kriːtl] *n.* decree, especially papal; *adj.* pertaining to decree. **decretist**, *n.* student of decretals. **decretive, decretory**, *adj.* pertaining to or like a decree.

decrudescence [ˌdiːkru'desns] *n.* diminution in disease.

decubitus [dɪ'kjuːbɪtəs] *n.* act or attitude of lying down. **decubital**, *adj.* pertaining to or resulting from this.

decumbence, decumbency [dɪ'kʌmbəns, –i] *n.* decubitus. **decumbent**, *adj.* **decumbiture**, *n.* confinement to bed.

decuple ['dekjupl] *adj.* tenfold; arranged in tens; *n.* such amount; *v.i.* & *t.* multiply by ten.

decurrent [dɪ'kʌrənt] *adj.* running downward; elapsing. **decurrence**, *n.*

decursive [dɪ'kɜːsɪv] *adj.* decurrent.

decurtate [dɪ'kɜːteɪt] *adj.* shortened; *v.t.* curtail. **decurtation**, *n.*

decurve [diː'kɜːv] *v.i.* & *t.* curve downward. **decurvation**, *n.*

decussate [dɪ'kʌseɪt, –ət] *adj.* X-shaped; [–eɪt] *v.i.* & *t.* cross in X-shape. **decussation**, *n.*

dedition [dɪ'dɪʃn] *n.* surrender.

deemster ['diːmstə] *n.* Manx judge.

de facto [deɪ 'fæktəʊ, diː–]] (*Latin*) 'in fact'; actual; done or existing whether rightfully or not.

defalcate ['diːfælkeɪt] *v.t.* embezzle. **defalcation**, *n.* embezzlement; amount embezzled.

defamation [ˌdefə'meɪʃn] *n.* injury to character; calumny. **defamatory** [dɪ'fæmətəri], *adj.*

defeasance [dɪ'fiːzns] *n.* *Law,* nullification; condition which if fulfilled, nullifies a provision. **defeasible** *adj.* able to be annulled; having such condition.

defecate ['defəkeɪt] *v.i.* & *t.* refine; remove impurities from; excrete. *adj.* purified. **defecant** *n.* purifying agent. **defecation, defecator** *n.*

defenestration [ˌdiːfenɪ'streɪʃn] *n.* throwing of a person or thing out of window.

deferrize [diː'feraɪz] *v.t.* remove iron from. **deferrization** *n.*

defervesce [ˌdiːfə'ves, ˌde–]] *v.t.* become cool; lose interest. **defervescence**; *n.* **defervescent**, *adj.* pertaining to or causing cooling; *n.* such drug.

defibrillate [diː'fɪbrɪleɪt] *v.t.* restore normal rhythm to (the heart) after a heart attack. **defibrillation**, *n.* **defibrillator**, *n.*

de fide [di 'faɪdi, deɪ 'fiːdeɪ] (*Latin*) 'of the faith': *Roman Catholic,* accepted and taught as essential doctrine.

defilade [ˌdefɪ'leɪd] *n.* protection provided by obstacles or fortifications against enemy fire; *v.t.* arrange (fortifications) for this purpose.

definiendum [dɪˌfɪni'endəm] *n.* (*pl.* **–da**) thing to be defined.

definiens [dɪ'fɪnienz] *n.* (*pl.* **–ientia** [–'enʃə]) something that defines.

deflagrate ['defləgreɪt] *v.i.* & *t.* burn up suddenly. **deflagration, deflagrator**, *n.*

deflocculate [diː'flɒkjuleɪt] *v.t.* disperse in fine particles. **deflocculant**, *adj.* & *n.*

deflorate [dɪ'flɔːreɪt] *v.t.* deflower. **defloration**, *n.*

deflower [diː'flaʊə, dɪ–] *v.t.* ravish; rupture hymen, especially as primitive ceremony; strip of flowers.

defluent ['defluənt] *adj.* flowing down. **defluxion** [dɪ'flʌkʃn], *n.* discharge of mucus from nose.

defoliate [diː'fəʊlieɪt] *v.i.* & *t.* lose, or strip of, leaves; *adj.* stripped of leaves. **defoliation, defoliator**, *n.* **defoliant**, *n.* chemical that does this.

dégagé [ˌdeɪgaː'ʒeɪ, deɪ'gaːʒeɪ] (*French*) *adj.* (*fem –ée*) 'disengaged'; at ease; unworried.

degauss [diː'gaʊs] *v.t.* demagnetize by surrounding with electrically charged wire or coil, especially ships to prevent their detonating magnetic mines.

deglutinate [diː'gluːtɪneɪt] *v.t.* unstick; remove glue or gluten from. **deglutination**, *n.*

deglutition [ˌdiːgluː'tɪʃn] *n.* act or power of swallowing. **deglutitious**, *adj.* **deglutitory**, *adj.* aiding swallowing.

de gratia [diː 'greɪʃiə, deɪ 'graːtiə] (*Latin*) 'by favour'.

degust, degustate [dɪ'gʌst, –eɪt] *v.t.* taste, savour. **degustation**, *n.*

dehiscent [dɪ'hɪsnt] *adj.* gaping; discharging contents (*e.g.* seeds) by bursting open. **dehiscence**, *n.*

dehydrate [ˌdiː'haɪdreɪt] *v.i.* & *t.* remove or lose water from; desiccate; remove or lose hydrogen and oxygen in amounts to form water. **dehydration, dehydrator**, *n.*

deicide ['deɪsaɪd, 'diː–]] *n.* killer or destroyer, or killing or destruction, of a god, especially of Christ.

deictic ['daɪktɪk] *adj.* directly proving or demonstrating.

Dei gratia [ˌdeɪiː 'graːtiə, ˌdiːaɪ 'greɪʃiə] (*Latin*) 'by the grace of God' (*abbreviation* **D.G.**).

Dei judicium [ˌdeɪiː dʒu'dɪkɪəm, ˌdiːaɪ dʒu'dɪʃiəm] (*Latin*) 'judgement of God'; trial by ordeal.

deiparous [deɪ'ɪpərəs, diː–]] *adj.* giving birth to god or Christ.

deipnosophist [daɪp'nɒsəfɪst] *n.* person expert in art of table talk. **deipnosophistic**, *adj.* **deipnosophism**, *n.*

deipotent [deɪ'ɪpətənt, diː–]] *adj.* with god-like power.

deism ['deɪɪzm, 'diː–]] *n.* belief in God's existence but not in revealed religion. **deist**, *n.* **deistic**, *adj.*

dejecta [dɪ'dʒektə] *n. pl. Medicine,* excrements. **dejectory**, *n.* & *adj.* purgative. **dejecture**, *n.* excrement.

déjeuner ['deɪʒəneɪ] (*French*) *n.* luncheon; breakfast. **petit déjeuner** breakfast.

de jure [deɪ 'dʒʊəri, diː–]] (*Latin*) 'by right'; rightful.

dekarch *see* **decarch**.

delactation [ˌdiːlæk'teɪʃn] *n.* weaning; cessation of milk flow.

delaminate [diː'læmɪneɪt] *v.t.* divide into thin layers.

delation [dɪ'leɪʃn] *n.* laying information against a person. **delator**, *n.* informer. **delatorian**, *adj.*

delectation [ˌdiːlek'teɪʃn] *n.* enjoyment.

delectus [dɪ'lektəs] *n.* chrestomathy.

delendum [dɪ'lendəm] *n.* (*pl.* **–da**) thing to be deleted.

deleterious [ˌdelɪ'tɪəriəs] *adj.* harmful.

delict [dɪ'lɪkt] *n. Scottish law,* offence giving a right to civil remedy.

deligation [ˌdelɪ'geɪʃn] *n.* bandaging.

delignate [diːˈlɪgneɪt] v.t. remove wood or woody matter from.

delimit [diːˈlɪmɪt] v.t. fix boundaries of. delimitation, n.

deliquesce [ˌdelɪˈkwes] v.i. melt away. deliquescence, n. deliquescent, adj.

delitescent [ˌdelɪˈtesnt] adj. latent. delitescence, n. Medicine, sudden disappearance of symptoms.

deloul [dɪˈluːl] n. quick-moving riding camel of Arabia.

Delphian, Delphic [ˈdelfiən, –ɪk] adj. pertaining to oracle of Delphi; ambiguous; having several senses.

delta [ˈdeltə] n. fourth letter of Greek alphabet (Δ δ); Δ–shaped area of alluvium at river-mouth. deltaic [–ˈteɪɪk], deltic, adj. deltification, deltation, n. formation of deltas. deltoid, adj. Δ–shaped; n. such shoulder muscle.

deltiology [ˌdelti ˈɒlədʒi] n. hobby of collecting post-cards.

demagogue [ˈdeməgɒg] n. orator addressing himself to, or using arguments such as to stir, the masses. demagogic [–ˈgɒgɪk, –ˈgɒdʒɪk], adj. demagogism [–gɪzm], demagogy [–gi, –dʒi], n.

demarcate [ˈdiːmɑːkeɪt] v.t. delimit. demarcation, n.

démarche [ˈdeɪmɑːʃ] (French) n. decisive step or action, especially diplomatic and initiating new policy.

demegoric [ˌdiːmɪˈgɒrɪk] adj. pertaining to demagogic speech.

démenti [deɪˈmɒnti] (French) n. official denial.

dementia [dɪˈmenʃə, –iə] n. insanity; impairment of cognitive and intellectual function because of damage to neurons in the brain. dementia praecox [–ˈpriːkɒks], schizophrenia.

demephitize [diːˈmefɪtaɪz] v.t. purify (air). demephitization, n.

demersal [dɪˈmɜːsl] adj. sinking to bottom. demersion, n.

demesne [dɪˈmeɪn, –ˈmiːn] n. estate; territory; unrestricted possession of land. demesnial, adj.

demijohn [ˈdemidʒɒn] n. large bottle with wicker case.

demi-monde [ˌdemiˈmɒnd] n. class of women of doubtful reputation. demi-mondain, adj. demi-mondaine, n. woman of that class.

demi-rep [ˈdemirep] n. demi-mondaine.

demisang(ue) [ˈdemisæŋ] n. half-breed; first cross.

demise [dɪˈmaɪz] n. death; act of conveying estate; v.t. convey estate, especially by will.

demit [dɪˈmɪt] v.t. & i. relinquish, abdicate. demission [dɪˈmɪʃn], n.

demiurge [ˈdemiɜːdʒ] n. inferior god who created world; creative power or spirit. demiurgeous, demiurgic, adj.

demivierge [ˌdemiviˈeəʒ] (French) woman who is sexually promiscuous but remains technically a virgin.

demogenic [ˌdeməˈdʒenɪk] adj. applied to societies based on citizenship rather than kinship.

demography [dɪˈmɒgrəfi] n. study of population statistics. demographer, demographist, n. demographic(al), adj.

demonetize [diːˈmʌnɪtaɪz] v.t. divest (coin, etc.) of its value or withdraw from circulation; abandon (gold, etc.) as currency. demonetization, n.

demonifuge [dɪˈmɒnɪfjuːdʒ] n. charm against evil spirits.

demonolatry [ˌdiːməˈnɒlətri] n. worship of demons, and good and evil spirits. demonolater, n. demon-worshipper. demonology n. study of demons.

demophil(e) [ˈdeməfɪl, –faɪl] n. friend of people; person fond of crowds or the masses. demophobe, n. person disliking the masses or crowds.

Demos [ˈdiːmɒs] n. personification of democracy or the masses.

demotic [dɪˈmɒtɪk] adj. pertaining to common people; applied to simplified style of Egyptian writing.

demulcent [dɪˈmʌlsnt] n. & adj. soothing (substance). demulsify v.t. extract from an emulsion. demulsion n. soothing.

demurrage [dɪˈmʌrɪdʒ] n. delay by charterer of a vehicle's or vessel's loading, departure, etc.; payment for such delay. demurrer, n. Law, objection to pleading.

denarius [dɪˈneəriəs] n. (pl. -rii) ancient Roman coin of silver or, later, copper; penny (abbreviation d.)

denary [ˈdiːnəri, ˈde–]] adj. of ten; tenfold; decimal n. ten; group of ten; one tenth.

dendrachate [ˈdendrəkeɪt] n. moss agate.

dendral [ˈdendrəl] adj. living in trees; arboreal. dendriform, adj. tree-like; branched.

dendrite [ˈdendraɪt] n. tree-shaped mark made by another mineral in stone or crystal; nerve-cell outgrowth conducting impulse inwards. dendritic [–ˈdrɪtɪk], adj. like a dendrite; tree-like.

dendrochronology [ˌdendrəʊkrəˈnɒlədʒi] n. analysis of the annual rings of trees to date past events.

dendrograph [ˈdendrəgrɑːf] n. instrument recording growth of tree's girth. dendrography n. such recording; treatise on trees.

dendroid [ˈdendrɔɪd] adj. tree-shaped.

dendrology [denˈdrɒlədʒi] n. study of or treatise on trees. dendrologic(al), dendrologous, adj. dendrologist, n.

dendrometer [denˈdrɒmɪtə] n. instrument measuring tree's height and girth.

dendron [ˈdendrɒn] n. dendrite (of nerve-cell).

dendrophilous [denˈdrɒfɪləs] adj. fond of or inhabiting trees.

denehole [ˈdiːnhəʊl] n. shaft, with chambers at base, sunk in chalk regions, of ancient origin.

dengue [ˈdeŋgi, –eɪ] n. kind of fever of hot regions; break-bone fever.

denier [ˈdeniə] n. originally a unit of weight (about 8⅕ troy grains) of silk, rayon, nylon, etc.; later, an indication of the fineness of such yarns, the lower the denier number the finer the yarn.

denigrate [ˈdenɪgreɪt] v.t. blacken; slander. denigration, denigrator, n.

denizen [ˈdenɪzən] n. inhabitant; naturalized person or thing; v.t. naturalize; people; colonize. denization, n.

denominate [dɪˈnɒmɪneɪt] v.t.. name, designate. denomination, n. designation; religious body or organisation; grade, degree.

denouement, dénouement [deɪˈnuːmɒn] n. resolution of the plot at the end of a play.

de nouveau [də ˈnuːvəʊ] (French) 'again'; afresh.

de novo [deɪ 'nəʊvəʊ, diː-]] (*Latin*) 'from the beginning'; afresh.

dentate ['denteɪt] *adj.* with toothed edge, or tooth-like prominences. **dentelated**, *adj.* with small notches.

denticle ['dentɪkl] *n.* small tooth or tooth-like part. **denticulated** ['den'tɪkjuleɪtɪd], *adj.* with small, tooth-like prominences.

dentigerous [den'tɪdʒərəs] *adj.* bearing teeth.

dentil ['dentɪl] *n.* small rectangular block, one of a row used as ornamentation, especially beneath a cornice.

dentilingual [ˌdentɪ'lɪŋgwəl] *n.* & *adj.* (sound) pronounced (as *th*) with tongue against teeth.

dentinasal [ˌdentɪ'neɪzl] *n.* & *adj.* (sound) pronounced (as *n*) with nasal passage open and tongue against upper teeth or teeth-ridge.

dentine ['dentiːn] *n.* bone-like substance forming tooth; dental ivory.

dentiphone ['dentɪfəʊn] *n.* audiphone.

dentition [den'tɪʃn] *n.* teeth development; characteristic arrangement or nature of animal's teeth.

denumeration [dɪˌnjuːmə'reɪʃn] *n.* *Mathematics,* determination of number of things able to fulfil certain conditions. **denumerable**, *adj.* countable.

deobstruent [diː'ɒbstruənt] *n.* & *adj.* (medicine) removing obstacles; purgative.

deodar ['diːədɑː] *n.* Indian cedar.

deontology [ˌdiːɒn'tɒlədʒi] *n.* science of moral duty. **deontological**, *adj.* **deontologist**, *n.*

deoppilate [di'ɒpɪleɪt] *v.i.* & *t.* remove obstructions (from). **deoppilant**, *n.* & *adj.* **deoppilation**, *n.* **deoppilative**, *adj.*

deordination [diˌɔːdɪ'neɪʃn] *n.* disorder; abnormality.

Deo volente [ˌdeɪəʊ və'lenti, ˌdiː-]] (*Latin*) 'God being willing' (*abbreviation* **D.V.**).

depascent [dɪ'pæsnt] *adj.* eating.

dépaysé [deɪ'peɪizeɪ] (*French*) *adj.* (*fem.* **-ée**) 'away from natural country or environment'; lost; out of one's element.

depilation [ˌdepɪ'leɪʃn] *n.* removal of hair. **depilous** ['dep-], *adj.* bald. **depilatory** [-'pɪl-], *adj.* used to remove hair. *n.* such substance.

deploy [dɪ'plɔɪ] *v.t.* & *t.* spread out into one line; organize for effective use. **deployment**, *n.*

deponent [dɪ'pəʊnənt] *n.* person giving evidence or making affidavit. *adj.* *Grammar*, applied to verbs with active meaning and passive form.

deposition [ˌdepə'zɪʃn, ˌdiː-]] *n.* *Law*, sworn testimony.

depotentiate [ˌdiːpə'tenʃieɪt] *v.t.* divest of power; weaken. **depotentiation**, *n.*

depredate ['deprədeɪt] *v.t.* plunder; ravage. **depredation**, *n.*

de profundis [ˌdeɪ prə'fundiːs, -ɪs] (*Latin*) 'from the depths'; *adv.* expressing deep misery; *n.* 130th Psalm.

depurate ['depjureɪt] *v.t.* purify. **depurant**, *n.* & *adj.* **depuration**, *n.* **depurative**, *n.* & *adj.*

deracinate [dɪ'ræsɪneɪt] *v.t.* uproot. **deracination**, *n.*

de règle [də 'reɪglə] (*French*) 'by rule'; according to custom or propriety.

dereliction [ˌderə'lɪkʃn] *n.* failure to perform duty.

de rigueur [də rɪ'gɜː] (*French*) according to or demanded by etiquette.

derma, dermis ['dɜːmə, -ɪs] *n.* layer of skin, containing nerves and blood vessels, beneath epidermis. **dermad**, *adj.* towards skin. **dermal, dermatic, dermatine**, *adj.* pertaining to skin.

dermatitis [ˌdɜːmə'taɪtɪs] *n.* inflammation of skin or derma.

dermatoglyphics [ˌdɜːmətə'glɪfɪks] *n.* (study of) lines forming fingerprints and other skin patterns. **dermatograph**, *n.* fingerprint or other impression of skin markings. **dermatography**, *n.* description of skin.

dermatoid ['dɜːmətɔɪd] *adj.* skin-like.

dermatology [ˌdɜːmə'tɒlədʒi] *n.* study of skin and skin diseases. **dermatological**, *adj.* **dermatologist**, *n.*

dermatome ['dɜːmətəʊm] *n.* instrument for cutting skin. **dermatomic** [-'tɒmɪk], *adj.*

dermatomycosis [ˌdɜːmətəmar'kəʊsɪs] *n.* skin disease due to vegetable parasite.

dermatopathy [ˌdɜːmə'tɒpəθi] *n.* skin disease. **dermatopathic**, *adj.*

dermatophyte ['dɜːmətəfaɪt] *n.* disease-causing fungus parasite of skin. **dermatophytic** [-'fɪtɪk], *adj.* **dermatophytosis**, *n.*

dermatoplasty ['dɜːmətəplæsti] *n.* plastic surgery of skin.

dermatosis [ˌdɜːmə'təʊsɪs] *n.* skin disease.

dermographia, dermographism [ˌdɜːmə'græfiə, dɜː'mɒgrəfɪzm] *n.* condition in which slight pressure, as of writing, on skin causes red mark. **dermographic**, *adj.*

dermoid ['dɜːmɔɪd] *adj.* skin-like.

dernier cri [ˌdeənieɪ 'kriː] (*French*) 'last cry'; latest fashion; newest discovery.

derogate ['derəgeɪt] *v.i.* & *t.* reduce value (of); detract from. **derogation**, *n.* **derogatory**, [dɪ'rɒgətəri] *adj.*, disparaging.

derringer ['derɪndʒə] *n.* short, wide-barrelled pistol.

desacralize [diː'seɪkrəlaɪz] *v.i.* & *t.* divest of supernatural qualities; remove tabu. **desacralization**, *n.*

desalination [ˌdiːsælɪ'neɪʃn] *n.* removal of salt from sea water to produce fresh water.

descant ['deskænt] *n.* *Music,* simple counterpoint sung by trebles above melody; counterpoint; treble; commentary; *v.i.* comment; discourse.

descry [dɪ'skraɪ] *v.t.* discern; detect.

deshabillé [ˌdezə'biːeɪ] (*French*) *adj.* partly clad; **deshabille** *n.* [-'biːl], such state.

desiccate ['desɪkeɪt] *v.t.* dry up; preserve by drying. **desiccant**, *n.* & *adj.* **desiccation, desiccator**, *n.* **desiccative, desiccatory**, *adj.*

desiderate [dɪ'zɪdəreɪt, -'sɪ-] (*Latin*) *v.t.* desire strongly; regard as lacking. **desideration**, *n.* **desiderative**, *adj.* **desideratum**, *n.* (*pl.* **desiderata**) desired thing; condition; thing regarded as lacking.

desiderium [ˌdezɪ'dɪəriəm, -sɪ-] (*Latin*) *n.* yearning.

desinent(ial) ['dezɪnənt, ˌdezɪ'nenʃl, -sɪ-] *adj.* terminal. **desinence**, *n.* ending.

desipient [dɪ'sɪpiənt] *adj.* foolish. **desipience**, *n.*

desition [dɪ'sɪʃn] *n.* ending; cessation. **desistive**, *adj.* final.

desman ['desmən] *n.* aquatic mole-like animal of Russia and Pyrenees; its fur.

desmid ['dezmɪd] *n.* species of algae. **desmidian,**

n. **desmiology,** *n.* study of such.

desmoid ['dezmɔɪd] *adj.* like a ligament.

desmology [dez'mɒlədʒi] *n.* study of ligaments or bandaging. **desmotomy,** *n.* cutting or anatomy of ligaments.

despiteous [dɪ'spɪtiəs] *adj.* spiteful, malevolent.

despumate [dɪ'spjuːmeɪt, 'despju–]] *v.i.* & *t.* remove scum; throw off like or in scum; foam. **despumation,** *n.*

desquamate ['deskwəmeɪt] *v.i.* & *t.* peel off, or cause to peel off in scales. **desquamation,** *n.* desquamatory, *adj.* & *n.* **desquamative,** *adj.*

desucration [ˌdiːsju'kreɪʃn, –su–] *n.* removal of sugar.

desuetude ['deswɪtjuːd] *n.* disuse; obsolescence.

desultory ['desltəri, 'dez–] *adj.* aimless; lacking method or application; digressive.

détente ['deɪtɒnt] *(French) n.* relaxation; ease of strained political relations.

detergence, detergency [dɪ'tɜːdʒəns, –i] *n.* power to clean. **detergent,** *n.* & *adj.*

determinism [dɪ'tɜːmɪnɪzm] *n.* philosophical theory that acts of will arise from deciding causes; fatalism; theory that present conditions are so by necessity.

detersion [dɪ'tɜːʃn] *n.* act of cleansing. **detersive,** *n.* & *adj.* detergent.

detinue ['detɪnjuː] *n. Law,* illegal detention of another's personal property; writ for recovering such detained property.

detoxicate [ˌdiː'tɒksɪkeɪt] *v.t.* remove poison or its effects from. **detoxicant,** *n.* & *adj.* **detoxication, detoxicator,** *n.*

detritus [dɪ'traɪtəs] *n.* debris; fragments worn away, especially of rock. **detrital,** *adj.* consisting of debris. **detrited,** *adj.* worn thin. **detrition** [–'trɪʃn], *n.*

de trop [də 'trəʊ] *(French)* 'too much'; unwanted; in the way.

detrude [dɪ'truːd] *v.t.* push down or out.

detruncate [dɪ'trʌŋkeɪt] *v.t.* cut short; lop. **detruncation,** *n.*

detrusion [dɪ'truːʒn] *n.* act of detruding. **detrusive,** *adj.*

deus ex machina [ˌdeɪəs eks 'mækɪnə, ˌdiː–] *(Latin)* 'a god from a machine'; interference by divine power to set right a situation; any artificial method of solving difficulty.

deuterium [djuː'tɪəriəm] *n.* heavy hydrogen, the oxide of which is heavy water used to slow down neutrons emitted in nuclear fission.

deuterogamy [ˌdjuːtə'rɒgəmi] *n.* remarriage after spouse's death. **deuterogamist,** *n.*

deuteron ['djuːtərɒn] *n.* a positively charged particle consisting of a proton and a neutron, equivalent to the nucleus of an atom of deuterium.

deuteropathy [ˌdjuːtə'rɒpəθi] *n.* secondary illness. **deuteropathic** [–'pæθɪk] *adj.*

deutoplasm ['djuːtəplæzm] *n.* yolk of egg. **deutoplasmic,** *adj.*

devaluate [diː'væljueɪt, dɪ–] *v.t.* reduce value of, especially of currency in terms of other currencies. **devaluation,** *n.*

devise [dɪ'vaɪz] *v.t. Law* bequeath (real estate) by will. **devisee** [dɪˌvaɪ'ziː], *n.* person to whom property is bequeathed. **devisor,** *n.* person bequeathing property.

devoir ['devwɑː] *(French) n.* duty; best of which one is capable; *pl.* respects; attentions; courtesy.

dewlap ['djuːlæp] *n.* loose skin hanging at throat.

dexter ['dekstə] *adj.* on right-hand side; presaging good; honest; *Heraldry,* on right-hand side of wearer of shield. **dexterity** [–'terəti] *n.* adroitness; deftness. **dexterous,** *adj* adroit; deft.

dextral ['dekstrəl] *adj.* on right-hand side. **dextrality** [–'stræl–], *n.* use of right limb, eye, etc., more than left. **dextrally,** *adv.* towards right-hand side.

dextrin ['dekstrɪn] *n.* gummy carbohydrate, manufactured from, and resulting from digestion of, starch; starch gum. **dextrinate,** *v.t.* make into or mix with dextrin. **dextrinous,** *adj.*

dextrocardia [ˌdekstrəʊ'kɑːdiə] *n.* condition in which the heart is on the right-hand side of the chest.

dextrocular [dek'strɒkjʊlə] *adj.* using right eye more than left. **dextrocularity** [–'lærəti], *n.*

dextrogyratory [ˌdekstrəʊdʒaɪ'reɪtəri] *adj.* turning to the right. **dextrogyration,** *n.*

dextrorotatory [ˌdekstrəʊrəʊ'teɪtəri] *adj.* turning to the right, especially turning plane of polarized light to right. **dextrorotation,** *n.*

dextrorse ['dekstrɔːs] *adj.* (of plants) spirally turning to the right. **dextrorsal,** *adj.*

dextrose ['dekstrəʊs] *n.* glucose; grape sugar.

dextrosinistral [ˌdekstrəʊ'sɪnɪstrəl] *adj.* extending to right and left; applied to the left-handed person using right hand for writing.

dextrous ['dekstrəs] *adj.* dexterous.

dextroversion [ˌdekstrə'vɜːʃn] *n.* turn to the right.

dhal [dɑːl] *n.* (purée of) Indian pulse.

dhobi ['dəʊbi] *n.* Indian washerman or woman.

dhole [dəʊl] *n.* Indian wild dog.

dhoti, dhooti, dhotie, ['dəʊti, 'duː–] *n.* Hindu loincloth.

dhow [daʊ] *n.* Arab sailing ship with lateen sails.

dhurra *see* **durra.**

diablerie [di'ɑːbləri] *(French) n.* 'devilry'; sorcery; black magic; mischievous act.

diabolism [daɪ'æbəlɪzm] *n.* devil worship; black magic; devilish behaviour. **diabolepsy,** *n.* devil-possession. **diabolic(al)** [–'bɒl–], *adj.* pertaining to devils. **diabolist,** *n.* student or teacher of diabolism. **diabology,** *n.* study of or belief in devils; doctrine about devils.

diabrosis [ˌdaɪə'brəʊsɪs] *n.* perforation, especially by ulcer. **diabrotic** [–'brɒtɪk], *n.* & *adj.* corrosive (thing).

diachoretic [ˌdaɪəkə'retɪk] *adj.* aperient.

diachronic [ˌdaɪə'krɒnɪk] *adj.* pertaining to the development of phenomena through time. **diachrony** [daɪ'ækrəni], *n.*

diachylon [daɪ'ækɪlən] *n.* kind of sticking plaster.

diaclasis [ˌdaɪə'kleɪsɪs] *n.* fracture; refraction. **diaclastic** [–'klæstɪk], *adj.*

diaconal [daɪ'ækənl] *adj.* pertaining to deacon. **diaconate,** *n.* deacon's jurisdiction or office; the order of deacons.

diacope [daɪ'ækəpi] *n.* deep incision.

diacrisis [daɪ'ækrəsɪs] *n. Medicine,* change in secretion during illness; discharge aiding diagnosis.

diacritic [ˌdaɪə'krɪtɪk] *n.* mark distinguishing sound of letter. **diacritical,** *adj.* pertaining to such marks; distinctive.

diactinic [ˌdaɪæk'tɪnɪk] *adj.* able to transmit actinic rays. **diactinism**, *n.*

diadem ['daɪədem] *n.* crown; fillet.

diaermic [ˌdaɪə'dɜːmɪk] *adj.* pertaining to penetration through skin.

diadromous [daɪ'ædrəməs] *adj.* migrating between fresh and salt water.

diaeresis, dieresis [daɪ'ɪərəsɪs, -'er-] *n.* (*pl.* **-ses**) mark ( ) placed over vowel to indicate change in pronunciation or that it is pronounced separately (*e.g.* naïve); such separate pronunciation of vowels. **diaeretic** [-'retɪk], *adj.* pertaining to diaeresis; dividing; caustic.

diaglyph ['daɪəglɪf] *n.* intaglio. **diaglyphic, diaglyptic,** *adj.*

diagraph ['daɪəgrɑːf] *n.* instrument for enlarging or reducing drawing, diagrams, etc.

dialectic(s) [ˌdaɪə'lektɪk, -s] *n.* art of logical and analytical argument. **dialectical,** *adj.* pertaining to or given to dialectic; logical. **dialectician** [-'tɪʃn], *n.* person skilled in dialectic.

diallelus [ˌdaɪə'liːləs] *n.* (*pl.* **-li**) arguing in a circle.

dialysis [daɪ'æləsɪs] *n.* separation of substances in a solution by diffusion through a membrane, especially such separation of waste products from blood in the kidneys. **dialyse,** *v.t.* **dialyser,** *n.* machine performing this function. **dialytic.**

diamb ['daɪæm] *n.* verse foot of two iambi.

diamesogamous [ˌdaɪəmɪ'sɒgəməs] *n. Botany,* not self-pollinated.

diamond ['daɪəmənd] *n.* size of type: 4 or 4½ point.

diandrous [daɪ'ændrəs] *adj. Botany,* having two stamens.

dianoetic [ˌdaɪənəʊ'etɪk] *adj.* pertaining to reasoning. **dianoia** [-'nɔɪə], *n.* faculty of discursive reasoning.

diapason [ˌdaɪə'peɪzn, -sn] *n.* loud, harmonious burst of music; entire gamut or compass; principal organ-stop.

diaper ['daɪəpə] *n.* linen with regular repetitive pattern; such pattern; *American,* nappy. *v.t.* ornament with such patterns.

diaphanous [daɪ'æfənəs] *adj.* transparent; filmy. **diaphaneity,** *n.* **diaphanometer** *n.*, instrument measuring transparency of air, etc. **diaphanoscopy,** *n.* illumination from within of body cavities for medical examination.

diaphoretic [ˌdaɪəfə'retɪk] *n. & adj.* (drug) causing perspiration. **diaphoresis** [-'riːsɪs], *n.* perspiration.

diaphragm ['daɪəfræm] *n.* vibrating disk in telephone, radio, etc.; muscular partition between abdomen and chest; any thin partition or dividing membrane. **diaphragmatic** [-fræg'mætɪk], *adj.*

diaplasis [daɪ'æpləsɪs] *n.* (*pl.* **-ses**) setting of fractured or dislocated bone.

diapnoic [ˌdaɪæp'nəʊɪk] *n. & adj.* mild(ly) diaphoretic.

diapositive [ˌdaɪə'pɒzətɪv] *n. Photography,* slide.

diapyesis [ˌdaɪəpaɪ'iːsɪs] *n.* discharge of pus. **diapyetic** [-'etɪk], *n. & adj.*

diarchy ['daɪɑːki] *n.* government by two rulers. **diarchial, diarchic,** *adj.*

diarthrosis [ˌdaɪɑːˈθrəʊsɪs] *n.* joint permitting free movement.

Diaspora [daɪ'æspərə] *n.* dispersal of the Jews after the Babylonian captivity; areas settled by Jews outside Israel.

diastase ['daɪəsteɪz, -eɪs] *n.* digestive ferment converting starch into sugar. **diastatic,** *adj.*

diastasis [daɪ'æstəsɪs] *n.* separation of bones without fracture; final phase of heart dilation.

diastole [daɪ'æstəli] *n.* heart dilatation alternating with systole. **diastolic** [ˌdaɪə'stɒlɪk], *adj.*

diastomatic [ˌdaɪəstə'mætɪk] *adj.* through pores.

diastrophe [daɪ'æstrəfi] *n. Geology,* deformation, upheaval, etc., of earth's crust. **diastrophic** [ˌdaɪə'strɒfɪk], *adj.* **diastrophism** [-'æs-], *n.* such geological process; result of diastrophe; any such process of upheaval or drastic change.

diasyrm ['daɪəsɜːm] *n.* rhetorical device of damning by faint praise.

diathermic [ˌdaɪə'θɜːmɪk] *adj.* transmitting heat rays. **diathermacy, diathermancy, diathermaneity,** *n.* **diathermanous, diathermous,** *adj.* **diathermotherapy,** *n.* medical treatment by diathermy. **diathermy,** *n.* heating, by electrical means, of subcutaneous tissues; electric current used in diathermy.

diathesis [daɪ'æθəsɪs] *n.* (*pl.* **-ses**) congenital susceptibility or aptitude; predisposing factor. **diathetic** [-'θetɪk], *adj.*

diatom ['daɪətɒm] *n.* species of algae. **diatomaceous** [-tə'meɪʃəs], *adj* containing many diatoms.

diatomic [ˌdaɪə'tɒmɪk] *adj.* comprising two atoms; bivalent. **diatomicity** [-'mɪsəti], *n.*

diatonic [ˌdaɪə'tɒnɪk] *n. Music,* containing no accidentals; denoting the standard 8-tone scale.

diatribe ['daɪətraɪb] *n.* violent speech or writing; denunciation.

dicaeology [ˌdaɪsi'ɒlədʒi] *n.* rhetorical device of defending oneself by pleading justification.

dicephalous [daɪ'kefələs, -'se-] *adj.* twoheaded. **dicephalism,** *n.* **dicephalus,** *n.* (*pl.* **-li**) such monster.

dicerous ['daɪsərəs] *adj.* having two antennae or horns.

dichogamy [daɪ'kɒgəmi] *n.* coming to maturity at different times of male and female elements of plant or animal, to avoid self-fertilization. **dichogamic** [-'gæmɪk], **dichogamous,** *adj.*

dichord ['daɪkɔːd] *n.* two-stringed musical instrument.

dichotomy [daɪ'kɒtəmi] *n.* division into two (opposed parts). **dichotomal, dichotomic** (om'ik), **dichotomous,** *adj.* **dichotomize,** *v.t.* divide into two or more parts; analyse.

dichromatic [ˌdaɪkrə'mætɪk] *adj.* of or in two colours; partially colour-blind. **dichromatism** [-'krəʊ-], *n.* substance's property of presenting different colours at different thicknesses.

dicotyledon [ˌdaɪkɒtɪ'liːdn] *n.* plant having two cotyledons. **dicotyledonary, dicotyledonous** [-'liː-, -'le-], *adj.*

dicrotic [daɪ'krɒtɪk] *adj.* (of the pulse) having a double beat. **dicrotism** ['daɪkrətɪzm, 'dɪ-], *n.*

dictum ['dɪktəm] *n.* (*pl.* **-ta**) axiom; saying; apophthegm.

didactic [daɪ'dæktɪk] *adj.* intended or intending to teach; moral. **didacticism** [-sɪzm], *n.* **didactics,** *n.* art of teaching.

didascalic, didascalar [ˌdɪdə'skælɪk, dɪ'dæskələ] *adj.* didactic; pertaining to teaching.

didelphian [daɪ'delfiən] *n. & adj.* marsupial.

didelphic, didelphous, *adj.*

didicoy, diddicoy ['dɪdɪkɔɪ] *n.* person who lives like a gypsy but is not a true Romany.

didymous, didymate ['dɪdɪməs, -ət] *adj.* growing in pairs.

diectasis [daɪ'ektəsɪs] *n.* lengthening verse line by introducing extra syllable.

dieldrin ['diːldrɪn] *n.* a persistent chemical pesticide, generally forbidden in the U.K. since 1964.

dielectric [,daɪ'lektrɪk] *n. & adj. Electricity,* nonconducting (substance). **dielectrical,** *adj.*

dies faustus [,diːeɪz 'faʊstəs, ,daɪiːz 'fɔːstəs] *(Latin)* 'auspicious or favourable day'. **dies infaustus,** 'unlucky day'.

dies irae [,diːeɪz 'ɪəreɪ, -aɪ] *(Latin)* 'day of wrath'; day of judgment; Latin hymn on that subject.

dies non (juridicus) [,daɪiːz 'nɒn (dʒuː'rɪdɪkəs), ,diːeɪz 'nəʊn] *(Latin)* *(pl. ... juridici* [-siː]), 'not lawful day'; day on which no law-court business takes place.

differentia [,dɪfə'renʃɪə] *n. (pl. -ae)* distinguishing mark.

diffident ['dɪfɪdənt] *adj.* shy; modest. **diffidence,** *n.*

diffinity [dɪ'fɪnəti] *n.* absence of affinity.

diffluent ['dɪfluənt] *adj.* flowing away or melting with ease. **diffluence,** *n.*

diffract [dɪ'frækt] *v.t.* break up into portions. **diffraction,** *n.* breaking up of light into coloured bands when it passes through narrow opening or by edge of solid body, etc. **diffraction grating,** fine grating causing diffraction of light.

diffrangible [dɪ'frændʒəbl] *adj.* able to be diffracted.

diffugient [dɪ'fjuːdʒɪənt] *adj.* dispersing.

digamma ['daɪ,gæmə, daɪ'gæmə] *n.* early Greek letter (F). **digammic,** *adj.*

digamy ['dɪgəmi] *n.* deuterogamy. **digamist,** *n.* **digamous,** *adj.*

digastric [daɪ'gæstrɪk] *adj.* biventral.

digenesis [daɪ'dʒensɪs] *n.* successive sexual and non-sexual reproduction. **digenetic** [-'netɪk], *adj.*

digeny ['dɪdʒəni] *n.* sexual reproduction. **digenous,** *adj.*

dight [daɪt] *adj. archaic,* clad; *v.t.* clothe.

digital ['dɪdʒɪtl] *adj.* (of a computer) calculating by numbers and not quantities.

digitalis [,dɪdʒɪ'teɪlɪs] *n.* heart stimulant obtained from foxglove leaves. **digitalism** ['dɪdʒɪtl-ɪzm], *n.* condition due to over-use of this.

digitate ['dɪdʒɪteɪt] *adj.* having or resembling fingers. **digitation,** *n.*

digitigrade ['dɪdʒɪtɪgreɪd] *adj.* walking on toes only; *n.* such animal.

digitize ['dɪdʒɪtaɪz] *v.t.* finger; point at; convert (data) into digital form.

digladiation [,daɪglædi'eɪʃn] *n.* fight; dispute.

diglossia [daɪ'glɒsiə] *n.* co-existence of a (in social and literary terms) higher and lower form of the same language.

diglot(tic) ['daɪglɒt, daɪ'glɒtɪk] *adj.* bilingual. **diglottist,** *n.* such person.

digoneutic [,daɪgə'njuːtɪk] *adj.* producing two broods in a year.

digonous ['dɪgənəs] *adj.* with two angles.

digraph ['daɪgrɑːf] *n.* two letters with one sound only (*e.g. ph*). **digraphic,** *adj.*

dihedral [daɪ'hiːdrəl] *n.* angle between an aircraft wing and the horizontal.

dilatory ['dɪlətəri] *adj.* procrastinating; slow.

dilettante [,dɪlə'tænti] *n. (pl. -ti)* amateur of fine arts; superficial lover or practiser of art. **dilettantism,** *n.*

dilogy ['dɪlədʒi] *n.* intentional ambiguity; emphatic repetition of word, etc.

diluent ['dɪljuənt] *n. & adj.* diluting (agent).

diluvial [dɪ'luːviəl] *adj.* pertaining to or caused by the Flood or any inundation. **diluvianism,** *n.* belief that certain geological facts are explainable by the Deluge.

dime [daɪm] *(American) n.* coin worth tenth part of dollar; ten-cent piece.

dimerous ['dɪmərəs] *adj.* arranged or divided in two parts.

dimeter ['dɪmɪtə] *n.* verse line of two feet. **dimetric** [daɪ'metrɪk], *adj.*

dimidiate [dɪ'mɪdieɪt, daɪ-] *v.t.* halve. **dimidiation,** *n.*

diminutive [dɪ'mɪnjutɪv] *n. & adj.* (word or form of word) signifying smallness; very small (person or thing).

dimissory ['dɪmɪsəri] *adj.* giving permission to go; dismissing.

dimorphism [daɪ'mɔːfɪzm] *n.* occurrence of noticeable differences between two creatures of

---

Different from...?

It is often claimed that *from* is the only preposition that can properly be used with *different*, and that *different to* and *different than* are 'incorrect'. The basis of this claim is that *differ* occurs only with *from* (a thing cannot *differ to* something else). But *different* is not the same word as *differ*, and there is no reason why it should take the same prepositions (one might just as well say that the equally related *difference* should not be used with *between*). In fact, the construction *different to* (perhaps modelled on *dissimilar to*) goes back at least to the 16th century, and has always been widely used by the best writers ('The party of prisoners lived ... with comforts very different to those which were awarded to the poor wretches

there,' William Thackeray, 1852). In present-day English it is commoner in Britain than in North America.

The case of *different than* is not so straightforward. When *different* is followed by a clause, one has the option of either introducing the somewhat inelegant *from/to what* or using *than* (*Her behaviour is different from what it used to be/different than it used to be*). The latter may seem preferable; certainly it is standard in American English. But the use of *different than* before a noun, with *than* functioning as a preposition (*Rabbits are a different species than hares*), is still widely objected to.

same species; dual personality. **dimorphic, dim-orphous,** *adj.*

dinic(al) ['dɪnɪk, –I] *adj.* pertaining to vertigo.

dioecious [daɪ'iːʃəs] *adj.* having male and female organs in separate individuals. **dioecism,** *n.*

dioestrum [daɪ'iːstrəm] *n.* period of sexual inactivity between 'heats'. **dioestrous,** *adj.*

dionym ['daɪənɪm] *n.* name containing two terms. **dionymal** [–'ɒnɪml], *adj.* binomial.

Dionysiac [ˌdaɪə'nɪziæk, –si–] *adj.* pertaining to Dionysus, ancient Greek god of wine, and his wild rites; bacchanalian.

dioptometer [ˌdaɪɒp'tɒmɪtə] *n.* instrument measuring refractive power of eye.

dioptre, diopter [daɪ'ɒptə] *n.* unit of power of lens, the reciprocal of the focal length in metres. **dioptric** [–'ɒptrɪk], *adj.* pertaining to refraction of light; transparent. **dioptroscopy,** *n.* measurement of refractive power of eye. **dioptrics,** *n.* study of refraction of light.

diorama [ˌdaɪə'rɑːmə] *n.* lighted painting(s) and figures so disposed and viewed as to appear real scenes; life-size museum exhibit. **dioramic** [–'ræmɪk], *adj.*

diorthosis [ˌdaɪɔː'θəusɪs] *n.* correction; straightening, especially of deformed limbs. **diorthotic** [–'θɒtɪk], *adj.*

diotic [daɪ'ɒtɪk, –'əutɪk] *adj.* affecting both ears.

diphyletic [ˌdaɪfaɪ'letɪk] *adj.* descended from two genealogical lines.

diphyodont ['dɪfɪədɒnt] *adj.* having two successive sets of teeth.

diplegia [daɪ'pliːdʒɪə] *n.* paralysis of corresponding parts on both sides of body.

diplocephalus [ˌdɪpləu'kefələs, –'se–] *n.* double-headed monster. **diplocephalous,** *adj.* **diplocephaly,** *n.*

diploid ['dɪplɔɪd] *adj.* double, especially having double normal chromosome number. **diploidy,** *n.* such state.

diplopia [dɪ'pləupɪə] *n.* double vision. **diplopic,** [–'ɒpɪk], *adj.*

diplopod ['dɪpləpɒd] *n.* millipede. **diplopodic,** *adj.*

dipnoous ['dɪpnəuəs] *adj.* having both lungs and gills. **dipnoan,** *n.* such fish; lungfish.

dipody ['dɪpədi] *n.* verse measure of two feet; dimeter.

dipole ['daɪpəul] *n. Electricity,* any object oppositely charged at its ends; a broadcast-receiving aerial consisting of a single metal rod.

dipsetic [dɪp'setɪk] *n. & adj.* (thing) causing thirst.

dipsomania [ˌdɪpsə'meɪnɪə] *n.* uncontrollable desire for drink, especially alcohol. **dipsomaniac,** *n.* sufferer from this. **dipsomaniacal** [–mə'naɪəkl], *adj.*

dipsosis [dɪp'səusɪs] *n.* great thirst due to disease.

dipterous ['dɪptərəs] *adj.* having two wings. **dipteral,** *adj.; Architecture,* having double colonnade. **dipteran,** *n.* such fly. **dipterology,** *n.* study of two-winged insects.

diptote ['dɪptəut] *n. Grammar,* noun with two cases only.

diptych ['dɪptɪk] *n.* paintings on a pair of hinged tablets used as altar-piece; pair of hinged wax writing tablets.

directoire [ˌdɪrek'twɑː] *adj.* signifying style of low-necked, high-waisted dress, and curving Oriental furniture, of the Directory period (1795–99)

in France.

dirigent ['dɪrɪdʒənt] *adj.* guiding.

dirigible ['dɪrɪdʒəbl] *adj.* capable of being steered; *n.* airship.

dirigisme ['dɪrɪʒɪzm] *(French) n.* state control of economic and social affairs. **dirigiste** [ˌdɪrɪ'ʒiːst], *adj. & n.*

diriment ['dɪrɪmənt] *adj. Law,* nullifying, especially as regards impediments to marriage.

disaffect [ˌdɪsə'fekt] *v.t.* alienate. **disaffected,** *adj.* discontented; rebellious.

disagio [dɪs'ædʒɪəu] *n.* charge made for exchanging depreciated or foreign money.

disburse [dɪs'bɜːs] *v.t.* pay out. **disbursement,** *n.*

discalced [dɪs'kælst] *adj.* bare-foot. **discalceate,** *n. & adj.* bare-foot (friar or nun).

discarnate [dɪs'kɑːnət] *adj.* having no body; [–eɪt], *v.t.* deprive of bodily existence.

discept [dɪ'sept] *v.i.* discuss; dispute. **disceptation, disceptator,** *n.*

discerp [dɪ'sɜːp] *v.t.* tear off, or to pieces. **discerptible,** *adj.* **discerption,** *n.*

discinct [dɪ'sɪŋkt] *adj.* partly or loosely clad; having belt removed.

discission [dɪ'sɪʃn] *n.* incision; open cut.

discobolus, discobolos [dɪ'skɒbələs] *n.* discus-thrower; famous ancient statue of discus-thrower.

discography [dɪ'skɒgrəfi] *n.* descriptive catalogue of gramophone records; list of recordings by one composer or performer.

discomfit [dɪs'kʌmfɪt] *v.t.* confuse, embarrass; thwart; defeat in battle.

discreet [dɪ'skriːt] *adj.* careful to avoid causing embarrassment or scandal; tactful; unobtrusive.

discrete [dɪ'skriːt] *adj.* separate; composed of separable parts; *v.t.* separate.

discretion [dɪ'skreʃn] *n.* discreet behaviour; prudence; freedom to act and make decisions.

disculpate ['dɪskʌlpeɪt] *v.t.* exculpate. **disculpation,** *n.* **disculpatory,** *adj.*

disembogue [ˌdɪsɪm'bəug, –em–] *v.i. & t.* debouch; discharge into sea, etc.; eject.

diseuse [diː'zɜːz] *(French) n. (masc.* **diseur** [–'zɜː]) reciter.

disgeneric [ˌdɪsdʒə'nerɪk] *adj.* of different kind or genus.

dishabille, deshabille [ˌdɪsə'biːl] *n.* déshabillé; negligée.

disinterested [dɪs'ɪntrəstɪd, –tərestɪd] *adj.* impartial; objective. (*as opposed to* **uninterested**).

disjecta membra [dɪsˌdʒektə 'membrə] *(Latin)* 'scattered fragments'; scattered or disjointed quotations.

disjection [dɪs'dʒekʃn] *n.* dispersion; scattering.

disjunction [dɪs'dʒʌŋkʃn] *n.* act of separating; state of being separated. **disjunctive,** *adj.* expressing or requiring alternation, separation or contrast; *n. Grammar,* such conjunction.

disomus [daɪ'səuməs] *n. (pl.* **–mi)** monster with two bodies. **disomatous** [–'sɒmətəs, –'səu–], *adj.* having two bodies.

disparate ['dɪspərət] *adj.* fundamentally different; unequal. **disparity** [–'pærəti], *n.*

dispendious [dɪ'spendɪəs] *adj.* extravagant; costly.

dispermous [daɪ'spɜːməs] *adj.* having two seeds. **dispermy** ['daɪspɜːmi], *n.* union of two sperm cells and one ovum.

disseminate [dɪ'semɪneɪt] *v.t.* spread; scatter;

broadcast; diffuse. **dissemination,** *n.* **disseminative,** *adj.*

dissepiment [dɪ'sepɪmənt] *n.* partition, especially of tissue. **dissepimental,** *adj.*

dissilient [dɪ'sɪliənt] *adj.* bursting open or apart.

dissimulate [dɪ'sɪmjuleɪt] *v.i.* & *t.* feign; pretend. **dissimulation,** *n.* **dissimulative,** *adj.*

dissociate [dɪ'səʊsieɪt, –ʃi–] *v.t.* separate into constituent parts; split up. **dissociation,** *n. Chemistry,* separation of a compound into components; *Psychology,* splitting of personality.

dissonant ['dɪsənənt] *adj.* discordant; harsh. **dissonance,** *n.*

distal ['dɪstl] *adj.* away from point of attachment or axis.

distich ['dɪstɪk] *n.* verse couplet. **distichous,** *adj.* arranged in two rows.

distrain [dɪ'streɪn] *v.i.* seize goods in default of payment. **distraint,** *n.*

distrait ['dɪstreɪ] *(French) adj.* inattentive; abstracted.

distributary [dɪ'strɪbjʊtəri] *n.* river branch flowing away from main stream.

disyllable [daɪ'sɪləbl, dɪ–] *n.* word or verse foot of two syllables. **disyllabic** [–'læbɪk], *adj.*

dit [diː] *(French) adj.* 'said'; commonly known as; reputed to be.

dithecal [daɪ'θiːkl] *adj.* having two cells. **dithecous,** *adj.*

ditheism ['daɪθiːɪzm] *n.* belief in two equal gods, especially one good and one evil. **ditheist,** *n.* **ditheistic(al),** *adj.*

dithyramb ['dɪθɪræm] *n.* Dionysiac song; ecstatic poem or harangue. **dithyrambic** [–'ræmbɪk], *adj.* wild and impassioned.

ditokous ['dɪtəkəs] *adj.* producing two offspring at a birth, or offspring of two kinds.

ditrichotomous [ˌdaɪtraɪ'kɒtəməs] *adj.* divided into two or three parts.

dittograph ['dɪtəgrɑːf] *n.* letter or word repeated unintentionally in writing or copying. **dittology** [dɪ'tɒlədʒi], *n.* two different interpretations of same text.

diuretic [ˌdaɪjʊ'retɪk] *n.* & *adj.* (drug) increasing urination. **diuresis,** *n.* copious urination.

diurnal [daɪ'ɜːnl] *adj.* daily; of a day or daylight; lasting one day; *Botany,* applied to flowers opening by day only. **diurnation,** *n.* sleeping or torpidity during daylight.

diuturnal [ˌdaɪju'tɜːnl] *adj.* lasting long time. **diuturnity,** *n.*

diva ['diːvə] *n.* prima donna.

divagate ['daɪvəgeɪt] *v.i.* wander; digress. **divagation,** *n.*

divaricate [daɪ'værɪkeɪt] *v.i.* bifurcate; *adj.* widespreading. **divarication,** *n.* bifurcation; straddling; disagreement; ambiguity.

diverticulum [ˌdaɪvə'tɪkjʊləm] *n.* blind passage or branch; caecum. **diverticular,** *adj.* **diverticulate,** *adj.* having such.

divertissement [ˌdiːveə'tiːsmɒn] *(French) n.* amusing diversion; light entertainment, play, music, etc.

divulse [daɪ'vʌls] *v.t.* rend apart. **divulsion,** *n.* **divulsive,** *adj.*

dixi ['dɪksiː] *(Latin)* 'I have spoken'; let that suffice or settle the matter. **dixit,** 'he has spoken'; person's statement, especially without corroboration.

DNA *abbreviation* of deoxyribonucleic acid (a nucleic acid present in every living cell, containing the genetic information that directs the sequence in which amino acids are arranged to form a protein).

docent ['dəʊsnt] *adj.* teaching; didactic; *n. American,* lecturer

docimasy ['dɒsɪməsi] *n.* experimental testing or inquiry. **docimology,** *n.* treatise on this, especially on assaying metals. **docimastic** [–'mæstɪk], *adj.*

doctrinaire [ˌdɒktrɪ'neə] *adj.* dogmatic; disregarding practical facts or difficulties in one's devotion to a theory or doctrine; *n.* such person. **doctrinairism,** *n.*

dodecafid [dəʊ'dekəfɪd] *adj.* divided into 12 parts.

dodecagon [dəʊ'dekəgən] *n.* 12-sided plane figure. **dodecagonal** [–'kægənl], *adj.*

dodecahedron [ˌdəʊdekə'hiːdrən] *n.* 12-sided solid figure. **dodecahedral, dodecahedric,** *adj.*

dodecarch ['dəʊdekɑːk] *n.* member of dodecarchy. **dodecarchy,** *n.* government by 12 persons.

dodecasyllable [ˌdəʊdekə'sɪləbl] *n.* word or verse line of twelve syllables. **dodecasyllabic** [–'læbɪk], *adj.*

doge [dəʊdʒ] *n.* former leading magistrate of Venice or Genoa. **dogaressa** [ˌdəʊgə'resə], *n.* doge's wife. **dogate** ['dəʊgeɪt], *n.* office of doge.

dokhma ['dɒkmə] *n.* structure on which Parsee dead are exposed; 'tower of silence'.

dol [dəʊl] *n.* basic and smallest unit for measuring the intensity of pain, equal to the faint sensation felt when heat rays are first applied to the skin.

dolabrate, dolabriform [dəʊ'leɪbreɪt, dəʊ'læbrɪfɔːm] *adj.* shaped like axe-head.

dolce far niente [ˌdɒltʃeɪ ˌfɑː ni'enteɪ] *(Italian)* 'sweet to do nothing'; pleasant idling.

doldrums ['dɒldrəmz] *n. pl.* area of calm and light winds about equator; mood of depression or boredom.

dolent ['dəʊlənt] *adj.* mournful.

dolichocephalic, dolichocephalous [ˌdɒlɪkəʊke'fælɪk, –sɪ–; –'kefələs, –'se–] *adj.* long-headed; having skull of which maximum breadth is less than 80 per cent of maximum length. **dolichocephalus** *n.* (*pl.* –li) such person. **dolichocephaly,** *n.*

dolichocercic [ˌdɒlɪkəʊ'sɜːsɪk] *adj.* having long forearms.

dolichocnemic [ˌdɒlɪkɒk'niːmɪk] *adj.* having long legs.

dolichofacial [ˌdɒlɪkəʊ'feɪʃl] *adj.* having long face.

dolichopodous [ˌdɒlɪ'kɒpədəs] *adj.* having long feet.

dolichoprosopic [ˌdɒlɪkəʊprə'səʊpɪk] *adj.* having very long and narrow face.

dolioform ['dəʊliəfɔːm] *adj.* shaped like a barrel.

dolman ['dɒlmən] *n.* long Turkish outer robe; short hussar's jacket worn over shoulder. **dolman sleeve,** large-armholed sleeve.

dolmen ['dɒlmen] *n.* cromlech. **dolmenic,** *adj.*

dolomite ['dɒləmaɪt] *n.* magnesian limestone containing white marble. **dolomitic** [–'mɪtɪk], *adj.*

dolorific [ˌdɒlə'rɪfɪk] *adj.* causing sorrow or pain.

dolorimetry [ˌdɒlə'rɪmətri] *n.* measurement of pain.

dolose, dolous ['dəʊləʊs, –əs] *adj. Law*, of evil intent.

dolus malus [,dəʊləs 'mæləs, –'meɪ–] (*Latin*) 'bad deceit'; fraud; evil intent. **dolus bonus,** 'good or permissible deceit'.

dominical [də'mɪnɪkl] *adj.* pertaining to Christ or Sunday. **dominical letter,** letter denoting Sunday and used in calculating Easter date.

dominie ['dɒmɪnɪ] (*Scottish*) *n.* school master; *archaic* ['dəʊ–] parson.

donga ['dɒŋgə] (*S African*) *n.* gully.

donjon ['dɒndʒən] *n.* castle keep.

dop [dɒp] (*S African*) *n.* kind of coarse brandy; cup for holding diamond during cutting.

doppelgänger ['dɒpl,gæŋə] *n.* ghostly double.

Doric ['dɒrɪk] *adj.* pertaining to Dorian race of ancient Greece; rustic; broad in speech; *n.* such dialect, especially N English or Scots. **dorism, doricism,** *n.* Doric idiom or custom.

dormer ['dɔːmə] *n.* window projecting vertically from roof with gable-like covering.

dormition [dɔː'mɪʃn] *n.* act of falling asleep; death. **dormitive** ['dɔː–], *n. & adj.* soporific.

dormy, dormie ['dɔːmɪ] *adj.* winning in golf by as many holes as remain to play.

dorsal ['dɔːsl] *adj.* pertaining to, on or at the back; *n.* dossal. **dorsad,** *adv.* towards the back.

dorsiventral, dorsoventral [,dɔːsɪ'ventrəl, –səʊ–] *adj.* having differentiated front and back, or upper and lower, surfaces. **dorsiventrality,** *n.*

doryphorus, doryphoros [də'rɪfərəs] *n.* sculptured figure of spear-bearer.

dos-à-dos [,dəʊsɪ'dəʊ, –ɑː–] (*French*) *adj.* back to back; *n.* such seat, etc.

dosimetry [dəʊ'sɪmətrɪ] *n.* measurement of doses; medical system in which very few drugs in strictly regulated doses are prescribed.

dossal ['dɒsl] *n.* ornamental hanging at the back of an altar or the sides of the chancel.

dosser ['dɒsə] *n.* covering for the back of a throne; bag or basket carried on the back; a person who sleeps in dosshouses.

dot [dɒt, dəʊt] (*French*) *n.* dowry. **dotal,** *adj.* **dotation,** *n.* endowment.

dotterel, dottrel ['dɒtrəl] *n.* several kinds of plover, including ringed plover.

dottle, dottel ['dɒtl] *n.* plug of tobacco left in a pipe after smoking.

douane [du'ɑːn] (*French*) *n.* customs house. **douanier** [–'ɑːnjeɪ], *n.* customs official.

doublette [du'blet] (*French*) *n.* artist's copy of own work.

douceur [duː'sɜː] (*French*) *n.* 'sweetness, sweetener'; bribe; gratuity; gentleness of manner.

doulocracy, dulocracy [du'lɒkrəsɪ] *n.* government by slaves.

do ut des [,dəʊ ʊt 'deɪz] (*Latin*) 'I give that you may give'; reciprocal agreement or concession.

dowager ['daʊədʒə] *n.* woman with title, etc., deriving from deceased husband.

dowel ['daʊəl] *n.* connecting pin, generally of wood.

doxastic [dɒk'sæstɪk] *adj.* pertaining to opinion.

doxography [dɒk'sɒgrəfɪ] *n.* ancient Greek collection of philosophical extracts. **doxographer,** *n.* **doxographical,** *adj.*

doxology [dɒk'sɒlədʒɪ] *n.* formula of praise to God, especially stanza beginning 'Glory be to the Father'. **doxological,** *adj.* **doxologize,** *v.i. & t.* give praise to God.

doyen ['dɔɪən] *n.* (*fem.* **doyenne** [dɔɪ'en]) senior member.

drachma ['drækmə] *n.* (*pl.* **–ae**) ancient Greek coin and weight; modern Greek coin.

dracone [dræ'kəʊn] *n.* towed flexible container for transporting liquids by water.

Draconian, Draconic [drə'kəʊnɪən, drə'kɒnɪk] *adj.* pertaining to Draco, Athenian law-giver (7th century BC) and his severe and cruel laws; harsh, oppressive.

draconic [drə'kɒnɪk] *adj.* like or pertaining to a dragon.

draconites, dracontites [,drækə'naɪtiːz, ,drækən'taɪtiːz] *n.* serpent-stone, a jewel supposed to be found in dragon's head.

dracontian, dracontine [drə'kɒnʃən, drə'kɒntaɪn] *adj.* draconic.

dragoman ['drægəmæn] *n.* (*pl.* **–mans** or **–men**) guide and interpreter. **dragomanic,** *adj.*

dragonnade [,drægə'neɪd] *n.* cruel persecution; violent invasion or punitive expedition.

dramamine ['dræməmiːn] *n.* chemical drug used against sea-sickness.

dramatis personae [,dræmətɪs pɜː'səʊnaɪ, –iː] (*Latin*) 'characters of the drama'.

dramaturgy ['dræmətɜːdʒɪ] *n.* composition and production of dramas. **dramaturgic,** *adj.* **dramaturge, dramaturgist,** *n.*

dree [driː] (*Scottish*) *v.i. & t.* endure. **dree one's weird,** endure one's fate; 'grin and bear it'.

drepaniform ['drepənɪfɔːm] *adj.* like a sickle in shape. **drepanoid,** *adj.* like a sickle.

dripstone ['drɪpstəʊn] *n.* stalactite or stalagmite; *Architecture*, stone projection for throwing off rain water.

droit [drɔɪt, drwɑː] (*French*) *n.* 'right'; law; justice. **droit du seigneur** [–duː seɪn'jɜː], feudal lord's right to enjoy female vassal on her wedding night. **droitural** ['drɔɪtjʊrəl], *adj.* pertaining to right to property.

dromic(al) ['drɒmɪk, –l] *adj.* pertaining to footrace course; *Architecture*, with long, narrow plan.

dromond ['drɒmənd, 'drʌ–] *n.* large medieval sailing ship.

dromos ['drɒmɒs] *n.* avenue or entrance-way to a building; passage to a tomb; ancient Greek race course.

droshki ['drɒʃkɪ] *n.* light one-horse four-wheeler Russian carriage, especially one in which passengers ride astride a saddle-like seat.

drosometer [drə'sɒmɪtə] *n.* instrument measuring amount of dew. **drosograph** ['drɒs–], *n.* such recording instrument.

drosophila [drə'sɒfɪlə] *n.* (*pl* **–las** or **–lae** the fruitfly, used in genetic experiments because of its quick breeding.

drugget ['drʌgɪt] *n.* coarse cloth used especially as floor-covering.

drumlin ['drʌmlɪn] *n.* long glacially-formed hill.

drupe [druːp] *n. Botany*, single-seeded stoned fruit with fleshy or dry covering, as cherry or almond. **drupelet, drupeole,** *n.* small drupe. **drupaceous,** *adj.* pertaining to, like, or bearing drupes.

dryad ['draɪæd] *n.* wood nymph. **dryadic,** *adj.*

dry-bob ['draɪbɒb] *n.* Etonian who plays cricket

or football.

drysalter ['draɪ,sɔːltə] *n.* dealer in dried goods, foods, chemicals, etc. **drysaltery,** *n.*

dualism ['djuːəlɪzm] *n. Philosophy,* theory that ultimate reality comprises two elements, *e.g.* mind and matter; *Theology,* belief in two equal and opposite principles, as good and evil, or in dual constitution of man, as composed of spirit and matter. **dualistic,** *adj.*

duarchy, *see* **diarchy.**

dubiety [djuˈbaɪəti] *n.* doubt; doubtful matter. **dubious** ['djuːbiəs], *adj.* doubtful; suspicious; questionable. **dubiosity,** *n.* **dubitation,** *n.* doubting; hesitation. **dubitative,** *adj.* signifying doubt.

ducat ['dʌkət] *n.* former gold and silver coin of several countries.

ductile ['dʌktaɪl] *adj.* easily hammered or drawn out into long thin strip; easily led. **ductility** [-'tɪl-], *n.*

ductless ['dʌktləs] *adj. Medicine,* endocrine.

dud(h)een [du'diːn] *(Irish) n.* clay pipe.

Duecento [,duːiˈtʃentəu] *(Italian) n.* the thirteenth century.

duenna [djuˈenə] *n.* chaperone; governess.

duffel ['dʌfl] *n.* coarse heavy-nap woollen cloth.

dug [dʌg] *n.* udder; teat; breast.

dugong ['duːgɒŋ] *n.* small seal-like aquatic mammal.

duiker ['daɪkə] *(S African) n.* cormorant; **duikerbok. duikerbok,** *n.* small African antelope.

dulce domum [,dulkeɪ 'dɒməm, ,dʌlsi 'dəu–] *(Latin)* 'sweet home'.

dulcify ['dʌlsɪfaɪ] *v.t.* sweeten; mollify. **dulcification,** *n.* **dulcigenic,** *adj.* yielding sweetness.

dulcimer ['dʌlsɪmə] *n. Music,* percussion instrument consisting of graduated strings stretched over a sounding board and struck with hammers.

dulia ['djuːliə] *n. Roman Catholic,* veneration accorded to saints.

dulosis [djuˈləusɪs] *n.* enslavement, especially of certain ant species. **dulotic** [-'lɒtɪk], *adj.*

dulse [dʌls] *n.* kind of red Scottish and Irish seaweed used as food.

duma ['duːmə] *n.* parliament of Tsarist Russia.

dumdum ['dʌmdʌm] *adj.* applied to bullet with soft nose, expanding on contact, first made at Dumdum, India.

dumose, dumous ['djuːməus, –əs] *adj.* bushy. **dumosity,** *n.*

dunlin ['dʌnlɪn] *n.* species of sandpiper.

dunnage ['dʌnɪdʒ] *n.* packing material for protecting cargo.

duodecillion [,djuːəudɪ'sɪljən] *n.* a million undecillions (10^{72}); *(American & French)* a thousand undecillions (10^{39}).

duodecimal [,djuːə'desɪml] *adj.* pertaining to twelve or twelfths; in groups of twelve. **duodecimal system,** arithmetical system similar to decimal but based on scale of twelve and twelfths. **duodecimo,** *n.* size of books, about 5¼ in. by 8 ⅛ in. *(abbr.* **12mo.).**

duodenum [,djuːə'diːnəm] *n.* part of small intestine leading from stomach. **duodenal,** *adj.* **duodenitis,** *n.* inflammation of duodenum.

duologue ['djuːəlɒg] *n.* (dramatic) dialogue between two people.

duomo ['dwəuməu] *(Italian) n.* cathedral.

duopoly [djuˈɒpəli] *n. Commerce,* market situation where there are only two producers or sellers. **duopsony,** *n.* situation with only two buyers.

Duralumin [djuˈræljumɪn] *n. trademark,* a very strong aluminium alloy.

dura mater [,djuərə 'meɪtə] *n.* outer membrane enclosing brain.

duramen [djuˈreɪmən] *n.* heartwood of tree.

durance ['djuərəns] *n.* imprisonment.

durbar ['dɜːbɑː] *n.* official reception given by native Indian ruler or Anglo-Indian official.

duress [dju'res] *n.* imprisonment; restraint; compulsion by threats.

durgah ['dɜːgə] *(Hindi) n.* Muslim saint's shrine or tomb.

durian, durion ['djuəriən, 'duə–] *n.* SE Asian fruit with prickly rind and pleasant edible pulp.

durity ['djuərəti] *n.* hardness. **durometer,** *n.* instrument measuring hardness.

durra ['durə] *(Arabic) n.* a kind of sorghum; Indian millet.

duumvir [djuˈʌmvə] *n.* (*pl.* **–i, duoviri**) member of duumvirate. **duumviral,** *adj.* **duumvirate,** *n.* governing body of two men.

dwaal [dwɑːl] *(S African) n.* state of befuddlement.

dwale [dweɪl] *n.* deadly nightshade.

dyad ['daɪæd] *n.* set of two; bivalent atom, etc.; *adj.* consisting of two; bivalent. **dyadic** [daɪ'ædɪk], *adj.*

dyarchy ['daɪɑːki] *n.* dual form of government. **dyarchic(al),** *adj.*

dygogram ['daɪgəgræm] *n.* graph showing amount, at all positions, of deflection of compass due to iron of ship.

dynameter [daɪ'næmɪtə] *n.* instrument measuring telescope's magnifying power.

dynamometer [,daɪnə'mɒmɪtə] *n.* instrument measuring power. **dynamometry,** *n.*

dynatron ['daɪnətrɒn] *n.* multi-electrode thermionic valve often used as an oscillator.

dyne [daɪn] *n.* unit of force: force causing mass of one gram to undergo acceleration of one centimetre per second.

dysaesthesia [,dɪses'θiːziə, –ʒə] *n.* loss of sense of touch. **dysaesthetic** [-'θetɪk], *adj.*

dysarthrosis [,dɪsɑː'θrəusɪs] *n.* diseased or abnormal condition of joint.

dyschroa, dyschroia [dɪs'krəuə, –'krɔɪə] *n.* skin discoloration.

dyschromatoptic [,dɪskrəumə'tɒptɪk] *adj.* colour-blind. **dyschromatopsia,** *n.*

dyschronous ['dɪskrənəs] *adj.* not synchronous.

dyscrasia [dɪs'kreɪziə, –ʒə] *n. Medicine,* constitutional weakness. **dyscrasic,** *adj.*

dysergia [dɪs'ɜːdʒiə] *n.* deficient muscular coordination.

dyskinesia [,dɪskɪ'niːziə, –kaɪ–, –ʒə] *n.* loss of power of voluntary movement. **dyskinetic** [-'netɪk], *adj.*

dyslexia [dɪs'leksiə] *n.* word-blindness; inability to associate letter symbols with sounds.

dyslogia [dɪs'ləudʒiə] *n.* inability to express ideas in speech due to mental deficiency.

dyslogy ['dɪslədʒi] *n.* unfavourable speech; censure. **dyslogistic,** *adj.*

dysmenorrhea [,dɪsmenə'riːə] *n.* painful menstruation. **dysmenorrheal,** *adj.*

dyspepsia [dɪs'pepsiə] *n.* severe indigestion, especially chronic. **dyspeptic,** *adj.*; *n.* person suffering from this.

dysphagic [dɪs'fædʒɪk, –'feɪ–] *adj.* having difficulty in swallowing. **dysphagia** [–'feɪdʒiə], *n.*

dysphasia [dɪs'feɪziə, –ʒə] *n.* impairment of speech co-ordination, due to brain disease or injury. **dysphasic,** *adj.*

dysphemia [dɪs'fiːmiə] *n.* stammering. **dysphemism,** *n.* substitution of a derogatory or offensive word for an ordinary one; word so substituted.

dysphonia [dɪs'fəʊniə] *n.* inability to pronounce sounds, due to physical abnormality or disease. **dysphonic** [–'fɒnɪk], *adj.*

dysphoria [dɪs'fɔːriə] *n.* generalized feeling of being ill or depressed. **dysphoric** [–'fɒrɪk], *adj.*

dyspnoea [dɪsp'niːə] *n.* difficult breathing.

dysteleology [ˌdɪsteli'ɒlədʒi] *n.* denial of a final cause or purpose of life.

dysthymia [dɪs'θaɪmiə] *n.* despondency. **dysthymic,** *adj.*

dystocia [dɪs'təʊsiə, –ʃə] *n.* difficult childbirth. **dystocial,** *adj.*

dystopia [dɪs'təʊpiə] *n.* opposite of utopia, imaginary place where everything is as bad as can be.

dystrophy, dystrophia ['dɪstrəfi, dɪs'trəʊfiə] *n.* malnutrition. **muscular dystrophy,** faulty nutrition of muscles, leading to paralysis. **dystrophic** [–ofɪk], *adj.*

E

eagre, eager ['eɪgə, 'iː–] *n.* tidal bore.
easement ['iːzmənt] *n. Law*, right over another's land.
eau-de-nil [ˌəʊdə'niːl] (*French*) 'water of Nile'; a light shade of green.
eau-de-vie [ˌəʊdə'viː] (*French*) *n.* brandy.
eau forte [ˌəʊ 'fɔːt] (*French*) *n.* aqua fortis; etching.
ebeneous [ɪ'biːniəs] *adj.* pertaining to or like ebony. **ébéniste**, *n.* cabinet-maker who veneers furniture; ebonist. **ebonist**, *n.* worker in ebony.
ebriose ['iːbriəʊs] *adj.* drunk. **ebriosity**, *n.*
ebullient [ɪ'bʌliənt, –'bʊ–] *adj.* boiling; effervescent; exhilarated. **ebullioscope**, *n.* instrument for determining boiling point. **ebullition, ebullience, ebulliency**, *n.* **ebullitive**, *adj.*
eburnean, eburneous [ɪ'bɜːniən, –əs] *adj.* like, pertaining to or made of ivory. **eburnated**, *adj.* like ivory. **eburnation**, *n.* disease in which cartilage or bone becomes very hard and dense like ivory.
ecbatic [ek'bætɪk] *adj. Grammar*, signifying result without intention.
ecbolic [ek'bɒlɪk] *n. & adj.* (drug) helping childbirth or causing abortion.
ecce homo [ˌeki 'həʊməʊ] (*Latin*) 'behold the man!'
ecchymosis [ˌekɪ'məʊsɪs] *n.* discoloured spot due to effusion of blood into tissue. **ecchymosed**, *adj.*
ecclesiarch [ɪ'kliːziɑːk] *n.* church ruler. **ecclesiarchy**, *n.* government by clerics.
ecclesiastry [ɪ'kliːziəstri] *n.* church affairs.
ecclesiolatry [ɪˌkliːzi'ɒlətri] *n.* worship of or undue devotion to church. **ecclesiolater**, *n.* such worshipper.
ecclesiology [ɪˌkliːzi'ɒlədʒi] *n.* study of ecclesiastical art, decoration, etc. **ecclesiological**, *adj.* **ecclesiologist**, *n.*
eccoprotic [ˌekə'prɒtɪk] *n. & adj.* purgative. **eccoprophoric**, *adj.* like a purgative in action.
eccrinology [ˌekrɪ'nɒlədʒi] *n.* study of excretion and secretion. **eccritic**, *n. & adj.* purgative.
ecdemic [ek'demɪk] *adj.* originating elsewhere; not endemic.
ecdysis ['ekdɪsɪs] *n.* moulting of outer skin, etc.
échelon ['eʃəlɒn] (*French*) *n.* step-like arrangement of troops with divisions parallel but offset diagonally to rear; a section of a military command or other organization.
echidna [ɪ'kɪdnə] *n.* spined, burrowing, egg-laying, ant-eating mammal of Australasia; spiny ant-eater.
echinal, echinoid [ɜk'ɪnəl, –ɔɪd] *adj.* pertaining to or like a sea urchin. **echinate(d)**, *adj.* prickly. **echinid(an)**, *n.* sea urchin.

echinoderm [ɪ'kaɪnədɜːm, 'ekɪ–] *n.* spiny-skinned marine animal, as sea urchin, starfish, etc. **echinology**, *n.* study of these.
echinulate [ɪ'kɪnjuleɪt, –'kaɪ–] *adj.* having small spines. **echinuliform**, *adj.* like small spines.
echinus [ɪ'kaɪnəs] *n.* (*pl.* **–ni**) hedgehog; sea urchin; *Architecture*, egg-and-dart ornament.
echolalia [ˌekəʊ'leɪliə] *n.* habitual repetition, like an echo, of others' remarks. **echolalic** [–'lælɪk], *adj.*
echometer [e'kɒmɪtə] *n.* device measuring the duration of sounds.
echopraxia [ˌekəʊ'præksiə] *n.* habitual repetition of others' actions.
éclaircissement [e'kleəsiːsmɒn] (*French*) *n.* full explanation; enlightenment.
eclampsia [ɪ'klæmpsiə] *n.* condition marked by high blood-pressure, excessive weight-gain and convulsions occurring in later stages of pregnancy.
éclat [eɪ'klɑː] (*French*) *n.* brilliancy; brilliant achievement; acclaimed success; exposure, especially scandalous.
eclectic [ɪ'klektɪk] *adj.* selecting, especially the best from a number of sources; comprising selected pieces. **eclecticism** [–sɪzm], *n.* compounding body of philosophical or religious doctrine from selected beliefs of other systems.
eclipsis [ɪ'klɪpsɪs] *n.* ellipsis, one of the consonantal mutations of Irish and Scottish Gaelic.
ecliptic [ɪ'klɪptɪk] *n. Astronomy*, celestial great circle along which sun apparently travels. **ecliptical**, *adj.*
eclogue ['eklɒg] *n.* pastoral poem.
ecophobia [ˌiːkə'fəʊbiə, ˌe–] *n.* dislike of home.
écru ['eɪkruː, 'ek–] *adj.* of a natural, unbleached shade.
ectasis ['ektəsɪs] *n.* dilatation. **ectatic** [ek'tætɪk], *adj.*
ecthlipsis [ek'θlɪpsɪs] *n.* (*pl.* **–ses**) in Latin, omission of final m.
ecthyma ['ekθɪmə, ek'θaɪmə] *n.* skin eruption bearing several pustules.
ectobatic [ˌektə'bætɪk] *adj.* efferent.
ectocranial [ˌektə'kreɪniəl] *adj.* pertaining to exterior of skull.
ectoderm ['ektədɜːm] *n.* outermost membrane and tissue. **ectodermal, ectodermic**, *adj.* **ectodermosis**, *n.* disease of the ectoderm.
ectogenesis [ˌektə'dʒenəsɪs] *n.* development outside body. **ectogenic** [–'tɒdʒ–], **ectogenous** [–'tɒdʒ–], *adj.*
ectomorph ['ektəmɔːf] *n.* psychophysical type with long thin bones and large surface relative to weight, often inhibited and shy. **ectomorphic**, *adj.* **ectomorphy**, *n.*

ectoparasite [,ektəʊ'pærəsaɪt] n. parasite on surface of animals. **ectophyte**, n. such plant parasite.

ectopia [ek'təʊpiə] n. Medicine, displacement of organs, etc. **ectopic** [–'tɒpɪk], adj. (of pregnancy) involving development of the foetus outside the uterus.

ectoplasm ['ektəplæzm] n. protoplasmic emanation from spiritualist medium; Biology, outer layer of protoplasm. **ectoplasmic**, adj. **ectoplasy** [–pleɪzi], n. formation of such emanation.

ectorhinal [,ektə'raɪnl] adj. pertaining to exterior of nose.

ectozoon [,ektə'zəʊɒn] n. (pl. **–zoa**) external parasite. **ectozoan, ectozoic**, adj.

ectype ['ektaɪp] n. copy; non-eternal being or idea. **ectypography**, n. etching in relief.

ecumenical [,i:kju'menɪkl, ,ek–] adj. worldwide; pertaining to whole church. **ecumenicalism**, n. promotion of Christian unity. **ecumenicity**, n.

edacious [ɪ'deɪʃəs] adj. jocular, pertaining to eating; gluttonous. **edacity** [–'dæs–], n.

edaphic [ɪ'dæfɪk] adj. pertaining to or conditioned by soil; indigenous. **edaphology**, n. study of soils. **edaphon** ['ed–], n. living organisms in soil.

edelweiss ['eɪdlvaɪs] n. small Alpine flower of Switzerland and New Zealand.

edema [iː'diːmə] n. swelling due to accumulation of watery fluid in a body cavity or in the spaces within connective tissue.

edentate [iː'denteɪt] adj. belonging to the order including anteaters, armadillos, and sloths, lacking incisor and canine teeth.

educe [ɪ'djuːs] v.t. bring out, develop; elicit. **educible**, adj. **educt**, n. substance separated out unchanged from another decomposing substance. **eduction**, n. act of educing; exhaust stroke of steam or internal-combustion engine. **eductive**, adj.

edulcorate [ɪ'dʌlkəreɪt] v.t. archaic, sweeten; purify, especially of acids; [–ət], adj. sweetened. **edulcoration, edulcorator**, n. **edulcorative**, adj.

effable ['efəbl] adj. able to be expressed in words.

effect [ɪ'fekt] n. result; ability to produce a result; impression produced on a spectator, auditor etc.; v.t. bring about; carry out, accomplish. (as opposed to affect). **effects**, n.pl. property; luggage; lighting, sound etc. accompanying a play or film.

effendi [e'fendi] (Turkish) n. title of respect; sir.

efferent ['efərənt] adj. carrying away; conveying outwards; n. such nerve, blood-vessel, etc.

effete [ɪ'fiːt] adj. degenerated; sterile; worn-out.

effleurage ['efləraːʒ] n. gentle stroking used in massage.

effloresce [,eflə'res] v.i. flower; burgeon; Chemistry, become powder when exposed to air; develop a powdery crust. **efflorescence**, n. **efflorescent**, adj.

effluent ['efluənt] adj. flowing out or away; n. such stream, drain, sewage, etc.; (liquid) waste. **effluence**, n. outflow; emanation. **effluvium**, n. (pl. **-via**) disgusting smell. **efflux, effluxion**, n.

effodient [e'fəʊdiənt] adj. burrowing.

effulgent [ɪ'fʌldʒənt] adj. radiant; bright. **effulgence**, n.

egest [ɪ'dʒest] v.t. excrete. **egesta**, n.pl. excrements. **egestion**, n. **egestive**, adj.

ego ['iːgəʊ, 'e–] n. I; self; personality. **egocentric**, adj. selfish; seeing only one's own or humankind's or individual's viewpoint. **egoism**, n. selfishness; conceit; egocentric philosophical or psychological theory. **egoist**, n. **egoistic**, adj.

egomania, n. excessive egoism. **egotism**, n. continuous speaking of oneself; self-praise; conceit. **egotist**, n. **egotistic**, adj.

egregious [ɪ'griːdʒəs] adj. outstanding; infamous.

egret ['iːgrət] n. white heron.

eidetic [aɪ'detɪk] adj. (of visual etc. images) exceptionally vivid; n. person having very vivid mental pictures.

eidolon [aɪ'dəʊlən] n. phantom. **eidolic** [–'dɒlɪk], adj. **eidolism**, n. belief in ghosts. **eidolology**, n. study of mental imagery.

eirenic, irenic [aɪ'renɪk, –'riː–] adj. promoting peace. **eirenicism** [–sɪzm], n. such state of mind. **eirenicon**, n. such act. **eirenics**, n. theology aiming at religious unity.

eisegesis [,aɪsɪ'dʒiːsɪs] n. incorrect explanation of text, especially of Bible, by distorting the meaning to fit preconceived ideas. **eisegetical**, adj.

eiusdem generis, ejusdem generis [eɪ,ʊsdem 'genərɪs, iː,ʌs–, 'dʒe–] 'of the same kind'.

ejecta(menta) [ɪ'dʒektə, ɪ,dʒektə'mentə] n. pl. ejected material, especially from volcano.

ekistics [ɪ'kɪstɪks] n. scientific study of human settlements.

elaeometer [,eli'ɒmɪtə] n. device measuring the specific gravity of oils.

élan [eɪ'lɒn] (French) n. eagerness; brilliancy of style; vivacity. **élan vital** creative or 'life' force, especially in Bergson's philosophy.

elastomeric [ɪ,læstə'merɪk] adj. denoting artificial fibres with rubber-like elasticity.

elaterid [ɪ'lætərɪd] n. click beetle. **elateroid**, adj.

elaterium [,elə'tɪəriəm] n. aperient extracted from a species of cucumber.

elaterometer [ɪ,lætə'rɒmɪtə] n. instrument measuring pressure of gas.

elchi, elchee ['eltʃi] (Turkish) n. ambassador.

eldritch, eldrich ['eldrɪtʃ] adj. weird; horrifying.

elecampane [,elɪkæm'peɪn] n. large yellow-flowered plant, with root from which sweet-meat is made.

electret [ɪ'lektrət] n. a non-conductor having permanent positive and negative poles, the electrostatic equivalent of a permanent magnet.

electrocardiogram [ɪ,lektrəʊ'kɑːdiəgræm] n. record of electric currents inducing heart-beat, used in diagnosis of heart disorder (abbr. E.C.G.). **electrocardiograph**, n. instrument for making such records. **electrocardiography**, n.

electroconvulsive [ɪ,lektrəʊkən'vʌlsɪv] adj. inducing a convulsion through electric shocks (to the brain). **electroconvulsive therapy**, such technique used to treat psychosis. (abbr. E.C.T.)

electrode [ɪ'lektrəʊd] n. elecric terminal; either pole of electrolytic cell.

electrodynamics [ɪ,lektrəʊdaɪ'næmɪks] n. study of electric currents.

electroencephalograph [ɪ,lektrəʊɪn'kefələgrɑːf, –'se–] n. apparatus which detects and records electric activity of the brain (abbr. E.E.G.). **electroencephalogram**, n. such record. **electroencephalographic**, adj. **electroencephalography**, n.

electrolier [ɪ,lektrə'lɪə] *n.* chandelier for electric lamps.

electrolysis [ɪ,lek'trɒlɪsɪs] *n.* decomposition of substance by elec. current. **electrolyse,** *v.t.* **electrolyte,** *n.* substance, especially dissolved in liquid, which is separated by current in electrolysis. **electrolytic** [-'lɪtɪk], *adj.*

electromerism [ɪ,lek'trɒmərɪzm] *n.* ionization of gases.

electrometer [ɪ,lek'trɒmɪtə] *n.* instrument measuring differences of electrical potential. **electrometric** [-'metrɪk], *adj.* **electrometry,** *n.*

electromotive [ɪ,lektrə'məʊtɪv] *adj.* pertaining to electric motion; causing electric current. **electromotive force,** amount of electric energy; voltage; potential (*abbr.* **e.m.f.**).

electronegative [ɪ,lektrəʊ'negətɪv] *adj.* negatively charged; passing to anode in electrolysis; acid; *n.* such substance.

electro-osmosis [ɪ,lektrəʊɒz'məʊsɪs] *n.* movement of a conducting liquid through a porous membrane due to a difference of potential between electrodes on opposite sides.

electrophoresis [ɪ,lektrəʊfə'riːsɪs] *n.* cataphoresis. **electrophoretic** [-'retɪk], *adj.*

electrophorus [ɪ,lek'trɒfərəs] *n.* (*pl.* **–ri**) instrument consisting of ebonite disc, electrified by friction, and metal plate in which positive electricity is induced from the disc. **electrophoric** [-'fɒrɪk], *adj.*

electropositive [ɪ,lektrəʊ'pɒzətɪv] *adj.* positively charged; passing to cathode in electrolysis; basic; *n.* such substance.

electroscope [ɪ'lektrəskəʊp] *n.* instrument determining electric charge and nature of it, especially by diverging gold-leaf strips, etc.

electrostatics [ɪ,lektrə'stætɪks] *n.* study of stationary (*i.e.* not current) electricity.

electrotherapy, **electrotherapeutics** [ɪ,lektrəʊ'θerəpi, –θerə'pjuːtɪks] *n.* use of electricity in medical treatment.

electrotype [ɪ'lektrətaɪp] *n.* plate for printing consisting of soft mould covered with metal electrolytically; *v.i. & t.* make electrotype (of). **electrotypy,** *n.*

electuary [ɪ'lektjʊəri] *n.* medical remedy in syrup.

eleemosynary [,eliiː'mɒzɪnəri] *adj.* pertaining to or like charity; giving, or given as, charity; dependent on charity.

elegiac [,elɪ'dʒaɪək] *n. Prosody,* verse line of five dactyls with marked caesura; *adj.* pertaining to or written in such verse line; mournful. **elegiac couplet,** dactylic hexameter followed by dactylic pentameter. **elegaics,** *n.* verses written in elegiac metre or couplets. **elegy,** *n.*

elenchus [ɪ'leŋkəs] *n.* syllogistic refutation. **Socratic elenchus,** use of question and answer to show untenability of opponent's position. **elenctic,** *adj.* refuting.

elephantiasis [,elɪfən'taɪəsɪs] *n.* disease causing skin, especially of legs, to become hard and thick, and limbs to swell. **elephantiac,** *n. & adj.* (person) suffering from this. **elephantous,** *adj.*

Eleusinian [,elju'sɪnɪən] *adj.* pertaining to Eleusis, in ancient Greece, and its religious mysteries of initiation.

eleutheromania [ɪ,luːθərə'meɪnɪə] *n.* strong desire for freedom. **eleutheromaniac,** *n. & adj.*

elide [ɪ'laɪd] *v.t.* suppress or omit in pronunciation. **elision,** *n.*

elixir [ɪ'lɪksə] *n.* highly purified spirit; substance thought to confer immortality or cure all diseases, or to transmute base metal into gold.

ellipsis [ɪ'lɪpsɪs] *n.* intentional omission of grammatically necessary words. **elliptic(al),** *adj.*

éloge [e'ləʊʒ] (*French*) *n.* eulogy; laudatory funeral oration.

elogy, elogium ['elədʒi, ɪ'ləʊdʒɪəm] *n.* éloge; laudatory obituary notice.

eluant, eluent ['eljuənt] *n.* solvent used in elution. **eluate,** *n.* solution resulting from elution.

elusory [ɪ'luːsəri, –'ljuː–] *adj.* evasive; difficult to grasp mentally.

elute [ɪ'ljuːt, ɪ'luːt] *v.t.* wash out; purify or separate by washing. **elution, elutor,** *n.* **elutriate,** *v.t.* purify by washing and straining. **elutriation, elutriator,** *n.*

eluvium [ɪ'luːvɪəm, –'ljuː–] *n.* detritus from weathering of rock. **eluvial,** *adj.*

elver ['elvə] *n.* young eel.

elydoric [,elɪ'dɒrɪk] *adj.* with both oil and water colours.

Elysian [ɪ'lɪzɪən] *adj.* pertaining to Elysium, the heaven of Greek mythology; ideally happy.

elytron, elytrum ['elɪtrɒn, –əm] *n.* (*pl.* **–ra**) insect's hardened forewing, forming case for hind wing. **elytral,** *adj.* **elytriferous, elytrigerous,** *adj.* bearing elytra. **elytriform,** *adj.* like elytra.

em [em] *n.* printer's unit of measurement: width of pica M (one-sixth of inch).

emarcid [ɪ'mɑːsɪd] *adj.* wilted.

emarginate [ɪ'mɑːdʒɪneɪt, –nət] *adj.* having notched edges. **emargination,** *n.*

emasculate [ɪ'mæskjuleɪt] *v.t.* castrate; weaken; deprive of vigour; render inoffensive. [–ət], *adj.* effeminate. **emasculation,** *n.* **emasculative, emasculatory,** *adj.*

embarras de richesses [ɑːnbæraː'də riːshəs'] (*French*) 'embarrassment of riches', embarrassing surplus. **embarras de choix** [–də shwaː], multitude difficult to choose from.

emblements ['embləmənts] *n. pl. Law,* growing crops.

emblic ['emblɪk] *n.* kind of myrobalan.

embolism ['embəlɪzm] *n. Medicine,* obstruction of vessel by clot, etc.; insertion of intercalary day(s), month, etc. **embolismic, embolic,** *adj.* **embolectomy,** *n.* removal of embolus. **emboliform,** *adj.* like a clot. **embolus,** *n.* (*pl.* **–li**) obstructive clot, foreign body, etc.; wedge.

embonpoint [,ɒmbɒn'pwæn] (*French*) *n.* corpulence.

embouchement [ɒm'buːfɒn] (*French*) *n.* opening of passage. **embouchure** [,ɒmbu'ʃʊə], *n.* river mouth; mouthpiece; placing of lips, etc., about mouthpiece of musical instrument.

embourgeoisé [,ɒmbʊəʒ'waːzeɪ] (*French*) *adj.* having become middle-class. **embourgeoisement** [–'waːzmɒn], *n.*

embow [ɪm'bəʊ] *v.t.* arch, vault. **embowed,** *adj.*

embracery [ɪm'breɪsəri] *n. Law,* offence of attempting to influence a jury or juror. **embrace,** *v.t.* **embracer,** *n.*

embranchment [ɪm'brɑːntʃmənt] *n.* branching out; branch, ramification.

embrangle [ɪm'bræŋgl] *v.t.* confuse, perplex.

embrasure [ɪm'breɪʒə] n. loophole in fortifications; window-opening with slanted sides.

emend [ɪ'mend] v.t. make alterations to (a text). emendation [,iːmen'deɪʃn], n.

emeritus [ɪ'merɪtəs] adj. retired, but retaining honorary office; n. (pl. –ti) such professor, etc.

emesis ['emǝsɪs] n. vomiting. emetic [ɪ'metɪk], n. & adj. (substance) causing vomiting. emetology, n. study of emetics and their action.

emiction [ɪ'mɪkʃn] n. urination; urine. emictory, n. & adj. (drug) promoting urination.

émigré ['emɪgreɪ] (French) n. (fem. –ée) person forced to flee, especially from revolution.

emmenagogue [ɪ'menǝgɒg, –'miː–] n. drug aiding menstruation. emmenagogic [–'gɒdʒɪk], adj. emmeniopathy, n. menstruation disorder. emmenology [,emǝ'nɒlǝdʒi], n. study of menstruation.

emmetropia [,emɪ'trǝupiǝ] n. perfect refraction of eye. emmetropic [–'trɒpɪk], adj.

emollient [ɪ'mɒliǝnt] n. & adj. softening or soothing (substance). emollescence, n.

emolument [ɪ'mɒljʊmǝnt] n. salary; profit.

empaestic, empaistic [em'piːstɪk] adj. embossed.

empasm [em'pæzm] n. scented powder concealing odour of perspiration.

empathy ['empǝθi] n. deep sympathetic understanding. empathic [–'pæθɪk], empathetic adj. empathize, v.i & t.

empennage ['ɒmpǝnɑːʒ, 'em–] n. tail assembly of an aircraft.

emphractic [em'fræktɪk] n. & adj. (substance) closing skin pores. emphraxia, emphraxis, n. obstruction, especially of pores.

emphysema [,emfɪ'siːmǝ, –'ziː–] n. Medicine, swollen state of tissue due to air or gas, especially in lungs. emphysematous [–'semǝtǝs, –'siː–], adj. so swollen; bloated; bladderlike.

emphyteusis [,emfɪ'tjuːsɪs] n. contract granting possession of land for long period on certain conditions. emphyteutic, adj.

empiric(al) [ɪm'pɪrɪk, –l] adj. relying on or derived from experiment or experience only; ignoring theory or science. empiric n. such thinker or scientist; quack. empiricism, empiricist, n.

emporeutic, emporetic [,empǝ'ruːtɪk, –'retɪk] adj. pertaining to trade; n. merchandise.

empressé [ɒm'preseɪ] (French) adj. (fem. –ée) in haste; eager. empressement [–'presmɒn], n. show of affection.

emption ['empʃn] n. buying.

empyema [,empaɪ'iːmǝ, –pi–] n. (pl. –ta) collection of pus in body cavity, especially in pleural cavity. empyemic, adj.

empyrean [,empɪ'riːǝn, –paɪ–] n. & adj. (pertaining to) the sky; heaven. empyreal [–'riːǝl], adj.

emulgent [ɪ'mʌldʒǝnt] adj. draining; purifying; pertaining to kidneys; n. drug stimulating bile.

emulsion [ɪ'mʌlʃn] n. milky fluid; suspension of oil or resin in watery liquid or vice versa; any dispersion of one liquid in another; coating, containing suspended silver salt, of photographic films and plates. emulsify [ɪ'mʌlsɪfaɪ], v.t convert into emulsion. emulsive, adj.

emunctory [ɪ'mʌŋktǝri] n. & adj. excretory (organ).

en [en] n. printer's unit of measurement, half the width of an em.

enallage [en'ælǝdʒi] n. Grammar, exchange of part of speech, gender, tense, etc., for another.

enantiomorph [en'æntiǝmɔːf] n. either of a pair of asymmetric figures that are mirror images of each other, e.g. a pair of hands.

enantiosis [en,ænti'ǝusɪs] n. rhetorical device of ironically stating the opposite of what is meant.

enarthrosis [,enɑː'θrǝusɪs] n. ball-and-socket joint.

enate ['iːneɪt] adj. growing out; n. relation on mother's side. enatic [iː'nætɪk], adj. related on mother's side; having same mother. enation, n. outgrowth; enatic relationship.

encaenia [en'siːniǝ] n. festival commemorating dedication or foundation.

encaustic [ɪn'kɔːstɪk] adj. burnt in; n. painting with wax colours fixed by heat.

enceinte [ɒn'sænt] (French) adj. pregnant; n. fortification enclosing fortress or town; cathedral close.

encephalitis [en,kefǝ'laɪtɪs, –,se–] n. inflammation of brain. encephalitis lethargica, sleeping sickness.

encephalon [en'kefǝlɒn, –'se–] n. (pl. –la) the brain. encephalograph, n. X-ray photograph of brain. encephaloid, adj. brain-like. encephaloma, n. brain tumour.

enchiridion [,enkaɪ'rɪdiǝn, –kɪ–] n. handbook.

enchorial, enchoric [en'kɔːriǝl, –'kɒrɪk] adj. native; domestic.

enchylema [,enkaɪ'liːmǝ] n. fluid part of protoplasm. enchylematous, adj.

en clair [ɒn 'kleǝ] (French) 'in clear', not in code.

enclave ['enkleɪv, 'ɒŋ–] n. part of a foreign country enclosed in native territory; [ɪn'kleɪv], v.t. surround land thus. enclavement, n.

enclitic [ɪn'klɪtɪk] adj. dependent, especially of word or particle attached to preceding word in pronunciation; n. such word or particle. enclisis ['eŋklɪsɪs], n. pronunciation of enclitic word.

encomic [en'kǝumɪk] adj. applied to closely curled woolly hair.

encomium [ɪn'kǝumiǝm] n. (pl. –ia) eulogy. encomiast, n. composer of such. encomiastic, adj.

encrypt [ɪn'krɪpt] v.t. put into code.

encyclical [ɪn'sɪklɪkl, en–, –'saɪ–] n. & adj. (publication) for wide distribution, especially Pope's letter to bishops.

endeictic [en'daɪktɪk] adj. demonstrating.

endemic [en'demɪk] adj. native; indigenous; generally present in a particular place or class; n. such disease. endemiology [–,diːmi'ɒlǝdʒi], n. study of such diseases. endemism ['endɪmɪzm], n.

endermic [en'dɜːmɪk] adj. acting by absorption through the skin.

endocardium [,endǝu'kɑːdiǝm] n. membrane lining heart cavities. endocardiac, endocardial, adj. endocarditis, n. inflammation of this.

endocrine ['endǝkraɪn, –rɪn] adj. secreting direct into the blood-stream; n. such gland. endocrinic [–'krɪnɪk], endocrinous [–'dɒkrɪnǝs], adj. endocrinology, n. study of endocrine glands and hormones. endocrinopathy, n. disease due to abnormal hormone secretion. endocrinotherapy, n. medical treatment with hormones.

endogamy [en'dɒgəmɪ] *n.* marriage to person of same tribe only. **endogamic** [–'gæmɪk], **endogamous**, *adj.*

endogeny [en'dɒdʒənɪ] *n.* growth from within. **endogenesis** [–'dʒenəsɪs], *n.* endogeny. **endogenetic** [–dʒə'netɪk], **endogenic** [–'dʒenɪk], *adj.* produced internally; pertaining to geological processes occurring within earth. **endogenous**, *adj.* developing or originating within.

endomorph ['endəmɔːf] *n.* psychophysical type, soft, rounded and fleshy, and often sociable and comfort-loving. **endomorphic**, *adj.* **endomorphy**, *n.*

endoparasite [,endəʊ'pærəsaɪt] *n.* internal parasite. **endoparasitic,** *adj.*

endophagy [en'dɒfədʒi] *n.* cannibalism among members of same tribe; erosion of internal tissue.

endophasia [,endəʊ'feɪzɪə, –ʒə] *n.* internalized, inaudible speech.

endophyte ['endəfaɪt] *n.* endoparasitic plant. **endophytic** [–'fɪtɪk], *adj.*

endoplasm ['endəplæzm] *n.* inner layer of cytoplasm. **endoplasmic,** *adj.*

endoscope ['endəskəʊp] *n.* instrument for medical examination of interior of organ. **endoscopic** [–'skɒpɪk], *adj.* **endoscopy** [en'dɒskəpɪ], *n.* such examination.

endoskeleton [,endə'skelɪtən] *n.* internal skeleton. **endoskeletal,** *adj.*

endosmosis [,endɒz'məʊsɪs] *n.* movement of substance into organ from surrounding fluid.

endosperm ['endəspɜːm] *n.* albumen in plant seed. **endospermic,** *adj.*

endothermy ['endəθɜːmi] *n.* surgical introduction of electric needle or knife into tissues to produce heat. **endothermic, endothermous,** *adj.* pertaining to absorption of heat.

enema ['enəmə] *n.* (*pl.* **–ta**) injection of liquid into rectum.

energumen [,enə'gjuːmen] *n.* person possessed by evil spirit; fanatic.

enervate ['enəveɪt] *v.t.* weaken. **enervation, enervator,** *n.* **enervative** [ɪ'nɜːvətɪv], *adj.*

enfant terrible [,ɒnfɒn tə'riːblə] (*French*) 'terrible child'; child causing embarrassment by its questions, remarks, etc.; any such rash person.

enfilade [,enfɪ'leɪd] *n.* arrangement in parallel rows or files; enfilading fire; *v.t.* fire upon from the flank.

enfleurage [,ɒnflɜː'rɑːʒ] *n.* exposure of oils to scent of fresh flowers in perfume-making.

engrail [ɪn'greɪl] *v.t.* decorate with curved notches; give serrated appearance to.

engram ['engræm] *n.* physical memory trace in brain. **engrammatic, engrammic,** *adj.* **engraphic** *adj.* producing engram. **engraphy,** *n.*

enjambement [ɪn'dʒæmmənt, ɒn'ʒɒmbmɒn] *n.* running-over of sense or sentence from one verse line to next.

ennead ['enɪæd] *n.* set of nine. **enneadic,** *adj.*

enneaeteric [,enɪə–'terɪk] *adj.* happening every ninth year.

enneagon ['enɪəgɒn] *n.* nine-sided plane figure. **enneagonal,** [,eni'ægənl], *adj.*

enneahedron [,enɪə'hiːdrən] *n.* nine-sided solid figure. **enneahedral,** *adj.*

enneatic [,eni'ætɪk] *adj.* happening once in every set of nine; every ninth.

ennui ['ɒnwiː] (*French*) *n.* boredom. **ennuyant**

[ɒn'wiːɒn], *adj.* boring. **ennuyé** [ɒn'wiːeɪ], *n.* & *adj.* (*fem.* **–uyée**) bored (person).

en pantoufles [,ɒn pɒn'tuːfl] (*French*) 'in slippers'; at ease; informal(ly).

enphytotic [,enfaɪ'tɒtɪk] *n.* & *adj.* endemic (disease) of plants.

en plein air [ɒn ,plen 'eə] (*French*) 'in the open air'. **en plein jour** [–,plæn 'ʒʊə], 'in open daylight'; openly.

en rapport [,ɒn ræ'pɔː] (*French*) 'in close relationship'; in sympathy; working together harmoniously.

en règle [ɒn 'reɪgl] (*French*) 'in rule'; in due order.

ensate, ensiform ['enseɪt, –ɪfɔːm] *adj.* swordshaped.

ensilage ['ensɪlɪdʒ] *n.* storing in silo; crops so stored. **ensilate, ensile,** *v.t.* store in silo. **ensilation,** *n.*

entablature [en'tæblətʃə] *n. Architecture,* wall resting on capitals of columns, comprising architrave, frieze and cornice.

entablement [en'teɪblmənt] *n.* platform of a pedestal, supporting a statue.

entail [ɪn'teɪl] *v.t. Law,* settle on a person and his descendants or certain of them; *n.* estate so settled; line of descendants to whom estate is limited.

entelechy [en'teləki] *n. Philosophy,* perfect realisation of end or cause.

enteric [en'terɪk] *n.* pertaining to intestines; *n.* typhoid fever. **enteritis,** *n.* inflammation of intestines. **enterography,** *n.* description of intestines. **enteroptosis,** *n.* dropping and protrusion of intestines.

enthetic [en'θetɪk] *adj.* (especially of infectious disease) introduced into the body from without.

enthymeme ['enθɪmiːm] *n.* argument or syllogism from which a premiss is omitted as self-evident.

entify ['entɪfaɪ] *v.t.* make or regard as separate substance or entity. **entifical,** *adj.* **entification,** *n.* **entitative** ['entɪtətɪv] *adj.* regarded as entity alone, apart from attendant circumstances.

entomic(al) [en'tɒmɪk, –l] *adj.* pertaining to insects.

entomology [,entə'mɒlədʒi] *n.* study of insects. **entomological,** *adj.* **entomologist,** *n.*

entomophagous [,entə'mɒfəgəs] *adj.* feeding on insects. **entomophilous,** *adj.* pollinated by insects.

entophyte ['entəfaɪt] *n.* parasitic plant living within another plant or animal. **entophytal, entophytic** [–'fɪtɪk], **entophytous** [–'tɒfɪtəs], *adj.*

entopic [en'tɒpɪk] *adj. Anatomy,* in the normal position.

entoptic [en'tɒptɪk] *adj.* pertaining to interior of eyeball. **entotic,** *adj.* pertaining to interior of ear.

entozoon [,entə'zəʊɒn] *n.* (*pl.* **–zoa**) internal parasite. **entozoal,** *adj.* **entozoan,** *n.* & *adj.* **entozoology,** *n.* study of these.

entrechat ['ɒntrəʃɑː] (*French*) *n.* dancer's leap in which legs are quickly crossed or heels tapped.

entrée ['ɒntreɪ] *n.* permission or right to enter; meat dish served before roast.

entre nous [,ɒntrə 'nuː] (*French*) 'between ourselves'.

entrepot ['ɒntrəpəʊ] (*French*) *n.* warehouse; importing for re-export.

entresol ['ɒntrəsɒl] (*French*) *n.* mezzanine floor.

entropy ['entrəpi] *n.* amount of unavailable energy in a thermodynamic system; (process of running down to a) static condition.

enuresis [‚enjuˈriːsɪs] *n.* inability to control urination; urine discharged involuntarily.

enzootic [‚enzəʊˈɒtɪk] *n. & adj.* (disease) attacking animals.

enzyme [ˈenzaɪm] *n.* organic catalyst, especially digestive. **enzymatic, enzymic,** *adj.*

eoan [iˈəʊən] *adj.* of dawn or east.

eolithic [‚iːəˈlɪθɪk] *adj.* pertaining to earliest Stone Age.

eonism [ˈiːənɪzm] *n.* adoption of opposite sex's manners, clothes and mentality, especially by a man. **eonist,** *n.* transvestite.

eozoic [‚iːəˈzəʊɪk] *adj.* containing earliest evidence of animal life.

epact [ˈiːpækt, ˈe–] *n.* difference, represented by a number, between solar and lunar year, or calendar and lunar month; age of moon at start of calendar year. **epactal,** *adj.* intercalary.

epagoge [ˈepəgəʊdʒi] *n.* inductive reasoning. **epagogic** [–ˈgɒdʒɪk], *adj.*

epanadiplosis [e‚pænədɪˈpləʊsɪs] *n. Rhetoric,* repetition at end of sentence of word used at beginning.

epanalepsis [‚epənəˈlepsɪs] *n. Rhetoric,* repetition. **epanaleptic,** *adj.*

epanodos [ɪˈpænədɒs] *n. Rhetoric,* return to theme from digression; repetition (of sentence) in reverse order.

epanorthosis [‚epənɔːˈθəʊsɪs] *n. Rhetoric,* emphatic substitution of more correct or stronger term.

epeiric [ɪˈpaɪrɪk] *adj.* (of sea) within the continental shelf.

epeirogeny [‚epaɪˈrɒdʒəni] *n.* geological formation of continents, oceans, etc. **epeirogenic** [–ˈdʒenɪk], *adj.*

epenthesis [eˈpenθəsɪs] *n.* (*pl.* **–ses**) introduction of sound into word; removal of vowel into preceding syllable. **epenthesize,** *v.t.* **epenthetic** [–ˈθetɪk], *adj.*

epergne [ɪˈpɜːn] *n.* central ornament on table.

ephectic [eˈfektɪk] *adj.* habitually suspending judgment.

ephelis [eˈfiːlɪs] *n.* (*pl.* **–lides,** [eˈfelɪdiːz]) freckle.

ephemeron [ɪˈfemərɒn, –ˈfiː–] *n.* (*pl.* **–ra**) thing, especially insect, living for a day only. **ephemeral, ephemerous,** *adj.* short-lived. **ephemerid,** *n.* may-fly. **ephemeris,** *n.* (*pl.* **–rides,** [‚efɪˈmerɪdiːz]) almanac showing daily positions of heavenly bodies.

ephod [ˈiːfɒd, ˈe–] *n.* garment of Jewish priest.

ephor [ˈiːfɔː, ˈe–] *n.* magistrate of Sparta. **ephoral, ephoric** [–ˈfɒrɪk], *adj.* **ephorate,** *n.* office of ephor; whole body of ephors.

epicedium [‚epɪˈsiːdɪəm] *n.* (*pl.* **–ia**) elegy; dirge. **epicedial,** *adj.*

epicene [ˈepɪsiːn] *adj.* having the characteristics of, or adapted for use by, both sexes; sexless; effeminate; *Grammar,* with one form signifying both male and female; *n.* epicene person.

epichorial [‚epɪˈkɔːrɪəl] *adj.* belonging to a particular area. **epichoric** [–ˈkɒrɪk], **epichoristic,** *adj.*

epichristian [‚epɪˈkrɪstʃən] *adj.* pertaining to the period immediately after Christ.

epicolic [‚epɪˈkɒlɪk] *adj.* applied to lower abdomen lying over the colon.

epicrisis [ɪˈpɪkrəsɪs] *n.* (*pl.* **–ses**) critical appreciation of literature; [ˈepi‚kraɪsɪs], *Medicine,* secondary crisis in disease.

epicritic [‚epɪˈkrɪtɪk] *adj.* responding to small variations in temperature and touch.

epicure [ˈepɪkjʊə] *n.* person taking care over the niceties of food and drink. **epicurean** [–ˈriːən], *adj.* luxurious; sensual; *n.* such person; follower of philosophy of Epicurus, who taught that ultimate moral good is happiness.

epicycle [ˈepɪ‚saɪkl] *n.* circle whose centre is on circumference of a greater circle. **epicyclic,** *adj.*

epideictic(al) [‚epɪˈdaɪktɪk, –l] *adj.* displaying.

epidermis [‚epɪˈdɜːmɪs] *n.* outermost layer of skin; *Botany,* plant's derma. **epidermal, epidermatic, epidermic, epidermous,** *adj.* **epidermoid,** *adj.* like this.

epidiascope [‚epɪˈdaɪəskəʊp] *n.* projector for use with opaque as well as translucent objects.

epididymis [‚epɪˈdɪdəmɪs] *n.* (*pl.* **–didymides**)

I wish I were a ...

Verbs have four different sets of forms (or 'moods,' as they are known technically; see **Grammar terms**). Most of the time they are used in the 'indicative' mood, which simply expresses actions, states, etc. They can also be used for giving orders, in the 'imperative' mood, and for asking questions, in the 'interrogative' mood. The fourth set of forms is called the '**subjunctive**' mood. It expresses states which do not actually exist.

There are two sorts of subjunctive in English: the present and the past. In form, the present subjunctive is the same as the infinitive of the verb, and it never varies. So the present subjunctives of *to be* and *to have* are *be* and *have* (*he be, she have*), and all other verbs do not add *-s* in the third singular (*it seem*). It is used in three main ways. First, after verbs, nouns and adjectives expressing a command,

suggestion, intention etc. (*I suggested that he reconsider; It would be fitting that she resign*). Second, in clauses expressing a condition or concession, commonly following conjunctions such as *if, though, whether, lest* (*Tie her up, lest she escape*). Both of these uses of the present subjunctive are commoner in American than in British English. Third, in various rather fixed and formulaic phrases such as *come what may, suffice it to say, heaven forbid* and *be that as it may*.

The past subjunctive is in practice limited to the verb *to be,* and consists of a single form: *were.* It is used to present hypothetical situations, and comes after the verbs *wish* and *suppose,* conjunctions such as *if, as though, whether,* and the phrases *would rather* and *would that* (*I wish she were here; I'd rather it were postponed*). In nonformal contexts, *were* is commonly replaced by *was* in the first and third persons singular.

convoluted duct at rear of testicle storing sperm.

epidural [ˌepɪ'djuərəl] *adj.* on, outside the dura mater; *n.* anaesthetic injection into the space around the spinal cord.

epigamic [ˌepɪ'gæmɪk] *adj.* attracting opposite sex at breeding time.

epigastrium [ˌepɪ'gæstrɪəm] *n.* part of abdomen lying over the stomach. **epigastrial, epigastric,** *adj.*

epigeal, epigean, epigeous [ˌepɪ'dʒiːəl, -ən, -əs] *adj.* living or growing near the ground.

epigenesis [ˌepɪ'dʒenəsɪs] *n.* biological theory of the development of the embryo, through progressive differentiation of originally undifferentiated cells. **epigenetic** [-'netɪk], *adj.* **epigenist** [e'pɪdʒənɪst], **epigenesist,** *n.*

epigenous [ɪ'pɪdʒənəs] *adj.* growing on the (upper) surface of an organism.

epiglottis [ˌepɪ'glɒtɪs] *n.* throat cartilage protecting the windpipe in swallowing. **epiglottal, epiglottic,** *adj.*

epigone, epigon ['epɪgəun, -gɒn] *n.* disciple, follower, imitator, especially in later generation.

epigraph ['epɪgrɑːf] *n.* inscription; quotation at beginning of work or chapter. **epigraphy** [ɪ'pɪgrəfɪ], *n.* study of ancient inscriptions.

epilate ['epɪleɪt] *v.t.* remove (hair). **epilation,** *n.*

epimorphic [ˌepɪ'mɔːfɪk] *adj.* passing several stages of growth in same form, especially of segmented insects. **epimorphosis,** *n.*

epimyth ['epɪmɪθ] *n.* moral of story.

epinician [ˌepɪ'nɪsɪən, -ʃn] *adj.* in celebration of victory. **epinicion,** *n.* song of victory or triumph.

epipastic [ˌepɪ'pæstɪk] *n.* medical dusting powder.

epiphenomenon [ˌepɪfɪ'nɒmɪnən] *n.* secondary phenomenon associated with and apparently due to another. **epiphenomenal,** *adj.*

epiphora [ɪ'pɪfərə] *n.* watering of eyes.

epiphysis [ɪ'pɪfəsɪs] *n.* (*pl.* **-ses**) separately ossified portion of bone, joining to main portion later. **epiphysis cerebri,** pineal body. **epiphysary, epiphyseal** [-'fɪzɪəl], *adj.*

epiphyte ['epɪfaɪt] *n.* non-parasitic plant growing on another. **epiphytal, epiphytic** [-'fɪtɪk], **epiphytous,** *adj.* **epiphytotic,** *n.* & *adj.* (disease) affecting many plants.

epiplexis [ˌepɪ'pleksɪs] *n. Rhetoric,* reproof. **epiplectic,** *adj.*

epiploce [ɪ'pɪpləsɪ] *n.* rhetorical crescendo.

epipolism [ɪ'pɪpəlɪzm] *n.* fluorescence. **epipolic** [-'pɒlɪk], *adj.* **epipolize,** *v.t.*

epipterous [e'pɪptərəs] *adj. Botany,* having wings or wing-like projections at apex.

episcopal [ɪ'pɪskəpl] *adj.* pertaining to or ruled by bishops. **episcopalian** [-'peɪlɪən], *adj.* pertaining to episcopal church or government; *n.* member of such church. **episcopacy** [-pəsɪ], *n.* rule by bishops; the body of bishops collectively. **episcopate,** *n.* office, see or whole body of bishops.

episematic [ˌepɪsɪ'mætɪk] *adj.* (of coloration) assisting recognition between members of same species.

episiotomy [ɪˌpɪzɪ'ɒtəmi, ˌepɪ-] *n.* cut made in perineum to ease childbirth.

epispastic [ˌepɪ'spæstɪk] *n.* & *adj.* (substance) causing blister as medical remedy.

epistasis [ɪ'pɪstəsɪs] *n.* act of suppressing secretion. **epistatic** [ˌepɪ'stætɪk], *adj.* suppressing,

especially the effect of another factor.

epistaxis [ˌepɪ'stæksɪs] *n.* nose-bleeding.

epistemology [ɪˌpɪstɪ'mɒlədʒi] *n.* branch of philosophy dealing with the study of knowledge. **epistemological,** *adj.* **epistemologist,** *n.* **epistemic** [-'stiːmɪk, -'stemɪk], **epistemonic,** *adj.* pertaining to knowledge; intellectual.

epistolary [ɪ'pɪstələri] *adj.* pertaining to letters. **epistolography,** *n.* art of letter-writing. **epistolarian** [-'leərɪən], *n.* & *adj.* (person) fond of letter-writing.

epistrophe [ɪ'pɪstrəfi] *n. Rhetoric,* repetition of same phrase at end of successive sentences. **epistropheal** [ˌepɪ'strəufɪəl], **epistrophic** [-'strɒfɪk], *adj.*

epitasis [ɪ'pɪtəsɪs] *n.* part of drama in which action is developed; crisis of disease.

epithalamium, epithalamion [ˌepɪθə'leɪmɪəm, -mɪən] *n.* (*pl.* **-ia**) wedding song or poem. **epithalamial, epithalamic** [-'læmɪk], *adj.* **epithalamiast,** *n.* composer of this. **epithalamy** [-'θæləmi], *n.* epithalamium.

epithelium [ˌepɪ'θiːlɪəm] *n.* (*pl.* **-ia**) cellular membrane covering surface or lining cavity or passage. **epithelial,** *adj.* **epithelioid,** *adj.* like epithelium.

epithet ['epɪθet] *n.* adjective describing a characteristic quality; descriptive word added to or substituted for a person's name.

epitimesis [ˌepɪtɪ'miːsɪs] *n.* adverse criticism; reproof.

epitome [ɪ'pɪtəmi] *n.* summary; collection of all characteristics, facts, etc., into small space; embodiment, essence. **epitomic(al)** [-'tɒm-], *adj.* **epitomize** [-'pɪt-], *v.t.* summarize; represent all essentials of; embody.

epitonic [ˌepɪ'tɒnɪk] *adj.* subjected to too great strain.

epitrope [ɪ'pɪtrəpi] *n. Rhetoric,* (ironical) giving of permission.

epizeuxis [ˌepɪ'zjuːksɪs] *n.* repetition for emphasis.

epizoon [ˌepɪ'zəuɒn] *n.* (*pl.* **-zoa**) external parasite. **epizoan,** *n.* & *adj.* **epizoic,** *adj.*

epizootic [ˌepɪzəu'ɒtɪk] *n.* & *adj.* (disease) epidemic among animals.

e pluribus unum [eɪ ˌpluərɪbəs 'uːnəm, -ʊm] (*Latin*) 'one out of many'; unity from combination of many parts.

eponym ['epənɪm] *n.* person or name from which name of race, family, etc., is derived; person whose name is used metaphorically to signify a quality or thing. **eponymic, eponymous** [e'pɒnɪməs], *adj.* **eponymy** [e'pɒnəmi], *n.*

epopee [e'pəpiː] *n.* epic poem or poetry. **epopean,** *adj.* **epopoist** [-'piːɪst], *n.* writer of epics.

epopt ['epɒpt] *n.* person initiated into mysteries. **epoptic,** *adj.*

epos ['epɒs] *n.* epic poem or poetry; collection of lays dealing with same theme.

epoxy [ɪ'pɒksi] *adj.* denoting chemical compounds in which oxygen is attached to two different atoms in a chain, *e.g.* epoxy resin.

epulary ['epjuləri] *adj.* pertaining to banquet. **epulation,** *n.*

epulosis [ˌepju'ləusɪs] *n.* formation of scar. **epulotic(al)** [-'lɒt-], *n.* & *adj.* (substance) aiding epulosis.

equilibrist [ɪ'kwɪlbrɪst] *n.* person who performs feats of balancing, tight-rope walker.

equine ['ekwaɪn, 'iː–] *adj.* pertaining to or like a horse.

equinox ['iːkwɪnɒks] *n.* date on which sun crosses equator. **autumnal equinox,** such date in autumn (about Sept. 23). **vernal equinox,** such date in spring (about March 21). **equinoctial,** *adj.* pertaining to equinox, or to place or time having day and night of equal length; equatorial. **equinoctial line,** celestial equator.

equipage ['ekwɪpɪdʒ] *n.* horse-drawn carriage; equipment and appurtenances; *archaic,* retinue.

equiparent [ɪ'kwɪpərənt] *adj.* having same mutual relationship. **equiparate** [–eɪt], *v.t.* level; equalize.

equipoise ['ekwɪpɔɪz, 'iː–] *n.* state of equilibrium; counterpoise; *v.t.* counterpoise.

equipollent [,iːkwɪ'pɒlənt, ,e–] *adj.* having equal force or power; having same meaning though differently expressed. **equipollence, equipollency,** *n.*

equiponderate [,iːkwɪ'pɒndəreɪt, ,e–] *v.t.* be equal in power, force, importance etc.; counterbalance. **equiponderance,** *n.* **equiponderant,** *adj.*

equisetum [,ekwɪ'siːtəm] *n.* (*pl.* **–ta**) horsetail (plant).

equitation [,ekwɪ'teɪʃn] *n.* horse-riding. **equitative** ['ek–], *adj.*

equivoque, equivoke ['ekwɪvəuk, 'iː–] *n.* pun; ambiguous remark.

equivorous [ɪ'kwɪvərəs] *adj.* eating horse-flesh.

Erastian [ɪ'ræstiən] *adj.* pertaining to Erastus (1524–83), Swiss theologian, and his doctrine of state government of ecclesiastical matters; *n.* adherent of that doctrine.

Erebian [e'riːbiən] *adj.* pertaining to Erebos, in Greek mythology a place of darkness leading to Hades; pitch dark.

eremic [ɪ'riːmɪk] *adj.* pertaining to sandy desert.

eremite ['erəmaɪt] *n.* hermit. **eremitage,** *n.* **eremitic(al)** [–'mɪt–], *adj.*

eremology [,erɪ'mɒlədʒi] *n.* study of deserts. **eremophyte** ['er–], *n.* plant living in desert.

erethism ['erəθɪzm] *n.* abnormal excitability. **erethismic, erethistic, erethitic,** *adj.*

erg [ɜːg] *n.* unit of energy: equal to the work done by a force of one dyne in moving its point of application one centimetre in the direction of that force.

ergo ['ɜːgəʊ] (*Latin*) *adv.* 'therefore'.

ergograph ['ɜːgəgrɑːf] *n.* instrument measuring work involved in contracting a muscle. **ergology,** *n.* study of work's effect on mind and body. **ergonomics,** *n.* scientific study of work conditions, equipment and operations, to promote efficiency. **ergophile,** *n.* lover of work. **ergophobia,** *n.* hatred of work.

ergosterol [ɜː'gɒstərɒl] *n.* chemical substance in the body developing into vitamin D on exposure to sunlight.

ergot ['ɜːgət] *n.* fungus disease of cereals, especially rye; dried fungus causing ergot, containing drug which contracts blood-vessels, nerves and uterus. **ergotic** [ɜː'gɒtɪk], *adj.* **ergotize,** *v.t.* **ergotism,** *n.* disease due to consuming ergotized grain, etc.

ericaceous [,erɪ'keɪʃəs] *adj.* pertaining to or like heath plant; belonging to the heath family of plants. **ericetal** [–'siːtl], *adj.* composed of heath plants. **ericeticolous** [,erəsɪ'tɪkələs], *adj.* living on heaths. **ericineous,** *adj.* ericaceous. **ericoid** [–kɔɪd], *adj.* like a heath plant. **ericophyte,** *n.* plant growing on heaths.

erinaceous [,erɪ'neɪʃəs] *adj.* like or pertaining to a hedgehog.

eriometer [,ɪərɪ'ɒmɪtə] *n.* optical instrument for measuring the diameters of fibres or particles by the diffraction of light.

eriophyllous [,ɪərɪəʊ'fɪləs] *adj.* with woolly leaves.

eristic [e'rɪstɪk] *adj.* pertaining to dispute or argument.

erne [ɜːn] *n.* golden or sea eagle.

erogenesis [,erəʊ'dʒenəsɪs] *n.* production of sexual desire. **erogeneity** [–dʒə'neɪəti, –'niː–], *n.* **erogenetic** [–dʒə'netɪk], **erogenic** [–'dʒen–], **erogenous** [ɪ'rɒdʒənəs], *adj.*

erotesis [,erəʊ'tiːsɪs] *n.* rhetorical questioning. **erotetic** [–'tetɪk], *adj.*

erotology [,erə'tɒlədʒi] *n.* study or description of sexual stimuli and behaviour. **erotological,** *adj.* **erotologist,** *n.*

erotomania [ɪ,rəʊtə'meɪniə, –,rɒ–] *n.* abnormally strong sexual desire. **erotomaniac,** *n.* & *adj.*

errant ['erənt] *adj.* wandering, especially seeking adventure; mistaking. **errantry,** *n.*

erratum [e'rɑːtəm] *n.* (*pl.* **–ta**) mistake, especially printer's or writer's.

errhine ['eraɪn] *n.* & *adj.* (substance) causing sneezing.

ersatz ['eəzæts] (*German*) *n.* & *adj.* substitute.

erubescent [,eru'besnt] *adj.* becoming red. **erubescence,** *n.*

eruca [ɪ'ruːkə] *n.* (*pl.* **–ae**) caterpillar. **eruciform** [–sɪfɔːm], *adj.* caterpillar-like. **erucivorous** [–'sɪvərəs], *adj.* feeding on caterpillars.

eructation [,iːrʌk'teɪʃn, ɪ,rʌk–] *n.* belching; belch. **eructative,** *adj.*

erumpent [ɪ'rʌmpənt] *adj.* bursting forth.

erysipelas [,erɪ'sɪpələs] *n.* disease marked by fever and inflammation of skin, especially of face; St. Anthony's fire. **erysipelatoid, erysipelatous** [–'pel–], *adj.* like erysipelas. **erysipeloid,** *n.* non-febrile disease resembling erysipelas.

erythema [,erɪ'θiːmə] *n.* inflammatory redness of skin. **erythemic, erythematous** [–'θemətəs], **erythematic** [–'mætɪk], *adj.*

erythraean, erythrean [,erɪ'θriːən] *adj.* red. **erythraemia,** *n.* excessive production of red blood corpuscles. **erythrism, erythrochroism,** *n.* excessive redness of hair, etc. **erythrocyte** [ɪ'rɪθrəsaɪt], *n.* red blood corpuscle. **erythrodermia,** *n.* reddening of skin. **erythroid,** *adj.* reddish. **erythrophobia,** *n.* fear of red light, or of blushing. **erythropia, erythropsia,** *n.* seeing all objects red.

escalade [,eskə'leɪd] *n.* act of scaling wall or crossing moat with ladder.

escalier [e'skælieɪ] (*French*) *n.* staircase. **escalier dérobé** [–deɪ'rəubeɪ], secret or back stairs.

escarp [ɪ'skɑːp] *n.* scarp. **escarpment,** *n.* cliff; cliff-like drop in ground round castle, etc.

eschar ['eskɑː, –kə] *n.* scab. **escharotic,** *n.* & *adj.* caustic (substance).

eschatology [,eskə'tɒlədʒi] *n.* religious doctrine concerning 'the last things', as death, resurrection, life hereafter, etc. **eschatological,** *adj.* **eschatologist,** *n.*

escheat [ɪs'tʃiːt, es–] *n.* reversion of land to feudal lord, crown or state, due to failure of heirs; *v.i. & t.* to revert or cause to revert. **escheatage,** *n.* right to receive by escheat.

eschew [ɪs'tʃuː] *v.t.* avoid, shun; abstain from.

escritoire [ˌeskrə'twɑː, –riː–] *n.* writing-table. **escritorial,** *adj.*

escrow ['eskrəʊ, ɪ'skrəʊ] *n. Law,* deed held by a third party until certain conditions are fulfilled. **in escrow,** held by a third party.

esculent ['eskjʊlənt] *n. & adj.* edible (thing).

escutcheon [ɪ'skʌtʃən] *n.* shield, etc., bearing coat of arms.

esker, eskar ['eskə] *n. Geology,* ridge of sandy soil sub-glacially deposited.

esodic [e'sɒdɪk] *adj.* afferent.

esophagus, [iː'sɒfəgəs, ɪ–] *n.* food passage between mouth and stomach.

esoteric [ˌesə'terɪk] *adj.* capable of being understood only by initiated; abstruse; confidential. **esoterica** *n.pl.* esoteric matters or details. **esotericism** [–sɪzm], **esoterism** [e'sɒtərɪzm], *n.*

esotropia [ˌesə'trəʊpiə] *n.* convergent squint. **esotrope,** *n.* person having this. **esotropic** [–'trɒpɪk], *adj.*

espalier [ɪ'spæliei, –iə] *n.* lattice, especially for trained fruit tree; such tree.

esparto [e'spɑːtəʊ, ɪ–] *n.* grass of Spain and N Africa, used in manufacture of paper, cordage, cloth, etc.

espièglerie [ˌespi'eɪgləri] (*French*) *n.* mischievousness; mischievous trick.

esprit [ɜspriː'] (*French*) *n.* wit; vivacity; quick intelligence. **esprit de corps** [–də kʊə'] loyalty to organization, corps or fellow-members; team spirit. **esprit de l'escalier,** 'wit of the staircase'; (witty) remark, retort one wishes one had thought of at the time. **esprit fort** [–fʊə'], religious freethinker.

essorant ['esərənt] *adj.* soaring.

estaminet [e'stæmɪneɪ] (*French*) *n.* small café.

estancia [ɪ'stænsiə, e–] (*Spanish-American*) *n.* ranch. **estanciero** [–si'eərəʊ], *n.* owner of ranch.

ester ['estə] *n. Chemistry,* salt-like compound formed by replacing acid hydrogen of acid with hydro-carbon radical. **esterify,** *v.t.* convert into this.

esthetic [iːs'θetɪk] *see* **aesthetic.**

estop [ɪ'stɒp] *v.t. Law,* preclude, especially by estoppel. **estoppage** [–ɪdʒ], **estoppel** [–l], *n.* principle preventing a person denying a fact he/she has previously alleged to be true.

estrade [e'strɑːd] (*French*) *n.* dais.

estreat [ɪ'striːt] *v.t. Law,* extract from court's records in order to prosecute; *n.* copy or extract of record, especially of fines, etc.

esurient [ɪ'sjʊəriənt] *adj.* hungry; starving; greedy; *n.* such person. **esurience, esuriency,** *n.*

et alibi [et 'ælɪbaɪ] (*Latin*) 'and elsewhere' (*abbr.* **et al.**). **et alii** (*fem.* **aliae**) [et 'æliiː, –aɪ], 'and others' (*abbr.* **et al.**).

etesian [ɪ'tiːziən, –ʒn] *adj.* occurring annually or periodically, especially such Mediterranean north wind in summer.

ether ['iːθə] *n.* the sky; space; *Chemistry,* distillation product of alcohol used as solvent, anaesthetic, etc.; *Physics,* medium supposed to fill space and transmit light, radio, etc., waves. **ethereal** [ɪ'θɪəriəl], *adj.* pertaining to ether; unearthly; delicate. **etheric** [ɪ'θerɪk], *adj.* **etherify,** *v.t.* convert into ether. **etherize,** *v.t.* administer ether as anaesthetic to.

ethmoid ['eθmɔɪd] *adj.* pertaining to bones forming nasal cavity and division between nostrils; of the nasal area; *n.* such bone. **ethmoidal,** *adj.*

ethnology [eθ'nɒlədʒi] *n.* study of human races. **ethnological,** *adj.* **ethnologist,** *n.* **ethnic,** *adj.* pertaining to race; characteristic of a particular group, race or (especially peasant) culture; pagan. **ethnocentric,** *adj.* believing in the superiority of one's own race, group etc. **ethnocentrism, ethnocentricity,** *n.* **ethnodicy,** *n.* comparative study of primitive laws. **ethnogeny,** *n.* study of origin of races. **ethnogeography,** *n.* study of geographical distribution of races. **ethnography,** *n.* study of racial relations, distribution and origin; description of human races. **ethnomaniac,** *n.* fanatical nationalist.

ethos ['iːθɒs] *n.* inherent spirit; character; ethical element in literature.

ethyl ['eθl] *n.* a univalent hydrocarbon radical.

etiolate ['iːtiəleɪt] *v.t.* make pale or sickly, especially by depriving of light. **etiolated,** *adj.* **etiolation,** *n.*

etiology [ˌiːti'ɒlədʒi] *see* **aetiology.**

etui [e'twiː] *n.* needle-case; small case for toilet articles, etc.

etymology [ˌetɪ'mɒlədʒi] *n.* derivation, origin or history of a word; study of words, their meanings and origins. **etymological,** *adj.* **etymologize,** *v.t.* **etymologist,** *n.* **etymon,** *n.* word from which another is derived.

eucaine [ju'keɪn, 'juːkeɪn] *n.* synthetic alkaloid used as local anaesthetic.

euchology [ju'kɒlədʒi] *n.* prayer-book. **euchological,** *adj.*

eucrasy, eucrasia ['juːkrəsi, ju'kreɪsiə, –ʃə, –ziə, –ʒə] *n.* state of general good health.

eudemon, eudaemon [ju'diːmən] *n.* good spirit. **eudemonic** [–dɪ'mɒnɪk], *adj.* causing happiness; pertaining to eudemonism. **eudemonics,** *n.* conduct based on eudemonism; art of being happy. **eudemonism,** *n.* philosophical theory that happiness is ultimate moral good and criterion.

eudiaphoresis [juˌdaɪəfə'riːsɪs] *n.* normal perspiration.

eudiometer [ˌjuːdi'ɒmɪtə] *n.* instrument measuring and analysing gases and purity of air. **eudiometric(al)** [–'met–], *adj.* **eudiometry,** *n.*

eudipleural [ˌjuːdɪ'plʊərəl] *n.* bilaterally symmetrical.

eugenesis [ju'dʒenəsɪs] *n.* fertility between hybrids. **eugenesic** [–'nes–], **eugenetic** [–'net–], *adj.*

eugenic [ju'dʒenɪk] *adj.* pertaining to improvement of hereditary characteristics; pertaining to production of healthy offspring. **eugenics,** *n.* study of influences promoting, and means to, such improvement and production. **eugenicist,** *n.*

euhemerism [ju'hiːmərɪzm, –'he–] *n.* belief that mythological gods were deified early heroes. **euhemerist,** *n.* **euhemeristic,** *adj.*

eulogy ['juːlədʒi] *n.* laudatory speech or writing; high praise. **eulogious** [–'ləʊdʒiəs], *adj.* **eulogize,**

v.t. praise highly. **eulogism, eulogist,** *n.* **eulogistic,** *adj.*

eumenorrhea [ˌjuːmenəˈriːə] *n.* normal menstruation.

eumerism [ˈjuːmərɪzm] *n.* collection of similar parts. **eumeristic,** *adj.*

eumoirous [juːˈmɔɪrəs] *adj.* happy because innocent and good. **eumoiriety** [-ˈraɪəti], *n.*

eunomy [ˈjuːnəmi] *n.* state of orderliness and good rule.

euonymous [juːˈɒnɪməs] *adj.* appropriately named. **euonymy,** *n.*

eupathy [ˈjuːpəθi] *n.* state of contentment and moderation.

eupatrid [juːˈpætrɪd] *n.* aristocrat, especially of ancient Greece.

eupeptic [juːˈpeptɪk] *adj.* having good digestion. **eupepsia,** *n.*

euphemism [ˈjuːfəmɪzm] *n.* mild or pleasant-sounding word or phrase, especially substituted for harsher or vulgar one; such substitution. **euphemize,** *v.i.* & *t.* **euphemist,** *n.* **euphemistic,** *adj.*

euphenics [juːˈfenɪks] *n.* biological improvement of human beings after birth.

euphony [ˈjuːfəni] *n.* pleasantness or harmony of sound, especially of words. **euphonic** [-ˈfɒnɪk], **euphonious** [-ˈfəʊnɪəs], *adj.* **euphonize,** *v.t.* **euphonism,** *n.* **euphonym,** *n.* euphonious synonym.

euphoric [juːˈfɒrɪk] *n.* having feeling of elation or well-being, especially for no particular reason. **euphoria,** [-ˈfɔːriə], **euphory** [ˈjuːfəri], *n.*

euphrasy [ˈjuːfrəsi] *n.* eyebright plant.

euphuism [ˈjuːfjuɪzm] *n.* affected style of writing full of high-flown language and far-fetched metaphors, especially in imitation of Lyly's *Euphues* (1579–80). **euphuist,** *n.* writer of such style. **euphuistic,** *adj.*

eupnoea [juːpˈniːə] *n.* normal breathing.

eupraxia [juːˈpræksiə] *n.* correct or normal action. **eupractic,** *adj.*

Eurasian [juːˈreɪʒn] *n.* & *adj.* (person) of mixed European and Asiatic parentage; common to both Europe and Asia; signifying Europe and Asia regarded as a whole.

eureka [juːˈriːkə] (*Greek*) 'I have found it!'

eurhythmic, eurythmic [juːˈrɪðmɪk] *adj.* well-proportioned; harmonious. **eurhythmal,** *adj.* **eurhythmy,** *n.* **eurhythmics,** *n.* art of graceful and harmonious movement, especially such free dancing, expressive of musical accompaniment.

euripus [juːˈraɪpəs] *n.* (*pl.* **-pi**) narrow channel with swift currents.

eurychoric [ˌjuərɪˈkɒrɪk] *adj.* (of plant, animal) widely distributed. **euryhaline** [-ˈheɪlaɪn] *adj.* tolerating wide range of salinity. **euryphagous** [juːˈrɪfəgəs], *adj.* eating a wide range of prey. **eurythermal,** *adj.* able to tolerate a wide range of temperature. **eurytopic** *adj.* able to tolerate wide variations in environment.

eustatic [juːˈstætɪk] *adj.* pertaining to worldwide changes in sea-level. **eustasy,** *n.*

eutaxy [ˈjuːtæksi] *n.* orderly management. **eutaxic,** *adj.*

eutectic [juːˈtektɪk] *n.* & *adj.* (alloy) having lowest possible melting point. **eutexia,** *n.* state of having low melting point.

euthenics [juːˈθenɪks] *n.* study of improvement of human conditions of life, especially to increase efficiency. **euthenist,** *n.*

euthermic [juːˈθɜːmɪk] *adj.* producing warmth.

eutony [ˈjuːtəni] *n.* pleasantness of sound of word.

eutrophy [ˈjuːtrəfi] *n.* state of being well nourished; (of area of water) state of being over-rich in organic and mineral nutrients which promote plant life at the expense of animal life. **eutrophic** [-ˈtrɒfɪk], *adj.*; *n.* tonic. **eutrophication,** *n.* process of becoming eutrophic, especially owing to pollution.

eutropic [juːˈtrɒpɪk] *adj.* turning with sun.

evagation [ˌiːvəˈɡeɪʃn] *n.* wandering; digression; departure from etiquette.

evaginate [ɪˈvædʒɪneɪt] *v.i.* & *t.* turn inside out; protrude by so turning; *adj.* evaginated. **evagination,** *n.*

evanesce [ˌevəˈnes] *v.i.* fade away; vanish. **evanescence,** *n.* **evanescent,** *adj.*

evangel [ɪˈvændʒəl] *n.* Gospel; creed; good news; evangelist. **evangelic(al)** [ˌiːvænˈdʒelɪk, -l] *adj.* pertaining or according to Gospel; Low Church; *n.* Low Church member. **evangelism** [-ˈvæn-], *n.* missionary work; adherence to Low Church. **evangelist,** *n.* writer or preacher of Gospel; missionary; revivalist. **evangelize,** *v.t.* convert to belief in Gospel.

evection [ɪˈvekʃn] *n.* alteration in moon's orbit caused by solar attraction. **evectional,** *adj.*

eventration [ˌiːvenˈtreɪʃn] *n.* protrusion of intestines from abdomen; dropped state of abdomen; evisceration.

everglade [ˈevəɡleɪd] (*American*) *n.* grassy, islanded swamp, especially of Florida.

evert [ɪˈvɜːt] *v.t.* turn inside out; turn outwards. **eversion,** *n.* **evertor,** *n.* muscle turning part outward.

eviscerate [ɪˈvɪsəreɪt] *v.t.* disembowel; divest of strength and force. **evisceration,** *n.*

evitable [ˈevɪtəbl] *adj.* avoidable. **evitation,** *n.* avoidance. **evite,** *v.t.* avoid.

evulgate [ɪˈvʌlɡeɪt] *v.t.* make widely known. **evulgation,** *n.*

evulsion [ɪˈvʌlʃn] *n.* act of uprooting or tearing out. **evulsive,** *adj.*

exallotriote [ˌeksəˈlɒtriəʊt] *adj.* foreign.

exanthema [ˌeksænˈθiːmə] *n.* (*pl.* **-ta**) (disease marked by) eruptions or rash, as measles. **exanthematic** [-θɪˈmætɪk], **exanthematous** [-ˈθemətəs], *adj.*

exarch [ˈeksɑːk] *n.* viceroy; travelling bishop of E Church. **exarchal,** *adj.* **exarchate,** *n.* office or jurisdiction of exarch.

exarticulate [ˌeksɑːˈtɪkjuleɪt] *v.t.* dislocate; cut off at joint. **exarticulation,** *n.*

exaugurate [ɪɡˈzɔːɡjureɪt] *v.t.* remove blessing from; profane. **exauguration,** *n.*

excalation [ˌekskəˈleɪʃn] *n.* omission or loss of part or unit from series.

ex cathedra [ˌeks kəˈθiːdrə] (*Latin*) *adj.* 'from the chair'; authoritatively; *Roman Catholic,* (of the Pope) pronouncing infallibly. **excathedral,** *adj.* authoritative.

excaudate [eksˈkɔːdeɪt] *adj.* tailless.

excelsior [ekˈselsiɔː] *adv.* onwards and upwards. *n. American,* wood shavings used as packing, stuffing, litter etc.

excise [ɪk'saɪz] *n. & v.t.* cut out. **excision** [–'sɪʒn], *n.* act of cutting out.

exclave ['ekskleɪv] *n.* part of a country surrounded by foreign territory.

exclosure [ɪk'skləʊʒə] *n.* area fenced to keep out unwanted animals.

excogitate [eks'kɒdʒɪteɪt] *v.t.* think up, devise; think out. **excogitation**, *n.* **excogitative**, *adj.*

excoriate [ɪk'skɔːrɪeɪt] *v.t.* remove skin from; flay; criticize savagely. **excoriation**, *n.*

excrement ['ekskrɪmənt] *n.* waste matter discharged from body. **excremental**, **excrementary**, **excrementitious**, *adj.*

excrescent [ɪk'skresnt] *adj.* growing out from main body; redundant. **excrescential**, *adj.* **excrescence**, *n.* such thing.

excrete [ɪk'skriːt] *v.t.* discharge from body. **excreta**, *n.pl.* excrements. **excretal**, *adj.* **excretion**, *n.* **excretionary**, **excretive**, **excretory**, *adj.*

exculpate ['ekskʌlpeɪt] *v.t.* clear of blame. **exculpation**, *n.* **exculpatory**, *adj.*

excursus [ek'skɜːsəs] *n.* lengthy discussion, especially appended to book; digression. **excursive**, *adj.* digressive, rambling.

exeat ['eksiæt] (*Latin*) 'let him go out'; permission to be absent or late.

execrate ['eksɪkreɪt] *v.t.* curse; loathe. **execrable**, *adj.* loathsome. **execration**, *n.* **execrative**, **execratory**, *adj.*

executant [ɪg'zekjʊtənt] *n.* performer. **executor** [ɪg'zekjuːtə], *n.* (*fem.* **executrix**) person carrying out provisions of will.

exegesis [,eksɪ'dʒiːsɪs] *n.* explanation, especially of Bible. **exegete**, *n.* expert in this. **exegetic(al)** [–'dʒet–], *adj.* **exegetics**, *n.* science of Biblical exegesis.

exemplum [ɪg'zempləm] (*Latin*) *n.* (*pl.* **–la**) example; moral anecdote. **exempli gratia** [–pli 'graːtiɑː, –'greɪʃiə], 'for sake of example'; for example (*abbr.* **e.g.**).

exenterate [ek'sentəreɪt] *v.t.* remove internal organ; disembowel.

exequatur [,eksɪ'kweɪtə] *n.* document recognizing foreign consular officer, or permitting Roman Catholic bishops to rule their church and publish papal bulls.

exequies ['eksɪkwɪz] *n. pl.* funeral ceremony. **exequial** [ek'siːkwɪəl], *adj.*

exercitor (maris) [ɪg'zɜːsɪtə, 'mærɪs, 'meə–] *n.* person having right to ship's profits. **exercitorial** [–'tɔːriəl], *adj.*

exergue [ek'sɜːg, 'eksɜːg] *n.* space at base of figure on coin containing date. **exergual** [ek'sɜːgl], *adj.*

exeunt ['eksɪʌnt, –eɪʊnt] (*Latin*) 'they go out'. **exeunt omnes** [–'ɒmneɪz, –iːz] 'all go out'.

exfoliate [eks'fəʊlɪeɪt] *v.i. & t.* flake or peel off; develop or unfold like leaves. **exfoliation**, *n.* **exfoliative**, *adj.*

ex gratia [eks 'greɪʃə, –iə] (*Latin*) 'by favour'; *Law.* implying the absence of legal obligation.

exheredate [eks'herɪdeɪt] *v.t.* disinherit. **exheredation**, *n.*

exigent ['eksɪdʒənt] *adj.* exacting; urgent. **exigible**, *adj.* chargeable. **exigence**, **exigency**, *n.* urgent need or requirement; necessary condition.

exiguous [ɪg'zɪgjuəs] *adj.* sparse; slender. **exiguity**,

n.

eximious [eg'zɪmiəs] *adj.* select; excellent.

existential [,egzɪ'stenʃl] *adj.* pertaining to existence. **existentialism**, *n.* philosophical theory stressing need for the individual to be intensely aware of his own existence and freedom, and of his own responsibility for the nature of his existence. **existentialist**, *n. & adj.*

ex jure [eks 'dʒʊəri, –'juːəreɪ] (*Latin*) 'by right'.

ex libris [eks 'liːbrɪs] (*Latin*) 'from the books (of)'; inscription on book-plate; a book-plate.

exobiology [,eksəʊbaɪ'ɒlədʒi] *n.* scientific study of the possibility of life outside the Earth. **exobiologist**, *n.*

exocentric [,eksəʊ'sentrɪk] *adj.* (of a phrase) having a different grammatical function from any of its constituent words.

exocrine ['eksəkraɪn, –ɪn] *adj.* secreting externally.

exoculate [eks'ɒkjuleɪt] *v.t.* blind. **exoculation**, *n.*

exodontia [,eksə'dɒnʃə, –iə] *n.* teeth extraction. **exodontist**, *n.*

exodromy [ek'sɒdrəmi] *n.* stabilizing movement of exchange. **exodromic** [–'drɒmɪk], *adj.*

ex officio [eks ə'fɪʃiəʊ] (*Latin*) 'from the office'; by virtue of one's office.

exogamy [ek'sɒgəmi] *n.* marriage to person not of same tribe, family, etc., only. **exogamic** [–'gæmɪk], **exogamous**, *adj.*

exogenous [ek'sɒdʒənəs] *adj.* growing or originating from outside, or due to external factors. **exogenetic** [–'netɪk], **exogenic** [–'dʒenɪk], *adj.*

exon ['eksɒn] *n.* one of four officers commanding the Yeomen of the Guard.

exopathic [,eksə'pæθɪk] *adj. Medicine,* due to external causes.

exophagy [ek'sɒfədʒi] *n.* cannibalism outside tribe or family. **exophagous** [–gəs], *adj.*

exophthalmic [,eksɒf'θælmɪk] *adj.* pertaining to or marked by protrusion of eyeball. **exophthalmos, exophthalmus**, *n.* such condition.

exorcize ['eksɔːsaɪz] *v.t.* expel (evil spirit) by rites or use of holy words. **exorcism**, *n.* **exorcist**, *n.*; *Roman Catholic*, member of a minor order.

exordium [ek'sɔːdiəm] *n.* (*pl.* **–ia**) opening portion of speech or writing. **exordial**, *adj.*

exoskeleton [,eksəʊ'skelɪtən] *n.* external skeleton, *e.g.* shell.

exosmosis [,eksɒz'məʊsɪs] *n.* osmosis outwards, especially from a cell or organism into its surrounding medium.

exosphere ['eksəʊsfɪə] *n.* outermost layer of the atmosphere.

exoteric [,eksə'terɪk] *adj.* popular; capable of being understood by uninitiated; *n.* uninitiated person. **exotericism** [–sɪzm], *n.*

exothermic [,eksəʊ'θɜːmɪk] *adj.* marked by production of heat. **exothermal**, **exothermous**, *adj.*

exotic [ɪg'zɒtɪk] *adj.* of foreign origin; attractively or bizarrely unusual; *n.* such plant.

exotropia [,eksə'trəʊpiə] *n.* outward squint.

ex parte [eks 'paːti] (*Latin*) 'from a side'; on or for one side only.

expatiate [ek'speɪʃieɪt] *v.i.* speak or write at length. **expatiation**, *n.* **expatiatory**, *adj.*

expatriate [eks'pætrieɪt, –'peɪ–] *v.t.* exile; [–iət] *adj.* resident abroad; exiled; *n.* such person. **expatriation**, *n.*

expedite ['ekspədaɪt] *v.t.* hasten; carry through quickly and efficiently. **expeditious** [–'dɪʃəs], *adj.* prompt (and efficient).

expergefacient [ek,spɜːdʒɪ'feɪʃnt] *adj.* awakening. **expergefaction** [–'fækʃn], *n.*

expiscate ['ekspɪskeɪt, ek'spɪs–] *v.t.* fish or search out. **expiscation, expiscator,** *n.* **expiscatory,** *adj.*

expletive [ɪk'spliːtɪv] *n.* & *adj.* (word) added to expand or fill up; swear-word. **expletory** ['eks–], *adj.*

explicandum [,eksplɪ'kændəm] *n.* (*pl.* **–da**) *Philosophy,* thing, e.g. term, to be explained. **explicans,** *n.* thing or part that explains or gives the meaning.

explication de texte [,eksplɪ,kæsjɒn də 'tekst] (*French*) *n.* (*pl.* **explications de texte**) piece of literary-critical close analysis.

exposé [ek'spəʊzeɪ] (*French*) *n.* exposure; full statement or explanation.

ex post facto [,eks pəʊst 'fæktəʊ] (*Latin*) 'from that which is done afterwards'; by virtue of a thing done later; retrospective.

exprobrate ['eksprəbreɪt] *v.t. archaic,* rebuke; reproach. **exprobration,** *n.*

expromissor [,eksprə'mɪsə] *n.* person relieving another of debt by taking it upon himself. **expromission,** *n.*

expropriate [ɪk'sprəʊprɪeɪt, ek–] *v.t.* deprive of; transfer ownership of. **expropriation, expropriator,** *n.*

expugnable [ek'spjuːnəbl, –'spʌg–] *adj.* capable of being captured by storm.

expunge [ɪk'spʌndʒ] *v.t.* blot, cross, rub or wipe out. **expunction,** *n.*

expurgate ['ekspəgeɪt] *v.t.* remove objectionable portions from; purify. **expurgation, expurgator,** *n.* **expurgatorial, expurgatory,** *adj.*

exsanguine [eks'sæŋgwɪn] *adj.* lacking blood. **exsanguinate,** *v.t.* drain blood from. **exsanguineous** [–'gwɪn–], **exsanguinious, exsanguinous** [–'sæŋ–], *adj.*

exscind [ek'sɪnd] *v.t.* cut out; uproot.

exsert [ek'sɜːt] *v.t.* thrust out. **exserted,** *adj.* protruding.

exsiccate ['eksɪkeɪt] *v.t.* desiccate. **exsiccation, exsiccator,** *n.* **exsiccative,** *adj.*

exstrophy ['ekstrəfi] *n. Medicine,* having organ, especially bladder, turned inside out.

exsuccous [eks'sʌkəs] *adj.* lacking sap.

exsufflate [eks'sʌfleɪt] *v.t.* blow away. **exsufflation,** *n.* blowing out; forced breathing.

extant [,ek'stænt, 'ekstənt] *adj.* existing.

extensor [ɪk'stensə, –ɔː] *n.* muscle extending limb.

extenuate [ɪk'stenjueɪt] *v.t.* reduce; weaken; excuse. **extenuation, extenuator,** *n.* **extenuative, extenuatory,** *adj.*

exterritorial [,eksterɪ'tɔːrɪəl] *adj.* outside territorial boundaries; beyond territorial jurisdiction. **exterritorialize,** *v.t.* **exterritoriality,** *n.* exemption from local laws.

extirpate ['ekstɜːpeɪt] *v.t.* destroy; banish; uproot. **extirpation, extirpator,** *n.* **extirpative, extirpatory,** *adj.*

extragalactic [,ekstrəgə'læktɪk] *adj.* beyond or outside our galaxy.

extramundane [,ekstrə'mʌndeɪn] *adj.* outside the known world or universe.

extramural [,ekstrə'mjuərəl] *adj.* outside the walls or fortifications; outside, but under the aegis of, a university or other institution.

extrasensory [,ekstrə'sensəri] *adj.* beyond the senses. **extrasensory perception,** unexplained phenomena such as clairvoyance, telepathy, etc., which are outside or beyond the scope of the senses.

extraterritorial [,ekstrəterɪ'tɔːrɪəl] *adj.* exterritorial. **extraterritoriality,** *n.*

extravasate [ek'strævəseɪt] *v.i.* & *t.* flow or filter out; expel from a vessel, especially blood; pour out; *n.* such fluid. **extravasation,** *n.*

extrinsic [eks'trɪnsɪk] *adj.* external; incidental.

extrorse [ek'strɔːs, 'ekstrɔːs] *adj.* facing away or out.

extrospection [,ekstrə'spekʃn] *n.* habitual interest in or examination of matters outside oneself. **extrospective,** *adj.*

exuviae [ɪg'zjuːviiː, eg–, –'zuː–] *n. pl.* cast-off skin, etc., of animal. **exuviable, exuvial,** *adj.* **exuviate,** *v.i.* & *t.* slough; shed.

ex-voto [eks 'vəʊtəʊ] *n.* & *adj.* votive (offering).

eyas ['aɪəs] *n.* unfledged bird, especially falcon.

eyot [eɪt] *n.* ait.

F

fabaceous [fə'beɪʃəs] *adj.* like a bean.
Fabian ['feɪbiən] *adj.* pertaining to Q. Fabius Maximus, Roman general, and his cautious tactics and avoidance of open battle. **Fabian Society**, society advocating a gradual approach to socialism.
fabiform ['feɪbɪfɔːm] *adj.* bean-shaped.
fabulist ['fæbjʊlɪst] *n.* recounter of fables; liar.
facetiae [fə'siːʃiiː] *n. pl.* humorous remarks or writings; pornographic books. **facetiation**, *n.* making such remark, etc.
facia ['feɪʃə] *n.* fascia.
facies ['feɪʃiiːz] *n. Medicine*, facial expression, as symptom; general aspect or appearance.
facile princeps [,fækɪleɪ 'prɪŋkeps, ,fæsɪli 'prɪnseps] (*Latin*) 'easily the first'. **facilis descensus Averno** or **Averni**, 'the road to evil, or Hell, is easy'.
facinorous [fə'sɪnərəs] *adj.* extremely wicked.
factice ['fæktɪs] *n.* vulcanized oil, used as substitute for rubber.
faction ['fækʃn] *n.* dissident or self-seeking group; clique; dissension. **factional, factious**, *adj.*
factitious [fæk'tɪʃəs] *adj.* artificial; spurious.
factitive ['fæktɪtɪv] *adj. Grammar*, signifying making something to be; applied to complementary object of such verb.
factoid ['fæktɔɪd] *n. & adj.* (assumption, speculation, etc.) presented, accepted or considered as a fact.
factotum [fæk'təʊtəm] *n.* servant of all work; general assistant. **Johannes Factotum**, Jack-of-all-trades.
faculty ['fæklti] *n.* talent; capability; branch of study and its students in university; governing body of university or college; body of teachers and administrators in a university; *Ecclesiastical*, permission to add to or alter fabric of church. **facultative**, *adj.* granting permission; optional; *Biology*, able to exist in different forms and conditions.
faeces ['fiːsiːz] *n. pl.* solid excrement; dregs. **faecal** ['fiːkl], *adj.* **faecaloid**, *adj.*
faex [fiːks] (*Latin*) *n.* dregs. **faex populi**, the rabble.
fagaceous [fə'geɪʃəs] *adj.* belonging to beech family of trees.
fagottist [fə'gɒtɪst] *n.* bassoon player.
faience [faɪ'ɒns] *n.* glazed decorative earthenware.
fainéant ['feɪniənt, –neɪɒn] *n. & adj.* idle (person). **fainéance, fainéancy** ['feɪniəns, –i], *n.*
fait accompli [,feɪt ə'kɒmpli, ,fet–, –'kʌ–] (*French*) 'accomplished deed'; thing done or completed, about which it is too late to argue.

fakir ['feɪkɪə] (*Indian*) *n.* ascetic or mendicant.
Falasha [fə'læʃə] *n.* member of black Jewish tribe of Ethiopia.
falcate ['fælkeɪt] *adj.* sickle-shaped.
falchion ['fɔːltʃən] *n.* broad curved sword.
falciform ['fælsɪfɔːm] *adj.* falcate. **falcular, falculate**, *adj.*
falderal, falderol ['fældəræl, –ɒl] *n.* trifle, gewgaw.
faldstool ['fɔːldstuːl] *n.* prayer desk; bishop's round armless chair.
Fallopian [fə'ləʊpiən] *adj.* discovered by Fallopius, 10th-century Italian physician. **Fallopian tube**, tube conveying egg from ovary to womb.
falsidical [fɔːl'sɪdɪkl] *adj.* giving false impression.
famulus ['fæmjʊləs] *n.* (*pl.* **–li**) attendant to a sorcerer, magician.
fanfaronade [,fænfærə'neɪd] *n.* boasting; bluster; blast on trumpets.
fanion ['fænjɒn] (*French*) *n.* small marking flag.
fan-tan ['fæntæn] (*Chinese*) *n.* gambling game in which bets are laid on number of objects (as beans) remaining after a known number has been removed.
fantassin ['fæntəsɪn, –æn] (*French*) *n.* infantryman.
fantoccini [,fæntə'tʃiːni] (*Italian*) *n. pl.* marionettes.
farad ['færəd, –æd] *n.* unit of electrical capacity: capacity of condenser, charged with one coulomb, giving potential difference of one volt. **faradaic, faradic**, *adj.* pertaining to inductive current. **faradism** *n.* medical application of induced electrical currents.
farceur [fɑː'sɜː] (*French*) *n.* joker.
farcy ['fɑːsi] *n.* disease affecting lymphatic glands of horses and cattle.
farina [fə'riːnə] *n.* flour or meal of cereals, nuts, etc. **farinaceous** [–ɪ'neɪʃəs], *adj.* like or consisting of flour. **farinose**, *adj.* like or yielding flour; mealy.
farouche [fə'ruːʃ, fæ–] (*French*) *adj.* wild; gauche; shy.
farrier ['færiə] *n.* horse-shoeing smith. **farriery**, *n.* art or place of shoeing horses.
farrow ['færəʊ] *v.i. & t.* give birth (of pigs); *n.* act of giving birth to pigs; litter.
farthingale ['fɑːðɪŋgeɪl] *n.* skirt or petticoat over hoops.
fasces ['fæsiːz] *n.* bundle of rods with an axe carried before ancient Roman magistrates, symbolizing authority.
fascia ['feɪʃə, 'fæ–] *n.* (*pl.* **–ae**) band of colour; band or layer of connective tissue; name-board over shop; dashboard. **fasciate, fasciated** *adj.* tied

round with a band or fillet; striped. **fasciation** *n.*

fascicle ['fæsɪkl] *n.* small bundle; part of book published separately; collection of written or printed sheets.

fascine [fæ'siːn, fə–] *n.* bundle of sticks used in building fortifications.

fasti ['fæstaɪ, –i] (*Latin*) *n. pl.* record; register; calendars of ancient Rome.

fastidious [fæ'stɪdɪəs] *adj.* very hard to please; particular about details; fussy and squeamish.

fastigate ['fæstɪgeɪt] *adj.* pointed. **fastigiate** [fæ'stɪdʒɪət], *adj.* narrowing at apex, **fastigium** [fæ'stɪdʒɪəm], *n.* (*pl.* **–gia**) roof; top; gable.

fastuous ['fæstjuəs] *adj.* arrogant; showy.

fata morgana [,fɑːtə mɔː'gɑːnə] *n.* mirage.

fatidic [feɪ'tɪdɪk, fə–] *adj.* pertaining to prophecy or fortune-telling. **fatidical**, *adj.* having fatidic powers.

fatwa ['fætwɑː, fʌ'twɑː] *n.* proscription pronounced by Islamic religious leader.

faucet ['fɔːsɪt] *n. American,* water tap.

faucial ['fɔːsɪəl, –ʃɪ] *adj.* pertaining to fauces. **faucitis**, *n.* inflammation of fauces.

fauna ['fɔːnə] *n.* (*pl.* **–ae**) animal life of region, period, etc. **faunal**, *adj.* **faunist**, *n.* expert on fauna. **faunology**, *n.* study of geographical distribution of animals.

faute de mieux [,fəut də 'mjɜː] (*French*) 'for want of better'.

fauteuil [fəu'tɜːi] (*French*) 'armchair'; stall seat in theatre; membership of French Academy.

faux pas [,fəu 'pɑː] (*French*) 'false step'; social solecism; embarrassing action.

faveolate [fə'viːəleɪt] *adj.* honey-combed. **faviform** ['feɪ–], *adj.* honeycomb-like.

favonian [fə'vəunɪən] *adj.* pertaining to Favonius, in Roman mythology the west wind; gentle; favourable.

favose ['feɪvəus] *adj.* faviform.

favus ['feɪvəs] *n.* contagious parasitic skin disease.

fealty ['fiːəlti] *n.* loyalty; duty, especially of vassal to feudal lord.

febricant ['febrɪkənt] *adj.* causing fever. **febricity**, *n.* feverishness. **febrific**, *adj.* feverish; febricant.

febrifuge ['febrɪfjuːdʒ] *n. & adj.* (drug) allaying fever. **febrifugal** [fe'brɪfjugl, ,febrɪ'fjuːgl], *adj.*

febrile ['fiːbraɪl, 'fe–] *adj.* characterized by or symptomatic of fever; feverish. **febrility** [fɪ'brɪləti], *n.*

fecit ['feɪkɪt, 'fiːsɪt] (*Latin*) 'made (it)'.

feculent ['fekjulənt] *adj.* containing or covered with filth; faecal; turbid. **feculence**, *n.*

fecund ['fekənd, 'fiː–] *adj.* fertile. **fecundate**, *v.t.* make fertile. **fecundity** [fɪ'kʌndəti], *n.*

fedora [fɪ'dɔːrə] (*American*) *n.* man's soft felt hat with curled brim; trilby.

fee [fiː] *n. Law,* heritable estate in land. **fee simple,** fee heritable without restrictions as to heirs; unconditional use. **fee tail,** entailed fee.

feedback ['fiːdbæk] *n.* return of a fraction of the energy output to the energy input in a transmission system; an arrangement by which a variation in output modifies the generation of energy; information or comments returned by users, respondents, etc.

feldspar ['feldspɑː] *n.* several minerals forming part of all crystalline rocks and decomposing into clay or china clay.

felicide ['fiːlɪsaɪd] *n.* killing of cat.

felicity [fə'lɪsəti] *n.* happiness; well-chosen word or phrase. **felicific** [,fiːlɪ'sɪfɪk], *adj.* making happy. **felicitate**, *v.t.* congratulate; make happy. **felicitation**, *n.* **felicitous**, *adj.* well chosen; apt.

feliform ['fiːlɪfɔːm] *adj.* cat-like. **feline**, *adj.*

felinophile [fɪ'laɪnəfaɪl] *n.* lover of cats. **felinophobe**, *n.* hater of cats.

fellah ['felə] *n.* (*pl.* **–een**) Egyptian peasant.

felloe, felly ['feləu, –li] *n.* wheel's rim or portion of it.

felo de se [,fiːləu di 'siː, ,fe–, –'seɪ] *n.* (*pl.* **felones ...**) self-murder or self-murderer.

felon ['felən] *n.* criminal. **felonious** [fə'ləunɪəs], *adj.* **felony**, *n.* serious crime.

felucca [fe'lʌkə, fə–] *n.* fast three-masted Mediterranean vessel, with lateen sails.

feme [fem] *n. Law,* woman. **feme covert** [–'kʌvət], married woman. **feme sole,** unmarried woman or widow.

femicide ['femɪsaɪd] *n.* killing or killer of woman.

femme [fæm] (*French*) *n.* woman. **femme fatale** [–fə'tɑːl], 'fatal woman'; woman exercising fatal fascination, or seemingly dogged by fate. **femme savante** [–'sævɒnt], learned woman; bluestocking.

femto- ['femtəu–] *prefix* of measurement meaning one thousand-million-millionth (10^{15}). (*abbr.* **f.**)

femur ['fiːmə] *n.* thigh bone; thigh. **femoral** ['fem–], *adj.*

fenestral [fə'nestrəl] *adj.* pertaining to windows; *n.* window, especially with paper, etc., instead of glass. **fenestrate**, *adj.* having many openings or windows. **fenestration**, *n.* state of being fenestrate; disposition of windows.

fennec ['fenek] *n.* small fox of Africa.

feoff [fiːf, fef] *n.* heritable land granted by feudal lord; lord's right in such land. **feoffee**, *n.* person to whom feoff is granted. **feoffor, feoffer**, *n.* grantor of feoff. **feoffment**, *n.* grant of feoff.

feracious [fə'reɪʃəs] *adj.* fecund. **feracity**, *n.*

feral ['ferəl, 'fɪə–] *adj.* wild; untamed; savage; (of animal species) living in the wild, especially after previously being domesticated; funereal. **ferae**, *n. pl.* carnivorous animals. **ferae naturae**, (*Latin*) 'of a wild nature'; animals living in the wild.

fer-de-lance [,feədə'lɑːns] *n.* large and poisonous snake of S and Central America.

feretory ['ferɪtəri] *n.* shrine; chapel for bier; bier.

feria ['fɪərɪə] *n.* (*pl.* **–ae**) feast day; holiday; *Ecclesiastical,* day neither feast nor fast. **ferial**, *adj.*

ferine ['fɪəraɪn] *adj.* feral.

feringhee, feringhi [fe'rɪŋgi] (*Indian*) *n.* European, especially Portuguese, born in India.

ferity ['ferəti] *n.* wild state; barbarism.

ferreous ['ferɪəs] *adj.* containing, like or pertaining to iron.

ferric, ferrous ['ferɪk, –əs] *adj.* pertaining to or containing iron. **ferriferous**, *adj.* yielding iron. **ferromagnetic**, *adj.* highly magnetic.

ferruginous [fe'ruːdʒɪnəs] *adj.* ferreous; pertaining to or coloured like iron rust. **ferruginate**, *v.t.* stain with iron compound.

ferule ['feruːl] *n.* rod or flat ruler for punishment. **ferulaceous**, *adj.* reed-like.

fervescent [fə'vesnt] *adj.* becoming feverish. **fervescence**, *n.*

Fescennine ['fesənaɪn] *adj.* pertaining to poetry and inhabitants of ancient Fescinnia, Italy; indecent; scurrilous.

fescue ['feskjuː] *n.* stick used by teacher as pointer; several tall kinds of grass.

fess, fesse [fes] *n.* horizontal band across a shield.

festina lente [fe,stiːnə 'lenteɪ, –,staɪ–, –ti] (*Latin*) 'make haste slowly'.

festination [,festɪ'neɪʃn] *n.* haste; hurrying walk, symptom of some nervous diseases.

Festschrift ['festʃrɪft] (*German*) *n.* collection of essays or articles published in honour of a distinguished scholar.

festucine ['festjusaɪn] *adj.* straw-coloured.

fête champêtre [,fet ʃɒm'petr, ,feɪt–] (*French*) 'country feast'; outdoor entertainment. **fête galante** [–'gælɒnt], (painting of) a scene of courtly romance in a pastoral setting.

fetial ['fiːʃl] *adj.* pertaining to declaration of war and peace; heraldic.

fetid ['fetɪd, 'fiː–] *adj.* stinking.

fetlock ['fetlɒk] *n.* tuft of hair on horse's leg immediately above hoof; part of leg bearing it.

fetor ['fiːtə, –ɔː] *n.* stench.

feudal ['fjuːdl] *adj.* pertaining to feoff or fee; pertaining to medieval social system of overlords and vassals. **feudatory**, *n. & adj.* (vassal) subject to feudal lord; (ruler) subject to overlord. **feudalism**, *n.* feudal system. **feudalist**, *n.* **feudalistic**, *adj.*

feu de joie [,fɜːdə'ʒwɑː] (*French*) 'fire of joy'; firing of guns as symbol of joy; bonfire.

feuilleton ['fɜːɪtɒn] (*French*) *n.* feature and criticism page of newspaper; instalment of serial story. **feuilletonist**, *n.* writer of matter in feuilleton or of serial story.

fiacre [fiˈɑːkr] (*French*) *n.* small hackney carriage.

fiat ['fiːæt, 'faɪ] *n.* decree; command; decision. **fiat lux**, (*Latin*), 'let there be light'.

fibrid ['faɪbrɪd] *n.* one of a type of synthetic fibrous particles used in bonding.

fibrin ['faɪbrɪn] *n.* fibrous protein in blood formed in clotting. **fibrination**, *n.* condition of having excessive fibrin in blood. **fibrinogen**, *n.* substance in blood producing fibrin. **fibrinosis**, *n.* disease marked by fibrination.

fibroid ['faɪbrɔɪd] *adj.* of or like fibre; *n.* non-malignant fibrous tumour.

fibroma [faɪ'brəʊmə] *n.* (*pl.* **–ta**) benign fibrous tumour. **fibromatous**, *adj.*

fibrosis [faɪ'brəʊsɪs] *n.* condition of excessive fibrous formation in organ. **fibrotic** [faɪ'brɒtɪk], *adj.*, **fibrositis** [,faɪbrə'saɪtɪs], *n.* inflammatory excess of fibrous tissue growth.

fibula ['fɪbjʊlə] *n.* (*pl.* **–ae**) outer, smaller bone of lower leg. **fibular**, *adj.*

fichu ['fiːʃuː, 'fɪ–] *n.* light shawl for shoulders.

ficiform ['fɪsɪfɔːm] *adj.* fig-shaped. **ficoid** ['faɪkɔɪd], *adj.* fig-like.

fictile ['fɪktaɪl] *adj.* pertaining to pottery; moulded; able to be moulded into shape or new shape. **fictility**, *n.*

fictive ['fɪktɪv] *adj.* imaginative; imaginary.

fideism ['fiːdeɪɪzm, 'faɪdi–] *n.* reliance on faith alone.

fidicinal [fɪ'dɪsɪnl] *adj.* pertaining to stringed musical instrument.

fiducial [fɪ'djuːʃl] *adj.* based on faith or trust; used as a standard of reference or measurement. **fiduciary**, *n. & adj.* (person) holding in trust; requiring trust; based on confidence, especially of public. **fiduciary issue**, currency issued beyond the amount backed by gold.

fief [fiːf] *n.* feoff; that which one rules.

figuline ['fɪgjulaɪn] *adj.* fictile; *n.* clay vessel, object. **figulate**, *adj.* made of clay; fictile.

figurant ['fɪgərənt, –rɒn] *n.* (*fem.* **figurante** [–'rɒnt]) ballet dancer who dances only with group; minor character in play.

figurate ['fɪgərət] *adj.* having a definite shape or form; *Music*, florid.

figurine ['fɪgəriːn, ,fɪgə'riːn] *n.* statuette.

filar ['faɪlə] *adj.* pertaining to thread; having threads across eye-piece. **filarial, filarian, filarious** [–'leə–], *adj.* pertaining or due to thread-worms. **filariasis** [–'raɪəsɪs], *n.* infestation with thread-worms. **filariform** [–'lær–], *adj.* thread-like.

filature ['fɪlətʃə] *n.* drawing out or reeling of silk threads; apparatus or factory for doing this.

filibeg ['fɪlɪbeg] (*Scottish*) *n.* kilt.

filibuster ['fɪlɪbʌstə] *n.* irregular soldier; freebooter; *American*, making of interminable obstructive speech; such speech or speaker; *v.i.* make such speech.

filicide ['fɪlɪsaɪd] *n.* killing or killer of own child.

filiciform [fɪ'lɪsɪfɔːm] *adj.* fern- or frond-shaped. **filicoid** ['fɪlɪkɔɪd], *adj.* fern-like.

filiferous [fɪ'lɪfərəs] *adj.* bearing threads. **filiform**, *adj.* thread-like. **filigerous**, *adj.* flagellate. **filipendulous**, *adj.* hanging by a thread.

filoselle ['fɪləsel] *n.* floss-like silk.

fils [fiːs] (*French*) *n.* son.

fimbrial ['fɪmbrɪəl] *adj.* pertaining to or having a fringe. **fimbriate**, *adj.* fringed; *v.t.* fringe; hem. **fimbriation**, *n.* **fimbricate**, *adj.* fringed. **fimbrillate**, *adj.* having small fringe.

fimetic [fɪ'metɪk] *adj.* pertaining to dung. **fimicolous**, *adj.* living in dung.

finagle [fɪ'neɪgl] *v.i. & t.* cheat, trick; *v.t.* obtain by trickery.

fin de siècle [,fæn də si'eklə] (*French*) 'end of century', especially of 19th century; decadent.

fingent ['fɪndʒənt] *adj.* moulding.

finial ['fɪniəl] *adj.* ornament at apex of gable, etc.; pinnacle.

firkin ['fɜːkɪn] *n.* small cask; measure of capacity: nine gallons.

firman ['fɜːmən, fə'mɑːn] *n.* Oriental ruler's edict, authorisation, etc.

fiscal ['fɪskl] *adj.* pertaining to public revenue. **fiscality**, *n.* avarice.

fission ['fɪʃn] *n.* *Physics*, splitting, especially of atomic nuclei, accompanied by release of immense energies. **fissionable**, *adj.* capable of being split, especially of unstable minerals used in atomic fission. **fissile**, *adj.* easily split; capable of nuclear fission. **fissiparous**, *adj.* reproducing by splitting into parts. **fissiped**, *adj.* having toes separated.

fistula ['fɪstjʊlə] *n.* pipe; very deep ulcer; pipe-like passage from ulcer to surface or between hollow organs. **fistuliform**, *adj.* like a fistula or pipe. **fistulous, fistular**, *adj.*

fitch [fɪtʃ] *n*. hair of polecat; brush of such hair. **fitchew** ['fɪtʃuː], *n*. polecat.

fixation [fɪk'seɪʃn] *n*. *Psychology*, establishment in childhood of mental attitude which persists through life; *popularly*, obsession, established habit.

fizgig ['fɪzgɪg] *n*. frivolous or coquettish girl.

flabellate [flə'belət, –eɪt] *adj*. fan-shaped. **flabelliform**, *adj*. **flabellation**, *n*. use of fan to cool.

flaccid ['flæksɪd, 'flæs–] *adj*. flabby. **flaccidity**, *n*.

flagellate ['flædʒəleɪt] *v.t*. whip; flog; *adj*. whip-shaped; having whip-like outgrowths. **flagellant**, *n. & adj*. (person) whipping himself as religious practice; lashing. **flagellum**, *n*. (*pl*. –la) whip-like outgrowth; runner of plant. **flagellation, flagellator**, *n*. **flagellatory**, *adj*.

flageolet [ˌflædʒə'let] *n*. small flute-like musical instrument.

flagitate ['flædʒɪteɪt] *v.t*. demand repeatedly. **flagitation**, *n*.

flagitious [flə'dʒɪʃəs] *adj*. heinous; villainous.

flagrante delicto [flə,grænti dɪ'lɪktəʊ] (*Latin*) 'the crime being still blazing'; in the act of committing crime.

flambé ['flɒmbeɪ] *adj*. served in flaming brandy.

flambeau ['flæmbəʊ] *n*. (*pl*. –beaux) burning torch.

flamen ['fleɪmen] *n*. pagan priest. **flamineous**, *adj*. pertaining to flamen. **flamenical**, *adj*.

flammeous ['flæmɪəs] *adj*. flame-coloured. **flammulated**, *adj*. ruddy. **flammulation**, *n*. flame-coloured or flame-shaped marking.

flâneur [flɑː'nɜː] (*French*) *n*. idler; trifler.

flatulent ['flætjʊlənt] *adj*. pertaining to or causing generation of gas in digestive tract; inflated; pretentious. **flatulence, flatulency**, *n*. **flatus** ['fleɪtəs], *n*. gas in intestines or stomach.

flautist ['flɔːtɪst] *n*. flute-player.

flavedo [flə'viːdəʊ] *n*. yellowness, especially of plants. **flavescent**, *adj*. turning yellow. **flavic(ant)** ['fleɪ–, 'flæ–], *adj*. yellow; yellowish. **flavid** ['fleɪ–], *adj*. golden yellow.

flense, flench [flens, flenz, flentʃ] *v.t*. cut up or skin, especially whale or seal.

fletcher ['fletʃə] *n*. arrow-maker.

fleurette [flɜː'ret] *n*. ornament in the shape of a small flower.

flews [fluːz] *n. pl*. pendulous lips; chops.

flexor ['fleksə, –ɔː] *n*. muscle bending limb. **flexion, flexure**, *n*. act or state of bending or being bent. **flexuose, flexuous**, *adj*. sinuous; zigzag.

floccose ['flɒkəʊs] *adj*. woolly.

flocculate ['flɒkjuleɪt] *v.i. & t*. collect into lumps or tufts; *adj*. having hairy tufts. **flocculent**, *adj*. woolly; consisting of soft flakes; tufted. **flocculence**, *n*. **flocculus**, *n*. (*pl*. –li) flake; small tuft. **flocculation**, *n*.

flora ['flɔːrə] *n*. (*pl*. –ae) plant life of region, period, etc.

florescence [flɔː'resns] *n*. state or time of flowering. **florescent**, *adj*.

floriated, floreated ['flɔːrieɪtɪd] *adj*. decorated with flowers and leaves.

florikan, floriken ['flɔːrɪkən] *n*. small Indian bustard.

florilegium [ˌflɔːrɪ'liːdʒɪəm] *n*. (*pl*. –gia) collection of flowers; description of flora; anthology.

floruit ['flɒruɪt, 'flɔː–] (*Latin*) 'he flourished'; period during which person lived (*abbr*. **fl.**); dates indicating when a person was active, especially in brackets after person's name.

flügelhorn ['fluːglhɔːn] *n*. bugle with keys; saxhorn-like musical instrument.

fluidic [flu'ɪdɪk] *adj*. pertaining to or like a fluid; operated by the flow of a liquid or gas. **fluidics**, *n*. study and application of fluidic operations.

fluminous, fluminose ['fluːmɪnəs, –əʊs] *adj*. pertaining to or having many rivers.

fluoresce [flɔː'res, ˌfluːə–] *v.i*. exhibit fluorescence. **fluorescence**, *n*. emission of radiation due to absorption of radiation of different wavelengths; light, etc., so emitted. **fluorescent**, *adj*. **fluoroscope**, *n*. instrument for observing fluorescence. **fluoroscopy**, *n*.

fluoride ['fluəraɪd, 'flɔː–] *n*. compound of fluorine, especially one introduced into public water supply to combat dental decay. **fluoridate** ['flɔːrɪdeɪt], *v.t*. introduce fluoride into. **fluoridation**, *n*.

fluorocarbon [ˌfluərəʊ'kɑːbən, ˌflɔː–] *n*. inert compound of carbon and fluoride used as lubricant and in manufacture of plastics and synthetic resins.

fluvial ['fluːvɪəl] *adj*. pertaining to rivers. **fluviatile**, *adj*. **fluviograph**, *n*. instrument recording river's rise and fall. **fluviology**, *n*. study of water-courses. **fluviometer**, *n*. device for measuring river levels.

fodient ['fəʊdɪənt] *adj*. pertaining to digging.

foehn [fɜːn] *n*. dry warm wind blowing down northern slopes of Alps.

foetid *see* fetid.

foliaceous [ˌfəʊli'eɪʃəs] *adj*. pertaining to, like or consisting of leaves or laminae.

foliate ['fəʊliət] *adj*. like or having leaves; [–eɪt], *v.i. & t*. divide into laminae; beat into thin plate; cover with thin coating. **foliation**, *n*. formation of leaves; state of being foliate; act of foliating; consecutive numbering of leaves of book; leaf-like ornamentation.

foliferous [fəʊ'lɪfərəs] *adj*. bearing leaves. **foliiform**, *adj*. leaf-shaped.

folio ['fəʊliəʊ] *n*. folded sheet of paper; leaf of book, etc.; largest size of book; *v.t*. number pages of.

foliolate ['fəʊliəleɪt] *adj*. pertaining to or having leaflets. **folioliferous**, *adj*. bearing leaflets.

follicle ['fɒlɪkl] *n*. small deep cavity or sac. **follicular** [fə'lɪkjulə], *adj*. **folliculate**, *adj*. having or enclosed in follicle. **folliculose, folliculous**, *adj*. like follicle.

fomes ['fəʊmiːz] *n*. (*pl*. –mites ['fɒmɪtiːz, 'fəʊ–]) substance carrying infection.

fons et origo [ˌfɒnz et ɒ'riːgəʊ] (*Latin*) 'source and origin'.

fontanelle [ˌfɒntə'nel] *n*. soft gap between the bones in a baby's skull.

fontinal ['fɒntɪnl] *adj*. growing by or in springs.

foramen [fə'reɪmen] *n*. (*pl*. –mina [–'ræmɪnə]) small orifice. **foraminate** [–'ræm–], *adj*. having such; *v.t*. pierce. **foraminous**, *adj*.

foraneous [fə'reɪnɪəs] *adj*. pertaining to forum.

force majeure [ˌfɔːs mæ'ʒɜː] (*French*) 'greater force'; compelling force; unavoidable circumstances.

forcipate ['fɔːsɪpeɪt] *adj.* like forceps.

forensic [fə'rensɪk] *adj.* pertaining to law courts, argument or rhetoric.

forfend [fɔː'fend] *v.i. & t.* defend; forbid.

forficate ['fɔːfɪkeɪt] *adj.* deeply forked. **forfication**, *n.*

formalin ['fɔːməlɪn] *n.* aqueous solution of formaldehyde, a chemical disinfectant and preservative.

form(e) [fɔːm] *n.* page of printed matter ready for impression.

formic ['fɔːmɪk] *adj.* pertaining to ants. **formicarian**, *adj.* pertaining to ant-hill. **formicary**, *n.* ant-hill. **formicate**, *v.i.* creep or swarm like ants. **formication**, *n.* feeling as of ants crawling over skin. **formicative**, *adj.* **formicide** [–saɪd], *n.* substance destroying ants. **formicivorous** [–'sɪvərəs], *adj.* feeding on ants.

fornicate ['fɔːnɪkeɪt] *v.i.* commit fornication; *adj.* vaulted; arched. **fornication**, *n.* sexual intercourse by an unmarried person; vaulting; vaulted building. **fornicator, fornicatrix**, *n.*

fortuitous [fɔː'tjuːɪtəs] *adj.* by or due to chance. **fortuitism**, *n.* theory that evolutionary adaptations are due to chance. **fortuitist**, *n.* **fortuity**, *n.* chance occurrence.

forum ['fɔːrəm] *n.* (*pl.* **–ra**) market place; general meeting place; place for discussion; law courts.

fossa ['fɒsə] *n.* (*pl.* **–sae**) depression or cavity, *e.g.* in bone.

fossick ['fɒsɪk] (*Australian*) *v.i. & t.* search for by turning or picking over, especially for gold; rummage. **fossicker**, *n.*

fossorial [fɒ'sɔːrɪəl] *adj.* for use in digging. **fossor**, *n.* grave-digger.

foudroyant [,fuːdrwɑː'jɒn, fu'drɔɪənt] *adj. Medicine*, beginning very suddenly and severely; dazzling.

fouetté ['fuːəteɪ] (*French*) *n.* ballet movement in which the dancer stands on one foot and makes a whip-like movement with the other.

foumart ['fuːmɑːt] *n.* polecat.

foveate, foveated ['fəuvɪeɪt, –ɪd] *adj.* pitted. **foveolate**, *adj.* bearing small pits.

fraenum, frenum ['friːnəm] *n.* fold of membrane restraining an organ, as beneath the tongue.

francolin ['fræŋkəlɪn] *n.* S Asiatic and African partridge.

franc-tireur [,frɒŋtiː'rɜː] (*French*) *n.* (*pl.* **francs-tireurs**) member of irregular infantry corps.

frangible ['frændʒəbl] *adj.* brittle.

fraternize ['frætənaɪz] *v.i.* be friendly, especially with residents in occupied enemy territory, enemy soldiers, etc. **fraternization**, *n.*

fratricide ['frætrɪsaɪd] *n.* killing or killer of brother or sister. **fratricidal**, *adj.*

Frau [frau] (*German*) *n.* (*pl.* **–en**) married woman; Mrs.

Fräulein ['frɔɪlaɪn] (*German*) *n.* unmarried woman; Miss.

freemartin ['friː,mɑːtɪn] *n.* sterile female twin calf.

Freiherr ['fraɪheə] (*German*) *n.* (*pl.* **–en**) baron.

fremitus ['fremɪtəs] *n.* vibration.

frenate ['friːneɪt] *adj.* having a fraenum.

frenetic [frə'netɪk] *n. & adj.* frantic (person).

fresco ['freskəu] *n.* water-colour painting on wet plaster; *v.t.* paint in fresco. **fresco secco**, such painting on dry plaster.

fretum ['friːtəm] *n.* (*pl.* **–ta**) constriction.

friable ['fraɪəbl] *adj.* easily crumbled.

fricative ['frɪkətɪv] *n. & adj.* (sound) made by friction of breath forced through narrow passage, as *s, f.*

frigoric [frɪ'gɒrɪk] *adj.* pertaining to cold. **frigiferous** [–'dʒɪf–], **frigorific**, *adj.* causing cold.

fringilline [frɪn'dʒɪlaɪn] *adj.* like a finch; belonging to finch family of birds. **fringillaceous, fringilliform, fringilloid**, *adj.* finch-like.

frisé ['frɪzeɪ] *n.* fabric with raised nap.

Geese, sheep, oxen, etc.

In Anglo-Saxon times, English had a wide range of ways to form the plural of nouns, but over the centuries they have been gradually narrowed down to one standard plural inflection: *-s.* This is added to most pluralizable nouns (*one dog, two dogs*). Nouns ending in *s, z, x, sh,* and *ch* add *-es* (*one match, two matches*). Nouns ending in *y* preceded by a consonant change the *y* to *i* and add *-es* (*one spy, two spies*). Most nouns ending in *o* add only *-s* in the plural (*one piano, two pianos*), but some add *-es* (*one potato, two potatoes*), and some can add either (*one volcano, two volcano(e)s*).

In many nouns that end in a voiceless consonant, this is voiced in the plural (*one calf, two calves; one path, two paths* (pronounced [pɑːðz]). Compound nouns usually add *-s* to their final element; but sometimes, when the final element is an adjective, adverb, or prepositional phrase, they add the *-s* to the first element (*attornies-general, passers-by*).

However, a few other sorts of plural survive from earlier times. Seven nouns change their vowel in the plural: *foot/feet, goose/geese, louse/lice, man/men, mouse/mice, tooth/teeth, woman/women.* Two nouns add *-en: child/children, ox/oxen.* One noun, *brother,* does both, but only in religious contexts: *brethren.*

Some nouns do not change at all in the plural. They include several animal names: some are always unchanged (*sheep, deer*); others are unchanged when the animals are considered en masse, but add *-s* when they are thought of as many individuals (*duck, antelope*). Also unchanged are nationality nouns ending in *-ese* (*Chinese, Portuguese*) and a range of nouns denoting quantity, when used together with other quantity words (*two foot tall, several thousand years, 500 head of cattle*).

Over the years English has borrowed many words from foreign languages that retain their original plurals. Most are Latin (*fungus/fungi, antenna/antennae, bacterium/bacteria, codex/codices*). But there are also Greek ones (*criterion/criteria*), French (*bureau/bureaux*), Italian (*tempo/tempi*).

frisette [frɪ'zet] *n.* curly fringe, often of artificial hair, worn on the forehead.

frisket ['frɪskɪt] *n.* parchment or paper mask used in printing or retouching work.

frisson ['friːsɒn] (*French*) *n.* thrill; shudder, shiver.

frit [frɪt] *n.* prepared material from which glass is made.

fritillary [frɪ'tɪləri] *n.* several kinds of spotted butterfly and bulbous plant.

frondesce [frɒn'des] *v.i.* open leaves. **frond-iferous, frondigerous,** *adj.* bearing leaves or fronds. **frondiform,** *adj.* frond-shaped. **frond-ivorous,** *adj.* feeding on leaves. **frondose,** *adj.* having or like leaves. **frondescence,** *n.* **frondescent,** *adj.*

frontogenesis [,frʌntə'dʒenəsɪs] *n.* meeting of two different air currents creating weather front.

frottage ['frɒtɑːʒ] *n.* rubbing, especially the making of rubbings on thin paper of objects underneath, *e.g.* ornamental brasses.

fructify ['frʌktɪfaɪ] *v.i. & t.* become or make fruitful. **fructiferous,** *adj.* bearing fruit. **fructification,** *n.* **fructiform,** *adj.* like fruit. **fructivorous,** *adj.* feeding on fruit.

frumenty ['fruːmənti] *n.* dish of hulled wheat boiled in milk, with sugar. **frumentaceous,** *adj.* like or made of grain.

frutescent [fru'tesnt] *adj.* like a shrub. **frutescence,** *n.* **fruticetum,** *n.* botanical garden of shrubs. **fruticose,** *adj.* **fruticulous,** *adj.* like a small shrub.

FSH *abbreviation* of Follicle-Stimulating Hormone (lack of which is a cause of infertility in women).

fucus ['fjuːkəs] *n.* (*pl.* **-ci** [-saɪ]) kind of flat seaweed; rockweed. **fucoid,** *n. & adj.* (plant) like seaweed. **fucous,** *adj.*

fugacious [fju'geɪʃəs] *adj.* elusive; ephemeral; volatile. **fugacity** [-'gæsəti], *n.*

fugleman ['fjuːglmən] *n.* soldier standing in front of others to demonstrate drill, etc.; model.

fugue [fjuːg] *n.* strictly contrapuntal and highly developed musical composition; *Psychology,* flight from one's own identity, often involving wandering away from one's usual surroundings.

fulcrum ['fʌlkrəm, 'fʊ-] *n.* (*pl.* **-ra**) support; point or support on which lever rests. **fulcral,** *adj.* **fulcrate,** *adj.* having a fulcrum.

fulgent ['fʌldʒənt] *adj.* radiant. **fulgid,** *adj.* glittering.

fulgurant ['fʌlgjʊrənt] *adj.* like lightning. **fulgurate,** *v.i.* flash. **fulgurating,** *adj. Medicine,* applied to intense sudden pains. **fulgurous,** *adj.* flashing.

fuliginous [fju'lɪdʒɪnəs] *adj.* like soot. **fuliginosity,** *n.*

fuliguline [fju'lɪgjulæn] *adj.* pertaining to or like a sea duck; belonging to sea duck family of birds.

fulmar ['fʊlmə] *n.* gull-like sea bird.

fulminate ['fʊlmɪneɪt, 'fʌ-] *v.i.* explode; thunder; denounce in loud or violent manner. **fulminant,**

adj. Medicine, developing suddenly. **fulmineous, fulminous,** *adj.* pertaining to or like thunder and lightning. **fulmination, fulminator,** *n.* **fulminatory,** *adj.*

fulvous ['fʌlvəs] *adj.* tawny. **fulvescent,** *adj.* somewhat tawny.

fumarole ['fjuːmərəʊl] *n.* volcano's smoke vent.

fumatory ['fjuːmətəri] *n.* place for fumigating. **fumiduct,** *n.* smoke vent.

funambulist [fju'næmbjʊlɪst] *n.* tight-rope walker. **funambulate,** *v.i.* **funambulation, funambulator, funambulism,** *n.* **funambulatory,** *adj.*

fundamentalism [,fʌndə'mentl–ɪzm] *n.* belief in the literal truth of all Biblical statements, miracles, etc. **fundamentalist,** *n.*

fundiform ['fʌndɪfɔːm] *adj.* sling-shaped.

fundus ['fʌndəs] *n.* base of an organ or part furthest from its opening.

fungible ['fʌndʒəbl] *n. & adj.* (thing) mutually interchangeable.

fungicide ['fʌndʒɪsaɪd] *n.* substance killing fungus. **fungistatic,** *n.* substance preventing fungus growth.

funicular [fju'nɪkjulə] *adj.* pertaining to small cord, rope or tension. **funicular railway,** cable mountain railway. **funiform,** *adj.* cord- or rope-like. **funipendulous,** *adj.* hanging by a rope.

furcate, furcal ['fɜːkeɪt, –kl] *adj.* branched. **furcellate,** *adj.* slightly branched. **furcation,** *n.*

furcula, furculum ['fɜːkjʊlə, –əm] *n.* (*pl.* **-lae** *or* **-la**) any forklike part, especially the wishbone.

furfur ['fɜːfə] *n.* scurf. **furfuraceous, furfurous,** *adj.* **furfuration,** *n.* falling of dandruff.

furibund ['fjʊərɪbʌnd] *adj.* furious.

furlough ['fɜːləʊ] *n.* leave; holiday.

furmety ['fɜːməti] *n.* frumenty.

furore [fjuˈrɔːri] *n.* outburst of public indignation; outburst of enthusiasm.

Fürst [fjʊəst] (*German*) *n.* (*pl.* **-en**) noble next in rank to duke; prince.

furuncle ['fjʊərʌŋkl] *n.* boil. **furuncular, furunculous,** *adj.* **furunculoid,** *adj.* like a boil. **furunculosis,** *n.* outbreak of boils.

fusarole ['fjuːzərəʊl] *n. Architecture,* decoration resembling a string of beads.

fuscous ['fʌskəs] *adj.* dark in colour; tawny.

fusee [fju'ziː] *n.* large-headed match; spirally grooved spindle used as counterweight in old clocks.

fusiform ['fjuːzɪfɔːm] *adj.* spindle-shaped. **fusoid,** *adj.*

fustian ['fʌstiən] *n.* coarse cotton cloth; bombast; *adj.* made of fustian; pompous.

fustic ['fʌstɪk] *n.* tropical American tree yielding yellow dye.

fustigate ['fʌstɪgeɪt] *v.t.* beat with a cudgel.

fusuma ['fjuːsəmɑː, 'fuː–] *n.* sliding paper screen separating rooms in Japanese house.

futon ['fuːtɒn] *n.* Japanese padded quilt unrolled on the floor as a bed.

fuzee *see* **fusee.**

G

gabbro ['gæbrəʊ] *n.* granular kind of igneous rock. **gabbroic** [gə'brəʊɪk], **gabbroitic** [–'ɪtɪk], *adj.*

gabelle [gə'bel] (*French*) *n.* tax on salt.

gabion ['geɪbɪən] *n.* wicker-work cylinder filled with earth or stones for building fortifications, harbour bars, etc. **gabionade**, *n.* structure made with gabions.

gadoid ['gædɔɪd] *n.* & *adj.* (fish) of the cod family.

gadroon [gə'druːn] *n.* form of fluting; *Architecture*, notched moulding.

gaduin ['gædjuɪn] *n.* substance occurring in cod-liver oil.

gaffe [gæf] *n.* blunder.

galactic [gə'læktɪk] *adj. Astronomy*, pertaining to a galaxy. **galactagogue**, *n.* & *adj.* (substance) promoting milk secretion. **galactoid**, *adj.* milk-like. **galactometer**, *n.* instrument measuring density of milk. **galactophore**, *n.* milk duct. **galactopherous**, *adj.* conveying milk. **galactophygous**, *adj.* preventing milk secretion. **galactopoiesis**, *n.* milk production and secretion. **galactopoietic**, *adj.* **galactorrhoea**, *n.* excessive milk flow.

galanty [gə'lænti] *n.* shadow play.

galaxy ['gæləksi] *n.* Milky Way; island universe, especially one to which solar system and all visible stars belong; collection of brilliant persons.

galbanum ['gælbənəm] *n.* asafoetida-like gum resin.

galea ['geɪlɪə] *n. Biology*, helmet-shaped structure. **galeate** [–eɪt], **galeiform** [gə'liːɪfɔːm], *adj.* helmet-shaped.

galena [gə'liːnə] *n.* natural lead sulphite, main source of lead. **galenic(al)** [–'len–], *adj.* **galenoid**, *adj.* like galena.

galericulate [ˌgælə'rɪkjʊlət] *adj.* having hat-like covering.

galilee ['gælɪliː] *n.* church porch, or chapel at entrance.

galingale ['gælɪŋgeɪl] *n.* ginger-like plant, or sedge, with aromatic root used in medicine.

galleass ['gælɪæs] *n.* large armed 16th-century vessel with oars and sails.

galliard ['gælɪɑːd, –ɪəd] *adj.* gay; gallant; *n.* lively 16th-century dance.

Gallice ['gælɪsi] *adv.* in French (style). **Gallicize**, *v.t.* make French. **Gallicism**, *n.* word or phrase borrowed from French; use of such words and phrases.

gallimaufry [ˌgælɪ'mɔːfri] *n.* hash of liver and other organs; hotch-potch.

gallinaceous [ˌgælɪ'neɪʃəs] *adj.* like pheasants and domestic fowls; belonging to the order of birds including those.

gallinule ['gælɪnjuːl] *n.* moor hen.

Gallionic, Gallionian [ˌgælɪ'ɒnɪk, –'əʊnɪən] *adj.* pertaining to Gallio (Acts xviii); careless; indifferent.

gallipot ['gælɪpɒt] *n.* small ceramic pot for medicine, etc.

gallivat ['gælɪvæt] *n.* E Indian galleass.

Gallomania [ˌgælə'meɪnɪə] *n.* fondness for French life, manners, etc. **Gallomaniac**, *n.* **Gallophile**, *n.* lover of France. **Gallophobe**, *n.* hater of France. **Gallophobia**, *n.*

galloway ['gæləweɪ] (*Scottish*) *n.* breed of small horse and black cattle.

galvanic [gæl'vænɪk] *adj.* pertaining to direct current from electric battery; giving or receiving shock. **galvanism**, *n.* current electricity; study of electric currents and their effects. **galvanize**, *v.t.* treat with galvanic current; stimulate into sudden excitement; coat with zinc. **galvanometer**, *n.* instrument measuring small electric currents. **galvanoscope**, *n.* instrument indicating presence and direction of small electric currents.

gambade, gambado [gæm'beɪd, –'bɑːd, gæm'beɪdəʊ] *n.* horse's leap; caper. **gambadoes**, *n. pl.* gaiters, especially attached to saddle.

gambier ['gæmbɪə] *n.* yellow dye and astringent substance obtained from a vine of Malaysia.

gamboge [gæm'bəʊdʒ, –'buːʒ] *n.* SE Asian yellow gum resin; reddish yellow colour. **gambogian**, *adj.*

gambrel ['gæmbrəl] *n.* horse's hock; kind of roof with pentagonal gable.

gamelan ['gæmələn] *n.* musical instrument like xylophone; percussion, string and flute orchestra of SE Asia.

gamelotte ['gæmələt] *n.* fibre for paper, etc., obtained from sedge.

gamete ['gæmiːt] *n.* sex cell, reproductive cell. **gametic** [–'metɪk], *adj.* **gametocyte**, *n.* cell producing gametes. **gametogenesis**, *n.* production of gametes. **gametophyll**, *n.* leaf bearing, sex organs. **gametophyte**, *n.* plant, or stage in plant growth, bearing sex organs.

gamic ['gæmɪk] *adj.* sexual; requiring or resulting from mating.

gamin ['gæmæn] (*French*) *n.* street urchin. **gamine** (*f.*), [–iːin]

gamma ['gæmə] *n.* third letter (Γ, γ) of Greek alphabet. **gamma globulin**, any of a group of globulins, including most antibodies, concerned with immunity. **gamma ray**, kind of radioactive ray resembling X-rays. **gammacism**, *n.* stuttering over *g* and *k*. **gammadion, gammation**, *n.* (*pl.* –dia, –tia,) cross, as swastika, formed of four capital gammas.

gamogenesis [ˌgæmə'dʒenəsɪs] *n.* sexual reproduction. **gamogenetic** [–dʒə'netɪk], *adj.*

gamut ['gæmət] *n.* whole range of musical notes; whole scale from doh to doh; entire range or compass.

gandoura, gandurah [gæn'dʊərə] *n.* short, loose, sleeveless garment of Levant and Asia Minor.

ganglion [gæŋ'glɪən] *n.* (*pl.* **–ia**) mass of nerve cells; nerve centre; small cyst in tendon sheath, especially at wrist or ankle. **ganglionectomy,** removal of ganglion. **ganglionitis,** *n.* inflammation of ganglion. **ganglial, gangliar, ganglionic,** *adj.* **gangliate(d), ganglionated,** *adj.* having ganglia. **gangliform, ganglioform, ganglioid,** *adj.* like ganglion.

gangrene ['gæŋgriːn] *n.* mortification of part of body; *v.i. & t.* suffer or cause this. **gas gangrene,** marked by impregnation of gas caused by bacillus. **gangrenous,** *adj.* **gangrenescent,** *adj.* tending to become gangrenous.

gangue [gæŋ] *n.* rock or earth yielding ore.

ganister ['gænɪstə] *n.* kind of flinty rock used for road faces and lining furnaces.

ganj *see* **gunge**.

ganja ['gændʒə] (*Anglo-Indian*) *n.* cannabis obtained from Indian hemp.

ganoid ['gænɔɪd] *adj.* applied to hard, smooth, bright fish-scales; having such scales; *n.* fish with such scales.

ganoin ['gænəʊɪn] *n.* (enamel-like substance forming) the surface of ganoid scales.

ganosis [gə'nəʊsɪs] *n.* reducing shine of marble, especially on naked parts of statue.

gantry ['gæntri] *n.* frame-like support, especially bridge for travelling crane or bearing railway signals.

garçon [gɑːr'swæn] (*French*) *n.* boy; waiter. **garçon d'honneur,** best man (at wedding).

garda ['gɑːdə] *n.* (*pl.* **gardaʃ** [gɑː'diː]) Irish policeman.

garderobe [ˌgɑːdə'rəʊb] *n.* wardrobe; private room, privy.

garganey ['gɑːgəni] *n.* kind of teal.

gargantuan [gɑː'gæntjuən] *adj.* vast.

gargoyle ['gɑːgɔɪl] *n.* grotesquely carved spout projecting from gutter; excessively ugly face or person. **gargoylism,** *n.* congenital abnormality characterized by extreme physical deformity and mental deficiency.

garnishee [ˌgɑːnɪ'ʃiː] *v.t. Law,* attach property by garnishment; *n.* person receiving garnishment. **garnishment,** *n.* legal notice requiring person liable to do so not to pay money, etc., to defendant in debt suit, but retain it on plaintiff's behalf; notice calling third party to appear in suit.

garniture ['gɑːnɪtʃə] *n.* embellishment, ornamentation.

garrotte [gə'rɒt] *v.t.* strangle; execute by strangling; *n.* killing by strangling.

garrulous ['gærələs, –rjʊ–] *adj.* talkative. **garrulity,** [gə'ruːləti], *n.*

gasconade [ˌgæskə'neɪd] *v.i. & n.* brag.

gasket ['gæskɪt] *n.* rope for tying furled sail; packing for pistons, etc.

gasogene, gazogene ['gæsədʒiːn, 'gæz–] *n.* apparatus for aerating liquids.

gasteropod, gastropod [gæs'tərəpod] *n.* kind of mollusc, including snail, slug, whelk, etc. **gasteropodous** [–op'ədəs], *adj.*

gastral ['gæstrəl] *adj.* pertaining to stomach. **gastralgia** [gæ'trældʒɪə], *n.* pain in stomach. **gastrectomy,** *n.* surgical removal of (part of) stomach.

gastric ['gæstrɪk] *adj.* pertaining to stomach.

gastriloquist [gæ'strɪləkwɪst] *n.* ventriloquist. **gastriloquial,** [–'ləʊkwɪəl], *adj.* **gastriloquism,** *n.*

gastritis [gæ'straɪtɪs] *n.* inflammation of stomach.

gastroenteritis [ˌgæstrəʊentə'raɪtɪs] *n.* inflammation of stomach and intestines.

gastrolater [gæ'strɒlətə] *n.* glutton. **gastrolatrous,** *adj.* **gastrolatry,** *n.* gluttony.

gastrology [gæ'strɒlədʒi] *n.* study of stomach and its diseases, etc. **gastrologer, gastrologist,** *n.* **gastrological,** *adj.*

gastronomy [gæ'strɒnəmi] *n.* science of food and cooking. **gastronome** [–nəʊm], **gastronomer, gastronomist,** *n.* **gastronomical,** *adj.*

gastropod *see* **gasteropod.**

gastroscope ['gæstrəskəʊp] *n.* instrument for examining interior of stomach. **gastroscopy,** *n.*

gastrosophy [gæ'strɒsəfi] *n.* gastronomy. **gastrosoph, gastrosopher,** *n.*

gastrostomy [gæ'strɒstəmi] *n.* making permanent incision into stomach.

gata ['gɑːtə] *n.* kind of shark of tropical Atlantic; nurse shark.

gauche [gəʊʃ] (*French*) *adj.* 'left-handed'; awkward; tactless. **gaucherie,** *n.* such act or remark.

gaucho ['gaʊtʃəʊ] (*Spanish*) *n.* S American cowboy.

gaudeamus [ˌgaʊdi'ɑːməs] (*Latin*) 'let us rejoice'; students' revelry. **gaudeamus igitur** [–'ɪgɪtʊə], 'let us then make merry'.

Gauleiter ['gaʊˌlaɪtə] (*German*) *n.* Nazi political governor of district or province.

gault [gɔːlt] *n.* heavy clay.

gauss [gaʊs] *n.* electrical unit of magnetic induction, formerly of magnetic intensity.

gavage [gæ'vɑːʒ] (*French*) *n.* forcible feeding.

gavel ['gævl] *n.* hammer used by auctioneer or chairman; rent; tribute.

gavial ['geɪvɪəl] *n.* kind of Indian alligator.

gavotte [gə'vɒt] *n.* high-stepping French dance.

gazebo [gə'ziːbəʊ] *n.* summerhouse; belvedere.

gazogene, *see* **gasogene.**

geal ['dʒiːəl] *adj.* pertaining to the earth.

gecko ['gekəʊ] *n.* kind of small harmless lizard of warm regions.

geest [giːst] *n.* old superficial alluvial soil.

gegenschein ['geɪgənʃaɪn] *n.* soft light in sky opposite sun; counter-glow.

Gehenna [gɪ'henə] *n.* Hell; place of torture.

Geiger-counter ['gaɪgəˌkaʊntə] *n.* instrument detecting presence, and recording intensity, of charged particles, radioactivity, cosmic rays, etc.

geisha ['geɪʃə] *n.* Japanese dancing or singing girl.

Geist [gaɪst] (*German*) *n.* spirit; intellectual capacity or bent.

geitonogamy [ˌgaɪtə'nɒgəmi] *n.* pollination of a flower by another on same plant. **geitonogamous,** *adj.*

gekkonid ['gekənɪd] *n.* gecko. **gekkonoid,** *adj.*

gelastic [dʒɪ'læstɪk] *adj.* pertaining to laughing.

gelid ['dʒelɪd] *n.* cold; frozen.

gelogenic [ˌdʒelə'dʒenɪk] *adj.* producing laughter.

gemel ['dʒeml] *adj.* in pairs; twin.

geminate ['dʒemɪneɪt] *v.i. & t.* double; arrange in pairs; [-ət/ *adj.* so arranged. **geminiflorous,** *adj.* having paired flowers. **geminiform,** *adj.* double. **geminous,** *adj.*

gemma ['dʒemə] *n.* (*pl.* **-ae**) kind of bud from which, when separated from parent, new plant can grow. **gemmaceous,** *adj.* **gemmiferous,** *adj.* bearing gemmae or gems. **gemmiform,** *adj.* like a gemma or bud. **gemmiparous,** *adj.* producing gemmae. **gemmate,** *adj.* **gemmation,** *n.* reproduction by gemmae or buds. **gemmoid,** *adj.* like a gemma.

gemmology [dʒe'mɒlədʒi] *n.* study of gems.

gemmule ['dʒemjuːl] *n.* small gemma. **gemmulation,** *n.* production of gemmule. **gemmuliferous,** *adj.* bearing gemmules.

genappe [dʒə'næp] *n.* kind of worsted used in fringes, etc.

genarch ['dʒenɑːk] *n.* head of family.

gendarme ['ʒɒndɑːm] (*French*) *n.* policeman trained and armed like soldier, especially in France. **gendarmerie,** *n.* corps of gendarmes.

genealogy [,dʒiːni'ælədʒi] *n.* lineage; family tree; study of these. **genealogical,** *adj.* **genealogist,** *n.* **genealogize,** *v.i. & t.*

generic [dʒə'nerɪk] *adj.* of, pertaining to or characterizing a genus, sort, or kind.

genesic [dʒə'nesɪk, -'niː-] *adj.* pertaining to generation or genital organs. **genesiology** [dʒə,niːsi'ɒlədʒi], *n.* study of heredity or procreation. **genesiurgic** [-'ɜːdʒɪk], *adj.* connected with generation.

genet ['dʒenɪt, dʒə'net] *n.* civet-like animal; its spotted fur.

genethliac(al) [dʒə'neθliæk, ,dʒenɪθ'laɪəkl] *adj.* pertaining to nativity and position of star at birth. **genethlialogy,** *n.* casting of nativities.

genetic [dʒə'netɪk] *adj.* pertaining to origin, reproduction and heredity. **genetic engineering,** manipulation of genetic material by biochemical techniques. **genetic fingerprint,** unique pattern of genetic material specific to an individual. **genetic fingerprinting,** identification of such patterns. **geneticism** [-sɪzm], *n.* theory referring to individual or racial history to explain existing conduct, etc. **geneticist,** *n.* believer in geneticism; expert on genetics. **genetics,** *n.* study of heredity.

genetotrophic [,dʒenɪtə'trɒfɪk] *adj.* denoting a defect in metabolism which prevents the normal assimilation of essential food elements.

genetous ['dʒenɪtəs] *adj.* congenital.

genetrix ['dʒenɪtrɪks] *n.* (*pl.* **-rices** [-'traɪsiːz]) mother.

geniculate [dʒə'nɪkjuleɪt] *adj.* abruptly bent. **geniculation,** *n.*

genital ['dʒenɪtl] *adj.* pertaining to reproduction or the sex organs.

genitive ['dʒenətɪv] *adj.* signifying possession or origin; *n.* such grammatical case. **genitival** [-'taɪvl], *adj.*

genocide ['dʒenəsaɪd] *n.* extermination of a race or people.

genome ['dʒiːnəʊm] *n.* complete set of chromosomes of a particular organism. **genomic** [dʒɪ'nəʊmɪk, -'nɒ-], *adj.*

genotype ['dʒenətaɪp, 'dʒiː-] *n.* constitution of an organism; group of organisms sharing this. .. RUNN: **genotypic,** *adj.*

genre ['ʒɒnrə] (*French*) *n.* kind; style; realistic painting of everyday scenes.

gens [dʒenz, genz] *n.* (*pl.* **gentes**) ancient Roman clan; group with common male ancestor.

gentilitial [,dʒentɪ'lɪʃl] *adj.* pertaining to nation or family; of high birth. **gentilitious,** *adj.*

gentoo ['dʒentuː] (*Anglo-Indian*) *n.* Hindu.

genuflect ['dʒenjuflekt] *v.i.* bend the knee in worship. **genuflection, genuflexion,** *n.* **genuflector,** *n.* **genuflectory,** *adj.* **genuflexuous,** *adj.* geniculate.

genus ['dʒiːnəs, 'dʒe-] *n.* (*pl.* **genera** ['dʒenərə]) class; kind; *Biology*, category between family and species.

geocentric [,dʒiːəʊ'sentrɪk] *adj.* pertaining to centre of earth; having earth as centre. **geocentricism** [-sɪzm], *n.* belief that earth is centre of universe.

geochemistry [,dʒiːəʊ'kemɪstri] *n.* chemical composition of the Earth's crust.

geochronology [,dʒiːəʊkrə'nɒlədʒi] *n.* measuring of geological time; ordering of past events using geological data. **geochronological,** *adj.* **geochronologist,** *n.*

geochrony [dʒiː'ɒkrəni] *n.* chronology used in geology. **geochronic** [,dʒiːə'krɒnɪk], *adj.*

geocyclic [,dʒiːəʊ'saɪklɪk] *adj.* pertaining to earth's rotation or revolution; revolving round earth.

geode ['dʒiːəʊd] *n.* cavity in stone lined with crystals.

geodesy [dʒiː'ɒdəsi] *n.* mathematical study of the earth, its shape, measurements, etc., and the position and area of points and parts of its surface. **geodete, geodesist,** *n.* student of geodesy. **geodetic** [-'detɪk], **geodesic** [-'diːsɪk, -'de-], *adj.* making allowance for earth's curvature.

geodynamic [,dʒiːəʊdaɪ'næmɪk] *adj.* pertaining to forces within the earth. **geodynamics,** *n.* study of such forces.

geognosy [dʒiː'ɒgnəsi] *n.* geological study of materials forming the earth. **geognost,** *n.* student of geognosy. **geognostic,** *adj.*

geogony [dʒiː'ɒgəni] *n.* theory or study of formation of the earth. **geogonic(al)** [-'gɒn-], *adj.*

geohydrology [,dʒiːəʊhaɪ'drɒlədʒi] *n.* study of subterranean water.

geoid ['dʒiːɔɪd] *n.* figure of the earth. **geoidal,** *adj.*

geomancy ['dʒiːəmænsi] *n.* divination by lines and figures. **geomantic,** *adj.*

geomorphic [,dʒiːə'mɔːfɪk] *adj.* pertaining to or like the form or figure of the earth. **geomorphogeny,** *n.* study of earth forms. **geomorphology,** *n.* study of form, nature and evolution on earth's surface.

geophagous [dʒiː'ɒfəgəs] *adj.* eating earth. **geophagia** [-'feɪdʒiə], **geophagism** [-dʒɪzm], **geophagy** [-dʒi], *n.*

geophilous [dʒiː'ɒfɪləs] *adj.* living in or on the ground; growing under the ground.

geophysics [,dʒiːəʊ'fɪzɪks] *n.* physics as applied to geology. **geophysical,** *adj.* **geophysicist** [-sɪst], *n.*

geophyte ['dʒiːəfaɪt] *n.* plant growing in earth.

geopolar [,dʒiːəʊ'pəʊlə] *adj.* pertaining to earth's pole(s).

geopolitics [,dʒiːəʊ'pɒlətɪks] *n.* study of relationship between geographical situation and politics of a nation.

geoponic(al) [,dʒiːə'pɒnɪk, –l] *adj.* agricultural. **geoponics,** *n.* science of agriculture.

georama [,dʒiːə'rɑːmə] *n.* map of world on inside of globe viewed from within.

georgic ['dʒɔːdʒɪk] *adj.* pertaining to agriculture; rural; *n.* such poem.

geoscopy [dʒi'ɒskəpi] *n.* examination of earth and soil. **geoscopic** [–'skɒpɪk], *adj.*

geoselenic [,dʒiːəusə'liːnɪk, –'le–] *adj.* pertaining to earth and moon.

geosphere ['dʒiːəsfɪə] *n.* solid part of the earth.

geostationary [,dʒiːəu'steɪʃənəri] *adj.* pertaining to an artificial satellite whose orbit corresponds to the earth's rotation, so it remains above the same point on the earth's surface.

geostrophic [,dʒiːə'strɒfɪk] *adj.* pertaining to deflection due to earth's rotation.

geosynchronous [,dʒiːəu'sɪŋkrənəs] *adj.* geostationary.

geotaxis, geotaxy [,dʒiːəu'tæksɪs, 'dʒiːəutæksi] *n. Biology,* movement directed by gravitation. **geotactic,** *adj.*

geotechnics [,dʒiːə'teknɪks] *n.* study of increasing the habitability of earth.

geotectonic [,dʒiːəutek'tɒnɪk] *adj.* pertaining to earth's structure. **geotectonics,** *n.* structural geology.

geothermal, geothermic [,dʒiːə'θɜːml, –mɪk] *adj.* pertaining to heat of earth's interior. **geothermometer,** *n.* instrument measuring such heat.

geotropism, geotropy [dʒi'ɒtrəpɪzm, –pi] *n. Biology,* growth or movement directed by gravitation, especially towards the earth. **geotropic** [–'trɒpɪk], *adj.*

gephyrophobia [,dʒefɪrə'fəubiə] *n.* morbid fear of bridges and passing over or under them.

geratic [dʒə'rætɪk] *adj.* pertaining to old age and decadence. **geratology,** *n.* biological study of decadence.

gerendum [dʒə'rendəm] *n.* (*pl.* **–da**) thing to be done.

gerent ['dʒɪərənt] *n.* manager.

gerfalcon ['dʒɜː,fɔːlkən] *n.* large Arctic falcon.

geriatrics [,dʒeri'ætrɪks] *n.* medical study of old age and its diseases.

german ['dʒɜːmən] *adj.* of same parents; of one's parent's brother or sister. **cousin-german,** first cousin.

germane [dʒɜː'meɪn] *adj.* relevant; apt.

germicide ['dʒɜːmɪsaɪd] *n.* substance destroying germs. **germicidal,** *adj.* **germifuge,** *n. & adj.* (substance) expelling germs.

germinal ['dʒɜːmɪnl] *adj.* pertaining to germ or germination; pertaining to embryo.

gerocomy, gerocomia [dʒə'rɒkəmi, ,dʒerə'kəumiə] *n.* medical study of old age. **gerocomical** [–'kɒmɪkl], *adj.*

geromorphism [,dʒerə'mɔːfɪzm] *n.* having appearance of age greater than one's real age.

gerontic, gerontal [dʒə'rɒntɪk, –tl] *adj. Biology,* pertaining to old age or decadence. **gerontism,** *n.* **gerontocracy,** *n.* government by old men. **gerontogeous** [–tə'dʒiːəs], *adj.* pertaining to Old World. **gerontology,** *n.* study of characteristics of old age.

gerrymander ['dʒerɪmændə] *v.t.* divide into electoral wards, etc., in such a way as to gain political advantage; distort or use facts, etc., to gain advantage.

gerund ['dʒerənd, –ʌnd] *n.* a kind of verbal noun. **gerundial** [dʒə'rʌndiəl], *adj.* **gerundive** [dʒə'rʌndɪv], *n.* gerundial adjective, expressing (in Latin) necessity.

Gesellschaft [gə'zelʃɑːft] (*German*) *n.* group whose concerns are of a formal and practical nature.

gesso ['dʒesəu] *n.* prepared gypsum or plaster of Paris used in painting; *v.t.* apply gesso to.

Gestalt [gə'ʃtælt] (*German*) *n.* (*pl.* **–en**) integral pattern or system of psychological events as a functional unit.

gestate [dʒe'steɪt, 'dʒesteɪt] *v.t.* carry in womb. **gestation,** *n.* such carrying or period of carrying. **gestational, gestative,** *adj.* **gestatorial,** *adj.* pertaining to ceremonial carrying-chair. **gestatory,** *adj.* pertaining to gestation; pertaining to carrying as exercise.

gestic(al) ['dʒestɪk, –l] *adj.* pertaining to motion of body, or gestures. **gesticulate** [–'stɪk–], *v.i.* gesture. **gesticulation,** *n.*

Gesundheit [gə'zunthaɪt] (*German*) *exclamation* 'good health'.

gharry ['gæri] (*Anglo-Indian*) *n.* light horse-drawn carriage.

ghat [gɑːt, gɔːt] (*Indian*) *n.* mountain pass or range; river steps.

ghazi ['gɑːzi] *n.* Muslim champion; highest Turkish title of honour.

ghee, ghi [giː] (*Hindi*) *n.* clarified butter.

giaour ['dʒauə] (*Turkish*) *n.* infidel; Christian.

gibbous ['gɪbəs] *adj.* convex; hump-backed; applied to moon between half and full. **gibbosity** [gɪ'bɒsəti], *n.* **gibbus,** *n.* hump.

gibus ['dʒaɪbəs] *n.* opera hat.

gid [gɪd] *n.* brain disease of sheep.

giga- ['gɪgə–, 'gaɪgə–, 'giːgə–] *prefix* of measurement meaning one thousand millions (10⁹). (*abbr.* **G.**)

gigantism [dʒaɪ'gæntɪzm] *n.* excessive growth; acromegaly. **giganticide,** *n.* killing or killer of giant. **gigantomachy,** *n.* battle of giants.

gigot ['dʒɪgət, 'ʒɪgəu] *n.* leg of mutton.

Gilbertian [gɪl'bɜːtiən] *adj.* absurd; topsy-turvy, like situations in Gilbert and Sullivan comic operas.

gillaroo [,gɪlə'ruː] (*Irish*) *n.* trout.

gillie, ghillie ['gɪli] (*Scottish*) *n.* attendant on hunter.

gilliver ['dʒɪlɪvə] *n.* wallflower.

gimbals ['dʒɪmblz, 'gɪm–] *n. pl.* contrivance of rings allowing supported body (*e.g.* ship's compass) to tip in any direction.

gingival [dʒɪn'dʒaɪvl, 'dʒɪndʒɪvl] *adj.* pertaining to gums; alveolar. **gingivalgia** [–'vældʒiə], *n.* pain in gums. **gingivitis,** *n.* inflammation of gums.

ginglymus ['dʒɪŋglɪməs, 'gɪŋ–] *n.* hinge joint. **ginglymoid,** *adj.* pertaining to or like a ginglymus.

ginkgo ['gɪŋkəu] *n.* rare Chinese temple tree; maidenhair tree.

ginseng ['dʒɪnseŋ] *n.* Chinese herb with root used in folk medicine.

girandole ['dʒɪrəndəul] *n.* cluster of water-jets or fireworks; fountain with spreading spray; any such radiating ornament.

girasol(e) ['dʒɪrəsɒl, –səul] *n.* heliotrope; sunflower; fire opal.

gittern ['gɪtn] *n.* cithern.

glabrous ['gleɪbrəs] *adj.* having smooth surface; hairless. **glabrate**, *adj.* **glabrescent**, *adj.* somewhat glabrous; tending to be glabrous.

glacis ['gleɪsɪs, 'glæ–] *n.* gentle slope, especially sloping bank of fortification.

gladiate ['glædɪeɪt, 'gleɪ–] *adj.* sword-shaped.

glair [gleə] *n.* white of egg; any similar substance; *v.t.* cover with glair. **glaireous** ['gleərɪəs], *adj.*

glanders ['glændəz] *n.* bacillary gland disease of horses.

glandiform ['glændɪfɔːm] *adj.* acorn-shaped. **glandiferous**, *adj.* bearing acorns.

glasnost ['glæsnɒst] (*Russian*) *n.* 'openness'; policy of openness followed by the Soviet government under Mikhail Gorbachev.

glaucescent [glɔː'sesnt] *adj.* somewhat glaucous.

glaucoma [glɔː'kəʊmə] *n.* excessive pressure of fluid within the eyeball. **glaucomatous**, *adj.*

glaucous ['glɔːkəs] *adj.* grey-green; green-blue; yellow-green.

glebe [gliːb] *n.* soil; land attached to benefice. **glebe house**, parsonage.

gleet [gliːt] *n.* mucous discharge, especially from urethra; *v.i.* emit such discharge.

glenoid ['gliːnɔɪd] *adj.* shaped like a shallow depression.

glirine ['glaɪrɪn] *adj.* dormouse-like. **gliriform**, *adj.*

glissade [glɪ'seɪd, –'saːd] *n.* slide down slope; sliding step; *v.i.* slide.

globigerina [gləʊ,bɪdʒə'raɪnə] *n.* (*pl.* **-ae**) protozoon living in surface waters of the sea. **globigerina ooze**, deposit of the chalky shells of globigerinae on the sea floor.

globulicide ['glɒbjʊlɪsaɪd] *n.* & *adj.* (substance) destroying blood corpuscles. **globulicidal**, *adj.* **globulimeter**, *n.* instrument measuring red corpuscles in blood. **globulin**, *n.* kind of protein in blood.

glochidiate, glochideous [gləʊ'lɪdɪət, iəɪt, iəs] *adj.* barbed; bristly.

glockenspiel ['glɒkənspiːl] *n.* xylophone-like musical instrument, especially with metal bars.

glomerate ['glɒməreɪt] *adj.* collected compactly together. **glomeration**, *n.*

glomerule ['glɒməruːl] *n.* compactly clustered flower-head. **glomerulate**, *adj.*

glomerulus [glɒ'merjʊləs] *n.* (*pl.* **-li**) intertwined cluster of organisms, nerve fibres, etc., especially capillaries in the kidney. **glomerular**, *adj.*

glossal ['glɒsl] *adj.* pertaining to tongue. **glossalgia** [–'sældʒɪə], *n.* pain in tongue. **glossator**, **glossographer**, *n.* writer of glosses or commentaries. **glossectomy**, *n.* removal of tongue. **glosseme**, *n.* smallest meaningful unit of a language. **glossitis**, *n.* inflammation of tongue. **glossoid**, *adj.* tongue-like. **glossolalia, glossolaly**, *n.* gift of tongues. **glossology**, *n.* terminology; study of language; medical study of tongue. **glossopathy**, *n.* disease of tongue. **glossophagine**, *adj.* feeding with tongue. **glossoplegia**, *n.* paralysis of tongue.

glottis ['glɒtɪs] *n.* chink-like space between the vocal cords. **glottal**, *adj.* **glottal stop**, closure and sudden explosive opening of glottis; sound thus caused (as *t* in Lowland Scots). **glottic, glottidean**, *adj.* **glottochronology** *n. Philology*, study of the rate at which changes take place in a language,

especially in divergent branches. **glottogonic**, *adj.* pertaining to origin of language. **glottology**, *n.* study of language.

glucagon ['gluːkəgən, –ɒn] *n.* pancreatic hormone which raises blood-sugar level and reduces appetite.

glucose ['gluːkəʊs, –əʊz] *n.* form of sugar; dextrose; kind of syrup made from this. **glucoside**, *n.* substance yielding glucose on hydrolysis.

glume [gluːm] *n.* dry bract of grass flower. **glumaceous, glumose**, *adj.* like or composed of glumes **glumiferous**, *adj.* bearing glumes.

gluside ['gluːsaɪd] *n.* saccharin.

gluteal ['gluːtɪəl] *adj.* pertaining to buttocks.

gluten ['gluːtn] *n.* sticky protein in flour; *adj.* containing little starch and much gluten. **glutenous**, *adj.* **glutinous**, *adj.* like or pertaining to glue.

glutition [glu'tɪʃn] *n.* act of swallowing.

glycaemia [glaɪ'kiːmɪə] *n.* presence of glucose in the blood.

glycogen ['glaɪkədʒən, –en] *n.* form of carbohydrate stored in body, found especially in liver. **glycogenesis**, *n.* formation of sugar from glycogen. **glycogenic, glycogenous** [–'kɒdʒənəs], *adj.*

glycose ['glaɪkəʊs] *n.* glucose. **glycosuria, glycuresis**, *n.* excretion of sugar in urine. **glycosuric**, *adj.*

glyph [glɪf] *n.* groove; ancient wall carving. **glyphic**, *adj.* pertaining to sculpture.

glyptic ['glɪptɪk] *adj.* pertaining to carving, especially of gems. **glyptics, glyptography**, *n.* gem-carving. **glyptology**, *n.* study of gem engravings.

gnathal, gnathic ['næθl, 'næθɪk] *adj.* pertaining to jaw. **gnathism**, *n.* formation of upper jaw; use of such formation as basis for classification. **gnathonic**, *adj.* flattering.

gneiss [naɪs] *n.* granite-like metamorphic rock. **gneissic, gneissitic, gneissose**, *adj.* **gneissoid**, *adj.* like gneiss.

gnomic ['nəʊmɪk] *adj.* pertaining to or like aphorisms; *Grammar*, signifying general truth. **gnomist**, *n.* writer of gnomic poetry. **gnomologic**, *adj.* aphoristic. **gnomology**, *n.* gnomic writing; collection of gnomic writings.

gnosis ['nəʊsɪs] *n.* spiritual knowledge or insight. **gnostic** ['nɒstɪk], *adj.* pertaining to knowledge or gnosticism; *n.* adherent of gnosticism. **gnosticism**, *n.* religious belief of those claiming gnosis or that freedom was possible through gnosis alone.

gnotobiosis [,nəʊtəʊbaɪ'əʊsɪs] *n.* rearing of organisms in germ-free environment. **gnotobiote**, *n.* germ-free animal. **gnotobiotic**, *adj.*

Gobinism ['gəʊbɪnɪzm] *n.* theory of the superiority of Aryan or Teutonic race, postulated by J. A. de Gobineau.

godet ['gəʊdeɪ] (*French*) *n.* panel inserted to make skirt flare.

godown ['gəʊdaʊn] (*Anglo-Indian*) *n.* warehouse.

goffer, gauffer ['gəʊfə] *v.t.* flute edges of crimp.

gombroon [gɒm'bruːn] *n.* kind of Persian pottery.

gomphosis [gɒm'fəʊsɪs] *n.* growth of tooth into bone cavity.

gonad ['gəʊnæd, 'gɒ–] *n.* sexual gland; ovary or testis. **gonadal** [–'næ–], **gonadial** [–'neɪ–], **gonadic** [–'næ–], *adj.* **gonadotrophic, gonadotropic**, *adj.* stimulating activity of the gonads. **gonadotrophin, gonadotropin**, *n.* gonadotrophic hormone.

gonalgia [gɒ'nældʒiə] *n.* pain in knee.

goneoclinic [ˌgɒniə'klɪnɪk] *adj.* applied to hybrid more like one parent than other.

gonfalon ['gɒnfələn] *n.* hanging banner. **gonfalonier**, *n.* standard-bearer; medieval Italian magistrate.

gonion ['gəʊniən] *n.* (*pl.* **–nia**) angle, especially of lower jaw. **goniometer**, *n.* instrument measuring angles. **goniometry**, *n.* trigonometry.

gonitis [gɒ'naɪtɪs] *n.* inflammation of knee.

gonoblast ['gɒnəblæst] *n.* reproductive cell. **gonochorism**, *n.* separation of sex, dioecism; development of sex differentiation. **gonocyte**, *n.* gamete-producting cell.

gonococcus [ˌgɒnə'kɒkəs] *n.* (*pl.* **–ci** [–saɪ]) bacterium causing gonorrhoea. **gonococcal, gonococcic,** *adj.*

gonorrhoea [ˌgɒnə'rɪə] *n.* bacterial disease of sexual and urinary tract. **gonorrhoeal, gonorrhoeic,** *adj.*

googol *n.* ten raised to the hundredth power (10^{100}). **googolplex**, *n.* ten raised to the power of a googol ($10^{10\ 100}$).

gopher ['gəʊfə] *n.* rat-like burrowing rodent of N America.

goral ['gɔːrəl] *n.* Asiatic goat antelope.

gorgon ['gɔːgən] *n.* extremely ugly or terrifying woman. **gorgonian** [gɔː'gəʊniən], *adj.*; *n.* form of horny coral. **gorgonize**, *v.t.* transfix with stare; petrify.

gormandize ['gɔːməndaɪz] *v.t. & i.* eat greedily or voraciously, *n.* gourmandise.

gorsedd ['gɔːseð] *n.* assembly for giving prizes, degrees, etc., at close of eisteddfod; meeting of bards and druids.

Götterdämmerung [ˌgɒtə'dæmərʊŋ] (*German*) *n.* 'twilight of the gods'.

gouache [gu'aːʃ] *n.* painting with pigments mixed with gum.

gourami [gʊ'raːmi] *n.* large freshwater SE Asian food fish.

gourmand ['gʊəmənd] *n. & adj.* gluttonous (person). **gourmandise, gourmandism,** *n.* gluttony.

gourmet ['gʊəmeɪ] (*French*) *n.* epicure.

governor ['gʌvənə] *n.* mechanical device, especially based on centrifugal action of two balls, for controlling speed, etc.

gracile ['græsaɪl] *adj.* slender. **gracility**, *n.*

gradatim [grə'deɪtɪm] (*Latin*) *adv.* 'step by step'.

gradin ['greɪdɪn] *n.* one of a tier of steps, seats, etc.

gradus ['grædəs, 'greɪ–] *n. abbreviation* of **gradus ad Parnassum**, dictionary used in composition of Latin verses.

Graf [graːf] (*German*) *n.* (*pl.* **–en**) title, equivalent of earl, in Germany and Sweden.

graffito [grə'fiːtəʊ] *n.* (*pl.* **–ti**) ancient wall drawing or writing; *usually pl.*, drawing or writing scratched, scribbled, or sprayed on a surface in a public place.

grallatory,   grallatorial   ['grælətəri, ˌgrælə'tɔːriəl] *adj.* pertaining to wading birds.

gramicidin [ˌgræmɪ'saɪdɪn, –'ɪs–] *n.* antibiotic produced by a bacterium and used against gram-positive bacteria.

graminaceous [ˌgræmɪ'neɪʃəs] *adj.* grass-like; pertaining to grass family of plants. **gramineal** [–'mɪn–], **gramineous**, *adj.* **graminivorous**, *adj.*

feeding on grass. **graminology**, *n.* study of grasses. **graminous**, *adj.* grassy.

grammalogue ['græməlɒg] *n.* word represented by one shorthand sign; such sign.

grammatolatry [ˌgræmə'tɒlətri] *n.* worship of words or letters, or the letter. **grammatolator**, *n.*

gram-positive [ˌgræm'pɒzətɪv] *adj.* denoting a class of bacteria stainable by method invented by H. J. C. Gram, Danish physician. **gram-negative**, *adj.* denoting class of bacteria not stainable thus.

grampus ['græmpəs] *n.* kind of small whale; blackfish; killer whale.

grandiloquent [græn'dɪləkwənt] *adj.* bombastic; using high-sounding language. **grandiloquence**, *n.* **grandiloquous**, *adj.*

grandisonant [græn'dɪsənənt] *adj.* sounding great; pompous. **grandisonous**, *adj.*

grangerize ['greɪndʒəraɪz] *v.t.* illustrate, especially by interleaving, with additional pictures. **grangerism**, *n.*

graniferous [grə'nɪfərəs] *adj.* bearing grain or grainlike seeds.

granivorous [grə'nɪvərəs] *adj.* feeding on grain or seeds.

granulocyte ['grænjʊləʊsaɪt] *n.* kind of white blood cell. **granulocytic**, *adj.*

graphology [græ'fɒlədʒi] *n.* study of and reading character from hand-writing. **graphologic(al)**, *adj.* **graphologist**, *n.*

graphometer [græ'fɒmɪtə] *n.* angle-measuring instrument.

graphospasm ['græfəspæzm] *n.* writer's cramp.

grapnel ['græpnəl] *n.* small anchor or hook.

graticulate [græ'tɪkjʊleɪt] *v.t.* divide (pattern, etc.) into squares for easiness of reproduction. **graticulation**, *n.* **graticule** ['grætɪkjuːl], *n.* grid of lines used with the eyepiece of a microscope, telescope, etc., for measuring or locating objects; grid of lines on a major chart.

gratuitous [grə'tjuːɪtəs] *adj.* done freely; needless; groundless. **gratuity**, *n.* gift of money; tip.

gratulatory ['grætjʊlətəri, ˌgrætju'leɪtəri] *adj.* congratulating. **gratulant**, *adj.* **gratulation**, *n.*

gravamen [grə'veɪmen] *n.* (*pl.* **–mina**) substance of a grievance or charge.

gravedo [grə'viːdəʊ] *n.* cold in the head.

gravid ['grævɪd] *adj.* pregnant. **gravida**, *n.* pregnant woman.

gravimetric(al) [ˌgrævɪ'metrɪk, – l] *adj.* pertaining to measurement by weight. **gravimeter**, *n.* instrument for measuring specific gravities; instrument for measuring variations in the earth's gravitational field. **gravimetry** [–'vɪmətri], *n.*

greave [griːv] *n.* armour covering lower leg. **greaves** [griːvz] *n.pl.* tallow refuse.

gregarious [grɪ'geəriəs] *adj.* living in herds; tending to flock together; fond of society. **gregarian**, *adj.* pertaining to the common herd.

gremial ['griːmiəl] *adj.* pertaining to bosom or lap; *n.* bishop's apron.

grenadine ['grenədiːn, ˌgrenə'diːn] *n.* sweet fruit syrup; light thin dress fabric.

gressorial, gressorious [gre'sɔːriəl, –iəs] *adj.* adapted for walking.

greywacke ['greɪwækə] *n.* coarse-grained sandstone.

grievance ['gri:vns] *n.* grounds, real or imaginary, for complaint; feeling of resentment, especially caused by treatment felt to be unfair.

grievous ['gri:vəs] *adj.* very severe or painful; causing grief or suffering, heinous. **grievous bodily harm,** *Law,* crime of inflicting serious physical injury on another person. (*abbr.* **GBH**)

griffe [grɪf] *n.* person of mixed American Indian and Negro blood. **griffado** [–aɪ'dəʊ], *n.* child of white and quadroon parents.

grilse [grɪls] *n.* young salmon.

grisaille [grɪ'zeɪl, –'zaɪ] (*French*) *n.* glass painted with grey pigment.

griseous ['grɪzɪəs, 'grɪs–] *adj.* grizzled.

grisette [grɪ'zet] (*French*) *n.* young working girl.

grisgris ['gri:gri:] *n.* African charm or amulet.

griskin ['grɪskɪn] *n.* lean loin of pork.

grivet ['grɪvɪt] *n.* black and white Abyssinian monkey.

grobian ['grəʊbɪən] *n.* lout. **grobianism,** *n.*

grognard ['grəʊnjɑː] (*French*) *n.* grouser; old soldier.

gromatic [grəʊ'mætɪk] *adj.* pertaining to surveying. **gromatics,** *n.* surveying, especially of camp.

grosbeak ['grəʊsbi:k] *n.* large-billed finch; hawfinch.

grossulariaceous [ˌgrɒsjʊleəri'eɪʃəs] *adj.* pertaining to or like a gooseberry; belonging to gooseberry family of plants. **grossularious,** *adj.*

groyne [grɔɪn] *n.* wooden breakwater.

gruine ['gru:aɪn] *adj.* like or pertaining to crane (bird).

grume [gru:m] *n.* clot; clotted liquid. **grumose,** *adj.* comprising a cluster of granules. **grumous,** *adj.* clotted.

gryllid ['grɪlɪd] *n.* cricket (insect); *adj.* pertaining to or like cricket; belonging to cricket family of insects.

grysbok ['graɪsbɒk, 'greɪs–] (*S African*) *n.* small reddish antelope.

guaiacum ['gwaɪəkəm] *n.* resin of a tropical American tree, used as rheumatic remedy.

guanaco [gwə'nɑːkəʊ, gwɑː–] *n.* S American llama-like animal.

Grammar terms

The basic structural element of discourse is the **clause**, which can be a main clause or a subordinate clause (see **Coping with clauses**). A main clause on its own is a **simple sentence**. A main clause with one or more subordinate clauses is a **complex sentence**.

Sentences are traditionally divided into **subject** and **predicate**. The subject is the part about which some statement is made in the sentence: in *Life is sweet, life* is the subject; in *The people who live next door are away, the people who live next door* is the subject. The predicate is the part which makes a statement about the subject. It may be just a verb: in *Life stinks, stinks* is the predicate. Or it may also include the object of the verb, a complement or an adverbial: in *She threw the flowers away, threw the flowers away* is the predicate.

Nouns are traditionally classified as **common nouns**, which denote any one of a class of things or beings, and do not usually have a capital letter (*dog, misery*) or **proper nouns,** which name a particular thing or person and usually do have a capital letter (*Russia, Gandhi*). Common nouns are further classified into **countable nouns,** which can have a plural (*one dog, two dogs*) and **uncountable nouns,** or **mass nouns,** which denote a concept or substance and generally do not have a plural (*misery, bread*). Nouns have the feature of **case**. In languages which indicate a noun's role in a sentence by means of a special suffix (such as Latin), there may be several cases (e.g. **nominative, accusative, genitive** *or* **possessive, dative, ablative, locative**); but in English, where this function is performed mainly by word order and prepositions, case is not so important.

Verbs have five distinct features. First, **number**: they may be **singular** (*I go*) or **plural** (*We go*). Second, **voice**: they may be **active** (*He made the tea*) or **passive** (*The tea was made by him*). Third, **mood**: they may be **indicative**, making a simple statement; **imperative**, giving a command; **interrogative**, asking a question; or **subjunctive** (see **I wish I were a...**). Fourth, **tense**: a range of forms and constructions indicating whether an event happened in the past, is happening at the present time, or will happen in the future. Fifth, **aspect**: indicating whether an action is beginning, is in progress, has finished, happens repeatedly, etc. (as in *She sings* versus *She is singing*).

There are four main categories of verb. First, **intransitive**, where the verb alone can constitute the entire predicate (*I object; You're lying*). Second, **transitive**, where the verb has an **object** to which the action of the verb is done (*I love you; He's killed it*). Third, **copulas** or **linking verbs**, which are followed by a **complement** that says something about the subject (*I am John; She seems happy*). Fourth, **auxiliary** verbs, which accompany or replace other verbs (e.g. *am* in *I am coming* and *do* in 'Who wants it?' 'I do'). A subcategory of auxiliary verbs is the **modal auxiliary**, such as *can, may, might, must,* which is used to indicate grammatical mood.

English verbs have two **participles**. The **present participle** ends in *-ing*. It is used in continuous tenses (*I was singing*) and as an adjective (*a singing bird*). The *-ing* form can also be used as a noun, known as a **verbal noun** or **gerund** (*I enjoy singing*). The **past participle** ends in *-(e)d* in regular verbs (in irregular ones it can have various forms, such as *come, forsaken, swum*). It is used in perfect tenses (*He has rejected it*) and as an adjective (*a rejected lover*).

Adjectives and adverbs have three different **degrees**: the **absolute** degree, which is shown by the ordinary form of the adjective or adverb (*a high mountain*); the **comparative** degree, which is shown by *more* or the suffix *-er* (*a higher mountain*); and the **superlative** degree, which is shown by *most* or the suffix *-est* (*the highest mountain*).

guano ['gwɑːnəʊ] *n.* sea-birds' excrement used as fertilizer. **guaniferous,** *adj.* yielding guano.

guava ['gwɑːvə] *n.* apple-like fruit of several tropical American shrubs.

gubernatorial [ˌguːbənə'tɔːriəl, ˌgjuː–] *adj.* pertaining to governor or government. **gubernatrix** [–'neɪtrɪks], *n.* female governor.

guepard(e) ['gepɑːd, ge'pɑːd] *n.* cheetah.

guerdon ['gɜːdn] *n.* & *v.t.* reward.

guillemot ['gɪlɪmɒt] *n.* kind of auk-like seabird.

guilloche [gɪ'lɒʃ] *n.* architectural ornament of intertwined curved lines or bands.

guimbard ['gɪmbɑːd] *n.* jew's-harp.

guipure [gɪ'pjʊə] *n.* kind of large-patterned heavy lace.

gulag ['guːlæg] *n.* system of prisons and labour camps in the former USSR; one of these camps.

gules [gjuːlz] *n.* & *adj. Heraldry,* red.

gulosity [gju'lɒsəti] *n.* greediness.

gumbotil ['gʌmbətɪl] *n.* dark sticky clay, formed by the weathering of boulder clay or glacial drift.

gunge [gʌndʒ] (*Anglo-Indian*) *n.* market; granary.

gunyah ['gʌnjə] (*Australian*) *n.* aborigine's hut.

gurgitate ['gɜːdʒɪteɪt] *v.i.* bubble. **gurgitation,** *n.* ebullition.

gurgulation [ˌgɜːgju'leɪʃn] *n.* gurgling sound; rumble.

gustation [gʌ'steɪʃn] *n.* act of tasting; sense of taste. **gustatory** ['gʌstətəri, gʌ'steɪt–], *adj.*

gutta ['gʌtə] *n.* (*pl.* **–ae**) drop. **gutta-percha,** *n.* rubber-like substance. **gutta rosacea,** acne rosacea. **gutta serena,** amaurosis. **guttate,** *adj.* like a drop; having spots like drops. **guttiferous,** *adj.* yielding gum. **guttiform,** *adj.* drop-shaped. **guttation,** *n.* exudation of drops of moisture.

guttule, guttula ['gʌtjuːl, –julə] *n.* small drop; spot like small drop. **guttulous,** *adj.*

gutturotetany [ˌgʌtərə'tetəni] *n.* throat spasm causing stammer.

gyle [gaɪl] *n.* a brewing of beer; wort; fermenting vat.

gymkhana [dʒɪm'kɑːnə] *n.* meeting for competitive sports events, especially equestrian competitions; public place for athletic displays and games.

gymnosophist [dʒɪm'nɒsəfɪst] *n.* ancient Indian ascetic philosopher; nudist. **gymnosophy,** *n.*

gymnosperm ['dʒɪmnəspɜːm] *n.* flowering plant with naked seed. **gymnospermous,** *adj.*

gynaecic [dʒɪ'niːsɪk, dʒaɪ–, gaɪ–] *adj.* female.

gynaecide ['gaɪnɪsaɪd, 'dʒaɪ–] *n.* killing or killer of women. **gynaecidal,** *adj.*

gynaecocentric [ˌgaɪnɪkəʊ'sentrɪk] *adj.* with the female element dominating.

gynaecocracy [ˌgaɪnɪ'kɒkrəsi] *n.* domination of society by women. **gynaecocratic** [–'krætɪk], *adj.*

gynaecolatry [ˌgaɪnɪ'kɒlətri] *n.* worship of women.

gynaecology [ˌgaɪnɪ'kɒlədʒi] *n.* branch of medicine dealing with diseases of women, especially disorders of the reproductive system. **gynaecologic(al),** *adj.* **gynaecologist,** *n.*

gynaecomania [ˌgaɪnɪkəʊ'meɪniə] *n.* sexual craving for women.

gynaecomastia, gynaecomasty [ˌgaɪnɪkəʊ'mæstiə, –'mæsti] *n.* abnormal enlargement of a man's breasts.

gynaecomorphous [ˌgaɪnɪkəʊ'mɔːfəs] *n.* having female form or characteristics.

gynaecopathy [ˌgaɪnɪ'kɒpəθi] *n.* any disease of women. **gynaecopathic** [–'pæθɪk], *adj.*

gynandroid [gaɪ'nændrɔɪd] *adj.* hermaphrodite; applied to woman of masculine physique. **gynandria, gynandrism, gynandry,** *n.* **gynandrous,** *adj.*

gynandromorph [gaɪ'nændrəmɔːf] *n.* animal having both male and female characteristics. **gynandromorphic,** *adj.* **gynandromorphism,** *n.*

gynarchy ['gaɪnɑːki] *n.* government by women. **gynarchic,** *adj.*

gyniatrics [ˌgaɪni'ætrɪks] *n.* treatment of women's diseases.

gynics ['gaɪnɪks] *n.* knowledge of women.

gynocracy [gaɪ'nɒkrəsi] *n.* gynaecocracy.

gynoecium [gaɪ'niːsiəm, dʒaɪ–] *n.* (*pl.* **–cia**) *Botany,* pistils collectively.

gypsum ['dʒɪpsəm] *n.* form of calcium sulphate used in making plaster of Paris; form of alabaster. **gypseous, gypsous,** *adj.* **gypsiferous,** *adj.* containing gypsum.

gyrfalcon *see* **gerfalcon.**

gyrinid [dʒɪ'raɪnɪd] *n.* whirligig beetle; *adj.* like or pertaining to this; belonging to the gyrinid family of beetles.

gyrocompass ['dʒaɪrəʊˌkʌmpəs] *n.* gyroscope with its axis kept horizontal, pointing always to true north.

gyrocopter ['dʒaɪrəkɒptə] *n.* combination of autogyro and helicopter, *i.e.* a rotorcraft having both drive to rotors and a normal propeller.

gyrograph ['dʒaɪrəgrɑːf] *n.* instrument recording wheel's revolutions.

gyromagnetic [ˌdʒaɪrəʊmæg'netɪk] *adj.* denoting the magnetic properties of the spinning electron in an atom.

gyropilot ['dʒaɪrəpaɪlət] *n.* automatic aircraft pilot comprising two gyroscopes.

gyroscope ['dʒaɪrəskəʊp] *n.* solid wheel rotating in a ring, with its axis free to turn; such apparatus with its axis fixed and acting as compass, stabilizer, etc. **gyroscopic** [–'skɒpɪk], *adj.*

gyrostatics [ˌdʒaɪrə'stætɪks] *n.* study of rotating bodies and their properties.

gyve [dʒaɪv] *n.* & *v.t.* fetter.

H

habanera [ˌhɑːbəˈneərə] *n.* slow Cuban dance.

habeas corpus [ˌheɪbiəs ˈkɔːpəs] (*Latin*) *n.* 'that you may have the body'; writ requiring presence of person before judge, court, etc., especially to investigate legality of his or her detention in custody.

habiliments [həˈbɪlɪmənts] *n. pl.* clothing, especially for a particular purpose; equipment, fittings.

habitant [ˈhæbɪtənt, ˌæbiːˈtɒn] (*French*) *n.* (descendant of) French settler in Canada or Louisiana.

habitué [həˈbɪtʃueɪ] (*French*) *n.* frequenter.

hachure [hæˈʃuə] *n.* line used in shading maps to indicate steepness of slope; *v.t.* shade with hachures.

hacienda [ˌhæsiˈendə] (*Spanish*) *n.* farm; estate.

hackle [ˈhækl] *n.* cock's long neck feather; part of angler's fly made from this.

Hades [ˈheɪdiːz] *n.* abode of dead, or king of underworld, of Greek myth; Hell. **Hadean**, *adj.*

hadj [hædʒ] (*Arabic*) *n.* pilgrimage, especially of Muslim to Mecca. **hadji**, *n.* Muslim who has made such pilgrimage.

hadron [ˈhædrɒn] *n.* one of a large class of sub-atomic particles that participate in the strong interaction that holds the atomic nucleus together

haecceity [hekˈsiːəti] *n.* 'thisness'; quality of being here at present.

haemachrome [ˈhiːməkrəʊm, ˈhem–] *n.* colouring matter of blood.

haemagogue [ˈhiːməgɒg, ˈhem–] *n. & adj.* (drug) promoting discharge of blood or menstrual flow. **haemagogic** [–ˈgɒdʒɪk], *adj.*

haemal [ˈhiːml] *adj.* pertaining to blood.

haemarthrosis [ˌhiːmɑːˈθrəʊsɪs, ˌhem–] *n.* extravasation of blood into joint.

haematal [ˈhiːmətl, ˈhem–] *adj.* haemal.

haematencephalon [ˌhiːmətenˈkefəlɒn, ˌhem–, –ˈsef–] *n.* haemorrhage into brain.

haematherm [ˈhiːməθɜːm] *n.* warm-blooded animal. **haemathermal, haemathermous, haematothermal,** *adj.*

haematic [hɪˈmætɪk] *n. & adj.* (drug) acting on blood; pertaining to, like, or coloured like, blood.

haematid [ˈhiːmətɪd, ˈhem–] *n.* red blood corpuscle.

haematite [ˈhiːmətaɪt, ˈhem–] *n.* reddish iron ore. **haematitic** [–ˈtɪtɪk], *adj.*

haematobic [ˌhiːməˈtəʊbɪk, ˌhem–] *n.* parasitic in blood. **haematobious**, *adj.* **haematobium**, *n.* (*pl.* –ia), such organism.

haematocele [ˈhiːmətəʊsiːl, ˈhem–] *n.* cavity or tumour containing blood.

haematocrit [ˈhiːmətəʊkrɪt, ˈhem–] *n.* instrument for separating red blood cells from plasma; ratio, by volume, of blood cells to whole blood.

haematocryal [ˌhiːməˈtɒkriəl, ˌhemə–, –təˈkraɪəl] *adj.* cold-blooded.

haematoid [ˈhiːmətɔɪd, ˈhem–] *adj.* like blood.

haematology [ˌhiːməˈtɒlədʒi, ˌhem–] *n.* study of blood. **haematologic(al)** *adj.* **haematologist**, *n.*

haematoma [ˌhiːməˈtəʊmə, ˌhem–] *n.* swelling containing blood; bruise.

haematonic [ˌhiːməˈtɒnɪk, ˌhem–] *n. & adj.* (drug) stimulating formation of blood.

haematopoiesis [ˌhiːmətəpɔɪˈiːsɪs, ˌhem–] *n.* formation of blood. **haematopoietic**, *adj.*

haematorrhoea [ˌhiːmətəˈriːə, ˌhem–] *n.* discharge of blood.

haematose [ˈhiːmətəʊs, ˈhem–] *adj.* full of blood.

haematuria [ˌhiːməˈtjʊəriə, ˌhem–] *n.* presence of blood in urine.

haemic [ˈhiːmɪk, ˈhem–] *adj.* haemal.

haemocyte [ˈhiːməsaɪt, ˈhem–] *n.* blood corpuscle.

haemogastric [ˌhiːməˈgæstrɪk, ˌhem–] *adj.* marked by gastric haemorrhage.

haemoglobin [ˌhiːməˈgləʊbɪn] *n.* colouring matter of blood's red corpuscles. **haemoglobinic, haemoglobinous,** *adj.*

haemoid [ˈhiːmɔɪd] *adj.* haematoid.

haemolysis [hiːˈmɒləsɪs] *n.* destruction of red blood corpuscles. **haemolytic** [–ˈlɪtɪk], *adj.*

haemophilia [ˌhiːməˈfɪliə, ˌhem–] *n.* condition marked by uncontrollable bleeding from smallest cuts. **haemophiliac, haemophile,** *n.* sufferer from this. **haemophilic,** *adj.*

haemophthalmia [ˌhiːmɒfˈθælmiə, ˌhem–] *n.* discharge of blood into eye.

haemoptysis [hɪˈmɒptɪsɪs] *n.* spitting of blood.

haemorrhage [ˈhemərɪdʒ] *n.* discharge of blood. **haemorrhagic,** *adj.*

haemorrhoids [ˈhemərɔɪdz] *n. pl.* piles.

haemospasia [ˌhiːməˈspeɪziə, ˌhem–, –ʒə] *n.* drawing of blood to part. **haemospastic,** *n. & adj.*

haemostasia, haemostasis [ˌhiːməˈsteɪziə, ˌhem–, –ʒə; hɪˈmɒstəsɪs] *n.* stopping of haemorrhage; blood stagnation. **haemostat,** *n.* instrument for stopping bleeding. **haemostatic** [–ˈstætɪk], *n. & adj.* (agent) for stopping bleeding; styptic.

haemotoxic [ˌhiːməˈtɒksɪk, ˌhem–] *adj.* causing blood-poisoning. **haemotoxin,** *n.*

haeremai [ˈhaɪrəmaɪ, ˈhe–] (*Maori*) *exclamation* welcome!

hageen [həˈdʒiːn] *n.* dromedary.

hagiarchy ['hægiɑːki, 'heɪdʒ–] *n.* government by priests. **hagiocracy** [–'ɒk–], *n.* government by holy persons.

hagiographa [,hægiɒ'grəfə, ,heɪdʒ–] *n. pl.* Old Testament Hebrew scriptures excluding Law and Prophets. **hagiographer, hagiographist,** *n.* writer of hagiographa; writer of saints' lives. **hagiographic,** *adj.* **hagiography,** *n.* hagiology.

hagiolatry [,hægi'ɒlətri, ,heɪdʒ–] *n.* worship of saints. **hagiolater,** *n.* such worshipper. **hagiolatrous,** *adj.*

hagiology [,hægiɒ'lədʒi, ,heɪdʒ–] *n.* description of holy persons or writings; study or writing of saints' lives; list of saints. **hagiologic(al),** *adj.* **hagiologist,** *n.*

hagioscope ['hægiəskəup, 'heɪdʒ–] *n.* opening in transept wall for viewing altar. **hagioscopic** [–'skɒpɪk], *adj.*

ha-ha ['hɑːhɑː] *n.* sunk fence.

haiku ['haɪkuː] *n.* Japanese poem of three lines of 5, 7 and 5 syllables.

hajib ['hɑːdʒɪb] (*Arabic*) *n.* Muslim court chamberlain.

hajj *see* **hadji**.

hakeem [hə'kiːm] (*Arabic*) *n.* Muslim physician.

Hakenkreuz ['hɑːkənkrɔɪts] (*German*) *n.* swastika.

hakim ['hɑːkɪm] *n.* Muslim judge or ruler; hakeem.

halation [hə'leɪʃn] *n.* spreading of light, seen as bright blur at edges in photographs.

halcyon ['hælsiən] *n.* sea bird supposed to calm the waves while nesting on them; kingfisher, especially Australian; *adj.* tranquil. **halcyon days,** calm period of 14 days at winter solstice; any peaceful period. **halcyonian** [–'əuniən], **halcyonic** [–'ɒnɪk]. *adj.*

halfpace ['hɑːfpeɪs] *n.* dais; small landing on staircase.

halibios [,hælɪ'baɪɒs] *n.* collective life of sea. **halibiotic** [–'ɒtɪk], *adj.*

halicore [hə'lɪkəri] *n.* dugong.

halide ['heɪlaɪd, 'hæ–] *n.* compound of halogen with other element or radical.

halieutic(al) [,hælɪ'juːtɪk, –l] *adj.* pertaining to fishing. **halieutics,** *n.* art of fishing.

halitosis [,hælɪ'təusɪs] *n.* foul breath.

halitus ['hælɪtəs] *n.* breath; exhalation. **halituous** [hə'lɪtjuəs], *adj.* **halituosity,** *n.*

hallel ['hælel, hə'leɪl] (*Hebrew*) *n.* psalm(s) of praise.

hallucinogen [,hæluː'sɪnədʒən, hə'luːsɪ–, –en] *n.* substance, especially a drug, that causes hallucinations. **hallucinogenic** [–'dʒenɪk], *adj.* **hallucinosis,** *n.* mental disorder characterized by hallucinations.

hallux ['hæləks] *n.* (*pl.* **–uces**) big toe; hind toe of birds. **hallucal** ['hæljukl], *adj.*

halobios [,hæləu'baɪɒs] *n.* halibios. **halobiotic** [–'ɒtɪk], *adj.*

halogen ['hælədʒen, –ən] *n.* any of a group of elements that unite directly with metal to form a salt, *e.g.* bromine, chlorine, fluorine, iodine.

haloid ['hælɔɪd] *adj.* like salt; *n.* halide. **halolimnic,** *adj.* applied to sea creatures adapted to fresh-water life. **halomancy,** *n.* divination by salt. **halometer,** *n.* device for measuring the crystals of salts. **halophilous,** *adj.* growing in salt water.

halophyte, *n.* plant growing in salty soil or water. **haloxene,** *adj.* unable to live in salt water.

halva(h) ['hælvə] *n.* confection of sesame seeds and honey.

hamadryad [,hæmə'draɪəd, –æd] *n.* wood nymph associated with one particular tree; king cobra.

hamal [hə'mɑːl] (*Turkish*) *n.* porter; litter-bearer; male servant.

hamartiology [hə,mɑːti'ɒlədʒi] *n.* division of theology dealing with sin. **hamartiologist,** *n.*

hamate ['heɪmeɪt] *adj.* hooked; hook-like. **hamiform,** *adj.* hook-shaped. **hamirostrate,** *adj.* with hooked beak.

hammam [hə'mɑːm] (*Turkish*) *n.* Turkish bath.

hamular ['hæmjulə] *adj.* hamate. **hamulate, hamulose, hamulous,** *adj.* having small hook. **hamulus,** *n.* (*pl.* **–li**) small hook-like projection from bristle, feather, etc.

handsel ['hænsl] *n.* gift, especially at New Year; first money taken at shop; earnest money; *v.t.* give handsel; inaugurate with gift, etc.; attempt for first time. **handseller,** *n.* cheap-jack.

hanif [hæ'niːf] (*Arabic*) *n.* orthodox Muslim. **hanifism,** *n.*

hapaxanthous [,hæpæk'sænθəs] *adj.* having one flowering period only.

hapax legomenon [,hæpæks lɪ'gɒmɪnən] (*Greek*) *n.* (*pl.* ... **legomena**) word or phrase of which there is only one recorded use.

haplography [hæ'plɒgrəfi] *n.* accidental omission of letters, words or lines in copying.

haploid ['hæplɔɪd] *adj.* single; *Biology*, having the specific chromosome number; *n.* such cell. **haploidy,** *n.* state of being haploid.

haplology, haplolaly [hæ'plɒlədʒi, –əli] *n.* omission of syllable(s) of word in pronunciation. **haplologic,** *adj.*

haplotype ['hæpləutaɪp] *n.* single species contained in a genus.

haptic ['hæptɪk] *adj.* pertaining to sense of touch. **haptics,** *n.* psychological study of sensations. **haptometer,** *n.* instrument measuring tactile sensitiveness.

hara-kiri [,hærə'kɪri] (*Japanese*) *n.* suicide by disembowelling.

harbinger ['hɑːbɪndʒə] *n.* person or thing that signals, or gives warning of, what is to come; precursor.

harengiform [hə'rendʒɪfɔːm] *adj.* shaped like a herring.

hariolate ['hæriəleɪt] *v.i.* prophesy; tell fortunes. **hariolation,** *n.*

harmattan [hɑː'mætn, ,hɑːmə'tæn] *n.* dry east wind blowing from Sahara.

harpagon, harpago ['hɑːpəgɒn, –gəu] *n.* grapnel; harpoon.

harquebus(e) *see* **arquebus(e)**.

hartal [hɑː'tɑːl] (*Hindi*) *n.* general strike.

hartebeest ['hɑːtɪbiːst] *n.* large S African antelope.

hartshorn ['hɑːtshɔːn] *n.* plantain; sal volatile.

haruspex [hə'rʌspeks, 'hærə–] *n.* (*pl.* **–pices**) soothsayer, especially divining by sacrifice's entrails. **haruspical, haruspicate,** *adj.* **haruspication, haruspicy.** [–ɪsɪ], *n.*

haslet ['heɪzlət, 'heɪs–] *n.* animal's fry or entrails, especially braised or compressed into a meat loaf.

haslock ['hæslɒk] *n.* wool on sheep's throat.

hastate ['hæsteɪt] *adj.* spear-shaped; like blade of halberd.

hatchment ['hætʃmənt] *n.* diamond-shaped escutcheon bearing deceased person's arms.

hauberk ['hɔːbɜːk] *n.* tunic-like coat of mail.

haulm [hɔːm] *n.* stalks of potatoes, beans, etc.

Hausfrau ['hausfrau] (*German*) *n.* housewife.

haustellum [hɔː'steləm] *n.* (*pl.* **–la**) sucking proboscis. **haustellate**, *adj.* having a haustellum, as a fly. **haustorium**, (*pl.* **–ia**) food-absorbing outgrowth from fungus or parasitic plant. **haustorial**, *adj.* haustellate.

haute couture [ˌəut ku'tjuə] (*French*) *n.* 'high fashion'; (fashion houses that produce) stylish, expensive clothing.

haute école [ˌəut eɪ'kɒl] (*French*) *n.* 'high school'; mastery of difficult horsemanship.

hauteur [əu'tɜː] *n.* haughty manner.

haut monde [ˌəu 'mɒnd] (*French*) *n.* 'high world'; high society. **haut ton** [–'tɒn], *n.* high fashion; bon ton.

havelock ['hævlɒk] *n.* cloth hanging from back of soldier's cap as protection against sun.

havildar ['hævɪldɑː] (*Anglo-Indian*) *n.* sepoy sergeant.

haysel ['heɪsl] *n.* haymaking season.

hebdomad ['hebdəmæd] *n.* (group of) seven; a week. **hebdomadal** [heb'dɒmədl] weekly; consisting of a week. **hebdomadary**, *adj.*

hebephrenia [ˌhiːbɪ'friːniə] *n.* schizophrenia occurring at puberty. **hebephrenic** [–'frenɪk], *adj.*

hebetate ['hebɪteɪt] *v.i. & t.* make or become blunt or dull; *adj.* dull-witted. **hebetation**, *n.* **hebetative**, *adj.*

hebetic [hɪ'betɪk] *adj.* pertaining to or occurring at puberty.

hebetude ['hebɪtjuːd] *n.* stupidity. **hebetudinous**, *adj.*

hecatomb ['hekətuːm, –əum] *n.* sacrifice of one hundred animals; wholesale slaughter

hecatontarchy [ˌhekə'tɒntɑːki] *n.* government by 100 persons.

hectic ['hektɪk] *adj.* habitual, especially in wasting diseases; consumptive; *popularly*, excited; feverish.

hectograph ['hektəgrɑːf] *n.* duplicating machine using gelatine slab; *v.t.* duplicate thus. **hectographic**, *adj.* **hectography**, *n.*

hederaceous [ˌhedə'reɪʃəs] *adj.* pertaining to or like ivy. **hederate**, *adj.* crowned with ivy. **hederic** [–'derɪk], *adj.* hederiferous, *adj.* bearing ivy. **hederiform**, *adj.* shaped like ivy leaves. **hederigerent**, *adj.* bearing or ornamented with ivy. **hederose**, *adj.* having much ivy.

hedonic [hɪdɒn'ɪk] *adj.* pertaining to pleasure. **hedonism** [hiː'dɒn–], *n.* philosophical doctrine that pleasure is sole moral good; life of pleasure. **hedonist**, *n.* **hedonistic**, *adj.* **hedonology**, **hedonics**, *n.* ethical or psychological study of pleasure.

hegemony [hɪ'gemənɪ, –'dʒe–] *n.* leadership; authority. **hegemonic** [–ɪ'mɒnɪk], *adj.*

Hegira, Hejira ['hedʒɪrə, hɪ'dʒaɪrə] *n.* Muslim era, dating from Mohammed's flight from Mecca, AD 622; flight.

heifer ['hefə] *n.* cow that has not calved.

heinous ['hiːnəs] *adj.* hateful; atrocious; unpardonable.

helcology [hel'kɒlədʒɪ] *n. Medicine*, study of ulcers. **helcoid**, *adj.* ulcer-like. **helcosis**, *n.* ulceration. **helcotic**, *adj.*

heliacal [hɪ'laɪəkl] *adj.* near or pertaining to sun.

helical ['helɪkl] *adj.* spiral; pertaining to helix. **heliciform** [he'lɪsɪfɔːm], **helicine** [–saɪn], **helicoid**, *adj.* **helicograph**, *n.* instrument for drawing spirals.

heliocentric [ˌhiːliəu'sentrɪk] *adj.* pertaining to centre of sun; having sun as centre.

helioelectric [ˌhiːliəuɪ'lektrɪk] *adj.* pertaining to electricity radiated from sun.

heliofugal [ˌhiːli'ɒfjugl, –iə'fjuːgl] *adj.* moving away from sun.

heliograph ['hiːliəgrɑːf] *n.* mirror apparatus for signalling by flashes of light; *v.i. & t.* signal with this. **heliogram**, *n.* message sent by heliograph. **heliographic**, *adj.*

helioid ['hiːliɔɪd] *adj.* like the sun.

heliolater [ˌhiːli'ɒlətə] *n.* sun-worshipper. **heliolatrous**, *adj.* heliolatry, *n.*

heliology [ˌhiːli'ɒlədʒɪ] *n.* astronomical study of sun. **heliologist**, *n.*

heliometer [ˌhiːli'ɒmɪtə] *n.* micrometer measuring short interstellar distances. **heliometric** [–'metrɪk], *adj.* **heliometry**, *n.*

heliophilous [ˌhiːli'ɒfɪləs] *adj.* attracted by sunlight. **heliophilia** [–'fɪliə], *n.* **heliophile**, **heliophiliac**, *n.*

heliophobia [ˌhiːliə'fəubiə] *n.* dread or avoidance of sunlight; excessive sensitiveness to sunlight. **heliophobe**, *n.* **heliophobic**, *adj.*

heliophyte ['hiːliəfaɪt] *n.* plant flourishing in sunlight. **heliophytic** [–'fɪtɪk], *adj.*

helioscope ['hiːliəskəup] *n.* instrument for observing sun. **helioscopic** [–'skɒpɪk], *adj.* **helioscopy** [–'ɒskəpɪ], *n.*

heliosis [ˌhiːli'əusɪs] *n.* sun scorching of plants; sunstroke.

heliostat ['hiːliəstæt] *n.* instrument using a mirror to reflect sunlight in a fixed direction, used for studying the sun or signalling messages.

heliotaxis [ˌhiːliəu'tæksɪs] *n.* movement towards or away from sunlight. **heliotactic**, *adj.*

heliotherapy [ˌhiːliəu'θerəpi] *n.* medical treatment by sunlight.

heliotropism [ˌhiːli'ɒtrəpɪzm, 'hiːliətrəup–] *n.* growth or movement directed by sunlight; growth towards the sun. **heliotropic** [–'trɒpɪk], *adj.*

helium ['hiːliəm] *n.* non-inflammable, lighter-than-air, inert gas.

helix ['hiːlɪks] *n.* (*pl.* **–ices** ['helɪsiːz]) any spiral-formed object; rim of outer ear; snail-shell; screw-thread.

hellebore ['helɪbɔː] *n.* several kinds of plant, especially the Christmas rose; alkaloid poison extracted from hellebore root.

Hellene ['heliːn] *n.* Greek. **Hellenic** [–'lenɪk], *adj.* Hellenism, *n.* Greek culture, idiom or language. **Hellenist**, *n.* expert on Greek literature. **Hellenize**, *v.t.* make Greek in manner or character.

helminth ['helmɪnθ] *n.* intestinal worm. **helminthagogue**, *n.* anthelmintic. **helminthiasis**, **helminthism**, *n.* infestation with helminths. **helminthic**, *adj.* **helminthoid**, *adj.* like helminth. **helminthology**, *n.* study of helminths. **helminthous**, *adj.* infested with helminths.

helobious [hɪ'ləubiəs] *adj.* dwelling in marshes. **helodes** [-'ləudiːz], *n.* marsh fever; *adj.* marshy.

heloma [hɪ'ləumə] *n. Medicine*, corn. **helosis**, *n.* state of having corns.

helot ['helət] *n.* slave, especially of Sparta. **helotism, helotry**, *n.* slavery.

helotomy [hɪ'lɒtəmi] *n.* cutting of corns.

helve [helv] *n.* handle; hilt.

Helvetian, Helvetic [hel'viːʃn, -'vetɪk] *n. & adj.* Swiss (person).

hematite, hemorrhage, etc., *n. see* **haematite, haemorrhage**, etc.

hemeralopia [ˌhemərə'ləupiə] *n.* ability to see only in faint or no light; day blindness. **hemeralope,** *n.* **hemeralopic** [-'lɒpɪk], *adj.*

hemerology, hemerologium [ˌhemər'ɒlədʒi, -ə'ləudʒiəm] *n.* calendar.

hemialgia [ˌhemi'ældʒiə] *n.* pain in one half of body or head. **hemianopsia, hemianopia,** *n.* blindness affecting half the field of vision. **hemicrania,** *n.* hemialgia of the head. **hemifacial,** *adj.* pertaining to one side of face. **hemiplegia,** *n.* paralysis of one half (left or right) of body.

hemiptera [hɪ'mɪptərə] *n. pl.* order of insects containing the bugs. **hemipteral, hemipteroid, hemipterous,** *adj.* **hemipteran, hemipteron,** *n.* bug. **hemipterology,** *n.* study of hemiptera.

hemistich ['hemɪstɪk] *n.* half a verse line. **hemistichal,** *adj.*

hemitery, hemiteria ['hemɪtəri, ˌhemɪ'tɪəriə] *n.* congenital malformation. **hemiteratic,** *adj.*

hendecagon [hen'dekəgən, -ɒn] *n.* 11-sided plane figure. **hendecahedron,** *n.* 11-sided solid figure. **hendecasyllable,** *n.* verse line of 11 syllables.

hendiadys [hen'daɪədɪs] *n.* use of two nouns joined by *and*, instead of a noun and an adjective.

henequen ['henɪkɪn] *n.* hard fibre from leaf of a Mexican agave, used for cords, rope, etc.; this plant.

henism ['henɪzm] *n.* philosophical belief that existence is of one kind only.

henogeny, henogenesis [he'nɒdʒəni, ˌhenə'dʒenəsɪs] *n.* ontogeny.

henotic [he'nɒtɪk] *adj.* promoting harmony or peace.

henry ['henri] *n.* unit of electrical inductance: inductance of circuit in which one volt is induced by current varying at one ampere per second.

heortology [ˌhiːɔː'tɒlədʒi] *n.* study of religious festivals, year, etc. **heortologion** [-'ləudʒiən], *n.* calendar of feast days.

hepatic [hɪ'pætɪk] *adj.* pertaining to or like liver; liver-coloured; *n.* liver medicine; liverwort. **hepatology,** *n.* botanical study of liverworts. **hepatitis,** *n.* inflammation of liver. **hepatoid,** *adj.* like liver.

hephaestic, hephaestian [hɪ'fiːstɪk, -'fes-, -tiən] *adj.* pertaining to Hephaestus, Greek god of fire and iron-working; pertaining to smiths.

heptachlor ['heptəklɔː] *n.* chemical pesticide forbidden in the U.K. since 1964.

heptachord ['heptəkɔːd] *n.* seven-tone musical scale; interval of a major seventh.

heptad ['heptæd] *n.* group of seven.

heptagon ['heptəgən] *n.* seven-sided plane figure. **heptagonal** [-'tægənl], *adj.*

heptahedron [ˌheptə'hiːdrən] *n.* seven-sided solid figure. **heptahedral,** *adj.*

heptameride [hep'tæməraɪd] *n.* writing in seven parts. **heptameter,** *n.* verse line of seven feet.

heptamerous, *adj.* having seven divisions; *Botany*, having the parts of flower in sevens. **heptapody,** *n.* heptameter.

heptarch ['heptɑːk] *n.* member of heptarchy. **heptarchal, heptarchic,** *adj.* **heptarchy,** *n.* government by seven persons; group of seven allied but independent kingdoms, especially of Anglo-Saxon England.

heptastich ['heptəstɪk] *n.* poem or stanza of seven lines.

heptasyllable ['heptəˌsɪləbl] *n.* verse line or word of seven syllables. **heptasyllabic** [-'læbɪk], *adj.*

heptateuch ['heptətjuːk] *n.* first seven books of Bible.

hepteris [hep'tɪərɪs] *n.* galley with seven banks of oars.

heraclean [ˌherə'kliːən] *adj.* herculean.

herbarium [hɜː'beəriəm] *n.* collection of dried plant specimens; museum or room holding it. **herbarial,** *adj.*

herbicide ['hɜːbɪsaɪd] *n.* weed-killer.

herbivorous [hɜː'bɪvərəs] *adj.* feeding on plants. **herbivore,** *n.* such animal. **herbivority,** *n.*

herculean [ˌhɜːkju'liːən, hɜː'kjuːliən] *adj.* pertaining to Hercules and his labours; of or requiring enormous strength. **herculanean, herculanian,** *adj.*

hereditament [ˌherə'dɪtəmənt] *n.* inheritance; hereditable property. **hereditable,** *adj.* capable of being inherited.

heresiarch [hə'riːsiɑːk, 'herəs-] *n.* leading heretic. **heresiography, heresiology,** *n.* study of or treatise on heresies.

heresy ['herəsi] *n.* unorthodox religious belief. **heretic** ['herətɪk]), *n.* **heretical** [hə'retɪkl], *adj.* **hereticate, hereticize,** *v.t.* denounce as heretic. **hereticide,** *n.* killer or killing of heretic.

heriot ['heriət] *n.* payment to feudal lord on death of tenant.

herisson ['herɪsn] *n.* pivoted beam with iron spikes, protecting wall, passage, etc.; soldier's punishment of being made to sit astride a herisson.

heritor ['herɪtə] *n.* owner; inheritor. **heretrix, heritrix,** *n.* heiress.

hermaphrodite [hɜː'mæfrədaɪt] *n. & adj.* (person, plant, etc.) with characteristics, especially generative organs, of both sexes. **hermaphrodite brig,** brigantine. **hermaphroditic** [-'dɪtɪk], *adj.* **hermaphroditism,** *n.*

hermeneutic [ˌhɜːmə'njuːtɪk] *adj.* explaining; interpreting. **hermeneutics,** *n.* definition of laws of interpretation of Scriptures.

hernia ['hɜːniə] *n.* rupture. **herniorrhaphy,** *n.* surgical operation for this. **herniate,** *v.i.* protrude as hernia. **herniation,** *n.*

herpes ['hɜːpiːz] *n.* disease caused by one of the herpes viruses, especially chicken pox, cold sores, genital herpes, shingles. **herpetic** [-'petɪk], *adj.* **herpetiform,** *adj.* like herpes; like a reptile. **herpetography,** *n.* study of herpetic disease; treatise on reptiles. **herpetology,** *n.* study of reptiles. **herpetophobia,** *n.* dread of reptiles.

Herrenvolk ['herənfolk] (*German*) *n.* 'master race'; superior nation.

hertz [hɜːts] *n.* unit of frequency, equal to one cycle per second (*abbr.* **Hz.**)

hertzian ['hɜːtsiən] *adj.* applied to electromagnetic waves of radio frequency, experimented on by Heinrich Hertz.

Herzog ['hɜːtsɒg] (*German*) *n.* (*pl.* **Herzöge**) duke.

Hesperian [he'spɪəriən] *adj.* pertaining to Hesperia (Italy or Spain) or Hesperus, the evening star; western.

hesperidium [,hespə'rɪdiəm] *n.* (*pl.* **–ia**) *Botany*, citrus-type fruit.

Hessian ['hesiən] *adj.* pertaining to Hesse; *n.* mercenary soldier. **Hessian boot**, high tasselled boot. **Hessian fly**, fly with larva harmful to wheat. **hessian**, *n.* kind of coarse sacking.

hesternal [he'stɜːnl] *adj.* pertaining to yesterday.

hesychastic [,hesɪ'kæstɪk] *adj.* soothing. **hesychasm**, *n.* omphaloskepsis.

hetaera, hetaira [hɪ'taɪrə] *n.* (*pl.* **–ae**, **–ai**) educated courtesan of ancient Greece; prostitute. **hetaeria**, *n.* (*pl.* **–ae**) society; club. **hetaerism**, *n.* concubinage; primitive communal ownership of women. **hetaerocracy**, *n.* government by courtesans, or by Fellows of college.

heterize ['hetəraɪz] *v.t.* transform. **heterism**, *n.* variation.

heterochiral [,hetərə'kaɪrəl] *adj.* laterally inverted.

heterochromatic ['hetərəkrəʊ'mætɪk] *adj.* pertaining to or having different colours. **heterochromia, heterochromy**, *n.* state of being heterochromatic. **heterochromous**, *adj.*

heterochthonous [,hetə'rɒkθənəs] *adj.* not autochthonous.

heteroclite ['hetərəklaɪt] *adj.* abnormal; irregular; *n.* such word, thing or person.

heterodox ['hetərədɒks] *adj.* not orthodox. **heterodoxy**, *n.* such belief or behaviour.

heterodyne ['hetərədaɪn] *n.* *Radio*, production of 'beats' by superimposition of oscillations of slightly different frequency upon the waves being received; use of this 'beat' frequency in radio reception; interference, especially whistle, due to heterodyne; *v.i.* produce heterodyne; cause interference thus.

heteroepy ['hetərəʊɪpi, ,hetə'rəʊɪpi] *n.* pronunciation different from standard. **heteroepic** [–'epɪk], *adj.*

heteroerotism [,hetərəʊ'erətɪzm] *n.* sexual love for another person. **heteroerotic** [–ɪ'rɒtɪk], *adj.*

heterogeneous [,hetərə'dʒiːniəs] *adj.* comprising different parts or qualities; diverse. **heterogeneity** [–dʒə'niːəti, –'neɪ–], *n.* **heterogenesis** [–'dʒenəsɪs], *n.* parthenogenesis; abiogenesis; alternation of generations. **heterogenous** [–'rɒdʒɪnəs], *adj.* originating elsewhere; of different origin. **heterogeny** [–'rɒdʒəni], *n.* heterogeneous collection.

heterograft ['hetərəʊgrɑːft] *n.* surgical graft or transplant in which donor and recipient belong to different species.

heterography [,hetə'rɒgrəfi] *n.* spelling different from standard, or in which same letter represents different sounds.

heterolateral [,hetərə'lætərəl] *adj.* pertaining to opposite sides.

heterologous [,hetə'rɒləgəs] *adj.* differing; comprising different parts or parts in different proportions. **heterologic(al)**, *adj.* **heterology**, *n.*

heteromorphic [,hetərə'mɔːfɪk] *adj.* of abnormal form; having different forms. **heteromorphism**, *n.* **heteromorphous**, *adj.*

heteronomous [,hetə'rɒnəməs] *adj.* not autonomous. **heteronomy**, *n.*

heteronym ['hetərənɪm] *n.* word having same spelling as, but different sound and meaning from, another; exactly equivalent word in other language. **heteronymous** [–'rɒnɪməs], *adj.*

heteroousia [,hetərəʊ'uːsiə, –'aʊ–] *n.* difference of substance. **heteroousian**, *adj.*; *n.* *Theology*, adherent of belief that Son is of different substance from Father.

heteropathy [,hetə'rɒpəθi] *n.* allopathy; excessive sensitivity. **heteropathic** [–'pæθɪk], *adj.*

heterophemy ['hetərəfiːmi] *n.* accidental speaking or writing of words different from those meant. **heterophemize**, *v.i.* **heterophemism**, **heterophemist**, *n.*

heterophoria [,hetərə'fɔːriə] *n.* squint due to weak muscle. **heterophoric** [–'fɒrɪk], *adj.*

heterophyte ['hetərəfaɪt] *n.* plant dependent on another. **heterophytic** [–'fɪtɪk], *adj.*

heterosexual [,hetərə'sekʃuəl, –sju–] *adj.* sexually attracted to persons of the opposite sex. **heterosexuality**, *n.* **heterosexism**, *n.* discrimination against homosexuals. **heterosexist**, *n. & adj.*

heterosis [,hetə'rəʊsɪs] *n.* tendency of a crossbred individual to show greater vigour and capacity for growth than its parents.

heterotaxis [,hetərə'tæksɪs] *n.* abnormality in arrangement. **heterotactic, heterotactous, heterotaxic**, *adj.*

heterotelic [,hetərə'telɪk, –'tiː–] *adj.* not autotelic.

heterotopia [,hetərə'təʊpiə] *n.* displacement of an organ from its normal position in the body. **heterotopic**, *adj.*

heterotrichosis [,hetərətrɪ'kəʊsɪs] *n.* having variegated coloured hair.

heterotropia [,hetərə'trəʊpiə] *n.* squint.

heterozygote [,hetərə'zaɪgəʊt] *n.* organism or cell have different alleles for a particular inherited characteristic; hybrid. **heterozygosis**, *n.* condition of being a heterozygote. **heterozygotic**, *adj.*

hetman ['hetmən] *n.* Cossack or Polish commander or ruler.

heuristic [hju'rɪstɪk] *adj.* revealing; leading to discovery; using trial and error to arrive at a solution; *n.* such argument or process. **heuristics**, *n.* in computing, process by which a program improves its performance by learning from its own experience.

hexachord ['heksəkɔːd] *n.* six-tone musical scale; interval of major sixth.

hexad ['heksæd] *n.* group of six. **hexadic**, *adj.*

hexaemeron, hexahemeron [,heksə'emərɒn, –'hem–] *n.* six days of Creation; treatise on or history of this. **hexaemeric** [–'merɪk], *adj.*

hexagon ['heksəgən] *n.* six-sided plane figure. **hexagonal** [–'sægənl], *adj.*

hexagram ['heksəgræm] *n.* six-pointed star.

hexahedron [,heksə'hiːdrən] *n.* six-sided solid figure. **hexahedral**, *adj.*

hexameron [hek'sæmərɒn] *n.* hexaemeron. **hexameral, hexamerous**, *adj.* having six parts; *Botany*, having parts of flower in sixes.

hexameter [hek'sæmɪtə] *n.* verse-line of six feet. **hexametral, hexametric** [–'met–], *adj.*

hexapod ['heksəpɒd] *n.* insect; *adj.* pertaining to insects; having six feet.

hexarchy ['heksɑːki] *n.* group of six allied but independent states.

hexastich ['heksəstɪk] *n.* poem or stanza of six lines. **hexastichic,** *adj.* **hexastichous,** *adj. Botany,* six-ranked.

hexasyllable ['heksə,sɪləbl] *n.* verse-line or word of six syllables. **hexasyllabic** [–'læbɪk], *adj.*

hexateuch ['heksətjuːk] *n.* first six books of Bible.

hexeris [hek'sɪərɪs] *n.* galley with six banks of oars.

hexicology [,heksɪ'kɒlədʒi] *n.* ecology.

hiatus [haɪ'eɪtəs] *n.* gap; pause, especially between vowels.

hibernacle ['haɪbənækl] *n.* winter quarters. **hibernacular** [–'nækjʊlə], *adj.* **hibernaculum,** *n.* (*pl.* **–la**) hibernacle; winter bud.

hibernal [haɪ'bɜːnl] *adj.* pertaining to winter.

Hibernian [haɪ'bɜːniən] *n.* & *adj.* Irish (person).

hic jacet [,hɪk 'jæket, –'dʒeɪsɪt] (*Latin*) 'here lies'; epitaph. **hic sepultus** [–sɪ'pʌltəs, –'pʊl–], 'here is buried'.

hidalgo [hɪ'dælgəʊ] (*Spanish*) *n.* gentleman; noble of lower rank.

hidrosis [hɪ'drəʊsɪs, haɪ–] *n.* perspiration, especially excessive. **hidrotic** [–'drɒtɪk], *n.* & *adj.* (drug) causing perspiration.

hiemal ['haɪəml] *adj.* pertaining to winter.

hieracosphinx [haɪ'reɪkəsfɪŋks] *n.* sphinx with head of hawk.

hierarch ['haɪrɑːk] *n.* chief priest. **hierarchal,** *adj.* **hierarchical,** *adj.* pertaining to a hierarchy. **hierarchy,** *n.* body of chief priests; body of persons in authority in ranks from highest to lowest; such ranking of officials, objects or facts.

hieratic [haɪ'rætɪk] *adj.* priestly, especially applied to ancient Egyptian writing used for religious works.

hierocracy [haɪ'rɒkrəsi] *n.* government by clerics. **hierocratic** [–'krætɪk], *adj.*

hierodule ['haɪrədjuːl, –duːl] *n.* ancient Greek temple slave. **hierodulic,** *adj.*

hieroglyph ['haɪrəglɪf] *n.* picture of object representing sound or word in ancient Egyptian writing. **hieroglyphic,** *n.* & *adj.* **hieroglyphics,** *n.* such picture-writing; illegible handwriting. **hieroglyphist,** *n.* writer of hieroglyphics. **hieroglyphology,** *n.* study of hieroglyphics. **hieroglyphy,** *n.* writing with hieroglyphics.

hierogram ['haɪrəgræm] *n.* sacred symbol. **hierogrammat(e),** *n.* writer of sacred annals or hieroglyphics.

hierography [haɪ'rɒgrəfi] *n.* writing on religious subjects. **hierology,** *n.* religious knowledge or tradition; hagiology.

hieromachy [haɪ'rɒməki] *n.* quarrel between clerics. **hieromancy,** *n.* divination by sacrificed objects.

Hieronymic, Hieronymian [,haɪrə'nɪmɪk, –iən] *n.* pertaining to or by St. Jerome (4th-5th century AD).

hierophant ['haɪrəfænt] *n.* priest; person engaged in or explaining religious mysteries. **hierophantic,** *adj.*

hierurgy ['haɪrɜːdʒi] *n.* religious worship or work. **hierurgical,** *adj.*

hinny ['hɪni] *n.* hybrid of stallion and she-ass.

hinterland ['hɪntəlænd] *n.* inland area behind coast or coastal town.

hippiater ['hɪpieɪtə] *n.* horse-doctor. **hippiatric** [–'ætrɪk], *adj.* **hippiatry** [–ætri, –'aɪətri], **hippiatrics,** *n.*

hippocampus [,hɪpə'kæmpəs] *n.* (*pl.* **–pi**) seahorse; part of the brain. **hippocampal, hippocampine,** *adj.*

hippocras ['hɪpəkræs] *n.* medieval spiced wine.

hippocrepiform [,hɪpə'krepɪfɔːm] *adj.* shaped like a horseshoe.

hippogriff, hippogryph ['hɪpəgrɪf] *n.* fabulous winged monster with body of horse.

hippoid ['hɪpɔɪd] *adj.* pertaining to or like a horse.

hippology [hɪ'pɒlədʒi] *n.* study of the horse. **hippological,** *adj.* **hippologist,** *n.*

hippophagous [hɪ'pɒfəgəs] *adj.* eating horseflesh. **hippophagi** [–dʒaɪ], *n.pl.* eaters of horseflesh. **hippophagism, hippophagy,** *n.*

hippophile ['hɪpəfaɪl] *n.* lover of horses or horseriding. **hippophobia,** *n.* dread of horses.

hippotomy [hɪ'pɒtəmi] *n.* horse's anatomy. **hippotomical** [–'tɒmɪkl], *adj.* **hippotomist,** *n.*

hircarra(h) [hə'kɑːrə] (*Persian*) *n.* spy; messenger.

hircine ['hɜːsaɪn, –sɪn] *adj.* pertaining to or like goats; indecent. **hircinous,** *adj.* with goat-like odour.

hirrient ['hɪriənt] *n.* & *adj.* trilled (sound), as *r.*

hirsute ['hɜːsjuːt] *adj.* hairy. **hirsuties** [–'sjuːʃiːz], **hirsutism,** *n.* undue hairiness.

hirudinean [,hɪru'dɪniən] *n.* & *adj.* (pertaining to) leech. **hirudine,** *adj.* **hirudinoid** [–'ruːdɪnɔɪd], *adj.* like a leech.

hirundine [hɪ'rʌndaɪn, –ɪn] *adj.* pertaining to or like a swallow; *n.* such bird. **hirundinous,** *adj.*

Hispanic [hɪ'spænɪk] *adj.* Spanish. **Hispanicism,** *n.* Spanish idiom. **Hispanophile,** *n.* & *adj.* (person) fond of Spain, Spanish life, etc.

hispid ['hɪspɪd] *adj.* bristly. **hispidity,** *n.* **hispidulate, hispidulous,** *adj.* with minute bristles.

histamine ['hɪstəmiːn] *n.* vasoconstrictive substance created in tissue at site of injury, ultimate cause of hay fever, nettlerash, and other allergic disorders.

histology [hɪ'stɒlədʒi] *n.* study of or treatise on organic tissue. **histological,** *adj.* **histologist,** *n.* **histography,** *n.* description of such tissues. **histolysis,** *n.* decay of same. **histopathology,** *n.* (study of) effects of disease on tissues.

historiographer [hɪ,stɒri'ɒgrəfə] *n.* historian, especially one specially appointed. **historiographic(al),** *adj.* **historiography,** *n.* **historiometry,** *n.* statistical study of history.

histrionic [,hɪstri'ɒnɪk] *adj.* pertaining to or like stage-acting; theatrical. **histrionicism** [–sɪzm], *n.* art of acting. **histrionism,** *n.* theatrical manner. **histrionics,** *n.pl.* theatrical presentation, behaviour or language.

hoatzin, hoactzin [həʊ'ætsɪn] *n.* S American crested bird; stinkbird.

hobson-jobson [,hɒbsn'dʒɒbsn] *n.* Anglicized word or language corrupted from Oriental word or words.

hodiernal [,həʊdi'ɜːnl] *adj.* pertaining to today.

How do you say ...?

amen [ɑː'men] is the standard pronunciation in Britain, although Roman Catholics tend to favour [eɪ'men]. In America [eɪ'men] is the usual pronunciation, but [ɑː'men] is used in singing.

aristocrat ['ærɪstəkræt] is the main pronunciation in Britain. Americans say mainly [ə'rɪstəkræt], which is also used in Britain.

centrifugal British speakers say mainly [ˌsentrɪ'fjuːgl̩], but they also use [sen'trɪfjəgl̩], which is the only American pronunciation.

consummate The verb is pronounced ['kɒnsəmeɪt]. The standard pronunciation of the adjective is [kən'sʌmət], but ['kɒnsəmeɪt] (or [–sjuː–, –sjə–, –mət]) is also used.

contrary In the sense 'opposite' it is pronounced ['kɒntrəri], in the sense 'perverse' [kən'treəri].

contribute The standard British pronunciation is [kən'trɪbjuːt]. ['kɒntrɪbjuːt] (after *contribution*) is increasingly heard, but widely disapproved of. Americans say only [kən'trɪbjuːt].

controversy The traditionally 'correct' pronunciation is ['kɒntrəvɜːsi], but it has now probably been overtaken in frequency in Britain by [kən'trɒvəsi]. Americans say only ['kɒntrəvɜːsi].

covert The traditional pronunciation is ['kʌvət], but an alternative pronunciation ['kəʊvɜːt] is increasingly heard, especially in contexts of espionage and other clandestine activities.

decade The standard way of saying it is ['dekeɪd]. The pronunciation [dɪ'keɪd], as if it rhymed with *decayed*, is widely used but often disapproved of.

deity Both ['deɪəti] and ['diːəti] are common and accepted pronunciations, the former perhaps more so.

demonstrable The commonest British pronunciation is probably [dɪ'mɒnstrəbl], although purists prefer ['demənstrəbl]. Americans only use the form stressed on the second syllable.

despicable By far the most usual pronunciation is [dɪ'spɪkəbl], but some purists try to maintain that the stress ought to be on the first syllable: ['despɪkəbl].

distribute The standard pronunciation is [dɪ'strɪbjuːt]. The pronunciation ['dɪstrɪbjuːt] (modelled on *distribution*) is quite common in Britain, even though it is widely felt to be 'incorrect'.

dynasty In Britain the standard pronunciation is ['dɪnəsti], in America ['daɪnəsti]. The broadcasting in Britain of the American soap opera *Dynasty* in the 1980s familiarised British speakers with the transatlantic version.

either The main British form is ['aɪðə], the main American form is ['iːðə], but each variety also uses the other alternative.

envelope Both ['envələʊp] and ['ɒnvələʊp] are regarded as acceptable, but the former is rather commoner than the latter, which is loosely based on the French pronunciation.

explicable Most people say [ɪk'splɪkəbl], but purists still continue to maintain that what one should say is ['eksplɪkəbl].

formidable Usage is fairly evenly split in British English between ['fɔːmɪdəbl] and [fə'mɪdəbl], although the former is regarded as the more 'correct'. Americans usually place the stress on the first syllable.

Gaelic The general and widespread pronunciation is ['geɪlɪk]. Some people use ['gælɪk] in connection with the language, people, and culture, but more general terms (e.g. *Gaelic coffee, Gaelic football*) are almost exclusively ['geɪlɪk].

garage There are several alternative pronunciations in British English: ['gærɑːdʒ, 'gærɑːʒ, 'gærɪdʒ, gə'rɑːʒ, gə'rɑːdʒ]. The first three are the commonest, with ['gærɪdʒ] being regarded by some people as substandard. Americans put the stress on the second syllable: [gə'rɑːʒ, gə'rɑːdʒ].

harass The traditional British pronunciation is ['hærəs], but in the 1970s the American [hə'ræs] began to appear, and has since become very common. Those who adhere to the traditional version tend to get annoyed by [hə'ræs].

homosexual This word has two pronunciations, [ˌhəʊmə'sekʃuəl] and [ˌhɒmə'sekʃuəl] (or [–sjuː–]). Purists prefer the second, on the grounds that the Greek source of the prefix *homo-* had a short vowel, but in practice [ˌhəʊm–] is probably commoner.

jejune The word is sometimes pronounced [dʒɪ'dʒɜːn], but in fact it has no connection with French *jeune* 'young'. Nor is there any justification for pronouncing it [ʒə'ʒuːn], as if it were a borrowing from French. The generally accepted pronunciation is [dʒɪ'dʒuːn] (or [dʒə–]).

junta The standard anglicised pronuciation in Britiain is ['dʒʌntə]. It is increasingly common to use an approximation to the original Spanish, ['hʊntə[(which is the main american pronunciation), but the halfway-house form ['dʒʊntə[has the advantages of neither tradition nor authenticity.

kilometer θhe traditional British pronunciation, ['kɪləmiːtə], has the advantage that it follows the pattern of *centimetre* and *millimetre*. However, the main American pronunciation, [kɪ'lɒmɪtə], appears to be gaining ground in Britain.

lichen The standard pronunciation is ['laɪkən], which corresponds to the word's Greek origin. However ['lɪtʃən] is also often heard in Britain, and may be regarded as acceptable.

margarine The original pronunciation was [ˌmɑːgə'riːn], reflecting the hard *g* of Greek *margaron* 'pearl', but it has been gradually supplanted by [ˌmɑːdʒə'riːn], and [ˌmɑːgə'riːn] has now almost disappeared. Americans say ['mɑːrdʒərən].

metallurgy British English has two pronunciations, [me'tælədʒi] and ['metəlɜːdʒi]. The former is generally regarded as standard, but

How do you say...?

the latter (which is the preferred American form) is also widely used.

migraine ['miːɡreɪn] is probably the main British pronunciation, but ['maɪɡreɪn] is also widespread. In America, the standard pronunciation is ['maɪɡreɪn]

patent The standard British pronunciation is ['peɪtnt]. In technical usage the word is often pronounced ['pætnt] when it refers to the protection of an invention, but even in this sense ['peɪtnt] is commoner in general usage. Americans use ['pætnt] for all senses of the word except 'obvious', for which they use ['peɪtnt].

pejorative The standard pronunciation is [pə'dʒɒrətɪv], but those who hanker after more traditional forms try to prolong the survival of ['piːdʒərətɪv].

privacy The main British pronunciation is ['prɪvəsi], but ['praɪvəsi] (which is the main American form) is also used.

proven The standard pronunciation is ['pruːvn], although in the context of Scots law (where juries may return a verdict of *not proven*) it is traditional to say ['prəuvn]. The latter is tending to become more widespread in the general language.

racist The accepted pronunciation of the word is ['reɪsɪst] (because it is based on *race*). The pronunciation ['reɪʃɪst] (probably formed by analogy with *racialist* or *fascist*) is generally regarded as incorrect.

research [rɪ'sɜːtʃ] is still regarded as the most acceptable pronunciation, although ['riːsɜːtʃ]

is increasingly common, particularly in America. Some people distinguish between [rɪ'sɜːtʃ] for the verb and ['riːsɜːtʃ] for the noun.

schism The traditional pronunciation is ['sɪzm], but it is now rapidly disappearing in the face of ['skɪzm]. It survives mainly amongst theologians and clergymen.

scone Neither [skɒn] nor [skəun] has any indisputable claim to be *the* 'correct' form, and the choice is largely a matter of personal preference. In Britain, [skɒn] is probably commoner, in America [skəun]. The word should not be confused with *Scone*, the name of a Scottish village, pronounced [skuːn].

swath The pronunciation is either [swɒθ] or [swɔːθ]; in the plural it is [swɒðs], [swɔːθs], or [swɔːðz]. It should not be confused with *swathe*, which is pronounced [sweɪð].

trauma The original English pronunciation is ['trɔːmə], but in recent years ['traumə] has become increasingly common, especially in psychoanalytic contexts. It probably arose partly from a general tendency to pronounce 'foreign'-looking words in a 'continental' way, partly from a specific subconscious association with German *Traum* 'dream.'

Uranus The traditional pronunciation is ['juərənəs]. This had been in long-term decline in the face of [jə'reɪnəs], but ['juərənəs] is now making a comeback (partly, it has been suggested, from a desire to avoid the element [−eɪnəs].

---

hodometry [hɒ'dɒmətri] *n.* measurement of length of ship's voyage. **hodometrical,** *adj.*

hogget ['hɒɡɪt] *n.* boar in its second year; year-old sheep or colt; fleece of year-old sheep.

hogmanay ['hɒɡməneɪ] (*Scottish*) *n.* New Year's Eve; gift, especially cake made on that day.

hoi polloi [ˌhɔɪ pə'lɔɪ] (*Greek*) 'the many'; the masses; the mob.

holagogue ['hɒləɡɒɡ] *n.* drug expelling all morbid humours.

Holarctic [hɒ'lɑːktɪk, həʊ–] *adj.* pertaining to or being the whole arctic region.

holism ['həʊlɪzm] *n.* philosophical theory that evolutionary factors are entities and not constituents; theory, that a complex system is more than the sum of its parts. **holistic,** *adj.* **holistic medicine,** medicine that considers the whole person, including psychological and social factors, rather than treating just the symptoms of a disease.

holm [həʊm] *n.* river island; river plain.

holobaptist [ˌhɒlə'bæptɪst, ˌhəʊl–] *n.* believer in baptismal immersion.

holocaust ['hɒləkɔːst] *n.* burnt-offering of whole animal; wholesale destruction or death. **holocaustal, holocaustic,** *adj.*

holocrine ['hɒləkraɪn, –krɪn] *adj.* applied to gland whose secretion is composed of its own disintegrated cells.

holocryptic [ˌhɒlə'krɪptɪk] *adj.* undecipherable.

hologram ['hɒləɡræm] *n.* photograph taken, without a lens, by the interference of two laser beams, one illuminating the object and the other directed

on to the film or plate; three-dimensional image produced from such a photograph. **holography** [−'lɒɡ–], *n.* **holographic,** *adj.*

holograph ['hɒləɡrɑːf] *n.* writing wholly in handwriting of its author. **holographic,** *adj.*

holophote ['hɒləfəʊt] *n.* apparatus for directing most or all of available light in one direction. **holophotal,** *adj.*

holophrase ['hɒləfreɪz] *n.* single word expressing complex idea. **holophrasis** [hə'lɒfrəsɪs], *n.* use of holophrase. **holophrastic** [−'fræstɪk], *adj.*

holophytic [ˌhɒlə'fɪtɪk] *adj.* obtaining food by photosynthesis. **holophyte,** *n.*

holoplexia [ˌhɒlə'pleksɪə, ˌhəʊ–] *n.* general paralysis.

holosteric [ˌhɒlə'sterɪk] *adj.* entirely solid.

holothurian [ˌhɒlə'θjʊərɪən] *n.* sea cucumber.

holotony, holotonia [hə'lɒtəni, ˌhɒlə'təʊnɪə] *n.* general tetanus. **holotonic** [−'tɒnɪk], *adj.*

holotype ['hɒlətaɪp] *n.* original type specimen used in defining and describing a species or variety. **holotypic,** *adj.*

holozoic [ˌhɒlə'zəʊɪk] *adj.* obtaining food by eating complex matter, in the manner of an animal.

hombre ['ɒmbreɪ] (*Spanish*) *n.* fellow; man.

homeostasis *see* homoeostasis.

Homeric [həʊ'merɪk] *adj.* pertaining to Homer, Greek epic poet; epic; heroic.

homily ['hɒməli] *n.* moral discourse; sermon. **homiletic(al),** *adj.* **homiletics,** *n.* study of sermons; art of preaching. **homiliarium, homiliary,** *n.* book of sermons. **homilist, homilite,** *n.* preacher.

hominal ['hɒmɪnl] *adj.* pertaining to mankind; human. **hominid** *n.* & *adj.* (pertaining to) a fossil ape-man. **hominiform**, *adj.* having human shape. **hominivorous**, *n.* man-eating. **hominoid**, *n.* & *adj.* man-like (animal).

homocentric(al) [,həʊmə'sentrɪk, -l] *adj.* concentric.

homochiral [,həʊmə'kaɪrəl] *adj.* identical in form.

homochromatic [,həʊməkrə'mætɪk] *adj.* pertaining to or having one colour. **homochromic**, **homochromous** [-'krəʊmɪk, -əs], *adj.* of same colour. **homochromy**, *n.*

homodyne ['həʊmədaɪn, 'hɒ-] *adj. Radio*, pertaining to detection of radio wave with wave of exactly same frequency.

homoeochromatic [,həʊmiəkrə'mætɪk] *adj.* having same or similar colour.

homoeochronous [,həʊmi'ɒkrənəs] *adj.* developing at same period of offspring's as of parent's life.

homoeogenous [,həʊmi'ɒdʒənəs] *adj.* of same or similar kind.

homoeopathy [,həʊmi'ɒpəθɪ] *n.* treatment of disease by medicines producing in a healthy body symptoms similar to those of disease treated; treatment by extremely small doses. **homoeopath, homoeopathician, homoeopathist,** *n.* **homoeopathic** [-ə'pæθɪk], *adj.*

homoeophony [,həʊmi'ɒfəni] *n.* similarity of sound.

homoeostasis [,həʊmiə'steɪsɪs] *n.* automatic maintenance by an organism of normal temperature, chemical balance, etc., within itself. **homoeostat**, *n.* machine capable of same kind of self-regulation.

homoeoteleutic [,həʊmiəʊte'luːtɪk] *adj.* having same or similar endings. **homoeoteleuton**, *n.* use of such words in close proximity.

homoeozoic [,həʊmiə'zəʊɪk] *adj.* having same or similar living organisms.

homoerotism [,həʊməʊ'erətɪzm] *n.* homosexuality.

homogeneous [,həʊmə'dʒiːniəs, ,hɒ-] *adj.* of same kind; comprising similar parts; uniform. **homogeneity**, *n.* **homogenesis** [-'dʒenəsɪs], *n.* reproduction with successive generations alike. **homogenize** [hə'mɒdʒənaɪz], *v.t.* make homogeneous, especially of milk, etc.

homogenous [hə'mɒdʒənəs] *adj.* having structural resemblance due to common ancestor. **homogeny**, *n.*

homograft ['həʊməɡrɑːft, 'hɒ-] *n.* & *adj.* (denoting) tissue graft taken from non-identical members of the same species; allograft. **homograft reaction**, rejection by the recipient's body of such a graft.

homograph ['hɒməɡrɑːf, 'həʊ-] *n.* word having same spelling as, but different meaning from, another. **homographic**, *adj.* having different symbol for each sound. **homography**, *n.*

homoiotherm [həʊ'mɔɪəθɜːm] *n.* warm-blooded animal; animal having a constant body temperature. **homoiothermal, homoiothermic,** *adj.* **homoiothermy**, *n.*

homoiousia [,həʊmɔɪ'uːsiə, -'aʊ-] *n.* similarity in substance. **homoiousian**, *adj.*; *n. Theology*, adherent to belief that Son is of essentially similar but not identical substance with Father.

homolateral [,həʊmə'lætərəl, ,hɒ-] *adj.* on the same side.

homologate [hə'mɒləɡeɪt] *v.i.* & *t.* confirm; approve; agree. **homologation**, *n.*

homologoumena [,həʊməʊlə'ɡuːmənə] *n. pl.* Biblical books included in early Christian canon.

homologous [hə'mɒləɡəs] *adj.* exactly or relatively corresponding in structure. **homologize**, *v.t.* make homologous. **homologue** ['hɒmələɡ], *n.* such thing. **homology** [-dʒi], *n.*

homomerous, homomeral [hə'mɒmərəs, -rəl] *adj.* having similar parts.

homomorphic [,hɒmə'mɔːfɪk, ,həʊ-] *adj.* similar in form. **homomorphism, homomorphy**, *n.* **homomorphous**, *adj.*

homonym ['hɒmənɪm] *n.* word of same pronunciation as, but different meaning from, another; namesake. **homonymic, homonymous**, [-'mɒnɪməs], *adj.* **homonymy**, *n.*

homoousia [,həʊməʊ'uːsiə, ,hɒ-] *n.* sameness of substance. **homoousian**, *adj.*; *n. Theology*, adherent to belief that Son is of same substance with Father.

homophone ['hɒməfəʊn] *n.* letter having same sound as another; word having same pronunciation as, but different spelling and meaning from, another. **homophonic** [-'fɒnɪk], **homophonous** [-'mɒfənəs], *adj.* **homophony**, *n.* sameness of sound.

homophylic [,həʊmə'fɪlɪk, ,hɒ-] *adj.* of same race. **homophyly** [-'mɒfɪli], *n.* similarity due to common ancestry.

homo sapiens [,həʊməʊ 'sæpienz, 'seɪp-, -iənz] (*Latin*) 'thinking man'; Man; the human species. **homo vulgaris** [-vʌl'ɡɑːrɪs], the common or average man.

homosexual [,həʊmə'sekʃuəl, ,hɒm-, -sju-] *n.* & *adj.* (person) having sexual desire for person of same sex. **homosexualism, homosexuality**, *n.* **homosexualist**, *n.*

homotaxis [,həʊmə'tæksɪs, ,hɒ-] *n.* similarity of arrangement. **homotactic, homotaxeous, homotaxial, homotaxic,** *adj.*

homotherm ['həʊməθɜːm, 'hɒ-] *n.* homoiotherm.

homozygote [,həʊmə'zaɪɡəʊt] *n.* organism or cell having the same alleles for a particular inherited characteristic. **homozygosis**, *n.* condition of being a homozygote. **homozygotic**, *adj.*

homunculus [hə'mʌŋkjʊləs] *n.* (*pl.* **-li**) little man; dwarf; human embryo. **homuncle**, *n.* **homuncular**, *adj.*

hong [hɒŋ] (*Chinese*) *n.* foreign trading establishment in China; warehouse.

honnête homme [,ɒnet 'ɒm] (*French*) 'honest man'; respectable middle-class man.

honorarium [,ɒnə'reəriəm] *n.* (*pl.* **-ia**) fee; gift of money. **honorary**, *adj.* given as an honour; without reward or salary.

hoopoe ['huːpuː, -əʊ] *n.* curved-billed, large-crested bird of Old World.

Hoosier ['huːʒə] (*American*) *n.* & *adj.* (native) of Indiana.

hoplite ['hɒplaɪt] *n.* armoured infantryman of ancient Greece. **hoplomachy**, *n.* fighting in heavy armour.

horal ['hɔːrəl] *adj.* pertaining to hour(s); hourly.

horary, *adj.* marking the hours; hourly; lasting for an hour only.

Horatian [hə'reɪʃn, –iən] *adj.* pertaining to Horace, Latin poet, and his elegant style.

hordeaceous [ˌhɔːdi'eɪʃəs] *adj.* pertaining to or like barley. **hordeiform** [–'diːɪfɔːm], *adj.* having shape of barley-grain.

horme ['hɔːmi] *n. Psychology*, vital energy directed to an active purpose. **hormic,** *adj.* **hormist,** *n.* believer in horme as fundamental psychological factor.

hornblende ['hɔːnblend] *n.* dark-coloured variety of amphibole, containing aluminium and iron.

hornbook ['hɔːnbʊk] *n.* ancient child's school-book comprising alphabet, digits, etc., on parchment covered with sheet of horn.

horography [hə'rɒgrəfi] *n.* account of the hours; art of constructing timepieces. **horographer,** *n.*

horologe ['hɒrəlɒdʒ] *n.* timepiece. **horologer, horologist** [–'rɒl–], *n.* watch-maker. **horologic** [–'lɒdʒɪk], *adj.* **horology** [–'rɒlədʒi], *n.* clock-making; science of measuring time. **horometry** [–'rɒmətri], *n.* measurement of time.

horrent ['hɒrənt] *adj. adj.* bristling. **horrescent,** *adj.* expressing horror.

horripilation [hɒˌrɪpɪ'leɪʃn] *n.* bristling of hair or creeping of flesh, due to cold, fright, etc. **horripilate,** *v.i. & t.* cause or suffer this.

horrisonant [hɒ'rɪsənənt] *adj.* making horrible sound.

hors de combat [ˌɔː də 'kɔːmbɑː] (*French*) 'out of the fight'; disabled.

hors d'oeuvre (*French*) *n.* (*pl.* **d'oeuvres** or **d'oeuvre**) savoury food served as appetizer.

horst [hɔːst] *n. Geology*, raised block of earth's crust between two parallel faults.

hortative ['hɔːtətɪv] *adj.* exhorting; urging. **hortatory,** *adj.* marked by exhortation.

hortensial, hortensian [hɔː'tensiəl, –iən] *adj.* pertaining to, grown in or suited to a garden.

hortulan ['hɔːtjʊlən] *adj.* pertaining to garden.

hortus siccus [ˌhɔːtəs 'sɪkəs] (*Latin*) 'dry garden'; herbarium.

hospice ['hɒspɪs] *n.* travellers' rest-house, especially kept by religious order; home caring for terminally ill patients.

hospitate ['hɒspɪteɪt] *v.i. & t.* welcome; be guest. **hospitation,** *n.*

hotchpot ['hɒtʃpɒt] *n. Law*, a returning to a common lot or fund for subsequent equal division, especially of advances received by children of person dying intestate.

hôtel de ville [əʊˌtel də 'viːl] (*French*) *n.* 'town-hall'. **hôtel Dieu** [–'djɜː], *hospital.

houbara [hu'bɑːrə] *n.* ruffed bustard.

houri ['hʊəri] *n.* beautiful nymph of Muslim paradise; alluring young woman.

housel ['haʊzl] *v.t.* administer Holy Communion to.

howadji [hə'wædʒi] (*Arabic*) *n.* traveller; merchant; Mr.

howdah ['haʊdə] *n.* seat on elephant.

hubris ['hjuːbrɪs] (*Greek*) *n.* arrogance, insolent conceit. **hubristic,** *adj.*

huguenot ['hjuːgənəʊ] *n.* French Protestant.

humanism ['hjuːmənɪzm] *n.* human nature; study of the humanities; Renaissance culture; philosophical doctrine concentrating on human ideals

and perfectibility. **humanist,** *n.*

humanities [hju'mænətiz] *n. pl.* human attributes; classical literature, especially Latin; learning concerned with human culture.

humectant [hju'mektənt] *n. & adj.* moistening (substance). **humectation,** *n.*

humerus ['hjuːmərəs] *n.* bone of upper arm. **humeral,** *adj.* pertaining to the shoulder; brachial.

humid ['hjuːmɪd] *adj.* moist. **humidity,** *n.*

humour ['hjuːmə] *n. Medicine*, body fluid; skin affection due to blood disorder; *archaic*, one of four body fluids—blood, phlegm, bile and atrabile—believed to determine health and character. **humoral,** *adj.*

humus ['hjuːməs] *n.* soil containing decayed vegetable matter. **humous,** *adj.*

hurgila [hə'giːlə] (*Hindi*) *n.* adjutant bird.

hurley, hurly ['hɜːli] (*Irish*) *n.* game like hockey; stick used in it.

hurling ['hɜːlɪŋ] *n.* hurley (the game).

hustings ['hʌstɪŋz] *n. pl.* platform or place for political electioneering speeches; election proceedings.

hyaline ['haɪəliːn, –lɪn] *adj.* glassy; transparent. **hyalescent,** *adj.* becoming or somewhat glassy. **hyalography,** *n.* engraving on glass. **hyaloid,** *adj.* like glass. **hyalopterous,** *adj.* with transparent wings.

hybris ['haɪbrɪs] *n.* hubris.

hydatid ['haɪdətɪd] *n.* fluid-filled cyst, especially containing tape-worm larva. **hydatidinous,** *adj.* **hydatiform,** *adj.* like a hydatid. **hydatigenous,** *adj.* producing hydatid.

hydra ['haɪdrə] *n.* many-headed monster in Greek mythology; small fresh-water polyp. **hydroid,** *n. & adj.* (like a) polyp.

hydracid [haɪ'dræsɪd] *n.* oxygen-less acid.

hydraemia [haɪ'driːmiə] *n.* excessively watery condition of blood. **hydraemic,** *adj.*

hydragogue ['haɪdrəgɒg] *n. & adj.* (drug) causing discharge of water.

hydrargiric [ˌhaɪdrɑː'dʒɪrɪk] *adj.* pertaining to mercury. **hydrargiria, hydrargiriasis, hydrargirism** [haɪ'drɑːdʒ–], [haɪ'drɑːdʒ–], hydrargirosis, *n.* mercurial poisoning.

hydrate ['haɪdreɪt] *n. Chemistry*, compound formed with water; [haɪ'dreɪt] *v.t. & i.* (cause to) combine with water. **hydric,** *adj.* pertaining to or containing hydrogen. **hydride,** *n.* compound formed with hydrogen.

hydraulic [haɪ'drɔːlɪk] *adj.* pertaining to moving fluids; pertaining to mechanical action of water; conveyed or worked by water. **hydraulics,** *n.* study of fluids in motion.

hydriotaphia [ˌhaɪdriə'tæfiə] *n.* urn burial.

hydro ['haɪdrəʊ] *n. abbreviation* of hydropathic.

hydrocarbon [ˌhaɪdrə'kɑːbən] *n.* compound of hydrogen and carbon.

hydrocephalus, hydrocephaly [ˌhaɪdrə'kefələs, –'se–, –li] *n.* water on the brain. **hydrocephalic** [–ke'fælɪk, –sɪ–], **hydrocephalous,** *adj.* **hydrocephaloid,** *adj.* like hydrocephalus.

hydroconion [ˌhaɪdrə'kəʊnɪən] *n.* atomizer.

hydrocortisone [ˌhaɪdrə'kɔːtɪzəʊn] *n.* steroid hormone produced by the adrenal gland, used in treating arthritis and skin disorders.

hydrocyanic [ˌhaɪdrəʊsaɪ'ænɪk] *adj.* prussic (acid).

hydrodynamics [,haɪdrəʊdaɪ'næmɪks] *n.* mechanical study of fluids, especially their motion and action.

hydroelectric [,haɪdrəʊɪ'lektrɪk] *adj.* pertaining to generation of, or generating, electricity by water-power. hydroelectricity, *n.*

hydrogenic [,haɪdrə'dʒenɪk] *adj. Geology*, formed by water. hydrogeology, *n.* study of geological action of water.

hydrognosy [haɪ'drɒgnəsi] *n.* historical description of earth's water surface.

hydrography [haɪ'drɒgrəfi] *n.* description, surveying and mapping of water surface of earth, with its depths, tides, etc. hydrographer, *n.* hydrographic, *adj.*

hydrokinetics [,haɪdrəʊkɪ'netɪks, –kaɪ–] *n.* study of changes of motion of fluids.

hydrology [haɪ'drɒlədʒi] *n.* study of water of earth's surface, especially subterranean. hydrologic(al), *adj.*

hydrolysis [haɪ'drɒləsɪs] *n.* (*pl.* –ses) chemical decomposition by addition of water. hydrolysate, *n.* product of hydrolysis. hydrolyse, *v.t.* hydrolytic, *adj.*

hydromancy ['haɪdrəmænsi] *n.* divination by water.

hydromechanics [,haɪdrəʊmɪ'kænɪks] *n.* study of laws of fluids in equilibrium and motion.

hydrometer [haɪ'drɒmɪtə] *n.* instrument measuring specific gravity and density of liquids. hydrometric(al) [–'met–], *adj.* hydrometry, *n.*

hydron ['haɪdrən] *n.* plastic which is rigid when dry and soft when wet.

hydropathy [haɪ'drɒpəθi] *n.* medical treatment by baths and mineral waters. hydropath, hydropathist, *n.* hydropathic [–'pæθɪk], *adj.*; *n.* establishment for such treatment; spa.

hydrophanous [haɪ'drɒfənəs] *adj.* becoming transparent when immersed in water. hydrophane, *n.* such kind of opal.

hydrophid ['haɪdrəfɪd] *n.* sea snake. hydrophoid, *adj.*

hydrophobia [,haɪdrə'fəʊbiə] *n.* morbid dread of water; rabies. hydrophobe, hydrophobist, *n.* hydrophobic, hydrophobous, *adj.*

hydrophone ['haɪdrəfəʊn] *n.* instrument for detecting sounds through water.

hydrophyte ['haɪdrəfaɪt] *n.* plant growing in or by water. hydrophytic [–'fɪtɪk], *adj.*

hydropic(al) [haɪ'drɒpɪk, –l] *adj.* dropsical. hydropigenous, *adj.* causing dropsy.

hydroplane ['haɪdrəpleɪn] *n.* fast flat-bottomed motor boat, skimming over water; seaplane.

hydroponics [,haɪdrə'pɒnɪks] *n.* cultivation of plants without soil, by supporting them in chemical solution containing all ingredients necessary for growth.

hydropot ['haɪdrəpɒt] *n.* water-drinker.

hydroscope ['haɪdrəskəʊp] *n.* instrument for seeing below the surface of water. hydroscopist *n.* water-diviner.

hydrosphere ['haɪdrəsfɪə] *n.* earth's envelope of watery vapour, or water surface.

hydrostatics [,haɪdrə'stætɪks] *n.* study of pressure and equilibrium of fluids.

hydrotaxis [,haɪdrə'tæksɪs] *n.* movement towards or away from water.

hydrotechny ['haɪdrətekni] *n.* use of water for

driving machinery, etc. hydrotechnic(al), *adj.* hydrotechnologist, *n.*

hydrotherapeutic [,haɪdrəʊθerə'pjuːtɪk] *adj.* hydropathic. hydrotherapeutics, hydrotherapy, *n.* hydropathy.

hydrothermal [,haɪdrə'θɜːml] *adj.* pertaining to hot water and its geological action.

hydrothorax [,haɪdrə'θɔːræks] *n.* water liquid in the pleural cavity.

hydrotic [haɪ'drɒtɪk] *n. & adj.* (drug) expelling water or phlegm.

hydrotimetry [,haɪdrə'tɪmətri] *n.* measurement of hardness of water. hydrotimeter, *n.* instrument used in this. hydrotimetric [–'metrɪk], *adj.*

hydrous ['haɪdrəs] *adj.* containing water.

hydrozoan [,haɪdrə'zəʊən] *n.* polyp. hydrozoal, hydrozoic, *adj.*

hyetal ['haɪətl] *adj.* pertaining to rain. hyetograph, *n.* rain gauge; chart of average rainfall. hyetography, *n.* study of rainfall distribution. hyetology, *n.* study of all precipitation. hyetometer, *n.* rain gauge. hyetometrograph, *n.* recording hyetometer.

hygiology [,haɪdʒi'ɒlədʒi] *n.* hygienic science. hygiologist, *n.*

hygric ['haɪgrɪk] *adj.* pertaining to moisture.

hygrometer [haɪ'grɒmɪtə] *n.* instrument measuring humidity of air. hygrograph, *n.* recording hygrometer.

hygrophanous [haɪ'grɒfənəs] *adj.* seeming transparent when wet, and opaque when dry. hygrophaneity [–'niːəti, –'neɪ–], *n.*

hygrophilous [haɪ'grɒfɪləs] *adj. Botany*, living in water or moist places.

hygrophthalmic [,haɪgrɒf'θælmɪk] *adj.* moistening the eye.

hygrophyte ['haɪgrəfaɪt] *n.* hygrophilous plant.

hygroscope ['haɪgrəskəʊp] *n.* instrument showing variations in humidity. hygroscopic [–'skɒpɪk], *adj.* absorbing moisture, especially of dust particles, etc., on which atmospheric moisture condenses to form rain and fog.

hygrostat ['haɪgrəstæt] *n.* apparatus for regulating humidity of air. hygrostatics, *n.* study of measurement of humidity.

hygrothermal [,haɪgrə'θɜːml] *adj.* pertaining to heat and humidity. hygrothermograph, *n.* instrument recording humidity and temperature.

hyle ['haɪli] (*Greek*) *n.* matter. hylic, *adj.* material. hylism *n.* materialism.

hylomorphism [,haɪlə'mɔːfɪzm] *n.* materialist conception of universe. hylomorphic(al), *adj.* hylomorphist, *n.* hylomorphous, *adj.* having material form.

hylopathism [haɪ'lɒpəθɪzm] *n.* belief in capability of matter to affect spirit. hylopathist, *n.*

hylophagous [haɪ'lɒfəgəs] *adj.* eating wood.

hylotheism [,haɪlə'θiːɪzm] *n.* identification of God with matter or universe. hylotheist, *n.* hylotheistic(al), *adj.*

hylotomous [haɪ'lɒtəməs] *adj.* cutting or boring in wood.

hylozoism [,haɪlə'zəʊɪzm] *n.* belief that all matter has life. hylozoist, *n.* hylozoistic(al), *adj.*

hymen ['haɪmen] *n.* membrane partly closing vagina; maidenhead. hymenal, *adj.*

hymeneal [,haɪmə'niːəl] *adj.* pertaining to Hymen, god of marriage; nuptial; *n.* nuptial song.

hymenopterous [ˌhaɪmˈnɒptərəs] *adj.* having four membranous wings. **hymenoptera,** *n. pl.* (*sing.* **hymenopteron**) order including such insects. **hymenopterist,** *n.* student of hymenoptera. **hymenopterology,** *n.* study of hymenoptera. .

hymenotomy [ˌhaɪməˈnɒtəmi] *n.* cutting of hymen.

hymnody ['hɪmnədi] *n.* hymns; hymn-singing; hymnology. **hymnography** *n.* hymn-writing. **hymnology** *n.* study of hymns; hymnography.

hyoid ['haɪɔɪd] *n. & adj.* (pertaining to) U-shaped bone at base of tongue.

hyoscine ['haɪəsiːn] *n.* sleep-inducing drug obtained from plants of nightshade family. **hyoscyamine** [-'saɪəmiːn], *n.* similar drug obtained from henbane.

hypaesthesia [ˌhɪpesˈθiːziə, ˌhaɪ-, -ʒə] *n.* incomplete sensory power.

hypaethral [hɪˈpiːθrəl, haɪ-] *adj.* roofless.

hypalgesia [ˌhɪpælˈdʒiːziə, ˌhaɪ-] *n.* diminished sensitivity to pain.

hyperacusis, hyperacusia [ˌhaɪpərəˈkjuːsɪs, -siə] *n.* abnormal keenness of hearing.

hyperaemia [ˌhaɪpərˈiːmiə] *n.* excess of blood in a part. **hyperaemic,** *adj.*

hyperaesthesia [ˌhaɪpəriːsˈθiːziə, -ʒə] *n.* excessive sensitivity. **hyperaesthetic** [-ˈθetɪk], *adj.*

hyperalgesia [ˌhaɪpərælˈdʒiːziə] *n.* undue sensitiveness to pain.

hyperaphia [ˌhaɪpərˈeɪfiə] *n.* abnormal keenness of touch.

hyperbaric [ˌhaɪpəˈbærɪk] *adj.* above normal atmospheric pressure, 'pressurized'.

hyperbaton [haɪˈpɜːbətən] *n.* (*pl.* **-ta**) inversion of normal word order. **hyperbatic** [-ˈbætɪk], *adj.*

hyperbola [haɪˈpɜːbələ] *n.* curve formed when cone is cut by plane which makes angle with the base greater than that made by side of cone.

hyperbole [haɪˈpɜːbəli] *n.* extravagant rhetorical exaggeration. **hyperbolical** [-ˈbɒlɪkl], *adj.* **hyperbolize,** *v.i. & t.* use hyperbole. **hyperbolism,** *n.*

hyperborean [ˌhaɪpəˈbɔːriən] *n. & adj.* (dweller) in extreme north or cold.

hyperbulia [ˌhaɪpəˈbjuːliə] *n.* undue eagerness for action; rashness.

hypercatalectic [ˌhaɪpəkætəˈlektɪk] *adj.* having extra syllable(s) at end of verse line. **hypercatalexis,** *n.*

hypercathexis [ˌhaɪpəkəˈθeksɪs] *n.* desire amounting to mania for an object.

hypercritical [ˌhaɪpəˈkrɪtɪkl] *adj.* excessively critical; captious. **hypercriticize** [-saɪz], *v.i. & t.*

hyperdulic [ˌhaɪpəˈdjuːlɪk] *adj.* venerating Virgin Mary highest of all human beings. **hyperdulia,** *n.*

hypergamy [haɪˈpɜːgəmi] *n.* marriage with person of same or higher caste only.

hyperglycaemia [ˌhaɪpəglaɪˈsiːmiə] *n.* excess sugar in the blood.

hypergolic [ˌhaɪpəˈgɒlɪk] *adj.* applied to rocket fuel which ignites spontaneously on contact with an oxidizing agent.

hyperkinesia, hyperkinesis [ˌhaɪpəkɪˈniːziə, -kaɪ-, -ʒə] *n.* muscle spasm; hyperactive condition of children.

hypermeter [haɪˈpɜːmɪtə] *n.* hypercatalectic verse line; person above average height. **hyper-**

metric(al) [-ˈmet-], *adj.*

hypermetropia [ˌhaɪpəmeˈtrəʊpiə] *n.* longsightedness. **hypermetropic(al)** [-ˈtrɒp-], *adj.* **hypermetropy** [-ˈmetrəpi], *n.*

hyperopia [ˌhaɪpərˈəʊpiə] *n.* hypermetropia. **hyperope,** *n.* **hyperopic** [-ˈrɒpɪk], *adj.*

hyperosmia [ˌhaɪpərˈɒzmiə] *n.* abnormal keenness of sense of smell. **hyperosmic,** *adj.*

hyperphagia [ˌhaɪpəˈfeɪdʒiə] *n.* bulimia

hyperphysical [ˌhaɪpəˈfɪzɪkl] *adj.* supernatural.

hyperpiesis, hyperpiesia [ˌhaɪpəpər'iːsɪs, -siə] *n.* high blood pressure. **hyperpietic** [-ˈetɪk], *adj.*

hyperpnoea [ˌhaɪpəpˈniːə, -əˈniːə] *n.* abnormally fast breathing.

hypersonic [ˌhaɪpəˈsɒnɪk] *adj.* pertaining to or denoting speed five or more times that of sound in the same medium.

hyperspace ['haɪpəspeɪs] *n.* space of more than three dimensions.

hypertension [ˌhaɪpəˈtenʃn] *n.* high blood pressure. **hypertensive,** *adj.*

hyperthyroidism [ˌhaɪpəˈθaɪrɔɪdɪzm] *n.* excessive thyroid activity, resulting in exophthalmic goitre.

hypertrichosis [ˌhaɪpətrɪˈkəʊsɪs] *n.* excessive hairiness.

hypertrophy [haɪˈpɜːtrəfi] *n.* excessive growth of a part; *v.i.* grow to abnormal size. **hypertrophic, hypertrophied,** *adj.*

hyphaema, hyphaemia [haɪˈfiːmə, -iə] *n.* anaemia; extravasation of blood.

hyphaeresis [haɪˈfɪərəsɪs, -ˈfer-] *n.* omission of sound, syllable or letter from word.

hypnaesthesis [ˌhɪpnesˈθiːsɪs] *n.* impaired sensitivity. **hypnaesthetic** [-ˈθetɪk], *adj.*

hypnagogic [ˌhɪpnəˈgɒdʒɪk] *adj.* causing sleep; occurring while falling asleep or waking.

hypnoanalysis [ˌhɪpnəʊəˈnæləsɪs] *n.* psychoanalysis of a patient under hypnosis.

hypnoetic [ˌhɪpnəʊˈetɪk] *adj.* pertaining to logical but unconscious mental processes.

hypnogenesis [ˌhɪpnəˈdʒenəsɪs] *n.* production of hypnosis. **hypnogenetic** [-dʒəˈnetɪk], *adj.*

hypnoid ['hɪpnɔɪd] *adj.* sleep-like.

hypnology [hɪpˈnɒlədʒi] *n.* study of sleep and hypnosis. **hypnologic(al),** *adj.* **hypnologist,** *n.*

hypnopedia [ˌhɪpnəˈpiːdiə] *n.* process of introducing information into the brain while asleep.

hypnopompic [ˌhɪpnəˈpɒmpɪk] *adj.* preventing or dispelling sleep; occurring while waking.

hypobole [haɪˈpɒbəli] *n.* rhetorical device of anticipating objections in order to refute them.

hypobulia [ˌhaɪpəʊˈbjuːliə] *n.* diminution in ability to act or decide. **hypobulic,** *adj.* lacking willpower.

hypocathexis [ˌhaɪpəʊkəˈθeksɪs] *n.* abnormal absence of desire for an object.

hypocaust ['haɪpəkɔːst] *n.* ancient air chamber or series of chambers for heating rooms.

hypochondria [ˌhaɪpəˈkɒndriə] *n.* morbid nervous depression; continual and causeless anxiety about one's health, especially concerning imaginary illnesses. **hypochondriac,** *adj.*; *n.* person suffering from hypochondria. **hypochondrial,** *adj.* **hypochondry,** *n.*

hypochondrium [ˌhaɪpəˈkɒndriəm] *n.* either of two regions of the upper part of the abdomen.

hypocorisma [ˌhaɪpəkəˈrɪzmə] *n.* pet name.

hypocoristic(al), *adj.*

hypodynamia [ˌhaɪpəʊdaɪ'neɪmɪə] *n.* diminution in strength. **hypodynamia cordis**, hypodynamia of the heart.

hypogastric [ˌhaɪpə'gæstrɪk] *adj.* pertaining to lower middle abdominal region. **hypogastrium**, *n.* that region.

hypogeal [ˌhaɪpə'dʒiːəl] *adj.* subterranean. **hypogean**, *adj.* growing underground. **hypogeic**, *adj.* **hypogeiody** [-'dʒaɪədi], *n.* surveying underground.

hypogene ['haɪpədʒiːn] *adj.* *Geology*, plutonic. **hypogenic** [-'dʒenɪk], *adj.*

hypogeous [ˌhaɪpə'dʒiːəs] *adj.* hypogean. **hypogeum**, *n.* (*pl.* **-gea**) underground part of building.

hypoglottis [ˌhaɪpə'glɒtɪs] *n.* underpart of tongue. **hypoglossitis**, *n.* inflammation of this.

hypoglycaemia [ˌhaɪpəʊglaɪ'siːmɪə] *n.* abnormally low levels of sugar in the blood.

hypohaemia [ˌhaɪpəʊ'hiːmɪə] *n.* anaemia.

hypolimnion [ˌhaɪpə'lɪmnɪən, -ɒn] *n.* lower, colder layer of water in a lake.

hypometropia [ˌhaɪpəʊme'trəʊpɪə] *n.* shortsightedness.

hyponasty ['haɪpənæsti] *n.* stronger growth on the under side of a plant part. **hyponastic**, *adj.*

hyponychial [ˌhaɪpəʊ'nɪkɪəl] *adj.* underneath finger- or toe-nail.

hypophonic, **hypophonous** [ˌhaɪpə'fɒnɪk, haɪ'pɒfənəs] *adj.* *Music*, acting as accompaniment.

hypophrenia [ˌhaɪpəʊ'friːnɪə] *n.* feeblemindedness. **hypophrenic** [-'frenɪk], *adj.*

hypophyll ['haɪpəfɪl] *n.* bract.

hypophysis [haɪ'pɒfəsɪs] *n.* pituitary gland. **hypophyseal**, **hypophysial** [-'fɪzɪəl], *adj.* **hypophysectomy**, *n.* removal of pituitary. **hypophyseoprivic**, **hypophyseoprivous**, *adj.* due to deficient pituitary secretion.

hypostasis [haɪ'pɒstəsɪs] *n.* (*pl.* **-ses**) support; hypostatised substance; essential substance; *Medicine*, sediment; hyperaemia of an organ; *Theology*, substance of the Trinity; person of the Trinity; whole personality of Christ. **hypostatic** [-'stætɪk], *adj.* **hypostatize**, *v.t.* regard as separate substance; assume (hypothetical thing) to be real.

hyposthenia [ˌhaɪpɒs'θiːnɪə] *n.* debility. **hyposthenic** [-'θenɪk], *adj.*

hypostrophe [haɪ'pɒstrəfi] *n.* *Medicine*, relapse or turning over; *Rhetoric*, return to main theme after digression.

hyposynergia [ˌhaɪpəʊsɪn'ɜːdʒɪə] *n.* incomplete co-ordination.

hypotenuse [haɪ'pɒtənjuːz] *n.* side opposite right angle in right-angled triangle.

hypothalamus [ˌhaɪpə'θæləməs] *n.* (*pl.* **-mi**) part of brain that controls body temperature, appetite, etc. **hypothalamic**, *adj.*

hypothecate [haɪ'pɒθəkeɪt] *v.t.* mortgage; deposit as security. **hypothecary**, *adj.* **hypothecation**, *n.* **hypothecatory**, *adj.*

hypothermal [ˌhaɪpəʊ'θɜːml] *adj.* tepid; pertaining to lowering of temperature. **hypothermia**, **hypothermy**, *n.* abnormally low body temperature. **hypothermic**, *adj.*

hypothesis [haɪ'pɒθəsɪs] *n.* (*pl.* **-ses**) assumption; conjecture; supposition; theory. **hypothesize**, *v.i.* & *t.* **hypothetical** [-'θetɪkl], *adj.*

hypothyroidism [ˌhaɪpəʊ'θaɪrɔɪdɪzm] *n.* deficient thyroid activity, resulting in cretinism.

hypotrichosis [ˌhaɪpəʊtrɪ'kəʊsɪs] *n.* lack of hair.

hypotrophy [haɪ'pɒtrəfi] *n.* incomplete growth; atrophy.

hypotyposis [ˌhaɪpətaɪ'pəʊsɪs] *n.* vivid description.

hypoxaemia [ˌhaɪpɒk'siːmɪə] *n.* insufficient oxygen in the blood. **hypoxia**, *n.* insufficient oxygen reaching the body tissues.

hypsiloid ['hɪpsɪlɔɪd, hɪp'saɪlɔɪd] (*Greek*) *adj.* like letter upsilon (Y).

hypsography [hɪp'sɒgrəfi] *n.* topographical relief, and its observation; the representation of this in maps. **hypsometry**, *n.* measurement of heights above sea-level. **hypsophobia**, *n.* dread of heights.

hyson ['haɪsn] *n.* kind of green tea of China.

hyssop ['hɪsəp] *n.* kind of mint, remedy for bruises.

hysteralgia [ˌhɪstə'rældʒɪə] *n.* neuralgia of womb. **hysterectomy**, *n.* removal of womb. **hysterodynia**, *n.* pain in womb.

hysteresis [ˌhɪstə'riːsɪs] *n.* lag in the effect of a change of force, especially in magnetization. **hysteretic** [-'retɪk], *adj.*

hysterogen(ic) ['hɪstərədʒen, ˌhɪstərə'dʒenɪk] *adj.* produced or developed later; causing hysteria.

hysteroid ['hɪstərɔɪd] *adj.* like womb or hysteria.

hysteron proteron [ˌhɪstərɒn 'prɒtərɒn] *n.* inversion of natural order or sense, especially of words; fallacy of proving or explaining a proposition with one presupposing or dependent on it.

hysteropathy [ˌhɪstə'rɒpəθi] *n.* disease of womb. **hysterorrhexia**, *n.* rupture of womb. **hysterotomy**, *n.* Caesarean cut.

I

iamatology [ˌaɪəmə'tɒlədʒi] *n.* medical study of remedies.

iamb(us) ['aɪæm, –b, aɪ'æmbəs] *n.* (*pl.* **–bi**) metrical foot of one short followed by one long syllable. **iambic,** *adj.* pertaining to or composed of iambi; *n.* line of iambi. **iambist,** *n.* writer of iambi.

iatric(al) [aɪ'ætrɪk, –l] *adj.* medical. **iatraliptics,** *n.* medical treatment by rubbing with oil. **iatrochemistry,** *n.* application of chemistry to medical theory and treatment. **iatrogenic,** *adj.* applied to a disease or condition induced in a patient by a doctor or medical treatment. **iatrology,** *n.* medical science or treatise. **iatrotechnics,** *n.* practical therapeutics.

Iberian [aɪ'bɪərɪən] *adj.* pertaining to Spanish-Portuguese peninsula; *n.* ancient inhabitant of that region.

ibex ['aɪbeks] *n.* wild goat, especially with long, backward-curved horns; bouquetin; aegagrus.

ibidem ['ɪbɪdem, ɪ'biː–, ɪ'baɪ–] (*Latin*) *adv.* 'in the same place' (*abbreviated as* **ibid.**).

ibis ['aɪbɪs] *n.* large heron-like wading bird, with down-curved bill.

Icarian [ɪ'keərɪən, aɪ–] *adj.* pertaining to Icarus in Greek mythology, who, in flying too near sun, met his death; flying dangerously high; over-ambitious.

ichabod ['ɪkəbɒd] (*Hebrew*) 'the glory has departed'.

ichneumon [ɪk'njuːmən] *n.* mongoose, especially Egyptian species believed to suck crocodiles' eggs. **ichneumon fly,** fly whose larva parasitizes other insect's larva. **ichneumous,** *adj.* parasitic.

ichnite ['ɪknaɪt] *n.* fossil footprint.

ichnography [ɪk'nɒgrəfi] *n.* map; ground plan; making of maps and plans. **ichnographic(al),** *adj.*

ichnology [ɪk'nɒlədʒi] *n.* geological study of fossil footprints. **ichnomancy,** *n.* divination by footprints.

ichor ['aɪkɔː] *n.* watery fluid discharged from wound; fluid supposed to fill veins of Greek and Latin gods. **ichorous,** *adj.* **ichorrhoea,** *n.* discharge of pus-like fluid.

ichthus, ichthys ['ɪkθəs, –ɪs] *n.* amulet or talismanic carving in shape of fish. **ichthyic** ['ɪkθiːɪk], *adj.* pertaining to fishes. **ichthyism,** *n.* fish-poisoning. **ichthyofauna,** *n.* fish life of region. **ichthyography,** *n.* treatise on fishes. **ichthyoid,** *adj.* fish-like. **ichthyolatry,** *n.* worship of fishes. **ichthyolite,** *n.* fossil fish. **ichthyology,** *n.* study of fishes. **ichthyomorphic,** *adj.* fish-shaped. **ichthyophagy,** *n.* eating of fish. **ichthyophagist,** *n.* **ichthyornis,** *n.* toothed fossil bird of America. **ichthyosaur(us),** *n.* large fossil marine reptile. **ichthyosis,** *n.* congenital disease characterized by thickened, scaly skin. **ichthyotoxism,** *n.* fish-poisoning.

icon ['aɪkɒn] *n.* sacred or monumental image, statue, painting, etc.; picture on computer monitor to represent command. **iconic** [aɪ'kɒnɪk], *adj.* **iconism,** *n.* worship of images. **iconoclasm** [aɪ'kɒnəklæzm], *n.* image-breaking; attacking of established beliefs. **iconoclast,** *n.* person practising iconoclasm. **iconography,** *n.* representation in art or diagrams; description of representational works of art. **iconolatry,** *n.* image-worship. **iconology,** *n.* study of icons; symbolism. **iconomachy,** *n.* objection to worship of icons. **iconomatic,** *adj.* pertaining to picture-writing in which characters represent names or phonetic values and not objects. **iconometer,** *n.* instrument finding distance or size of object by measuring its image; instrument for finding photographic focus; direct view-finder. **iconoplast,** *n.* image-maker. **iconoscope,** *n.* part of television camera where light is converted into electric waves. **iconostasis,** *n.* screen bearing icons, separating sanctuary from nave in Eastern churches.

icosahedron [ˌaɪkɒsə'hiːdrən] *n.* 20-sided solid figure. **icosahedral,** *adj.* **icosian,** *adj.* pertaining to 20. **icositetrahedron,** *n.* 24-sided solid figure.

icteric [ɪk'terɪk] *adj.* pertaining to jaundice; *n.* remedy for jaundice. **icterine, icteritious, icteritous,** *adj.* yellowish. **icteroid,** *adj.* like jaundice; yellow. **icterus** ['ɪktərəs], *n.* jaundice.

ictus ['ɪktəs] *n.* stress in verse; *Medicine*, fit; sudden pulsation or stroke. **ictic,** *adj.*

id [ɪd] *n. Psychology*, instinctive energies and tendencies; sub-conscious mind.

ideate ['aɪdieɪt] *v.t. & i.* form ideas; imagine; conceive. **ideation,** *n.* **ideational, ideative,** *adj.*

idée fixe [ˌiːdeɪ 'fɪks, –'fiːks] (*French*) *n.* 'fixed idea'; obsession; musical motif.

idem ['ɪdem, 'aɪ–] (*Latin*) 'the same' (*abbr.* **id.**).

ideogeny [ˌaɪdi'ɒdʒəni, ˌɪ–] *n.* study of origin of ideas. **ideogenetic** [–ədʒə'netɪk], *adj.* initiating ideas. **ideogenical,** *adj.* **ideogenous,** *adj.* of mental origin.

ideogram, ideograph ['ɪdiəgræm, 'aɪ–, –grɑːf] *n.* symbol in picture-writing representing idea of thing; any symbol universally recognized. **ideography,** *n.*

ideology [ˌaɪdi'ɒlədʒi, ˌɪd–] *n.* science of ideas; theory, especially impractical; body of ideas on a subject or of a class, race, political party, etc. **ideological,** *adj.*

ides [aɪdz] *n. pl.* 13th or 15th day of month in ancient Roman calendar. **ides of March,** unlucky or fatal day.

id est [ˌɪd 'est] (*Latin*) 'that is' (*abbr.* **i.e.**).

idiasm ['ɪdiæzm] *n.* idiosyncrasy.

idioblast ['ɪdɪəblæst] *n.* isolated cell differing greatly from surrounding cells or tissue. **idioblastic,** *adj.*

idiochromatic [,ɪdɪəkrəʊ'mætɪk] *adj.* having characteristic coloration.

idiocrasy, idiocrasis [,ɪdi'ɒkrəsi, ,ɪdiə'kreɪsɪs] *n.* constitutional peculiarity. **idiocratic,** *adj.*

idioelectric(al) [,ɪdiəʊɪ'lektrɪk, –l] *adj.* able to be electrified by friction.

idioglossia [,ɪdiə'glɒsiə] *n.* secret speech or language, especially invented by children; psychological condition in which speech is so distorted as to be unintelligible.

idiograph ['ɪdiəgrɑːf] *n.* trademark. **idiographic(al),** *adj.* pertaining to or dealing with the individual or unique.

idiolect ['ɪdiəlekt] *n.* personal speech pattern.

idiologism [,ɪdi'ɒlədʒɪzm] *n.* idiolect.

idiom ['ɪdiəm] *n.* language or dialect peculiar to a people, region, class, etc.; linguistic expression peculiar to itself in form, grammar, etc.; style of artistic expression characteristic of a person, period, medium etc. **idiomatic,** *adj.* **idiomology,** *n.* study of idioms.

idiomorphic, idiomorphous [,ɪdiə'mɔːfɪk, –əs] *adj.* having its own peculiar or proper form.

idiopathy [,ɪdi'ɒpəθi] *n.* peculiar characteristic; disease not caused by another. **idiopathetic, idiopathic(al),** *adj.*

idioplasm ['ɪdiəplæzm] *n.* part of protoplasm bearing hereditary characteristics; germ plasm. **idioplasmatic, idioplasmic,** *adj.*

idiospasm ['ɪdiəspæzm] *n.* localized cramp. **idiospastic,** *adj.*

idiosyncrasy [,ɪdiə'sɪŋkrəsi] *n.* mental or physical peculiarity; eccentricity; special sensitivity to a drug. **idiosyncratic(al)** [–'kræt–], *adj.*

idiothermous, idiothermic [,ɪdiə'θɜːməs, –ɪk] *adj.* warm-blooded. **idiothermy,** *n.*

idioticon [,ɪdi'ɒtɪkən] *n.* dialect dictionary.

idiot savant [,ɪdiəʊ 'sævɒn] *n.* (*pl.* ...savants, idiots savants) mentally retarded person with exceptional talent in one field.

idolothyte [aɪ'dɒləθaɪt] *n. & adj.* (sacrifice) offered to idol. **idolothytic** [–'θɪtɪk], *adj.*

idolum [aɪ'dəʊləm] *n.* (*pl.* –la) phantom; fallacy.

idoneous [aɪ'dəʊniəs] *adj.* appropriate. **idoneity** [,aɪdə'niːɪti, –'neɪ–], *n.*

ignavy, ignavia ['ɪgnəvi, ɪg'neɪviə] *n.* laziness.

igneous ['ɪgniəs] *adj.* pertaining to fire; *Geology;* produced by action of heat within the earth; formed by solidification of molten magma. **ignescent,** *n. & adj.* (substance) throwing off sparks when struck; sparkling; inflamed. **ignicolist,** *n.* fire-worshipper.

ignis fatuus [,ɪgnɪs 'fætjuəs] (*Latin*) (*pl.* ignes fatui) 'foolish fire'; light produced over marshland; will-o'-the wisp; any misleading idea or thing.

ignominy ['ɪgnəmɪni] *n.* dishonour. **ignominious,** *adj.*

ignorantism ['ɪgnərəntɪzm] *n.* obscurantism.

iguana [ɪ'gwɑːnə] *n.* large lizard, especially of tropical America. **iguanian,** *adj.* **iguanodon,** *n.* kind of dinosaur.

ileum ['ɪliəm] *n.* last part of small intestine. **ileac,** *adj.* **ileitis,** *n.* inflammation of ileum. **ileus,** *n.* complete obstruction of intestine.

ilex ['aɪleks] *n.* holm-oak; holly genus. **ilicic** [aɪ'lɪsɪk], *adj.* pertaining to holly.

ilium ['ɪliəm] *n.* (*pl.* ilia) bone forming part of pelvis; hip bone. **iliac,** *adj.* pertaining to the loins. **iliacus** [ɪ'laɪəkəs], *n.* flexor muscle of thigh.

illation [ɪ'leɪʃn] *n.* inference; act of inferring. **illative** ['ɪlətɪv, ɪ'leɪtɪv], *adj.; n.* such word (as *therefore*).

illinition [,ɪlɪ'nɪʃn] *n.* act of rubbing on.

illuminati [ɪ,luːmɪ'nɑːtiː] *n. pl.* persons claiming special enlightenment.

illuvium [ɪ'luːviəm] *n.* (*pl.* –iums, –ia) material removed from soil layer by rainwater and deposited in lower layer. **illuvial,** *adj.* **illuviate,** *v.i.* undergo illuviation. **illuviation,** *n.* accumulation of illuvium.

imagism ['ɪmɪdʒɪzm] *n.* poetical doctrine of the use of precise images but entire freedom of form and subject-matter. **imagist,** *n.*

imago [ɪ'meɪgəʊ, –'mɑː–] *n.* (*pl.* –es, –gines), adult form of insect.

imam, imaum [ɪ'mɑːm] (*Arabic*) *n.* priest in charge of Muslim mosque; title of several Muslim rulers or leaders. **imamah,** *n.* office of imam. **imamate,** *n.* jurisdiction of imam. **imamic,** *adj.*

imbat ['ɪmbæt] (*Turkish*) *n.* periodical cool wind of Cyprus and Levant.

imbreviate [ɪm'briːvieɪt] *v.t.* draw up as a brief; enrol.

imbricate ['ɪmbrɪkeɪt] *adj.* overlapping; *v.i. & t.* be or make imbricate. **imbrication,** *n.* intricacy. **imbricative,** *adj.*

imbroglio [ɪm'brəʊliəʊ] *n.* confused or embarrassing situation or state.

imbrue [ɪm'bruː] *v.t.* dye; soak.

imbrute [ɪm'bruːt] *v.t. & i.* degrade; become brutish.

imbue [ɪm'bjuː] *v.t.* soak; dye; impregnate; permeate.

immanent ['ɪmənənt] *adj.* indwelling; inherent; all-pervading. **immanence,** *n*

immeability [,ɪmiə'bɪləti] *n.* state of being impassable or lacking power to pass.

immerge [ɪ'mɜːdʒ] *v.t. & i.* plunge in; immerse oneself in something. **immergence,** *n.*

imminent ['ɪmɪnənt] *adj.* happening in near future; threatening. **imminence,** *n.*

imminution [,ɪmɪ'njuːʃn] *n.* diminution.

immolate ['ɪmələɪt] *v.t.* sacrifice, especially by killing. **immolation, immolator,** *n.*

immortelle [,ɪmɔː'tel] *n.* everlasting dried flower.

immunoassay [,ɪmjunəʊ'æseɪ, ɪ,mjuː–] *n.* determination of presence and quantity of a substance through its action as an antigen.

immunocompromised [,ɪmjunəʊ'kɒmprəmaɪzd, ɪ,mjuː–] *adj.* immunosuppressed.

immunogen [ɪ'mjuːnədʒən, –en] *n.* antigen. **immunogenesis,** *n.* production of immune response. **immunogenic,** *adj.* **immunogenetics,** *n.* study of immunity as affected by heredity. **immunogenetic,** *adj.*

immunology [,ɪmjuː'nɒlədʒi] *n.* study of immunity. **immunological,** *adj.* **immunologist,** *n.*

immunosuppressed [,ɪmjunəʊsə'prest, ɪ,mjuː–] *adj.* lacking a fully effective immune system; having the normal immune response suppressed. **immunosuppressant,** *n.* drug causing immunosuppression, especially to prevent rejection of a transplanted organ. **immunosuppression**, *n*. **immunosuppressive**, *adj*.

immunotherapy [ˌɪmjunəʊ'θerəpi, ɪ,mjuː–] *n*. medical treatment by exploiting immunological principles, *e.g.* by arousing antibodies through introducing antigens, or by causing tissue rejection through a graft. **immunotherapeutic**, *adj*.

immure [ɪ'mjʊə] *v.t.* imprison; entomb.

impacable [ɪm'peɪkəbl, –'pæ–] *adj*. not pacifiable.

impaction [ɪm'pækʃn] *n*. obstruction, or lodgement of matter, in passage.

impactite ['ɪmpæktaɪt, ɪm'pæk–] *n*. slag-like glassy object found on surface of the earth, probably formed from rock melted by the impact of a meteor.

impair [æm'peə, ɪm–] *n*. odd number; (wager on) odd numbers in roulette.

impanation [ˌɪmpə'neɪʃn] *n*. introduction or embodiment of Christ's body in Communion bread. **impanate** [–'peɪneɪt], *adj*.

imparity [ɪm'pærəti] *n*. disparity. **imparisyllabic** [ˌɪmpærɪsɪ'læbɪk], *n. & adj.* (word) having different number of syllables in different cases.

impasse [æm'pɑːs, 'ɪmpɑːs] *n*. deadlock; blind alley.

impasto [ɪm'pæstəʊ] *n*. application of pigment thickly, in painting; such pigment.

impavid [ɪm'pævɪd] *adj*. without fear. **impavidity**, *n*.

impeccable [ɪm'pekəbl] *adj*. without fault. **impeccant**, *adj*. without sin.

impecunious [ˌɪmpɪ'kjuːniəs] *adj*. poor. **impecuniosity**, *n*.

impedance [ɪm'piːdns] *n*. *Electricity*, apparent resistance to flow of alternating current.

impediment [ɪm'pedɪmənt] *n*. obstacle, hindrance; speech defect. **impedimenta** [–'mentə], *n. pl.* luggage. **impedimental, impedimentary**, **impeditive**, *adj*. hindering.

impennate [ɪm'peneɪt] *adj*. flightless; pertaining to penguins; *n*. penguin.

imperator [ˌɪmpə'rɑːtɔː] *n*. commander, ruler.

imperscriptible [ˌɪmpə'skrɪptəbl] *adj*. not recorded.

impetigo [ˌɪmpɪ'taɪgəʊ] *n*. pustulous skin disease. **impetiginous** [–'tɪdʒɪnəs], *adj*.

impetrate ['ɪmpɪtreɪt] *v.t.* ask for; obtaining by asking. **impetration**, *n*. **impetrator**, *n*. **impetrative**, *adj*.

impi ['ɪmpi] *n*. formation of African, especially Zulu, warriors.

impignorate [ɪm'pɪgnəreɪt] *v.t.* mortgage; pawn; [–ət], *adj*. pawned. **impignoration**, *n*.

implacable [ɪm'plækəbl] *adj*. not to be appeased; irreconcilable.

implement ['ɪmplɪment] *v.t.* carry out, perform; fulfil; [–mənt], *n*. tool; utensil. **implemental**, *adj*. useful, effective. **implementation**, *n*.

implicit [ɪm'plɪsɪt] *adj*. implied though not expressed; without question or doubt.

implode [ɪm'pləʊd] *v.t. & i.* burst inwards. **implosive**, *n*. **implosive**, *adj*.

imponderable [ɪm'pɒndərəbl] *adj*. incapable of being weighed or evaluated; *n*. such thing, especially spiritual value. **imponderous**, *adj*. weightless.

importune [ˌɪmpə'tjuːn, –pɔː–] *v.i. & t.* urge or ask persistently; solicit for immoral or sexual purposes. **importunate** [ɪm'pɔːtjʊnət], *adj*. urgent, pressing; making persistent requests. **importunity** [–'tjuːn–], *n*.

impostumate, imposthumate [ɪm'pɒstjumeɪt] *v.i. & t.* form or inflict an abscess. **impostumation**, *n*.

impotent ['ɪmpətənt] *adj*. weak; powerless; sexually incapable.

imprecate ['ɪmprɪkeɪt] *v.i. & t.* pray for (evil); curse. **imprecation**, *n*. **imprecatory**, *adj*.

impregnable [ɪm'pregnəbl] *adj*. able to withstand attack; capable of being fertilized; able to become or be made pregnant.

impresario [ˌɪmprə'sɑːriəʊ] *n*. manager of entertainment.

impressionism [ɪm'preʃn–ɪzm] *n*. artistic doctrine of expressing without detail the artist's subjective impression of subject. **impressionist**, *n*.

imprimatur [ˌɪmprɪ'mɑːtə, –'meɪtə] *n*. licence to print; approval.

imprimis [ɪm'praɪmɪs, –'priː–] (*Latin*) *adv*. 'in the first place'.

improcreant [ɪm'prəʊkriənt] *adj*. sexually impotent.

impromptu [ɪm'prɒmptjuː] *n. & adj.* extempore (composition).

impropriate [ɪm'prəʊprieɪt] *v.t.* transfer (ecclesiastical revenue) to layman. **impropriation, impropriator, impropriatrix**, *n*.

improvise ['ɪmprəvaɪz] *v.i. & t.* invent or compose without forethought; extemporize. **improvisate** [–'prɒvɪzeɪt], *v.i. & t.* **improvisation, improvisator**, *n*. **improvisatorial, improvisatory**, *adj*.

impudicity [ˌɪmpjuː'dɪsəti] *n*. shamelessness.

impugn [ɪm'pjuːn] *v.t.* challenge; call in question; oppose; attack by argument. **impugnable**, *adj*. **impugnment**, *n*.

impunity [ɪm'pjuːnəti] *n*. exemption from punishment.

imshi ['ɪmʃi] (*Arabic*) *exclamation*, go away!

inamorato [ɪnˌæmə'rɑːtəʊ] (*Italian*) *n. (fem.* **–ta**) lover; beloved person.

inanition [ˌɪnə'nɪʃn] *n*. emptiness; starvation; exhaustion.

in articulo mortis [ɪn ɑːˌtɪkjuləʊ 'mɔːtɪs] (*Latin*) 'at the point of death'.

incalescent [ˌɪnkə'lesnt] *adj*. becoming warm or warmer. **incalescence, incalescency**, *n*.

in camera [ɪn 'kæmərə] (*Latin*) 'in private chamber'; in secret; in private.

incandesce [ˌɪnkæn'des] *v.i. & t.* become white, glow, or make to glow, with heat. **incandescence**, *n*. **incandescent**, *adj*.

incanous [ɪn'keɪnəs] *adj*. covered with soft white hairs.

incarcerate [ɪn'kɑːsəreɪt] *v.t.* imprison. **incarceration, incarcerator**, *n*.

incardinate [ɪn'kɑːdɪneɪt] *v.t.* make cardinal; receive (priest) from another diocese.

incarnadine [ɪn'kɑːnədaɪn] *adj*. crimson; fleshcoloured; *v.t.* dye crimson.

inchoate ['ɪnkəʊeɪt] *v.t.* begin; inaugurate; initiate; [–ət], *adj*. just begun; imperfect. **inchoacy**, *n*. **inchoation**, *n*. beginning. **inchoative**, *adj*. signifying commencement.

incipient [ɪn'sɪpiənt] *adj*. beginning; in initial stage. **incipience, incipiency**, *n*.

incipit ['ɪŋkɪpɪt, 'ɪns–] (*Latin*) 'here begins'.

incisor [ɪn'saɪzə] *n.* cutting tooth at front of mouth. **incisorial, incisory,** *adj.*

inclination [ˌɪnklɪ'neɪʃn] *n.* angle between horizon and magnetic needle moving vertically; magnetic dip.

incognito [ˌɪnkɒg'niːtəu, ɪn'kɒgnɪtəu] *adj.* & *adv.* (*fem.* **-ta**) with identity concealed; under assumed name; *n.* such person (*abbr.* **incog.**).

incommunicado [ˌɪnkəmjuːnɪ'kɑːdəu] *adj.* prevented from communicating, in solitary confinement.

incondite [ɪn'kɒndɪt, -aɪt] *adj.* badly composed or put together; unpolished.

inconnu [ˌæŋkɒ'njuː] (*French*) *n.* (*fem.* **-ue**) unknown person; stranger.

incrassate [ɪn'kræseɪt] *v.t.* thicken; *adj.* thickened. **incrassation,** *n.* **incrassative,** *adj.*

incretion [ɪn'kriːʃn] *n.* internal secretion; hormone. **incretionary, incretory,** *adj.*

incroyable [ˌæŋkrwæ'jɑːblə] (*French*) *n.* fop.

incubus ['ɪŋkjubəs] (*Latin*) *n.* (*pl.* **-bi**) 'nightmare'; burden; oppression; *Medicine,* nightmare; demon taking on male form to have sexual intercourse with a woman in her sleep.

inculcate ['ɪnkʌlkeɪt] *v.t.* impress on mind by frequent repetition. **inculcation,** *n.* **inculcative, inculcatory,** *adj.*

inculpate ['ɪnkʌlpeɪt] *v.t.* blame; involve in blame. **inculpation,** *n.* **inculpative, inculpatory,** *adj.*

incumbent [ɪn'kʌmbənt] *adj.* lying; resting upon as a duty; *n.* holder of benefice; vicar. **incumbency,** *n.*

incunabula [ˌɪnkju'næbjulə] *n. pl.* (*sing.* **-lum**) early printed books, especially printed before AD 1500; any early or beginning period. **incunabulist,** *n.* student of these. **incunabular,** *adj.*

incur [ɪn'kɜː] *v.t.* become liable for; bring upon oneself. **incurrence,** *n.* **incurrent,** *adj.* running or flowing inwards.

incuse [ɪn'kjuːz] *n.* & *adj.* (impression, especially on coin) stamped in.

indaba [ɪn'dɑːbə] (*Zulu*) *n.* palaver; conference.

indagate ['ɪndəgeɪt] *v.t.* investigate. **indagation,** *n.* **indagator,** *n.* **indagative,** *adj.*

indenture [ɪn'dentʃə] *n.* written agreement, originally torn or cut into two parts along a jagged line; *pl.,* agreement between master and apprentice; *v.t.* notch; wrinkle; bind by contract.

Index Librorum Prohibitorum ['ɪndeks lɪ,brɔːrəm prəhɪbɪ'tɔːrəm] (*Latin*) 'list of forbidden books' of the Roman Catholic Church. **Index Expurgatorius** [-,ekspɜːgə'tɔːriəs], list of books allowed only in expurgated form.

indicia [ɪn'dɪʃiə] (*Latin*) *n. pl.* identifying marks; signs. **indicial,** *adj.*

indict [ɪn'daɪt] *v.t.* accuse. **indiction** [-'dɪkʃn], *n.* ancient Roman tax; property tax or assessment. **indictive** *adj.* **indictment** [ɪn'daɪtmənt], *n.*

indigenous [ɪn'dɪdʒənəs] *adj.* native; aboriginal; inherent. **indigenal,** *adj.* **indigine,** *n.* native. **indigeneity,** *n.*

indigent ['ɪndɪdʒənt] *adj.* poor; destitute. **indigence,** *n.*

indigo ['ɪndɪgəu] *n.* dark blue colour and dye; plant yielding it. **indigoferous** [-'gɒfərəs], *adj.* yielding indigo. **indigotic** [-'gɒtɪk], *adj.*

indite [ɪn'daɪt] *v.t.* compose; write down; describe. **inditement,** *n.*

indoles ['ɪndəliːz] *n.* inherent disposition.

induciae [ɪn'djuːʃiiː] (*Latin*) *n. pl.* armistice.

induction [ɪn'dʌkʃn] *n. Electricity,* production of electrified or magnetic state in body by the near presence of a charged or magnetized body; production of a current in a circuit by a variation in the magnetic field linked with it or in current in an adjacent circuit; *Logic,* reasoning from particular to general; establishment of general rules from observation of individual cases; installing in office, position, etc. **inductive,** *adj.*

indue [ɪn'djuː] *v.t.* put on; assume; endow; supply.

indumentum [ˌɪndju'mentəm] *n.* (*pl.* **-ta, -ums**) thick, woolly or hairy covering.

induna [ɪn'duːnə] (*Zulu*) *n.* S African chief or councillor.

indurate ['ɪndjureɪt] *v.i.* & *t.* harden. **induration,** *n.* **indurative,** *adj.*

ineffable [ɪn'efəbl] *adj.* indescribable; unspeakable.

ineluctable [ˌɪnɪ'lʌktəbl] *adj.* irresistible; unavoidable. **ineluctability,** *n.*

inept [ɪ'nept] *adj.* inappropriate; weak; silly.

inerm(ous) [ɪ'nɜːm, -əs] *adj. Botany,* without prickles.

inert [ɪ'nɜːt] *adj.* not capable of motion or action; inactive, especially chemically.

inertia [ɪ'nɜːʃiə, -iə] *n.* matter's property of remaining at rest or of continuing to move in same straight line; tendency to be inactive; sluggishness.

in esse [ɪn 'esi] (*Latin*) 'in existence'.

inexorable [ɪn'eksərəbl] *adj.* unalterable; relentless. **inexorability,** *n.*

in extenso [ɪn ek'stensəu, -ɪk-] (*Latin*) extended to full length.

in extremis [ɪn ek'striːmɪs, -ɪk-] (*Latin*) on point of death; at last extremity.

in facie curiae [ɪn ˌfeɪʃiiː 'kjuərniː, -,fækieɪ 'kjuəriaɪ] (*Latin*) 'in the presence of the court'.

infanta [ɪn'fæntə] *n.* daughter of Spanish or Portuguese sovereign. **infante** [-teɪ], *n.* younger son of Spanish or Portuguese sovereign.

infarct ['ɪnfɑːkt] *n.* portion of dead and scarred tissue in an organ resulting from congestion or blockage of a blood vessel serving it. **infarction,** *n.*

inferiae [ɪn'fɪəriiː] (*Latin*) *n. pl.* sacrifices to beings of underworld.

infeudation [ˌɪnfju'deɪʃn] *n.* granting of feoff; transfer of tithes to layman.

in fieri [ɪn 'faɪəri, -fi'eəri] (*Latin*) 'pending'.

in fine [ɪn 'faɪn, -i] (*Latin*) 'at the end'; finally.

in flagrante [ˌɪn flə'grænti] (*Latin*) 'in blazing crime'; in the act of committing a crime or offence; in the act of having illicit sexual intercourse.

inflorescence [ˌɪnflə'resns] *n.* flowering; arrangement of flowers in a plant; flower cluster or head. **inflorescent,** *adj.*

in foro [ɪn 'fɔːrəu] (*Latin*) 'in the forum'; before the court.

infra ['ɪnfrə] (*Latin*) *adv.* 'below', later; afterwards. **infra dignitatem,** beneath one's dignity (*abbreviated as* **infra dig.**).

infract [ɪn'frækt] *v.t.* infringe. **infraction,** *n.* violation, especially of law.

infumate(d) [ɪn'fjuːmeɪt, -ɪd] *adj.* blackish; smoky.

infundibular, infundibulate [‚ɪnfʌn'dɪbjʊlə, –ət] *adj.* funnel-shaped. **infundibuliform** [–'dɪbjʊlɪfɔːm], *adj.* **infundibulum**, *n.* (*pl.* **-la**) *Anatomy*, funnel-shaped part.

infuscate(d) [ɪnfʌs'keɪt, –ɪd] *adj.* brownish; obscured.

infusoria [‚ɪnfju'zɔːriə, –'sɔː–] *n. pl.* (*sing*, **-ian**) class of protozoa found in water. **infusorial, infusorian**, *adj.* **infusoriform, infusorioid**, *adj.* like an infusorian.

ingeminate [ɪn'dʒemɪneɪt] *v.t.* reiterate. **ingemination**, *n.*

in genere [ɪn 'dʒenəri, –'genəreɪ] (*Latin*) 'in kind'; in general.

ingénue ['ænʒənjuː] (*French*) *n.* guileless girl, especially such stage rôle.

ingenuous [ɪn'dʒenjuəs] *adj.* innocent; guileless. **ingenuousness**, *n.*

ingest [ɪn'dʒest] *v.t.* take in as food; digest. **ingesta**, *n. pl.* ingested matter. **ingestion**, *n.* **ingestive**, *adj.*

ingluvies [ɪn'gluːviiːz] *n.* bird's crop. **ingluvial**, *adj.*

ingrate ['ɪngreɪt] *n.* ungrateful person.

ingravescent [‚ɪngrə'vesnt] *adj.* continually becoming more severe.

ingress ['ɪngres] *n.* entrance; right of entering. **ingression**, *n.*

inguinal ['ɪŋgwɪnl] *adj.* pertaining to or near the groin.

ingurgitate [ɪn'gɜːdʒɪteɪt] *v.i. & t.* swallow up; guzzle. **ingurgitation**, *n.*

inhere [ɪn'hɪə] *v.i.* belong intimately and by nature; be a part of. **inhesion, inherence**, *n.* **inherent**, *adj.* innate; fixed; settled; constituting an inseparable part or attribute.

in hoc [ɪn 'hɒk] (*Latin*) 'in this (respect)'.

inhume [ɪn'hjuːm] *v.t.* bury. **inhumation**, *n.*

inimical [ɪ'nɪmɪkl] *adj.* hostile; unfavourable. **inimicality**, *n.*

in initio [ɪn ɪ'nɪʃiəʊ] (*Latin*) 'in the beginning'.

iniquitous [ɪ'nɪkwɪtəs] *adj.* unjust; wicked. **iniquity**, *n.*

in loco [ɪn 'ləʊkəʊ] (*Latin*) 'in the (proper) place'. **in loco parentis** [–pə'rentɪs], in place or position of a parent.

in medias res [ɪn ‚miːdɪæs 'reɪz, –‚meɪ–] (*Latin*) 'into the midst of things'; beginning in the middle or at the most important part.

in memoriam [ɪn mɪ'mɔːriəm] (*Latin*) 'in memory (of)'.

innate [ɪ'neɪt] *adj.* inborn; forming natural or constitutional part; inherited.

innervate, innerve ['ɪnɜːveɪt, ɪ'nɜːv] *v.t.* supply with nerves; stimulate. **innervation**, *n.*

innocuous [ɪ'nɒkjuəs] *adj.* harmless.

innovate ['ɪnəveɪt] *v.t. & i.* introduce something new; make changes; introduce as new. **innovation**, *n.* **innovator**, *n.*

innoxious [ɪ'nɒkʃəs] *adj.* harmless.

innuendo [‚ɪnju'endəʊ] *n.* (*pl.* **-es**) allusion; insinuation, especially unpleasant.

inopinate [ɪ'nɒpɪneɪt] *adj.* unexpected.

inosculate [ɪ'nɒskjuleɪt] *v.i. & t.* unite; combine; blend. **inosculation**, *n.*

in posse [ɪn 'pɒsi] (*Latin*) 'in possibility'.

in principio [ɪn prɪn'sɪpiəʊ, –'kɪ–] (*Latin*) 'in the beginning'.

inquiline ['ɪnkwɪlaɪn, –lɪn] *adj.* living in another's nest or dwelling; *n.* such animal. **inquilinism, inquilinity**, *n.* **inquilinous**, *adj.*

inquinate ['ɪnkwɪneɪt] *v.t.* corrupt. **inquination**, *n.*

in re [ɪn 'riː, –'reɪ] (*Latin*) (*pl.* ... **rebus**) 'in the thing'; in reality; concerning.

inscenation [‚ɪnsɪ'neɪʃn] *n.* mise en scène.

insectivorous [‚ɪnsek'tɪvərəs] *adj.* feeding on insects. **insectivore**, *n.* such animal.

inseminate [ɪn'semɪneɪt] *v.t.* sow; impregnate. **insemination**, *n.*

insidious [ɪn'sɪdiəs] *adj.* treacherous; sly; lying in wait to capture; *Medicine*, more serious than it appears.

insignia [ɪn'sɪgniə] *n. pl.* badges of office; any distinctive emblems.

insipience [ɪn'sɪpiəns] *n.* stupidity. **insipient**, *adj.*

in situ [ɪn 'sɪtjuː, –'saɪ–] (*Latin*) 'on the site'; in original position.

insolate ['ɪnsəleɪt] *v.t.* expose to sunlight. **insolation**, *n.* such exposure; sunstroke; medical treatment by sun-bathing; radiation from sun.

insouciance [ɪn'suːsiəns, æn'suːsiəns] *n.* indifference; carefreeness. **insouciant**, *adj.*

inspissate [ɪn'spɪseɪt] *v.t.* thicken. **inspissant**, *n. & adj.* thickening (substance). **inspissation, inspissator**, *n.*

in statu quo (ante) [ɪn ‚stætjuː 'kwəʊ ('ænti), –‚steɪ–] (*Latin*) 'in same state (as before)'.

instauration [‚ɪnstɔː'reɪʃn] *n.* restoration to former excellence. **instaurator**, *n.*

insufflate ['ɪnsəfleɪt, ɪn'sʌf–] *v.t.* blow on or into; breathe upon. **insufflation**, *n.* **insufflator**, *n.*

insular ['ɪnsjulə] *adj.* pertaining to island; narrow-minded. **insularity**, *n.*

intaglio [ɪn'tɑːliəʊ] *n.* engraved pattern in cavo relievo, especially on gem; gem bearing such. **intagliate**, *v.t.* incise. **intagliation**, *n.*

intarsia [ɪn'tɑːsiə] *n.* pattern of inlaid wood; art of making such patterns. **intarsiate**, *adj.*

integer ['ɪntɪdʒə] *n.* whole number; entity; *adj.* whole. **integral**. *adj.* essential; constituent; whole. **integrant**, *n. & adj.* component; essential (part).

intellection [‚ɪntɪ'lekʃn] *n.* superhuman knowledge; act or exercise of intellect; synecdoche.

intelligentsia [ɪn‚telɪ'dʒentsiə, –'ge–] *n.* intellectual persons; 'highbrows'.

intemerate [ɪn'temərət] *adj.* undefiled.

intempestive [‚ɪntem'pestɪv] *adj.* inopportune; out of season. **intempestivity**, *n.*

intenerate [ɪn'tenəreɪt] *v.t.* soften. **inteneration**, *n.*

intension [ɪn'tenʃn] *n.* intensity; intensification; exertion of mind or will; *Logic*, properties implied by a concept or term.

inter alia [‚ɪntə 'eɪliə, –'ɑː–] (*Latin*) 'among other (things)'. **inter alios**, 'among other (persons)'.

interamnian [‚ɪntər'æmniən] *adj.* between rivers.

intercalary [‚ɪntə'kæləri] *adj.* inserted in the calendar; bissextile; leap (year); interpolated. **intercalate** [ɪn'tɜːkəleɪt, ‚ɪntəkə'leɪt], *v.t.* **intercalation**, *n.*

intercardinal [‚ɪntə'kɑːdɪnl] *n. & adj.* (point) half-way between two cardinal points of compass.

interciliary [ˌɪntəˈsɪlɪəri] *adj.* between eyebrows.
intercolline [ˌɪntəˈkɒlaɪn] *adj.* between hills.
intercosmic [ˌɪntəˈkɒzmɪk] *adj.* between or among stars.
intercostal [ˌɪntəˈkɒstl] *adj.* between ribs.
interdict [ˌɪntəˈdɪkt] *v.t.* forbid; [ˈɪntədɪkt], *n.* prohibition. **interdiction**, *n.* **interdictive, interdictory**, *adj.* **interdictor**, *n.*
interdigitate [ˌɪntəˈdɪdʒɪteɪt] *v.t.* interlock; intertwine. **interdigitation**, *n.*
interested [ˈɪntrəstɪd, –təres–] *adj.* showing curiosity or concern about; involved or implicated in (and therefore not impartial).
interfenestral [ˌɪntəfəˈnestrəl] *n.* between windows. **interfenestration**, *n.* such distance.
interferometer [ˌɪntəfəˈrɒmɪtə] *n.* instrument measuring wavelengths of light and analysing spectra. **interferometric**, *adj.* **interferometry**, *n.*
interfluvial [ˌɪntəˈfluːvɪəl] *adj.* between two rivers flowing in same direction. **interfluve**, *n.* such area.
interjacent [ˌɪntəˈdʒeɪsnt] *adj.* situated between; intervening. **interjacence, interjacency**, *n.*
interlocutor [ˌɪntəˈlɒkjʊtə] *n.* (*fem.* **–tress, –trice, –trix**) speaker in conversation; interpreter. **interlocution**, *n.* conversation; interruption. **interlocutory**, *adj.*; *Law*, done during action; intermediate.
interlunar [ˌɪntəˈluːnə] *adj.* pertaining to period between old and new moon. **interlunation**, *n.* such period; interval of darkness.
intern(e) [ˈɪntɜːn] (*American*) *n.* hospital physician, surgeon or student.

I write pyjamas and you write pajamas

There are several significant differences between the British and American spelling systems. In particular, six distinct word elements are consistently spelled differently in a wide range of words (British precedes American in all the examples that follow):

l -ll at the end of certain words: *fulfil/fulfill, instil/instill*, etc.

ll -l in inflected forms of verbs and certain other words: *marvelling/marveling, woollen/woolen*, etc.

lyse -lyze: analyse/analyze, paralyse/paralyze, etc.

ogue -og: catalogue/catalog, monologue/mono-log, etc.

our -or: colour/color, humour/humor, etc.
re –er: centre/center, fibre/fiber etc.

Traditionally, British English has used the spellings *ae, oe* in words of Latin and Greek origin (*mediaeval, foetus*), whereas American uses the simplified *e* for both (*medieval, fetus*). However, there is a rapidly increasing tendency for British to adopt the American convention. On the transatlantic differences between *-ise* and *-ize*, see **'-ise' or '-ize'**.

There are many other one-off items in which spelling differs. These are the most important:

BRITISH	AMERICAN
axe	also *ax*
cheque(*book*)	*check*(*book*)
chequer (pattern)	*checker*
chilli	*chili*
cigarette	also *cigaret*
defence	also *defense*
disc (except in computers)	*disk*
doughnut	also *donut*
draught	*draft*
gauge	also *gage*
grey	*gray*
jewellery	*jewelry*
kerb	*curb*
mould	*mold*
mollusc	also *mollusk*
moult	*molt*
moustache	also *mustache*
offence	also *offense*
pyjamas	*pajamas*
plough	also *plow*
pretence	also *pretense*
programme (except in computers)	*program*
sceptic	also *skeptic*
smoulder	*smolder*
storey (of building)	*story*
sulphur	also *sulfur*
tyre	*tire*
vice (tool)	*vise*
waggon	also *wagon*

internecine [,Intə'niːsaɪn] *adj.* causing death and destruction, especially mutual.

internuncio [,Intə'nʌnʃiəʊ] *n.* go-between; papal emissary.

interoceptor [,Intərəʊ'septə] *n.* sensory receptor responding to stimuli arising within the body, especially the viscera. **interoceptive,** *adj.*

interosculate [,Intər'ɒskjuleɪt] *v.i.* intermix; have common biological characteristics. **interosculant,** *adj.* intersecting. **interosculation,** *n.*

interpellate [ɪn'tɜːpəleɪt, ,Intə'peleɪt] *n.* arraign or question for explanation. **interpellant,** *adj.* interrupting; *n.* person interpellating. **interpellation,** *n.* interpellating; interruption. **interpellator,** *n.*

interpolate [ɪn'tɜːpəleɪt] *v.t.* insert; introduce; interject; alter or falsify (text etc.) by inserting new material; estimate (intermediate values) from known values in a mathematical range or series. **interpolation,** *n.* **interpolative,** *adj.* **interpolator,** *n.*

interregnum [,Intə'regnəm] *n.* (*pl.* **-na**) interval, especially between two successive reigns. **interrex,** *n.* (*pl.* **-reges**) ruler during such.

inter se [,Intə 'seɪ, -'siː] (*Latin*) 'among themselves'.

interstice [ɪn'tɜːstɪs] *n.* small opening or space, especially intervening. **intersitial,** *adj.*

intertessellation [,Intətesə'leɪʃn] *n.* complicated interrelationship.

intertonic [,Intə'tɒnɪk] *adj.* between accented sounds or syllables.

intertrigo [,Intə'traɪgəʊ] *n.* inflammation of skin caused by friction between moist surfaces. **intertriginous** [-'trɪdʒɪnəs], *adj.*

intestate [ɪn'testeɪt] *n.* & *adj.* (person dying) without having made a valid will. **intestacy,** *n.*

intima ['ɪntɪmə] *n.* (*pl.* **-ae**) *Anatomy,* inner lining of organ or vessel.

intorsion [ɪn'tɔːʃn] *n.* twisting, twining. **intort,** *v.i.*

in toto [ɪn 'təʊtəʊ] (*Latin*) 'entirely'.

intrados [ɪn'treɪdɒs] *n.* interior curve of arch.

intramural [,Intrə'mjʊərəl] *adj.* within the walls; taking place within, or confined to, a college, institution, etc.

intransigent [ɪn'trænsɪdʒənt, -'trænz-] *n.* & *adj.* uncompromising (person); radical. **intransigence,** *n.*

intravasation [ɪn,trævə'seɪʃn] *n.* *Medicine,* entrance of externally formed matter into vessels.

intravenous [,Intrə'viːnəs] *adj.* into a vein.

intra-vitam [,Intrə'viːtæm, -'vaɪ-] *adj.* during life.

intrinsic [ɪn'trɪnsɪk] *adj.* inward; inherent.

introit ['ɪntrɔɪt] *n.* psalm or hymn chanted at approach to altar of celebrant priest; first part of Roman Catholic Mass.

introjection [,Intrə'dʒekʃn] *n.* incorporation of external ideas and attitudes into one's own personality. **introject,** *v.t.*

intromit [,Intrə'mɪt] *v.t.* insert; admit. **intromission,** *n.* **intromittent,** *adj.*

introrse [ɪn'trɔːs] *adj.* inward facing.

introspection [,Intrə'spekʃn] *n.* looking inward; self-examination; intense, sometimes morbid, interest in one's own mental processes and emotions. **introspect,** *v.t.* & *i.* **introspective,** *adj.*

intumesce [,Intju'mes] *v.i.* swell; bubble, especially owing to heat. **intumescence,** *n.* **intumescent,** *adj.*

intussusception [,Intəsə'sepʃn] *n.* movement or slipping of a part into another, especially of small into large intestine. **intussuscept,** *v.t.* **intussusceptive,** *adj.*

inula ['ɪmjʊlə] *n.* elecampane. **inulaceous, inuloid,** *adj.* like inula.

inunct [ɪ'nʌŋkt] *v.t.* anoint. **inunction,** *n.* act of anointing; ointment; rubbing of ointment into skin. **inunctum,** *n.* lanolin ointment.

invaginate [ɪn'vædʒɪneɪt] *v.i.* & *t.* sheathe; infold; draw part of tube, etc., inside other part. **invagination,** *n.* act of invaginating; part invaginated; intussusception.

inveigh [ɪn'veɪ] *v.i.* attack with words.

inveigle [ɪn'veɪgl, -'viː-] *v.t.* entice; persuade by flattery, guile, etc. **inveiglement,** *n.*

invenit [ɪn'veɪnɪt, -'viː-] (*Latin*) 'invented (it)'.

inveterate [ɪn'vetərət] *adj.* confirmed; long-established. **inveteracy,** *n.*

invictive [ɪn'vɪktɪv] *adj.* not defeatable.

invidious [ɪn'vɪdiəs] *adj.* tending to provoke envy or ill-will or give offence.

invigilate [ɪn'vɪdʒɪleɪt] *v.i.* supervise closely, especially candidates in examination. **invigilation,** *n.* **invigilator,** *n.*

invination [,Invaɪ'neɪʃn] *n.* inclusion or embodiment of blood of Christ in Communion wine.

inviscate [ɪn'vɪskeɪt] *v.t.* make sticky; entrap with sticky substance. **inviscation,** *n.*

in vivo [ɪn 'viːvəʊ, -'vaɪ-] (*Latin*) 'in living (creature)'. **in vitro** [-'viːtrəʊ], 'in glass'; in test-tube or laboratory experiment. **in vitro fertilization,** union of eggs and sperm to form embryos, in the laboratory.

involucre ['Invəluːkə] *n.* covering, especially whorl of bracts in plant. **involucral,** *adj.* like an involucre. **involucrate,** *adj.* having an involucre.

involute ['Invəluːt] *adj.* curved spirally inwards; complicated. **involution,** *n.*

invultuation [ɪn,vʌltju'eɪʃn] *n.* stabbing of wax image of person to be injured as form of witchcraft.

iodoform [aɪ'ɒdəfɔːm, -'əʊ-] *n.* antiseptic made from iodine and alcohol. **iodotherapy,** *n.* medical treatment with iodine.

ion ['aɪən, -ɒn] *n.* electrically charged particle or atom. **ionization,** *n.* **ionize,** *v.t.* convert into ion; make conductive by forming ions in. **ionophoresis,** *n.* electrophoresis, especially of small ions. **ionosphere** [aɪ'ɒnəsfɪə], *n.* region of the atmosphere, from 40 km./25 miles up, in which air is ionized by sun's ultra-violet rays and reflects radio waves back to earth. **iontophoresis,** *n.* introduction of ions into body as medical treatment.

iota [aɪ'əʊtə] *n.* ninth letter of Greek alphabet (I, ι); jot; atom.

ipecacuanha [,ɪpɪkækju'ænə] *n.* dried roots of S American plant used as expectorant, etc. (*abbreviated as* **ipecac.**).

ipse dixit [,ɪpsi 'dɪksɪt] (*Lat*) 'himself he said (it)'; dogmatic statement; dictum.

ipseity [ɪp'siːəti] *n.* selfhood.

ipso facto [,ɪpsəʊ 'fæktəʊ] (*Latin*) 'by that fact'; by virtue of that very fact or case.

IQSY *abbreviation* of International Quiet Sun Years.

irade [ɪ'rɑːdi] *n.* Muslim edict, especially sultan's decree.

irascent [ɪ'ræsnt, aɪ-] *adj.* becoming angry. **irascible**, *adj.* easily angered; irritable. **irascibility**, *n.*

irenic(al) *see* eirenic.

iridescent [ˌɪrɪ'desnt] *adj.* glittering with rainbow-like colours. **iridescence, iridescency**, *n.*

iridic [ɪ'rɪdɪk, aɪ-] *adj.* containing iridium; pertaining to iris of eye.

iridium [ɪ'rɪdiəm, aɪ-] *n.* rare, hard, platinum-like metal.

iridization [ˌɪrɪdaɪ'zeɪʃn, ˌaɪ-] *n.* iridescence.

iridology [ˌɪrɪ'dɒlədʒi, ˌaɪ-] *n.* diagnosis based on examining iris of eye. **iridologist**, *n.*

irisation [ˌaɪrɪ'seɪʃn] *n.* iridescence. **iriscope**, *n.* apparatus producing iridescence.

iritis [aɪ'raɪtɪs] *n.* inflammation of iris of eye. **iritic** [aɪ'rɪtɪk], *adj.*

irrecusable [ˌɪrɪ'kjuːzəbl] *adj.* not to be rejected.

irredenta [ˌɪrɪ'dentə] (*Italian*) *adj.* 'unredeemed'; applied to part of country under another's rule. **irredential**, *adj.* **irredentism**, *n.* policy of attempting to recover such region to country that has lost it. **irredentist**, *n.*

irrefragable [ɪ'refrəgəbl] *adj.* indisputable; unbreakable.

irrefrangible [ˌɪrɪ'frændʒəbl] *adj.* unbreakable; incapable of being refracted.

irremeable [ɪ'remiəbl, -'riː-] *adj.* allowing of no return; irrevocable.

irrevocable [ɪ'revəkəbl] *adj.* incapable of being recalled or revoked; unalterable.

irrupt [ɪ'rʌpt] *v.i.* burst in; enter violently. **irruption**, *n.* **irruptive**, *adj.*

isagoge [ˌaɪsə'gəʊdʒi] *n.* introduction. **isagogic(al)** [-'gɒdʒ-], *adj.* **isagogics**, *n.* introductory study of Bible.

isallobar [aɪ'sæləbɑː] *n.* line on map passing through all places with equal changes in pressure over a certain period.

isanemone [aɪ'sænɪməʊn] *n.* line on map connecting all places with same wind velocity.

isarithm [ˈaɪsərɪðm] *n.* line on map passing through places of same density of population.

ischaemia [ɪ'skiːmiə] *n.* localized anaemia or deficiency of blood. **ischaemic**, *adj.*

ischialgia [ˌɪski'ældʒiə] *n.* sciatica. **ischialgic**, *adj.*

ischidrosis [ˌɪski'drəʊsɪs] *n.* suppression of perspiration.

ischium [ˈɪskiəm] *n.* (*pl.* **–ia**) bone forming base of each half of pelvis.

ischuria, ischury [ɪ'skjʊəriə, 'ɪskjʊri] *n.* retention of urine. **ischuretic** [-'retɪk], *n.* & *adj.* (agent) causing this.

isinglass [ˈaɪzɪŋglɑːs] *n.* form of gelatine made from fishes' air bladders; agar-agar.

ism [ˈɪzm] *n.* doctrine, especially a foolish one. **ismal, ismatic(al)**, *adj.*

isobar [ˈaɪsəbɑː] *n.* line on map passing through all places with same barometric pressure. **isobaric** [-'bærɪk], adj.

isobath [ˈaɪsəbæθ] *n.* line of map passing through all points of equal depth below water.

isocheim [ˈaɪsəkaɪm] *n.* line on map passing through all places with same average winter temperature. **isocheimal, isocheimenal, isocheimic,** *adj.*

isochromatic [ˌaɪsəʊkrə'mætɪk] *adj.* of the same colour.

isochronous [aɪ'sɒkrənəs] *adj.* lasting equal time; recurring at equal intervals. **isochronal, isochronic(al),** *adj.* **isochronize,** *v.t.* **isochronism,** *n.* **isochronon,** *n.* chronometer.

isochroous [aɪ'sɒkrəʊəs] *adj.* of uniform colour.

isoclinal [ˌaɪsəʊ'klaɪnl] *n.* & *adj.* (line on map passing through all places) with same magnetic dip; having equal inclination. **isoclinic** [-'klɪnɪk], *adj.*

isocracy [aɪ'sɒkrəsi] *n.* equal rule; possession of equal power by all. **isocrat,** *n.* **isocratic,** *adj.*

isocryme [ˈaɪsəʊkraɪm] *n.* isotherm for coldest period of year. **isocrymal, isocrymic** [-'krɪmɪk], *adj.*

isodiabatic [ˌaɪsəʊdaɪə'bætɪk] *adj.* pertaining to equal heat transmission

isodynamic [ˌaɪsəʊdaɪ'næmɪk] *adj.* pertaining to or having equal force. **isodynamia** [-'neɪmiə], *n.*

isogenesis [ˌaɪsəʊ'dʒenəsɪs] *n.* sameness of origin. **isogenetic,** [-dʒə'netɪk], **isogenic, isogenous** [-'sɒdʒənəs], *adj.* **isogeny,** *n.*

isogeotherm [ˌaɪsə'dʒiːθɜːm] *n.* line connecting points of equal temperature below the earth's surface.

isogloss [ˌaɪsə'glɒs] *adj.* a line of a dialect map delimiting localities in which some feature of speech is found. **isoglossal** [ˌaɪsə'glɒsl] *adj.*

isogonal [aɪ'sɒgənl] *adj.* having equal angles. **isogonic** [-'gɒnɪk], *adj.*; *n.* line on map passing through all places with same magnetic declination.

isogram [ˈaɪsəgræm] *n.* line on map passing through all places with same conditions or figures for the subject in question, as temperature, rainfall, etc.

isography [aɪ'sɒgrəfi] *n.* imitation of other person's hand writing. **isographic(al),** *adj.*

isohel [ˈaɪsəhel] *n.* line on map passing through all places with same hours of sunshine.

isohyet [ˌaɪsə'haɪət] *n.* line on map passing through all places with same rainfall. **isohyetal,** *adj.*

isokeraunic [ˌaɪsəʊkə'rɔːnɪk] *n.* & *adj.* (line on map connecting places) with equal or simultaneous occurrence of thunderstorms.

isomer [ˈaɪsəmə] *n.* compound of same elements in same proportions by weight as another, but having different structure and properties. **isomeric** [-'merɪk], *adj.* **isomerize** [-'sɒməraɪz], *v.t.* **isomerism,** *n.* **isomerous,** *adj.* having same number of parts, peculiarities, etc.

isometric [ˌaɪsə'metrɪk] *adj.* of equal measure. **isometrics** *n.* system of muscular exercises without apparatus, *e.g.* by opposing one set of muscles to another. **isometry,** *n.* equality of measure.

isomorphic [ˌaɪsə'mɔːfɪk] *adj.* of same or similar form. **isomorphism,** *n.* **isomorphous,** *adj.*

isonomy [aɪ'sɒnəmi] *n.* equality of legal rights. **isonomic** [-'nɒmɪk], **isonomous,** *adj.*

isonym [ˈaɪsənɪm] *n.* word of same derivation or form as another; cognate word. **isonymic,** *adj.* **isonymy** [-'sɒnəmi], *n.*

isopiestic [ˌaɪsəʊpaɪ'estɪk] *n.* & *adj.* isobar(ic)

isopleth ['aɪsəpleθ] *n*. line on map passing through places with same numerical values for a meteorological feature.

isopod ['aɪsəpɒd] *n*. crustacean with flattened body and seven pairs of legs. *e.g.* woodlouse.

isopolity [ˌaɪsə'pɒləti] *n*. equality of political rights. **isopolitical,** *adj*.

isopsephic [ˌaɪsɒp'siːfɪk, –'se–] *adj*. numerically equal. **isopsephism,** *n*.

isopycnic [ˌaɪsə'pɪknɪk] *n*. & *adj*. (line passing through points) of equal density.

isorropic [ˌaɪsə'rɒpɪk] *adj*. of equal value.

isosceles [aɪ'sɒsəliːz] *adj*. having two sides equal.

isoseismal [ˌaɪsə'saɪzməl] *n*. & *adj*. (line on map passing through places) of same intensity of earthquake shock. **isoseismic(al),** *adj*.

isostasy [aɪ'sɒstəsi] *n*. state of equilibrium due to equal pressure on all sides. **isostatic,** *adj*.

isothere ['aɪsəθɪə] *n*. isotherm for average summer temperature. **isotheral** [–'sɒθərəl], *adj*.

isotherm ['aɪsəθɜːm] *n*. line on map passing through places with same temperature. **isothermal, isothermic, isothermous,** *adj*.

isotope ['aɪsətəʊp] *n*. form of an element having same atomic number but different atomic weight and different radioactivity. **radioactive isotope,** form of an element made radioactive and used in medical diagnosis and treatment, etc. **isotopic** [–'tɒpɪk]), *adj*. **isotopy** [aɪ'sɒtəpi, 'aɪsətəʊpi], *n*.

isotron ['aɪsətrɒn] *n*. device for separating isotopes.

isotropic [ˌaɪsə'trɒpɪk] *adj*. having same properties in every direction. **isotrope,** *adj*. **isotropism, isotropy** [–'sɒt–], *n*. **isotropous,** *adj*.

iterate ['ɪtəreɪt] *v.t.* & *i*. repeat. **iterant,** *adj*. repeating. **iterance, iterancy, iteration,** *n*. **iterative,** *adj*.

iterum ['ɪtərəm] (*Latin*) 'again'; afresh.

ithyphallic [ˌɪθɪ'fælɪk] *adj*. indecent; pertaining to verse line of three trochees.

itinerant [aɪ'tɪnərənt, ɪ–] *adj*. journeying from place to place; *n* wanderer; traveller. **itinerancy,** *n*. **itinerary,** *n*. journey; route; guide book; *adj* pertaining to journey. **itinerate,** *v.i.* journey from place to place, especially preaching. **itineration,** *n*.

ixia ['ɪksiə] *n*. iris-like S African plant; corn lily.

ixiodic [ˌɪksi'ɒdɪk] *adj*. pertaining or due to ticks. **ixiodian** [–'ɒdiən], **ixiodid,** *n*. & *adj*. (pertaining to) a tick.

J

jabot ['ʒæbəʊ] (*French*) *n*. long frill in front of bodice.

jacamar ['dʒækəmɑː] *n*. long-billed brightly-coloured bird of tropical S America.

jacinth ['dʒæsɪnθ, 'dʒeɪ–] *n*. orange-coloured variety of the gem hyacinth. **jacinthe**, *n*. orange colour.

Jacobin ['dʒækəbɪn] *n*. extreme revolutionary, especially of French revolution of 1789. **Jacobinic(al)**, *adj*. **Jacobinism**, *v.t*. **Jacobinize**, *n*.

jaconet ['dʒækənet] *n*. kind of thin cotton fabric, especially with one side glazed.

Jacquerie ['ʒækriː] (*French*) *n*. peasant revolt, especially of French in 1358; peasant class.

jactancy ['dʒæktənsi] *n*. boasting. **jactation** [dʒæk'teɪʃn], *n*. boasting; *Medicine*, tossing or shaking of body.

jactitation [,dʒæktɪ'teɪʃn] *n*. jactation; false claim. **jactitation of marriage**, false claim to be married to a person.

jaculation [,dʒækju'leɪʃn] *n*. hurling or darting, as of spears. **jaculiferous**, *adj*. with arrow-like prickles. **jaculatory**, *adj*.

j'adoube [ʒæ'duːb] (*French*) 'I adjust'; call when merely adjusting, and not moving, a piece in chess, etc.

jaeger ['jeɪɡə, 'dʒeɪ–] *n*. gull-like bird of prey, also called skua.

jagannath ['dʒʌɡənɔːt] *n*. juggernaut.

jai alai [,haɪ ə'laɪ, 'haɪlaɪ] (*Spanish*) *n*. rackets-like game of Spain and Spanish America.

jalap ['dʒæləp] *n*. root of Mexican plant used as purgative.

jalop(p)y [dʒə'lɒpi] *n*. worn-out motor-car or air-craft.

jalouse [dʒə'luːz] *v.t*. be jealous of; grudge; *Scottish*, suspect.

jalousie ['ʒæluziː] (*French*) *n*. blind or shutter with slats slanting upwards and inwards.

jambolan ['dʒæmbələn] *n*. plum-like tree of Java with fruit used as astringent and drug. **jambool, jambul**, *n*. jambolan.

jampan ['dʒæmpæn] (*Anglo-Indian*) *n*. kind of sedan chair.

Janiform ['dʒænɪfɔːm] *adj*. like the Roman god Janus; two-faced.

janissary, janizary ['dʒænɪsəri, –zəri] *n*. member of certain Turkish infantry corps.

jannock ['dʒænək] (*dialect*) *adj*. pleasant; outspoken; honest; generous.

jardinière [,ʒɑːdɪni'eə] (*French*) *n*. ornamental flower stand.

jarrah ['dʒærə] *n*. Australian eucalyptus tree with mahogany-like timber; red gum tree of Australia.

jarvey ['dʒɑːvi] *n*. Irish jaunting-car driver; hackney coachman.

jaspé ['dʒæspeɪ] *adj*. mottled or streaked with colour.

jaspideous, jaspidean [dʒæ'spɪdiəs, –iən] *adj*. like or containing jasper.

jecoral ['dʒekərəl] *adj*. pertaining to the liver. **jecorize**, *v.t*. impregnate with ultra-violet rays; make similar in value to cod-liver oil.

jehad, jihad [dʒɪ'hæd, –'hɑːd] *n*. Muslim religious war; crusade.

jejune [dʒɪ'dʒuːn] *adj*. empty; sterile; dry; naïve; immature. **jejunity**, *n*. **jejunum**, *n*. middle part of small intestine.

jellab [dʒɪ'lɑːb] *n*. loose hooded cloak of Morocco, etc.

jelutong ['dʒelətɒŋ] *n*. Malayan tree yielding rubbery resin; this resin.

jemadar ['dʒemədɑː] (*Indian*) *n*. sepoy lieutenant; any military or police leader.

je ne sais quoi [,ʒə nə seɪ 'kwɑː] (*French*) 'I do not know what'; indescribable attribute or quality; a certain 'something'.

jennet ['dʒenɪt] *n*. small Spanish horse; she-ass.

jentacular [dʒen'tækjulə] *adj*. pertaining to breakfast.

jequirity [dʒɪ'kwɪrəti] *n*. seed of Indian liquorice used as weight, rosary-bead, etc.

jerboa [dʒɜː'bəʊə] *n*. jumping rat, especially of N Africa.

jeremiad [,dʒerɪ'maɪəd, –æd] *n*. mournful prophecy, story or complaint.

jerque [dʒɜːk] *v.t*. examine ship's papers for smuggling attempts, etc. **jerquer**, *n*. customs officer who jerques ships.

jess [dʒes] *n*. ringed strap round hawk's leg.

jesuitry ['dʒezjuːtri, –ʒu–] *n*. casuistry. **jesuitical** [–'ɪt–], *adj*. cunning. **jesuitism**, *n*. jesuitry; quibble.

jetsam ['dʒetsəm] *n*. goods thrown overboard, especially when found cast up on shore.

jettison ['dʒetɪsən] *v.t*. throw overboard to lighten ship; cast off as nuisance; discard; *n*. such act; jetsam.

jeu d'esprit [ʒɜː des'priː] (*French*) 'game of wit'; light, humorous work; witty sally.

jeune premier [,ʒɜːn 'premieɪ] (*French*) (*fem.* **–ière** [–i'eə]) juvenile lead in musical play, etc.

jeunesse dorée [,ʒɜːnes 'dɔːreɪ] (*French*) 'gilded youth'; rich young people.

jihad see jehad.

jinn [dʒɪn] *n. pl*. (*sing.* **jinni, jinnee**) in Muslim mythology, class of spirits, lower than angels, able to take on human and animal form.

jodhpurs ['dʒɒdpəz] *n. pl*. riding breeches fitting lower leg tightly.

joie de vivre [ˌʒwɑː də 'viːv, –rə] (*French*) 'joy of living'; zest.

jointure ['dʒɔɪntʃə] *n.* settlement of estate on wife to become effective on death of husband; *v.t.* settle jointure on. **jointress, jointuress,** *n.* woman holding jointure.

jongleur [ʒɒŋ'glɜː] (*French*) *n.* medieval wandering minstrel; troubadour; juggler.

jorum ['dʒɔːrəm] *n.* large bowl containing drink; its contents.

joule [dʒuːl] *n.* unit of energy or work: equal to work done when force of one newton moves its point of application one metre.

Judaize ['dʒuːdeɪaɪz] *v.i.* & *t.* make or become Jewish; keep Jewish observances; convert to Jewish beliefs. **Judaic,** *adj.* **Judaism,** *n.*

Judophobism, Judophobia [dʒu'dɒfəbɪzm, ˌdʒuːdə'fəʊbiə] *n.* anti-Semitism.

jugal ['dʒuːgl] *adj.* pertaining to cheek or cheek bone.

jugate ['dʒuːgeɪt] *adj.* in pairs; applied to two overlapping heads on coin. **jugation,** *n.*

juggernaut ['dʒʌgənɔːt] (*Hindi*) *n.* huge Indian idol of Vishnu, drawn at festivals on a cart beneath whose wheels worshippers were erroneously believed to throw themselves to death; any belief or object needing or receiving sacrifice of themselves by believers; anything that crushes all in its path; very large lorry.

jugular ['dʒʌgjʊlə] *adj.* pertaining to neck or throat; *n.* such vein. **jugulate,** *v.t.* kill by cutting throat or strangling; check by drastic measures.

julep ['dʒuːlɪp] *n.* sweet medicated beverage.

jumelle [dʒuˈmel] (*French*) *adj.* in or with pairs.

juncaceous [dʒʌŋ'keɪʃəs] *adj.* pertaining to or like a rush; belonging to rush family of plants.

juncture ['dʒʌŋktʃə] *n.* junction; joint; critical moment of time.

Jungfrau ['juŋfraʊ] (*German*) *n.* young woman; maiden.

Junker ['juŋkə] (*German*) *n.* landed aristocrat, especially of Prussia. **Junkerdom, Junkerism,** *n.*

junta ['dʒʌntə, 'hun–] (*Spanish*) *n.* council; any administrative body; clique. **junto,** *n.* clique; faction.

jural ['dʒʊərəl] *adj.* pertaining to law or legal rights. **juramentum,** (*Latin*) *n.* (*pl.* **-ta**) oath. **jurant,** *n.* & *adj.* (person) taking oath. **jurat,** *n.* sworn public officer; magistrate; municipal officer of Cinque Ports; statement at end of affidavit showing circumstances in which it was sworn. **juration,** *n.* swearing. **juratorial,** *adj.* pertaining to jury. **juratory,** *adj.* pertaining to oath.

jurisconsult [ˌdʒʊərɪskən'sʌlt] *n.* legal expert.

jurisdiction [ˌdʒʊərɪs'dɪkʃn] *n.* legal authority or administration; extent or area of such authority. **jurisdictive,** *adj.*

jurisprudence [ˌdʒʊərɪs'pruːdns] *n.* science of law; knowledge of law. **jurisprudent,** *n.* & *adj.* (person) expert in this.

jurist ['dʒʊərɪst] *n.* jurisconsult. **juristic,** *adj.* pertaining to jurist; pertaining to or permissible by law.

jus [dʒʌs, jus] (*Latin*) *n.* (*pl.* **jures**) law; legal power or right. **jus gentium** [–'gentiəm, –'dʒenʃiəm], law of nations. **jus inter gentes** [–ˌɪntə 'genteɪz, –'dʒentiːz], international law. **jus primae noctis** [–ˌpriːmaɪ 'nɒktɪs, –ˌpraɪmiː–], droit du seigneur. ·

jusqu'au bout [ˌʒuskəʊ 'buː] (*French*) 'to the end'. **jusqu'au boutist,** *n.* radical; one willing to go to the bitter end.

jussive ['dʒʌsɪv] *adj. Grammar,* signifying command.

juvenescent [ˌdʒuːvə'nesnt] *adj.* becoming young. **juvenescence,** *n.*

juvenilia [ˌdʒuːvə'nɪliə] (*Latin*) *n. pl.* writer's or artist's youthful, early works.

juxtapose [ˌdʒʌkstə'pəʊz] *v.t.* place side by side or next to. **juxtaposition** [–pə'zɪʃn], *n.*

jyngine ['dʒɪndʒaɪn] *adj.* pertaining to or like a wryneck; belonging to wryneck subfamily of birds.

K

kabbadi [kə'bɑːdi, -'bʌ-] *n.* Indian game of tag, played by two teams.

kabuki [kə'buːki] *n.* Japanese popular traditional drama, with male actors only.

kaddish ['kædɪʃ] *n.* Jewish prayers for the dead.

kadi *see* cadi.

kaka ['kɑːkɑː] talking parrot of New Zealand. **kakapo,** ['kɑːkəpəu] *n.* ground-owl-parrot of New Zealand

kakemono [ˌkækɪ'məunəu] *n.* Japanese vertical wall-picture or inscription mounted on a roller.

kakidrosis [ˌkækɪ'drəusɪs] *n.* secretion of malodorous perspiration.

kakistocracy [ˌkækɪ'stɒkrəsi] *n.* government by worst people.

kaleidoscope [kə'laɪdəskəup] *n.* instrument containing fragments of coloured glass, etc., which are reflected in mirrors to produce a multitude of patterns; any many-coloured, changing pattern or scene. **kaleidoscopic** [-'skɒpɪk] *adj.*

kalends *see* calends.

kampong ['kæmpɒŋ] *n.* Malay village.

kanaka [kə'nækə] *n.* South Sea islander.

Kannada ['kɑːnədə, 'kæ-] *n.* S Indian language also called Kanarese.

kanya ['kænjə] *n.* shea tree and butter.

kaolin ['keɪəlɪn] *n.* china clay, used in porcelain manufacture and in medicine.

kaon ['keɪɒn] *n. Physics,* elementary particle of the meson family.

Kapellmeister [kə'pel,maɪstə] *(German) n. Music,* conductor (and leader) of an orchestra.

kapok ['keɪpɒk] *n.* soft fibre of silk-cotton tree, used to fill cushions, etc.; the silk-cotton tree, its seeds and oil.

kappa ['kæpə] *n.* tenth letter of Greek alphabet (κ, Κ).

karaka [kə'rækə] *(New Zealand) n.* tree with edible seeds and fruit.

karakul ['kærəkl] *n.* sheep of Central Asia; curled black fleece of its lambs.

karaoke [ˌkæri'əuki] *(Japanese) n* entertainment of singing popular songs to pre-recorded backing tape.

karma ['kɑːmə, 'kɜː-] *n.* destiny; in Buddhist belief, actions of one incarnation determining nature of next; religious rite. **karmic,** *adj.*

karri ['kæri] *n.* W Australian giant gum tree, with red timber.

karroo [kə'ruː] *n.* dry terrace-like plateau of S Africa.

karst [kɑːst] *n.* limestone region with underground streams, potholes, etc.

karyokinesis [ˌkæriəukɪ'niːsɪs, -kaɪ-] *n.* cell division, especially of nucleus. **karyoplasm** ['kæriəplæzm], *n.* protoplasm of cell nucleus.

karyotin ['kæriətɪn], *n.* sustainable matter of nucleus.

kashrut(h) ['kæʃruːt] *(Hebrew) n.* condition of being kosher; Jewish religious law concerning food.

katabasis [kə'tæbəsɪs] *n.* military retreat. **katabatic** [ˌkætə'bætɪk] *adj.* moving downhill, sinking (of winds).

kathakali [ˌkɑːtə'kɑːli] *n.* highly stylized form of S Indian drama, using dance and mime.

katharometer [ˌkæθə'rɒmɪtə] *n.* instrument measuring alterations in composition of gas mixture.

katipo ['kætɪpəu] *n.* venomous black spider of New Zealand.

katydid ['keɪtɪdɪd] *n.* large green grasshopper of America.

kauri ['kauri] *n.* gum- and timber-yielding tree of New Zealand; its white timber; its resin found in lumps in ground.

kava ['kɑːvə] *n.* kind of pepper plant of Australasia, with root from which strong drink is made.

kayak ['kaɪæk] *n.* Eskimo canoe.

kazoo [kə'zuː] *n.* musical toy that makes a vibrating sound when hummed into.

kea ['kiːə, 'keɪə] *n.* large green parrot of New Zealand, said to kill sheep.

keddah ['kedə] *(Indian) n.* elephant trap.

kedge [kedʒ] *n.* small anchor; *v.t.* move (ship) by hauling on anchor dropped ahead from boat.

keelhaul ['kiːlhɔːl] *v.t.* haul under keel of ship as punishment.

keelson ['kelsn, 'kiːlsn] *n.* wooden or steel structure lengthwise within ship's frame to bear and distribute stress.

kef [kef] *(Arabic) n.* sleepiness, caused by drugs; hashish, etc.

kefir [kə'fɪə] *n.* koumiss-like drink of Caucasus.

kelim [kɪ'lɪm] *n.* woven rug, made in W Asia.

keloid ['kiːlɔɪd] *n.* fibrous skin tumour, especially over scar; raised scars forming pattern on body, in certain African tribes.

kelp [kelp] *n.* seaweed ashes, yielding iodine; several large brown seaweeds.

kelpie ['kelpi] *n.* water spirit in Gaelic mythology; *Australia,* kind of sheep- or cattle-dog, derived partly from dingo.

kelson *see* keelson.

kelt [kelt] *n.* salmon after spawning.

kenosis [kɪ'nəusɪs] *n. Theological,* action of Christ in humbling Himself, or divesting Himself of divine attributes, in becoming man. **kenotic** [kɪ'nɒtɪk], *adj.; n.* believer in kenosis. **kenoticism, kenotism,** *n.*

kepi, ké- ['keɪpi] *n.* soldier's peaked cap with high

flat crown.

kerasine ['kerəsɪn] *adj.* horny.

keratin ['kerətɪn] *n.* protein from which horns, nails, hair and similar tissues develop. **keratinize** [kə'rætɪnaɪz], *v.i.* & *t.* become or make horny. **keratinous** [-'rætɪnəs] *adj.* horny.

keratogenic [ˌkerætə'dʒenɪk] *adj.* able to cause growth of horn, skin, hair, etc. **keratogenous** [ˌkerə'tɒdʒənəs], *adj.* horn-producing. **keratoid** ['kerətɔɪd], *adj.* horny. **keratode** ['kerətəud], *n.* keratose substance. **keratose** ['kerətəus], *n.* & *adj.* (substance) of horny fibres. **keratosis** [-'təusɪs], *n.* excessive growth of horny tissue of skin.

keraunograph [kə'rɔːnəgrɑːf] *n.* instrument detecting distant thunderstorm; pattern made by lightning on struck object. **keraunoscopia**, **keraunoscopy**, *n.* divination by thunder.

kermes ['kɜːmiːz] *n.* red cochineal-like dye made from dried bodies of certain female insects of Mediterranean; evergreen oak on which these insects feed.

kerogen ['kerədʒən, –en] *n.* kind of bitumen found in oil shale. **kerosene** ['kerəsiːn], *n.* fuel oil also called paraffin.

kerygmatic [ˌkerɪg'mætɪk] *adj.* pertaining to preaching, especially of gospel.

ketch [ketʃ] *n.* two-masted fore-and-aft rigged sailing vessel.

ketone ['kiːtəun] *n.* chemical compound of carbon, obtained by distilling salts of organic acids. **ketonaemia** [-'niːmiə], *n.* presence of ketone, especially acetone, in blood. **ketonic** [-'tɒnɪk], *adj.* **ketonize** [-tənaɪz], *v.t.* convert into ketone. **ketogenesis**, *n.* production of ketone, especially in diabetes. **ketosis** [-'təusɪs], *n.* presence of excess of ketone in body.

khamsin, khamseen ['kæmsɪn, kæm'siːn] (*Arabic*) *n.* hot wind of Egypt blowing from Sahara; dust storm.

khan [kɑːn] (*Turkish*) *n.* prince; Tartar emperor; *Arabic*, caravanserai. **khanate**, *n.* khan's office or jurisdiction. **khanjee**, *n.* keeper of caravanserai.

Khedive [kɪ'diːv] *n.* Turkey viceroy of Egypt. **Khedival**, *adj.*

khoja(h) ['kəudʒə] *n.* title of respect for teacher or wise man.

kiang [ki'æŋ] *n.* wild ass of Tibet.

kia ora [ˌkiːə 'ɔːrə] (*Maori*) 'be well'; good health!

kibe [kaɪb] *n.* chapped place on skin; ulcerated chilblain.

kibitzer ['kɪbɪtsə] (*Yiddish*) *n.* giver of unwanted advice; interfering onlooker.

kieselguhr ['kiːzlguə] *n.* powdery substance, mainly silica, used in filters, explosives, etc.

kilderkin ['kɪldəkɪn] *n.* measure of capacity, about 18 gallons; cask holding that amount.

kinesalgia [ˌkɪnɪ'sældʒiə] *n.* muscular pain. **kinesiatrics** [-i'ætrɪks], *n.* medical treatments by muscular movements.

kinetic [kɪ'netɪk, kaɪ–] *adj.* of or due to movement. **kinesics** [-'niːzɪks], *n.* study of body movements as means of communication. **kinesis** [-'niːsɪs] *n.* movement. **kinetics**, *n.* study of changes of motion under forces. **kinetogenic**, *adj.* causing movement.

kinin ['kaɪnɪn, 'kɪ–] *n.* hormone causing contrac-

tion of smooth muscle; hormone that promotes cell division and development in plants.

kinkajou ['kɪŋkədʒuː] *n.* raccoon-like animal of Central and S America.

kino ['kiːnəu] *n.* red gum containing tannin, obtained from several tropical trees.

kir [kɪə] *n.* drink consisting of white wine and blackcurrant liqueur.

kirsch [kɪəʃ] (*German*) *n.* clear brandy made from cherries.

kismet ['kɪzmet] *n.* fate.

kit-cat ['kɪtkæt] *n.* & *adj.* not quite half-length (portrait).

klepht [kleft] (*Greek*) *n.* brigand. **klephtic**, *adj.* **klephtism**, *n.*

kleptomania [ˌkleptə'meɪniə] *n.* uncontrollable desire to steal. **kleptomaniac** [-æk], *n.* & *adj.*

klong [klɒŋ] (*Thai*) *n.* canal.

kloof [kluːf] (*S African*) *n.* ravine.

knout [naut] *n.* whip with leather and wire thongs; *v.t.* flog with a knout.

knur [nɜː] *n.* knob; knot in wood.

knurl [nɜːl] *n.* small knob.

koala [kəu'ɑːlə] *n.* Australian tree bear.

koan ['kəuæn] (*Japanese*) *n.* puzzle with no logical solution used in Zen Buddhism to develop intuitive thought.

kobold ['kəubɒld, –əuld] *n.* sprite in German folklore.

koftgari [ˌkɒftgə'riː] (*Urdu*) *n.* inlaying of gold on steel.

kohl [kəul] *n.* dark eye make-up used in Asia.

kohlrabi [kəul'rɑːbi] *n.* kind of cabbage with a turnip-like stem.

Koine ['kɔɪneɪ] *n.* Greek dialect used throughout E Mediterranean in Hellenistic and Roman times; (**koine**) any lingua franca.

kolkhoz [ˌkɒl'kɒz] (*Russian*) *n.* collective farm.

komatik [kəu'mætɪk] *n.* long Eskimo sledge.

koniology [ˌkəuni'ɒlədʒi] *n.* study of dust and germs in atmosphere. **koniometer, koniscope**, *n.* instrument measuring amount of dust in air.

kookaburra ['kukəbʌrə] *n.* Australian kingfisher with a harsh laughing call, also called the laughing jackass.

kopek, kopeck ['kəupek] *n.* Russian coin worth one-hundredth part of rouble.

kopje ['kɒpi] (*S African*) *n.* hillock.

Koran [kɔː'rɑːn] *n.* holy scriptures of Islam.

korfball ['kɔːfbɔːl] *n.* basketball-like game played between two teams of six men and six women each.

kosher ['kəuʃə] (*Hebrew*) *adj.* permitted by, or prepared according to, Jewish religious law.

koumiss ['kuːmɪs] *n.* intoxicating drink made from fermented mare's milk.

kourbash ['kuəbæʃ] *n.* whip of hide; *v.t.* flog with a kourbash.

krait [kraɪt] *n.* very poisonous Indian snake.

krasis ['kreɪsɪs] *n.* addition of water to Communion wine.

Kriegspiel ['kriːgʃpiːl] (*German*) *n.* 'war game', played by moving on a board pieces, flags, etc., representing armed forces.

krill [krɪl] *n.* shrimp-like crustacean of the Antarctic.

kris [kriːs, krɪs] *n.* Malay dagger with scalloped blade.

krona ['krəunə] *n.* (*pl.* **kronor**) money unit of Sweden worth 100 øre; **króna,** (*pl.* **kronur**) money unit of Iceland worth 100 aurar.

krone ['krəunə] *n.* (*pl.* **kroner**) money unit of Denmark and Norway worth 100 ore.

krypton ['krɪptɒn] *n.* colourless and odourless rare gas which occurs in the atmosphere.

kudos ['kjuːdɒs] *n.* glory; fame; reward.

kudu ['kuːduː] *n.* larged curled-horned African antelope.

Ku Klux Klan [ˌkuː klʌks 'klæn] *n.* white supremacist secret society of S USA.

kukri ['kʊkri] *n.* broad curved Gurkha knife.

kulak ['kuːlæk] (*Russian*) *n.* rich peasant or farmer.

Kultur [kʊl'tuə] (*German*) *n.* 'culture', especially representing civilization of a nation.

kumiss *see* **koumiss.**

kumquat ['kʌmkwɒt] *n.* very small citrus fruit.

Kursaal ['kɜːzl, 'kuəzaːl] (*German*) *n.* entertainment hall, public room or hotel at spa or seaside resort.

kvas(s) [kvaːs] *n.* thin weak Russian beer.

kvetch [kvetʃ] *v.i.* complain habitually or at length.

kwashiorkor [ˌkwɒʃi'ɔːkɔː] *n.* disease of children in W Africa caused by lack of proteins and vitamins.

kymatology [ˌkaɪmə'tɒlədʒi] *n.* study of wave motion.

kymograph ['kaɪməgrɑːf] *n.* instrument recording pressure curves, etc. **kymographic,** *adj.*

kyphosis [kaɪ'fəusɪs] *n.* inward curvature of the spine. **kyphotic** [–'fɒtɪk], *adj.*

kyrie eleison [ˌkɪrieɪ ɪ'leɪsɒn] (*Greek*) 'Lord, have mercy'; words from the Mass often set to music.

L

laager ['lɑːgə] (*S African*) *n.* camp of wagons drawn into circle; *v.i. & t.* make such camp.

laagte ['lɑːgtə, 'lɑːx–] (*Dutch*) *n.* valley; dry river bed.

labanotation [ˌlɑːbənəʊ'teɪʃn] *n.* a method of writing down the movements, etc., of ballet diagrammatically.

labefact, labefy ['læbɪfækt, –fæɪ] *v.t.*, weaken. **labefactation, labefaction,** *n.*

labellate [lə'belət] *adj.* lipped. **labelloid,** *adj.* lip-like. **labellum,** *n.* (*pl.* –la) lip of flower's corolla.

labia ['leɪbiə] *n. pl.* (*sing.* **labium**) lip-like folds of female genital organs. **labia majora** [–mə'dʒɔːrə] outer folds. **labia minora** [–mɪ'nɔːrə] inner folds.

labial ['leɪbiəl] *adj.* pertaining to lips or labia; pronounced with lips; *n.* such sound, as *p, w.* **labiate,** *adj.* lipped; *v.t.* labialize. **labialize,** *v.t.* make labial in pronunciation. **labialism,** *n.*

labidophorous [ˌlæbɪ'dofərəs] *adj.* with a pair of pincer-like organs.

labile ['leɪbaɪl] *adj.* liable to err or change; unstable. **lability** [leɪ'bɪləti], *n.* **labilize,** *v.t.*

labiodental [ˌleɪbɪəʊ'dentl] *adj.* pertaining to or pronounced with lips and teeth; *n.* such sound, as *f.* **labiomancy,** *n.* lip-reading. **labionasal,** *n. & adj.* (sound) pronounced with lips and nasal passage, as *m.* **labiovelar,** *n. & adj.* (sound) pronounced with rounded lips and back of tongue raised, as *w.*

labret ['leɪbret] *n.* ornamental insertion in lip.

labrose ['leɪbrəʊs] *adj.* thick-lipped.

labyrinth ['læbərɪnθ] *n.* maze; internal ear. **labyrinthian, labyrinthic, labyrinthine,** *adj.* **labyrinthitis,** *n.* inflammation of internal ear.

lac *see* **lakh.**

lacerate ['læsəreɪt] *v.t.* tear; mangle; wound. **laceration,** *n.* **lacerative,** *adj.*

lacertilian [ˌlæsə'tɪliən] *n. & adj.* (pertaining to or like a) lizard. **lacertian,** *n. & adj.* **lacertiform,** *adj.* lizard-shaped. **lacertine, lacertoid,** *adj.* lizard-like.

laches ['lætʃɪz] *n.* negligence; carelessness.

lachrymal ['lækrɪməl] *adj.* pertaining to tears and weeping; *n.pl.* organs secreting tears; crying fits. **lachrymary,** *adj.* **lachrymation,** *n.* **lachrymator,** *n.* substance or gas causing tears. **lachrymatory,** *n.* narrow-necked vase; tear-bottle. **lachrymiform,** *adj.* tear-shaped. **lachrymist,** *n.* weeper. **lachrymogenic,** *adj.* causing tears. **lachrymose,** *adj.* tearful.

laciniate [lə'sɪnieɪt] *adj.* fringed; jagged, slashed. **laciniform,** *adj.* like a fringe. **laciniose,** *adj.* **lacinulate,** *adj.* with fine or small fringe. **laciniation,** *n.*

lacis ['leɪsɪs] *n.* network; filet lace.

laconic [lə'kɒnɪk] *adj.* curt; in few words; unemotional. **laconicism** [–sɪzm], **laconism,** *n.*

lacrimal ['lækrɪməl] *adj.* lachrymal.

lactarium [læk'teəriəm] *n.* dairy. **lactary** ['læktəri], *adj.* pertaining to milk.

lactate ['lækteɪt] *v.i.* secrete milk; suckle young; *n.* salt or ester of lactic acid. **lactation,** *n.*

lacteal ['læktiəl] *adj.* pertaining to milk; *n. & adj.* (vessel) conveying chyle. **lactean,** *adj.* milky.

lactescent [læk'tesnt] *adj.* like milk; secreting milk; yielding milky substance. **lacteous,** *adj.* milky. **lactescence,** *n.*

lactic ['læktɪk] *adj.* pertaining to milk or sour milk. **lactiferous,** *adj.* yielding or conveying milk or milky substance. **lactific,** *adj.* producing milk. **lactifluous,** *adj.* full of milk. **lactiform,** *adj.* like milk.

lactometer [læk'tɒmɪtə] *n.* instrument measuring the purity of milk. **lactoscope,** *n.* instrument measuring amount of cream in milk.

lactose ['læktəʊs] *n.* sugar occurring in milk.

lacuna [lə'kjuːnə] *n.* (*pl.* –ae) gap; interval; hiatus. **lacunal, lacunose, lacunar, lacunary,** *adj.*

lacuscular [lə'kʌskjʊlə] *adj.* pertaining to pools.

lacustrine [lə'kʌstraɪn, –rɪn] *adj.* pertaining to lakes. **lacustral,** *adj.* **lacustrian,** *adj.*; *n.* lake-dweller.

Ladino [lə'diːnəʊ] *n.* language of Sephardic Jews, based on Spanish, written in Hebrew characters.

ladrone [lə'drəʊn] (*Spanish*) *n.* robber. **ladronism,** *n.* brigandage.

laevoduction [ˌliːvə'dʌkʃn] *n.* movement leftwards. **laevogyrate, laevorotatory,** *adj.* turning to left, especially plane of polarized light. **laevoversion,** *n.* turning of eyes to left. **laevulose,** *n.* kind of very sweet sugar obtained from sucrose.

lagan ['lægən] *n.* goods lying on sea-bed, often at marked spot.

lagena [lə'dʒiːnə] (*Latin*) *n.* (*pl.* –ae) flask. **lageniform,** *adj.* flask-shaped.

lagnappe, lagniappe ['lænjæp, læn'jæp] *n.* *American,* gratuity; small gift, especially given to a customer.

lagophthalmus, lagopthalmos [ˌlægɒf'θælməs] *n.* condition of incomplete closure of eye. **lagopthalmic,** *adj.*

laic ['leɪɪk] *adj.* not clerical or ecclesiastical; lay. **laicism** [–sɪzm], *n.* anticlericalism. **laicize** [–saɪz], *v.t.* divest of ecclesiastical nature; give over to lay control.

laissez faire [ˌleɪseɪ 'feə] (*French*) 'let be' or 'act'; policy of non-intervention by government in industry or industrial conditions.

lakh [lɑːk, læk] (*Hindi*) *n.* one hundred thousand (rupees).

lallation [læ'leɪʃn] *n.* infant's talk, or speech similar to it; pronunciation of *r* as *l*.

laloplegia [ˌlælə'pliːdʒɪə] *n.* loss of speech caused by paralysis.

lama ['lɑːmə] *n.* Tibetan monk or priest. **lamaic** [lə'meɪɪk], **lamaistic**, *adj.* **lamaism, lamaist,** *n.* **lamasery** ['lɑːməsəri], *n.* lama monastery.

lambda ['læmdə] *n.* eleventh letter of Gr. alphabet (Λ, λ). **lambdacism**, *n.* undue use of *l* sound in speech, etc.; incorrect pronunciation of *l*; pronunciation of *r* as *l*. **lambdoid**, *adj.* shaped like Λ.

lambent ['læmbənt] *adj.* shining gently or playing about surface; flickering; gently radiant. **lambency,** *n.*

lambert ['læmbət] *n.* unit of brightness: brightness of surface radiating one lumen per square centimetre.

lambrequin ['læmbrɪkɪn, 'læmbəkɪn] *n.* ornamental hanging over upper part of window or along the edge of a shelf; border pattern with draped effect used in ceramics; covering for helmet.

lamella [lə'melə] *n.* (*pl.* **–ae**) thin plate or layer. **lamelloid,** *adj.* like lamella. **lamellose, lamellar, lamellary,** *adj.* **lamellated,** *adj.* composed of such. **lamellation,** *n.*

lamia ['leɪmɪə] *n.* mythical monster with snake's body and woman's head and breasts.

lamiaceous [ˌleɪmɪ'eɪʃəs] *adj.* pertaining to or like mint; belonging to mint family of plants.

lamina ['læmɪnə] *n.* (*pl.* **–ae**) thin plate or layer; flake. **laminal, laminose, laminous, laminar, laminary,** *adj.* **laminate,** *v.i.* & *t.* split into laminae; bond several laminae together; plate with metal; *adj.* shaped like or composed of laminae. **lamination,** *n.*

lammergeier ['læməgaɪə] *n.* eagle- and vulture-like bird of prey, largest of Europe; bearded vulture.

lampadedromy [læmpədəd'rəmɪ] *n.* foot race with lighted torches, especially relay race in which torch is passed on. **lampadephore** [–æd'ɪfor], *n.* torchbearer.

lampion ['læmpiən] *n.* small crude lamp.

lampoon [læm'puːn] *n.* written satire on a person; *v.t.* satirize. **lampooner, lampoonist,** *n.* writer of lampoon.

lamprey ['læmpri] *n.* slender eel-like fish with toothed sucking mouth.

lamprophony [læm'prɒfəni] *n.* speaking in clear, loud voice.

lampyrid ['læmpərɪd] *n.* & *adj.* (pertaining to) glow-worm or fire-fly. **lampyrine,** *adj.*

lanameter ['lænəmiːtə] *n.* mechanical means of determining quality of wool. **lanate** ['leɪneɪt], *adj.* woolly.

lanceolate ['lɑːnsiəleɪt] *adj.* having shape of lance-head, especially tapering at each end. **lanceolation,** *n.*

lancet ['lɑːnsɪt] *n.* pointed surgical instrument; pointed window or arch.

lancinate ['lɑːnsɪneɪt] *v.t.* lacerate; pierce. **lancination,** *n.*

landau ['lændɔː] *n.* four-wheeler carriage with folding hood and removable top. **landaulette,** *n.* coupé with folding hood.

landes [lɒnd] (*French*) *n. pl.* desert or marshy lowlands beside sea.

landfall ['lændfɔːl] *n.* the sighting of land from sea.

landgrave ['lændgreɪv] *n.* kind of German count. **landgraviate,** *n.* jurisdiction of landgrave. **landgravine** [–viːn], *n.* wife of landgrave; woman having position of landgrave.

Landwehr ['læntveə] (*German*) *n.* reserve of men who have completed conscription service in army.

languet(te) ['læŋgwet] *n.* tongue-like appendage or outgrowth.

laniary ['leɪnɪəri, 'læ–] *adj.* & *n.* canine (tooth). **laniariform,** *adj.*

lanolin ['lænəlɪn] *n.* fat extracted from wool and used in ointments and cosmetics. **lanose,** *adj.* woolly.

lanugo [lə'njuːgəʊ] *n.* woolly down, especially covering human foetus. **lanuginose** [–dʒɪnəʊs], **lanuginous** [–dʒɪnəs], *adj.* downy.

Laodicean [ˌleɪəʊdi'siːən] *adj.* pertaining to Laodicea and its 'lukewarm' Christians (Rev. iii); zeal-less; *n.* such person.

lapactic [lə'pæktɪk] *n.* & *adj.* purgative. **laparectomy, laparotomy** [ˌlæpə'rɒtəmi], *n.* operation for removal of part of wall of abdomen.

lapicide ['læpɪsaɪd] *n.* stone-cutter.

lapidary ['læpɪdəri] *adj.* pertaining to or engraved on stone; (of style) elegant and precise; *n.* gem engraver. **lapidarian,** *adj.* pertaining to or inscribed on stone. **lapidarist,** *n.* expert on gems and gem cutting.

lapidate ['læpɪdeɪt] *v.t.* stone to death. **lapidation, lapidator,** *n.*

lapideous [lə'pɪdɪəs] *adj.* of or cut in stone. **lapidicolous,** *adj.* living under stones. **lapidific,** *adj.* forming stone. **lapidify,** *v.t.* turn into stone.

lapillus [lə'pɪləs] *n.* (*pl.* **–li**) small stone, especially ejected by volcano. **lapilliform,** *adj.* like small stones.

lapis lazuli [ˌlæpɪs 'læzjuli, aɪ] *n.* rich blue stone.

lappaceous [læ'peɪʃəs] *adj.* prickly.

lappet ['læpɪt] *n.* flap or fold (on garment); fleshy lobe.

lapsus linguae [ˌlæpsəs 'lɪŋgwaɪ, –wiː] (*Latin*) (*pl.* **lapsus....**) 'slip of the tongue'. **lapsus calami** [–'kæləmaɪ, –iː], slip of the pen. **lapsus memoriae** [–mə'mɔːriaɪ], slip of memory.

Laputan [lə'pjuːtn] *adj.* pertaining to Laputa, island of philosophers in Swift's *Gulliver's Travels*; absurd; fantastic.

larboard ['lɑːbəd] *n.* & *adj.* archaic, port.

lares ['lɑːreɪz, 'leəriːz] (*Latin*) *n. pl.* local or tutelary gods. **lares and penates,** household gods.

largesse [lɑː'dʒes] *n.* bountiful gift of money; generosity. **largition,** *n.* giving of largesse.

larine ['lærɪn, –rɪn] *adj.* pertaining to or like gulls.

larithmics [lə'rɪðmɪks] *n.* study of population statistics.

larmoyant [lɑː'mɔɪənt] *adj.* tearful; weeping.

larva ['lɑːvə] *n.* (*pl.* **–ae**) form of insect after hatching from egg and before pupation; earliest form of animal's young. **larval,** *adj.* **larvate,** *adj.* hidden. **larviparous,** *adj.* bringing forth larvae. **larvivorous,** *adj.* feeding on larvae.

larynx ['lærɪŋks] *n.* (*pl.* **–nges**) upper part of windpipe; voice organ. **laryngal** [lə'rɪŋgl],

laryngeal [lə'rɪndʒəl, ˌlærɪn'dʒiːəl], **laryngic**, *adj.* **laryngismus**, *n.* spasm closing larynx, with croup-like effect. **laryngitis**, *n.* inflammation of larynx. **laryngology** [ˌlærɪŋ'gɒlədʒi], *n.* study of larynx. **laryngoscope** , *n.* instrument for viewing larynx. **laryngotomy**, *n.* incision into larynx.

lascar ['læskə] (*E Indian*) *n.* native sailor or soldier.

lascivious [lə'sɪvɪəs] *adj.* lustful; lecherous.

lasher ['læʃə] *n.* weir; water in or pool below weir.

lassitude ['læsɪtjuːd] *n.* tiredness.

latebricole [lə'tebrɪkəʊl] *adj.* living in holes.

lateen [lə'tiːn, læ–] *adj.* applied to triangular sail rigged on spar forming angle of 45° with mast. **lateener**, *n.* lateen-rigged vessel.

latent ['leɪtnt] *adj.* lying concealed or dormant. **latency**, *n.*

laterigrade ['lætərɪgreɪd] *n.* & *adj.* (animal) moving sideways or crab-wise.

laterite ['lætəraɪt] *n. Geology*, red clay formed by weathering of oxide-bearing rocks. **lateritic**, *adj.* **lateritious**, *adj.* brick-red in colour.

lateroversion [ˌlætərəʊ'vɜːʃn] *n. Medicine*, sideways displacement of organ.

latescent [leɪ'tesnt] *adj.* becoming latent.

lathi ['lɑːti] *n.* Indian policeman's long staff, used for crowd control, as weapon, etc.

laticostate [ˌlætɪ'kɒsteɪt] *adj.* having broad ribs. **latidentate**, *adj.* having broad teeth. **latipennate** , *adj.* having broad wings. **latirostrate**, *adj.* having broad beak.

latitudinarian [ˌlætɪtjuːdɪ'neərɪən] *n.* & *adj.* (person) having broad and free views, especially religious. **latitudinarianism**, *n.*

latitudinous [ˌlætɪ'tjuːdɪnəs] *adj.* (of attitude, interpretation) having breadth.

latrant ['leɪtrənt] *adj.* barking. **latration**, *n.*

latticinio [ˌlætɪ'tʃɪnɪəʊ] (*Italian*) *n.* kind of glass with white veins.

laud [lɔːd] *v.t.* & *n.* praise. **laudation**, *n.* **laudatory**, **laudative**, *adj.* expressing praise.

laudanum ['lɔːdənəm, 'lɒ–] *n.* tincture of opium.

laudator temporis acti [lɔːˌdɑːtɔː ˌtempərɪs 'æktiː, –ˌdeɪ–] (*Latin*) 'praiser of past time'; die-hard; Conservative.

laureate ['lɔːrɪət, 'lɒ–] *adj.* crowned with laurel wreath as prize or sign of distinction; *n.* such person, especially poet; prize-winner; [–ieɪt], *v.t.* bestow laurel wreath on. **laureation**, *n.*

laurustinus, **laurustine** [ˌlɔːrə'staɪnəs, 'lɔːrəstɪn] *n.* evergreen shrub, species of viburnum, with white or pink flowers.

lavabo [lə'vɑːbəʊ, –'veɪ–] *n.* (*pl.* **–boes**) *Roman Catholic*, rite of washing hands by celebrant priest, while reciting Psalm xxvi, 6-12; towel or basin used in this; wash-basin.

lavage ['lævɪdʒ, læ'vɑːʒ] *n.* washing (out). **lavation**, *n.*

laverock ['lævərək] (*Scottish*) *n.* skylark.

laxation [læk'seɪʃn] *n.* act of loosening; state of being loosened.

layette [leɪ'et] *n.* clothing, bedding, etc., for newborn child.

lazar ['læzə, 'leɪ–] *n.* leper; any plague-stricken person. **lazaretto** [ˌlæzə'retəʊ], *n.* leper hospital.

lazarole ['læzərəʊl] *n.* medlar.

lazuli ['læzjuli, –aɪ] *n.* lapis lazuli. **lazuline**, *adj.*

Lebensraum ['leɪbənzraʊm] (*German*) *n.* 'living space'; territory claimed to be necessary for national self-sufficiency.

lecanomancy ['lekənəmænsi] *n.* divination by water in basin. **lecanoscopy**, *n.* staring at water in basin, as form of self-hypnotism.

lecithal ['lesɪθl] *adj.* having yolk. **lecithity**, *n.*

lectern ['lektən] *n.* reading desk. **lection**, *n.* variant reading in a particular edition of a text.

lectionary ['lekʃənəri] *n.* list of parts of Scriptures ordered to be read in churches.

lectual ['lektjuəl] *adj.* necessitating confinement to bed.

legate ['legət] *n.* papal envoy; ambassador. **legation** [lɪ'geɪʃn], *n.* dispatch of legate; embassy.

legerdemain [ˌledʒədə'meɪn] *n.* sleight of hand.

leguleian [ˌlegju'liːən] *adj.* like lawyer; pettifogging; *n.* lawyer. **leguleious**, *adj.*

Coping with clauses

A **clause** is the basic building block of sentences. It consists of a **subject** (typically a noun, noun phrase, or pronoun) and a **predicate** (typically a verb, often followed by its object). So in the clause *She switched off the TV, she* is the subject and *switched off the TV* is the predicate. (See also **Grammar terms**.)

This clause can stand on its own as a sentence, so it is called a **main clause**. However, there are clauses that cannot be used alone (e.g. *where we went last year*). These are called **subordinate** or **dependent clauses**. There are three sorts: noun clauses, adverbial clauses, and adjectival clauses. **Noun clauses** can be used in place of a noun, as the subject of a verb or the object of a verb or preposition: so instead of the noun object in *I remember our holiday*, you could use a noun clause, as in *I remember where we went last year*.

Adverbial clauses perform the role of an adverb, typically in qualifying a verb, as in *Come and see me when you're in London* (the adverbial clause is *when you're in London*).

Adjectival clauses qualify nouns. They are usually called **relative clauses**, and there are two types: **restrictive** or **defining** relative clauses and **nonrestrictive** or **nondefining** relative clauses.

The former specifies a particular instance of the noun, and the sentence would be incomplete without it: *The zebra which the lion picked on was clearly sick.* The second merely gives extra information, and is dispensable: *The zebra, which lives in southern Africa, is related to the horse.* Both types of relative clause can be introduced by *which, who, whom,* and *whose,* but *that* is usually used only in restrictive clauses. Nonrestrictive clauses are usually enclosed within commas, but restrictive clauses are not.

leguminous [lɪ'gjuːmɪnəs] *adj.* applied to plants with seeds in pods. **legume** ['legjuːm], *n.* vegetable; leguminous plant grown as forage; pod. **leguminiform**, *adj.* pod-shaped. **leguminose**, *adj.*

lei [leɪ, 'leɪɪ] (*Hawaiian*) *n.* garland of flowers.

leiotrichous [laɪ'ɒtrɪkəs] *adj.* smooth-haired. **leiotrichy**, *n.* **leiophyllous**, *adj.* smooth-leaved.

leister ['liːstə] *adj.* trident for spearing fish.

leitmotif, leitmotiv ['laɪtməʊ,tiːf, –,məʊtɪv] (*German*) *n.* recurring musical theme with definite association with a person, idea, event, etc.

lemma ['lemə] *n.* (*pl.* **–mas, –mata**) *Logic*, major premise; (argument or theme used as) the title of a composition; *Botany*, flowering glume of grass.

lemming ['lemɪŋ] *n.* rat of polar regions.

lemnaceous [lem'neɪʃəs] *adj.* pertaining to or like duckweed; belonging to duckweed family of plants.

lemur ['liːmə] *n.* large-eyed, monkey-like animal of Madagascar, etc. **flying lemur**, E Indian cat-like animal, with fold of skin on both sides of body enabling it to make long leaps. **lemuriform**, **lemuroid** ['lemjurɔɪd], *adj.* like lemur.

lemures ['lemjuriːz] (*Latin*) *n. pl.* spirits of dead.

lenitive ['lenətɪv] *n. & adj.* soothing (drug); gentle laxative; palliative. **lenity**, *n.* gentleness; leniency.

lentic ['lentɪk] *adj.* pertaining to or living in still water.

lenticular [len'tɪkjʊlə] *n.* shaped like lentil or convexo-convex lens; *n.* such lens. **lentiform**, *adj.*

lentigo [len'taɪgəʊ] *n.* (*pl.* **–tigines** [–'tɪdʒəniːz]) freckle or freckle-like condition. **lentiginous** [–'tɪdʒənəs], *adj.* freckly; scurfy.

lentiscus [len'tɪskəs] *n.* mastic tree. **lentiscine**, *adj.*

lentisk ['lentɪsk] *n.* lentiscus.

lentitude ['lentɪtjuːd] *n.* slowness; lethargy. **lentitudinous**, *adj.*

lentoid ['lentɔɪd] *adj.* lens-shaped.

leonine ['liːənaɪn] *adj.* like a lion. **leonine partnership**, one in which partner bears losses but receives no profits. **Leonine** (verse), *n.* Latin verse line with internal rhyme.

leontiasis [,liːən'taɪəsɪs] *n.* kind of leprosy giving leonine appearance to face. **leontiasis ossea**, hypertrophy of facial bones.

lepidopterous [,lepɪ'dɒptərəs] *adj.* having four scale-covered wings. **lepidopteran, lepidopteron**, *n.* (*pl.* **–ra**) such insect, as moth or butterfly. **lepidopterology**, *n.* study of such insects. **lepidopterologist**, *n.*

lepidosis [,lepɪ'dəʊsɪs] *n.* scaly skin disease. **lepidote**, *adj.* scurf-covered.

leporid ['lepərɪd] *adj.* pertaining or belonging to the family comprising rabbits and hares; *n.* animal of this family. **leporine**, *adj.* pertaining to or like a hare.

lepra ['leprə] *n. Medicine*, leprosy.

leprechaun ['leprəkɔːn] *n.* fairy in shape of old man, in Irish folklore.

lepric ['leprɪk] *adj.* pertaining to leprosy. **leproid**, *adj.* **leprology**, *n.* study of leprosy. **leprose**, *adj.* scurfy.

leptocephalous [,leptə'kefələs, –'se–] *adj.* having very narrow head. **leptocephalia** [–ke'feɪlɪə, –sɪ–], *n.* such condition. **leptocephalus**, *n.* (*pl.* **–li**) larva of conger eel; conger eel; leptocephalous person.

leptochroous [lep'tɒkrəʊəs] *adj.* having very thin skin. **leptochroa**, *n.*

leptophyllous [,leptə'fɪləs] *adj.* having long thin leaves.

leptorrhine ['leptəraɪn] *n. & adj.* (person) with long thin nose. **leptorrhinism**, *n.*

Lesbian ['lezbɪən] *adj.* pertaining to Lesbos (Mytilene), and the sexual practices of its ancient inhabitants; (**lesbian**) *n.* homosexual woman. **Lesbian rule**, rule or standard alterable to suit circumstances. **lesbianism**, *n.* homosexuality between women.

lèse-majesté, lese-majesty, leze-majesty [,leɪz'mædʒəsteɪ, –ti] *n.* treason; crime against sovereign's person.

lesion ['liːʒn] *n.* injury, especially causing structural changes; injured area.

lestobiosis [,lestəʊbaɪ'əʊsɪs] *n.* (*pl.* **–ses**) mode of life characterized by furtive stealing, especially as found where two species of ant live side by side.

lethargy ['leθədʒi] *n.* sleepy state. **lethargic** [lə'θɑːdʒɪk], *adj.* **lethargize**, *v.t.*

Lethe ['liːθi] *n.* river of Hades in Greek mythology, whose waters grant oblivion; forgetfulness of past; peace of mind. **Lethean** [–'θiːən], *adj.* **lethiferous**, *adj.* deadly.

lethologica [,liːθə'lɒdʒɪkə] *n.* forgetfulness of words.

lettre de cachet [,letrə də 'kæʃeɪ] *n.* (*pl.* **lettres...**), 'sealed letter'; monarch's written edict; order for imprisonment.

leucocyte ['luːkəsaɪt] *n.* white corpuscle of blood. **leucocytic** [–'sɪtɪk], *adj.* **leucocytoid**, *adj.* **leucocytosis**, *n.* increase in number of leucocytes in blood.

leucoma [luˈkəʊmə] *n.* whiteness and thickening of cornea. **leucomatous** [–'kɒmətəs], *adj.*

leucomelanous, leucomelanic [,luːkəʊ'melənəs, –me'lænɪk] *adj.* having dark hair and eyes, and fair skin.

leucopenia [,luːkə'piːnɪə] *n.* decrease in number of leucocytes in blood. **leucopenic** ['pɒnɪk], *adj.*

leucophyllous [,luːkə'fɪləs] *adj.* with white leaves.

leucopoiesis [,luːkəʊpɔɪ'iːsɪs] *n.* formation of leucocytes. **leucopoietic**, *adj.*

leucorrhoea [,luːkəˈrɪə] *n.* vaginal discharge of whitish mucus. **leucorrheal**, *adj.*

leucotomy [luˈkɒtəmi] *n.* lobotomy.

leucous ['luːkəs] *adj.* white; fair; albino.

leukaemia, leukemia [luˈkiːmɪə] *n.* presence of excess leucocytes in blood due to affection of organs making blood. **leukaemic**, *adj.*

leuko- ['luːkəʊ] *prefix* leuco-.

Levant [lə'vænt] *n.* the East, especially the eastern end of Mediterranean. **Levanter**, *n.* E wind of Mediterranean. **Levantine**, *n. & adj.*

levant [lə'vænt] *v.i.* flee from creditors.

levator [lə'veɪtə] *n.* (*pl.* **levatores** [,levə'tɔːriːz]), muscle raising limb or part.

levee ['levi] *n.* monarch's reception held after rising or, in Britain, for men only in the afternoon; *American*, river embankment; quay.

leveret ['levərət] *n.* young hare.

leviathan [lə'vaɪəθən] *n.* sea monster mentioned in Bible; any gigantic creature or work.

levigate ['levɪgeɪt] *v.t.* make smooth; polish; mix thoroughly; reduce to powder or paste; *adj.* smooth. **levigation, levigator**, *n.*

levirate ['levərett, 'liː–] *n.* custom requiring a man to marry his brother's widow.

levitate ['levɪteɪt] *v.i & t.* rise; float; cause to rise or float. **levitation**, *n.* raising of body without support, especially by spiritualistic means; illusion of floating. **levitative**, *adj.*

levo- ['liːvəʊ] *prefix American*, laevo-.

lewisite ['luːɪsaɪt] *n. Chemistry*, blistering liquid, derived from arsenic and acetylene, used in war; *Geology*, yellow or brown mineral containing antimony.

lex [leks] (*Latin*) *n.* (pl. **leges** ['liːdʒiːz]) law. **lex domicilii**, law of the country where a person is domiciled. **lex fori**, law of the country where an action is brought. **lex loci**, law of the country where a transaction, tort, etc. occurs. **lex non scripta**, unwritten law. **lex talionis**, law of an eye for an eye; law of equal retaliation.

lexicon ['leksɪkən] *n.* dictionary; vocabulary of a language, individual or group. **lexical**, *adj.* pertaining to lexicon. **lexicography**, *n.* compilation of dictionaries. **lexicology**, *n.* study of words, their meanings and origins.

lexigraphy [lek'sɪgrəfɪ] *n.* art of definition of words; writing with characters each one representing a word. **lexigraphic(al)**, *adj.*

lexiphanic [‚leksɪ'fænɪk] *adj.* using many long words; bombastic. **lexiphanism** [–sɪzm], *n.*

li [liː] (*Chinese*) *n.* unit of weight (equivalent of decigram) or measure (equivalent of millimetre, kilometre or centiare).

liaise [li'eɪz] *v.i.* establish and maintain contact; co-operate. **liaison** [li'eɪzɒn], *n.* communication, contact and co-operation; illicit sexual relationship; thickening agent for soups and sauces; pronunciation of normally silent final consonant before word beginning with a vowel.

liana [li'ɑːnə] *n.* climbing plant with roots in ground; vine.

lias ['laɪəs] *n.* kind of fossiliferous limestone. **liassic** [laɪ'æsɪk], *adj.*

libanophorous [‚lɪbə'nɒfərəs] *adj.* yielding incense. **libaniferous, libanotophorous**, *adj.*

libation [laɪ'beɪʃn] *n.* offering of drink to gods; act of pouring out such. **libationary, libatory**, *adj.*

libeccio, libecchio [lɪ'betʃəʊ] (*Italian*) *n.* southwest wind.

liber ['laɪbə] *n.* bast.

liberticide [lɪ'bɜːtɪsaɪd] *n.* destruction or destroyer of liberty. **liberticidal**, *adj.*

libertine ['lɪbətiːn] *n.* freethinker; lecher; *adj.* freethinking; lecherous. **libertinage, libertinism**, *n.*

libido [lɪ'biːdəʊ] *n.* sexual desire; vital motive force deriving from sex or life instinct. **libidinal** [–'bɪd–], *adj.* **libidinous** [–'bɪd–], *adj.* lecherous.

librate [laɪ'breɪt] *v.i.* oscillate before settling into equilibrium; be poised; balance. **libration**, *n. Astronomy*, apparent swinging of moon's visible surface. **libratory**, *adj.*

libretto [lɪ'bretəʊ] *n.* (pl. **–ti**) book or words of opera, etc. **librettist**, *n.* writer of this.

libriform ['lɪbrɪfɔːm] *adj.* like liber.

licentiate [laɪ'senʃiət] *n.* certificated member; person with licence to practise. **licentiation**, *n.*

licentious [laɪ'senʃəs] *adj.* sexually immoral; unrestrained.

lichen ['laɪkən] *n.* lowly grey-green flowerless plant encrusting rocks, trees, etc.; encrusting skin disease. **lichenic** [–'kenɪk], **lichenoid, lichenose, lichenous**, *adj.* **lichenography**, *n.* description of or treatise on lichens. **lichenology**, *n.* study of these.

licit ['lɪsɪt] *adj.* lawful.

lickerish ['lɪkərɪʃ] *adj.* greedy; lecherous.

lickspittle ['lɪk‚spɪtl] *n.* toady, flatterer.

lictor ['lɪktə] *n.* magistrate's attendant bearing fasces in ancient Rome. **lictorian** [–'tɔːrɪən], *adj.*

lidar ['laɪdɑː] *n.* system of using lasers in the same way as radar: *acronym* of Light Detection and Ranging.

Lied [liːd] (*German*) *n.* (pl. **–er** [–ə]) song, especially short and expressing emotion.

lien ['liːən] *n.* right over property or services.

lienal [laɪ'iːnl] *adj.* pertaining to spleen. **lienic** [–'enɪk], *adj.* **lienitis**, *n.* inflammation of spleen.

lientery ['laɪəntərɪ] *n.* diarrhoeal discharge of incompletely digested food. **lienteric** [–'terɪk], *adj.*

lierne [li'ɜːn] *n. Architecture*, short secondary rib connecting principal ribs especially in Gothic vaulting.

ligament ['lɪgəmənt] *n.* bond; bandage; band of tissue connecting bones, etc. **ligamental, ligamentary, ligamentous**, *adj.*

ligate ['laɪgeɪt] *v.t.* tie. **ligation**, *n.* **ligature**, *n.* tie; link; bandage; two conjoined letters, as *fl.*

ligneous ['lɪgniəs] *adj.* wood-like; containing wood. **lignescent**, *adj.* rather woody. **lignicolous**, *adj.* living in wood. **lignify**, *v.i. & t.* become or make woody. **ligniperdous**, *adj.* destroying wood. **lignite**, *n.* woody brown coal. **lignum vitae** [‚lɪgnəm 'vaɪtɪ], *Latin*, 'wood of life'; several W Indian and other varieties of guaiacum tree.

ligule ['lɪgjuːl] *n.* thin outgrowth at junction of leaf and leafstalk. **ligulate**, *adj.* having ligule; strap-shaped. **liguloid**, *adj.* like ligule.

Lilliputian [‚lɪlɪ'pjuːʃn] *adj.* pertaining to Lilliput, a country of pygmies in Swift's *Gulliver's Travels*; small; weak; *n.* very small or puny person.

limacine ['lɪməsaɪn] *adj.* pertaining to slugs. **limaceous**, *adj.* **limacoid** [–kɔɪd], *adj.* sluglike.

limation [laɪ'meɪʃn] *n.* polishing; smoothing; correction of astronomical errors.

limbate ['lɪmbeɪt] *adj.* having border, especially (*Botany*) of different colour from the rest. **limbation**, *n.*

limbo ['lɪmbəʊ] *n.* oblivion; place for unwanted or neglected things; dwelling-place of souls of persons excluded from heaven but not through sin, as unbaptized infants, etc.

limbus ['lɪmbəs] *n.* border.

limen ['laɪmen] *n.* (pl. **limens, limina** ['lɪmɪnə]) *Psychology*, threshold; limit below which a stimulus becomes imperceptible.

limes ['laɪmiːz] *n.* (pl. **limites** ['lɪmɪtiːz]) ancient Roman fortified boundary.

limicolous [laɪ'mɪkələs] *adj.* living in mud. **limicoline**, *adj.* living on shore; pertaining to wading birds.

liminal ['lɪmɪnl] *adj.* pertaining to or at threshold.

limitarian [‚lɪmɪ'teərɪən] *n. & adj.* (person) who believes that salvation is limited to a certain section of mankind.

limitrophe ['lɪmɪtrəʊf] *adj.* situated on border or along boundary; adjacent.

limivorous [laɪ'mɪvərəs] *adj.* swallowing mud.

limn [lɪm] *v.t.* portray; paint; delineate. **limner**, *n.*

limnetic [lɪm'netɪk] *adj.* pertaining to or inhabiting fresh water. **limnobiology**, *n.* study of freshwater life. **limnology**, *n.* general study of lakes and ponds. **limnophilous**, *adj.* inhabiting freshwater ponds.

limoniad [laɪ'məʊniæd] *adj.* meadow nymph.

limpid ['lɪmpɪd] *adj.* pellucid. **limpidity**, *n.*

limuloid ['lɪmjulɔɪd] *n.* & *adj.* (pertaining to) king crab.

linaceous [laɪ'neɪʃəs] *adj.* pertaining to or like flax; belonging to the flax family of plants.

linctus ['lɪŋktəs] *n.* medicated syrup for throat.

linden ['lɪndən] *n.* lime tree.

lineal ['lɪnɪəl] *n.* pertaining to or composed of lines; in direct line of descent. **lineage**, *n.* descent from ancestor; family tree. **linear**, *adj.* **lineate**, *v.t.* mark with lines. **lineation**, *n.* outline; arrangement by or in lines. **lineolate**, *adj.* marked with fine lines.

lineaments ['lɪnɪəmənts] *n. pl.* facial features or outline; distinctive characteristics. **lineamental**, *adj.*

lingua franca [ˌlɪŋgwə 'fræŋkə] *n.* any language used as a means of communication among speakers of other languages.

linguiform ['lɪŋgwɪfɔːm] *adj.* tongue-shaped.

liparian [lɪ'peərɪən] *n.* & *adj.* (pertaining to a) sea-snail.

liparoid ['lɪpərɔɪd] *adj.* fatty. **lipase**, *n.* enzyme hydrolysing fats. **lipogenous**, *adj.* fat-producing.

lipogram ['lɪpəgræm, 'laɪ–] *n.* composition in which all words containing a certain letter or letters are omitted.

lipography [lɪ'pɒgrəfɪ, laɪ–] *n.* accidental omission of a letter or syllable.

lipoid ['lɪpɔɪd, 'laɪ–] *adj.* like fat. **lipoidal, lipoidic**, *adj.* **lipolysis**, *n.* disintegration of fat. **lipoma**, *n.* (*pl.* **–mata**) fatty tumour. **lipomatosis**, *n.* presence of many lipomata; obesity.

lipothymy, lipothymia [lɪ'pɒθɪmɪ, ˌlɪpə'θaɪmɪə] *n.* swoon. **lipothymial, lipothymic**, *adj.*

lippitude ['lɪpɪtjuːd] *n.* soreness or bleariness of eyes.

lipsanographer [ˌlɪpsə'nɒgrəfə] *n.* writer about relics. **lipsanotheca**, *n.* holder for relics.

liquate ['laɪkweɪt] *v.t.* separate or purify (metals) by heating to liquify certain components.

liquefacient [ˌlɪkwɪ'feɪʃnt] *n.* liquifying agent; drug increasing liquid excretions. **liquefaction**, *n.*

liquescent [lɪ'kwesnt] *adj.* melting. **liquescence, liquescency**, *n.*

lissotrichous [lɪ'sɒtrɪkəs] *adj.* having straight hair. **lissotrichan, lissotrichian**, *adj.* **lissotrichy**, *n.*

literati [ˌlɪtə'rɑːtɪ] *n. pl.* learned or literary people.

literatim [ˌlɪtə'rɑːtɪm, –'reɪ–] (*Latin*) *adv.* letter by or for letter; literally.

literation [ˌlɪtə'reɪʃn] *n.* representation of sounds by letters.

litharge ['lɪθɑːdʒ] *n.* lead monoxide.

lithiasis [lɪ'θaɪəsɪs] *n.* formation of calculi in body.

lithic ['lɪθɪk] *adj.* pertaining to stone, or stone in the bladder. **lithify** *v.i.* & *t.* solidify into rock.

lithochromy ['lɪθəkrəʊmɪ] *n.* painting on stone. **lithochromatics**, *n.* chromolithography.

lithoclase ['lɪθəkleɪs] *n. Geology*, crack in rock. **lithoclast**, *n.* stone breaker; stone-breaking instrument.

lithogenesis [ˌlɪθə'dʒenəsɪs] *n.* study of rock formation; calculi formation. **lithogenetic** [–dʒə'netɪk], *adj.* **lithogenous** [–'θɒdʒənəs], *adj.* producing stone.

lithograph ['lɪθəgrɑːf] *v.t* draw or reproduce on stone or metal plate with greasy substance, from which impressions are taken; *n.* impression so taken (*abbreviated* as **litho** ['laɪθəʊ]). **lithographer, lithography** *n.* **lithographic**, *adj.*

lithoid(al) ['lɪθɔɪd, –l] *adj.* stone-like. **litholatry**, *n.* worship of stones. **lithology**, *n.* study of rocks or calculi. **lithontriptic**, *n.* & *adj.* (substance) dissolving stones in bladder. **lithophagous**, *adj.* swallowing or burrowing in, stone **lithophilous**, *adj.* growing among stones. **lithophyte**, *n.* plant growing on rock. **lithopone**, *n.* white pigment used in paints consisting of a mixture of zinc sulphide and barium sulphate. **lithosphere**, *n.* earth's outer crust. **lithotomy**, *n.* cutting for stone in bladder. **lithotrity**, *n.* breaking up stone in bladder.

litigate ['lɪtɪgeɪt] *v.i* & *t.* go to law (about). **litigant**, *n.* & *adj.* (person) engaged in lawsuit. **litigious** [–'tɪdʒəs], *adj.* habitually engaging in lawsuits; quarrelsome; involved in litigation. **litigation**, *n.*

litmus ['lɪtməs] *n.* dye obtained from lichens, used in chemical tests, being turned red by acid and blue by alkali.

litotes ['laɪtətiːz, laɪ'təʊ–] *n.* rhetorical device of understatement.

littérateur [ˌlɪtərə'tɜː] (*French*) *n.* a literary person.

littoral ['lɪtərəl] *adj.* pertaining to or on seashore; *n.* such region

liturate ['lɪtjureɪt] *adj.* spotted.

liturgy ['lɪtədʒɪ] *n.* body of church services and ritual. **liturgical** [lɪ'tɜːdʒɪkl], *adj.* **liturgician**, *n.* student of this. **liturgics**, *n.* study of liturgy and worship. **liturgiology**, *n.* study of or treatise on liturgy. **liturgism**, *n.* keeping strictly to liturgy.

livedo [lɪ'viːdəʊ] *n.* blueness of skin due to congestion.

lixiviate [lɪk'sɪvɪeɪt] *v.t.* separate by washing with solvent; treat with lye, etc. **lixiviation**, *n.* **lixiviator**, *n.* **lixivium**, *n.* solution resulting from lixiviation; lye.

llanero [ljə'neərəʊ] (*Spanish*) *n.* cowboy; plainsman.

loadstar, loadstone *see* **lodestar, lodestone.**

lobate ['ləʊbeɪt] *adj.* having lobes. **lobal, lobar**, *adj.* lobe-like.

lobotomy [lə'bɒtəmɪ] *n.* surgical incision to sever nerve fibres in the frontal lobe of the brain, to change the behaviour of severely mentally disturbed patients. **lobotomize** *v.t.*

lobule *n.* small lobe. **lobular, lolulate(d)** *adj.* having lobules.

locale [ləʊ'kɑːl] *n.* locality; scene

locative ['lɒkətɪv] *n.* & *adj. Grammar*, (case) signifying place where.

locellus [lə'seləs] *n.* (*pl.* **–li**) compartment of cell. **locellate**, *adj.* divided into locelli.

lochetic [lə'ketɪk] *adj.* waiting for prey; in ambush.

loco ['ləʊkəʊ] (*Spanish*) *adj.* insane. **loco disease**, kind of nervous disease of cattle, sheep and horses due to eating loco weed.

loco citato [,ləʊkəʊ kɪ'tɑːtəʊ, –sɪ–] 'in the place (or passage) quoted' (*abbr.* **loc. cit.**).

locomobile [,ləʊkə'məʊbaɪl, –iːl] *n.* & *adj.* self-propelling (machine).

locoum, lokoum [lə'kuːm] *n.* Turkish delight.

loculus ['lɒkjʊləs] *n.* (*pl.* **–li**) cell; cavity; compartment. **locular, loculate,** *adj* having or divided into loculi. **loculation,** *n.*

locum tenens [,ləʊkəm 'tenenz, 'tiː–] (*Latin*) 'holding place'; deputy.

locus ['ləʊkəs, 'lɒ–] *n.* (*pl.* **–ci** [–saɪ, –kiː]) place; point; *Mathematics*, path of moving point or curve. **locus citatus,** *see* **loco citato. locus classicus,** authoritative and often-cited passage on a subject. **locus standi,** (*Latin*), 'place of standing'; legal status; right to be heard in law-court.

locution [lə'kjuːʃn] *n.* manner of speech; phrase.

lode [ləʊd] *n.* vein of ore. **lodestar,** *n.* pole-star; guiding star. **lodestone,** *n.* magnetic iron oxide; magnet.

loess ['ləʊes] *n.* deposit of rich loam soil occurring in belt in N hemisphere. **loessal, loessial, loessic,** *adj.*

loggia ['lɒdʒiə] *n.* verandah; open arcade.

logia ['lɒgiə, 'ləʊdʒiə] (*Greek*) *n. pl.* (*sing.* **–ion**) sayings, especially of Christ.

logistics [lə'dʒɪstɪks] *n.* billeting, supply and transport of troops; organizational aspects of any complex operation.

logogogue ['lɒgəgɒg] *n.* person laying down law about words.

logogram, logograph ['lɒgəgræm, –grɑːf] *n.* sign representing word. **logogrammatic,** *adj.* **logography,** *n.* reporting, as of speeches, etc., in longhand by relays of writers.

logomachy [lɒ'gɒməki] *n.* battle of words; dispute about words. **logomacher, logomachist,** *n.* **logomachic** [–'mækɪk], *adj.*

logometer [lɒ'gɒmɪtə] *n.* device or scale for measuring chemical equivalents. **logometric** [–'metrɪk], *adj.*

logopaedics, logopaedia [,lɒgə'piːdɪks, –diə] *n.* study of speech defects.

logorrhoea [,lɒgə'riːə] *n.* excessive or incoherent talking.

logos ['lɒgɒs, 'ləʊ–] (*Greek*) *n.* divine rational principle; the Word of God.

logotype ['lɒgətaɪp] *n.* single body of type containing frequently occuring word or syllable; logo. **logotypy,** *n.*

loimic ['lɔɪmɪk] *adj.* pertaining to plague. **loimology,** *n.* study of plague.

lollapalooza [,lɒləpə'luːzə] *n. American slang,* excellent thing.

longanimity [,lɒŋgə'nɪməti] *n.* long-suffering; forebearance.

longe [lʌndʒ] *n.* rope or place for training horses.

longeron ['lɒndʒərən] (*French*) *n.* structure running length of aircraft fuselage.

longevity [lɒn'dʒevɪti] *n.* long life; length of life. **longevous** [–'dʒiːvəs], *adj.*

longiloquence [lɒn'dʒɪləkwəns] *n.* long-winded speech

longitudinal [,lɒndʒɪ'tjuːdɪnl] *adj.* pertaining to longitude or length; lengthwise.

longueur [lɒŋ'gɜː] *n.* boring stretch of time, passage in work, etc.

loquacious [lə'kweɪʃəs] *adj.* talkative. **loquacity** [–'kwæsəti], *n.*

loquat ['ləʊkwɒt] *n.* plum-like fruit of evergreen tree of Asia.

loquitur ['lɒkwɪtə] (*Latin*) *v.i.* 'he (she) speaks'.

lorate ['lɔːreɪt] *adj.* ligulate.

lorch(a) ['lɔːtʃ, 'lɔːtʃə] *n.* light Pacific vessel with two or three masts.

lordosis [lɔː'dəʊsɪs] *n.* forward spinal curvature. **lordotic** [–'dɒtɪk], *adj.*

lore [lɔː] *n.* space between eye and beak or snout. **loral,** *adj.* **loreal,** *n.* & *adj.* (scale, etc.) situated on the lore.

Lorelei ['lɒrəlaɪ, 'lɔː–] (*German*) *n.* siren, especially of the Lorelei rock in the Rhine.

lorgnette [lɔːn'jet] *n.* pair of spectacles or opera glasses on a handle.

loricate ['lɒrɪkeɪt] *v.t.* cover with protective layer; encrust; plate. **lorication,** *n.*

loris ['lɔːrɪs] *n.* lemur of India, E India and Ceylon.

lory ['lɔːri] *n.* small Australasian parrot, feeding on flower nectar. **lorikeet** ['lɒrɪkiːt], **lorilet** [,lɒrə'let], *n.* species of lory.

lota(h) ['ləʊtə] *n.* globular brass waterpot, used in India.

Lothario [lə'θɑːriəʊ, –'θeə–] *n.* seducer in Rowe's play *The Fair Penitent;* rake; seducer.

lotic ['ləʊtɪk] *adj.* pertaining to or living in fast-flowing water.

lotophagous [ləʊ'tɒfəgəs] *adj.* lotus-eating; indolent. **lotophagi** [–dʒaɪ], *n. pl.* lotus-eaters; day-dreamers.

louche [luːʃ] *adj.* disreputable; morally dubious.

louping-ill ['luːpɪŋ ɪl, 'laʊ–] *n.* paralytic disease of sheep.

loxodograph [lɒk'sɒdəgrɑːf] *n.* device for recording ship's course. **loxodrome,** *n.* line on globe equally oblique to all meridians. **loxodromics,** *n.* sailing on loxodromes.

loxophthalmus [,lɒksɒf'θælməs] *n.* squint.

loxotic [lɒk'sɒtɪk] *adj.* oblique; distorted. **loxotomy,** *n.* oblique cut in amputation.

lubra ['luːbrə] (*Australian*) *n.* aborigine woman or girl.

lubricity [lu'brɪsəti] *n.* slipperiness; wiliness; indecency; **lubricious** [–'brɪʃəs], **lubricous** ['luːbrɪkəs], *adj.*

lucarne [lu'kɑːn] *n.* dormer window.

lucent ['luːsnt] *adj.* shining; clear. **lucence, lucency,** *n.*

lucernal [lu'sɜːnl] *adj.* pertaining to lamp.

lucerne [lu'sɜːn] *n.* alfalfa, also called purple medic.

luciferous [lu'sɪfərəs] *adj.* illuminating. **luciform,** *adj.* like light. **lucifugal, lucifugous,** *adj.* avoiding light. **lucimeter,** *n.* instrument measuring intensity of light, or sunlight's power of evaporation.

lucre ['luːkə] *n.* money; gain. **lucrative,** *adj.* yielding profit.

lucubrate ['luːkjʊbreɪt] *v.i.* study laboriously, especially at night; work by artificial light. **lucubration,** *n.* act or result of lucubrating; over-elaborated literary work. **lucubrator,** *n.* **lucubratory,** *adj.* pertaining to night work; laborious.

luculent ['luːkjʊlənt] *adj.* lucid; shining.

lucullan, lucullean, lucullian [luˈkʌlən, –iən] *adj.* pertaining to Lucullus, ancient Roman consul noted for his elaborate banquets.

lues ['luːiːz] *n.* syphilis; any similar disease. **luetic** [luˈetɪk], *adj.*

lugubrious [ləˈguːbriəs, lu–] *adj.* mournful.

lumbar ['lʌmbə] *adj.* pertaining to the lower part of the torso.

lumbrical ['lʌmbrɪkl] *adj. & n.* (pertaining to) small muscle of palm or sole.

lumbricine ['lʌmbrɪsaɪn, –sɪn] *adj.* pertaining to or like an earthworm. **lumbriciform, lumbricoid** [–kɔɪd], *adj.* like an earthworm. **lumbricosis, *n.*** infestation with intestinal round-worms.

lumen ['luːmɪn] *n. (pl. –mina)* unit of light: luminous energy emitted per second in a unit solid angle by a source of one candela.

luminescence [ˌluːmɪˈnesns] *n.* any emission of light not due to incandescence. **luminescent,** *adj.*

lumpen ['lʌmpən] *adj.* pertaining to the lowest strata of society; degraded; stupid.

lunate ['luːneɪt] *adj.* crescent-shaped. **lunation,** *n.* changes of moon; interval between successive new moons.

lunette [luˈnet] *n.* crescent-shaped ornament or object; opening or window in vault.

lunistice ['luːnɪstɪs] *n.* time each month at which moon is farthest north or south. **lunistitial,** *adj.*

lunula, lunule ['luːnjʊlə, –juːl] *n.* cresent-shaped mark or organ; 'half-moon' on finger nail. **lunulate,** *adj.* bearing lunula; like a small crescent. **lunulet,** *n.* crescent-shaped spot.

lupanar [luˈpeɪnə] *n.* brothel.

lupine ['luːpaɪn] *adj.* pertaining to wolves. **lupicide,** *n.* killing of wolf.

lupulin ['luːpjʊlɪn] *n.* yellow powder on hop cones, used as sedative. **lupuline, lupulinous,** *adj.* like a hop-cluster. **lupulinic,** *adj.* pertaining to lupulin or hops.

lupus ['luːpəs] *n.* tuberculous skin disease, with red patches or ulcers on face. **lupous,** *adj.* pertaining to or affected with lupus.

lurdan(e) ['lɜːdn] *n. & adj.* dull and lazy (person). **lurdanism,** *n.*

lusory ['luːsəri] *adj.* playful.

lustration [lʌˈstreɪʃn] *n.* purifying rite, especially washing. **lustral, lustrical,** *adj.* used in lustration. **lustrate,** *v.t.* purify.

lustrine ['lʌstrɪn] *n.* lustrous silk or cotton material.

lustrum ['lʌstrəm] (*Latin*) *n. (pl. –ra)* period of five years; purification of Roman nation every five years; census.

lusus naturae [ˌluːsəs nəˈtuərai, –ri] (*Latin*) *n.* 'sport of nature'; freak.

lutaceous [luˈteɪʃəs] *adj.* pertaining to or made of mud.

lute, luting [luːt, 'luːtɪŋ] *n.* mixture of cement and clay used to seal joints in pipes, etc.

luteous ['luːtiəs] *adj.* yellow; yellowish. **luteolous,** *adj.* somewhat yellow. **lutescent,** *adj.* yellowish.

luthern ['luːθɜːn] *n.* lucarne.

lutose ['luːtəʊs] *adj.* covered with mud or clay.

lutrine ['luːtraɪn, –rɪn] *adj.* pertaining to or like an otter; belonging to the otter subfamily of animals.

lutulent ['luːtjʊlənt] *adj.* thick; muddy. **lutulence,** *n.*

luxate [lʌkˈseɪt, 'lʌkseɪt] *v.t.* displace; dislocate. **luxation,** *n.*

lycanthrope ['laɪkənθrəʊp, laɪˈkæn–] *n.* werewolf. **lycanthropic** [–ˈθrɒpɪk], **lycanthropous** [–ˈkænθrəpəs], *adj.* **lycanthropize,** *v.i.* change from human to wolf's shape. **lycanthropy,** *n.* change to wolf's shape or characteristics; form of insanity in which person believes himself to be a wolf.

lycée ['liːseɪ] (*French*) *n.* secondary school. **lyceal,** *adj.* **lyceum** [laɪˈsiːəm] *n.* place of instruction, especially in philosophy.

lycoperdon [ˌlaɪkəˈpɜːdn] *n.* puffball fungus. **lycoperdaceous, lycoperdoid,** *adj.*

lycopod ['laɪkəpɒd] *n.* club moss. **lycopodiaceous,** *adj.*

lycosid [laɪˈkəʊsɪd] *n.* wolf spider.

lyddite ['lɪdaɪt] *n.* high explosive for shells, largely picric acid.

Lydian ['lɪdiən] *adj.* pertaining to ancient Lydia, noted for its wealth and voluptuousness; luxurious; effeminate.

lye [laɪ] *n.* strong alkaline solution, especially made from wood ashes; lixiviation solution.

lymph [lɪmf] *n.* colourless blood-like fluid containing leucocytes, conveying nourishment to, and collecting waste products from, tissues. **lymphadenitis,** *n.* inflammation of lymph glands. **lymphadenopathy,** *n.* swelling of lymph nodes. **lymphangial,** *adj.* pertaining to lymph vessels. **lymphangitis,** *n.* inflammation of these. **lymphatic,** *adj.* pertaining to or conveying lymph; pale; lifeless; indolent; *n.* vessel conveying lymph **lymphyatism,** *n.* hypertrophy of lymph tissues; lymphatic character. **lymphocyte,** *n.* lymph cell. **lymphocytosis,** *n.* unusually large number of lymphocytes in the blood. **lymphoid, lymphous,** *adj.* like lymph. **lymphoma,** *n.* lymphoid tumour.

lyncean [lɪnˈsiːən] *adj.* pertaining to or like a lynx; keen-sighted.

lypemania [ˌlaɪpɪˈmeɪniə] *n.* intense nervous depression.

lypothymia [ˌlaɪpəˈθaɪmiə] *n.* lypemania.

lysimeter [laɪˈsɪmɪtə] *n.* device measuring percolation of water through soils and the removal of soluble constituents.

lysis ['laɪsɪs] *n. Chemistry,* disintegration or destruction of cells; *Medicine,* gradual recovery from disease. **lysigenic, lysigenous,** *adj.* formed by lysis. **lysin,** *n.* substance causing lysis. **lysogen,** *n.* antigen increasing lysin production.

lyssa ['lɪsə] *n.* rabies or hydrophobia. **lyssic,** *adj.* **lyssophobia,** *n.* dread of going insane.

lyterian [laɪˈtɪəriən] *adj. Medicine,* pertaining to lysis.

M

maar [mɑː] *n.* volcanic crater without a cone, usually filled by a lake.

macabre [məˈkɑːbə, –brə] *adj.* gruesome; pertaining to death.

macaco [məˈkeɪkəʊ] *n.* species of lemur and S American monkey. **macaco worm**, parasitic larva of S American botfly.

macaque [məˈkɑːk] *n.* short-tailed monkey of Asia; Barbary ape.

macarism [ˈmækərɪzm] *n.* pleasure in another's joy; a beatitude. **macarize**, *v.t.* pronounce blessed; praise; congratulate.

macaronic [ˌmækəˈrɒnɪk] *adj.* mixing words from different languages, especially Latin with vernacular or Latinized vernacular words; *n.* verse of this type. **marcaronicism** [–sɪzm], *n.*

macedoine [ˌmæsɪˈdwɑːn] *n.* mixed diced vegetables; mixed fruit in syrup of jelly.

macerate [ˈmæsəreɪt] *v.i. & t.* soften and separate by soaking; grow or make lean. **maceration**, *n.* **macerator**, *n.*

machairodont [məˈkaɪrədɒnt] *n. & adj.* sabretoothed (animal).

machete [məˈʃeti, –ˈʃet] *n.* long, heavy knife, with swordlike blade.

Machiavellian [ˌmækɪəˈveliən] *adj.* pertaining to Niccolo Machiavelli, 15th-century Italian statesman; unscrupulously cunning. **Machiavellianism, Machiavellism,** *n.*

machicolation [məˌtʃɪkəˈleɪʃn] *n.* apertures in parapet or floor of gallery for firing upon persons below. **machicolate,** *v.t.* furnish with these

machination [ˌmækɪˈneɪʃn] *n.* device; plot. **machinate,** *v.i. & t.* plot. **machinator,** *n.*

machinule [ˈmækɪnjuːl] *n.* surveyor's instrument for obtaining right angle.

Mach number [mɑːk] *n.* measure of speed of aircraft, in which speed of sound (about 770 m.p.h.) is Mach One. **Mach meter,** instrument showing speeds as fractions and multiples of speed of sound.

Machtpolitik [ˈmɑːxtpɒlɪˌtiːk] (*German*) *n.* 'power politics'.

mackle [ˈmækl] *n.* blurred or double impression in printing.

maconochie [məˈkɒnəki] *n.* army tinned stew.

macradenous [mæˈkrædnəs] *adj.* with large glands.

macrencephalic, **macrencephalous** [ˌmækrensɪˈfælɪk, –ˈsefələs] *adj.* having large brain pan.

macrobian [mæˈkrəʊbiən] *adj.* longevous. **macrobiosis,** *n.* **macrobiote,** *n.* longevous person. **macrobiotic,** *adj.* longevous, or promoting longevity; involving the use or consumption of whole grains and organically grown vegetables. **macrobiotics,** *n.* art of increasing length of life; macrobiotic dietary system.

macrocephalous [ˌmækrəˈsefələs] *adj.* largeheaded. **macrocephalus,** *n.* (*pl.* **–li**) such person.

macrocosm [ˈmækrəkɒzm] *n.* universe; world; large entity. **macrocosmic(al),** *adj.* **macrocosmology,** *n.* description of this.

macrocyte [ˈmækrəsaɪt] *n.* abnormally large red blood corpuscle. **macrocythaemia, macrocytosis,** *n.* presence of these in blood.

macrodont [ˈmækrədɒnt] *adj.* large-toothed. **macrodontia, macrodontism,** *n.*

macroeconomics [ˌmækrəʊiːkəˈnɒmɪks, –ek–] *n.* study of aspects of the economy as a whole. **macroeconomic,** *adj.*

macrograph [ˈmækrəɡrɑːf] *n.* reproduction of object natural size or larger. **macrographic,** *adj.* **macrography,** *n.* large handwriting; viewing of object with naked eye.

macrology [mæˈkrɒlədʒi] *n.* redundancy, especially pleonasm.

macromania [ˌmækrəˈmeɪniə] *n.* delusion in which things seem larger than natural size. **macromaniacal** [–aɪˈəkl], *adj.*

macrometer [mæˈkrɒmɪtə] *n.* instrument for finding size and distance of distant objects.

macron [ˈmeɪkrɒn, ˈmæk–] *n.* mark (ˉ) placed over long vowels.

macrophallic [ˌmækrəʊˈfælɪk] *adj.* having an unusually large phallus.

macrophotograph [ˌmækrəˈfəʊtəɡrɑːf] *n.* enlarged photograph. **macrophotography,** *n.*

macropsia, macropsy [mæˈkrɒpsiə, –si] *n.* disease of eye causing objects to seem very large.

macropterous [mæˈkrɒptərəs] *adj.* large-winged; large-finned.

macroscian [mæˈkrɒʃiən] *n. & adj.* (person) casting long shadow; inhabitant of polar region.

macroscopic [ˌmækrəˈskɒpɪk] *adj.* observable with naked eye; seen as a whole or in the large.

macroseism [ˈmækrəʊˌsaɪzm] *n.* severe earthquake. **macroseismic,** *adj.* **macroseismograph,** *n.* instrument recording this.

macrotia [mæˈkrəʊʃiə] *n.* largeness of ears. **macrotous,** *adj.* large-eared.

macrotome [ˈmækrətəʊm] *n.* instrument for making large sections for anatomical study.

macrural [mæˈkrʊərəl] *adj.* pertaining to, like or belonging to the crustacean division including lobsters, prawns, etc. **macruran,** *n.* **macrurous,** *adj.* having long tail.

mactation [mækˈteɪʃn] *n.* killing, especially sacrificial.

macula ['mækjʊlə] *n.* (*pl.* **-ae**) coloured spot. **macular,** *adj.* **maculate(d),** *adj.* bearing maculae; spotted; defiled. **maculation,** *n.*

macule ['mækjuːl] *n.* macula; mackle. **maculiferous,** *adj.* bearing macules. **maculose,** *adj.* spotted.

madar [mə'dɑː] *see* **mudar.**

madarosis [,mædə'rəʊsɪs] *n.* loss of eyelashes or eyebrows. **madarotic** [-'rɒtɪk], *adj.*

madcap ['mædkæp] *adj* & *n.* impulsive and reckless (person).

madescent [mə'desnt] *adj.* growing damp.

madrasah [mə'dræsə] *n.* Islamic college, or school attached to mosque.

madrepore ['mædrɪpɔː] *n.* stony coral. **madreporian, madreporic, madreporiform,** *adj.*

madrigal ['mædrɪgl] *n.* unaccompanied polyphonic part song, in five or six parts. **madrigalian** [-'eɪliən], *adj.* **madrigalist,** *n.* composer of madrigal.

madroña, madroño [mə'drəʊnə] *n.* N American evergreen tree. **madroña apples,** red berries of the **madroña.**

Maecenas [maɪ'siːnæs] *n.* generous patron of the arts, like Gaius Maecenas, patron of Virgil and Horace.

maelstrom ['meɪlstrɒm] *n.* whirlpool, especially off W coast of Norway.

maenad ['miːnæd] *n.* (*pl.* **-es**) bacchante; wildly excited woman. **maenadic,** *adj.* **maenadism,** *n.*

maestro ['maɪstrəʊ] (*Italian*) *n.* (*fem.* **-tra**) teacher; master, especially of music. **maestro di capella,** musician in charge of an orchestra in the Baroque period.

magada ['mægədə] *n.* bridge of stringed musical instrument. **magadis** ['mægədɪs], *n.* monochord; ancient bridged instrument for playing octaves.

magi ['meɪdʒaɪ] *n. pl.* (*sing.* **-gus** [-gəs]) ancient Persian priests; the wise men present at Epiphany. **magian,** *n.* & *adj.*

magirics [mə'dʒaɪrɪks] *n.* art of cookery. **magirology** [,mædʒɪ'rɒlədʒi], *n.*

magisterial [,mædʒɪ'stɪəriəl] *adj.* authoritative; master-like; dictatorial. **magisteriality** *n.* **magisterium,** *n. Roman Catholic,* teaching function of the Church.

magistral ['mædʒɪstrəl] *adj.* made up in accordance with a prescription.

magistrand ['mædʒɪstrænd] (*Scottish*) *n.* university student in fourth year.

magma ['mægmə] *n.* (*pl.* **-ta**) paste of mixed solid materials; *Geology,* molten rock within the earth. **magmatic** [-'mætɪk], *adj.*

magnanerie [mæn'jænəri] (*French*) *n.* art or place of rearing silkworms.

magnanimous [mæg'nænɪməs] *adj.* high-minded; noble; generous and forgiving. **magnanimity** [-ə'nɪməti], *n.*

magnesia [mæg'niːʃə] *n.* magnesium oxide, used as antacid and insulating material. **magnesia alba,** a carbonate of magnesium, used as mild purge. **magnesia magma,** milk of magnesia. **magnesian,** *adj.* **magnesic,** *adj.*

magneto [mæg'niːtəʊ] *n.* small dynamo generating current producing spark that ignites fuel vapours in internal combustion engine.

magnetohydrodynamic [mæg,niːtəʊ,haɪdrədaɪ'næmɪk] *adj.* pertaining to a method of generating electricity directly by

passing an ionized gas through a magnetic field at an extremely high temperature. *abbr.* MHD.

magnetometer [,mægnɪ'tɒmɪtə] *n.* instrument measuring magnetic forces. **magnetograph,** *n.* recording instrument of the same kind. **magnetogram,** *n.* recording made by such instrument. **magnetometry,** *n.*

magneton ['mægnɪtɒn] *n.* unit of magnetic moment.

magnetron ['mægnɪtrɒn] *n.* thermionic valve for generating very high frequency oscillations.

magniloquent [mæg'nɪləkwənt] *adj.* using high-flown language; bombastic. **magniloqence,** *n.*

magnum ['mægnəm] *n.* bottle holding twice as much as an ordinary bottle; large-calibre or more than usually powerful firearm. **magnum opus** [-'əʊpəs], *Latin,* 'great work'; finest achievement, especially literary.

maharishi [,mɑːhə'rɪʃi] *n.* Hindu teacher of spiritual or mystical knowledge.

mahatma [mə'hætmə] *n.* wise man; person of noble intellect. **mahatmaism,** *n.*

Mahdi ['mɑːdi] *n.* Islamic Messiah.

mahlstick ['mɔːlstɪk] *n.* maulstick.

mahout [mə'haʊt] *n.* driver of elephant.

mahseer, mahsir, mahsur ['mɑːsɪə, -sɔː] *n.* Indian freshwater food fish.

maidan [maɪ'dɑːn] *n.* (in India) open space used as park, parade ground, etc.

maieutic [meɪ'juːtɪk] *adj.* pertaining to Socratic method. **maieutics,** *n.* Socratic method; midwifery.

maigre ['eɪgə] *adj. Roman Catholic,* not containing meat or its juices, thus permissible on days of abstinence; (of a day) on which abstinence is enjoined.

mainour ['meɪnə] *n.* stolen property discovered on thief's person. **in** or **with the mainour,** in the act; red-handed.

maître ['meɪtrə] (*French*) *n.* master; title of respect for barristers, etc. (*abbr.* Mᵉ). **maître d'armes** [-'dɑːrm], fencing master. **maître de ballet** [də bæ'leɪ], trainer of ballet dancers. **maître d'hôtel** [- dəʊ'tel], major-domo.

majolica [mə'dʒɒlɪkə] *n.* elaborate, highly-coloured, glazed Italian pottery; faience. **majolist,** *n.* maker of majolica.

major-domo [,meɪdʒə'dəʊməʊ] *n.* steward; head servant; butler.

majuscule ['mædʒəskjuːl] *n.* capital or other large letter. **majuscular,** *adj.*

mako ['mɑːkəʊ] *n.* large shark of Australasia, also called blue pointer. **mako-mako,** *n.* wineberry tree or bellbird of New Zealand.

malachite ['mæləkaɪt] *n.* green ornamental stone, an ore of copper.

malacia [mæ'leɪʃiə] *n.* softening of tissue; craving for a certain food. **malacodermous,** *adj.* having soft skin. **malacology,** *n.* study of molluscs. **malacophonous,** *adj.* soft-voiced. **malactic,** *adj.* emollient.

maladroit [,mælə'drɔɪt] *adj.* awkward; gauche.

mala fide [,mælə 'fiːdeɪ] (*Latin*) 'in bad faith'. **mala fides** [-iːz], bad faith.

Malagasy [,mælə'gæsi] *n.* native or language of Madagascar.

malagma [mə'lægmə] *n.* (*pl.* **-ta**) emollient plaster.

malaise [mæ'leɪz] *n.* uneasiness; indefinable feeling of illness or discomfort.

malapropos [,mæləprə'pəʊ] *adj. & adv.* not apropos; inopportune(ly); *n.* such thing or remark. **malapropism,** *n.* ludicrous misuse of long words, or such word misused, as by Mrs. Malaprop in Sheridan's *The Rivals*.

malar ['meɪlə] *adj.* pertaining to cheek(-bone).

malax ['meɪlæks] *v.t.* soften by kneading or diluting. **malaxage** ['mæl–], *n.* such softening of clay. **malaxate,** *v.t.* **malaxation, malaxator,** *n.*

mal de mer [,mæl də 'meə] (*French*) *n.* seasickness. **mal du pays** [–də peɪ'iː], homesickness.

malediction [,mælɪ'dɪkʃn] *n.* curse. **maledictive, maledictory,** *adj.*

malefaction [,mælɪ'fækʃn] *n.* evil-doing.

malefic(ent) [mə'lefɪk, –snt] *adj.* evil; harmful. **maleficence,** *n.*

malevolent [mə'levələnt] *adj.* malicious; *Astrology*, exerting evil influence on. **malevolence,** *n.*

malfeasance [mæl'fiːzns] *n.* misconduct by official. **malfeasant,** *n. & adj.*

malgré ['mælgreɪ] (*French*) *prep.* in spite of. **malgré lui** [–lwiː], in spite of himself; against his desires or beliefs.

maliferous [mæ'lɪfərəs] *adj.* harmful; unhealthy.

malinger [mə'lɪŋgə] *v.i.* feign illness, especially to evade duty. **malingerer,** *n.*

malism ['meɪlɪzm] *n.* belief that world is bad or evil.

malison ['mælɪzn] *n.* curse.

malleable ['mælɪəbl] *adj.* capable of being hammered or pressed into shape; pliable; weak-willed. **malleability,** *n.* **malleation,** *n.* dent.

mallee ['mæli] (*Australian*) *n.* a eucalyptus shrub; thick growth of such shrubs; area covered by such growth.

malleiform [mə'liːɪfɔːm, 'mælɪɪ–] *adj.* hammer-shaped.

mallophagan [mə'lɒfəgən] *n.* bird louse. **mallophagous,** *adj.*

malmsey ['mɑːmzi] *n.* sweet Madeira wine.

malo animo [,mæləʊ 'ænɪməʊ] (*Latin*) 'with evil intent'.

malvaceous [mæl'veɪʃəs] *adj.* pertaining to or like a mallow; belonging to mallow family of plants.

malvasia [,mælvə'siːə] *n.* grape from which malmsey is made. **malvasian,** *adj.*

malversation [,mælvə'seɪʃn] *n.* misconduct; corruption; misuse of public or other funds.

malvoisie ['mælvɔɪzi, –vɔzi] *n.* malmsey.

mamba ['mæmbə, –ɑː] *n.* venomous cobra-like snake of Africa; tree-cobra.

mameluke ['mæmɪluːk] *n.* member of ruling class of Egypt from 13th to 19th cent.; (in Muslim countries) a slave.

mamma ['mæmə] *n.* (*pl.* –ae) milk-secreting gland; breast; teat. **mammary,** *adj.* pertaining to mamma. **mammiferous** [mæ'mɪfərəs], *adj.* having breasts. **mammiform,** *adj.* shaped like breast or nipple.

mammilla [mæ'mɪlə] *n.* (*pl.* –ae) nipple. **mammilliform, mammilloid,** *adj.* like nipple. **mammillar, mammillary,** *adj.* **mammillate,** *adj.* having mammillae, or similar outgrowths. **mammilation,** *n.*

mammography [mæ'mɒgrəfi] *n.* X-ray scanning for early detection of breast cancer.

mana ['mɑːnə, –ɑː] *n.* spirit of nature as object of veneration.

manakin ['mænəkɪn] *n.* small brightly-coloured S American bird; manikin.

mañana [mæn'jɑːnə] (*Spanish*) *n. & adv.* tomorrow.

manatee [,mænə'tiː] *n.* sea-cow.

mancinism ['mænsɪnɪzm] *n.* left-handedness.

manciple ['mænsɪpl] *n.* college or monastery steward.

Mancunian [mæn'kjuːnɪən] *n. & adj.* (resident or native) of Manchester.

mandala ['mændələ] *n.* Hindu or Buddhist symbol representing the universe.

mandament ['mændəmənt] *n.* command.

mandamus [mæn'deɪməs] (*Latin*) *n.* 'we command'; *Law*, Crown writ commanding performance of an action.

mandarin ['mændərɪn] *n.* higher public official of Chinese empire; chief dialect of China; small Chinese orange. **madarinate,** *n.* office, rule or body of mandarin(s). **mandarinic,** *adj.* **mandarinism,** *n.* rule by mandarins; bureaucracy.

mandat ['mɒndɑː] (*French*) *n.* order; mandate; proxy; currency bill issued during French revolution.

mandate ['mændeɪt] *n.* commission to perform act or rule for another; command; instruction, especially to political representative. **mandated,** *adj.* held or ruled under mandate. **mandatary,** *n.* holder of mandate. **mandative,** *adj.* pertaining to command. **mandatory,** *adj.* obligatory.

mandible ['mændɪbl] *n.* lower jaw; either part of bird's beak or insect's mouth parts. **mandibular** [–'dɪbjʊlə], *adj.* **mandibulate,** *adj.* having mandible.

mandil ['mændɪl] (*Arabic*) *n.* turban.

mandorla (*Italian*) *n.* any almond-shaped object or ornament, especially (in painting, sculpture) area of light surrounding the risen Christ.

mandragora [mæn'drægərə] *n.* mandrake.

mandrake ['mændreɪk] *n.* plant with large forked root, believed to aid conception.

mandrel ['mændrəl] *n.* spindle supporting work in lathe, etc.

mandriarch ['mændriɑːk] *n.* founder or head of monastic order.

mandrill ['mændrɪl] *n.* W African baboon with blue markings on face and red posterior.

manducate ['mændjukeɪt] *v.t.* masticate; eat. **manducation,** *n.* **manducatory,** *adj.*

mane ['mɑːneɪ] (*Latin*) *adv.* in the morning.

manège [mæ'neɪʒ] (*French*) *n.* horsemanship; teaching or school of horsemanship.

manent ['mænent] (*Latin*) 'they remain'.

manes ['mɑːneɪz] (*Latin*) *n. pl.* spirits of dead; ghosts.

manet ['mænet] (*Latin*) 'he (she) remains'.

mangel-wurzel ['mæŋglwɜːzl] *n.* kind of large beet.

mangold ['mæŋgəʊld] *n.* mangel-wurzel.

mangosteen ['mæŋgəstiːn] *n.* large reddish orange-like fruit of E Indies.

mangrove ['mæŋgrəʊv] *n.* tropical swamp tree with aerial roots.

manicate ['mænɪkeɪt] *adj.* having dense woolly growth which can be peeled off.

manichord ['mænɪkɔːd] n. clavichord.

maniform ['mænɪfɔːm] adj. hand-shaped.

manikin ['mænɪkɪn] n. dwarf; Medicine, anatomical model; mannequin.

manioc ['mæniɒk, 'meɪ–] n. cassava.

maniple ['mænɪpl] n. narrow embroidered band worn hanging from left arm by celebrant priest; subdivision of Roman legion consisting of 120 to 200 men.

manism ['maːnɪzm] n. belief in mana; ancestorworship.

manjak ['mændʒæk] n. kind of asphalt of Barbados.

mannequin ['mænɪkɪn] n. fashion model; tailor's dummy; lay figure.

manometer [mə'nɒmɪtə] n. instrument measuring pressure of gases, or blood-pressure. manometric(al) [–'metrɪk, –l], adj. manometry, n.

manque [mɒŋk] (French) n. bet in roulette on low numbers, from 1 to 18.

manqué ['mɒŋkeɪ] (French) adj. (fem. –ée) 'lacking'; defective; having failed to achieve ambition; falling short of hopes or expectations.

mansard ['mænsɑːd] n. kind of roof with two slopes, the upper being the less steep; garret formed within such roof.

mansuetude ['mænswɪtjuːd] n. sweetness of temper; tameness.

mantic ['mæntɪk] adj. pertaining to or having powers of prophecy or divination; divinely inspired. manticism [–sɪzm], n. divination.

manticore ['mæntɪkɔː] n. fabulous monster with man's head, lion's body and dragon's tail.

mantid ['mæntɪd] n. & adj. (pertaining to) mantis.

mantilla [mæn'tɪlə] n. light cloak, cape or veil, especially of Spain.

mantis ['mæntɪs] n. (pl. –tes) grasshopper-like insect, having forelegs folded as if in prayer.

mantissa [mæn'tɪsə] n. decimal part of logarithm.

mantistic [mæn'tɪstɪk] adj. mantic.

mantra ['mæntrə] n. sacred word or syllable.

manubrial [mæ'njuːbrɪəl] adj. handle-shaped. manubrium n. (pl. –bria) handle-shaped part.

manuduction [,mænju'dʌkʃn] n. careful guidance; leading by the hand; introduction; guide. manuductory, adj.

manuka [mə'nuːkə, 'maːnəkə] (Maori) n. bush with tea-like leaves; 'tea-tree'.

manumit [,mænju'mɪt] v.t. liberate (slave). manumission, n. manumissive, adj.

manu propria [,mænjuː 'prəʊprɪə] (Latin) 'with one's own hand'.

manustupration [,mænjuːstju'preɪʃn] n. masturbation.

maquette [mæ'ket] (French) n. rough sketch or model.

maqui(s) [mæ'kiː, 'mækiː] n. thicket of shrubs of Mediterranean coastland and central Corsica, refuge of outlaws; underground resistance movement in German-occupied France and Belgium (1940–45). maquisard [–'zaː], n. member of maquis.

marabou ['mærəbuː] n. stork-like bird; adjutant bird; its down used in millinery; thin, downy silk.

marabout ['mærəbuː, –t] n. Muslim monk, saint or hermit; shrine or grave of such.

marantic [mə'ræntɪk] adj. marasmic.

marasca [mə'ræskə] n. bitter wild cherry. maraschino [–ə'skiːnəʊ], n. liqueur distilled from juice of this.

marasmus [mə'ræzməs] n. intense emaciation due to malnutrition. marasmic, marasmous, adj. marasmoid, adj. like this.

marcasite ['maːkəsaɪt] n. crystallized iron pyrites, used in jewellery. marcasitic [–'sɪtɪk], adj.

marcescent [maː'sesnt] n. & adj. (plant with leaves) withering but remaining on plant. marcescence, n.

march [maːtʃ] n. frontier; (disputed) border area; v.i. border (on). marcher, n. inhabitant of march.

Märchen ['meəkən] (German) n. fairy or folk tale.

marcor ['maːkɔː] n. marasmus.

Mardi gras [,maːdi 'graː] (French) 'fat Tuesday'; Shrove Tuesday, a carnival day.

mare ['maːreɪ, 'mæ–, –i] n. (pl. maria ['maːrɪə, 'mæ–]) huge dark-coloured plain on the moon, formerly thought to be a sea. mare clausum ['klɔːsəm, 'klaʊ–] (Latin) 'closed sea'; territorial waters. mare liberum [–'lɪbərəm, 'laɪ–], 'open sea'; sea outside territorial waters. mare nostrum [–'nɒstrəm], 'our sea'; Roman name for Mediterranean.

maremma [mə'remə] (Italian) n. (pl. –me) marsh; landes; miasma. maremmatic, adj.

margaritaceous [,maːgərɪ'teɪʃəs] adj. pearllike. margaritiferous, adj. yielding pearls.

margin ['maːdʒɪn] n. Commercial, deposit of cash held by broker as security or instalment of purchase price; amount remaining to, or to be paid by, client at termination of account; profit; minimum return required for profitability. marginal, adj. marginal utility, Economics, minimum usefulness that will cause production of commodity, etc., to continue.

marginalia [,maːdʒɪ'neɪlɪə] (Latin) n. pl. notes in margin.

margrave ['maːgreɪv] (German) n. title of nobility, equivalent of marquess. margravial, adj. margraviate, n. jurisdiction of margrave. margravine, n. margrave's wife or woman having power of margrave.

maricolous [mə'rɪkələs] adj. inhabiting the sea.

marigenous, adj. produced by or in sea.

marigraph ['mær–], n. tide gauge.

marimba [mə'rɪmbə] n. kind of xylophone.

marinade [,mærɪ'neɪd] n. mixture, typically of oil, wine and vinegar with herbs and spices, in which meat, fish, etc. is steeped before cooking; food so steeped; v.t. steep in such mixture.

marinate ['mærɪneɪt] v.t. marinade.

Mariolater [,meəri'ɒlətə] n. worshipper of the Virgin Mary. mariolatrous, adj. mariolatry, n.

marital ['mærɪtl] adj. connubial; pertaining to husband. maritality, n. excessive fondness for husband.

markhor ['maːkɔː] n. wild goat of NW India.

marline ['maːlɪn] n. line of two loosely twisted strands.

marlinspike, marlinespike ['maːlɪnspaɪk] n. pointed tool used to separate strands of rope and for other purposes.

marmarize ['maːməraɪz] v.t. transform into marble. marmarosis, n.

marmoreal [mɑː'mɔːriəl] *adj.* pertaining to or like marble. **marmaraceous,** *adj.* **marmorate,** *adj.* veined like marble. **marmoric,** *adj.* pertaining to marble.

marmot ['mɑːmət] *n.* squirrel-like rodent of Pyrenees and Alps; woodchuck.

marque [mɑːk] *n.* (emblem of) brand, make; taking possession of object as pledge or reprisal. **letters of marque,** authorisation by Crown of seizure of foreign goods, etc., as reprisal; privateer's commission.

marquetry ['mɑːkɪtri] *n.* art of inlaying; inlaid work.

marrano [mə'rɑːnəʊ] (*Spanish*) *n.* Jew converted to Christianity, especially merely to evade persecution. **marranize,** *v.t.* **marranism,** *n.*

marron ['mærən] (*French*) *n.* chestnut. **marrons glacés** [–'glæseɪ], chestnuts preserved or coated with sugar.

marsala [mɑː'sɑːlə] *n.* sweet dark dessert wine of Sicily.

marsupium [mɑː'suːpiəm] *n.* (*pl.* **–ia**) pouch of skin in which marsupial carries young.

martello tower [mɑː'teləʊ] *n.* small round coastal-defence fort.

marten ['mɑːtɪn] *n.* large weasel-like animal, with fine fur; its fur, called sable. **pine-marten,** marten of European pine woods; American sable. **stone-marten,** marten of European beech woods.

martinet [,mɑːtɪ'net] *n.* strict enforcer of discipline.

martingale ['mɑːtɪŋgeɪl] *n.* check-rein holding horse's head down; betting system, especially of doubling stakes.

martlet ['mɑːtlət] *n.* martin (bird); *Heraldry,* footless, beakless bird, denoting fourth son.

martyrolatry [,mɑːtə'rɒlətri] *n.* excessive veneration of martyrs. **martyrology,** *n.* study of, treatise on, or list of, martyrs. **martyry,** *n.* shrine.

mascle ['mæskl] *n.* diamond-shaped scale or plate; *Heraldry,* lozenge with lozenge-shaped opening in centre. **mascled,** *adj.* covered with mascles.

maser ['meɪzə] *n.* intensely concentrated beam of coherent microwaves; device for producing such beam. *abbreviation* of Microwave Amplification by Stimulated Emission of Radiation.

mashie ['mæʃi] *n.* broad-bladed iron golf club. **mashie niblick,** club with head partaking of both mashie and niblick.

masjid ['mʌsdʒɪd] *n.* mosque.

masseter [mə'siːtə] *n.* muscle raising lower jaw.

massif ['mæsɪf, mæ'siːf] *n.* main mountain group or region.

massotherapy [,mæsə'θerəpi] *n.* medical treatment by massage.

mastaba, mastabah ['mæstəbə] *n.* structure originally of mud bricks above tombs of earlier dynasties in ancient Egypt.

mastectomy [mæ'stektəmi] *n.* surgical removal of a breast.

mastic ['mæstɪk] *n.* resin of S European tree, used in varnishes, etc.; any sticky paste.

mastigophoric [,mæstɪgə'fɒrɪk] *adj.* carrying a whip.

mastitis [mæ'staɪtɪs] *n.* inflammation of breast or milk gland.

mastodon ['mæstədən] *n.* extinct elephant-like animal.

mastoid ['mæstɔɪd] *adj.* nipple- or breast-like; denoting such bony outgrowth behind ear. **mastoidectomy,** *n.* operation to remove mastoid bone. **mastoiditis,** *n.* inflammation of mastoid cells. **mastoidotomy,** *n.* surgical incision into mastoid.

mastology [mæ'stɒlədʒi] *n.* mammalogy.

matara(h) ['mætərə] (*Arabic*) *n.* water-bottle or -skin.

maté ['mæteɪ, 'mɑːt–] *n.* Paraguay tea (plant and beverage).

matelassé [mæt'lɑːseɪ] (*French*) *adj.* with quilting-like ornamentation.

Mater dolorosa [,meɪtə ,dɒlə'rəʊsə, ,mɑː–] (*Latin*) 'sorrowing mother'; the Virgin Mary.

materfamilias [,meɪtəfə'mɪliæs] *n.* (*pl.* **matresfamilias** [,meɪtreɪz–]) mother or female head of family.

materia [mə'tɪəriə] (*Latin*) *n.* matter. **materia ex qua,** material out of which (something is made). **materia in qua,** material in which (something subsists). **materia medica,** study of medical remedies.

matériel, materiel [mə,tɪəri'el] *n.* equipment and materials used in an operation (especially military).

mathesis [mə'θiːsɪs] *n.* learning; wisdom; mathematics. **mathetic** [–'θetɪk], *adj.*

matin ['mætɪn] *adj.* pertaining to morning. **matinal,** *adj.* **matins,** *n.* morning prayer.

matrass, mattrass ['mætræs] *n.* long-necked round-bodied chemical flask; closed glass tube.

matriarch ['meɪtriɑːk] *n.* women ruling family or group. **matriarchal,** *adj.* **matriarchate,** *n.* **matriarchy,** *n.* inheritance in female line; society dominated by women.

matric(al) ['meɪtrɪk, 'mætrɪkl] *adj.* pertaining to matrix or womb.

matricide ['meɪtrɪsaɪd] *n.* killing or killer of own mother. **matricidal,** *adj.*

matriclinous [,meɪtrɪ'klaɪnəs, ,mæ–] *adj.* showing inherited characteristics of the female parent. **matricliny,** *n.*

matricular [mæ'trɪkjʊlə] *adj.* matric.

matriculate [mə'trɪkjuleɪt] *v.i.* & *t.* admit, or obtain admission by passing examination, to university as student. **matriculant,** *n.* matriculating student. **matriculation,** *n.* act of matriculating; examination necessary to matriculate. **matriculatory,** *adj.*

matriherital [,meɪtrɪ'herɪtl, ,mæ–] *adj.* pertaining to inheritance in female line. **matrilineal,** *adj.* tracing descent in female line. **matrilocal,** *adj.* pertaining to marriage in which husband goes to reside with wife and her family. **matripotestal,** *adj.* pertaining to mother's power.

matrix ['meɪtrɪks] *n.* (*pl.* **–ices**) womb; mould for casting; cement.

matroclinous [,meɪtrə'klaɪnəs, ,mæ–] *adj.* matriclinous.

mattock ['mætək] *n.* pick-like digging tool.

mattoid ['mætɔɪd] *n.* congenital idiot.

maturate ['mætjʊreɪt] *v.i.* & *t.* become mature or ripe; cause to suppurate. **maturation,** *n.* **maturative,** *adj.*

maturescent [,mætjʊ'resnt] *adj.* becoming mature. **maturescence,** *n.*

matutinal [,mætjuː'taɪnl, mə'tjuːtɪnl] *adj.* pertaining to or occurring in morning.

maudlin ['mɔːdlɪn] *n.* sentimental; tearful, especially when drunk.

maugre, mauger ['mɔːgə] *prep. archaic* in spite of.

maulstick ['mɔːlstɪk] *n.* painter's stick for steadying the hand.

maund [mɔːnd] *n.* measure of weight in Asia, equivalent of from 25 to 82 lbs.

maundy ['mɔːndi] *n. originally*, ceremony of washing of feet of poor by sovereign; *modern*, alms-giving by sovereign in its stead. **Maundy money**, such alms. **Maundy Thursday,** Thursday before Easter, on which the ceremony was performed and the money is distributed.

mausoleum [,mɔːsə'liːəm] *n.* monumental tomb, especially elaborate. **mausolean,** *adj.*

mauvais ['məʊveɪ] (*French*) *adj.* (*fem.* **-se**) bad; wicked. **mauvaise foi,** 'bad faith'. **mauvais quart d'heure,** brief bad or embarrassing experience. **mauvais sujet** [-'suːʒeɪ], 'bad or wicked subject' or person.

mavis ['meɪvɪs] *n.* song- or misselthrush.

maxilla [mæk'sɪlə] *n.* (*pl.* **-ae**) jawbone, especially bearing upper molars and canines. **maxillary** ['mæks–], *adj.*

maximalism ['mæksɪməlɪzm] *n.* uncompromising adherence to maximum demands, as in trade dispute, etc. **maximalist,** *n.* radical; extremist.

maxwell ['mækswəl] *n.* unit of magnetic flux.

maya ['maɪə, 'mɑːjə] (*Hindu*) *n.* magic; creative power of universe; God's power of manifestation.

mayhem ['meɪhem] *n. Law*, maiming; violent confusion.

mazarine [,mæzə'riːn] *n.* & *adj.* (of) reddish-blue hue.

mazurka [mə'zɜːkə] *n.* Polish dance in slow waltz time.

mazzard ['mæzəd] *n.* wild sweet cherry; *archaic*, head.

meable ['miːəbl] *adj.* easily penetrable.

mea culpa [,meɪə 'kʊlpə] (*Latin*) 'my fault'.

mead [miːd] *n.* strong drink of fermented honey and water.

meatus [mi'eɪtəs] *n.* passage of the body. **meatal,** *adj.*

mechanolater [,mekə'nɒlətə] *n.* worshipper of machines. **mechanomorphic,** *adj.* having form of machine. **mechanotherapy,** *n.* medical treatment by mechanical means.

mecometer [mɪ'kɒmɪtə] *n.* length-measuring instrument. **mecometry,** *n.*

meconium [mɪ'kəʊniəm] *n.* mucoid substance in new-born baby's intestines, excreted as first faeces.

meconology [,miːkə'nɒlədʒi] *n.* treatise on opium. **meconophagist,** *n.* consumer of opium.

médaillon [me'daɪɒn] (*French*) *n.* round thin slice of meat, vegetable, etc.

meden agan [,meɪden æ'gɑːn] (*Greek*) 'nothing too much'; the golden mean.

medianic [,miːdi'ænɪk] *adj.* pertaining to spiritualist medium, or prophet. **medianimic,** *adj.* **medianimity, medianity,** *n.*

mediastinum [,miːdiə'staɪnəm] *n.* (*pl.* **-na**) chest cavity containing heart. **mediastinal,** *adj.* **mediastinitis,** *n.* inflammation of tissue enclosing organs in mediastinum.

medicaster [,medɪ'kæstə] *n.* quack doctor.

medlar ['medlə] *n.* crab-apple-like fruit and tree.

medresseh [me'dreseɪ] *n.* madrasah.

medulla [me'dʌlə] *n.* marrow or pith. **medulla oblongata,** posterior part of brain joining it to spinal cord. **medulla spinalis,** spinal cord. **medullose, medullary,** *adj.*

meerkat ['mɪəkæt] *n.* S African mongoose-like animal; suricate.

meerschaum ['mɪəʃəm] *n.* white fine clayey silicate of magnesium; smoking pipe made or partly made of this.

megacephalic [,megəsə'fælɪk] *adj.* having large head. **megacephaly,** *n.*

megaceros [me'gæsərəs] *n.* extinct giant deer; Irish elk.

megachiropteran [,megəkaɪə'rɒptərən] *n.* & *adj.* (pertaining to a) fruit bat. **megachiropterous,** *adj.*

megadeath ['megədeθ] *n.* million fatalities, used in estimating consequences of a nuclear attack.

megadont ['megədɒnt] *adj.* having large teeth.

megalith ['megalɪθ] *n.* any large prehistoric stone monument. **megalithic,** *adj.*

megalocyte ['megələsaɪt] *n.* macrocyte.

megalomania [,megələ'meɪniə] *n.* form of insanity in which patient believes him- or herself to be person of great importance; mania for doing grand actions. **megalomaniac,** *n.* **megalomaniacal,** [-'aɪəkl], *adj.*

megalophonous [,megə'lɒfənəs] *adj.* high-sounding; having loud voice. **megalophonic** [-ə'fɒnɪk], *adj.*

megalophthalmus [,megələf'θælməs] *n.* state of having large eyes. **megalopic** [-'lɒpɪk], *adj.* large-eyed; pertaining to megalops.

megalopolis [,megə'lɒpəlɪs] *n.* vast city. **megalopolitan** [-'pɒlɪtən], *adj.*

megalops ['megəlɒps] *n.* larval stage of crab.

megalosaur(us) ['megələsɔː, -'sɔːrəs] *n.* huge carnivorous dinosaur. **megalosaurian, megalosauroid,** *adj.*

megameter [me'gæmɪtə] *n.* instrument for finding longitude from stellar observations.

megapod ['megəpɒd] *adj.* having large feet. **megapode** *n.* such bird of Australasia, as jungle fowl, brush turkey, etc.

megaprosopous [,megə'prɒsəpəs] *adj.* having large face.

megapterine [me'gæptəraɪn, -rɪn] *n.* & *adj.* (pertaining to a) humpback whale.

megascope ['megəskəʊp] *n.* magnifying magic lantern. **megascopic** [-'skɒpɪk], *adj.* magnified; macroscopic.

megaseism ['megəsaɪzm] *n.* macroseism.

megatherium [,megə'θɪəriəm] *n.* fossil sloth-like animal. **megathere,** *n.* **megatherian, megatherine, megatherioid,** *adj.*

megatherm ['megəθɜːm] *n.* plant thriving only in tropical heat and moisture. **megathermic,** *adj.*

megaton ['megətʌn] *n.* measure of explosive force of atomic and hydrogen bombs, equal to that of 1 million tons of T.N.T.

megohm ['megəʊm] *n.* electrical unit, equivalent of one million ohms.

megrim ['miːgrɪm] *n.* migraine; whim. **megrims,** *n.pl.* low spirits.

mehari [mə'hɑːri] *n.* racing dromedary. **meharist,** *n.* soldier riding one.

meinie, meiny ['meɪni] *n.* household, retinue.

meiosis [maɪ'əʊsɪs] *n.* litotes; misrepresentation

of thing as being less than its actual size or importance; *Biology*, nuclear division with halving of chromosome number. **meiotic** [–'ɒtɪk], *adj*.

mekometer [mɪ'kɒmɪtə] *n*. kind of range-finder.

melaena [mɪ'liːnə] *n*. black vomit or bowel discharge. **melaenic**, *adj*.

melalgia [mɪ'lældʒɪə] *n*. pain in limbs.

melampodium [ˌmelæm'pəʊdɪəm] *n*. Christmas rose.

mélange [meɪ'lɑːnʒ] (*French*) *n*. mixture.

melanin ['melənɪn] *n*. dark or black pigment of body. **melanian** [–'eɪnɪən], **melanic** [–'lænɪk], *adj*. dark-skinned. **melaniferous**, *adj*. containing melanin. **melanism**, *n*. abnormal blackness of skin or plumage; extreme darkness of complexion and hair. **melano**, *n*. person or animal having unnaturally dark pigmentation. **melanocomous**, **melanotrichous**, *adj*. dark-haired. **melanoderma**, **melanodermia**, *n*. abnormal blackness of skin. **melanoid**, *adj*. **melanoma**, *n*. tumour made up of dark-pigmented cells. **melanopathy**, **melanosis**, *n*. disease marked by deposition of melanin in tissues. **melanous**, *adj*. with black hair and skin.

melasma [mɪ'læzmə] *n*. dark patch of skin.

meldometer [mel'dɒmɪtə] *n*. instrument for finding melting points.

meleagrine [ˌmeli'ægraɪn, –rɪn] *adj*. pertaining to or like a turkey; belonging to turkey genus of birds.

mêlée ['meleɪ] *n*. confused fight; struggling crowd.

melic ['melɪk] *adj*. pertaining to song; lyric; *n*. such poetry, especially of ancient Greece.

meliceris, **melicera** [ˌmelɪ'sɪərɪs] *n*. tumour or exudation of honey-like matter. **meliceric**, **melicerous**, *adj*.

melichrous ['melɪkrəs] *adj*. honey-coloured.

melinite ['melɪnaɪt] *n*. explosive resembling lyddite.

meliorism ['miːlɪərɪzm] *n*. belief that world and humankind tend to grow better. **meliorist**, *n*. **melioristic**, *adj*. **meliority**, *n*. improved state.

meliphagous [me'lɪfəgəs] *adj*. feeding on honey.

melisma [me'lɪzmə] *n*. (*pl*. **–ta**) melody; song; melodic ornamentation. **melismatic** [–'mætɪk], *adj*. in florid style, especially of singing one syllable on a number of notes. **melismatics**, *n*. such florid singing.

melitaemia, **melithaemia** [ˌmelɪ'tiːmɪə] *n*. presence of excess of sugar in blood.

melittology [ˌmelɪ'tɒlədʒɪ] *n*. study of bees. **melittologist**, *n*.

melituria [ˌmelɪ'tjurɪə] *n*. sugar diabetes. **melituric**, *adj*.

mellaginous [me'lædʒɪnəs] *adj*. pertaining to or like honey. **melleous**, *adj*. like or containing honey.

mellifluent, **mellifluous** [me'lɪfluənt, –əs] *adj*. sweet-sounding; flowing with honey. **melliferous**, *adj*. honey-producing. **mellisonant**, *adj*. sweet-sounding. **mellivorous**, *adj*. eating honey.

melologue ['melalɒg] *n*. recitation with musical accompaniment. **melomania**, *n*. mania for music.

melongena [ˌmelən'dʒiːnə] *n*. egg-plant.

melophonic [ˌmelə'fɒnɪk] *adj*. pertaining to music. **melopoeia** [–'piːə], *n*. composition of music.

melton ['meltən] *n*. short-napped woollen tailoring material. **meltonian** [–'təʊnɪən], *adj*. pertaining to Melton Mowbray, Leicestershire, and its hunting; hunter.

memento mori [mɪ,mentəʊ 'mɒri] (*Latin*) 'remember you must die'; *n*. reminder of death, or of shortness of life.

memorabilia [ˌmemərə'bɪlɪə] (*Latin*) *n*. *pl*. memorable things; records.

memoriter [me'mɒrɪtə] (*Latin*) *adv*. from memory; by heart.

memsahib ['memsɑːb] (*Indian*) *n*. title of respect for white women; madam.

ménage [me'nɑːʒ] (*French*) *n*. household; art of housekeeping. **ménage à trois** (menaz a trwa), household consisting of married couple and the lover of either.

menald ['menld] *adj*. speckled.

menarche [me'nɑːki] *n*. first appearance of menses.

mendacious [men'deɪʃəs] *adj*. telling lies, especially habitually. **mendacity** [–'dæsəti], *n*.

Mendelian [men'diːlɪən] *adj*. pertaining to Gregor Mendel, and his theory of inheritance; *n*. believer in his theory. **Mendelism** ['mendl–ɪzm], *n*.

mendicant ['mendɪkənt] *n*. beggar; *adj*. begging. **mendicity** [–'dɪsəti], **mendicancy**, *n*.

menhir ['menhɪə] *n*. upright monolith.

meninges [me'nɪndʒiːz] *n*. *pl*. membranes enclosing brain. **meningeal**, **meningic**, *adj*. **meningitis**, *n*. inflammation of meninges.

The media are ... or is?

Most English nouns clearly take either a singular or a plural verb (*a dog is; dogs are*). But some can do both. Collective nouns behave like this: if they are used to denote an entire entity they take a singular verb, but if one has the individual members in mind they take a plural verb (*the committee is/are*). (See **A clutch of collectives**.)

There are some nouns that have a plural ending but can also take a singular verb (*The barracks has/have been demolished; Where is/are your headquarters?*). Some of them have Latin plural endings, and these can cause problems: *data, media, strata*. Purists say that these should be used only with a plural verb. But uses such as

Your data is inconclusive and *The media distorts the truth* are now very well established (*They come from every strata of society* perhaps less so). Apparently similar is the case of the Greek plural ending in *criteria* and *phenomena* which are often treated in English as if they were singular. But in fact this is a slightly different phenomenon; these words appear to have been genuinely misapprehended as fully countable singulars (*a criteria, a phenomena*) with even the possibility of being pluralized (*criterias, phenomenas*) whereas *data* and *media* are more collective singulars – one would be unlikely to encounter *a data* or *a media*.

meniscus [mə'nɪskəs] *n.* (*pl.* **-ci**) crescent-shaped object, especially cartilage of knee; concavo-convex lens; curved surface of liquid in a tube. **meniscal, meniscate, meniscoid,** *adj.* **menisciform,** *adj.* shaped like meniscus. **meniscitis,** *n.* inflammation of meniscus of knee.

menology [me'nɒlədʒi] *n.* calendar of months; calendar of saints' days.

menorrhagia [,menə'reɪdʒiə] *n.* excessive bleeding during menstruation. **menhorrhoea** [,menə'riːə], *n.* normal menstrual bleeding. **menoschesis,** *n.* temporary suppression of menstruation. **menostaxis** [,menə'stæksɪs], *n.* abnormally long period.

mensal ['mensl] *adj.* pertaining to or for table; monthly.

menses ['mensiːz] *n. pl.* monthly discharge of blood, etc., from womb.

mens rea [,menz 'riːə] *n.* criminal intent, knowledge that an act is wrong.

menstruum ['menstruəm] *adj.* (*pl.* **-ua**) solvent.

mensual ['mensjuəl] *adj.* pertaining to month; monthly.

mensuration [,mensjə'reɪʃn] *n.* calculation of measurements. **mensurable,** *adj.* measurable; *Music,* rhythmic; composed in first ancient form of notation. **mensurative,** *adj.* of use in measuring.

mentation [men'teɪʃn] *n.* cerebration. **mentiferous,** *adj.* telepathic.

mentor ['mentɔː] *n.* adviser; teacher. **mentorial,** *adj.*

mepacrine ['mepəkriːn, –ɪn] *n.* synthetic anti-malarial drug formerly called atebrin.

mephitis [mɪ'faɪtɪs] *n.* foul exhalation from earth; stink. **mephitic** [–'fɪtɪk], *adj.* **mephitic air,** air devoid of oxygen. **mephitism,** *n.* poisoning by mephitis.

meralgia [mə'rældʒiə] *n.* neuralgia of thigh.

mercantile ['mɜːkəntaɪl] *adj.* pertaining to trading and merchants. **mercantile system,** economic or political system aiming at increase in national strength through trade. **mercantilism,** *n.* commercial practice; practice of mercantile system. **mercantility,** *n.*

mercer ['mɜːsə] *n.* dealer in textiles. **mercerize,** *v.t.* make stronger and lustrous by treating with caustic alkali. **mercery,** *n.*

mercurial [mɜː'kjuəriəl] *adj.* pertaining to or containing mercury; lively in mind; volatile. **mercurous,** *adj.* pertaining to mercury.

merdivorous [mɜː'dɪvərəs] *adj.* eating dung.

meretricious [,merɪ'trɪʃəs] *adj.* superficially attractive or ornamented; gaudy; pertaining to prostitution. **meretrix,** *n.* (*pl.* **-rices**) prostitute.

merganser [mɜː'gænsə] *n.* hooked-billed crested duck.

meridian [mə'rɪdiən] *n.* highest point; *Geography,* circle passing through both poles and any given place; *adj.* pertaining to midday or zenith. **meridional,** *adj.* pertaining to meridian; southern.

merino [mə'riːnəʊ] *n.* breed of heavy-fleeced white sheep, especially of Australia.

merisis ['merəsɪs] *n. Biology,* growth by cell division. **merismatic.** *adj.* dividing into segments by internal partitions. **meristem,** *n.* embryonic plant tissue capable of growth by division. **meristic,** *adj.* divided into segments; pertaining to number or variation of body parts.

merkin ['mɜːkɪn] *n.* pubic wig.

merlon ['mɜːlən] *n.* narrow wall between embrasures in battlements.

merogenesis [,merəʊ'dʒenəsɪs] *n.* segmentation. **merogenetic,** *adj.* **merogony,** *n.* growth of embryo from part of egg. **meromorphic,** *adj.* fractional. **meropia,** *n.* partial blindness.

mesa ['meɪsə] *n.* flat-topped steep-sided mountain.

mésalliance [me'zæliəns] (*French*) *n.* mistaken marriage; marriage into lower social class.

mescalin ['meskəlɪn] *n.* crystalline alkaloid extracted from a Mexican cactus producing hallucinations when taken as a drug.

mesencephalon [,mesen'sefəlɒn] *n.* midbrain. **mesencephalic** [–sɪ'fælɪk], *adj.*

mesentery ['mesntəri] *n.* membrane enclosing intestines. **mesenterial** [–'tɪəriəl], **mesenteric** [–'terɪk], *adj.* **mesenteritis,** *n.* inflammation of mesentery

mesial ['miːziəl] *adj.* middle. **mesiad,** *adv.* towards the middle.

mesic ['miːzɪk] *adj.* adapted to conditions with a balanced supply of moisture.

mesocardia [,mesəʊ'kɑːdiə, ,miː–] *n.* placing of heart in middle of thorax.

mesocephalic [,mesəʊsɪ'fælɪk, ,miː–] *adj.* having medium-sized head. **mesocephalus** [–'sefələs], *n.* (*pl.* **-li**) such person.

mesochroic [,mesə'krəʊɪk, ,miː–] *adj.* having colour of skin midway between light and dark races.

mesode ['mesəʊd] *n.* part of ode between strophe and antistrophe.

mesodont ['mesədɒnt, 'miː–] *adj.* with teeth of medium size.

mesognathism [me'sɒgnəθɪzm, mɪ–] *n.* state of having jaws of medium size. **mesognathic** [–'næθɪk], **mesognathous,** *adj.*

mesology [me'sɒlədʒi, miː–] *n.* ecology.

mesomorph ['miːsəmɔːf] *n.* psychophysical type showing predominance of muscle, bone and connective tissue, often aggressive and self-assertive. **mesomorphic,** *adj.* **mesomorphy,** *n.*

meson ['miːsɒn] *n.* unstable subatomic particle with a mass between that of an electron and a photon, found in cosmic radiation.

mesoprosopic [,mesəprə'səʊpɪk, ,miː–] *adj.* with face of medium width.

mesotherm ['mesəθɜːm, 'miː–] *n.* plant thriving only in moderate temperature.

mesquite [me'skiːt] *n.* prickly shrub, forming thickets, of Mexico and SW United States.

messuage ['mesjuɪdʒ] *n.* house with its land and outbuildings.

mestizo [me'stiːzəʊ] (*Spanish*) *n.* half-breed.

metabasis [me'tæbəsɪs] *n.* transition; transfer. **metabatic** [–'bætɪk], *adj.*

metabiosis [,metəbaɪ'əʊsɪs] *n.* reliance by an organism on another to produce favourable environment; change due to external agency. **metabiotic** [–'ɒtɪk], *adj.*

metabolism [mə'tæbəlɪzm] *n.* continuous process of chemical change in cells, with assimilation of foodstuffs and release of energy. **metabolic** [–'bɒlɪk], *adj.* **metabolize,** *v.i.* & *t.* perform or subject to metabolism. **metabolite,** *n.* product of metabolism.

metacarpus [ˌmetəˈkɑːpəs] *n.* hand between wrist and base of fingers. **metacarpal**, *adj.*; *n.* bone of the metacarpus.

metachemistry [ˌmetəˈkemɪstri] *n.* speculative or theoretical, or subatomic, chemistry.

metachromatism [ˌmetəˈkrəʊmətɪzm] *n.* change of colour.

metachronism [meˈtækrənɪzm] *n.* anachronism dating thing later than its correct date.

metachrosis [ˌmetəˈkrəʊsɪs] *n.* ability to change colour voluntarily.

metage [ˈmiːtɪdʒ] *n.* official measurement; fee paid for this.

metageometry [ˌmetədʒiˈɒmɪtri] *n.* non-Euclidean geometry.

metagnomy [meˈtægnəmi] *n.* divination.

metagnostic [ˌmetægˈnɒstɪk] *adj.* beyond understanding.

metagraphy [meˈtægrəfi] *n.* transliteration.

metalanguage [ˈmetəˌlæŋgwɪdʒ] *n.* language or symbols used to describe, classify etc. (another) language or set of symbols.

metalepsis [ˌmetəˈlepsɪs] *n.* rhetorical device of changing figurative sense by metonymy. **metaleptic(al)**, *adj.*; *Medicine*, applied to muscle associated with others in action.

metallogeny [ˌmetəˈlɒdʒəni] *n.* study of origin of ores. **metallogenic** [-ˈdʒenɪk], **metallogenetic** [-dʒəˈnetɪk], *adj.*

metallography [ˌmetəˈlɒgrəfi] *n.* study of structure of metals and alloys. **metallographist**, *n.*

metallurgy [meˈtælədʒi] *n.* art of extracting and refining metals. **metallurgical** [-ˈlɜːdʒɪkl], *adj.* **metallurgist**, *n.*

metameric [ˌmetəˈmerɪk] *adj.* pertaining to serial segmentation of body; isomeric. **metamerism** [-ˈtæmərɪzm], **metamery**, *n.* **metamerous** [-ˈtæmərəs], *adj.*

metamorphic [ˌmetəˈmɔːfɪk] *adj.* changing in form; *Geology*, changing or changed in composition, especially to more solid and crystalline form. **metamorphism**, *n.*

metamorphose [ˌmetəˈmɔːfəʊz] *v.i. & t.* transform or be transformed. **metamorphotic**, **metamorphous**, *adj.* **metamorphosis**, *n.* (*pl.* **-ses**) complete transformation.

metanoia [ˌmetəˈnɔɪə] *n.* penitence; spiritual conversion.

metaphony [meˈtæfəni] *n.* umlaut. **metaphonic(al)**, *adj.* **metaphonize**, *v.t.*

metaphrase [ˈmetəfreɪz] *n.* literal translation; *v.t.* translate literally; paraphrase. **metaphrast**, *n.* person putting verse into different metre, or prose into verse. **metaphrastic**, *adj.*

metaphysics [ˌmetəˈfɪzɪks] *n.* philosophical study of first principles, such as being, the nature of reality, etc.; ontology; any abstract or abstruse philosophical study. **metaphysical**, *adj.* **metaphysician**, *n.*

metaphysis [meˈtæfəsɪs] *n.* metamorphosis. **metaphyseal** [-ˈfɪziəl], *adj.*

metaplasia [ˌmetəˈpleɪʒiə] *n.* change of one kind of tissue into another.

metaplasm [ˈmetəplæzm] *n.* lifeless matter in cell; *Grammar*, alteration in spelling of word. **metaplastic**, *adj.* pertaining to metaplasm or metaplasia.

metapolitics [ˌmetəˈpɒlətɪks] *n.* theoretical political study. **metapolitical** [-ˈlɪtɪkl], *adj.* **metapolitician** [-ˈtɪʃn], *n.*

metapsychical [ˌmetəˈsaɪkɪkl] *adj.* beyond, or unexplainable by, psychology; spiritualistic. **metapsychology**, *n.* speculative psychological theory. **metapsychosis**, *n.* telepathy.

metasomatosis [ˌmetəsəʊməˈtəʊsɪs] *n. Geology*, chemical metamorphism. **metasomasis** [-ˈsɒməsɪs], **metasomatism**, *n.* **metasomatic** [-ˈmætɪk], *adj.*

metastasis [meˈtæstəsɪs] *n. Rhetoric*, change of subject; movement to another part of body of agent causing disease; *archaic*, metabolism. **metastasize**, *v.i.* **metastatic**, *adj.*

metasthenic [ˌmetəˈsθenɪk] *adj* having strong hindquarters.

metastrophe [meˈtæstrəfi] *n.* mutual exchange. **metastrophic** [-ˈstrɒfɪk], *adj.*

metatarsus [ˌmetəˈtɑːsəs] *n.* foot between ankle and base of toes; instep. **metatarsal**, *adj.*; *n.* bone of metatarsus.

metathesis [meˈtæθəsɪs] *n.* (*pl.* **-ses**) transposition of letters or sounds in a word. **metathesize**, *v.t.* **metathetic(al)** [-ˈθetɪk, -l], *adj.*

métayer [meˈteɪə, ˌmeteɪˈeɪ] (*French*) *n.* person doing agricultural work for a share of the yield. **métayage** [-ɪdʒ, -ˈjɑːʒ], *n.* such system.

metazoa [ˌmetəˈzəʊə] *n.* pl. (*sing.* **-zoon**) all animals except protozoa. **metazoal**, **metazoic**, *adj.* **metazoan**, *n. & adj.*

metel [ˈmiːtel] *n.* thorn apple.

metempiric [ˌmetemˈpɪrɪk] *adj.* transcending but associated with empirical knowledge. **metempiricism** [-sɪzm], *n.* **metempirics**, *n.* study of metempiric ideas.

metempsychosis [ˌmetemsaɪˈkəʊsɪs, -mp-] *n.* (*pl.* **-ses**) passage of soul into another body at death. **metempsychose**, *v.t.* transfer a soul.

metemptosis [ˌmetempˈtəʊsɪs] *n.* omission of day from calendar (as of intercalary day once in 134 years) to correct date of new moon.

metensomatosis [ˌmetensəʊməˈtəʊsɪs] *n.* passage into another body of soul after or before death.

methadone [ˈmeθədəʊn] *n.* synthetic pain-relieving drug, slightly more potent than morphine.

metheglin [meˈθeglɪn] *n.* mead.

métier [ˈmetieɪ] (*French*) *n.* profession; vocation; forte.

métis [meɪˈtiːs, -iː] (*French*) *n.* (*fem.* **-sse**) half-breed.

metonymy [meˈtɒnəmi] *n.* figurative use of a word for another closely associated with it, especially of attribute for its subject (as *the crown* for *the sovereign* or *monarchy*). **metonymical** [-ˈnɪmɪkl], **mentonymous**, *adj.*

metopic [meˈtɒpɪk] *adj.* pertaining to forehead. **metopomancy** [ˈmet-], *n.* divination by face or forehead.

metritis [mɪˈtraɪtɪs] *n.* inflammation of womb.

metrology [mɪˈtrɒlədʒi] *n.* study of weights and measures. **metrological**, *adj.* **metrologist**, **metrologue**, *n.*

metromania [ˌmetrəʊˈmeɪniə] *n.* mania for composing verse. **metromaniac**, *n.*

metronome [ˈmetrənəʊm] *n.* adjustable pendulum marking musical tempo. **metronomic** [-'nɒmɪk], *adj.*

metronymic [,metrə'nɪmɪk, ,miː–] *n. & adj.* (name) derived from mother's or ancestress's name; pertaining to descent in the female line. **metronymy** [–'trɒnəmɪ], *n.* metronymic usage.

metropolis [mə'trɒpəlɪs] *n.* capital city; see of metropolitan. **metropolitan** [–'pɒlɪtən], *adj.* pertaining to metropolis; *n.* archbishop or bishop of ecclesiastical province. **metropolitanate**, *n.* jurisdiction or see of metropolitan. **metropolite** [–'trɒpəlaɪt], *n.* metropolitan.

meubles ['mɜːblə] (*French*) *n. pl.* 'movables'; furniture. **meublé**]] [–leɪ], *adj.* furnished.

meum et tuum ['meɪəm et 'tuːəm] (*Latin*) 'mine and thine'.

meunière [,mɜːni'eə] (*French*) *adj.* (of fish) coated with flour, fried in butter and served with a butter, lemon and parsley sauce.

meuse [mjuːz] *n.* gap through which wild animal's track passes.

mezereon [mə'zɪərɪən] *n.* small purple-flowered shrub. **mezereum**, *n.* its bark used in medicine.

mezuzah [mə'zuzə] *n.* (*pl.* –zuzahs, –zuzoth) (metal case containing) a piece of parchment inscribed with Biblical texts, attached to the doorpost in Jewish homes.

mezzanine ['metsəniːn] *n.* storey between two others, especially between ground and first floor; such storey not extending throughout building.

mezzo-relievo [,metzəʊ-rɪ'liːvəʊ, –rɪl'jeɪv–] *n.* (carving in) relief between alto-relievo and bas-relief.

mezzotint ['metzəʊtɪnt] *n.* engraving on roughened metal, which is smoothed and polished to produce light and shade.

mho [məʊ] *n.* unit of electrical conductance, opposite of ohm.

miamia ['maɪəmaɪə, 'maɪmaɪ] *n.* Australian aborigine's hut.

miasma [maɪ'æzmə] *n.* (*pl.* –mas or –mata) noxious exhalation from swamps, etc.; any such exhalation or atmosphere. **miasmal, miasmous, miasmatic,** *adj.*

mi-carême [,miː–kæ'reɪm, –'rem] (*French*) *n.* Sunday in mid-Lent, a festival day.

MICR *abbreviation* of Magnetic Ink Character Readers (letters and figures readable by a computer, as on cheque forms)

micrander [maɪ'krændə] *n.* dwarf male plant. **micrandrous,** *adj.*

microbiology [,maɪkrəʊ–baɪ'ɒlədʒi] *n.* study of micro-organisms and their effects on humans. **microbiological,** *adj.* **microbiologist,** *n.*

microbiota [,maɪkrəʊ–baɪ'əʊtə] *n.* microscopic life of a region. **microbiotic** [–'ɒtɪk], *adj.*

microcephalic, microcephalous [,maɪkrəʊsɪ'fælɪk –'sefələs] **microcephalus,** *n.* (*pl.* –li) such person.

microclimate ['maɪkrəʊ,klaɪmət] *n.* climate of a small area or of a particular habitat. **microclimatology** *n.* study of these.

microcopy ['maɪkrə,kɒpi] *n.* microphotograph.

microcosm ['maɪkrə,kɒzm] *n.* miniature representation of something vast, especially universe; man as epitome of universe. **microcosmal, microcosmian, microcosmic(al),** *adj.*

microdont ['maɪkrədɒnt] *adj.* with small teeth.

microdontism, *n.* **microdontous,** *adj.*

microdot ['maɪkrəʊdɒt] *n.* photograph reduced to the size of a dot.

microeconomics [,maɪkrəʊiːkə'nɒmɪks, –ek–] *n.* economies dealing with individual units, as households, firms, etc.

microencapsulation [,maɪkrəʊenkæpsju'leɪʃn] *n.* preparation of a substance (*e.g.* a medical drug) in the form of particles or droplets each enclosed in a permeable or dissoluble capsule.

micrograph ['maɪkrəgrɑːf] *n.* instrument for writing or engraving on microscopic scale; drawing or photograph of object as seen through microscope. **micrographic,** *adj.* **micrography** ([-'krɒgrəfi], *n.*

micrology [maɪ'krɒlədʒi] *n.* excessive devotion to minute details; art of using the microscope.

micromania [,maɪkrə'meɪniə] *n.* form of insanity in which patient constantly depreciates himself, or imagines that he has become very small. **micromaniac,** *n.*

micrometer [maɪ'krɒmɪtə] *n.* instrument for measuring minute distances. **micrometric(al)** [-'metrɪk, –l], *adj.* **micrometry,** *n.*

micron ['maɪkrɒn] *n.* millionth part of a metre (symbol μ)

micronometer [,maɪkrə'nɒmɪtə] *n.* instrument measuring minute intervals of time.

microphagous [maɪ'krɒfəgəs] *adj.* feeding on small objects. **microphagy** [–dʒi], *n.*

microphotograph [,maɪkrə'fəʊtəgrɑːf] *n.* minute photograph; *erroneously,* photomicrograph.

microphyllous [,maɪkrə'fɪləs] *adj.* having minute leaves.

microphyte ['maɪkrəfaɪt] *n.* microscopic vegetable organism. **microphytal, microphytic,** [–'fɪtɪk], *adj.* **microphytology,** *n.* study of these.

micropodal, micropodous [maɪ'krɒpədl, –əs] *n.* having extremely small feet.

micropsia [maɪ'krɒpsiə] *n.* optical defect causing objects to appear smaller than their real size.

micropterous [maɪ'krɒptərəs] *adj.* having small wings or fins. **micropterygious,** *adj.* having small fins.

micropyle ['maɪkrəpaɪl] *n.* microscopic orifice in plant ovule or female cell. **micropylar,** *adj.*

microseism ['maɪkrə,saɪzm] *n.* small earth tremor. **microseismic(al),** *adj.* **microseismology,** *n.* study of these. **microseismometer,** *n.* instrument measuring these.

microsomatous, [,maɪkrə'səʊmətəs] *adj.* having small body.

microstomatous, microstomous [,maɪkrə'stɒmətəs –ɒstəməs] *adj.* having small mouth. **microstome,** *n.* small opening.

microtherm ['maɪkrəθɜːm] *n.* plant thriving only in very low temperature. **microthermic,** *adj.*

microtia [maɪ'krəʊʃiə] *n.* abnormal smallness of ear.

microtome ['maɪkrətəʊm] *n.* instrument for cutting minute sections. **microtomic(al)** [–'tɒmɪk, –l], *adj.* **microtomy** [–'krɒtəmi], *n.*

micrurgy ['maɪkrɜːdʒi] *n.* art of dissecting, etc., under microscope. **micrurgic(al),** *adj.* **micrurgist,** *n.*

micturition [,mɪktju'rɪʃn] *n.* urination, especially abnormally frequent. **micturate,** *v.i.*

midden ['mɪdn] *n.* dung- or refuse-heap.

Midi [mɪ'diː] (*French*) *n.* the South (of France).
midinette [ˌmɪdɪ'net] (*French*) *n.* shop-girl.
mignon ['mɪnjɒn] (*French*) *adj.* (*fem.* **mignonne**) small and dainty.
miles gloriosus [ˌmiːleɪz glɔːri'əʊsəs] (*Latin*) 'braggart soldier'.
miliaria [ˌmɪli'eəriə] *n.* prickly heat. **miliary,** *adj.* (characterized by a rash) like millet seeds.
milieu ['miːljɜː] (*French*) *n.* surroundings; environment.
militate ['mɪlɪteɪt] *v.t.* be influential, have an effect.
millefiori, millefiore [ˌmɪlɪfi'ɔːri] *n.* & *adj.* (ornamental glassware) of fused coloured glass rods embedded in clear glass.
millennium [mɪ'leniəm] *n.* (*pl.* **-ia**) period of one thousand years; thousandth anniversary; future period of ideal happiness on earth, especially that foretold in Revelations XX. **millenarian,** *adj.* pertaining to millennium; believing in its occurrence in near future; *n.* such believer. **millenarianism,** *n.* such belief. **millenary** ['mɪl–], *adj.* pertaining to or consisting of a thousand men; *n.* a thousand (years); thousandth anniversary. **millennial,** *adj.*; *n.* thousandth anniversary. **millennian,** *adj.* & *n.* millenarian. **millenniary,** *adj.*
millepede, millipede ['mɪlɪpiːd] *n.* long cylindrical many-legged insect.
millesimal [mɪ'lesɪml] *n.* & *adj.* (pertaining to) thousandth part.
milliad ['mɪlɪæd] *n.* a thousand years.
milliard ['mɪlɪɑːd] *n.* one thousand millions.
milliary ['mɪliəri] *adj.* pertaining to miles, especially ancient Roman.
millipore ['mɪlɪpɔː] *n.* kind of branching coral. **milliporite,** *n.* fossil millipore.
milt [mɪlt] *n.* fish's spawn; *v.t.* impregnate with this. **milter,** *n.* male fish, especially in spawning time.
mimesis [maɪ'miːsɪs] *n.* imitation, especially in literature and art or by animal of its surroundings, etc. **mimetic** [–'metɪk], *adj.* **mimetism** (['mɪmɪtɪzm, 'maɪ–], *n.* mimicry.
mimography [maɪ'mɒɡrəfi] *n.* representation in writing of language of signs.
minatory ['mɪnətəri] *n.* threatening. **minatorial,** *adj.*
miniaceous [ˌmɪni'eɪʃəs] *adj.* having colour of red lead. **miniate,** *v.t.* paint with red lead; decorate with red letters or rubrics; illuminate (manuscripts). **miniator,** *n.*
minify ['mɪnɪfaɪ] *v.t.* minimize; diminish the size or importance of.
minikin ['mɪnɪkɪn] *adj.* & *n.* delicate, dainty or affected (person).
minimalism ['mɪnɪml–ɪzm] *n.* (advocacy of) use of a minimum of resources, materials, etc. **minimalist,** *n.*
minimifidian [ˌmɪnɪmɪ'fɪdiən] *adj.* having smallest possible degree of faith. **minimifidianism,** *n.*
minion ['mɪnjən] *n.* size of type (7-point); favourite; hanger-on.
minium ['mɪniəm] *n.* vermilion; red lead.
miniver ['mɪnɪvə] *n.* unspotted ermine fur; any white fur.
minnesinger ['mɪnɪˌsɪŋə] *n.* troubadour-like poet of medieval Germany.
minuend ['mɪnjuend] *n.* number from which

another has to be subtracted.
minuscule ['mɪnəskjuːl, mɪ'nʌs–] *n.* small simple handwriting, especially of ancient times; such letter; lower-case letter; *adj.* small; petty; diminutive. **minuscular,** *adj.*
minutia [mɪ'njuːʃiə] *n.* (*pl.* **-ae**) minute detail; triviality. **minutiose, minutious,** *adj.* paying undue attention to these.
miosis, myosis [maɪ'əʊsɪs] *n.* excessive contraction of the pupil of the eye. **miotic** *adj.* & *n.* (substance) causing this.
miothermic [ˌmaɪə'θɜːmɪk] *adj.* *Geology,* pertaining to present temperature conditions.
mirabile dictu [mɪˌrɑːbɪli 'dɪktjuː] (*Latin*) 'wonderful to relate'. **mirabilia,** *n.pl.* wonders. **mirabiliary,** *n.* miracle worker.
mirador [ˌmɪrə'dɔː] *n.* watch-tower, or other architectural feature with fine view.
mirepoix [ˌmɪə'pwɑː] (*French*) *n.* sautéed vegetables used as base for braising meat, etc.
mirific(al) [mɪ'rɪfɪk, –l] *adj.* wonder-working; miraculous.
mirliton ['mɜːlɪtən, 'mɪə–] *n.* reed pipe.
mirza ['mɜːzə, 'mɪə–] (*Persian*) *n.* title of honour; prince.
misalliance [ˌmɪsə'laɪəns] *n.* mésalliance.
misandry ['mɪsændri] *n.* hatred of men by woman.
misanthrope ['mɪsənθrəʊp] *n.* hater of people. **misanthropic** [–'θrɒpɪk], *adj.* **misanthropy** [–'ænθrəpi], *n.*
miscegenation [ˌmɪsɪdʒə'neɪʃn] *n.* racial interbreeding, especially between blacks and whites. **miscegenetic,** *adj.* **miscegenate** ['mɪs–], *v.i.* & *t.* practise, or produce by, miscegenation; *n.* halfcaste. **miscegenator,** *n.*
misdemeanant [ˌmɪsdɪ'miːnənt] *n.* person guilty of misdemeanour.
mise en scène [ˌmiːz ɒn 'seɪn, –'sen] (*French*) *n.* staging, scenery, etc., of play; setting; locality; surroundings.
misfeasance [mɪs'fiːzəns] *n.* misuse of legal power; illegal performance of legal act. **misfeasor,** *n.* person guilty of this.
misocapnic [ˌmɪsə'kæpnɪk, ˌmaɪ–] *adj.* hating tobacco smoke. **misocapnist,** *n.*
misogallic [ˌmɪsə'ɡælɪk, ˌmaɪ–] *adj.* hating the French.
misogamy [mɪ'sɒɡəmi, maɪ–] *n.* hatred of marriage. **misogamic** [–'ɡæmɪk], *adj.* **misogamist,** *n.*
misogyny [mɪ'sɒdʒəni, maɪ–] *n.* hatred of women by men. **misogynic(al)** [–'dʒɪnɪk, –l], **misogynous,** *adj.* **misogynist, misogynism,** *n.*
misology [mɪ'sɒlədʒi, maɪ–] *n.* hatred of reason, knowledge or argument. **misologist,** *n.*
misoneism [ˌmɪsə'niːɪzm, ˌmaɪ–] *n.* hatred of change or novelty. **misoneist,** *n.*
misopaedia [ˌmɪsə'piːdiə, ˌmaɪ–] *n.* hatred of children, especially one's own. **misopaedism,** *n.* **misopaedist,** *n.*
misopolemical [ˌmɪsəpə'lemɪkl, ˌmaɪ–] *adj.* hating war.
misosophy [mɪ'sɒsəfi, maɪ–] *n.* hatred of wisdom. **misosopher, misosophist,** *n.*
misotheism [ˌmɪsə'θiːɪzm, ˌmaɪ–] *n.* hatred of gods or God. **misotheist,** *n.*
misprision [mɪs'prɪʒn] *n.* error of omission or commision; misdemeanour; contempt, scorn. **misprise** [–'praɪz], *v.t.* & *n.* scorn.

missa ['mɪsə] n. (pl. –ae) Roman Catholic, service of mass. missa bassa, low mass. missa cantata, missa media, sung mass, without deacon or high-mass ceremonial. missa privata, low mass, or one at which only priest communicates. missa publica, mass at which all faithful may communicate. missa solemnis, high mass.

missal ['mɪsl] n. Roman Catholic service-book.

misspell [,mɪs'spel] v.t. & t. to spell (a word) incorrectly. misspelling, n.

mistral ['mɪstrəl, mɪ'straːl] n. strong cold north wind of S France.

mithridatism ['mɪθrədeɪtɪzm] n. immunity from poison obtained by consuming series of small doses. mithridatic [–'dætɪk], adj. mithridatize, v.t.

mitigate ['mɪtɪgeɪt] v.t. make less harsh or severe; moderate. mitigable, adj. mitigation, n. mitigative, adj.

mitochondria [,maɪtə'kɒndrɪə] n. pl. (sing. –rion) minute bodies in the living cell in which the final stages of the breakdown of carbohydrates and fats to release energy take place. mitochondrial, adj.

mitosis [maɪ'təʊsɪs] n. cell division, with division of nucleus first. mitotic [–'tɒtɪk], adj.

mitraille [miː'traɪ] (French) n. grape and other small shot. mitrailleur [–'ɜː], n. machine-gunner. mitrailleuse [–'ɜːz], n. machine-gun.

mitral ['maɪtrəl] adj. mitre- or bonnet-shaped. mitriform, adj. mitre-shaped.

mittimus ['mɪtɪməs] (Latin) 'we send'; n. writ for committing to prison or removing records to other court; congé.

mneme ['niːmi] n. Psychology, persisting effect of memory of past events. mnemic, adj. mnemist, n.

mnemonic [nɪ'mɒnɪk] adj. pertaining to or aiding memory; n. device to aid memory. mnemonical, adj. mnemonize ['niː–], v.t. make into a mne-monic. mnemonism, n. practice of mnemonics. mnemonics, mnemotechny, n. system of improving memory.

mnesic ['niːsɪk] adj. pertaining to memory. mnestic, adj. pertaining to memory or mneme.

moa ['məʊə] n. extinct ostrich-like flightless bird of New Zealand.

mockado [mə'kaːdəʊ] n. ancient woollen fabric; inferior material; tawdry.

modal ['məʊdl] adj. pertaining to or having form rather than substance. modality, n.

module ['mɒdjuːl] n. unit of measurement or means of measuring; standard or self-contained unit of construction; self-contained section of edu-cational course.

modus operandi [,məʊdəs ɒpə'rændaɪ] (Latin) 'method of operating or proceeding'. modus vivendi, 'method of living'; compromise adopted until final settlement is reached.

mogadore ['mɒgədɔː] n. ribbed silk necktie material.

mogigraphia, mogigraphy [,mɒdʒɪ'græfɪə, –ɪgrəfɪ] n., writing only with difficulty. mogilalia, [–'leɪlɪə], n. speaking only with difficulty.

moho ['məʊhəʊ] n. boundary between the crust and upper mantle of the Earth: abbreviation of Mohorovic discontinuity. mohole, n. borehole into the Earth's crust as far as the moho.

mohur ['məʊhɜː] (Indian) n. gold coin worth 15 rupees.

moidore ['mɔɪdɔː] n. ancient Portuguese gold coin.

moiety ['mɔɪətɪ] n. half; small portion.

moire [mwaː] (French) n. watered silk or other fabric. moiré ['mwaːreɪ], adj. with watered pat-tern; n. such pattern.

molimen [mə'laɪmen] n. strenuous effort or labour.

molinary ['mɒlɪnərɪ, 'məʊ–] adj. pertaining to mills or grinding.

mollescent [mə'lesənt] adj. softening. mollify, v.t. soften; appease. mollipilose [,mɒlɪ'paɪləʊs], adj. downy. mollities [–'lɪʃiːɪz], n. Medicine, softness. mollitious, adj. softening; voluptuous.

Moloch ['məʊlɒk] n. deity mentioned in Old Tes-tament, to whom children were sacrificed; any-thing requiring human sacrifice; Australian spiny lizard.

molossus [mə'lɒsəs] n. verse foot of three long syllables.

molybdenum [mə'lɪbdnəm] n. iron-like white metal used in steel manufacture and dyeing. molybdic, molybdious, molybdenic, molybdenous, adj.

momentaneous [,məʊmən'teɪnɪəs] adj. Gram-mar, signifying action completed in a moment.

momism ['mɒmɪzm] n. American, excessive devo-tion to mother.

Momus ['məʊməs] (Greek) n. god of ridicule; carping critic; satirist. disciple, son, etc., of Momus, person continually poking fun.

monachal ['mɒnəkl] adj. monastic. monachate, n. period of monkhood. monachize, v.i. & t. become or cause to become a monk or monkish. mona-chism, n.

monad ['mɒnæd, 'məʊ–] n. unit; atom; microcos-mic element underlying reality; God. monadic, adj. monadism, n. philosophic theory that uni-verse is composed of such elements.

monandry [mə'nændrɪ] n. marriage to only one man at a time. monandric, monandrous, adj.

monanthous [mə'nænθəs] adj. single-flowered.

monarticular [,mɒnɑː'tɪkjʊlə] adj. of or affect-ing only one joint.

monatomic [,mɒnə'tɒmɪk] adj. having one atom, or only one atom in molecule; uni-valent. monatomicity [–'mɪsətɪ], monatomism [–'ætəmɪzm], n.

monaural [,mɒn'ɔːrəl] adj. pertaining to, having or for one ear only; monophonic.

monde [mɒnd] (French) n. 'world', especially of fashion; one's own little world.

monepic [mɒn'epɪk] adj. comprising one word, or single-worded sentences.

monetize ['mʌnɪtaɪz] v.t. convert into or adopt as currency, or as currency standard.

mongo, mongoe ['mɒŋgəʊ] n. mungo.

monial ['məʊnɪəl] n. nun.

moniliform [mə'nɪlɪfɔːm] adj. having narrow intervals or joints resembling a string of beads.

monism ['mɒnɪzm, 'məʊ–] n. philosophical belief that matter, mind, etc., consist of one substance only, which is the only reality. monist, n. monistic, adj.

monition [mə'nɪʃn] n. caution; warning, espe-cially legal. monitory ['mɒnɪtərɪ], adj.; n. letter containing a monition.

monitor ['mɒnɪtə] *v.t.* maintain continuous observation of, as a check on output, efficiency, etc.; *n.* recording device or display for this purpose.

monoblepsia, monoblepsis [ˌmɒnə'blepsiə, –sɪs] *n.* normality of vision with one eye, but confusion when both are used; colour-blindness for all but one colour.

monocarpic [ˌmɒnə'kɑːpɪk] *adj.* fruiting only once.

monoceros [mə'nɒsərəs] *n.* unicorn; swordfish. **monocerous**, *adj.* having one horn only.

monochord ['mɒnəkɔːd] *n.* musical instrument with one string; similar apparatus determining musical intervals; clavichord.

monochrome ['mɒnəkrəʊm] *n.* work of art in one colour; black and white (photograph); *adj.* in black and white. **monochroic, monochromatic, monochromic(al)**, *adj.* **monochromatism**, *n.* complete colour-blindness. **monochromist, monochromy**, *n.*

monochronic [ˌmɒnə'krɒnɪk] *adj.* relating to one period of time.

monocline ['mɒnəklaɪn] *n. Geology*, single upward band or fold. **monoclinal**, *adj.*

monocoque ['mɒnəkɒk] *n. & adj.* (denoting) aircraft structure in which the outer skin carries all or most of the torsional and bending stresses; (denoting) car structure in which the body is integral with and shares the stresses with the chassis.

monocotyledon [ˌmɒnəkɒtə'liːdn] *n.* plant having single cotyledon. **monocotyledonous** [-'ledənəs], *adj.*

monocracy [mə'nɒkrəsi] *n.* autocracy. **monocrat** ['mɒn–], *n.* **monocratic**, *adj.*

monocular [mə'nɒkjʊlə] *adj.* having, pertaining to, or for one eye only. **monoculist, monoculus**, *n.* one-eyed person. **monoculous**, *adj.*

monodont ['mɒnədɒnt] *adj.* one-toothed.

monodrama ['mɒnəˌdrɑːmə] *n.* play acted by one person only; dramatic account of thoughts of one person. **monodramatic** [-'drəmætɪk], *adj.*

monodromic [ˌmɒnə'drɒmɪk] *adj.* uniform in value. **monodromy** [mə'nɒdrəmi], *n.*

monody ['mɒnədi] *n.* song on one note or by one voice; dirge; melody.

monodynamic [ˌmɒnədaɪ'næmɪk] *adj.* having only one power or ability. **monodynamism**, *n.* belief in one force causing all activity.

monoecious [mə'niːʃəs] *adj.* having male and female organs in same organism, especially having male and female flowers on same plant. **monoecism**, *n.*

monogamy [mə'nɒgəmi] *n.* marriage to only one person at a time. **monogamic** [-'gæmɪk], **monogamous**, *adj.* **monogamist**, *n.*

monogenesis [ˌmɒnə'dʒenəsɪs] *n.* singleness of origin; theory that all human beings derive from one man and woman, or that all life derives from a single cell; asexual reproduction; development without change of form. **monogeneous**, [-'dʒiːniəs], **monogenetic** [-dʒən'etɪk], **monogenic, monogenous** [-'ɒdʒənəs], *adj.* **monogenism**, [-'ɒdʒənɪzm], **monogeny** [-i] *n.*

monoglot ['mɒnəglɒt] *n. & adj.* (person) knowing one language only; *adj.* written in one language only.

monogoneutic [ˌmɒnəgə'njuːtɪk] *adj.* single-brooded.

monogony [mə'nɒgəni] *n.* non-sexual reproduction.

monograph ['mɒnəgrɑːf] *n.* treatise on one subject; any learned treatise. **monographic**, *adj.* **monographist**, *n.*

monogyny [mə'nɒdʒəni] *n.* marriage to only one woman at a time, or to one chief wife, with other consorts. **monogynic** [-'dʒɪnɪk], **monogynious, monogynous**, *adj.*

monoideism [ˌmɒnəʊ'aɪdiːɪzm] *n.* obsession with a single idea. **monoideic**, *adj.* **monoideist**, *n.*

monolatry [mə'nɒlətri] *n.* worship of one god only out of many believed to exist. **monolater, monolatrist**, *n.* **monolatrous**, *adj.*

monolingual [ˌmɒnə'lɪŋgwəl] *adj.* monoglot. **monolinguist**, *n.*

monoliteral [ˌmɒnə'lɪtərəl] *adj.* comprising one letter only.

monolith ['mɒnəlɪθ] *n.* single monumental stone or pillar, especially of prehistoric orgin; any object, organization, etc. that appears uniform and uniformly unchangeable. **monolithic**, *adj.*

monology [mə'nɒlədʒi] *n.* soliloquy; monopoly of the conversation. **monologian, monologist**, *n.* **monologic(al)**, *adj.* **monologize**, *v.i.*

monomachy [mə'nɒməki] *n.* duel. **monomachist**, *n.*

monomania [ˌmɒnə'meɪniə] *n.* insanity on one subject only; obsession to insane degree with one subject. **monomaniac**, *n.* **monomaniacal** [-'naɪəkl], *adj.*

monomer ['mɒnəmə] *n.* simple unpolymerized form of a chemical compound, of comparatively low molecular weight.

monometallism [ˌmɒnə'metl–ɪzm] *n.* use of one metal as currency standard; theory advocating this. **monometallist**, *n.*

monomial [mɒ'nəʊmiəl] *n. & adj.* (name or expression) comprising one term only.

monomorphic [ˌmɒnə'mɔːfɪk] *adj.* having same form throughout life. **monomorphism**, *n.* **monomorphous**, *adj.*

mononym ['mɒnənɪm] *n.* monomial name or term. **mononymic**, *adj.* **mononymize** [-'nɒnɪmaɪz], *v.t.* **mononymy**, *n.*

monoousian [ˌmɒnəʊ'uːsiən, –'aʊ–] *adj.* having same subtance.

monophagous [mə'nɒfəgəs] *adj.* eating one kind of food only. **monophagia** [ˌmɒnə'feɪdʒiə], **monophagism** [-fədʒɪzm], **monophagy** [-fədʒi], *n.*

monophobia [ˌmɒnə'fəʊbiə] *n.* dread of solitude.

monophonous [mə'nɒfənəs] *adj.* representing same sound, as *f* and *ph*; giving tones singly.

monophthalmus [ˌmɒnɒf'θælməs] *n.* congenital absence of one eye. **monopthalmic**, *adj.*

monophthong ['mɒnəfθɒŋ] *n.* single vowel sound. **monophthongal**, *adj.* **monophthongize**, *v.t.* pronounce as monophthong.

monophyletic [ˌmɒnəfɪ'letɪk] *adj.* derived from one common parental stock. **monophyleticism** [-sɪzm], *n.*

monoplasmatic [ˌmɒnəplæz'mætɪk] *adj.* of one substance. **monoplastic**, *adj.* of one form.

monoplegia [ˌmɒnə'pliːdʒiə] *n.* paralysis of one part of body only, especially such one limb. **monoplegic**, *adj.*

monopode ['mɒnəpəʊd] *n. & adj.* (creature) with one foot, especially such fabulous Ethiopian race.

monopodial, monopodic [-'pɒdɪk], monopodous [-'nɒpədəs], adj. monopodium, n. (pl. -dia) Botany, main axis of growth. monopody [-'nɒpədi], n. verse measure of one foot.

monopolylogue [,mɒnə'pɒlɪlɒg] n. dramatic entertainment with interpretation of many rôles by one person. monopolylogist [-'lɪlədʒɪst], n.

monopsony [mə'nɒpsəni] n. market situation where there is only one buyer for a product.

monopsychism [,mɒnə'saɪkɪzm] n. belief in one universal soul.

monopteros [mə'nɒptərɒs] n. (pl. - tera) building with single ring of columns supporting a roof. monopteral, adj.

monoptic(al) [mə'nɒptɪk, -l] adj. one-eyed.

monoptote ['mɒnəptəʊt] n noun (or adjective) occurring in a single oblique case. monoptotic [-'tɒtɪk], adj.

monopyrenous [,mɒnəpaɪ'riːnəs] adj. applied to single-stoned or single-kernelled fruit.

monoschemic [,mɒnə'skiːmɪk] adj. using same metrical foot throughout.

monosemy ['mɒnəsiːmi, mə'nɒsəmi] n. fact of having only one meaning. monosemous, adj.

monospermous, monospermal [,mɒnə'spɜːməs, -əl] adj. single-seeded. monospermy, n. fertilization of egg by one sperm cell only.

monostich ['mɒnəstɪk] n. one verse line; poem of one verse line. monostichous [-'nɒstɪkəs], adj. in one line or row.

monostrophe [mə'nɒstrəfi] n. poem with all stanzas of same form. monostrophic [-'trɒfɪk], adj.

monotheism ['mɒnə,θiːɪzm] n. belief in one God only. monotheist, n. monotheistic, adj.

monothelious [,mɒnə'θiːliəs] adj. polyandrous.

monotic [mə'nɒtɪk] adj. affecting one ear only.

monotocous [mə'nɒtəkəs] adj. laying one egg, or bringing forth one young, only.

monotreme ['mɒnətriːm] n. primitive Australian egg-laying mammal, e.g. duck-billed platypus. monotrematous, adj.

monotrophic [mɒnə'trɒfɪk] adj. monophagous.

monoxide [mə'nɒksaɪd] n. oxide with one oxygen atom in molecule.

monozygotic [,mɒnəzaɪ'gɒtɪk] adj. developed from one zygote only.

mons [mɒnz] (Latin) n. mountain. mons pubis, hair-covered eminence in male pubic region. mons Veneris, 'mountain of Venus'; fatty eminence in female pubic region.

monstrance ['mɒnstrəns] n. Ecclesiastical, vessel for exposing eucharist.

montage [mɒn'tɑːʒ] (French) n. a composite picture made up of many pictures artistically blended or laid out; any similar blending of scenes, sounds, etc.; manner of artistically constructing sequence of scenes in film.

mont-de-piété [,mɒn-də-piːe'teɪ] (French) n. 'mount, or bank, of piety'; public pawnbroker's.

montero [mɒn'teərəʊ] (Spanish) n. huntsman; his cap.

montgolfier [mɒnt'gɒlfiə, mɒŋ-, -ieɪ] (French) n. hot-air balloon.

monticle, monticule ['mɒntɪkl, -juːl] n. hillock. monticulate, monticulous, adj. hillocky.

moolvee ['muːlvi] n. doctor of Islamic law; title of respect for learned man or teacher.

moong [muŋ] see mung.

mopoke ['məʊpəʊk] n. morepork.

moquette [mə'ket] n. thick-piled upholstery fabric or carpet.

mora ['mɔːrə] n. (pl. -ae) unit of metre in prosody, equivalent of one short syllable; Law, postponement; default.

moraine [mə'reɪn] n. detritus deposited by glacier. morainal, morainic, adj.

moratorium [,mɒrə'tɔːriəm] n. (pl. -ria) lawful suspension. moratory ['mɒrətəri], adj. pertaining to moratorium or delay.

morbid ['mɔːbɪd] adj. Medicine, unhealthy; diseased. morbific, adj. causing disease. morbiferal, morbiferous, adj. carrying disease. morbidezza [-'detsə], (Italian) n. softness in artistic representation of flesh. morbidity, n.

morbilli [mɔː'bɪli] n. pl. measles. morbillary, morbilliform, adj. like measles. morbillous, adj.

morbus ['mɔːbəs] (Latin) n. disease. morbus Gallicus, 'French disease'; syphilis.

morcellate ['mɔːsəleɪt] v.t. divide into small portions. morcellation, n.

mordacious [mɔː'deɪʃəs] adj. tending to bite; caustic, sarcastic. mordacity, n.

mordant ['mɔːdnt] adj. biting; corrosive; caustic; stinging; n. corrosive substance; colour fixative. mordancy, n.

mordent ['mɔːdnt] n. musical device of alternating quickly a tone with another a half-tone lower.

more ['mɔːri] (Latin) adv. 'in the manner or style'. more suo, 'in his own manner or fashion'.

morel [mə'rel] n. kind of edible fungus; black night-shade. morello, n. dark-coloured cultivated cherry.

morepork ['mɔːpɔːk] n. New Zealand, kind of owl; Tasmania, night-jar; Australia, several birds with cry sounding like 'more pork'.

mores ['mɔːriːz] (Latin) n. pl. manners and customs.

morganatic [,mɔːgə'nætɪk] adj. pertaining to or denoting marriage of person of royal blood to person of inferior rank, by which the latter does not receive the royal spouse's rank nor do the children inherit his or her titles or property. morganatical, adj.

morganize ['mɔːgənaɪz] v.t. do away with secretly; burke.

moribund ['mɒrɪbʌnd] adj. about to die; half-dead; n. such person. moribundity, n.

moriform ['mɒrɪfɔːm] adj. mulberry-shaped.

morigerous [mə'rɪdʒərəs] adj. obsequiously obedient.

morology [mə'rɒlədʒi] n. nonsense. morological, adj. morologist, n.

morpheme ['mɔːfiːm] n. smallest element of language to have meaning or grammatical function. morphemic, adj.

Morpheus ['mɔːfjuːs, -iəs] n. god of dreams. morphean, adj. morphetic, adj. pertaining to sleep.

morphogenesis, morphogeny [,mɔːfə'dʒenəsɪs, -ʒini] n. development of morphological characteristics. morphogenetic [-dʒə'netɪk], morphogenic [-'dʒenɪk], adj.

morphography [mɔː'fɒgrəfi] n. morphological description or study. morphographer, n. artist portraying forms. morphographic(al), adj. morphographist, *n*.

morphology [mɔːˈfɒlədʒi] *n*. biological or philological study of forms and structures; form and structure of an organism, word, etc. **morphological**, *adj*. **morphologist**, *n*.

morphometry [mɔːˈfɒmətri] *n*. measurement of form. **morphometric(al)** [ˌmɔːfəˈmetrɪk, –l], *adj*.

morphonomy [mɔːˈfɒnəmi] *n*. morphological biological laws. **morphonomic** [ˌmɔːfəˈnɒmɪk], *adj*.

morphosis [mɔːˈfəʊsɪs] *n*. manner of development. **morphotic** [–ˈfɒtɪk], *adj*. pertaining to morphosis or formation.

morphous [ˈmɔːfəs] *adj*. having definite form.

morro [ˈmɒrəʊ] *n*. rounded hill or headland.

morsal [ˈmɔːsl] *adj*. pertaining to cutting edge.

morse [mɔːs] *n*. walrus.

mortician [mɔːˈtɪʃn] (*American*) *n*. funeral undertaker.

mortmain [ˈmɔːtmeɪn] *n*. *Law*, state of being held inalienably by a corporation; *v.t.* alienate into corporation's possession.

mortorio [mɔːˈtɔːriəʊ] (*Italian*) *n*. sculpture of the dead Christ.

moschate [ˈmɒskeɪt] *adj*. musk-like in odour. **moschiferous**, *adj*. producing musk. **moschine**, *adj*. pertaining to musk deer.

mot [məʊ] (*French*) *n*. 'word'; pithy saying; bon mot. **mot juste** [–ʒuːst], word or phrase exactly expressing an idea.

motatory, motarious [ˈməʊtətəri, –ːriəs] *adj*. continually moving.

motet [məʊˈtet] *n*. kind of unaccompanied part-song or anthem.

motif, motiv [məʊˈtiːf] *n*. recurrent or dominating feature or theme.

motile [ˈməʊtaɪl, –tl] *adj*. able to move spontaneously; causing motion; *n*. person whose mental processes emerge in, or are best stimulated by, motion or action. **motility**, *n*.

motmot [ˈmɒtmɒt] *n*. jay-like S American bird.

motorium [məʊˈtɔːriəm] *n*. division of nervous system concerned with movement.

motricity [ˌməʊtəˈrɪsəti] *n*. function of movements, especially muscular.

motu proprio [ˌməʊtjuː ˈprəʊpriəʊ] (*Latin*) 'by its or one's own motion'; by own desire or impulse.

moucharaby [muːˈʃærəbi] *n*. projecting latticed window in Muslim architecture; such balcony of castle.

mouchard [muːˈʃɑː] (*French*) *n*. police spy.

moue [muː] (*French*) *n*. pout; grimace.

mouflon, moufflon [ˈmuːflɒn] *n*. horned wild sheep of Mediterranean islands.

mouillé [ˈmwiːeɪ, ˈmuːjeɪ] (*French*) *adj*. 'wet'; made soft or palatal in pronunciation, as *ll* in *mouillé*, *ñ* in *cañon*, etc. **mouillation, mouillure**, *n*.

moujik [ˈmuːʒɪk] *n*. Russian peasant; lady's loose fur cape.

mournival [ˈmɔːnɪvl] *n*. set of four, especially set of four court cards in one hand.

mousseline [ˌmuːsəˈliːn] (*French*) *n*. French dress fabric; hollandaise sauce with whipped cream or egg whites added. **mousseline de laine** [–də ˈlen], light woollen fabric. **mousseline de soie** [–də ˈswɑː], gauzy silk or rayon fabric.

moutonnée [muːˈtɒneɪ] (*French*) *adj*. applied to rocks with rounded outlines like backs of flock of sheep.

moxa [ˈmɒksə] *n*. down from various plants used as cauterizing agent and counterirritant by being burned on the skin.

Mozarab [məʊˈzærəb] *n*. Christian in Moorish Spain.

mozzetta, mozetta [məʊˈzetə] (*Italian*) *n*. *Roman Catholic*, short cape with hood worn by Pope, cardinals, etc.

mu [mjuː, muː] *n*. twelfth letter of Gr. alphabet (M, μ); symbol for micron; *Electricity*, factor of amplification.

mucago [mjuːˈkeɪgəʊ] *n*. mucilage; mucus.

mucedine [ˈmjuːsədɪn] *n*. mould or mildew fungus. **mucedinaceous, mucedineous, mucedinous** [mjuːˈsedɪnəs], *adj*. mildew-like.

muchacha [muːˈtʃɑːtʃɑ] (*Spanish*) *n*. girl; female servant. **muchacho**, *n*. boy; manservant.

mucid [ˈmjuːsɪd] *adj*. slimy; mouldy, musty.

muciferous [mjuːˈsɪfərəs] *adj*. secreting or stimulating secretion of mucus. **mucific, mucigenous**, *adj*.

mucilage [ˈmjuːsɪlɪdʒ] *n*. gummy or adhesive substance. **mucilaginous** [–ˈlædʒɪnəs], *adj*.

mucivore [ˈmjuːsɪvɔː] *n*. insect feeding on plant juices. **mucivorous** [–ˈsɪvərəs], *adj*.

muckna [ˈmʌknə] *n*. male elephant lacking, or having only rudimentary, tusks; spurless cock.

mucocele [ˈmjuːkəsiːl] *n*. cyst containing mucus; swelling due to accumulation of mucus. **mucoid(al)**, *adj*. like mucus. **mucopus**, *n*. mixture of mucus and pus. **mucorrhoea**, *n*. abnormal discharge of mucus. **mucosa**, *n*. mucous membrane. **mucous**, *adj*. secreting, like, or covered with mucus.

mucronate [ˈmjuːkrəneɪt] *adj*. terminating in sharp point. **mucroniferous**, *adj*. like a sharp point. **mucronulate** [–ˈkrɒnjuleɪt], *adj*. terminating in small sharp point. **mucronation**, *n*.

muculent [ˈmjuːkjulənt] *adj*. slimy; like mucus.

mucus [ˈmjuːkəs] *n*. viscous fluid secreted by membranes lining body cavities.

mudar [məˈdɑː] *n*. E Indian fibre-yielding shrub with root and bark used in medicine.

mudir [muːˈdɪə] (*Arabic*) *n*. governor of Egyptian province. **mudiria, mudirieh**, *n*. jurisdiction of mudir.

mudra [ˈmʊdrə] *n*. ritual hand movement in classical Indian dancing.

muezzin [muˈezɪn] *n*. person calling Muslim faithful to prayer.

mufti [ˈmʌfti] *n*. person learned in Islamic law; civilian dress.

mugger, muggar, muggur [ˈmʌgə] (*Indian*) *n*. crocodile.

mugient [ˈmjuːdʒiənt] *adj*. bellowing, especially like cattle. **mugience, mugiency**, *n*.

mugiloid [ˈmjuːdʒɪlɔɪd] *n*. & *adj*. (fish) like grey mullet, or belonging to grey mullet family of fishes. **mugiliform**, *adj*.

mugwump [ˈmʌgwʌmp] *n*. political independent or neutral. **mugwumpery, mugwumpism**, *n*. **mugwumpish**, *adj*.

mukluk [ˈmʌklʌk] *n*. eskimo's soft (especially sealskin) boot.

mulatto [mjuˈlætəʊ] *n*. (*pl*. **–os**) offspring of a pure negro and a white parent; *adj.* having yellowish-brown skin.

mulct [mʌlkt] *v.t.* rob of; deprive of; fine; *n.* fine. **mulctation,** *n.* **mulctative, mulctatory,** *adj.* **mulctuary,** *adj.* punishable by fine.

muliebrile [ˌmjuːliˈiːbraɪl, –ˈeb–] *adj.* feminine. **muliebrity,** *n.* womanliness; womanhood. **muliebrous,** *adj.* effeminate.

mulier [ˈmjuːliə] *n.* woman; wife; legitimate child. **mulier puisne** [–ˈpjuːni], younger legitimate son. **mulierose,** *adj.* fond of women.

mullah [ˈmʌlə] *n.* Islamic teacher of law and theology.

mullid [ˈmʌlɪd] *n.* & *adj.* (fish) like red mullet, or belonging to red mullet family of fishes.

mullion [ˈmʌliən] *n.* upright division, especially of stone, between panes of window.

mulse [mʌls] *n.* boiled wine with honey.

multeity [mʌlˈtiːəti] *n.* state of being, or thing comprising, many.

multifid [ˈmʌltɪfɪd] *adj.* having many divisions.

multigravida [ˌmʌltɪˈɡrævɪdə] *n.* woman pregnant for at least the third time.

multilateral [ˌmʌltɪˈlætərəl] *adj.* many-sided; involving several parties, nations, etc.

multilinguist [ˌmʌltɪˈlɪŋɡwɪst] *n.* speaker of many languages. **multilingual,** *adj.*

multiliteral [ˌmʌltɪˈlɪtərəl] *adj.* having many letters or unknown quantities.

multilocation [ˌmʌltɪləˈkeɪʃn] *n.* appearance in many places at the same time.

multiloquent [mʌlˈtɪləkwənt] *adj.* talkative. **multiloquious** [ˌmʌltɪˈləukwiəs], **multiloquous,** *adj.* **multiloquence, multiloquy,** *n.*

multinomial [ˌmʌltɪˈnəumiəl] *n.* & *adj.* (expression) containing three or more terms.

multipara [mʌlˈtɪpərə] *n.* mother of two or more children. **multiparity** [ˌmʌltɪˈpærəti], *n.* state of being multipara; act of giving birth to two or more offspring. **multiparous,** *adj.*

multiplepoinding [ˌmʌltɪplˈpɔɪndɪŋ] *n. Scottish Law,* action by holder of property, etc., requiring claimants upon it to appear and settle claims in court.

multiplex [ˈmʌltɪpleks] *adj.* multiple; (of telecommunications channel) able to carry two or more signals at a time; *n.* such channel or its use; *v.t.* send via a multiplex channel.

multiplicand [ˌmʌltɪplɪˈkænd] *n.* number or amount to be multiplied.

multipotent [mʌlˈtɪpətənt] *adj.* having many powers.

multisonous [mʌlˈtɪsənəs] *adj.* producing many or loud sounds. **multisonant,** *adj.*

multitarian [ˌmʌltɪˈteəriən] *adj.* having many forms but one essence.

multivalent [mʌlˈtɪvələnt, ˌmʌltɪˈveɪlənt] *adj.* having valency of more than two; having more than one valency. **multivalence, multivalency,** *n.*

multiversity [ˌmʌltɪˈvɜːsəti] *n. American,* university with many campuses or attached institutions.

multivious [mʌlˈtɪviəs] *adj.* leading in many directions; having many ways.

multivocal [mʌlˈtɪvəkl] *adj.* having many meanings.

multivolent [mʌlˈtɪvələnt] *adj.* not in agreement; not of one mind.

multivoltine [ˌmʌltɪˈvɒltaɪn, –iːn] *adj.* having many broods in one season.

multum in parvo [ˌmʌltəm ɪn ˈpɑːvəu] (*Latin*) 'much in little'; compression of much into little space; summary.

multure [ˈmʌltʃə] *n.* miller's fee for grinding corn.

mumchance [ˈmʌmtʃɑːns] *adj.* silent; tongue tied; *n. obsolete,* masquerade.

mummer [ˈmʌmə] *n.* actor in folk play; mimer. **Mummerset.** *n. jocular,* rustic accent or dialect for the stage. **mummery,** *n.* performance by mummers; empty ceremonial.

mump [mʌmp] *v.i.* sulk; be silent; beg. **mumper,** *n.* **mumpish,** *adj.*

mumsy [ˈmʌmzi] *adj.* old-fashioned; drab.

mundane [mʌnˈdeɪn] *adj.* worldly; earthly; everyday; secular. **mundanity** [–ˈdænɪti], *n.*

mundify [ˈmʌndɪfaɪ] *v.t.* cleanse; heal. **mundificant,** *n.* & *adj.* **mundification, mundifier,** *n.*

mung [mʌŋ] (*Indian*) *n.* fibre-yielding vetch. **mung bean,** bean-like food plant of Asia.

mungo [ˈmʌŋɡəu] *n.* fabric made from felted woollen rags.

muniments [ˈmjuːnɪmənts] *n. pl.* legal records, as deeds, etc.

munj [mʊndʒ] *n.* mung.

munjeet [mʌnˈdʒiːt] *n.* dye-yielding madder plant of Bengal; dye obtained from its roots.

muntjak [ˈmʌntdʒæk] *n.* small tusked deer of SE Asia; barking deer.

murage [ˈmjuːrɪdʒ] *n.* rate levied for upkeep of city's walls.

mural [ˈmjuərəl] *adj.* pertaining to or on a wall; *n.* wall-painting.

murex [ˈmjuəreks] *n.* (purple dye obtained from) tropical mollusc.

muriate [ˈmjuəreɪt] *n.* chloride, especially of potassium. **muriated,** *adj.* impregnated with chloride, especially silver chloride; pickled; briny. **muriatic** [–ˈætɪk], *adj.* hydrochloric.

muricate [ˈmjuərɪkeɪt] *adj.* prickly. **muriculate,** *adj.* having small prickles.

murid [muˈriːd] (*Arabic*) *n.* Muslim disciple. **muridism,** *n.*

murine [ˈmjuəraɪn, –rɪn] *n.* & *adj.* (animal) belonging to rats and mice family of rodents. **muriform,** *adj.* like rat or mouse; like courses of bricks.

murrain [ˈmʌrɪn] *n.* plague, especially of cattle.

murre [mɜː] *n.* kind of guillemot or auk. **murrelet,** *n.* several small sea-birds of N Pacific.

murrhine [ˈmɜːraɪn, –rɪn] *adj.* applied to transparent glassware containing pieces of coloured glass; *n.* such vase, or one made of valuable stone or porcelain.

musaceous [mjuˈzeɪʃəs] *adj. Botany,* belonging to the banana and plantain family.

musal [ˈmjuːzl] *adj.* pertaining to poetry or the Muses.

musang [mjuˈsæŋ] *n.* civet-like animal of E Indies.

muscae volitantes [ˌmʌski ˌvɒlɪˈtæntiːz] (*Latin*) 'flying flies'; spots, lines, etc., seen before the eyes, caused by particles in the vitreous humour of the eye.

muscari [mʌˈskeəri] *n.* grape hyacinth. **muscariform** [mʌˈskærɪfɔːm], *adj.* brush-shaped. **muscarine** [ˈmʌskəriːn], *n.* poisonous alkaloid in fly agaric.

muscicide ['mʌsɪsaɪd] *n.* substance killing flies.

muscid ['mʌsɪd] *n. & adj.* (a member) of the family including the housefly.

muscology [mʌ'skɒlədʒɪ] *n.* study of mosses. **muscoid, muscose,** *adj.* moss-like. **muscologic(al),** *adj.* **muscologist,** *n.*

muscovado [ˌmʌskə'vɑːdəʊ] *n.* unrefined sugar.

museology [ˌmjuːzɪ'ɒlədʒɪ] *n.* science of collecting and arranging objects for museums. **museologist,** *n.*

musette [mjuː'zet] *n.* small French bagpipe; air or dance performed on or to this; soldier's provision wallet; small bag worn over shoulder, especially by cyclist.

musicale [ˌmjuːzɪ'kɑːl] *n.* musical evening; private concert.

mussitate ['mʌsɪteɪt] *v.i.* mutter. **mussitation,** *n.*

must [mʌst] *n.* newly pressed grape juice; musth.

mustee [mʌ'stiː] *n.* octoroon; half-breed.

musteline ['mʌstɪlaɪn, –lɪn] *n. & adj.* (animal) belonging to family of animals including otters, badgers, weasels, mink, etc. **mustelinous,** *adj.*

musth [mʌst] *n. Zoology,* state of frenzied sexual excitement.

mutable ['mjuːtəbl] *adj.* capable of being changed, especially for the worse; fickle. **mutability,** *n.*

mutant ['mjuːtnt] *adj.* resulting from or undergoing mutation; *n.* mutated organism.

mutation [mjuː'teɪʃn] *n.* change; *Biology,* sudden variation from type, due to change in genes. **mutational,** *adj.* **mutationism,** *n.* belief that mutation is important in evolution of species.

mutatis mutandis [mjuːˌtɑːtɪs mjuː'tændɪs, -ˌteɪ–] (*Latin*) with suitable or necessary alterations.

mutative ['mjuːtətɪv] *adj. Grammar,* expressing change of place or state.

mutch [mʌtʃ] *n.* Scottish woman's close-fitting cap. **mutchkin,** *n.* Scottish liquid measure of approximately three-quarters of an imperial pint.

mutic ['mjuːtɪk] *adj. Zoology,* lacking normal defensive parts, as claws, etc. **muticous,** *adj.* lacking a point.

mutive ['mjuːtɪv] *adj.* tending to alter. **mutivity,** *n.*

muzhik, mujik ['muːʒɪk] *see* **moujik.**

myalgia [maɪ'ældʒɪə] *n.* muscular rheumatism.

myalism ['maɪəlɪzm] *n.* magic cult among W Indian blacks.

myall ['maɪɔːl] *n.* Australian acacia tree.

mycelium [maɪ'siːlɪəm] *n.* (*pl.* **–ia**), web of spore-bearing filaments of fungi; 'spawn'. **mycelial, mycelian, mycelioid, myceloid,** *adj.*

mycetism ['maɪsɪtɪzm] *n.* fungus poisoning. **mycetoid, mycetous,** *adj.* fungus-like. **mycetophagous,** *adj.* eating fungi.

mycoderma [ˌmaɪkə'dɜːmə] *n.* membrane formed on fermenting liquid; 'mother'; kind of fungus forming scum on liquid. **mycodermic, mycodermatoid, mycodermatous,** *adj.*

mycoid ['maɪkɔɪd] *adj.* fungus-like.

mycology [maɪ'kɒlədʒɪ] *n.* study of fungi. **mycological,** *adj.* **mycologist,** *n.*

mycophagous [maɪ'kɒfəgəs] *adj.* eating mushrooms. **mycophagist,** *n.* **mycophagy,** *n.*

mycorrhiza, mycorhiza [ˌmaɪkə'raɪzə] *n.* association in symbiosis of certain fungi with roots of certain plants and trees. **mycorrhizal,** *adj.*

mycosis [maɪ'kəʊsɪs] *n.* (*pl.* **–ses**) infestation with fungi. **mycotic** [–'kɒtɪk], *adj.*

mycteric [mɪk'terɪk] *adj.* pertaining to cavities of nose. **mycterism,** *n.* sneering.

mydriatic [ˌmɪdri'ætɪk] *n. & adj.* (substance) causing dilatation of pupil of eye. **mydriasis** [mɪ'draɪəsɪs], *n.* such excessive dilatation.

myectopy, myectopia [maɪ'ektəpi, –əʊpiə] *n.* dislocation of muscle.

myelic [maɪ'elɪk] *adj.* pertaining to spinal cord. **myelencephalous,** *adj.* having brain and spinal cord. **myelitis,** *n.* inflammation of spinal cord or marrow of bones. **myelocyte,** *n.* nerve-cell of brain or spinal cord. **myeloid,** *adj.* myelic. **myeloma,** *n.* tumour of bone marrow. **myelon,** *n.* spinal cord. .

myentasis [maɪ'entəsɪs] *n.* surgical stretching of muscle.

mygale ['mɪgəli] *n.* shrew mouse.

myiasis ['maɪəsɪs, maɪ'aɪə–] *n.* disease due to flies' larvae in body.

myoglobin [ˌmaɪə'gləʊbɪn] *n.* protein carrying oxygen to muscle as haemoglobin carries it to blood.

myograph ['maɪəgrɑːf] *n.* instrument recording strength of muscular contraction. **myography,** *n.* description of muscles.

myoid ['maɪɔɪd] *adj.* muscle-like.

myology [maɪ'ɒlədʒɪ] *n.* study of muscles. **myologic(al),** *adj.* **myologist,** *n.*

myopia, myopy [maɪ'əʊpiə, –'maɪəpi] *n.* short-sightedness. **myope,** *n.* person suffering from this. **myopic** [–'ɒpɪk], *adj.*

myosis [maɪ'əʊsɪs] *n.* miosis. **myotic,** *adj.*

myositis [ˌmaɪə'saɪtɪs] *n.* inflammation of muscles. **myositic** [–'sɪtɪk], *adj.*

myosotis [ˌmaɪə'səʊtɪs] *n.* forget-me-not.

myothermic [ˌmaɪə'θɜːmɪk] *adj.* pertaining to heat due to muscular contraction.

myotonia, myotonus, myotony [ˌmaɪə'təʊniə, –ɒtənəs, –ni] *n.* muscular spasm or rigidity.

myoxine [maɪ'ɒksaɪn, –sɪn] *adj.* pertaining to dormice.

myriacanthous [ˌmɪriə'kænθəs] *adj.* having many prickles.

myriapod ['mɪriəpɒd] *n.* millepede or centipede. **myriapodan** [–'æpədən], **myriapodous** [–əs], *adj.*

myringa [mɪ'rɪŋgə] *n.* ear drum. **myringitis** [–ˌmɪrɪn'dʒaɪtɪs], *n.* inflammation of myringa.

myristicaceous [mɪˌrɪstɪ'keɪʃəs] *adj.* like or pertaining to nutmeg tree; belonging to nutmeg family of plants. **myristicivorous** [–'sɪvərəs], *adj.* feeding on nutmegs.

myrmecoid ['mɜːmɪkɔɪd] *adj.* ant-like. **myrmecology,** *n.* study of ants. **myrmecophagous,** *adj.* ant-eating. **myrmecophyte,** *n.* plant living in symbiosis with ants.

myrmidon ['mɜːmɪdən] *n.* follower; hireling.

myrobalan [maɪ'rɒbələn] *n.* prune-like tannin-containing fruit, used in tanning and dyeing; Indian tree bearing this.

myrtaceous [mɜː'teɪʃəs] *adj.* belonging to myrtle family of plants. **myrtiform,** *adj.* myrtle-like.

mysophobia [ˌmaɪsə'fəʊbiə] *n.* dread of dirt. **mysophilia,** *n.* unnatural attraction to dirt.

mystacial [mɪ'steɪʃl] *adj.* having moustache-like stripe. **mystacal, mystacine, mystacinous**

[ˌmɪstə'saɪnəs], *adj.* **mystax,** *n.* mouth-hairs of insects.

mystagogue ['mɪstəgɒg] n instructor in mystical doctrines or of those being initiated into religious mysteries. **mystagogic,** *adj.* **mystagogy,** *n.*

mysticete ['mɪstɪsiːt] *n.* Arctic right whale. **mysticetous,** *adj.*

mythoclast ['mɪθəklæst] *n.* destroyer of myths. **mythoclastic,** *adj.* **mythogony,** *n.* study of myths' origins. **mythography,** *n.* descriptive study or artistic representation, of myths. **mythomania,** *n.* desire or aptitude for telling lies.

mythopoeic, *adj.* myth-making. **mythopoesis,** *n.* composition of myths.

mytilid ['maɪtɪlɪd] *n.* mussel. **mytiliform, mytiloid,** *adj.*

myxoedema [ˌmɪksɪ'diːmə] *n.* skin disease, marked by swelling and dryness, due to insufficient thyroid secretion. **myxoedemic, myxoedematoid, myxoedematous,** *adj.*

myxoid *adj.* mucoid. **myxoma,** *n.* soft mucoid tumour. **myxomatosis,** *n.* fatal contagious disease of rabbits.

N

naartjie ['nɑːtʃi] (*S African*) *n*. tangerine.

nabob ['neɪbɒb] *n*. Indian or Mogul governor; wealthy person, especially retired Anglo-Indian.

nacelle [nə'sel] *n*. airship passenger compartment; structure on aircraft wing containing engine.

nachtmaal ['nɑːktmɑːl] (*S African*) *n*. evening meal; Lord's Supper.

nacre ['neɪkə] *n*. mother-of-pearl; shellfish bearing it. **nacreous, nacrine,** *adj*.

nadir ['neɪdɪə] *n*. point opposite zenith; lowest point. **nadiral,** *adj*.

naevus ['niːvəs] *n*. small mark on skin; birthmark; tumour of small blood vessel. **naevoid,** *n*. like this.

nagana [næ'gɑːnə] *n*. tropical disease of cattle transmitted by tsetse fly.

nagor ['neɪgɔː] *n*. S African reed-buck.

naiad ['naɪæd, 'neɪ–] *n*. (*pl*. **-es,** [-ez] water-nymph; fresh-water mussel; aquatic larva of dragonfly.

nainsook ['neɪnsuk] *n*. Indian fabric of fine cotton.

naissant ['neɪsnt] *adj*. nascent; *Heraldry*, rising.

namaqua [nə'mɑːkwə] *n*. kind of African dove.

nanism ['neɪnɪzm] *n*. state of being a dwarf. **nanization,** *n*. art of dwarfing (plants).

nannander [næ'nændə] *n*. dwarf male plant. **nannandrous,** *adj*.

nano- ['nænəʊ–, 'neɪnəʊ–] *prefix* of measurement meaning one thousand millionth (10-9) *abbr*. **n.**

nanocephalous [,nænə'sefələs, ,neɪ–] *adj*. having abnormally small head. **nanoid,** *adj*. dwarfish. **nanomalous,** *adj*. having abnormally short limbs.

naology [neɪ'ɒlədʒi] *n*. study of ecclesiastical buildings. **naological,** *adj*.

napellus [nə'peləs] *n*. aconite

napery ['neɪpəri] *n*. table and other household linen.

naphtha ['næfθə] *n*. volatile petroleum-like liquid. **naphthalic, naphthous,** *adj*. **naphthaline, naphthalene,** *n*. hydrocarbon obtained from coal tar and used in dyeing, etc.

napiform ['neɪpɪfɔːm] *adj*. turnip-shaped.

naprapathy [nəpræpəθi] *n*. medical treatment by manipulation of spine, thorax or pelvis.

narceine ['nɑːsiiːn, –ɪn] *n*. narcotic alkaloid found in opium.

narcissism [nɑː'sɪsɪzm, 'nɑːs–] *n*. excessive self-concern or self-admiration; sexual love of, or excitement aroused by, one's own body. **narcissist,** *n*. **narcissistic,** *adj*.

narcohypnia [,nɑːkə'hɪpnɪə] *n*. numb feeling experienced on awakening.

narcolepsy ['nɑːkəlepsi] *n*. condition marked by short fits of heavy sleep. **narcoleptic,** *adj*.

narcoma [nɑː'kəʊmə] *n*. coma caused by narcotics. **narcomatous,** *adj*.

narcosis [nɑː'kəʊsɪs] *n*. stupor induced by narcotics. **narcose,** *adj*. in a stupor.

narcotherapy [,nɑːkəʊ'θerəpi] *n*. treatment of mental disturbance by prolonged drug-induced sleep.

narcotism ['nɑːkətɪzm] *n*. narcosis; tendency to fall asleep; abuse of narcotics. **narcotine,** *n*. alkaloid found in opium. **narcotize,** *v.t*. induce narcosis in.

narcous ['nɑːkəs] *adj*. narcose.

nard [nɑːd] *n*. spikenard; ointment made of it. **nardine,** *adj*.

nares ['neəriːz] *n. pl*. nostrils.

narghile ['nɑːgɪleɪ, –li] *n*. Oriental tobacco pipe in which smoke is drawn through water by a long tube; hookah; hubble-bubble.

narial, naric ['neərɪəl –'nærɪk] *adj*. pertaining to nostrils. **nariform,** *adj*. nostril-like. **narine,** *adj*. pertaining to nostrils.

narthex ['nɑːθeks] *n*. church porch; vestibule. **narthecal** [–'θiːkl], *adj*.

narwhal ['nɑːwəl] *n*. kind of greyish dolphin with one long tusk; sea-unicorn.

nascent ['næsnt] *adj*. being born; beginning to grow; having enhanced chemical activity at moment of liberation from compound. **nascency,** *n*.

nasicorn ['neɪzɪkɔːn] *adj*. having horn(s) on nose; *n*. rhinoceros. **nasicornous,** *adj*.

nasillate ['neɪzɪleɪt] *v.i*. speak or sing nasally. **nasillation,** *n*.

nasitis [neɪ'zaɪtɪs] *n*. nasal inflammation.

nasology [neɪ'zɒlədʒi] *n*. study of noses.

nasute ['neɪzjuːt, neɪ'sjuːt] *adj*. having large nose. **nasutiform,** *adj*. nose-like.

natable ['neɪtəbl] *adj*. able to float. **natability,** *n*.

natal ['neɪtl] *adj*. pertaining to birth; native; pertaining to nates. **natality,** *n*. birth-rate; birth.

natant ['neɪtnt] *adj*. swimming or floating.

natation [neɪ'teɪʃn] *n*. swimming. **natator,** *n*. **natatorial, natatory,** *adj*. **natatorium,** *n*. (*pl*. **-ia**) swimming pool.

nates ['neɪtiːz] *n. pl*. buttocks. **natiform,** *adj*. like nates.

natricine ['nætrɪsaɪn, –sɪn] *adj*. belonging to genus of snakes including grass and water snakes; *n*. such snake.

natron ['neɪtrɒn] *n*. natural carbonate of soda.

natterjack ['nætədʒæk] *n*. yellowish-brown European toad.

natura naturans [næ'tjʊərə 'nætjʊrænz] *n*. creative nature; Creator; God. **natura naturata,** created nature.

naturopathy [ˌneɪtʃəˈrɒpəθi] *n.* medical treatment by methods believed to aid nature. **naturopath, naturopathist,** *n.*

naumachy, naumachia [ˈnɔːməki, -eɪkiə] *n.* mock sea-battle; arena for it.

naupathia [nɔːˈpæθɪə] *n.* sea-sickness.

nauplius [ˈnɔːpliəs] *n.* (*pl.* **-ii**) first larval form of crustacean. **nauplial, naupliform, nauplioid,** *adj.*

nautch [nɔːtʃ] *n.* Indian dancing performance.

nautics [ˈnɔːtɪks] *n.* art of navigation; *n.pl.* water sports.

nautilus [ˈnɔːtɪləs] *n.* kind of mollusc of Pacific. **paper nautilus,** eight-tentacled mollusc with thin papery shell; argonaut. **pearly nautilus,** nautilus with pearly inner shell.

navarch [ˈneɪvɑːk] *n.* fleet-commander. **navarchy,** *n.*

navarin [ˈnævərɪn, -æn] (*French*) *n.* stew of mutton and vegetables.

navicular [nəˈvɪkjʊlə] *adj.* pertaining to or like a boat; *n.* boat-shaped bone of wrist. **naviculoid, naviform,** *adj.* boat-shaped.

nawab [nəˈwɔːb] *n.* Indian nobleman or governor; nabob.

nazim [ˈnɑːzɪm] (*Arabic*) *n.* Indian military governor.

nazir [ˈnɑːzɪə] (*Arabic*) *n.* Indian court treasurer; Muslim official.

neanic [niˈænɪk] *adj.* young; brephic.

neat [niːt] *n. archaic,* ox, bullock or cow. **neatherd,** *n.* cow-herd.

nebula [ˈnebjʊlə] *n.* (*pl.* **-ae**) vast gaseous area of universe. **spiral nebula,** a galaxy, or island universe. **nebulize,** *v.t.* vaporize; atomize. **nebulose, nebulous,** *adj.* cloudy; vague. **nebular,** *adj.*

necessitarian [nɪˌsesɪˈteərɪən] *n. & adj. Philosophy,* fatalist. **necessitarianism,** *n.*

necessitous [nəˈsesɪtəs] *adj.* needy; destitute.

necrobiosis [ˌnekrəʊbaɪˈəʊsɪs] *n.* normal process of decay of body cells. **necrobiotic,** *adj.*

necrogenic, necrogenous [ˌnekrəˈdʒenɪk, -ɒdʒɪnəs] *adj.* pertaining to or derived from dead bodies.

necrolatry [neˈkrɒlətri] *n.* worship of the dead.

necrology [neˈkrɒlədʒi] *n.* death-roll; obituary. **necrologic(al),** *adj.* **necrologist,** *n.* **necrologue,** *n.* obituary.

necromancy [ˈnekrəmænsi] *n.* black magic; divination by communication with spirits. **necromancer,** *n.* **necromantic,** *adj.*

necromorphous [ˌnekrəˈmɔːfəs] *adj.* feigning death.

necropathy [neˈkrɒpəθi] *n.* necrotic disease.

necrophagous [neˈkrɒfəgəs] *adj.* feeding on dead bodies.

necrophilia [ˌnekrəˈfɪliə] *n.* sexual attraction to or intercourse with dead bodies. **necrophile, necrophiliac,** *adj. & n.* **necrophilous** [-ˈkrɒfɪləs], *adj.* fond of dead creatures as food.

necrophobia [ˌnekrəˈfəubiə] *n.* dread of dead bodies or death. **necrophobic,** *adj.*

necropolis [neˈkrɒpəlɪs] *n.* large cemetery. **necropolitan** [-ˈpɒlɪtən], *adj.*

necropsy [ˈnekrɒpsi] *n.* post-mortem examination. **necroscopy,** *n.* necropsy.

necrosis [neˈkrəʊsɪs] *n.* mortification of tissue. **necrotic** [-ˈkrɒtɪk], *adj.* **necrotize, necrose,** *v.i. & t.* suffer or cause to suffer necrosis.

necrotomy [neˈkrɒtəmi] *n.* dissection of dead bodies; removal of necrosed part. **necrotomic** [-ˈtɒmɪk], *adj.* **necrotomist,** *n.*

necrotype [ˈnekrətaɪp] *n.* extinct creature or species. **necrotypic** [-ˈtɪpɪk], *adj.*

nectar [ˈnektə] *n.* sugary liquid secreted by flowers; divine drink. **nectareal, nectarean, nectareous, nectarial, nectarian, nectarous,** *adj.* **nectariferous, nectiferous,** *adj.* yielding nectar. **nectarine,** [-iːn, -ɪn] *n.* smooth-skinned variety of peach. **nectarium** (*pl.* **-ia**), **nectary,** *n.* plant's gland secreting nectar. **nectarivorous,** *adj.* feeding on nectar.

nectopod [ˈnektəpɒd] *n.* swimming limb.

ne exeat [ˌneɪ ˈeksɪæt, ˌniː-] (*Latin*) 'let him not go out'; writ forbidding person to leave country or court's jurisdiction.

nefandous [nɪˈfændəs] *adj.* unspeakable.

nefarious [nɪˈfeərɪəs] *adj.* evil.

negatron [ˈnegətrɒn] *n.* hypothetical atomic particle with mass equal to that of a proton, but with a negative charge equal to that of an electron.

négligé(e) [ˈneglɪʒeɪ] (*French*) *n.* easy, comfortable dress; partly-undressed state; loose robe.

negotiable [nɪˈgəʊʃiəbl] *adj. Commerce,* transferable; capable of being exchanged for cash.

negrillo [nɪˈgrɪləʊ] *n.* African pygmy. **negrito** [-ˈgriːt-], *n.* SE Asian pygmy.

negus [ˈniːgəs] *n.* drink of wine, hot water and spices; title of Abyssinian ruler.

nek [nek] (*S African*) *n.* mountain pass.

nekton [ˈnektɒn] *n.* swimming creatures of open sea. **nektonic,** *n.*

nemaline [ˈneməlaɪn] *adj.* thread-like.

nematoceran [ˌneməˈtɒsərən] *n. & adj.* (insect) belonging to the suborder of flies including mosquitoes. **nematocerous,** *adj.*

nematode [ˈnemətəʊd] *n.* parasitic round-worm. **nematodiasis,** *n.* infestation with these. **nematocide,** *n.* substance killing these. **nematology,** *n.* study of these.

Nemesis [ˈnemɪsɪs] (*Greek*) *n.* goddess of revenge; retribution; inevitable consequence. **nemesic** [-ˈmesɪk], *adj.*

nemoral [ˈnemərəl] *adj.* pertaining to or living in a forest or wood. **nemophilous,** *adj.* fond of forests or woods. **nemoricolous, nemoricoline,** *adj.* living in forests or groves.

nenuphar [ˈnenjufɑː] *n.* white or yellow water-lily.

neoblastic [ˌniːəˈblæstɪk] *adj.* pertaining to new growth.

neoclassicism [ˌniːəʊˈklæsɪsɪzm] *n.* revival of classical style in art, especially in the art and architecture of the late 18th and early 19th centuries. **neoclassical,** *adj.*

neocolonialism [ˌniːəʊkəˈləʊniəlɪzm] *n.* maintenance by a former imperial power of economic and political influence over liberated peoples.

neolatry [niˈɒlətri] *n.* worship of novelty. **neolater,** *n.*

neolithic [ˌniːəˈlɪθɪk] *adj.* pertaining to the later Stone Age. **neolith,** *n.* stone tool of this period.

neologism [niˈɒlədʒɪzm] *n.* use or coining of a new word; such new word; *Theology,* new doctrine, especially rationalism. **neologian** [ˌniːəˈləʊdʒiən], *n. Theology,* rationalist. **neologic(al),** *adj.* **neology, neologist,** *n.* **neologize,** *v.t.*

neomenia [ˌniːəˈmiːniə] *n.* time of new moon. **neomenian**, *adj.*

neomorphic [ˌniːəˈmɔːfɪk] *adj.* developed suddenly and not inherited. **neomorph**, *n.* **neomorphism**, *n.*

neomycin [ˌniːəʊˈmaɪsɪn] *n.* an antibiotic drug used against some intestinal diseases.

neonate [ˈniːəneɪt] *n.* new-born child. **neonatal**, *adj.* **neonatology**, *n.* care and treatment of neonates.

neonomian [ˌniːəˈnəʊmiən] *n.* adherent of new law, especially of that of the New Testament. **neonomianism**, *n.*

neophilia [ˌniːəʊˈfɪliə] *n.* love of novelty and new things, ideas, etc. **neophobia** [–ˈfəʊbiə], *n.* dread of the new.

neophrastic [ˌniːəˈfræstɪk] *adj.* pertaining to use of neologisms.

neophyte [ˈniːəfaɪt] *n.* recent convert; novice; beginner. **neophytic** [–ˈfɪtɪk], *adj.* **neophytism**, *n.*

neoplasm [ˈniːəplæzm] *n.* abnormal new growth, especially of tumours. **neoplastic**, *adj.* **neoplasty**, *n.* formation of part afresh by plastic surgery.

neoprene [ˈniːəpriːn] *n.* a type of artificial rubber.

neorama [ˌniːəˈrɑːmə] *n.* view of interior of building.

neossology [ˌniːɒˈsɒlədʒi] *n.* study of nestling birds. **neossoptile**, *n.* newly hatched bird's downy feather.

neoteny [nɪˈɒtəni] *n.* indefinite prolongation of period of immaturity; retention of infantile or juvenile characteristics into adulthood. **neotenous**, *adj.*

neoteric [ˌniːəˈterɪk] *adj.* new; modern; *n.* such thing. **neoterism** [nɪˈɒtərɪzm], *n.* neologism. **neoterist**, *n.* **neoteristic**, *adj.* **neoterize**, *v.t.*

neotropical [ˌniːəˈtrɒpɪkl] *adj.* occurring in or pertaining to tropical part of New World.

nepenthe [nɪˈpenθi] *n.* drug destroying sorrow. **nepenthes** [–iːz], *n.* pitcher-plant.

nephalism [ˈnefəlɪzm] *n.* teetotalism. **nephalist**, *n.*

nepheligenous [ˌnefəˈlɪdʒənəs] *adj.* discharging smoke in clouds. **nephelognosy**, *n.* observation of clouds. **nepheloid**, *adj.* cloudy. **nephelometer**, *n.* instrument measuring cloudiness. **nephelorometer**, *n.* instrument measuring clouds'

direction and velocity. **nepheloscope**, *n.* instrument demonstrating formation of clouds.

nephology [nɪˈfɒlədʒi] *n.* study of clouds. **nephogram**, *n.* cloud photograph. **nephoscope**, *n.* instrument measuring direction, velocity, etc., of clouds.

nephrectomy [neˈfrektəmi] *n.* surgical removal of kidney. **nephrectomize**, *v.i. & t.*

nephria [ˈnefriə] *n.* Bright's disease. **nephric**, *adj.* pertaining to kidneys. **nephrism**, *n.* chronic kidney disease.

nephrite [ˈnefraɪt] *n.* kind of jade used as charm against kidney disease; kidney stone.

nephritis [nɪˈfraɪtɪs] *n.* inflammation of kidneys. **nephritic** [–ˈfrɪtɪk], *adj.* pertaining to nephritis or kidneys; *n.* person suffering from nephritis.

nephroid [ˈnefrɔɪd] *adj.* kidney-shaped. **nephrolith**, *n.* stone of the kidney. **nephrology**, *n.* study of kidneys. **nephrolysis**, *n.* destruction of tissue of kidneys. **nephropathy**, *n.* kidney disease. **nephropexy**, *n.* surgical fixing of floating kidney. **nephroptosis**, *n.* floating kidney. **nephrosis**, *n.* degeneration of kidneys. **nephrotomy**, *n.* incision into kidney. **nephrotoxic**, *adj.* poisoning the kidneys.

nepionic [ˌnepiˈɒnɪk] *adj.* very young; at stage immediately following embryo.

ne plus ultra [ˌneɪ plʊs ˈʊltrɑː, ˌniː plʌs ˈʌltrə] (*Latin*) 'no more beyond'; highest or furthest attainable.

nepotism [ˈnepətɪzm] *n.* favouring of relatives in giving appointments and offices. **nepotal**, *adj.* pertaining to nephew. **nepotic** [–ˈpɒtɪk], *adj.* **nepotist**, *n.*

neptunium [nepˈtjuːniəm] *n.* one of the transuranic elements.

nereid [ˈnɪəriɪd] *n.* sea-nymph; sea-centipede.

neritic [nɪˈrɪtɪk] *n.* pertaining to shallow coastal waters.

Neronian, Neronic [nɪˈrəʊniən, –ɒnɪk] *n.* like Nero, Roman emperor infamous for cruelty and vice. **Neronize**, *v.i. & t.*

nerval [ˈnɜːvəl] *adj.* neural; *n.* ointment for sinews. **nervation**, *n.* arrangement of nerves or veins.

nervine [ˈnɜːvaɪn, –iːn] *n. & adj.* (drug) affecting, especially soothing, nerves.

nescient [ˈnesiənt] *adj.* lacking or disclaiming knowledge; *n.* agnostic. **nescience**, *n.*

A not uncommon problem

The use of two or more negative words (*not, never, nothing* etc.) together in the same clause or sentence is traditionally regarded as an error in modern standard English, although from AngloSaxon times until the 18th century it was quite usual and acceptable to add extra negatives for emphasis ('He nevere yet no vileynye ne sayde/In all his lyf unto no maner wight [person],' Chaucer, Prologue, *Canterbury Tales*). Today such emphatic use (as in 'I wouldn't never tell you a lie') is largely restricted to certain dialects, and although it seldom leads to misunderstandings, the weight of objection to it is so heavy that it is widely avoided, particularly in written English.

However, there are other, less obvious sorts of double negative which are not so easy to avoid. For example, it is quite common for expressions like 'I shouldn't be surprised if' and 'I shouldn't wonder if' to be followed by a further negative clause ('I shouldn't be surprised if they weren't late') even when the intended meaning is positive. And words with an underlying negative connotation (e.g. *deny*) can attract a superfluous extra negative ('I can't deny there isn't some possibility of failure'). Constructions of this sort are frowned upon by purists, who however find nothing to quarrel with in expressions like 'a not uncommon problem', in which the positive is expressed by *not* and a negative adjective.

nesiote ['niːsiəut] *adj.* living on an island.

nestitherapy [ˌnestɪ'θerəpi] *n.* medical treatment by reducing food taken.

netsuke ['netski, –suːkeɪ] (*Japanese*) *n.* kind of carved button of wood, ivory, bone, etc.

neural ['njuərəl] *adj.* pertaining to nerves; dorsal.

neuralgia [nju'rældʒiə] *n.* pain along nerve. **neuralgiac,** *n.* person suffering from neuralgia. **neuralgic,** *adj.* **neuralgiform,** *adj.* like neuralgia.

neurasthenia [ˌnjuərəs'θiːniə] *n.* nervous debility or breakdown. **neurasthenic** [–'θenɪk], *n. & adj.*

neuration [nju'reɪʃn] *n.* nervation.

neurergic [nju'rɜːdʒɪk] *adj.* pertaining to nerve action.

neuric ['njuərɪk] *adj.* pertaining to or having nerves.

neurilemma [ˌnjuərɪ'lemə] *n.* outer nerve sheath. **neurilemmal, neurilemmatic, neurilemmatous,** *adj.* **neurilemmitis,** *n.* inflammation of nerve sheath.

neurine ['njuəriːn, –aɪn] *n.* poison arising in decaying flesh.

neuritis [nju'raɪtɪs] *n.* inflammation of nerve.

neurogram ['njuərəgræm] *n.* modification in nerve structure to which memory is due. **neurogrammic,** *adj.* **neurography,** *n.* formation of neurograms; descriptive neurology.

neuroid ['njuərɔɪd] *n.* nerve-like.

neuroleptic [ˌnjuərə'leptɪk] *adj.* capable of having an effect on the brain, especially tranquillising; *n.* such drug.

neurology [nju'rɒlədʒi] *n.* study of nerves and brain. **neurological,** *adj.* **neurologist,** *n.*

neurolysis [nju'rɒləsɪs] *n.* disintegration of nerve substance; surgical liberation of nerve.

neuroma [nju'rəumə] *n.* nerve tumour. **neuromatous,** *adj.* **neuromatosis,** *n.*

neuromimesis [ˌnjuərəmaɪ'miːsɪs] *n.* imitation of symptoms of disease by neurotic person. **neuromimetic** [–'metɪk], *adj.*

neuron(e) ['njuərɒn, –rəun] *n.* nerve cell. **neuronal, neuronic,** *adj.* **neuronism,** *n.* theory that neurons of brain are most important in mental processes.

neuropath ['njuərəpæθ] *n.* person believing that majority of diseases have nervous origin; sufferer from nervous disease. **neuropathic,** *adj.* **neuropathology,** *n.* pathology of nervous system. **neuropathy** [–'rɒpəθi], *n.* morbid condition of nerve.

neuropterous [nju'rɒptərəs] *adj.* pertaining or belonging to insect order including lace-wing flies. **neuropteran, neuropteron** (*pl.* –ra), *n.* such insect. **neuropterist,** *n.* student of these insects. **neuropterology,** *n.* study of such.

neurosis [nju'rəusɪs] *n.* (*pl.* –ses) relatively mild mental disturbance; disorder of nervous system. **neurotic** [–'rɒtɪk], *n. & adj.* (person) suffering from nervous disease; (drug) acting on nerves.

neurotomy [nju'rɒtəmi] *n.* dissection of or incision into nerve. **neurotomical** [ˌnjuərə'tɒmɪkl], *adj.* **neurotomist,** *n.*

neurotoxin ['njuərə,tɒksɪn] *n.* poison that attacks the nervous system. **neurotoxic,** *adj.*

neurypnology [ˌnjuərɪp'nɒlədʒi] *n.* study of hypnotism and of sleep.

neuston ['njuːstɒn] *n.* minute organisms on the surface film of open water; ecosystem of surface film.

neutrino [nju'triːnəu] *n.* uncharged atomic particle of less mass than neutron.

neutron ['njuːtrɒn] *n.* uncharged proton-like particle of atom.

névé ['neveɪ] *n.* grainy snow in the process of becoming glacial ice.

newel ['njuːəl] *n.* post at foot or head of stairs, or about which spiral staircase turns.

nexus ['neksəs] *n.* bond; tie; interconnected group.

niblick ['nɪblɪk] *n.* iron-headed golf club with steeply angled face, for playing out of bunkers.

niccolic, niccolous ['nɪkəlɪk, –əs] *n.* of nickel.

nichevo [ˌnɪtʃɪ'vɔː, –'vəu] (*Russian*) *exclamation* 'it doesn't matter'.

nicolo, niccolo ['nɪkələu] *n.* blue-black variety of onyx.

nicotian [nɪ'kəuʃiən] *n.* tobacco-user.

nictate [nɪk'teɪt] *v.i.* nictitate. **nictation,** *n.*

nictitate ['nɪktɪteɪt] *v.i.* wink or blink. **nictitant,** *adj.* winking. **nictitating membrane,** membrane of certain animals and birds that can be drawn across eyeball; **nictitating spasm,** spasm of eyelid. **nictitation,** *n.*

nidatory ['nɪdətəri] *adj.* pertaining to nests. **nidicolous,** *adj.* living in nests. **nidificate, nidify,** *v.i.* construct nest. **nidifugous,** *adj.* leaving nest at early stage. **nidology,** *n.* study of nests. **nidulant,** *adj.* nestling. **nidus** ['naɪdəs], *n.* (*pl.* –di) nest; place of breeding or origin.

niello [ni'eləu] *n.* (*pl.* –li) black alloy used to fill engraved designs on metal; work or object decorated with this; *v.i.* decorate with this. **niellist,** *n.*

nigrescent [nɪ'gresnt] *adj.* becoming or somewhat black. **nigrescence,** *n.* **nigrine,** *adj.* black. **nigrities,** *n.* unusually dark colouring. **nigritude,** *n.* blackness. **nigrous** ['naɪgrəs], *adj.*

nihilism ['naɪlɪzm] *n.* extreme anarchism; terrorism; *Philosophy,* denial that anything has real existence. **nihilist,** *n.* **nihility,** *n.* nothingness; thing of no worth.

nilgai ['nɪlgaɪ] *n.* blue-grey short-horned Indian antelope.

nimbus ['nɪmbəs] *n.* (*pl.* –bi) halo; cloud of glory; low, black rain-cloud. **nimbose,** *adj.* cloudy.

nimiety [nɪ'maɪəti] *n.* excess.

nirvana [nɜː'vɑːnə] *n.* oblivion; loss of identity at death by union with Brahma. **nirvanic,** *adj.*

nisi ['naɪsaɪ] (*Latin*) *conj.* 'unless'. **decree nisi,** order, especially of divorce, to become effective at certain future time, unless reasons against it appear in the meantime. **nisi prius** [– 'praɪəs], 'unless before'; formerly, writ summoning jurors to Westminster unless in the meantime judges of assize had come to county in question; now, trial by jury before a single judge, in London or at assizes.

nisus ['naɪsəs] *n.* effort, especially to evacuate faeces; desire, especially sexual of birds.

nitchevo *see* **nichevo.**

nitid ['nɪtɪd] *adj.* shining.

nitre ['naɪtə] *n.* saltpetre (potassium nitrate). **cubic nitre,** sodium nitrate. **nitrate,** *n.* salt of nitric acid; *v.t.* treat with nitric acid. **nitric,** *adj.* **nitrify,** *v.t.* **nitrophilous,** *adj.* flourishing in soil rich in nitrogen. **nitrophyte,** *n.* nitrophilous plant. **nitrous,** *adj.*

nival ['naɪvl] *adj.* marked by, or living in, snow.

nivellate ['nɪvəleɪt] *v.t.* level. **nivellation, nivellator,** *n.*

niveous ['nɪvɪəs] *adj.* snowy. **nivosity,** *n.*

nix [nɪks] *n. (fem. –ie)* water sprite.

nizam [nɪ'zɑːm, naɪ–, –'zæm] *(Urdu) n.* title of former ruler of Hyderabad; Turkish soldier.

Noachian, Noachic [nəʊ'eɪkɪən, –ɪk] *adj.* pertaining to Noah and his period.

nobiliary [nə'bɪlɪəri] *n.* pertaining to nobility. **nobiliary particle,** preposition indicating nobility, *e.g. de* (French) or *von* (German).

noblesse [nəʊ'bles] *(French) n.* noble birth; nobility. **noblesse oblige** [–ɒb'liːʒ], 'nobility obliges'; obligation upon persons of high birth to act nobly.

nocent ['nəʊsnt] *adj.* harmful; criminal.

noctambulant [nɒk'tæmbjʊlənt] *adj.* walking by night or in one's sleep. **noctambulation, noctambulism,** *n.* **noctambulist,** *n.* sleep-walker. **noctambulous,** *adj.*

noctidiurnal [ˌnɒktɪdaɪ'ɜːnl] *adj.* comprising one day and night.

noctiflorous [ˌnɒktɪ'flɔːrəs] *adj.* flowering at night.

noctiluca [ˌnɒktɪ'luːkə] *n. (pl. –cae)* luminescent sea creature. **noctilucal, noctilucent,** *adj.* luminescent (applied to living organisms only). **noctilucence,** *n.* **noctilucous,** *adj.* shining at night; luminescent.

noctivagant [nɒk'tɪvəgənt] *adj.* wandering about at night. **noctivagation,** *n.* **noctivagous,** *adj.*

noctovision ['nɒktəvɪʒn] *n.* transmission by infrared rays of image of object invisible through darkness.

noctuid ['nɒktjuɪd] *n.* night-flying moth.

nocturia [nɒk'tjuərɪə] *n.* abnormal urination at night.

nocuous ['nɒkjuəs] *adj.* harmful.

nodus ['nəʊdəs] *n. (pl. –di)* crucial or difficult point; knot.

noegenesis [ˌnəʊɪ'dʒenəsɪs] *n.* production of new knowledge. **noegenetic** [–dʒə'netɪk], *adj.*

noesis [nəʊ'iːsɪs] *n.* pure knowledge; cognition. **noetic** [–'etɪk], *n. & adj.* **noetics,** *n.* laws of logic.

Noetic [nəʊ'etɪk] *adj.* Noachian.

noggin ['nɒgɪn] *n.* small cup or quantity; gill.

nogging ['nɒgɪn] *n.* masonry or brickwork between wooden frame.

noisette [nwɑː'zet] *n.* small thick round slice of boneless meat, especially lamb; hazelnut (chocolate).

noisome ['nɔɪsəm] *adj.* foul-smelling.

nolens volens [ˌnəʊlenz 'vəʊlenz] *(Latin)* willynilly.

noli me tangere [ˌnəʊli meɪ 'tæŋgəri, ˌnəʊlaɪ miː 'tændʒ–] *(Latin)* 'do not touch me'.

nolition [nə'lɪʃn] *n.* unwillingness.

nolle prosequi ['nɒli 'prɒsɪkwaɪ] *(Latin)* 'to be unwilling to prosecute'; withdrawal of suit by plaintiff.

nom [nɒm] *(French) n.* 'name'. **nom de guerre** [–də 'geə], 'war name'; pseudonym. **nom de plume** [–də 'pluːm], 'pen name'; writer's pseudonym.

nomenclature [nəʊ'meŋklətʃə, 'nəʊmənkleɪtʃə] *n.* system or arrangement of names; terminology of a science. **nomenclator,** *n.*

lexicographer; announcer or inventor of names. **nomenclatorial, nomenclatural,** *adj.*

nomial ['nəʊmɪəl] *n.* single term.

nomic ['nɒmɪk, 'nəʊ–] *adj.* customary; conventional; *n.* such non-phonetic spelling.

nominalism ['nɒmɪnl–ɪzm] *(Philosophy) n.* doctrine that universal terms and abstractions are mere names and have no reality. **nominalist,** *n.*

nominative ['nɒmɪnətɪv] *n. & adj. Grammar,* (case) signifying subject of sentence.

nomism ['nəʊmɪzm] *n.* acceptance of moral law as basis of conduct. **nomistic,** *adj.*

nomocracy [nə'mɒkrəsi] *n.* government based on legal system.

nomogenist [nə'mɒdʒənɪst] *n.* believer in nonmiraculous origin of life. **nomogenous,** *adj.* **nomogeny,** *n.*

nomography [nə'mɒgrəfi] *n.* drafting of laws; treatise on this. **nomographer,** *n.* **nomographic(al),** *adj.*

nomology [nə'mɒlədʒi] *n.* science of law. **nomological,** *adj.* **nomologist,** *n.*

nomothetic [ˌnəʊmə'θetɪk] *adj.* legislative; based on law. **nomothetes** [nə'mɒθɪtiːz], *Greek n. pl. –tai)* law-giver.

nonage ['nəʊnɪdʒ] *n.* state of being under age.

nonagenarian [ˌnəʊnədʒə'neərɪən] *n. & adj.* (person) in from ninetieth to hundredth year. **nonagesimal,** *adj.* ninetieth.

nones [nəʊnz] *n. pl.* ninth day before ides in ancient Roman calendar; *Ecclesiastical,* office said at ninth hour.

non est [nɒn est] *(Latin)* '(it) is not'; non-existent; lacking. **non est disputandum,** not to be disputed. **non esse,** non-existence.

nonfeasance [nɒn'fiːzns] *n.* failure to perform an act or obligation.

nonferrous [nɒn'ferəs] *adj.* not pertaining to or including iron; pertaining to metals other than iron.

non grata [nɒn 'grɑːtə] *(Latin)* 'not welcome'; not acceptable to society or by authority.

nonillion [nə'nɪljən] *n.* a million octillions (10^{54}); *(French & American)* a thousand octillions (10^{30}).

nonjuror [ˌnɒn'dʒuərə] *n.* person refusing to take oath, especially of allegiance to William and Mary (1688). **nonjurant,** *adj.* **nonjurism,** *n.*

non libet [ˌnɒn 'laɪbet, 'lɪb–] *(Latin)* 'it is not pleasing'. **non licet** [–'laɪset, 'lɪs–], 'it is not lawful'. **non liquet** [–'laɪkwet, 'lɪk–], 'it is not clear'.

non obstante [ˌnɒn ɒb'stænti] *(Latin)* notwithstanding *(abbr.* **non obst.**).

nonpareil [ˌnɒnpə'reɪl] *n.* size of type: 6-point; *n. & adj.* unique (thing or person).

nonparous [ˌnɒn'pærəs] *adj.* having not given birth to any offspring.

non placet [ˌnɒn 'plækət, –'pleɪsɪt] *(Latin)* '(it) does not please'; negative vote, especially at university, etc.

non possumus [ˌnɒn 'pɒsuməs, –ju–] *(Latin)* 'we cannot'; plea of inability; refusal.

non prosequitur [ˌnɒn prəʊ'sekwɪtə] '(he *or* she) does not prosecute'; judgement against plaintiff on his non-appearance in court *(abbr.* **non pros.**).

non sequitur [ˌnɒn 'sekwɪtə] *(Latin)* '(it) does not follow'; illogical deduction; fallacy; anacoluthon.

nonsuit ['nɒnsuːt] *n. Law,* judge's dismissal of suit when plaintiff fails to show good cause or produce evidence; *v.t.* dismiss a suit thus.

nonuple ['nɒnjupl] *adj.* ninefold; consisting of, or in sets of, nine.

non-user [ˌnɒn'juːzə] *n. Law,* failure to use, or exercise right.

noology [nəʊ'ɒlədʒi] *n.* study of intuition and reason. **nooscopic,** *adj.* pertaining to examination of mind.

nopal ['nəʊpl] *n.* prickly pear; cochineal fig.

nordcaper ['nɔːdkeɪpə] *n.* right whale.

normocyte ['nɔːməsaɪt] *n.* red blood corpuscle.

nosism ['nəʊzɪzm] *n.* conceit on part of a group; use of 'we' in speaking of oneself.

nosocomial [ˌnɒsə'kəʊmiəl] *adj.* (of a disease) contracted in hospital.

nosology [nɒ'sɒlədʒi, nəʊ–] *n.* classification of diseases. **nosography,** *n.* descriptive nosology. **nosomania,** *n.* delusion of suffering from imaginary disease. **nosophobia,** *n.* morbid dread of disease.

nostology [nɒ'stɒlədʒi] *n.* study of senility. **nostologic,** *adj.*

nostopathy [nɒ'stɒpəθi] *n.* morbid fear of returning to familiar places. **nostomania** [–ə'meɪniə], *n.* abnormally strong desire to return to familiar places; longing for one's home.

nostrification [ˌnɒstrɪfɪ'keɪʃn] *n.* acceptance of foreign university degrees as equal with native.

nostrum ['nɒstrəm] *n.* illusive remedy or scheme; quack medicine.

nota bene [ˌnəʊtə 'beni, –'biːni] (*Latin*) 'note well' (*abbr.* N.B.).

notabilia [ˌnəʊtə'bɪliə] *pl. n.* things worth noting.

notacanthous [ˌnəʊtə'kænθəs] *adj.* spiny-backed.

notal ['nəʊtl] *adj.* dorsal. **notalgia,** *n.* pain in back.

notandum [nəʊ'tændəm] (*Latin*) *n.* (*pl.* **-da**) thing to be noted.

notary ['nəʊtəri] *n.* (public) law officer certifying deeds, affidavits, etc. **notarial,** *adj.* **notarize,** *v.t.*

nothosaur ['nəʊθəsɔː] *n.* plesiosaurus-like fossil reptile. **nothosaurian,** *n. & adj.*

nothous ['nəʊθəs] *adj.* spurious; bastard.

notochord ['nəʊtəkɔːd] *n.* backbone-like series of cells in lowest vertebrates. **notochordal,** *adj.*

notornis [nə'tɔːnɪs] *n.* domestic-fowl-like bird of New Zealand

noumenon ['nuːmɪnɒn] *n.* (*pl.* **-mena**) object perceived by intellect or reason alone. **noumenal,** *adj.* **noumenalism,** *n.* belief in existence of noumena.

nous [naʊs, nuːs] *n.* pure intellect; reason; commonsense.

nouveau riche [ˌnuːvəʊ 'riːʃ] (*French*) (*pl.* **nouveaux riches;** *fem.* **nouvelle.** ......) newly-rich person.

nova ['nəʊvə] *n.* (*pl.* **-ae**) star suddenly increasing in brightness for short time.

novella [nə'velə] *n.* (*pl.* **-las, -le**) long short story; short novel.

novenary [nə'viːnəri, 'nɒvə–] *adj.* pertaining to or consisting of nine; *n.* set of nine. **novendial,** *n. & adj.* (festival) lasting nine days. **novennial,** *adj.* happening every ninth year.

novercal [nə'vɜːkl] *adj.* pertaining to stepmother.

novolescence [ˌnəʊvə'lesns] *n.* state of being new or up to date.

noxal ['nɒksl] *adj.* noxious; pertaining to damage.

noxious ['nɒkʃəs] *adj.* harmful.

noyade [nwaɪ'ɑːd, –'æd] (*French*) *n.* drowning, especially of many persons together as form of execution.

nu [njuː, nuː] *n.* thirteenth letter (N, *v*) of Gr. alphabet; /nū/ (*French*) *adj.* naked.

nuance ['njuːɑːns] (*French*) *n.* slight shade or difference.

nubia ['njuːbiə] *n.* cloud; lady's fleecy head-wrap. **nubilate,** *v.t.* obscure.

nubile ['njuːbaɪl] *adj.* marriageable (applied to women only). **nubility,** *n.*

nubilous ['njuːbɪləs] *adj.* cloudy; vague.

nucal ['njuːkl] *adj.* of nuts.

nuchal ['njuːkl] *adj.* pertaining to nape of neck; *n.* such bone, etc. **nuchalgia** [–'kældʒiː], *n.* pain in nape.

nuciferous [njuː'sɪfərəs] *adj.* yielding nuts. **nuciform,** *adj.* nut-shaped. **nucivorous,** *adj.* nut-eating.

nuclide ['njuːklaɪd] *n.* an atom of specified atomic number and mass number.

nudicaudate [ˌnjuːdɪ'kɔːdeɪt] *adj.* with hairless tail. **nudicaulous.** *adj.* with leafless stems. **nudiflora,** *adj.* flowering before leaves appear. **nudiflorous,** *adj.* with naked flowers. **nudiped,** *n. & adj.* (animal) with naked feet.

nugacious [njuː'geɪʃəs] *adj.* unimportant. **nucity,** *n.* triviality; futility. **nugae** ['njuːdʒiː], (*Latin*) *n.pl.* trifles.

nugatory ['njuːgətəri] *adj.* futile; powerless; null; nugacious.

nullah ['nʌlə] *n.* (in India) dry watercourse; gully; stream.

nulla-nulla ['nʌlə,nʌlə] *n.* Australian aborigine's club.

nullibist ['nʌlɪbɪst] *n.* person denying soul's existence in space.

nullifidian [ˌnʌlɪ'fɪdiən] *n. & adj.* sceptic(al).

nulliparous [nʌ'lɪpərəs] *adj.* having borne no children. **nullipara,** *n.* such woman. **nulliparity** [–'pærəti/, *n.*

nullius filius [ˌnʌliəs 'fɪliəs] (*Latin*) 'nobody's son'; bastard.

numen ['njuːmen] *n.* (*pl.* **-mina**) local or presiding divinity; god in human form. **numinism,** *n.* belief in numina. **numinous,** *adj.* pertaining to numina; awe-inspiring; supernatural.

numerology [ˌnjuːmə'rɒlədʒi] *n.* study of mystic meanings in numbers. **numerologist, numerist,** *n.*

numismatic [ˌnjuːmɪz'mætɪk] *adj.* pertaining to coins. **numismatics, numismatology,** *n.* study and collection of coins and medals. **numismatician, numismatist,** *n.* **numismatography,** *n.* description of coins.

nummary ['nʌməri] *adj.* pertaining to coin. **nummiform,** *adj.* coin-shaped.

nummular(y) ['nʌmjulə, –ri] *adj.* nummary; nummiform. **nummulite,** *n.* coin-like fossil shell.

Nunc Dimittis [ˌnʌŋk dɪ'mɪtɪs] (*Latin*) 'now thou lettest depart'; canticle (Luke ii, 29-32) sung at Evensong; permission to depart; congé.

nuncio ['nʌnsiəʊ] *n.* papal envoy. **nunciate,** *n.* messenger. **nunciative,** *adj.* bearing messages. **nunciature,** *n.* office of nuncio.

nuncupate [ˈnʌŋkjʊpeɪt] *v.t.* declare verbally; dedicate. **nuncupation,** *n.* **nuncupator,** *n.* **nuncupative, nuncupatory,** *adj.* oral; not written down; designative.

nundinal [ˈnʌndɪnl] *n.* one of first eight letters of alphabet, indicating day of week in ancient Rome; *adj.* pertaining to such; pertaining to market or market-day. **nundination,** *n.* trading. **nundine,** *n.* market-day, held in ancient Rome every eighth day.

nuptial [ˈnʌpʃl] *adj.* pertaining to wedding. **nuptiality,** *n.* wedding; marriage- rate. **nuptials,** *n. pl.* wedding.

nuque [njuːk] (*French*) *n.* nape.

nutation [njuːˈteɪʃn] *n.* nodding; such motion of earth's axis. **nutant,** *adj.* nodding or drooping. **nutal,** *adj.*

nutria [ˈnjuːtrɪə] *n.* coypu; its fur; browny-grey colour.

nutrice [ˈnjuːtrɪs] *n.* nurse. **nutricial,** *adj.*

nux vomica [ˌnʌks ˈvɒmɪkə] *n.* strychnine-containing seed of Asiatic tree.

nychthemer(on) [ˈnɪkθɪmə, nɪkˈθiːmərɒn] *n.* period of one night and day. **nychthemeral,** *adj.*

nyctalopia [ˌnɪktəˈləʊpɪə] *n.* condition of seeing poorly at night or in partial darkness, while day sight is normal; *erroneously,* the opposite condition. **nyctolope,** *n.* person suffering from this. **nyctolopic** [-ˈlɒpɪk], *adj.*

nyctophobia [ˌnɪktəˈfəʊbɪə] *n.* dread of darkness.

nycturia [nɪkˈtjʊərɪə] *n.* nocturia.

nylghau, nylghai [ˈnɪlgɔː, -gaɪ] *n.* nilgai.

nymphet [ˈnɪmfet] *n.* young girl sexually attractive to older men.

nymphitis [nɪmˈfaɪtɪs] *n* inflammation of inner lips of vulva. **nympholepsy,** *n.* emotional frenzy, especially desire for the unattainable. **nympholept** *n.* **nymphomania,** *n.* sexual mania in female. **nymphomaniac,** *adj. & n.* **nymphotomy,** *n. Medicine,* removal of inner lips of vulva.

nystagmus *n.* involuntary lateral movement of the eyeballs. **nystagmic,** *adj.*

O

oakum ['əʊkəm] n. fibre of old untwisted ropes.

obbligato [ˌɒblɪ'ɡɑːtəʊ] adj. & n. Music, accompanying, or accompaniment, by solo instrument other than piano.

obdormition [ˌɒbdɔː'mɪʃn] n. numbness or 'going to sleep' of a limb, etc.

obdurate ['ɒbdjʊrət] adj. obstinate; hardhearted. **obduracy,** n.

obeah ['əʊbiə] n. W African, W Indian, N and S American (among black people) magic cult; magical spell.

obeisance [əʊ'beɪsns] n. bow or curtsey; paying of homage. **obeisant,** adj.

obeism ['əʊbiːzm] n. practice of obeah.

obelisk ['ɒbəlɪsk] n. tapering rectangular stone pillar. **obeliskoid,** adj.

obelize ['ɒbəlaɪz] v.t. mark with obelus; especially to mark as spurious.

obelus ['ɒbələs] n. (pl. **obeli**), mark of reference; mark or ÷ signifying spurious passage in manuscript, etc.

obfuscate ['ɒbfʌskeɪt] v.t. make dark or obscure; confuse. **obfuscatory,** adj. **obfuscation,** n.

obi ['əʊbi] (Japanese) n. wide Japanese girdle; obeah.

obiit ['ɒbiɪt, 'əʊ–] (Latin) 'died' (abbr. **ob.**). **obiit sine prole** [–ˌsɪni 'prəʊli, –ˌsaɪ–], 'died without issue' (abbr. **o.s.p.**).

obit ['əʊbɪt] n. death; funeral or memorial service; obituary.

obiter dictum [ˌɒbɪtə 'dɪktəm, ˌəʊ–] (Latin) n. (pl. **obiter dicta**) 'thing said in passing'; casual or incidental remark or opinion.

obituary [ə'bɪtʃʊəri] n. death-record or roll; biographical notice of recently dead person; adj. pertaining to person's death. **obituarist,** n. writer of obituaries.

objet d'art [ˌɒbʒeɪ 'dɑː] (French) (pl. **objets d'art**) thing of artistic value.

objicient [əb'dʒɪʃiənt] n. objector.

objurgate ['ɒbdʒəɡeɪt] v.t. rebuke; scold. **objurgation,** n. **objurgatory,** adj.

oblate ['ɒbleɪt] n. & adj. dedicated (person); adj. Geometry, flattened at poles. **oblation,** n. offering; sacrifice. **oblational,** adj.

oblique [ə'bliːk] adj. slanting; indirect; underhand. **obliquity** [ə'blɪkwəti], n. deviation from straight line or moral code.

oblivion [ə'blɪvɪən] n. complete forgetfulness or forgottenness. **oblivescence,** n. fact or state of forgetting. **oblivious,** adj. **obliviscence,** n. forgetfulness.

obloquy ['ɒbləkwi] n. abuse; disgrace. **oblocutor** [–'lɒkjʊtə], n. one who denies or disputes.

obreption [ɒ'brepʃn] n. attempt to obtain ecclesiastical dispensation, etc., fraudulently. **obreptitious,** adj. performed in underhand fashion.

obrogate ['ɒbrəɡeɪt] v.t. alter (law) by passing new law. **obrogation,** n.

obscurantism [ˌɒbskjuː'ræntɪzm] n. prevention of enlightenment. **obscurantic** [–'ræntɪk], adj. **obscurantist,** n.

obsecrate ['ɒbsɪkreɪt] v.t. beseech. **obsecration,** n.

obsequies ['ɒbsəkwiz] n. pl. funeral. **obsequious** [əb'siːkwiəs], adj. servile.

obsidian [əb'sɪdiən] n. dark-coloured volcanic glass.

obsidional, obsidionary [ɒb'sɪdiənl, –nəri] adj. pertaining to siege.

obsolescent [ˌɒbsə'lesnt] adj. becoming obsolete. **obsolescence,** n. **obsolete,** adj. disused; out-ofdate. **obsoletism,** n. obsolete thing.

obstetric(al) [əb'stetrɪk, –l] adj. pertaining to childbirth or midwifery. **obstetrician, obstetrist,** n. expert in obstetrics. **obstetrics,** n. midwifery.

obstipation [ˌɒbstɪ'peɪʃn] n. complete constipation.

obstreperous [əb'strepərəs] adj. noisy, exuberant; unruly.

obstriction [əb'strɪkʃn] n. obligation.

obstruent ['ɒbstruənt] (Medicine) n. & adj. blocking up body passage. Phonetics/Linguistics, sound characterized by obstruction of the airstream: a plosive, fricative, or affricate.

obtenebrate [ɒb'tenɪbreɪt] v.t. darken; cast shadow over.

obtest [ɒb'test] v.t. beseech; invoke; adjure. **obtestation,** n.

obtrude [əb'truːd] v.i. & t. thrust (oneself) forward in an annoying way; thrust (something) out or forward. **obtrusive,** adj. **obtrusion,** n.

obtruncate [ɒb'trʌŋkeɪt] v.t. behead. **obtruncation,** n.

obtund [ɒb'tʌnd] v.t. blunt; dull. **obtundent,** n. & adj. (drug) dulling pain.

obturate ['ɒbtjʊreɪt] v.t. stop up, especially **obturation, obturator,** n.

obumbrate [ɒb'ʌmbreɪt] adj. obsolete, darkened; hidden under a projection. **obumbrant,** adj. overhanging.

obvallate [ɒb'væleɪt] adj. walled in.

obvention [ɒb'venʃn] n. casual or occasional happening or gift.

obverse ['ɒbvɜːs] n. front or top side; 'head' of coin; counterpart; adj. facing observer; with top wider than base.

obvert [ɒb'vɜːt] v.t. turn; alter. **obversion,** n.

obviate ['ɒbvieɪt] v.t. anticipate and so avoid the need for.

obvolute ['ɒbvəluːt] *adj.* over-lapping; twisted. **obvolution**, *n.*

ocarina [ˌɒkə'riːnə] *n.* egg-shaped whistle-like musical instrument.

Occam's razor, Okham's razor [ˌɒkəmz 'reɪzə] *n.* rule that scientific and philosophic theories should be kept as simple as possible, disregarding unknown quantities.

occamy ['ɒkəmi] *n.* alloy imitating silver or gold.

occident ['ɒksɪdənt] *n.* the west; the West. **occidental**, *adj.*

occiput ['ɒksɪpʌt] *n.* back of head. **occipital** [ɒk'sɪpɪtl], *adj.*; *n.* such bone.

occlude [ə'kluːd] *v.t.* shut up, in or out; *v.i.* shut mouth so that teeth meet. **occludent**, *n.* & *adj.* **occlusal**, *adj.* pertaining to cutting edge of tooth. **occlusion, occlusor**, *n.* **occlusive**, *adj.*; *n.* sound (as *t*) made by stopping breath.

occult [ə'kʌlt] *adj.* mysterious; hidden; magical; supernatural; *v.t. Astrononomy*, obscure (object) by passing between it and observer. **occultation**, *n.*

oceanology [ˌəʊʃə'nɒlədʒi] *n.* study of economic geography of the sea.

ocellus [əʊ'seləs] *n.* (*pl.* –li) small eye; eye-like coloured spot. **ocellar**, *adj.* **ocellated**, *adj.* bearing ocelli. **ocellation**, *n.*

ocelot ['ɒsəlɒt, 'əʊ–] *n.* yellow, spotted, wild cat of S and Central America, and its fur.

oche ['ɒki] *n.* mark on floor behind which darts player must stand.

ochlesis [ɒ'kliːsɪs] *n.* unhealthy condition due to over-crowding.

ochlocracy [ɒ'klɒkrəsi] *n.* mob rule. **ochlocrat**, *n.* **ochlocratic**, *adj.* **ochlophobia**, *n.* dread of crowds.

ochre ['əʊkə] *n.* red or yellow iron-containing earth used as pigment; yellowish-brown hue. **ochreous, ochrous, ochry**, *adj.* **ochroid**, *adj.* like ochre.

ocracy ['ɒkrəsi] *n.* government.

octactinal [ˌɒkt'æktɪnl] *adj.* eight-rayed.

octad ['ɒktæd] *n.* group of eight.

octagon ['ɒktəgən] *n.* eight-sided plane figure. **octagonal** [ɒk'tægənl], *adj.*

octahedron [ˌɒktə'hiːdrən] *n.* eight-sided solid figure. **octahedral**, *adj.*

octamerous [ɒk'tæmərəs] *adj.* having its parts in eights.

octameter [ɒk'tæmɪtə] *n.* verse-line of eight feet.

octane ['ɒkteɪn] *n.* liquid hydrocarbon of paraffin series. **octane number**, number representing anti-knock property of petrol. **high octane**, denoting petrol having high anti-knock properties.

octant ['ɒktənt] *n.* eighth part of circle (45°); angle-measuring instrument with that arc.

octapla ['ɒktəplə] *n.* multilingual book in eight texts, especially part of Bible.

octapody [ɒk'tæpədi] *n.* octameter.

octarchy ['ɒktɑːki] *n.* government by eight persons; alliance of eight independent governments.

octastich ['ɒktəstɪk] *n.* poem or stanza of eight lines.

octateuch ['ɒktətjuːk] *n.* series of eight books; first eight books of Old Testament.

octave ['ɒktɪv] *n.* group of eight; *Ecclesiastical*, week following feast day; eighth day (including feast day) after feast day; *Music*, interval comprising eight tones; *Literature*, first eight lines of sonnet; eight-line stanza. .

octavo [ɒk'teɪvəʊ] *n.* book size: **foolscap octavo**, 6¾ in. × 4¼ in.; **crown octavo**, 7½ in. × 5 in.; **large crown octavo**, 8 × 5¼ in.; **demy octavo**, 8¾ in. × 5⅝ in.; **medium octavo**, 9½ in. × 6 in.; **royal octavo**, 10 in. × 6¼ in.; **super royal octavo**, 10¼ in. × 6⅞ in.; **imperial octavo**, 11 in. × 7½ in. (*abbr.* **8vo.**).

octennial [ɒk'teniəl] *adj.* happening in every eighth year; lasting eight years.

octillion [ɒk'tɪljən] *n.* a million septillions (10^{48}); (*French & American*) a thousand septillions (10^{27}).

octodecimo [ˌɒktə'desɪməʊ] *n.* book size. **demy octodecimo**, 5¾ in. × 3¾ in. (*abbr.* **18mo.**).

octogenarian [ˌɒktədʒə'neəriən] *n.* & *adj.* (person) in from eightieth to ninetieth year.

octonary ['ɒktənəri] *adj.* pertaining to or consisting of eight; in groups of eight; *n.* stanza of eight lines.

octoploid, octaploid ['ɒktəplɔɪd] *adj.* eight-fold; having eight times basic number of chromosomes; *n.* such cell.

octopod ['ɒktəpɒd] *n.* & *adj.* (mollusc) belonging to the order of cephalopods having eight arms. **octopodan, octopodous** [–'tɒp–], *adj.*

octoroon [ˌɒktə'ruːn] *n.* child of quadroon and white.

octosyllable ['ɒktə‚sɪləbl] *n.* verse line or word of eight syllables. **octosyllabic** [–'læbɪk], *adj.*

octroi ['ɒktrɔɪ, –trwɑː] (*French*) *n.* trading privilege; concession; monopoly; tax on goods imported into town, and place where it is collected.

octuple ['ɒktjʊpl] *adj.* in groups of eight; eight-fold. *v.i.* & *t.* multiply eightfold.

ocular ['ɒkjʊlə] *adj.* pertaining to eyes; visual. **oculate**, *adj.* having eyes. **oculist**, *n.* opthalmologist. **oculus**, *n. Architecture*, any eye-like feature, especially window.

odalisque ['əʊdəlɪsk] *n.* woman of harem.

odium ['əʊdiəm] *n.* hatred; reproach. **odious**, *adj.* hateful, repugnant.

odograph ['əʊdəgrɑːf] *n.* instrument recording distance travelled, especially by pedestrian. **odometer**, *n.*

odontology [ˌəʊdɒn'tɒlədʒi] *n.* study of teeth. **odontalgia**, *n.* toothache. **odontiasis**, *n.* teething. **odontognathous**, *adj.* pertaining to extinct toothed birds. **odontography**, *n.* description of or treatise on teeth. **odontoid**, *adj.* tooth-like. **odontoma**, *n.* dental tumour. **odontosis**, *n.* dentition. **odontotomy**, *n.* incision into tooth.

odorivector [əʊ'dɒrɪvektə] *n.* substance causing odour.

odyssey ['ɒdəsi] *n.* protracted, wandering journey.

oecist ['iːsɪst] *n.* colonist.

oecumenical *see* ecumenical.

Oedipus ['iːdɪpəs] *n.* prince of Thebes in Greek legend, who unknowingly murdered his father and married his mother, and who answered the riddle of the Sphinx. **Oedipus complex**, *Psychology*, fixation on one's mother, especially with hatred of father.

oeil-de-boeuf [ˌɜːi-də-'bɜːf] (*French*) *n.* (*pl.* **oeils-de-boeuf**) round or oval window.

oeillade [ɜː'jɑːd] (*French*) *n.* glance, ogle.

oenology [iː'nɒlədʒi] *n.* study of wines. **oenological**, *adj.* **oenologist**, *n.* **oenophilist**, *n.* wine-lover.

oenopoetic, *adj.* pertaining to wine-making.

oenomel ['iːnəmel] *n.* ancient Greek drink of wine and honey.

oersted ['ɜːsted] *n.* unit of magnetic field strength or intensity.

oesophagus [iːˈsɒfəgəs] *n.* food passage between mouth and stomach.

oestrogen ['iːstrədʒən] *n.* any of several steroid hormones or drugs connected with reproduction in females.

oestrus ['iːstrəs] *n.* period of sexual heat; frenzy. **oestrous**, *adj.* **oestruate**, *v.i.* be on heat. **oestruation**, *n.*

offal ['ɒfl] *n.* refuse; garbage; edible animal entrails and organs.

officinal [əˈfɪsɪnl] *adj.* used in medicine, art or industry; stocked by pharmacists; *n.* such drug.

ogam *see* **ogham**.

ogdoad ['ɒgdəʊæd] *n.* eight; group of eight.

ogee ['əʊdʒiː] *n.* moulding with S-shaped section; *adj.* S-shaped. **ogee arch**, pointed arch with ogee curve on either side.

ogham, ogam ['ɒgəm] *n.* ancient British alphabet of notches; character of ogam. **ogamic**, *adj.*

ogive ['əʊdʒaɪv] *n.* pointed arch; vault's diagonal rib. **ogival**, *adj.*

ohm [əʊm] *n.* unit of electrical resistance: resistance of circuit in which current of one ampere is produced by one volt. **ohmage**, *n.* resistance in ohms.

okapi [əʊˈkɑːpi] *n.* African animal like short-necked giraffe, with whitish face and black-striped whitish legs.

oleaginous [ˌəʊliˈædʒɪnəs] *adj.* oily.

oleander [ˌəʊliˈændə] *n.* poisonous white- or red-flowered evergreen shrub of East Indies.

oleaster [ˌəʊliˈæstə] *n.* yellow-flowered, olive-like shrub of S Europe; *erroneously*, wild olive.

olecranon [əʊˈlekrənɒn, ˌəʊlɪˈkreɪnən] *n.* projecting bone of elbow; 'funny-bone'. **olecranal**, *adj.*

oleic [əʊˈliːɪk] *adj.* pertaining to or derived from oil. **oleiferous**, *adj.* oil-producing.

olent ['əʊlənt] *adj.* archaic, fragrant.

oleograph ['əʊliəɡrɑːf] *n.* lithographic reproduction of oil painting. **oleography**, *n.*

oleometer [ˌəʊliˈɒmɪtə] *n.* oil hydrometer; instrument measuring amount of oil in substance.

oleraceous [ˌɒləˈreɪʃəs] *adj.* potherb-like; edible.

olfaction [ɒlˈfækʃn] *n.* sense of smell; act or process of smelling. **olfactible**, *adj.* capable of being smelt. **olfactology**, *n.* study of smells. **olfactometer**, *n.* instrument measuring keenness of sense of smell, and olfactibility of odours. **olfactory**, *adj.* pertaining to sense of smell.

olid ['ɒlɪd] *adj.* evil-smelling.

oligarch ['ɒlɪgɑːk] *n.* member of oligarchy. **oligarchic(al)**, *adj.* **oligarchy**, *n.* government by the few.

oligist ['ɒlɪdʒɪst] *n.* haematite.

Oligocene ['ɒlɪgəʊsiːn] *n. & adj.* (pertaining to) third epoch of Tertiary period.

oligochronometer [ˌɒlɪgəʊkrəˈnɒmɪtə] *n.* instrument measuring very short time intervals.

oligocythaemia [ˌɒlɪgəʊsaɪˈθiːmiə] *n.* deficiency of red corpuscles in blood.

oligodontous [ˌɒlɪgəʊˈdɒntəs] *adj.* having few teeth.

oligodynamic [ˌɒlɪgəʊdaɪˈnæmɪk] *adj.* pertaining

to effect of small quantities; having effect in small quantities only.

oligomycin [ˌɒlɪgəʊˈmaɪsɪn] *n.* antibiotic used against plant fungi.

oligophagous [ˌɒlɪˈgɒfəgəs] *adj.* eating a few sorts of food only.

oligophrenia [ˌɒlɪgəʊˈfriːniə] *n.* feeble-mindedness.

oligopoly [ˌɒlɪˈgɒpəli] *n.* market dominated by a few producers.

oligosyllable [ˌɒlɪgəʊˈsɪləbl] *n.* word of few syllables.

olio ['əʊliəʊ] *n.* miscellany; hotch-potch; rich Spanish stew.

olitory ['ɒlɪtəri] *adj.* archaic, pertaining to pot-herbs or kitchen garden.

oliver ['ɒlɪvə] *n.* treadle-hammer.

olivet ['ɒlɪvet] *n.* artificial pearl; olive grove; Mount of Olives.

olla-podrida [ˌɒləpəˈdriːdə] *n.* olio.

oloroso [ˌɒləˈrəʊsəʊ] *n.* full-bodied sherry, usually sweet.

olympiad [əˈlɪmpiæd] *n.* interval of four years between Greek Olympic games; *modern*, Olympic games.

Olympian [əˈlɪmpiən] *adj.* pertaining to Olympus, abode of Greek gods; divine; magnificent; magnanimous.

omasum [əʊˈmeɪsm] *n.* (*pl.* **omasa**) third stomach of ruminants. **omasitis**, *n.* inflammation of omasum.

ombre ['ɒmbə] (*Spanish*) *n.* eighteenth-century card game for three persons.

ombré ['ɒmbreɪ] (*French*) *n. & adj.* shaded (fabric). **ombres chinoises** [ˌɒmbrə ʃiːnˈwɑːz], 'Chinese shadows'; shadow-play.

ombrology [ɒmˈbrɒlədʒi] *n.* study of rain. **ombrograph**, *n.* recording ombrometer. **ombrometer**, *n.* rain gauge. **ombrophile**, *n.* plant flourishing in extremely rainy conditions. **ombrophobe**, *n.* plant thriving only in desert conditions.

ombudsman ['ɒmbʊdzmən] *n.* commissioner appointed by a legislature to investigate complaints by private citizens against government officials or agencies.

omega ['əʊmɪgə] *n.* last (twenty-fourth) letter (Ω, ω) of Greek alphabet; ending. **omegoid**, *adj.* Ω-shaped.

omentum [əʊˈmentəm] *n.* (*pl.* **omenta**) fold of the peritoneum. **great omentum**, fat-filled sac covering small intestines. **lesser omentum**, omentum joining stomach with liver. **omental**, *adj.*

omer ['əʊmə] *n.* ancient Hebrew unit of dry capacity, about four litres.

omicron [əʊˈmaɪkrɒn, 'ɒmɪ–] *n.* fifteenth letter (O, o) of Greek alphabet; short o.

omneity [ɒmˈniːɪti, –ˈneɪ–] *n.* state of including all things. **omnes** [ɒmneɪz, –iːz], Latin *n. pl.* 'all (persons)'. **omniana**, *n.* scraps of information of every kind.

omnicompetent [ˌɒmnɪˈkɒmpɪtənt] *adj.* legally competent in all matters. **omnifarious**, *adj.* of all kinds. **omnific, omnificient**, *adj.* creating all things. **omnify**, *v.t.* make large or universal. **omnigenous** [ɒmˈnɪdʒənəs], *adj.* of all kinds. **omnipotent** [ɒmˈnɪpətənt], *adj.* all-powerful. **omnipresent**, *adj.* present everywhere. **omniscient** [ɒmˈnɪsɪənt], *adj.* knowing everything. **omnium,**

n. Commerce, total of parts of fund or stock.

omnium gatherum, *n.* miscellaneous collection, especially of persons. **omnivorous** [ɒm'nɪvərəs], *adj.* feeding on all kinds of food.

omodynia [,əumə'dɪnɪə] *n.* pain in shoulder.

omophagy, **omophagia** [əu'mɒfədʒɪ, ,əumə'feɪdʒɪə] *n.* eating of raw flesh. **omophagic** [–'fædʒɪk], **omophagous** [əu'mɒfəgəs], *adj.*

omoplate ['əuməupleɪt] *n.* shoulder blade.

omphalos ['ɒmfəlɒs] (*Greek*) *n.* (*pl.* **–li**) navel; central point. **omphaloskepsis**, *n.* meditation while gazing at one's navel. **omphalic** [–'fælɪk], *adj.* **omphaloid**, *adj.* like a navel.

onager ['ɒnədʒə] *n.* (*pl.* **–gri**) wild ass of Asia. **onagraceous**, *adj.* belonging to evening primrose family of plants.

onanism ['əunənɪzm] *n.* masturbation. **onanist**, *n.* **onanistic**, *adj.*

oncology [ɒŋ'kɒlədʒɪ] *n.* study of tumours. **oncologic(al)**, *adj.* **oncometer**, *n.* instrument measuring changes in internal organs' size. **oncogenesis**, *n.* development of tumours. **oncogenic, oncogenous**, *adj.* **oncogene**, *n.* gene (in some viruses) that causes cancer. **oncotomy**, *n.* incision into tumour or abscess.

ondatra [ɒn'dætrə] *n.* musk-rat.

on dit [,ɒn 'diː] (*French*) 'one says'; rumour; hearsay.

ondograph ['ɒndəgrɑːf] *n.* instrument measuring variations in wave formation of electric current. **ondogram**, *n.* record of ondograph. **ondoscope**, *n.* instrument showing such wave form.

ondoyant [ɒn'dwaɪɒn] (*French*) *adj.* wavy.

oneiric [əu'naɪrɪk] *adj.* pertaining to dreams. **oneirocritic**, *n.* interpreter of dreams. **oneiromancy**, *n.* divination through dreams.

onerous ['əunərəs, 'ɒn–] *adj.* burdensome; weighty.

oniomania [,əunɪə'meɪnɪə] *n.* mania for making purchases. **oniomaniac**, *n.*

onomancy ['ɒnəmænsɪ] *n.* divination from letters of a name.

onomasiology [,ɒnəmeɪzɪ'ɒlədʒɪ] *n.* branch of semantics dealing with related words and their meanings.

onomastic [,ɒnə'mæstɪk] *adj.* pertaining to or consisting of names; applied to autograph signature in one hand on document written in another. **onomastics** (*n. pl.*) study of proper names. **onomasticon** *n.* vocabulary of proper names. **onomatology**, *n.* science of names. **onomatomania**, *n.* irresistible desire to repeat certain words continually, especially words of something to be remembered.

onomatopoeia [,ɒnəmætə'piːə] *n.* use or formation of words which attempt to imitate the sound of what they describe or stand for. **onomatopoeic, onomatopoetic** *adj.*

ontogeny, **ontogenesis** [ɒn'tɒdʒənɪ, ,ɒntə'dʒenɪsɪs] *n.* life history of individual organism. **ontogenetic** [–dʒən'etɪk], **ontogenic** [–'dʒenɪk], *adj.*

ontology [ɒn'tɒlədʒɪ] *n.* branch of philosophy dealing with the ultimate nature of reality or being. **ontologic(al)**, *adj.* **ontologism**, *n.* ontological doctrine. **ontic, ontal**, *adj.* having or pertaining to real existence.

onus ['əunəs] *n.* burden; responsibility; obligation. **onus probandi**, obligation to prove.

onychia, onychitis [əu'nɪkɪə, ,əunɪ'kaɪtɪs] *n.* inflammation of root or side of nail. **onychauxis**, *n.* hypertrophy of nails. **onychoid**, *adj.* fingernail-like. **onychophagia**, *n.* nail-biting. **onychosis**, *n.* disease of nail.

onyxis [əu'nɪksɪs] *n.* ingrowing nail.

oogamete [,əuə'gæmiːt, –gə'miːt] *n.* female gamete. **oogenesis**, *n.* egg-formation. **oogamous**, *adj.* heterogamous.

ooid(al) ['əuɔɪd, əu'ɔɪdl] *adj.* egg-shaped.

oolite ['əuəlaɪt] *n.* limestone comprising small egg-like grains. **oolitic** [–'lɪtɪk], *adj.*

oology [əu'ɒlədʒɪ] *n.* collection and study of birds' eggs. **oologic(al)**, *adj.* **oologize**, *v.i.* search for birds' eggs. **oologist**, *n.*

oolong ['uːlɒŋ] *n.* dark China tea, partly fermented before drying.

oometer [əu'ɒmɪtə] *n.* egg-measuring instrument.

ooscope ['əuəskəup] *n.* instrument for examining interior of egg.

oosperm ['əuəspɜːm] *n.* fertilized egg. **oospore**, *n.* spore arising from fertilized egg cell.

ootheca [,əuə'θiːkə] *n.* firm-walled egg-case of some molluscs and insects.

opacity [əu'pæsətɪ] *n.* quality or state of being opaque. **opacify**, *v.* make or become opaque.

opah ['əupə] *n.* large brightly-coloured fish.

opalescent [,əupə'lesnt] *adj.* iridescent. **opalescence**, *n.*

opaque [əu'peɪk] *adj.* not transparent; dark; stupid.

op(tical) art ['ɒp ɑːt, 'ɒptɪkl–] *n.* non-representational art in which straight or curved lines and geometrical patterns are used to produce an optical illusion.

op. cit. [,ɒp 'sɪt] (*Latin*) *abbreviation* for 'opere citato'; in the work already mentioned.

ope et consilio [,əupi et kɒn'sɪlɪəu] (*Latin*) 'with aid and advice'.

opeidoscope [əu'paɪdəskəup] *n.* instrument showing sound vibrations by vibrating mirror.

operculum [əu'pɜːkjuləm] *n.* (*pl.* **–s** or **–la**) lid-like organ, as of moss capsule and mollusc shell; fish's gill cover. **opercular**, *adj.* **operculate**, *adj.*

opere citato [,ɒpəri kɪ'tɑːtəu, –sɪ–] (*Latin*) 'in the work quoted' (*abbr.* **op. cit.**).

operon ['ɒpərɒn] *n.* group of genes operating as a unit.

operose ['ɒpərəus] *adj.* requiring effort; working hard.

ophelimity [,əufə'lɪmətɪ] *n.* economic satisfaction.

ophiasis [əu'faɪəsɪs] *n.* baldness in wavy bands.

ophic ['ɒfɪk] *adj.* pertaining to serpents. **ophism**, *n.* snake-worship.

ophicleide ['ɒfɪklaɪd] *n.* bass bugle-like keyed brass musical instrument. **ophicleidean**, *adj.* **ophicleidist**, *n.*

ophidian ['ɒfɪdɪən] *n. & adj.* (reptile) belonging to order of reptiles including snakes; like snakes. **ophidioid**, *adj.* snake-like. **ophiolog**, *n.* study of snakes. **ophiomorphic**, *adj.* snake-shaped.

ophthalmia [ɒf'θælmɪə] *n.* inflammation of eye. **ophthalmic**, *adj.* pertaining to eye. **ophthalmology**, *n.* study of eye and its diseases. **ophthalmometer**, *n.* instrument for measuring eye, especially for astigmatism. **ophthalmoplegia**, *n.* paralysis of ocular muscles. **ophthalmoscope**, *n.* instrument for examinining inner eye.

opiate ['əʊpɪət, –eɪt] *n.* & *adj.* (drug or thing) inducing sleep or soothing pain; [–eɪt] *v.t.* impregnate with opium; treat with opiate; soothe or dull. **opiatic** [–'ætɪk], *adj.*

opine [ə'paɪn] *v.* state (as) an opinion.

opisometer [ˌɒpɪ'sɒmɪtə] *n.* instrument measuring curved lines.

opisthenar [əʊ'pɪsθənɑː] *n.* back of hand. **opisthognathous**, *adj.* with receding jaws. **opisthograph**, *n.* ancient tablet or manuscript bearing writing on both sides. **opisthosomal**, *adj.* pertaining to posteriors.

opopanax [ə'pɒpənæks] *n.* aromatic gum resin formerly used in medicine.

opossum [ə'pɒsm] *n.* small grey American marsupial, and its fur. **playing opossum** *or* **'possum**, feigning death; remaining silent or concealed.

oppidan ['ɒpɪdən] *adj.* pertaining to town; *n.* town-dweller; student at Eton boarding in the town.

oppilate ['ɒpɪleɪt] *v.t. Medicine,* stop up. **oppilation**, *n.* **oppliative**, *adj.*

opprobrium [ə'prəʊbrɪəm] *n.* reproach; abuse; disgrace. **opprobrious**, *adj.*

oppugn [ə'pjuːn] *v.i.* & *t.* call in question; deny; resist; conflict with. **oppugnant**, *adj.* hostile, combative.

opsimath ['ɒpsɪmæθ] *n.* mature student; late learner.

opsonin ['ɒpsənɪn] *n.* substance of blood serum making bacteria vulnerable to phagocytic action.

optative [ɒp'teɪtɪv, 'ɒptə–] *n.* & *adj. Grammar,* (mood) expressing wish.

optician [ɒp'tɪʃn] *n.* maker or seller of optical instruments, spectacles, etc. **optics**, *n.* study of light and vision.

optimum ['ɒptɪməm] *n.* (*pl.* –ma) the best; *adj.* best; producing best result.

optogram ['ɒptəgræm] *n.* image fixed on retina. **optometry**, *n.* measuring range of vision; eye-testing. **optophone**, *n.* instrument enabling blind to read by transforming light into sound. **optotypes**, *n. pl.* varying-sized print for eye-testing.

opulent ['ɒpjʊlənt] *adj.* rich. **opulence**, *n.*

opus ['əʊpəs, 'ɒ–] (*Latin*) *n.* (*pl.* **opera** ['ɒpərə]) 'work'; musical work or set of works (*abbr.* **op.**). **magnum opus**, *see* **magnum.**

opuscule [əʊ'pʌskjuːl] *n.* minor composition or work. **opuscular**, *adj.*

orache ['ɒrɪtʃ] *n.* plant of the goosefoot family, especially one grown as a vegetable.

oracular [ɒ'rækjʊlə] *adj.* like an oracle; sententious; prophetic; ambiguous.

orant ['ɔːrənt] *n.* representation of a praying figure.

ora pro nobis [ˌɔːrɑː prəʊ 'nəʊbɪs] (*Latin*) 'pray for us'.

orarian [ə'reərɪən] *n.* & *adj.* (dweller) of the seashore.

oratio recta [ɒˌreɪʃɪəʊ 'rektə, ɒˌrɑːti–] (*Latin*) 'direct speech'. **oratio obliqua** [–ə'bliːkwə], 'indirect speech'.

orbicular [ɔː'bɪkjʊlə] *adj.* spherical; circular. **orbiculate**, *adj.* **orbiculation**, *n.*

orbific [ɔː'bɪfɪk] *adj.* world-creating.

orbis terrarum [ˌɔːbɪs te'rɑːrəm] (*Latin*) 'orb of lands'; world; globe.

orc [ɔːk] *n.* grampus; monster. **orca**, *n.* killer whale.

orchesis [ɔː'kiːsɪs] *n.* art of dancing in Greek chorus.

orchidaceous [ˌɔːkɪ'deɪʃəs] *adj.* pertaining to or like an orchid; exceptionally beautiful; ostentatious; gaudy.

orchil ['ɔːkɪl, 'ɔːtʃɪl] *n.* archil.

orchitis [ɔː'kaɪtɪs] *n.* inflammation of testicles. **orchidectomy** [ˌɔːkɪ'dektəmi], *n.* removal of testicle(s).

ordinal ['ɔːdɪnl] *n.* & *adj.* (number) signifying position in series, as *third*; ordination service book; Roman Catholic service book.

ordinance ['ɔːdɪnəns] *n.* decree.

ordinate ['ɔːdɪnət] *adj.* in rows.

ordnance ['ɔːdnəns] *n.* military stores or supplies; artillery.

Ordovician [ˌɔːdə'vɪʃn, –ɪən] *n.* & *adj.* (pertaining to) second period of Palaeozoic era.

ordure ['ɔːdjʊə] *n.* dung; filth

oread ['ɔːrɪæd] *n.* mountain nymph.

orectic [ɔː'rektɪk] *adj.* pertaining to desires and their satisfaction. **orexis**, *n.* mental desire; effort.

orfe [ɔːf] *n.* small yellow fish kept in aquariums.

organdy ['ɔːgəndi] *n.* fine, transparent, rather stiff cotton material.

organic [ɔː'gænɪk] *adj.* structural; of or derived from living organisms; *Medicine,* of or affecting organ of body; *Chemistry,* of carbon compounds. **organogenesis**, *n.* a development of bodily organs. **organogenic**, *adj.* derived from organic substance. **organography**, *n.* description of organs of plants or animals. **organoleptic**, *adj.* affecting whole organ or organism. **organotherapy**, *n.* medical treatment with animal organs.

organum, organon ['ɔːgənəm, –ɒn] *n.* logical system or method for investigating phenomena.

orgasm ['ɔːgæzm] *n.* emotional paroxysm. **orgasmic, orgastic**, *adj.*

oriel ['ɔːrɪəl] *n.* projecting window or part of building containing window.

orient ['ɔːrɪənt] *n.* the East; pearl's lustre; *adj.* applied to rising sun; being born; lustrous; brilliant; *v.t.* point towards east; discover compass-bearings of; adjust to suit situation. **oriental**, *adj.* **orientate**, *v.t.* to orient. **orientation**, *n.*

orienteering [ˌɔːrɪən'tɪərɪŋ, –ien–⁻] *n.* a form of cross-country running in which competitors have to find their way by map and compass to a series of check-points on a course over rough terrain.

orifice ['ɒrəfɪs] *n.* opening for entrance or exit.

oriflamme ['ɒrɪflæm] (*French*) *n.* royal red banner; battle standard.

oriform ['ɒrɪfɔːm] *adj.* mouth-shaped.

origami [ˌɒrɪ'gɑːmi] *n.* Japanese art of paper folding.

orismology [ˌɔːrɪz'mɒlədʒi, ˌɒ–] *n.* technical definition or terminology. **orismologic**, *adj.*

orison ['ɒrɪzn] *n.* prayer.

orlop ['ɔːlɒp] *n.* ship's lowest deck.

ormolu ['ɔːməluː] *n.* gilt metal; gold-like brass ornament of furniture.

ornis ['ɔːnɪs] *n.* avifauna.

ornithology [ˌɔːnɪ'θɒlədʒi] *n.* study of birds. **ornithological**, *adj.* **ornithologist**, *n.* **ornithic**, *adj.*

Suffixes

-able capable of doing or being done: *electable, undrinkable*

-age action; state; cost: *peerage, postage*

-al of or pertaining to; action: *sentimental, revival*

-an of or from; expert in: *Australian, historian*

-ant doing or being: *expectant, resultant.* Hence **-ance**: *reliance* and **-ancy**: *vibrancy*

-ar of or pertaining to; = **-er**; *columnar, beggar*

-archy government, rule: *monarchy, oligarchy*

-arian person connected with or in favour of: *antiquarian, egalitarian*

-ary (person or thing) connected with: *functionary, monetary*

-ate full of; cause to become; group of people; rank or degree: *passionate, activate, directorate, doctorate*

-ation act, process, or result of: *inspiration, realisation*

-ative liking or tending to do: *argumentative, causative*

-cide killing: *ecocide, genocide*

-cy quality, state; rank: *celibacy, baronetcy*

-dom condition; rank; set of people: *serfdom, earldom, officialdom*

-ectomy surgical removal: *mastectomy, tonsillectomy*

-ee person who is or has: *interviewee, escapee*

-eer person who does; do the stated action: *mountaineer, profiteer*

-en made of; (cause to) be: *silken, darken*

-ent = **-ant**: *resident.* Hence **-ence, -ency**

-er person or thing that does or is; person who comes from: *cricketer, screwdriver, Dubliner*

-ery condition; place of action or residence: *buffoonery, winery, rookery*

-ese (people or language) of the stated country, place, or group: *Vietnamese, Milanese, legalese*

-esque in the style of; like: *Junoesque, statuesque*

-ess female: *waitress, tigress*

-ette small; female; imitation: *kitchenette, suffragette, flannelette*

-ey = **-y**: *clayey*

-fold multiplied by: *twofold, thousandfold*

-ful full of, containing; amount that fills a container etc.: *painful, roomful*

-gamy marriage: *bigamy, monogamy*

-genarian stated number of decades old: *septuagenarian*

-gon geometrical figure with stated number of sides: *pentagon*

-gram message delivered as a surprise: *kissagram, strippagram*

-hood condition: *fatherhood, falsehood*

-ible = **-able**: *contemptible*

-ic(al) of or pertaining to: *poetic, zoological*

-icide = **-cide**: *germicide*

-ie nice small one: *auntie*

-ify make or become: *unify, Frenchify*

-ine of or pertaining to: *bovine, labyrinthine*

-ion act, condition, or result: *abstention, rejection*

-ise make or become; put into: *anonymise, nationalise, hospitalise*

-ish (people or language) of the stated country; somewhat: *British, reddish*

-ism movement, religion; state, quality; discrimination: *Republicanism, hooliganism, racism*

-ist follower, student, player etc. of; unfairly discriminating: *Buddhist, violinist, sexist*

-ite (follower or inhabitant) of: *Thatcherite, Canaanite*

-itis inflammation: *gastritis, laryngitis*

-itude state or quality: *disquietude, promptitude*

-ity state or quality: *acidity, similarity*

-ive (person or thing) that does or tends to: *assertive, consumptive*

-ize = **-ise**

-latry worship: *idolatry, bardolatry*

-less without: *brainless, sunless*

-let small kind: *flatlet, tartlet*

-ling small, young, or unimportant one: *duckling, groundling*

-ly in the stated way; at the stated intervals: *easily, monthly*

-ment act, result, or condition: *involvement, measurement*

-monger seller; promulgator, advocate: *fishmonger, warmonger*

-ness condition: *drunkenness, fondness*

-nik person connected with or enthusiastic about: *computernik, peacenik*

-ocracy rule, government: *democracy, gerontocracy.* Hence **-ocrat** ruler: *autocrat*

-oid like: *asteroid, hemispheroid*

-ology study: *musicology, theology.* Hence **-ological, -ologist**

-or = **-er**: *inventor, surveyor*

-ory place used for; that does: *lavatory, conciliatory*

-osis disease: *byssinosis, tuberculosis.* Hence **-otic**: *neurotic*

-ous causing or having: *adventurous, rapturous*

-phile or **-phil** person who likes: *Francophile, oenophile.* Hence **-philia**: *Anglophilia*

-phobe person who dislikes or is afraid of: *ailurophobe, Russophobe.* Hence **-phobia**: *xenophobia*

-ship rank, position; skill; group: *directorship, musicianship, readership*

-some causing, tending to; group of: *meddlesome, foursome*

-ster person who does or is: *prankster, youngster*

-ule small: *spherule, valvule*

-ure act, condition: *composure, seizure*

-ward(s) in the direction of: *homewards, southward*

-ways in the direction of: *lengthways, sideways*

-wise in connection with; = **-ways**: *lengthwise, taxwise*

-y full of: like; tending to; nice small one; act, action: *filthy, summery, curly, pussy, inquiry*

---

pertaining to birds. **ornithocopros,** *n.* guano. **ornithoid,** *adj.* bird-like. **ornithomancy,** *n.* divination from flight of birds. **ornithomyzous,** *adj.* parasitic on birds. **ornithon,** *n.* aviary. **ornithophilous,** *adj.* applied to flowers pollinated by birds; bird-

loving. **ornithopter,** *n.* aircraft propelled by flapping wings. **ornithorhyncus,** *n.* duck-bill. **ornithoscopy,** *n.* bird-watching; ornithomancy. **ornithotomy,** *n.* anatomy or dissection of birds.

orobathymetric [ˌɔːrəbæθɪˈmetrɪk] *adj.* pertaining to map showing sea depths or submerged heights.

orogeny, orogenesis [ɔː'rɒdʒəni, ˌɔːrə'dʒenəsis] *n.* formation of mountains. **orogenic,** *adj.*

orograph ['ɔːrəgrɑːf] *n.* machine recording heights and distances traversed. **orographic,** *adj.* showing heights. **orography,** *n.* study of mountains.

orology [ɒ'rɒlədʒi, ɔː–] *n.* study of mountains. **orometer,** *n.* barometer showing height above sea-level.

orotund ['ɒrətʌnd, 'ɔː–] *adj.* using high-flown language; speaking or singing clearly and strongly. **orotundity,** *n.*

orphic ['ɔːfɪk] *adj.* mystic, oracular; pertaining to Orpheus.

orphrey ['ɔːfri] *n.* gold-embroidered band on ecclesiastical robes.

orpiment ['ɔːpɪmənt] *n.* yellow compound of arsenic, used as pigment, etc.

orpine ['ɔːpaɪn] *n.* kind of stone-crop; *British,* livelong; *American,* live-forever.

orrery ['ɒrəri] *n.* moving model of solar system.

orris ['ɒrɪs] *n.* kind of iris, and its rootstock used in perfumery, medicine, etc.

orthoclase ['ɔːθəkleɪz] *n.* feldspar.

orthodontia, orthodontics [ˌɔːθə'dɒnʃiə, –ʃə, –'dɒntɪks] *n.* correction of irregularity of teeth. **orthodontic,** *adj.* **orthodontist,** *n.*

orthodox ['ɔːθədɒks] *adj.* having correct or accepted opinions; approved; in accordance with standard or authorized practice. **orthodoxy,** *n.*

orthodromy, orthodromics [ɔː'θɒdrəmi, ˌɔːθə'drɒmɪks] *n.* navigation by great circle.

orthoepy [ɔː'θəʊɪpi, 'ɔːθəʊˌepi] *n.* correct pronunciation; study of pronunciation. **orthoepic,** *adj.* **orthoepist,** *n.*

orthogenesis [ˌɔːθə'dʒenəsis] *n.* (belief that) biological variation results in new species, always along same path; belief that the development of civilization always proceeds in same way. **orthogenetic,** *adj.* **orthogenic,** *adj.* pertaining to correction of children's mental defects.

orthognathism [ɔː'θɒgnəθɪzm] *n.* state of having straight jaws. **orthognathous,** *adj.* **orthognathy,** *adj.*

orthogonal [ɔː'θɒgənl] *adj.* right-angled. **orthogonality,** *n.*

orthograde ['ɔːθəgreɪd] *adj.* walking with the body upright.

orthography [ɔː'θɒgrəfi] *n.* correct spelling. **orthographer, orthographist,** *n.* **orthographize,** *v.i.*

orthometopic [ˌɔːθəʊmɪ'tɒpɪk] *adj.* having vertical forehead.

orthopaedic [ˌɔːθə'piːdɪk] *adj.* correcting physical deformities, originally of children. **orthopaedist, orthopaedics,** *n.*

orthopnoea [ˌɔːθɒp'niːə, ɔː'θɒpniə] *n.* ability to breathe in upright position only.

orthopraxy ['ɔːθəpræksi] *n.* correct action.

orthopsychiatry [ˌɔːθəʊsaɪ'kaɪətri, –sɪ–] *n.* preventive psychiatry for young people.

orthopter [ɔː'θɒptə] *see* **ornithopter**

orthopterous [ɔː'θɒptərəs] *adj.* pertaining or belonging to insect order including grasshoppers, crickets, etc. **orthopteran,** *n. & adj.* **orthopterist,** *n.* student of insects. **orthopteron,** *n.* such insect.

orthoptic [ɔː'θɒptɪk] *adj.* pertaining to correct vision.

orthoscope ['ɔːθəskəʊp] *n. obsolete,* instrument for examining exterior of eye. **orthoscopic,** *adj.* producing normal image.

orthosis [ɔː'θəʊsɪs] *n.* correction of neurotic state.

orthostatic [ˌɔːθə'stætɪk] *adj* pertaining to erect or standing position. **orthotic,** *adj.*

orthotonus [ɔː'θɒtənəs] *n.* spasmic bodily rigidity due to tetanus.

orthotropism [ɔː'θɒtrəpɪzm] *n.* vertical growth. **orthotropic,** *adj.*

ortolan ['ɔːtələn] *n.* kind of bunting (bird) esteemed as food.

orts [ɔːts] *n. pl. archaic,* crumbs, scraps.

oryctognosy [ˌɒrɪk'tɒgnəsi] *n.* mineralogy. **oryctognostic(al)** [əˌrɪktəg'nɒstɪk, –l], *adj.* **oryctology,** *n.* mineralogy.

oryx ['ɒrɪks] *n.* large straight-horned African antelope.

oryzivorous [ˌɒrɪ'zɪvərəs] *adj.* rice-eating.

os [ɒs] (*Latin*) *n.* (*pl.* **ossa** ['ɒsə]) bone; (*pl.* **ora** ['ɔːrə]) mouth.

oscillograph [ə'sɪləgrɑːf] *n.* instrument recording electrical oscillations, *e.g.* A.C. current wave forms.

oscillometer [ˌɒsɪ'lɒmɪtə] *n.* instrument measuring ship's rollings, etc.; instrument measuring blood pressure variations. **oscillometric,** *adj.*

oscilloscope [ə'sɪləskəʊp] *n.* instrument showing variations in electric potential, on a fluorescent screen by means of deflection of a beam of electrons.

oscine ['ɒsɪn, –aɪn] *n. & adj.* (bird) belonging to sub-order of birds including singing birds.

oscitance, oscitancy ['ɒsɪtəns, –i] *n.* yawning; sleepiness; dullness. **oscitant,** *adj.* **oscitation,** *n.*

osculate ['ɒskjuleɪt] *v.i. & t.* make contact; coincide; *jocular,* kiss. **osculant, osculatory, oscular,** *adj.* pertaining to mouth or kissing. **osculation** *n.*

Osmanli [ɒz'mænli, ɒs–] *adj.* of Turkish Empire; Ottoman; *n.* Western Turk.

osmatic [ɒz'mætɪk] *adj.* relying on smell for orientation. **osmesis,** *n.* act of smelling. **osmics,** *n.* study of sense of smell. **osmidrosis,** *n.* secretion of strong-smelling perspiration.

osmosis [ɒz'məʊsɪs, ɒs–] *n.* passage of solvent through a separating membrane between two solutions of different strengths. **osmose,** *v.i.* undergo osmosis. **osmotic,** *adj.* **osmometer,** *n.* instrument for measuring osmotic pressure.

osophy ['ɒsəfi] *n.* belief or doctrine; ism.

osphresis [ɒs'friːsɪs] *n.* sense of smell. **osphretic,** *adj.*

osprey ['ɒspri, –eɪ] *n.* large fish-eating hawk; *erroneously,* egret feather.

osseous ['ɒsɪəs] *adj.* bony. **ossicle,** *n.* small bone, especially of ear.

ossifrage ['ɒsɪfrɪdʒ] *n.* lammergeier; osprey.

ossify ['ɒsɪfaɪ] *v.i.* change into bone; become set in one's ways. **ossification,** *n.*

ossuary ['ɒsjuəri] *n.* charnel-house.

osteal ['ɒstɪəl] *adj.* pertaining to or like bone. **osteitis,** *n.* inflammation of bone. **ostosis,** *n.* bone formation.

ostensible [ɒ'stensəbl] *adj.* apparent, professed.

osteology [ˌɒsti'ɒlədʒi] *n.* study of bones; bony structure. **osteoarthritis**, *n.* degenerative arthritis. **osteoblastic**, *adj.* pertaining to formation of bone. **osteochondrous**, *adj.* pertaining to bone and cartilage. **osteoclasis**, *n.* surgical breaking of bone. **osteodermatous**, *adj.* having bone-like skin. **osteogenesis**, *n.* bone formation. **osteography**, *n.* descriptive osteology. **osteoid**, *adj.* bone-like. **osteoma**, bone tumour. **osteometry**, *n.* measurement of bones or skeleton. **osteopath**, *n.* one who treats disease by osteopathy. **osteopathy**, *n.* medical treatment by manipulation of bones. **osteophyte**, *n.* bony outgrowth. **osteoporosis**, *n.* disease affecting especially older women making bones brittle. **osteosclerosis**, *n.* hardening of bone. **osteotomy**, *n.* surgical cutting into, or removal of a piece of, bone.

ostiary ['ɒstiəri] *n.* door-keeper, especially of church.

ostinato [ˌɒstɪ'nɑːtəʊ] *n.* recurring musical phrase.

ostiole ['ɒstiəʊl] *n.* small orifice, pore.

ostracize ['ɒstrəsaɪz] *v.t.* exile from society. **ostracism**, *n.*

ostreiform ['ɒstriɪfɔːm] *adj.* oyster-shaped or -like. **ostreiculture**, *n.* oyster-breeding. **ostreoid**, *adj.* oyster-like. **ostreophagous**, *adj.* oyster-eating.

otacoustic [ˌəʊtə'kuːstɪk] *n.* & *adj.* (instrument) aiding hearing.

otalgia [əʊ'tældʒiə] *n.* earache. **otalgic**, *n.* & *adj.* (curative) of earache.

otiant ['əʊtiənt, –ʃi–] *adj.* idle; resting.

otic ['əʊtɪk, 'ɒ–] *adj.* pertaining to the ear. **otitis**, *n.* inflammation of the ear. **otolith**, *n.* concretion or 'stone' of ear. **otology**, *n.* study of ear and its diseases. **otorhinolaryngology, otolaryngology**, *n.* study of ear, nose and throat. **otoscope**, *n.* instrument for examining ear. **otosclerosis**, *n.* growth of new bone in inner ear, leading to deafness. **otosis**, *n.* mishearing of speech.

otiose ['əʊtiəʊs, –ʃi–] *adj.* idle; useless; futile. **otiosity**, *n.*

otto ['ɒtəʊ] *n.* attar.

Ottoman ['ɒtəmən] *adj.* pertaining to Turks or Turkish Empire.

oubliette [ˌuːbli'et] *n.* dungeon with entrance in roof.

ounce [aʊns] *n. Zoology*, snow-leopard of Tibet and Siberia.

ousel ['uːzl] *n.* blackbird. **ring ousel**, European thrush with white collar.

oust [aʊst] *v.t.* force out, dispossess; supplant. **ouster**, *n. Law*, wrongful dispossession or eviction.

outrance *see* à **outrance**.

outré ['uːtreɪ] (*French*) *adj.* unconventional; exaggerated.

outspan ['aʊtspæn] (*S African*) *v.i.* & *t.* remove harness (from); *n.* halting- or camping-place.

ouzel *see* **ousel**.

ouzo ['uːzəʊ] *n.* aniseed-flavoured Greek liqueur.

ovary ['əʊvəri] *n.* female egg-producing organ.

ovarian, *adj.* **ovariectomy**, *n.* removal of ovary. **ovaritis**, *n.* inflammation of ovary.

overt [əʊ'vɜːt, 'əʊvɜːt] *adj.* unconcealed.

overweening [ˌəʊvə'wiːnɪŋ] *adj.* arrogantly excessive.

ovicide ['əʊvisaɪd] *n.* substance killing eggs, especially of insects. **ovicidal**, *adj.*

oviduct ['əʊvidʌkt] *n.* passage conveying eggs to exterior or place of fertilization; Fallopian tube. **oviductal, oviducal**, *adj.*

ovine ['əʊvaɪn] *adj.* pertaining to or like sheep; *n.* such animal. **oviform**, *adj.* sheep- or egg-like.

oviparous [əʊ'vɪpərəs] *adj.* producing offspring in eggs. **ovipositor**, *n.* insect's tube-like organ for depositing eggs. **oviparity**, *n.*

ovoid ['əʊvɔɪd] *adj.* egg-shaped.

ovopyriform [ˌəʊvəʊ'pɪrifɔːm] *adj.* between pear-shaped and egg-shaped.

ovoviviparous [ˌəʊvəʊvɪ'vɪpərəs, –əʊvaɪ–] *adj.* producing offspring in eggs that hatch within parent's body. **ovoviviparity**, *n.*

ovum ['əʊvəm] *n.* (*pl.* **ova**) female's germ-cell from which, after fertilization, embryo develops. **ovule** ['ɒvjuːl], *n.* unfertilized seed. **ovulate** ['ɒvjuleɪt, –jə–], *v.i.* discharge eggs from ovary.

oxalidaceous [ɒkˌsæli'deɪʃəs] *adj.* pertaining to or like wood sorrel (plant); belonging to wood sorrel family of plants. **oxalic** [ɒk'sælɪk], *adj.* of or from wood sorrel; **oxalic acid**, poisonous acid used in dyeing, etc.

oxide ['ɒksaɪd] *n.* compound of oxygen. **oxidize**, *v.i.* & *t.* combine or cause to combine with oxygen; coat with oxide; rust or make rusty; give (metal) dull lustre or aged appearance by treating with chemicals. **oxidation**, *n.*

oxyacanthous [ˌɒksiə'kænθəs] *adj.* with sharp thorns. **oxyaesthesia**, *n.* extreme acuteness of sensation. **oxyaphia**, *n.* sensitivity of touch sense. **oxyblepsia**, *n.* keen-sightedness. **oxygeusia**, *n.* extreme sensitivity of taste sense.

oxymoron [ˌɒksi'mɔːrɒn, –ən] *n.* rhetorical device of conjoining contradictory words.

oxyopia [ˌɒksi'əʊpiə] *n.* abnormal keen-sightedness. **oxyosphresia**, *n.* extreme sensitivy of smell sense. **oxyphonia**, *n.* shrillness of voice. **oxyrhinch**, *adj.* sharp-nosed. **oxytocia**, *n.* quickness of child-birth. **oxytocic**, *adj.* hastening child-birth.

oxytocin [ˌɒksi'təʊsɪn] *n.* a pituitary hormone causing contraction of the uterus in childbirth.

oxytone ['ɒksitəʊn] *adj.* in ancient Greek, bearing acute accent on last syllable; *n.* such word.

ozocerite [əʊ'zəʊkəraɪt, –sə–, ˌəʊzəʊ'sɪəraɪt] *n.* kind of waxy mineral.

ozone ['əʊzəʊn] *n.* form of oxygen, and strong oxidizing agent, present in atmosphere, produced by electric sparks. **ozonic, ozonous**, *adj.* **ozoniferous**, *adj.* producing ozone.

ozonosphere [əʊ'zəʊnəsfɪə] *n.* region in upper atmosphere where most atmospheric ozone is concentrated.

ozostomia [ˌəʊzə'stəʊmiə] *n.* foul-smelling breath.

P

pabulum ['pæbjʊləm] n. food.
pacable ['peɪkəbl, 'pæk–] adj. capable of being pacified.
pace ['peɪsɪ] (*Latin*) prep. 'by permission of'; with reference to.
pachisi [pə'tʃiːzɪ] n. backgammon-like Indian game.
pachyderm ['pækɪdɜːm] n. thick-skinned animal, especially elephant. pachydermal, pachydermatous, pachydermous, adj. pachydermia, n. elephantiasis. pachyglossal, adj. thick-tongued. pachymenia, n. thickening of skin or membrane. pachymeninx, n. dura mater. pachymeter, n. thickness-measuring instrument.
paciferin [pə'sɪfərɪn] n. an infection-resisting factor found in natural foods.
pacific adj. conciliatory; soothing; peaceable.
paddock n. archaic, frog or toad.
paddymelon ['pædɪmelən] (*Australian*) n. small wallaby.
padishah ['pædɪʃɑː] (*Persian*) n. emperor; Shah of Iran; *Indian*, Emperor of India.
padmasana [pʌd'mɑːsənə] n. Buddha-like manner of sitting cross-legged; lotus seat.
padre ['pɑːdreɪ] n. minister of religion, especially chaplain of forces.
padrone [pə'drəʊneɪ, –nɪ] (*Italian*) n. (*pl.* –ni) master; inn-keeper; *American*, employment agent for (Italian) immigrants.
paduasoy n. corded silk; garment of this.
paean ['piːən] n. thanksgiving song.
paedarchy ['piːdɑːkɪ] n. government by children. paederasty, n. pederasty. paediatrics, n. study of children's diseases. paedobaptism, n. infant baptism. paedodontics, n. care of children's teeth. paedology, n. child study. paedomorphism, n. continuance of infantile characteristics in adult. paedophilia, n. sexual love of children. paedopsychologist, n. expert on child psychology.
paella n. Spanish rice dish with shellfish, chicken, vegetables, etc.
paeon ['piːən] n. metrical foot of one long and three short syllables or one stressed and these unstressed syllables. paeonic [pi'ɒnɪk], n. & adj.
paginate ['pædʒɪneɪt] v.t. arrange and number pages of (book). paginal, adj. pertaining to or consisting of pages; page for page. pagination, n.
pagurian [pə'gjʊərɪən] n. & adj. (crab) belonging to hermit crab family. pagurid, n.
paideia [paɪ'deɪə] n. education aimed at forming an enlightened, mature mind.
paillasse ['pælɪæs] n. palliasse.
pakeha ['pɑːkɪhɑː] (*Maori*) n. white man; foreigner.

paladin ['pælədɪn] n. medieval champion or knight, especially of court of Charlemagne; hero.
palaeoanthropic [ˌpælɪəʊæn'θrɒpɪk, ˌpeɪ–] adj. pertaining to earliest form of humankind. palaeobiology, n. study of fossil life. palaeobotany, n. study of fossil plants. palaeocene, n. & adj. (pertaining to) earliest epoch of Tertiary period. palaeodendrology, n. study of fossil trees. palaeoethnic, adj. pertaining to earliest races of Man. palaeogenetic, adj. of past origin. palaeography, n. study of ancient writings. palaeolithic, adj. pertaining to early Stone Age. palaeology, n. study of antiquities. palaeontography, n. description of fossils. palaeontology, n. study of past life and fossils. palaeophile, n. antiquarian. palaeoornithology, n. study of fossil birds. palaeozoic, n. & adj. (pertaining to). geological era extending from beginning of Cambian to end of Permian periods. palaeozoology, n. study of fossil animals.
palaestra, palestra [pə'lestrə] n. wrestling; gymnasium. palaestral, palestral, adj.
palamate ['pæləmeɪt] adj. webfooted.
palanquin [ˌpælən'kiːn] n. litter for one in E Asia, carried on the shoulders.
palatine ['pælətaɪn] adj. having royal authority over a certain locality. count palatine, such count. county palatine, jurisdiction of count palatine. palatinate [–'lætɪnət], n. jurisdiction of count palatine.
paleaceous [ˌpeɪlɪ'eɪʃəs] adj. chafflike.
paletot ['pælɪtəʊ] n. loose outer garment; overcoat.
palfrey ['pɔːlfrɪ] n. quiet-moving saddle horse.
palilogy [pə'lɪlədʒɪ] n. emphatic repetition of word.
palimpsest ['pælɪmpsest] n. parchment, etc., of which first writing has been erased to enable it to be used again. palimpsestic, adj.
palindrome ['pælɪndrəʊm] n. word, phrase, etc., reading the same backwards or forwards. palindromic [–'drɒmɪk], adj.
palingenesis [ˌpælɪn'dʒenəsɪs] n. resuscitation; rebirth; metempsychosis; exact reproduction of ancestral characteristics. palingenesian [–dʒə'niːzɪən], palingenetic [–dʒə'netɪk], adj. palingenesist, n.
palinode ['pælɪnəʊd] n. recantation, especially in verse. palinodist, n.
Palladian [pə'leɪdɪən] adj. pertaining to or like classical architural style of Andrea Palladio, 16th-century Italian architect; pertaining to Pallas Athena, Greek goddess of wisdom; wise; learned. palladium, n. (*pl.* –ia) safeguard; protection.
pallaesthesia [ˌpæles'θiːʒɪə] n. sense of vibration.

palletron ['pælɪtrɒn] *n.* a cyclotron-like apparatus accelerating atomic particles up to a level of one million electron volts.

palliasse ['pælɪæs] *n.* hard straw mattress.

palliate ['pælɪeɪt] *v.t.* mitigate; ease; relieve but not cure; excuse. **palliation**, *n.* **palliative**, *n. & adj.* **palliatory**, *adj.*

pallium ['pælɪəm] *n. (pl. -ia) Roman Catholic*, white woollen band worn round shoulders by pope and archbishops; *Medicine*, cerebral cortex.

pallograph ['pæləgrɑːf] *n.* instrument measuring steam ship's vibration.

palma Christi [,pælmə 'krɪsti] (*Latin*) *n.* 'hand of Christ'; castor-oil plant.

palmary ['pælməri] *adj.* meriting highest prize; principal.

palmate ['pælmeɪt] *adj.* like hand, especially with fingers spread; webfooted. **palmation**, *n.*

palmetto [pæl'metəu] *n.* fan palm and its leaves.

palmiped ['pælmɪped] *n. & adj.* web-footed (bird).

palmus ['pælməs] *n.* palpitation; twitching; nervous tic. **palmodic**, *adj.*

palmyra [pæl'maɪrə] *n.* tall African palm, yielding timber, thatching leaves, edible fruit, sugar and wine.

palomino [,pælə'miːnəu] *n.* horse of Arab descent, light-cream or tan-coloured with a pale-coloured mane and tail.

palpable ['pælpəbl] *adj.* tangible; provable; obvious. **palpability**, *n.*

palpate [pæl'peɪt, 'pælpeɪt] *v.t.* examine by touching. **palpation**, *n.* **palpatory**, *adj.*

palpebra ['pælpɪbrə] *n. (pl. -ae)* eyelid. **palpebra**, *adj.* **palpebrate**, *adj.* having palpebrae; *v.i.* wink.

palpi ['pælpaɪ] *n. pl. (sing. -pus)* insect's or crustacean's feelers.

palter ['pɔːltə] *v.i.* act or talk deceitfully.

paludal [pə'luːdl, 'pæljudl] *adj.* pertaining to marshes. **paludicolous** [,pælju'dɪkələs], *adj.* inhabiting marshes. **paludous**, ['pæl–], *adj.* marshy; living in marshes; malarial. **paludrine**, *n.* synthetic anti-malarial drug.

palynology [,pælɪ'nɒlədʒi] *n.* study of pollen and spores living and fossil.

pampas ['pæmpəs] *n. pl.* grassy plains of Argentina. **pampean**, *n. & adj.* (inhabitant) of the pampas. **pampero**, *n.* cold west wind of the pampas.

pampiniform [pæm'pɪnɪfɔːm] *adj.* like a tendril.

pan [pɑːn] (*Hindi*) *n.* betel-nut.

panacea [,pænə'siːə] *n.* universal cure. **panacean**, *adj.*

panache [pə'næʃ] *n.* plume on helmet; verve flamboyance. **panached**, *adj.* having coloured stripes.

panaché [pə'næʃeɪ] (*French*) *adj.* composed of various different foods.

panada [pə'nɑːdə] *n.* sauce base made from flour or bread crumbs plus water or stock.

panarchy ['pænɑːki] *n.* universal rule.

panarthritis [,pænɑː'θraɪtɪs] *n.* arthritis of all joints of body, or of whole of one joint.

panary ['pænəri] *adj.* pertaining to bread and baking.

panchromatic [,pænkrə'mætɪk] *adj.* sensitive to light of every colour; *n.* such photographic film. **panchromatism**, *n.*

pancosmism [,pæn'kɒzmɪzm] *n.* belief that nothing exists beyond the material universe.

pancosmic, *adj.* pertaining to pancosmism, or to universe in its entirety.

pancratic [pæn'krætɪk] *adj.* athletic; pertaining to or having ability in all matters.

pancreas ['pæŋkrɪæs] *n.* large digestive gland behind stomach; sweetbread. **pancreatic** [–'ætɪk], *adj.* **pancreatitis**, *n.* inflammation of pancreas.

pancyclopaedic [,pænsaɪklə'piːdɪk] *adj.* encyclopaedic.

panda ['pændə] *n.* **giant** *or* **great panda**, rare black and white bear-like Tibetan animal; **lesser** *or* **red panda**, raccoon-like animal of Himalayas.

pandects ['pændekts] *n. pl.* complete summary of ancient Roman legal decisions. **pandect**, *n. sing.* legal code; any summary of or treatise on whole of subject.

pandemic [pæn'demɪk] *adj.* universal; affecting majority of people of an area; epidemic everywhere. **pandemia** [–'diːmiə], *n.* pandemic disease.

pandemoniac [,pændɪ'məuniæk] *adj.* pertaining to general tumult. **pandemonium**, *n.* riotous uproar or place.

pander ['pændə] *n.* someone who panders; pimp. *v.i.* help to gratify unworthy desires of others.

pandiculation [pæn,dɪkju'leɪʃn] *n.* act of stretching oneself.

pandit ['pændɪt, 'pʌn–] *n.* (honorary title for) wise man in India.

panegyric [,pænɪ'dʒɪrɪk] *n.* eulogy. **panegyrical**, *adj.* **panegyrize** ['pæn–], *v.t.* praise highly. **panegyrist**, *n.*

paneity [pə'niːəti] *n. Theology*, state of being merely bread.

panentheism [pæn'enθiɪzm] *n.* belief that world is part of God.

pangamy ['pæŋgəmi] *n.* marriage without limitation as to spouses. **pangamic** [–'gæmɪk], *adj.*

pangenesis [pæn'dʒenəsɪs] *n.* theory that reproductive cells contain particles from all parts of parents.

Panglossian [pæŋ'glɒsiən] *adj.* pertaining to Pangloss, character in Voltaire's *Candide*, and his optimism.

pangolin [pæŋ'gəulɪn, 'pæŋgə–] *n.* scaly anteater of Asia and Africa.

pangrammatist [pæn'græmətɪst] *n.* person composing sentences, verses, etc., containing all letters of alphabet.

panicle ['pænɪkl] *n.* loose much-branched flowerhead, especially of grasses; compound raceme. **paniculate**, *adj.* having or arranged in panicles.

panification [,pænɪfɪ'keɪʃn] *n.* transformation into bread.

panivorous [pə'nɪvərəs] *adj.* bread-eating.

panmixy, panmixia ['pænmɪksi, pæn'mɪksiə] *n.* interbreeding without limitation. **panmictic**, *adj.*

panmnesia [pæn'niːʒiə] *n.* belief that every mental impression continues in memory.

pannage ['pænɪdʒ] *n.* pigs' food in woods, as nuts, etc.; right to, or fee paid for, feeding pigs in woods.

pannicular [pæ'nɪkjulə] *adj.* pertaining to or like a sheet or thin layer.

pannose ['pænəus] *adj.* felt-like.

panoply ['pænəpli] *n.* complete and splendid array; full suit of armour.

panoptic(al) [pæn'ɒptɪk, –l] *adj.* giving view of whole at once. **panopticon**, *n.* such optical instrument; exhibition; building, as prison, whole of interior of which can be watched from one point.

panorpid [pə'nɔːpɪd] *n.* scorpion fly. **panorpine**, *adj.*

panpsychism [ˌpæn'aɪkɪzm] *n.* theory that all objects have minds or souls.

pansexualism [ˌpæn'seksjuəlɪzm] *n.* obsession with sex in all activities; belief that sexual instinct is basis of all activity. **pansexuality**, *n.*

pansophism ['pænsəfɪzm] *n.* claim to know everything. **pansophist**, *n.* **pansophy**, *n.* knowledge of everything.

pantagamy [pæn'tægəmi] *n.* marriage in which all spouses are held in common; free love.

pantarchy ['pæntɑːki] *n.* government by all.

pantechnicon [pæn'teknɪk] *adj. n.* removal van.

pantheism ['pænθiɪzm] *n.* belief that universe is God; worship of many or all gods. **pantheist**, *n.* **pantheistic(al)** *adj.*

pantheon ['pænθiən] *n.* temple to all gods; body of a nation's gods; temple of fame containing remains of nation's great men and women.

pantisocracy [ˌpæntɪ'sɒkrəsi] *n.* anarchistic community. **pantisocratic**, *adj.*

pantochronometer [ˌpæntəkrə'nɒmɪtə] *n.* combined sundial and compass, showing time in all parts of world.

pantoglot ['pæntəglɒt] *n.* speaker of all languages.

pantograph ['pæntəgrɑːf] *n.* instrument for copying maps, etc., on any scale; device for taking electric current from overhead wires to motor of train, etc. **pantographic**, *adj.*

pantology [pæn'tɒlədʒi] *n.* system of universal knowledge. **pantologist**, *n.*

pantometer [pæn'tɒmɪtə] *n.* device measuring all angles of elevations and distances.

pantomorphic [ˌpæntə'mɔːfɪk] *adj.* taking on all shapes.

pantothenic [ˌpæntə'θenɪk] *adj.* denoting an acid which is a growth-promoting vitamin of vitamin B complex.

pantropic [pæn'trɒpɪk] *adj.* pertaining to life found throughout the tropics; pertaining to a virus affecting all tissues.

panurgic [pæ'nɜːdʒɪk] *adj.* adept at all kinds of work.

panzootic [ˌpænzəʊ'ɒtɪk] *adj.* applied to disease attacking animals of many kinds.

paparchy ['peɪpɑːki] *n.* government by pope. **paparchical**, *adj.*

papaveraceous [pəˌpævə'reɪʃəs] *adj.* pertaining to or like a poppy; belonging to the poppy family of plants.

papilionaceous [pəˌpɪliə'neɪʃəs] *adj.* shaped like a butterfly.

papilla [pə'pɪlə] *n.* (*pl.* **-ae**) nipple; projection shaped like nipple. **papilliform**, *adj.* nipple-shaped. **papilloma**, *n.* small tumour, *e.g.* wart. **papillary** ['pæp–], *adj.* **papillate**, **papillose**, *adj.* having papillae.

papolatry [peɪ'pɒlətri] *n.* excessive reverence paid to pope.

papoose [pə'puːs] *n.* N American Indian baby.

pappus ['pæpəs] *n.* (*pl.* **-pi**) downy tuft on plant seed; down. **pappescent**, *adj.* producing pappi. **pappose**, **pappous**, *adj.* having or like pappi.

paprika ['pæprɪkə, pə'priːkə] *n.* kind of pepper.

papule ['pæpjuːl] *n.* pimple. **papular**, **papulate**, **papuliferous**, *adj.* pertaining to or bearing papules. **papulous**, *adj.* pimply.

papyrus [pə'paɪrəs] *n.* (*pl.* **-ri**) kind of sedge from which paper-like material was made; writing on papyrus. **papyraceous**, *adj.* like or pertaining to papyrus. **papyrology**, *n.* study of papyrus.

parabiosis [ˌpærəbaɪ'əʊsɪs] *n.* union of two organisms sharing blood circulation, etc. **parabiotic**, *adj.*

parablepsy, **parablepsia** [ˌpærə'blepsi, -iə] *n.* false vision.

parabola [pə'ræbələ] *n.* curve formed by cutting of cone by plane parallel to its side. **parabolic** [-'bɒlɪk], *adj.* pertaining to parabola; like or described in a parable. **parabolist**, *n.* teller of parables.

paracentesis [ˌpærəsen'tiːsɪs] *n.* tapping of body fluid.

paracentral [ˌpærə'sentrəl] *adj.* situated near centre.

parachronism [pæ'rækrənɪzm] *n.* error of chronology, especially placing event at date later than it actually happened. **parachronistic**, *adj.*

paraclete ['pærəkliːt] *n.* advocate; Holy Ghost.

paracme [pæ'rækmi] *n.* stage following acme; decline.

paracusia, **paracusis** [ˌpærə'kjuːsiə, -sɪs] *n.* abnormality of hearing. **paracusic**, *adj.*

paradigm ['pærədaɪm] *n.* example, especially of grammatical inflections. **paradigmatic(al)** [-ɪg'mætɪk, –l], *adj.*

parados ['pærədɒs] *n.* band behind trench etc., giving protection from the near.

paradox ['pærədɒks] *n.* apparently self-contradictory statement; heterodox statement. **paradoxical**, *adj.* **paradoxist**, **paradoxology**, *n.* use of paradox.

paradromic [ˌpærə'drɒmɪk] *adj.* adjacent; side by side. **paradromism**, *n.*

paraenesis [pə'renəsɪs, -'riː–] *n.* advice; exhortation. **paraenetic** [ˌpærɪ'netɪk], *adj.*

paraesthesia [ˌpæres'θiːʒiə] *n.* tingling sensation on skin. **paraesthetic** [-'θetɪk], *adj.*

paragenesis [ˌpærə'dʒenəsɪs] *n.* order in which minerals together in rock were formed.

parageusia [ˌpærə'gjuːsiə] *n.* abnormality in taste sense.

paragoge [ˌpærə'gəʊdʒi] *n.* addition of sound at end of word. **paragogic(al)** [-'gɒdʒɪk, –l], *adj.*

paragon ['pærəgən] *n.* model of perfection; *v.t.* compare; regard as paragon.

paragraphia [ˌpærə'græfiə] *n.* writing of unintended words or letters.

parakinesis, **parakinesia** [ˌpærəkɪ'niːsɪs, -siə] *n.* abnormality of nervous control over movement; production of movements.

paralalia [ˌpærə'leɪliə] *n.* abnormality of speech sounds.

paralanguage ['pærəˌlæŋgwɪdʒ] *n.* non-verbal elements which affect meaning of speech, as intonation, etc.

paraldehyde [pə'rældɪhaɪd] *n.* sleep-inducing drug.

paraleipsis,   paralepsis,   paralipsis

[ˌpærə'laɪpsɪs, -'lep-] *n*. rhetorical device of emphasising thing by omitting it or mentioning it only cursorily.

paralexia [ˌpærə'leksɪə] *n*. transposition of words or syllables in reading, due to brain damage.

paralipomena [ˌpærəlɪ'pɒmənə] *n. pl*. things added as supplement to main text.

parallax ['pærəlæks] *n*. apparent difference in object's position or direction as viewed from different points. **parallactic**, *adj*.

parallelepiped, parallelopiped [ˌpærəlelə'paɪped] *n*. solid figure with every side a parallelogram.

paralogism [pæ'rælədʒɪzm] *n*. illogical or fallacious deduction. **paralogical, paralogistic**, *adj*. **paralogize**, *v.i*. be illogical; draw unwarranted conclusions. **paralogist**, *n*.

paramagnetic [ˌpærəmæg'netɪk] *adj*. having a weak magnetic susceptibility.

paramatta [ˌpærə'mætə] *n*. cotton or silk and wool dress material.

paramedian [ˌpærə'miːdiən] *adj*. near middle line.

paramedic(al) [ˌpærə'medɪkl] *n. & adj*. (person) supplementing work of medical doctors.

paramenia [ˌpærə'miːniə] *n*. abnormality of menstruation.

parameter [pə'ræmɪtə] *n*. *Mathematics*, a quantity that is constant in the case considered, but varies in other cases; a variable by the functions of which other variables can be expressed; *generally*, a measurement to which other measurements can be compared, a dimension. **parametric** [ˌpærə'metrɪk], *adj*.

paramnesia [ˌpæræm'niːʒiə] *n*. abnormality of memory, especially forgetting of meaning of words; illusion of having experienced before events which are being experienced for the first time.

paramour ['pærəmʊə] *n*. illicit lover; mistress.

paranephric [ˌpærə'nefrɪk] *adj*. near kidney; suprarenal.

parang ['pɑːræŋ] *n*. large Malay or Dyak sheath-knife.

paranoia [ˌpærə'nɔɪə] *n*. form of insanity in which patients believe themselves to be people of great importance, or think themselves persecuted by everyone. **paranoiac, paranoic**, *n. & adj*. **paranoid**, *adj*.

paranormal [ˌpærə'nɔːml] *adj*. supernatural.

paranymph ['pærənɪmf] *n*. *archaic*, best man; bridesmaid.

paraparesis [ˌpærəpə'riːsɪs] *n*. paralysis of lower limbs.

paraph ['pærəf] *n*. a flourish made after a signature.

paraphasia [ˌpærə'feɪʒiə] *n*. mental disorder marked by constant talking with misuse of words. **paraphasic**, *adj*.

paraphrase ['pærəfreɪz] *v.t*. restate in different words; *n*. such restatement. **paraphrasia**, *n*. incoherence. **paraphrastic** [-'fræstɪk], *adj*.

paraphrenia [ˌpærə'friːniə] *n*. the group of paranoid illnesses.

paraplegia [ˌpærə'pliːdʒiə] *n*. paralysis of lower half of body. **paraplegic**, *adj. & n*.

parapraxis [ˌpærə'præksɪs] *n*. committing of blunders.

parapsychology [ˌpærəsaɪ'kɒlədʒi] *n*. study of psychic phenomena.

paraquat ['pærəkwæt] *n*. herbicide that kills green vegetation by interfering with photosynthesis.

pararthria [pæ'rɑːθriə] *n*. incoherence.

paraselene [ˌpærəsə'liːni] *n*. bright spot on moon's halo.

parasigmatism [ˌpærə'sɪgmətɪzm] *n*. inability to pronounce sound of *s*.

parasynthesis [ˌpærə'sɪnθəsɪs] *n*. adding of prefix or suffix to compound to form new word.

parataxis [ˌpærə'tæksɪs] *n*. unconnected arrangement; *Grammar*, omission of connectives between related sentences. **paratactic**, *adj*.

parathyroid [ˌpærə'θaɪrɔɪd] *adj*. near thyroid gland, especially applied to such small glands whose hormone controls calcium content of body; *n*. such gland.

paratonic [ˌpærə'tɒnɪk] *adj*. resulting from external impulse.

paratyphoid [ˌpærə'taɪfɔɪd] *n. & adj*. (fever) resembling typhoid but caused by different bacillus.

paravane ['pærəveɪn] *n*. knife-bearing torpedo-like device for cutting mines adrift.

paravent ['pærəvent] *n*. wind-screen.

parbuckle ['pɑːbʌkl] *n*. rope sling used to lift or lower heavy cylindrical objects.

parcener ['pɑːsənə] *n*. co-parcener.

pardine ['pɑːdaɪn] *adj*. pertaining to or like a leopard; spotted.

paregoric [ˌpærə'gɒrɪk] *n*. drug soothing pain.

parenchyma [pə'reŋkɪmə] *n*. fundamental or essential tissue of organ or plant. **parenchymatous** [-'kɪmətəs], *adj*.

parentelic [ˌpærən'tiːlɪk, -'te-] *adj*. related by blood.

parenteral [pæ'rentərəl] *adj*. entering body by injection rather than through digestion.

parenthesis [pə'renθəsɪs] *n*. (*pl*. **-ses**) word, statement, etc., inserted incidentally into sentence; round bracket (), containing such word, etc. **parenthetic(al)** [-'θetɪk, -l], *adj*.

parergon [pæ'rɜːgɒn] *n*. subordinate work; accessory.

paresis [pə'riːsɪs, 'pærəsɪs] *n*. partial paralysis. **paretic**, [-'retɪk, -'riː-], *n. & adj*.

pareunia [pə'ruːniə] *n*. coitus.

parget ['pɑːdʒɪt] *n. & v.t*. plaster, whitewash, rough-cast, etc. **pargeting**, *n*.

parhelion [pɑː'hiːliən] *n*. (*pl*. **-ia**) halo-like light seen at point opposite sun; mock sun. **parhelic**, *adj*.

pariah [pə'raɪə, 'pæriə] *n*. low caste Indian; outcast; mongrel stray dog of streets.

paries ['pæriiːz] *n*. (*pl*. **-rietes**) wall of hollow organ or cavity.

parietal [pə'raɪətl] *adj*. pertaining to wall of cavity or body. **parietal bone**, bone of top and sides of cranium.

pari mutuel [ˌpæri 'mjuːtʃuəl] (*French*) *n*. 'mutual bet'; form of betting whereby winners receive share of all stakes placed; totalizator or pool betting.

parine ['peəraɪn, -rɪn] *adj*. like or pertaining to titmouse.

pari passu ['pæri 'pæsjuː] (*Latin*) 'at equal pace'; in equal degree, proportion, etc.

paristhmion [pæ'rɪsθmiən] *n.* tonsil.

parisyllabic [ˌpærɪsɪ'læbɪk] *n.* & *adj.* (word) having same number of syllables in all forms.

parkin ['pɑːkɪn] *n.* moist ginger cake made with treacle and oatmeal.

Parkinson's law ['pɑːkɪnsnz lɔː] *n. Economics, jocular,* work expands to fill the time available.

Parnassian [pɑː'næsiən] *adj.* pertaining to Greek mountain sacred to Muses and Apollo; poetic; *n.* member of 19th-century French school of classical poets.

parochial [pə'rəʊkiəl] *adj.* of a parish; narrow, limited, local. **parochialism,** *n.* narrow outlook.

paroemia [pə'riːmiə] *n.* proverb. **paroemiac,** *adj.* **paroemiography,** *n.* collection of proverbs. **paroemiology,** *n.* study of proverbs.

paromology [ˌpærə'mɒlədʒi] *n.* apparent concession of opponent's point which in reality strengthens one's own argument.

paronomasia [ˌpærənə'meɪʒiə] *n.* pun; punning. **paronomastic,** *adj.*

paronychia [ˌpærə'nɪkiə] *n.* whitlow.

paronym ['pærənɪm] *n.* word having same derivation as another, or formed from foreign word, or having same form as cognate foreign word. **paronymic** [–'nɪmɪk], **paronymous** [–'rɒnɪməs], *adj.*

parorexia [ˌpærə'reksiə] *n.* desire to eat strange foods.

parosmia [pæ'rɒzmiə] *n.* desire for strange scents.

parotic [pə'rɒtɪk] *n.* adjacent to ear. **parotid,** *adj.* pertaining to salivary gland below ear; *n.* such gland. **parotitis,** *n.* mumps.

parous ['pærəs] *adj.* bringing forth, or having borne, offspring.

parousia [pæ'ruːziə] *n.* coming, especially second coming of Christ.

paroxysm ['pærəksɪzm] *n.* sudden convulsion or fit. **paroxysmal, paroxysmic,** *adj.*

paroxytone [pə'rɒksɪtəʊn] *n.* & *adj.* (word) having acute accent on last syllable but one.

parr [pɑː] *n.* young salmon.

parrhesia [pə'riːʒiə] *n.* outspokenness.

parricide ['pærɪsaɪd] *n.* killer or killing of parent, close relative, or king, etc. **parricidal,** *adj.*

parsec ['pɑːsek] *n.* astronomical measure of distance, approximately equivalent to 19.5 billion miles.

parsimony ['pɑːsɪməni] *n.* stinginess; economy. **parsimonious** [–'məʊniəs], *adj.*

parthenian [pɑː'θiːniən] *adj.* pertaining to virgin. **parthenocarpy** [–θən–], *n.* bearing of fruit without fertilization. **parthenogenesis,** *n.* reproduction without fertilization; virgin birth. **parthenoparous,** *adj.* bearing offspring without fertilization.

participle ['pɑːtɪsɪpl] *n.* verbal adjective. **participial** [–'sɪpiəl], *adj.*

particulate [pɑː'tɪkjʊlət] *n.* & *adj.* (substance) made up of particles.

parti pris [ˌpɑːti 'priː] (*French*) 'side taken'; prejudice; preconception.

partisan [ˌpɑːtɪ'zæn] *n.* adherent or follower of a party, person, or principle; member of armed resistance group in enemy-occupied country; *adj.* devotedly adhering to a party, etc.; strongly biased.

parton ['pɑːtɒn] *n. Physics,* elementary particle

theoretically held to be a constituent of protons and neutrons.

parturition [ˌpɑːtju'rɪʃn] *n.* bringing forth of young. **parturient,** *adj.* **parturifacient,** *n.* & *adj.* (drug) inducing parturition.

parulis [pə'ruːlɪs] *n.* gumboil.

parure [pæ'rʊə] (*French*) *n.* set of jewels or other ornaments.

parvenu ['pɑːvənjuː] *n.* vulgar newly-rich person; upstart.

parvipotent [pɑː'vɪpətənt] *adj.* having little power. **parviflorous,** *adj.* having small flowers.

parvis ['pɑːvɪs] *n.* enclosed area in front of church.

parvule ['pɑːvjuːl] *n.* minute pill.

pas [pɑː] (*French*) *n.* 'step'; dance step or figure. **pas de deux** [–də 'dɜː], dance (figure) for two. **pas seul** [–'sɜːl], solo dance (figure).

PASCAL [pæ'skæl] *n.* high-level computer-programming language.

paschal ['pæskl] *adj.* pertaining to Easter, or Passover. **paschal letter,** bishop's letter of ancient Church concerning next Easter date. **paschal moon,** new moon of vernal equinox.

pascual ['pæskjuəl] *adj.* pertaining to pasture.

pasha ['pɑːʃə, pə'ʃɑː] *n.* Turkish title of high military rank. **pashalik,** *n.* jurisdiction of pasha.

pasigraphy [pə'sɪgrəfi] *n.* universal written language, especially using symbols for ideas rather than words. **pasigraphic(al),** *adj.*

pasque-flower ['pæsk,flaʊə] *n.* white- or purple-flowered anemone-like plant.

pasquinade [ˌpæskwɪ'neɪd] *n.* lampoon, especially exhibited in public place.

passacaglia [ˌpæsə'kɑːliə] *n.* old slow Italian or Spanish dance; variations on a theme over a continuously repeated ground bass.

passado [pə'sɑːdəʊ] *n.* forward thrust in fencing.

passé ['pæseɪ] (*French*) *adj.* 'past'; worn out; out of date; antiquated.

passementerie [pæs'mɒntri] (*French*) *n.* bright trimmings of gilt, tinsel, etc.

passe partout [ˌpæs pɑː'tuː, ˌpɑːs–] *n.* picture-frame, especially of adhesive cloth holding together glass, picture and back; universal passport; master-key.

passerine ['pæsəraɪn, –rɪn] *n.* & *adj.* (bird) belonging to the bird order including perching birds. **passeriform,** *adj.*

passible ['pæsɪbl] *adj.* capable of feeling; impressionable.

passim ['pæsɪm] (*Latin*) *adv.* 'everywhere'; recurring frequently or here and there.

passometer [pæ'sɒmɪtə] *n.* pedometer.

passus ['pæsəs] *n.* canto of poem.

pastel ['pæstl, pæ'stel] *n.* crayon of powdered pigment; crayon-drawing; light literary work; *adj.* delicately coloured.

pastern ['pæstən] *n.* part of horse's foot between fetlock joint and upper edge of hoof.

pasteurize ['pɑːstʃəraɪz, 'pæs–] *v.t.* sterilize partially, by heating to, and maintaining at, a high temperature. **pasteurization,** *n.*

pasticcio [pæ'stiːtʃəʊ] (*Italian*) *n.* (*pl.* **–ci**) medley; pot-pourri, pastiche.

pastiche [pæ'stiːʃ] *n.* work of art or literature in imitation of, or satirizing, another's style. **pasticheur** [–'ʃɜː], *n.* maker of pastiche.

pastose ['pæstəʊs] *adj.* painted thickly.

pastrami [pə'strɑːmi] *n.* highly seasoned smoked beef.

patagium [pə'teɪdʒiəm] *n.* web of skin between forelimbs and hind-limbs of tree-dwelling creatures, that acts as a wing.

patamar, pattamar ['pætəmɑː] *n.* Indian messenger or mail-boat; W Indian lateen-rigged boat.

patavinity [,pætə'vɪnəti] *n.* use of dialect.

patchouli ['pætʃʊli] *n.* kind of E Indian mint, and strong perfume obtained from it.

pâté de foie gras [,pæteɪ də fwɑː 'grɑː] (*French*) paste made of fattened goose's liver.

patella [pə'telə] *n.* kneecap. **patelliform,** *adj.* limpet-shaped. **patellar,** *adj.* **patellate,** *adj.* having shape of patella.

paten ['pætn] *n.* Communion bread plate.

patera ['pætərə] *n.* decorative round or oral medallion used in ornamental bas reliefs, etc.

pateriform ['pætərɪfɔːm] *adj.* saucer-shaped.

paternoster [,pætə'nɒstə] *n.* Lord's Prayer, or recital of it; rosary bead on which this is said; curse or spell; bead-like moulding; doorless, continuously moving lift/elevator.

pathodontia [,pæθə'dɒnʃiə] *n.* study of dental diseases.

pathogen ['pæθədʒən] *n.* disease-causing agent such as virus. **pathogenic,** *adj.* causing disease.

pathogenesis [,pæθə'dʒenəsɪs] *n.* origin or development of disease. **pathogenetic** [–dʒə'netɪk], *adj.*

pathognomic, pathognomonic [pə'θɒgnəmi] *adj.* aiding diagnosis; distinctive.

pathology [pə'θɒlədʒi] *n.* study of disease; condition due to disease. **pathological,** *adj.* **pathologist,** *n.*

pathy ['pæθi] *n.* medical treatment; nostrum.

patina ['pætɪnə] *n.* film formed on exposed metals, etc., especially green film on copper or bronze; any such sign of mellowing or old age. **patinous,** *adj.* bearing patina. **patinate,** *v.i. & t.*

patisserie [pə'tiːsəri] (*French*) *n.* pastry shop.

patois ['pætwɑː] *n.* dialect; jargon.

patrial ['peɪtrɪəl] *adj.* pertaining to, derived from, or signifying native country. *n. British,* person having at least one parent or grandparent born in Britain.

patriarch ['peɪtrɪɑːk] *n.* tribal elder, ruler or father; any venerable ancient man; *Roman Catholic,* bishop; metropolitan; bishop next below pope in rank. **patriarchate,** *n.* office of patriach. **patriarchal,** *adj.* **patriarchy,** *n.* social system marked by supremacy of father and male line.

patrician [pə'trɪʃn] *n. & adj.* (person) of noble birth. **patriciate,** *n.* position of patrician; nobility.

patricide ['pætrɪsaɪd] *n.* killing or killer of own father; traitor or act of treason. **patricidal,** *adj.*

patrilineal [,pætrɪ'lɪniəl] *adj.* pertaining to or descending in male line.

patrimony ['pætrɪməni] *n.* inherited property. **patrimonial** [–'məʊniəl], *adj.*

patriolatry [,pætrɪ'ɒlətri] *n.* excessive devotion to native country.

patristic [pə'trɪstɪk] *adj.* pertaining to the Fathers of the Church. **patristics,** *n.* study of the Fathers' lives and works.

patrix ['peɪtrɪks] *n.* die from which matrix is made.

patroclinous, patriclinous [,pætrə'klaɪnəs] *adj.* pertaining to, or having, inherited paternal characteristics.

patrology [pə'trɒlədʒi] *n.* patristics.

patronymic [,pætrə'nɪmɪk] *n. & adj.* (name) derived from father or ancestors; surname, especially formed by addition of suffix (as *-son,* etc.) to father's name.

patten ['pætn] *n.* wooden sole, or clog, for raising foot above wet.

pattu ['pætuː] *n.* woollen cloth or shawl of Kashmir.

patulous ['pætjʊləs] *adj.* wide-spreading or wide open.

pauca verba [,pɔːkə 'vɜːbə, ,paʊ–] (*Latin*) 'few words'. **paucis verbis** [–sɪs 'vɜːbɪs], 'in few words'.

pauciloquy [pɔː'sɪləkwi] *n.* brevity in speech.

paucity ['pɔːsəti] *n.* state of being few or small; scarcity; lack.

pavane [pə'væn] *n.* slow stately dance.

pavé ['pæveɪ] *n.* (uneven) paved surface; method of setting gem stones very close together so that base is hidden.

paviour ['peɪvjə] *n.* labourer doing, or tool for, paving work.

pavonated ['pævəneɪtɪd] *adj.* peacock blue. **pavonine,** *adj.* like or coloured like a peacock.

pawky ['pɔːki] *adj.* sly; coy; dry.

pawl [pɔːl] *n.* lever which engages with a ratchet wheel so as to permit movement in one direction only.

pax [pæks] (*Latin*) *n.* 'peace'. **pax vobiscum,** 'peace (be) with you'.

paynim ['peɪnɪm] *n. archaic* pagan.

payola [peɪ'əʊlə] *n. slang,* bribe, especially secret payment as inducement to mention a product, personality, etc., on radio and television programme or in a newspaper.

paysage [peɪ'zɑːʒ] (*French*) *n.* landscape. **paysagist** ['peɪzədʒɪst], *n.* painter of paysage.

peccable ['pekəbl] *adj.* liable to sin. **peccadillo,** *n.* (*pl.* **-es**) minor sin. **peccant,** *adj.* sinning; *n.* sinner.

peccary ['pekəri] *n.* American wild pig.

peccavi [pe'kɑːvi] (*Latin*) 'I have sinned'; *n.* confession of sin.

pecksniffian [pek'snɪfiən] *adj.* sanctimoniously hypocritical.

pecten ['pekten] *n.* (*pl.* **-tines**) scallop; comb-like membrane of eye of birds and reptiles.

pectin ['pektɪn] *n.* principle in fruit causing jam, etc., to set. **pectinaceous, pectic** *adj.*

pectinate ['pektɪnl] *adj.* comb-shaped; toothed. **pectineal,** *adj.* pertaining to public bone. **pectiniform,** *adj.* like a comb or a scallop shell.

pectinous ['pektɪnəs] *adj.* pertaining to pectin. **pectize,** *v.t.* cause to set.

pectoral ['pektərəl] *adj.* pertaining to or worn on breast or chest; *n.* breast-plate; muscle of breast. **pectoriloquy,** *n.* clear hearing of patient's voice in auscultation.

peculate ['pekjuleɪt] *v.i. & t.* embezzle. **peculation, peculator,** *n.*

pecuniary [pɪ'kjuːniəri] *adj.* pertaining to money.

pedagogue ['pedəgɒg] *n.* schoolteacher, pedant. **pedagogic(al)** [–'gɒdʒɪk, –l], *adj.* **pedagogics** [–'gɒdʒɪks], **pedagogy** [–ɒdʒi], *n.* art of teaching;

instruction in such art.

pedant ['pednt] *n.* person making display of his or her learning; learned person paying excessive attention to details; precisian. **pedantic** [-'dæntik], *adj.* **pedanticism, pedantry,** *n.*

pedate ['pedeit] *adj.* like a foot; having feet.

pederast, paederast ['pedəræst] *n.* person having sexual intercourse with boy(s). **pederasty,** *n.*

pedialgia [,pedi'æ1dʒiə] *n.* pain in foot.

pedicel ['pedisel] *adj.* short, thin stalk; footstalk. **pedicle,** *n.* **pedicellate,** *adj.* having pedicel. **pedicelliform,** *adj.* like a pedicel.

pedicular [pi'dikjulə] *adj.* pertaining to or having lice. **pediculicide,** *n.* substance destroying lice. **pediculosis,** *n.* infestation with lice. **pediculous,** *adj.*

pedicure ['pedikjuə] *n.* chiropody. **pedicurist,** *n.*

pediform ['pedifɔːm] *adj.* footshaped. **pedigerous,** *adj.* having feet. **pediluvium,** *n.* foot-bath.

pediment ['pedimənt] *n.* triangular space at end of gable, especially ornamented; such space over door, window, etc. **pedimental,** *adj.*

pedometer [pi'domitə] *n.* instrument measuring distance traversed by walker by recording number of steps. **pedograph,** *n.* instrument recording nature of ground passed over.

peduncle [pi'dʌŋkl] *n.* flower stalk; stem. **peduncular,** *adj.* **pedunculate,** *adj.* having peduncles.

peekaboo [,piːkə'buː] *adj.* (of clothing) of transparent material; of fabric covered with small holes.

peen [piːn] *n.* rounded or wedge-shaped end of head of hammer.

peepul ['piːpl] *n.* holy Indian fig-tree; bo-tree.

peignoir ['peinwaː] (*French*) *n.* loose dress; negligée.

peine [pein] *n.* 'pain'. **peine forte et dure** [-,fɔːt ei 'duə], 'pain strong and hard'; execution by crushing to death under heavy weights.

pejorate ['piːdʒəreit] *v.t.* depreciate; worsen. **pejoration,** *n.* change for worse. **pejorative,** *n.* & *adj.* disparaging (word or suffix, etc.).

pekoe ['piːkəu] *n.* sort of black tea.

pelage ['pelidʒ] *n.* animal's coat.

pelagic [pə'lædʒik] *adj.* pertaining to or found in open sea, or near surface of sea. **pelagial** [-'leidʒ-], *adj.* **pelagian** [-'leidʒ-], *n.* & *adj.* pelagic (animal).

pelargic [pə'laːdʒik] *adj.* like or pertaining to a stork.

pelargonium [,pelə'gəuniəm] *n.* geranium.

pelerine ['peləriːn, -rin] *n.* woman's short cape with tippets in front.

pelisse [pi'liːs] *n.* long outer mantle.

pellagra [pə'lægrə] *n.* nervous and digestive disease due to deficiency of nicotinic acid in diet. **pellagragenic,** *adj.* causing pellagra. **pellagrin,** *n.* person suffering from pellagra. **pellagrous,** *adj.*

pellicle ['pelikl] *n.* membrane; film. **pellicular,** *adj.* **pelliculate,** *adj.* covered with pellicle.

pellitory ['pelitəri] *n.* one of several wall-growing plants, including one with root used in dentifrices.

pellucid [pe'luːsid] *adj.* clear; transparent. **pellucidity,** *n.*

pelma ['pelmə] *n.* impression showing shape of sole.

pelota [pə'lɒtə, pe'ləu-] (*Spanish*) *n.* 'ball'; several tennis-like Spanish games, and fives-like Basque game.

pelotherapy [,piːlə'θerəpi, ,pel-] *n.* medical treatment by mud baths.

peltast ['peltæst] *n.* ancient Greek soldier with light shield. **peltate, peltiform,** *adj.* shield-shaped. **peltiferous,** *adj.* bearing a shield.

pelvis ['pelvis] *n.* (*pl.* –**ves**) bony structure forming frame of abdominal cavity. **pelvic,** *adj.* **pelviform,** *adj.* basin-shaped.

pemmican ['pemikən] *n.* pounded, pressed, dried meat.

penates [pe'naiteiz] (*Latin*) *n. pl.* household gods.

penchant ['pɒnʃɒn] (*French*) *n.* inclination; liking.

pendent, pendant ['pendənt] *adj.* dangling; suspended; jutting; overhanging.

pendente lite [pen,denti 'laiti] (*Latin*) 'during the lawsuit'; until completion of litigation.

pendulous ['pendjuləs] *adj.* hanging down; free to swing.

peneplain ['piːniplein] *n.* land reduced to plain level by erosion. **peneplanation,** *n.*

penetralia [,peni'treiliə] (*Latin*) *n. pl.* private places; secrets.

penetrometer [,peni'trɒmitə] *n.* instrument measuring the penetrability or firmness of a substance by driving a needle into it; instrument measuring the penetrativeness of X-rays, etc.

penicillate [,penə'silət] *adj.* terminating in tuft of hairs. **penicilliform,** *adj.*

penicillin [,penə'silin] *n.* antibiotic of wide use, produced by species of penicillium mould.

penis ['piːnis] *n.* (*pl.* –**nes**) male copulative organ. **penial, penile,** *adj.*

penna ['penə] *n.* any of a bird's larger feathers, covering most of its body. **pennaceons,** *adj.*

pennant ['penənt] *n.* pennon-shaped flag, especially on ships or boats.

pennate ['peneit] *adj.* having or like wings or feathers. **penniferous, pennigerous,** *adj.* feather-bearing. **penniform,** *adj.* feather-like.

pennon ['penən] *n.* long flag coming to a point or swallowtail, especially attached as banner to head of lance; pennant.

penology [piː'nɒlədʒi] *n.* study of criminal punishment. **penologic(al),** *adj.* **penologist,** *n.*

pensile ['pensail] *adj.* hanging; building a hanging nest. **pensility,** *n.*

pentachord ['pentakɔːd] *n.* five-stringed musical instrument; series of five tones.

pentacle ['pentəkl] *n.* pentagram. **pentacular** [-'tækjulə], *adj.*

pentad ['pentæd] *n.* five; group of five.

pentadactyl [,pentə'dæktil] *adj.* having five fingers or toes to each hand or foot. **pentadactylate,** *adj.* **pentadactylism,** *n.*

pentadecagon [,pentə'dekəgən] *n.* 15-sided plane figure.

pentaglot ['pentəglɒt] *n.* & *adj.* (book, speaker, etc.), in or of five languages.

pentagon ['pentəgən] *n.* five-sided plane figure. **pentagonal** [-'tægənl], *adj.*

pentagram ['pentəgræm] *n.* five pointed star, especially as magic symbol. **pentagrammatic,** *adj.*

pentahedron [,pentə'hiːdrən] *n.* five-sided solid figure. **pentahedral,** *adj.*

pentalogy [pen'tælədʒi] *n.* state of being fivefold or in five parts.

pentalpha [pen'tælfə] *n.* pentagram.

pentamerous [pen'tæmərəs] *adj.* in five parts; *Botany*, having its parts in fives. **pentameral,** *adj.* **pentamerism,** *n.*

pentameter [pen'tæmitə] *n.* verse line of five feet. **pentametrist** [-'metrist], *n.*

pentangle ['pentæŋgl] *n.* pentagon. **pentangular,** *adj.*

pentapody [pen'tæpədi] *n.* verse line of five feet.

pentapolis [pen'tæpəlis] *n.* group or alliance of five cities. **pentapolitan,** [-'polɪtən], *adj.*

pentarch ['pentɑːk] *n.* member of pentarchy. **pentarchy,** *n.* government by five persons; alliance between five powers.

pentastich ['pentəstɪk] *n.* stanza of five lines. **pentastichous** [-'tæstɪkəs], *adj.* arranged in five rows. **pentastichy,** *n.*

pentasyllable ['pentə,sɪləbl] *n.* word, verse-line, etc., of five syllables. **pentasyllabic** [-'læbɪk], *adj.*

Pentateuch ['pentətjuːk] *n.* first five books of Old Testament; books of Moses. **Pentateuchal,** *adj.*

pentathlon [pen'tæθlən] *n.* athletic contest consisting of five different events competed in by all contestants.

Pentecost ['pentɪkɒst] *n.* Jewish festival, like harvest thanksgiving, on fiftieth day after second day of Passover; *modern*, Whit Sunday, or the event which it commemorates. **Pentecostal,** *adj.* **Pentecostalism,** *n.* charismatic, fundamentalist variety of Christian worship.

pentimento [,penti'mentəu] *n.* (*pl.* **–ti**) trace of earlier painting showing through layer(s) of paint added later.

pentobarbitone [,pentə'bɑːbɪtəun] *n.* *British*, barbiturate drug formerly used in sedatives.

penult [pə'nʌlt] *n.* last but one, especially such syllable. **penultimate,** *n.* & *adj.*

penumbra [pə'nʌmbrə] *n.* partly light margin surrounding complete shadow, especially during an eclipse. **penumbral,** *adj.*

penurious [pə'njuəriəs] *adj.* poor; mean. **penury** ['pen–], *n.* poverty.

peon ['piːən] *n.* *Spanish-American*, agricultural labourer; person bound to service for debt; *Indian*, infantryman; native policeman; office attendant or messenger. **peonage, peonism,** *n.*

peotomy [pi'ɒtəmi] *n.* surgical removal of penis.

peplos ['peplɒs] *n.* short tunic-like garment for women in ancient Greece.

peplum ['pepləm] *n.* flounce at waistline of blouse, dress, etc.

pepsin ['pepsɪn] *n.* gastric digestive juice. **pepsinate,** *v.t.* treat or mix with pepsin. **pepsiniferous,** *adj.* yielding pepsin. **peptic,** *adj.* pertaining to pepsin or digestion; aiding or capable of digestion; pertaining to, or in, stomach and duodenum; *n.* aid to digestion. **peptone,** *n.* substance resulting from digestion of protein by pepsin. **peptonize,** *v.t.* convert into peptone; pre-digest.

peracute [,pɜːrə'kjuːt] *adj.* very acute.

percale [pə'keɪl] *n.* closely woven cotton used especially for sheets.

per capita [pə 'kæpitə] (*Latin*) 'by heads'; shared or sharing equally among individuals; per unit of population.

percheron ['pɜːʃərɒn] *n.* kind of dappled or black heavy carthorse.

perciform ['pɜːsɪfɔːm] *adj.* like a perch (fish).

percurrent [pə'kʌrənt] *adj.* extending whole length (of a leaf).

percuss [pə'kʌs] *v.i.* & *t.* strike, tap, especially part of body in medical diagnosis. **percussion,** *n.* act of striking violently; impact of violent sound on ear; musical instrument as drums, etc., sounded by being struck. **percussive,** *adj.*

percutaneous [,pɜːkju'teɪniəs] *adj.* taking effect through the skin.

perdition [pə'dɪʃn] *n.* damnation; hell.

perdu [pɜː'djuː] *adj.* (*fem.* **–e**) out of sight; lost; reckless.

peregrinate ['perəgrɪneɪt] *v.i.* & *t.* wander (through). **peregrination,** *n.* **peregrinatory,** *adj.*

peregrine ['perəgrɪn, –riːn] *n.* kind of falcon used in sport.

peremptory ['perəmptəri, pə'rem–] *adj.* commanding; allowing no denial, refusal, or delay; arrogant.

perennial [pə'reniəl] *adj.* everlasting; *n.* plant flowering every year.

perfidy ['pɜːfədi] *n.* treachery; breaking of promise. **perfidious,** *adj.*

perfunctory [pə'fʌŋktəri] *adj.* mechanical, routine, cursory.

perfuse [pə'fjuːz] *v.t.* suffuse, permeate. **perfusion,** *n.* **perfusive,** *adj.*

pergameneous [,pɜːgə'miːniəs] *adj.* resembling parchment.

per gradus [pɜː 'grædəs] (*Latin*) '(step) by step'.

peri ['pɪəri] (*Persian*) *n.* fairy, especially excluded from paradise; beautiful woman.

perianth ['periænθ] *n.* external part of flower, including corolla and calyx. **perianthial,** *adj.*

periapt ['periæpt] *n.* amulet.

pericardium [,peri'kɑːdiəm] *n.* (*pl.* **–ia**) membranous sac containing heart. **pericardiac, pericardial,** *adj.* **pericarditis,** *n.* inflammation of pericardium.

pericarp ['perikɑːp] *n.* seed-vessel of plant. **pericarpial, pericarpic,** *adj.*

pericope [pə'rɪkəpi] *n.* selection or quotation from book. **pericopal, pericopic** [-'kopɪk], *adj.*

pericranium [,peri'kreɪniəm] *n.* membrane covering skull. **pericranial,** *adj.*

peridot ['peridɒt] *n.* gemstone, pale green variety of olivine.

perigee ['peridʒiː] *n.* point in orbit nearest earth. **perigeal, perigean,** *adj.*

perihelion [,peri'hiːliən] *n.* point in orbit nearest sun. **perihelial, perihelian,** *adj.*

perilune ['periluːn] *n.* point in the path of a body orbiting the moon that is nearest to the centre of the moon.

perimeter [pə'rɪmɪtə] *n.* outer boundary, and its length. **perimetric** [,peri'metrɪk], *adj.* **perimetrium** [-'metriəm], *n.* part of peritoneum round uterus.

perineum [,peri'niːəm] *n.* region of body between anus and genitals especially in pregnant females.

periodontal [,periə'dɒntl] *adj.* round tooth or teeth. **periodontics** *n. pl.* **periodontia, periodontology,** *n.* study of diseases of such tissues.

perioeci [,peri'iːsi] *n. pl.* (*sing.* **–cus**) persons living in same latitude on opposite sides of earth.

perioecic, *adj.*

periosteal [ˌperi'ɒstiəl] *adj.* round a bone. **periosteum,** *n.* such membranous tissue.

periotic [ˌperi'ɒtɪk, -'əʊ-] *adj.* round the ear.

peripatetic [ˌperɪpə'tetɪk] *adj.* walking about or from place to place; *British,* travelling to teach in several schools; belonging to Aristotle's school of philosophy; *n.* such person.

peripety, peripetia, peripeteia [pə'rɪpɪti, ˌperɪ'piːtiə, -pə'tiːə] *n.* sudden and violent change in circumstances, especially in drama.

periphery [pə'rɪfəri] *n.* perimeter, especially of round object or surface; area of termination of nerves. **peripheral,** *adj.* pertaining to periphery; of lesser importance or significance; *n.* additional device linked to computer. **peripheric** [-'ferɪk], *adj.*

periphrasis [pə'rɪfrəsɪs] *n.* (*pl.* **–ses**) circumlocution. **periphrastic** [-'fræstɪk], *adj.*; *Grammar,* formed with auxiliaries, prepositions, etc.

periplus ['perɪpləs] *n.* tour round, circumnavigation; account of such tour.

peripteral [pə'rɪptərəl] *adj.* with row of columns on every side; pertaining to air about moving body. **periptery** *n.* region round moving body in air.

periscian [pə'rɪsiən, -'rɪʃ-] *n.* person living in polar circle.

peristalith [pə'rɪstəlɪθ] *n.* prehistoric stone circle.

peristalsis [ˌperɪ'stælsɪs] *n.* (*pl.* **–ses**) wave-like movement of intestines forcing contents onward. **peristaltic,** *adj.*

peristeronic [pəˌrɪstə'rɒnɪk] *adj.* pertaining to pigeons.

peristyle ['perɪstaɪl] *n.* row of columns, especially on all sides of court, etc.; area enclosed by it.

peritoneum [ˌperɪtə'niːəm] *n.* membranous sac lining abdominal cavity. **peritoneal,** *adj.* **peritonitis,** *n.* inflammation of peritoneum.

perityphlic [ˌperɪ'tɪflɪk] *adj.* round caecum. **perityphlitis,** *n.* inflammation of perityphlic tissue.

perlaceous [pɜː'leɪʃəs] *adj.* pearly. **perligenous,** *adj.* producing pearls.

perlite ['pɜːlaɪt] *n.* volcanic glass forming, when expanded by heat, an insulating material and a light-weight aggregate added to concrete and plaster or used as soil conditioner. **perlitic** [-'lɪtɪk], *adj.* having perlite-like texture.

perlustrate [pə'lʌstreɪt] *v.t.* inspect with care. **perlustration,** *n.*

permafrost ['pɜːməfrɒst] *n.* layer of permanently frozen subsoil in polar regions.

permalloy ['pɜːmələɪ, pɜːm'ælɔɪ] *n.* alloy of nickel and iron, most easily magnetized of all materials.

permeate ['pɜːmieɪt] *v.i. & t.* diffuse through. **permeable,** *adj.*

Permian ['pɜːmiən] *adj. & n.* (pertaining to) last period of Palaeozoic era.

permutation [ˌpɜːmju'teɪʃn] *n.* transformation; change in order of objects, etc., or number of such possible changes. **permute** [-'mjuːt], *v.t.* arrange (especially a sequence) in different order. **permutate,** *v.t.* change the arrangement of.

pernancy ['pɜːnənsi] *n. Law,* receiving.

pernicious [pə'nɪʃəs] *adj.* deadly, highly destructive; malicious, evil.

pernine ['pɜːnaɪn] *adj.* pertaining to honey buzzard.

pernoctation [ˌpɜːnɒk'teɪʃn] *n.* act of spending the night.

pernor ['pɜːnə, -ɔː] *n.* person taking or receiving.

peroneal [ˌperə'niːəl] *adj.* pertaining to fibula.

peroral [pər'ɔːrəl] *adj.* through the mouth.

perorate ['perəreɪt] *v.i.* make grandiloquent speech; bring speech to close. **peroration,** *n.* final passage of speech. **perorative, peroratory,** [pə'rɒrətəri], *adj.*

peroxide [pə'rɒksaɪd] *n.* oxide containing large proportion of oxygen, especially peroxide of hydrogen.

per procurationem [pɜː ˌprɒkjureɪʃi'əʊnem] 'by agency'; by agent or proxy (*abbr.* **p.p.** *or* **per pro.**).

perquisite ['pɜːkwɪzɪt] *n.* something held to be a right.

perry ['peri] *n.* cider-like drink made from pears.

per se [pɜː 'seɪ] (*Latin*) 'by itself'; of or in itself; essentially; by virtue of its own essence. **perseity** *n.* self-sufficiency.

perseverate [pə'sevəreɪt] *v.i.* repeat action, etc., continually; recur persistently. **perseveration,** *n.*

persiennes [ˌpɜːsi'enz] *n. pl.* kind of Venetian blinds; outside shutters with movable slats.

persiflage ['pɜːsɪflɑːʒ] *n.* raillery; idle chatter.

persimmon [pə'sɪmən] *n.* orange-coloured plum-like fruit.

persona [pə'səʊnə] *n.* facade presented by individual to other people, in Jungian psychology.

persona grata [pəˌsəʊnə 'grɑːtə] (*Latin*) 'welcome or acceptable person'. **persona non grata,** unwelcome or unacceptable person.

personalia [ˌpɜːsə'neɪliə] (*Latin*) *n. pl.* personal details or anecdotes; personal belongings.

personalty ['pɜːsn–əlti] *n.* personal property.

perspicacious [ˌpɜːspɪ'keɪʃəs] *adj.* clear-sighted; having discernment. **perspicacity** [-'kæsəti], *n.*

perspicuous [pə'spɪkjuəs] *adj.* easily understood; clearly expressed. **perspicuity,** *n.*

pertinacity [ˌpɜːtɪ'næsəti] *n.* persistence; tenacity. **pertinacious,** *adj.*

pertussis [pə'tʌsɪs] *n.* whooping-cough. **pertussal,** *adj.*

peruke [pə'ruːk] *n.* wig.

peruse [pə'ruːz] *v.t.* read through thoroughly. **perusal,** *n.*

pervious ['pɜːviəs] *adj.* permeable; open-minded.

perwitsky [pə'wɪtski] *n.* pole-cat of N Asia and its fur.

pessary ['pesəri] *n.* supporting instrument or suppository introduced into vagina.

pestiferous [pe'stɪfərəs] *adj.* carrying infection or plague; noxious. **pesticide,** *n.* pest-killing substance. **pestology,** *n.* scientific study of insect pests.

petard [pe'tɑːd] *n.* bomb attached to, and for bursting open, gates, etc. **hoist with own petard,** blown up by own bomb; damaged by own devices to injure others.

pethidine ['peθɪdiːn] *n.* pain-relieving drug used in childbirth, etc.

petiole ['petiəʊl] *n.* leaf-stalk. **petiolar,** *adj.* **petiolate,** *adj.* having petiole. **petiolule,** *n.* petiole of a leaflet.

petitio principii [pɪˌtɪʃiəu prɪn'sɪpiaɪ, -'kɪpiiː] (*Latin*) 'begging the question'.

petrel ['petrəl] *n.* small dark seabird. **stormy** *or* **storm petrel**, such bird of the Atlantic and Mediterranean; person fond of, or whose presence heralds, strife.

petricolous [pe'trɪkələs] *adj.* inhabiting rocks.

pétrissage ['petrɪsɑːʒ] (*French*) *n.* kneading (in massage).

petrogenesis [ˌpetrə'dʒenəsɪs] *n.* origin or development of rocks. **petrogenic**, *adj.* **petroglyph**, *n.* ancient rock-carving. **petrography**, *n.* description and classification of rocks. **petrolithic**, *adj.* as hard as rock, applied to road surface. **petrology**, *n.* geological study of rocks. **petrophilous**, *adj.* living on rocks. **petrous**, *adj.* rocky; hard as stone.

pettitoes ['petɪtəuz] *n. pl.* pig's trotters.

petto ['petəu] (*Italian*) *n.* breast. **in petto**, in mind; in secret thoughts.

phacometer [fæ'kɒmɪtə] *n.* lens-measuring instrument.

phaeton ['feɪtn] *n.* light two-horse four-wheeled open carriage.

phagedaena [ˌfædʒɪ'diːnə] *n.* gangrene; extensive ulceration. **phagedaenic** *adj.*

phagocyte ['fægəsaɪt] *n.* leucocyte destroying harmful bacteria, etc. **phagocytic** [-'sɪtɪk], *adj.* **phagocytosis**, *n.* destruction of harmful elements by phagocytes.

phalacrosis [ˌfælə'krəusɪs] *n.* baldness.

phalanger [fə'lændʒə] *n.* several kinds of long-tailed Australian marsupial.

phalanges [fə'lændʒiːz] *n. pl.* (*sing.* **–nx**) bones of finger or toe. **phalangeal**, *adj.* **phalangigrade**, *adj.* walking on phalanges

phalanx ['fælæŋks] *n.* closely-ranked infantry formation; any such closely packed or organized body.

phalarope ['fælərəup] *n.* small sandpiper-like shore bird.

phallus ['fæləs] *n.* (*pl.* **–li**) representation of penis, symbol of generative power, as object of worship. **phallic**, *adj.* **phallicism, phallism**, *n.* phallic worship.

phanerogam ['fænərəgæm] *n.* (old term) flowering plant. **phanerogamic, phanerogamous** [-'rɒgəməs], *adj.*

phaneromania [ˌfænərə'meɪniə] *n.* habit of biting nails, picking at scars, etc.

phantasm ['fæntəm] *n.* figment of imagination, an illusion; ghost. **phantasmal, phantasmic**, *adj.*

phantasmagoria [ˌfæntæzmə'gɔːriə] *n.* crowd of phantoms; series of shifting images or scenes. **phantasmagoric(al)**, *adj.*

pharisee ['færɪsiː] *n.* Jewish religious adherent to ritual formalities; person ostentatiously religious, or self-righteous; hypocrite. **pharisaic(al)** [-'seɪɪk, -l], *adj.* **pharisaism** ['fær-], *n.*

pharmaceutical [ˌfɑːmə'suːtɪkl] *adj.* pertaining to pharmacy; *n.* drug used in medicine. **pharmacal**, *adj.* **pharmaceutics**, *n.* preparation, dispensing and selling of drugs. **pharmacist**, *n.* practiser of pharmacy. **pharmacognosy**, *n.* study of medicinal drugs from plants, etc. **pharmacology**, *n.* study of medicinal drugs and their properties. **pharmacon**, *n.* drug; poison. **pharmacopaedics**, *n.* study of drugs. **pharmacopoeia**, *n.* official list of drugs. **pharmacy**, *n.* pharmaceu-

tics; chemist's shop.

pharmacodynamic [ˌfɑːməkəudaɪ'næmɪk] *adj.* pertaining to action of drugs on body.

pharos ['feərɒs] *n.* lighthouse. **pharology**, *n.* study of lighthouses.

pharynx ['færɪŋks] *n.* (*pl.* **–nges**) part of throat between mouth and oesophagus. **pharyngeal**, *adj.* **pharyngismus**, *n.* spasm of pharynx. **pharyngitis**, *n.* inflammation of pharynx. **pharyngology** [-'gɒlədʒi], *n.* medical study of pharynx. **pharyngoscope** [-gəskəup], *n.* instrument for viewing pharynx.

phatic ['fætɪk] *adj.* denoting speech as a means of sharing feelings or establishing sociability rather than for the communication of information and ideas.

phellem ['felem] *n.* cork. **phellogen**, *n.* tissue producing cork.

phenakistoscope [ˌfenəkɪstəskəup] *n.* apparatus or instrument in which figures on a moving dial, etc., seem to move when viewed through a slit; earliest form of cinematograph.

phenobarbitone [ˌfiːnəu'bɑːbɪtəun] *n.* sedative and sleep-inducing drug.

phenogenesis [ˌfiːnə'dʒensɪs] *n.* origin of races. **phenogenetic** [-dʒə'netɪk], *adj.* **phenogenology**, *n.* study of relations between recurring biological activities and climate.

phenomenon [fə'nɒmɪnən] *n.* (*pl.* **phenomena**) any fact or happening; anything perceived by the senses; remarkable thing or person, or rare event. **phenomenal**, *adj.* **phenomenology**, *n.* description and classification of phenomena.

phenotype ['fiːnətaɪp] *n.* characteristics of an organism resulting from interaction between genetic and environmental factors.

pheromone ['ferəməun] *n.* hormone-like substance which, when secreted by an animal, can directly influence other animals of the same species, by contact, odour, etc.

philabeg ['fɪləbeg] *see* **filibeg.**

philadelphian [ˌfɪlə'delfiən] *adj.* pertaining to or exercising brotherly love.

philander [fɪ'lændə] *v.i.* (of man) flirt. **philanderer**, *n.*

philately [fɪ'lætəli] *n.* stamp-collecting. **philatelic** [-'telɪk], *adj.* **philatelist**, *n.*

philematology [fɪˌliːmə'tɒlədʒi] *n.* art or science of kissing.

philhellene [ˌfɪl'heliːn] *n.* lover of Greece or things Greek. **philhellenic**, *adj.* **philhellenism** [-'helɪnɪzm], **philhellenist**, *n.*

philippic [fɪ'lɪpɪk] *n.* diatribe; abusive speech.

phillumenist [fɪ'luːmənɪst] *n.* collector of matchbox labels.

philocaly [fɪ'lɒkəli] *n.* love of beauty. **philocalic** [-'kælɪk], *adj.* **philocalist**, *n.*

philodemic [ˌfɪlə'demɪk] *adj.* fond of the common people.

philodox ['fɪlədɒks] *n.* dogmatic person; person fond of opinions, especially their own.

philogynist [fɪ'lɒdʒɪnɪst] *n.* lover of women. **philogynous**, *adj.* **philogyny**, *n.*

philology [fɪ'lɒlədʒi] *n.* study of language. **philological**, *adj.* **philologist**, *n.*

philomel ['fɪləmel] *n.*, nightingale.

philometrist [ˌfɪlə'metrɪst] *n.* collector of envelopes, etc., for their postal meter impressions.

philoprogenitive [ˌfɪləprəʊ'dʒenətɪv] *adj.* having many children; fond of children.

philotheism [ˌfɪlə'θiːɪzm] *n.* love of God. **philotheist,** *n.*

philtre ['fɪltə] *n.* love potion.

phlebology [flɪ'baɪtɪs] *n.* science of veins. **phlebitis,** *n.* inflammation of vein. **phlebitic** [-'bɪtɪk], *adj.*

phlebotomy [flɪ'bɒtəmi] *n.* blood-letting; venesection. **phlebotomize,** *v.i. & t.* **phlebotomist,** *n.*

phlegmagogue ['flegməgɒg] *n.* phlegm-expelling drug. **phlegmasia,** *n.* inflammation. **phlegmon,** *n.* boil.

phlegmatic [fleg'mætɪk] *adj.* unexcitable; having a stolid or sluggish nature.

phloem ['fləʊɪm] *n.* bast tissue. **phloic,** *adj.*

phlogiston [flə'dʒɪstən] *n.* principle of combustibility once supposed to exist in all inflammable substances. **phlogogenetic, phlogogenic** [ˌflɒg–], *adj.* causing inflammation. **phlogistic,** *adj.* pertaining to inflammation.

phobia ['fəʊbiə] *n.* fear; dread. **phobic,** *adj.* **phobiac,** *n.*

phocine ['fəʊsaɪn] *adj.* pertaining to seals (animals).

Phoebe ['fiːbi] *n. Literature,* moon.

phoenicopter, phenicopter ['fiːnɪkɒptə, 'fen–] *n.* flamingo. **phoenicurous,** *adj.* having red tail. **phoenix,** *n.* mythical bird reborn from ashes.

phon [fɒn] *n.* unit of loudness of sound.

phonal ['fəʊnl] *adj.* vocal; phonetic. **phonate,** *v.i.* speak or sing. **phonation,** *n.*

phoneme ['fəʊniːm] *n.* collective variations of a sound pronounced with slight differences in differing circumstances. **phonemic,** *adj.*

phonetic [fə'netɪk] *adj.* pertaining to or showing speech sound. **phonetics,** *n.* study of vocal sounds and their representation; the speech sounds of a language collectively. **phonetician, phoneticist, phonetist,** *n.* **phoneticize,** *v.t.* spell in phonetic alphabet.

phonic ['fɒnɪk, 'fəʊ–] *adj.* phonetic; acoustic. **phoniatrics,** *n.* study and correction of speech defects. **phonics,** *n.* phonetics; acoustics; study of phonetic method of teaching reading.

phonogram ['fəʊnəgræm] *n.* symbol representing sound, syllable or word. **phonograph,** *American, n.* gramophone. **phonography,** *n.* system of spelling or shorthand based on speech sounds.

phonology [fə'nɒlədʒi] *n.* study of speech sounds in a language; such speech sounds. **phonological,** *adj.* **phonologist,** *n.*

phonometry [fə'nɒmətri] *n.* measurement of intensity, etc., of sounds. **phonometer,** *n.* instrument used in phonometry. **phonometric** [–'metrɪk], *adj.*

phonophorous [fə'nɒfərəs] *adj.* able to transmit sound waves. **phonophore,** *n.* system of hearing for the deaf conducting sounds to the teeth; device for sending telephonic and telegraphic messages over same line simultaneously.

phonotype ['fəʊnətaɪp] *n.* printing type of phonetic alphabet; a character of phonotype. **phonotypic** [–'tɪpɪk], *adj.* **phonotypy,** *n.* transcription into phonetic spelling advocated for ordinary use.

phorometry [fɔː'rɒmətri] *n.* study and correction of abnormalities of muscles of eye. **phorometer,** *n.* instrument used in phorometry.

phosgene ['fɒzdʒiːn, 'fɒs–] *n.* colourless poison gas made from chlorine and carbon monoxide.

phosphate ['fɒsfeɪt] *n.* salt of phosphoric acid; non-biodegradable ingredient in some detergents; fertilizer containing phosphorus. **phosphatic** [–'fætɪk], *adj.*

phosphene ['fɒsfiːn] *n.* sensation of seeing lights in darkness or when lids are closed.

phosphorescence [ˌfɒsfə'resns] *n.* light without heat, continuing after exposure to radiation which causes it; faint glow in dark without apparent cause. **phosphorescent** *adj.*

phossy jaw ['fɒsi] *adj. n.* necrosis of jaw among workers handling phosphorus.

phot [fɒt, fəʊt] *n.* unit of illumination of a surface.

photic ['fəʊtɪk] *adj.* pertaining to or penetrated by light. **photics,** *n.* study of light.

photoautotrophic [ˌfəʊtəʊɔːtə'trɒpɪk] *adj.* (of plants, etc.) capable of using light to synthesize food from inorganic substances.

photobathic [ˌfəʊtə'bæθɪk] *adj.* pertaining to sea depths penetrated by sunlight. **photobiotic,** *adj.* thriving only in light.

photochemistry [ˌfəʊtəʊ'kemɪstri] *n.* science, processes and properties of chemical changes effected by light.

photochromism [ˌfəʊtə'krəʊmɪzm] *n.* property of changing colour on exposure to light or other radiation and of reverting to original colour immediately the light or radiation source is removed. **photochromic,** *adj.*

photocoagulation [ˌfəʊtəkəʊˌægjʊ'leɪʃn] *n.* surgical coagulation of tissue by means of a laser beam.

photocomposition [ˌfəʊtəʊkɒmpə'zɪʃn] *n.* typesetting directly onto film; film-setting.

photoelectric [ˌfəʊtəʊɪ'lektrɪk] *adj.* pertaining to discharge of electrons by, or decrease in resistance in, certain substances when exposed to light. **photoelectricity,** *n.*

photofission [ˌfəʊtə'fɪʃn] *n.* nuclear fission induced by gamma rays.

photogenic [ˌfəʊtə'dʒenɪk] *adj.* generating light; suitable for being photographed.

photogrammetry [ˌfəʊtə'græmətri] *n.* photographic means of obtaining reliable measurements, e.g. by superimposing photographs of an area or object taken from different angles.

photogravure [ˌfəʊtəgrə'vjʊə] *n.* printing from engraved plates photographically prepared.

photogyric [ˌfəʊtə'dʒaɪrɪk] *adj.* turning towards light.

photokinesis [ˌfəʊtəkɪ'niːsɪs] *n.* activity caused by light. **photokinetic** [–'netɪk], *adj.*

photolithography [ˌfəʊtəʊlɪ'θɒgrəfi] *n.* printing process using photographically prepared plates (*abbr.* **photolitho**).

photolysis [fəʊ'tɒləsɪs] *n.* decomposition caused by light. **photolytic** [–'lɪtɪk], *adj.*

photometer [fəʊ'tɒmɪtə] *n.* instrument measuring intensity, etc., of light. **photometric** [–'metrɪk], *adj.* **photometry,** *n.*

photomicrograph [ˌfəʊtəʊ'maɪkrəgraːf] *n.* enlarged photograph of minute object; photograph taken through microscope.

photon ['fəʊtɒn] *n.* quantum (smallest possible unit) of electromagnetic radiation, considered as an elementary particle with zero charge and rest mass.

photonasty ['fəʊtənæsti] *n. Botany*, adoption of certain position due to effect of light on growth. **photonastic**, *adj.*

photonosus [fə'tɒnəsəs] *n.* morbid condition due to exposure to light. **photopathy**, *n.* any such disease.

photophile ['fəʊtəfaɪl] *n. & adj.* (organism) loving light. **photophilous** [–'tɒfɪləs], *adj.* **photophily** [–'tɒfɪli], *n.* **photophobia**, *n.* dislike or dread of light. **photophobic**, *adj.* **photophygous** [–'tɒfɪgəs], *adj.* avoiding or disliking light.

photopia [fəʊ'təʊpiə] *n.* normal day vision. **photopic**, *adj.*

photoscope ['fəʊtəskəʊp] *n.* apparatus for observing light, especially changes in its intensity, or magnifying photographs.

photosensitive [ˌfəʊtə'sensətɪv] *adj.* sensitive to light, especially sunlight. **photosensitize** *v.t.*

photosphere ['fəʊtəsfɪə] *n.* sun's luminous envelope. **photospheric** [–'sferɪk], *adj.*

photostat ['fəʊtəstæt] *n.* photographic copy of document, etc. **photostatic**, *adj.*

photosynthesis [ˌfəʊtə'sɪnθəsɪs] *n.* formation of carbohydrates by chlorophyll-containing cells of plant exposed to light. **photosynthesize**, *v.i. & t.* **photosynthetic** [–'θetɪk], *adj.*

phototaxis [ˌfəʊtə'tæksɪs] *n.* growth or movement directed by light. **phototactic**, *adj.*

phototherapy [ˌfəʊtə'θerəpi] *n.* medical treatment by means of light. **phototherapeutic**, *adj.*

photothermic [ˌfəʊtə'θɜːmɪk] *adj.* pertaining to heat and light.

phototonus [fəʊ'tɒtənəs] *n.* sensitivity to light.

phototropism [ˌfəʊtəʊ'trəʊpɪzm, fəʊ'tɒtrə–] *n.* movement directed by light; heliotropism. **phototropic** [–'trɒpɪk], *adj.*

phototypesetting [ˌfəʊtəʊ'taɪpsetɪŋ] *n.* photocomposition.

photovoltaic [ˌfəʊtəʊvɒl'teɪɪk] *adj.* pertaining to or producing electric current caused by electromagnetic radiation, such as light.

phratry ['freɪtri] *n.* clan; tribe. **phrator**, *n.* member of phratry. **phratric**, *adj.*

phreatic [fri'ætɪk] *adj.* pertaining to wells and subterranean water.

phrenetic, [frə'netɪk] *see* **frenetic.**

phrenic ['frenɪk] *adj.* pertaining to diaphragm.

phrenology [fre'nɒlədʒi] *n.* study of outline of skull giving supposed indication of mental ability and characteristics. **phrenological**, *adj.* **phrenologist**, *n.*

phrontistery ['frɒntɪstəri] *n.* place for study.

phthiriasis [θaɪ'raɪəsɪs, θɪ–] *n.* infestation with lice. **phthirophagous**, *adj.* eating lice.

phthisis ['θaɪsɪs, 'taɪ–, 'fθaɪ–] *n.* tuberculosis of lungs. **phthisical**, *adj.*

phycology [faɪ'kɒlədʒi] *n.* study of seaweeds or algae.

phylactery [fɪ'læktəri] *n.* small leather box containing scriptural extracts worn by Jews at prayer on head and arm; relic-container; amulet; reminder; record; in medieval art, words in a balloon-like circle drawn issuing from mouth.

phylactic [fɪ'læktɪk] *adj.* defending against disease.

phylliform ['fɪlɪfɔːm] *adj.* leaf-shaped. **phylline**, *adj.* leaf-like. **phyllode** (-d), *n.* flattened stem functioning as leaf. **phyllogenetic**, *adj.* pertaining to production of, or producing, leaves. **phylloid**, *adj.* phylline. **phyllomania**, *n.* abnormal leaf-production. **phyllomorph**, *n.* artistic leaf-like detail. **phyllophagous**, *adj.* leaf-eating. **phyllophorous**, *adj.* bearing leaves. **phyllotaxy**, *n.* arrangement of leaves of plant.

phylloxera [fɪ'lɒksərə, ˌfɪlək'sɪərə] *n.* plant-louse harmful to vines.

phylogeny [faɪ'lɒdʒəni] *n.* history or development of a race, species, etc. **phylogenetic(al)** [–dʒə'netɪk, –l], **phylogenic** [–'dʒenɪk], *adj.*

phylum ['faɪləm] *n.* (*pl.* **-la**) largest subdivision of natural kingdom.

phyma ['faɪmə] *n.* (*pl.* **-ta**) skin tumour. **phymatic** [–'mætɪk], *adj.* **phymatosis**, *n.* disease characterised by phymata.

physagogue ['faɪsəgɒg, 'fɪs–] *n. & adj.* (drug) expelling wind.

physiatrics [ˌfɪzi'ætrɪks] *n. American*, physiotherapy.

physiocracy [ˌfɪzi'ɒkrəsi] *n.* government that does not interfere with the operation of supposed natural laws. **physiocrat**, *n.* advocate (especially French, 18th-century) of physiocracy.

physiognomy [ˌfɪzi'ɒnəmi, –'ɒgnə–] *n.* face; facial expression; divination of character or fortune from face. **physiognomic** [–'nɒmɪk], *adj.* **physiognomist**, *n.*

physiography [ˌfɪzi'ɒgrəfi] *n.* physical geography; topography; description of natural phenomena. **physiographer**, *n.* **physiographic(al)**, *adj.*

physiolatry [ˌfɪzi'ɒlətri] *n.* nature worship. **physiolater**, *n.* **physiolatrous**, *adj.*

physiology [ˌfɪzi'ɒlədʒi] *n.* study of functions of healthy living organism; such functions collectively. **physiological**, *adj.* **physiologist**, *n.*

physiotherapy [ˌfɪziəʊ'θerəpi] *n.* medical treatment by physical means: (massage, exercises, electricity, etc.)

physitheism [ˌfɪzɪ'θiːɪzm] *n.* nature worship; ascription to God of physical shape.

physiurgic [ˌfɪzi'ɜːdʒɪk] *adj.* due to natural causes.

phytivorous [faɪ'tɪvərəs] *adj.* feeding on plants.

phytogamy [faɪ'tɒgəmi] *n. Botany*, cross-fertilization. **phytogenesis**, *n.* development and origin of plants. **phytogenic**, *adj.* derived from plants. **phytography**, *n.* descriptive botany. **phytoid**, *adj.* plant-like. **phytophagic**, **phytophagous**, *adj.* phytivorous. **phytophilous**, *adj.* fond of plants. **phytosis**, *n.* infection or disease caused by parasitic plant. **phytosociology**, *n.* branch of ecology dealing with plant communities. **phytotomy**, *n.* anatomy of plants. **phytotoxin**, *n.* poison produced by plant.

phytotron ['faɪtətrɒn] *n.* a botanical laboratory comprising a series of chambers reproducing any condition of temperature, humidity, illumination, or other plant-growth factor.

pi [paɪ] sixteenth letter (Π, π) of Gr. alphabet; *Mathematics*, ratio (3.1416) of circumference to diameter of circle.

piacular [paɪ'ækjʊlə] *adj.* expiatory; sinful.

pia mater [ˌpaɪə 'meɪtə] *n.* inner membrane enclosing brain.

pibroch ['pi:brɒx] *n.* piece of music for bagpipe.

pica ['paɪkə] *n.* (12-point) size of type; *Medicine,* abnormal craving to eat unusual things such as chalk or hair. **small pica,** 11-point. **double pica,**

Prefixes

a- (or, before a vowel, **an-**) not; lacking: *amoral, atypical, anaerobic.*

ambi- all round; on both sides; both: *ambilateral, ambisexual, ambisonics.*

ante- before: *antedate, antenuptial, anteprandial.* Compare **anti-.**

anthropo- human beings: *anthropocentric, anthropology, anthropomorphism.*

anti- against: *anticlerical, anti-federal, anti-war.*

arch- greatest (and worst); of highest rank: *archdruid, arch-enemy, arch-villain.*

auto- self; automatic: *autobiography, autodestruct, autotimer.*

bi- two; double: *bicentenary, bilateral, bisexual.*

bio- living things: *biochemistry, biorhythm, biotechnology.*

cardio- heart: *cardiology, cardiometry, cardiovascular.*

cent(i)- hundred; hundredth part: *centigrade, centilitre, centipede.*

chrono- time: *chronological, chronometer, chronoscope.*

circum- all round: *circumambient, circumlocution, circumnavigate.*

co- with; together: *co-author, co-defendant, co-operate.*

contra- against; opposite: *contraception, contracyclical, contra-indication.*

crypto- hidden; secret: *cryptarchy, crypto-Communist, cryptonym.*

de- removal; reduction: *deindustrialize, deselect, devalue.*

deca- ten: *decade, decapod, decasyllable.*

deci- tenth part: *decibel, decigram, decilitre.*

di- two; double: *digraph, dimorphic, diplegia.* Compare **bi-.**

dis- not; removal: *disculpate, dislike, distrust.*

extra- outside; beyond: *extramarital, extrasensory, extraterrestrial.*

geo- earth: *geocentric, geomorphology, geophagous.*

hecto- hundred: *hectogram, hectolitre, hectometre.*

hetero- different: *heterochromatic, heterogeneous, heterosexual.*

homo- same: *homolateral, homophone, homotaxis.*

hydro- water: *hydroelectric, hydropathy, hydroplane.*

hyper- more than normal: *hypercritical, hyperinflation, hyperosmia.*

hypo- less than normal: *hypobulia, hypoglycaemia, hypothermia.*

in- (or **il-, im-, ir-**) not: *ineffective, illogical, impossible, irresponsible.*

infra- below: *infrahuman, infraorbital, infrasonic.*

inter- between; among: *interbreed, intercosmic, inter-war.*

intra- inside: *intracardiac, intramuscular, intrauterine.*

iso- equal: *isobar, isoglossal, isotherm.*

kilo- thousand: *kilobyte, kilogram, kilometre.*

macro- large; all-embracing: *macrocephalous, macroeconomics, macrotia.*

mal- bad(ly): *maladministration, malformation, malodorous.*

mega- million; extremely large: *megabyte, megacycle, megastore.*

meta- beyond: *metachemistry, metagnostic, metaphysical.*

micro- millionth part; extremely small: *microgram, microprocessor, microskirt.*

milli- thousandth part: *milligram, millilitre, millisecond.*

mis- bad(ly); wrong(ly): *mismanage, mistreat, misunderstand.*

mono- one: *monocarpic, monogamy, monolingual.*

neo- new; revived: *neoblastic, neoclassical, neoteric.*

neuro- nerves: *neurologist, neuropathology, neurotomy.*

non- not: *nonferrous, nonparous, nonsense.*

omni- all: *omnicompetent, omnipresent, omnivorous.*

palaeo- very ancient: *palaeobotany, palaeodendrology, palaeontology.*

pan- all-inclusive: *panarthritis, pandemic, panivorous.*

para- beyond (normal): *paracusia, parakinesis, parapsychology.*

penta- five: *pentagamist, pentaglot, pentapody.*

photo- light: *photometer, photosensitive, photosynthesis.*

poly- many: *polyandry, polyethnic, polyphagia.*

post- after: *postexilic, postnuul, postprandial.*

pre- before: *preadamic, prefabricated, pretonic.*

pro- in favour of: *pro-abortion, pro-British, pronuclear.*

proto- original: *protomartyr, protoplasm, prototype.*

quasi- to a certain degree: *quasi-autonomous, quasijudicial, quasi-stellar.*

re- again: *re-evaluate, resubmit, rewrite.*

retro- backwards; back to an earlier (and worse) state: *retrograde, retrorocket, retrospection.*

semi- half; partly: *semicircle, semi-divine, semiprecious.*

step- related through a remarried parent: *stepmother.*

sub- below; worse than: *subhuman, submarine, subterranean.*

tele- long distance: *telecommunications, telekinesis, telemetry.*

trans- across: *transfluent, translucent, transmigrate.*

tri- three: *triennial, trigonous, trinoctial.*

ultra- beyond; extremely: *ultra-difficult, ultramicroscope, ultrasonic.*

un- not; reversal: *unbelievable, unfunny, unlock.*

vice- next below in rank: *vice-chancellor, vice-president, vice-regent.*

22-point.

picador ['pɪkədɔː] *n.* mounted bull-fighter with lance.

picaro [pɪ'kɑːrəʊ] (*Spanish*) *n.* (*fem.* **picara**) rogue. **picaresque**, *adj.* pertaining to rogues, especially applied to literature about rogues and vagabonds. **picaroon**, *n.* rogue; thief; pirate.

picayune [ˌpɪkə'juːn] *adj.* American, petty, trivial.

piceous ['paɪsɪəs, 'pɪs–] *adj.* like pitch; inflammable.

piciform ['paɪsɪfɔːm, 'pɪs–] *adj.* like a woodpecker. **picine**, *adj.* pertaining to woodpeckers.

pickerel ['pɪkərəl] *n.* young pike (fish); small American freshwater fish.

Pickwickian [pɪk'wɪkɪən] *adj.* benevolent and naïve; (of words) used strangely; not (to be) taken literally.

pico- ['piːkəʊ–, 'paɪkəʊ–] *prefix* of measurement meaning one million-millionth (10^{-12}) (*abbr.* p.)

picot ['piːkəʊ] *n.* one of series of small loops forming ornamental edging to ribbon, lace, etc. **picotee**, *n.* flower with petal margins of different colour.

picric acid ['pɪkrɪk] *n.* yellow, bitter, poisonous acid used as dye and disinfectant and in manufacture of explosives.

pidan [piː'dɑːn] *n.* preserved Chinese duck's eggs.

piddock ['pɪdək] *n.* rough-shelled, boring, marine bivalve.

pidgin ['pɪdʒɪn] *n.* restricted language system used for communication between people who have no common language.

pièce de résistance [pi,es də re'zɪstɒns] (*French*) *n.* 'piece of resistance'; culminating or main item. **pièce d'occasion** [–dɒ'kɑːzjɒn], *n.* piece written or composed for a special occasion; bargain.

pied-à-terre [pi,eɪd–ɑː–'teə] (*French*) *n.* 'foot on the ground'; temporary or subsidiary home.

Pierian [paɪ'ɪərɪən] *adj.* pertaining to Pieria, Macedonia, where the Muses were worshipped; pertaining to the Muses or poetry.

pierid ['paɪərɪd] *n. & adj.* (butterfly) belonging to the family including cabbage and other butterflies. **pieridine** [–'erɪdaɪn], *adj.*

pietà [ˌpiːe'tɑː] (*Italian*) *n.* 'piety'; representation of the dead Christ held and mourned by the Virgin Mary.

pietism ['paɪətɪzm] *n.* unquestioning religious devotion; priggishness. **pietist,** *n.*

piezochemistry [paɪ,iːzəʊ'kemɪstri, pi,eɪz–] *n.* study of chemical effects of pressure. **piezoelectricity,** *n.* production of electric charges on certain crystals when under pressure; slight change in shape of crystal when in electric field. **piezometer,** *n.* instrument measuring compressibility of liquids.

pignorate ['pɪgnəreɪt] *v.t.* pawn; take in pawn. **pignoration,** *n.*

pilaster [pɪ'læstə] *n.* rectangular pillar projecting from and supporting wall. **pilastered,** *adj.*

pile [paɪl] *n.* in nuclear physics, controlled arrangement of fissionable material for producing a chain reaction.

pileus ['paɪlɪəs, 'pɪl–] *n.* (*pl.* **–ei**) cap- or umbrella-like top of mushroom. **pileate(d),** *adj.* having pileus; with crest on pileum. **pileiform,** *adj.*

shaped like pileus. **pileolus,** *n.* (*pl.* **–li**) small pileus. **pileum,** *n.* top of bird's head.

pilose ['paɪləʊs] *adj.* hairy. **piliferous,** *adj.* bearing hair. **piliform,** *adj.* like a (long) hair. **pilosis,** *n.* over-growth of hair. **pilosity,** *n.* hairiness.

pilular ['pɪljʊlə] *adj.* pertaining to or like a pill. **pillule,** *n.* small pill.

pimento [pɪ'mentəʊ] (*Spanish*) *n.* pepper; allspice.

pinaceous [paɪ'neɪʃəs] *adj.* pertaining to or like a pine tree; belonging to the pine family of trees.

pinaster [paɪ'næstə, pɪ–] *n.* cluster pine.

pinchbeck ['pɪntʃbek] *n.* gold-like alloy of copper and zinc; tawdry jewellery; *adj.* spurious; trashy.

Pindaric [pɪn'dærɪk] *adj.* having complex metrical structure, as in Pindar's Odes.

pineal ['pɪnɪəl] *adj.* pertaining to or like a pine cone. **pineal body** *or* **gland,** small gland-like process of brain cavity.

pinguefy ['pɪŋgwɪfaɪ] *v.i. & t.* become or make fat or rich. **pinguid,** *adj.* fatty; oily; rich.

pink [pɪŋk] *v.t.* prick with sword, etc.; decorate with perforations; cut with special scissors to make zigzag edge. *v.i.* (of internal-combustion engine) make a metallic noise as a result of faulty combustion.

pinnate ['pɪneɪt] *adj.* like a feather; with leaflets on either side of a leafstalk. **pinnatifid,** divided pinnately. **pinnation,** *n.*

pinochle ['piːnʌkl] *n.* bezique-like American card game.

pintle ['pɪntl] *n.* usually upright pin acting as hinge or pivot.

pinxit ['pɪŋksɪt] (*Latin*) 'painted (it)'.

pipal ['piːpl] *see* peepul.

pip emma [ˌpɪp 'emə] *adj. & adv.* World War One signaller's slang for post meridiem.

piperaceous [ˌpaɪpə'reɪʃəs] *adj.* pertaining to or like pepper plant; belonging to pepper family of plants.

pipette [pɪ'pet] *n. Chemistry,* narrow tube into which liquids are sucked for measurement, etc.

pipistrelle [ˌpɪpɪ'strel] *n.* brown bat.

pipit ['pɪpɪt] *n.* several lark-like singing birds; titlark.

pipkin ['pɪpkɪn] *n.* small pot.

pique [piːk] *n.* hurt pride, resentful irritation; *v.t.* cause pique; pride (oneself) on something.

pis aller [ˌpiːz 'æleɪ] (*French*) *n.* 'go worst'; last resort; something done or accepted for lack of anything better; less desirable alternative.

piscary ['pɪskəri] *n.* fishing rights or place.

piscatology [ˌpɪskə'tɒlədʒi] *n.* art or science of fishing. **piscator** [pɪ'skeɪtə], *n.* angler. **piscatorial, piscatory,** *adj.* pertaining to fishing.

piscine ['pɪsaɪn] *adj.* pertaining to fish. **pisciculture,** *n.* fish breeding. **piscifauna,** *n.* fish life of a region. **pisciform,** *adj.* fish-shaped. **piscivorous,** *adj.* fish-eating. **piscina** [pɪ'siːnə], *n.* water basin in church sanctuary. **piscinity,** *n.*

pisiform ['paɪsɪfɔːm] *adj.* like pea(s).

pismire ['pɪsmaɪə, 'pɪz–] *n. dialect or archaic,* ant.

pistil ['pɪstɪl] *n.* plant's ovary with style and stigma. **pistilline,** *adj.* **pistillate,** *adj.* having pistils. **pistilloid,** *adj.* like a pistil.

Pithecanthropus [ˌpɪθɪ'kænθrəpəs, -kæn'θrəʊ–] *n.* one of former genus of ape-like men, now included in *Homo*. **Pithecanthropus erectus,** such creature whose remains were discovered in Java: now called 'Java man'.

pithecoid ['pɪθɪkɔɪd, pɪ'θiː–] *adj*. pertaining to anthropoid apes. **pithecism,** *n*. pithecoid characters in Man. **pithecomorphic,** *adj*. like anthropoid apes.

pituitary [pɪ'tjuːɪtəri] *adj*. denoting or pertaining to ductless gland at base of brain secreting a hormone controlling bone growth and activity of thyroid and reproductive glands, and another controlling blood pressure and activity of involuntary muscles.

pityriasis [ˌpɪtɪ'raɪəsɪs] *n*. scaly skin infection. **pityriasic** [–'æsɪk], *adj*.

pixel ['pɪksl, –sel] *n*. any of number of minute units making up a picture on *e.g.* a computer screen.

pixilated ['pɪksɪleɪtɪd] *adj*. as if bewitched by fairies; slightly crazy or dunk.

placate [plə'keɪt] *v.t*. soothe; appease. **placatory,** *adj*.

placebo [plə'siːbəʊ] (*Latin*) 'I will please'; *n*. *Roman Catholic,* Vespers for dead; something given to please or quiet, especially medicine given merely to please patient; dummy medicine given to 'controls' in medical experiment.

placenta [plə'sentə] *n*. (*pl.* –ae) mammal's organ attached to and nourishing foetus in womb; afterbirth. **placental,** *adj*.; *n*. mammal having placenta. **placentate,** *adj*. having placenta. **placentation,** *n*. structure or attachment of placenta. **placentatoid,** *adj*. like placenta.

placer ['plæsə] *n*. gold deposit other than vein, *e.g.* where it is obtained by washing.

placet ['plæket, 'pleɪsɪt] (*Latin*) 'it pleases'; *n*. assenting vote or expression.

placoid ['plækɔɪd] *adj*. pertaining to or like teeth-like scales.

plage [plɑːʒ] (*French*) *n*. sea beach; seaside resort.

plagiarism ['pleɪdʒərɪzm] *n*. copying another's words, ideas, etc., and publishing them as one's own. **plagiarist,** *n*. **plagiarize,** *v.i. & t*.

plagiograph ['pleɪdʒəgrɑːf] *n*. kind of pantograph.

plagiotropic [ˌpleɪdʒɪə'trɒpɪk] *adj*. (of plant) growing away from vertical.

planarian [plə'neəriən] *n*. kind of flatworm.

planchette [plɑːn'ʃet] (*French*) *n*. board supported on two wheels and a pencil, which is supposed to write spirit messages.

planetarium [ˌplænə'teəriəm] *n*. (*pl.* –ia) model of solar system; (building containing) apparatus for projecting moving images of stars, planets, etc. on inside of a dome. **planetesimal,** *adj*. pertaining to minute bodies moving in space, supposed by some to have joined to form planets. **planetoid,** *n*. asteroid. **planetology,** *n*. study of planets' surface.

plangent ['plændʒənt] *n*. deep- or loud-sounding. **plangency,** *n*. **plangorous,** *adj*. mournful.

planimeter [plə'nɪmɪtə] *n*. instrument measuring plane figure's area. **planimetry,** *n*. such measurement.

planipennate [ˌpleɪnɪ'peneɪt] *adj*. having flat, broad wings. **planirostral,** *adj*. having such beak. **planisphere,** *n*. map of heavens on plane surface.

plankton ['plæŋktən] *n*. floating or minute swimming organisms of ocean. **planktonic,** *adj*. **plankter,** *n*. planktonic organism **planktology,** *n*. study of plankton.

planography [plæ'nɒgrəfi] *n*. printing from flat surface. **planometry,** *n*. gauging of plane surface.

plantaginaceous [plænˌtædʒɪ'neɪʃəs] *adj*. pertaining to or like plantain; belonging to plantain family of plants.

plantigrade ['plæntɪgreɪd, 'plɑːn–] *n. & adj*. (animal) walking on sole of foot, as Man.

plantivorous [plɑːn'tɪvərəs] *n*. plant-eating.

plasma ['plæzmə] *n*. fluid part of blood, etc; an ionized gas. **plasmatic** [–'mætɪk], **plasmic,** *adj*. **plasma cell,** *n*. white blood corpuscle. **plasmophagous,** *adj*. consuming plasma.

plasmapheresis [ˌplæzməfə'riːsɪs, –'ferəs–] *n*. process of separating plasma from red blood cells in blood from donor, and returning red blood cells to donor.

plastic ['plæstɪk] *adj*. moulding; forming; capable of being moulded; *n*. such synthetic organic substance. **plastometer,** *n*. instrument for measuring plasticity.

plastid ['plæstɪd] *n*. minute mass of protoplasm in cell.

plastron ['plæstrɒn] *n*. breast-pad or plate for protection; shell protecting under side of tortoise, etc.; false shirt-front.

plataleiform [ˌplætə'liːɪfɔːm] *adj*. spoonbilled.

platelet ['pleɪtlət] *n*. tiny cell fragment in blood which helps it to clot.

platen ['plætn] *n*. plate pressing paper against type in printing machine; roller of typewriter.

platitude ['plætɪtjuːd] *n*. trite statement. **platitudinarian,** *n. & adj*. (person) habitually uttering platitudes. **platitudinize,** *v.i*. utter platitudes. **platitudinous** *adj*.

Platonic [plə'tɒnɪk] *adj*. pertaining to Plato, Greek philosopher, and his doctrines; ideal; spiritual; theoretical.

platycephaly [ˌplætɪ'sefəli] *n*. flatness of crown of head. **platycephalic** [–sə'fælɪk], **platycephalous,** *adj*. **platydactyl,** *adj*. having flat digits. **platypodous,** *adj*. having broad, flat feet. **platypodia,** *n*. flat-footedness. **platypus,** *n*. duckbill. **platyrrhinian,** *n. & adj*. (person) with short, flat nose.

plebeian [plə'biːən] *n. & adj*. (person) of common people or lower classes; vulgar. **plebiscite** ['plebɪsaɪt, –sɪt], *n*. nation's or district's direct vote on a specific measure. **plebs** [plebz], (*Latin*) *n*. the common people.

plectrum ['plektrəm] *n*. (*pl.* –ra) implement for plucking strings of musical instrument. **plectridial,** *adj*. drumstick-shaped.

pledget ['pledʒɪt] *n*. small wound dressing.

pleiobar ['plaɪəbɑː] *n*. isobar or area of high atmospheric pressure. **pleiophylly,** *n*. abnormal increase in number of leaves.

Pleistocene ['plaɪstəsiːn] *n. & adj*. (pertaining to) first epoch of Quaternary period.

plenary ['pliːnəri, 'ple–] *adj*. full; entire; unlimited; with all members present.

plenilunar [ˌpliːnɪ'luːnə, ˌple–] *adj*. like or pertaining to full moon.

plenipotentiary [ˌplenɪpə'tenʃəri] *n. & adj*. (envoy) having full power.

plenitude ['plenɪtjuːd] *n.* fullness; sufficiency; abundance; entirety.

plenum ['pliːnəm, 'ple–] *n.* (*pl.* **–na**) space full of matter; plenary meeting.

pleochroic [,pliːə'krəʊɪk] *adj.* showing different colours when viewed in different directions. **pleochrous,** *adj.* **pleochroism,** *n.*

pleonasm ['pliːənæzm] *n.* use of unnecessary words; redundancy. **pleonastic,** *adj.*

pleonectic [,pliːə'nektɪk] *adj.* covetous. **pleonexia,** *n.*

plesiosaurus [,pliːziə'sɔːrəs] *n.* extinct long-necked swimming reptile.

plethora ['pleθərə] *n.* excess, superfluity.

pleura ['plʊərə] *n.* (*pl.* **–ae**) membrane lining half of thorax. **pleural,** *adj.* **pleurisy,** *n.* inflammation of pleura. **pleuritic,** *adj.* **pleurogenic,** *adj.* formed in pleura.

pleurodynia [,plʊərə'dɪniə] *n.* pain in muscles of chest or side.

pleuronectid [,plʊərəʊ'nektɪd] *n.* & *adj.* (pertaining to) flat-fish.

plexus ['pleksəs] *n.* network. **plexiform,** *adj.* like plexus. **plexure,** *n.* inter-weaving.

plicate [plaɪ'keɪt] *v.t.* pleat; plait; fold; *adj.* pleated; plaited. **plication,** *n.*

Pliocene ['plaɪəsiːn] *n.* & *adj.* (pertaining to) last epoch of Tertiary period.

plinth [plɪnθ] *n.* rectangular base of column, pedestal, etc.

pliofilm ['plaɪəfɪlm] *n.* *trademark,* thin transparent waterproof sheet used for packaging, etc.

pliosaurus [,plaɪə'sɔːrəs] *n.* shorter-necked plesiosaurus.

pliothermic [,plaɪə'θɜːmɪk] *adj.* *Geology,* pertaining to periods of temperature above average.

plosive ['pləʊsɪv] *n.* & *adj.* *Phonetics,* explosive (sound), as *p.*plosion, *n.*

plumbago [plʌm'beɪgəʊ] *n.* graphite; *Botany,* leadwort. **plumbaginous** [–'bædʒɪnəs], *adj.*

plumbeous ['plʌmbiəs] *adj.* leaden. **plumbic, plumbous,** *adj.* **plumbiferous, plumbism,** *n.* lead-poisoning.

plumose ['pluːməʊs] *adj.* feathered; feathery.

pluperfect [,pluː'pɜːfɪkt] *n.* & *adj.* (grammatical tense) signifying completion of action before a certain point in past time.

pluralism ['plʊərəlɪzm] *n.* *Philosophy,* belief that ultimate reality is of several kinds, or consists of several entities; holding of more than one office. **pluralist,** *n.*

plurilateral [,plʊərɪ'lætərəl] *adj.* of more than two sides or parties. **pluriliteral,** *adj.* of more than three letters. **plurinominal,** *adj.* of more than one name. **pluriparous,** *adj.* bringing forth more than one at a birth. **plurisyllable,** *n.* word of more than one syllable.

plutocracy [pluː'tɒkrəsi] *n.* government by wealthy class. **plutocrat,** *n.* **plutocratic,** *adj.* **plutolatry,** *n.* worship of riches. **plutology,** *n.* study of wealth.

Plutonian [pluː'təʊniən] *adj.* pertaining to the underworld, ruled by Pluto.

plutonic [pluː'tɒnɪk] *adj.* of volcanic or deep-seated origin.

plutonium [pluː'təʊniəm] *n.* one of the transuranic elements, product of decay of neptunium, used in the atomic bomb.

plutonomy [pluː'tɒnəmi] *n.* economics.

pluvial ['pluːviəl] *adj.* pertaining or due to rain; having much rain. **pluvine,** *adj.* **pluviography,** *n.* recording of rainfall. **pluviometer,** *n.* rain gauge. **pluvious, pluviose,** *adj.* rainy.

pneuma ['njuːmə] *n.* soul, spirit.

pneumatic [nju'mætɪk] *adj.* pertaining to, using or worked by air pressure. **pneumatics,** *n.* study of mechanics of gases. **pneumatographer,** *n.* person receiving and writing spirit messages. **pneumatology,** *n.* pneumatics; doctrine about spirits or Holy Ghost. **pneumatomachy,** *n.* denial of Holy Ghost's divinity. **pneumatometer** instrument indicating the strength of the lungs by measuring the quantity of air inhaled and exhaled at a breath. **pneumatophany,** *n.* appearance of spirit or Holy Ghost. **pneumatophony,** *n.* sound caused by spirit. **pneumatosis,** *n.* presence of gas in body.

pneumonia [nju'məʊniə] *n.* inflammation of lungs. **pneumonic** [–'mɒnɪk], *adj.* **pneumoconiosis,** *n.* lung disease due to inhaling metallic, etc., particles. **pneumograph,** *n.* **pneumology,** *n.* study of lungs. **pneumonography,** *n.* taking of X-ray photographs of lungs. **pneumothorax,** *n.* presence or introduction of air in thorax, causing collapse of lung.

pnigophobia [,naɪgə'fəʊbiə] *n.* morbid fear of being smothered.

poaceous [pəʊ'eɪʃəs] *adj.* pertaining to or like grass; belonging to the grass family of plants.

pochard ['pɒtʃəd, 'pəʊ–] *n.* kind of redheaded duck.

pococurante [,pəʊkəʊ–kju'rænti] *n.* & *adj.* (person) lacking interest; indifferent; apathetic. **pococurantism,** *n.*

poculiform ['pɒkjulɪfɔːm] *adj.* cup-shaped.

podagra [pɒ'dægrə] *n.* gout. **podagral, podagric, podagrous,** *adj.*

podalic [pə'dælɪk] *adj.* pertaining to feet.

podesta [,pɒde'stɑː] (*Italian*) *n.* Italian mayor or chief magistrate.

podex ['pəʊdeks] *n.* (*pl.* **–dices**) posterior. **podical** ['pɒd–], *adj.* pertaining to podex

podiatry [pə'daɪətri] *n.* *Medicine,* study of abnormalities of feet. **podology,** *n.* physiological study of feet. **podoscaph** ['pɒd–], *n.* boat-shaped boot for walking on water; boat with bicycle mechanism.

poetaster [,pəʊɪ'tæstə] *n.* poor or unimportant poet. **poetastery,** *n.*

pogoniasis [,pəʊgə'naɪəsɪs] *n.* overgrowth of beard; growth of beard in woman. **pogonology,** *n.* book on beards. **pogonophobia,** *n.* morbid fear of beards. **pogonotomy,** *n.* cutting of beard; shaving. **pogonotrophy,** *n.* growing of a beard.

pogrom ['pɒgrəm, –ɒm] *n.* wholesale massacre of a class or race, especially of Jews in Russia.

poiesis [pɔɪ'iːsɪs] *n.* creation. **poietic** [–'etɪk], *adj.*

poikilothermic [,pɒɪkɪlə'θɜːmɪk] *adj.* cold-blooded. **poikilothermism,** *n.* **poikilothermous,** *adj.*

poilu ['pwæluː] (*French*) *adj.* 'hairy'; *n. slang,* infantry soldier in World War One.

poimenics [pɔɪ'menɪks] *n.* pastoral theology.

point [pɔɪnt] *n.* measure of depth of letter in printing: one seventy-second of an inch.

point d'appui [ˌpwæn dæ'pwiː] (*French*) 'point of support'; (formerly) base for military operations.

pointillism ['pɔɪntɪlɪzm, 'pwæn–] *n.* method of painting in dots of colour. **pointillist,** *n.*

poise [pwaːz] *n.* unit of viscosity.

polarimeter [ˌpəʊlə'rɪmɪtə] *n.* instrument measuring amount of polarized light or rotation of plane of polarized light. **polariscope** [ˈlærɪskəʊp], *n.* instrument for studying polarized light or objects in it. **polarize,** *v.t.* modify normally transverse light vibrations so that they are confined to one plane. **polarization,** *n.*

polder ['pəʊldə] (*Dutch*) *n.* piece of land reclaimed from sea.

polemic [pə'lemɪk] *adj.* disputatious; pertaining to argument *n.* dispute; aggressive attack or refutation. **polemicist** [–sɪst], *n.* **polemics,** *n.* art of controversy.

poliomyelitis [ˌpəʊliəʊmaɪə'laɪtɪs] *n.* virus disease of the spinal cord, often causing paralysis; infantile paralysis (*abbr.* **polio**).

poliosis [ˌpɒli'əʊsɪs] *n.* greyness of hair.

politic ['pɒlətɪk] *adj.* wise, prudent, expedient; artful, devious; shrewd.

politicaster [pə'lɪtɪkæstə] *n.* minor or petty politician; dabbler in politics.

polity ['pɒləti] *n.* political organization or constitution of a state, church, etc.

poll [pəʊl] *n.* head, especially top or back part of head of animal; striking face of hammer.

pollack ['pɒlæk] *n.* cod-like food fish.

pollard ['pɒlɑːd, –ləd] *v.t.* cut off top of (tree); *n.* pollarded tree; animal without its usual horns, antlers, etc.

pollen ['pɒlən] *n.* yellowish dust, each grain containing male reproductive element, of plants.

pollex ['pɒleks] *n.* (*pl.* **–lices**) thumb. **pollical,** *adj.*

pollice verso, (*Latin*) with thumb turned down, indicating condemnation, especially to death. **pollicitation,** *n.* offer not accepted.

pollinate ['pɒlɪneɪt] *v.t.* fertilize with pollen. **pollination,** *n.* **–linic,** *adj.* **polliniferous, polliniferous,** *adj.* pollen bearing. **pollinosis,** *n.* hay fever.

polonaise [ˌpɒlə'neɪz] *n.* stately Polish dance; dress-like garment worn over skirt.

polony [pə'ləʊni] *n.* sort of sausage.

poltergeist ['pɒltəgaɪst] *n.* active manifestation o. spirit in rappings, moving of furniture, etc.; such manifested spirit.

poltophagy [pɒl'tɒfədʒi] *n.* lengthy mastication of food reducing it to semi-liquid state. **poltophagic** [–'fædʒɪk], *adj.* **poltophagist,** *n.*

poltroon [pɒl'truːn] *n.* abject coward.

polyamide [ˌpɒli'æmaɪd] *n.* compound characterized by more than one amide group, a polymeric amide.

polyandry [ˌpɒli'ændri] *n.* marriage of one woman to two or more men at same time. **polyandric, polyandrous,** *adj.* **polyandrist,** *n.*

polyarchy ['pɒliɑːki] *n.* government by many persons.

polychaete ['pɒlikiːt] *n. & adj.* (pertaining to) marine worm. **polychaetous,** *adj.*

polychotomy [pɒli'kɒtəmi] *n.* division into many parts. **polychotomous,** *adj.*

polychrest ['pɒlikrest] *n.* remedy for several diseases. **polychrest,** *adj.* **polychresty,** *n.*

polychrome ['pɒlɪkrəʊm] *n. & adj.* work of art in many colours. **polychromatic** [–ə'mætɪk], **polychromic, polychromous,** *adj.* many-coloured. **polychromia,** *n.*, *Medicine*, excessive coloration. **polychromy,** *n.*

polycythaemia [ˌpɒlisaɪ'θiːmiə] *n.* blood condition with abnormal numbers of red blood cells.

polydactyl [ˌpɒli'dæktɪl] *n. & adj.* (animal or human) having too many fingers or toes.

polydemic [ˌpɒli'demɪk] *adj.* native to several countries.

polydipsia [ˌpɒli'dɪpsiə] *n.* abnormal thirst.

polyeidic [ˌpɒli'aɪdɪk] *adj.* applied to insects with conspicuous metamorphosis. **polyeidism,** *n.*

polyelectrolyte [ˌpɒliː'lektrəlaɪt] *n.* a jelly-like plastic compounded of two polymers, one charged positively and one negatively.

polyethnic [ˌpɒli'eθnɪk] *adj.* derived from or containing many races.

polygamy [pə'lɪgəmi] *n.* marriage to more than one spouse at same time. **polygamic** [–'gæmɪk], **polygamous,** *adj.* **polygamist,** *n.*

polygenesis [ˌpɒli'dʒenəsɪs] *n.* derivation from many origins. **polygenesic, polygenetic, polygenic,** *adj.* **polygenism** [–'lɪdʒɪnɪzm], *n.* theory of polygenesis of Man.

polyglot ['pɒliglɒt] *adj.* in or pertaining to several languages; *n.* person speaking or book printed in several languages. **polyglottal, polyglottic, polyglottous,** *adj.*

polygon ['pɒlɪgən] *n.* many-sided plane figure. **polygonal** [–'lɪgənl], *adj.*

polygraph ['pɒligrɑːf] *n.* device for recording simultaneously bodily activities such as pulse rate, blood pressure, etc., especially to detect lies. **polygraphic,** *adj.*

polygyny [pə'lɪdʒəni] *n.* marriage of man to several wives at once. **polygynist,** *n.* **polygynous,** *adj.*

polyhedron [ˌpɒli'hiːdrən] *n.* many-sided solid figure. **polyhedral,** *adj.*

polyhidrosis [ˌpɒlihɪ'drəʊsɪs] *n.* excessive perspiration.

polyhistor [ˌpɒli'hɪstə] *n.* person of exceptionally wide knowledge; polymath.

polylith ['pɒliliθ] *n.* prehistoric monument of many stones. **polylithic,** *adj.*

polymath ['pɒlimæθ] *n.* person of wide learning. **polymathic,** *adj.* **polymathy** [–'lɪməθi], *n.*

polymer ['pɒlɪmə] *n.* a compound of the same elements in the same proportion by weight, but of different molecular weights. **polymeric** [–'merɪk], *adj.* **polymerize** ['pɒl–], *v.t.* change into polymeric compound, especially one of higher molecular weight and different properties.

polymorphic, polymorphous ['pɒlimɔːfɪk, ˌpɒli'mɔːfəs] *adj.* having many forms or functions. **polymorphism,** *n.*

polymythy, ['pɒlimɪθi] *n.* use of many plots in one story. **polymythic,** *adj.*

polyneuritis [ˌpɒlinju'raɪtɪs] *n.* neuritis of many nerves simultaneously. **polyneuritic** [–'rɪtɪk], *adj.*

polynomial [ˌpɒli'nəʊmiəl] *n. & adj.* *Mathematics*, (expression) of more than one term; *Biology*, (name) of more than three terms.

polyonymy [ˌpɒli'ɒnəmi] *n.* use of many names for same thing; use of polynomial term or name. **polyonymous,** *adj.*

polyopia [ˌpɒliˈəupiə] *n.* multiple vision. **polyopic** [-ˈɒpɪk], *adj.*

polyp [ˈpɒlɪp] *n.* hollow-bodied, tentacled marine invertebrate, as coral, sea-anemone, etc. small growth on mucous membrane. **polypoid, polypous** *adj.*

polyphagia [ˌpɒliˈfeɪdʒiə] *n.* eating of excessive amount, or many different kinds, of food. **polyphagic** [-ˈfædʒɪk], **polyphagous** [-ˈlɪfəgəs], *adj.* **polyphagy** [-ˈlɪfədʒi], *n.*

polypharmacy [ˌpɒliˈfɑːməsi] *n.* treatment with many medicines for same disease. **polypharmacon,** *n.* medicine containing many ingredients.

polyphony [pəˈlɪfəni] *n. Music,* composition in separate, but simultaneous and harmonizing, parts; counterpoint; *Phonetics,* use of one symbol for several sounds. **polyphonic** [-ˈfɒnɪk], *adj.* **polyphonist** [-ˈfəʊnɪst], *n.* composer of polyphony.

polyphyletic [ˌpɒlifaɪˈletɪk] *adj.* having more than one original type. **polyphylesis** [-ˈliːsɪs], *n.* such descent.

polyploid [ˈpɒliplɔɪd] *n. & adj.* (cell, individual, generation) having more than twice the basic number of chromosomes.

polypnea [ˌpɒlɪpˈniːə] *n.* rapid breathing. **polypneic,** *adj.*

polypod [ˈpɒlipɒd] *n. & adj.* many-legged (animal).

polypragmatist [ˌpɒliˈprægmətɪst] *n.* busybody. **polypragmatism,** *n.*

polypsychic [ˌpɒliˈsaɪkɪk] *adj.* having several souls. **polypsychism,** *n.*

polypus [ˈpɒlɪpəs] *n.* (*pl.* **–pi**) nasal, etc., polyp.

polyseme [ˌpɒliˈsiːmænt] *n.* word with many meanings. **polysemantic,** *adj.* **polysemous,** *adj.* having many meanings. **polysemy,** *n.*

polystachious [ˌpɒliˈstækiəs] *adj.* many-spiked.

polystichous [pəˈlɪstɪkəs] *adj.* in several rows.

polystomatous [ˌpɒlɪˈstɒmətəs, -ˈstəʊ-] *adj.* many-mouthed.

polystyle [ˈpɒlistaɪl] *n. & adj.* (building) with many columns.

polysyllable [ˈpɒliˌsɪləbl] *n.* many-syllabled word. **polysyllabic** [-ˈlæbɪk], *adj.* being or using polysyllables.

polysyndeton [ˌpɒliˈsɪndətən] *n.* rhetorical device of repeating conjunction for emphasis. **polysyndetic** [-ˈdetɪk], *adj.*

polysynthetic [ˌpɒlisɪnˈθetɪk] *adj.* of languages where whole phrases are combined into one word.

polythalamous [ˌpɒliˈθæləməs] *adj.* having many chambers.

polytheism [ˈpɒliθiːɪzm] *n.* belief in several gods. **polytheist,** *n.* **polytheistic,** *adj.*

polytocous [pəˈlɪtəkəs] *adj.* bringing forth many young at once.

polytomous [pəˈlɪtəməs] *adj.* divided into several parts. **polytomy,** *n.*

polyunsaturated [ˌpɒliʌnˈsætʃəreɪtɪd] *adj.* (of vegetable & animal fats) having many double and triple chemical bonds, and without cholesterol.

polyuria [ˌpɒliˈjuəriə] *n.* excessive urination. **polyuric,** *adj.*

polyvalent [ˌpɒliˈveɪlənt] *adj. Chemistry,* having multiple valency; *Medicine,* effective against more than one toxin or strain of micro-organism. **polyvalence,** *n.*

polyvinyl [ˌpɒliˈvaɪnl, -ɪl] *adj.* denoting a group of plastics used as adhesives, for waterproofing, insulating, etc.

pomace [ˈpʌmɪs] *n.* crushed apples in cider-making. **pomaceous** [-ˈmeɪʃəs], *adj.* pertaining to apples or similar fruit.

pomatum [pɒˈmeɪtəm] *n.* hair pomade.

pomelo [ˈpɒmələʊ] *n.* fruit like a grapefruit; shaddock.

pomfret [ˈpɒmfrɪt] *n.* large black marine food fish.

pomiculture [ˈpəʊmɪˌkʌltʃə] *n.* fruit growing. **pomiform,** *adj.* apple-shaped. **pomology,** *n.* science of fruit growing.

poncho [ˈpɒntʃəʊ] (*Spanish*) *n.* simple kind of cloak with slit for head.

ponderable [ˈpɒndərəbl] *adj.* having weight; capable of being evaluated; *n.* substantial thing. **ponderability,** *n.* **ponderal,** *adj.* pertaining to weight. **ponderous,** *adj.* weighty; heavy.

pone [pəʊn, ˈpəʊni] *n.* card player on dealer's right, who cuts the cards.

ponerology [ˌpɒnəˈrɒlədʒi] *n.* division of theology dealing with evil.

pongee [ˌpɒnˈdʒiː] *n.* thin, soft silk from China, naturally coloured beige or tan; cotton or rayon imitation of this.

pons [pɒnz] (*Latin*) *n.* (*pl.* **–ntes**) 'bridge'. **pons asinorum** [-ˌæsɪˈnɔːrəm], 'bridge of asses'; test of ignorant person's ability. **pontine,** *adj.*

pood [puːd] (*Russian*) *n.* weight, equivalent of 36 lb.

pooja [ˈpuːdʒɑː] *see* **puja.**

popliteal [ˌpɒplɪˈtiːəl, pɒˈplɪtiəl] *adj* pertaining to the back of the knee.

popple [ˈpɒpl] *v.i.* (of water) bubble, toss, heave; flow tumbling over rocks.

porbeagle [ˈpɔːbiːgl] *n.* voracious Atlantic and Pacific shark.

porcine [ˈpɔːsaɪn, -sɪn] *adj.* pertaining to or like pigs.

porism [ˈpɔːrɪzm] *n.* geometric proposition that it is possible, in certain conditions, for a problem to have any number of solutions.

porogamy [pɔːˈrɒgəmi] *n.* fertilization of seed plants. **porogamic** [-ˈgæmɪk], **porogamous,** *adj.*

porphyry [ˈpɔːfəri] *n.* rock composed of crystals in purple-coloured matrix; any rock of like composition. **porphyritic,** *adj.* **porphyrogenitic,** *adj.* royal-born. **porphyrogenitism,** *n.* succession to throne of son born after his father's accession in preference to elder son not so born.

porraceous [pəˈreɪʃəs, pɒ-] *adj.* like leek in colour.

porrect [pəˈrekt] *adj.* stretched at length.

porrigo [pəˈraɪgəʊ] *n.* scalp disease causing baldness. **porriginous** [pəˈrɪdʒənəs], *adj.*

portamento [ˌpɔːtəˈmentəʊ] *n.* (*pl.* **–ti**), gliding movement in music from one note to another.

portend [pɔːˈtend] *v.t.* bode, foreshadow; signify. **portent,** *n.* **portentous,** *adj.*

portfolio [ˌpɔːtˈfəʊliəʊ] *n.* case for carrying papers; office of cabinet minister. **minister without portfolio,** cabinet minister not having charge of a state department.

portière [ˌpɔːtiˈeə] *n.* curtain covering door or across doorway.

portmanteau [pɔːtˈmæntəʊ] *n.* travelling trunk that opens into two equal parts.

portreeve ['pɔːtriːv] *n.* formerly, in England, mayor.

poseur [pəʊ'zɜː] (*French*) *n.* (fem. **-euse**), person who poses or pretends; affected person.

posit ['pɒzɪt] *v.t.* postulate.

positivism ['pɒzɪtɪvɪzm] *n. Philosophy*, doctrine excluding everything not an observable natural phenomenon.

positron ['pɒzɪtrɒn] *n.* positively charged atomic particle of same mass as electron, emitted by transuranic elements and found in cosmic rays.

posology [pə'sɒlədʒi] *n.* study of medical doses. **posologist**, *n.*

posset ['pɒsɪt] *n.* hot spiced drink of milk and wine.

'possum ['pɒsəm] *see* **opossum.**

post [pəʊst] (*Latin*) *prep.* 'after'. **post bellum**, after the war. **post diem**, after the appointed day. **post factum**, after the event; late; retrospective. **post hoc**, after this. **post hoc ergo propter hoc**, after this therefore on account of this; fallacy that because one event follows another the second must be caused by the first. **post meridiem**, after noon (*abbr.* **p.m.**). **postmortem**, after death; examination of dead body to determine cause of death. **post-obit**, following death; becoming effective after death; postmortem. **post partum**, after childbirth. **post rem**, after the thing or matter.

postament ['pəʊstəment] *n.* pedestal; frame.

postcenal [,pəʊst'siːnl] *adj.* post-prandial.

postcibal [,pəʊst'saɪbl] *adj.* after a meal.

postconnubial [,pəʊstkə'njuːbiəl] *adj.* after marriage.

postdiluvian [,pəʊstdɪ'luːviən] *adj.* after the flood.

posteen [pɒ'stiːn] (*Anglo-Indian*) *n.* Afghan leather jacket.

poste restante [,pəʊst 'restɒnt] (*French*) department of post office holding letters until called for.

posterity [pɒ'sterəti] *n.* later generation(s); one's descendants.

postern ['pɒstən] *n. archaic*, back door.

postexilic [,pəʊsteg'zɪlɪk] *adj.* after exile, especially after Babylonian captivity of Jews.

posthumous ['pɒstjuməs] *adj.* after person's death; born after father's death; published after author's death. **posthuma**, *n. pl.* posthumous writings.

postiche [pɒ'stiːʃ] (*French*) *n.* & *adj.* artificial or spurious (thing); false (hair); (ornament) added, especially inappropriately, to finished thing.

postil ['pɒstɪl] *n.* note in margin; comment.

postilion, postillion [pɒ'stɪljən] *n.* person who rides near horse of those drawing coach etc. and acts as guide to the whole team.

postjacent [,pəʊst'dʒeɪsnt] *adj.* posterior.

postlude ['pəʊstluːd] *n.* concluding piece of music as at end church service; closing phase of period, literary work, etc.

postmundane [,pəʊst'mʌndeɪn] *adj.* after the (end of the) world.

postnatal [,pəʊst'neɪtl] *adj.* after birth. **postnati**, *n.pl.* (*sing.* **-tus**) persons born after a certain event.

postprandial [,pəʊst'prændiəl] *adj.* after dinner.

postrorse ['pɒstrɔːs] *adj.* turned, or bent, backwards.

posttonic [,pəʊst'tɒnɪk] *adj.* after accent or accented syllable.

postulate ['pɒstjuleɪt] *v.t.* require or assume as necessary or true; *n.* assumption; necessary condition; axiom. **postulant**, *n.* candidate for religious order. **postulation**, *n.* **postulatory**, *adj.*

postvocalic [,pəʊstvə'kælɪk] *adj.* after a vowel.

potable ['pəʊtəbl] *adj.* drinkable; *n.* beverage.

potamic [pə'tæmɪk] *adj.* pertaining to rivers. **potamology**, *n.* study of rivers.

potation [pəʊ'teɪʃn] *n.* act of drinking; drinking bout; thing drunk. **potatory**, *adj.*

pot-au-feu [,pɒt–əʊ'-fɜː] (*French*) 'pot on fire'; stew of vegetables and meat.

poteen, potheen [pɒ'tiːn] *n.* illicitly distilled Irish whisky.

potential [pə'tenʃl] *adj.* possible; latent; having power to become; *n. Electricity*, degree of electrification; work done in bringing a unit positive charge to a point from infinity. **potential difference**, voltage. **potentiality**, *n.* **potentiate**, *v.t.* make possible.

potentiometer [pə,tenʃi'ɒmɪtə] *n.* instrument measuring electromotive force or potential difference by comparison with a known voltage.

potomania [,pɒtə'meɪniə] *n.* dipsomania.

potpourri [,pəʊpə'riː] *n.* mixture of dried petals & spices to scent a room; miscellany of music or literature, etc.; medley.

pottle ['pɒtl] *n.* half-gallon (pot).

Poujadist [,puː'ʒɑːdɪst] *adj.* denoting a right-wing bourgeois political movement in France in the 1950s led by Pierre Poujade.

poulard [puː'lɑːd] *n.* sterilized or fat pullet.

poult [pəʊlt] *n.* young fowl, especially turkey.

poult-de-soie [,puː-də-'swɑː] *n.* finely corded silk fabric.

pounce [paʊns] *n.* fine powder formerly spread on writing paper to arrest running of ink; powder for tracing perforated design, or such design.

poundal ['paʊndl] *n.* unit of force: force imparting to one pound mass acceleration of one foot per second.

pour ainsi dire [puər,ænsiː'diə] (*French*) 'so to speak'.

pourboire [puə'bwɑː] (*French*) *n.* tip; gratuity.

pourparler [puə'pɑːleɪ] (*French*) *n.* preliminary or informal discussion.

pour rire [puə'riə] (*French*) 'for laughing'; not serious.

pou sto [puː stəʊ, paʊ–] (*Greek*) 'where I may stand'; place to stand; basis; locus standi.

practice ['præktɪs] *n.* (period of) exercise to develop a skill; condition of having such a skill through exercise; application of a skill, etc. as opposed to theory; customary action or proceeding; procedure; professional business and clientele of a doctor, lawyer, etc. (*as opposed to* **practise**)

practise ['præktɪs] *v.i.* & *t.* do regular exercises (in); be engaged in (a profession); *v.t.* perform habitually; carry out in practice; *v.i.* take advantage of. (*as opposed to* **practice**) **practised**, *adj.* experienced; expert. **practising**, *adj.* active as. **practitioner**, *n.* person who practises a profession, skill, etc.

praedial, predial ['priːdiəl] *adj.* of land, farming, etc.

praetor ['priːtə, -ɔː] *n*, ancient Roman magistrate of high rank. **praetorian,** *adj*. pertaining to praetors; belonging to or forming Roman emperor's bodyguard.

pragmatic(al) [præg'mætɪk, -l] *adj*. matter-of-fact; practical; dogmatic. **pragmatic sanction,** decree of head of state having force of law. **pragmatism,** *n*. Philosophy, doctrine emphasizing practical bearing or value of philosophy. **pragmatist,** *n*. **pragmatize,** *v.t.* materialize; represent as factual.

praline ['prɑːliːn] *n*. sweetmeat made of sugar and nuts.

prandial ['prændiəl] *adj*. pertaining to or at dinner.

pratincolous [prə'tɪŋkələs] *adj*. inhabiting meadows.

praxinoscope [præk'sɪnəskəup] *n*. instrument with mirrors in which a series of moving drawings appear as a continuously moving picture; early form of cinematograph.

praxis ['præksɪs] *n*. practice (of profession, science, etc.) as opposed to theory; accepted practice.

preadamic [,priːə'dæmɪk] *adj*. before Adam. **preadamite** [-'ædəmaɪt], *n*. person living before Adam; believer in such persons.

preagonal [priː'ægənl] *adj*. immediately preceding death throes. **preagony,** *n*. such period.

preamble [priː'æmbl, 'priː-] *n*. preface; introduction. **preambulation,** *n*. making a preamble. **preambulatory,** *adj*.

prebend ['prebənd] *n*. *Ecclesiastical*, stipend of member of chapter. **prebendal,** *adj*. **prebendary,** *n*. holder of prebend.

Precambrian *n*. & *adj*. (of) earliest geological era.

precative, precatory ['prekətɪv, -əri] *adj*. beseeching.

precentor [prɪ'sentə] *n*. (*fem*. **-tress, -trix**) leader of singing. **precentorial,** *adj*.

precept ['priːsept] *n*. rule of conduct; law; command. **preceptive,** *adj*. **preceptor,** *n*. (*fem*. **-ress**) teacher. **preceptual,** *adj*. conveying precept(s).

precession [prɪ'seʃn] *n*. preceding. **precession of equinoxes,** westward movement of equinoctial points, bringing equinox to meridian earlier every day. **precessional,** *adj*.

preciation [,priːʃi'eɪʃn] *n*. determination of value or price.

precinct ['priːsɪŋkt] *n*. ground belonging to ecclesiastical or other building; surroundings; (*American*), police-district.

preciosity [,preʃi'ɒsəti] *n*. excessive elegance, especially of literary style.

precipitate [prɪ'sɪpɪtət] *adj*. hasty, abrupt; falling away steeply;

precipitous [prɪ'sɪpɪtəs] *adj*. like a precipice; precipitate.

précis ['preɪsiː] *n*. summary; *v.t.* summarize.

precisian [prɪ'sɪʒn] *n*. person excessively devoted to minute observance of rules. **precisianism,** *n*. **precisive** [-'saɪsɪv], *adj*. separating; defining; exact.

preclude [prɪ'kluːd] *v.t.* make impossible in advance.

precocial [prɪ'kəuʃl] *adj*. applied to birds having downy young, able to run immediately they are hatched.

preconize ['priːkənaɪz] *v.t.* proclaim; publish publicly. **preconization,** *n*.

predacious, predaceous [prɪ'deɪʃəs] *adj*. pertaining to preying; living on prey. **predacity,** *n*.

predatory ['predətəri] *adj*. pertaining to or living by plundering; destructive. **predation,** *n*. **predative,** *adj*.

predella [prɪ'delə] *n*. (*pl*. **-le**) platform for altar; work of art on predella.; portable altar or decoration on it; shelf behind altar.

predial *see* **praedial**.

predicable ['predɪkəbl] *n*. & *adj*. affirmable (thing); attribute. **predicability,** *n*.

predicate ['predɪkeɪt] *v.t.* affirm; preach; state; [ət], *n*. attribute affirmed; *Grammar*, part of sentence containing statement about subject. **predicant,** *n*. & *adj*. preaching (friar). **predication, predicator,** *n*. **predicative** [-'dɪkətɪv], **predicatory,** *adj*.

predilection [,priːdɪ'lekʃn] *n*. preference.

preemption [prɪ'empʃn] *n*. first right to purchase; appropriation. **preemptive,** *adj*. pertaining to preemption; seizing for oneself by preventing others from acting. **preemptor,** *n*. **preemptory,** *adj*.

preexilian, preexilic [,priːeg'zɪliən, -ɪk] *adj*. before exile, especially Babylonian captivity of Jews.

prehensile [prɪ'hensaɪl] *adj*. capable of or adapted for grasping. **prehensity, prehension,** *n*. **prehensive, prehensorial, prehensory,** *adj*.

prelapsarian [,priːlæp'seəriən] *adj*. pertaining to time before Man's fall.

prelect [prɪ'lekt] *v.i.* deliver lecture. **prelection,** *n*. lecture. **prelector,** *n*. lecturer.

premiate ['priːmieɪt] *v.t.* give prize or premium for.

première ['premieə] (*French*) *n*. first performance. **première danseuse** [-dɑːn'sɜːz], first or leading dancer (female).

premise ['premɪs] *n*. (*British also* **premiss**) proposition, condition or statement from which conclusion is drawn; thing previously stated; *v.t.* (prɪmaɪz), set out before, or as preface; presuppose.

premolar [,priː'məulə] *n*. & *adj*. (tooth) in front of molars, or between molars and canines.

premorse [prɪ'mɔːs] *adj*. bitten off short; as if bitten off.

premundane [,priː'mʌndeɪn] *adj*. before creation of world.

prenarial [,priː'neəriəl] *adj*. pertaining to or in front of nostrils.

prenatal [,priː'neɪtl] *adj*. before birth.

prepense [prɪ'pens] *adj*. deliberate; premeditated.

prepollent [prɪ'pɒlənt] *adj*. predominant.

prepotent [priː'pəutnt] *adj*. very or more powerful; predominant. **prepotency,** *n*.; *Biology*, propensity for transmitting certain heritable characteristics.

preprandial [,priː'prændiəl] *adj*. before dinner or eating a meal.

prepsychotic [,priːsaɪ'kɒtɪk] *adj*. having predisposition to mental disorder.

prepuce ['priːpjuːs] *n*. foreskin. **preputial,** *adj*.

prerogative [prɪ'rɒgətɪv] *n*. right or power peculiar to a person or office.

prerupt [prɪ'rʌpt] *adj*. abrupt; steep.

presage ['presɪdʒ] v.t. portend; give a warning of; n. portent; foreboding. **presageful**, adj.

presbycousis [,prezbɪ'kuːsɪs] n. hardness of hearing in old age. **presbyophrenia**, n. loss of memory in old age. **presbyopia, presbytia**, n. long-sightedness in old age.

prescience ['presɪəns] n. foreknowledge; foresight. **prescient**, adj.

prescind [prɪ'sɪnd] v.i. & t. abstract or separate (oneself). **prescission**, n.

prescribe [prɪ'skraɪb] v.t. ordain; direct; order; confine; outlaw. **prescript** ['priː-], n. & adj. (thing) prescribed. **prescription**, n. act of prescribing; thing prescribed; establishment of claim by proof of long use or exercise of right. **prescriptive**, adj. prescribing; based on long use; customary; traditional.

presentient [priː'senʃnt] adj. having premonition.

presidial [prɪ'sɪdɪəl] adj. presidential.

presimian [,priː'sɪmɪən] adj. before occurrence of anthropoid apes.

prestidigitator [,prestɪ'dɪdʒɪteɪtə] n. juggler; conjuror. **prestidigitate**, v.i. perform juggling or conjuring tricks. **prestidigitation**, n.

prêt-à-porter [,pretɑː'pɔːteɪ] adj. French, 'ready to wear'; (of clothes) off the peg.

preterhuman [,priːtə'hjuːmən] adj. beyond what is human.

preterite ['pretərɪt] adj. Grammar, signifying past time; aorist; n. such tense. **preterition**, n. passing over or omission.

preterlabent [,priːtə'leɪbənt] adj. flowing by.

pretermit [,priːtə'mɪt] v.t. omit; neglect; interrupt. **pretermission**, n.

pretone ['priːtəun] n. syllable or vowel before accented syllable. **pretonic** [-'tɒnɪk], adj.

pretzel ['pretsl] n. a dry, salted biscuit of figure-8 or similar shape.

prevenient [prɪ'viːnɪənt] adj. preceding; anticipating; having foresight; preventing. **prevenience**, n.

prevernal [priː'vɜːnl] adj. flowering or foliating early.

prevocalic [,priːvə'kælɪk] adj. before a vowel.

prevoyant [prɪ'vɔɪənt] adj. having foresight. **prevoyance**, n.

priapic, priapean [praɪ'æpɪk, ,praɪə'piːən] adj. pertaining to Priapus, Greek god of male reproductive power; phallic. **priapism** ['praɪ-], n. obscenity; obscene act; persistent erection of penis.

prie-dieu [,priː'djɜː] (French) n. praying-desk.

prima facie [,praɪmə 'feɪʃi] (Latin) 'at first sight'; on the face of it; enough to cause fact to be presumed true.

primate ['praɪmeɪt] n. Ecclesiastical, archbishop; Zoology, member of highest order of mammals. **primatial**, adj.

primavera [,priːmə'veərə] (Italian) n. spring (season).

primipara [praɪ'mɪpərə] n. (pl. **–rae**), woman bearing first child, or having borne only one child. **primiparous**, adj. **primiparity** [-'pærəti], n.

primitiae [prɪ'mɪtɪaɪ, praɪ'mɪʃiiː] (Latin) n. pl. first fruits; annates. **primitial**, adj.

primogeniture [,praɪməu'dʒenɪtʃə] n. principle of inheritance by eldest child; state of being eldest child. **primogenial**, adj. first to be formed; original. **primogenital, primogenitary**, adj. **primogenitor**, n. ancestor.

primordial [praɪ'mɔːdɪəl] adj. pertaining to, or having existed from, beginning; in original form; first; primary. **primordiality**, n.

primum mobile [,priːməm 'məubɪleɪ, ,praɪməm 'mɒbɪli] (Latin) in ancient astronomy, outermost sphere of heaven bearing fixed stars.

primus inter pares [,priːməs ɪntə 'paːreɪz, ,praɪməs-, -'peərɪːz] (Latin) (fem. **prima** :.....) 'first among his/her equals'.

princeps ['prɪnseps] (Latin) n. chief, headman; first edition of book.

principal ['prɪnsɪpəl] adj. chief; main; Finance, relating to a capital sum lent or invested; n. head, especially of a school, college, etc.; leading actor, singer or orchestral player; Law, person for whom another acts as agent; person responsible for a crime; Finance, capital sum as opposed to interest or income; main rafter or girder; combatant in a duel. (as opposed to **principle**)

principle ['prɪnsɪpl] n. fundamental truth or law; law of nature, physics, etc.; fundamental source; code of personal conduct; morality; (pl.) moral standards or rules. (as opposed to **principal**) **in principle**, in theory; essentially. **on principle**, on moral or ethical grounds. **principled**, adj. based on moral principles.

prion ['praɪɒn] n. minute micro-organism thought to cause some diseases of the nervous system.

pristine ['prɪstiːn, –aɪn] adj. primitive; ancient; unspoiled.

privateer [,praɪvə'tɪə] n. privately owned ship commissioned by government to attack enemy vessels; captain or seaman of privateer.

privative ['prɪvətɪv] adj. depriving; signifying negation or deprivation; n. such prefix (as un-) or suffix (as -less).

privity ['prɪvəti] n. private knowledge; connivance.

proa ['prəuə] n. kind of Malay sailing boat.

proairesis, proaeresis [prəu'eərəsɪs, –'ɪə–] n. deliberate choice.

probate ['prəubeɪt] n. proving of a will.

probative, probatory ['prəubətɪv] adj. substantiating; testing. **probate**, n. proving of a will.

probity ['prəubəti] n. integrity of character.

pro bono publico [prəu ,bəunəu 'pʊblɪkəu, -'pʌb–] (Latin) 'for the public good'.

proboscis [prə'bɒsɪs] n. (pl. **–cises** or **–cides**) long snout; prominent nasal organ. **proboscidal, proboscidiform**, adj. like a proboscis. **proboscidate, proboscidial, proboscidiferous**, adj. having a proboscis. **proboscidean, proboscidian**, n. & adj. (animal) with proboscis.

probouleutic [,prəubuː'luːtɪk] adj. pertaining to prior discussion and deliberation.

procacious [prə'keɪʃəs] adj. insolent. **procacity**, n.

procatalectic [,prəukætəl'ektɪk] adj. with unaccented part of first metrical foot lacking.

procathedral [,prəukə'θiːdrəl] n. parish church used as cathedral.

proceleusmatic [,prəusɪluːs'mætɪk] adj. exhorting; encouraging; n. metrical foot of four short syllables.

procellous [prə'seləs] adj. stormy.

procephalic [ˌprəʊsɪˈfælɪk] *adj.* pertaining to front of head.

procès-verbal [ˌprəʊseɪ-ˈveəbɑːl] (*French*) *n.* official report or memorandum; minutes of meeting.

prochronism [ˈprəʊkrənɪzm] *n.* error of assigning to an event a date before its real date.

procidence [ˈprəʊsɪdəns, ˈprɒs-] *n.* prolapse. **procident**, *adj.*

proclinate [ˈprəʊklɪneɪt] *adj.* directed forward.

proclitic [ˌprəʊˈklɪtɪk] *adj.* applied to naturally unaccented words dependent for pronunciation and accent on following word; *n.* such word. **proclisis** [ˈprəʊ-, ˈprɒ-], *n.* such pronunciation.

proclivity [prəˈklɪvəti] *n.* tendency; natural bent. **proclivitous**, *adj.* steep. **proclivous** [-ˈklaɪvəs], *adj.* bending forward at an angle.

procrastinate [prəˈkræstɪneɪt] *v.i.* delay or defer action; be dilatory. **procrastination, procrastinator**, *n.* **procrastinative, procrastinatory**, *adj.*

procreate [ˌprəʊkriˈeɪt] *v.i. & t.* produce young. **procreation, procreator**, *n.* **procreant, procreative**, *adj.*

Procrustean [prəˈkrʌstiən] *adj.* ruthlessly enforcing conformity to a policy etc. without regard for individual differences.

procryptic [prəˈkrɪptɪk] *adj.* pertaining to or having protective coloration. **procrypsis**, *n.*

proctal [ˈprɒktl] *adj.* pertaining to or near anus or rectum. **proctoclysis**, *n.* injection of fluid into rectum. **proctology**, *n.* medical study of anus and rectum.

proctor [ˈprɒktə] *n.* disciplinary officer of university. **proctorship**, *n.* **proctoral, proctorial**, *adj.*

procumbent [prəʊˈkʌmbənt] *adj.* lying flat; trailing along ground.

procurator [ˈprɒkjʊreɪtə] *n.* governor of territory; agent; manager of another's affairs. **procuratorial**, *adj.*

procurer [prəˈkjʊərə] *n.* (*fem.* **-ess**) (person) supplying women to brothels, etc.

prodigal [ˈprɒdɪgl] *adj.* wasteful; extravagant; lavish; generous; *n.* such person; spendthrift. **prodigality**, *n.*

prodigy [ˈprɒdədʒi] *n.* marvel; extraordinary thing or person. **prodigious** [-ˈdɪdʒəs], *adj.* extraordinary, especially in size.

prodrome [ˈprəʊdrəʊm] *n.* symptom appearing before setting in of disease. **prodromal** [ˈprɒdrəməl], **prodromic**, *adj.* **prodromus** [ˈprɒd-], *n.* prefatory work.

proem [ˈprəʊem] *n.* preface. **proemial** [-ˈiːmiəl], *adj.*

proemptosis [ˌprəʊempˈtəʊsɪs] *n.* addition once in every three centuries of one day to lunar calendar.

proethnic [prəʊˈeθnɪk] *adj.* prior to division into smaller ethnic groups.

profligate [ˈprɒflɪgət] *adj.* immoral; dissolute; *n.* such person. **profligacy**, *n.*

profluent [ˈprɒfluənt] *adj.* flowing, abundant; exuberant. **profluence**, *n.*

pro forma [ˌprəʊ ˈfɔːmə] (*Latin*) 'according to the form'; as a matter of form or formality.

progamic [prəʊˈgæmɪk] *adj.* before fertilization. **progamete**, *n.* germ or sperm cell.

progenitive [prəˈdʒenətɪv] *n.* reproductive. **progenital**, *adj.* **progenitor**, *n.* (*fem.* **-tress, -trix**)

ancestor.

progeny [ˈprɒdʒəni] *n.* offspring

progeria [prəʊˈdʒɪəriə] *n.* premature senility.

progesterone [prəˈdʒestərəʊn] *n.* female reproductive hormone.

prognathism [ˈprɒgnəθɪzm] *n.* state of having projecting jaws. **prognathic** [-ˈnæθɪk], **prognathous**, *adj.*

prognosis [prɒgˈnəʊsɪs] *n.* (*pl.* **-ses**) forecast, especially of development of disease. **prognostic** [-ˈnɒstɪk], *adj.* **prognosticate**, *v.i. & t.* predict; presage.

projectile [prəˈdʒektaɪl] *n.* thing thrown forwards; self-propelling missile; *adj.* pertaining to this; thrusting or projecting forwards.

projicient [prəʊˈdʒɪʃnt] *adj.* projecting; communicating between organism and its surroundings.

prolapse, prolapsus [ˈprəʊlæps, prəʊˈlæpsəs] *n.* falling (of bodily organ) forward or downward, especially of the uterus.

prolate [ˈprəʊleɪt] *adj.* having flattened sides due to lengthwise elongation.

prolegomena [ˌprəʊləˈgɒmɪnə] *n. pl.* (*sing.* **-non**) introductory remarks. **prolegomenist**, *n.* **prolegomenous**, *adj.*

prolepsis [prəʊˈliːpsɪs, -ˈlep-] *n.* (*pl.* **-ses**) rhetorical device of weakening objections by anticipating them; use of adjective that anticipates result of verb; prochronism; assumption. **proleptic**, *adj.*; *Medicine*, recurring at decreasing intervals. **proleptical**, *adj.* prehistoric. **proleptics** *n.* prognosis.

proletariat [ˌprəʊləˈteəriət] *n.* working classes. **proletarian**, *n. & adj.* (member) of proletariat.

prolicide [ˈprəʊlɪsaɪd] *n.* killing or killer of own offspring. **prolicidal**, *adj.*

proliferate [prəˈlɪfəreɪt] *v.i. & t.* produce (offspring, cells or buds) in large numbers at short intervals; grow by such reproduction of parts. **proliferation**, *n.* **proliferative, prolific, proliferous**, *adj.*

proligerous [prəʊˈlɪdʒərəs] *adj.* bearing offspring.

prolix [ˈprəʊlɪks] *adj.* long-winded; verbose. **prolixity**, *n.*

prolocutor [prəʊˈlɒkjʊtə] *n.* presiding officer; chair, especially of lower house of convocation.

prolusion [prəʊˈluːʒn] *n.* preliminary trial; tentative introductory essay. **prolusory**, *adj.*

Promethean [prəˈmiːθiən] *adj.* pertaining to Prometheus, Greek god who brought fire to human beings; original, creative; life-enhancing; *n.* such person.

promiscuous [prəˈmɪskjuəs] *adj.* mixed in haphazard fashion; indiscriminate. **promiscuity**, *n.* such mixing or mixture; indiscriminate sexual activity.

promissory [ˈprɒmɪsəri] *adj.* promising. **promissory note**, written promise to pay sum of money; I.O.U.

promulgate [ˈprɒmlgeɪt] *v.t.* publish; announce; put into action. **promulgation, promulgator**, *n.*

promuscis [prəˈmʌsɪs] *n.* proboscis, especially insect's. **promuscidate**, *adj.* having this.

pronation [prəʊˈneɪʃn] *n.* turning of hand and forearm so that palm is downward; procumbency. **pronator**, *n.* muscle used in pronation.

prone [prəʊn] *adj.* lying face down.

pronograde ['prəʊnəgreɪd] *adj.* walking with body parallel to ground.

pronominal [prə'nɒmɪnl] *adj.* pertaining to a pronoun.

prooemium [prəʊ'iːmɪəm] *n.* proem. **prooemiac,** *adj.*

propaedeutic(al) [,prəʊpɪ'djuːtɪk, -l] *adj.* preliminary, especially of instruction; *n.* introductory part of science or art; preliminary course of study. **propaedeutics,** *n.* preliminary instruction.

propensity [prə'pensəti] *n.* natural inclination or tendency.

prophylactic [,prɒfə'læktɪk] *n.* & *adj.* preventive against disease; protective. **prophylaxis,** *n.* such knowledge, act or treatment.

propinquity [prə'pɪŋkwəti] *n.* nearness.

propitiate [prə'pɪʃieɪt] *v.t.* appease; conciliate. **propitiatory,** *adj.* **propitiation,** *n.* act of propitiating; expiatory sacrifice.

proplasm ['prəʊplæzm] *n.* mould; preliminary model.

propolis ['prɒpəlɪs] *n.* resin of tree buds collected by bees; bee glue. **propolize,** *v.t.* cement with this.

proponent [prə'pəʊnənt] *n.* proposer; person arguing in favour of something.

propound [prə'paʊnd] *v.t.* put forward for consideration.

proprioceptor [,prəʊprɪə'septə, ,prɒ–] *n.* sense organ receptive to stimuli from within the body. **proprioceptive,** *adj.* **proprioception,** *n.*

proprio motu [,prəʊprɪəʊ 'məʊtuː, -tjuː] (*Latin*) 'by one's own motion'; of own initiative. **proprio vigore,** 'by (its) own force'; independently.

proptosis [prɒp'təʊsɪs] *n.* prolapse of eyeball.

propugnation [,prəʊpʌg'neɪʃn] *n.* *obsolete,* defence.

pro rata [prəʊ 'rɑːtə, 'reɪtə] (*Latin*) 'in proportion'.

pro re nata [prəʊ ,reɪ 'nɑːtə, –,riː 'neɪtə] (*Latin*) 'for the thing born'; to meet an emergency.

proreption [prəʊ'repʃn] *n.* *obsolete,* slow secret advance; creeping attack.

prorogue [prə'rəʊg] *v.t.* end session (of Parliament); postpone (meeting). **prorogation** [,prəʊrə'geɪʃn], *n.*

prosaic [prə'zeɪɪk] *adj.* like prose; commonplace. **prosaist** *n.* such a person.

proscenium [prəʊ'siːnɪəm] *n.* part of stage before curtain.

proscribe [prəʊ'skraɪb] *v.t.* outlaw; prohibit; condemn as harmful. **proscription,** *n.* **proscriptive,** *adj.*

proselyte ['prɒsəlaɪt] *n.* convert, especially to Jewish faith. **proselytic** [-'lɪtɪk], *adj.* **proselytize,** *v.i.* & *t.* **proselytism,** *n.*

prosenchyma [prɒ'seŋkɪmə] *n.* supporting plant tissue containing little protoplasm. **prosenchymatous,** *adj.*

prosilient [prəʊ'sɪlɪənt] *adj.* jumping forth; conspicuous.

prosit ['prəʊsɪt] (*Latin*) 'may it do good'; good health!

prosody ['prɒsədi] *n.* study or art of versifying, especially of metre, rhyme and stanza-form; method of versifying. **prosodial** [-'səʊdɪəl], **prosodic** [-'sɒdɪk], *adj.*

prosopic [prə'səʊpɪk, –'sɒ–] *adj.* pertaining to face. **prosopography,** *n.* description of face. **prosopopoeia,** *n.* personification; speaking or acting as if by imaginary or absent person.

prospice ['prɒspɪkeɪ, –siː] (*Latin*) 'look forward'.

prostaglandin [,prɒstə'glændɪn] *n.* hormone-like compound found in body tissues of mammals.

prostate ['prɒsteɪt] *adj.* applied to gland at head of urethra in men, discharging mucoid fluid. **prostatic** [–'stætɪk], *adj.* **prostatism,** *n.* disease of prostate gland.

prosthesis [prɒs'θiːsɪs, 'prɒsθəsɪs] *n.* (*pl.* **–es,** /iːz/]) replacement of lost part of body with artificial substitute; addition of sound at beginning of word. **prosthetic** [–'θetɪk], *adj.* **prosthetist,** *n.* branch of surgery or dentistry dealing with provision of artificial body parts. **prosthetics** *n.* **prosthodontics,** *n.* provision of artificial teeth etc.

prostitute ['prɒstɪtjuːt] *v.t.* debase for gain; make bad use of.

prostyle ['prəʊstaɪl] *n.* & *adj.* (building) with columns in front only.

protagonist [prəʊ'tægənɪst] *n.* principal character in play, etc.; supporter; contender.

protandry [prəʊ'tændri] *n.* development of male organs before female to avoid self-fertilization. **protandric, protandrous,** *adj.*

protanopia [,prəʊtə'nəʊpiə] *n.* colour blindness towards red. **protanope,** *n.* **protanopic** [–'nɒpɪk], *adj.*

protasis ['prɒtəsɪs] *n.* introductory and explanatory part of drama; subordinate clause in conditional sentence. **protatic** [–'tætɪk], *adj.*

protean [prəʊ'tiːən, 'prəʊtiən] *adj.* pertaining to or like Roman god Proteus, who was able to assume any shape; versatile.

protégé ['prɒtəʒeɪ] *n.* (*fem.* **–ée**) person under another's protection, or in whose career another takes an interest.

protein, proteid ['prəʊtiːn, –iːd] *n.* organic compound of carbon, hydrogen, oxygen and nitrogen, with other elements, essential to life in food and as part of every living cell. **proteinaceous, proteinous,** *adj.*

pro tempore [,prəʊ 'tempəri] (*Latin*) 'for the time (being)'.(*abbr.* **pro tem.**).

protensive [prəʊ'tensɪv] *adj.* extensive in time or lengthwise. **protensity,** *n.*

proteogenous [,prəʊti'ɒdʒənəs] *adj.* derived from protein. **proteolysis,** *n.* disintegration of protein. **proteose,** *n.* substance derived from protein in digestion.

proteranthous [,prəʊte'rænθəs] *adj.* with flowers appearing before leaves.

protervity [prə'tɜːvəti] *n.* petulance.

prothalamion, prothalamium [,prəʊθə'leɪmɪən, –əm] *n.* (*pl.*) **–mia**), song in honour of a marriage.

prothesis ['prɒθəsɪs] *n.* addition of a sound to beginning of a word.

prothorax [prəʊ'θɔːræks] *n.* front segment of thorax.

protocanonical [,prəʊtəʊkə'nɒnɪkl] *adj.* pertaining to the first canon of the bible.

protocol ['prəʊtəkɒl] *n.* preliminary draft of treaty; collection of formulae; rules of procedure and etiquette of state ceremonies, diplomatic exchanges, etc.

protogalaxy [,prəʊtəʊ'gæləksi] *n.* hypothetical

cloud of gas from which present galaxies are thought to have formed.

protogenic [,prəʊtə'dʒenɪk] *adj. Geology*, formed at beginning.

protograph ['prəʊtəgrɑːf] *n.* holograph.

protogyny [prəʊ'tɒdʒɪni] *n.* development of female organs before male to avoid self-fertilization. **protogynous,** *adj.*

protolithic [,prəʊtə'lɪθɪk] *adj.* pertaining to earliest Stone Age.

protomartyr [,prəʊtəʊ'mɑːtə] *n.* first martyr.

protomorphic [,prəʊtə'mɔːfɪk] *adj.* primitive.

proton ['prəʊtɒn] *n.* positively charged particle of atom nucleus.

protonotary, prothonotary [prəʊ'tɒnətəri, ,prəʊtə'nəʊt–] *n. Roman Catholic,* official keeper of canonization records and signatory to papal bull.

protopathic [,prəʊtə'pæθɪk] *adj.* pertaining to reception by nerves, etc. of only coarse stimuli such as heat, pain, etc.; pertaining to such nerves.

protophyte ['prəʊtəfaɪt] *n.* unicellular plant. **protophytic** [–'fɪtɪk], *adj.*

protoplasm ['prəʊtəplæzm] *n.* essential semi-fluid living substance of cells. **protoplasmal, protoplasmatic,** *adj.* **protoplast,** *n.* first-formed person or thing; original ancestor; protoplasmic content of cell. **protoplastic,** *adj.*

prototrophic [,prəʊtə'trɒfɪk] *adj.* feeding directly on uncombined elements.

prototype ['prəʊtətaɪp] *n.* original model or type. **prototypal, prototypic(al)** [–'tɪpɪk, –l], *adj.*

protozoa [,prəʊtə'zəʊə] *n. pl. (sing. –zoon)* the microscopic unicellular animals. **protozoal,** *adj.* **protozoan,** *n.* **protozoology,** *n.* study of these.

protreptic [prə'treptɪk] *adj.* hortatory; doctrinal.

protrusile [prəʊ'truːsaɪl] *adj.* able to be thrust forward (as a frog's tongue).

provection [prə'vekʃn] *n.* carrying forward of sound at end of word to beginning of next (as *a newt* from original form *an ewt*).

proveditor [prə'vedɪtə] *n.* purveyor of supplies.

provedore, providore ['prɒvɪdɔː] *n.* proveditor; steward.

provenance ['prɒvənəns] *n.* source; origin. **provenience** [–'viːniəns], *n.* **provenient,** *adj.* issuing forth.

provident ['prɒvɪdənt] *adj.* prudent, far-sighted; thrifty. **providential,** *adj.* lucky, opportune.

proviso [prə'vaɪzəʊ] *n.* stipulation. **provisory,** *adj.*

provost ['prɒvəst] *(Scottish) n.* mayor; head of cathedral or college. **provost marshal** [prə,vəʊ–], head of military police.

proxenete ['prɒksɪniːt] *n.* procurer; marriage broker.

proxime accessit [,prɒksɪmeɪ ə'kesɪt, –mi æk'se–] *(Latin)* '(he or she) came nearest'; *n.* competitor next to prize-winner.

proximo ['prɒksɪməʊ] *adj.* of next month *(abbr.* **prox.**).

proxy ['prɒksi] *n.* authority giving person power to vote, etc. on behalf of another; such an authorized person.

pruinose ['pruːɪnəʊs] *adj.* bearing whitish dust; hoary. **pruinescence,** *n.* **pruinous,** *adj.*

prurient ['pruərɪənt] *adj.* having indecent desires; lascivious; curious about lewd subjects. **prurience,** *n.*

prurigo [pru'raɪgəʊ] *n.* skin disease with small itching pustules. **pruriginous** [–'rɪdʒɪnəs]

pruritus ['pruərɪtəs] *n.* (condition of) itching of skin. **pruritic** ['rɪtɪk], *adj.*

psaltery ['sɔːltəri] *n.* ancient zither-like musical instrument.

psammophyte ['sæməfaɪt] *n.* plant of arid, sandy soil. **psammophytic** [–'fɪtɪk], *adj.*

psellism ['selɪzm] *n.* defective pronunciation.

psephology [sɪ'fɒlədʒi, siː–] *n.* scientific analysis of political elections and polls. **psephologist,** *n.*

pseudaesthesia [,sjuːdes'θiːʒə, ,suː–] *n.* imaginary feeling, as of pain, etc.

pseudandry ['sjuːdændri, 'suː–] *n.* use by woman of man's name as assumed name.

pseudaposematic [,sjuːdæpəsɪ'mætɪk, ,suː–] *adj.* imitating in colour, etc., a dangerous animal.

pseudepigrapha [,sjuːdɪ'pɪgrəfə, ,suː–] *n. pl.* spurious books supposed to be written by or about Biblical persons but not contained in Apocrypha. **pseudepigraphal,** *adj.* **pseudepigraphic** [–'græfɪk], *adj.* pertaining to pseudepigrapha or pseudepigraphy. **pseudepigraphous,** *adj.* bearing wrong name; wrongly attributed. **pseudepigraphy,** *n.* mistaken attribution of works to wrong authors.

pseudoblepsia [,sjuːdə'blepsiə, ,suː–] *n.* false or imaginary vision.

pseudocarp ['sjuːdəkɑːp, 'suː–] *n.* fruit, as apple, comprising more than mere seeds. **pseudocarpous,** *adj.*

pseudochromaesthesia [,sjuːdəkrəʊmes'θiːʒə, ,suː–] *n.* mental association of sounds with colours. **pseudochromia,** *n.* false colour perception.

pseudochronism [sjuː'dɒkrənɪzm, suː–] *n.* error in date. **pseudochronologist,** *n.* person making this.

pseudocyesis [,sjuːdəʊsaɪ'iːsɪs, ,suː–] *n.* false pregnancy, with symptoms only.

pseudodox ['sjuːdədɒks, 'suː–] *n. & adj.* false (doctrine or opinion).

pseudograph ['sjuːdəgrɑːf, 'suː–] *n.* spurious writing; forgery. **pseudographer,** *n.*

pseudogyny [sjuː'dɒdʒɪni, suː–] *n.* use by man of woman's name as assumed name.

pseudohermaphroditism [,sjuːdəhɜː'mæfrədaɪθɪzm, ,suː–] *n.* congenital abnormality where interior sexual organs are of one sex, external ones the other, or characteristic of both.

pseudology [sjuː'dɒlədʒi, suː–] *n.* telling of lies. **pseudological,** *adj.* wildly exaggerated or untrue. **pseudologue,** *n.* mania for lying.

pseudomonas [,sjuːdə'məʊnəs, ,suː–] *n. (pl. -ades)* any of a genus of rod-like bacteria, many of which cause disease in plants or animals.

pseudomorph ['sjuːdəmɔːf, 'suː–] *n.* false or abnormal form. **pseudomorphic, pseudomorphous,** *adj.* **pseudomorphism,** *n.* **pseudomorphose,** *v.t.* make into this. **pseudomorphosis,** *n.*

pseudonym ['sjuːdənɪm, 'suː–] *n.* assumed name. **pseudonymous** [–'dɒnɪməs], *adj.* **pseudonymity,** *n.*

pseudopodium [,sjuːdə'pəʊdiəm, ,suː–] *n. (pl. -dia),* temporary projection of amoeba, etc. for use as foot or mouth.

pseudopsia [sjuː'dɒpsiə, suː–] *n.* optical illusion.

pseudoscope ['sjuːdəskəʊp, 'suː–] *n.* instrument

producing images in reversed relief. **pseudoscopic** [-'skɒpɪk], *adj.* **pseudoscopy** [-'dɒskəpi], *n.*

pseudovum [sjuː'dəʊvəm, suː-] *n.* (*pl.* **-va**) parthenogenetic egg.

psi [psaɪ, saɪ, psiː] *n.* 23rd letter (Ψ, ψ) of Greek alphabet.

psilanthropy [saɪ'lænθrəpi] *n.* denial of divinity of Christ. **psilanthropic** [-'θrɒpɪk], *adj.* **psilanthropism, psilanthropist,** *n.*

psilosis [saɪ'ləʊsɪs] *n.* falling of hair; sprue.

psittaceous [sɪ'teɪʃəs] *adj.* like or pertaining to parrot; belonging to parrot family of birds. **psittacine** ['sɪt-], *adj.* **psittacism,** *n.* parrot-like repetition in speech. **psittacosis,** *n.* contagious parrot disease, causing fever and pneumonia in humans.

psoas ['səʊəs] *n.* loin muscle; tender-loin. **psoatic,** *adj.*

psora ['sɔːrə] *n.* several itching skin diseases.

psoriasis [sə'raɪəsɪs] *n.* skin disease with white-scaled red eruptions. **psoriatic** [ˌsɔːri'ætɪk], *n. & adj.* (person) suffering from this.

psorophthalmia [ˌsɔːrɒf'θælmiə] *n.* scurfy inflammation of the eyes.

psoroptic [sɔː'rɒptɪk] *adj.* pertaining to scab mite.

psychaesthesia [ˌsaɪkes'θiːʒiə] *n.* sensation in relation to feeling and thought.

psychagogic [ˌsaɪkə'gɒdʒɪk] *adj.* attractive; encouraging. **psychagogy** ['saɪkəgəʊdʒi], *n.* psychiatric treatment by persuading patient to adopt an absorbing interest or life work.

psychalgia [saɪ'kældʒiə] *n.* mental pain or distress.

psychasthenia [ˌsaɪkæs'θiːniə] *n.* acute apathetic neurasthenic condition. **psychasthenic** [-'θenɪk], *adj.*

psyche ['saɪki] *n.* soul; ego; mind.

psychedelic [ˌsaɪkɪ'delɪk] *adj.* 'mind-expanding', denoting drugs or other stimulants producing a state of intensified sensual perception.

psychiatry [saɪ'kaɪətri, sə-] *n.* medical study and treatment of mental disorders. **psychiatrist,** *n.* expert in this. **psychiatric** [-'ætrɪk], *adj.*

psychic ['saɪkɪk] *adj.* pertaining to spirit or mind; having mediumistic powers. **psychical,** *adj.* mental; psychic. **psychicism** [-sɪzm], *n.* research on spiritualistic subjects; mentality.

psychoanalysis [ˌsaɪkəʊə'næləsɪs] *n.* treatment of neurotic persons by the analysis of their neuroses and revelation of their origins; system of such treatment, and body of theories related to it. **psychoanalyse** [-'ænəlaɪz], *v.t.* treat patient in this way. **psychoanalyst,** *n.* **psychoanalytic(al)** [-'lɪtɪk, -l], *adj.*

psychodrama ['saɪkəʊˌdrɑːmə] *n.* psychotherapeutic acting out, especially of situations from patient's earlier life.

psychodynamic [ˌsaɪkədaɪ'næmɪk] *adj.* pertaining to psychological motives and causation.

psychogalvanic [ˌsaɪkəʊgæl'vænɪk] *adj.* pertaining to change in electrical resistance of skin resulting from mental processes which cause alterations in secretion of perspiration. **psychogalvanometer,** *n.* instrument measuring such electric change; lie detector.

psychogenesis [ˌsaɪkə'dʒenəsɪs] *n.* origin in internal or mental state. **psychogenetic** [-dʒə'netɪk], *adj.* **psychogenetics,** *n.* study of this. **psychogenic,** *adj.* derived from the mind.

psychognosis, psychognosy [ˌsaɪkɒg'nəʊsɪs, saɪ'kɒgnəsi] *n.* study of mentality or character. **psychognostic** [-'nɒstɪk], *adj.*

psychogram ['saɪkəgræm] *n.* spirit message; psychological description of person; mental picture. **psychograph,** *n.* instrument recording spirit messages; photographic plate recording spirit image. **psychography,** *n.*

psychokinesis [ˌsaɪkəʊkɪ'niːsɪs, -kaɪ-] *n.* maniacal fit due to inhibitions; psychical production of physical motion.

psycholepsy ['saɪkəlepsi] *n.* period of intense nervous depression and apathy.

psycholinguistics [ˌsaɪkəʊlɪŋ'gwɪstɪks] *n.* psychological study of language.

psychology [saɪ'kɒlədʒi] *n.* study of the mind; mental equipment or state of a person, etc. **psychological,** *adj.* **psychologize,** *v.i. & t.* study psychology; explain in psychological terms. **psychologism,** *n.* doctrine applying psychology to other subjects. **psychologist,** *n.*

psychomachy [saɪ'kɒməki] *n.* conflict of the soul.

psychometer [saɪ'kɒmɪtə] *n.* instrument measuring duration and intensity of mental states.

psychometrics [ˌsaɪkə'metrɪks] *n.* design and use of psychological tests, including statistical techniques. **psychometry** [-'kɒm-], *n.* measurement of mental aptitudes and intelligence; supposed

---

Putting a full stop to it

The full stop (or period, as it is usually called in American English), is the most decisive of punctuation marks. It brings a clause emphatically to a close, signalling the end of the sentence. Material that follows it must begin with a capital letter.

But the full stop does have other roles. In particular, it signals an abbreviation (for example, *abbr.* or *abbrev.* for *abbreviation*). There is a growing tendency, though, to omit this full stop. In particular, abbreviations consisting of capital letters may have none (*ITV, OED, SW*). The same applies to acronyms (*NATO, USDAW*). Remember that the full stop can only come after a letter that represents a full word – so *TV*, for example, should not have a full stop after either the *T* or the *V*.

Abbreviations that end with the final letter of the abbreviated word are sometimes regarded as 'contractions' rather than abbreviations, and some people consider that they should not have a full stop (*Dr, Mrs*).

The full stop is also used to denote decimal places. In handwriting and print it is often raised above the line (2·65), but in typewritten text it usually stays on the line (2.65). In American English, it is standard to put the decimal point on the line.

ability to discover facts about events or people by touching objects relating to them. **psychometrist,** *n.*

psychomorphism [,saɪkə'mɔːfɪzm] *n.* attribution of human mentality to inanimate objects. **psychomorphic,** *adj.*

psychomotor [,saɪkəu'məutə] *adj.* pertaining to physical action as immediate result of mental act.

psychonomics [,saɪkə'nɒmɪks] *n.* psychology.

psychopannychism [,saɪkə'pænɪkɪzm] *n.* belief in sleep of souls from death to bodily resurrection. **psychopannychist, psychopannychite,** *n.*

psychopathy [saɪ'kɒpəθi] *n.* mental disorder. **psychopath,** *n.* dangerously violent person suffering from severe mental disorder. **psychopathic,** *adj.* **psychopathology,** *n.* scientific study of mental disorders.

psychophysics [,saɪkəu'fɪzɪks] *n.* study of relationship between mental and physical processes. **psychophysical,** *adj.* **psychophysicist** [-sɪst], *n.*

psychopomp ['saɪkəpɒmp] *n.* one who conducts souls of dead to afterworld, as Charon.

psychoprophylaxis [,saɪkəuprɒfə'læksɪs] *n.* use of relaxation techniques, etc. to avoid or lessen pain in childbirth.

psychorrhagy [saɪ'kɒrədʒi] *n.* temporary sighting of soul separate from body.

psychosis [saɪ'kəusɪs] *n.* (*pl.* **-ses**) major mental disorder or disease. **psychotic,** *adj.*

psychosomatic [,saɪkəsə'mætɪk] *adj.* pertaining to mind and body as a whole; pertaining to physical disorder etc. caused by stress etc. **psychosome,** ['saɪkəsəum], **psychosoma,** *n.* unit formed by mind and body.

psychosophy [saɪ'kɒsəfi] *n.* doctrine concerning the soul.

psychotaxis [,saɪkə'tæksɪs] *n.* involuntary alteration of mental outlook for the satisfaction of the personality.

psychotechnology [,saɪkəu'teknɒlədʒi] *n.* practical use of psychology in solving problems etc. **psychotechnological,** *adj.*

psychotheism [,saɪkə'θiːɪzm] *n.* belief in pure spirituality of God.

psychotherapy [,saɪkə'θerəpi] *n.* treatment of mental disease using psychological methods. **psychotherapeutic,** *adj.* **psychotherapeutics,** *n.* science of psychotherapy. **psychotherapist,** *n.*

psychotic [saɪ'kɒtɪk] *n. & adj.* (person) affected with psychosis; insane (person). **psychotomimetic,** *adj.* (of drugs) bringing on psychotic behaviour.

psychotoxic [,saɪkə'tɒksɪk] *adj.* damaging to the mind, especially of such addictive drugs.

psychotropic [,saɪkə'trɒpɪk, -'trəu-] *adj.* (of drug) acting on the mind.

psychrometer [saɪ'krɒmɪtə] *n.* wet and dry bulb hygrometer. **psychrometry,** *n.*

psychrophile ['saɪkrəfaɪl] *n.* plant thriving in cold. **psychrophilic** [-'fɪlɪk], *adj.*

psychrophobia [,saɪkrə'fəubiə] *n.* dread of cold.

psychrophyte ['saɪkrəfaɪt] *n.* alpine or arctic plant.

psychurgy ['saɪkɜːdʒi] *n.* mental energy or function.

ptarmic ['tɑːmɪk] *n. & adj.* (substance) causing sneezing.

ptarmigan ['tɑːmɪgən] *n.* kind of northern grouse with white winter plumage and feathered feet.

pteric ['terɪk] *adj.* alar.

pteridium [te'rɪdiəm] *n.* (*pl.* **-ia**) bracken. **pteridography,** *n.* description of ferns. **pteridology,** *n.* study of ferns. **pteridophyte,** *n.* fern.

pterocarpous [,terə'kɑːpəs] *adj* with winged fruits.

pterodactyl [,terə'dæktɪl] *n.* extinct featherless flying reptile. **pterodactylian, pterodactylic, pterodactylid, pterodactylous,** *adj.* **pterodactyloid,** *adj.* like a pterodactyl.

pterography [te'rɒgrəfi] *n.* treatise on or description of feathers. **pterographic(al),** *adj.* **pteropaedes,** *n.pl.* birds capable of flying soon after hatching.

pteropid ['terəpɪd] *n. & adj.* (pertaining to) fruit bat.

pteropod ['terəpɒd] *n.* small swimming mollusc, often shell-less. **pteropodan** [-'rɒpədən], *adj.*

pterospermous [,terə'spɜːməs] *adj.* with winged seeds.

pterygium [te'rɪdʒiəm] *n.* (*pl.* **-ia**) fleshy growth over inner corner of eyeball, common in old age; overgrowth of cuticle. **pterygial,** *adj.*

pterygoid ['terɪgɔɪd] *adj.* wing-like.

pterygote ['terɪgəut] *n. & adj.* (any) of a subclass of insects, comprising winged insects, fleas, etc.

pterylosis [,terɪ'ləusɪs] *n.* arrangement of bird's feathers. **pterylology,** *n.* study of this. **pteryla,** *n.* (*pl.* **-lae,**) any of the feathered areas of a bird's body.

ptilosis [tɪ'ləusɪs] *n.* plumage; loss of eyelashes.

ptisan [tɪ'zæn, 'tɪzn] *n.* kind of barley-water; tisane.

ptochocracy [təu'kɒkrəsi] *n.* government by the poor.

ptomaine ['təumeɪn] *n.* poisonous alkaloid in decaying matter. **ptomainic,** *adj.*

ptosis ['təusɪs] *n.* prolapse; drooping of eyelid. **ptotic** ['təutɪk], *adj.*

ptyalin ['taɪəlɪn] *n.* enzyme, acting on starch, of saliva. **ptyalagogue** [-'ælədɒg], *n.* substance promoting salivation. **ptyalism,** *n.* salivation, especially excessive.

puberty ['pjuːbəti] *n.* time of reaching sexual maturity. **pubertal,** *adj.*

puberulent [pjuː'berʊlənt] *adj.* covered with minute down.

pubes ['pjuːbiːz] *n.* lower abdominal region; hair growing in that region. **pubic,** *adj.* **pubigerous,** *adj.* hairy. **pubis,** *n.* (*pl.* **-bes**) fore-bone of pelvis. **pubescent** [-'besnt], *adj.* reaching or having reached puberty; covered with soft down; *n.* youth at puberty. **pubescence,** *n.*

pucka *adj. see* **pukka.**

pudency ['pjuːdnsi] *n.* modesty; prudery. **pudendal** [-'dendl], *adj.* pertaining to reproductive organs. **pudendum,** *n.* (*pl.* **-da**) external reproductive organ, especially of female. **pudibund,** *adj.* bashful; prudish. **pudic,** *adj.* pudendal. **pudicity,** *n.* modesty; chastity.

pueblo ['pwebləu] (*Spanish*) *n.* town; native tenement house of New Mexico.

puerile ['pjuːəraɪl] *adj.* childish. **puerilism,** *n.* childish conduct. **puerility,** *n.* **puericulture,** *n.* bringing up of children; antenatal care.

puerperal [pjuː'ɜːpərəl] *adj.* pertaining to childbirth. **puerperium** [,pjuːə'pɪəriəm], *n.* condition immediately following childbirth.

pug [pʌg] *n.* any of a breed of small dog with flattened, unwrinkled nose; such a nose; footprint of wild animal. *v.t.* plug or pack with clay etc.; knead clay with water.

pugnacious [pʌg'neɪʃəs] *adj.* eager to fight; belligerent.

puisne ['pjuːni] *adj.* inferior; junior.

puissant ['pwiːsɒnt, 'pwɪsnt] *adj.* powerful. **puissance,** *n.*

puja, pooja ['puːdʒɑː] *n.* Hindu rite or act of worship.

pukka ['pʌkə] (*Anglo-Indian*) *adj.* good; sound; reliable; genuine.

puku ['puːkuː] *n.* red Central African antelope.

pulchritude ['pʌlkrɪtjuːd] *n.* physical beauty. **pulchritudinous,** *adj.*

pulicine ['pjuːlɪsaɪn] *adj.* pertaining to fleas. **pulicose, pulicous,** *adj.* infested with fleas. **pulicosity,** *n.* such infestation. **pulicid,** *n.* & *adj.* **pulicide,** *n.* substance killing fleas. **pulicoid,** *adj.* flea-like.

pullulate ['pʌljuleɪt] *v.i.* sprout forth; bud; teem. **pullulant,** *adj.* **pullulation,** *n.*

pulmogastric [ˌpʌlmə'gæstrɪk] *adj.* pertaining to lungs and stomach.

pulmometry [pʌl'mɒmətri] *n.* measurement of lungs' capacity.

pulmonary ['pʌlmənəri] *adj.* pertaining to or like lungs; having lungs. **pulmonate,** *adj.* having lungs. **pulmonic** [–'mɒnɪk], *adj.* pulmonary; affecting lungs; pneumonic; *n.* medicine for, or person with, lung disease.

pulque ['pʊlki, 'pʊlkeɪ] (*Spanish*) *n.* Mexican fermented drink made from agave.

pulsar ['pʌlsɑː] *n.* a heavenly body emitting radio pulses of extreme regularity.

pulsatile ['pʌlsətaɪl] *adj.* vibrating; pulsating; *Music,* percussive; *n.* percussion instrument. **pulsatility,** *n.*

pulsatilla [ˌpʌlsə'tɪlə] *n.* pasqueflower.

pulsimeter [pʌl'sɪmɪtə] *n.* pulse measuring instrument.

pultaceous [pʌl'teɪʃəs] *adj.* pulpy; like porridge.

pultun, pultan ['pʌltən] (*Indian*) *n.* native infantry regiment.

pulverize ['pʌlvəraɪz] *v.t.* reduce to powder or fragments; grind; smash. **pulveraceous, pulverous, pulverulent** [–'verʊlənt], *adj.* covered with dust; dusty; crumbling into dust. **pulverulence,** *n.*

pulvillus [pʌl'vɪləs] *n.* pad on feet of flies. **pulvillar,** *adj.* like a cushion or pad. **pulvilliform,** *adj.* pulvillar. **pulvinate** *adj.* swelling; pulvillar. **pulvination,** *n.* swelling; bulge. **pulviniform,** *adj.*

pulwar ['pʌlwɑː] *n.* light flat-bottomed Indian river boat.

pumpernickel ['pʌmpənɪkl, 'pʊm–] (*German*) *n.* kind of rye bread.

punaluan [ˌpuːnɑː'luːən] *adj.* pertaining to primitive group marriage of a number of brothers to a number of sisters.

puncheon ['pʌntʃən] *n.* large cask, with capacity of seventy gallons; engraved punch or die; short upright timber for load-bearing.

punctate ['pʌŋkteɪt] *adj.* like or ending in a point; like a dot; bearing spots; pitted. **punctal,** *adj.* like a point. **punctatim,** (*Latin*) *adv.* 'point for point'. **punctation,** *n.* **puncticular, puncticulate,** *adj.* bearing small spots. **punctiform,** *adj.* pointlike.

punctilio [pʌŋk'tɪliəu] *n.* small point or detail of conduct; close observance of such points. **punctilious,** *adj.*

punctulate ['pʌŋktjulət] *adj.* bearing small spots. **punctule,** *n.* small spot. **punctulation,** *n.*

pundigrion [pʌn'dɪgriən] *n. obsolete,* play on words; pun.

pundit ['pʌndɪt] *n.* learned man, especially Hindu; critic, authority. **punditry,** *n.*

pungent ['pʌndʒənt] *adj.* having sharp, bitter flavour or acid smell; incisive, caustic (of wit etc.);- *Botany,* ending in a sharp point. **pungency,** *n.*

puniceous [pju'nɪʃəs] *adj.* bright or purplish red.

punitive ['pjuːnətɪv] *adj.* pertaining to or inflicting punishment. **punitory,** *adj.*

punk [pʌŋk] *n.* decayed wood; tinder made from dried fungus impregnated with saltpetre.

punkah ['pʌŋkə] *n.* large fan, especially moved by rope. **punkah-wallah,** *n.* servant moving this.

punnet ['pʌnɪt] *n.* shallow fruit basket.

punto ['pʌntəu] (*Italian*) *n.* hit as in fencing.

pupa ['pjuːpə] *n.* (*pl.* **-ae**) quiescent stage of insect's development betweenlarval and adult stages; chrysalis. **pupal,** *adj.* **pupiform,** *adj.* like a pupa. **pupate,***v.i.* pass chrysalis stage. **pupation,** *n.*

pupillage ['pjuːpɪlɪdʒ] *n.* state of being a pupil or under age. **pupillary,** *adj.* pertaining to pupil or guardianship; pertaining to pupil of eye.

purblind ['pɜːblaɪnd] *adj.* half-blind; dull-witted; obtuse.

purdah ['pɜːdə] *n.* curtain concealing some Indian women of high birth; system of concealing such women from public gaze.

purée ['pjʊəreɪ] (*French*) *n.* pulpy mixture; boiled and sieved food; thick soup.

purfle ['pɜːfl] *v.t.* ornament edges of, especially with embroidery; *n.* such edge ortrimming. **purfling,** *n.*

purgatory ['pɜːgətəri] *n.* place of suffering or purification; *Roman Catholic,* stateintermediate between death and Heaven where sin is punished. **purgatorial,** *adj.*

puriform ['pjʊərɪfɔːm] *adj.* like pus.

Purim ['pʊərɪm, pu'riːm] (*Hebrew*) *n.* Jewish festival (14th day of Adar) celebrating deliverance of Jews from Haman.

purl [pɜːl] *v.i.* (of stream etc.) ripple along, murmuring; *n.* this sound; a knitting stitch; gold or silver thread; decorative, often lacy, border.

purlicue ['pɜːlɪkjuː] (*Scottish*) *n.* space between extended thumb and index finger; curl or flourish in writing;summary of speeches; peroration; *pl.* caprices.

purlieus ['pɜːljuːz] *n. pl.* neighbourhood; suburb(s).

purport ['pɜːpɔːt] *n.* conveyed or implied meaning; [pə'pɔːt] *v.t.* profess, seem to mean.

purpresture [pə'prestʃə] *n.* wrongful seizing of, or encroachment on, other's or common land.

purpura ['pɜːpjʊrə] *n.* any of several blood diseases causing purplish patches on skin. **purpura haemorrhagica,** purpura with severe haemorrhage; similar fever of horses.

purpureal, purpureous [pɜː'pjʊəriəl, -iəs] *adj.* purple. **purpurescent,** *n.* becoming or somewhat purple. **purpurogenous,** *adj.* causing purple colour.

pur sang [ˌpuə 'sɒŋ] (*French*) 'pure blood'; *adj.* pure-blooded.

pursuivant ['pɜːsɪvənt, –swɪ–] *n.* official of College of Heralds inferior to herald.

pursy ['pɜːsɪ] *adj.* short-winded, especially because stout.

purulent ['pjuərulənt] *adj.* pertaining to, containing or discharging pus. **puruloid,** *adj.* like pus. **purulence,** *n.*

purview ['pɜːvjuː] *n.* scope or range of operation; range of vision or comprehension.

pusillanimity [ˌpjuːsɪlæn'ɪmɪtɪ] *n.* cowardice; mean-spiritedness. **pusillanimous** [–'lænɪməs], *adj.*

pustule ['pʌstjuːl] *n.* pus-containing pimple. **pustulant,** *n. & adj.* (medicine) producing pustules. **pustular, pustulatous, pustulose, pustulous,** *adj.* **pustulate,***v.i. & t.*

putamen [pjuː'teɪmen] *n.* fruit stone; membrane lining eggshell. **putaminous** [–'tæmɪnəs], *adj.*

putative ['pjuːtətɪv] *adj.* supposed; believed.

putid ['pjuːtɪd] *adj.* worthless; fetid.

putrefy ['pjuːtrɪfaɪ] *v.i. & t.* rot; decay; fester. **putrefacient, putrefactive,** *adj.* pertaining to or causingputrefaction; *n.* such thing. **putrefaction,** *n.* **putresce,** *v.i. & t.* **putrescent,** *adj.* decaying; tending to decay. **putrescence,** *n.* **putrid,** *adj.* decayed; fetid; morally corrupt. **putrilage,** *n.* thing decaying; products of decay. **putrilaginous,** *adj.*

Putsch [putʃ] (*German*) *n.* rebellion; rising.

puttee ['pʌtɪ] *n.* long strip of cloth wound round lower leg, especially as part of army uniform.

putti ['putɪ] (*Italian*) *n. pl.* (*sing.* **–to**) figures of naked children or cherubsin art.

pyaemia, pyemia [paɪ'iːmɪə] *n.* blood-poisoning accompanied by widespread abscesses. **pyaemic, pyemic,** *adj.*

pyarthrosis [ˌpaɪɑː'θrəusɪs] *n.* suppuration in joint.

pycnometer [pɪk'nɒmɪtə] *n.* kind of bottle for measuring specific gravities or densities. **pycnomorphic, pycnomorphous,** *adj.* (of nerve cells) compact.

pyedog ['paɪdɒɡ] (*Anglo-Indian*) *n.* stray or pariah dog.

pyelitis [ˌpaɪə'laɪtɪs] *n.* inflammation of the kidney outlet.

pygal ['paɪɡl] *adj.* pertaining to rump. **pygalgia** [–'ɡældʒɪə], *n.* pain in rump.

pyic ['paɪɪk] *adj.* pertaining to or discharging pus.

pyknic ['pɪknɪk] *adj.* short, stocky, often fat (person).

pylon ['paɪlən, –ɒn] *n.* towered gateway; any tower-like erection.

pylorus [paɪ'lɔːrəs] *n.* opening from stomach into intestine. **pyloric** [–'lɒrɪk], *adj.*

pyoderma [ˌpaɪə'dɜːmə] *n.* any skin disease resulting in pustules and/or pus.

pyoid ['paɪɔɪd] *adj.* pus-like. **pyogenic,** *adj.* producing pus. **pyorrhoea,** *n.*discharge of pus, especially in inflammation of tooth sockets. **pyosis,***n.* suppuration.

pyracanth ['paɪərəkænθ] *n.* small white-flowered red-berried evergreen shrub; firethorn.

pyranometer [ˌpaɪrə'nɒmɪtə] *n.* instrument measuring solar radiation.

pyrenocarp [paɪ'riːnəkɑːp] *n.* drupe. **pyrenocarpous,** *adj.*

pyrethrum [paɪ'riːθrəm, –'reθ–] *n.* chrysanthemum-like garden plant; kind of insect powder.

pyretic [paɪ'retɪk] *adj.* pertaining to fever. **pyrosis,** *n.* heartburn. **pyretogenic,** *adj.* inducingfever. **pyretology,** *n.* medical study of fevers. **pyretotherapy,** *n.* medical treatment by causing fever.

pyrexia [paɪ'reksɪə] *n.* fever. **pyrexial, pyrexic,** *adj.*

pyrgeometer [ˌpaɪədʒi'ɒmɪtə] *n.* instrument measuring radiation from earth.

pyrgoidal [pɜː'ɡɔɪdl] *adj.* tower-shaped.

pyrheliometer [ˌpaɪəhiːli'ɒmɪtə] *n.* instrument measuring sun's heat. **pyrheliometric** [–'metrɪk], *adj.* **pyrheliometry,***n.*

pyridine ['pɪrɪdiːn] *n.* nitrogenous base used as antiseptic, etc. **pyridic** [paɪ'rɪdɪk], *adj.*

pyriform ['pɪrɪfɔːm] *adj.* pearshaped.

pyrite(s) ['paɪraɪt, –s, paɪ'raɪtiːz] *n.* sulphide of a metal with metallic appearance. **pyritic(al)** [–'rɪtɪk, –l], *adj.* **pyritiferous,** *adj.* yielding pyrites. **pyritize** ['pɪr–], *v.t.* convert into pyrite(s). **pyritoid,** *adj.* like pyrite(s). **pyritology,** *n.* study of pyrites.

pyroelectricity [ˌpaɪrəuɪlek'trɪsəti] *n.* electric charge produced in some crystals by temperature changes.

pyrogen [ˌpaɪrədʒɪ'neɪʃn] *n.* substance inducing fever. **pyrogenesis,** *n.* production of heat. **pyrogenation,** *n.* subjection to heat. **pyrogenic, pyrogenous,** *adj.* due to heat or fever.

pyrognomic [ˌpaɪrəɡ'nɒmɪk] *adj.* easily made incandescent. **pyrognostic,** *adj.* pertaining to, characteristics produced byheat, especially as shown by blowpipe analysis.

pyrography [paɪ'rɒɡrəfɪ] *n.* tracing of designs by burning; 'poker work'. **pyrographer,** *n.* **pyrographic,** *adj.* **pyrogravure,***n.* design traced by pyrography.

pyrolatry [paɪ'rɒlətrɪ] *n.* fire-worship. **pyrolater,** *n.*

pyroligneous *adj.* produced by action of heat on wood.

pyrology [paɪ'rɒlədʒɪ] *n.* study of heat or fever and its effects. **pyrological,** *adj.* **pyrologist,** *n.*

pyrolysis [paɪ'rɒləsɪs] *n.* decomposition due to heat. **pyrolytic** [–'lɪtɪk], *adj.*

pyromachy [paɪ'rɒməkɪ] *n.* use of fire in fighting.

pyromancy ['paɪrəmænsɪ] *n.* divination by flames or fire. **pyromancer,** *n.* **pyromantic,** *adj.*

pyromania [ˌpaɪrə'meɪnɪə] *n.* mania for setting fire to things. **pyromaniac,** *n.* **pyromaniacal,** *adj.*

pyrometer [paɪ'rɒmɪtə] *n.* instrument measuring very high temperatures. **pyrometric** [–'metrɪk], *adj.* **pyrometry,** *n.*

pyrophanous [paɪ'rɒfənəs] *adj.* becoming transparent when heated.

pyrophobia [ˌpaɪrə'fəubɪə] *n.* dread of fire.

pyrophorus [paɪ'rɒfərəs] *n.* (*pl.* **–ri**) substance igniting when exposed to air. **pyrophoric** [–'fɒrɪk], **pyrophorous,** *adj.*

pyroscope ['paɪrəskəup] *n.* kind of optical thermometer or pyrometer.

pyrosis [paɪ'rəusɪs] *n.* heartburn.

pyrostat ['paɪrəstæt] *n.* automatic fire-alarm and

extinguisher; thermostat.

pyrotechnics, pyrotechny [ˌpaɪrə'teknɪks, 'paɪrətekni] *n.* manufacture or display of fireworks. **pyrotechnic(al),** *adj.* **pyrotechnist,** *n.*

pyrotoxin [ˌpaɪrə'tɒksɪn] *n.* pyrogen.

pyrrhic ['pɪrɪk] *n.* ancient Greek war dance; metrical foot of two short syllables; *adj.* pertaining to such dance or foot, or to Pyrrhus, king of Epirus. **Pyrrhic victory,** victory like that of Pyrrhus of Epirus over Romans in 279 BC., when his army sustained tremendous losses; fruitless victory.

Pyrrhonian [pɪ'rəʊnɪən] *adj.* pertaining to Pyrrho, Greek sceptic philosopher of 4th century BC; extremely sceptical. **Pyrrhonism** ['pɪrənɪzm], *n.*

pyrrhotism ['pɪrətɪzm] *n.* red-hairedness.

pythogenic [ˌpaɪθə'dʒenɪk, ˌpɪθ–] *adj.* due to or causing dirt or decay. **pythogenesis,** *n.* **pythogenetic** [–dʒə'netɪk], *adj.*

pythonic *adj.* like a python; like an oracle. **pythonism** ['paɪθən–ɪzm, 'pɪθ–], *n.* possession by oracular spirit; prophecy. **pythoness,** *n.* female seer; prophesying priestess at oracle of Apollo. **pythonist,** *n.* soothsayer.

pyx *n.* vessel for reservation of Eucharist; box containing specimens of newly-minted coins. **trial of the pyx,** test for weight, etc., of newly-minted coins.

Q

qua [kweɪ, kwɑː] (*Latin*) *conj.* 'as'; in capacity of.

quad [kwɒd] *n. abbreviation* of quadrat; *v.t.* fill with quadrats.

quadra ['kwɒdrə] *n.* plinth; square frame.

quadragenerian [ˌkwɒdrədʒə'neəriən] *n. & adj.* (person) in from fortieth to fiftieth year.

Quadragesima [ˌkwɒdrə'dʒəsimə] *n.* first Sunday of Lent. **Quadragesimal,** *adj.* pertaining to Lent; consisting of forty, especially consisting of, or lasting, forty days.

quadragintesimal [ˌkwɒdrədʒin'tesiml] *adj.* in forty parts; forty-fold.

quadral ['kwɒdrəl] *adj.* in four parts.

quadrant ['kwɒdrənt] *n.* quarter of circumference of circle; instrument for measuring altitudes. **quadrantal** [-'dræntl], *adj.*

quadrat ['kwɒdrət] *n.* small square area or block, especially used as space in printing (*abbr.* quad).

quadrate ['kwɒdreɪt] *v.i. & t.* square; agree; make to agree; *n. & adj.* ['kwɒdrət], square; oblong; *Astronomy,* distant 90° from each other. **quadratic** [-'drætɪk], *adj.* square; applied to algebraic expression containing square but no higher power of unknown quantity; *n.* such equation. **quadratics,** *n.* algebra dealing with quadratic equations.

quadrature ['kwɒdrətʃə], *n.* problem or act of finding square with area equal of another known figure; act of determining areas; *Astronomy,* relation of quadrate heavenly bodies.

quadrel ['kwɒdrəl] *n.* small block (of stone, wood etc.).

quadrennial [kwɒ'dreniəl] *adj.* lasting four years; occurring every fourth year; *n.* fourth anniversary. **quadrennium,** *n.* (*pl.* **–nia**) period of four years.

quadricentennial [ˌkwɒdrisen'teniəl] *n. & adj.* (pertaining to) four hundredth anniversary.

quadriceps ['kwɒdriseps] *n.* thigh muscle extending leg.

quadrifid ['kwɒdrɪfɪd] *adj.* divided into four portions.

quadriform ['kwɒdrɪfɔːm] *adj.* having fourfold form; square.

quadriga [kwɒ'driːgə, –'draɪ–] *n.* (*pl.* **–ae**) four-horse chariot.

quadrigamist [kwɒ'drɪgəmɪst] *n.* person married four times, especially having four spouses at once.

quadrigeminal, quadrigeminous [ˌkwɒdrɪ'dʒeminl] *adj.* in four similar or equal parts; having two parts, each equally or similarly divided.

quadrilateral [ˌkwɒdrɪ'lætərəl] *n. & adj.* four-sided (figure).

quadrilin ['kwɒdrɪlɪn] *n.* fourfold vaccine, especially giving protection against poliomyelitis, diphtheria, whooping cough, and tetanus.

quadrilingual [ˌkwɒdrɪ'lɪŋgwəl] *adj.* in or speaking four languages.

quadriliteral [ˌkwɒdrɪ'lɪtərəl] *n. & adj.* (form) of four letters or consonants.

quadrille [kwə'drɪl, kwɒ–] *n.* square dance for four or more couples; music for this; 18th-century card-game for four.

quadrillion [kwɒ'drɪljən] *n.* a million trillions (10^{21}); (*American & French*) a thousand trillions (10^{15}).

quadrimum [kwɒ'draɪməm] (*Latin*) *n.* best or oldest wine. **quadrimum merum,** four-years-old wine.

quadrinomial [ˌkwɒdrɪ'nəumiəl] *n. & adj.* (expression) consisting of four terms. **quadrinominal** [–'nɒmɪnl], *adj.*

quadripartite [ˌkwɒdrɪ'pɑːtaɪt] *adj.* pertaining to or for four parts or parties. **quadripartition,** *n.*

quadriplegia [ˌkwɒdrɪ'pliːdʒiə] *n.* paralysis of all four limbs.

quadrisect [ˌkwɒdrɪ'sekt] *v.t.* divide into four equal parts. **quadrisection,** *n.*

quadrisyllable ['kwɒdrɪˌsɪləbl] *n.* word of four syllables. **quadrisyllabic** [–'læbɪk], *adj.*

quadrivalent [ˌkwɒdrɪ'veɪlənt] *adj.* having valency of four.

quadrivial [kwɒ'drɪvɪəl] *adj.* leading in four directions; pertaining to meeting of four ways.

quadrivium [kwɒ'drɪvɪəm] *n.* (*pl.* **–ia**) higher division of seven liberal arts studied in Middle Ages: arithmetic, music, astronomy, geometry.

quadrivoltine [ˌkwɒdrɪ'vɒltaɪn] *adj.* having four broods in one year; *n.* such creature.

quadroon [kwɒ'druːn] *n.* child of white and mulatto parents, having one quarter black ancestry.

quadrual ['kwɒdruəl] *n. & adj.* (number) denoting four.

quadrumanous [kwɒ'druːmənəs] *adj.* (of apes, etc.) with all four feet adapted for use as hands.

quadruped ['kwɒdruped] *n. & adj.* four-footed (mammal). **quadrupedal** [–'druːpɪdl], *adj.*

quaestor ['kwiːstə, 'kwaɪ–] *n.* ancient Roman public treasurer or assistant military commander. **quaestorial,** *adj.*

quaestuary ['kwiːstjuərɪ, 'kwes–] *n. & adj. archaic,* (person) in business for profit, or having profit as sole aim.

quaff [kwɒf, kwɑːf] *v.* drink deeply; drink in long draughts; *n.* a long draught.

quagga ['kwægə] *n.* extinct zebra-like wild ass of S Africa.

quagmire ['kwægmaɪə, 'kwɒ–] *n.* patch of boggy ground; predicament. **quaggy,** *adj.*

quale ['kweɪli] *n.* (*pl.* **–lia**) thing having quality; sensation considered in virtue of its own quality alone; quality having independent existence.

quant [kwɒnt] *n.* punting pole; *v.t.* propel with quant.

quantulum ['kwɒntjʊləm] *n.* small quantity.

quantum ['kwɒntəm] *n.* (*pl.* **–ta**) large, necessary or allotted amount; share; unit of energy in quantum theory. **quantum leap**, sudden, momentous advance or breakthrough; *Physics*, abrupt transition from one energy level to another. **quantum theory**, theory that atoms emit or absorb energy by steps, each of which is the emission or absorption of a discrete amount of energy (the quantum).

quaquaversal [,kweɪkwə'vɜːsl] *adj.* dipping in all directions; dome-like.

quarantine ['kwɒrəntiːn] *n.* time for which, and place where, ships, persons or animals suspected of infection are isolated; *v.t.* place in quarantine.

quarender, quarenden ['kwɒrəndə, –ən] *n.* kind of dark red apple.

quark [kwaːk] *n.* hypothetical sub-atomic entity with fractional electric charge, the supposed material from which hadrons are built up.

quartan ['kwɔːtn] *n. & adj.* (fever) recurring after approximately seventy-two hours.

quarto ['kwɔːtəʊ] *n.* book size made by folding sheet into four leaves: **foolscap quarto**, 8½ in. × 6¾ in.; **crown quarto**, 10 in. × 7½ in.; **demy quarto**, 11¼ in. × 8¼ in.; **royal quarto**, 12½ in. × 10 in.; **imperial quarto**, 15 in. × 11 in. (*abbr.* **4to**).

quasar ['kweɪzaː, –saː] *n.* a heavenly body, from 4,000 million to 10,000 million light years distant, that is a powerful source of radio energy: *abbreviation* of quasi-stellar radio source.

quasi ['kweɪzaɪ, 'kweɪs–, 'kwaːz–, –i] *adj. & adv.* as if; seemingly; in a manner.

quassia ['kwɒʃə] *n.* drug obtained from certain tropical American trees, used as tonic, insecticide, etc.

quatercentenary [,kwætəsen'tiːnəri, ,kweɪ–] *n.* four-hundredth anniversary.

quaternary [kwə'tɜːnəri] *n.* four; set of four; *adj.* in four parts; in sets of four; *Geology*, applied to period following Tertiary. **quaternion**, *n.* set of four; *Mathematics*, quotient of two vectors, or factor changing (by multiplication) one vector into another. **quaternity**, *n.* state of being fourfold.

quatorzain [kə'tɔːzeɪn, 'kætə–] *n.* 14-line poem; sonnet.

quatrain ['kwɒtreɪn] *n.* stanza of four lines.

quatrefoil ['kætrəfɔɪl] *n.* any figure like leaf or flower with four leaflets. **quatrefoliated**, *adj.*

quattrocento [,kwætrəʊ'tʃentəʊ, ,kwaː–] (*Italian*) *n. & adj.* 15th century.

quean [kwiːn] *n.* virago; lewd woman; (*Scottish*) unmarried woman or girl.

quebracho [keɪ'braːtʃəʊ] *n.* several tropical American trees and their timber or bark.

quenelle [kə'nel] *n.* fish or meat forcemeat ball.

quenouille [kə'nwiː] (*French*) *adj.* applied to training of trees, etc., into cone-like outline.

quercetum [kwɜː'siːtəm] *n.* oak plantation.

querimony ['kwerɪməni] *n.* complaint. **querimonious** [–'məʊniəs], *adj.*

quern [kwɜːn] *n.* hand-power grinding mill.

querulent ['kwerʊlənt, –jʊ–] *n. & adj.* habitually and abnormally suspicious (person). **querulous**, *adj.* peevish; fretful; complaining.

question   extraordinaire   [,kestjɒn ,ekstrəɔːdɪ'neə] (*French*) *n.* final or severest torture.

quidam ['kwiːdæm, 'kwaɪ–] (*Latin*) *pron.* somebody; unknown person.

quiddity ['kwɪdəti] *n.* quintessence; equivocation; triviality. **quidditative**, *adj.*

quidnunc ['kwɪdnʌŋk] *n.* gossiper; inquisitive person.

quid pro quo [,kwɪd prəʊ 'kwəʊ] (*Latin*) 'what for which'; equivalent; thing given in return.

quiescent [kwi'esnt, kwaɪ–] *adj.* resting; dormant. **quiescence, quiescency**, *n.*

quietism ['kwaɪətɪzm] *n.* kind of mysticism in which indifference to world is obtained by passive contemplation of divinity; passivity. **quietist**, *n.*

quietus [kwaɪ'iːtəs] *n.* receipt; release; act of dispatching or disposing of; knock-out or fatal blow; death.

qui-hi [kə'haɪ] (*Indian*) *n.* Anglo-Indian call for a

Quoting from memory

Quotation marks, or **inverted commas**, have three main uses. The commonest is the marking off of words that are not the author's own: 'Are you coming?' asked Jack (the words are Jack's, not the writer's). This way of showing what is said is known as **reported speech**, or **direct speech**, and contrasts with **indirect speech**, where quotation marks are not used: Jack asked if I was coming. Their second use is around the names of short poems, short stories, articles, parts of books, short pieces of music, etc.: Keats's 'Ode to Autumn'. By contrast, the names of books, plays, films, long poems and pieces of music, etc. are usually italicized. The third use of quotation marks is to mark words that do not quite fit precisely or in the expected way into the context in which they are used: for instance, words used ironically (With 'friends' like that, who needs enemies?), or words from a different level of the language (Readers need a regular 'fix' of excitement).

In British printed texts it is usual to use single quotation marks (' '), in American printed texts, double quotation marks (" "). In handwritten and typed texts, double quotation marks are normal. For quotes within quotes, the contrasting quotation mark is used ('Who was it who said "I want to be alone"?' he asked).

In American English, commas and full stops always come before the closing quotation mark ("I thought as much," she mused). British English usually follows this order before a verb phrase that presents direct speech such as *she mused*, but in other circumstances commas and full stops often come after the closing quotation mark (With such 'friends', who needs enemies?)

servant.

quillet ['kwɪlɪt] *n. archaic,* quibble; small tube.

quinary ['kwaɪnəri] *adj.* pertaining to or comprising five; in fives; *Mathematics,* having five as base.

quincentenary [ˌkwɪnsen'tiːnəri] *n. & adj.* (pertaining to) five hundredth anniversary.

quincunx ['kwɪŋkʌnks] *n.* four corners and centre of rectangle; arrangement of five things in those positions. **quincuncial** [–'kʌnʃl], *adj.*

quindecagon [kwɪn'dekəgən] *n.* 15-sided plane figure. **quindecasyllabic,** *adj.* having 15 syllables. **quindecennial,** *adj.* pertaining to 15 years.

quinquagenarian [ˌkwɪŋkwədʒə'neəriən] *n. & adj.* (person) in from fiftieth to sixtieth year. **quinquagenary,** [–'kwædʒɪnəri], *adj.* fifty-year-old; *n.* 50th anniversary.

Quinquagesima [ˌkwɪŋkwə'dʒesɪmə] *n.* Sunday before Lent. **Quinquagesimal,** *adj.* pertaining to fifty days.

quinquennial [kwɪŋ'kweniəl] *adj.* lasting five years; occurring every fifth year. **quinquennium,** *n.* (*pl.* **–nia**) period of five years.

quinsy ['kwɪnzi] *n.* severe inflammation of tonsils and throat.

quintain ['kwɪntən] *n.* object, or target, tilted at; tilting at quintain.

quintal ['kwɪntl] *adj.* hundred weight; 100 lb; metric unit of 100 kg.

quintan ['kwɪntən] *n. & adj.* (fever) recurring after five days (*i.e.* every fourth day).

quintant ['kwɪntənt] *n.* instrument having arc of fifth part of circumference of circle for taking altitudes.

quintessence [kwɪn'tesns] *n.* purest essence. **quintessential** [–'senʃl], *adj.*

quintic ['kwɪntɪk] *adj. Mathematics,* of or pertaining to fifth degree.

quintillion [kwɪn'tɪljən] *n.* a million quadrillions (10³⁰); (*American & French*) a thousand quadrillions (10¹⁸).

quintroon [kwɪn'truːn] *n.* child of white and octoroon.

quipu ['kiːpuː] *n.* device of knotted cords, used by Incas of Peru to calculate or order information.

quire [kwaɪə] *n.* two dozen sheets of paper.

Quirinal ['kwɪrɪnl] (*Italian*) *adj.* Italian court or government.

quisling ['kwɪzlɪŋ] *n.* traitor collaborating with enemy occupiers of his or her country.

quitrent ['kwɪtrent] *n.* small nominal rent commuting feudal services.

qui vive [ˌkiː 'viːv] (*French*) 'who goes there?'**on the qui vive,** on the alert.

quixotic [kwɪk'sɒtɪk] *adj.* idealistic; altruistic; unpractical. **quixotism, quixotry,** *n.*

quod erat demonstrandum [ˌkwɒd ˌeræt demən'strændəm] (*Latin*) 'which was to be demonstrated' (*abbr.* **Q.E.D.**). **quod erat faciendum** [–fæki'endəm, –feɪʃ–], 'which was to be done' (*abbr.* **Q.E.F.**).

quodlibet ['kwɒdlɪbet] (*Latin*) 'what you like'; moot or subtle point; fruitless or pedantic argument.

quod vide [ˌkwɒd 'vɪdeɪ, –'vaɪdi] (*Latin*) (*pl.* **quae vide**) 'which see' (*abbr.* **q.v.**; **pl.** *abbr.* **qq.v.**).

quoin [kɔɪn, kwɔɪn] *n.* angle; wedge; cornerstone.

quondam ['kwɒndæm] (*Latin*) *adv.* 'formerly'; *adj.* former.

quorum ['kwɔːrəm] *n.* minimum number of members whose presence is necessary at a meeting; select body of persons. **quorate,** *adj.*

quota ['kwəʊtə] *n.* due share; amount allowed to be imported from a certain country.

quotidian [kwə'tɪdiən] *adj.* daily; *n.* fever recurring daily.

quotient ['kwəʊʃnt] *n.* answer of division sum.

quo vadis [ˌkwəʊ 'vɑːdɪs] (*Latin*) 'whither goest thou?'

R

rabbet ['ræbɪt] *n.* groove into which projection fits; frame against which door, etc., closes; *v.t.* cut such groove; join with a rabbet.

rabbinical [ræ'bɪnɪkl] *adj.* pertaining to rabbis and Talmud; denoting a kind of simplified Hebrew alphabet. **rabbinism**, *n.* teaching of rabbis and Talmud.

rabboni [ræ'bəʊnaɪ] (*Hebrew*) *n.* 'my great master', as title of respect.

Rabelaisian [ˌræbə'leɪzɪən] *adj.* pertaining to or like the coarse, uproarious humour of François Rabelais (16th century French writer).

rabid ['ræbɪd, 'reɪ–] *adj.* furious; fanatical; mad; pertaining to rabies. **rabidity**, *n.*

rabies ['reɪbiːz] *n.* infectious madness in dogs; hydrophobia. **rabic, rabietic** [–i'etɪk], *adj.* **rabific, rabigenic**, *adj.* causing rabies. **rabiform**, *adj.* like rabies.

raccoon [rə'kuːn] *n.* squirrel-like animal of N America and Mexico, and its fur.

raceme ['ræsiːm] *n.* kind of inflorescence with flowers borne on footstalks up a central stem, as in lily of valley. **racemiferous**, *adj.* bearing racemes. **racemiform**, *adj.* like raceme. **racemose, racemous** ['ræs–], *adj.*.

rach(e) [rætʃ] *n.* dog hunting by scent.

rachis ['reɪkɪs] *n.* (*pl.* **–ides**) spine; central axis. **rachialgia**, *n.* pain in spine. **rachidian**, *adj.* **rachiform**, *adj.* like rachis. **rachiometer**, *n.* instrument measuring spinal curvature.

rachitis [rə'kaɪtɪs] *n.* inflammation of spine; rickets. **rachitic** [–'kɪtɪk], *adj.* pertaining to or having rachitis. **rachitogenic**, *adj.* causing rachitis.

rackrent ['rækrent] *n.* reasonable rent, equivalent of two-thirds or more of annual value of building for which it is paid; *popularly* excessive rent.

raconteur [ˌrækɒn'tɜːr] (*French*) *n.* (*fem.* **–euse,**) [–'tɜːz] anecdote-teller.

racoon *see* **raccoon.**

radectomy [rə'dektəmi] *n.* removal of part of tooth root.

radical ['rædɪkl] *adj.* pertaining to, like, deriving from or striking at root; fundamental; extreme; *Mathematics*, pertaining to radix; *n.* root; fundamental principle; advocate of radical, especially socialistic, policy; basic constituent of chemical compound; group of atoms replaceable by single atom. **radical sign**, *Mathematics*, sign √ indicating extraction of root.

radicel ['rædɪsel] *n.* rootlet.

radicle ['rædɪkl] *n.* rootlike organ or part; *Botany*, portion of seed developing into root; *Chemical*, radical. **radicolous**, *adj.* living on roots. **radicular**, *adj.* **raduculitis**, *n.* inflammation of nerve root. **radiculose**, *adj.* having many rootlets.

radioastronomy [ˌreɪdɪəʊə'strɒnəmi] *n.* branch of astronomy studying the sources of radio waves reaching earth from outer space.

radiocarbon [ˌreɪdɪəʊ'kɑːbən] *n.* radioisotope of carbon, especially carbon-14. **radiocarbon dating**, estimation of age of organic matter by measuring carbon-14 content.

radiodontia [ˌreɪdɪə'dɒnʃɪə] *n.* making and study of X-ray photographs of teeth. **radiodontic**, *adj.* **radiodontist**, *n.*

radio galaxy ['reɪdɪəʊ ˌgæləksi] *n.* galaxy that is a strong source of radio waves.

radiogenic [ˌreɪdɪəʊ'dʒenɪk] *adj.* produced by radioactive decay; suitable for radio broadcasting.

radiogoniometer [ˌreɪdɪəgəʊni'ɒmɪtə] *n.* radio direction-finding apparatus. **radiogoniometry**, *n.*

radiogram ['reɪdɪəgræm] *n.* telegram transmitted by radio; combined gramophone and radio receiver; radiograph.

radiography [ˌreɪdɪ'ɒgrəfi] *n.* making and study of X-ray photographs. **radiograph**, *n.* X-ray photograph or image. **radiographer, radiographic(al)**, *adj.*

radio-heliograph [ˌreɪdɪəʊ'hiːlɪəgrɑːf] *n.* arrangement of radio-telescopes for receiving and recording the radio waves emitted by the sun.

radioisotope [ˌreɪdɪəʊ'aɪsətəʊp] *n.* radioactive isotope; radioactive form of an element.

radiology [ˌreɪdɪ'ɒlədʒi] *n.* science of X-rays and their medical application. **radiological**, *adj.* **radiologist**, *n.*

radiolucent [ˌreɪdɪəʊ'luːsnt] *adj.* penetrable by X-rays.

radiometer [ˌreɪdɪ'ɒmɪtə] *n.* instrument measuring energy emitted by radioactive substance, or sun's radioactivity. **radiometric** [–'metrɪk], *adj.* **radiometry**, *n.*

radiomicrometer [ˌreɪdɪəʊmaɪ'krɒmɪtə] *n.* instrument measuring intensity of radioactivity.

radionuclide [ˌreɪdɪəʊ'njuːklaɪd] *n.* a radioactive nuclide.

radiopaque [ˌreɪdɪəʊ'peɪk] *adj.* not allowing passage of X-rays. **radiopacity**, *n.*

radiopraxis [ˌreɪdɪəʊ'præksɪs] *n.* medical use of radioactivity.

radioscope ['reɪdɪəskəʊp] *n.* instrument detecting radioactivity. **radioscopy** [–'ɒskəpi], *n.* examination of opaque bodies by X-rays.

radiosonde ['reɪdɪəʊsɒnd] *n.* radio transmitter, borne into and from upper atmosphere by balloon and parachute, sending out information on atmospheric conditions.

radio-telescope [ˌreɪdɪəʊ'telɪskəʊp] *n.* device, often a large parabolic reflector, for receiving and focusing radio waves from outer space.

radiotherapy [ˌreɪdɪəʊ'θerəpɪ] *n.* medical treatment by X-rays. **radiotherapeutics**, *n.* **radiotherapist**, *n.*

radiotropism [ˌreɪdɪ'ɒtrəpɪzm] *n.* direction of growth by radioactivity. **radiotropic** [–ə'trɒpɪk], *adj.*

radium ['reɪdɪəm] *n.* rare radioactive metallic element found in pitchblende, etc. **radiumtherapy**, *n.* medical treatment by radium.

radix ['reɪdɪks] *n.* (*pl.* **–dices**) root; *Mathematics,* base of a numerical system, as 10 is of decimal system.

radome ['reɪdəʊm] *n.* protective housing for radar antenna.

radon ['reɪdɒn] *n.* gaseous emanation of radium.

radula ['rædjʊlə] *n.* (*pl.* **–ae**) rasp-like toothed band of tissue in mollusc's mouth. **radular,** *adj.* **radulate,** *adj.* having radula. **raduliform,** *adj.* rasp-like.

raga ['rɑːɡə, rɑːɡ] *n.* traditional melody used as basis for improvisation in Indian music; piece based on raga.

ragout [ræ'ɡuː] *n.* highly seasoned stew of vegetables and meat.

rail [reɪl] *n. Ornithology,* kind of small crane-like wading bird. **land rail,** corncrake.

rais [raɪs] (*Arabic*) *n.* chief; captain.

raison d'être [ˌreɪzɒn 'detr] (*French*) *n.* 'reason for being'; justification for existence. **raison d'état** [–'deɪ'tɑː], 'reason of state'.

raisonné ['reɪzɒneɪ] (*French*) *adj.* systematically arranged; ordered.

raj [rɑːdʒ] (*Hindi*) *n.* rule. **rajah,** *n.* prince; king; ruler. **rajput,** *n.* member of N Indian ruling caste.

rale [rɑːl] *n.* sound symptomatic of disease heard in auscultation.

ralliform ['rælɪfɔːm] *adj.* like the rails (birds). **ralline,** *adj.* pertaining to rails.

ramage ['ræmɪdʒ] *n.* boughs of tree. **ramal, rameal** ['reɪ–], *adj.* pertaining to branch.

ramekin, ramequin ['ræmɪkɪn] *n.* small baking dish or mould for individual portion; food cooked in such dish.

ramellose ['ræmələʊs] *adj.* having small branches.

ramentaceous [ˌræmən'teɪʃəs] *adj.* bearing, like or consisting of small shavings or chaffy scales. **ramental** [–'mentl], *adj.* **ramentiferous,** *adj.* bearing such scales. **ramentum,** *n.* (*pl.* **–ta**) shaving; chaffy scale on young ferns.

rameous ['reɪmɪəs] *adj.* ramal.

ramex ['reɪmeks] *n.* hernia.

ramie ['ræmɪ] *n.* fibre-yielding E Asiatic plant; its fibre, used in manufacture of gas-mantles, etc.; China grass.

ramiferous [rə'mɪfərəs] *adj.* bearing branches. **ramiform** ['ræm–], *adj.* branch-like.

ramify ['ræmɪfaɪ] *v.i. & t.* branch out; make complex. **ramification,** *n.*

ramoneur [ˌræməʊ'nɜː] (*French*) *n.* chimney-sweep.

ramose ['ræməʊs] *adj.* branched. **ramous** ['reɪməs], *adj.* ramose; ramiform.

rampant ['ræmpənt] *adj. Heraldry,* rearing up on hind legs; fierce; dominating; exuberant; unrestrained; rank; *Architecture,* having one abutment higher than other. **rampancy,** *n.*

rampion ['ræmpɪən] *n.* kind of campanula with root used in salad.

ramsons ['ræmzɒnz] *n. pl.* kind of garlic with root used in salad.

ramulus ['ræmjʊləs] *n.* (*pl.* **–li**) small branch. **ramular,** *adj.* **ramuliferous,** *adj.* bearing ramuli. **ramulose, ramulous,** *adj.* having many ramuli.

ramus ['reɪməs] *n.* (*pl.* **–mi**) branch, especially of nerve; barb of feather; mandible.

rana ['rɑːnɑː] (*Hindi*) *n.* prince.

ranarium [rə'neərɪəm] *n.* (*pl.* **–ia**) place for rearing frogs.

rand [rænd] (*S African*) *n.* mountains flanking river valley; unit of S African currency. **the Rand,** gold-mining district about Johannesburg.

randan ['rændæn, ræn'dæn] *n.* boat for three oarsmen, *viz.* one sculler with two oars in middle and an oarsman with one oar fore and aft; such style of rowing. **randem,** *adv.* with three horses in single file.

ranee, rani ['rɑːniː] (*Hindi*) *n.* queen or princess; wife of rajah.

rangiferine [ræn'dʒɪfəraɪn] *adj.* pertaining to or like reindeer; belonging to animal genus containing reindeer.

ranine ['reɪnaɪn] *adj.* pertaining to or like frogs; belonging to subfamily of amphibians including frogs. **raniform,** *adj.* frog-like.

ranula ['rænjʊlə] *n.* (*pl.* **–ae**) small cyst on tongue. **ranular,** *adj.*

ranunculaceous [rəˌnʌnkju'leɪʃəs] *adj.* pertaining to or like buttercups; belonging to buttercup family of plants. **ranunculus,** *n.* (*pl.* **–li**) buttercup, especially cultivated.

rapacious [rə'peɪʃəs] *adj.* greedy; obtaining by extortion; predacious; ravenous. **rapacity** [–'pæsəti], *n.*

rapine ['ræpaɪn] *n.* pillaging.

rapparee [ˌræpə'riː] (*Irish*) *n.* irregular soldier; vagabond.

rappee [ræ'piː] *n.* kind of strong snuff.

rapport [ræ'pɔː] *n.* relationship, especially harmonious. **en rapport** [ɒn–], (*French*) 'in rapport'.

rapprochement [ræ'prɒʃmɒn] (*French*) *n.* resumption of or improvement in relations between countries or persons.

raptorial, raptatorial, raptatory [ræp'tɔːrɪəl, ˌræptə'tɔːrɪəl, 'ræptətəri] *adj.* predatory; pertaining to birds of prey.

raptus ['ræptəs] *n.* trance; rapture; seizure.

rara avis [ˌreərə 'eɪvɪs] (*Latin*) *n.* (*pl.* **rarae aves**) 'rare bird'; any unusual person or thing, especially of excellence.

rarefy [ˌreərɪfaɪ] *v.t.* make thin, rare or tenuous. **rarefaction,** *n.*

ras [rɑːs] *n.* headland; Abyssinian prince.

rasorial [rə'sɔːrɪəl] *adj.* scratching ground for food; pertaining to domestic fowls.

ratafia [ˌrætə'fiə] *n.* almond-flavoured liqueur or biscuit.

ratel ['reɪtl, 'rɑː–] *n.* badger-like S African and Indian animal.

Rathaus ['rɑːthaʊs] (*German*) *n.* (*pl.* **–häuser**, [–hɔɪzə]) town hall.

ratify ['rætɪfaɪ] *v.t.* confirm, approve formally. **ratification,** *n.*

ratihabition [ˌrætɪhə'bɪʃn] *n.* ratification.

ratiocinate [ˌrætɪ'ɒsɪneɪt] *v.i.* reason; argue logically. **ratiocinant,** *adj.* reasoning. **ratiocination,** *n.* **rationcinator,** *n.* **ratiocinative,** *adj.*

rationale [,ræʃə'nɑːl] n. fundamental principles or reasons; logical basis.

rationalism ['ræʃn–əlɪzm] n. belief in truth and supreme power of reason; philosophical theory of reason as source of knowledge; deductive method. **rationalist**, n. **rationalistic**, adj.

ratite ['rætaɪt] adj. having flat breastbone; n. such flightless bird, as ostrich, emu, etc.

ratline ['rætlɪn] n. small rope forming rung of rope ladder.

rattan [rə'tæn] n. kind of palm with long jointed stems used for walking-sticks, etc.

ratten ['rætn] v.t. compel to obey trade union by damaging or depriving of machinery, tools, etc.

rauwolfia [rɔː'wulfiə] n. tropical tree or shrub used as source of various drugs, especially reserpine.

ravelin ['rævlɪn] n. projecting out-work in fortification, having two embankments forming salient angle; 'half-moon'.

ravissant [,rævɪ'sɒn] (French) adj. (fem. **-e**, [–ɒnt]) ravishing; causing rapture.

reagent [ri'eɪdʒənt] n. Chemistry, substance used in detecting, measuring, etc. other substances by their reaction with it.

realism ['rɪəlɪzm] n. rationalism; acceptance of existing positions and things, and repudiation of idealism; truth to real life; Philosophy, doctrine of the separate and real existence of universal qualities, or of objects of cognition. **realist**, n. **realistic**, adj.

Realpolitik [reɪ'ɑːlpɒlɪ,tiːk] (German) n. practical politics, especially belief that might is right. **Realpolitiker**, n. believer in Realpolitik.

realty ['rɪəlti] n. real estate, i.e. houses and land. **realtor**, n. American dealer in realty.

Réaumur ['reɪəmjuə] adj. pertaining to temperature scale or thermometer having freezing point of water at 0° and boiling point at 80°.

rebarbative [rɪ'bɑːbətɪv] adj. repulsive.

rebec(k) ['riːbɛk] n. ancient three-stringed violin.

reboant(ic) ['rebəuənt, ,rebəu'æntɪk] adj. reverberating.

rebus ['riːbəs] n. picture puzzle representing word.

recalcitrant [rɪ'kælsɪtrənt] n. & adj. disobedient or stubborn (person). **recalcitrance, recalcitration**, n.

recalesce [,riːkə'les] v.i. liberate heat suddenly when cooling through certain temperature. **recalescent**, adj. **recalescence**, n.

recapitulate [,riːkə'pɪtʃuleɪt] v.i. & t. repeat; summarize. **recapitulation**, n. **recapitulation theory**, theory that in its development an individual organism passes through all the stages of the history of the race to which it belongs. **recapitulative, recapitulatory**, adj.

recension [rɪ'senʃn] n. revision; revised text. **recense**, v.t. make recension of.

recessional [rɪ'seʃn–əl] n. & adj. (hymn) sung during withdrawal of clergy and choir at end of service; concluding voluntary.

réchauffé [reɪ'ʃəufeɪ] (French) n. & adj. warmed-up (dish); rehash.

recherché [rə'ʃeəʃeɪ] (French) adj. refined; carefully done; curious; far-fetched; extravagant.

recidivism [rɪ'sɪdɪvɪzm] n. state of returning habitually to crime. **recidivist**, n. **recidivate**,

recidive ['resɪdɪv], v.i. relapse; recur. **recidivous**, adj.

reciprocal [rɪ'sɪprəkl] adj. mutual; complementary; interchangeable; n. Mathematics, expression the product of which and another is 1. **reciprocate**, v.i. & t. return equally; interchange; alternate; move backwards and forwards. **reciprocation, reciprocity**, [,resɪ'prɒsəti] n.

recision [rɪ'sɪʒn] n. rescission.

recitative [,resɪtə'tiːv] n. speechlike declamatory song in opera, oratorio, etc.

réclame [reɪ'klɑːm] (French) n. publicity.

reclinate ['reklɪneɪt] adj. bending backwards or downwards.

recoct [riː'kɒkt] v.t. cook again; concoct; improvise.

recognisance [rɪ'kɒgnɪzəns, –'kɒn–] n. person's promise to court or magistrate to observe some obligation; sum of money as pledge of this.

recondite ['rekəndaɪt] adj. concealed; abstruse; erudite.

reconnaissance [rɪ'kɒnɪsns] n. military survey of country, disposition of forces, etc.; act of spying out land. **reconnoitre** [,rekə'nɔɪtə], v.i. & t. make reconnaissance (of).

recreant ['rekrɪənt] n. & adj. cowardly or renegade (person). **recreancy**, n.

recrement ['rekrɪmənt] n. redundant matter; dross; Medicine, secretion of body absorbed again by body. **recremental, recrementitial**, adj.

recriminate [rɪ'krɪmɪneɪt] v.t. make countercharge; utter mutual accusations or abuse. **recrimination, recriminator**, n. **recriminative, recriminatory**, adj.

recrudesce [,riːkruː'des] v.i. grow up or break out again. **recrudescence, recrudescency**, n. **recrudescent**, adj.

rectigrade ['rektɪgreɪd] adj. moving in straight line.

rectilinear [,rektɪ'lɪnɪə] adj. pertaining to or bounded by straight lines; rectigrade. **rectilineal**, adj. **rectilinearity**, n.

rectirostral [,rektɪ'rɒstrəl] adj. having straight beak.

rectiserial [,rektɪ'sɪərɪəl] adj. in vertical ranks.

recto ['rektəu] n. right-hand page; front of printed or manuscript page.

rectrices ['rektrɪsiːz] n. pl. (sing. **rectrix**) quill feathers of bird's tail. **rectricial** [–'trɪʃl], adj.

rectum ['rektəm] n. last part of large intestine, leading to anus. **rectal**, adj.

rectus ['rektəs] n. (pl. **-ti**,) straight muscle.

recumbent [rɪ'kʌmbənt] adj. lying at ease. **recumbency**, n.

recusant ['rekjuzənt] n. person refusing to obey command, especially to attend Anglican Church service; adj. disobedient; nonconformist. **recusance, recusancy**, n.

redaction [rɪ'dækʃn] n. preparing for publication; editing; new edition. **redactor**, n. **redactorial**, adj.

redan [rɪ'dæn] n. fieldwork in fortification, with two parapets making salient angle.

redhibition [,redɪ'bɪʃn, –hɪ–] n. cancellation of sale of defective article with its return to vendor. **redhibitory** [–'hɪb–], adj.

redintegrate [rɪ'dɪntɪgreɪt] v.t. make whole again; restore. **redintegration**, n.; Psychology, revival of whole of previous mental state at recurrence of part of it. **redintegrative**, *adj*.

redivivus [,redɪ'vaɪvəs] *adj*. living again.

redolent ['redələnt] *adj*. smelling or smacking (of). **redolence, redolency**, *n*.

redoubt [rɪ'daʊt] *n*. fortification within an outwork.

reductio ad absurdum [rɪ,dʌktiəu æd əb'sɜːdəm, -ʃi-] (*Latin*) *n*. 'reduction to absurdity'; proving a proposition by showing that its opposite is absurd; disproving a proposition by deducing from it an absurd conclusion; such conclusion.

reeve [riːv] *n*. chief magistrate; bailiff; *Canadian*, rural council's president; *Ornithology*, female ruff (bird); *v.t.* pass (rope) through ring; fasten by reeving.

refection [rɪ'fekʃn] *n*. light meal; refreshment. **refectory**, *n*. dining room of monastery, college, etc.

reflet [rə'fleɪ] (*French*) *n*. lustre, irridescence, esp. on pottery.

reflex ['riːfleks] *adj*. turned back; reflected; resulting from reaction; *Psychology*, resulting directly, without conscious will, from a stimulus; *n*. reflected light, etc.; image; involuntary act. **conditioned reflex**, *Psychology*, reflex transferred to new or different stimulus. **reflex angle**, angle greater than 180°. **reflexive**, *adj*. reflex; reflective; *Grammar*, signifying action directed or done to subject; *n*. *Grammar*, such verb or pronoun. **reflexology**, *n*. psychological theory of the reflex nature of all behaviour; treatment of illness and stress by massaging specific points on soles of feet. **reflexologist**, *n*.

refluent ['refluənt] *adj*. flowing back or backward. **refluence**, *n*. **reflux**, *n*. refluence; *Chemistry*, boiling of liquid in flask with condenser attached to minimise evaporation; *v.t. & i.* boil (liquid) thus.

refract [rɪ'frækt] *v.t.* deflect (ray of light etc.) on its passage from a medium to another of different density, with, usually, dispersion or splitting up of the ray; distort. **refraction**, *n*. **refractor**, *n*. **refractional, refractive**, *adj*. **refractometer**, *n*. instrument measuring amount of refraction.

refractory [rɪf'ræktəri] *adj*. stubborn; disobedient; immune; *n*. material resistant to heat, corrosion, fusion, etc.

refrangible [rɪ'frændʒəbl] *adj*. capable of being refracted. **refrangent**, *adj*. refracting.

refringent [rɪ'frɪndʒənt] *adj*. refracting. **refringence, refringency**, *n*.

refulgent [rɪ'fʌldʒənt] *adj*. brightly shining. **refulgence**, *n*.

refute [rɪ'fjuːt] *v.t.* prove to be false or wrong. **refutation** [,ref-], *n*. **refutative, refutatory**, *adj*.

regalism ['riːgl-ɪzm] *n*. doctrine of supremacy of sovereign, especially in ecclesiastical matters.

regardant [rɪ'gɑːdnt] *adj*. *Heraldry*, in profile and looking to rear.

regelation [,riːdʒə'leɪʃn] *n*. freezing again, especially of water from ice melted by pressure when pressure is relieved. **regelate**, *v.t. & i.*

regicide ['redʒɪsaɪd] *n*. killing or killer of king; person who signed death-warrant of Charles I of England, or Louis XVI of France. **regicidal**, *adj*.

régime [reɪ'ʒiːm] (*French*) *n*. system, especially of government.

regimen ['redʒɪmən] *n*. system, especially of diet or way of life. **regiminal** [-'dʒɪmɪnl], *adj*.

regina [rɪ'dʒaɪnə] (*Latin*) *n*. queen. **reginal**, *adj*.

regius ['riːdʒiəs] *adj*. royal. **regius professor**, one holding professorship founded by royalty.

reglementation [,regləmen'teɪʃn] *n*. regulation.

regnal ['regnl] *adj*. pertaining to reign. **regnancy**, *n*. rule. **regnant**, *adj*. reigning.

regurgitate [rɪ'gɜːdʒɪteɪt] *v.i. & t.* throw or pour back, or be thrown or poured back, especially from crop or stomach into mouth; vomit. **regurgitant**, *adj*. **regurgitation**, *n*.

Reichstag ['raɪkstɑːg] (*German*) *n*. German parliament (1867-1933) and parliament building.

reify ['reɪfaɪ, 'riː-] *v.t.* make concrete; materialize. **reification**, *n*.

reimburse [,riːɪm'bɜːs] *v.t.* repay. **reimbursement**, *n*.

re infecta [,riː ɪn'fektə, ,reɪ-] (*Latin*) 'the matter being not completed'.

reis *see* **Rais**.

reiterate [rɪ'ɪtəreɪt] *v.t.* repeat many times. **reiterant**, *adj*. **reiteration**, *n*. **reiterative**, *adj*.; *n*. word signifying repetition of action.

reive [riːv] *v.i. & t.* rob; plunder; carry off. **reiver**, *n*.

rejectamenta [rɪ,dʒektə'mentə] *n. pl.* rejected things; excrement.

rejoinder [rɪ'dʒɔɪndə] *n*. reply to an answer; *Law* defendant's reply to plaintiff's replication.

rejuvenate [rɪ'dʒuːvəneɪt] *v.i. & t.* become or make young again. **rejuvenescence, rejuvenation**, *n*. **rejuvenator**, *n*.

relativity [,relə'tɪvəti] *n*. *Phyics*, principle, formulated by Einstein, and based primarily on the constancy of the velocity of light, denying the absoluteness of space and time and establishing time as 'fourth dimension'. **special theory of relativity**, as above. **general theory of relativity**, conclusions from special theory as it affects gravitation, which is identified with inertia and interpreted by the varying geometrical structure of the space in which masses are moving. **relativity of knowledge**, *Philosophy*, doctrine that knowledge is limited by nature of mind, which is unable to perceive the reality of, but only the relations between, objects.

relegate ['relɪgeɪt] *v.t.* banish; assign, especially to less important place or person. **relegation**, *n*.

relict ['relɪkt] *n*. widow; survivor; *adj*. pertaining to land bared by reliction. **reliction**, *n*. recession of sea leaving land bare; land so left.

religate ['relɪgeɪt] *v.t.* tie together; restrain. **religation**, *n*.

religiose [rɪ'lɪdʒiəus] *adj*. excessively or sentimentally religious; over-pious. **religiosity**, *n*.

reliquary ['relɪkwəri] *n*. container for holy relics.

reliquiae [rɪ'lɪkwiaɪ] (*Latin*) *n. pl.* 'remains'. **reliquian**, *adj*. **reliquism** ['rel-], *n*. worship of relics.

relucent [rɪ'luːsnt] *adj*. reflecting; refulgent.

reluctance [rɪ'lʌktəns] *n*. *Electricity*, magnetic resistance. **reluctivity**, *n*. amount of this.

rem [rem] *n*. unit dose of ionising radiation, equal to that having the same biological effect as one röntgen of X-rays.

remanent ['remənənt] *adj.* remaining; residual. remanence, *n.*

remiform ['remɪfɔːm] *adj.* oar-shaped. remigate, *v.i.* row. remiges, *n. pl.* (*sing.* remex) quill feathers of bird's wing. remiped, *n. & adj.* (creature) having legs or feet adapted for propelling it through water.

remigrate [ˌriːmaɪ'greɪt] *v.i.* migrate again; return. remigrant, *n.* one who returns. remigration, *n.*

remontant [rɪ'mɒntənt] *n. & adj.* (rose) flowering more than once in season.

rémoulade [ˌreməˈleɪd, –ˈlɑːd] *n.* cold sauce of mayonnaise flavoured with herbs, capers, etc.

renaissance [rɪ'neɪsns] *n.* revival, especially of art, architecture and literature in 14th-16th centuries in Europe.

renal ['riːnl] *adj.* pertaining to kidneys.

renascence [rɪ'næsns] *n.* re-birth; revival; renaissance. renascent, *adj.*

rencontre [renˈkɒntə, rɒnˈkɒntr] *n.* meeting; encounter; duel.

rendezvous ['rɒndɪvuː] *n.* meeting or meeting-place; assignation; *v.i.* meet by arrangement.

rendition [renˈdɪʃn] *n.* surrender; (manner of or item in) performance; interpretation.

renegade ['renɪgeɪd] *n.* deserter; turncoat; *adj.* pertaining to a renegade or traitor; *v.i.* become a renegade.

renege [rɪ'niːg, –'neɪg, –'neg, –'nɪg] *v.i.* revoke (in card-playing); break promise.

reniform ['renɪfɔːm, 'riːn–] *adj.* kidney-shaped.

renitent [rɪ'naɪtnt, 'renɪtənt] *adj.* resisting; refactory. renitence, renitency, *n.*

rennet ['renɪt] *n.* contents or part of stomach, or preparation therefrom, of young animal, used to curdle milk. rennin, *n.* gastric enzyme curdling milk.

renography [rɪ'nɒgrəfi] *n.* treatise on or description of kidneys.

rentes [rɒnt] (*French*) *n. pl.* government stock, bonds, etc. rentier [–tieɪ], *n.* owner of rentes; one living on income from investments; one living on fixed income.

renvoi [renˈvɔɪ] (*French*) *n.* expulsion of alien from country; *Law*, referral of dispute to another jurisdiction.

reparation [ˌrepəˈreɪʃn] *n.* compensation. reparable, reparative, *adj.*

repatriate [ˌriːˈpætrieɪt] *v.t.* restore to, or re-establish in, native land; *n.* repatriated person. repatriation, *n.*

repertoire ['repətwɑː] *n.* list of plays, pieces, etc., which company or person can perform; range or store of techniques, skills, capabilities, etc. repertorial, *adj.* repertory, *adj.* pertaining to or having a permanent acting company which plays through and continually adds to its repertoire; *n.* repertoire; repertory company; repertory theatre.

repetend ['repətend] *n.* digit(s) repeated in recurring decimal; repetition of same or similar word in sentence; refrain.

replete [rɪ'pliːt] *adj.* full. repletion, *n.* repletive, *adj.*

replevin [rɪ'plevɪn] *n. Law*, repossession of goods wrongfully taken, with pledge to return them if defeated in lawsuit on the matter; writ or action in such case. repleviable, replevisable,

adj. replevisor, *n.* plaintiff in replevin action. replevy, *v.t.*

replica ['replɪkə] *n.* exact copy, especially made by artist who made the original. replicate, *adj.* folded back; repeated; *v.t.* fold back; repeat; reproduce. replication, *n.* making of replica; reply; echo; *Law*, reply of plaintiff to defendant's plea. replicative, *adj.*

répondez s'il vous plaît [reɪˌpɒndeɪ siːl vuː 'pleɪ] (*French*) 'reply, if you please' (*abbr.* R. S V.P.).

repoussé [rəˈpuːseɪ] (*French*) *adj.* shaped in relief by being beaten up from under or reverse side; *n.* such artistic work. repoussage [–ˈsɑːʒ], *n.* art of doing such work.

reprehend [ˌreprɪ'hend] *v.t.* rebuke. reprehensible, *adj.* deserving rebuke. reprehension, *n.* reprehensive, *adj.* rebuking.

reprisal [rɪ'praɪzl] *n.* securing of redress or compensation by violent measure; act of retaliation in same kind or to same degree as offence.

reprobate ['reprəbeɪt] *v.t.* rebuke; disapprove of; reject; abandon; *adj.* sinful; depraved; *n.* hardened sinner. reprobation, *n.* reprobative, reprobatory, *adj.*

reptant ['reptənt] *adj.* creeping. reptation, *n.* reptatorial, reptatory, *adj.*

repugn [rɪ'pjuːn] *v.t.* oppose. repugnance, [–'pʌg–], repugnancy, *n.* aversion; inconsistency; incompatibility. repugnant, *adj.* distasteful; disgusting; contradictory; incompatible; resisting.

requiem ['rekwiəm, –em] *n.* Mass or dirge for the dead.

requiescat [ˌrekwi'eskæt] (*Latin*) 'may he (or she) rest'; *n.* prayer for dead. requiescat in pace, [–'paɪtʃeɪ], 'may he (or she) rest in peace' (*abbr.* R.I.P.).

reredos ['rɪədɒs] *n.* screen behind altar; *erroneously*, choir screen.

rerum cognoscere causas [ˌreərəm kɒgˈnɒskəri 'kausæs] (*Latin*) 'to know the causes of things'.

rescind [rɪ'sɪnd] *v.t.* cancel; revoke. rescission, *n.* rescissory, *adj.*

rescript ['riːskrɪpt] *n.* decree; rewriting or rewritten thing. rescriptive, *adj.*

réseau ['reɪzəʊ] (*French*) *n.* network, especially of lines on astronomical photograph.

resect [rɪ'sekt] *v.t. Surgery*, remove part of organ. resection, *n.* such surgical operation; determination of position by drawing lines on map from two or more known objects.

reserpine ['resəpiːn, rɪ'sɜːp–] *n.* sedative drug.

res gestae [ˌreɪz 'gestaɪ] (*Latin*) *n. pl.* 'things done'; matters incident to question in lawsuit.

residue ['rezɪdjuː] *n.* remainder. residual, residuary [rɪ'zɪdjuəl, –əri], *adj.* pertaining to or receiving residue. residuent, *n.* by-product. residuum, *n.* (*pl.* –ua.) residue. .

resile [rɪ'zaɪl] *v.i.* draw back; return to first position or shape. resilient [–'zɪl–], *adj.* elastic; recovering quickly from shock, illness, etc. resilience, *n.*

resipiscent [ˌresɪ'pɪsnt] *adj.* returning to one's senses, or to wiser course; reforming. resipiscence, resipiscency, *n.*

resorb [ˌriːˈsɔːb] *v.t.* reabsorb. resorbent, resorptive, *adj.* resorbence, resorption, *n.*

respirator ['respəreɪtə] *n.* device worn over face to prevent inhalation of fumes dust, etc.; apparatus for artificial respiration. **respirometer** *n.* apparatus for measuring breathing.

responsions [rɪ'spɒnʃnz] *n. pl.* first examination for B.A. degree at Oxford University.

ressala(h) [rɪ'sɑːlə] *n.* Indian native cavalry squadron. **ressaldar,** *n.* Indian native cavalry captain.

restaurateur [ˌrestərə'tɜː] (*French*) *n.* restaurant-keeper.

restive ['restɪv] *adj.* fidgety; uneasy; obstinate; unmanageable; refusing to go forward.

résumé ['rezjumeɪ] (*French*) *n.* summary; *v.t.* summarize.

resupinate [rɪ'suːpɪneɪt, -'sjuː-, -nət] *adj.* upside down. **resupine,** *adj.* supine. **resupination,** *n.*

resurgam [rɪ'sɜːgæm, reɪ-] (*Latin*) 'I shall rise again'.

resurgent [rɪ'sɜːdʒənt] *adj.* rising again. **resurgence,** *n.*

resuscitate [rɪ'sʌsɪteɪt] *v.i. & t.* restore, or return, to life. **resuscitation,** *n.* **resuscitator,** *n.* **resuscitative,** *adj.*

rete ['riːti] *n.* (*pl.* **-tia,** ['riːʃiə], network; net. **retecious** [rɪ'tiːʃəs], **retial, retiary,** *adj.*

reticulate [rɪ'tɪkjuleɪt] *v.t.* mark with network-like lines; *adj.* like network. **reticular,** *adj.* net-like; intricate. **reticulation,** *n.* reticulate marking. **reticule** ['retɪkjuːl], *n.* handbag, especially of net. **reticulose,** *adj.* reticulated. **reticulum,** *n.* (*pl.* **-la**) network; second stomach of ruminant. **retiform,** *adj.* net-like; reticulate.

retina ['retɪnə] *n.* (*pl.* **-ae**) membrane at back of eye receiving image. **retinal,** *adj.* **retinitis,** *n.* inflammation of retina. **retinoscopy,** *n.* examination of eye by observing changing light and shadow on retina.

retine ['retiːn] *n.* substance in animal tissue which retards tissue growth.

retinoid ['retɪnɔɪd] *adj.* like resin.

retortion [rɪ'tɔːʃn] *n.* turning or twisting back; retaliation.

retrad ['riːtræd, 're–] *adv.* backwards. **retrahent,** *adj.* drawing back. **retral,** *adj.* backward; at the back.

retrench [rɪ'trentʃ] *v.i. & t.* reduce; economize. **retrenchment,** *n.*

retribution [ˌretrɪ'bjuːʃn] *n.* just punishment or reward; requital. **retributive, retributory** [–'trɪb–], *adj.*

retro ['retrəʊ] (*Latin*) *adv.* backwards.

retroact [ˌretrəʊ'ækt] *v.i.* act backwards or opposite; react. **retroaction,** *n.* **retroactive,** *adj.* taking effect as from a previous date.

retrocede [ˌretrəʊ'siːd] *v.i. & t.* go back or inwards; cede back. **retrocession,** *n.* **retrocessive,** *adj.*

retrochoir ['retrəʊˌkwaɪə] *n.* space in choir behind high altar.

retrograde ['retrəʊgreɪd] *adj.* moving or directed backwards; deteriorating; *v.i.* move backwards; revert. **retrogress,** *v.i.* retrograde; degenerate. **retrogression,** *n.* **retrogressive,** *adj.*

retroject [ˌretrə'dʒekt] *v.t.* throw back. **retrojection,** *n.*; *Medicine,* washing of cavity from within.

retrometer [rɪ'trɒmɪtə] *n.* device for transmitting sound by modifying a beam of light.

retromingent [ˌretrəʊ'mɪndʒənt] *n. & adj.* (ani-

mal) urinating rearwards.

retromorphosis [ˌretrəmɔː'fəʊsɪs] *n.* degenerative metamorphosis; change for the worse.

retrorocket ['retrəʊˌrɒkɪt] *n.* rocket with thrust directed in reverse direction to travel, used to slow down space craft.

retrorse [rɪ'trɔːs] *adj.* turned back or down.

retrospect ['retrəspekt] *n.* act of, or view seen on, looking back. **retrospection,** *n.* act of looking back to past. **retrospective,** *adj.* pertaining to retrospection; retroactive.

retrostalsis [ˌretrə'stælsɪs] *n.* reversed peristalsis. **retrostaltic,** *adj.*

retroussé [rə'truːseɪ] *adj.* turned up (applied to nose only).

retrovert [ˌretrə'vɜːt] *v.t.* turn back. **retroverse,** *adj.* turned back. **retroversion,** *n.*

retrovirus ['retrəʊˌvaɪrəs] *n.* virus that synthesises DNA from RNA rather than the usual reverse.

retuse [rɪ'tjuːs] *adj.* having a blunt end with a central notch, as some leaves.

revalescent [ˌrevə'lesnt] *adj.* convalescent. **revalescence,** *n.*

revalorize [ˌriː'væləraɪz] *v.t.* restore to original value, especially such monetary unit.

revanche [rə'vɑːnʃ] (*French*) *n.* revenge; desire to regain lost territory; favour done in return. **revanchism,** *n.* policy of aggressively seeking recovery of lost territory. **revanchist,** *n.*

revehent ['revɪhənt, rɪ'viː-] *adj.* carrying back.

reveille [rɪ'væli] *n.* signal to waken soldiers, sounded on drum or bugle.

revenant ['revənənt] *n.* person returning after supposed death or long absence; ghost.

revenons à nos moutons [ˌrəvənɒn ɑ: nəʊ 'muːtɒn] (*French*) 'let us return to our sheep'; let us return to the subject in hand.

revers [rɪ'vɪə] *n.* tuned-back edge or part of garment.

revetment [rɪ'vetmənt] *n.* masonry etc. facing of embankment or trench. **revet,** *v.t.*

revirescent [ˌrevɪ'resnt] *adj.* growing young or strong again. **revirescence,** *n.*

reviviscent [ˌrevɪ'vɪsnt] *adj.* capable of causing revival. **reviviscence,** *n.*

revolute ['revəluːt] *adj.* rolled back, especially at edges.

rhabdomancy ['ræbdəmænsi] *n.* divination by means of rod; water-divining. **rhabdos,** *n.* magic wand.

rhabdomyoma [ˌræbdəʊmaɪ'əʊmə] *n.* tumour of striated muscle.

Rhadamanthus [ˌrædə'mænθəs] *n.* in Greek mythology a judge of the souls of the dead; stern judge. **Rhadamanthine,** *adj.*

rhaebosis [rɪ'bəʊsɪs] *n.* curvature; bandiness.

rhamphoid ['ræmfɔɪd] *adj.* beak-shaped.

rhapontic [rə'pɒntɪk] *n.* knapweed; rhubarb.

rhea ['riːə] *n.* S American flightless bird like small ostrich.

rhema ['riːmə] (*Greek*) *n.* word; verb. **rheme,** *n.* speech element expressing an idea. **rhematic** [–'mætɪk], *adj.* pertaining to formation of words; derived from verbs. **rhematology,** *n.* study of rhemes.

rheology [ri'ɒlədʒi] *n.* study of flow of matter. **rheometer,** *n.* instrument measuring or controlling currents. **rheophile** ['riː–], *adj.* living in running water. **rheophore**, *n.* wire connection of electrical apparatus. **rheoscope**, *n.* galvanoscope. **rheostat**, *n.* variable electrical resistor. **rheotaxis**, *n.* direction of movement by water. **rheotrope**, *n.* commutator reversing electric current. **rheotropism**, *n.* direction of growth by water.

rhesus ['riːsəs] *n.* species of small Indian monkey. **rhesus factor**, agglutinating substance present in red blood cells of most human beings and higher animals. (*abbr.* **Rh**). **Rh-positive**, *adj.* having blood containing the rhesus factor. **Rh-negative**, *adj.* having blood which does not contain the rhesus factor and is liable to react unfavourably to its introduction.

rhetoric ['retərɪk] *n.* art of effective expression in words; oratory; bombastic language. **rhetorical** [–'tɒr–], *adj.* pertaining to rhetoric. **rhetorical question**, question used merely for effect and not expecting an answer. **rhetorician** [–'rɪʃn], *n.*

rheum [ruːm] *n.* watery discharge from eyes and nose. **rheumic**, **rheumy**, *adj.* pertaining to or causing rheum; damp.

rhexis ['reksɪs] *n.* rupture.

rhigosis [rɪ'gəʊsɪs] *n.* sensation of cold; ability to feel cold. **rhigotic** [–'gɒtɪk], *adj.*

rhinal ['raɪnl] *adj.* nasal. **rhinalgia** [–'nældʒɪə], *n.* pain in nose. **rhinencephalon**, *n.* olfactory lobe of brain. **rhinenchysis** [,raɪnən'kaɪsɪs], *n.* injection into nose. **rhinitis**, *n.* inflammation of nose or its mucous membrane. **rhinodynia**, *n.* rhinalgia. **rhinogenic**, **rhinogenous**, *adj.* deriving from nose. **rhinolalia**, *n.* nasal speech. **rhinology**, *n.* medical study of the nose. **rhinophyma**, *n.* acne of the nose. **rhinoplasty**, *n.* plastic surgery of nose. **rhinorrhagia**, *n.* nose-bleeding. **rhinorrhoea**, *n.* continuous nasal catarrh. **rhinoscopy**, *n.* medical examination of nose.

rhipidate ['rɪpɪdeɪt] *adj.* fan-shaped.

rhizanthous [raɪ'zænθəs] *adj.* with flowers emerging from root.

rhizocarpous [,raɪzə'kɑːpəs] *adj.* with perennial root, etc., but annual foliage and stems.

rhizogenic [,raɪzə'dʒenɪk] *adj.* root-producing. **rhizogenous** [–'zɒdʒənəs], *adj.*

rhizoid ['raɪzɔɪd] *n.* thin root-like filament of fern, etc.; *adj.* root-like.

rhizome, **rhizoma** ['raɪzəʊm, raɪ'zəʊmə] *n.* root-like underground stem; root-stock. **rhizomatic** [–'mætɪk], **rhizomatous** [–'zɒm–, –'zəʊm–], **rhizomic**, *adj.* **rhizomorphous**, *adj.* root-like.

rhodocyte ['rəʊdəsaɪt] *n.* red blood corpuscle.

rhomb(us) [rɒm, 'rɒmbəs] *n.* equilateral oblique-angled parallelogram. **rhombic(al)**, **rhombiform**, *adj.* **rhombohedron**, *n.* (*pl.* **–dra**) six-sided prism with each face a parallelogram. **rhomboid**, *n.* oblique-angled and non-equilateral parallelogram; *adj.* like rhomb or rhomboid.

rhonchus ['rɒŋkəs] *n.* whistling sound heard in auscultation. **rhonchial**, *adj.*

rhotacism ['rəʊtəsɪzm] *n.* mispronunciation or overuse of sound *r*. **rhotacise**, *v.i.* **rhotacistic**, *adj.*

rhumb [rʌm] *n.* point of compass; loxodrome.

rhyparography [,raɪpə'rɒgrəfi] *n.* painting or description of mean or sordid things; still-life or genre painting. **rhyparographer**, **rhyparographist**, *n.* **rhyparographic**, *adj.*

rhysimeter [raɪ'sɪmɪtə] *n.* instrument measuring

speed of current or ship.

ria ['riːə] (*Spanish*) *n.* long, wide creek.

riant ['raɪənt] *adj.* laughing; jolly.

ribald ['rɪbld] *adj.* low; indecent. **ribaldry**, *n.*

riboflavin [,raɪbə'fleɪvɪn] *n.* B vitamin involved in energy production.

ribonucleic acid [,raɪbəʊnju'kliːɪk] *n.* RNA.

ribosome ['raɪbəsəʊm] *n.* minute angular or spherical particle in the living cell, composed of protein and RNA.

ricochet ['rɪkəʃeɪ] *n.* glancing rebound; *v.i.* move in or like this.

rictus ['rɪktəs] *n.* orifice; mouth, especially gaping; fixed grin or grimace. **rictal**, *adj.*

rideau ['riːdəʊ] *n.* ridge or mound of earth, especially as protection.

ridel, **riddel** ['rɪdl] *n.* altar-curtain.

ridibund ['rɪdɪbʌnd] *adj.* easily moved to laughter.

rigadoon [,rɪgə'duːn] *n.* ancient lively skipping dance.

rigescent [rɪ'dʒesnt] *adj.* becoming numb or stiff. **rigescence**, *n.*

rigor ['rɪgə, 'raɪgɔː] *n.* shiver; chill; rigidity; *abbreviation* of rigor mortis. **rigor mortis**, stiffening of body for period shortly after death. **rigorism**, *n.* extreme strictness. **rigorist**, *n.*

rima ['raɪmə] *n.* (*pl.* **–ae**) narrow fissure. **rima oris**, space between lips. **rimal**, *adj.* **rimose**, **rimous**, *adj.* having many rimae. **rimulose**, *adj.* having many small rimae. **rimate**, *adj.* having rima.

rime [raɪm] *n.* frost; hoar-frost; ice formed from supercooled fog or cloud; *v.t.* cover with rime. **rimy**, *adj.*

rinderpest ['rɪndəpest] ((*S African*)) *n.* cattle plague.

riparian [raɪ'peərɪən, rɪ–] *adj.* pertaining to or on river bank or lake shore; *n.* person living on or owning river bank. **riparial**, **riparious**, **ripicolous**, *adj.* living on river banks.

riposte [rɪ'pɒst, –'pəʊst] *n.* quick return thrust or reply; *v.i.* make a riposte.

risala [rɪ'sælə] *see* ressala.

risible ['rɪzɪbl] *adj.* pertaining to or capable of laughter; used in laughing; laughable. **risibles**, *n.pl.* sense of humour; inclination to laugh. **risibility**, *n.*

risorgimento [rɪ,sɔːdʒɪ'mentəʊ] (*Italian*) *n.* revival; Italian renaissance; 19th-century Italian liberal and national political movement.

risorial [raɪ'sɔːrɪəl] *adj.* pertaining to or causing laughter.

risqué ['rɪskeɪ, 'riː–] (*French*) *adj.* improper; mildly indecent.

ritornel(le), **ritornello** [,rɪtə'nel, –əʊ] *n.* short prelude or interlude for musical instrument in song or opera.

Ritter ['rɪtə] (*German*) *n.* knight.

riverain, **riverine** ['rɪvəreɪn, –aɪn] *n.* & *adj.* riparian.

rivière [,rɪvi'eə] (*French*) *n.* necklace of precious stones, especially having more than one string.

rivose ['raɪvəʊs] *adj.* bearing winding furrows. **rivulation**, *n.* having irregular marks of colour. **rivulose**, *adj.* bearing winding and haphazard lines.

riziform ['rɪzɪfɔːm] *adj.* like a rice grain.

Roots

cede or **ceed** come (from Latin *cedere* to come, yield): *accede, antecedent, concede, exceed, intercede, precede, proceed, recede, secede, succeed*

chron time (from Greek *chronos* time): *anachronism, chronicle, chronology, chronometer, synchronic*

cise cut (from Latin *caedere* to cut): *circumcise, concise, excise, incise, precise*

crease or **cresc** grow (from Latin *crescere* to grow): *crescent, decrease, excrescence, increase*

dic or **dict** say (from Latin *dicere* to say): *abdicate, contradict, dedicate, dictate, diction, dictionary, edict, indicate, indict, predicament, predicate, predict, verdict*

duce or **duct** lead (from Latin *ducere* to lead): *abduct, conduce, conduct, deduce, deduct, ductile, educe, induce, induct, introduce, produce, product, reduce, seduce, traduce*

fer carry (from Latin *ferre* to carry): *circumference, confer, defer, differ, fertile, infer, offer, prefer, refer, suffer, transfer*

gen offspring (from Latin *genus* kin): *congenital, degenerate, engender, gender, generate, generic, genital, genitive, indigenous, ingenious, ingenuous, progenitor, progeny, regenerate*

grad or **gress** step (from Latin *gradi* to step): *aggression, congress, degrade, digress, egress, grade, gradient, gradual, progress, regress, retrograde, transgress*

ject throw (from Latin *jacere* to throw): *abject, adjective, conjecture, deject, eject, inject, interjection, object, project, reject, subject, trajectory*

jur swear (from Latin *jurare*): *abjure, adjure, conjure, injure, jurisdiction, jury, objurgation, perjure*

lect read, collect (from Latin *legere* to collect, read): *collect, elect, lecture, neglect, predilection, select*

loc or **loqu** speak (from Latin *loqui* to speak): *circumlocution, colloquy, elocution, eloquent, loquacious, obloquy, soliloquy, ventriloquist*

log say, word (from Greek *logos* saying): *analogy, apology, catalogue, dialogue, epilogue, eulogy, logarithm, logic, monologue, prologue*

lude play (from Latin *ludere* to play): *allude, collude, delude, elude, ludicrous, prelude*

man hand (from Latin *manus* hand): *amanuensis, manacle, manage, manifest, manipulate, manoeuvre, manual, manufacture, manure, manuscript*

mit send (from Latin *mittere* to send): *admit, commit, emit, omit, permit, remit, submit, transmit*

nat born (from Latin *natus* born): *cognate, impregnate, innate, natal, nation, native, nature*

ped foot (from Latin *ped-* foot): *biped, impede, pedal, pedestal, pedestrian, pedigree, quadruped*

pel send (from Latin *pellere* to drive, send): *appellant, compel, dispel, expel, impel, interpellate, propel, repel*

pend hang (from Latin *pendere* to hang): *append, depend, pendant, pendulous, pendulum, perpendicular*

port carry (from Latin *portare* to carry): *comport, deport, disport, export, import, porter, portfolio, purport, report, support, transport*

posit place (from Latin *positus* placed): *apposite, composite, deposit, exposition, imposition, opposite, position, positive, proposition, repository, supposition, transposition*

prim first (from Latin *primus* first): *prime, primeval, primitive, primrose*

rect rule (from Latin *rectus* ruled): *correct, direct, erect, insurrection, rectangle, rectify, rectitude, resurrection*

rog ask (from Latin *rogare* to ask): *abrogate, derogate, interrogate, prerogative, surrogate*

rupt break (from Latin *ruptus* broken): *abrupt, corrupt, disrupt, erupt, interrupt, rupture*

scrib or **script** write (from Latin *scribere* to write, *scriptus* written): *ascribe, circumscribe, conscript, describe, inscribe, prescribe, proscribe, rescript, script, scripture, subscribe, transcribe.*

sec or **sequ** follow (from Latin *sequi* to follow): *consecutive, consequence, obsequious, persecute, prosecute, second, sect, sequal, sequence, subsequent.*

spec look (from Latin *specere* to look): *aspect, circumspect, expect, inspect, perspective, prospect, respect, special, specify, specimen, specious, spectacle, spectator, speculate, suspect*

tain hold (from Latin *tenere* to hold): *abstain, contain, detain, entertain, obtain, pertain, retain, sustain*

tend extend (from Latin *tendere* to extend): *attend, contend, distend, extend, intend, portend, pretend, tendon*

tract pull (from Latin *tractus* pulled): *abstract, attract, contract, detract, distract, extract, protract, retract, subtract, tractable*

val be strong (from Latin *valere* to be strong): *convalesce, valiant, valid, valour, value*

ven come (from Latin *venire* to come): *advent, adventure, avenue, contravene, convene, convenient, event, intervene, invent, prevent, revenue, souvenir*

vert turn (from Latin *vertere* to turn): *advert, avert, convert, divert, invert, pervert, revert, subvert, vertebra, vertigo*

vis see (from Latin *visus* seen): *advise, improvise, proviso, revise, supervise, visible, vision, visit, visual*

viv live (from Latin *vivere* to live): *convivial, revive, survive, vivacity, vivid, vivisection*

voc or **vok** voice (from Latin *voc-* voice): *advocate, convoke, evoke, invoke, provoke, revoke, vocal, vociferous.*

RNA *abbreviation* of ribonucleic acid (which in the living cell transmits the genetic information coded in the DNA and acts as template for protein synthesis).

robinet ['rɒbɪnet] *n.* chaffinch; robin; ancient light cannon.

roble ['rəʊbleɪ] *n.* several kinds of New World oak, or other hard-timbered tree.

roborant ['rɒbərənt] *n. & adj.* tonic. **roborate,** *v.t.* strengthen; corroborate. **roborative,** *adj.*

roborean [rə'bɔːriən] *adj.* like an oak; strong. **roboreous,** *adj.*

roc [rɒk] *n.* mythical Arabian bird of great size. **roc's egg,** unattainable object.

rocaille [rɒ'kaɪ] *(French) n.* florid, shell-like, 18th-century ornamentation; rococo scroll ornamentation.

roche moutonnée [ˌrɒʃ muːˈtɒneɪ] *(French) n.* (*pl.* **roches moutonnées**) 'sheep-like rock'; rock rounded by glacial action.

rochet ['rɒtʃɪt] *n.* bishop's or abbot's vestment resembling surplice; red gurnard.

rococo [rə'kəʊkəʊ] *n. & adj.* (pertaining to or like) 18th-cent. style of ornamentation with florid, unsymmetrical curves and shell-work; showy; fantastic.

rodomontade [ˌrɒdəmɒn'taːd, –'teɪd] *n.* bragging talk; rigmarole; *v.i.* brag. **rodomontadist, rodomontador,** *n.*

roentgen ['rɒntgən] *see* **röntgen.**

rogation [rə'geɪʃn] *n.* special prayer for Rogation Days. **Rogation Days,** three days before Ascension Day.

roi [rwaː] *(French) n.* king. **le roi le veult** [lə ˌrwaː lə 'vɜː], 'the king wills it'; signification of royal assent to Act of parliament. **roi fainéant** [–,feɪneɪ'ɒn], powerless king.

roil [rɔɪl] *v.t.* make turbid by stirring up sediment; agitate. **roily,** *adj.* turbid, muddy.

roinek ['rɔɪn'ek] *(S African) n.* 'red neck'; new immigrant, especially British; greenhorn.

rojo ['rəʊhəʊ] *(Spanish) adj.* red; *n.* Mexican Indian.

rolley ['rɒli] *n.* lorry; trolley.

romal [ru'maːl] *(Indian) n.* silk or cotton fabric; handkerchief of this.

roman [rəʊ'maːn, –'mɒn] *(French) n.* ancient French saga-like poem; novel; romance. **roman-à-clef,** *n.* novel or real people given fictitious names. **roman policier** [–pə'liːsjeɪ], detective story.

romaunt [rəʊ'mɒnt, –'mɔːnt] *n.* ancient romance in verse.

rondeau ['rɒndəʊ] *n.* (*pl.* **–aux,**) thirteen-lined poem with two rhymes and refrain. **rondel,** *n.* such poem of fourteen lines.

rondo ['rɒndəʊ] *n.* musical composition with main theme occurring three or more times, interspersed with minor themes.

röntgen, roentgen ['rɒntgən] *n.* unit of dose of ionising radiation, *e.g.* X-rays or gamma rays. **röntgen rays,** *n. pl.* X-rays. **röntgenogram, röntgenograph,** *n.* X-ray photograph. **röntgenology,** *n.* radiology. **röntgenoscopy,** *n.* X-ray examination.

rood [ruːd] *n.* crucifix or cross; one-quarter of acre; seven or eight yards. **rood screen,** screen bearing crucifix.

rooinek ['ruːɪnek] *(S African) n.* roinek. **rooibok,** *n.* impala.

roomaul [ru'maːl] *n.* romal.

roric ['rɔːrɪk] *adj.* dewy.

rorqual ['rɔːkwəl] *n.* large whale-bone whale; finback.

rorulent ['rɔːrulənt] *adj.* covered with dew.

rosace ['rəʊzeɪs] *n.* rose-window; rose-shaped ornament. **rosacea,** *n.* acne rosacea. **rosaceous,** *adj.* pertaining to roses; belonging to rose family of plants.

rosarium [rəʊ'zeəriəm] *n.* rose garden. **rosarian,** *n.* cultivator of roses.

Roscius ['rɒskiəs, –ʃi–] *n.* famous ancient Roman actor; great actor.

roseola [rəʊ'ziːələ] *n.* rash of rose-coloured patches; rose rash. **roseoliform, roseolous, roseolar,** *adj.*

rosin ['rɒzɪn] *n.* solid resin; *v.t.* rub with rosin.

rosmarine ['rɒzməriːn, –raɪn] *n.* walrus; mythical walrus-like sea animal believed to feed on dew; sea dew.

rosorial [rəʊ'sɔːriəl] *adj.* pertaining to rodents; gnawing.

rostel(lum) ['rɒstl, rɒ'steləm] *n.* small beak or beak-like outgrowth. **rostellar,** *adj.* **rostellate,** *adj.* having rostellum. **rostelliform,** *adj.* like rostellum.

rostrum ['rɒstrəm] *n.* (*pl.* **–ra**) beak; prow of ancient warship; platform or pulpit for speaking; musical conductor's dais; any beak-like part or thing. **rostral,** *adj.* **rostrate,** *adj.* beaked. **rostriform, rostroid,** *adj.* beak-like. **rostrulum,** *n.* (*pl.* **–la**) small rostrum.

rosular, rosulate ['rɒzjulə, –lət; 'rəʊ–] *adj.* in rosettes.

rota ['rəʊtə] *n.* roster; Roman Catholic tribunal; *Music,* round. **rotameter,** *n.* instrument measuring length of curved lines.

rotacism ['rəʊtəsɪzm] *see* **rhotacism.**

rotifer ['rəʊtɪfə] *n.* microscopic, multicellular, fresh-water creature with rotating cilia at one end. **rotiferal, rotiferous,** *adj.* **rotiform,** *adj.* wheel-shaped.

rotisserie [rəʊ'tɪsəri, –'tiːs–] *(French) n.* shop selling roast meat, especially restaurant where meat is roasted in view of diners; rotating spit for roasting meat.

rotograph ['rəʊtəɡraːf] *n.* photograph of manuscript, etc., made direct on bromide paper without negative.

rotor ['rəʊtə] *n.* rotating part of machine, especially of electricity-generating machine; rotating wing of helicopter.

rotula ['rɒtjulə] *n.* kneecap. **rotulian, rotular,** *adj.* **rotuliform,** *adj.* like rotula.

rotunda [rə'tʌndə] *n.* circular domed building or room. **rotundate,** *adj.* rounded.

roué ['ruːeɪ] *(French) n.* debauched man; lecher. **rouérie,** *n.*

rouge-et-noir [ˌruːʒ–eɪ–'nwaː] *(French) n.* 'red-and-black'; gambling game of betting on those colours; trente et quarante.

roulade [ru'laːd] *n.* arpeggio-like musical figure sung to one syllable; rolled slice of meat.

rounceval ['raunsɪvl] *adj.* large; *n.* marrowfat pea.

roundel ['raundl] *n.* rondeau; any round thing; badge, on aircraft, of concentric coloured rings.

roup [ruːp] *n.* poultry disease with mucous discharge and hoarseness. **roupy,** *adj.*

rouseabout ['rauzəbaut] *(Australian) n.* odd-job man, especially helping sheep-shearers.

roustabout ['raustəbaut] *n.* labourer on oil-rig; *American,* unskilled labourer; *American,* dock hand; *Australian,* rouseabout.

rubedinous [ru'bedɪnəs] *adj.* ruddy. **rubedity,** *n.*

rubefacient [ˌruːbɪ'feɪʃnt] *n. & adj.* (substance) causing redness of skin. **rubefaction,** *n.*

rubella [ru'belə] *n.* German measles.

rubeola [ru'bi:ələ] *n.* measles. **rubeoloid,** *adj.* like rubeola. **rubeolar,** *adj.*

rubescent [ru'besnt] *adj.* reddening; flushing. **rubescence,** *n.*

rubiaceous [,ru:bi'eiʃəs] *adj.* like or pertaining to madder plant; belonging to madder family of plants.

rubican ['ru:bɪkən] *adj.* red bay; sorrel.

Rubicon ['ru:bɪkən, -ɒn] *n.* river between Italy and Cisalpine Gaul, the crossing of which by Julius Caesar began civil war and made him dictator. **to cross the Rubicon,** make a fateful and irrevocable decision.

rubific [ru'bɪfɪk] *n.* & *adj.* rubefacient. **rubification,** *n.* **rubificative,** *adj.*

rubiginous [ru'bɪdʒɪnəs] *adj.* rust-coloured; rusty. **rubiginose,** *adj.*

rubineous, rubious [ru'bɪniəs] *adj.* ruby-coloured.

rubor ['ru:bɔɪ] *n.* redness due to excess of blood in part.

rubric ['ru:brɪk] *n.* passage in book printed in red or other distinctive type, especially such direction in service book; any direction to conduct or ceremony; title; heading. **rubrical,** *adj.* **rubricality,** *n.* ceremony. **rubricate,** *v.t.* mark in red; fix like a ritual. **rubrication,** *n.* **rubrician** [-'brɪʃn], *n.* student of rubrics. **rubricism, rubricity,** *n.* strict adherence to rubric; formalism. **rubricose,** *adj.* ruddy.

rubrific [ru'brɪfɪk] *adj.* rubefacient.

rucervine [ru'sɜːvaɪn] *adj.* pertaining to or like Indian swamp deer.

ruderal ['ru:dərəl] *adj. Botany,* growing in refuse or waste ground.

rudiment ['ru:dɪmənt] *n.* elementary principle; undeveloped part or organ. **rudimental, rudimentary,** *adj.*

rufescent [ru'fesnt] *adj.* ruddy; bronzy. **rufescence,** *n.*

ruff [rʌf] *n. Ornithology,* sandpiper.

rufous ['ru:fəs] *adj.* reddish; tawny; red-haired.

rufulous, *adj.* somewhat rufous.

rugose ['ru:gəʊs] *adj.* ridged; wrinkled. **rugate, rugous,** *adj.* **rugulose,** *adj.* having small or fine wrinkles. **rugosity,** *n.*

rumal [ru'maɪl] *n.* romal

rumchunder [rʌm'tʃʌndə] *n.* fine Indian silk.

rumen ['ru:men] *n.* (*pl.* **-mina**) first stomach of ruminant; cud. **rumenitis,** *n.* inflammation of rumen. **rumenotomy,** *n.* incision into rumen.

ruminate ['ru:mɪneɪt] *v.i.* chew the cud; ponder. **ruminant,** *n.* & *adj.* (animal) that chews the cud; pondering. **rumination,** *n.* **ruminative,** *adj.*

runcinate ['rʌnsɪnət] *adj.* pinnate with lobes pointing downwards.

rune [ru:n] *n.* character of simple ancient Teutonic alphabet; magical mark or sign; magic. **runic,** *adj.* **runiform,** *adj.* like rune. **runology,** *n.* study of runes.

rupestrian [ru'pestriən] *n.* made of, or written on, rock. **rupestral,** *adj.* **rupestrine,** *adj.* living on or in rocks.

rupicoline, rupicolous [ru'pɪkəlaɪn, -əs] *adj.* rupestrine.

ruridecanal [,ruərɪdɪ'keɪnl] *adj.* pertaining to rural dean and his jurisdiction.

rusine ['ru:saɪn] *adj.* pertaining to E Indian maned deer.

rus in urbe [,rʊs ɪn 'ɜːbi, ,rʌs-] (*Latin*) 'countryside in the town'.

rusticate ['rʌstɪkeɪt] *v.i.* & *t.* live in country; make rustic; punish by expelling from university for a period; *Architecture,* face with large, boldly textured blocks with deep grooves between. **rustication,** *n.*

rutidosis [,ru:tɪ'dəʊsɪs] *n.* wrinkling.

rutilant ['ru:tɪlənt] *adj.* shining red. **rutilous,** *adj.*

rynchosporous [,rɪŋkə'spɔːrəs] *adj.* having beaked fruit.

ryot ['raɪət] *n.* Indian peasant. **ryotwar,** *adj.* pertaining to system of rent- or tax-collecting with direct settlement between goverment and ryot. **ryotwary,** *n.* & *adj.*

S

sabbat ['sæbət] *n.* witches' midnight assembly or sabbath.
sabbatarian [,sæbə'teəriən] *n. & adj.* (person) devoted to strict keeping of sabbath. **sabbatarianism**, *n.*
sabbatic(al) [sə'bætɪk, –l] *adj.* pertaining to or suitable for sabbath. **sabbatical**, *n. & adj.* (peroid of paid leave) granted to academic staff approximately every seventh year. **sabbatical year**, every seventh year when ancient Jews ceased tilling; year's paid leave for academic. **sabbatism**, *n.* freedom from work on sabbath; sabbatarianism.
sabicu ['sæbɪkuː, –juː] *n.* mahogany-like W Indian tree and timber.
sabot ['sæbəʊ] *n.* wooden shoe; clog.
sabra ['saːbrə] *n. Hebrew,* a native-born Israeli.
sabretache ['seɪbətæʃ] *n.* satchel suspended by straps from cavalry officer's belt.
sabulous ['sæbjʊləs] **sabulose** [–əʊs] *adj.* sandy. **sabuline**, *adj.* **sabulosity**, *n.*
saburra [sə'bʌrə] *n. Medicine,* granular matter deposited in the body. **saburral**, *adj.* **saburration** [,sæb–], *n. Medicine,* arenation.
sac [sæk] *n.* any membranous bag or cavity.
sacatra ['sækətrə] *n.* person of one-eighth white and seven-eighths negro blood.
saccade [sæ'kɑːd] *n.* jerky movement of the eye moving from one fixation point to another, as in reading. **saccadic**, *adj.* jerky, twitching.
saccate ['sækeɪt] *adj.* sac-like.
saccharine ['sækərɪn, –riːn] *adj.* very sweet; cloying; pertaining to sugar. **saccharic** [–'kærɪk], *adj.* pertaining to saccharine substances. **sacchariferous**, *adj.* containing sugar. **saccharify**, **saccharise**, *v.t.* transform into, or impregnate with, sugar. **saccharimeter**, *n.* polarimeter measuring amount, and kind, of sugar in a solution. **saccharoid**, *adj.* sugary; granular. **saccharometer**, *n.* hydrometer measuring amount of sugar in a solution.
sacciferous [sæ'kɪfərəs] *adj.* bearing sac(s). **sacciform**, *adj.* sac-shaped.
saccular ['sækjʊlə] *adj.* sac-like. **sacculate** [–ət], *adj.* having sacs; *v.t.* [–eɪt] enclose in sac. **saccule**, **sacculus**, *n.* little sac.
sacerdotal [,sæsə'dəʊtl] *adj.* pertaining to priest, especially sacrificial; granting or believing in mysterious or miraculous priestly powers. **sacerdocy**, *n* priesthood. **sacerdotalism**, *n.*
sachem ['seɪtʃəm] *(American) n.* Indian chieftain; boss. **sachemic** [–'tʃemɪk], *adj.*
sackbut ['sækbʌt] *n.* ancient trombone-like musical instrument.
sacral ['seɪkrəl] *adj.* pertaining to sacrum; pertaining to sacred rites.

sacrarium [sə'kreəriəm] *n. (pl.* **–craria**) *Ecclesiastical,* sanctuary; *Roman Catholic,* basin, etc. for disposal of ablutions after rite; ancient Roman depository for sacred objects.
sacrilege ['sækrɪlɪdʒ] *n.* violation of sacred place or object; stealing from a church. **sacrilegious** [–'lɪdʒəs], *adj.*
sacring ['seɪkrɪŋ] *n.* hallowing; consecration; ordination. **sacring bell**, bell rung at moment of elevation of the Host.
sacristan ['sækrɪstən] *n.* ecclesiastical official having care of sacred objects; sexton. **sacristy**, *n.* sacristan's room in church; vestry.
sacrum ['seɪkrəm] *n. (pl.* **–ra**) flat triangular bone at base of spine.
sadhu ['saːduː] *n.* Hindu holy man.
saeculum ['sekjʊləm] *(Latin) n. (pl.* **–la**) 'generation'; age; aeon.
saffian ['sæfiən] *n.* brightly-coloured goatskin or sheepskin leather.
sagacious [sə'geɪʃəs] *adj.* wise; perspicacious. **sagacity** [–'gæs–], *n.*
sagamore ['sægəmɔː] *n.* sachem.
saggar, sagger ['sægə] *n.* clay box in which delicate ceramics are fired.
sagittal ['sædʒɪtl] *adj.* pertaining to or like an arrow. **sagitate**, *adj.* arrowhead-shaped.
sainfoin ['sænfɔɪn] *n.* pink-flowered forage plant; 'French clover'.
sake ['saːki] *(Japanese) n.* Japanese beer made from rice.
saki ['saːki] *n.* white-bearded and -ruffed S American monkey.
sakia, sakieh, sakiyeh ['saːkɪə] *n.* bucket-bearing wheel used in Egypt for raising water.
salacious [sə'leɪʃəs] *n.* obscene; lascivious. **salacity** [–'læs–], *n.*
salamander ['sæləmændə] *n.* lizard-like amphibian animal, fabled to live in fire; utensil for browning pastry, etc.; portable stove. **salamandriform**, *adj.* salamander-shaped. **salamandrine**, **salamandroid**, *adj.* like salamander; able to withstand fire.
salchow ['sælkəʊ] *n.* ice-skating leap with turns from inner backward edge of one skate to outer backward edge of other.
salep ['sælep] *n.* dried root of species of orchid, used as food, etc.
saleratus [,sælə'reɪtəs] *n.* sodium bicarbonate; baking powder.
salic ['sælɪk] *adj.* Frankish. **salic law**, exclusion of women from succession to throne.
salicaceous [,sælɪ'keɪʃəs] *adj.* pertaining to or like a willow; belonging to the willow family of plants.

salient ['seɪlɪənt] *adj.* leaping; outstanding; pointing outwards; *n.* such angle or curve, especially in battle-line. **salience,** *n.*

saliferous [sə'lɪfərəs] *adj.* containing salt. **salify,** *v.t.* form salt with; transform into salt.

salina [sə'laɪnə] *n.* salt lake, spring or marsh; salt pan.

saline ['seɪlaɪn] *adj.* salty; *n.* metallic salt; soluble salt; solution of salt and water. **saliniform,** *adj.* like salt. **salinity** [-'lɪn-], *n.* **salinometer,** *n.* hydrometer measuring amount of salt in a solution.

salivant ['sælɪvənt] *n.* & *adj.* (substance) promoting secretion of saliva. **salivate,** *v.i.* & *t.* secrete saliva; cause excessive saliva in. **salivous** [sə'laɪvəs], *adj.*

salle [sæl] (*French*) *n.* 'room'. **salle à manger** [-ɑː 'mɒnʒeɪ] 'dining-room'.

sallyport ['sælipɔːt] *n.* opening in fortifications from which defenders may make a sally.

salmagundi [,sælmə'gʌndi] *n.* highly seasoned mixed dish of meat, eggs, etc.

salmi ['sælmi] *n.* ragout, especially of game.

salon ['sælɒn] (*French*) *n.* 'drawing-room'; reception at which famous persons are present; hostess's circle of fashionable or famous acquaintances.

saloop [sə'luːp] *n.* salep; sassafras; drink made of salep and milk.

salopettes [,sælə'pets] *n. pl.* quilted skiing trousers with shoulder straps.

salpinx. ['sælpɪŋks] *n.* (*pl.* **-nges**) Eustachian or Fallopian tube. **salpingian,** [-'pɪndʒ-], *adj.* **salpingitis,** *n.* inflammation of salpinx. **salpingectomy,** *n.* surgical removal of Fallopian tube.

salsify ['sælsɪfi] *n.* purple-flowered plant, with root (called 'oyster plant') boiled as vegetable.

salsuginous, salsuginose [sæl'suːdʒɪnəs, -əus; -'sjuː-] *adj. Botany,* thriving in salt-impregnated soil.

saltant ['sæltənt] *adj.* leaping; dancing; *Biology,* exhibiting saltation. **saltation,** *n.* act of leaping or dancing; spurt; sudden metamorphosis; mutation. **saltativeness,** *n.* ability to jump. **saltatorial, saltatory,** *adj.* pertaining to leaping or dancing; taking place by leaps and bounds.

saltigrade ['sæltɪgreɪd] *adj.* having leaping legs; *n.* such spider.

saltire ['sɔːltaɪə, 'sæl-] *n.* X-shaped cross. **saltirewise,** *adj.*

saltpetre [,sɔːlt'piːtə] *n.* potassium nitrate; nitre. **saltpetrous,** *adj.*

salubrious [sə'luːbrɪəs] *adj.* health-giving; respectable, wholesome. **salubrify,** *v.t.* make salubrious **salubrity,** *n.*

saluki [sə'luːki] *n.* greyhound-like Arab dog; gazelle hound.

salutary ['sæljʊtəri] *adj.* having good results; healthy; wholesome.

salvific(al) [sæl'vɪfɪk, -l] *adj.* tending to save.

salvo ['sælvəu] *n. pl.* **-s**) proviso let-out clause; evasion; means of saving one's pride or reputation.

sal volatile [,sæl və'lætəli] *n.* ammonium carbonate as smelling-bottle.

salwar [sʌl'waː] *n.* loose, light, oriental trousers.

samara ['sæmərə, sə'maːrə] *n.* propeller-like winged fruit, as of ash; key fruit. **samariform** [-'mær-], **samaroid,** *adj.* like this in shape.

sambuca [sæm'bjuːkə] *n.* ancient triangular stringed instrument; Roman siege engine.

sambur ['saːmbuə] *n.* Indian elk and its hide.

samiel ['sæmjel] (*Turkish*) *n.* simoom.

samisen ['sæmɪsen] (*Japanese*) *n.* banjo-like instrument.

samite ['sæmaɪt] *n.* ancient rich silk fabric.

samizdat [,sæmɪz'dæt] *n.* (system for distributing) underground literature in former USSR.

samlet ['sæmlət] *n.* young salmon.

samogon [,sæmə'gɒn] (*Russian*) *n.* illicitly-distilled vodka.

samovar ['sæməvaː] (*Russian*) *n.* tea-urn.

samoyed(e) [sə'mɔɪed, ,sæmə'jed] (*Russian*) *n.* white sledge-dog.

sampan ['sæmpæn] *n.* small Chinese river boat.

samphire ['sæmfaɪə] *n.* fleshy sea-coast plant; glasswort.

samshu ['sæmʃuː] *n.* Chinese liquor distilled from rice.

samurai ['sæmuraɪ] *n.* (member of) ancient Japanese military caste; military officer.

sanative ['sænətɪv] *adj.* healing. **sanatorium,** *n.* (*pl.* **-ria**) hospital, especially for tuberculosis. **sanatory,** *adj.* producing health.

sanbenito [,sænbə'niːtəu] *n.* Spanish Inquisition garment resembling scapular, either yellow with red St. Andrew's crosses for penitent heretics or black and decorated with friars and devils for impenitent heretics at an auto-da-fé.

sanction ['sæŋkʃn] *n.* ratification; permission; penalty incurred or reward lost by breaking law; *v.t.* permit. **sanctionative,** *adj.*

sanctum ['sæŋktəm] *n.* (*pl.* **-ta**) holy or private place. **sanctum sanctorum,** 'holy of holies'; holiest, innermost or most private room.

sanctus ['sæŋktəs] *n.* part of Communion service beginning 'Holy, Holy, Holy'. **sanctus bell,** bell rung as sanctus is said.

sangaree [,sæŋgə'riː] *n.* drink of spiced wine and water.

sang-froid [,sɒŋ'frwaː] (*French*) 'cold blood'; calmness in danger; levelheadedness.

sangria ['sæŋgrɪə, sæn'griːə] *n.* Spanish drink of red wine, fruit juice, sugar and soda water.

sanguinary ['sæŋgwɪnəri] *adj.* bloody; bloodthirsty; causing bloodshed. **sanguinaceous, sanguine,** *adj.* hopeful; optimistic; blood-red. **sanguineous,** *adj.* bloody; pertaining to, containing or having blood; full-blooded; blood-red. **sanguinolent,** *adj.* containing blood; bloodthirsty. **sanguisugous,** *adj.* blood-sucking.

sanhedrin ['sænədrɪn] *n.* highest court of ancient Jerusalem. **sanhedrist,** *n.* member of this.

sanies ['seɪniiːz] *n. Medical,* discharge from ulcers, etc. **sanious,** *adj.*

sanitarium [,sænə'teərɪəm] (*American,*) *n.* (*pl.* **-ria**) sanatorium.

sanjak [sæn'dʒæk] *n.* division of a vilayet. **sanjakbeg, sanjakbey,** *n.* governor of sanjak.

sannup ['sænʌp] *n.* American Indian man, especially married.

sans [sænz, sɒn] (*French*) *prep.* 'without'. **sans-culotte,** 'without trousers'; violent or low-class

French revolutionary. **sans gêne**, 'without trouble'; unembarrassed; familiarity. **sans peur et sans reproche**, 'without fear and without reproach', applied to perfect knight of chivalry. **sans serif**, 'without serif'. **sans souci**, 'without worry'; condition of indifference or carefreeness.

santonin(e) ['sæntənɪn] *n.* anthelmintic extracted from worm-wood or derived from naphthalene.

sapajou ['sæpədʒuː, –ʒuː] (*French*) *n.* capuchin or spider monkey.

sapele [sə'piːli] *n.* species of African mahogany.

saphena [sə'fiːnə] *n.* one of two main superficial veins of leg. **saphenous,** *adj.*

sapid ['sæpɪd] *adj.* pleasantly flavoured; having flavour; agreeable. **sapidity,** *n.*

sapient ['seɪpiənt] *adj.* wise; pretending to be wise. **sapiential** [–'enʃl], *adj.* providing wisdom. **sapience,** *n.*

sapodilla [ˌsæpə'dɪlə] *n.* large tropical evergreen chicle-yielding tree; naseberry.

saponaceous [ˌsæpə'neɪʃəs] *adj.* soapy; slippery. **saponification,** *n.* act of making (into) soap; hydrolysis of a fat.

sapor ['seɪpə, –ɔː] *n.* quality perceived by taste; flavour. **saporific,** *adj.* having flavour. **saporous,** *adj.* tasty; pleasant in taste.

sapota [sə'pəʊtə] *n.* sapodilla. **sapotaceous,** *adj.* pertaining to or like sapota; belonging to sapota family of trees.

Sapphic ['sæfɪk] *adj.* pertaining to Sappho, ancient Greek poetess of Lesbos, and her love poems; erotic. **sapphism,** *n.* lesbianism. **sapphics,** *n. pl.* verses by Sappho or like hers in form.

sapraemia [sæ'priːmiə] *n.* blood-poisoning with bacterial products in blood. **sapraemic,** *adj.*

saprodontia [ˌsæprə'dɒnʃiə] *n.* decay of teeth.

saprogenic [ˌsæprə'dʒenɪk] *adj.* causing decay; produced in decaying matter. **saprogenous** [–'rɒdʒ–], *adj.*

sapropel ['sæprəpel] *n.* ooze composed mainly of decaying organic matter. **sapropelic,** *adj.* living in this. **sapropelite,** *n.* coal formed of this.

saprophagous [sæ'prɒfəgəs] *adj.* feeding on decaying matter. **saprophilous,** *adj.* flourishing in decaying matter.

saprophyte ['sæprəfaɪt] *n.* plant living on dead or decaying matter. **saprophytic** [–'fɪt–], *adj.* **saprophytism,** *n.*

saprostomous [sæ'prɒstəməs] *adj.* having foul breath.

saprozoic [ˌsæprə'zəʊɪk] *adj.* applied to animals living on dead or decaying matter.

sapsago [sæp'seɪgəʊ, 'sæpsə–] *n.* hard green Swiss cheese.

sapwood ['sæpwʊd] *n.* soft tissues immediately beneath bark of tree.

saraband(e) ['særəbænd] *n.* stately Spanish dance.

sarafan ['særəfɑːn] *n.* national dress of Russian peasant woman.

sarangousty [ˌsærən'guːsti] *n.* waterproof stucco.

sarcenet ['sɑːsnət] *n.* soft lining silk fabric; *adj.* soft; gentle.

sarcoid ['sɑːkɔɪd] *adj.* flesh-like; *n.* formation of nodules in skin, leaving scars. **sarcoidosis,** *n.* condition characterised by formation of nodules, *especially* in lymph nodes and lungs. **sarcoline,**

adj. flesh-coloured. **sarcology,** *n.* anatomy of flesh.

sarcoma [sɑː'kəʊmə] *n.* (*pl.* **–ta**) cancerous tumour arising in connective tissue. **sarcomatoid,** *adj.* like sarcoma. **sarcomatosis,** *n.* condition of having sarcoma. **sarcomatous,** *adj.*

sarcophagus [sɑː'kɒfəgəs] *n.* (*pl.* **–gi**) coffin of stone. **sarcophagal,** *adj.* **sarcophagous,** *adj.* feeding on flesh; like a sarcophagus. **sarcophagic** [–'fædʒɪk], *adj.* feeding on flesh.

sarcoptid [sɑː'kɒptɪd] *n.* itch mite. **sarcoptic,** *adj.*

sarcotic [sɑː'kɒtɪk] *n. & adj.* (medicine) promoting growth of flesh.

sarcous ['sɑːkəs] *adj.* pertaining to flesh or muscle.

sard [sɑːd] *n.* deep orange-coloured kind of chalcedony.

sardonic [sɑː'dɒnɪk] *adj.* bitterly or evilly humorous; grimly mocking. **sardonicism** [–sɪzm], *n.*

sardonyx ['sɑːdənɪks, sɑː'dɒ–] *n.* onyx with alternate layers of sard and other mineral.

sargasso [sɑː'gæsəʊ] *n.* kind of floating seaweed; gulfweed. **Sargasso Sea,** area of N Atlantic covered with mass of this.

sarmentum [sɑː'mentəm] *n.* (*pl.* **–ta**) *Bot.*, runner. **sarmentaceous, sarmentiferous, sarmentose, sarmentous,** *adj.* producing sarmenta.

sarong [sə'rɒŋ] *n.* Malayan skirt-like garment, of long strip cloth wound round body.

saros ['seərɒs] *n.* cycle of about 6,585 days after which a sequence of eclipses repeats itself.

sarrusophone [sə'ruːzəfəʊn, –'rʌs–] *n.* double-reeded bassoon-like musical instrument.

sarsaparilla [ˌsɑːspə'rɪlə] *n.* kind of smilax; drink made from its root or with its flavour.

sarsen ['sɑːsn] *n.* sandstone boulder of S England; such stone used in prehistoric monument.

sarsenet *see* **sarcenet.**

sartorial [sɑː'tɔːriəl] *adj.* pertaining to tailoring or men's clothes.

sassafras ['sæsəfræs] *n.* kind of laurel and its root-bark, used medicinally.

sassenach ['sæsənæk] (*Scottish*) *n.* Saxon; Englishman; Lowland Scottish.

satiate ['seɪʃieɪt] *v.t.* fill to brim; cloy; glut; *adj.* surfeited. **satient,** *adj.* causing satiety. **satiety** [sə'taɪəti], **satiation,** *n.*

satisdation [ˌsætɪs'deɪʃn] *n. Law,* security, or the giving of it.

satrap ['sætræp] *n.* ancient Persian ruler of province; despot, especially in petty position. **satrapal,** *adj.* **satrapy,** *n.*

saturnalia [ˌsætə'neɪliə] *n. pl.* ancient Roman festival in honour of Saturn; orgy. **saturnalian,** *adj.*

saturnian [sæ'tɜːniən] *adj.* pertaining to Saturn or the golden age; denoting very early Latin verse form with stress accent.

saturnine ['sætənaɪn] *adj.* melancholy; taciturn; *Medicine,* pertaining to lead poisoning. **saturninity,** *n.* **saturnism,** *n. arch.,* lead poisoning.

satyr ['sætə] *n.* half-animal follower of Bacchus, in ancient mythology; obscene or bestial man. **satyresque,** *adj.* **satyress,** *n.* female satyr. **satyriasis,** *n.* insatiable sexual desire in male. **satyric** [–'tɪrɪk], *adj.* **satyrism,** *n.* uncontrolled licentiousness.

saurian ['sɔːriən] *n.* & *adj.* (animal) belonging to order including crocodiles, lizards, etc. **saurophagous,** *adj.* eating lizards.

sauterelle [,səʊtə'rel] (*French*) *n.* mason's angle-making instrument.

sautoir [səʊ'twaː] *n.* long chain necklace.

sauve qui peut [,səʊv kiː 'pɜː] (*French*) '(let him) save (himself) who can'; every man for himself; rout.

savannah [sə'vænə] *n.* open grassy plain of tropical America.

savant ['sævnt] (*French*) *n.* learned man.

savarin ['sævəræn] (*French*) *n.* ring-shaped cake (tin).

savoir faire [,sævwaː 'feə] (*French*) 'to know how to do'; knowledge of correct action; tact; adroitness. **savoir vivre** [–'viːvr], 'to know how to live'; good behaviour or breeding.

saxatile ['sæksətaɪl] *adj.* pertaining to or living in rocks. **saxicavous,** *adj.* boring into rocks. **saxicole, saxicoline, saxigenous,** *adj.* growing in rocks. **saxifrage,** *n.* kind of rock plant. **saxifragous,** *adj.* breaking stone.

scaberulous [skə'berʊləs] *adj.* bearing small raised roughnesses.

scabies ['skeɪbiːz] *n.* the itch; mange. **scabietic** [–i'etɪk], *adj.* **scabious,** *adj.* pertaining to scabies or scabs.

scabrous ['skreɪbrəs] *adj.* having rough or scurfy surface; scaly; full of difficulties; risqué; obscene. **scabrate,** *adj.* **scabrescent,** *adj.* scaberulous. **scabrid,** *adj.* somewhat scabrous. **scabrities,** *n.* scabby skin condition.

scacchic ['skækɪk] *adj.* like or pertaining to chess.

scagliola [skæl'jəʊlə] (*Italian*) *n.* stonelike plasterwork for interior decoration. **scagliolist,** *n.*

scalar ['skeɪlə] *adj.* like a ladder; denotable by a number. **scalariform** [–'lær–], *adj.* like a ladder.

scalene ['skeɪliːn, skeɪ'liːn] *adj.* *Geom.*, have three sides of different length; *n.* such triangle. **scalenous,** *adj.*

scallion ['skæljən] *n.* shallot; leek.

scalpriform ['skælprɪfɔːm] *adj.* like chisel in shape.

scammony ['skæməni] *n.* kind of convolvulus of Near East, with root yielding resin used as purge. **scammoniate** [–'məʊniət], *adj.*

scandaroon [,skændə'ruːn] *n.* kind of homing pigeon.

scandent ['skændənt] *adj.* *Botany*, climbing.

scansion ['skænʃn] *n.* determination of metre of verse; prosody.

scansorial [skæn'sɔːriəl] *adj.* *Zoology*, climbing; used for climbing.

scantling ['skæntlɪŋ] *n.* small amount; small beam; trestle.

scaphion ['skeɪfiən] *n.* kind of sundial. **scaphism** ['skæf–], *n.* mode of execution by smearing criminals with honey and exposing them to insects.

scaphoid ['skæfɔɪd] *adj.* boat-shaped; such bone of carpus or tarsus.

scapiform ['skeɪpɪfɔːm] *adj.* like a stalk. **scapoid,** *adj.* **scapose,** *adj.* bearing stalks.

scapula ['skæpjʊlə] *n.* (*pl.* **-ae**) shoulder-blade. **scapular,** *adj.*; *n.* cowl-bearing part of monk's habit; badge, worn over shoulders, of monastic order; feather on bird's shoulder. **scapulary,** *n.* & *adj.* scapular; shoulder strap.

scarab(aeus) ['skærəb, ,skærə'biːəs] *n.* large black Mediterranean dung beetle, held sacred by ancient Egyptians; gem cut in shape of scarab. **scarabaeid,** *n.* member of beetle family that includes dung beetles and chafers. **scarabaeiform,** *adj.* like scarab. **scaraboid,** *n.* & *adj.* (gem) like scarab.

scaramouch(e) ['skærəmuːtʃ, –uːʃ, -aʊʃ] *n.* boastful coward in Commedia dell'Arte; ne'er-do-well.

scarcement ['skeəsmənt] *n.* narrow ledge on wall.

scarify ['skærɪfaɪ] *v.t.* scratch; cut; scar. **scarification, scarificator, scarifier,** *n.*

scarious ['skeəriəs] *adj.* thin and tough; bract-like. **scariose,** *adj.*

scarlatina [,skaːlə'tiːnə] *n.* *Medicine*, scarlet fever.

scaroid ['skeərɔɪd] *n.* & *adj.* (fish) like parrot fish, or belonging to parrot fish family of fishes.

scarp [skaːp] *n.* steep drop; cliff; *v.t.* make steep.

scatology [skə'tɒlədʒi] *n.* study of excrement or obscenity. **scatologic(al),** *adj.* **scatophagous,** *adj.* eating dung. **scatoscopy,** *n.* examination of faeces.

scaturient [skə'tjʊəriənt] *adj.* gushing.

scaurie ['skɔːri] (*Scottish*) *n.* young gull.

scazon ['skeɪzɒn] *n.* limping verse; choliamb. **scazontic,** *adj.*

scelalgia [se'lældʒiə] *n.* pain in leg.

scend [send] *v.i.* be heaved upwards, especially by wave; *n.* upward surge of vessel; lifting force of wave.

scenography [siː'nɒgrəfi] *n.* representation of object in perspective. **scenograph, scenographer,** *n.* **scenographic(al),** *adj.*

Schadenfreude ['ʃaːdn,frɔɪdə] (*German*) *n.* glee at others' misfortunes.

schapska ['ʃæpskə] *n.* flat-topped cavalry helmet.

schediasm ['ʃiːdiæzm] *n.* impromptu work; jotting. **schediastic,** *adj.*

schematograph [skɪ'mætəgraːf] *n.* instrument tracing reduced outline of person. **schematonics,** *n.* art of gesture expressing tones, etc.

schesis ['skiːsɪs] *n.* rhetorical device of weakening force of opponent's arguments by reference to his or her habit of thought.

schiller ['ʃɪlə] *n.* & *adj.* (having) bronzy lustre. **schillerise,** *v.t.*

schipperke ['ʃɪpəki, 'skɪ–] *n.* small black Belgian canal-boat dog.

schism [skɪzm, sɪzm] *n.* division, especially of church, into two parties. **schismatic(al),** *adj.* pertaining to or causing schism; *n.* , person involved in or promoting schism. **schismatise,** *v.i.* & *t.* **schismatism,** *n.*

schist [ʃɪst] *n.* foliated metamorphic crystalline rock. **schistaceous,** *adj.* slate-coloured. **schistic, schistose,** *adj.* **schistoid,** *adj.* like schist. **schistosis,** *n.* fibrosis of lungs from inhaling slate dust.

schistosome ['ʃɪstəsəʊm] *n.* disease-causing blood fluke. **schistosomiasis,** *n.*

schizocarp ['skɪtsəkaːp, 'skɪz–] *n.* compound fruit splitting into several one-seeded ones. **schizocarpic, schizocarpous,** *adj.* **schizogenesis, schizogony,** *n.* reproduction by division. **schizoid,** *adj.* pertaining to, like or suffering from schizophrenia. **schizophrenia,** *n.* mental disorder with 'splitting' of personality and separation from environment. **schizophyte** *n.* , plant reproducing only by multiple fission. **schizothymia**, *n.* schizophrenia-like mental disorder. **schizotrichia**, *n.* splitting of hair.

schlemiel, schlemihl [ʃləˈmiːl] *n. American slang*, unlucky or incompetent person who is often duped.

schlenter [ˈʃlentə] (*S African*) *n. & adj.* imitation (diamond).

schlepp [ʃlep] *v.i. & t. American slang*, drag (about); *n.*, wearisome task or journey.

schlieren [ˈʃliərən] *n.* visible streaks of different density in a fluid; streaks of different colour or composition in igneous rock.

Schloss [ʃlɒs] (*German*) *n.* (*pl.* **Schlösser**) castle

schnauzer [ˈʃnautsə, ˈʃnauzə] *n.* blackish German terrier.

schoenobatic [ˌskiːnəˈbætɪk] *adj.* pertaining to rope-walking. **schoenobatist** [-ˈnɒbət-], *n.*

scholium [ˈskəʊliəm] *n.* (*pl.* **-ia**) marginal note, especially by ancient grammarian. **scholiast**, *n.* writer of scholia.

schorl [ʃɔːl] *n.* tourmaline. **schorlaceous, schorlous, schorly**, *adj.*

schottische [ʃɒˈtiːʃ] *n.* polka-like 19th-cent. dance.

scialytic [ˌsaɪəˈlɪtɪk] *adj.* dispelling shadows. **sciagraphy**, *n.* art of shading; X-ray photography. **sciamachy**, *n.* mock battle; fighting with shadows or imaginary enemies. **sciapodous**, *adj.* with large feet. **sciatheric**, *adj.* pertaining to measurement of time by shadow, as in sundial.

sciatic [saɪˈætɪk] *adj.* pertaining to hip. **sciatica**, *n.* neuralgia of hip and thigh.

scibile [ˈskiːbɪleɪ, ˈsɪbɪli] *n.* thing which it is possible to know.

scientia [skiˈentɪə, siˈenʃɪə] (*Latin*) *n.* science; knowledge. **scientia scientiarum**, 'science of sciences'; philosophy.

scilicet [ˈsɪlɪset, ˈsaɪ-, ˈskiːlɪket] (*Latin*) *adv.* 'that is to say'; namely (*abbreviated* as **sc.**)

scintilla [sɪnˈtɪlə] *n.* (*pl.* **-ae**) spark; atom. **scintillant**, *adj.* sparkling. **scintillescent**, *adj.* twinkling. **scintillometer**, *n.* instrument measuring scintillation of star. **scintillate**, *v.i.* sparkle. **scintillation**, *n.*

sciolism [ˈsaɪəlɪzm] *n.* pretence to wisdom; conceit due to it. **sciolist**, *n.* **sciolistic**, *adj.*

sciomancy [ˈsaɪəmænsi] *n.* divination by reference to spirits of dead. **sciomantic**, *adj.*

scion [ˈsaɪən] *n.* young member of family; shoot of plant, especially taken for grafting.

sciophilous [saɪˈɒfɪləs] *adj.* applied to shade-loving plants. **sciophyte**, *n.* such plant.

scioptic [saɪˈɒptɪk] *adj.* pertaining to formation of images in darkened room, as in camera obscura. **scioptics**, *n.* **scioptric**, *adj.*

scirrhus [ˈsɪrəs, ˈskɪ-] *n.* (*pl.* **-hi**) hard tumour. **scirrhoid**, *adj.* **scirrhous**, *adj.*

scissile [ˈsɪsaɪl] *adj.* easily cut or split. **scission**, *n.* act of cutting or dividing; schism.

scissure, scissura [ˈsɪʃə, sɪˈsjuərə] *n.* cleft; fissure; scission.

sciurine [ˈsaɪjuraɪn, -rɪn] *adj.* pertaining to or like squirrels; belonging to squirrel division of rodents. **sciuroid**, *adj.* like a squirrel or a squirrel's tail.

sclera [ˈskliərə] *n.* dense white coat of eyeball. **scleral**, *adj.* **sclerectomy**, *n.* removal of sclera.

sclerema, *n.* induration. **sclerenchyma**, *n.* thickened and woody tissue of plants. **scleriasis**, *n.* induration, especially of edge of eyelid.

scleroderma [ˌsklɪərəˈdɜːmə, ˌskler-] *n.* disease marked by hardening of skin. **sclerodermic, sclerodermous, sclerodermatous**, *adj.* hardskinned; having bony armour.

sclerogenous [sklɪəˈrɒdʒɪnəs, sklie-] *adj.* producing hard tissue. **sclerogenic** [-ˈdʒenɪk], *adj.* **scleroid** [ˈsklɪə-], *adj.* indurated. **scleroma**, *n.* induration. **sclerometer**, *n.* instrument measuring hardness. **scleronychia**, *n.* hardening of nails.

sclerosis [sklɪəˈrəusɪs, skle-] *n.* (*pl.* **-ses**) hardening. **sclerotic** [-ˈrɒtɪk], *adj.* hard; pertaining to sclera; *n.* sclera. **sclerotitis**, *adj.* inflammation of sclera. **sclerotomy**, *n.* incision into sclera. **sclerous** [ˈsklɪə-], *adj.* hard.

scobiform [ˈskəʊbɪfɔːm] *adj.* like sawdust.

scolex [ˈskəʊleks] *n.* (*pl.* **-leces**) head of tapeworm. **scoleciasis**, *n.* infestation with tapeworms. **scolecid**, *adj.* **scoleciform**, *adj.* like scolex.

scoliometer [ˌskəʊliˈɒmɪtə] *n.* instrument measuring curvature. **scoliographic**, *adj.* marked by oblique lines. **scoliosis**, *n.* lateral spinal curvature.

scolopaceous [ˌskɒləˈpeɪʃəs] *adj.* snipe-like. **scolopacine**, *adj.* belonging to snipe family of birds.

scombriform [ˈskɒmbrɪfɔːm] *adj.* like mackerel; belonging to mackerel division of fishes. **scombroid**, *n. & adj.* (fish) like mackerel.

scopa [ˈskəʊpə] *n.* brush-like tuft on back legs or abdomen of bees.

scopic [ˈskɒpɪk] *adj.* visual.

scopodromic [ˌskɒpəˈdrɒmɪk] *adj.* pertaining to or denoting guided missiles travelling on a homing course.

scopolamine [skəˈpɒləmiːn, -ɪn] *n.* sleep-inducing drug obtained from nightshade family of plants.

scopula [ˈskɒpjulə] *n.* brush-like tuft of hairs on legs of some spiders.

scorbutic [skɔːˈbjuːtɪk] *n. & adj.* (person) suffering from scurvy; pertaining to or like scurvy.

scoria [ˈskɔːriə] *n.* (*pl.* **-ae**) slag; slag-like mass of lava. **scoriac, scoriaceous, scorious**, *adj.* **scoriform**, *adj.* like slag. **scorify**, *v.t.* reduce to slag.

scorpioid [ˈskɔːpiɔɪd] *adj.* scorpion-like; curved at end.

scortation [skɔːˈteɪʃn] *n.* fornication. **scortatory**, *adj.*

scoter [ˈskəʊtə] *n.* black sea duck; coot.

scotodinia [ˌskəʊtəˈdɪniə] *n.* dizziness together with headache and loss of vision. **scotograph**, *n.* instrument for writing without seeing; X-ray photograph. **scotoma**, *n.* (*pl.* **-ata**) blind spot. **scotophobia**, *n.* dread of darkness. **scotopia**, *n.* ability of eye to adjust to seeing in dark. **scotoscope**, *n.* instrument detecting objects in darkness.

scow [skau] *n.* large blunt-ended, flat-bottomed boat; refuse lighter.

scrannel [ˈskrænl] *adj.* weak; thin; harshsounding.

scrapie [ˈskreɪpi] *n.* disease of sheep, marked by progressive degeneration of the nervous system.

scree [skriː] *n.* steep slope with loose soil and stones.

screed [skriːd] *n.* lengthy (and dull) speech or piece of writing; guide to obtaining uniform thickness in plastering; instrument for levelling or mix for surfacing concrete.

scrim [skrɪm] *n.* (stage curtain made of) open-weave fabric.

scrimshaw ['skrɪmʃɔː] *n.* carving on bone, ivory, etc. as done by sailors.

scriniary ['skrɪnɪərɪ] *n.* keeper of archives.

scrip [skrɪp] *n. Comm.*, document showing entitlement to receive something; share certificate, especially preliminary issued on payment of first instalment; certificate transferable into share issued as dividend. **scripophily,** *n.* hobby of collecting bonds and share certificates.

scriptorium [skrɪp'tɔːrɪəm] *n.* (*pl.* **-ia**) writing room, especially of scribes in medieval monastery.

scriptory ['skrɪptərɪ] *adj.* pertaining to writing; in writing; *n.* scriptorium.

scripturient [skrɪp'tjʊərɪənt] *n.* having violent desire to write. **scripturiency,** *n.*

scrivello [skrɪ'veləʊ] *n.* elephant's tusk.

scrivener ['skrɪvənə] *n.* writer-out of documents; lawyer. **scrivener's palsy,** writer's cramp. **scrivenery,** *n.*

scrobiculate [skrəʊ'bɪkjʊlət, −eɪt] *adj.* pitted. **scrobicule, scrobiculus,** *n.* small depression. **scrobiculus cordis,** pit of stomach.

scrod [skrɒd] (*American,*) *n.* young cod or haddock, especially split and bound for cooking.

scrofula ['skrɒfjʊlə] *n.* tuberculous condition, especially of children, with enlargement of lymphatic glands of neck; king's evil. **scrofulism, scrofulosis,** *n.* **scrofulitic, scrofulous,** *adj.*

scrophulariaceous [,skrɒfjʊlərɪ'eɪʃəs] *adj.* pertaining to or like figwort; belonging to figwort family of plants, which includes veronica, antirrhinum, etc.

scrotum ['skrəʊtəm] *n.* (*pl.* **-ta**) bag of flesh containing testicles. **scrotal,** *adj.* **scrotiform,** *adj.* pouch-shaped.

scrutable ['skruːtəbl] *adj.* understandable upon close examination.

scrutator [skruː'teɪtə] *n.* one who scrutinises or investigates. **scrutineer,** [−'nɪə], *n.* person scrutinising votes.

scullion ['skʌlɪən] *n.* scullery servant; washer of dishes; *adj.* menial; wretched.

sculpsit ['skʌlpsɪt] (*Latin*) 'carved (it)'; 'engraved (it)'.

scumble ['skʌmbl] *v.t.* overlay with thin layer of paint to soften shade, line, etc.

scuncheon ['skʌntʃn] *n.* bevelled inner edge of door jamb or window frame.

scunner ['skʌnə] *n.* strong dislike.

scupper ['skʌpə] *n.* gap in ship's bulwarks for drainage of water.

scurrilous ['skʌrələs] *adj.* abusive; ribald; obscene. **scurrility,** *n.*

scurvy ['skɜːvɪ] *n.* disease, due to deficiency of vitamin C, marked by skin haemorrhage, anaemia, spongy gums, etc.

scutal ['skjuːtl] *adj.* pertaining to shield. **scutate,** *adj.* shield- or buckler-shaped; having horny scales. **scute, scutum,** *n.* large scale, as of reptile's head. **scutella,** *n.* (*pl.* **-ae**) small scute. **scutellate, scutulate,** *adj.* shaped like platter; covered with scutellae. **scutelligerous,** *adj.* bearing scutellae.

scutiferous, *adj.* bearing a shield or scutes. **scutiform,** *adj.* shield-shaped. **scutigerous,** *adj.* bearing scutes.

scuttlebutt ['skʌtlbʌt] *n.* cask of drinking water on ship's deck; *American,* rumour, gossip.

scyphate ['saɪfeɪt] *adj.* cup-shaped. **scyphiform,** *adj.*

sebaceous [sɪ'beɪʃəs] *adj.* fatty; greasy; secreting oily substance. **seborrhagia, seborrhoea** [,seb−], *n.* excessive secretion of sebaceous glands. **sebum** ['siː−], *n.* fatty substance secreted by sebaceous glands.

SECAM ['siːkæm] *abbreviation* of French Système en Couleurs à Mémoire (French colour television transmission system).

secant ['siːkənt] *n. & adj.* cutting (line), especially one cutting curve at two points; radius produced through one end of arc to meet tangent drawn to other end; ratio of this line to radius (*abbreviated* as **sec.**).

secco ['sekəʊ] (*Italian*) *n.* painting on dry plaster.

secern [sɪ'sɜːn] *v.i. & t.* secrete; separate; discriminate. **secernent,** *n. & adj.* (thing) secreting or causing secretion. **secernment,** *n.*

secodont ['sekədɒnt] *adj.* having cutting teeth.

secque [sek] *n.* light sabot; clog.

secreta [sɪ'kriːtə] *n. pl.* products of secretion.

secretaire [,sekrə'teə] *n.* writing desk.

secrete [sɪ'kriːt] *v.t.* conceal; discharge; emit. **secretion,** *n.* **secretional, secretionary, secretory,** *adj.*

secretum [sɪ'kriːtəm] *n.* (*pl.* **-ta**) private seal.

sectarian [sek'teərɪən] *n. & adj.* (person) belonging to religious sect; bigot(ed). **sectarianism,** *n.* **sectary,** *n.* (zealous) adherent of sect.

sectile ['sektaɪl] *adj.* capable of being cut, especially cleanly; cut into small divisions. **sectility,** *n.*

sectorial [sek'tɔːrɪəl] *adj.* pertaining to sectors; adapted for cutting; *n.* such tooth.

secular ['sekjʊlə] *adj.* worldly; non-religious; not belonging to religious order; lasting for centuries; occurring once in a century. **secularise,** *v.t.* make secular. **secularity,** *n.*

secund ['siːkənd] *adj.* on one side only. **secundiflorous,** *adj.* having such flowers. **secundines** ['sekəndaɪnz, −iːnz] *n. pl.* afterbirth. **secundipara** [,sekən'dɪpərə] *n.* woman having had two child-deliveries. **secundiparous,** *adj.* **secundiparity** [−'pær−], *n.*

secundogeniture [sɪ,kʌndəʊ'dʒenɪtʃə] *n.* state of being second eldest child; custom whereby such child inherits parent's property.

secundum [sɪ'kʌndəm] (*Latin*) *prep.* 'according to'. **secundum legem,** according to law.

securiform [sɪ'kjʊərɪfɔːm] *adj.* axe-shaped. **securigerous,** *adj.* bearing an axe.

secus ['siːkəs] (*Latin*) *adv.* 'otherwise'.

sedent ['siːdnt] *adj.* in sitting position.

sedentary ['sedntərɪ] *adj.* habitually sitting; done while sitting; stationary. **sedentation,** *n.*

sederunt [sɪ'dɪərənt] (*Latin*) 'they were sitting'; session of court; gathering; long discussion.

sedilia [sɪ'dɪlɪə, −'diːl−] *n. pl.* (*sing.* **-le**) clergy's stone seats in chancel wall.

sedition [sɪ'dɪʃn] *n.* incitement to rebellion. **seditionary, seditious,** *adj.*

sedulous ['sedjʊləs] *adj.* taking great care; assiduous. **sedulity,** *n.*

seersucker ['sɪəsʌkə] *n.* light puckered linen or cotton fabric.

segue ['seɪgweɪ, 'seg–, –wi] *v.i. Music,* proceed from one piece or section to another without a break.

seicento [seɪ't ʃentəʊ] *(Italian) n. & adj.* 17th century.

seiche [seɪʃ] *n.* rocking movement of surface of lake or inland sea.

Seidel ['zaɪdl] *(German) n.* large beer mug with lid.

seigneur [seɪ'njɜ:] *n.* lord, especially of manor. **seigneurial, seigniorial, seignorial,** *adj.* **seigniorage, seignioralty, seigniory, seigneury,** *n.* lordship; dominion; brassage; mining royalty.

seine [seɪn] *n.* large vertical fishing net; *v.i. & t.* catch (fish) with seine.

seisin ['si:zɪn] *n.* freehold possession of land.

seismic ['saɪzmɪk] *adj.* pertaining to earthquakes. **seismicity,** *n.* **seismal, seismatical, seismetic,** *adj.* **seismism,** *n.* seismic phenomena. **seismograph,** *n.* instrument recording earthquakes. **seismology,** *n.* study of earthquakes. **seismometer,** *n.* sort of seismograph measuring movements of ground in earthquake. **seismoscope,** *n.* instrument merely showing occurrence of earthquake. **seismotectonic,** *adj.* pertaining to geological features related to earthquakes. **seismotherapy,** *n.* medical treatments by vibrations. **seismotic,** *adj.* causing earthquakes.

seity ['seɪəti, 'si:–] *n.* personality; 'selfness'.

seizin ['si:zɪn] *see* **seisin.**

sejant ['si:dʒənt] *(Heraldry) adj.* sitting.

sejugate ['sedʒugeɪt] *v.t.* separate.

selachian [sɪ'leɪkɪən] *n. & adj.* (fish) like shark or ray; belonging to shark family of fishes; a shark or ray.

selah ['si:lə] *(Hebrew) n.* pause; kind of musical sign of Psalms.

selenian [sɪ'li:nɪən] *adj.* lunar. **selenic** [–'lenɪk], *adj.* like the moon; containing selenium. **selenite** ['sel–], *n.* dweller on moon; kind of gypsum. **selenitic,** *adj.* pertaining to or affected by moon; of or pertaining to selenite. **selenium,** *n.* nonmetallic solid element used in photoelectric cells. **selenocentric,** *adj.* pertaining to moon's centre; having moon as centre. **selenodont,** *n. & adj.* (animal) having crescent-shaped ridges on the crowns of the molar teeth. **selenography,** *n.* study of moon's surface. **selenology,** *n.* study of moon. **selenomancy,** *n.* divination by the moon. **selenoscope,** *n.* instrument for viewing moon.

selliform ['selɪfɔ:m] *adj.* saddle-shaped. **sellate,** *adj.* having saddle.

semanteme [sɪ'mænti:m] *n.* sememe. **semantic,** *adj.* pertaining to meaning. **semantics,** *n.* science of meanings of words.

semasiology [sɪ,meɪzɪ'ɒlədʒi, -si–] *n.* semantics. **semasiological,** *adj.* **semasiologist,** *n.*

sematic [sɪ'mætɪk] *adj. Zoology,* (of coloration) serving as a warning. **sematography,** *n.* writing in signs and not letters. **sematology,** *n.* semantics.

semeiography, semeiology *see* **semiography, semiology.**

semelincident [,semə'lɪnsɪdənt] *adj.* occurring only once in same person.

sememe ['si:mi:m] *n.* smallest unanalysable unit of linguistic meaning (e.g. a word or affix).

semester [sɪ'mestə] *(American) n.* academic half-year.

semibreve ['semɪbri:v] *n. Musical,* longest generally used note, having twice length of minim and half that of breve.

semic ['si:mɪk] *adj.* pertaining to a sign.

semi-conductor [,semikən'dʌktə] *n.* solid which is an electrical non-conductor in its pure state or at low temperatures and becomes a conductor when impure or at higher temperatures.

seminal ['semɪnəl, 'si:m–] *adj.* pertaining to semen; pertaining to seed; capable of development; having wide creative influence. **semination,** *n.* sowing of seed. **seminative,** *adj.* producing growth. **seminiferal, seminiferous, seminific(al),** *adj.* producing seed or semen. **seminivorous,** *adj.* seed-eating. **seminule,** *n.* small seed; spore.

semiography [,semi'ɒgrəfi] *n.* description of signs and symptoms. **semiology,** *n.* semiotics; system of signs. **semiotic,** *adj.* pertaining to signs, symbols or symptoms or the study of these. **semiotician,** *n.* **semiotics,** *n.* study of signs and symbols, especially the relations between language and its referents; *Medical,* symptomatology. .

semiology [,semi'ɒlədʒi, ,si:m–] *n.* semiotics; system of signs. **semiotic,** *adj.* pertaining to signs, symbols or symptoms or the study of these. **semiotician,** *n.* **semiotics,** *n.* study of signs and symbols, *especially* the relations between language and its referents; *Medicine,* symptomatology.

semioviparous [,semiəu'vɪpərəs] *adj.* bringing forth young in incompletely developed state.

semiped ['semɪped] *n.* half a metrical foot. **semipedal,** *adj.*

semiquote ['semikwəut] *n.* single quotation mark or inverted comma (' ').

semitaur ['semitɔ:] *n.* mythological creature, half-man and half-bull.

semper ['sempə] *(Latin) adv.* 'always'. **semper fidelis,** 'always faithful'. **semper idem** (*feminine* **semper eadem**), 'always the same'.

sempiternal [,sempɪ'tɜ:nl] *adj.* eternal. **sempiternity,** *n.*

senary ['si:nəri] *adj.* having six as base; six-fold. **senarius,** *n.* (*pl.* **–rii**) verse of six feet.

senectitude [sɪ'nektɪtju:d], **senectude** [–tju:d] *n.* old age. **senectuous,** *adj.* old.

senescent [sɪ'nesnt] *adj.* growing old. **senescence,** *n.*

seneschal ['senɪʃl] *adj.* steward, especially of ancient palace or manor.

senicide ['si:nɪsaɪd] *n.* killing off of old men.

sennet ['senɪt] *n.* fanfare, especially on Elizabethan stage.

sennight ['senaɪt] *n.* week.

sennit ['senɪt] *n.* plaited rope, straw, etc.

senocular [siː'nɒkjʊlə] *adj.* having six eyes.

sensate ['senseɪt] *adj.* perceived by senses; endowed with senses.

sensillum [sen'sɪləm] *n.* (*pl.* **–la**) simple sense organ consisting of one or a few receptor cells at the end of a nerve connection.

sensorium [sen'sɔ:riəm] *n.* (*pl.* **–riums** or **–ria**) part of brain that receives and processes sensory stimuli.

sententia [sen'tenʃiə] *n.* (*pl.* **–ae**) aphorism; opinion. **sententiary,** *n.* speaker of sententiae.

sententious, *adj.* aphoristic; full of aphorisms; pompously moralising.

sentient ['senʃnt, 'sentiənt] *adj.* capable of feeling. **sentience,** *n.*

sentisection [ˌsentɪ'sekʃn] *n.* vivisection without use of anaesthetic.

sepal ['sepl, 'siː–] *n.* portion of calyx. **sepaline, sepaloid,** *adj.* like sepal.

sepia ['siːpiə] *n.* cuttle-fish; inky secretion of cuttle-fish; rich brown pigment obtained from this. **sepic** ['siːpɪk, 'sep–], *adj.* done in sepia colour. **sepiarian, sepiary,** *n.* & *adj.* (pertaining to) cuttle-fish.

sepicolous [sɪ'pɪkələs] *adj.* dwelling in hedges. **sepiment** ['sep–], *n.* hedge.

sepoy ['siːpɔɪ] *n.* formerly, Indian native soldier in British service.

seppuku [se'puːkuː] (*Japanese*) hara-kiri.

sepsis ['sepsɪs] *n.* state of poisoning in part of body or blood stream.

sept [sept] *n.* division of tribe; clan.

septaemia [sep'tiːmiə] *n.* septicaemia.

septal ['septl] *adj.* pertaining to sept or septum.

septan ['septən] *n.* & *adj.* (fever) recurring after seven days (*i.e.* every sixth day).

septate ['septeɪt] *adj.* having septum. **septation,** *n.*

septave ['septeɪv] *n.* seven-tone musical scale.

septemfluous [sep'temfluəs] *adj.* in seven streams. **septemfoliate,** *adj.* having seven leaves.

septemplicate [sep'templɪkət] *n.* one of seven copies.

septemvir [sep'temvə] *n.* member of septemvirate. **septemvirate,** *n.* government by, or group of, seven men.

septenary [sep'tiːnəri, 'septən–] *adj.* pertaining to seven; *n.* seven; set of seven. **septenate,** *adj.* divided into seven portions.

septendecimal [ˌsepten'desɪml] *adj.* pertaining to seventeen.

septennary [sep'tenəri] **septennial** [–iəl] *adj.* lasting for seven years; occurring every seven years. **septennate, septennium** (*pl.* –nia) *n.* period of seven years.

septentrional [sep'tentriənl] *adj.* pertaining to north. **septentrionality,** *n.* **septentrionic** [–i'ɒnɪk], *adj.*

septicaemia [ˌseptɪ'siːmiə] *n.* blood-poisoning with presence of bacteria and their toxins in blood. **septopyaemia,** *n.* combination of septicaemia and pyaemia.

septilateral [ˌseptɪ'lætərəl] *adj.* having seven sides.

septillion [sep'tɪljən] *n.* a million sextillions (10⁴²); *American & French,* a thousand sextillions (10²⁴).

septimal ['septɪml] *adj.* pertaining to seven.

septimanal [ˌseptɪ'meɪnl] *adj.* weekly.

septisyllable ['septɪˌsɪləbl] *n.* word of seven syllables. **septisyllabic** [–'læbɪk], *adj.*

septuagenarian [ˌseptjuədʒə'neəriən] **septuagenary** [–'dʒiːn–] *n.* & *adj.* (person) in from seventieth to eightieth year.

Septuagesima [ˌseptjuə'dʒesɪmə] *n.* third Sunday before Lent; period of seventy days. **septuagesimal,** *adj.*

Septuagint ['septjuədʒɪnt] *n.* Greek version of Old Testament, supposedly translated by seventy scholars.

septum ['septəm] *n.* (*pl.* –ta) *Biology, Anatomy,* partition. **septulum,** *n.* (*pl.* –la) small septum.

sepulchre ['seplkə] *n.* tomb. **whited sepulchre,** hypocrite; seemingly holy but really evil person or thing. **sepulchral** [–'pʌlkrəl], *adj.* pertaining to tombs; gloomy; hollow.

sepulture ['sepltʃə] *n.* interment. **sepultural** [–'pʌltʃərəl], *adj.*

sequacious [sɪ'kweɪʃəs] *adj.* easily led or moulded; servile; logical. **sequacity** [–'kwæs–], *n.*

sequela [sɪ'kwiːlə] *n.* (*pl.* –ae) *Medicine,* consequential effect of a disease, condition, etc., complication. **sequelant,** *n.*

sequent ['siːkwənt] *adj.* following in sequence or as consequence. **sequential** [–'kwenʃl], *adj.*

sequester [sɪ'kwestə] *v.t.* set apart; seclude. **sequestrate** ['siː–], *v.t.* confiscate; set apart income of estate to meet claims. **sequestration,** *n.* **sequestrator,** *n.*

sequitur ['sekwɪtə] (*Latin*) '(it) follows'; natural or logical consequence or deduction.

sequoia [sɪ'kwɔɪə] *n.* gigantic redwood or 'big tree' of California.

sérac [se'ræk] (*French*) *n.* ice pinnacle among glacier crevasses.

seraglio [sə'rɑːljəʊ] *n.* (*pl.* –li, -yē) harem; palace of sultan.

serai [sə'raɪ] *n.* caravanserai.

serape [sə'rɑːpi] *n.* Spanish-American shawl.

sere [sɪə] *n.* sequence of changes in population during ecological development of an area.

serein [sə'ræn, –'reɪn] *n.* fine rain falling from an apparently cloudless sky.

serendipity [ˌserən'dɪpəti] *n.* propensity for finding things by chance or in unexpected places.

seriatim [ˌsɪəri'eɪtɪm] (*Latin*) *adv.* in series; point by point.

sericate ['serɪkət], **sericeous** [sɪ'rɪʃəs] *n.* silky; bearing silky hairs. **serictery,** *n.* caterpillar's silk-producing gland. **sericulture,** *n.* breeding of silkworms for silk production.

serif ['serɪf] *n.* minute fine line, especially horizontal, of a letter, as at top and bottom of verticals in 'h'.

serific [sɪ'rɪfɪk] *adj.* silk-producing. **serigraph,** *n.* silk-screen print. **serimeter,** *n.* instrument for testing silk.

serin ['serɪn] *n.* small finch.

serment ['sɜːmənt] *n.* oath.

sermuncle ['sɜːmʌŋkl] *n.* short sermon.

serology [sɪə'rɒlədʒi] *n.* study of serums. **serologic(al),** *adj.* **serologist,** *n.*

serositis [ˌsɪərə'saɪtɪs] *n.* inflammation of serous membrane. **serosity** [–'rɒs–], *n.* state of being serous; serous fluid.

serotine ['serətaɪn] *n.* brown bat; *adj.* serotinous.

serotinous [sə'rɒtɪnəs] *adj.* flowering late.

serotonin [ˌsɪərə'təʊnɪn] *n.* adrenalin-like crystalline compound occurring in the brain, intestines, and blood platelets, that induces contraction of muscles and blood vessels.

serous ['sɪərəs] *adj.* pertaining to or like serum; thin and watery; producing such fluid.

serpette [sɜː'pet] (*French*) *n.* kind of pruning knife.

serpiginous [sə'pɪdʒɪnəs] *adj.* *Med.,* spreading by creeping. **serpigo** [–'paɪgəʊ], *n.* such disease; ringworm.

serpivolant [sə'pɪvələnt] *n.* flying serpent.

serpolet ['sɜːpələt] *n.* wild thyme.

serrate ['sereɪt] *adj.* having notched or toothed edge. **serradentate,** *adj.* having serrations which are themselves serrate. **serratic** [–'rætɪk], *adj.* like a saw. **serration, serrature,** *n.*

serried ['serid] *adj.* densely-packed; in close formation.

serriferous [se'rɪfərəs] *adj.* having a saw-like organ. **serriform,** *adj.* like a saw.

serrulate ['serʊleɪt] *adj.* finely serrate. **serrulation,** *n.*

serrurerie [se,rʊərə'riː] (*French*) *n.* wrought-iron work.

sertule ['sɜːtjuːl], **sertulum** [–əm] *n.* umbel; scientific collection of plants. **sertum,** *n.* treatise on such a collection.

serum ['sɪərəm] *n.* (*pl.* **–s, –ra**) watery part of bodily fluid, especially blood, separated in coagulation; such fluid containing antibodies.

serval ['sɜːvl] *n.* African wild cat and its fur. **servine,** *adj.*

servile ['sɜːvaɪl] *adj.* pertaining to or like a slave; slavish; cringing. **servilism,** *n.* slavery; advocation of slavery. **servility** [–'vɪl–], *n.*

servomotor ['sɜːvəʊ,məʊtə] *n.* small auxiliary electrical motor operating a control, or carrying out subsidiary operation in a machine. **servomechanism,** *n.* control system where a small-input mechanism regulates a large-output mechanism.

sesame ['sesəmi] *n.* E Indian seed-yielding plant. **open sesame,** spell opening door in story of Ali Baba and the Forty Thieves; any master-key or magical command. **sesamoid,** *adj.* pertaining to mass of bone or cartilage in a tendon, as kneecap.

sesquialteral [,seskwi'æltərəl] *adj.* one and a half times as big; having ratio 3:2.

sesquicentennial [,seskwisen'teniəl] *adj.* pertaining to 150 years; *n.* 150th anniversary.

sesquiduplicate [,seskwi'djuːplɪkət] *adj.* having ratio of 5:2.

sesquipedalian [,seskwɪpɪ'deɪliən] *adj.* a foot and a half long; using very long words; *n.* such thing or word. **sesquipedalianism, sesquipedality,** *n.*

sesquiquartal [,seskwi'kwɔːtl] *adj.* having ratio 5:4. **sesquintal,** *adj.* having ratio 6:5.

sesquiseptimal [,seskwi'septɪml] *adj.* having ratio 8:7. **sesquisextal,** *adj.* having ratio 7:6.

sesquitertian [,seskwi'tɜːʃn] *adj.* having ratio 4:3.

sessile ['sesaɪl] *adj.* attached by base without a stalk; attached permanently. **sessility,** *n.*

sestet [,ses'tet] *n.* sextet; six-lined stanza; final six lines of sonnet.

sestina [se'stiːnə] *n.* (*pl.* **–ne**) poem of six-lined stanzas with six end-words repeated in each stanza and in the envoi.

seta ['siːtə] *n.* (*pl.* **–ae**) bristle; any bristle-like organ. **setaceous** [sɪ'teɪʃəs], *adj.* bristly. **setal,** *adj.* **setarious,** *adj.* like a bristle. **setiferous,** *adj.* bearing bristles; pertaining to swine.

seton ['siːtn] *n.* thread passed under skin acting as channel for discharge.

setose ['siːtəʊs] *adj.* bristly.

settecento [,seti'tʃentəʊ] (*Italian*) *n.* & *adj.* 18th century.

setula ['setjulə] *n.* (*pl.* **–ae**) small seta. **setule,** *n.* **setuliform,** *adj.* like setula. **setulose, setulous,** *adj.* having setulae.

sève [sev, seɪv] (*French*) *n.* wine's distinctive bouquet; sap.

severy ['severi] *n.* compartment of vaulted ceiling.

sevum [sɪ'vəm] *n.* suet in pharmaceutics.

sexadecimal [sɜksəd3s'ɪməl] *adj.* pertaining to sixteen; sixteenth.

sexagenarian [sɜksəjɪnəə'ɪən] *n.* & *adj.* (person) in from sixtieth to seventieth year. **sexagenary** [–æj'ɪnərɪ], *n.*; *adj.* pertaining to sixty; proceeding by sets of sixty.

Sexagesima [sɜksəjɜs'ɪmə] *n.* second Sunday before Lent. **sexagesimal,** *adj.* pertaining to sixty.

sexcentenary [sɜkssɜntɪ'nərɪ] *adj.* pertaining to six hundred (years); *n.* six hundredth anniversary.

sexenary [sɜks'ɪnərɪ] *adj.* six-fold. **sexennial,** *adj.* lasting six years; occurring every six years; *n.* such occurrence. **sexennium,** *n.* (*pl.* **–nia**) period of six years.

sexipara [sɜksɪp'ərə] *n.* woman having had six child-deliveries. **sexiparous,** *adj.* **sexiparity** [–ær'ɪtɪ], *n.*

sextain [sɜks'teɪn] *n.* sestina; sestet.

Avoiding sexism in English

The pronoun problem. English does not have a non-sex-specific third-person singular pronoun. When talking about someone, you have to plump for either *he* or *she.* When you are referring to people in general, or to a person of unknown sex, this involves an invidious choice. The traditional practice is to use the masculine pronoun ('Someone's left his book behind'), but this is open to the objection that it is demeaning to women. In many contexts it is possible to use *he or she* instead, although if it is repeated several times within a few sentences it begins to sound very cumbersome. The plural but non-sex-specific *they* is often used as an alternative ('Someone's left their book behind'). This is still regarded by purists as 'incorrect', but is increasingly prevalent in the spoken language and it has much to recommend it. Another option is, of course, to reformulate your sentence so as to avoid the choice ('Someone's left a book behind').

The -man suffix. Many English words, particularly names of occupations, contain the final element *-man.* This is open to the objection that it excludes women from the category denoted by the word. The notion of replacing it with a nonsex-specific element, such as *person,* met with much heavy-handed sarcasm at first, but the last quarter of the 20th century has seen the evolution of a range of alternative options that are becoming established in usage (if not always in people's affections): for example, *fire-fighter* for *fireman, chair* for *chairman, humankind* for *mankind,* and even *spokesperson* for *spokesman.*

sextan [sɔks'tən] *n. & adj.* (fever) recurring after six days (*i.e.* every fifth day).

sextant [sɔks'tənt] *n.* sixth part of circle; nautical instrument with that arc for measuring altitudes.

sextennial [sɔkstɛn'ɪəl] *adj.* sexennial.

sextern [sɔks'tən] *n.* quire of six sheets.

sextillion [sɔkstɪl'yən] *n.* a million quintillions (10³⁶); *American & French*, a thousand quintillions (10²¹).

sextodecimo [sɔkstədɛs'ɪməu] *n.* book size 55/8 x 43/8 ins. (*abbreviated* as **16mo.**).

sextumvirate [sɔkstʌm'vɪrət] *n.* government by six men.

sforzando [sfuɔtsæn'dəu] (*Italian*) *adj. Music,* accented (*abbreviated* as **sf, sfz**).

sfumato [sfuːmaː'to] (*Italian*) *adj.* misty; *n.* painting technique of blending tones to produce soft outlines.

sgraffito [zgraːfiː'təu] (*Italian*) *n.* pottery decoration by scratching through surface to reveal a differently-coloured ground.

shabash [shaː'baːsh] (*Persian*) *exclamation* bravo!

shabrack [shæb'ræk] *n.* saddle-cloth.

shad [shæd] *n.* deep-bodied herring-like marine fish, spawning in rivers.

shaddock [shæd'ək] *n.* grape-fruit-like tree and fruit.

shadoof, shaduf [shaː'duːf'] *n.* method of raising water in Egypt in a counterpoised bucket at end of a long pole.

shagreen [shəgriːn'] *n.* untanned leather bearing many small round protuberances, especially dyed green; shark-skin.

shagroon [shəgruːn'] (*New Zealand*) *n.* non-English, especially, Australian, settler on S Island.

shahin [shaː'hiːn'] (*Pers.*) *n.* kind of Indian falcon.

shahzada(h) [shaːzaː'də] (*Hindu*) *n.* king's son.

shaitan [sheɪtaːn'] (*Arabic*) *n.* the Devil; evil spirit; *Indian*, duststorm.

shake [sheɪk] *n.* unit of time equal to a hundred-millionth of a second, used in describing nuclear processes.

shako [shəkəu'] *n.* soldier's high crowned peaked cap.

shale [sheɪl] *n.* laminated rock of consolidated clay or mud.

shallop [shæl'əp] *n.* light river boat with sail and oars.

shalom [shaːləum', shɔː'–] (*Hebrew*) *n.* peace (Jewish greeting). **shalom aleihem** [–aːleɪ'kɜm], 'peace be unto you'.

shalwar *see* **salwar**.

shama [shaː'mə] *n.* Indian millet-like cereal; Indian song-bird.

shaman [shaː'mən, shæm'–] *n.* medicine man; witch doctor. **shamaness**, *n.* female shaman. **shamanic**, *adj.* **shamanism**, *n.* primitive religion in which shamans are much venerated as having power to communicate with gods and spirits. **shamanistic**, *adj.*

shandrydan [shæn'drɪdæn] *n.* Irish two-wheeled cart; *jocular*, any worn-out antique vehicle.

shanghai [shænghaɪ'] *v.t.* drug and ship aboard a vessel as a sailor.

shard [shaːd] *n.* piece of broken pottery; elytrum.

shashlik, shashlick [shæʃ'lɪk] *n.* kebab.

shawm [shɔːm] *n.* ancient oboe-like musical instrument.

shea [shɪː] *n.* African tree with seeds yielding a white fat. **shea butter**, such fat.

sheading [shiː'dɪng] *n.* administrative division of Isle of Man.

shearling [shɪə'lɪng] *n.* one-year-old sheep, from which one crop of wool has been taken.

shearwater [shɪə'wɔːtə] *n.* gull-like oceanic bird of the petrel family.

shebang [shɪbæng'] (*American*) *n.* hut; outfit; contrivance; business.

shebeen [shɪbiːn'] (*Irish*) *n.* unlicensed liquor-selling place.

Shelta ['ʃeltə] *n.* secret slang of wandering tinkers and similar groups.

Sheol ['ʃiːɒl, –əul] (*Hebrew*) *n.* Hell; the underworld; the grave. **sheolic**, *adj.*

sherardise ['ʃerədaɪz] *v.t.* coat with zinc by process invented by Sherard Cowper-Coles.

sherd [ʃɜːd] *n.* shard.

sherif [ʃə'riːf] *n.* Arab prince; Muslim ruler. **sherifate**, *n.* sherif's jurisdiction or office. **sherifian**, *adj.*

shibah ['ʃibaː, 'ʃivə] (*Hebrew*) *n.* seven days' mourning.

shibboleth ['ʃɪbəleθ] *n.* slogan; watchword; anything forming test of loyalty, nationality, etc., or distinguishing a party or denomination; linguistic peculiarity. **shibbolethic**, *adj.*

shikar [ʃɪ'kaː] (*Indian*) *n.* hunting; game; *v.i. & t.* hunt (animal) as sport. **shikaree, shakari, shakary**, *n.* (big game) hunter.

shiksa ['ʃɪksə] *n.* (often derogatory) non-Jewish girl.

shillelagh [ʃɪ'leɪlə] (*Irish*) *n.* cudgel.

shirakashi [ˌʃɪrə'kaːʃi] (*Japanese*) *n.* Japanese evergreen oak.

shirr [ʃɜː] *v.t. & i.* gather fabric in parallel rows, especially using elastic thread. **shirring**, *n.* such gathers as decoration.

shivaree [ˌʃɪvə'riː] *n.* charivari.

shoat [ʃəut] *n.* recently weaned piglet.

shogun ['ʃəugʌn] (*Japanese*) *n.* one of a series of Japanese military governors exercising imperial powers until 19th century. **shogunal**, *adj.* **shogunate**, *n.*

shola ['ʃəulə] *n.* jungle of S India.

shrievalty ['ʃriːvltɪ] *n.* sheriff's office or jurisdiction.

shrive [ʃraɪv] *v.t.* give absolution to after confession. **shrift**, *n.* absolution.

shtick [ʃtɪk] *n. slang* comedian's routine.

shuck [ʃʌk] *n. & v.t.* husk, pod.

shulwar *see* **salwar**.

shyster ['ʃaɪstə] (*American*) *n.* dishonest lawyer; swindler.

sial ['saɪæl] *n.* siliceous rock; outer part of earth's surface.

sialagogic [ˌsaɪələ'gɒdʒɪk] *n. & adj.* (substance) promoting salivation. **sialogogue**, *n.* **sialoid**, *adj.* like saliva.

sib [sɪb] *n.* kindred; kinsman; brother or sister; descendants from a common ancestor; *adj.* blood-related.

sibilant ['sɪbɪlənt] *n. & adj.* hissing (sound). **sibilate**, *v.i. & t.* pronounce like sibilant. **sibilation, sibilance, sibilancy**, *n.* **sibilatory, sibilous**, *adj.*

sibling ['sɪblɪŋ] *n.* one of several children of the same parents; brother or sister.

sic [sɪk] (*Latin*) *adv.* 'thus'; appearing thus in the original.

sicarian [sɪ'keəriən] *n.* murderer.

siccation [sɪ'keɪʃn] *n.* act of drying. **siccative**, *adj.*

siccimeter [sɪk'sɪmɪtə] *n.* instrument measuring evaporation from liquid surface.

sice [saɪs] *n.* six on a dice; syce.

sideration [ˌsɪdə'reɪʃn] *n.* use of green manure.

sidereal [saɪ'dɪəriəl] *adj.* pertaining or according to stars; measured by stellar motion. **siderean**, *adj.* **siderism** ['sɪd–], *n.* belief in influence of stars on human affairs.

siderography [ˌsɪdə'rɒgrəfi] *n.* art of steel engraving, or copying such engravings.

sideromancy ['sɪdərəmænsi] *n.* divination by the stars.

sideroscope ['sɪdərəskəup] *n.* instrument detecting presence of iron magnetically. **siderose**, *adj.* like or containing iron. **siderous**, *adj.* like iron.

siderurgy, *n.* metallurgy of iron.

sidi ['sɪdi] *n.* African negro; African Muslim title of respect.

sierra [si'erə, –'eərə] *n.* rugged mountain chain. **sierran**, *adj.*

siesta [si'estə] (*Spanish*) *n.* short rest, especially at midday.

siffilate ['sɪfɪleɪt] *v.t.* whisper.

siffleur [si'flɜːr] (*French*) *n.* (*fem.* **–euse**, [–'flɜːz]) whistler.

sigil ['sɪdʒɪl] *n.* seal; image. **sigillary**, **sigillistic**, *adj.* **sigillate**, *adj.* bearing seal-like marks; *v.t.* seal. **sigillation**, *n.* **sigillative**, *adj.* causing or tending to scar-formation. **sigillography**, *n.* study of seals. **sigillum**, *n.* (*pl.* **–lla**) seal, especially of confession. .

sigla ['sɪglə] *n. pl.* (list of) abbreviations, symbols, etc. denoting words.

sigma ['sɪgmə] *n.* eighteenth letter (Σ, σ) of Greek alphabet; thousandth part of second. **sigmate**, *adj.* having shape of Σ or S; *v.t.* add *-s* in tense formation. **sigmatism**, *n.* inability to pronounce sibilants.

sigmatron ['sɪgmətrɒn] *n.* machine generating high-potential X-rays.

sigmoid ['sɪgmɔɪd] *adj.* S-shaped. **sigmoid flexure**, such portion of intestine between descending colon and rectum.

signate ['sɪgneɪt] *adj.* distinct; distinguished; having letter-like marks. **signation**, *n.* act of signing. **signatory**, *n.* & *adj.* (person or state) who has signed a treaty, etc.

silage ['saɪlɪdʒ] *n.* green fodder preserved for winter in silo by fermentation.

silentiary [saɪ'lenʃiəri] *n.* person maintaining or bound to silence; confidant; privy councillor.

silenus [saɪ'liːnəs] *n.* (*pl.* **–ni**) satyr-like woodland god; attendant of Bacchus; tipsy person.

silica ['sɪlɪkə] *n.* silicon compound occurring in flint, quartz and sand. **siliceous** [–'lɪʃəs], **silicic** [–'lɪsɪk], *adj.* **silicicolous**, *adj.* growing in flinty soil. **siliciferous**, *adj.* producing silica or silicon. **silicify**, *v.t.* convert into silica. **silicon**, *n.* very common non-metallic element, obtained from silica. **silicone**, *n.* oily or plastic compound of silicon used in lubricants, polishes, paints, waterproofing, etc. **silicosis**, *n.* lung disease due to inhaling siliceous rock dust. **silicate**, *v.t.* combine or coat with silica.; *n.* salt of silicic acid.

siliqua ['sɪlɪkwə], **silique** [sɪ'liːk, 'sɪlɪk] *n.* long dry seed capsule of e.g. wallflower.

sillabub ['sɪləbʌb] *n.* cream, etc., curdled with wine, or whipped to stiff froth; frothy language or thing.

sillograph ['sɪləgrɑːf] *n.* writer of satires. **sillographer**, *n.*

sillometer [sɪ'lɒmɪtə] *n.* instrument measuring ship's speed.

silo ['saɪləu] *n.* storage pit or building for silage.

silva *see* **sylva.**

silvics ['sɪlvɪks] *n.* study of tree's life. **silvical**, *adj.* **silvicolous**, *adj.* living in woods. **silviculture**, *n.* forestry.

sima ['saɪmə] *n.* lower layer of earth's crust, underlying oceans.

simian ['sɪmiən] *n.* & *adj.* (like) ape or monkey. **simiad**, **simial**, *adj.*

simile ['sɪmɪli] *n.* literary device of comparing one thing with another, using *like* or *as.* **similia**, *n.pl.* similar things. **similiter**, (*Latin*) *adv.* in similar manner.

simioid ['sɪmiɔɪd], **simious** [–əs] *adj.* simian.

simony ['saɪməni] *n.* buying and selling of ecclesiastical preferments. **simoniac** [sɪ'məuniæk], *n.* **simoniacal** [–ə'naɪəkl], *adj.* **simonism**, **simonist**, *n.*

simoom [sɪ'muːm] *n.* dry hot dusty wind of deserts.

simous ['saɪməs] *adj.* having flat, upturned nose.

simulacrum [ˌsɪmju'leɪkrəm] *n.* (*pl.* **–ra**) image; semblance; vague likeness; sham. **simulacral**, *adj.*

simulant ['sɪmjulənt] *adj.* that simulates or resembles. **simular**, *n.* & *adj. archaic*, sham.

simulate ['sɪmjuleɪt] *v.i.* & *t.* pretend; imitate. **simulation**, **simulator**, *n.* **simulative**, **simulatory**, *adj.*

sinal ['saɪnl] *adj.* pertaining to sinus.

sinapise ['sɪnəpaɪz] *v.t.* sprinkle; powder. **sinapism**, *n.* mustard-plaster.

sinciput ['sɪnsɪpʌt] *n.* forehead; part of head from crown to forehead. **sincipital** [–'sɪpɪtl], *adj.*

sindon ['sɪndən] *n.* fine linen fabric; thing made of it, as altar frontal, winding-sheet, etc.

sine ['sɪni, 'saɪni] (*Latin*) *preposition* 'without'. **sine die** [–'daɪiː, –'diːeɪ], 'without a day or date'; indefinitely. **sine mora**, 'without delay'. **sine qua non**, 'without which not'; essential adjunct or condition.

sinecure ['sɪnɪkjuə, 'saɪn–] *n.* office involving no toil or duties. **sinecural**, *adj.* **sinecurist**, *n.*

singhara [sɪŋ'gɑːrə] *n.* Indian water chestnut and edible nut.

singillatim [ˌsɪŋgɪ'leɪtɪm, ˌsɪndʒɪ–] (*Latin*) *adv.* 'singly'.

singultus [sɪŋ'gʌltəs] *n. Medicine*, hiccup(s). **singultous**, *adj.*

Sinicism ['sɪnɪsɪzm] *n.* Chinese peculiarity, etc. **sinicise**, **sinify**, *v.t.* make Chinese. **sinism**, *n.*

sinistrad ['sɪnɪstræd] *adv.* towards left. **sinistral**, *adj.* pertaining to left; left-handed; illegitimate. **sinistration**, *n.* **sinistrogyrate**, **sinistrogyric**, *adj.* moving to left. **sinistromanual**, *adj.* left-handed. **sinistrorse**, *adj.* (of plant) climbing spirally from right to left. **sinistrous**, *adj.* sinister; baleful; sinistral.

Sino- ['saɪnəʊ–, 'sɪ–] *prefix*, Chinese. **Sinogram**, *n.* character in Chinese alphabet. **Sinology**, *n.* study of Chinese history, literature, etc. **Sinophile**, *n.* lover or supporter of China.

sinter ['sɪntə] *n.* iron dross; *Geology*, deposit of hot siliceous springs; *v.i.* & *t.* agglomerate by heating.

sinuate ['sɪnjueɪt] *adj.* wavy; *v.i.* curve. **sinuation**, *n.*

sinus ['saɪnəs] *n.* cavity, especially of skull bone. **sinusitis**, *n.* inflammation of sinuses.

siphonogam ['saɪfənəgæm, saɪ'fɒn–] *n.* seed plant. **siphonogamic, siphonogamous** [–'nɒg–], *adj.*

sipid ['sɪpɪd] *adj.* sapid. **sipidity**, *n.*

sippet ['sɪpɪt] *n.* small piece of something, *especially* crouton or piece of bread to dip in gravy.

sirdar ['sɜːdɑː, sɜː'dɑː] *n.* British general formerly commanding Egyptian army.

sirenian [saɪ'riːnɪən] *n.* & *adj. Zoology*, (animal) belonging to an order of aquatic mammals including the manatee and dugong.

sirenic [saɪ'renɪk] *adj.* like a siren, alluring; melodious, sweet-sounding.

siriasis [sɪ'raɪəsɪs] *n.* sunstroke. **siriometer**, *n. Astronomy*, unit of distance, equiv. of one million times mean distance of earth from sun.

sirocco [sɪ'rɒkəʊ] *n.* hot wet, or dry dusty, southerly wind of Italy, etc., blowing from N Africa.

siskin ['sɪskɪn] *n.* small green-yellow European finch.

sissoo ['sɪsuː] *n.* E Indian tree with hard timber and leaves used as fodder.

Sisyphean [ˌsɪsɪ'fiːən] *adj.* pertaining to Sisyphus, in Greek mythology king of Corinth, condemned in underworld to roll huge stone to top of hill from which it constantly fell back; laborious and fruitless; endless.

sitology [saɪ'tɒlədʒɪ] *n.* treatise on food or diet; science of diet. **sitomania**, *n.* abnormal craving for food. **sitophobia**, *n.* morbid dread of eating; aversion to food; loss of appetite. **sitotoxism**, *n.* vegetable-food poisoning.

sitringee [sɪ'trɪndʒɪ] *n.* oriental striped cotton carpet.

sittine ['sɪtaɪn] *adj.* pertaining to or like a nuthatch; belonging to nuthatch family of birds.

situs ['saɪtəs] *n.* (*pl.* **situs**) (usual or correct) position.

sitz bath ['sɪts bɑːθ] *n.* bath in which one bathes sitting.

sitzkrieg ['sɪtskriːg] *n.* (virtual) stalemate in warfare.

sizar ['saɪzə] *n.* Cambridge undergraduate receiving allowance for expenses from college. **sizarship**, *n.*

sjambok ['ʃæmbɒk] (*S African*) *n.* heavy whip; *v.t.* flog with it.

skald [skɔːld] *n.* ancient Scandinavian bard. **skaldic**, *adj.*

skat [skæt] *n.* card game for three persons, resembling solo whist.

skatology *see* **scatology.**

skean [skiːn, 'skiːən] (*Gael.*) *n.* dagger. **skean dhu** [–'duː], Scottish Highlander's dagger.

skeet [skiːt] *n.* form of clay-pigeon shooting.

skeg [skeg] *n.* short fin, projection or brace at rear of keel of a sailing boat; fin at rear of surfboard.

skelic ['skelɪk] *adj.* pertaining to skeleton. **skelic index**, figure resulting from division of length of leg by length of trunk.

skellum ['skeləm] *n. archaic, dialect* or *S African*, rogue.

skep [skep] *n.* farm basket, *especially* of wicker or straw; beehive, *especially* domed and made of straw.

skerry ['skeri] (*Scottish*,) *n.* rocky island.

skeuomorph ['skjuːəmɔːf] *n.* ornament representing vessel or tool. **skeuomorphic**, *adj.*

skewbald ['skjuːbɔːld] *adj.* bearing patches of white and some colour not black.

skiascope ['skaɪəskəʊp] *n.* instrument for testing refractive power of eye.

skijoring ['skiːˌdʒɔːrɪŋ] *n.* sport of being drawn on skis over snow by horse or motor.

skimble-scamble ['skɪmbl,skæmbl] *adj. archaic*, rambling; jumbled.

skink [skɪŋk] *n.* tropical lizard.

skippet ['skɪpɪt] *n.* small round box for keeping document or seal.

skirr [skɜː] *v.i.* move, fly etc. rapidly; *v.t. archaic*, traverse rapidly; scour.

skive [skaɪv] *v.t.* remove surface of leather; *v.t. slang*, shirk; evade work, duty etc. **skiver**, *n.*

skoal [skəʊl] (*Nor.*) *n.* 'cup'; good health!

skua ['skjuːə] *n.* large, predatory gull.

sleave [sliːv] *n.* anything tangled, *especially* thread; *v.t.* disentangle; separate into filaments.

sleekit ['sliːkɪt] (*Scottish*,) *adj.* crafty, sly; smooth.

slew, slue [sluː] (*American*) *n.* great many.

slivovitz ['slɪvəvɪts] *n.* E European plum brandy.

sloid, sloyd [slɔɪd] *n.* Swedish system of manual training, especially in woodcarving.

slubber ['slʌbə] *v.t.* stain, sully; do carelessly. **slubberdegullion**, [–dɪ'gʌlɪən] *n. archaic*, slovenly person.

slumgullion [slʌm'gʌljən] (*American*,) *n.* meat and vegetable stew; watery soup or drink; offal.

smalt [smɔːlt] *n.* deep-blue pigment.

smalto ['zmaːltəʊ] (*Italian*) *n.* (*pl.* **–ti**) piece of coloured glass in mosaic.

smaragd ['smærægd] *n.* emerald. **smaragdine**, *adj.*

smectic ['smektɪk] *adj. Archaic* purifying; *Crystallography* arranged in layers.

smegma ['smegmə] *n.* soapy matter of sebaceous gland. **smegmatic**, *adj.* like soap; cleansing.

smew [smjuː] *n.* smallest merganser.

smilax ['smaɪlæks] *n.* tropical climbing shrub of family including sarsaparilla; S African greenhouse plant with bright green leaves.

smithsonite ['smɪθsənaɪt] *n.* natural zinc carbonate; calamine.

snaffle ['snæfl] *n.* light bridle bit.

snell [snel] *n.* short line with which fish-hook is fastened to line.

snickersnee [ˌsnɪkə'sniː, 'snɪk–] *n. jocular*, large knife, cutlass etc.; knife fight.

sniggle ['snɪgl] *v.i.* fish for eels by lowering baited hook into possible hiding place.

snood [snuːd] *n.* snell; hair net.

soboles ['sɒbəliːz] *n. Botany*, sucker; shoot. **soboliferous**, *adj.* producing these.

sobriquet ['səʊbrɪkeɪ, 'suː–] *n.* nickname.

sociogenetic [ˌsəʊsɪəʊdʒə'netɪk] *adj.* pertaining to social development. **sociogenic**, *adj.* arising from or affected by social factors. **sociogram**, *n.*

diagram of social relationships within a group.
sociolinguistics, *n.* study of language in a social
context. **sociologism,** [–'ɒl–] *n.* interpretation
emphasizing social factors. **sociometry,** [–'ɒm–]
n. study of sociological relationships and attitudes, especially as expressed by preferences.
sociopath, *n.* person hostile to society.
socius ['səʊʃiəs] *n.* (*pl.* **–ii**) member; companion;
associate; individual. **socius criminis,** accomplice
in crime.
socle ['sɒkl] *n. Architecture,* moulded member at
base of plinth or pedestal.
Socratic [sə'krætɪk] *adj.* pertaining to Socrates,
Greek philosopher, and his method of argument.
Socratic irony, method of argument by pretending
ignorance and asking seemingly simple questions
in order to draw opponent into making errors or
rash statements. **Socratic method,** instruction by
asking questions.
sodality [sə'dæləti] *n.* association; union; brother-
hood. **sodalist** ['səʊ–], *n.* member of this.
soffit ['sɒfɪt] *n. Architecture,* underside of auxiliary part of building, as arch, staircase, etc.
soi-disant [,swaː'diːzɒn] (*French*) 'calling himself'; self-styled; would be.
soigné ['swaːnjeɪ] (*French*) *adj.* (*fem.* **–ée**)
'carefully done'; well-groomed.
soirée ['swaːreɪ] (*French*) *n.* 'evening'; evening
party.
soka ['səʊkə] (*Hindu*) *n.* blight; drought.
sola ['səʊlə] *n.* Indian plant with stems containing pith. **sola topi** [–'təʊpi], sun-helmet made
of sola pith.
solan ['səʊlən] *n.* gannet.
solanaceous [sɒlə'neɪʃəs] *adj.* pertaining to or
like a potato or nightshade plant; belonging to the
potato or nightshade family of plants. **solaneous,**
adj.
solano [sə'laːnəʊ] *n.* hot East wind of Mediterranean Spanish coast.
solarise ['səʊləraɪz] *v.i. & t.* expose to sunlight;
subject to or be affected by solarisation. **solarisation,** *n.* reversal of gradation sequence in
photographic image after very long or intense
exposure.
solaristics [,səʊlə'rɪstɪks] *n.* study of relation
between sun and its radiation and earth.
solarium [sə'leəriəm] *n.* (*pl.* **–ia**) room, porch,
etc., exposed to sunshine.
solatium [sə'leɪʃiəm] *n.* (*pl.* **–ia**) compensation,
especially for hurt feelings.
soldan ['sɒldən] *n.* sultan.
solecism ['sɒlɪsɪzm] *n.* ignorant error, *especially* in
grammar. **solecise,** *v.i.* **solecist,** *n.* **solecistic(al),**
adj.
soleiform [sə'liːɪfɔːm] *adj.* shaped like a slip-
per.
solenitis [,sɒlɪ'naɪtɪs, ,səʊ–] *n.* inflammation of
duct.
solenium [sə'liːniəm] *n.* stolon. **solenial,** *adj.*
solenoid ['sɒlənɔɪd, 'səʊ–] *n.* tubular coil of wire
producing magnetic field. **solenoidal,** *adj.* pertaining to solenoid or tube.
solfatara [,sɒlfə'taːrə] (*Italian*) *n.* vent for sulphurous volcanic gases. **solfataric,** *adj.*
solfeggio [sɒl'fedʒəʊ, –iəʊ] *n.* (*pl.* **–ggi**) tonic sol-
fa system or scale.
solidago [,sɒlɪ'deɪgəʊ] *n.* golden rod plant.

solidary ['sɒlɪdəri] *adj. Law,* having joint interests
or obligations.
solidum ['sɒlɪdəm] *n.* total; pedestal's dado.
solidungular [,sɒlɪ'dʌŋgjʊlə], **solidungulate,** [–ət]
solidungulous [–əs] *adj.* having single hoof on
each foot.
solidus ['sɒlɪdəs] *n.* (*pl.* **–di**) oblique line (/); slash.
solifidian [,sɒlɪ'fɪdiən] *n.* believer that faith alone
will ensure salvation. **solifidianism,** *n.*
soliform ['səʊlɪfɔːm] *adj* sun-like.
soliped ['sɒlɪped] *n. & adj.* solidungular (animal).
solipedal, solipedous [–'liːp–], *adj.*
solipsism ['sɒlɪpsɪzm] *n.* belief that all reality is
subjective, or that the self can know no more
that its own states. **solipsismal,** *adj.* **solipsist,** *n.*
solipsistic *adj.*
soliterraneous [,sɒlɪte'reɪniəs] *adj.* pertaining to
sun and earth, especially their joint meteorological effect. **solitidal,** *adj.* pertaining to tides caused
by sun.
solivagant [sə'lɪvəgənt] *adj.,* **solivagous** [–əs] *n.*
wandering alone.
solmisate ['sɒlmaɪzeɪt] *v.i. & t.* sing or set to sol-fa
notation. **solmisation,** *n.*
solonist ['səʊlənɪst] *n.* wise man.
solstice ['sɒlstɪs] *n.* point or time when sun is furthest from Equator. **summer solstice,** such time in
summer in Northern latitudes. (about June 22).
winter solstice, such time in winter (about Dec.
22). **solstitial,** *adj.*
solus ['səʊləs] (*Latin*) *adj.* 'alone'.
solute ['sɒljuːt] *n.* in a solution, the substance
which is dissolved.
solvent ['sɒlvənt] *adj. Commerce,* able to pay
debts; *Chemistry,* dissolving; *n.* such substance.
solvency, *n.* **solvolysis,** *n.* decomposition of dissolved substance.
soma ['səʊmə] *n.* E Indian vine with milky juice;
ancient Indian drink made from it; *Anatomy,*
(*pl.* **–ata**) body of an organism excluding germ
or reproductive cells. **somatic,** [səʊ'mætɪk], *adj.*
pertaining to body or trunk. **somatasthenia,** *n.*
bodily weakness. **somatism,** *n.* **somatognosis,** *n.*
diagnosis of bodily conditions. **somatology,** *n.*
anthropological study of structure, etc., of human
body. **somatopsychic,** *adj.* pert to person's ideas
of or attitude towards his own body. **somatotonic**
adj. Psychology, having aggressive, self-assertive
temperament associated with mesomorphy. y. y.
somascope ['səʊməskəʊp] *n.* instrument detecting disease of the internal organs by 'echo-
sounding' methods and producing images of the
diseased tissue on a television screen.
sommelier [sɒ'meliə, ,sʌm'ljeɪ] (*French*) *n.* butler; wine waiter; cellarman.
somnambulate [sɒm'næmbjuleɪt] *v.i.* walk in
one's sleep. **somnambulic, somnambulistic,** *adj.*
somnambulism, somnambulist, *n.*
somnifacient [,sɒmnɪ'feɪʃnt] *n. & adj.* soporific.
somniferous, *adj.* inducing sleep. **somniloquence,
somniloquy,** *n.* talking in one's sleep. **somnipathy,**
n. hypnotic sleep.
somnolent ['sɒmnələnt] *adj.* sleepy; causing, or
resembling, sleep. **somnolescent,** *adj.* becoming
sleepy. **somnolence,** *n.* **somnorific,** *adj.* soporific.
sonant ['səʊnənt, 'sɒn–] *adj.* sounding; *Phon.,*
voiced. **sonantal, sonantic,** *adj.* **sonable,** *adj.*
capable of being sounded **sonance,** *n.*

sonata [sə'nɑːtə] *n.* instrumental composition in three or more movements. **sonata da camera,** chamber sonata. **sonata da chiesa,** church sonata. **sonatina,** *n.* short sonata.

sonation [sə'neɪʃn] *n.* sounding. **sondation,** [sɒn'deɪʃn], *n.* sounding, *especially* by boring, of the earth.

sonde [sɒnd] *n.* device sent up to observe the upper atmosphere.

soniferous [sɒ'nɪfərəs] *adj.* producing sound. **sonification,** *n.* act of producing sound.

sonorescent [,sɒnə'resnt] *adj.* emitting sound under influence of some radiation. **sonorescence,** *n.*

soojee ['suːdʒi] *n.* flour from Indian wheat.

sophiology [,sɒfi'ɒlədʒi] *n.* science of ideas. **sophiologic,** *adj.*

sophism ['sɒfɪzm] *n.* deceptive or fallacious argument. **sophist,** *n.* fallacious arguer. **sophistic(al),** *adj.* **sophisticate,** *v.i.* make artificial or worldly; corrupt. **sopyistry,** *n.* sophism, or use of sophism; mere empty argument.

sophomore ['sɒfəmɔː] (*American*) *n.* college student in second year. **sophomoric,** *adj.* adolescent; immature; pompous.

sopor ['səupə] *n.* unusually deep sleep or lethargy. **soporific,** *n. & adj.* (drug) inducing sleep. **soporiferous,** *adj.* **soporose,** *adj.* abnormally sleepy; comatose.

soral ['sɔːrəl] *adj.* pertaining to sorus.

sorbefacient [,sɔːbɪ'feɪʃnt] *n. & adj.* (substance) promoting absorption.

sorbile ['sɔːbaɪl] *adj.* that can be sipped or drunk.

sordes ['sɔːdiːz] *n.* foul or excreted matter. **sordor,** *n.* refuse; sordidness.

sordino [sɔː'diːnəu] *n.* (*pl.* **–ni**) *Music,* mute.

sorghum ['sɔːgəm] *n.* kind of tropical forage grass, yielding syrup. **sorgo,** *n.* sweet sorghum.

soricid ['sɒrɪsɪd] *n. & adj.* (pertaining to) shrew (animal). **soricine,** *adj.* pertaining to or like a shrew. **soricident** [–'rɪs–], *adj.* having teeth like shrew's.

sorites [sə'raɪtiːz] *n.* series of syllogisms following one from another, with the first and last closely linked; collection of facts, things, etc. **soritic(al)** [–'rɪt–], *adj.*

sororal [sə'rɔːrəl] *adj.* pertaining to sisters. **sororate,** *n.* custom of marriage to sister, *especially* to younger sister after wife's death. **sororicide,** *n.* killing or killer of own sister. **sorority,** *n.* sisterhood; *American,* club of college girls.

sorosis [sə'rəusɪs] *n.* kind of fruit in which many flowers are united, as in pineapple.

sortes ['sɔːtiːz] *n. pl.* (*sing.* **sors**) lot; drawing lots. **sortes Vergilianae,** divination by reference to book of Virgil's poems opened at random.

sortie ['sɔːti] *n.* sally by beleaguered troops.

sortilege ['sɔːtɪlɪdʒ] *n.* divination by casting lots; witchcraft; enchantment. **sortilegic, sortilegious** [–'liːdʒ–], *adj.* **sortileger,** *n.*

sortition [sɔː'tɪʃn] *n.* casting of, or assignment by lots.

sorus ['sɔːrəs] *n.* cluster of spore cases on fern fronds; 'fruit dots'.

soterial [sə'tɪəriəl] *adj.* pertaining to salvation. **soteriology,** *n.* theological study of salvation; treatise on hygiene.

sottise [sɒ'tiːz] (*French*) *n.* stupid or blundering act.

sotto voce [,sɒtəu 'vəutʃi] (*It.,*) 'under the voice'; in a whisper or undertone; secretly.

sou [suː] *n.* former French coin, one-twentieth part of franc; any coin or amount of minimum value.

soubise [su'biːz] *n.* onion sauce.

soubrette [su'bret] *n.* role of light-hearted or coquettish girl in drama; actress playing such part.

soubriquet ['suːbrɪkeɪ] *see* **sobriquet.**

soucar ['saukə] *n.* Hindu usurer or banker.

souchong [suː'tʃɒŋ, –'ʃɒŋ] *n.* high grade black China tea.

soufflé ['suːfleɪ] *adj.* decorated with scattered spots of colour; puffed out by cooking; *n.* such light dish; any light, delicate mixture.

soupçon ['suːpsɒn] (*French*) *n.* 'suspicion'; faint flavour or trace.

sousaphone ['suːzəfəun] *n.* large-belled, bass brass instrument with circular horn placed round player's body.

soutane [su'tɑːn] *n.* Roman Catholic priest's cassock.

sovkhoz ['sɒvxɒz] *n.* Soviet co-operative farm.

spadassin ['spædəsɪn, ,spædæ'sæn] (*French*) *n.* swordsman; fighter.

spadiceous [spə'dɪʃəs] *adj.* chestnut-coloured; pertaining to spadix. **spadicifloral, spadiciflorous,** *adj.* having flowers in a spadix. **spadicose,** *adj.* **spadix,** *n.* (*pl.* **–dices**) flower-spike covered by large leaf, as of arum plant.

spado ['speɪdəu] *n.* (*pl.* **–ones**) impotent person; castrated animal.

spahi ['spɑːhi] *n.* Algerian cavalryman in French army.

spallation [spɔː'leɪʃn] *n.* splitting into numerous fragments of the nucleus of an atom by high-energy bombardment.

spanaemia [spæ'niːmiə] *n.* anaemia. **spanaemic,** *adj.*

spandrel ['spændrəl] *n.* triangular space between curve of arch and right angle enclosing it; design in corner of postage stamp.

spanopnoea [,spænɒp'niːə] *n.* slow deep breathing as a morbid condition.

sparadrap ['spærədræp] *n.* medical plaster.

sparge [spɑːdʒ] *v.t.* sprinkle; scatter; *n.* sprinkling. **spargefication,** *n.*

spargosis [spɑː'gəusɪs] *n. Medicine,* swelling

sparid ['spærɪd], **sparoid** [–ɔɪd] *adj.* pertaining to or like sea bream.

sparsim ['spɑːsɪm] (*Latin*) *adv.* 'here and there'.

Spartacist ['spɑːtəsɪst] *n.* member of German socialist party formed in 1918; any extreme socialist. **Spartacism,** *n.*

Spartan ['spɑːtən] *adj.* pertaining to ancient Sparta, famous for its severity and discipline; hardy; harsh; fearless.

spatchcock ['spætʃkɒk] *n.* roughly prepared and cooked fowl; *v.t.* prepare and cook as this; interpolate unnecessarily or inappropriately; patch in or together.

spathe [speɪð] *n.* large sheath-like bract or leaf, as of arum plant. **spathaceous, spathal, spathose, spathous,** *adj.*

spatiate ['speɪʃieɪt] *v.i.* ramble; saunter. **spatiation,** *n.*

spatiotemporal [ˌspeɪʃɪəu'tempərəl] *adj.* pertaining to or having space and time.

spatula ['spætjulə] *n.* broad thin flexible knife. **spatuliform, spatulose, spatular, spatulate,** *adj.* like spatula.

spavin ['spævɪn] *n.* tumour on horse's leg. **bogspavin,** spavin on hock. **bone-spavin,** bony outgrowth on hock. **spavined,** *adj.* affected with spavin; worn-out.

spay [speɪ] *v.t.* render (female animal) sterile.

specie ['spiːʃi] *n.* coined money.

specious ['spiːʃəs] *adj.* plausible; superficial. **speciosity,** *n.*

spectrum ['spektrəm] *n.* (*pl.* **-ra**) series of images, colours, etc., formed when ray of radiant energy is dispersed into its component parts. **spectrobolograph,** *n.* photogographic record of lines of infra-red spectrum. **spectrogram,** *n.* representation of a spectrum. **spectrograph,** *n.* instrument showing spectrum. **spectroheliogram,** *n.* photograph made by spectroheliograph. **spectroheliograph,** *n.* instrument that photographs light of a particular wavelength from sun to show details of sun's surface. **spectrorohelioscope,** *n.* instrument for making spectroheliographic observations of sun. **spectorology,** *n.* chemical analysis by means of spectrum. **spectrometer,** *n.* instrument measuring refractive indices, and wave-lengths of rays of a spectrum. **spectroscope,** *n.* instrument for forming spectrum by dispersing ray. **spectroscopy,** *n.* production and study of spectra.

speculum ['spekjuləm] *n.* (*pl.* **-la**) mirror; reflector; instrument for examining body passages; coloured patch on bird's wing.

Speisekarte ['ʃpaɪzəˌkɑːtə] (*German*) *n.* menu

spelaean, spelean [spɪ'liːən] *adj.* pertaining to or living in caves. **speleology** [ˌspiːli'ɒlədʒi], *n.* study and exploration of caves. **speleologist,** *n.*

spelt [spelt] *n.* kind of wheat.

spelter ['speltə] *n.* zinc

speluncar [spɪ'lʌŋkə] *adj.*, **speluncean** [-'lʌnsɪən] *adj.* pertaining to or like a cave.

spermaceti [ˌspɜːmə'siːti] *n.* wax-like substance used in candles, ointments, etc., obtained from oil of sperm-whale, etc.

spermatic [spə'mætɪk] *adj.* pertaining to or like sperm. **spermatise,** ['spɜːm-], *v.t.* impregnate with sperm. **spermatism,** *n.* emission of sperm. **spermatoblast,** *n.* sperm-producing cell. **spermatocyte,** *n.* cell producing spermatozoa. **spermatogenesis,** *n.* formation of spermatozoa. **spermatoid,** *adj.* like sperm. **spermatorrhoea,** *n.* involuntary and frequent spermatism. **spermatozoon,** *n.* (*pl.* **-oa**) male sexual cell, which fertilises egg.

spermology [spə'mɒlədʒi] *n.* bot. study of seeds. **spermological,** *adj.* **spermologist,** *n.*

spermophile ['spɜːməfaɪl] *n.* gopher.

sphacel ['sfæsl] *n.* gangrene. **sphacelate,** *v.i.* & *t.* affect with gangrene; mortify; *adj.* gangrenous. **sphacelation, sphacelism,** *n.* **sphacelous,** *adj.* **sphacelus,** *n.* gangrene; necrosis.

sphagnum ['sfægnəm] *n.* (*pl.* **-na**) peat or bog moss. **sphagnicolous,** *adj.* growing in this. **sphagnology,** *n.* study of this. **sphagnous,** *adj.*

sphenic ['sfenɪk] *adj.* wedge-shaped; *Mathematics,* having three different prime numbers as its

factors. **sphenocephaly,** *n.* state of having sphenic head. **sphenogram** ['sfiː-], *n.* cuneiform character. **sphenography,** *n.* art of using or interpreting sphenograms. **sphenoid** ['sfiː-], *adj.*

spheroid ['sfɪərɔɪd] *n.* sphere-like figure. **spheroidal, spheroidic,** *adj.* **spherometer,** *n.* instrument measuring curvature. **spherule** ['sferuːl], *n.* small sphere or spheroid.

sphincter ['sfɪŋktə] *n.* ring-like muscle closing body passage. **sphincteral, sphincteric,** *adj.* **sphincterate,** *adj.* having sphincter; contracted as if by sphincter.

sphingal ['sfɪŋgl] *adj.* like sphinx.

sphingid ['sfɪndʒɪd] *n.* hawk moth. **sphingiform, sphingine,** *adj.* like sphingid or sphinx.

sphragistic [sfrə'dʒɪstɪk] *adj.* pertaining to or like a seal or signet ring. **sphragistics,** *n.* study of these.

sphygmic ['sfɪgmɪk] *adj.* pertaining to pulse (of heart). **sphygmochronograph,** *n.* instrument recording pulse. **sphygmodic,** *adj.* pulsating. **sphygmograph,** *n.* instrument recording pulse of artery. **sphygmoid,** *adj.* like a pulse. **sphygmology,** *n.* study of pulse. **sphygmomanometer,** *n.* instrument registering blood pressure. **sphygmophone,** *n.* instrument for hearing the pulse. **sphygmus,** *n. Med.,* the pulse. e.

spicate ['spaɪkeɪt] *adj.* having, like or in a spike. **spical, spicant, spiciferous, spiciform, spicigerous, spicose, spicous,** *adj.* having spikes. **spicula, spicule** ['spɪk-], *n.* small spike; small spiky body in sponges and similar creatures.

spifflicate, spifflicate ['spɪflɪkeɪt] *v.t. jocular & slang,* beat up; trounce.

spigot ['spɪgət] *n.* bung; plug of a tap; end of smaller pipe when inserted into larger one to form a junction.

spikenard ['spaɪknɑːd] *n.* ancient sweetly scented ointment; Indian plant yielding it.

spiloma [spaɪ'ləumə] *n.* birthmark; naevus. **spilomalus,** *n.* (*pl.* **-li**) naevus.

spinaceous [spɪ'neɪʃəs] *adj.* pertaining to or like spinach; belonging to spinach family of plants.

spindrift ['spɪndrɪft] *n.* sea spray.

spinel [spɪ'nel, 'spɪnl] *n.* ruby-like precious stone.

spinescent [spɪ'nesnt] *adj.* becoming or tending to be spiny; tapering. **spinescence,** *n.*

spinnaker ['spɪnəkə] *n.* large triangular sail on side opposite mainsail.

spinneret ['spɪnəret] *n.* insect's or spider's silk-spinning organ.

spinthariscope [spɪn'θærɪskəup] *n.* instrument demonstrating the emission of alpha rays by radium compound.

spintherism ['spɪnθərɪzm] *n.* seeing of sparks before the eyes.

spiracle ['spaɪrəkl] *n.* air-hole. **spiracular** [-'rækjulə], *adj.* **spiraculate, spiraculiferous,** *adj.* having these.

spirant ['spaɪrənt] *n.* & *adj.* (consonant) pronounced with friction of breath against part of mouth, as *f* or *s.*; fricative. *Obsolete,* **spirate,** *adj.* voiceless. **spiration,** *n.* act of breathing.

spirochaete ['spaɪrəkiːt] *n.* spirally-moving, disease-producing organism. **spirochaetaemia,** *n.* presence of these in blood. **spirochaeticide,** *n.* substance killing these. **spirochaetosis,** *n.* infection by these.

spirograph ['spaɪrəgrɑːf] *n.* instrument recording movements of breathing. **spirogram**, *n.* record made by this. **spirometer**, *n.* instrument recording volume of air taken in by lungs or volume of gas.

spirulate ['spɪrʊlət, -jʊ-] *adj.* spirally arranged.

spissated [spɪ'seɪtɪd] *adj.* thickened. **spissitude**, *n.*

spitchcock ['spɪtʃkɒk] *n.* eel split and grilled or fried.

splanchnic ['splæŋknɪk] *adj.* visceral. **splanchnology**, *n.* study of viscera. **splanchnopathy**, *n.* disease of viscera. **splanchnotomy**, *n.* incision into viscera.

spleen [spliːn] *n.* gland-like organ near stomach, concerned in blood-cell production; malice; anger. **splenectomy**, *n.* surgical removal of the spleen. **splenetic** [splə'netɪk], *adj.* ill-tempered; crabbed. **splenic** ['splenɪk], *adj.* pertaining to spleen. **splenisation**, *n.* congestion of tissue which becomes spleen-like. **splenitive**['splen–], *adj.* fiery; splenetic. **splenomegaly**, *n.* enlargement of the spleen.

spodium ['spəʊdiəm] *n.* bone charcoal. **spodogenic, spodogenous**, *adj.* pertaining to or due to waste matter. **spodomancy**, *n.* divination by study of ashes.

spokeshave ['spəʊkʃeɪv] *n.* plane or knife for rounding spokes or spoke-like objects.

spoliation [ˌspəʊli'eɪʃn] *n.* pillage. **spoliative**, *adj.* robbing; diminishing. **spoliator**, *n.* robber. **spoliatory**, *adj.*

spondee ['spɒndiː] *n.* metrical foot of two long syllables. **spondaic** [–'deɪ–], **spondean**, *adj.*

spondyl(e) ['spɒndɪl, –aɪl] *n.* vertebra. **spondylexarthrosis**, *n.* displacement of this. **spondylic, spondylous**, *adj.* **spondylitis**, *n.* inflammation of this. **spondylotherapeutics**, *n.* medical treatment by manipulating spine. .

sponsion ['spɒnʃn] *n.* act of taking pledge or becoming surety for a person.

sponson ['spɒnsn] *n.* projection from side of ship, as protection, gun platform, etc.

spontoon [spɒn'tuːn] *n.* short pike carried by 18th-century infantry officer.

spoondrift ['spuːndrɪft] *n.* spindrift.

sporangium [spə'rændʒɪəm] *n.* (*pl.* **-gia**) spore case or receptacle of ferns, fungi, etc. **sporangial**, *adj.* **sporangiferous**, *adj.* having sporangia. **sporangiform**, *adj.* like sporangium. **sporangiophore**, *n.* stalk bearing sporangium.

spore [spɔː] *n.* plant's or protozoan's reproductive body. **sporiferous**, *adj.* producing spores. **sporocarp**, *n.* body producing spores. **sporogenesis**, *n.* reproduction by, or production of, spores. **sporogony**, *n.* reproduction by spores. **sporophorous**, *adj.* sporiferous. **sporophyll**, *adj.* sporiferous leaf. **sporophyte**, *n.* spore-bearing phase of plant. **sporozoan**, *n.* parasitic spore-producing kind of protozoan. n. n.

sporulate ['spɔːruleɪt] *v.i.* & *t.* form (into) spores. **sporule**, *n.* small spore. **sporuliferous**, *adj.* producing sporules. **sporuloid**, *adj.* like a sporule. **sporulation**, *n.*

Sprachgefühl ['ʃprɑːxgəˌfjuːl] (*German*) *n.* instinctive grasp of a language and it usage.

sprag [spræg] *n.* bar, stake etc. used as a chock to stop a vehicle rolling back; pitprop.

Sprechgesang ['ʃprexgəˌzaŋ] (*German*) *n.* mode of voice production between singing and recita-

tion used in some 20th-century operas.

sprew [spruː] (*S African*), **spreeuw** ['spreɪuː] *n.* African starling.

springbok ['sprɪŋbɒk] (*S African*) *n.* white-striped and -rumped S African gazelle.

spritzer ['sprɪtsə] *n.* drink of (white) wine and soda water.

sprue [spruː] *n.* tropical inflammatory disease of digestive tract.

spruit [spreɪt] (*S African*) *n.* small stream flowing only in wet season.

spumescent [spju'mesənt] *adj.* foaming; foamy. **spumescence**, *n.*

sputnik ['spʊtnɪk, 'spʌt–] (*Russian*) *n.* a satellite, spacecraft.

sputum ['spjuːtəm] *n.* saliva or mucus spat out. **sputative**, *adj.* habitually spitting.

squab [skwɒb] *n.* young pigeon; nestling; stuffed lower cushion of chair; sofa.

squadrism ['skwɒdrɪzm] *n.* government by armed squadrons of supporters or party members.

squaliform ['skweɪlɪfɔːm] *adj.* shark-shaped. **squaloid**, *adj.* like a shark.

squamaceous [skwə'meɪʃəs] *adj.* scaly. **squamate, squameous, squamose, squamous**, *adj.* like, having or covered with scales. **squamellate, squamelliferous, squamulate, squamulose**, *adj.* having small scales. **squamoid** ['skweɪmɔɪd], *adj.* like a scale.

squatinid ['skwætɪnɪd] *n.* & *adj.* (pertaining to an) angelfish.

squill [skwɪl] *n.* sea onion, used as expectorant, etc.

squinancy ['skwɪnənsi] *n.* wild plant believed to cure quinsy.

squinch [skwɪntʃ] *n.* arch, etc., across corner of room.

SST *abbreviation* of Super-Sonic Transport (aircraft).

Stabat Mater [ˌstɑːbæt 'mɑːtə] (*Latin*) 'the mother stood'; hymn describing the Virgin Mary at the Cross.

stabile ['steɪbaɪl, –iːl] *adj.* stationary; *n.* stationary abstract sculpture similar to a mobile.

staccato [stə'kɑːtəʊ] *adv.* & *adj.* *Music*, with notes sharply separated.

stactometer [stæk'tɒmɪtə] *n.* glass for measuring drops.

stadiometer [ˌsteɪdi'ɒmɪtə] *n.* kind of theodolite; wheel by which length of line is measured.

stagiary ['steɪdʒɪəri] *n.* resident canon; law student.

Stagirite ['stædʒəraɪt] *n.* native or inhabitant of ancient Stagira, Macedonia; Aristotle. **Stagiritic** [–'rɪtɪk], *adj.*

stagmometer [stæg'mɒmɪtə] *n.* device for measuring number of drops in certain volume of liquid.

stagnicolous [stæg'nɪkələs] *adj.* living in stagnant water.

Stakhanovism [stə'kænəvɪzm, –'kɑːn–] (*Russian*) *n.* voluntary system in former USSR of increasing production through hard work, efficiency, teamwork, and competition. **Stakhanovite**, *n.* worker honoured for success in the system.

Stalag ['stælæg] (*German*) *n.* (*abbreviation* of *Stammlager*), prisoner-of-war camp for non-commissioned officers and men.

stalagmometer [ˌstæləg'mɒmɪtə] *n.* drop-meas-

How do you spell ... ?

A compendium of over a hundred of the most commonly misspelt words in the English language:

abhorrent
abominable
abscess
accommodate
acquaintance
acquiesce
acquire
address
advisable
aficionado
ageing *or* aging
align
all right
ancillary
artefact *or* artifact
attach
believe
benefited
biased *or* biassed
budgeted
buoy
bureaucracy
calendar
Caribbean
changeable
coloration
commemorate
committee
competent
concede
concise
consensus
debtor
dependant *noun*/dependent *adjective*
diarrhoea
dichotomy
dilapidated
dilettante
disappointed
dismissal
dispatch *or* despatch
dissatisfied
dissect
eczema
enforceable
expatriate
feasible
foreign
foresee
freight
fuchsia
fulfil
gauge
genealogy
grievance
haemorrhage
harass
hygiene
idiosyncrasy
impresario
incurred

indigenous
indispensable
innovate
inoculate
jewellery
liaise
lightning
liquefy
liqueur
maintenance
manageable
manoeuvre
Mediterranean
millennium
mineralogy
miniature
minuscule
mischievous
misspell
mortgage
necessary
noticeable
occasion
occurred
omitted
parallel
pavilion
pejorative
penicillin
perennial
permanent
personnel
pharaoh
Portuguese
practice *noun*/practise *verb*
practitioner
precede
principal *adjective, noun*/principle *noun*
privilege
proceed
prophecy *noun*/prophesy *verb*
rarefied
receipt
receive
recommend
referred
rhythm
saccharin
sacrilege
seize
separate
skilful
stationary *adjective*/stationery *noun*
subtle
supersede
threshold
transferred
truly
variegated
weird
withhold

uring instrument.

stamen ['steɪmən] *n.* (*pl.* **–mina**), flower's pollen-bearing organ, comprising filament and anther. **staminal,** *adj.* **staminate,** *adj.* having stamen. **stamineal, stamineous,** *adj.* pertaining to or having stamen.

stanchion ['stɑ:nʃən] *n.* upright support or post.

stanhope ['stænəp] *n.* high four-wheeled driving carriage.

stannary ['stænəri] *n.* tin-mine or -works. **stannic,** *adj.* pertaining to tin; *Chemistry,* in which tin has valency of four. **stannous,** *adj.* pertaining to tin; *Chemistry,* in which tin has valency of two.

stapes ['steɪpi:z] *n.* innermost bone of ear; stirrup bone. **stapedectomy,** *n.* removal of stapes and insertion of an artificial replacement to relieve deafness. **stapedial,** *adj.* pertaining to stapes. **stapediform,** *adj.* like a stapes or stirrup.

staphylic [stə'fɪlɪk] *adj.* pertaining to alveolar arch. **staphylorrhaphy** [–'lɒrəfi], *n.* surgical union of cleft palate.

staphylococcus [ˌstæfɪlə'kɒkəs] *n.* (*pl.* **–ci**) a pus-producing bacterium occurring in clusters.

stasis ['steɪsɪs] *n.* (*pl.* **–ses**), stoppage in circulation; stagnation.

statant ['steɪtnt] (*Heraldry*) *adj.* in profile with all four feet on the ground.

statics ['stætɪks] *n.* study of bodies and forces in equilibrium.

statism ['steɪtɪzm] *n.* concentrating economic and political power in the organs of the state. **statist,** *adj.*; *n.* believer in this; statistician.

stative ['steɪtɪv] *adj.* (of a verb) denoting a state rather than an action; *n.* such verb.

statocyst ['stætəsɪst] *n.* organ of balance in some invertebrates.

statolith ['stætəlɪθ] *n.* calcium granule in statocyst, whose movement stimulates sensory cells; solid, free-moving particle in plant cytoplasm, thought to influence changes in plant's orientation.

stator ['steɪtə] *n.* stationary part of motor.

statoscope ['stætəskəup] *n.* kind of aneroid barometer recording minute barometric changes.

status quo (ante) [ˌsteɪtəs 'kwəu ('ænti)] *see in* **statu quo (ante).**

staurolatry [stɔ:'rɒlətri] *n.* worship of the cross or crucifix.

stavesacre ['steɪvzˌeɪkə] *n.* kind of larkspur, from which ointment for lice is obtained.

stearin ['stɪərɪn] *n.* hard fat. **stearic** [–'ærɪk], *adj.* **steariform,** *adj.* like stearin.

steatite ['stɪːətaɪt] *n.* soapstone. **steatitic** [–'tɪtɪk], *adj.* **steatogenous,** *adj.* fat-producing. **steatolysis,** *n.* breaking down of fats. **steatopathic,** *adj.* pertaining to disease of sebaceous glands. **steatopygic** [–'pɪdʒɪk], **steatopygous** [–'paɪgəs], *adj.* having excessively fat buttocks. **steatorrhea,** *n.* fattiness of faeces; seborrhoea. **steatosis,** *n.* adiposity.

stechados ['stekədɒs] *n.* French lavender.

steeve [sti:v] *n.* long spar with pulley used to stow cargo in ship's hold; *v.t.* stow (cargo).

steganography [ˌstegə'nɒgrəfi] *n.* cryptography.

stegnosis [steg'nəusɪs] *n.* constipation. **stegnotic** [–'nɒtɪk], *n.* & *adj.* (medicine) causing constipation.

stegophilist [ste'gɒfɪlɪst] *n.* person whose pastime is climbing the outside of buildings.

stein [staɪn] (*German*) *n.* large earthenware beer-mug.

steinbok ['staɪnbɒk] *n.* small S African antelope.

stele ['sti:li] *n.* (*pl.* **–lae**) carved or painted stone pillar or slab; central part of plant's stem. **stelar,** *adj.*

stella ['stelə] (*Latin*) *n.* 'star'. **stella maris,** 'star of the sea'; Virgin Mary. **stella polaris,** Pole Star. **stelliferous,** *adj.* having many stars. **stellify,** *v.t.* place among stars; glorify. **stellular,** *adj.* like a star; having star-like spots. **stellar,** *adj.* **stellate,** *adj.* star-like.

stemma ['stemə] *n.* (*pl.* **–mas, –mata**) family tree; genealogy of literary text; simple eye of insect.

stemson ['stemsən] *n.* curved timber joining stem of ship to kelson.

stenocardia [ˌstenə'kɑ:diə] *n.* angina pectoris. **stenocardiac,** *adj.* **stenocephaly,** *n.* narrowness of head. **stenochoric,** *adj.* not widely distributed. **stenochromy,** *n.* printing of many-coloured pattern at one impression.

stenometer [ste'nɒmɪtə] *n.* distance-measuring instrument.

stenopaic, stenopaeic [ˌstenə'peɪɪk, –'pi:ɪk] *adj.* with narrow aperture. **stenopetalous,** *adj.* with narrow petals. **stenophagous,** *adj.* eating only a narrow range of food. **stenophyllous,** *adj.* with narrow leaves. **stenophobia** *n.* morbid fear of narrow places.

stenosis [stɪ'nəusɪs] *n.* narrowing of an orifice. **stenotic** [–'nɒtɪk], *adj.* **stenotypy,** *n.* type of short-hand using ordinary characters.

stentor ['stentɔ:] *n.* loud-voiced person. **stentorian, stentorious, stentorophonic,** *adj.*

stercoraceous [ˌstɜ:kə'reɪʃəs] *adj.* pertaining to dung. **stercoral, stercorous,** *adj.* **stercorary** ['stɜ:kərəri], *n.* place for dung. **stercoricolous,** *adj.* living in dung.

stereobate ['steriəbeɪt, 'stɪə–] *n.* masonry platform used as foundation for a building. **stereobatic** [–'bætɪk], *adj.*

stereochemistry [ˌsteriəu'kemɪstri, ˌstɪə–] *n.* chemical study of arrangement of molecules and atoms.

stereochromy ['steriəkrəumi, 'stɪə–] *n.* kind of wall painting. **stereochrome,** *n.* **stereochromic,** *adj.*

stereognosis [ˌsteriəg'nəusɪs, ˌstɪə–] *n.* ability to perceive weight, form, etc., of a body by touch. **sterognostic,** *adj.*

stereography [ˌsteri'ɒgrəfi, ˌstɪə–] *n.* representation of solid bodies on plane surface. **sterogram,** *n.* representation giving impression of solidity of object. **sterograph,** *n.* picture used in stereoscope. **stereographic,** *adj.*

stereometry [ˌsteri'ɒmətri, ˌstɪə–] *n.* measurement of volumes, etc., of solid figures. **stereometric(al)** [–'metrɪk, –l], *n.*

stereomonoscope [ˌsteriə'mɒnəskəup, ˌstɪə–] *n.* instrument projecting image with appearance of solidity, by means of two lenses.

stereoplasm ['steriəplæzm, 'stɪə–] *n.* solid protoplasm.

stereopsis [ˌsteri'ɒpsɪs, ˌstɪə–] *n.* stereoscopic vision.

stereoscope ['steriəskəup, 'stɪə–] *n.* instrument with two lenses combining images of two almost identical pictures to give effect of solidity and distance. **stereoscopic** [–'skɒpɪk], *adj.* pertaining to stereoscope or stereoscopy. **stereoscopy** [–'ɒskəpi], *n.* use of the stereoscope; seeing or representation of objects with the effect of solidity and distance.

stereostatic [,steriə'stætɪk, ,stɪə–] *adj.* geostatic. **stereostatics**, *n.* statics of solids.

stereotomy [,steri'ɒtəmi, ,stɪə–] *n.* cutting of solids, especially stone. **stereotomical** [–'tɒmɪkl], *adj.* **stereotomist**, *n.*

stereotype ['steriətaɪp, 'stɪə–] *n.* metal printing plate cast from a mould of the set-up type; standardised or hackneyed image or concept; *v.t.* make stereotype of; fix permanently; make trite; repeat without alteration. **stereotypic** [–'tɪpɪk], *adj.* **stereotypy**, *n.*

steric(al) ['sterɪk, –l] *adj.* stereochemical.

sterlet ['stɜːlət] *n.* small sturgeon yielding best caviare.

sternson ['stɜːnsən] *n.* timber joining sternpost of ship to kelson.

sternum ['stɜːnəm] *n.* (*pl.* –na) breastbone. **sternal**, *adj.*

sternutation [,stɜːnju'teɪʃn] *n.* sneezing. **sternutative, sternutatory**, *n.* & *adj.* (substance) causing sneezing.

steroid ['sterɔɪd, 'stɪə–] *n.* any of a large group of fat-soluble organic compounds, including bile acids and hormones, having specific physiological action; a synthetic hormone.

sterol ['sterɒl, 'stɪə–] *n.* organic solid alcohol.

stertor ['stɜːtə] (*Medicine*) *n.* snoring. **stertorous**, *adj.* breathing loudly or hoarsely; snoring.

stet [stet] (*Latin*) 'let it stand'; direction to ignore alteration; *v.t.* mark with such direction.

stethometer [ste'θɒmɪtə] *n.* instrument measuring chest expansion in breathing. **stethoscopy** [–'θɒskəpi] *n.* examination with a stethoscope. **stethospasm**, *n.* spasm of chest muscles.

stevedore ['stiːvədɔː] *n.* dock labourer loading or unloading ship. **stevedorage**, *n.*

sthenia ['sθiːniə] *n.* (unusual or abnormal) strength. **sthenic** ['sθenɪk], *adj.* (unusually) strong.

stibial ['stɪbiəl] *adj.* pertaining to antimony. **stibiated**, *adj.* containing antimony.

stibnite ['stɪbnaɪt] *n.* natural compound of antimony from which it is obtained.

stich [stɪk] *n.* line of verse. **stichic**, *adj.* **stichometry**, *n.* measurement by counting lines, especially of books or documents; division of written or printed matter into lines, *especially* in accordance with the sense. **stichomythia**, *n.* alternating single lines of dialogue in poetic drama.

stifle ['staɪfl] *n.* joint above hock of horse, equivalent of human knee.

stigma ['stɪgmə] *n.* (*pl.* –ata), mark; spot; stain; disgrace; mark representing wound of Christ; *Botany*, part of pistil, *especially* end of style, on which pollen germinates. **stigmal, stigmatic, stigmatiform**, *adj.* **stigmatise**, *v.t.* mark with a spot or stain; brand as infamous or evil. **stigmatism**, *n.* correct focusing power of lens or eye.

stilliform ['stɪlɪfɔːm] *adj.* drop-shaped.

stimie *see* **stymie**.

stingo ['stɪŋgəʊ] *n.* strong (Yorkshire) beer.

stipe [staɪp] *n. Botany*, short stalk.

stipend ['staɪpend] *n.* salary. **stipendiary**, *n.* & *adj.*

(person) receiving stipend.

stipes ['staɪpiːz] *n.* stock; stalk. **stipiform**, *adj.* like a stalk. **stipitate**, *adj.* borne on a stipe.

stipple ['stɪpl] *v.t.* mark, paint etc. with dots; dab on; *n.* this method of painting; stippled effect.

stipulate ['stɪpjuleɪt] *v.i.* & *t.* bargain; guarantee; demand as a condition. **stipulation**, *n.* **stipulator**, *n.* **stipulatory**, *adj.*

stipule ['stɪpjuːl] *n.* one of a pair of leaf-like appendages at base of leaf. **stipuliferous**, *adj.* producing this. **stipuliform**, *adj.* like this.

stirpiculture ['stɜːpɪ,kʌltʃə] *n.* breeding of special stocks. **stirps**, *n.* (*pl.* –pes) family line; stock; biological category.

stithy ['stɪði] *n.* blacksmith's anvil or forge.

stiver ['staɪvə] *n.* Dutch coin worth about one penny; thing of little or no value.

stoa ['stəʊə] *n.* (*pl.* –as, –ae) covered walk with colonnade(s).

stochastic [stə'kæstɪk] *adj.* pertaining to random variables in statistics and their interrelations with the laws of probability.

stoep [stuːp] (*S African*) *n.* verandah.

stogy ['stəʊgi] *n.* cheap cigar.

stoichiology [,stɔɪki'ɒlədʒi] *n.* physical study of composition of animal tissues. **stoichiometry**, *n. Chemistry*, calculation of elements' combining weights; study of chemical composition and combination.

STOL [stɒl] *abbreviation* of Short Take-Off and Landing (aircraft).

stolon ['stəʊlən, –ɒn] *n.* runner of plant. **stolonate**, *adj.* having stolon. **stoloniferous**, *adj.* producing stolon.

stoma ['stəʊmə] *n.* (*pl.* –ata), mouth; orifice; breathing pore of plants. **stomatal**, *adj.* **stomatic**, *adj.* pertaining to stoma.; *n.* & *adj.* (medicine) used for disorders of mouth. **stomatiferous**, *adj.* having stoma. **stomatitis**, *n.* inflammation of mouth. **stomatology**, *n.* medical study of mouth. **stomatose, stomatous**, *adj.* having stoma.

stope [stəʊp] *n.* step-like working in a mine to extract ore; *v.t.* excavate in stopes.

stopple ['stɒpl] *n.* stopper; plug.

storge ['stɔːdʒiː, –geɪ] *n.* parental instinct.

storiate ['stɔːrieɪt] *v.t.* ornament with historical designs. **storiation**, *n.*

storiology [,stɔːri'ɒlədʒi] *n.* study of folk-lore. **storiological**, *adj.* **storiologist**, *n.*

stovaine ['stəʊveɪn] *n.* anaesthetic cocaine-substitute, chiefly injected into spine.

strabismus [strə'bɪzməs] *n.* squint. **strabismal, strabismic(al)**, *adj.* **strabismometer**, *n.* instrument measuring degree of strabismus.

stramineous [strə'mɪniəs] *adj.* like straw or its colour; worthless.

stramonium [strə'məʊniəm] *n.* thorn apple, and its leaves used in medicine.

strandlooper ['strænd,luːpə] (*S African*) *n.* Bushman; native beachcomber.

strappado [stræ'peɪdəʊ, –'pɑː–] *n.* form of torture in which victim was let fall the length of a rope tied to his wrists, etc.

strata *see* **stratum**.

strath [stræθ, strɑːθ] (*Scottish*) *n.* wide river valley. **strathspey**, *n.* reel-like Scottish dance.

stratification [,strætɪfɪ'keɪʃn] *n.* arrangement in layers or strata. **stratiform**, *adj.* like a stratum.

stratigraphy [strə'tɪgrəfi] *n.* study of geological strata; stratification. **stratigrapher, stratigraphist,** *n.* **stratigraphic,** *adj.*

stratocracy [strə'tɒkrəsi] *n.* military rule. **stratocrat,** *n.* **stratocratic,** *adj.* **stratography,** *n.* art of directing an army.

stratocumulus [ˌstreɪtəʊ'kjuːmjʊləs, ˌstræ–] *n.* uniform stretch of grey cloud in lines or waves.

stratosphere ['strætəsfɪə] *n.* upper atmosphere, from about 7 miles/11 km. up. **stratospheric(al),** *adj.*

stratum ['strɑːtəm, 'streɪ–] *n.* (*pl.* **–ta**) layer, especially of earth's crust. **stratose,** *adj.* in strata. **stratous,** *adj.* in strata; like stratus.

stratus ['strɑːtəs, 'streɪ–] *n.* (*pl.* **–ti**) sheet of cloud covering sky at height of 2,000 to 7,000 ft./610 to 2,135 km.

strepor ['strepə] *n.* noise. **strepent, strepitant, strepitous,** *adj.*

strepsis ['strepsɪs] *n.* twisting.

streptococcus [ˌstreptə'kɒkəs] *n.* (*pl.* **–cci**) harmful bacterium occurring in chains. **streptococcal,** *adj.*

streptomycin [ˌstreptə'maɪsɪn] *n.* antibiotic produced by a soil fungus, used chiefly against tuberculosis.

stretcher ['stretʃə] *n.* brick placed lengthwise in brick-laying.

stria ['straɪə] *n.* (*pl.* **–ae**) line; small groove; flute of column; scratch; band; stripe. **striate,** *v.t.* mark with striae. **striation,** *n.*

strickle ['strɪkl] *n.* scythe-sharpening instrument; template; instrument for levelling off material, especially grain, in a container.

stricture ['strɪktʃə] *n.* harsh criticism; *Med.*, contraction; constriction of body passage; constricted passage.

stridor ['straɪdə] *n.* harsh noise; whistling sound in breathing. **stridulate** ['strɪdjʊleɪt], *v.i.* make a shrill or harsh noise. **stridulation,** *n.* **stridulator,** *n.* **stridulous,** *adj.* squeaky.

striga ['straɪgə] *n.* (*pl.* **–ae**) stria; plant's stiff bristle. **strigal,** *adj.* **strigate,** *adj.* having striga.

strigil ['strɪdʒɪl] *n.* instrument used to scrape down skin in Greek and Roman baths.

strigilation [ˌstrɪdʒɪ'leɪʃn] *n.* scraping.

strigine ['strɪdʒaɪn] *adj.* pertaining to or like an owl.

strigose [straɪgəʊs] *adj.* having strigae.

stringent ['strɪndʒənt] *adj.* strict; tight; cogent. **stringency,** *n.*

striola ['straɪələ] *n.* (*pl.* **–ae**) small or weak stria. **striolate,** *adj.* having striolae.

strobic ['strɒbɪk] *adj.* spinning; like a top.

strobile ['strəʊbaɪl, –bɪl], **strobilus** [–ɪləs] *n.* cone-like inflorescence, especially of hop. **strobilaceous, strobiline, strobiloid,** *adj.*

stroboscope ['strəʊbəskəʊp] *n.* instrument for studying periodic motion by illuminating object with flashes at same frequency as that of its motion. **stroboscopic** [–'skɒpɪk], *adj.* **stroboscopy** [–'bɒskəpi], *n.*

strombuliform [strɒm'bjuːlɪfɔːm] *adj.* like a spinning top or screw.

strongyle ['strɒndʒɪl] *n.* parasitic roundworm; spicule. **strongylate,** *adj.* having these. **strongylidosis, strongylosis,** *n.* infestation with these.

strophe ['strəʊfi] *n.* section of Greek ode sung by

chorus when moving from right to left; stanza. **strophic** ['strɒfɪk], *adj.* **strophosis,** *n.* twist; turn.

strudel ['struːdl] (*German*) *n.* kind of tart with fruit between layers of very thin pastry. **apfelstrudel,** strudel containing apple.

struma ['struːmə] *n.* (*pl.* **–ae**) goitre. **strumectomy,** *n.* surgical removal of struma. **strumose, strumous, strumatic,** *adj.*

strumpet ['strʌmpɪt] *n.* prostitute.

struthian ['struːθɪən] *adj.* ratite. **struthiform,** *adj.* like an ostrich. **struthionine, struthious,** *adj.*

stucco ['stʌkəʊ] *n.* (*pl.* **–oes**) kind of plaster for exteriors of buildings, especially highly ornamented.

stulm [stʌlm] *n.* adit.

stultify ['stʌltɪfaɪ] *v.t.* make to seem foolish; frustrate; make futile. **stultification,** *n.*

stupa ['stuːpə] *n.* dome-like Buddhist shrine.

stupe [stjuːp] *n.* flannel for fomentation; pledget.

stupefacient [ˌstjuːpɪ'feɪʃnt] *adj.* stupefying; *n.* narcotic. **stupefy,** *v.t.* make stupid; daze.

stupeous ['stjuːpɪəs] *adj.* tow-like. **stupose,** *adj.* having tow-like tufts.

stupration [stju'preɪʃn] *n.* rape.

stupulose ['stjuːpjʊləʊs] *adj.* downy.

Sturm und Drang [ˌʃtʊəm ʊnt 'dræŋ] (*German*) 'storm and stress'; nationalist literary movement of 18th-century Germany.

sturnine ['stɜːnaɪn] *adj.* pertaining to starlings. **strunoid,** *adj.* like a starling.

Stygian ['stɪdʒɪən] *adj.* pertaining to Styx, river of the mythical underworld; murky; applied to solemn, unbreakable vow.

style [staɪl] *n.* ancient writing instrument with one sharp and one blunt end; *Botany* stalk-like outgrowth of ovary bearing stigma. **stylate, styliferous,** *adj.* bearing a style. **styliform,** *adj.* like a style. **styline,** *adj.* **stylite,** *n.* ascetic saint living on top of pillar.

stylobate ['staɪləbeɪt] *n.* coping, etc., supporting colonnade.

stylograph ['staɪləɡrɑːf] *n.* fountain pen with needle-like point. **stylography** *n.* writing with a style on wax tablet, etc. **stylographic** *adj.*

stylometer [staɪ'lɒmɪtə] *n.* column-measuring instrument.

stylus ['staɪləs] *n.* style; gramophone needle; any pointed tracer or indicator.

stymie ['staɪmi] *n.* obstruction of golfer's putt by opponent's ball; *v.t.* obstruct putt in this way; thwart.

styptic ['stɪptɪk] *n.* & *adj.* (substance) checking bleeding by constricting blood vessels. **stypsis,** *n.* use of this.

stythe [staɪð] *n.* choke-damp.

suasion ['sweɪʒn] *n.* persuasion; advice.

sub [sʌb] (*Latin*) *preposition* 'under'. **sub judice** [–'dʒuːdɪsi], still under judicial consideration. **sub plumbo,** 'under lead'; under the Pope's seal. **sub rosa,** in confidence; secret. **sub sigillo,** 'under seal'; in strict confidence. **sub silentio** [–sɪ'lenʃɪəʊ, –ti–], secret; tacit. **sub specie aeternitatis,** 'under the aspect of eternity'; in respect of its essential nature or worth. **sub voce,** under that word; in the place where that subject is considered (*abbreviated* as **s.v.**).

subacid [sʌb'æsɪd] *adj.* slightly acid.

subacute [ˌsʌbə'kjuːt] *adj.* applied to diseases

between acute and chronic.

subaerial [sʌb'eəriəl] *adj.* in open air; on surface of ground.

subahdar [ˌsuːbə'dɑː] (*Anglo-Indian*) *n.* viceroy; provincial governor; sepoy company commander.

subalary [sʌb'æləri] *adj.* beneath wings.

subalpine [sʌb'ælpaɪn] *adj.* of higher mountain slopes below timber line.

subangular [sʌb'æŋgjʊlə], **subangulate** [-ət] *adj.* somewhat angular.

subarid [sʌb'ærɪd] *adj.* slightly arid.

subarrhation [ˌsʌbə'reɪʃn] *n.* betrothal, with gift from man to woman.

subastral [sʌb'æstrəl] *adj.* sublunary.

subaudition [ˌsʌbɔː'dɪʃn] *n.* understanding of something not expressed; thing so understood. **subaudible**, *adj.* hardly audible. **subauditur**, *n.* thing understood; implication.

subboreal [sʌb'bɔːriəl] *adj.* very cold.

subcentral [sʌb'sentrəl] *adj.* beneath the centre; not exactly central.

subcontinent [ˌsʌb'kɒntɪnənt] *n.* mass of land almost as large as a continent. **subcontinental**, *adj.*

subcutaneous [ˌsʌbkju'teɪniəs] *adj.* beneath the skin.

subdecimal [sʌb'desɪml] *adj.* applied to quotient of division by a multiple of ten. **subdecuple**, *adj.* containing one part of ten.

subduct [səb'dʌkt] *v.t.* draw or turn downwards; deduct. **subduction**, *n.* turning downward; *Geology*, movement of one part of earth's crust beneath another.

subduplicate [ˌsʌb'djuːplɪkət] *adj.* expressed by square root.

subereous [sju'bɪəriəs] *adj.* pertaining to or like cork. **suberise**, *v.t.* convert into corky tissue. **suberose**, *adj.* like cork.

subfluvial [ˌsʌb'fluːviəl] *adj.* beneath, or at bottom of, a river.

subfocal [sʌb'fəʊkl] *adj.* of which one is not entirely conscious.

subfusc ['sʌbfʌsk, sʌb'fʌsk] *adj.* dusky drab; *n.* formal academic dress at Oxford University.

subglacial [ˌsʌb'gleɪʃl] *adj.* beneath, or at bottom of, a glacier.

subinfeudate [ˌsʌbɪn'fjuːdeɪt] *v.i.* & *t.* grant to another land held from feudal lord; sublet. **subinfeudation, subinfeudatory**, *n.*

subitaneous [ˌsʌbɪ'teɪniəs] *adj.* sudden.

subito ['suːbɪtəʊ, 'sʊb-] (*Latin* & *It.*) *adv.* 'at once'; immediately; suddenly.

subjacent [sʌb'dʒeɪsnt] *adj.* lying or situated below.

subjectivism [səb'dʒektɪvɪzm] *n.* philosophical doctrine that all knowledge is merely subjective, or that attaches great importance to subjective experiences.

subjunctive [səb'dʒʌŋktɪv] *n.* & *adj. Grammar*, (pertaining to) mood of verb expressing possibility, desire, etc., and not actuality or fact.

sublate [sʌb'leɪt] *v.t.* deny; cancel; reduce, especially an idea to subordinate part of a greater unity. **sublation**, *n.* **sublative**, *adj.* tending to remove.

sublethal [ˌsʌb'liːθl] *adj.* not quite fatal.

sublimate ['sʌblɪmeɪt] *v.t.* vaporise substance and

allow to solidify; *Psychology*, direct instinctive energy to higher plane; *adj.* refined; *n.* product of sublimating. **sublimation**, *n.* **sublimatory**, *adj.*

subliminal [ˌsʌb'lɪmɪnl] *adj. Psychology*, present though unknown to conscious mind; too weak, small, or rapid to be consciously noticed.

sublineation [ˌsʌblɪni'eɪʃn] *n.* act of underlining.

sublunary [sʌb'luːnəri] *adj.* of the world; terrestrial.

subluxation [ˌsʌblʌk'seɪʃn] *n.* state of being almost dislocated.

submaxillary [ˌsʌbmæk'sɪləri] *adj.* beneath lower jaw. **submaxillary gland**, salivary gland discharging beneath tongue.

submerse [səb'mɜːs] *v.t.* & *i.* submerge. **submersible**, *adj.*; *n.* vessel used for undersea exploration or maintenance. **submersion**, *n.*

submicron [ˌsʌb'maɪkrɒn] *n.* ultra-microscopic particle.

submiliary [ˌsʌb'mɪliəri] *adj.* smaller than a millet seed.

subminiature [ˌsʌb'mɪnətʃə, -niə-] *adj.* (especially of electronic components) very small. **subminiaturise**, *v.t.* reduce to a very small size.

subminimal [ˌsʌb'mɪnɪml] *adj.* less than minimum necessary; subliminal.

submontane [sʌb'mɒnteɪn] *adj.* at foot of mountain.

submultiple [sʌb'mʌltɪpl] *n.* & *adj.* (quantity) dividing into another exactly.

subnubilar [ˌsʌb'njuːbɪlə] *adj.* under clouds. **subnuvolar**, *adj.*

suboctuple [sʌb'ɒktjʊpl] *adj.* containing one part of eight; related as I is to 8.

suborn [sə'bɔːn] *v.t.* induce, especially to commit crime; procure. **subornation**, *n.* **subornative**, *adj.* **suborner**, *n.*

subpoena [sə'piːnə, ˌsʌb-] *n.* writ calling person to attend at court; *v.t.* serve subpoena on. **subpoenal**, *adj.* under penalty.

subquintuple [sʌb'kwɪntjʊpl] *adj.* having ratio of I to 5.

subreptary [sə'breptəri] *adj.* adapted to crawling. **subreption**, *n.* false or unfair deduction or representation due to suppression of truth. **subreptitious**, *adj.* pertaining to subreption.

subrident [sə'braɪdnt] *adj.* smiling. **subrision**, *n.*

subrogate ['sʌbrəgeɪt] *v.t.* substitute. **subrogation**, *n.*

subserve [səb'sɜːv] *v.t.* be useful to; promote. **subservient**, *adj.* servile.

subsextuple [sʌb'sekstjʊpl] *adj.* related as I is to 6.

subsist [səb'sɪst] *v.i.* (be able to) continue to exist; consist; *Philosophy*, be conceivable; feed and clothe. **subsistence**, *n.* (continuing) existence; (means of obtaining) the bare necessities of life. **subsistent(ial)**, *adj.*

subsolar [sʌb'səʊlə] *adj.* beneath the sun; sublunary; between tropics.

subsonic [sʌb'sɒnɪk] *adj.* pertaining to or at a speed less than the speed of sound in air.

substantive [səb'stæntɪv, 'sʌbstən-] *adj.* pertaining to or like a substance or entity; existing alone; independent; substantial; solid; essential; real, actual; *Grammar*, expressing existence; *n.* noun or pronoun. **substantival** [-'taɪvl], *adj.*

substituent [səb'stɪtjuənt] *n.* thing, especially

atom, substituted for another.

substratum ['sʌb,strɑːtəm, –,streɪ–] *n*. (*pl.* –**ta**) underneath layer; foundation. **substratal, substrative,** *adj*. **substrate,** *n*. **substratose,** *adj*. imperfectly stratified.

subsultus [səb'sʌltəs] *n*. convulsive movement. **subsultory,** *adj*. leaping.

subsume [səb'sjuːm, –'suːm] *v.t*. include within a larger entity or under a broader heading. **subsumption,** *n*. **subsumptive,** *adj*.

subtend [səb'tend] *v.t*. extend beneath or opposite to. **subtense,** *adj*. pertaining to object of known length by which distances are measured.

subterfuge ['sʌbtəfjuːdʒ] *n*. means of evading; trick.

subtopia [sʌb'təʊpiə] *n*. deceptively spacious subrural suburban paradise.

subtrahend ['sʌbtrəhend] *n*. amount to be subtracted.

subtrist [sʌb'trɪst] *adj*. rather sad.

subturbary [sʌb'tɜːbəri] *adj*. beneath turf.

subulate ['sjuːbjʊlət, 'suː–, –juleɪt] *adj*. long and tapering; awl-shaped. **subulicorn,** *adj*. having such horns or antennae. **subuliform,** *adj*.

subungual [sʌb'ʌŋgwəl], **subunguial** [–wiəl] *adj*. beneath a nail or hoof.

suburbicarian [sə,bɜːbɪ'keəriən] *adj*. pertaining to suburbs, especially of Rome.

subvention [səb'venʃn] *n*. subsidy. **subvene,** *v.t*. support; aid; happen to help.

subvert [səb'vɜːt] *v.t*. overthrow; pervert; destroy. **subversion,** *n*. **subversive,** *adj*. tending to overthrow existing order.

subvocal [sʌb'vəʊkl] *adj*. put into words but not spoken.

succedaneum [,sʌksɪ'deɪniəm] *n*. (*pl.* –**ea**) substitute; remedy. **succendaneous,** *adj*.

succent [sək'sent] *v.t*. sing second part. **succentor,** *n*. deputy precentor.

succès d'estime [,sʌkseɪ de'stiːm, sək,seɪ–] (*French*) 'success of esteem'; state of being highly praised or respected but not a financial success. **succès fou** [–'fuː], 'mad success'; tremendous success.

succinct [sək'sɪŋkt] *adj*. concise; curt.

succiniferous [,sʌksɪ'nɪfərəs] *adj*. producing amber.

succise [sək'saɪs] *adj*. having appearance of having lower part cut off.

succorrhoea [,sʌkə'riːə] *n*. excessive secretion.

succory ['sʌkəri] *n*. chicory.

succubus ['sʌkjubəs] *n*. (*pl.* –**bi**) demon, especially one taking on female form to have sexual intercourse with man in his sleep; harlot. **succubine,** *adj*.

succursal [sə'kɜːsl] *adj*. like a branch or outgrowth; subordinate.

succus ['sʌkəs] *n*. (*pl.* –**cci**) juice. **succus entericus,** digestive secretion of small intestine.

succuss [sə'kʌs] *v.t*. shake violently, *especially Medicine*, to detect presence of fluid. **succussation, succussion,** *n*. **succussatory, succussive,** *adj*.

sucrose ['suːkrəʊs, 'sjuː–] *n*. cane or beet sugar.

suctorial [sʌk'tɔːriəl] *adj*. pertaining to, or for, sucking; having such organs. **suctorian,** *n*. such animal.

sudamen [sju'deɪmən, su–] *n*. (*pl.* –**mina**) eruption due to retention of sweat under skin.

sudarium [sju'deəriəm, su–] *n*. (*pl.* –**ia**) handkerchief or cloth for wiping away sweat, especially St. Veronica's, on which portrait of Christ is supposed to have been impressed; sudatorium. **sudatorium,** *n*. (*pl.* –**ia**) sweating room of a bath.

sudatory ['sjuːdətəri, 'suː–] *adj*. sweating; sudorific; *n*. sudatorium; sudarium.

sudd [sʌd] *n*. mass of floating weed blocking the Nile.

sudiform ['sjuːdɪfɔːm, 'suːd–] *adj*. having shape of stake.

sudor ['sjuːdɔː, 'suː–] (*Latin*) *n*. sweat. **sudoral, sudoric,** *adj*. **sudoresis,** *n*. copious sweating. **sudoriferous, sudoriparous,** *adj*. sweat-producing. **sudorific,** *n. & adj*. (drug) promoting perspiration.

Suecism ['swiːsɪzm] *n*. peculiarity of Swedish speech, thought, life, etc.

suffiaminate [sə'flæmɪneɪt] *v.t*. check; obstruct. **suffamination,** *n*.

sufflation [sə'fleɪʃn] *n*. afflatus.

suffragan ['sʌfrəgən] *adj*. *Ecclesiastical*, subordinate; *n*. assistant bishop. **suffraganal, suffraganeous,** *adj*. **suffraganate, suffragancy,** *n*. office or jurisdiction of suffragan.

suffrage ['sʌfrɪdʒ] *n*. vote; right to vote; supplication. **suffragial** [–'freɪ–], *adj*. **suffragist,** *n*. believer in extension of suffrage.

suffrutescent [,sʌfru'tesnt] *adj*. having woody base. **suffruticose, suffruticous,** *adj*. applied to such perennial plant, remaining herbaceous in upper part.

suffuse [sə'fjuːz] *v.t*. spread from within; fill with fluid. **suffusion,** *n*. **suffusive,** *adj*.

sugent ['sjuːdʒənt, 'suː–] *adj*. suctorial. **sugescent,** *adj*.

suggilate ['sʌdʒɪleɪt] *v.t*. beat black and blue; slander. **suggilation,** *n*.

sui generis [,suːaɪ 'dʒenərɪs, ,sjuː–, –iː–, –'geː–] (*Latin*) 'of its, his or her own kind'; unique. **sui juris,** 'in his or her own right'; having full legal rights.

suilline ['sjuːɪlaɪn, su–] *n. & adj*. (person or animal) like a pig.

suint [swɪnt] *n*. sheep's dried perspiration in wool.

sukiyaki [,suːki'jɑːki] *n*. Japanese dish of thin slices of meat, bean curd and vegetables with soy sauce cooked at the table.

sulcate ['sʌlkeɪt] *adj*. having grooves; furrowed; *v.t*. furrow. **sulcation,** *n*. **sulcus,** *n*. groove, furrow, especially on surface of brain.

sullage ['sʌlɪdʒ] *n*. refuse; sewage; pollution; silt.

sulpha-drugs ['sʌlfə–drʌgz] *n. pl*. group of synthetic chemical drugs also called sulphonamides, including **sulphadiazine** [–'daɪəziːn] for pneumonia; **sulphaguanidine** [–'gwɑːnɪdiːn] for intestinal infections; **sulphanilamide** [–'nɪləmaɪd] for throat infections, blood-poisoning, etc.; and others.

sulphate ['sʌlfeɪt] *n*. salt of sulphuric acid. **sulphide,** *n*. compound of sulphur. **sulphite,** *n*. salt of sulphurous acid.

sulphonal ['sʌlfənl] *n*. kind of sedative drug. **sulphonalism,** *n*. condition due to abuse of this.

sulphonamide [sʌl'fonəmaɪd] *n*. sulpha-drug.

sulphurate ['sʌlfəreɪt, –ju–] *v.t*. impregnate with sulphur. **sulphureous,** *adj*. pertaining to or like sulphur. **sulphuretted**, *adj.* impregnated with sulphur. **sulphuric**, *adj.* containing sulphur in higher valency. **sulphurous**, *adj.* containing sulphur in lower valency; pertaining to hellfire; scathing; profane.

sumi ['suːmi] *n.* Japanese black ink in block form.

summa ['sʌmə, 'sʊmə] *n.* (*pl.* **-ae**) comprehensive treatise. **summa cum laude**, 'with the highest praise'; highest distinction in some academic examinations. **summa rerum**, 'sum of things'; great public interest. **summa summarum**, 'sum of sums'; consummation.

summand ['sʌmænd, sʌ'mænd] *n.* number, quantity to be added in a sum.

summation [sʌ'meɪʃn] *n.* total; addition; summing up. **summative, summatory**, *adj.*

summum bonum [ˌsʌməm 'bəʊnəm, ˌsʊ–] (*Latin*) 'highest good'. **summum jus**, exact legal right.

sumpitan ['sʌmpɪtən] *n.* E Indian poisoned-arrow blow-pipe.

sumpter ['sʌmptə] *n.* pack; pack horse; beast of burden.

sumptuary ['sʌmptʃʊəri] *adj.* regulating expenditure.

sunn [sʌn] *n.* E Indian plant yielding hemp-like fibre.

Sunna ['sʊnə] *n.* body of traditional Islamic law and custom based on words and deeds of Mohammed.

Suomic ['swəʊmɪk] *adj.* Finnish.

supari [su'pɑːri] (*Hindu*) *n.* betel nut.

superannuate [ˌsuːpər'ænjueɪt, ˌsjuː–] *v.t.* discharge as too old; pension off. **superannuation**, *n.* retirement pension.

supercargo [ˌsuːpə'kɑːgəʊ, ˌsjuː–] *n.* (*pl.* **-oes**) ship's official in charge of business affairs.

superciliary [ˌsuːpə'sɪliəri, ˌsjuː–] *adj.* pertaining to brows or eyebrows. **supercilious**, *adj.* haughty; contemptuous.

supercrescent [ˌsuːpə'kresnt, ˌsjuː–] *adj.* parasitic.

supererogate [ˌsuːpər'erəgeɪt, ˌsjuː–] *v.i.* do more than necessary. **supererogation, supererogator**, *n.* **supererogative, supererogatory** [–'rɒg–], *adj.*

superfetate [ˌsuːpə'fiːteɪt, ˌsjuː–] *v.i.* conceive during pregnancy. **superfetation**, *n.* such conception; cumulative growth by accretion; overproduction.

superficies [ˌsuːpə'fɪʃiiːz, ˌsjuː–] *n.* surface; surface area. **superficiary**, *adj.* built on another's land.

superheterodyne [ˌsuːpə'hetərədaɪn, ˌsjuː–] *adj. Radio*, applied to reception in which oscillations of slightly different frequency are imposed on the received oscillations, producing beats of a frequency above audio-frequency which are easily amplified.

superhumeral [ˌsuːpə'hjuːmərəl, ˌsjuː–] *n.* garment, especially ecclesiatical, worn over shoulders.

superincumbent [ˌsuːpərɪn'kʌmbənt, ˌsjuː–] *adj.* lying on top of; overhanging. **superincumbence, superincumbency**, *n.*

superinduce [ˌsuːpərɪn'djuːs, ˌsjuː–] *v.t.* bring as addition. **superinduction**, *n.*

superjacent [ˌsuːpə'dʒeɪsnt, ˌsjuː–] *adj.* lying

over or above.

superlative [su'pɜːlətɪv, sju–] *n.* & *adj.* (of) the highest degree.

superlunary [ˌsuːpə'luːnəri, ˌsjuː–, –'ljuː–] *adj.* above the moon; other-worldly.

supermaxillary [ˌsuːpəmæk'sɪləri, ˌsjuː–] *adj.* pertaining to the upper jaw.

supernal [su'pɜːnl, sju–] *adj.* heavenly.

supernatant [ˌsuːpə'neɪtnt, ˌsjuː–] *adj.* floating on surface. **supernatation**, *n.*

supernova [ˌsuːpə'nəʊvə, ˌsjuː–] *n.* star that suddenly increases immensely in brightness, emitting up to 100 million times its normal light.

supernumerary [ˌsuːpə'njuːmərəri, ˌsjuː–] *n.* & *adj.* (person) in addition to usual or necessary number.

superphosphate [ˌsuːpə'fɒsfeɪt, ˌsjuː–] *n.* acid phosphate.

superscribe [ˌsuːpə'skraɪb, ˌsjuː–] *v.t.* write on top or at head. **superscript**, *adj.* written above. **superscription**, *n.*

supersensible [ˌsuːpə'sensəbl, ˌsjuː–] *adj.* beyond physical perception; spiritual.

supersolid ['suːpəˌsɒlɪd, 'sjuː–] *n.* magnitude of more than three dimensions.

supersonic [ˌsuːpə'sɒnɪk, ˌsjuː–] *adj.* denoting speed greater than speed of sound; pertaining to vibrations above the audible limit.

superstratum [ˌsuːpə'strɑːtəm, –'streɪ–; ˌsjuː–] *n.* (*pl.* **-ta**) overlying layer.

superterranean [ˌsuːpətə'reɪnɪən, ˌsjuː–], **superterraneous** [–ɪəs] *adj.* above or on surface of earth. **superterrene**, *adj.*

supervene [ˌsuːpə'viːn, ˌsjuː–] *v.i.* occur in addition or unexpectedly; follow close upon. **supervenient**, *adj.* **supervenience, supervention**, *n.*

supinate ['suːpɪneɪt, 'sjuː–] *v.i.* & *t.* lie or make lie on back; turn arm so that palm is upward. **supination**, *n.* **supinator**, *n.* muscle producing supination.

supine [su'paɪn, sju–] *adj.* lying flat on back; sluggish; lazy; ['suːpaɪn, 'sjuː–], *n. Grammar*, kind of Latin verbal noun.

suppedaneum [ˌsʌpɪ'deɪnɪəm] *n.* (*pl.* **-ea**) support for feet, especially on cross for crucifixion. **suppedaneous**, *adj.*

suppletion [sə'pliːʃn] *n. Philology*, use of a word form as tense, inflection etc. of another, different word form, as e.g. *worse* as comparative of *bad*. **suppletive**, *adj.* **suppletory**, *adj.* supplementary.

suppliant ['sʌpliənt] *n.* & *adj.* beseeching (person). **supplicate**, *v.i.* & *t.* beseech; beg. **supplication**, *n.*

suppository [sə'pɒzɪtəri] *n.* soluble medical remedy introduced into orifice.

suppressio veri [səˌpresɪəʊ 'veəriː, –'vɪəraɪ] (*Latin*) 'suppression of truth'.

suppurate ['sʌpjʊreɪt] *v.i.* fester; discharge pus. **suppuration**, *n.* **suppurative**, *adj.*

supra ['suːprə, 'sjuː–. –ɑː] (*Latin*) *adv.* 'above'; previously. **vide supra**, 'see above' (*abbreviated* as **v.s.**)

supraliminal [ˌsuːprə'lɪmɪnl, ˌsjuː–] *adj.* conscious.

supraorbital [ˌsuːprə'ɔːbɪtl, ˌsjuː–] *adj.* above the eye socket.

suprarenal [ˌsuːprə'riːnl, ˌsjuː–] *adj.* above the kidneys; adrenal.

surah ['suərə, 'sjuərə] *n.* soft silk fabric.

sural ['sjuərəl, 'suə–] *adj.* pertaining to calf of leg.

surcease [sɜː'siːs] *v.i. & t.* cease; stop; *n.* cessation.

surcingle ['sɜː,sɪŋgl] *n.* band fastening anything on horse's back; girdle or belt worn with cassock.

surculose ['sɜːkjuləus] *adj.* producing suckers. **surculous,** *adj.* **surculus,** *n.* (*pl.* **-li**) sucker.

surd [sɜːd] *adj.* deaf; senseless; *Phonetics,* unvoiced; *n. Mathematics,* irrational number, as π. **surdimutism,** *n.* state of being deaf and dumb. **surdomute,** *n.* deaf and dumb person.

suricate ['suərɪkeɪt, 'sjuə–] *n.* mongoose-like animal of S Africa.

surma ['suərmɑː, –mə] (*Indian*) *n.* eye-shadow.

surmullet [sə'mʌlɪt] *n.* red mullet.

surnominal [sɜː'nɒmɪnl] *adj.* pertaining to surnames.

surrebutter [,sɜːrɪ'bʌtə] *n. Law,* plaintiff's reply to defendant's rebutter. **surrebuttal,** *n.* giving evidence in support of this.

surrejoinder [,sɜːrɪ'dʒɔɪndə] *n. Law,* plaintiff's reply to defendant's rejoinder.

surrogate ['sʌrəgət] *n.* substitute; deputy, especially for bishop; *adj.* substitute; deputizing. **surrogation,** *n.*

sursum corda [,sɜːsəm 'kɔːdə] (*Latin*) 'lift up your hearts'; versicle in church service.

surveillance [sə'veɪləns] *n.* observation; watch. **surveillant,** *n. & adj.*

suscept [sə'sept] *n.* parasite's host.

suscitate ['sʌsɪteɪt] *v.t.* stimulate. **suscitation,** *n.*

suspensus per collum [sə,spensəs pɜː 'kɒləm] (*Latin*) 'hung by the neck'; executed (*abbreviated* as **sus. per coll.**).

suspire [sə'spaɪə] *v.i.* breathe; sigh. **suspiration,** *n.* **suspirative,** *adj.*

sustentation [,sʌsten'teɪʃn] *n.* sustaining; maintenance; sustenance. **sustentative,** *adj.*

susurrate ['sjuːsəreɪt, 'suː–] *v.i.* whisper. **susurrant,** *adj.* **susurrous,** *adj.* rustling. **susurrus,** *n.* whispering sound. **susurration,** *n.*

sutler ['sʌtlə] *n.* camp-follower vending provisions. **sutlery,** *n.*

suttee ['sʌtiː, sʌ'tiː] *n.* Hindu woman, or custom of women, committing suicide on husband's funeral pyre. **sutteeism,** *n.*

suture ['suːtʃə, 'sjuː–] *n.* stitching up of wound; seam-like joint between parts; connection; *v.t.* stitch up. **sutural,** *adj.* **suturation,** *n.*

suum cuique [,suːəm 'kwiːkwi, ,sjuː–] (*Latin*) 'to each his own'.

suzerain ['suːzəreɪn, 'sjuː–] *n. & adj.* sovereign. **suzerainty,** *n.*

svelte [svelt] *adj.* slim and attractive; sophisticated.

swage [sweɪdʒ] *n.* groove; metal-worker's grooved shaping tool; *v.t.* shape with this.

swale [sweɪl] *n.* meadow; marshy hollow.

swami ['swɑːmi] (*Hindu*) *n.* lord; learned master.

swaraj [swə'rɑːdʒ] (*Hindu*) *n.* self-government. **swarajist,** *n.*

swipple ['swɪpl] *n.* blade of a flail.

sybarite ['sɪbəraɪt] *n.* inhabitant of Sybaris, S Italy; person excessively fond of luxury. **sybaritic** [–'rɪtɪk], *adj.*

sybil ['sɪbl] *n.* prophetess; hag. **sybillic, sybillline,** *adj.* like sybil or oracle; mysterious. **sybilllism,** *n.*

prophecy by sybil.

sybotic [saɪ'bɒtɪk] *adj.* pertaining to swineherd. **sybotism,** *n.*

syce [saɪs] *n.* Indian groom or mounted attendant.

syconium [saɪ'kəuniəm] *n.* form of fruit with ovaries on enlarged receptacle, as fig.

sycophant ['sɪkəfənt, –fænt] *n.* flatterer; parasite. **sycophantic** *adj.* **sycophancy, sycophantry,** *n.*

sycosis [saɪ'kəusɪs] *n.* inflammatory pustular disease of facial hair follicles. **sycosiform,** *adj.*

syllabary ['sɪləbəri] (*Latin*) *n.* set of symbols for syllables. **syllabatim** [–'beɪtɪm], *adv.* syllable by syllable.

syllepsis [sɪ'lepsɪs] *n.* (*pl.* **-ses**) use of word agreeing with only one of them to govern two or more words; use of word in figurative and literal senses in same phrase. **sylleptic(al),** *adj.*

syllogism ['sɪlədʒɪzm] *n.* argument in which conclusion is deduced from two premises. **syllogise,** *v.i. & t.* **syllogistic(al),** *adj.*

sylph [sɪlf] *n.* spirit of air; slim girl. **sylphic, sylphid,** *adj.*

sylva ['sɪlvə] *n.* tree of a region; treatise on trees; anthology. **sylvan, sylvestral,** *adj.*

symbiosis [,sɪmbaɪ'əusɪs, –bi–] *n.* living together of two organisms of different kinds, especially to their mutual benefit. **symbion, symbiont, symbiote,** *n.* such organism. **symbiotic** [–'ɒtɪk], *adj.* **symbiotics,** *n.* study of symbiosis.

symbolaeography [,sɪmbəliːˈɒɡrəfi] *n.* drawing up of legal documents.

symbolofideism [,sɪmbələu'faɪdiɪzm] *n.* having faith in symbols. **symbolatry,** *n.* worship of symbols.

symphily ['sɪmfɪli] *n.* living together to their mutual benefit of insects and other organisms. **symphilic, symphilous,** *adj.*

symphonious [sɪm'fəuniəs] *adj.* harmonious.

symphysis ['sɪmfɪsɪs] *n.* (*pl.* **-ses**) fixed articulation of two bones, especially by cartilaginous pad. **symphysis menti,** symphysis of two lower jawbones at chin. **symphysis pubis,** symphysis of two pubic bones. **symphytic** [–'fɪtɪk], *adj.*

symploce ['sɪmpləsi] *n.* repetition of initial and concluding phrases or words of a sentence at beginning and end of following sentence.

symposium [sɪm'pəuziəm] *n.* (*pl.* **-ia**) collection of opinions; discussion. **symposiac(al)** [–ziæk, –'zaɪəkl], *adj.* **symposiarch,** *n.* leader of symposium. **symposiast,** *n.* contributor to symposium.

symptosis [sɪmp'təusɪs] *n.* emaciation.

synactic [sɪ'næktɪk] *adj.* acting in addition or together; cumulative.

synaeresis [sɪ'nɪərəsɪs] *n.* pronunciation as one of two vowels usually pronounced separately.

synaesthesia [,sɪniːs'θiːʒiə] *n.* sensation occurring in part distant from part stimulated; association of sensation, as colour, etc., with other sensation. **synaesthetic** [–'θetɪk], *adj.*

synallagmatic [,sɪnəlæg'mætɪk] *adj.* bilateral; reciprocal.

synaloepha [,sɪnə'liːfə] *n.* contraction of two syllables into one by omission of vowel.

synanthesis [sɪ'nænθəsɪs] *n.* synchronous maturity of male and female elements of plant. **synanthetic** [–'θetɪk], *adj.* **synanthy,** *n.* growing together of two flowers.

synapse ['saɪnæps] *n.* place of passage of impulse

from one neurone to next.

synarchy ['sɪnɑːki] *n.* joint rule. **synarchical**, *adj.*

synartesis [,sɪnɑː'tiːsɪs] *n.* close junction. **synarthrosis**, *n.* (*pl.* **–ses**) fixed articulation of bones.

synastry [sɪ'næstri, 'sɪn–] *n.* conjunction of stellar influences on person.

syncategorematic [,sɪnkætɪgɒrɪ'mætɪk] *adj.* having meaning only in conjunction with another word.

synchoresis [,sɪnkə'riːsɪs] *n.* rhetorical device of apparently conceding point to strengthen argument.

synchronous ['sɪŋkrənəs] *adj.* pertaining to or happening at same time. **synchronal, synchronic**, *adj.* **synchronise**, *v.i. & t.* occur or make occur simultaneously. **synchronism**, *n.*

synchroscope ['sɪŋkrəskəup] *n.* device indicating the degree of synchronism of associated machines or moving parts.

synchrotron ['sɪŋkrətrɒn] *n.* apparatus, combination of betatron and cyclotron, for accelerating charged particles for atomic fission experiments.

synchysis ['sɪŋkɪsɪs] *n.* confusion.

synclastic [sɪn'klæstɪk] *adj.* curved in all directions towards same point.

syncline ['sɪnklaɪn] *n. Geology*, downward fold. **synclinal, synclinical**, *adj.*

syncopate ['sɪŋkəpeɪt] *v.t.* omit part from interior of; *Music*, begin rhythm on unaccented beat. **syncope** [–pi], *n.* omission of sound from word; *Medicine*, fainting. **syncopation**, *n.*

syncrasy ['sɪŋkrəsi] *n.* combination.

syncretism ['sɪŋkrətɪzm] *n.* combination of different religious beliefs; eclecticism; compromise. **syncretise**, *v.i. & t.* become or cause to become fused. **syncretist**, *n.* **syncretistic**, *adj.*

syndactyl(e) ['sɪndæktɪl] *n. & adj.* (animal) with digits joined together. **syndactylia, syndactylism** [–'dæk–], syndactyly, *n.* **syndactylic, syndactylous**, *adj.*

syndetic(al) [sɪn'detɪk, –l] *adj.* connective.

syndic ['sɪndɪk] *n.* magistrate; member of committee. **syndical**, *adj.* **syndicalism**, *n.* theory of obtaining control of means of production by workers' organisations.

syndrome ['sɪndrəum] *n.* group of things, especially medical symptoms, happening together.

synecdoche [sɪ'nekdəki] *n. Literature* device of signifying thing by its part, or part by whole, etc. **synecdochic(al)** [–'dɒk–], *adj.* **synecdochism**, *n.*

synechiology [sɪ,neki'ɒlədʒi] *n.* doctrine of the continuity or union of things. **synechiological**, *adj.*

synechthry ['sɪnekθri] *n.* living together of hostile species.

synecology [,sɪnɪ'kɒlədʒi] *n.* study of ecological communities.

synectics [sɪ'nektɪks] *n.* problem-solving by creative and lateral thinking among a diverse group of people.

synergetic [,sɪnə'dʒetɪk] *adj.* co-operating. **synergise**, *v.i.* **synergism**, *n.* synergy; *Religion*, doctrine of co-operation of human will with divine grace. **synergy**, *n.* combined action of drugs, muscles, units, etc. to produce an effect greater than the sum of its parts.

synesis ['sɪnɪsɪs] *n. Grammar*, construction in

which grammatical agreement is according to sense rather than syntax.

synethnic [sɪn'eθnɪk] *adj.* of same race or country.

syngamy ['sɪŋgəmi] *n.* conjunction of gametes, etc. **syngamic** [–'gæmɪk], **syngamous**, *adj.*

syngenesis [sɪn'dʒenəsɪs] *n.* sexual reproduction. **syngenetic** [–dʒə'netɪk], *adj.*

synizesis [,sɪnɪ'ziːsɪs] *n.* contraction of two syllables by combining pronunciation of successive vowels.

synkinesis [,sɪŋkɪ'niːsɪs] *n.* movement of part when another is moved.

synod ['sɪnəd, –ɒd] *n.* assembly or council, especially of Church. **synodal, synodic(al)**, *adj.*; *Astronomy*, between two conjunctions with sun.

synoecious [sɪ'niːʃəs] *adj.* having male and female flowers in same inflorescence. **synoecise**, *v.t.* join together. **synoecism** *n.* **synoecy**, *n.* association of species with benefit to one and neither harm nor benefit to other.

synonym ['sɪnənɪm] *n.* word having same meaning as another. **synonymic, synonymous** [–'nɒnɪməs], *adj.* **synonymy** [–'nɒnəmi], *n.* use for emphasis of several synonyms.

synopsis [sɪ'nɒpsɪs] *n.* (*pl.* **–ses**) summary; outline. **synoptic(al)**, *adj.* giving or pertaining to synopsis; taking the same view; **synoptic Gospels**, those according to Matthew, Mark and Luke. **synoptist**, *n.* writer of synoptic Gospel.

synoptophore [sɪ'nɒptəfɔː] *n.* instrument correcting defects in eye muscle.

synorthographic [,sɪnɔːθə'græfɪk] *adj.* spelt alike.

synovia [saɪ'nəuviə] *n.* lubricating fluid secreted by certain membranes. **synovial**, *adj.* **synoviparous**, *adj.* producing this. **synovitis**, *n.* inflammation of synovial membrane.

syntagma [sɪn'tægmə] *n.* a systematic collection.

syntax ['sɪntæks] *n.* sentence-construction; systematic arrangement. **syntactic(al)**, *adj.*

syntectic [sɪn'tektɪk] *adj.* pertaining to syntexis.

synteresis [,sɪntə'riːsɪs] *n.* intuitive knowledge of right and wrong; 'divine spark' of the soul.

syntexis [sɪn'teksɪs] *n.* wasting or melting away.

synthermal [sɪn'θɜːml] *adj.* having same temperature.

syntony ['sɪntəni] *n.* tuning wireless instrument to same wavelength. **syntonic** [–'tɒnɪk], *adj.* pertaining to syntony; *Psychology*, in harmony with one's surroundings. **syntonize**, *v.t.*

sypher ['saɪfə] *v.t.* (of boards) join edge to edge or overlap to form a level surface.

syringadenous [,sɪrɪŋ'gædɪnəs] *adj.* pertaining to sweat glands.

syrinx ['sɪrɪŋks] *n.* (*pl.* **–nges**) tubular object; bird's vocal organ; Pan's pipes.

systaltic [sɪ'stæltɪk] *adj.* pulsatory.

systatic [sɪ'stætɪk] *adj.* bringing together.

systemic [sɪ'stiːmɪk, –'stem–] *adj.* affecting the whole organism; (of a pesticide) making the whole plant toxic to pests.

systole ['sɪstəli] *n.* contraction, alternating with diastole, in pulsation of heart; shortening of long syllable. **systolic** [–'stɒlɪk], *adj.*

syzygy ['sɪzədʒi] *n.* conjunction or opposition of celestial body with the sun. **syzygial**, *adj.*

T

Taal [tɑːl] (*S African*) *n*. the Afrikaans language.
tabacosis [ˌtæbə'kəʊsɪs] *n*. tobacco-poisoning.
tabagie [ˌtæbə'ʒiː] (*French*) *n*. smoking-room or -party.
tabard ['tæbɑːd] *n*. herald's sleeveless tunic; coat worn over armour.
tabaret ['tæbərət] *n*. striped material of watered silk and satin.
tabasco [tə'bæskəʊ] *n*. kind of pepper sauce.
tabasheer [ˌtæbə'ʃɪə] *n*. hard substance extracted from bamboo joints and used medicinally; sugar of bamboo.
tabefaction [ˌtæbɪ'fækʃn] *n*. emaciation.
tabellion [tə'beljən] *n*. scrivener.
tabes ['teɪbiːz] *n*. wasting or emaciation of body or organ. **tabes dorsalis**, *n*. locomotor ataxia. **tabetic** [–'betɪk], **tabid** ['tæbɪd], *adj*. **tabescent** [–'besnt], *adj*. wasting away. **tabescence**, *n*.
tabinet ['tæbɪnət] *n*. silk-and-wool watered material.
tabitude ['tæbɪtjuːd] *n*. tabes.
tablature ['tæblətʃə] *n*. *Music*, notation, especially for the lute; mental image; description; picture; any plate-like surface or object.
tableau ['tæbləʊ] *n*. (*pl*. –x) graphic description; dramatic or artistic grouping, especially at the end of a scene on stage. **tableau vivant**, 'living picture'; pose reproducing a well-known painting, sculpture, scene, etc.
table d'hôte [ˌtɑːbl 'dəʊt] (*French*) 'table of the host'; restaurant menu with limited choice of dishes at fixed price.
tabor ['teɪbə, –ɔː] *n*. small drum.
tabouret ['tæbərət] *n*. low stool; small tabor; embroidery frame.
tabula rasa [ˌtæbjʊlə 'rɑːzə] (*Latin*) 'smoothed tablet'; condition of mind free from ideas or impressions.
tace ['teɪkeɪ, 'teɪsɪ] (*Latin*) 'be silent'. **tacet**, 'it, he or she is silent'.
tacheometer [ˌtæki'ɒmɪtə] *n*. tachymeter.
tachistoscope [tə'kɪstəskəʊp] *n*. instrument exposing visual signals, *e.g.* colours or shapes, for very short periods of time, especially one showing words and phrases at increasing speeds, to accelerate reading.
tachograph ['tækəgrɑːf] *n*. instrument installed in vehicle recording distance travelled, number and length of stops, speeds, and similar data.
tachometer [tæ'kɒmɪtə] *n*. instrument indicating engine speed in revolutions per minute. **tachometry**, *n*. measurement of speed.
tachycardia [ˌtæki'kɑːdɪə] *n*. abnormally rapid heart beat. **tachycardiac**, *adj*.
tachygraphy [tæ'kɪgrəfi] *n*. shorthand; shortened cursive writing. **tachygrapher, tachygraphist,** *n*. **tachygraphical,** *adj*.
tachymeter [tæ'kɪmɪtə] *n*. instrument for making quick surveys.
tachyphylaxis [ˌtækɪfɪ'læksɪs] *n*. rapid development of immunity to the effects of a drug, especially to those of a poison through previous ingestion of small amount of same.
tachypn(o)ea [ˌtækɪp'niːə] *n*. abnormally rapid breathing.
tachytelic [ˌtækɪ'telɪk] *adj*. pertaining to abnormally rapid evolution.
tacit ['tæsɪt] *n*. silent; unspoken; merely implied. **taciturn,** *adj*. silent; morose. **taciturnity,** *n*.
tactile ['tæktaɪl] *adj*. pertaining to sense of touch; tangible; *n*. person whose mental processes are stimulated most by sense of touch. **tactility,** *n*. **taction,** *n*. touching. **tactual,** *adj*. **tactus,** *n*. sense of touch; stroke in beating time.
taedium vitae [ˌtiːdɪəm 'viːtaɪ, ˌtaɪ–] (*Latin*) 'weariness of life'.
taenia ['tiːnɪə] *n*. (*pl*. –ae) band; fillet; tapeworm. **taeniacide, taenicide,** *n*. substance destroying tapeworms. **taeniafuge, taenifuge,** *n*. substance expelling tapeworms. **taenial,** *adj*. **taeniasis** [–'naɪəsɪs], *n*. infestation with tapeworms. **taeniform, taeniate,** *adj*. ribbon-like. **taenioid,** *adj*. like a ribbon or tapeworm.
taffrail ['tæfreɪl] *n*. rail round ship's stern.
tagmeme ['tægmiːm] *n*. smallest meaningful unit of grammatical form.
tahsil [tə'siːl] *n*. administrative district in India. **tahsildar,** *n*. tax-collector.
taiga ['taɪgə] *n*. subarctic coniferous forest.
taipan ['taɪpæn] *n*. rich merchant in China; highly poisonous Australian snake.
taj [tɑːdʒ] (*Arabic*) *n*. cap, especially of dervish.
talalgia [tə'lældʒɪə] *n*. pain in heel or ankle.
talapoin ['tæləpɔɪn] *n*. Buddhist monk; species of monkey of W Africa.
talar ['teɪlə] *n*. ankle-length robe. **talaria** *n*. *pl*. winged sandals. **talaric** [tə'lærɪk], *adj*. pertaining or reaching to ankles.
taligrade ['tælɪgreɪd] *n*. & *adj*. (animal) walking on outer side of foot.
talionic [ˌtæli'ɒnɪk] *adj*. retaliatory.
talipes ['tælɪpiːz] *n*. clubfoot. **taliped,** *n*. person with talipes.
talipot ['tælɪpɒt] (*S Indian*) *n*. palm tree with huge leaves.
talisman ['tælɪzmən] *n*. thing believed to have magical power. **talismanic(al)** [–'mæn–], *adj*.
tallith ['tælɪθ, 'tɑːlɪs] *n*. Jewish prayer-shawl.
Talmud ['tælmʊd] *n*. Jewish scriptures. **Talmudic,** *adj*.

talpa ['tælpə] *n. Medicine*, mole.

taluk ['tɑːlʊk] (*Indian*) *n.* estate. **talukdar**, *n.* owner of taluk.

talus ['teɪləs] *n.* (*pl.* **-li**) ankle bone; slope; *Geology*, rock detritus at base of slope.

tamandu(a) ['tæmənduː, tə'mænduə] *n.* small anteater of Central and S America. **tamanoir**, *n.* ant bear.

tamaricaceous [ˌtæmərɪ'keɪʃəs] *adj.* pertaining to or like tamarisk; belonging to tamarisk family of trees.

tamarind ['tæmərɪnd] *n.* cultivated tropical tree, with edible leaves and flowers, and fruit used as medicine, flour and in preserves.

tamarisk ['tæmərɪsk] *n.* heathlike shrub or tree of warm regions.

tamasha [tə'mɑːʃə] (*Indian*) *n.* show; important occasion; commotion.

tambour ['tæmbʊə] *n.* drum; embroidery frame; sloping buttress or fortification.

tamis ['tæmi, -ɪs] *n.* woollen cloth for straining.

tampan ['tæmpən] *n.* venomous S African tick.

tampon ['tæmpɒn, -ən] *n.* surgical plug of cotton-wool; double-headed drumstick. **tamponage**, *n.* use of tampons.

tanager ['tænədʒə] *n.* finch-like American bird.

tanagra ['tænəgrə] *n.* brown madder; terracotta statuette, especially found at Tanagra, Greece.

tangram ['tæŋgræm] *n.* puzzle or toy made by cutting square into seven pieces, which are fitted together to form other shapes.

tannin ['tænɪn] *n.* highly astringent substance obtained from many plants. **tannic**, *adj.* **tanniferous**, *adj.* yielding tannin. **tannoid**, *adj.* like tannin.

tantalus ['tæntələs] *n.* case or stand, fitted with a lock, for wine or spirit bottles.

tantivy ['tæntəvɪ, tæn'tɪvɪ] *adv.* at full gallop.

tant mieux [ˌtɒn 'mjɜː] (*French*) 'so much the better'.

tant pis [ˌtɒn 'piː] (*French*) 'so much the worse'.

taphephobia [ˌtæfɪ'fəʊbɪə] *n.* dread of being buried alive.

tapinosis [ˌtæpɪ'nəʊsɪs] *n.* use of degrading diction about a subject.

tapir ['teɪpə] *n.* ant-eater with short proboscis.

tapis ['tæpi] (*French*) *n.* 'carpet'. **on the tapis**, under discussion.

tapotement [tæ'pɒtmɒn] (*French*) *n.* use of percussion in massage.

tarantas(s) [ˌtærən'tæs] *n.* low four-wheeled Russian carriage.

tarantella [ˌtærən'telə] *n.* fast violent S Italian dance. **tarantism**, *n.* nervous disease marked by desire to dance.

tarantula [tə'ræntjʊlə] *n.* poisonous spider of S Europe. **tarantulous, tarantular**, *adj.*

taraxacum [tə'ræksəkəm] *n.* dandelion, and its dried roots used in medicine.

tarboosh [ˌtɑː'buːʃ] *n.* fez.

tardigrade ['tɑːdɪgreɪd] *adj.* slow-moving. **tardiloquous**, *adj.* slow in speech. **tardive**, *adj.* unpunctual.

tarlatan, tarletan ['tɑːlətən] *n.* kind of thin stiff muslin.

tarpon ['tɑːpən] *n.* large American marine game fish.

tarsier ['tɑːsɪə] *n.* large-eyed squirrel-like E Indian animal.

tarsus ['tɑːsəs] *n.* (*pl.* **-si**) ankle and bones supporting it. **tarsal**, *adj.*

tartar ['tɑːtə] *n.* crust-like deposit of grape juice on wine casks; incrustation on teeth. **tartareous** [-'teərɪəs], **tartaric** [-'tærɪk], *adj.*

tartarology [ˌtɑːtə'rɒlədʒɪ] *n.* doctrine about Hell.

tartrate ['tɑːtreɪt] *n.* salt of tartaric acid.

tasimetry [tə'sɪmətrɪ] *n.* measurement of pressures. **tasimeter**, *n.* instrument measuring temperature changes by responding to minute changes of air pressure due to expansion and contraction of solid bodies.

tassie ['tæsi] (*Scottish*) *n.* small cup.

tatami [tə'tɑːmi] (*Japanese*) *n.* (*pl.* **-mi, -mis**) straw mat of standard size.

tatou ['tætuː] *n.* armadillo. **tatouay**, *n.* large S American armadillo.

tau [tɔː, taʊ] *n.* nineteenth letter (T, τ), of Greek alphabet; any T-shaped thing.

taupe [təʊp] *n.* mole-colour.

taurian ['tɔːrɪən] *adj.* pertaining to bull. **tauricide**, *n.* killing or killer of bull. **tauriform**, *adj.* bull-like. **taurine**, *adj.* **tauromachy**, *n.* bullfight.

tautology [tɔː'tɒlədʒɪ] *n.* repetition of sense of word(s) in other unnecessary words. **tautological**, *adj.* **tautologize**, *v.i.*

tautomerism [tɔː'tɒmərɪzm] *n. Chemistry*, possession by a substance of more than one structure. **tautomer**, *n.* **tautomeric**, *adj.*.

taws(e) [tɔːz] *n.* thong for punishment.

taxaceous [tæk'seɪʃəs] *adj.* pertaining to or like yew; belonging to the yew family of trees. **taxine**, *adj.*

taxeme ['tæksiːm] *n.* linguistic feature (*e.g.* difference in stress, pronunciation or word-order) differentiating otherwise identical utterances.

taxonomy [tæk'sɒnəmi] *n.* classification, especially of animals and plants. **taxonomic(al)**, [-'nɒm-], *adj.* **taxonomist**, *n.*

tazza ['tætsə, 'taɪ-] *n.* cup with saucer-shaped bowl on a pedestal.

teapoy ['tiːpɔɪ] *n.* three-legged stand or table.

tebbad ['tebæd] *n.* simoom of Central Asia.

technocracy [tek'nɒkrəsi] *n.* government by technical experts. **technocrat**, *n.* **technography**, *n.* description of arts and crafts. **technolithic**, *n.* pertaining to implements of stone. **technonomy**, *n.* laws of industrial arts. **technophobia**, *n.* fear of using technological devices or of the impact of technology on society.

tecnology [tek'nɒlədʒi] *n.* study of children.

tectiform ['tektɪfɔːm] *adj.* rooflike.

tectonic [tek'tɒnɪk] *adj.* structural; *Geology*, pertaining to deformation of earth's crust. **tectonics**, *n.* science of construction; *Geology*, study of structure of earth's crust.

tectorial [tek'tɔːrɪəl] *adj.* acting as covering.

tectrix ['tektrɪks] *n.* (*pl.* **-rices**) bird's wing or tail covert. **tectricial**, *adj.*

ted [ted] *v.t.* spread out for drying.

tedesco [te'deskəʊ] (*Italian*) *adj.* (*feminine* **-ca**) German. **tedescan**, *adj.*

Te Deum [ˌtiː'diːəm, ˌteɪ 'deɪ-] (*Latin*) *abbreviation* of **te deum laudamus**, 'we praise thee, O God'; *n.* ancient Christian hymn sung at morning service; any song of praise or thanks.

teg [teg] *n.* sheep, and fleece, in second year.

tegestologist [ˌtegeˈstɒlədʒɪst] *n.* collector of beer mats.

tegmen [ˈtegmen] *n.* (*pl.* **–mina**) covering. **tegminal, tegmental,** *adj.*

tegula [ˈtegjʊlə] *n.* (*pl.* **–ae**) tile. **tegular,** *adj.* **tegulated,** *adj.* made of overlapping plates.

tegument [ˈtegjʊmənt] *n.* integument. **tegumental, tegumentary,** *adj.*

te igitur [ˌteɪ ˈɪgɪtʊə, ˌtiː ˈɪdʒɪtə] (*Latin*) 'thee therefore'; first words of Canon of Roman Mass; binding oath.

teil [tiːl] *n.* lime tree.

teinoscope [ˈtaɪnəskəʊp] *n.* prism telescope.

tektite [ˈtektaɪt] *n.* small glassy body found on the surface of the Earth in large numbers and many forms, of uncertain origin but probably from outer space, perhaps debris from the moon or from a comet.

telacoustic [ˌteləˈkuːstɪk] *adj.* pertaining to telaesthesia by sound.

telaesthesia [ˌteliːsˈθiːʒiə] *n.* perception of events or objects not actually present or near, *e.g.* clairvoyance.

telamon [ˈteləmɒn] *n. Archtitecture,* male figure supporting entablature.

telarian [tɪˈleəriən] *n.* & *adj.* (spider) spinning web. **telary** [ˈteləri, ˈtiː–], *adj.* web-spinning.

telautograph [teˈlɔːtəgrɑːf] *n.* telecommunication system reproducing handwriting, drawings, etc.

telecast [ˈtelɪkɑːst] *n.* television broadcast. **telecaster,** *n.*

telechiric [ˌtelɪˈkaɪrɪk] *adj.* & *n.* (pertaining to) machine able to grasp and manipulate objects at a distance.

teledu [ˈtelɪduː] *n.* Javanese skunk.

telegenic [ˌtelɪˈdʒenɪk] *adj.* looking attractive on television.

telegnosis [ˌtelɪgˈnəʊsɪs] *n.* clairvoyance. **telegnostic** [–ˈnɒstɪk], *adj.*

telegony [tɪˈlegəni] *n.* supposed influence of female's first mate on offspring of her later matings with other males. **telegonic** [–ˈgɒnɪk], **telegonous,** *adj.*

telekinesis [ˌtelɪkaɪˈniːsɪs, –kɪ–] *n.* causing objects to move by mind power. **telekinetic** [–ˈnetɪk], *adj.*

telelectric [ˌtelɪˈlektrɪk] *adj.* pertaining to electrical transmission over long distance. **telectrograph,** *n.* instrument transmitting a picture electrically.

telemark [ˈtelɪmɑːk] *n.* method of turning in skiing.

telemechanics [ˌtelɪmɪˈkænɪks] *n.* transmission of power, or control of machinery, over a distance, especially by radio.

telemeter [tɪˈlemɪtə] *n.* distance- or strain-measuring instrument; instrument recording a measurement of quantity and transmitting it over a distance. **telemetric** [–ˈmetrɪk], *adj.* **telemetrograph,** *n.* telescopic instrument for measuring and drawing distant objects. **telemetry,** *n.*

telenergy [teˈlenədʒi] *n.* application of spiritualistic energy at a distance. **telenergic** [–ˈnɜːdʒɪk], *adj.*

teleology [ˌtiːliˈɒlədʒi, ˌte–] *n.* fact of being directed to an end, as by Providence; doctrine as to the purposes of nature; explanation of a phenomenon by reference to its purpose. **teleological,** *adj.* **teleologist,** *n.*

teleorganic [ˌteliɔːˈgænɪk] *adj.* necessary to organic life.

teleost(ean) [ˈteliɒst, ˌteliˈɒstiən] *adj.* pertaining to the bony fishes.

telephotography [ˌtelɪfəˈtɒgrəfi] *n.* photography of distant objects with telescopic lens; electrical transmission of photographs.

teleplasm [ˈtelɪˌplæzm] *n.* ectoplasm. **teleplasmic, teleplastic,** *adj.*

teleprompter [ˈtelɪˌprɒmptə] *n.* device unrolling a magnified script visible to speakers on a television programme but invisible to viewers.

teleran [ˈteləræn] *n.* navigation system transmitting ground-based radar scan to aircraft by television.

telergy [ˈtelədʒi] *n.* force that effects telepathy. **telergic** [–ˈlɜːdʒɪk], *adj.* effective at a distance.

teleseism [ˈtelɪˌsaɪzm] *n.* tremor due to distant earthquake. **teleseismic,** *adj.* **teleseismology,** *n.* study of teleseism.

telestich [ˈtelɪstɪk, təˈlestɪk] *n.* acrostic-like poem, etc., in which last letters of lines spell a name.

teletactor [ˈtelɪˌtæktə] *n.* instrument enabling deaf to feel sound vibrations with finger tips. **teletactile,** *adj.*

teletherapy [ˌtelɪˈθerəpi] *n.* medical treatment by telepathy.

telic [ˈtelɪk, ˈtiː–] *adj.* purposive; *Grammar,* signifying intention.

tell [təl] *n.* mound of accumulated debris over site of ancient settlement.

tellurian [teˈlʊəriən, –ˈljʊə–] *adj.* pertaining to the earth; *n.* dweller on the earth. **telluric,** *adj.* **tellurion,** *n.* instrument showing how night and day alternate and the seasons change owing to the obliquity of Earth's axis. **tellurism,** *n.* disease production by the soil. **tellurometer** *n.* electronic instrument for surveying and measuring large areas of the Earth's surface.

telmatology [ˌtelməˈtɒlədʒi] *n.* study of peat-bogs. **telmatological,** *adj.*

telodynamic [ˌtelədaɪˈnæmɪk] *adj.* pertaining to transmission of power to a distance.

telopsis [teˈlɒpsɪs] *n.* visual telaesthesia. **teloptic,** *adj.*

telpher [ˈtelfə] *n.* electrically propelled light car on overhead cable. **telpherage,** *n.* transportation by telpher

telson [ˈtelsn] *n.* last segment of crustacean, etc.

telurgy [ˈtelədʒi] *n.* telepathy.

temerity [təˈmerəti] *n.* boldness. **temerarious,** *adj.*

tempera [ˈtempərə] *n.* painting with white of egg or similar medium replacing oil.

temperative [ˈtempərətɪv] *adj.* moderating; soothing.

template, templet [ˈtempleɪt, –lət] *n.* bezel; supporting beam, etc.; shaped plate used as gauge or pattern.

temporal [ˈtempərəl] *adj.* pertaining to time; earthly; secular; pertaining to temples of head. **temporality,** *n.* property or revenue of religious body.

tempore [ˈtempəri] (*Latin*) *adv.* 'in the time of'.

temporize [ˈtempəraɪz] *v.i.* procrastinate; delay; comply with circumstances.

tempus fugit [ˌtempəs ˈfjuːdʒɪt, –ˈfuːg–] (*Latin*)

'time is fleeting'.

tenable ['tenəbl] *adj.* that can be held or maintained. **tenability**, *n.*

tenacious [tɪ'neɪʃəs] *adj.* grasping firmly; clinging closely; not quickly relinquishing or forgetting. **tenacity** [–'næsəti], *n.*

tendentious [ten'denʃəs] *adj.* tending to uphold or advance a cause; not impartial. **tendential**, *adj.*

tendinous ['tendɪnəs] *adj.* pertaining to or like a tendon; sinewy.

tendresse [tɒn'dres] (*French*) *n.* tender feeling; care; delicacy.

tenebra ['tenɪbrə] (*Latin*) *n.* (*pl.* **–ae**) 'darkness'; *pl.*, *Roman Catholic*, matins and lauds for last three days of Holy Week. **tenebrific**, *adj.* making dark. **tenebrious, tenebrose, tenebrous**, *adj.* dark; gloomy. **tenebrity, tenebrosity**, *n.*

tenesmus [tɪ'nezməs] *n. Medicine*, ineffective urge or straining to empty bowels or bladder. **tenesmic**, *adj.*

tenet ['tenɪt] *n.* doctrine; dogma.

tenon ['tenən] *n.* projecting part of joint for inserting into mortise.

tenonectomy [ˌtenə'nektəmi] *n.* surgical removal of tendon. **tenonitis, tenositis**, *n.* inflammation of tendon. **tenorrhaphy**, *n.* surgical stitching of tendon. **tenotomy**, *n.* surgical incision into tendon.

tensile ['tensaɪl] *adj.* pertaining to tension; that can be stretched. **tensile strength**, ability to endure lengthwise pull without breaking. **tensible**, *adj.* **tensive**, *adj.* causing tension. **tensor**, *n.* stretching muscle.

tentamen [ten'teɪmen] (*Latin*) *n.* (*pl.* **–mina**) experiment; attempt. **tentation**, *n.* experiment by trial and error.

tenue [tə'nju:] (*French*) *n.* general appearance or manner.

tenuous ['tenjuəs] *adj.* thin; sparse; rarefied. **tenuity**, *n.*

tepary ['tepəri] *n.* kind of hardy bean of southern USA and Mexico.

tepefy ['tepɪfaɪ] *v.t.* make tepid. **tepefaction**, *n.*

tephrosis [tɪ'frəʊsɪs] *n.* incineration.

tepor ['ti:pə, –ɔ:] *n.* tepidness.

tera- ['terə–] *prefix* of measurement meaning one million millions (10¹²) *abbrev.* as T).

teramorphous [ˌterə'mɔ:fəs] *adj.* monstrous; of abnormal form.

teraph ['terəf] *n.* (*pl.* **–phim**) ancient Jewish household god.

teratism ['terətɪzm] *n.* monstrosity; love of monsters or marvels. **teratical** [–'ræt–], *adj.* **teratogen**, *n.* substance that can cause foetal deformities if absorbed during pregnancy. **teratogenesis**, **teratogeny**, *n.* production of malformations in a foetus or of biological monstrosities. **teratoid**, *adj.* abnormal. **teratology**, *n.* composition of fantastic stories; study or description of, or doctrine about, miracles; study of freaks, monsters, and physical abnormalities. **teratosis**, *n.*

tercel ['tɜ:sl] *n.* male hawk.

tercentenary [ˌtɜ:sen'ti:nəri] *adj.* pertaining to or lasting 300 years; *n.* 300th anniversary. **tercentennial** [–'teniəl], **tercentenarian**, *adj.*

tercet ['tɜ:sɪt] *n.* set of three rhyming verse-lines.

terdiurnal [ˌtɜ:daɪ'ɜ:nl] *adj.* three times per day.

terebinth ['terəbɪnθ] *n.* tree yielding turpentine. **terebinthine**, *adj.*

terebrant ['terəbrənt] *adj.* boring (hole in); pertaining to long thin sharp sea-shell. **terebrate**, *v.t.* bore. **terebration**, *n.*

teredo [tə'ri:dəʊ] *n.* ship worm.

terek ['terek] *n.* kind of sandpiper.

terephah [tə'reɪfə] (*Hebrew*) *n.* unclean or forbidden meat.

terete ['teri:t] *adj.* round and tapering.

tergal ['tɜ:gl] *adj.* pertaining to back.

tergiversation [ˌtɜ:dʒɪvɜ:'seɪʃn] *n.* act or state of being apostate or renegade; equivocation. **tergiversator**, *n.* **tergiversatory**, *adj.*

termagant ['tɜ:məgənt] *n.* virago.

terminus ad quem [ˌtɜ:mɪnəs æd 'kwem] (*Latin*) *n.* 'end to which'; aim; terminal or latest point in time.

terminus a quo [ˌtɜ:mɪnəs aɪ 'kwəʊ] (*Latin*) *n.* 'end from which'; starting point.

termitarium [ˌtɜ:mɪ'teəriəm] *n.* termites' nest.

termitarium [ˌtɜ:mɪ'teəriəm] *n.* termites' nest.

To boldly go

When scholars of the 17th century laid down the rules of English grammar, they used as their model the grammar of classical Latin. They did this because they thought Latin was as near perfect a language as one could get, and therefore worthy of emulation. Now the infinitive form of Latin verbs is a single indivisible word (*amare* to love, *venire* to come etc.). But in English, the infinitive is often expressed by putting *to* in front of the verb. So these early grammarians recommended that because the Latin infinitive could not be broken up, the English infinitive should not be either, by placing a word between *to* and the following verb. Latin is of course a completely different language from English, and its grammar is structured along different lines, so there is no reason why its rules should determine the rules of English. Nevertheless, this injunction against the so-called 'split infinitive' took,

and continues to have, a strong hold. Even if one knows that the 'rule' is illogical, expressions like *to boldly go where no man has gone before* (perhaps the most famous of all 'split infinitives', from the television series *Startrek*) can jar, and make one wish the adverb could have gone somewhere else. This inculcated caution about the placement of adverbs can even make people go to the ludicrous lengths of avoiding an adverb in other verb phrases, notably the passive, about which there is no 'rule' – thus preferring, say, the ponderous *It ought rigorously to be avoided* to the natural and perfectly acceptable *It ought to be rigorously avoided*. In most instances the unsplittable infinitive is merely a harmless shibboleth, but there are some contexts in which it can lead to ambiguity: does *I have decided definitely to go*, for instance, mean that my decision is definite or that my going is definite?

ternary ['tɜːnəri] *adj.* triple; pertaining to or consisting of three(s); in threes; having three as base; *n.* set of three. **ternion,** *n.* three; set of three.

Terpsichore [tɜːp'sɪkəri] *n.* muse presiding over the dance. **Terpsichoreal, Terpsichorean** [-'riː-], *adj.* pertaining to Terpsichore or dancing.

terra ['terə] (*Latin & Italian*) *n.* 'earth'. **terra alba,** 'white earth'; gypsum, kaolin, magnesia, etc. **terra cotta,** glazed earthenware and its reddish colour. **terra firma,** dry land. **terra incognita,** unknown land.

terraceous [te'reɪʃəs] *adj.* earthen.

terramara [ˌterə'mɑːrə] *n.* kind of earthy fertilizer; neolithic pile dwelling.

terramycin [ˌterə'maɪsɪn] *n.* antibiotic produced by a soil fungus.

terrane ['tereɪn] *n.* geological formation; area covered by certain type of rock. **terranean, terraneous,** *adj.* pertaining to earth.

terrapin ['terəpɪn] *n.* kind of edible N American turtle.

terraqueous [te'reɪkwɪəs] *adj.* amphibious; consisting of land and water.

terrarium [tə'reəriəm] *n.* (*pl.* **-riums, -ria**) enclosure for small land animals; glass container for growing plants.

terrazzo [te'rætsəʊ] *n.* flooring of marble chips.

terrene ['teriːn] *adj.* pertaining to or consisting of earth; mundane.

terricolous [te'rɪkələs] *adj.* living in or on ground.

terrigenous [te'rɪdʒənəs] *adj.* produced by earth.

terrine [te'riːn] *n.* earthenware jar or dish; tureen; ragout.

territelarian [ˌterɪtə'leəriən] *n.* & *adj.* (pertaining to) trap-door spider.

terry ['teri] *n.* & *adj.* (cloth) with pile of uncut loops.

tertian ['tɜːʃn] *n.* & *adj.* (fever) recurring after three (*i.e.*, every two) days. **tertiary,** *adj.* of third degree; *n.* member of third monastic order. **tertium quid,** *n.* 'third something', not included in simple classification; intermediate or anomalous thing. **tertius,** *n.* third of the name; 'minimus'.

terza rima [ˌteətsə 'riːmə, ˌtɜː-] (*Italian*) 'third rhyme'; rhyming scheme of linked tercets. **terzet, terzetto,** *n.* trio.

tessara ['tesərə] *n. pl.* quadrilaterals. **tessaraglot,** *adj.* pertaining to, in or speaking four languages.

tesselated ['tesəleɪtɪd] *adj.* chequered; pertaining to or like mosaic. **tesselation,** *n.*

tessera ['tesərə] *n.* (*pl.* **-ae**) small block of stone, tile, etc., used in mosaic; piece of wood, bone, etc., used in ancient times as a token, voucher, tally, etc. **tesseral, tessular,** *adj.*

test [test] *n. Zoology,* shell of invertebrate. **testacean,** *n.* shell-fish. **testaceous,** *adj.* pertaining to, like or bearing a test.

testa ['testə] *n.* (*pl.* **-tae**) hard external covering of a seed.

testa ['testə] *n.* hard external covering of a seed.

testacy ['testəsi] *n.* dying testate.

testamur [te'steɪmə] *n.* certificate of passing university examination.

testate ['testeɪt] *n.* & *adj.* (person) dying leaving a valid will. **testation,** *n.* **testator, testatrix,** *n.* **testatory,** *adj.*

tester ['testə] *n.* bed canopy.

testicle ['testɪkl] *n.* male reproductive gland. **testicular,** *adj.* **testiculate,** *adj.* like a testicle in shape.

testis ['testɪs] *n.* (*pl.* **-tes**) testicle.

testudinal [te'stjuːdɪnl] *adj.* pertaining to or like tortoise or tortoiseshell. **testudinarious,** *adj.* **testudinate,** *adj.* like tortoiseshell; arched; *n.* turtle.

testudo [te'stjuːdəʊ] *n.* cover, especially of overlapping shields, used by Roman army against attack from above.

tetanus ['tetənəs] *n.* muscular spasm due to a soil bacillus; lockjaw. **tetanic(al)** [-'tæn-], *adj.* **tetanize,** *v.t.* cause tetanus in. **tetanoid,** *adj.* like tetanus. **tetany,** *n.* state resembling tetanus.

tête-à-tête [ˌteɪt-ə-'teɪt, -ɑː-] (*French*) 'head to head'; *n.* & *adj.* (meeting or conversation) of two persons; *adj.* & *adv.* (in) private; confidentially.

tethydan [tɪ'θaɪdn] *n.* ascidian.

tetrabrach ['tetrəbræk] *n.* metrical foot, or word, of four short syllables.

tetrachord ['tetrəkɔːd] *n.* musical scale of four tones, or instrument with four strings. **tetrachordal,** *adj.*

tetrachotomous [ˌtetrə'kɒtəməs] *adj.* divided into fours.

tetrachromatic [ˌtetrəkrə'mætɪk] *adj.* having four colours; denoting or pertaining to theory that there are four primary colours.

tetracycline [ˌtetrə'saɪkliːn, -ɪn] *n.* antibiotic drug used against many infections.

tetrad ['tetræd] *n.* four; set of four.

tetradactyl(e) [ˌtetrə'dæktɪl, -aɪl] *n.* & *adj.* (animal) with four digits. **tetradactylous,** *adj.*

tetraglot ['tetrəglɒt] *adj.* in four languages. **tetraglottic(al),** *adj.*

tetragon ['tetrəgən] *n.* four-sided plane figure. **tetragonal** [-'træg-], *adj.*

tetragram ['tetrəgræm] *n.* word of four letters; quadrilateral. **tetragrammaton,** *n.* four Hebrew consonants (JHWH) forming name of Creator (Jahweh, or Jehovah).

tetrahedron [ˌtetrə'hiːdrən] *n.* four-sided solid figure. **tetrahedral,** *adj.*

tetralemma [ˌtetrə'lemə] *n.* dilemma-like position with four alternatives.

tetralogy [te'trælədʒi] *n.* set of four connected works of literature or music.

tetramerous [te'træmərəs] *adj.* having four parts; *Botany,* having parts in fours. **tetrameral, tetrameric** [-'merɪk], *adj.*

tetrameter [te'træmɪtə] *n.* verse line of four feet.

tetrapla ['tetrəplə] *n.* edition of book, especially Old Testament, with four texts.

tetraplegia [ˌtetrə'pliːdʒiə] *n.* paralysis of all four limbs.

tetrapod ['tetrəpɒd] *n.* & *adj.* quadruped; caltrop; four-armed concrete structure used in sea defences.

tetrapody [te'træpədi] *n.* verse of four feet. **tetrapodic** [-'pɒdɪk], *adj.*

tetrapolis [te'træpəlɪs] *n.* group of four cities. **tetrapolitan** [-'pɒlɪtən], *adj.*

tetrapous ['tetrəpəs] *adj.* four-footed.

tetrapteran [te'træptərən] *adj.* four-winged. **tetrapteron,** *n.* (*pl.* **-ra**) such insect. **tetrapterous,** *adj.*

tetraptych [te'træptɪk] *n.* painting in four parts, especially hinged.

tetrarch ['tetrɑːk] *n.* ruler of quarter of a province; member of tetrarchy. **tetrarchic**, *adj.* **tetrarchy**, *n.* jurisdiction or office of a tetrarch; rule by four persons.

tetrastich ['tetrəstɪk] *n.* four-lined poem or stanza. **tetrastichal** [–'træst–], **tetrastichic**, *adj.* **tetrastichous** [–'træst–], *adj.* in four rows.

tetrasyllable ['tetrə‚sɪləbl] *n.* word of four syllables. **tetrasyllabic** [–'læbɪk], *adj.*

tetravalent [‚tetrə'veɪlənt, te'trævələnt] *adj.* quadrivalent.

tetter ['tetə] *n.* any of several kinds of skin disease, as eczema, etc. **tetterous**, *adj.*

thalamus ['θæləməs] *n.* (*pl.* **–mi**) part of brain with a co-ordinating and relaying function. **thalamic** [–'læmɪk], *adj.*

thalassa [θə'læsə] (*Greek*) *n.* 'the sea', especially exclamation of the Greek soldiers on seeing the Black Sea in the Anabasis. **thalassaemia**, *n.* hereditary anaemia common especially in Mediterranean regions. **thalassian**, *n.* sea turtle. **thalassic**, *adj.* pertaining to the sea, especially to small or inland seas. **thalassiophyte**, *adj.* seaweed. **thalassocracy**, *n.* supremacy at sea. **thalassography**, *n.* study and mapping of (especially coastal and smaller) seas. **thalassometer**, *n.* tide gauge. **thalassophilous**, *adj.* living in or fond of the sea. **thalassophobia**, *n.* dread of the sea. **thalassotherapy**, *n.* medical treatment by sea baths, etc.

Thalian [θə'laɪən, 'θeɪlɪən] *adj.* pertaining to Thalia, muse of comedy.

thallus ['θæləs] *n.* (*pl.* **–li**) frond-like body of lower plants, as lichens, algae, etc. **thalliform**, *adj.* shaped like a thallus. **thalline**, **thallodal** [–'ləʊdl], **thallodic** [–'lɒdɪk], **thalloid**, **thallose**, *adj.* **thallogen**, **thallophyte**, *n.* plant having thalli.

thalposis [θæl'pəʊsɪs] *n.* sensation of warmth. **thalpotic** [–'pɒtɪk], *adj.*

thamuria [θə'mjʊərɪə] *n.* abnormally frequent micturition.

thanatography [‚θænə'tɒgrəfi] *n.* description of person's death. **thanatognomonic** [–təʊnə'mɒnɪk], *adj.* indicating death. **thanatoid**, *adj.* apparently dead. **thanatology**, *n.* study, description or theory of death. **thanatophidian**, *n.* venomous snake. **thanatopsis**, *n.* meditation on death. **thanatosis**, *n.* necrosis; state imitating death. **thanatousia**, *n.* funeral rites.

thaumaturgy ['θɔːmətɜːdʒi] *n.* miracle-working; magic. **thaumaturge**, **thaumaturgist**, **thaumaturgus**, *n.* miracle-worker; saint. **thaumaturgic**, *adj.* **thaumaturgics**, **thaumaturgism**, *n.* **thaumatology**, *n.* study of thaumaturgy.

THC *abbreviation* of tetrahydrocannabinol (chief intoxicant in marijuana).

theaceous [θi'eɪʃəs] *adj.* pertaining to or like tea-plant; belonging to tea family of plants.

theandric [θi'ændrɪk] *adj.* pertaining to combination of divine and human; Christ-like. **theanthropic**, *adj.* pertaining to god-like human being; theandric. **theanthropism**, *n.* state of being both God and man; anthropomorphism. **theanthropos**, *n.* god-man; Christ.

thearchy ['θiːɑːki] *n.* government by or power of God; theocracy.

thebaine [tiː'beɪiːn] *n.* poisonous alkaloid obtained from opium.

theca ['θiːkə] *n.* (*pl.* **–ae**) spore-case; capsule; sheath. **thecal**, *adj.* **thecate**, *adj.* having thecae.

thé dansant [‚teɪ 'dɑːnsɒn] (*French*) (*pl.* **thés dansants**) 'tea dance'.

theiform ['θiːɪfɔːm] *adj.* like tea or tea plant. **theine**, *n.* caffeine.

theism ['θiːɪzm] *n.* belief in God, especially one God; *Medicine*, condition due to excessive tea-drinking. **theistic**, *adj.*

thelemite [θə'liːmaɪt] *n.* libertine.

thelyotoky, **thelytoky** [‚θeli'ɒtəki, θe'lɪtəki] *n.* production of females parthenogenetically. **thely(o)tokous**, *adj.*

theobromine [‚θiːə'brəʊmiːn] *n.* caffeine-like alkaloid in cocoa beans.

theocentric [‚θiːə'sentrɪk] *adj.* having God or divine being as central fact. **theocentrism**, *n.*

theocracy [θi'ɒkrəsi] *n.* government of a state by priests or according to religious law. **theocratic**, *adj.* **theocrasy**, *n.* worship of a mixture of gods.

theodicy [θi'ɒdəsi] *n.* proof of God's justice; theological study of God's government, especially over the soul. **theodicean**, *adj.*

theodolite [θi'ɒdəlaɪt] *n.* surveyor's angle-measuring swivel-telescope. **theodolitic** [–'lɪtɪk], *adj.*

theody ['θiːədi] *n.* hymn in praise of God.

theogamy [θi'ɒgəmi] *n.* marriage of gods.

theogony [ti'ɒgəni] *n.* doctrine of origin of gods. **theogonal**, **theogonic** [–'gɒnɪk], *adj.* **theogonism**, *n.* belief in a theogony.

theoktony [θi'ɒktəni] *n.* death of gods. **theoktonic** [–'tɒnɪk], *adj.*

theomachy [θi'ɒməki] *n.* battle between or against gods. **theomachist**, *n.*

theomancy ['θiːəmænsi] *n.* divination by divinely inspired oracles. **theomantic** [–'mæntɪk], *adj.*

theomania [‚θiːə'meɪnɪə] *n.* delusion that one is God or inspired.

theomastix [‚θiːə'mæstɪks] *n.* punishment, or punisher, of mortals sent by God.

theomicrist [θi'ɒmɪkrɪst] *n.* person belittling God.

theomorphic [‚θiːə'mɔːfɪk] *adj.* god-like. **theomorphism**, *n.*

theonomy [θi'ɒnəmi] *n.* government by God.

theopantism [‚θiːə'pæntɪzm] *n.* belief that God is the only reality.

theopathy [θi'ɒpəθi] *n.* mystical religious experience; entire devotion to religion. **theopathetic**, **theopathic** [–'pæθɪk], *adj.*

theophagy [θi'ɒfədʒi] *n.* eating of god, or of thing symbolising god, as a sacrament. **theophagic** [–'fædʒɪk], **theophagous**, *adj.* **theophagite**, *n.*

theophany [θi'ɒfəni] *n.* manifestation of a god. **theophanic** [–'fænɪk], **theophanous**, *adj.* **theophanism**, *n.*

theophilanthropism [‚θiːəfɪ'lænθrəpɪzm] *n.* love of God and Man. **theophilanthropic** [–'θrɒpɪk], *adj.* **theophilanthropist**, *n.* **theophilanthropy**, *n.*

theophile ['θiːəfaɪl] *n.* person loving, or loved by, God.

theophobia [‚θiːə'fəʊbiə] *n.* fear or hatred of God.

theophorous [θi'ɒfərəs] *adj.* having name of a god; derived from god's name. **theophoric** [–'fɒrɪk], *adj.*

theopneustic [ˌθiːɒpˈnjuːstɪk] *adj.* divinely inspired. **theopneusty,** *n.*

theorbo [θiˈɔːbəʊ] *n.* 17th-century double-necked lute.

theosophy [θiˈɒsəfi] *n.* supposed mystical or philosophical knowledge of God, especially of a Buddhist-like sect, 'The Theosophical Society'. **theosophical,** *adj.* **theosophist,** *n.*

theotechny [ˈθiːətekni] *n.* supernatural beings involved in the action of a poem, play, etc.; introduction of such beings**theotechnic,** *adj.*

theotherapy [ˌθiːəˈθerəpi] *n.* faith-healing.

thereoid [ˈθɪərɪɔɪd] *adj.* bestial; savage.

thereology [ˌθɪəriˈɒlədʒi] *n.* therapeutics.

theriac(a) [ˈθɪəriæk, θəˈraɪəkə] *n.* antidote to poison; treacle. **theriacal, therial,** *adj.* medicinal.

therianthropic [ˌθɪəriænˈθrɒpɪk] *adj.* half-man half-animal; pertaining to such gods. **therianthropism** [-ˈænθrəpɪzm], *n.*

theriodic [ˌθɪəriˈɒdɪk] *adj.* malignant.

theriomorphic [ˌθɪəriəˈmɔːfɪk] *adj.* having form of an animal. **theriomorphism,** *n.* such representation of a god. **theriomorphous,** *adj.*

thermae [ˈθɜːmiː] (*Latin*) *n. pl.* warm public baths.

thermaesthesia [ˌθɜːmiːsˈθiːziə] *n.* sensitivity to heat.

thermantidote [θəˈmæntɪdəʊt] *n.* air-cooling apparatus.

thermatology [ˌθɜːməˈtɒlədʒi] *n.* study of heat as medical remedy. **thermatologic,** *adj.* **thermatologist,** *n.*

thermion [ˈθɜːmiən, –aɪən] *n.* ion emitted by incandescent object or substance. **thermionic** [-ˈɒnɪk], *adj.* **thermionic valve,** vacuum tube with several electrodes – cathode, anode, and grid(s) – the heated cathode emitting electrons.

thermistor [θɜːˈmɪstə, ˈθɜːmɪstə] *n.* electrical resistor, the resistance of which varies with changes of temperature.

thermit(e) [ˈθɜːmɪt, –aɪt] *n.* heat-producing mixture of powdered aluminium and iron oxide, used in welding and incendiary bombs.

thermocline [ˈθɜːməklaɪn] *n.* intermediate layer of water in lake, sea, etc. with steep temperature gradient.

thermocouple [ˈθɜːməˌkʌpl] *n.* device for measuring temperature thermoelectrically by the junction of two dissimilar metallic conductors.

thermoduric [ˌθɜːməˈdjʊərɪk] *adj.* resistant to high temperatures.

thermodynamics [ˌθɜːmədaɪˈnæmɪks] *n.* study of relationships of heat and mechanical energy.

thermoelectricity [ˌθɜːməʊɪlekˈtrɪsəti] *n.* electricity due directly to action of heat. **thermoelectric,** *adj.*

thermogenesis [ˌθɜːməˈdʒenəsɪs] *n.* production of heat; spontaneous combustion. **thermogenetic** [-dʒəˈnetɪk], **thermogenic, thermogenous** [-ˈmɒdʒ–], *adj.*

thermogram [ˈθɜːməgræm] *n.* record made by a thermograph

thermograph [ˈθɜːməgrɑːf] *n.* recording thermometer. **thermographic,** *adj.* **thermography** *n.* writing or printing process in which heat is used; the making of a photographic record of the surface temperature of the human body, used in diagnosing disease.

thermolabile [ˌθɜːməʊˈleɪbaɪl] *adj.* easily decomposed by heat.

thermology [θɜːˈmɒlədʒi] *n.* study of heat. **thermological,** *adj.*

thermolysis [θɜːˈmɒləsɪs] *n.* disintegration by heat; loss of body heat. **thermolyze,** *v.t.* **thermolytic** [-ˈlɪtɪk], *adj.*

thermonasty [ˈθɜːmənæsti] *n.* abnormality in position of plant organs due to heat. **thermonastic,** *adj.*

thermonous [ˈθɜːmənəs] *adj.* pertaining to stimulation by heat.

thermonuclear [ˌθɜːməʊˈnjuːkliə] *adj.* pertaining to fusion of atomic nuclei brought about by, and producing, intense heat, as in hydrogen bomb.

thermophile [ˈθɜːməfaɪl] *n.* organism thriving in high temperatures. **thermophilic** [-ˈfɪlɪk], **thermophilous** [-ˈmɒfɪləs], *adj.*

thermophore [ˈθɜːməfɔː] *n.* heat-conveying apparatus.

thermopile [ˈθɜːməpaɪl] *n.* instrument consisting of several linked thermocouples used to generate electricity or measure radiant heat.

thermoplastic [ˌθɜːməˈplæstɪk] *n. & adj.* (substance) becoming soft and mouldable when heated.

thermopolypnoea [ˌθɜːməpɒlɪpˈniːə] *n.* rapid respiration due to heat. **thermopolypnoeic,** *adj.*

thermoscope [ˈθɜːməskəʊp] *n.* instrument indicating, but not measuring, changes of temperature. **thermoscopic** [-ˈskɒpɪk], *adj.*

thermosetting [ˈθɜːməʊˌsetɪŋ] *adj.* becoming permanently hard and rigid when heated.

thermosphere [ˈθɜːməsfɪə] *n.* region of the Earth's atmosphere beyond about 50 miles/80 km above the surface, in which the temperature steadily increases with height.

thermostat [ˈθɜːməstæt] *n.* automatic apparatus for regulating temperature, or for actuating a mechanism at a pre-set temperature. **thermostatic,** *adj.* **thermostatics,** *n.* study of thermal equilibrium.

thermotaxis [ˌθɜːməˈtæksɪs] *n.* movement controlled or influenced by heat. **thermotactic,** *adj.*

thermotherapy [ˌθɜːməˈθerəpi] *n.* medical treatment by heat. **thermotherapeutics,** *n.*

thermotic(al) [θɜːˈmɒtɪk, –l] *adj.* thermal. **thermotics,** *n.* thermology.

thermotropism [θɜːˈmɒtrəpɪzm] *n.* growth influenced by temperature. **thermotropic** [-ˈtrɒpɪk], *adj.*

theroid [ˈθɪərɔɪd] *adj.* feral. **therology,** *n.* study of wild mammals. **theromorphism,** *n.* reversion to animal type in human being.

therophyte [ˈθɪərəfaɪt] *n. Botany,* annual.

thersitical [θɜːˈsɪtɪkl] *adj.* like Thersites, an ugly and scurrilous Greek in Greek legend; scurrilous; violent in speech.

thesmothete(s) [ˈθesməθiːt, θezˈmɒθətiːz] (*Greek*) *n.* (*pl.* **–tae**) lawgiver.

Thespian [ˈθespiən] *adj.* pertaining to Thespis, supposed founder of Greek drama; pertaining to drama; *n.* actor or actress.

theta [ˈθiːtə] *n.* eighth letter (θ, Θ) of Greek alphabet.

thetic [ˈθetɪk] *adj.* prescriptive; pertaining to metrical stress.

theurgy ['θiːɜːdʒi] *n.* art of persuading benefi-cent divinity to perform desired act; supernatu-ral intervention in human affairs. **theurgic,** *adj.* **theurgist,** *n.*

thionate ['θaɪəneɪt] *v.t.* combine with sulphur. **thionic** [-'ɒnɪk], *adj.* pertaining to or contain-ing sulphur.

thixotropy [θɪk'sɒtrəpi] *n.* property of some gels of becoming fluid when stirred or shaken, and setting to gel again when allowed to stand. **thixotropic** [,θɪksə'trɒpɪk], *adj.*

thlipsis ['θlɪpsɪs] *n. Medicine* , compression.

thole [θəʊl] *n.* upright peg in boat's gunwale against which oar is worked; *v.i.* & *t. dia-lect,* endure.

thooid ['θəʊɔɪd] *adj.* like a wolf.

thorax ['θɔːræks] *n.* (*pl.* **–races**) cavity between neck and abdomen, containing lungs, heart, etc.; chest. **thoracic** [-'ræsɪk], *adj.* **thoracoscope,** *n.* stethoscope; instrument for viewing thorax.

thranite ['θreɪnaɪt] *n.* rower in ancient galley. **thranitic** [θrə'nɪtɪk], *adj.*

thrasonical [θrə'sɒnɪkl] *adj.* boasting.

thremmatology [,θremə'tɒlədʒi] *n.* science of breeding domesticated animals and plants.

threnetic(al) [θrə'netɪk] *adj.* mournful.

threnody ['θrenədi] *n.* lament; dirge. **threnodial** [-'nəʊdiəl], **threnodic** [-'nɒdɪk], *adj.* **threnodist,** *n.*

threpsology [θrep'sɒlədʒi] *n.* science of nutrition. **threptic,** *adj.* pertaining to rearing of young.

thrombin ['θrɒmbɪn] *n.* substance in blood help-ing to form fibrin in clotting. **thrombogen,** *n.* sub-stance from which thrombin is derived.

thrombus ['θrɒmbəs] *n.* (*pl.* **–bi**) clot of blood; tumour in blood vessel. **thrombogenic,** *adj.* pro-ducing thrombus. **thromboid,** *adj.* like a throm-bus. **thrombosis,** *n.* formation of thrombi.

thrum [θrʌm] *n.* (any of) a fringe of warp threads left on the loom after weaving.

thuggee ['θʌgiː] *n.* robbery and murder as prac-tised by Indian sect of Thugs.

Thule [θjuːl, 'θjuːli] *n.* northernmost region in ancient geography. **ultima Thule,** furthest Thule; any very distant or unknown region; distant objec-tive or end.

Thummim ['θʌmɪm] *n.* one of the sacred instru-ments (Urim and Thummim) of ancient Jews, worn by high priest in breastplate in some cer-emonies.

thurible ['θjʊərɪbl] *n.* censer. **thurifer,** *n.* car-rier of a thurible. **thuriferous,** *adj.* yielding frankincense. **thurify,** *v.t.*

Thyestean [θaɪ'estiən] *adj.* pertaining to Thyestes, in Greek legend, whose sons were killed and served to him at a banquet by his brother. **Thyestean banquet,** one at which human flesh is eaten.

thylacine ['θaɪləsiːn] *n.* Tasmanian wolf.

thymus ['θaɪməs] *n.* lymphoid gland in lower part of throat, disappearing in adult. **thymic,** *adj.* **thymopathy,** *n.* mental disorder; disease of thymus.

thyratron ['θaɪrətrɒn] *n.* gas-discharge triode used as a relay or electronic switch, and in tele-vision as voltage generator.

thyristor [θaɪ'rɪstə] *n.* electronic switch without moving parts.

thyroid ['θaɪrɔɪd] *adj.* & *n.* (denoting or per-taining to) large ductless gland of the neck, the hormone of which influences growth, etc. **thyroidism,** *n.* deficient thyroid action. **thyrocale,** *n.* goitre. **thyrogenic,** *adj.* due to thyroid action. **thyrotherapy,** *n.* medical treatment by thyroid extract. **thyroxine,** *n.* hormone of thyroid gland.

thyrsus ['θɜːsəs] *n.* (*pl.* **–si**) ornamented staff carried by Bacchus; *Botany,* mixed cymose and racemose inflorescence, as of lilac. **thyrsoid,** *adj.* like a thyrsus.

tibia ['tɪbiə] *n.* shin-bone; kind of ancient flute. **tibial,** *adj.*

tic ['tɪk] *n.* involuntary nervous movement. **tic douloureux** [–duːlə'rɜː], neuralgia with tic of facial muscles.

tichorrhine ['tɪkəraɪn] *n.* woolly rhinoceros.

ticpolonga [,tɪkpə'lɒŋgə] *n.* venomous Indian snake; Russell's viper.

tierce [tɪəs, tɜːs] *n.* three or third; sequence of three playing cards of same suit; ecclesiastical ser-vice sung at third hour (9 a.m.).

tiercel ['tɪəsl] *n.* tercel.

Tiergarten ['tɪə,gɑːtn] (*German*) *n.* zoological garden.

tiffany ['tɪfəni] *n.* light gauzy material.

tiffin ['tɪfɪn] (*Anglo-Indian*) *n.* light meal; lunch.

tigella [tɪ'dʒelə] *n. Botany,* short stem. **tigellate,** *adj.*

tika ['tiːkə] *n.* tilka.

tiki ['tiːki] *n.* carved figure of ancestor, worn as an amulet.

til [tɪl, tiːl] (*Hindi*) *n.* sesame.

tilak ['tɪlək] *n.* tilka.

tilbury ['tɪlbəri] *n.* kind of two-wheeled carriage.

tilde ['tɪldə, –eɪ] *n.* wavy mark (˜) indicating *ny* sound of Spanish ñ (as in *cañon* or *canyon.*)

tileaceous [,tɪli'eɪʃəs] *adj.* pertaining to or like linden tree; belonging to linden family of trees.

tilka ['tɪlkə] *n.* Hindu caste-mark on forehead.

timbal ['tɪmbl] *n.* kettledrum.

timbre ['tæmbr, 'tæmbə] (*French*) *n.* distinctive quality of a sound.

timbrel ['tɪmbrəl] *n.* tambourine.

timocracy [tɪ'mɒkrəsi] *n.* state in which pos-session of property is required for partici-pation in government; ideal state in which love of honour is ruling principle. **timocratic,** *adj.*

timpani ['tɪmpəni] (*Italian*) *n. pl.* (*singular* **–no**) set of kettledrums. **timpanist,** *n.* player of tim-pani.

tinction ['tɪŋkʃn] *n.* act of dyeing. **tinctorial,** *adj.* pertaining to tinction or colours. **tinctumutation,** *n.* change of colour.

tincture ['tɪŋktʃə] *n.* colour; dye; slight amount; extract of medicinal principle of a plant; *v.t.* stain; imbue.

tine [taɪn] *n.* prong.

tinea ['tɪniə] *n.* ringworm, or similar disease. **tin-eal,** *adj.*

tinnitus [tɪ'naɪtəs, 'tɪnɪ–] *n.* ringing sound in the head.

tintinnabulate [,tɪntɪ'næbjuleɪt] *v.i.* ring; tinkle. **tintinnabulant, tintinnabular(y), tintinnabulous,** *adj.* **tintinnabulation,** *n.*

tiqueur [tɪ'kɜː] *n.* person suffering from tics.

tirade [taɪ'reɪd] *n.* long, violent speech.

tirailleur [ˌtɪəreɪˈjɜː, tɪˈrælʒɜː] (*French*) *n.* infantry soldier.

tiro [ˈtaɪrəʊ] *n.* beginner. **tirocinium**, *n.* (*pl.* **-ia**) first experience.

tisane [tɪˈzæn] *n.* medicinal beverage of barley, camomile, etc.; ptisan.

Titan [ˈtaɪtn] *n.* one of a race of giants in Greek mythology; giant; genius. **titanic** [-ˈtænɪk], *adj.*

tithe [taɪð] *n.* tenth part; tax payable to church.

Titian [ˈtɪʃn] *adj.* reddish-brown.

titillate [ˈtɪtɪleɪt] *v.t.* tickle; stimulate. **titillant**, *adj.* **titillation**, *n.* **titillator**, *n.* **titillative**, **titillatory**, *adj.*

titivate [ˈtɪtɪveɪt] *v.t.* smarten up.

titrate [taɪˈtreɪt] *v.t. Chemistry*, determine strength of, or analyse, etc., by finding the smallest amount of the substance that will produce a given effect with another known quantity. **titre** [ˈtaɪtə], *n.* such smallest amount. **titrimetry** [-ˈtrɪm-], *n.* measuring by such means. **titration**, *n.*

tittup [ˈtɪtəp] *v.i.* prance.

titubant [ˈtɪtjʊbənt] *adj.* staggering. **titubancy**, *n.*

tmesis [ˈtmiːsɪs] *n.* introduction of word, etc., between parts of a compound word.

toadstone [ˈtəʊdstəʊn] *n.* any stone or stone-like concretion believed to be formed in a toad and to have magic powers.

toccata [təˈkɑːtə] (*Italian*) *n.* brilliant, quick, fantasia-like musical composition.

tocology [təˈkɒlədʒi] *n.* midwifery. **tocological**, *adj.* **tocologist**, *n.*

tocsin [ˈtɒksɪn] *n.* alarm bell.

tody [ˈtəʊdi] *n.* very small, long-billed W Indian bird.

toga praetexta [ˌtəʊgə praɪˈtekstə] (*Latin*) *adj.* toga with broad purple border, worn by magistrates, etc.

togated [təʊˈgeɪtɪd] *adj.* wearing toga; dignified.

toga virilis [ˌtəʊgə vɪˈriːlɪs] (*Latin*) *n.* toga adopted as sign of manhood.

tohubohu [ˌtəʊhuːˈbəʊhuː] (*Hebrew*) *n.* chaos.

toison [ˈtwæzɒn] (*French*) *n.* sheep's fleece. **toison d'or**, Golden Fleece.

toluene [ˈtɒljuiːn] *n.* light liquid hydrocarbon, obtained from coal tar and used in dye manufacture.

tomalley [ˈtɒmæli] *n.* fat or 'liver' of lobster, eaten as a delicacy.

tombac [ˈtɒmbæk] *n.* alloy of zinc and copper used for cheap jewellery, etc.; Dutch gold.

tombolo [ˈtɒmbələʊ] *n.* narrow spit linking an island with another island or the mainland.

tomentose, **tomentous** [təˈmentəʊs, -təs] *adj.* bearing thickly matted hairs. **tomentulose**, *adj.* slightly tomentose. **tomentum**, *n. Botany*, covering of matted woolly hairs; *Anatomy*, network of minute blood vessels in the brain.

tomography [təˈmɒgrəfi] *n.* X-ray photography in which parts of body in front of, or behind, the part under examination are not shown. **tomogram**, *n.* such photograph. **tomographic(al)**, *adj.*

tonant [ˈtəʊnənt] *adj.* making loud, deep noise.

tondo [ˈtɒndəʊ] *n.* a circular painting or relief sculpture.

tonetics [təˈnetɪks] *n.* study of intonation in languages. **tonetician** [ˌtəʊnɪˈtɪʃn, ˌtɒ-], *n.*

tonga [ˈtɒŋgə] *n.* light Indian two-wheeled carriage; tonka.

tonic [ˈtɒnɪk] *adj. Medicine*, pertaining to tension, especially muscular; improving muscular condition; invigorating; *Music*, pertaining to keynote; *n. Medicine*, tonic medicine; *Music*, keynote. **tonicity**, *n.*

tonitruous [təˈnɪtruəs] *adj.* thundering. **tonitruone**, *n.* musical instrument imitating thunder.

tonka [ˈtɒŋkə] (*American*) *n.* bean-like tree and seed, used in perfumes, vanilla extract, etc.

tonneau [ˈtɒnəʊ] *n.* rear seating compartment of car.

tonometer [təˈnɒmɪtə] *n.* instrument measuring pitch of tones; *Medicine*, instrument measuring tension or pressure. **tonograph** [ˈtɒn-], *n.* recording tonometer.

tonsillectomy [ˌtɒnsɪˈlektəmi] *n.* surgical removal of tonsils. **tonsillotomy**, *n.* removal of part or all of tonsils.

tonsorial [tɒnˈsɔːriəl] *adj.* pertaining to barber or hairdressing.

tontine [ˈtɒntaɪn, tɒnˈtiːn] *n.* allocation of certain benefits, as annuities, etc., among a group of persons such that at the death of one member the remainder share his or her portion; annuity, etc., so shared.

tonus [ˈtəʊnəs] *n.* normal response to stimuli; muscular spasm.

toparch [ˈtɒpɑːk] *n.* ruler, especially of toparchy. **toparchy**, *n.* petty state under a toparch.

tope [təʊp] *n.* small shark.

topee [ˈtəʊpiː] *see* **topi**.

tophaceous [təˈfeɪʃəs] *adj.* gritty. **tophus** [ˈtəʊfəs], *n.* (*pl.* **-phi**) tufa; bodily concretion.

topi, **topee** [ˈtəʊpiː] *n.* sola topi.

topiary [ˈtəʊpiəri] *n.* & *adj.* (pertaining to) art of clipping shrubs, etc., into ornamental shapes. **topiarian**, *adj.* **topiarist**, *n.* expert in topiary.

topography [təˈpɒgrəfi] *n.* geography of a locality; configuration of a land surface; arrangement of physical features. **topographer**, *n.* **topographic(al)**, *adj.*

topology [təˈpɒlədʒi] *n. Mathematics*, study or theory of the properties of a figure that is not affected by deformation; topographical study of one place; regional anatomy. **topological**, *adj.* **topologist**, *n.*

toponym [ˈtɒpənɪm] *n.* name of, or designating, a place; name derived from a place-name. **toponymic**, *adj.* **toponymics**, *n.* study of place-names. **toponymy** [-ˈpɒnəmi], *n.* region's place-names.

topophobia [ˌtɒpəˈfəʊbiə] *n.* dread of certain places.

toque [təʊk] *n.* woman's turban-like brimless hat.

Torah [ˈtɔːrə] (*Hebrew*) *n.* law; revelation; Pentateuch.

torchon [ˈtɔːʃɒn] *n.* kind of coarse lace or paper.

torcular [ˈtɔːkjʊlə] *n.* tourniquet.

tore [tɔː] *n.* torus.

toreutic [təˈruːtɪk] *adj.* pertaining to metal ornamented with small engraved patterns; chased. **toreutics**, *n.* art of doing such work.

torii [ˈtɔːriiː] *n.* Japanese gateway of curved posts and lintel only.

tormentum [tɔːˈmentəm] *n.* (*pl.* **-ta**) ancient catapult-like war machine.

tormina [ˈtɔːmɪnə] (*Latin*) *n. pl.* gripes. **torminal**, **torminous**, *adj.*

tornote ['tɔːnəut] adj. with blunt extremities.

torose ['tɔːrəus] adj. bulging, knobbly; muscular. torous, adj. torosity [-'rɒsəti], n.

torpid ['tɔːpɪd] n. numb; sleepy; dull. torpidity, n. torpify, v.t. make torpid. torpor, n. torpid state; apathy. torporific, adj. torpifying.

torque [tɔːk] n. collar, especially of twisted metal; force tending to produce rotation. torquate(d), adj. having a collar.

torrid ['tɒrɪd] n. dried up; very hot; tropical. torrefy, torrify, v.t. scorch; parch.

torsade [tɔː'seɪd, -'saːd] n. twisted cord.

torsion ['tɔːʃn] n. act of twisting; state of being twisted. torsibility, n. tendency to untwist. torsile, adj. torsive, adj. spirally twisted.

tort [tɔːt] n. civil injury, excluding breach of contract, actionable for damages. tort-feasor, person committing tort.

torticollis [,tɔːtɪ'kɒlɪs] n. Medicine, condition in which neck is permanently twisted and head held at an unusal angle.

tortile ['tɔːtaɪl] adj. twisted; capable of being twisted. tortility, n.

tortious ['tɔːʃəs] adj. causing or committing tort.

torulose, torulous ['tɒruləus, -ləs] adj. slightly torose.

torus ['tɔːrəs] n. (pl. -ri) rounded swelling; Archtitecture, such lowest moulding of column; Botany, receptacle; Geometry, ring shape as of quoit or doughnut formed by rotation of a circle about an axis in its own plane. toric, adj.

torvous ['tɔːvəs] adj. stern. torvity, n.

totara ['təutərə] n. timber tree, with reddish wood, of NZ.; mahogany pine.

totem ['təutəm] n. animal or plant adopted as ancestor by savage tribe, and held in great veneration. totemic [-'temɪk], adj. totemism, n.

toties quoties [,tɒtieɪz 'kwɒtieɪz, ,təuʃiːɪz 'kwəuʃiːɪz] (Latin) adv. 'as often as'; repeatedly; n. Roman Catholic, indulgence obtainable as often as desired.

touché ['tuːʃeɪ] (French) adj. 'touched' by opponent's rapier in fencing; hit; defeated in argument.

tourbillion [tuə'bɪljən] n. whirlwind; any whirling object.

tourmaline ['tuəməliːn, -ɪn] n. kind of black, blue, red and green silicate cut as gem.

tourniquet ['tɔːnɪkeɪ, 'tuə-] n. device to stop bleeding, as a bandage twisted tight by a stick, etc.

tournure ['tuənjuə] (French) n. grace; poise; expressive phrase.

tout [tuː, -t] (French) n. & adj. 'all'. tout à fait [,tuːt aː 'feɪ], 'entirely'. tout à l'heure [,tuːt aː 'lɜː], 'in a moment'; 'a moment ago'. tout court [,tuː 'kuə], 'quite short'; simply; without any addition. tout de suite [,tuːt 'swiːt], 'immediately'. tout ensemble [,tuːt ɒn'sɒmbl], 'all together'; general effect; outfit.

tovarish, tovarisch [tə'vaːrɪʃ] (Russian) n. 'comrade'.

toxaemia [tɒk'siːmiə] n. blood poisoning due to toxins in blood.

toxic ['tɒksɪk] adj. poisoning; pertaining to or due to poison. toxicity, n. toxicogenic, adj. producing or produced by poison. toxicology, n. study of poisons. toxicopathy, n. disease due to poison.

toxicophagy, n. eating of poisons. toxicosis, n. condition due to poisoning.

toxin ['tɒksɪn] n. poison, especially one produced by a living organism.

toxiphobia [,tɒksɪ'fəubiə] n. dread of being poisoned.

toxoid ['tɒksɔɪd] n. toxin treated to reduce toxicity and used in immunisation.

toxophily [tɒk'sɒfəli] n. archery. toxophilite, n. person fond of toxophily. toxophilous, adj.

trabeate(d) ['treɪbieɪt, -ɪd] adj. constructed of horizontal beams. trabeation, adj.

trabecula [trə'bekjulə] n. (pl. -ae) small bar, rod, etc. trabecular, adj. trabeculate, adj. crossbarred.

trachea [trə'kiːə] n. (pl. -ae) windpipe. tracheitis [,træk-, ,treɪk-], n. inflammation of trachea. tracheotomy, n. making of incision into trachea. tracheal, tracheary, adj.

trachoma [trə'kəumə] n. chronic form of conjunctivitis. trachomatous, adj.

trachycarpous [,trækɪ'kaːpəs, ,treɪ-] adj. rough-fruited. trachyglossate, adj. rough-tongued. trachyphonia, n. roughness of voice. trachyspermous, adj. rough-seeded.

tractable ['træktəbl] n. easily managed or led; obedient; malleable. tractability, n.

tractarian [træk'teəriən] n. writer of tracts; Anglo-Catholic, especially member of Tractarian movement at Oxford in 1833-41.

tractile ['træktaɪl] adj. ductile. tractility [-'tɪləti], n.

tractive ['træktɪv] adj. pulling.

traduce [trə'djuːs] v.t. slander. traduction, traducement, n.

tragacanth ['trægəkænθ] n. valuable gum exuded by Indian tree, used in medicine.

tragopan ['trægəpæn] n. kind of bright-hued Asiatic pheasant.

tragus ['treɪgəs] n. (pl. -gi) prominence in front of opening of ear.

tralatition [,trælə'tɪʃn] n. metaphor. tralatious, adj. metaphorical; handed down from father to son.

trammel ['træml] n. net to catch fish, birds, etc.; shackle on horse's leg; check; obstacle; instrument for drawing ellipses; v.t. restrain; hamper.

tramontane [trə'mɒnteɪn] adj. (from) across the mountains; transalpine.

transalpine [trænz'ælpaɪn] adj. on the other (i.e. the north) side of the Alps; crossing the Alps.

transcalent [trænz'keɪlənt] adj. pervious to heat. transcalescent, adj. transcalency, n.

transceiver [trænz'siːvə] n. combined radio transmitter and receiver.

transcend [træn'send] v.t. pass beyond or over; surpass; lie outside; excel. transcendence, transcendency, n. transcendent, adj. transcendental, adj. beyond human understanding; supernatural; not founded on experience; theoretical. transcendentalism, n. philosophical theory emphasising that which transcends knowledge or sense perception, or the importance of spiritual over material things.

transcribe [træn'skraɪb] v.t. make a written or typewritten copy of; Music, arrange for other instrument(s) or voice(s); Radio, prerecord for sound broadcasting. transcript, n. such copy, arrangement, or recording. transcription, n.

transducer [trænz'djuːsə] *n.* electronic device transmitting received energy in a different form.

transect [træn'sekt] *v.t.* cut across; *n.* cross section. **transection**, *n.*

transept ['trænsept] *n.* transverse part of church at right angles to and between nave and choir. **transeptal**, *adj.*

transfluent [trænz'fluːənt] *adj.* flowing across. **transflux**, *n.*

transforation [ˌtrænzfə'reɪʃn] *n.* perforation.

transgenic [ˌtrænz'dʒenɪk] *adj.* which has had a foreign gene added to it.

transhume [træns'hjuːm] *v.t.* move (cattle) to summer pastures or winter quarters. **transhumance**, *n.*

transient ['trænzɪənt] *adj.* fleeting. **transience**, *n.*

transilient [træn'sɪlɪənt] *adj.* passing abruptly from one state to another. **transilience**, *n.*

transilluminate [ˌtrænzɪ'luːmɪneɪt, -'ljuː-] *v.t.* pass light through, especially through body past for medical examination..

transire [træns'aɪri] *n.* ship's document for customs declaration, showing cargo, etc.

transition [træn'zɪʃn] *n.* act or state of passing from one condition or time to another. **transitional**, *adj.* **transitive**, *adj. Grammar,* requiring direct object. **transitory**, *adj.* transient.

transliterate [trænz'lɪtəreɪt] *v.t.* write in letters of another alphabet. **transliteration**, *n.* **transliterator**, *n.*

translucent [trænz'luːsnt, -'ljuː-] *adj.* shining through; permitting the passage of light but not transparent. **translucid**, *adj.* **translucence**, *n.*

translunary [trænz'luːnəri] *adj.* beyond the moon; spiritual; unearthly.

transmarine [ˌtrænzmə'riːn] *adj.* across or beyond the sea.

transmigrate [ˌtrænzmaɪg'reɪt] *v.i. & t.* pass from one body or place into another; transfer. **transmigration**, *n.* **transmigrative**, *adj.*

transmogrify [trænz'mɒɡrɪfaɪ] *v.t.* transform. **transmogrification**, *n.*

transmute [trænz'mjuːt] *v.t.* change into another substance or species. **transmutation**, *n.* **transmutative**, *adj.*

transom ['trænsəm] *n.* horizontal or transverse beam or bar.

transpadane ['trænzpədeɪn] *adj.* on the other (*i.e.* the north) side of the river Po.

transpicuous [træn'spɪkjuəs] *adj.* easily seen through or understood. **transpicuity**, *n.*

transpire [træn'spaɪə] *v.i. & t.* exhale; give off or escape as vapour; become known; happen. **transpiratory**, *adj.* **transpiration**, *n.*

transponder [træn'spɒndə] *n.* radio or radar transceiver, automatically transmitting a reply to a certain signal.

transpontine [trænz'pɒntaɪn] *adj.* on the other (*i.e.* the south) side of the bridges over the Thames; pertaining to or like the lurid melodrama played in theatres there in the 19th century.

transrhenane [trænz'riːneɪn] *adj.* on the other (*i.e.* the east) side of the river Rhine; German.

transubstantiate [ˌtrænsəb'stænʃɪeɪt] *v.t.* transmute. **transubstantiation**, *n.; Theology,* conversion of Communion bread and wine into body and blood of Christ.

transude [træn'sjuːd] *v.i.* be exuded. **transudate**, *n.* such substance. **transudation**, *n.* **transudative**, **transudatory**, *adj.*

transumptive [træn'sʌmptɪv] *adj.* transferred; metaphorical.

transuranic [ˌtrænzju'rænɪk] *adj.* denoting any chemical element having atomic number beyond uranium (92), not occuring in nature but artificially produced by bombardment of atoms.

transvection [trænz'vekʃn] *n.* flying by supernatural means, *e.g.* like a witch.

transverbate ['trænzvəbeɪt] *v.t.* translate word for word. **transverbation**, *n.*

transverberate [trænz'vɜːbəreɪt] *v.t.* pierce. **transverberation**, *n.*

transvolation [ˌtrænzvə'leɪʃn] *n.* flying higher than normal.

transvest [trænz'vest] *v.i. & t.* disguise; wear clothes of another, especially of other sex. **transvestism**, *n.* **transvestite**, *n. & adj.*

trapezium [trə'piːzɪəm] *n.* (*pl.* **-ia**) quadrilateral with two parallel sides; any irregular quadrilateral; *American,* trapezoid. **trapezial**, **trapeziform**, *adj.* **trapezoid** ['træp-], *n.* quadrilateral with no sides parallel; *American,* trapezium.

traulism ['trɔːlɪzm] *n.* stammering.

traumatology [ˌtrɔːmə'tɒlədʒi] *n.* scientific description of wounds.

travail ['træveɪl] *n.* painful or arduous labour; suffering; labour pains; *v.i.* toil; suffer; be in labour. **travailous**, *adj.*

trave ['treɪv] *n.* crossbeam; space between crossbeams. **travated**, *adj.*

travertine ['trævətɪn, -iːn] *n.* crystalline calcium carbonate, deposit of hot springs; onyx marble.

trebuchet ['trebjuʃet] *n.* large sling-like medieval engine for hurling stones.

trecento [treɪ'tʃentəʊ] (*Italian*) *n. & adj.* thirteenth century. **trecentist**, *n.* writer or artist of that period.

trechometer [tre'kɒmɪtə] *n.* device measuring distance travelled by a vehicle.

treen [triːn] *adj.* made of wood. **treenware**, *n.* cups, dishes etc. made of wood.

trefoil ['trefɔɪl] *n.* clover, or other plants with leaf divided into three lobes; architectural ornament of that shape.

trematode ['tremətəʊd, 'triː-] *n.* kind of parasitic flatworm.

trenchant ['trentʃənt] *adj.* sharp; cutting.

trente et quarante [ˌtrɒnt eɪ 'kærɒnt] (*French*) 'thirty and forty'; gambling card game with betting on red and black.

trepan [trɪ'pæn] *n.* surgical saw for incision into skull; *v.t.* use trephine on; decoy; swindle. **trepanation** [ˌtrep-], *n.*

trepang [trɪ'pæŋ] *n.* sea cucumber.

trephine [trɪ'fiːn] *n.* form of trepan; *v.t.* use trephine on. **trephination** [ˌtref-], *n.*

tressilate ['tresɪleɪt] *v.i.* quiver. **tressilation**, *n.*

trey [treɪ] *n.* card, domino, etc., bearing three pips.

triad ['traɪæd] *n.* group of three; *Music,* chord of three notes. **triadic**, *adj.*

triage ['triːɑːʒ] *n.* sorting into order of urgency, as with battlefield casualties.

triagonal [traɪ'ægənl] *adj.* triangular.

triarch ['traɪɑːk] *n.* triumvir. **triarchy**, *n.*

tribade ['trɪbəd] *n.* homosexual woman. **tribad-**

ism, *n.*

tribology [traɪˈbɒlədʒi trɪ–] *n.* scientific study of friction and lubrication.

tribrach [ˈtrɪbræk, traɪ–] *n.* verse foot of three syllables; object, etc., with three branches. **tribrachial** [–ˈbreɪk–], **tribrachic**, *adj.*

tribuloid [ˈtrɪbjulɔɪd] *adj.* yielding prickly fruit.

tribune [ˈtrɪbjuːn] *n.* tribal chief; representative of a section of people; demagogue; platform; dais.

tricenary [traɪˈsiːnəri] *adj.* pertaining to or consisting of thirty; lasting thirty days.

tricephalous [ˌtraɪˈsefələs] *adj.* having three heads. **tricephalus**, *n.* (*pl.* –**li**) such monster.

triceps [ˈtraɪseps] *n.* muscle of back of upper arm with three points of attachment.

trichiasis [trɪˈkaɪəsɪs] *n.* ingrowing eyelashes.

trichinosis [ˌtrɪkɪˈnəʊsɪs] *n.* disease due to eating pork infested with certain kind of nematode worms. **trichinize**, *v.t.* infest with such worms. **trichinotic** [–ˈnɒtɪk], **trichinous**, *adj.*

trichoid [ˈtrɪkɔɪd] *adj.* hair-like. **trichology**, *n.* study of hair. **trichome**, *n.* hair-like outgrowth on the surface of a plant. **trichosis**, *n.* any disease of the hair.

trichotomy [traɪˈkɒtəmi, trɪ–] *n.* division into three parts or categories. **trichotomic** [–ˈtɒmɪk], **trichotomous**, *adj.*

trichromatic [ˌtraɪkrəˈmætɪk] *adj.* pertaining to or in three colours; having normal colour vision. **trichromatism**, *n.* use of the three primary colours for colour reproduction; normal colour vision.

tricipital [traɪˈsɪpɪtl] *adj.* pertaining to triceps; tricephalous.

triclinic [traɪˈklɪnɪk] *adj.* having three unequal axes meeting at oblique angles.

tricorn [ˈtraɪkɔːn] *adj.* having three corners or horns. **tricorne**, *n.* three-cornered hat.

tricot [ˈtrɪkəʊ, ˈtriː–] *n.* silk, rayon, nylon or woollen fabric resembling knitting. **tricotine** [ˌtrɪkəˈtiːn], *n.* double-twilled worsted fabric.

tridactyl [ˌtraɪˈdæktɪl] *n.* having three fingers or toes. **tridentate**, *adj.* having three teeth. **tridigitate**, *adj.* tridactyl.

tridiurnal [ˌtraɪdaɪˈɜːnl] *adj.* lasting three days; happening every three days.

triennial [traɪˈeniəl] *adj.* happening every three years; lasting three years; *n.* such plant; third anniversary.

trieteric [ˌtraɪɪˈterɪk] *n.* & *adj.* (festival) occurring each third year (*i.e.* in alternate years).

trifarious [traɪˈfeəriəs] *adj.* facing three ways.

trifid [ˈtraɪfɪd] *adj.* divided into three parts.

triforium [traɪˈfɔːriəm] *n.* gallery over nave and choir. **triforial**, *adj.*

trifurcate [ˈtraɪfɜːkeɪt, –ˈfɜː–] *v.t.* divide into three forks; *adj.* so dividing. **trifurcation**, *n.*

trigamy [ˈtrɪgəmi] *n.* state of being married to three living spouses. **trigamist**, *n.* **trigamous**, *adj.*

trigeminal [traɪˈdʒemɪnl] *adj.* pertaining to pair of nerves from cranium to jaw. **trigeminous**, *adj.* (one of) three born together; threefold.

trigeneric [ˌtraɪdʒəˈnerɪk] *adj.* belonging to three kinds or genera; having three genders.

triglot [ˈtraɪglɒt] *n.* & *adj.* (book) in three languages.

triglyph [ˈtrɪglɪf, ˈtraɪ–] *n.* architectural ornament of tablet bearing two V-shaped channels. **triglyphal**, **triglyphic**, *adj.*

trigonal [ˈtrɪgənəl] *adj.* pertaining to or having three angles.

trigonometry [ˌtrɪgəˈnɒmətri] *n.* mathematical study of triangles and measurement by deducing unknown from known sides and angles. **trigonometric** [–ˈmetrɪk], *adj.*

trigonous [ˈtrɪgənəs] *adj.* having triangular cross-section.

trigram [ˈtraɪgræm] *n.* figure of three lines; inscription of three letters. **trigrammatic**, *adj.*

trigraph [ˈtraɪgræf] *n.* three letters having one sound, as *eau.* **trigraphic**, *adj.*

trihedron [traɪˈhiːdrən] *n.* solid figure of three planes. **trihedral**, *adj.*

trihoral [traɪˈhɔːrəl] *adj.* happening every three hours.

trijugate [ˈtraɪdʒugeɪt] *adj.* with three pairs of leaflets.

trilabiate [ˌtraɪˈleɪbieɪt] *adj.* having three lips. **trilaminar**, *adj.* having three layers.

trilateral [ˌtraɪˈlætərəl] *n.* & *adj.* three-sided (figure).

trilemma [traɪˈlemə] *n.* dilemma-like position offering three choices.

trilinear [ˌtraɪˈlɪniə] *adj.* pertaining to, having or bounded by three lines.

trilingual [ˌtraɪˈlɪŋgwəl] *adj.* pertaining to, in or speaking three languages.

triliteral [ˌtraɪˈlɪtərəl] *n.* & *adj.* (word) of three letters.

trilith(on) [ˈtraɪlɪθ, –ɒn] *n.* ancient monument of two upright stones bearing one transverse stone.

trillion [ˈtrɪljən] *n.* a million billions (10^{18}); (*American & French*) a thousand billions (10^{12}).

trilobite [ˈtraɪləbaɪt] *n.* oval, flattened fossil with trifid body. **trilobitic** [–ˈbɪtɪk], *adj.*

trilocular [traɪˈlɒkjulə] *adj.* having three cells. **triloculate**, *adj.*

trimacer [ˈtrɪməsə] *n.* metrical foot of three long syllables.

trimacular, **trimaculate** [ˌtraɪˈmækjulə, –leɪt] *adj.* bearing three spots.

trimensual [ˌtraɪˈmensjuəl] *adj.* happening every three months.

trimerous [ˈtrɪmərəs] (*Botany*) *adj.* having its parts in threes.

trimester [traɪˈmestə] *n.* period of three months. **trimestral**, **trimestrial**, *adj.*

trimeter [ˈtrɪmɪtə] *n.* verse-line of three feet. **trimetric** [traɪˈmetrɪk], *adj.*

trimorph [ˈtraɪmɔːf] *n.* substance crystallising into three forms. **trimorphism**, *n.* **trimorphous**, *adj.*

trin [trɪn] *n.* triplet. **trinal** [ˈtraɪnl], **trine** [traɪn], *adj.* threefold. **trinary** [ˈtraɪnəri], *n.* group of three.

tringoid [ˈtrɪŋgɔɪd] *adj.* pertaining to sandpipers.

trinitrotoluene [ˌtraɪˌnaɪtrəʊˈtɒljuiːn] *n.* high explosive obtained from toluene (*abbr.* **T.N.T.**).

Trinkgeld [ˈtrɪŋkgelt] (*German*) *n.* 'drink money'; tip; gratuity. **Trinklied** [–liːt], *n.* 'drinking song'.

trinoctial [traɪˈnɒkʃl] *adj.* lasting three nights.

trinomial [traɪˈnəʊmiəl] *adj.* pertaining to or using three names; having name of three terms; pertaining to such scientific nomenclature; *n.* mathematical expression of three terms joined by + or –. **trinominal** [–ˈnɒmɪnl], *adj.*

trioecious [traɪˈiːʃəs] *adj.* having male, female

and hermaphrodite flowers on different plants. **trioecism**, *n*.

triolet ['triːəlet, –leɪ; 'traɪələt] *n*. eight-lined poem, with repetition of first line as fourth and seventh, and of second line as eighth; and with first, third, fourth, fifth and seventh lines, and second, sixth and eighth lines, rhyming.

tripara ['trɪpərə] *n*. woman who has had three childbirths.

tripartite [traɪ'pɑːtaɪt] *adj*. in three parts; between three parties or States. **tripartient** [–'pɑːʃiənt], *adj*. dividing into three parts. **tripartition**, *n*.

tripedal ['traɪˌpedl, 'trɪpɪdl] *adj*. having three feet.

triphibian [traɪ'fɪbiən] *adj*. equipped to operate from land or water and in the air; triphibous. **triphibious**, *adj*. involving land, sea and air forces.

triphthong ['trɪfθɒŋ] *n*. three vowel sounds pronounced as one.

triphyllous [traɪ'fɪləs] *adj*. three-leaved.

triplegia [traɪ'pliːdʒiə] *n*. hemiplegia with paralysis of a part on the other side.

triplopia [trɪ'pləupiə] *n*. triple vision.

tripody ['trɪpədi] *n*. verse measure of three feet.

tripos ['traɪpɒs] *n*. honours examination at Cambridge University.

tripsis ['trɪpsɪs] *n*. act of rubbing or grinding; massage.

triptote ['trɪptəut] *n*. & *adj*. *Grammar*, (noun) with three cases only.

triptych ['trɪptɪk] *n*. painting in three parts, especially altar piece with one central and two hinged side panels.

triptyque [trɪp'tiːk] (*French*) *n*. customs pass for importing motor car.

triquetra [traɪ'kwetrə, –'kwiː–] *n*. triangular-shaped pattern, object, etc. **triquetral, triquetric, triquetrous**, *adj*.

trireme ['traɪriːm] *n*. ancient galley with three banks of oars.

trisect [traɪ'sekt] *v.t*. cut into three equal parts. **trisection, trisector**, *n*.

triskelion [trɪ'skeliɒn, –iən] *n*. pattern of three curved branches, especially of three bent legs as badge of Isle of Man.

trismus ['trɪzməs] *n*. lockjaw. **trismic**, *adj*.

tristachyous [traɪ'steɪkiəs] *adj*. three-spiked.

triste [triːst] (*French*) *adj*. 'sad'. **tristesse**, *n*. sadness.

tristich ['trɪstɪk] *n*. stanza of three lines. **tristichic**, *adj*. **tristichous**, *adj*. in three rows.

tristiloquy [trɪ'stɪləkwi] *n*. mournful manner of speech. **tristisonous**, *adj*. mournful-sounding.

trisulcate [traɪ'sʌlkeɪt] *adj*. with three ridges, forks or furrows.

trisyllable [ˌtraɪ'sɪləbl] *n*. word of three syllables. **trysyllabic** [–'læbɪk], *adj*.

tritanopia [ˌtraɪtə'nəupiə, ˌtrɪ–] *n*. inability to distinguish properly between blue and yellow. **tritanope**, *n*. sufferer from this.

tritheism ['traɪθiːɪzm] *n*. belief that members of Trinity are three separate gods. **tritheist**, *n*.

triticism ['trɪtɪsɪzm] *n*. trite remark.

triticoid ['trɪtɪkɔɪd] *adj*. like wheat.

tritium ['trɪtiəm] *n*. isotope of hydrogen of mass number 3.

triton ['traɪtɒn] *n*. positively charged atomic particle consisting of a proton and two neutrons, equivalent to the nucleus of an atom of tritium.

triturate ['trɪtjureɪt] *v.t*. rub; bruise; grind to powder. **tritural**, *adj*. of use in grinding. **trituration**, *n*. **triturator**, *n*.

triumvir [traɪ'ʌmvə] *n*. (*pl*. –**ri**) member of triumvirate. **triumvirate**, *n*. ruling body of three men.

triune ['traɪjuːn] *adj*. three in one. **triunity**, *n*.

trivalent [ˌtraɪ'veɪlənt, 'trɪvə–] *adj*. having valency of three.

trivirgate [traɪ'vɜːgeɪt] *adj*. bearing three linear markings.

trivium ['trɪviəm] *n*. lower division (i.e. grammar, rhetoric, logic) of the seven liberal arts as taught in medieval universities.

trocar ['trəukɑː] *n*. surgical instrument with sharp point for inserting drainage tube into body cavity.

trochaic [trəu'keɪk] *adj*. pertaining to or consisting of trochees; *n*. such verse line.

trochal ['trəukl] *adj*. wheel-shaped.

troche ['trəuki] *n*. circular lozenge, especially for throat affection.

trochee ['trəukiː] *n*. verse foot of one long and one short syllable.

trochilic [trə'kɪlɪk] *adj*. rotary; able to turn. **trochilics**, *n*. study of rotary motion.

trochiline, trochilidine ['trɒkɪlaɪn, –ɪlɪdɪn] *adj*. pertaining to or like a humming-bird; belonging to humming-bird family of birds. **trochilus**, *n*. humming-bird; crocodile bird; gold-crest.

trochlea ['trɒkliə] *n*. pulley-like structure of shoulder, thigh, or orbit of eye. **trochleiform, trochlear, trochleariform, trochleate**, *adj*. like a pulley.

trochocephalic [ˌtrɒkəsɪ'fælɪk] *adj*. having abnormally round head. **trochocephalia** [–'feɪliə], **trochocephalus, trochocephaly** [–'sef–], *n*. such condition.

troglodyte ['trɒglədaɪt] *n*. cave-dweller. **troglodytal, troglodytic** [–'dɪtɪk], *adj*.

trogon ['trəugɒn] *n*. brightly coloured bird of American, African and Indian jungle.

trompe-l'oeil [ˌtrɒmp'lɔɪ] (*French*) 'deceives the eye'; *n*. type of painting exactly imitating reality, and of interior decoration producing an illusion of space, height, length, etc.

tronc [trɒŋ] (*French*) *n*. 'alms-box'; system of pooling tips among waiters.

trope [trəup] *n*. figure of speech; heading; *Music*, interpolation into a plainsong setting of the Mass.

trophic ['trɒfɪk, 'trəu–] *adj*. pertaining to nutrition. **trophesy**, *n*. disease due to fault in such nerves. **trophism**, *n*. nutrition. **trophogenic**, *adj*. due to differences in food. **trophopathy**, *n*. disorder of nutritional processes. **trophoplasm**, *n*. nutritive substance of cell. **trophotropism**, *n*. growth direction by nutritional factors.

tropism ['trəupɪzm] *n*. movement of an organism, especially direction of growth of plant, in response to a stimulus; innate inclination. **tropismatic, tropistic**, *adj*.

tropology [trə'pɒlədʒi] *n*. figurative style of writing; interpretation of Bible stressing figurative nature of language. **tropological**, *adj*.

tropometer [trə'pɒmɪtə] *n*. instrument measuring rotation.

tropopause ['trɒpəpɔːz, 'trəu–] *n*. level where troposphere ends and stratosphere begins.

tropophilous [trə'pɒfɪləs] *adj*. flourishing in

seasonal extremes of climate. **tropophyte** ['trɒpəfaɪt], *n.* such plant.

troposphere ['trɒpəsfɪə, 'trəʊ–] *n.* all the atmosphere below the stratosphere.

trotyl ['trəʊtɪl] *n.* trinitrotoluene.

troubadour ['truːbəduə, –dɔː] *n.* medieval romantic poet; wandering minstrel.

trouvaille [truːˈvaɪ] *n.* lucky find; ingenious idea.

trouvère [truːˈveə] (*French*) *n.* troubadour of N France.

trovatore [ˌtrəʊvəˈtɔːri, –eɪ] (*Italian*) *n.* (*pl.* **–ri**) troubadour.

trucidation [ˌtruːsɪˈdeɪʃn] *n.* slaughter.

truculent ['trʌkjʊlənt] *adj.* bellicose; cruel; savage. **truculence,** *n.*

trumeau ['truːməʊ] *n.* (*pl.* **–eaux**) pier glass; pillar supporting tympanum of doorway.

truncate [trʌŋˈkeɪt] *v.t.* & *adj.* cut off. **truncation, truncator,** *n.*

trunnion ['trʌnɪən] *n.* one of a pair of projecting pivots.

truttaceous [trʌˈteɪʃəs] *adj.* pertaining to or like trout.

tryma ['traɪmə] *n.* kind of nut-like fruit, as walnut.

trypanosome ['trɪpənəsəʊm] *n.* parasitic protozoan, especially causing sleeping sickness. **trypanosomiasis** [–səˈmaɪəsɪs], *n.* infestation with these.

trypsin ['trɪpsɪn] *n.* pancreatic enzyme digesting protein. **tryptic,** *adj.*

tsetse ['tetsi] *n.* African fly carrying trypanosome that causes sleeping sickness.

tsiology [tsiˈɒlədʒi] *n.* treatise on tea.

tsunami [tsuˈnɑːmi] (*Japanese*) *n.* 'storm wave', a tidal wave caused by seismic disturbance of the ocean floor.

tuan [tuˈɑːn] (*Malay*) *n.* sir.

tuber ['tjuːbə] *n.* fleshy underground stem, as potato. **tuberaceous,** *adj.* pertaining to fungus family having tubers. **tuberation,** *n.* formation of tubers.

tubercle ['tjuːbəkl] *n.* small knob or outgrowth; small tuber; *Medicine,* small diseased nodule, especially of tuberculosis. **tubercular** [–ˈbɜːkjʊlə], *adj.* pertaining to tubercles or tuberculosis. **tuberculation,** *n.* formation of tubercles. **tuberculin,** *n.* culture of products of tubercular bacilli used as test for tuberculosis. **tuberculous,** *adj.*

tubicinate [tjuˈbɪsɪneɪt] *v.i.* blow a trumpet. **tubicination,** *n.*

tubicolous [tjuˈbɪkələs] *adj.* spinning a tubular web; living in a self-constructed tube.

tubicorn(ous) ['tjuːbɪkɔːn, ˌtjuːbɪˈkɔːnəs] *adj.* hollow-horned. **tubifacient,** *adj.* constructing a tube. **tubifex,** *n.* freshwater tubicolous worm used as bait. **tubiform,** *adj.* tube-like. **tubinarial,** *adj.* with tubular nostrils. **tubiparous,** *adj.* secreting matter used in making tube.

tubulure ['tjuːbjələ] *n.* tubular opening.

tucket ['tʌkɪt] *n.* flourish on trumpet.

tucuma ['tuːkʊmə] *n.* fibre-yielding Brazilian palm.

tufa ['tjuːfə] *n.* porous calcareous rock deposited by springs, etc.; rock composed of fine volcanic detritus. **tufaceous,** *adj.*

tufthunter ['tʌft,hʌntə] *n.* toady.

tuism ['tjuːɪzm] *n.* use of second person (*thou, you*); philosophical theory stressing existence of a second, or other, self.

tulwar [tʌlˈwɑː] *n.* Indian sabre.

tumbak(i), tumbek(i) [tʌmˈbæk, –i; –ˈbek, –i] *n.* kind of coarse tobacco of Persia.

tumblehome ['tʌmblhəʊm] *n.* inward curve of a ship's side near the stern.

tumbrel ['tʌmbrəl] *n.* farm-cart, especially as used to carry condemned persons to the guillotine in French revolution.

tumid ['tjuːmɪd] *adj.* swollen; bombastic. **tumidity,** *n.* **tumefacient,** *adj.* producing swelling. **tumefy,** *v.t.* swell. **tumescent,** *adj.* somewhat tumid.

tump, tumpline [tʌmp, 'tʌmplaɪn] *n.* *American,* band across forehead or chest to aid in carrying or hauling a load.

tumulus ['tjuːmjələs] *n.* (*pl.* **–li**) mound over ancient grave; barrow. **tumular,** *adj.* **tumulose,** *adj.* having many small mounds.

tundra ['tʌndrə] *n.* arctic plain with mosses, shrubs, etc.

tungsten ['tʌŋstən] *n.* white metal, also called wolfram, with highest melting point of all metals, used in filaments of electric lamps, steel alloys, etc. **tungstenic** [–'stenɪk], **tungstic,** *adj.*

tunicate ['tjuːnɪkət, –eɪt] *n.* one of a class of marine animals, including ascidians; *adj.* covered with layers.

tup [tʌp] *n.* ram; head of pile-driver, steamhammer, *v.t.* mate with.

tuque [tjuːk] *n.* Canadian knitted winter cap.

tu quoque [ˌtuː ˈkwəʊkwi, ˌtjuː–] (*Latin*) 'thou also'; act of imputing to one's accuser the same fault as that with which one is charged.

turbary ['tɜːbəri] *n.* land from which peat may be cut.

turbellarian [ˌtɜːbəˈleəriən] *n.* kind of flatworm.

turbid ['tɜːbɪd] *adj.* muddy; not clear. **turbidity,** *n.*

turbinate ['tɜːbɪnət] *adj.* spirally rolled; like a spinning-top in shape; *v.t.* spin; whirl. **turbinal,** *adj.* **turbination,** *n.*

turbit ['tɜːbɪt] *n.* kind of fancy pigeon.

turdiform ['tɜːdɪfɔːm] *adj.* like a thrush. **turdoid,** *adj.*

turgid ['tɜːdʒɪd] *adj.* swollen; inflated; bombastic. **turgescent,** *adj.* becoming turgid. **turgidity,** *n.* **turgor,** *n.* normal rigid state of a cell; turgidity.

turmeric ['tɜːmərɪk] *n.* plant with rootstock yielding dye, or used ground as condiment.

turpeth ['tɜːpɪθ] *n.* root of tropical plant used as purge; Indian jalap.

turpitude ['tɜːpɪtjuːd] *n.* depravity.

turrical ['tʌrɪkl] *adj.* turret-like. **turricular, turriculate,** *adj.* **turriferous,** *adj.* bearing towers.

tussis ['tʌsɪs] *n.* *Medicine,* cough. **tussal, tussive,** *adj.* **tussicular,** *adj.* pertaining to slight cough.

tutelage ['tjuːtɪlɪdʒ] *n.* guardianship. **tutelary,** *adj.* protecting.

tutti-frutti [ˌtuːtiˈfruːti] (*Italian*) 'all fruits'; mixture of, or flavoured with, fruits of many kinds.

tychism ['taɪkɪzm] *n.* theory that chance plays an active role in the universe, especially such theory of evolution.

tympanum ['tɪmpənəm] *n.* (*pl.* **–na**) ear-drum; *Architecture,* triangular face of pediment; space within arch. **tympanal, tympanic** [-'pænɪk], *adj.* **tympani,** *n.pl. (sing.* **-no)** timpani. **tympaniform,** *adj.* like a tympanum. **tympanist,** *n.* timpanist. **tympanites** [-'naɪtiːz], *n.* distention of abdomen by flatulence. **tympanitis,** *n.* inflammation of the tympanum. **tympany,** *n.* inflation; turgidity.

Tynwald ['tɪnwəld, 'taɪ-] *n.* legislature of Isle of Man.

typhlitis [tɪ'flaɪtɪs] *n.* inflammation of caecum; *archaic*, appendicitis.

typhlology [tɪ'flɒlədʒi] *n.* study of blindness. **typhlosis,** *n.* blindness.

typhogenic [,taɪfə'dʒenɪk] *adj.* causing typhoid fever or typhus.

typhonic [taɪ'fɒnɪk] *adj.* pertaining to or like a typhoon.

typography [taɪ'pɒgrəfi] *n.* art of printing; style and layout of printed matter. **typographer,** *n.* **typographic(al),** *adj.*

typology [taɪ'pɒlədʒi] *n.* study of types; theological doctrine of symbolization of New Testament events in the Old Testament. **typologist,** *n.*

typothetae [taɪ'pɒθɪti, ,taɪpə'θiːti] *n.pl. American,* (an association of) printers.

typtology [tɪp'tɒlədʒi] *n.* theory concerning rappings by spirits. **typtological,** *adj.* **typtologist,***n.*

tyrannicide [tɪ'rænɪsaɪd, taɪ-] *n.* killing or killer of tyrant.

tyremesis [taɪ'reməsɪs] *n.* vomiting of curd-like matter.

tyro ['taɪrəʊ] *see* **tiro.**

tyroma [taɪ'rəʊməʊv] *n.* (*pl.* **-ata**) cheese-like matter. **tyromatous,** *adj.*

U

uberous ['juːbərəs] *adj.* abundant; fruitful. **uberty**, *n.*

ubiety [ju'baɪəti] *n.* state of being in a place; 'thereness'; position.

ubiquity [ju'bɪkwəti] *n.* state of being everywhere. **ubiquitous**, *adj.*

udometer [ju'dɒmɪtə] *n.* rain gauge. **udograph**, *n.* recording udometer. **udometric** [–'metrɪk], *adj.* **udometry**, *n.*

ufology [ˌjuː'fɒlədʒi] *n.* study of unidentified flying objects. **ufologist** *n.*

uhlan ['uːlɑːn, 'juːlən] (*German*) *n.* kind of lancer.

uitlander ['eɪtlændə, 'aʊt–] (*S African*) *n.* 'foreigner'; British resident in former Boer state.

ukase [ju'keɪz, –'keɪs] (*Russian*) *n.* decree; proclamation.

uliginose, uliginous [ju'lɪdʒɪnəus] *adj.* marshy; muddy.

ulitis [ju'laɪtɪs] *n.* inflammation of gums.

ullage ['ʌlɪdʒ] *n.* lack; deficiency; amount by which a quantity, especially of liquor, is short of full measure; dregs. **ullaged**, *adj.* not full measure.

ulna ['ʌlnə] *n.* (*pl.* –ae) inner of two bones of forearm. **ulnad**, *adv.* towards the ulna. **ulnar**, *adj.*

uloid ['juːlɔɪd] *adj.* like a scar.

ulotrichous [ju'lɒtrɪkəs] *adj.* having woolly hair. **ulotrichan**, *n.* such person. **ulotrichy**, *n.* such state.

ulterior [ʌl'tɪəriə] *adj.* further; beyond; not seen or avowed; secret.

ultimo ['ʌltɪməʊ] *adv.* of last month (*abbr.* **ult.**).

ultimogeniture [ˌʌltɪməʊ'dʒenɪtʃə] *n.* inheritance by the youngest son.

ultra ['ʌltrə] *n.* & *adj.* extremist. **ultraism**, *n.*

ultracrepidarian [ˌʌltrəkrepɪ'deəriən] *adj.* venturing beyond one's province; presuming. **ultracrepidate**, *v.i.*

ultrafidian [ˌʌltrə'fɪdiən] *adj.* going beyond faith.

ultramarine [ˌʌltrəmə'riːn] *adj.* beyond the sea; *n.* & *adj.* (of) greenish-blue colour or pigment.

ultramicroscope [ˌʌltrə'maɪkrəskəʊp] *n.* instrument for viewing particles too small to be seen by ordinary microscope. **ultramicroscopic** [–'skɒpɪk], *adj.* pertaining to or visible only with ultramicroscope. **ultramicroscopy** [–'krɒskəpi], *n.*

ultramontane [ˌʌltrə'mɒnteɪn] *adj.* beyond (*i.e.* south of) the Alps; supporting the supremacy of the Pope; *n.* such person. **ultramontanism**, *n.*

ultramundane [ˌʌltrə'mʌndeɪn] *adj.* beyond the world; spiritual.

ultrasonic [ˌʌltrə'sɒnɪk] *adj.* denoting air-waves or vibrations with frequencies higher than those audible to the human ear, *i.e.* more than about 20,000 cycles per second. **ultrasonics**, *n.* study and use of such waves.

ultra vires [ˌʌltrə 'vaɪriːz] (*Latin*) 'beyond strength'; beyond or exceeding the authority of a person, court, etc.

ultroneous [ʌl'trəʊniəs] *adj.* spontaneous, voluntary.

ululate ['juːljuleɪt] *v.i.* howl. **ululant, ululatory**, *adj.* howling. **ululation**, *n.*

umbel ['ʌmbl] *n.* umbrella-like inflorescence with stalks of equal length springing from one point, as in carrot. **umbellar, umbellate, umbelliferous**, *adj.* having flowers in this shape. **umbellifer**, *n.* plant having umbel, or belonging to carrot family.

umber ['ʌmbə] *n.* reddish-brown pigment.

umbilicus [ʌm'bɪlɪkəs, ˌʌmbɪ'laɪkəs] *n.* (*pl.* –ci) navel; navel-like growth. **umbilical**, *adj.* pertaining to navel or umbilical cord; central; related on mother's side. **umbilicate, umbiliform**, *adj.* navel-like.

umbo ['ʌmbəʊ] *n.* (*pl.* –ones) boss of shield; any rounded projection. **umbonal, umbonic** [–'bɒnɪk], *adj.* **umbonate**, *adj.* having umbo.

umbrage ['ʌmbrɪdʒ] *n.* offence; shade; foliage. **umbrageous** [–'breɪdʒəs], *adj.* shady; offended. **umbratile**, *adj.* shadowy; unreal; secluded; giving shade. **umbriferous**, *adj.* giving shade. **umbrous**, *adj.* shady.

umiak ['uːmɪæk] *n.* large, open Eskimo boat.

umlaut ['umlaʊt] (*German*) *n.* vowel change due to following sound; diaeresis marking such changed vowel in German

unasinous [ju'næsɪnəs] *adj.* being equally stupid.

uncate ['ʌŋkeɪt] *adj.* hooked.

uncial ['ʌnsiəl, 'ʌnʃl] *n.* & *adj.* (letter or manuscript) written in large rounded script of before 10th century AD; majuscule; capital.

unciform ['ʌnsɪfɔːm] *adj.* hook-like. **uncinate**, *adj* hooked.

unco ['ʌŋkəʊ] (*Scottish*) *adj.* strange; foreign; extraordinary. **unco guid** [–'gɪd], strictly moral.

unconscionable [ʌn'kɒnʃn–əbl] *adj.* unreasonable; against the conscience.

unction ['ʌŋkʃn] *n.* act of, or oil used in, anointing; fervour; oiliness; simulated emotion. **unctuous**, *adj.* oily; greasy; soothing; suave; smug.

undecagon [ʌn'dekəgən] *n.* eleven-sided plane figure.

undecennial [ˌʌndɪ'seniəl] *adj.* happening every, or lasting, eleven years.

undecillion [ˌʌndɪ'sɪljən] *n.* a million decillions (10^{66}); (*American & French*) a thousand decillions (10^{36}).

undecimal [ʌn'desɪml] *adj.* in eleven parts.

undine ['ʌndiːn] *n.* water spirit.

und so weiter [ʊnt zəʊ 'vaɪtə] (*German*) 'and so forth'; et cetera (*abbr.* **usw**).

ungual ['ʌŋgwəl] *adj.* pertaining to or like nail, hoof or talon.

unguent ['ʌŋgwənt] *n.* soothing ointment. **unguentary,** *adj.*

unguiculate [ʌŋ'gwɪkjuleɪt] *adj.* having claws or nails.

unguinous ['ʌŋgwɪnəs] *adj.* oily; fatty.

ungulate ['ʌŋgjuleɪt] *n.* & *adj.* hoofed (mammal). **unguligrade,** *adj.* walking on hoofs.

unicameral [,juːnɪ'kæmərəl] *adj.* having one legislative chamber. **unicity** [–'nɪs–], *n.* one-ness; state of being unique. **unidextral,** *adj.* using one hand more deftly than other. **unifarious,** *adj.* in one row or series. **unifilar,** *adj.* having or using one thread or wire. **unifoliate,** *adj.* with one leaf only. **unigenesis,** *n.* non-sexual reproduction. **unigenital,** *adj.* only-begotten. **unigenous,** *adj.* of same kind. **unilateral,** *adj.* one-sided; done by one of two or more contracting parties. **unilingual,** *adj.* in one language only. **uniliteral,** *adj.* having one letter only. **uninominal,** *adj.* pertaining to or consisting of one name only. **unipara,** *n.* woman having had one childbirth only. **uniparous,** *adj.* producing only one at a birth. **uniped,** *n.* & *adj.* one-legged or one-footed (person). **unipotent,** *adj.* powerful in one direction only. **unireme,** *n.* & *adj.* (galley) with one bank of oars. **unisonous,** *adj.* in unison; agreeing. **unitarian,** *n.* & *adj.* (person) denying doctrine of Trinity. **univalent,** *adj.* single; having valency of one. **univocal,** *adj.* unmistakable; pertaining to things of same kind. **univoltine,** *adj.* single-brooded. **univorous,** *adj.* applied to parasites living on one host only.

uninterested [ʌnɪ'trɪstɪd, –tərɪs–] *adj.* not eager to know of or learn about; unconcerned. (*as opposed to* **disinterested**).

Unterseeboot ['ʊntəzeɪ,bəʊt] (*German*) *n.* submarine (*abbrev.* **U-Boot,** *English,* **U-Boat**).

untoward [,ʌntə'wɔːd, –'təʊəd] *adj.* unlucky; awkward; inconvenient; improper.

upas ['juːpəs] *n.* poison-yielding tree of Java.

upher ['juːfə] *n.* rough scaffolding pole of fir.

upsilon [juːp'saɪlən, 'juːpsɪlɒn] *n.* twentieth letter Y, υ of Greek alphabet.

uraemia [ju'riːmiə] *n.* accumulation in the blood of urinary products normally excreted.

uraeus [ju'riːəs] *n.* representation of the sacred asp as emblem of supreme power, especially on headdress of Egyptian rulers.

uranism ['jʊərənɪzm] *n.* homosexuality in males. **uranist,** *n.* of this.

uranography [,jʊərə'nɒgrəfi] *n.* description or mapping of heaven(s). **uranolatry,** *n.* worship of heavenly bodies. **uranology,** *n.* treatise on or study of heavens. **uranometry,** *n.* chart or measurement of heavenly bodies. **uranoscopy,** *n.* star-watching.

urbacity [ɜː'bæsɪti] *n.* excessive civic pride.

urbanism ['ɜːbənɪzm] *n.* characteristic way of life in cities; study of this. **urbanist,** *n.* expert on town-planning. **urbanite,** *n.* town-dweller.

urbarial [ɜː'beəriəl] *adj.* founded on landed property register. **urbicolous,** *adj.* city-dwelling.

urceus ['ɜːsiəs] *n.* single-handed jug; urn. **urceolate,** *adj. Botany,* shaped like a pitcher.

ure [jʊə] *n.* custom; use.

urea [ju'riːə] *n.* crystalline constituent of urine. **ureal,** *adj.* **ureic,** *adj.*

uredinous [ju'riːdɪnəs] *adj.* pertaining or belonging to rusts (fungus); *Medicine,* pertaining to or like uredo. **uredinoid,** *adj.* like rusts. **uredinology,** *n.* study of rusts.

uredo [ju'riːdəʊ] *n.* burning feeling of skin.

ureter ['jʊərɪtə] *n.* duct through which urine enters bladder. **ureteral, ureteric,** *adj.* **urethra,** *n.* duct through which urine leaves bladder. **urethral,** *adj.*

uretic [ju'retɪk] *n.* & *adj.* (medicine) affecting urination.

Urgrund ['ʊəgrʊnt] (*German*) *n.* basis; primary principle, cause or factor.

uric ['jʊərɪk] *adj.* pertaining to or contained in urine. **uridrosis,** *n.* excretion of perspiration containing urinary products.

Urim ['jʊərɪm] *see* **Thummim.**

uro- ['jʊərəʊ–] *prefix* pertaining to urine or the urinary tract. **urochrome,** *n.* yellowish pigment colouring urine. **urogenital,** *adj.* pertaining to organs used for urination and reproduction. **urogenous,** *adj,* producing, or produced by, urine. **urolith,** *n.* calculus in urinary tract. **urology,** *n.* medical study of urinary organs. **uroscopy,** *n.* examination of urine in diagnosis. **urosis,** *n.* disease of urinary organs.

uro- ['jʊərəʊ–] *prefix* pertaining to tail, rump. **urochord** *n.* notochord, confined to tail area, of

---

Coping with commas

The comma is the all-purpose workhorse of punctuation marks, separating off distinct portions of a sentence, typically mirroring the pauses of speech. It can come after a clause (*I never met him, but I admired him*) or after a phrase (*Such a position is, in the long run, untenable*). It can also divide up lists of items (*a cat, a dog, a rabbit*). When the final item in the list is preceded by *and*, the comma is commonly omitted in British English (*a cat, a dog and a rabbit*), but American English standardly retains it.

A common error is to link two main clauses with a comma, as in *We saw John last night, it was good to see him again*. There is a signifi-

cant break between these two clauses, and they should at least be separated by a semicolon. One could even regard them as two sentences, and put a full stop after *night*.

The comma can also be used in separating the elements of large numbers. In numbers over five digits, it is customary to divide the figures into groups of three. This is traditionally done with a comma (*1,000,000,000*), but now the practice of doing it with a space is on the increase (*1 000 000 000*). In four-digit numbers the comma is optional (*1,000* or *1000*); but a comma is not used in four-figure dates, page numbers, house numbers, or room numbers.

tunicate larvae. **urodele** *n.* amphibian, e.g. newt, that retains its tail through life.

uropygium [ˌjʊərə'pɪdʒiəm] *n.* rear part of bird's body from which tail feathers grow. **uropygial**, *adj.* **uropygial gland**, gland at base of tail feathers secreting fluid used in preening.

ursine ['ɜːsaɪn] *adj.* pertaining to or like a bear. **ursiform**, *adj.* bear-shaped. **ursoid**, *adj.* like a bear.

urticaceous [ˌɜːtɪ'keɪʃəs] *adj.* pertaining to or like nettles; belonging to nettle family of plants. **urticant**, *n. & adj.* stinging (substance). **urticaria**, *n.* nettle-rash. **urticate**, *v.t.* sting; cause wheals; flog. **urticose**, *adj.* full of nettles.

usance ['juːzns] *n. Commerce*, time allowed for payment of a bill of exchange; interest on loan.

user ['juːzə] *n. Law*, continued use; right to use.

usine [ju'ziːn] (*French*) *n.* factory.

usitative ['juːzɪtətɪv] *adj.* signifying usual act.

usquebaugh ['ʌskwɪbɔː] *n.* whiskey; kind of Irish cordial.

ustulate ['ʌstjuleɪt] *v.t.* give burned appearance to; *adj.* scorched. **ustulation**, *n.* roasting; lust.

usufruct ['juːsjufrʌkt, 'juːz–] *n.* right to enjoy property. **usufructuary**, *n. & adj.*

usurer ['juːʒərə] *n.* moneylender, especially one demanding very high interest. **usurious**, *adj.* **usury**, *n.*

ut [ʊt] (*Latin*) *conj.* 'as'. **ut infra**, as below. **ut supra**, as above.

uti possidetis [ˌjuːtaɪ ˌpɒsɪ'diːtɪs] *n.* principle of international law allowing a belligerent to claim the territory it occupies at the end of a war.

Utopian [ju'təupiən] *adj.* pertaining to or like Utopia, imaginary country where life is perfect; ideal; impracticable.

utraquist ['juːtrəkwɪst] *n.* person speaking two or both languages, or believing that both kinds of Sacrament should be administered.

utricle ['juːtrɪkl] *n.* small cavity or sac. **utricular**, **utriculate**, *adj.* **utriculitis**, *n.* inflammation of inner ear.

utriform ['juːtrɪfɔːm] *adj.* like a leather bottle.

uvula ['juːvjʊlə] *n.* (*pl.* **–ae**) fleshy outgrowth at back of soft palate. **uvulitis**, *n.* inflammation of uvula. **uvular**, *adj.*

uxorial [ʌk'sɔːriəl] *adj.* wifely. **uxoricide** *n.* killing or killer of own wife. **uxorious**, *adj.* loving wife to excess; submissive to wife.

V

vaccinia [væk'sɪnɪə] *n.* cow-pox.

vacillate ['væsɪleɪt] *v.i.* waver; fluctuate. **vacillation, vacillator,** *n.* **vacillatory,** *adj.*

vacuity [væ'kjuːəti] *n.* emptiness; void; inanity, fatuousness; inane thing, thought or saying. **vacuole,** *n.* small air- or fluid-containing cavity. **vacuous,** *adj.* empty; inane, fatuous.

vade-mecum [,vɑːdi 'meɪkəm, ,veɪdi 'miː–] (*Latin*) 'come with me'; *n.* guide-book; manual. **vade retro,** 'go behind'; 'get thee behind me'.

vadose ['veɪdəʊs] *adj.* pertaining to water above the water table.

vagary ['veɪgəri] *n.* whim, caprice. **vagarious** *adj.* erratic.

vagile ['vædʒaɪl] *adj.* able to move about freely.

vaginate ['vædʒɪnət] *adj.* sheathed.

vaginismus [,vædʒɪ'nɪzməs] *n.* painful contraction of the vagina.

vagitus [və'dʒaɪtəs] *n.* new-born child's cry.

vale ['vɑːleɪ, 'veɪli] (*Latin*) 'farewell'. **valediction,** *n.* bidding farewell. **valedictory,** *adj.*

valency ['veɪlənsi] *n.* element's power to combine, measured by number of atomic weights of other elements with which the atomic weight of the element will combine. **valence,** *n.* **valent,** *adj.*

valetudinarian [,vælɪtjuːdɪ'neərɪən] *n.* hypochondriac; sickly person. **valetudinarianism,** *n.* **valetudinary,** *adj.*

valgus ['vælgəs] *n. & adj.* clubfoot; bow-legged or knock-kneed (condition). **valgoid,** *adj.* like valgus.

vallate ['væleɪt] *adj.* having a raised rim. **vallated,** *adj.* having a rampart. **vallation,** *n.* rampart.

vallecular [və'lekjʊlə] *adj.* pertaining to or like a groove. **valleculate,** *adj.* bearing grooves.

valorize ['væləraɪz] *v.t.* fix arbitrary price of. **valorization,** *n.*

vapid ['væpɪd] *adj.* dull; uninteresting; insipid. **vapidity,** *n.*

vaquero [væ'keərəʊ] (*Spanish*) *n.* cowboy.

varec ['værek] *n.* seaweed; kelp.

varia ['veərɪə] (*Latin*) *n. pl.* miscellany.

varication [,værɪ'keɪʃn] *n.* varicose state.

varicella [,værɪ'selə] *n.* chicken-pox. **varicellous,** *adj.*

varicose ['værɪkəʊs] *adj.* swollen, especially in irregular lumps and twists. **varicotomy,** *n.* incision into varicose vein. **varicosis,** *n.* state of being varicose. **varicosity,** *n.*

varietal [və'raɪətl] *adj.* pertaining to a variety. **varietist,** *n.* person who chooses variety in the satisfaction of (sexual) desire.

variola [və'raɪələ] *n.* smallpox. **variolic, variolar,** *adj.* **varioloid,** *adj.* like smallpox; *n.* mild form of same. **variolate,** *v.t.* inoculate with smallpox.

variole ['veərɪəʊl] *n.* small depression resembling pockmark; *Geology,* small light-coloured sphere found in type of igneous rock. **variolite,** *n.* such rock. **variolitic,** *adj.*

variometer [,veərɪ'ɒmɪtə] *n.* instrument measuring variations in magnetic force; variable inductor with one coil rotating within another.

variorum [,veərɪ'ɔːrəm] *n. & adj.* (edition) with comments by various critics, or containing various versions of text.

varistor [væ'rɪstə] *n.* semiconductor with resistance varying in accordance with voltage.

varix ['veərɪks] *n.* (*pl.* **–rices**) varicose swelling; ridge on surface of e.g. snail's shell.

varsovienne [vɑː'səʊvjen] *n.* polka-like Polish dance.

varus ['veərəs] *n. & adj.* pigeon-toed (person or condition).

vas [væs] *n.* (*pl.* **vasa**) *Medicine,* duct; vessel. **vas deferens,** spermatic duct. **vasal,** *adj.* **vascular, vasculose, vasculous,** *adj.* pertaining to fluid-conveying vessels. **vasculature,** *n.* arrangement of blood vessels. **vasculiform,** *adj.* flowerpot-shaped. **vasiferous,** *adj.* bearing a vas.

vasoconstriction [,veɪəʊkən'strɪkʃn] *n.* constriction of blood vessels. **vasodilatation,** *n.* dilatation of blood vessels. **vasomotor,** *adj.* applied to nerves controlling constriction and dilatation of blood vessels.

vastate ['væsteɪt] *v.t.* make immune. **vastation,** *n.* purification.

Vaterland ['fɑːtəlænd] (*German*) *n.* 'fatherland'.

vatic(al) ['vætɪk, –l] *adj.* pertaining to prophecy. **vaticide,** *n.* killing or killer of a prophet.

vaticinate [væ'tɪsɪneɪt] *v.i. & t.* prophesy. **vaticinal, vaticinatory,** *adj.* prophetic. **vaticination, vaticinator,** *n.*

vection ['vekʃn] *n.* infection with disease. **vector,** *n.* disease-carrying insect; *Mathematics,* symbol of quantity having magnitude and direction; compass direction of aircraft.

vedette [vɪ'det] *n.* outpost mounted sentry. **vedette boat,** small boat or ship for watching enemy.

vegetal ['vedʒɪtl] *adj.* pertaining to or like a vegetable; lacking feelings. **vegetant,** *adj.* vegetable-like; causing growth; tonic. **vegetative,** *adj.* growing; plant-like; fertile; pertaining to unconscious life processes, as growth, digestion, etc. **vegetivorous,** *adj.* eating vegetables.

velamen [vɪ'leɪmen] *n.* (*pl.* **–mina**) water-absorbing outer covering of aerial roots of certain orchids. **velamentous,** *adj.* pertaining to or like a thin membrane.

velar ['viːlə] *adj.* pertaining to soft palate; pronounced with back of tongue touching soft palate, as k, ng, etc.; n. such sound. **velate,** adj. having veil or velum. **velation,** n. act of veiling; secrecy. **velic,** adj. pertaining to velum. **veliferous, veligerous,** adj. bearing a sail or velum.

velitation [,velɪ'teɪʃn] n. skirmish; minor argument.

velleity [ve'liːətɪ] n. state of desiring faintly; slight wish.

vellicate ['velɪkeɪt] v.t. pinch; tickle; make to twitch. **vellication,** n. **vellicative,** adj.

vellum ['veləm] n. calf or lamb gut or skin prepared for writing on; parchment.

velocious [və'ləuʃəs] adj. jocular, with great speed.

velocipede [və'lɒsəpiːd] n. old-fashioned bicycle. **velocipedist,** n.

velodrome ['viːlədrəum] n. cycle-racing track, or building containing one.

velouté [və'luːteɪ] n. rich white sauce or soup.

velum ['viːləm] n. (pl. **-la**) veil-like membrane; soft palate.

velutinous [və'luːtɪnəs] adj. having downy covering; velvety.

venal ['viːnl] adj. capable of being bribed or corrupted; based on bribery or corruption; mercenary. **venality,** n. **venalize,** v.t.

venatic(al) [vɪ'nætɪk, -l] adj. pertaining to, used in, or fond of hunting.

venation [viː'neɪʃn, və-] n. arrangement of veins on leaf or wing of insect.

vendeuse [vɒn'dɜːz] (French) n. saleswoman.

vendible ['vendəbl] adj. capable of being sold; venal.

vendue [ven'djuː] n. auction.

venenation [,venɪ'neɪʃn] n. poisoning; poisoned state.

venenose ['venɪnəus] adj. poisonous.

venereology [və,nɪəri'ɒlədʒi] n. study of venereal diseases. **venereologist,** n.

venery ['venəri] n. hunting; game (animals); sexual intercourse. **venerer,** n. huntsman.

venesect [,venɪ'sekt] v.i. & t. open vein in blood-letting. **venesection,** n.

venial ['viːniəl] adj. forgivable; not criminal. **veniality,** n.

venin ['venɪn, 'viː-] n. poisonous substance in snake venom.

veni, vidi, vici [,veɪni ,viːdi 'viːki] (Latin) 'I came, I saw, I conquered'.

venous ['viːnəs] adj. pertaining to the veins; applied to blood carried by veins to heart, containing impurities. **venostasis,** n. constricting veins to check blood.

ventage ['ventɪdʒ] n. small vent, as finger hole on a wind instrument.

venter ['ventə] n. Zoology, abdomen, belly; Law, womb, whence wife or mother.

ventiduct ['ventɪdʌkt] n. air-pipe. **ventifact,** n. stone rounded by wind action.

ventral ['ventrəl] adj. pertaining to the belly.

ventricle ['ventrɪkl] n. cavity, especially of heart from which blood enters arteries. **ventricose,** adj. swollen on one side; big-bellied. **ventricular,** adj.

ventricumbent [,ventrɪ'kʌmbənt] adj. lying on front. **ventriduct,** v.i. turn towards belly. **ventrine,** adj. ventral.

ventripotent [ven'trɪpətənt] adj. big-bellied; gluttonous.

venule ['venjuːl] n. small vein. **venulose, venulous,** adj. having many venules.

veracious [və'reɪʃəs] adj. truthful; true; exact. **veracity** [-'ræs-], n.

verbigerate [vɜː'bɪdʒəreɪt] v.i. involuntarily repeat certain words, phrases, etc. **verbigeration,** n. **verbigerative,** adj.

verbile ['vɜːbaɪl] n. person whose mental processes are most easily stimulated by words.

verboten [fə'bəutn] (German) adj. 'forbidden'; prohibited.

verbum sapienti (sat est) [,vɜːbəm sæpi'enti] (Latin) 'a word (is enough) to the wise' (abbr. **verb. sap.**).

verd-antique [,vɜːd-æn'tiːk] n. kind of green mottled marble.

verecund ['verɪkənd] adj. shy. **verecundity,** n.

vergiform ['vɜːdʒɪfɔːm] adj. like a rod.

veridic(al) [və'rɪdɪk, -l] adj. veracious; genuine. **veridicality,** n.

verisimilitude [,verɪsɪ'mɪlɪtjuːd] n. appearance of being true. **verisimilar,** adj.

verjuice ['vɜːdʒuːs] n. sour juice; sourness.

vermeil ['vɜːmeɪl, -mɪl] n. & adj. vermilion; n. gilded metal.

vermian ['vɜːmiən] adj. like a worm.

vermicelli [,vɜːmɪ'tʃelɪ, -'selɪ] n. fine variety of spaghetti.

vermicide ['vɜːmɪsaɪd] n. substance killing worms. **vermicular, vermiform,** adj. worm-like. **vermiculate,** v.t. decorate with worm-like markings; adj. worm-like; worm-eaten. **vermifugal,** adj. expelling worms. **vermifuge,** n. vermifugal substance. **vermigerous,** adj. infested with worms. **vermigrade,** adj. creeping in worm-like manner. **vermiparous,** adj. producing worms. **vermivorous,** adj. feeding on worms.

vermiculite [vɜː'mɪkjulaɪt] n. any of a group of hydrous silicates of mica, used as heat-insulation, etc.

vernacular [və'nækjulə] adj. native; common; everyday; local; n. such language.

vernal ['vɜːnl] adj. pertaining or belonging to spring (season).

vernalize ['vɜːnəlaɪz] v.t. to cause (plants) to come to early maturity, especially by chilling seeds, bulbs etc. **vernalization,** n.

vernicose ['vɜːnɪkəus] adj. covered with natural varnish.

vernier ['vɜːniə] n. short sliding scale indicating fractions of a graduation; additional control for obtaining fine adjustments.

vernissage [,vɜːnɪ'sɑːʒ] n. preview or opening of an art exhibition.

veronal ['verənl] n. hypnotic drug, also called barbital.

verricule ['verɪkjuːl] n. tuft of bristles, hairs, etc. **verriculate,** adj. having verricules.

verruca [ve'ruːkə] n. wart. **verrucated,** adj. bearing wart-like prominences. **verrucose, verrucous,** adj. covered with warts. **verruculose,** adj. having very small warts or wart-like prominences.

versant ['vɜːsnt] n. slope of a mountain (range); general slope of a region.

versicle ['vɜːsɪkl] n. short verse; Ecclesiastical, short verse followed by response. **versicular,** adj. pertaining to or marking verses.

versicolour ['vɜːsɪ,kʌlə] adj. of various or

varying colours.

vers libre [ˌveə 'liːbr] (*French*) 'free verse'. **verslibrist**, *n*. writer of such.

verso ['vɜːsəʊ] *n*. left-hand page or back cover of book; reverse of coin.

verst [vɜːst] (*Russian*) *n*. unit of distance, equivalent of two-thirds of a mile.

vertebra ['vɜːtɪbrə] *n*. (*pl.* **-ae**) segment of backbone. **vertebral**, *adj*. **vertebrate**, *n*. & *adj*. (animal) having a backbone. **vertebration**, *n*. division into segments; firmness.

vertex ['vɜːteks] *n*. (*pl.* **-tices**) apex.

verticil ['vɜːtɪsɪl] *n*. *Botany*, whorl.

vertiginous [vɜː'tɪdʒɪnəs] *adj*. having or causing vertigo; whirling.

vervain ['vɜːveɪn] *n*. verbena plant.

vervet ['vɜːvɪt] *n*. small monkey of S and E Africa.

vesicle ['vesɪkl] *n*. small blister; bladder-like or rounded cavity; cell; cyst. **vesical**, *adj*. pertaining to bladder; oval. **vesicant**, **vesicatory**, *adj*. raising blisters. **vesicate**, *v.t.* blister. **vesicular**, *adj*. like a vesicle or bladder; bearing many vesicles.

vespal ['vespl] *adj*. pertaining to wasps. **vespacide**, *n*. substance or person killing wasps.

vespertine ['vespətaɪn] *adj*. in or of the evening; setting at same time as, or just after, the sun.

vespiary ['vespɪəri] *n*. wasps' nest. **vespid**, *n*. social wasp. **vespine**, *adj*. pertaining to or like wasps.

vesta ['vestə] *n*. wax-match.

vestal ['vestl] *adj*. having taken vows of chastity; *n*. such virgin.

vestiary ['vestɪəri] *adj*. pertaining to clothes or dress.

vesuvian [və'suːvɪən, -'sjuːv-] *n*. old-fashioned kind of match; fusee. **vesuviate**, *v.i.* erupt; burst with heat.

vetanda [ve'tændə] (*Latin*) *n*. *pl.* forbidden things.

veterinary ['vetərənəri, 'vetn–əri] *adj*. pertaining to diseases of domestic animals.

vetitive ['vetətɪv] *adj*. having power to forbid or veto.

vexillary ['veksɪləri] *adj*. pertaining to regimental colours or standard; *n*. standard-bearer. **vexillology**, *n*. study of flags.

viable ['vaɪəbl] *adj*. born alive and able to live; able to exist alone.

via media [ˌvaɪə 'miːdɪə, ˌviːə 'meɪdɪə] (*Latin*) 'middle way'.

viands ['vaɪəndz] *n. pl.* food.

viatic(al) [vaɪ'ætɪk, -l] *adj*. pertaining to roads or travel. **viaticum**, *n*. Holy Communion administered to dying person; travelling provisions or expenses. **viator**, *n*. traveller. **viatorial**, *adj*. travelling.

vibrissa [vaɪ'brɪsə] *n*. (*pl.* **-ae**) sensitive whisker on animal's face. **vibrissal**, *adj*.

viburnum [vaɪ'bɜːnəm] *n*. kind of shrub or tree including guelder-rose, etc.

vicarial [vɪ'keərɪəl] *adj*. pertaining to vicar or delegate. **vicarious**, *adj*. acting for another; enjoyed or suffered for, or through, another; substituted.

vice ['vaɪsi] (*Latin*) *prep*. 'in place of'; succeeding to.

vicegerent [ˌvaɪs'dʒerənt, -'dʒɪə-] *n*. & *adj*. (person) representing a ruler or God. **vicegerency**,

n. **vicegeral**, *adj*.

vicenary ['vɪsɪnəri] *adj*. pertaining to or consisting of 20; having 20 as a base. **vicennial**, *adj*. lasting, or happening every, 20 years.

viceroy ['vaɪsrɔɪ] *n*. ruler having king's authority. **viceroyalty**, *n*. **viceregal**, *adj*. **vicereine**, *n*. viceroy's wife; female viceroy.

vicinage ['vɪsɪnɪdʒ] *n*. neighbourhood. **vicinal**, *adj*. neighbouring; local.

vicissitude [vaɪ'sɪsɪtjuːd, vɪ–] *n*. change of fortune; alternation. **vicissitudinous**, *adj*.

victoria [vɪk'tɔːrɪə] *n*. light open two-seater four-wheeled carriage, with raised driver's seat.

victual ['vɪtl] *v.i.* & *t.* provision; *n.pl.* food. **victualler**, *n*. licensee of public house.

vicuna [vɪ'kjuːnə, -'kuːnjə] *n*. wild wool-bearing llama-like animal of the Andes.

vide ['vɪdeɪ, 'vaɪdi] (*Latin*) 'see'. **vide infra**, 'see below' (*abbr.* **v.i.**). **vide supra**, 'see above' (*abbr.* **v.s.**). **videlicet** [vɪ'diːlɪset], *adv*. namely (*abbr.* **viz.**). **videtur**, 'it seems'.

viduage ['vɪdjuɪdʒ] *n*. widowhood. **viduity**, *n*.

vi et armis [ˌviː et 'ɑːmɪs, ˌvaɪ–] (*Latin*) 'by force and arms'.

vieux jeu [ˌvjɜː 'ʒɜː] (*French*) 'old game'; antiquated or worn-out subject.

vigentennial [ˌvɪdʒen'tenɪəl, ˌvaɪ–] *adj*. lasting, or happening every, twenty years; *n*. twentieth anniversary.

vigesimal [vaɪ'dʒesɪml] *adj*. pertaining to or based on number twenty; twentieth.

vigintillion [ˌvɪdʒɪn'tɪljən] *n*. a million novemdecillions (10^{120}); (*American & French*) a thousand novemdecillions (10^{63}).

vignette [vɪn'jet] *n*. small, ornamental illustration without frame or with background shaded off; slight portrait or character sketch.

vilayet [vɪ'lɑːjet] *n*. Turkish province.

vilify ['vɪlɪfaɪ] *v.t.* slander; degrade. **vilification**, *n*. **vilipend**, *v.t.* speak slightingly of. **vilipenditory**, *adj*. despising.

villanelle [ˌvɪlə'nel] (*French*) *n*. poem of three tercets and a quatrain, with special rhyming scheme.

villar ['vɪlə] *adj*. pertaining to feudal manor or village; *n*. villein. **villatic**, *adj*. rural; pertaining to villa.

villeggiatura [vɪˌledʒə'tʊərə] (*Italian*) *n*. stay at country seat.

villein ['vɪleɪn, -ən] *n*. free villager; serf. **villeinage**, *n*.

villus ['vɪləs] *n*. (*pl.* **-li**) small vein-like outgrowth; soft hair. **villiform**, *adj*. like villus; with velvety surface. **villose**, **villous**, *adj*. bearing soft hairs. **villosity**, *n*.

vimen ['vaɪmen] *n*. (*pl.* **-mina**) long thin branch or twig. **vimineous**, *adj*. pertaining to or made of twigs.

vinaceous [vaɪ'neɪʃəs] *adj*. pertaining to or like grapes or wine; wine-coloured.

vinaigrette [ˌvɪneɪ'gret, -nə-] *n*. bottle of smelling-salts; salad dressing made of oil and vinegar. **vinaigrous**, *adj*. like vinegar; sour in manner.

vincular ['vɪŋkjʊlə] *adj*. connective. **vinculum**, *n*. (*pl.* **-la**) bond, tie; *Mathematics*, horizontal line over figures with the same function as brackets.

vindemiate [vɪn'diːmɪeɪt] *v.i.* gather in fruit, or

the vintage. **vindemiation**, *n.* **vindemiatory**, *adj.*

vingt-et-un [ˌvænt-eɪ-'ɜːn] (*French*) 'twenty-one'; *n.* card game the object of which is to obtain cards with values adding up to twenty-one.

vin ordinaire [ˌvæn ɔːdɪ'neə] (*French*) *n.* 'common wine'; ordinary, cheap wine, especially cheap claret.

vinous ['vaɪnəs] *adj.* pertaining to or like wine; fond of wine; wine-coloured. **vinosity**, *n.*

vintner ['vɪntnə] *n.* wine-seller.

virago [vɪ'rɑːgəʊ] *n.* nagging or abusive woman.

virelay ['vɪrɪleɪ] *n.* old French poem with refrain and various special rhyming schemes.

virescent [vɪ'resnt] *n.* becoming or slightly green. **virescence**, *n.*

virgal ['vɜːgl] *adj.* composed of twigs. **virgate**, *adj.* like a rod; having many twigs; *v.i.* branch off.

virginals ['vɜːdʒɪnlz] *n.* kind of spinet of 16th and 17th centuries.

virgule ['vɜːgjuːl] *n.* slanting mark (/) indicating pause, hyphen, or alternative. **virgulate**, *adj.* rod-like.

viridescent [ˌvɪrɪ'desnt] *adj.* greenish. **viridigenous**, *adj.* producing greenness. **viridity**, *n.* greenness; freshness.

virilescence [ˌvɪrə'lesns] *n.* acquisition by females of male characteristics. **virilia**, *n.* male reproductive organs. **virilism**, *n.* masculinity in women, especially with secondary male characteristics.

viripotent [vɪ'rɪpətənt] *adj.* (sexually) potent.

virology [vaɪ'rɒlədʒi, vɪ-] *n.* study of viruses and viral diseases.

virose ['vaɪrəus] *adj.* poisonous; foul-smelling.

virtu, vertu [vɜː'tuː] *n.* objects of art; antiques; love or study of such objects; artistic value. **virtuoso**, *n.* (*fem.* –**sa**; *pl.* –**si**) technically brilliant performer, especially musical. **virtuosity**, *n.* skill of virtuoso.

visage ['vɪzɪdʒ] *n.* face. **visagiste** *n.* make-up artist.

visard ['vɪzəd] *n.* mask; visor.

vis à vis [ˌviːzə'viː] *adv., adj. & prep.* facing; opposite; regarding; *n.* person facing one.

viscera ['vɪsərə] *n. pl.* internal organs; intestines. **visceral, viscerous,** *adj.* **visceroptosis**, *n.* prolapse of visceral organs.

viscerotonic [ˌvɪsərə'tɒnɪk] *adj. Psychology*, having sociable, comfort-loving temperament associated with endomorphy.

viscid ['vɪsɪd] *adj.* viscous. **viscose**, ['vɪskəus], *n.* cellulose prepared for use as rayon, etc. **viscous**, *adj.* thick and sticky like glue or treacle. **viscosity**, [–'skɒs–], *n.* treacliness; force opposing flow.

visile ['vɪzaɪl] *n. & adj.* (person) with mental processes most readily stimulated by visual impressions.

vis major [ˌvɪs 'meɪdʒə] (*Latin*) 'greater force'; act of God; unavoidable accident.

vitalism ['vaɪtl–ɪzm] *n.* philosophical doctrine that life processes are not entirely explicable, or bound, by scientific laws. **vitalist**, *n.* **vitalistic**, *adj.*

vitascope ['vaɪtəskəup] *n.* moving picture projector.

vitative ['vaɪtətɪv] *adj.* fond of life.

vitellus [vɪ'teləs] *n.* yolk of egg. **vitelline**, *adj.* pertaining to or coloured like egg yolk. **vitelline membrane,** sac surrounding fertilized ovum. **vitellin**, *n.* protein in egg yolk.

vitiate ['vɪʃieɪt] *v.t.* impair; spoil; debase; make useless or impure. **vitiation, vitiator,** *n.*

viticulture ['vɪtɪˌkʌltʃə, 'vaɪ–] *n.* vine-growing. **vitiferous,** *adj.* bearing vines.

vitiligo [ˌvɪtɪ'laɪgəʊ] *n. Medicine*, condition characterized by smooth white patches on skin.

vitrail [vɪ'traɪ] (*French*) *n.* (*pl.* –**aux**) stained glass.

vitreous ['vɪtriəs] *adj.* pertaining to or like glass. **vitreal,** *adj.* **vitrescent,** *adj.* becoming vitreous; able to be made into glass. **vitrescible,** *adj.* vitrifiable. **vitric,** *adj.* glassy. **vitrics,** *n.* study of glassware. **vitrifacture,** *n.* making of glassware. **vitriform,** *adj.* glassy. **vitrify,** *v.i. & t.* make or become vitreous. **vitrine,** *n.* glass case.

vitriol ['vɪtrɪəl] *n.* sulphuric acid; several sulphates of metals. **vitriolic,** *adj.* like vitriol; corrosive; caustic, scathing.

vittate ['vɪteɪt] *adj.* striped length-wise.

vituline ['vɪtjulaɪn] *adj.* pertaining to or like calf, or veal.

vituperate [vaɪ'tjuːpəreɪt] *v.i. & v.t.* speak bitterly, harshly or abusively (of). **vituperation, vituperator,** *n.* **vituperative, vituperatory,** *adj.*

viva ['viːvə] (*Italian*) *exclamation* 'long live'; hurrah.

vivandière [vɪˌvɒndi'eə] (*French*) *n.* woman camp-follower supplying provisions.

vivarium [vɪ'veərɪəm] *n.* (*pl.* –**ia**) place or box, etc., for keeping living animals.

vivat ['vaɪvæt, 'viː–] (*Latin*) 'may he or she live'; long live; hurrah.

viva voce [ˌvaɪvə 'vəusi] (*Latin*) 'by word of mouth'; oral(ly); *n.* oral examination (*abbr.* **viva**).

vive [viːv] (*French*) 'long live'.

viverrine [vaɪ'veraɪn] *adj.* pertaining to or like a civet; belonging to civet family; *n.* civet.

vives [vaɪvz] *n.* swelling of horse's submaxillary glands.

viveur [viː'vɜː] (*French*) *n.* person who lives (well); person indulging in pleasures.

The semicolon

Take two main clauses (say, *She was free* and *Her heart leapt*), and put them together. What punctuation mark do you put between them? You could use a full stop, but with short clauses like these, that would create a rather abrupt effect. If you think there is some sort of logical link between the two clauses, you could use a colon. A comma is possible, but disliked by purists. But the usual mark between two main clauses is a semicolon: *She was free; her heart leapt.*

Those who think that sentences should not begin with *and, but* and *or* apply the same 'rule' to clauses following a semicolon; but in fact it is perfectly natural English to start a clause in this way when you want to give particular weight to it, and there is no reason why a semicolon should not precede it.

vivify ['vɪvɪfaɪ] *v.t.* make alive or vivid; animate; sharpen. **vivification,** *n.*

viviparous [vɪ'vɪpərəs] *adj.* bringing forth live young. **viviparism, viviparity** [–'pær–], *n.*

vivisect ['vɪvɪsekt] *v.t.* experiment on by dissecting, while alive. **vivisection,** *n.* **vivisepulture,** *n.* burying alive.

vizard ['vɪzəd] *n.* mask; visor.

vizier [vɪ'zɪə] *n.* Muslim minister of state.

vocable ['vəʊkəbl] *n.* word; name; sound. **vocabular** [–'kæb–], *adj.*

vocalic [və'kælɪk] *adj.* pertaining to or like vowels.

vocative ['vɒkətɪv] *adj.* used when addressing a person; *n.* such grammatical case.

vociferate [və'sɪfəreɪt] *v.i.* & *t.* shout loudly or repeatedly. **vociferant, vociferous,** *adj.* **vociferation, vociferator,** *n.*

voetsak ['futsæk] (*S African*) *exclamation* go away.

voilà [vwæ'lɑː] (*French*) *exclamation* 'see there'; behold; there is or are. **voilà tout,** that is all.

voivode ['vɔɪvəʊd] *n.* former Russian military governor.

volant ['vəʊlənt] *adj.* flying; able to fly; quick.

volar ['vəʊlə] *adj.* pertaining to palm or sole; pertaining to flight.

volary ['vəʊləri, 'vɒl–] *n.* aviary.

volatile ['vɒlətaɪl] *adj.* light-hearted; changeable; readily evaporating; ephemeral. **volatility,** *n.* **volatilize,** *v.t.* vaporize.

volation [və'leɪʃn] *n.* ability to fly.

volcanology [,vɒlkə'nɒlədʒi] *n.* vulcanology.

volent ['vəʊlənt] *adj.* exercising will power.

volitate ['vɒlɪteɪt] *v.i.* fly about; flutter. **volitant,** *adj.* able to fly; flying. **volitation,** *n.*

volition [və'lɪʃn] *n.* act of willing; will. **volitional, volitionary,** *adj.* **volitive,** *adj.* pertaining to or derived from the will; *Grammar,* expressing desire or permission.

volitorial [,vɒlɪ'tɔːriəl] *adj.* able to fly.

volk [fɒlk] (*S African,*) *n.* people, nation, especially the Afrikaner nation.

volplane ['vɒlpleɪn] *v.i.* glide through air.

volte-face [,vɒlt'fɑːs] *n.* change to opposite opinion or direction.

volucrine ['vɒljukraɪn] *adj.* pertaining to birds.

volumetric [,vɒlju'metrɪk] *adj.* pertaining to measurement by volume.

voluntary ['vɒləntəri] *n.* *Music,* (improvised) music introducing or closing performance or church service.

voluptuary [və'lʌptjuəri] *n.* person excessively devoted to luxury. **voluptuous,** *adj.* luxurious; given up to luxury; sensuous. **volupty,** *n.* sexual pleasure.

volute [və'luːt, –'ljuːt] *n.* & *adj.* spiral (object or ornament). **volutate** ['vɒljuteɪt] *v.i.* roll. **volution,** *n.* twist; convolution.

vomer ['vəʊmə] *n.* thin bone separating nasal passages.

vomitory ['vɒmɪtəri] *n.* emetic; vessel for receiving vomit; passageway leading to a tier of seats, especially in Roman amphitheatre.

vomiturition [,vɒmɪtju'rɪʃn] *n.* retching; unsuccessful attempt to vomit; easy vomiting.

voracious [və'reɪʃəs] *adj.* greedy; ravenous. **voracity** [–'ræs–], *n.*

vortex ['vɔːteks] *n.* (*pl.* **–tices**) whirlpool. **vortical, vorticose, vorticular, vortiginous,** *adj.* whirling. **vorticist** [–sɪst], *n.* painter whose theory of art was that it should express the complexity of modern machinery, etc.

votary ['vəʊtəri] *n.* person vowed or devoted to God, etc. **votaress,** *n.* such woman or girl.

votive ['vəʊtɪv] *adj.* fulfilling a vow; done in devotion.

voussoir [vuː'swɑː] *n.* any wedge-shaped stone forming part of arch, vault, etc.

vox populi [,vɒks 'pɒpjulaɪ, –liː] (*Latin*) 'the voice of the people'; public verdict. **vox populi vox Dei** [–'deiiː], 'the voice of the people (is) the voice of God'.

vrouw [frau] (*S African*) *n.* housewife; woman.

VTOL ['viːtɒl] *abbreviation* of Vertical Take-Off and Landing (aircraft).

vulcanize ['vʌlkənaɪz] *v.i.* harden (rubber) by chem. process. **vulcanite,** *n.* hardened rubber.

vulcanology [,vʌlkə'nɒlədʒi] *n.* study of volcanic activity.

vulgarian [vʌl'geərɪən] *n.* vulgar person, especially one who is rich or has pretensions to taste.

vulgarism ['vʌlgərɪzm] *n.* coarse, substandard or obscene expression; vulgarity.

Vulgate ['vʌlgeɪt, –gət] *n.* 4th-century Latin translation of Scriptures; generally accepted text or version.

vulgus ['vʌlgəs] *n.* the common people; school composition in Latin verse.

vulnerary ['vʌlnərəri] *n.* & *adj.* (remedy) that heals wounds.

vulpicide ['vʌlpɪsaɪd] *n.* killing or killer of fox, except by hunting. **vulpecular,** *adj.* pertaining to young fox. **vulpine,** *adj.* fox-like; cunning.

vulturn ['vʌltən] (*Australian*) *n.* brush turkey.

vulva ['vʌlvə] *n.* external portion of female reproductive organs. **vulval, vulvar,** *adj.* **vulvate, vulviform,** *adj.* shaped like vulva. **vulvitis,** *n.* inflammation of vulva.

W

waddy ['wɒdi] *n.* war-club of aborigines.

wadi ['wɒdi] (*Arabic*) *n.* valley; stream; watercourse drying up in summer; oasis.

wagon-lit [ˌvægɒn-'liː] (*French*) *n.* sleeping compartment of railway train.

wain [weɪn] *n.* farm wagon. **wainwright,** *n.* maker or repairer of carts.

waldgrave ['wɔːldɡreɪv] *n.* former German title of count; head forest ranger. **waldgravine,** *n.* wife of a waldgrave.

wallah ['wɒlə] (*Anglo-Indian*) *n.* person employed in certain capacity or connected with a certain thing or activity; –worker; –carrier.

wallaroo [ˌwɒlə'ruː] *n.* large species of kangaroo.

wall-eye ['wɔːlaɪ] *n.* eye with light grey or whitish iris or cornea, or showing abnormal amount of white by turning outwards. **wall-eyed,** *adj.*

wampum ['wɒmpəm] (*N American Indian*) *n.* beads used as money.

wamus ['wɔːməs] (*American*) *n.* heavy knitted cardigan.

wanderoo ['wɒndəruː, ˌwɒndə'ruː] *n.* kind of monkey of Sri Lanka with purple face, or of India with lion-like tail.

wapentake ['wɒpənteɪk] *n.* subdivision of certain counties; court or bailiff of such area.

wapiti ['wɒpəti] (*American*) *n.* elk.

wappenshaw ['wæpənʃɔː] *n.* muster of men with their weapons formerly held in certain areas of Scotland.

warble ['wɔːbl] *n.* small tumour of horse, especially under saddle, or caused by warble fly. **warble fly,** fly with larvae living under skin of cattle, etc.

warison ['wɒrɪzn] *n.* bugle call ordering the attack.

warlock ['wɔːlɒk] *n.* wizard.

warp [wɔːp] *n.* in weaving, lengthwise threads in loom.

warranty ['wɒrənti] *n.* guarantee as to the fitness for use of thing sold, with undertaking to repair defects, etc. *Law*, covenant by which vendor guarantees security of title to real estate conveyed; understanding given by insured as to truth of statements regarding risk; act of warranting.

wassail ['wɒseɪl] *n.* toast to a person; festive drink, especially spiced ale; revelry; *v.i.* carouse; go carol-singing.

wayzgoose ['weɪzɡuːs] *n.* annual outing or dinner of employees, especially of printing firm.

wazir [wə'zɪə] *n.* vizier.

weasand ['wiːznd] *n.* throat; gullet; wind-pipe.

weatherometer [ˌweðə'rɒmɪtə] *n.* device measuring the weather resistance of paint.

weft [weft] *n.* woof; woven thing; web; film.

Wehrmacht ['veəmɑːxt] (*German*) *n.* 'defence force'; the armed forces of Germany.

Weltanschauung ['veltæn,ʃauʊŋ] (*German*) *n.* 'world view'; personal philosophy of life. **Weltpolitik** [–'tiːk], (*German*) *n.* international politics; policy towards the world. **Weltschmerz** [–ʃmeəts], (*German*) *n.* 'world sorrow'; sadness at the world's woes; pessimism.

werewolf ['wɪəwulf] *n.* human being transformed into wolf.

wergild ['wɜːɡɪld] *n.* value of a man's life, payable to his family by his murderer.

wet-bob ['wetbɒb] *n.* Etonian adopting rowing as his sport.

wether ['weðə] *n.* castrated ram.

When to use a capital letter

Starting a sentence. Always use a capital for the first letter of the first word of a sentence. It is usual to use a capital for the first word of each line of a poem, whether or not it begins a sentence.

Proper nouns. Use a capital letter for a noun that is the name of a person, place, thing, or organization: *Helen, Glasgow, Boeing 747, Federal Bureau of Investigation*. Use a capital letter for the names of days and months, for the names of special days and religious festivals, and for particular periods and events in history: *Monday, July, Christmas, First World War, Bronze Age*. Use a capital for the names of languages and ethnic groups: *Urdu, British, Chinese*.

Common nouns. Use a capital letter for a common noun when it is (part of) a person's title or part of the name of a place or institution: *Auntie Joan, President Roosevelt, the Queen, River Thames, Harvard University, United Biscuits, Church of England*.

Titles and headings. The convention in English is to capitalize the first and last word of the title of literary and artistic works, and all the words in between except *a(n)*, *the*, and short prepositions and conjunctions: *The Lord of the Rings, A Study in Scarlet, The Old Man and the Sea*. The first word of a heading is capitalized; subsequent ones may be, and if they are, they follow the rule for titles.

wharfinger ['wɔːfɪndʒə] *n.* owner or manager of a wharf.

whicker ['wɪkə] *v.i.* whinny, neigh.

whiffle ['wɪfl] *v.i.* blow in puffs or gusts; make a light whistling sound; be evasive; vacillate. **whiffler** *n.* evasive or vacillating person; attendant who cleared the way for a procession.

whigmaleerie [,wɪgmə'lɪəri] *n.* whim, caprice.

whilom ['waɪləm] *adv.* once, formerly; *adj.* former.

whim-wham ['wɪmwæm] *n.* trifle; knick-knack.

whin [wɪn] *n.* gorse. **whinchat**, *n.* small brown and buff song-bird.

whippoorwill ['wɪpəwɪl] *n.* N American nightjar.

whisht [hwɪʃt] (*Scottish*) *exclamation* hush.

whitlow ['wɪtləʊ] *n.* abscess on finger, especially round nail.

widdershins ['wɪdəʃɪnz] *adv.* anticlockwise; backwards, in the reverse order or direction to normal.

widgeon ['wɪdʒən] *n.* kind of fresh-water duck with light crown.

wie geht's [,viː 'geɪts] (*German*) 'how goes it?'; how do you do?

wimble ['wɪmbl] *n.* boring tool, *e.g.* gimlet, brace and bit.

wimple ['wɪmpl] *n.* women's head covering worn round neck and chin, as by nuns.

windage ['wɪndɪdʒ] *n.* deflection of projectile by the wind.

window ['wɪndəʊ] *n.* in space research, period of time within which a rocket or spacecraft must be launched to accomplish a particular mission; area at the limit of the Earth's atmosphere through which a spacecraft must pass for successful reentry; *Computing*, section of a VDU screen displaying a particular type of information.

wingding ['wɪŋdɪŋ] (*American*) *n.* noisy party.

witan ['wɪtn] *n.* early English King's council.

witenagemot ['wɪtənəgɪməʊt] *n.* early English national council; witan.

withe [wɪθ, waɪð] *n.* tough, flexible branch or twig, especially one used for binding.

withershins ['wɪðəʃɪnz] *adv.* widdershins.

withhold [wɪð'həʊld] *v.t.* not give or grant; restrain; deduct; *v.i.* refrain (from).

withy ['wɪði] *n.* willow; withe.

wittol ['wɪtl] *n.* complacent cuckold.

wivern ['waɪvn] *n.* winged dragon in heraldry.

wobbegong ['wɒbigɒŋ] (*Australian*) *n.* carpet shark.

wolfram ['wʊlfrəm] *n.* tungsten.

wolverine ['wʊlvəriːn] (*American*) *n.* shaggy-furred animal of weasel family.

wombat ['wɒmbæt] (*Australian*) *n.* bear-like marsupial; Australian badger.

woof [wuːf] *n.* threads crossing warp in weaving; weft.

word [wɜːd] *n.* in computers, a block of data made up of many 'bits'.

wort [wɜːt] *n.* infusion of malt before fermentation.

wrack [ræk] *n.* sea-weed cast up on shore; wreckage; vestige.

wrangler ['ræŋglə] *n.* at Cambridge University, an honours graduate in first class in mathematics tripos. **senior wrangler**, first on list of such graduates.

wrasse [ræs] *n.* a bright-hued marine fish of Atlantic and Mediterranean.

wroth [rəʊθ] *adj. archaic* angry.

wuther ['wʌðə] *v.i.* (of the wind) blow strongly, bluster.

wynd [waɪnd] (*Scottish*) *n.* alley.

X

xanthic ['zænθɪk] *adj.* yellow; yellowish. **xanthochroid**, *n. & adj.* fair-haired and pale-skinned (person). **xanthochroism**, *n.* condition in which all skin pigments except yellow and orange disappear. **xanthoma**, *n.* skin disease causing yellow patches. **xanthopsia**, *n.* optical defect causing everything to seem yellow. **xanthous**, *adj.* yellow- or red-haired; yellow-skinned.

xebec ['ziːbek] *n.* ancient three-masted Mediterranean pirate ship.

xenial ['ziːnɪəl] *adj.* pertaining to hospitality, or relations with friendly visitors. **xenian**, *adj.*

xenodocheionology [ˌzenəʊdəʊkɪə'nɒlədʒi] *n. jocular*, love of hotels and inns.

xenogamy [zɪ'nɒgəmi] *n.* cross-fertilization. **xenogenesis**, *n.* production of offspring unlike the parent. **xenograft**, *n.* heterograft. **xenolith**, *n.* rock particle included in another rock. **xenomorphic**, *adj.* with a form not its own.

xenophobia [ˌzenə'fəʊbɪə] *n.* hatred or dread of foreigners.

xerarch ['zɪərɑːk] *adj.* growing in dry places. **xerasia**, *n.* morbid dryness of hair. **xeric**, *adj.* pertaining to or adapted to dry conditions.

xeroderma, *n.* morbid dryness of skin. **xerography**, *n.* method of reproducing illustrations, text, etc., electrostatically, by attraction of ink powder to positively charged sheet of selenium metal. **xerophagy**, *n.* strict fast of Eastern Church during Holy Week. **xerophilous**, *adj.* resisting drought. **xerophobous**, *adj.* unable to survive drought. **xerophthalmia**, *n. Medicine*, abnormal dryness of the eyeball. **xerophyte**, *n.* plant thriving in desert conditions. **xerosis**, *n. Medicine*, abnormal dryness. **xerostoma**, *n.* dryness of mouth. **xerotic**, *adj.* dry.

xi [saɪ, zaɪ, ksiː] *n.* fourteenth letter (Ξ ξ) of Greek alphabet.

xiphoid ['zɪfɔɪd] *adj.* sword-like. **xiphoid process**, lowest division of sternum; king-crab's tail. **xiphophyllous**, *adj.* with sword-shaped leaves.

xylem ['zaɪləm, –em] *n.* woody tissue of plants. **xylocarp**, *n.* woody fruit.

xylograph ['zaɪləgrɑːf] *n.* wood-engraving; print made from a wood block. **xylography**, *n.*

xyloid ['zaɪlɔɪd] *adj.* like wood. **xylonite**, *n.* celluloid. **xylophagous**, *adj.* destroying or boring in wood. **xylophilous**, *adj.* living on or in wood. **xylotomous**, *adj.* boring into or cutting wood.

Y

yaffle ['jæfl] *n.* green woodpecker.

yahoo [jɑːˈhuː, ˈjɑːhuː] *n.* member of brutish, quasi-human species in Swift's *Gulliver's Travels*; depraved person.

yamen ['jɑːmən] (*Chinese*) *n.* official residence.

yammer ['jæmə] *v.i.* complain peevishly; whine; howl.

yarborough ['jɑːbərə] *n.* hand of cards containing no card above a nine.

yare [jeə] *adj.* nimble, brisk; ready.

yarmulke ['jɑːmlkə] *n.* skullcap worn by orthodox Jewish males.

yashmak ['jæʃmæk] *n.* veil of Muslim women.

yataghan ['jætəgæn] *n.* Muslim long curved knife.

yaw [jɔː] *v.i.* & *t.* move or deviate from course; move in a zigzag; *n.* such deviation or movement.

yawl [jɔːl] *n.* ship's small rowing-boat; small sailing vessel with from one to three lugsails; small fore-and-aft rigged vessel with mizzen-mast abaft rudder post.

yaws [jɔːz] *n.* contagious skin disease resembling syphilis.

yean [jiːn] *v.i.* & *t.* bring forth (lamb or kid). **yeanling,** *n.* lamb or kid.

yerba (maté) ['jeəbə, 'jɜː– ('mæteɪ)] *n.* Paraguay tea. **yerbal,** *n.* plantation of yerba.

yom [jɒm] (*Hebrew*) *n.* 'day'. **yom Kippur,** 'day of atonement', a solemn Jewish fast. **yom Tob,** 'good day'; religious festival; Sabbath.

ypsiliform [ɪpˈsɪlɪfɔːm] *adj.* shaped like Greek upsilon Y. **ypsiloid,** *adj.*

yurt [juət] *n.* tent consisting of a framework of poles covered by skins or felt, used by Mongol nomads.

Z

zaibatsu [zaɪˈbætsuː] (*Japanese*) *n.* large industrial and financial combines.

zamindar [zəˈmiːndɑː] (*Hindi*) *n.* landowner. **zamindari**, *n.* land or jurisdiction of a zamindar.

zariba, zareba [zəˈriːbə] *n.* protective hedge, etc., round Sudanese village; fortified camp.

zebrule, zebrula [ˈzebruːl, –rʊlə; ˈziːb–] *n.* hybrid of male zebra and female horse.

zebu [ˈziːbjuː] *n.* humped ox of the East and E Africa.

zeigarnik [tsaɪˈgɑːnɪk] *n.* *Psychology*, tendency to remember an uncompleted rather than a completed task.

Zeitgeist [ˈzaɪtgaɪst, ˈtsaɪ–] (*German*) *n.* 'spirit of the age'; philosophy or outlook of a particular period.

zenana [zɪˈnɑːnə] *n.* harem; system of segregating women in harems.

zenography [zɪˈnɒgrəfi] *n.* study or description of planet Jupiter. **zenographic(al)**, *adj.*

zeta [ˈziːtə] *n.* sixth letter (Z ζ) of Greek alphabet.

zetetic [zɪˈtetɪk] *adj.* proceeding by inquiry.

zeugma [ˈzjuːgmə, ˈzuː–] *n.* literary device of using word to modify two other words with only one of which it is correctly used. **zeugmatic**, *adj.*

zibeline, zibelline [ˈzɪbəlaɪn] *adj.* pertaining to sables.

zibet [ˈzɪbet] *n.* Indian civet.

Zigeuner [tsɪˈgɔɪnə] (*German*) *n.* 'gypsy'.

zingaro [ˈzɪŋgərəʊ, ˈtsiːŋ–] (*Italian*) *n.* (*pl* **–ri**) 'gypsy'.

zircon [ˈzɜːkɒn] *n.* brownish or greyish mineral used as gem. **zirconiferous**, *adj.*

zither [ˈzɪðə] *n.* musical instrument of strings stretched over a horizontal sounding board and plucked with a plectrum.

zoanthropy [zəʊˈænθrəpi] *n.* delusion of a person who believes himself changed into an animal.

zoea [zəʊˈiːə] *n.* early larva of crab and other crustaceans. **zoeal**, *adj.*

zoetrope [ˈzəʊitrəʊp] *n.* device whereby a series of drawings are made to seem, by revolving them, one continuous moving picture.

zoic [ˈzəʊɪk] *adj.* showing traces of life; containing organic remains. **zoism**, *n.* doctrine that life depends on a peculiar vital principle.

Zollverein [ˈtsɒlfəˌraɪn] (*German*) *n.* 'customs-union' as organized by Prussia in the 1830s.

zombie [ˈzɒmbi] *n.* in voodoo worship, a corpse made by witchcraft to move and walk as if alive; *slang*, a person of the lowest order of intelligence.

zomotherapy [ˌzəʊməˈθerəpi] *n.* medical treatment by raw meat or meat juice. **zomotherapeutic**, *adj.*

zoogamy [zəʊˈɒgəmi] *n.* sexual reproduction of animals. **zoogenous** [–ˈɒdʒ–], *adj.* originating in animals. **zoography**, *n.* description of animals.

zooid [ˈzəʊɔɪd] *n.* organism resembling animal, especially asexually produced; sperm cell. **zooidal**, *adj.*

zoolite, zoolith [ˈzəʊəlaɪt, –lɪθ] *n.* fossil animal.

zoometry [zəʊˈɒmətri] *n.* measurement of animals. **zoomimetic**, *adj.* imitating an animal or part of an animal. **zoomorph**, *n.* object in form of animal. **zoomorphism**, *n.* representation of god as lower animal.

zoonic [zəʊˈɒnɪk] *adj.* pertaining to or derived from animals. **zoonosis**, *n.* disease that can be communicated among animals or from animal to man.

zoopery [zəʊˈɒpəri] *n.* experimenting on lower animals. **zooperal**, *adj.* **zooperist**, *n.*

zoophile [ˈzəʊəfaɪl] *n.* lover of animals; plant pol-

'-ise' or '-ize'

The choice between *-ise* and *-ize* in verbs like *nationalise*/*-ize* and *realise*/*-ize* often causes difficulty. The current state of affairs is that *-ise* is the commoner form in British English, although *-ize* is quite widespread too (it is used, for instance, by *The Times* newspaper), while American English uses almost exclusively *-ize*. It is sometimes claimed that one or other form is more historically 'correct', but neither proposition really holds water. To be sure, the suffix comes ultimately from Greek *-izein* (although the actual Greek letter was not of course *z* but ζ), but many of these suffixed verbs reached English via French, which always has *-iser*; so the historical case for *s* and *z* is in most instances equally good.

There are some verbs for which you can *only* use *-ise*: they include *advertise, advise, chastise, circumcise, enfranchise, improvise, merchandise, supervise, televise*. The only common verb for which you can only use *-ize* is *capsize*.

The distinction in usage between *-lyse* and *-lyze* is much stricter: British English uses only *-lyse* (*analyse*), while American English overwhelmingly favours *-lyze* (*analyze*). (The related noun has *s* in both varieties *-analysis*.)

linated by animals. **zoophilia, zoophilist** [–'ɒf–], *n*. **zoophilous** [–'ɒf–], *adj*. **zoophobia,** *n*. dread of animals.

zoophorus, zophorus [zəʊ'ɒfərəs, 'zəʊf–] *n*. sculptured relief frieze with a continuous pattern of men or animals.

zoophyte ['zəʊəfaɪt] *n*. plant-like animal, as coral, sea anemone, etc. **zoophytal** [–'faɪtl], **zoophytic** [–'fɪtɪk], *adj*. **zoophytology,** *n*. study of such.

zooscopy [zəʊ'ɒskəpi] *n*. hallucination of seeing animals. **zooscopic** [–'skɒpɪk], *adj*.

zootechny, zootechnics [,zəʊə'tekni] *n*. breeding and taming of animals. **zootechnic,** *adj*.

zootomy [zəʊ'ɒtəmi] *n*. study of animal anatomy. **zootomic(al)** [–'tɒm–], *adj*. **zootomist,** *n*.

zootrophy [zəʊ'ɒtrəfi] *n*. feeding of animals. **zootrophic** [–'trɒfɪk], *adj*.

zouave [zu'ɑːv] *n*. French-Algerian infantry soldier; woman's short jacket.

zwitterion ['zwɪtər,aɪən, 'tsvɪt–] *n*. ion charged both positively and negatively.

zygal ['zaɪgl] *adj*. H-shaped. **zygodactyl(ic),** *adj*. having toes in two pairs, one behind the other.

zygomorphic, *adj*. bilaterally symmetrical.

zygophyte ['zaɪgəfaɪt] *n*. plant with reproduction by union of two similar cells. **zygospore,** *n*. spore formed by such union.

zygote ['zaɪgəʊt] *n*. cell formed by union of two gametes; fertilized egg. **zygotic** [–'gɒtɪk], *adj*.

zymase ['zaɪmeɪs] *n*. enzyme converting sugar to alcohol and carbon dioxide.

zymogenic [,zaɪmə'dʒenɪk] *adj*. causing fermentation. **zymogenous** [–'mɒdʒ–], *adj*.

zymology [zaɪ'mɒlədʒi] *n*. study of or treatise on fermentation. **zymologic(al),** *adj*. **zymologist,** *n*.

zymolysis [zaɪ'mɒləsɪs] *n*. action of enzymes.

zymoplastic [,zaɪmə'plæstɪk] *adj*. partaking in the production of enzymes.

zymosis [zaɪ'məʊsɪs] *n*. fermentation; process resembling fermentation in development of infectious disease.

zymotic [zaɪ'mɒtɪk] *adj*. pertaining to fermentation; due to development of germs entering body from outside; *n*. contagious or infectious disease.